The Arthurian Encyclopedia

Norris J. Lacy, *Editor*

with Associate Editors Geoffrey Ashe,
Sandra Ness Ihle, Marianne E. Kalinke,
and Raymond H. Thompson

GARLAND PUBLISHING, INC.
NEW YORK & LONDON   1986

Library of Congress Cataloging-in-Publication Data
Main entry under title:

The Arthurian encyclopedia.

(Garland reference library of the humanities ;
vol. 585)
 Bibliography: p.
 1. Arthur, King—Dictionaries, indexes, etc.
2. Arthur, King—Bibliography. 3. Arthurian romances—
Dictionaries. 4. Arthurian romances—Bibliography.
I. Lacy, Norris J. II. Ashe, Geoffrey. III. Series:
Garland reference library of the humanities ; v. 585.
DA152.5.A7A78 1986   809′.93351   84-48864
ISBN 0-8240-8745-3 (alk. paper)

Design by Jonathan Billing
Cover design by Donna Montalbano

Printed on acid-free, 250-year-life paper

Manufactured in the United States of America

ℑ Contents

✣ Preface

Few legends have been recast more often or in more forms than that of Arthur. From *dux bellorum* to immortal king, from medieval romance to Broadway stage, from Malory to Monty Python and Tennyson to television, Arthur has been familiar to many centuries and in numerous languages and media. The Arthurian tradition is rich and complex, with every generation, indeed every writer and artist, reinterpreting the material in the light of contemporary conceptions of the King or current artistic, ideological, or even political views. In part, it is this "transposability" of the legend that explains, or at least permits, its popularity. Arthur can be a military leader of early Britain, he can be the patriarch of medieval romance or a romantic hero, or he can be a timeless ideal, born in the Middle Ages but living anywhere, at any time. And that "any time" has included even the future, as Arthur's return is an event frequently predicted and anticipated. He is indeed "once and future."

The scope of the Arthurian legend (that is, both the number of Arthurian works and their geographical and cultural dispersion) is likely to surprise even those who have studied Arthur in detail. In addition to the chronicles and romances of Western Europe, during the Middle Ages and beyond, and the extensive reworkings of the legend during the nineteenth and twentieth centuries (especially in England and America), there are Serbo-Croatian, Greek, Japanese, and Tagalog texts; there are also tapestries and embroideries; murals, mosaics, and miniatures; paintings and depictions in stained glass.

Given the richness of the tradition dealing with Arthur and his world, we have surprisingly few reference works devoted to the subject. In recent years, scholars have begun to remedy that situation, particularly in regard to bibliographies: in addition to the annual bibliography of Arthurian literature published since 1949 by the International Arthurian Society, we now have *Arthurian Legend and Literature: An Annotated Bibliography. I: The Middle Ages*, by Edmund Reiss, Louise Horner Reiss, and Beverly Taylor (Garland, 1984), and *The Arthurian Bibliography*, prepared by C.E. Pickford, R.W. Last, and C.R. Barker (Boydell and Brewer, 1981, 1983). Among other recent reference tools is Charles and Ruth Moorman's *An Arthurian Dictionary* (University Press of Mississippi, 1978). Until the publication of the present volume, however, we have not had a reference work that offers, in encyclopedic form, a comprehensive and critical treatment of Arthurian subjects, artists, and works.

It is unfortunate that Arthurian specialists themselves have, somewhat arbitrarily, erected partitions at certain points within Arthurian studies and have all too often neglected important developments of the legend. Medievalists may well be more culpable in this regard than others. Owing to the legend's development and remarkable diffusion during the Middle Ages, Arthurian studies have been dominated by medievalists, who have often chosen to ignore (perhaps as decadent or contaminated) postmedieval Arthuriana. But if the modern period represents the decadence of earlier tradition, we might argue with equal justification that texts of the late Middle Ages contaminate the Arthurian legend of the twelfth century, or even that twelfth-century romance distorts or abases earlier history and chronicle. Indeed, even the very first texts we have represent an obvious and considerable embellishment on the skeletal Arthurian "fact." Whatever one's own tastes and preferences, it is apparent that the survival and the constant evolution of the Arthurian legend into our own time provide evidence not of decadence and decay but rather of the vitality and appeal of Arthur. *The Arthurian Encyclopedia* accordingly deals with Arthuriana of all periods, from the earliest tales and texts to the present. Similarly, alongside literature we have included history and chronicle, archaeology, art, film, and other media.

This volume thus intends to be comprehensive, but it is not exhaustive. Given the extraordinary dimensions of the Arthurian legend, readers will certainly be able to identify omissions. Many of these are intentional. We have not dealt (except in passing) with writers, like Rabelais, who make frequent and extensive reference to Arthurian romances but who have not provided an actual recasting of the legend. In such cases, our test has simply been the question: "Is this a genuine Arthurian text?" We have therefore thought it reasonable to exclude a number of medieval romances that become marginally "Arthurian" because the heroes, at some point in their adventures, stop briefly at Arthur's court. Included, on the other hand, are a small number of "non-Arthurian" (mostly Italian) texts in which there is unmistakable Arthurian influence, as indicated by explicit reference to characters or motifs. Decisions to include or exclude works were not always easy. An example is Bernard

Malamud's novel *The Natural* (and the film made from it). The Perceval story provides an obvious structure for it, and the parallels are often striking; yet after some hesitation we chose not to include it. After similar hesitation, we did include Nabokov's story "Lance," in which structural or thematic parallels may be less immediately apparent to many readers, but in which the author makes explicit reference to Lancelot, the Sword Bridge, and a specific Old French text.

Other intentional omissions are a number of names and motifs. Major Arthurian characters (e.g., Arthur, Lancelot, Tristan, Perceval, Merlin) have their own entries, but most secondary figures are omitted. Similarly, we include a certain number of motifs and themes (e.g., the Grail, the Sword in the Stone) but have not sought to be exhaustive in the treatment of such material. Nor have we attempted to deal with every country or language in regard to a particular subject; thus, for example, there are entries on British and American book illustration but not that of other countries. Also omitted are a certain number of textual fragments and some translations that, while historically important, make no significant contribution to the Arthurian corpus. Finally, in entries dealing with Arthurian texts the reader will find references in varying detail to subject matter and theme, but it has not been our intention to provide consistent and thorough plot summaries. On the other hand, we have attempted to be far more complete in the treatment of authors and artists, texts and artifacts, and the historical and archaeological basis for the Arthurian legend.

In addition to the large number of brief and informative entries devoted to particular subjects, the volume includes a number of extended essays, of two sorts. The first are those that treat major texts or authors (e.g., Malory, Tennyson, Chrétien de Troyes); these not only provide the necessary information about their subjects but also offer analyses and critical evaluations. Second, we offer a number of surveys and essays on broader subjects (e.g., Arthur in the Visual Arts, Arthur in Medieval German Literature, Arthurian Scholarship). Within those essays, authors have been free to choose their method and focus, which may thus vary from one entry to another. For example, the survey of French Arthurian literature is relatively brief and to the point, with detailed presentation of most subjects reserved for individual entries; the medieval German essay, on the other hand, concentrates on the figure of Arthur and offers more extensive discussions of a number of texts. We have, in other words, been less concerned with uniformity than with the availability and accessibility of material.

The organization of the volume is intended to be simple and logical. Entries are alphabetized under their most obvious or distinctive element; for example, the article on Arthur in the Visual Arts can be found under VISUAL ARTS, with a cross-reference under ARTS. Individual works are listed by author or artist, rather than by title; thus, *Idylls of the King* is treated under TENNYSON, but to assist the reader in locating less well known authors or subjects we include listings by title, with appropriate cross-references. The few exceptions to this practice concern works of disputed or tentative authorship, those attributed to a translator rather than to an author or adapter, and (of course) anonymous works; in those cases, we give the entry under the title, with a cross-reference from the author's or translator's name, if it is known. Within entries, cross-references have been kept to a minimum; virtually all names and titles mentioned in a given entry can be found under their own headings.

Names of characters naturally varied a good deal from language to language and even within the literature of a single country. We have tried to list them under the most familiar form or, where that is in doubt, the form most prevalent in English. In practice, the spelling under which we list names will not often cause difficulties, and cross-references are rarely necessary. Within entries, we have generally kept names (e.g., Perceval or Parsifal, Guinevere or Guenevere) as they occur in the author or work in question.

In most cases, names of medieval authors who identify themselves by their places of origin are alphabetized under their first names; thus, Chrétien de Troyes is found under the letter "C." Custom has dictated a different system for a few names, however, and Jacob van Maerlant is under "M" rather than "J." In general, we have not cross-referenced such items: when a name is not initially found, the alternative will be obvious. For medieval works, such as the *Roman de Brut*, which might be alphabetized under "R" or "B," we have taken the "Roman de" as an identification of genre rather than as part of the title; that work will thus be listed as *BRUT, LE ROMAN DE.* For more recent works, "Roman" or "Romance" has been considered inseparable from the rest of the title. To facilitate attempts to locate material, we include a list of entries grouped by subject and by language.

The authorship of entries is indicated by initials at the end of each entry; a list of contributors follows this introduction. Most entries are followed by one or more bibliographical references that give the source of the material in question or suggest further reading. In addition, we offer a general bibliography. A word of explanation may be in order about its comparative brevity. Our intention has been simply to provide the reader with a list of some major contributions to Arthurian studies, and as a result we have been quite selective. Moreover, because entries within the encyclopedia include bibliographical references, we have minimized duplication by exercising even greater selectivity in regard to individual writers in the volume's bibliography. Thus, despite the importance of such writers as Malory or Wolfram von Eschenbach, we include there only one or two references to each of them.

That this encyclopedia is—and had to be—a collaborative effort is obvious. Some aspects of that collaboration deserve note here. Our contributors include a number of scholars whose assistance went far beyond what we could reasonably have asked of them. Debra Mancoff, of Beloit College, provided invaluable advice in preparing the list of entries and the plates for Arthurian art, a complex area that, except for the Loomises' 1938 book, has been largely neglected until recently; she also wrote the general essay on visual arts and a number of other entries. Similarly, Christopher Kleinhenz, of the University of Wisconsin, Madison, offered substantial assistance in regard to Italian Arthuriana. We also owe a debt of gratitude to Leslie Alcock for his expert advice concerning Arthurian archaeology. We are pleased to express our gratitude to them, and if it is with some hesitation that we single these persons out for acknowledgment, it is only because that acknowledgment does an injustice to many others who contributed not only a number of entries but also extremely valuable counsel about entries, approaches, and the solution of various problems.

Finally, we are grateful to the University of Kansas for a grant that materially facilitated the general editor's work, and to Gary Kuris, of Garland Publishing, for the assistance and informed advice he offered at every turn.

Lawrence, Kansas   N.J.L.
January 1985

1 Arthur, King of Britain. Manuscript illumination. Pierpont Morgan Library 805: Lancelot Proper (fol. 34v). Courtesy Pierpont Morgan Library.

❖The Contributors

NJL Norris J. Lacy, *Editor*
University of Kansas

GA Geoffrey Ashe, *Associate Editor*
Glastonbury, Somerset, England

SNI Sandra Ness Ihle, *Associate Editor*
University of Wisconsin

MEK Marianne E. Kalinke, *Associate Editor*
University of Illinois

RHT Raymond H. Thompson, *Associate Editor*
Acadia University

LA Lilian Armstrong
Wellesley College

CLB Cynthia L. Barnett
University of Chicago

MSB M.S. Batts
University of British Columbia

RB Robert Baudry
Université Nationale, Lubumbashi, Zaire

BB Bart Besamusca
University of Utrecht

FWB Foster W. Blaisdell
Indiana University

FB Fanni Bogdanow
University of Manchester

NB-C Nancy Bradley-Cromey
Sweet Briar College

CONTRIBUTORS

EJB	E. Jane Burns *University of North Carolina*	**MCH**	Margaret C. Hunt *Indiana University*
KB	Keith Busby *University of Utrecht*	**CSJ**	C. Stephen Jaeger *Bryn Mawr College*
JPC	James P. Carley *University of Rochester*	**SMJ**	Sidney M. Johnson *Indiana University*
MDC	Mark Cumming *Memorial University of Newfoundland*	**BK**	Beverly Kennedy *Marianopolis College*
RGD	R.G. Dahms *University of Waterloo*	**EDK**	Edward Donald Kennedy *University of North Carolina*
JRD	Janine R. Dakyns *University of East Anglia*	**WWK**	William W. Kibler *University of Texas*
MLD	Mildred Leake Day *Quondam et Futurus*	**RWK**	Richard W. Kimpel *University of Western Ontario*
PD	Patrick Deane *University of Western Ontario*	**CK**	Christopher Kleinhenz *University of Wisconsin*
PJCF	Peter J.C. Field *University College of North Wales*	**NK**	Naomi Kline *Plymouth State College*
PKF	Patrick K. Ford *University of California, Los Angeles*	**ESK**	Erik S. Kooper *University of Utrecht*
MF	Maureen Fries *Fredonia State University College*	**JK**	Julia Kurtz *Lake Forest College*
AEG	Aubrey E. Galyon *Iowa State University*	**VML**	Valerie M. Lagorio *University of Iowa*
LRG	L.R. Galyon *Iowa State University*	**JL**	Joanne Lukitsh *Eastman House*
FGG	Francis G. Gentry *University of Wisconsin*	**WCM**	William C. McDonald *University of Virginia*
KHG	K.H. Göller *Universität Regensburg*	**JPM**	J. Paul McRoberts *Pennsylvania State University*
MAG	Alice Grellner *Rhode Island College*	**KGM**	Kenneth G. Madison *Iowa State University*
JLG	John L. Grigsby *Washington University*	**DBM**	Dhira B. Mahoney *University of Arizona*
KRG	Karin R. Gürttler *University of Montreal*	**DNM**	Debra N. Mancoff *Beloit College*
CBH	Constance B. Hieatt *University of Western Ontario*	**UM**	Ulrich Müller *Universität Salzburg*
DLH	Donald L. Hoffman *Northeastern Illinois University*	**LAM**	Louis A. Murillo *University of California, Berkeley*
LH	Linda Hughes *Washburn University*	**HN**	Helmut Nickel *Metropolitan Museum of Art*
		SJN	Susan J. Noakes *University of Kansas*

JN	James Noble *University of Western Ontario*	**CNS**	Christopher Smith *University of East Anglia*
JFO'G	James F. O'Gorman *Wellesley College*	**JWS**	James W. Spisak *Virginia Polytechnic Institute and State University*
RFO'G	Richard F. O'Gorman *University of Iowa*	**DS**	David Staines *University of Ottawa*
JPal	Joseph Palermo *Virginia Polytechnic Institute and State University*	**MS**	Marilyn Stokstad *University of Kansas*
MJP	Marylyn J. Parins *University of Arkansas*	**MAS**	M. Alison Stones *University of Pittsburgh*
JP	Jocelyn Price *University of Liverpool*	**PWT**	Petrus W. Tax *University of North Carolina*
VCR	Virginia C. Raguin *College of the Holy Cross*	**BT**	Beverly Taylor *University of North Carolina*
SRR	Stephen R. Reimer *University of Toronto*	**HT**	Hilary Thompson *Acadia University*
IJR	Isidro J. Rivera *University of Illinois*	**FLT**	Frederick L. Toner *Montana State University*
BFR	Brynley F. Roberts *University College of Wales*	**C-AVC**	Colette-Anne Van Coolput *Vlaamse Economische Hogeschool, Brussels*
RJR	Robert J. Rodini *University of Wisconsin*	**SLW**	Stephen L. Wailes *Indiana University*
AAR	Amelia Rutledge *George Mason University*	**PAW**	Patricia A. Ward *Wheaton College*
VJS	Vincent J. Scattergood *University of Dublin*	**JW**	Jean Watson *Rhodes College*
RCS	Roger C. Schlobin *Purdue University*	**MAW**	Muriel A. Whitaker *University of Alberta*
SSch	Siegrid Schmidt *Universität Salzburg*	**JKW**	John Keith Wikeley *University of Alberta*
JAS	James A. Schultz *Yale University*	**CCW**	Charity Cannon Willard *Ladycliff College*
HLS	Harvey L. Sharrer *University of California, Santa Barbara*	**LDW**	Lenora D. Wolfgang *Lehigh University*
TLS	Thomas L. Sloan *Northeastern Illinois University*	**JW-M**	Joanna Woods-Marsden *University of California, Los Angeles*
JLS	Janet L. Smarr *University of Illinois*	**LJW**	Leslie J. Workman *Studies in Medievalism*

✨ List of Entries
Arranged by Category

The following list contains all the entries of the Encyclopedia, arranged by category. Works by a known author are discussed in the author's entry. In general, chronicles are listed with HISTORY, LEGEND, ARCHAEOLOGY, rather than with the literature of the language in which they were written. In some cases, where those chronicles offer a clear literary, as well as historical, interest, they are also included under the appropriate literary category. A number of other duplications occur, the most common ones being the listing of place-names under HISTORY and PLACES. Owing to the large number of entries on literature in English, they have been divided into Medieval and Postmedieval (although that division is general and not determined by a specific date).

ARTS

Archer, James
Arthurian Revival
Blank, Richard
Book Illustration (American)
Book Illustration (British)
Boorman, John
Boston Public Library Murals
Boughton, Rutland

Bresson, Robert
Burghley Nef
Burne-Jones, Edward
Caen Capital
Cameron, Julia Margaret
Chausson, Ernest
Chertsey Abbey Tiles
Crane, Walter

LIST OF ENTRIES

Decorative Arts (Medieval)
Dent *Morte D'arthur*
Doré, Gustave
Draeseke, Felix August Bernhard
Dunlop Windows
Embroidery
Films
Fuseli, Henry
Goldmark, Karl
Hughes, Arthur
Ivory
Jones, Inigo
Kent, William
Lerner, Alan Jay
Louvre Tray
Manuscripts, Arthurian Illuminated
Martin, Frank
Misericords
Modena Archivolt
Monty Python and the Holy Grail
Morris, William
Mortimer, John
Moxon Tennyson
Murals (Medieval)
Nine Worthies
Otranto Mosaic
Oxford Union Murals
Pageant Design (British)
Perros Relief
Pisano, Antonio
Pre-Raphaelites
Princeton University Chapel Windows
Purcell, Henry
Queen's Robing Room
Rohmer, Eric
Rossetti, Dante Gabriel
Runkelstein Murals
Smith, John Moyr
Stained Glass
Stanmore Hall Tapestries
Sullivan, Sir Arthur
Syberberg, Hans Jurgen
Tapestry
Television Series
Tournament Books
Visual Arts, Arthurian Legend in
Von Fürstenberg, Veith
Wagner, Richard
Wynkyn de Worde

CHARACTERS

Agravain
Arthur, Character of
Balin and Balan
Bedivere
Bran
Elaine of Astolat
Elaine of Corbenic
Fisher King
Galahad
Gareth
Gawain
Guenevere
Hoël
Igerne
Isolde of the White Hands
Joseph of Arimathea
Kay
Lady of the Lake
Lancelot
Lohengrin
Lot
Mark
Merlin
Mordred
Morgan le Fay
Pendragon
Perceval
Taliesin
Tristan and Isolde
Uther Pendragon
Vortigern
Vortimer
Yvain

HISTORY, LEGEND, ARCHAEOLOGY

Ambrosius Aurelianus
Anglo-Saxon Chronicle
Annales Cambriae
Arthur, Origins of Legend
Aurelius Ambrosius
Avalon
Badon
Bede
Bek, Thomas, of Castelford
Brittany

LITERATURE
CELTIC

DUTCH

✣ List of Plates

LIST OF PLATES

✵ Select Bibliography

The following bibliography is selective and comparatively brief; it is intended to offer suggestions for further reading. For additional information, the reader may consult the bibliographical information appended to most entries.

Several periodicals or series are devoted entirely to Arthurian subjects. The oldest of these is of course the Bibliographical Bulletin of the International Arthurian Society *(ed. Douglas Kelly), an annual that lists all the preceding year's publications on medieval Arthurian literature; it also includes several articles, a list of members of the Society, and Arthurian news.* Arthurian Interpretations *(ed. Henry Hall Peyton III) offers studies of Arthurian literature, both medieval and modern; similarly,* Avalon to Camelot *(ed. Freya Reeves Lambides) deals with modern as well as earlier subjects, providing studies of Arthurian literature, archaeology, history, and art.* Quondam et Futurus *(ed. Mildred L. Day) is a newsletter that provides news of conferences, publications, etc. and that includes some articles and reviews.* Tristania *(ed. Lewis Sumberg) focuses on all aspects of the Tristan legend. Finally,* Arthurian Literature *(ed. Richard Barber) offers extended studies, editions, and translations of Arthurian literature.*

I. BIBLIOGRAPHY

Bulletin Bibliographique de la Société Internationale Arthurienne, Bibliographical Bulletin of the International Arthurian Society, 1 (1949)–35 (1983).

Pickford, Cedric E., and Rex Last, eds. *The Arthurian Bibliography, I: Author Listing.* Cambridge: Brewer, 1981.

———, ———, and C. R. Barker, eds. *The Arthurian Bibliography, II: Subject Index.* Cambridge: Brewer, 1983.

Last, Rex, ed. *The Arthurian Bibliography, 3.* Cambridge: Brewer, 1985.

Reiss, Edmund, Louise Horner Reiss, and Beverly Taylor. *Arthurian Legend and Literature: An Annotated Bibliography. I: The Middle Ages.* New York and London: Garland, 1984.

II. History and Legend

Alcock, Leslie. *Arthur's Britain: History and Archaeology A.D. 367–634.* London: Penguin, 1971.

Alcock, Leslie. *"By South Cadbury Is That Camelot . . .": Excavations at Cadbury Castle 1966–70.* London: Thames and Hudson, 1972.

Ashe, Geoffrey, ed. *The Quest for Arthur's Britain.* London and New York: Praeger, 1968.

——— . "'A Certain Very Ancient Book': Traces of an Arthurian Source in Geoffrey of Monmouth's *History.*" *Speculum,* 56 (1981), 301–23.

——— . *Avalonian Quest.* London: Methuen, 1982.

——— . *A Guidebook to Arthurian Britain.* Wellingborough: Aquarian, 1983.

——— . *The Discovery of King Arthur.* Garden City, N.Y.: Anchor/Doubleday, 1985.

Barber, R.W. *Arthur of Albion.* London: Barrie and Rockliff, 1961.

——— . *King Arthur in Legend and History.* London: Cardinal, 1973.

Bromwich, Rachel. "Scotland and the Earliest Arthurian Tradition." *Bibliographical Bulletin of the International Arthurian Society,* 15 (1963), 85–95.

Chambers, E.K. *Arthur of Britain.* London: Sidgwick and Jackson, 1927.

Darrah, John. *The Real Camelot: Paganism and the Arthurian Romances.* London: Thames and Hudson, 1981.

Fletcher, R.H. *The Arthurian Material in the Chronicles, Especially Those of Great Britain and France.* Boston: Ginn, 1906; 2nd ed. Roger Sherman Loomis. New York: Franklin, 1966.

Jenkins, Elizabeth. *The Mystery of King Arthur.* New York: Coward, McCann and Geoghegan, 1975.

Jones, W. Lewis. *King Arthur in History and Legend.* Cambridge: Cambridge University Press, 1911.

Lindsay, Jack. *Arthur and His Times.* London: Muller, 1958.

Loomis, Roger Sherman. *Celtic Myth and Arthurian Romance.* New York: Columbia University Press, 1927.

——— . *Wales and the Arthurian Legend.* Cardiff: University of Wales Press, 1956.

Morris, John. *The Age of Arthur.* New York: Scribner, 1973.

Newstead, Helaine. *Bran the Blessed in Arthurian Romance.* New York: Columbia University Press, 1939.

Paton, L.A. *Studies in the Fairy Mythology of Arthurian Romance.* Boston: Ginn, 1903.

Radford, C.A. Ralegh, and Michael J. Swanton. *Arthurian Sites in the West.* Devon: University of Exeter, 1975.

Schirmer, W.F. *Die frühen Darstellungen des Arthurstoffes.* Cologne: Opladen, 1958.

Treharne, R.F. *The Glastonbury Legends.* London: Cresset, 1967.

Williams, Mary. "King Arthur in History and Legend." *Folklore,* 73 (1962), 73–88.

III. ARTHUR AND ARTHURIAN CHARACTERS

App, August J. *Lancelot in English Literature: His Role and Character.* Washington, D.C.: Catholic University of America Press, 1929.

Baker, Imogene. *The King's Household in the Arthurian Court from Geoffrey of Monmouth to Malory.* Washington, D.C.: Catholic University of America Press, 1937.

Busby, Keith. *Gauvain in Old French Literature.* Amsterdam: Rodopi, 1980.

Eisner, Sigmund. *The Tristan Legend: A Study in Sources.* Evanston, Ill.: Northwestern University Press, 1969.

Fox, Marjorie. "Merlin in the Arthurian Prose Cycle." *Arthuriana,* 2 (1929–30), 20–29.

Jarman, A.O.H. *The Legend of Merlin.* Cardiff: University of Wales Press, 1960.

Kennedy, Elspeth. "King Arthur in the First Part of the *Prose Lancelot.*" In *Medieval Miscellany Presented to Eugène Vinaver.* Manchester: Manchester University Press, 1965, pp. 186–95.

Morris, Rosemary. *The Character of King Arthur in Medieval Literature.* Cambridge: Brewer, 1982.

Nitze, William A. "The Character of Gauvain in the Romances of Chrétien de Troyes." *Modern Philology,* 50 (1952–53), 219–25.

Noble, Peter. "The Character of Guinevere in the Arthurian Romances of Chrétien de Troyes." *Modern Language Review,* 67 (1972), 524–35.

Owen, D.D.R. "The Development of the Perceval Story." *Romania,* 80 (1959), 473–92.

Schoepperle, Gertrude. *Tristan und Isolt: A Study of the Sources of the Romance.* 2 vols. Frankfurt, 1913; 2nd ed. New York: Franklin, 1959.

Soudek, Ernst. *Studies in the Lancelot Legend.* Houston: Rice University Press, 1972.

Tyson, Diana B. "King Arthur as a Literary Device in French Vernacular History Writing of the Fourteenth Century." *Bibliographical Bulletin of the International Arthurian Society,* 33 (1981), 237–57.

Weston, Jessie L. *The Legend of Sir Gawain: Studies upon Its Original Scope and Significance.* London: Nutt, 1897.

———. *The Legend of Sir Lancelot du Lac.* London: Nutt, 1901.

———. *The Legend of Sir Perceval: Studies upon Its Origin, Development and Position in the Arthurian Cycle.* 2 vols. London: Nutt, 1906, 1909.

Zumthor, Paul. *Merlin le prophète: Un thème de la littérature polémique de l'historiographie et des romans.* Lausanne: Payot, 1943.

IV. Literature

Benson, Larry D. *Art and Tradition in Sir Gawain and the Green Knight.* New Brunswick, N.J.: Rutgers University Press, 1965.

———. *Malory's "Morte Darthur."* Cambridge, Mass.: Harvard University Press, 1976.

Brinkley, Roberta F. *Arthurian Legend in the Seventeenth Century.* Baltimore: Johns Hopkins Press, 1932.

Bruce, James Douglas. *The Evolution of Arthurian Romance from the Beginnings Down to the Year 1300.* 2nd ed. 2 vols. Baltimore: Johns Hopkins Press, 1928.

Entwistle, W.J. *Arthurian Legend in the Literatures of the Spanish Peninsula.* London: Dent, 1925.

Faral, Edmond. *La Légende arthurienne: Études et documents.* 3 vols. Paris: Champion, 1929.

Frappier, Jean. *Chrétien de Troyes.* Paris: Hatier, 1957.

———. *Amour courtois et Table Ronde.* Geneva: Droz, 1973.

Gardner, E.G. *The Arthurian Legend in Italian Literature.* London: Dent, 1930.

Jackson, W.T.H. *The Anatomy of Love: The Tristan of Gottfried von Strassburg.* New York: Columbia University Press, 1971.

Kalinke, Marianne E. *King Arthur, North-by-Northwest: The "matière de Bretagne" in Old Norse–Icelandic Romances.* Copenhagen: Reitzel, 1981.

Köhler, Erich. *Ideal und Wirklichkeit in der höfischen Epik.* Tübingen: Niemeyer, 1956; 2nd ed. 1970.

Lazar, Moshé. *Amour courtois et fin'amors dans la littérature du XIIe siècle.* Paris: Klincksieck, 1964.

Loomis, Roger Sherman, ed. *Arthurian Literature in the Middle Ages: A Collaborative History.* Oxford: Clarendon, 1959.

———. *The Development of Arthurian Romance.* New York: Harper and Row, 1963.

Loth, Joseph. *Contributions à l'etude des romans de la Table Ronde.* Paris, 1912.

Lumiansky, R.M., ed. *Malory's Originality.* Baltimore: Johns Hopkins Press, 1964.

Marx, Jean. *Nouvelles Recherches sur la littérature arthurienne.* Paris: Klincksieck, 1965.

Merriman, James Douglas. *The Flower of Kings: A Study of the Arthurian Legend in England Between 1485 and 1835.* Lawrence: University Press of Kansas, 1973.

Owen, D.D.R., ed. *Arthurian Romance: Seven Essays.* New York: Barnes and Noble, 1971.

Poag, James F. *Wolfram von Eschenbach.* New York: Twayne, 1972.

Rosenberg, John D. *The Fall of Camelot: A Study of Tennyson's Idylls of the King.* Cambridge, Mass.: Belknap, 1973.

Schmolke-Hasselmann, Beate. *Der Arthurische Versroman von Chrestien bis Froissart.* Tübingen: Niemeyer, 1980.

Schultz, James A. *The Shape of the Round Table: Structures of Middle High German Arthurian Romance.* Toronto: University of Toronto Press, 1983.

Staines, David. *Tennyson's Camelot: The Idylls of the King and Its Medieval Sources.* Waterloo, Ont.: Wilfrid Laurier University Press, 1983.

Starr, Nathan Comfort. *King Arthur Today: The Arthurian Legend in English and American Literature, 1901–1953.* Gainesville: University of Florida Press, 1954.

Stevens, John. *Medieval Romance: Themes and Approaches.* London: Hutchinson, 1973.

Taylor, Beverly, and Elisabeth Brewer. *The Return of King Arthur: British and American Arthurian Literature Since 1800.* Woodbridge, Suffolk: Boydell and Brewer, 1983.

Thompson, Raymond H. *The Return from Avalon: A Study of the Arthurian Legend in Modern Fiction.* Westport, Conn.: Greenwood, 1985.

Varty, Kenneth, ed. *An Arthurian Tapestry: Essays in Memory of Lewis Thorpe.* Glasgow: French Department of the University, 1981.

Vinaver, Eugène. *Form and Meaning in Medieval Romance.* Leeds: Maney, 1966.

———— . *The Rise of Romance.* Oxford: Clarendon, 1971.

Wapnewski, Peter. *Hartmann von Aue.* 3rd ed. Stuttgart: Metzler, 1967.

V. ARTS

Gerould, G.H. "Arthurian Romance and the Date of the Relief at Modena." *Speculum,* 10 (1935), 355–76.

Haug, Walter. *Das Mosaik von Otranto: Darstellung, Deutung, und Bilddokumentation.* Wiesbaden: Riechert, 1977.

Loomis, Roger Sherman, and Laura Hibbard Loomis. *Arthurian Legends in Medieval Art.* London: Oxford University Press, 1938.

Mancoff, Debra N. *The Arthurian Revival in Victorian Painting.* 2 vols. Ann Arbor, Mich.: University Microfilms International, 1982.

Newman, Ernest. *The Wagner Operas.* New York: Knopf, 1949.

Olschki, Leonardo. "La cattedrale di Modena e il suo rilievo arturiano." *Archivum Romanicum,* 19 (1935), 145–82.

Scherer, Margaret R. *About the Round Table.* New York: Metropolitan Museum of Art, 1945.

VI. THEMES, SYMBOLS, MOTIFS

Adolf, Helen. *Visio Pacis: Holy City and Grail: An Attempt at an Inner History of the Grail Legend.* State College: Pennsylvania State University Press, 1960.

Brown, Arthur C.L. "The Bleeding Lance." *PMLA,* 25 (1910), 1–59.

———— . *The Origin of the Grail Legend.* Cambridge, Mass.: Harvard University Press, 1943.

Bruce, James Douglas. "The Development of the Mort Arthur Theme in Mediaeval Romance." *Romanic Review,* 4 (1913), 403–71.

Cosman, Madeleine Pelner. *The Education of the Hero in Arthurian Romance.* Chapel Hill: University of North Carolina Press, 1966.

Frappier, Jean. "Le Graal et la chevalerie." *Romania,* 75 (1954), 165–210.

Harward, Vernon J., Jr. *The Dwarfs of Arthurian Romance and Celtic Tradition.* Leiden: Brill, 1958.

Holmes, Urban Tigner, Jr., and M. Amelia Klenke. *Chrétien, Troyes, and the Grail.* Chapel Hill: University of North Carolina Press, 1959.

Jonin, Pierre. *Les Personnages féminins dans les romans français de Tristan au XII siècle: Études des influences contemporaines.* Aix: Ophrys, 1958.

Kahn Blumstein, Andrée. *Misogyny and Idealization in the Courtly Romance.* Bonn: Bouvier Verlag Herbert Grundmann, 1977.

Kennedy, Angus. "The Hermit's Role in French Arthurian Romance (c. 1170–1530)." *Romania,* 95 (1974), 54–83.

Lewis, Gertrud Jaron. *Das Tier und seine dichterische Funktion in Erec, Iwein, Parzival und Tristan.* Berne and Frankfurt: Lang, 1974.

Loomis, Laura Hibbard. "Arthur's Round Table." *PMLA,* 41 (1926), 771–84.

Loomis, Roger Sherman. "The Visit to the Perilous Castle: A Study of the Arthurian Modifications of an Irish Theme." *PMLA,* 48 (1933), 1000–35.

————. "Arthurian Tradition and Folklore." *Folklore,* 69 (1958), 1–25.

————. "The Legend of Arthur's Survival." In *Arthurian Literature in the Middle Ages: A Collaborative History.* Oxford: Clarendon, 1959.

————. *The Grail: From Celtic Myth to Christian Symbol.* Cardiff: University of Wales Press, 1963.

Marx, Jean. *La Légende arthurienne et le Graal.* Paris: Presses Universitaires, 1952.

Mott, Lewis F. "The Round Table." *PMLA,* 20 (1905), 231–64.

Muir, Lynette R. "The Questing Beast: Its Origin and Development." *Orpheus,* 4 (1957), 24–32.

Nelli, René, ed. *Lumière du Graal: Études et Textes.* Paris: Cahiers du Sud, 1951.

Newstead, Helaine. "The Besieged Lady in Arthurian Romance." *PMLA,* 63 (1948), 803–30.

Nitze, William A. "The Fisher King in the Grail Romances." *PMLA,* 24 (1909), 365–418.

————. "The Wasteland: A Celtic Arthurian Theme." *Modern Philology,* 43 (1945–46), 58–62.

Nutt, Alfred. *Studies on the Legend of the Holy Grail.* London: Nutt, 1888.

Owen, D.D.R. *The Evolution of the Grail Legend.* Edinburgh and London: Oliver and Boyd, 1968.

Pickford, Cedric E. "Camelot." In *Mélanges de langue et de littérature médiévales offerts à Pierre Le Gentil.* Paris: SEDES, 1973.

Vinaver, Eugène. "King Arthur's Sword, or the Making of a Medieval Romance." *Bulletin of the John Rylands Library,* 40 (1957–58), 513–26.

Weston, Jessie. *From Ritual to Romance.* Cambridge: Cambridge University Press, 1920.

✸ The Arthurian Encyclopedia

ABBEY, EDWIN AUSTIN: *see* BOSTON PUBLIC LIBRARY MURALS.

ABENDLÄNDISCHE TAUSEND UND EINE NACHT: see LYSER, JOHANN PETER.

ACHIEVEMENT OF SIR GALAHAD ACCOMPANIED BY SIR PERCIVAL AND SIR BORS, THE: see STANMORE HALL TAPESTRIES.

ACCOLON OF GAUL: see CAWEIN, MADISON J.

ACCUSER, THE: see FIELD, MICHAEL.

ACTS OF KING ARTHUR AND HIS NOBLE KNIGHTS, THE: see STEINBECK, JOHN.

ADVENTURES OF SIR LANCELOT, THE: see TELEVISION SERIES.

1

AFALLENNAU: see MERLIN.

AGRAVAIN, brother of Gawain, son of Lot and Morgause (or Anna), nicknamed *aux dures mains* ("of the hard hands"). He plays a prominent role in the Old French Prose *Lancelot* and *Mort Artu*, and subsequently in the various romances derived and adapted from these, including the Prose *Tristan* and Malory's *Morte Darthur*. His most significant deed is probably the public exposure of the affair of Lancelot and Guenevere, in which he is aided and abetted by Arthur's son, Mordred, and which is one of the catalysts in the downfall of the Round Table. His name in Old French already has overtones of "aggravation." [KB]

ALBRECHT VON SCHARFENBERG, author of *Der jüngere Titurel*. Composed around 1270, the work was inspired by Wolfram von Eschenbach's *Titurel* fragments, which focus on the love of Sigune and Schionatulander, two characters appearing in *Parzival*. The *Jüngerer Titurel*, consisting of some 6,000 stanzas that are imitative of Wolfram's so-called *Titurel* stanzas, tells in leisurely fashion the entire life history of both Sigune and Schionatulander. The enormous novel, which has intimidated critics and editors alike, transforms courtly romance into a vehicle of didacticism that instructs by means of exempla. Throughout the work, the author assumes the identity of Wolfram von Eschenbach; he steps forward as "ich, Wolfram" and is addressed as "her Wolfram" who hails from "Eschenbach." Not until almost the very end, in stanza 5883, does the author reveal that he is one "Albreht," whom scholars identify with Albrecht von Scharfenberg, a pious, clerically oriented man—to judge by the tenor of his work—whose patron was Ludwig II of Bavaria. Because Albrecht used the persona of Wolfram throughout most of the *Jüngerer Titurel*, the work was attributed in the Middle Ages—and even as late as the nineteenth century—to Wolfram. It is plausible that the author's identification of himself in stanza 5883 may have been interpreted as an indication that Wolfram had left the work incomplete and that it was finished by Albrecht. Although the pious tone and extraordinary verbosity of the *Jüngerer Titurel* strike modern critics as tedious, the compendious narrative was extremely popular in the Middle Ages. Berthold von Regensburg, who died in 1272, already knew the work and quoted from it in his German sermons. One of Albrecht's Arthurian episodes, in which the knights' virtue or lack thereof is revealed when they cross a magic bridge, inspired Hans Sachs to compose a *Meisterlied* on the subject. [MEK]

Albrecht von Scharfenberg. *Der jüngere Titurel*, ed. K. A. Hahn. Quedlinburg: Basse, 1842.
———. *Albrechts von Scharfenberg Jüngerer Titurel*, ed. Werner Wolf. 3 vols. Berlin: Akademie, 1955, 1964, 1968.
Parshall, Linda B. *The Art of Narration in Wolfram's* Parzifal *and Albrecht's* Jüngerer Titurel. Cambridge: Cambridge University Press, 1981.
Wolf, Werner. "Wer war der Dichter des Jüngeren Titurel?" *Zeitschrift für deutsches Altertum und deutsche Literatur*, 84 (1953), 309–46.

ALLITERATIVE *MORTE ARTHURE,* a long narrative poem in Middle English (4,346 lines), composed near the end of the fourteenth century, possibly 1400. It survives in a unique manuscript, Lincoln Cathedral Library 91, a miscellany compiled ca. 1440 by the Yorkshire scribe Robert Thornton. The poet is unknown, and the dialect of the original text not easily identifiable; it may be West Midlands, or, more likely, Northeast Midlands, passing through two stages of transcription.

Like other examples of the Alliterative Revival of the fourteenth century in England, the *Morte Arthure* uses the unrhymed alliterative long line, strongly resembling that of Old English poetry. The line falls regularly into two half-lines, the A-verse and the B-verse, linked by the alliteration of stressed syllables. There are usually two (sometimes three) stressed syllables in the A-verse and one (sometimes two) in the B-verse, while the fourth stressed syllable remains unalliterated. The number of unstressed syllables varies. Thus, the most common alliterative pattern in the poem is aa/ax, but the poet manipulates the conventions with freedom and artistry, achieving a wide range of variations from the norm for different effects. Sometimes, he creates blocks of sound by running the same initial alliteration through several successive lines.

The poet also uses a highly specialized vocabulary, archaic terms associated with battle subjects, and technical terms describing armor, costume, cuisine, and so on. He employs frequent alliterative collocations (associational word clusters bound by ties of alliteration), drawing from a stock common to alliterative poets of the period. Though not itself composed orally, the poem may have been influenced by the techniques of oral-formulaic composition. Yet, despite the conventional features, the poet achieves great variation in his descriptions, being as adept at static pictures of idyllic landscapes as at scenes of violent action on the battlefield or at sea. His battle descriptions are both stylized and particularized, with vivid, concrete details, accurate references to contemporary fashion in armor or costume, and graphic portrayals of the brutality of war.

The structure of the poem is clear and well balanced, the narrative falling into four parts. Arthur, holding court at Carlisle, receives a demand from the emperor Lucius that he pay homage as a vassal of Rome. After his own vassals have pledged their support and made their battle vows, Arthur defies Lucius, and both sides prepare for war. Leaving Mordrede, his sister's son, as regent of England, Arthur embarks for France, dreaming a prophetic dream in which a dragon defeats a bear. Arriving in Brittany, he singlehandedly kills the giant of St. Michael's Mount, who has abducted and raped the Duchess of Brittany.

After two separate engagements with the emperor's forces and pagan allies, in which Gawayn and Cador each distinguishes himself against heavy odds, Arthur's forces meet the emperor's in a decisive battle. Lucius is killed and the vows made in council at Carlisle fulfilled, though Kayous, Bedwere, and many other British knights are lost. Instead of tribute, Arthur sends to Rome the coffins of his enemies.

Arthur then successfully besieges a disloyal vassal, the Duke of Lorraine, at Metz. During the siege, Gawayn slips away from the foraging party and meets in single combat Priamus, a Saracen knight, who converts to Christianity and brings his men over to Gawayn's side in the ensuing battle. Arthur continues southward into Italy, conquering Italian towns until the Romans offer him the imperial crown.

At his peak of success, Arthur dreams that Fortune is turning him on her wheel and dashing him down. Next morning, he hears that Mordrede has usurped both his crown and his queen. Returning immediately to England, Arthur defeats Mordrede's pagan allies in a great sea battle, but in the ensuing land battle Gawayn's forces are outnumbered and he is killed. Arthur bitterly laments the death of his sister's son and vows vengeance on Mordrede. In the final battle in Cornwall, Arthur kills Mordrede but is himself fatally wounded. He is buried at Glastonbury, having appointed Cador's son Constantyne as his successor.

The poem clearly belongs to the Arthurian chronicle tradition, deriving ultimately from Geoffrey of Monmouth's *Historia Regum Britanniae*, transmitted through the *Bruts* of Wace and Layamon. The poet may have used as his sources all three chronicles, as well as that by Robert Mannyng of Brunne. The Charlemagne romance of *Sir Fierabras* (or the Middle English redaction *Sir Ferumbras*) may have suggested the Gawayn–Priamus episode, and the Alexandrian romance *Li Fuerres de Gadre* the foraging expedition. The motifs of the Nine Worthies and the avowing patterns may derive from the Alexandrian *Voeux du Paon*, or the Middle English *Parlement of the Thre Ages*. It has also been argued that the poet is alluding to contemporary history, especially the military campaigns of Edward III.

The genre of the *Morte Arthure* is difficult to define. It has been called a romance, an epic, a *chanson de geste*, a tragedy of Fortune, and a "mirror" for kings. The difficulty of classifying the poem is related to the difficulty of interpreting its theme. It has been argued that Arthur's fall is the result not only of Fortune's capriciousness but also of his own moral degeneration from a champion of Christendom to an ambitious aggressor pursuing unjust wars. At what point Arthur's wars become unjust, however, is a matter of disagreement. Though the poem celebrates the heroic virtues of courage against odds, of loyalty to leader and fellows, of desire for fame, the poet appears at the same time to be ambivalent, even ironic (it has been argued), about war in general. Perhaps he is simply displaying the medieval ability to hold conflicting viewpoints in tension without their invalidating each other.

The *Morte Arthure* has influenced other works, such as the *Awntyrs off Arthure* and most notably Sir Thomas Malory's *Le Morte Darthur*. Malory's "Noble Tale of King Arthur and the Emperor Lucius" (Caxton's Book V) is a free prose rendering, much condensed, of the first two-thirds of the poem, ending with Arthur's triumphal coronation in Rome. [DBM]

&⸱ Hamel, Mary, ed. *Morte Arthure: A Critical Edition*. New York and London: Garland, 1984.

Krishna, Valerie, ed. *The Alliterative Morte Arthure: A Critical Edition.* New York: Franklin, 1976.

Perry, George, ed. *Morte Arthure.* London: Kegan Paul, Trench, Trübner, 1865; rev. Edmund Brock, 1871.

The Thornton Manuscript (Lincoln Cathedral MS. 91). Introduction by D.S. Brewer and A.E. Owen. London: Scolar, 1975; rev. 1977.

Göller, Karl Heinz, ed. *The Alliterative Morte Arthure: A Reassessment of the Poem.* Woodbridge, Suffolk: Boydell and Brewer, 1981.

Matthews, William. *The Tragedy of Arthur: A Study of the Alliterative "Morte Arthure."* Berkeley: University of California Press, 1960.

ALTAR OF THE LEGION, THE: *see* BISHOP, FARNHAM.

AMADÍS DE GAULA: *see* MONTALVO, GARCÍ RODRÍGUEZ DE.

AMBROSIUS AURELIANUS, a fifth-century British leader. He is the historical prototype of one of Geoffrey of Monmouth's kings, Aurelius Ambrosius, who checks the Saxon invasion unleashed by the policies of the previous king, Vortigern. In Welsh, the name *Ambrosius* becomes *Emrys*, and many Welshmen are still so called.

Ambrosius Aurelianus is the only fifth-century Briton actually named in the *De Excidio* of Gildas, written during the 540s or thereabouts. Gildas tells of Saxon mercenaries settling in Britain under the aegis of a *superbus tyrannus*, or "preeminent ruler," with whom Vortigern is usually identified. The Saxons revolted, raiding and ravaging everywhere. Their onslaught caused a migration of Britons overseas (the reference here is to the move to Armorica in northwest Gaul, which began the conversion of part of it into the Lesser Britain, or Brittany). Finally, the marauders withdrew to their settlements in the east of the island. Then, says Gildas, the surviving Britons recovered and launched a counteroffensive. Ambrosius enters his narrative as the war-leader who organizes it.

Gildas presents him as a "Roman," the son of parents who had "worn purple" and died in the Saxon devastation. "Wearing purple" suggests an emperor but could mean merely that his father was of senatorial rank, like many imperial citizens of all nationalities. Gildas puts his counterattack after the British emigration, which can be roughly dated to the late 450s, so that the counterattack itself doubtless began in the 460s. The allusion to Ambrosius as a Roman has no ethnic content and probably points to a political leaning. Across the Channel in northern Gaul, a general named Aegidius had been attempting (with no help from the hapless emperors) to uphold the imperial system against barbarian pressures. His son Syagrius carried on his work, ruling from Soissons and at some point adopting the remarkable title "king of the Romans." Though Britain was now outside the Empire, there are indications that the

Britons who made new homes in Armorica may have done so through some agreement with these authorities; and the proimperial campaign of the king called Riothamus a few years after shows that the dominant Britons of the 460s had Roman rather than barbarian sympathies.

According to Gildas, Ambrosius's action against the Saxon settlements led to a period of doubtful warfare, culminating in a British success at the siege of Mount Badon somewhere about the year 500. Nothing shows when he ceased to be active personally. It has been thought that he was still in command at Badon, but Gildas does not name the commander on that occasion, and the only individual who is ever connected with it—admittedly, not till centuries afterward—is Arthur. In general, the rally that Ambrosius launched is associated with Arthur, too. Early materials shed no real light on the relation between them but hardly support the theory that they are the same person under different names.

Nennius mentions Ambrosius in the *Historia Brittonum*. Confusingly, he ignores him as a leader of anti-Saxon resistance, allotting that role first to Vortimer and later to Arthur. Ambrosius is spoken of as a rival whom Vortigern feared and then, after Vortigern's death, as a king holding paramountcy over lesser rulers. The only episode dealing with him at length is legendary—a story that introduces him in his youth as having prophetic gifts, displayed before Vortigern. At the end of it, he is made to say that his father was a Roman consul: perhaps an echo of Gildas, though it conflicts with the rest of the tale, which depends on his father being unknown.

In the same passage, Nennius calls him *Emrys gwledig* and says that Vortigern, awed by his prophecies, gave him the overlordship of western Britain—thus (it would seem) starting him on the career that made him formidable. Here, Nennius may at least be recording his true status, rather than when he calls him a paramount king. *Emrys gwledig* is the way Ambrosius is styled in Welsh tradition generally. The word *gwledig* comes to mean simply "prince," but its basic sense is "land-holder"; and in its application to fifth-century figures it reflects a political reality of the time. Parts of Britain were governed by army commanders vested with regional powers. Ambrosius appears to have been one of them. Nennius is probably wrong to locate him in the west, which would mean essentially Wales. In some notes at the end of Nennius's main text, Ambrosius is stated to have fought Vitalinus (otherwise unknown) at Wallop in Hampshire, twelve years "from the reign of Vortigern"—a phrase taken to mean from the reign's beginning, which the same notes assign to 425. This suggests that he was asserting authority over the south or some part of it in 437. If so, he was already middle-aged at the time of his generalship against the Saxons, and he can scarcely have been the Britons' leader at Badon.

As to his position in the anti-Saxon campaign, Alcock plausibly pictures him as appointed to supreme command in the service of a high king, one of two or three who apparently reigned in Britain during the fifth century. He may be commemorated by a few place-names, such as Amesbury in Wiltshire, originally *Ambres-byrig*. In the Late Roman period, military forces were occasionally called after their leaders or nominal leaders. Ambrosius's men might have been the Ambrosiani; their chief's name could have been given to bases they used.

A Welsh Triad of uncertain provenance calls Ambrosius a fleet-owner. Conjecturally, he assembled shipping for the movement of Britons to Armorica, which developed from a flight of refugees into a more considered colonization, though not yet on a large scale. Some kind of British fleet existed in 468, when the army of the "king of the Britons" called Riothamus crossed to the Continent. Fleuriot has argued that this king actually was Ambrosius Aurelianus, "Riothamus" being a title. He draws attention to Breton place-names with *Aurilian* in them, and to traces of a tradition locating Ambrosius temporarily in Brittany. But there is no real evidence for Ambrosius's having held the sort of kingship implied, and a supervisory role in the overseas settlement would be enough to account for the facts. [GA]

Gildas. *De Excidio Britanniae*, Chapter 25.

Nennius. *Historia Brittonum*, Chapters 31, 40–42, 48, 66.

Alcock, Leslie. *Arthur's Britain*. London: Penguin, 1971.

Bromwich, Rachel. *Trioedd Ynys Prydein*. Cardiff: University of Wales Press, 1961.

Fleuriot, Léon. *Les Origines de la Bretagne*. Paris: Payot, 1980.

Morris, John. *The Age of Arthur*. New York: Scribner, 1973.

AMERICAN ARTHURIAN LITERATURE: *see* ENGLISH AND AMERICAN ARTHURIAN LITERATURE (MODERN).

AMMANN, JOSEPH-HURTER: *see TRISTAN,* MODERN GERMAN VERSIONS OF GOTTFRIED'S.

AMOROSA VISIONE: see BOCCACCIO, GIOVANNI.

ANATHEMATA, THE: see JONES, DAVID.

ANDREAS CAPELLANUS, author of *De Amore* (Latin prose, ca. 1185). This important (if not entirely serious) treatise on courtly love includes a brief story about a young knight who must win the prize hawk from Arthur's court for his lady—but first he must slay two knights in double combat, obtain the hawk's gauntlet, and finally prove his lady's greater beauty in jousts at Arthur's court. When the knight finally achieves the hawk, he finds a parchment tied to it on which are written the rules of love. (*See also* COURTLY LOVE.) [MLD]

Andreas Capellanus. *De Amore*, ed. E. Trojel. Copenhagen, 1892; 2nd ed. Munich: Eidos, 1964.

ANDREW OF WYNTOUN: *see* SCOTTISH ARTHURIAN CHRONICLES.

ANGLICA HISTORIA: *see* VERGIL, POLYDORE.

ANGLO-SAXON CHRONICLE, THE (ninth century?), contains no specifically Arthurian material but offers indirect support to statements in Gildas and Nennius that Saxon advances were halted early in the sixth century. There is no mention of Saxon progress for a long time beginning with 527, a date too late to square exactly with Gildas and Nennius. [AEG]

Plummer, C., ed. *Anglo-Saxon Chronicle*. London, 1899.

ANNALES CAMBRIAE ("Annals of Wales"). This Latin chronicle records the battles of Badon and Camlann. It is attached to Nennius's *Historia Brittonum* in the Harley manuscript, and its date probably lies within the range 960–80. However, the text is a composite formed by transcription of items from older chronicles. Several early entries are from Irish sources. The first that concern Britain are the ones mentioning Arthur. There are other copies with additional matter but nothing Arthurian.

The framework is a table of 533 years, against some of which events are noted. The years are numbered from a Year 1 best taken as A.D. 447. On that basis, the Arthurian entries come in 518 and 539. The first is: "The battle of Badon, in which Arthur carried the cross of Our Lord Jesus Christ on his shoulders for three days and three nights and the Britons were victors." The second is: "The strife of Camlann, in which Arthur and Medraut fell. And there was plague in Britain and in Ireland."

Odd as the Badon entry looks, it can be rationalized. "Shoulders" may mistranslate a Welsh word meaning "shield," so that the cross could be an emblem. Nevertheless, the "three days and nights" have a legendary air, and the date seems incompatible with the testimony of Gildas, who wrote when the battle was within living memory.

The second entry is the earliest known reference to Camlann and to Medraut, otherwise Mordred. Unlike other Welsh matter introducing Arthur, it looks like a plain statement, free from legend, and it has sometimes therefore been singled out as the only trustworthy evidence for him. But the late date, 539, casts serious doubt on it, and it hangs in a void unrelated to history. A claim that it proves Arthur's reality because it must have been posted from a contemporary record is no longer pressed. However, since everyone else who is mentioned in the *Annales* did exist, there is a certain presumption that a real Arthur must underlie these questionable phrases. [GA]

Annales Cambriae, in Nennius, ed. and trans. John Morris under the title *British History and the Welsh Annals*. In *History from the Sources*. Chichester: Phillimore, 1980, Vol. 8.

Alcock, Leslie. *Arthur's Britain*. London: Penguin, 1971.

ANSPACHER, LOUIS K. (1878–1947), American author of *Tristan and Isolde* (1904), a verse tragedy in which Tristan and Isolde fall in love but remain chaste until they drink the love potion. Stabbed by a jealous Cornish lord, Tristan perishes, and Isolde dies by his side. King Mark says that he would have given up Isolde had he known all. [AEG]

🍂 Anspacher, Louis K. *Tristan and Isolde*. New York: Brentano, 1904.

APOLLINAIRE, GUILLAUME (1880–1918), published *L'Enchanteur pourrissant* ("The Rotting Enchanter") in 1904; a new version appeared in 1909 with woodcuts by Derain. It is a fascinating but confused work, owing no doubt to the fact that it was one of the twenty-four-year-old author's earliest prose compositions.

The enchanter of the title is Merlin, whose fate, according to the author, was to be imprisoned by the spells he had imprudently revealed to Viviane, or Évïène, the Lady of the Lake. Apollinaire was inspired by the *Premier volume de Lancelot nouvellement imprimé à Paris suivi du second et du tiers volume*, edited in 1533 by Philippe Le Noir. Apollinaire's story provides a continuation of the *Roman de Merlin l'Enchanteur*. In it we find an elaborate procession of characters and representatives of multiple mythologies (oriental, Greek, Hebraic, Scandinavian, Christian, Celtic) and a fantastic bestiary—all parading before the sepulcher of the immortal necromancer. Gauvain, for example, passes by, still linked to his solar mythology. All come in vain, however, since the charms transmitted by Merlin are by their nature invincible. We remain aware that their quest is condemned to failure from the start. The tedious impression is that of a surging mass, a kaleidoscope of conflicting mythologies. For Apollinaire offers us a curious mixture: erudition, a perceptive sense of diverse myths, and a propensity to treat them as an intellectual game, thereby precluding the expected effect of wonder and the supernatural.

In Merlin, Apollinaire may have wanted to represent his own fate as a "fatherless child"; in Viviane, the perfidy of woman toward the "Mal-Aimé." The author also suggests a number of his other personal obsessions (e.g., concerning menstrual blood) in the work. He doubtless wanted to recount an "inverted" quest: a pilgrimage of the "Magi" not to the cradle of a son of God but to the tomb of a son of the Devil. Attached to the work are some other fragments: e.g., the "Onirocritique," in which we recognize Orqueneseles, the city that Gauvain sees and of which Guiromélans declares himself master, at the end of Chrétien's *Perceval*. [RB]

🍂 Apollinaire, Guillaume. *L'Enchanteur pourrissant*, ed. Jean Burgos. Paris: Minard, 1972.
   Baudry, Robert. "La Tradition du merveilleux et l'Enchanteur pourrissant." *Essays in French Literature*, 17 (1980), 36–49.

ARCHER, JAMES (1823–1904), was characteristic of painters of the Arthurian Revival in that his interpretation was synthetic, drawing subjects from Tennyson and Malory. His extensive involvement with the Arthurian narrative is known through the lists of the Royal Scottish Academy and the Royal Academy of Arts in London, for many of his paintings are at present unlocated.

His earliest Arthurian painting was *La Mort D'Arthur* (1861, Manchester City Galleries), a theme he was to return to with subtle variations. His other works suggest that he sought to paint a full narrative of the legend; they include *King Arthur Obtains the Mystic Sword Excalibur* (1862, known through engraving), *Sir Lancelot Looks on Queen Guinevere* (1863, Private Collection), *The Parting of Arthur and Guinevere* (1865, known through oil study, Private Collection), *How Sir Lancelot and His Eight Fellows of the Round Table Carried Queen Guinevere from Almesbury to Glastonbury* (1869, unlocated), *The Death of Arthur* (1872, Private Collection), *The Dying King Arthur on the Island of Avalon Has a Vision of the San Grail* (1880, unlocated), *King Arthur in the Quest of His Mystic Sword Excalibur* (1880, unlocated), and *La Mort D'Arthur* (1897, unlocated). Archer's style was typical of the mid–Arthurian Revival, drawing upon both the Robing Room frescoes and the work of the Pre-Raphaelites as prototypes. [DNM]

❧ Mancoff, Debra N. *The Arthurian Revival in Victorian Painting.* 2 vols. Ann Arbor, Mich.: University Microfilms International, 1982, Vol. 2, pp. 474–80.

ARDEN, JOHN, and MARGARETTA D'ARCY, authors of *The Island of the Mighty*, "a play on a traditional British theme in three parts": "Two Wild Young Noblemen," "O the Cruel Winter," and "A Handful of Watercress." Part 1 is a confusing mélange of the adventures of Balin, Knight of the Two Swords, and his brother, Balan; King Arthur, cast as the Imperial General (in his late sixties), and his chief poet, Merlin; the Prince of Strathcylde and his chief poet, Taliesin; assorted Round Table knights; and the nexus of King Pellam, Garlon, the Dolorous Stroke, and the Sacred Spear. Part 2 focuses on Arthur's refusal to admit that his army's power is at an end. Leaving Medraut in charge of his forces, Arthur goes to meet with the Prince of Gododdin, while Gwenhwyvar allies herself with the evil Medraut. The act ends with Medraut and Arthur killing each other at Camlann and Merlin going mad. Part 3 concerns Merlin's madness, which is an objective correlative for the chaotic proceedings.

According to the authors, the play is not only an encomium to bards and an analysis of exploitive myths but also an attack on imperialism, with Arthur a murderous, ugly military commander; the flower of chivalry, more like weeds; and the little people, as always, the sufferers. As one reviewer noted: "What starts out to be sensational theatre turns into a shaggy-dog story. *The Island of the Mighty* is scintillating for one hour, interesting after two, sinking in three, and sunk by the finale." [VML]

❧ Arden, John, and Margaretta D'Arcy. *The Island of the Mighty. Plays and Players*, February 1973, 1–32 (Parts 1 and 2), and March 1973, 1–14 (Part 3).
   Gems, Pam. "The Island of the Ardens." *Plays and Players*, February 1973, 16–19, 36.

ARIOSTO, LUDOVICO (1474–1533), a member of the Este court in Ferrara and a major figure in the evolution of vernacular theater in modern Europe.

He completed the first edition of the *Orlando Furioso* early in the sixteenth century (published in 1516) and revised it for a second edition published in 1522; major emendations and additions were incorporated into the final edition of 1532. A continuation of Matteo Maria Boiardo's *Orlando Innamorato*, the *Orlando Furioso* is recognized as the masterpiece of Italian chivalric romance, a blend of medieval Carolingian epic, *matière de Bretagne*, and the popular narrative traditions (*cantari*) of the Italian late Middle Ages. Structured upon three basic narrative lines—the war between Christian and pagan forces; the pursuit of the elusive Angelica by the love-crazed protagonist, Orlando; and the encomiastic celebration of the Este line in the marriage of Ruggiero and Bradamante—the forty-six–canto poem in octaves (*ottave*) is richly imbued with the structural and thematic elements of Arthurian romance. Borrowing from Italian versions of Arthurian literature—in particular the *Vita di Merlino*, *Palamedes, Tristan,* the *Tavola Ritonda*, and the Prose *Lancelot*—the poem centers on the vagaries and vicissitudes of numerous victims of love, using the motif to underscore the multifaceted nature of human emotions and as a metaphor for the dichotomy between the ideals of chivalric tradition and the realities of a politically unstable Italy in the early decades of the sixteenth century. The titular hero, driven mad by a frustrated love and modeled after, among others, the lover of Iseult in the Prose *Tristan*, embarks upon a series of quests that, like those of his comrades Rinaldo and Ruggiero, reflect a personal voyage toward understanding, maturation, and, in his particular case, disillusionment. Ariosto borrows structural techniques from Arthurian tradition, especially interlace and a complex system of thematic cross-referencing. Of particular significance is the Arthurian tradition of enchantment and magic, which in Ariosto underscores the relativity and variable nature of the world. Numerous episodes derive directly from Arthurian sources in late medieval *cantari*, including Rinaldo's adventures in the Caledonian Wood (Canto IV), based on Tristan's sojourn in the Forest of Danantes; names, such as that of the heroine Ginevra, whose story in Canto IV also contains numerous Arthurian elements; and figures with magical powers, such as the Arthurian sage Merlin. [RJR]

&⁂ Ariosto, Ludovico. *Orlando Furioso*, ed. Giuseppe Campari and Angelo Ottolini. Milan: Hoepli, 1926.

Gardner, Edmund G. *The Arthurian Legend in Italian Literature.* London: Dent, 1930.

Rajna, Pio. *Le Fonti dell' "Orlando Furioso."* Florence: Sansoni, 1876, 1900.

ARMING AND DEPARTURE OF THE KNIGHTS, THE: *see* STANMORE HALL TAPESTRIES.

ARMS AND ARMOR. Though Arthurian stories abound with battles and tournaments, factual descriptions of the arms and armor used are relatively rare. To a knightly audience, these would be thoroughly familiar and not need to be explained, except under special circumstances, such as to emphasize the richness of a champion's armament.

Three such descriptions of the arming of a knight are of special interest: first, the arming of King Arthur at the eve of the battle of Badon, in Geoffrey of Monmouth's *Historia Regum Britanniae* (ca. 1135); second, the arming of Erec in borrowed armor before the Joust of the Sparrowhawk, in Chrétien de Troyes's *Erec et Enide* (ca. 1170); finally, the arming of Sir Gawain in *Sir Gawain and the Green Knight* (ca. 1400).

The armings of Erec and Gawain give accurate accounts of the armor used during the twelfth and fourteenth centuries; they also demonstrate the proper way a knight should be armed, namely from his feet upward, in order to avoid unnecessary tiring and top-heaviness. Erec's armor consists of mail leggings (*chausses*) reinforced by separately buckled-on knee cops (*genouillières*) of solid plate, a mailshirt (*hauberk*), a helmet, and a shield. The term *hauberk* (from German *Halsberge* 'neck cover'), and the detail that Enide fastens Erec's *aventail* for him, indicate that this mailshirt had a hood (*coif*) with a face-covering flap, the *aventail*, and also mail mittens in one piece with its long sleeves, which made it impossible for Erec to tie the laces of the *aventail* himself. The helmet would have been a conical steel cap with a simple noseguard; the shield would be of the almond-shaped "Norman" type, with rounded top and drawn-out lower point covering the knight's entire left side from eye to knee.

Gawain, on the other hand, is being armed in the much more complicated armor of mail (*paunce*, related to German *Panzer*) and plates developed in the second half of the fourteenth century: articulated iron shoes (*sabatouns*), shin defenses (*greaves*), knee cops (*poleyns*), and thigh defenses (*cuishes*). After these, he dons mailshirt (*byrnie*); emblazoned surcoat (*cote-armure*); and arm defenses of *vambraces* for the forearms, *cowters* for the elbows, *rerebraces* for the upper arms, and *pauldrons* for the shoulders. The last items to be put on are the sword belt; the helmet, which now has an attached mail cape (*camail* and/or *aventail*) to replace the older *coif*; and finally the armored gloves (*gauntlets*). It was understood that proper arming of a knight could be done only with the help of a squire (or an obliging damsel, as in Erec's case). When the knight was in the saddle, his shield and lance would be handed to him by his squire (French *écuyer* 'shield bearer,' from *écu* 'shield'; German *Schildknappe* 'shield boy').

In striking contrast to these two descriptions, the arming of King Arthur in Geoffrey's *Historia* is not done in contemporary arms but with "a leather jerkin [*lorica*] worthy of so great a king. On his head . . . a golden helmet with a crest carved in the shape of a dragon; and across his shoulders a circular shield called Pridwen, on which was painted the likeness of the Blessed Mary, Mother of God." These elements—leather *lorica*, dragon-crested helmet, circular shield— correspond to actual weapons found in the seventh-century ship burial of Sutton Hoo, now in the British Museum. The faithful preservation of these details over a period of at least 500 years is another clue that Geoffrey had access to some earlier source, quite possibly "a very ancient book in the British language." High-ranking officers in the Late Roman army bore portraits of their emperors on their shields, as represented on the consular diptych of the commander-in-chief Stilicho (killed in A.D. 408); the icon of the Virgin Mary on Arthur's shield was a logical alternative for a Christian commander without an emperor above him.

Geoffrey also states that, when the Romans withdrew from Britain (assumed date A.D. 410), they left behind samples of their armor and weapons as models for the Britons to copy for their self-defense (Book VI, Chapter 3). After almost four centuries of Roman occupation, the tribal military traditions of Britain had dwindled away. Former Roman magistrates became local chieftains, or even kings, and organized their followers as best as they could. The wealthier among them would have helmets (*cassis* or *galea*), and short-sleeved mailshirts (*lorica hamata*), but the shield (Latin *scutum*; Welsh *ysquit*) would have been the main defense for practically every fighting man, with the possible exception of archers, who needed both hands to draw their bows. Shields were made of half-inch-thick wooden boards, covered with glued-on leather against splitting under a heavy blow and reinforced around the rim with bronze or iron mountings. Circular or oval in shape, they had a central handgrip. To accommodate the holding hand, a hole was cut into the shield board, covered by the iron shield boss (*umbo*).

Spears, bows and arrows, and swords—the latter mostly longer (ca. three feet) versions of the Roman *gladius*—were the weapons of offense.

The King Arthur of legend is the leader of the knights of the Round Table; the "historical Arthur" is generally thought to have been a Romanized British war-leader, who revived half-forgotten Roman cavalry tactics in order to repel the hit-and-run raids of sea-borne Saxon pirates.

The last surviving muster roll of the Roman army, the *Notitia Dignitatum*, of ca. A.D. 425, shows that there was an unusual concentration of Roman cavalry in Britain. The only two active regiments of heavy-armored cavalry, *cataphractarii*, were stationed in Britain, one of them at Binchester/*Vinovia*. This was probably the *Castell Guinnion* in Nennius's Battle List (ca. A.D. 800). In this list of Arthur's twelve victories over the Saxons, most battle sites are at rivers, where pirate raids were to be expected, but three of them are places that were garrisons of Roman heavy cavalry. One of them, *Bregomion*, is probably Ribchester/*Bremetennacum*, the settlement of the *cuneus veteranorum Sarmatorum*, the troop of Sarmatian veterans. The Sarmatians were horse nomads from the eastern steppes; in A.D. 175 Emperor Marcus Aurelius had 5,500 of them transferred from Pannonia, today's Hungary, to northern Britain to fight the Picts. They were the first heavy-armored cavalry known to western Europe, with body armor of horn or metal scales and similar armor for their horses. Their helmets were *spangenhelms*, built from bronze straps and iron filling plates. Their equipment was in fact the model for the *cataphractarii* of the Late Roman and Byzantine armies. They carried long lances (*kontus*) and long double-edged swords; the swords were often worn in pairs, one on either hip. Their battle standard was a windsock-like dragon on a pole, and their tribal god of war was worshiped as a naked sword planted upright in the ground or a platform. The Sarmatians in Britain were attached as auxiliaries to the Sixth Legion; its *praefectus* was a certain Lucius Artorius Castus, who had served in

13

ARMS AND ARMOR

3 Arms and armor (drawings by Helmut Nickel).

British weapons (left): spear, shield, sword of gladius type

Germanic weapons (right): ango, shield, long axe, two swords, francisca, scramasax, seax with scabbard.

Saxon and British warriors.

"Barbarian" armor in Late Roman style, from ship burial of Sutton Hoo (ca. seventh century).

Erec and Enide (ca. 1170).

Gawain arming (ca. 1370).

Pannonia earlier in his career. It is thinkable that his name, like Caesar's, became a title among the Sarmatian troopers. After 250 years in Britain, they were still referred to as the Sarmatian veterans, which indicates that they must have preserved their tribal identity reasonably intact. When the regular army withdrew from Britain, the Sarmatian veterans, who had been settled in Ribchester to guard the Lancashire coast against Irish pirates, seem to have stayed. They might have become the cavalry of the "historical Arthur," when worse danger threatened from the Saxons. (See "The Sarmatian Connection," by C. Scott Littleton and Ann C. Thomas, in *Journal of American Folklore*, 1978.)

Archaeological evidence for Romano-British arms is scarce. The Britons were Christians, who did not believe in warlike gravegoods as did the Saxons. The latter were pagans who could look forward to a warrior's afterlife in Valhalla till Ragnarök. The main defense of a Saxon thegn was a round shield, of basically the same construction as the British type, though Saxon shields could have an extra carrying sling for the forearm; they also could have sharply pointed bosses to be used as effective weapons in counterattack. Body armor consisted of mailshirts, produced in the formerly Roman industrial centers of the Rhinelands, and *spangenhelms*, the "barbarian" helmet type, introduced into central Europe by eastern nomads, such as Sarmatians, Alani, and Huns. A particularly splendid type of *spangenhelm* seems to have been made at the court workshop of the Ostrogothic kings of Italy, at Ravenna, and distributed all over continental Europe, probably as diplomatic presents. Anglo-Saxon *spangenhelms* were distinguished by having crests, either dragon (Sutton Hoo helmet) or boar figurines (Benty Grange helmet); visor masks (*grim*) either covered the entire face or were frames around eyes and nose. However, not a single Germanic (or Viking) helmet with horns or wings has been found so far, though there are pre-Roman British and Gaulish horned helmets! The name of the Saxons is derived from *seax*, a machete-like long-knife, both tool and weapon; its sword-length version was the *scramasax* ("wound-knife"). The name of the Angles is probably related to *ango*, a barbed throwing spear or harpoon. A much-favored weapon that also was a handy tool on shipboard was the battle-axe, which also gave name to a tribe of the continental Saxons, the Longobards ("Long-axes"). The Franks were feared for their short-handled throwing axes, the *francisca*. The most treasured of weapons of a Germanic warrior was the sword (*spatha*); beautifully pattern-welded blades, whose surface markings evoked comparisons with dragon skin or twisting snakes, were produced in the Rhinelands, where mythical smiths, such as Wayland or Regin, to whom Siegfried once was apprenticed, were located, and where the cutlery center of Solingen still flourishes. Famous swords were given personal names; *Balmung* = Siegfried's sword, *Mimung* and *Nagelring* = products of Wayland, *Durendal* = Roland's sword, and of course Arthur's *Excalibur/Caliburnus*. (The intricate cross-cultural relations of the Migration Period and the so-called Dark Ages are shown in these sword names: *Balmung* is probably related to *Avalon*, where Geoffrey has Arthur's *Caliburnus* forged, whose name is derived from Latin *chalybs* 'steel,' which in turn comes from the *Kalybes*, a Sarmatian tribe of smiths in the Caucasus.) To enhance the value of a cherished sword, the maker richly mounted its hilt and scabbard in silver and gold. Ritual deposits of swords in sacred lakes are known from the province Angeln, the homeland of the Angles, at the Danish-German border. The motif of the Sword in the Lake might have its historical background in remembered occasions, when a priestess in charge of such a sacred lake would have retrieved a sword for a champion, to be returned after the hero's death. (*See also* HERALDRY; ROUND TABLES; TOURNAMENT BOOKS.) [HN]

Gamber, Ortwin. "Some Notes on the Sutton Hoo Military Equipment." *Journal of the Arms and Armour Society*, 10 (December 1982), 208–16.

Nickel, Helmut. "About Arms and Armor in the Age of Arthur." *Avalon to Camelot*, 1 (Fall 1983), 19–21.

Norman, A.V.B., and Don Pottinger. *Warrior to Soldier: English Weapons and Warfare, 449–1660.* London: Weidenfeld and Nicolson, 1966.

Robinson, H. Russell, and Ronald Embleton. *What the Soldiers Wore on Hadrian's Wall.* Newcastle-upon-Tyne: Graham, 1976.

Simkins, Michael, and Ronald Embleton. *The Roman Army from Hadrian to Constantine.* London: Osprey, 1979.

Wise, Terence. *Saxon, Viking and Norman.* London: Osprey, 1979.

ARMSTEAD, H. H.: *see* QUEEN'S ROBING ROOM.

ARNOLD, MATTHEW (1822–1888), wrote the first English modernization of the Tristan story, *Tristram and Iseult* (1852). His chief source was Dunlop's *History of Prose Fiction* (1814), which recounted Tristan's birth, voyage to Ireland disguised as a harper, wooing of Iseult for Mark, drinking of the love potion, secret meetings, marriage to Iseult of Brittany (Iseult of the White Hands), and deathbed reunion with Queen Iseult. From Southey's Malory, Arnold took the form of the hero's name, the Roman Wars episode (in which Malory's Tristram did not participate), and the phrase "passing weary" to describe Vivian's attitude to Merlin. The story of Merlin and Vivian came from Villemarqué's "Visite au Tombeau de Merlin" (*Revue de Paris*, 1837). Arnold's theme is the destructive power of love. He also seeks to evoke the ethos of Celtic poetry as defined in *On the Study of Celtic Literature* (1867): "the magical charm of nature" and the passionate melancholy of the characters' "adverse destiny."

In Part I, "Tristram" (373 lines of predominantly trochaic tetrameter), the hero in a delirious dream recalls his life with Iseult of Ireland, while his wife, "the sweetest Christian soul alive," watches by his bed. Part II, "Iseult of Ireland" (193 lines), consists of a rhapsodic duet in quatrains as the lovers are reunited. The exchange is soon terminated by their deaths. Part III, "Iseult of Brittany" (224 lines in heroic couplets), takes place a year later, after the lovers have been buried at Tintagel. The widowed Iseult tells her children (Arnold's addition) "an old world Breton history," the story of Merlin's beguilement. For the sexually frustrated heroine, Vivian's ability to enslave Merlin may be a wish-fulfilling dream of female power. Her patient suffering, loneliness, and social isolation represent a characteristic Arnoldian mode. [MAW]

≈ Arnold, Matthew. *The Poetical Works of Matthew Arnold*, ed. C.B. Tinker and H.F. Lowry. London: Oxford University Press, 1960.

Buckler, William E. *On the Poetry of Matthew Arnold: Essays in Critical Reconstruction*. New York: New York University Press, 1982.

ART: *see* DECORATIVE ARTS (MEDIEVAL); VISUAL ARTS.

ARTHOUR AND MERLIN, the earliest English verse romance about Merlin. It emphasizes his role as Arthur's mage, with only fleeting references to his connection with the Holy Grail. Drawn from a chronicle of Arthur's career and the French Vulgate Cycle, and written as early as the middle or third quarter of the thirteenth century, the poem (ca. 9,900 lines) concerns the miraculous birth of Merlin, his aid to Uther Pendragon, the founding of the Round Table, and his great service to the young King Arthur.

A later rendition of this romance, the so-called "jüngere version" (ca. 2,000 lines) contained in four varying fifteenth-century manuscripts, recounts the history only up until the death of Pendragon, Uther's brother, so that it concentrates on Merlin, the mage, and his pre-Arthurian activities. There is also an interesting colophon giving Glastonbury as the burial site for Pendragon, whereas in the earlier version both Pendragon and Uther are buried at Stonehenge. The poem offers an interesting contrast with the two later English translations of the Merlin saga, Lovelich's *Merlin* and the Prose *Merlin*, both of which concern Merlin's role as the prophet of the Holy Grail. An English chapbook version, *A Lytel Treatyse of þe Byrth and Prophecye of Marlyn*, appeared in 1510. [VML]

≈ Kölbing, Eugen, ed. *Arthour and Merlin*. Heilbronn: Henniger, 1890.

Ackerman, R.W. "English Rimed and Prose Romances." In *Arthurian Literature in the Middle Ages*, ed. Roger Sherman Loomis. Oxford: Clarendon, 1959, pp. 485–86.

ARTHUR, an early fifteenth-century English verse chronicle (642 lines), is an interpolation in a Latin chronicle of the kings of Britain found in Longleat MS 55. Based upon some version of Wace's *Brut*, it tells of Arthur's war against the Romans. Details not in known versions of Wace include Arthur's burial at Glastonbury and the inscription on Arthur's tomb ("Hic jacet Arthurus, rex quondam rexque futurus"), which are also found in the Thornton Manuscript of the Alliterative *Morte Arthure* and in Malory's *Morte Darthur*. [EDK]

≈ Furnivall, Frederick J., ed. *Arthur*. London: Oxford University Press, 1864.

Finlayson, J. "The Source of 'Arthur,' an Early Fifteenth-Century Verse Chronicle." *Notes and Queries*, n.s., 7 (1960), 46–47.

Göller, K. H. *König Arthur in der englischen Literatur des späten Mittelalters*. Göttingen: Vandenhoeck and Ruprecht, 1963, pp. 57–66.

ARTHUR, CHARACTER OF. Although attempts to identify the historical Arthur continue, the King is largely a creation of romance, and it is hardly surprising that his character changes and grows and that he presents occasional inconsistent traits from text to text. In pseudo-chronicles (e.g., Wace), the depiction is understandably that of a military leader, since the legend of Arthur was just being forged and developed and since his prestige would henceforth be based in large part on his having subjugated much of the world and imposed himself as its leader. Even in such texts, however, Arthur's concern for peace and justice balances his warlike traits; it is in Wace that, having brought an extended period of peace to the world, he establishes the Round Table to promote equality and harmony.

Much of Arthurian literature is only marginally, if at all, about Arthur. In the course of the Middle Ages, emphasis shifts quickly to Lancelot and Guenevere, to Perceval, Galahad, or Gawain, to Tristan and Isolde. However, in Celtic material more than in French or other romances, Arthur does often play the central and dominant role, undertaking wars, hunts, and quests, succeeding thereby in gaining both glory and territory for himself. At the same time, in works like *Culhwch and Olwen*, Arthur (although a glorious and famous king) is closely associated with magic and the supernatural: the Welsh Arthur, not surprisingly, participates extensively in the Celtic mythological tradition.

Beyond the chronicles, the Celtic material, and certain other texts (e.g., the Middle English works), the emphasis on Arthur as warrior and conqueror is reduced. Romance authors generally abandon interest in large-scale wars in favor of more localized battles, tourneys, and (especially) the presentation of Arthur as sovereign and patriarch rather than warrior. He is most consistently presented as wise, generous, and magnanimous. He is kind and forgiving, trustworthy and loyal. On the other hand, he is sometimes seen as indecisive or, conversely, petulant and stubborn, even when his own interests or those of the court may be compromised. For example, in Chrétien de Troyes's *Erec et Enide* Arthur insists on conducting the hunt for the white stag, even though he is told—and does not appear to doubt—that the hunt will inevitably lead to dissension and trouble at court.

Arthur may act hastily, but he rarely reacts in anger, other than righteous indignation. An exception is offered by the Alliterative *Morte*, but most often he is presented as even-tempered to the point of blandness. In the *Mort Artu*, we may be startled by an absence of outrage when Arthur is told of Lancelot's sin with Guenevere: he becomes pale, comments that all this is *merveilles*, and lapses into silence. Of course, his passivity may be less a function of his traditional character than of the *Mort Artu* poet's individual presentation—the King will react with near indifference even to the Queen's death—but in most texts he is shown to be even-tempered, even-handed, and calm.

The King appears on occasion to be a somewhat feeble patriarch. In Chrétien's *Yvain*, for example, Arthur is unable to stay awake after a feast; he retires to the Queen's chamber for a nap, causing puzzlement and grumbling on the part of his knights. The essential fact here and in other texts, however, is that his prestige is never—or almost never—compromised by his personal weaknesses. Whether he is nodding off at awkward moments, suffering fools (like Kay) a bit too gladly, or risking the harmony of the court by commanding everyone to play his white-stag game, his authority and glory remain intact. Indeed, they remain intact even when the ethic and efficacy of the Arthurian court itself are questioned. (It should be noted that occasional works, such as Robert Biket's *Lai du cor* and other settings of chastity tests, often indulge in humor at Arthur's expense; this is, however, a minority view of the King.)

As Rosemary Morris notes, Arthur was an ideal Christian hero, and in various texts, such as *Culhwch and Olwen*, he is presented as God's elect. In some works that recount the withdrawal of the Sword in the Stone, it is by that phenomenon that God chooses Arthur as king. Yet, as early as Chrétien, authors begin to hint that the court and its kind of chivalry are ineffective or flawed ideals. Once the Grail quest becomes a preoccupation of Chrétien and his successors, the writers imply—and sometimes indicate explicitly—that the quest can be accomplished only by a renunciation of Arthurian chivalry and adherence to a higher code.

Nevertheless, it is only by implication (however clear) that Arthur is himself diminished, and within the context of his court and world he remains respected and revered. It appears that there are in a sense two Arthurs: one of them is a human being (illustrious, wise, but quite human nonetheless); the other is an image, identified with the ideals of Camelot and the Round Table. The natural, if rare, frailties of the human king seldom compromise the image, even when the distinction between the two widens progressively, and the most fascinating settings of the Arthurian legend are often those that show Arthur as human and imperfect.

If later authors have not often made fundamental changes in the character of Arthur, they have in a number of cases concentrated more heavily on one side of that character than on the other. Some accounts have deified him and thereby robbed him of most of his humanity, but other writers have success-fully resisted that temptation, presenting Arthur as subject to doubts, fears, and jealousies. Among many notable treatments of the monarch, we might conclude with two. Thomas Berger comically traces Arthur's development from a naïve youth (and a pompous one, who reacts to the news that he will be king by immediately adopting the royal "we") to a great ruler who nonethe-less retains his human traits; and T.H. White shows us, far better than most writers, an Arthur who is at the end an old man, feeble and exhausted, sad and near despair, an old man sustained—but barely—by hope. [NJL]

  Morris, Rosemary. *The Character of King Arthur in Medieval Literature.* Cambridge: Boydell and Brewer, 1982.

  Thompson, Raymond H. *The Return from Avalon: A Study of the Arthurian Legend in Modern Fiction.* Westport, Conn.: Greenwood, 1985.

ARTHUR, ORIGINS OF LEGEND. Though the legend of Arthur is a phenomenon of history, taking shape over a roughly known period, historical research alone fails to establish how it began. With (for example) Alexander and Charlemagne, who likewise inspired medieval romance, history gives a simple answer: the hero was a real person, with a documented career. The question "Was Arthur a real person?" cannot be answered in the same direct manner. His reality is not proved, or for that matter disproved, by the strictly historical evidence. Barring some new discovery, the only way to arrive at even a cautious conclusion is to appraise this in conjunction with data of other types.

A manifest obstacle is that the medieval authors who developed the Matter of Britain had little interest in authenticity. They were not writing historical fiction in the modern sense. Like all medieval storytelling based on ancient material, Arthurian romance updated it, portraying kingship, warfare, costume, and much else in contemporary terms, however idealized and fantasized, and giving pride of place to themes of contemporary interest, such as chivalry and courtly love. There is no direct route from the romances back to any underlying reality. Geoffrey of Monmouth, who prepared the ground by creating Arthur's official biography, is an author of a different kind: he undoubtedly *uses* history and is somewhat closer to whatever facts there may be. But he, too, updates, as in his description of Arthur's court at Caerleon, and where he can be checked, as in his version of the preceding Roman period, his fictionalization is so palpable as to deprive him of any credit as a historian. Nothing he says can be trusted by itself as a statement of fact.

Most investigators who have sought a "historical Arthur" by historical methods have dismissed Geoffrey and the romancers from any consideration at all. That exclusion has led in practice to another. It is assumed that there can be no evidence directly concerning Arthur outside Britain, because his activities overseas, however important and circumstantial Geoffrey and some romancers make them, are part of the literary fantasy. (The possibility of Breton information, handed down from emigrant Britons in Arthur's time, has generally been ignored.) Within the tacitly agreed limits, the evidence is twofold. First, there is a miscellany of data, almost entirely of Welsh provenance, showing the nature of the tradition before Geoffrey. Second, there is another body of data, augmented by archaeology, from which a vague picture can be formed of the course of events in Britain during the fifth and sixth centuries A.D., when Arthur supposedly lived. Historians have tried to evaluate the former and bring it into relation with the latter.

An early Welsh allusion occurs in the *Gododdin* series of poems, composed toward 600 and ascribed to the northern bard Aneirin. The poems commemorate the fallen in a battle against the Angles at *Catraeth*, probably Catterick in Yorkshire. Arthur is mentioned in passing as proverbial for martial prowess. It is not implied that he was one of the northern warriors himself, or contemporary with them. The line may be an interpolation, but no cogent reason exists for thinking so, and even if it is it must still be quite early. Other poems, in the so-called Book of Taliesin and the Black Book of Carmarthen, also name Arthur as a famous warrior and refer to a band of followers. The "Stanzas of the Graves" say his grave is a mystery, and in this connection a Cornish anecdote told by Hermann of Tournai attests a folk-belief in his immortality. The cryptic Welsh verses entitled *The Spoils of Annwfn* involve him and his followers in an otherworld quest, a possible Celtic antecedent of the quest of the Grail.

Such bardic and folkloric items, though not numerous in the early centuries, demonstrate a rooted tradition that the Welsh developed from older materials—perhaps from heroic lays current among their forebears, the Celtic inhabitants of Britain before the Saxon ascendancy. Arthur's appearances in several fabulous "Lives" of Welsh saints also make him a military figure, with troops at his command and sometimes a royal title, if a rather uncertain one. The Triads, and the *Mabinogion* tale *Culhwch and Olwen*, show that by the late eleventh century a Welsh Arthurian saga had grown up portraying him as a formidable warrior-prince with a large entourage comprising historical, quasi-historical, and purely fantastic characters.

While these poems and stories may be thought to give a cumulative impression of a real original, a great man remembered and glorified, the factual element in them must be scanty. But Wales supplies two Latin texts giving what looks like substantiation. These are the ninth-century *Historia Brittonum*, ascribed to Nennius, and the tenth-century *Annales Cambriae*. The former speaks of Arthur as *dux bellorum*, the war-leader of the kings of the Britons, and lists twelve battles that he won against the Saxons and probably their Pictish allies. The twelfth battle is Badon, a major victory attested by Gildas much earlier, though Gildas does not name the Britons' commander. The *Annales* also refer to Badon and add the "strife of Camlann" in which Arthur fell, together with Medraut (Mordred).

Some historians have accepted Nennius and the *Annales* as more or less reliable here. The chief justification for doing so is plausibility. The other body of data, on the post-Roman situation in general, suggests that an Arthur who led antibarbarian resistance can at least be credibly fitted in. Britain was separated from the Empire in 410 and passed into a long phase of transition and trouble. Though the wilder jeremiads of Gildas can be discounted, there is no good reason to doubt that Saxon auxiliaries stationed in Britain did revolt toward the middle of the fifth century; that a period of widespread raiding, which involved Picts as well, was followed by a respite and partial British recovery; that, while subsequent Saxon land-taking progressed without conflict in many places, a fluctuating warfare continued for years in others; and that in the first half of the sixth century, after the British success at Badon, all major Saxon encroachment ceased for a time. Alone among Rome's provincials, the Britons became self-governing before the barbarians moved in, fought back when they did, and more than once appeared to have halted their advance. This pattern of rescue-from-disaster would accord with Arthur's career in Nennius. As British war-leader, he could have been, at some crucial stage, the principal rescuer. For this reason, the Britons' resurgence has been described as the "Arthurian Fact," meaning the fact of history that he came to symbolize, whether he existed or not.

Scholars favoring the view that he did exist, on the basis of the Welsh matter, made various suggestions during the 1930s and decades ensuing. R.G. Collingwood envisaged Arthur as holding the Late Roman military office of *Comes Britanniarum*, Count of the Britains, and employing cavalry to defeat the pedestrian Saxons. The cavalry theory has outlived Collingwood's presentation of it. Much of its original force depended on the assumption that all the battles in Nennius's list were genuine, the inference being that, as they are apparently widely scattered, Arthur must have been mobile and ubiquitous. Kenneth Jackson, while rejecting most of Collingwood's thesis, found likely locations for some of the battles, which confirmed that Arthur's activities were believed to have ranged far and wide. Jackson regarded him as probably though not certainly real; if real, he was a "supreme British commander of genius" active principally in southern Britain. Leslie Alcock, having shown that Cadbury Castle (allegedly Camelot) was reoccupied and refortified in about the right period, interpreted Arthur much as Jackson did and proposed Cadbury as a base from which he operated. During this phase of scholarship, his royal status was usually regarded as a product of legend, but in 1973 John Morris presented him as a sort of emperor.

Four years later, the use of the Welsh matter as historical evidence was crushingly criticized by David Dumville, and the pursuit of Arthur along this line came to a virtual halt. Alcock retired into agnosticism. The documents, it must be acknowledged, are inadequate. They may contain factual material, but they are insufficient for proof or even convincing reconstruction. They supply no reference to Arthur that comes anywhere near to being contemporary, except perhaps the *Gododdin* line, and that is uncertain and uninformative. They offer or imply hopelessly inconsistent dates for him, spreading him out, as an active campaigner, over a stretch of eighty or ninety years. They never give a chronological fix: that is, they never synchronize him with known history outside Britain. Moreover, not a single Welsh text makes a plain historical statement about him, acceptable as free from legend. Even Nennius's fairly sober account is called in question by the assertion that Arthur singlehandedly slew 960 enemies at Badon, a feat that shows him to be already legendary.

One or two historians have picked out the Camlann entry in the *Annales* as a solitary scrap of firm evidence. But it was written in the tenth century; it cannot be related to known history; and the late date that it gives, 539, can hardly be reconciled with the rest of Arthur's quasi-historical record. The only logical way to handle it would be to drop the rest altogether and postulate an Arthur doing nothing of note at all but perish at Camlann fighting another Briton. That step has occasionally been taken. But it seems a *reductio ad absurdum*, implying that the whole Arthurian legend grew round a petty chief—one among dozens—with no victories to his credit, no role in the struggle against the Saxons, and an inglorious exit. To confine Arthur to Camlann merely replaces one mystery with another.

The failure of the purely historical approach is proved in the end by the contradictions among those who have attempted it. Some have made Arthur a local leader, some a national one. Some have put him in the fifth century, some around the beginning of the sixth, some, by a radical reinterpretation, toward the end of it. N.K. Chadwick even hazarded the notion—if noncommittally— that the only original Arthur was a Scottish prince in Argyll, who was probably born about 570. Fully as daunting are the disagreements over Arthur's home territory. An influential school of thought has favored the north, mainly on the ground that the oldest poetic allusions to him are northern. But there need not be more in this than the fact that the first memorable poets in Welsh happened to be northerners. Opponents have retorted that Arthur is far more believable as a leader in the south, where Saxons were numerous and aggressive, and have pointed out that, while stories of him occur widely, the only ones identifying a birthplace, a headquarters, or a grave all belong to Cornwall and Somerset.

In the midst of these perplexities, one fact does emerge, the significance of Arthur's name. It is the Welsh form of the Roman name Artorius, and clearly suggests a real person born in the fifth century, when the custom of giving children Roman names still flourished among the Britons. Furthermore, a revival of this particular name late in the sixth century, when the custom in general was almost defunct, strongly hints that, somewhat earlier, an Arthur had flourished who had become a national hero.

The name tells against the conjecture, which the character of the Welsh matter has sometimes encouraged, that Arthur is not a man but a myth: perhaps a Celtic god, euhemerized. Plainly, such a figure is not likely to have borne a Roman name, and a human one at that. Advocates of the myth theory have failed to find a god called Artorius or to give "Arthur" a viable alternative etymology. Arthur's saga certainly involved touches of what may be described as mythification—he may, for instance, owe something to Bran— but the notion of him as wholly mythical or divine has proved unsustainable. Would-be reconstructions by Raglan, Darrah, and others are more completely incompatible than their historical counterparts. No one who definitely denies Arthur has succeeded in accounting for the facts without him. Most followers of the long debate have been inclined, after all, to conclude that there is a real person lurking somewhere. Despite the difficulties, it is easier on balance to believe that he did exist than that he did not.

Given such an outcome—only barely positive and in the eyes of skeptics not even that—an issue that arises is whether the starting point might be reached by some other path. If so, the figure of Arthur might come into better focus, and the ostensibly historical data might be better assessed. The question "Was he a real person?" leads to no certain answer, but the question "How did his legend originate, what facts is it rooted in?" can broaden the scope of the inquiry by taking the literary process into account, with the hope of attaining fresh historical insight by way of it. In particular, this question brings Geoffrey of Monmouth back into the discussion. Rightly ruled out as a historian, he can return as an imaginative writer who uses history. The nature of the history that he uses is a proper subject to explore.

It might be supposed that this exploration can shed no further light, because, when Geoffrey wrote of Arthur, he merely adopted him from the Welsh and inflated the Welsh material already reviewed. That is one frequent assumption; another is that his notorious claim to have drawn on an additional work, an "ancient book in the British language," is bogus. Yet, whether or not he had an ancient book, the assumption about his sources is questionable. The Arthur story contrasts eloquently with other parts of the text. His narrative of the villain Vortigern is indeed purely Welsh, an expansion of Nennius. But his narrative of the hero Arthur is a great deal more. Welsh quasi-historical matter underlies only about one-fifth of it. The rest is quite different in substance and atmosphere, and different also from the Welsh Arthur saga, which he hardly seems to know. The anti-Saxon campaign, which for Nennius is the whole point, is not central but introductory. Promoting Arthur to a kingship without parallel, Geoffrey devotes half the story of his reign to embroilments with the Empire and warfare in Gaul, of which the Welsh give no hint.

Also, Geoffrey transforms the denouement. When he first foreshadows Arthur's career, in the *Prophetiae Merlini*, he seems to picture it as ending in Gaul. When he comes to compose the actual narrative, he does bring in the Welsh tradition, returning Arthur to Britain to fall at Camlann. But, in defiance of the Welsh, he makes Mordred a traitorous deputy ruler who intrigues with barbarians. The disaster is still intertwined with the Gallic warfare, and Arthur's final destination is *Insula Avallonis*, which does not precisely Latinize the Welsh *Avallach* but does echo the name of a real place in Burgundy—Avallon.

As remarked, since Arthur's activities overseas have normally been dismissed as invention, it has been taken for granted that no relevant historical sources exist outside Britain. But Geoffrey's account of the Gallic warfare suggests that this is another assumption that may fairly be challenged. In view of the climactic importance he gives it, and the lack of any Welsh prototype, it is reasonable to wonder whether he found materials for it in continental records. Vital here are his indications of date. Curiously, he supplies what the Welsh matter never does, a chronological fix. Arthur's Gallic campaigning occurs (as he says three times) in the reign of Leo, clearly the eastern emperor Leo I, who reigned from 457 to 474. Similar if less certain clues narrow the range to 468–74 and may even reduce it to 469–70. This agrees with the observation of Sharon Turner, as long ago as 1799, that Geoffrey's Arthur is based—here at least—on the "king of the Britons" called Riothamus who led a British army through Gaul at exactly that time, playing a part in the last agonies of the western Empire.

Other features of his career, pieced together from Jordanes, Sidonius, and Gregory of Tours, confirm Geoffrey's use of it and the likelihood of a lost historical source (even an "ancient book") assembling the scattered details. Riothamus advanced to the neighborhood of Burgundy. He was betrayed by a deputy ruler who treated with barbarian enemies. He is last located in Gaul among the Burgundians. He disappears after a fatal battle with no recorded death. The line of his retreat shows him moving in the direction of the actual

Avallon. All these themes are introduced in Geoffrey's account of Arthur, and so, if garbled, are several contemporary names besides Leo's. While the politics of the war are different, its true character is still vestigially visible.

Riothamus means "supreme king" or "supremely royal" and was probably a title or honorific applied to a British high king, so that the personal name of the man thus styled is unknown. There are signs that, in fictionalizing him under the name of Arthur and implying his identity with the war-leader of the Welsh, Geoffrey was not indulging in fancy without precedent. The author of the Breton *Legend of St. Goeznovius* apparently refers to the same king and calls him Arthur, and at least five chroniclers give dates and particulars for Arthur, not derived from Geoffrey, that point the same way. Credibly, "Arthur" (Artorius) was Riothamus's name or at any rate was supposed to have been his name long before Geoffrey, who used a source, probably Breton, affirming the identity.

Riothamus existed, and therefore supplies a point of origin for at least part of the legend, the Gallic part. The further question is whether the Welsh tradition requires a separate Arthur-figure, real or fictitious, or whether, as Geoffrey and others would imply, Riothamus-called-Arthur could account for this, too. Any answer must be speculative, since nothing is known of his activities in Britain before he shipped his army to Gaul. However, in the situation of the 450s and 460s he could have fought the Britons' enemies at all the more-or-less identified places on Nennius's list. The most relevant archaeological site is Cadbury-Camelot, and on the basis of Alcock's revised assessment (1982) Riothamus is the only documented person who qualifies as its royal refortifier.

As Arthur-Riothamus (to coin a term), hypothetically high king in succession to Vortigern, he is an arguable original for the insular legend as well as the continental. The other military leader, Ambrosius, might have been a general in his service while he reigned in Britain and regent during his absence abroad. More important to the case than guesswork like this is the question whether a fifth-century high king could have been transformed by bards and storytellers into the Arthur of the Welsh, who is less clearly royal and, though undatable, is sometimes associated with persons belonging to the sixth century. The parallel here might be the treatment by German minstrels of Theodoric, the great Gothic king of Italy, who in the *Nibelungenlied* is reduced to the warlike noble Dietrich of Bern and made anachronistically a companion of Attila. On this showing, Geoffrey reunited a figure who had been split up, though the result was a literary creation, not a reinstatement of historical truth.

If the question "Was Arthur a real person?" is pressed, a defensible answer would be: "The Arthur of Geoffrey and the romancers is a legend, but he has a real original, the British high king who went to Gaul." The feasibility of regarding this man as the *only* original must remain an open question. King Arthur may be a composite like Merlin. Certainly, Riothamus, who fades from the scene about 470, cannot explain the association of Arthur with Badon and Camlann. He can explain another seeming anomaly, the date 542, which

Geoffrey gives for Arthur's passing, because recognized processes of error could have derived it from 470. But Badon and Camlann might be thought to demand a second Arthur-figure. This, however, is far from definite. To judge from a Welsh poem about a battle at *Llongborth* (Portchester?), a military body called Arthur's Men existed, or was believed to have existed, independently of his presence and perhaps after his departure. Poetic allusions to Arthur's Men at Badon, Camlann, and indeed other battles, might have been misconstrued as implying that Arthur was there in person: a misconstruction that is demonstrably possible, because it has been laid on the Llongborth poem itself. Obviously, this is only one of many problems remaining unsolved. (*See also* CHRONICLES, ARTHUR IN; *GOEZNOVIUS, LEGEND OF ST.*; LEO I; LUCIUS; RIOTHAMUS; SCHOLARSHIP, MODERN ARTHURIAN; SULPICIUS.) [GA]

Alcock, Leslie. *Arthur's Britain*. London: Penguin, 1971.

Ashe, Geoffrey. "A Certain Very Ancient Book." *Speculum*, 56 (April 1981), 301–23.

——— . *The Discovery of King Arthur*. New York: Doubleday, 1985.

Chambers, E.K. *Arthur of Britain*. London: Sidgwick and Jackson, 1927.

Collingwood, R. G., and J.N.L. Myres. *Roman Britain and the English Settlements*. London and New York: Oxford University Press, 1937.

Dumville, David. "Sub-Roman Britain: History and Legend." *History*, 62 (1977), 173–92.

Jackson, Kenneth Hurlstone. Chapters 1 and 2. In *Arthurian Literature in the Middle Ages*, ed. Roger Sherman Loomis. Oxford: Clarendon, 1959.

Morris, John. *The Age of Arthur*. New York: Scribner, 1973.

ARTHUR, A TRAGEDY: see BINYON, LAURENCE.

ARTHUR AND GORLAGON, Latin prose, whose extant text dates from the early fourteenth century. Arthur's queen tells him that he does not know the heart, nature, or ways of women. Challenged by her, Arthur goes on a quest for the answer, an answer that Gorlagon gives him by telling the story of a king (Gorlagon himself) who is turned into a werewolf by his lecherous, traitorous wife. Analogues for the story of the werewolf exist in Celtic and in oriental folktales. [MLD]

Kittredge, G.L., ed. *Arthur and Gorlagon. Harvard Studies and Notes in Philology and Literature*, 8 (1903), 149–273.

ARTHUR MASTER: *see* MODENA ARCHIVOLT.

ARTHUR, MONARCH OF THE BRITONS, A TRAGEDY: see HILTON, WILLIAM.

ARTHUR OF LITTLE BRITAIN. The hero of this sixteenth-century prose translation by Sir John Bourchier, Lord Berners, of the French romance *Artus de la Petite Bretagne* is the son of the Duke of Brittany. The best knight in the world, Arthur demonstrates his prowess in feats of arms and encounters with marvelous creatures. He ends the enchantments of the Port Noire and wins the hand of the fair Florence, daughter of King Emendus. [JN]

  Utterson, E.V., ed. *The History of the Valiant King Arthur of Little Britain*. London: White, Cochrane, 1814.

ARTHUR OF THE BRITONS: *see* TELEVISION SERIES.

ARTHUR, OR THE NORTHERN ENCHANTMENT IN SEVEN BOOKS: *see* HOLE, RICHARD.

ARTHUR REX: *see* BERGER, THOMAS.

ARTHURIAD, THE: *see* BADGER, JOHN D'ARCY.

ARTHURIAN REVIVAL. The renewed interest in Arthurian literature in the early nineteenth century did not significantly affect the visual arts until the reign of Queen Victoria. The Arthurian Revival in the arts was in fact a Victorian phenomenon, built upon the ideas and sensibilities of the Gothic Revival but endowed with the high moral values and modernized chivalric ideals of the subsequent era. The course of the Arthurian Revival followed Victorian history, flowering shortly after the coronation, developing through the reign, and waning at the end of the epoch. In this way, the Arthurian Revival reflected the rise and decline of the idealism of the Victorian era.

After centuries of neglect, the Arthurian legend was introduced into the repertoire of the British painter as a patriotic allegory. In 1848, the government, upon the suggestion of Prince Albert, requested that William Dyce design and execute a program of frescoes based on the Arthurian legend in the Queen's Robing Room in the new palace at Westminster. Using Malory as his text, Dyce personified the ideal qualities of British manhood in the heroes of the legend, and his moral stance foreshadowed Tennyson's interpretation in the *Idylls of the King*. The frescoes provided the absent prototype, both in heroic form and didactic interpretation, that endured through the course of the Revival.

The Robing Room frescoes stimulated wide interest in Arthurian iconography in the 1850s. The Pre-Raphaelites, already drawn to the poetry of Tennyson, addressed the new subject with energy and ingenuity. Tennyson's influence was in ascendance, and the Moxon Tennyson disseminated Arthurian interest. The first publication of the *Idylls*, in 1859, placed him on an equal footing with Malory as a literary source for the arts.

Arthurian interest came to fruition in the 1860s and 1870s; every sector of the Victorian art world embraced the expanding iconography. Academic artists, including James Archer, Joseph Noël Paton, and Thomas Woolner, followed the example set by Dyce, depicting monumental figures engaged in noble action, while the Pre-Raphaelites, notably Edward Burne-Jones, Dante Gabriel Rossetti, and Arthur Hughes, preferred poignant vignettes of love. Overall, the favored subjects included Sir Galahad, Elaine of Astolat, the adventures of Sir Lancelot, and the death of Arthur. Narrative interpretation supplanted allegorical personification, but Dyce's moral didacticism and physical types were maintained. Sources from Tennyson and Malory were freely mixed, and new subjects were invented, such as Arthurian landscape, depicting archaeological sites, and portraits of legendary *femmes fatales*, inspired by the work of Dante Gabriel Rossetti. Book illustration enjoyed enormous popularity, especially editions of Tennyson's poetry, illustrated by Gustave Doré and Julia Margaret Cameron. During these decades, the visual arts caught up with the literary tradition and enjoyed a parallel course of equal strength and invention.

During the last decades of the century, Arthurian art betrayed the decline of Victorian aspiration. Subjects implying the failure of the vision, particularly the Lady of Shalott and the death of Arthur, drew unprecedented attention, especially in the circle of Academic artists, such as John Lyston Byam Shaw, Frank Dicksee, and John William Waterhouse. The heroic figure type was replaced with an attenuated, even androgynous, form, seen in the work of Burne-Jones and especially Aubrey Beardsley. By the turn of the century, Arthurian interest was vestigial, as seen in late Pre-Raphaelite imitators like Sidney Meteyard and in decadent aesthetes like Frank Cadogan Cowper. The tragedy of World War I dealt the death blow to the last shreds of Victorian idealism and likewise to the Arthurian Revival.

The Arthurian Revival shared only the basic subject matter with the medieval development in the arts. In origin, in form, and in meaning, it was distinct. Brought into being as inspirational allegory, it maintained a moral implication and a monarchical association to the end of its course. The aesthetic was medieval only in superficial details of costume and setting; it reflected instead current taste. Visual conventions allowed the viewer to read the narrative, and a specific iconography was codified. Ultimately, even the subject matter was contemporary, incorporating new writings and revised interpretations of traditional materials. These differences distinguish the Arthurian Revival as a revival in the fullest sense, not simply imitating the past but revitalizing the tradition itself. (*See also* MEDIEVALISM.) [DNM]

ىۈ Mancoff, Debra N. *The Arthurian Revival in Victorian Painting.* 2 vols. Ann Arbor, Mich.: University Microfilms International, 1982.

ARTHURIAN TORSO: *see* LEWIS, C.S.; WILLIAMS, CHARLES.

ARTMANN, HANS CARL, a contemporary Viennese poet who is one of the most versatile and adventuresome Austrian authors. He repeatedly employs characters and storylines from Arthurian literature in his poems, such as a brief cycle written in 1953–54. The poem found at the center of this cycle, "ginevra verrät sich im schlaf und der könig antwortet ihr mit einem gedicht" ("Guinevere reveals herself while asleep, and the king responds with a poem"), shows Artmann's playful mastery of language, being composed in a form of pseudo-Cymric. [UM/WCM]

ᐒ Donnenberg, Josef, ed. *Pose, Possen und Poesie: Zum Werke Hans Carl Artmanns.* Stuttgart: Akademischer Heinz, 1981.

ARTORIUS: *see* HEATH-STUBBS, JOHN.

ARTORIUS REX: *see* GLOAG, JOHN.

ARTUS DE LA PETITE BRETAGNE, a fourteenth-century French prose romance, concerning the quest undertaken by Artus (who is not Arthur but is named after him) to liberate an enchanted castle and to win love. It was translated into English in the sixteenth century, as *Arthur of Little Britain*, by John Bourchier, Lord Berners. [NJL]

ᐒ *Le Livre du vaillant et preux chevalier Artus, fils du duc de Bretagne.* Lyon: Jean de la Fontaine, 1493.

ASHTON, WINIFRED: *see* DANE, CLEMENCE.

ASPIRATIONS OF CHIVALRY: *see* PRINCETON UNIVERSITY CHAPEL WINDOWS.

ASSERTIO INCLYTISSIMI ARTURII REGIS BRITANNIAE: *see* LELAND, JOHN.

ATRE PÉRILLEUX, L' ("The Perilous Cemetery"), an anonymous verse romance of 6,676 lines dating from about the middle of the thirteenth century. The hero is Gauvain, who sets out in search of Arthur's abducted cupbearer after Keu has unsuccessfully made the attempt. Three maidens tell Gauvain (incognito) that they are lamenting his own death at the hands of three wicked knights. Gauvain does not reveal his identity but promises to "avenge" the victim, eventually forcing one of the killers to bring him back to life. He beheads a devil who has imprisoned a damsel in a tomb in the Perilous Cemetery and then kills the knight, Escanor, who had abducted the cupbearer. Gauvain is incognito for most of the romance and is known as *cil sans nom* ("he without a name").

The author of *L'Atre périlleux* seems to have drawn on *La Vengeance Raguidel* and *Meraugis de Portlesguez*, as well as Chrétien's *Yvain* and *Lancelot*. Many of the motifs and incidents are familiar from other romances: Gauvain's false death, his incognito, his being loved for his reputation alone, his succeeding where Keu fails. *L'Atre périlleux* is a successful romance remarkable for being one of the few poems (along with the *Mériadeuc*) of which Gauvain is actually the hero rather than an important adjunct figure. [KB]

⁂ Woledge, Brian, ed. *L'Atre périlleux*. Paris: Champion, 1936.

ATWOOD, MARGARET (ELEANOR), a contemporary Canadian poet, fiction writer, and literary critic, employed the Arthurian myth in "Avalon Revisited" (1963), an early sequence of seven short poems: "The Kings," "Recollections of Vivien," "The Betrayal of Arthur," "Elaine in Arcadia," "The Rider," "The Apotheosis of Guinevere," and "The King." Reflecting a young poet's exploration of the possibilities of recreating myth, the seven impressionistic reworkings are less interesting for their vague Arthurian origin than for the theme of loneliness and isolation so prevalent in Atwood's later work. Atwood's postgraduate studies in English at Harvard University centered on Victorian literature, and the Victorian poets, especially Tennyson, stand behind these brief forays into Arthurian legend. [DS]

⁂ Atwood, Margaret Eleanor. "Avalon Revisited." *The Fiddlehead*, 55 (1963), 10–13.

AU CHÂTEAU D'ARGOL: see GRACQ, JULIEN.

AURELIUS AMBROSIUS, Arthur's uncle in Geoffrey of Monmouth. He is based on the historical figure Ambrosius Aurelianus. In Geoffrey's narrative, Aurelius and his brother Uther are sons of King Constantine. As children, they live after Constantine's death at the Breton court, where their guardians have taken them to keep them safe from the usurper Vortigern. Growing up, Aurelius becomes renowned for his generosity, truthfulness, and skill with weapons. He returns to Britain with Uther, and the Britons acknowledge him as their rightful sovereign.

Aurelius besieges Vortigern in a fort; it catches fire and Vortigern perishes. Next, he defeats the Saxons whom the usurper allowed to settle in Britain, captures their leader Hengist, and executes him for his many atrocities. He restores the churches destroyed in the Saxon ravaging. Wishing to set up a monument for 460 nobles whom Hengist massacred, he sends Uther to Ireland with Merlin to bring back a megalithic circle called the Giants' Ring. Merlin dismantles it by his arts, the stones are shipped to Britain, and he reassembles them on Salisbury Plain—the origin of Stonehenge. Aurelius does not live much longer. When he is ill, a vengeful son of Vortigern hires a Saxon to pose as a doctor and give him poison. He is buried at Stonehenge and Uther succeeds him.

The connection with the actual Ambrosius Aurelianus—or with the little that is known of him—is tenuous. Gildas, the sole early authority, speaks of him as a war-leader only. Nennius, however, calls him a king in passing, doubtless a sufficient hint. Geoffrey seems to put the whole reign in the 430s, whereas Gildas implies that Ambrosius was alive much later. Even if Geoffrey was aware of the discrepancy, it was forced on him by the invented family relationships, within an original scheme in which Arthur was a contemporary of the emperor Leo I. [GA]

&. Geoffrey of Monmouth. *Historia Regum Britanniae*, Book VI, Chapters 5 and 8; Book VIII, Chapters 1–16.

"AUSGLEICHUNG, DIE" ("The Adjustment"). Clemens Brentano's and Achim von Arnim's famous collection of folksongs *Des Knaben Wunderhorn* (1806–08) contains one Arthurian ballad, "Die Ausgleichung." The ballad is an adaptation and conflation of matter first attested in Robert Biket's *Lai du cor* and *Le Mantel mautaillié*. In the ballad, King Arthur obtains a magic mantle from a fay for the express purpose of testing Guinevere. The Queen, in turn, obtains from a dwarf a magic drinking horn to prove her husband. When King and Queen are disgraced by horn and mantle, the royal couple demand that those present also be tested. The only faithful pair are an old knight and his young wife. They turn out to be a fay and a dwarf, presumably the very ones who had provided the mantle and the drinking horn in the first place. The dwarf and fay return the mantle and horn to Arthur and Guinevere—but only after having emptied the horn and spilled a drop of the wine on the mantle. Now King and Queen and all present can make use of the objects without embarrassment: the horn does not spill and the mantle fits. The ballad ends, however, on a sour note: in the course of the years, the stain on the mantle widens and the horn rings ever more hollow. [MEK]

&. Von Arnim, Ludwig Achim, and Clemens Brentano, eds. "Die Ausgleichung." In *Des Knaben Wunderhorn: Alte deutsche Lieder*. Berlin: Rütten and Loening, 1966, Vol. 1, pp. 333–35.

AVALON. Geoffrey of Monmouth gives the name *Avalon* to an otherworldly island of Celtic mythology. In his Latin, it is *Insula Avallonis*. He mentions the place twice in the *Historia Regum Britanniae*, saying that Arthur's sword was forged there and that he was carried there after his last battle so that his wounds might be attended to. The meaning Geoffrey attaches to the name emerges in his poetic *Vita Merlini*, where he introduces the island as the *Insula Pomorum*, or "isle of apples," which, he adds, is called Fortunate. It lies vaguely over western waters and is the home of Morgan—i.e., Morgan le Fay—here depicted as a kindly enchantress heading a sisterhood of nine. In Geoffrey's poem, the bard Taliesin tells how Arthur was taken there after Camlann in a boat piloted by Barinthus, an authority on seafaring who also figures in the Irish tale of St. Brendan's Voyage. Morgan placed Arthur on a bed made of gold, examined his major wound, and undertook to heal him if he would stay in Avalon for a long time under her care.

This account is related to much older beliefs, and even realities. Geoffrey pictures Avalon as one of the Fortunate Isles of classical myth. He speaks of self-sown grain, vines that flourish without tending, and inhabitants who live for a century or more. But he combines all this with genuine Celtic motifs. The nine sisters are like the nine maidens who have custody of the magic cauldron in *The Spoils of Annwfn*. Moreover, the first-century geographer Pomponius Mela refers to a group of nine virgin priestesses actually living on the Ile de Sein off the coast of Brittany. Reputedly, they could cure the sick, foretell the future, control the weather, and assume animal disguises. Their talents resemble Morgan's as Geoffrey describes them. She herself, in her origins, is a Celtic goddess.

In Welsh, Geoffrey's island is *Ynys Avallach*. His "apple" etymology is probably right, the apples being paradisal or magical fruit like those of the Hesperides, or of Celtic otherworld regions portrayed elsewhere. However, a king called Avallach (variously spelled) occurs in Welsh genealogical and legendary matter and is supposed to rule over the island and to be Morgan's father. There may be nothing more here than coincidence followed by confusion. Another curious point is that Geoffrey's spelling of the name, whether or not he invented it, would scarcely be a true Latin equivalent for the Welsh. His *Insula Avallonis* is influenced—perhaps through Breton channels—by the name of a real place in Burgundy, Avallon. This is of Gaulish derivation and certainly does have the "apple" meaning. Geoffrey's use of it, coupled with hints in his *Prophetiae Merlini* and elsewhere, may indicate a different version of Arthur's passing.

Apart from what Geoffrey transmits himself, little is known of the way the island was regarded before him. The Irish sea-god Manannan ruled over an elysian otherworld isle to which the epithet *ablach* was given, meaning "rich in apple-trees." There is obviously some connection, but the Irish parallel remains unenlightening. Some have thought that Avalon was an abode of departed spirits. Evidence is lacking, and indeed, as the story of Arthur's sojourn develops, the whole point is that he is not a departed spirit; he is still alive through enchantment and will continue in Avalon till the day comes for his return. Wace and Layamon note this as a Breton belief, and several authors follow inventively in the same path.

Their Avalon tends to drift into other climes, and Morgan goes with it. Étienne de Rouen in *Draco Normannicus* (ca. 1169) takes Arthur to the Antipodes, though his intention may be satirical. Others do not venture so far. The author of *Floriant et Florete* (ca. 1250) seems to identify Avalon with Sicily, an opinion that passes from romance into folklore. The resulting Sicilian presence of Morgan is the reason for the term *Fata Morgana* applied to a mirage phenomenon in the Straits of Messina. A fourteenth-century poem about the hero Ogier places Avalon in the East near the Earthly Paradise, and a Danish redaction of it points to India. But the chronicler Jean des Preis, or d'Outremeuse, toward 1400, tells of Ogier's meeting with Arthur in a Mediterranean Avalon, where Morgan houses them in a palace surrounded by pools and fruit-trees, and both enjoy immortality and perpetual youth. The Majorcan poet Guillem Torroella, in *La Faula* (1360–70), describes a voyage on a whale's back to an island that is likewise in the Mediterranean and is clearly meant to be Avalon. The narrator enters Morgan's palace, and she shows him paintings of Arthurian characters. A young man in her company turns out to be Arthur. He has healed his wounds by bathing in the water of the River Tigris, which flows from the Earthly Paradise, and his youth is annually restored by visits of the Holy Grail.

Back in England, a different story was told at Glastonbury. The monks of its abbey claimed that Glastonbury itself was Avalon, in a comparatively mundane sense, as Arthur's last earthly destination where he died and was buried. It is not known whether they said this before 1191, when they announced that they had exhumed him, together with a cross bearing the island's name in the form *Avalonia*. At all events, the equation was widely publicized after that, and accepted by Giraldus Cambrensis, Robert de Boron, and the anonymous author of *Perlesvaus*. It was probably helped by a lingering sense of "otherness" at Glastonbury, rooted in its strange topography and non-Christian associations.

Malory is unclear about Arthur's end. The King is carried off in a barge by a company of ladies including Morgan, apparently Avalon-bound, but Malory allows that he *may* have been buried at Glastonbury and that the ladies *may* simply have brought his body there, in which case the Avalon = Glastonbury equation holds. Tennyson rules it out. Arthur goes away over the water to a sort of paradise:

> . . . the island-valley of Avilion
> Where falls not hail, or rain, or any snow,
> Nor ever wind blows loudly; but it lies
> Deep-meadow'd, happy, fair with orchard-lawns
> And bowery hollows crown'd with summer sea.

This is to come full circle, more or less, to Geoffrey's Fortunate Isle. [GA]

❧ Geoffrey of Monmouth. *Historia Regum Britanniae*, Book IX, Chapter 4; Book XI, Chapter 2; *Vita Merlini*, ll. 908–40.

Ashe, Geoffrey. *Avalonian Quest*. London: Methuen, 1982; rev. ed. London: Fontana, 1984.
Bromwich, Rachel. *Trioedd Ynys Prydein*. Cardiff: University of Wales Press, 1961.
Cavendish, Richard. *King Arthur and the Grail*. London: Weidenfeld and Nicolson, 1978.
Loomis, Roger Sherman, ed. *Arthurian Literature in the Middle Ages*. Oxford: Clarendon, 1959.

AVALON: see BOUGHTON, RUTLAND.

"AVALON REVISITED": *see* ATWOOD, MARGARET.

AVOWING OF KING ARTHUR, SIR GAWAIN, SIR KAY, AND BALD-WIN OF BRITAIN, THE, a stanzaic tail-rhyme romance of 1,148 lines, extant only in the Liverpool Ireland Manuscript of post-1450, though written somewhat earlier and farther south in the West Midlands.

Arthur, accompanied by Kay, Gawain, and Baldwin, hunts a ferocious boar in Inglewood Forest. He vows to slay and cut it up, Gawain and Kay vow vigil and errantry overnight, and Baldwin vows never to be jealous of any woman, nor fear death, nor deny hospitality. Arthur accomplishes his vow; Kay fails in combat with Sir Menealf over a captured maiden, but is avenged by Gawain, who wins the maiden. Having submitted to Guinevere, Menealf becomes a Round Table knight.

Arthur sends a roadside ambush and a minstrel-spy to test Baldwin and then visits him himself. Baldwin fulfills all his vows, even though the King sets up an elaborately misleading situation in his wife's chamber. "Explaining" his triple vow, Baldwin tells Arthur three stories of his campaign experiences in a Spanish castle.

A fearless, genial hunter and host, Baldwin is reminiscent of the Green Knight in *Sir Gawain and the Green Knight*, with which this romance also shares a predilection for triadic arrangements, fitt divisions, a difficult boar hunt, and a preoccupation with the meaning and application of chivalric institutions. The vows move from response to a specific adventure to chivalry's characteristic construction of relations (where the maiden can become an object of pledge for the knights, like the boar with which she is carried to court), to Baldwin's larger perspective. His vows are conditions of life, not specific acts. His awareness of female competition for survival contrasts with Arthur's naïveté, but his exemplary stories give no guarantees or explanations, showing only that chivalric codes may as well be adhered to as not, since defining the appropriate moment to fear death, be jealous, or withhold food is not obvious or easy in the light of experience. [JP]

⁇ Dahood, Roger, ed. *The Avowing of King Arthur*. New York and London: Garland, 1984.
French, W.H., and C.B. Hale, eds. *Middle English Metrical Romances*. New York: Russell and Russell, 1930 (but see also R. Dahood, "Dubious Readings in the French and Hale Text of *The Avowing of King Arthur*." *Notes and Queries*, n.s., September 1971, 323–26).

AWNTYRS OFF ARTHURE AT THE TERNE WATHELYN, THE, a somewhat unusual English Arthurian poem of the late fourteenth century (the four manuscripts, however, all date from the fifteenth century). The poem consists of fifty-five stanzas of thirteen lines each (715 lines in all) and has a highly intricate structure. The rhyme scheme is abababababcdddc; the first nine lines are four-beat and the final four (the "wheel") are two-beat alliterating lines. The stanzas are linked by the repetition of a word or phrase from the last line of one stanza in the first line of the next (stanza linking or iteration). A similar phenomenon occurs between the two parts of a stanza, though less regularly.

The poem itself consists of two parts, not very convincingly linked. In the first half, the ghost of Guinevere's mother, emerging from Tarn Wadling, appears to Guinevere and Gawain. She warns them that the sumptuousness of the court will lead to damnation. Gawain anxiously inquires what will happen to those who have taken other kings' lands without any right. The spirit then prophesies that Arthur's covetousness, and Fortune's Wheel, will cause his fall. The second part seems to provide an exemplum that justifies the ghost's accusations. Galeron, a Scottish knight whose lands had been won by Arthur (through deceit, he says), fights with Gawain, to whom they had been given. Arthur stops the combat when Gawain is about to win; Galeron resigns his claim, is made a knight of the Round Table, and is restored his lands.

The source for the second part is unknown, but the first part goes back to the *Trentals of St. Gregory* (also known in a Middle English version). The topographical names relate the story to the north (Cumberland). Its author was influenced by *Sir Gawain and the Green Knight*, which he may be "citing" when he says that Galeron wounded Gawain, dressed in green, on his neck with a sword. Remarkable is the social criticism implied by Gawain's question to the spirit and her reply. [ESK]

ᐁ Gates, Robert J., ed. *The Awntyrs off Arthure at the Terne Wathelyne*. Philadelphia: University of Pennsylvania Press, 1969.

Hanna, Ralph, III, ed. *The Awntyrs off Arthure at the Terne Wathelyn*. Manchester: Manchester University Press, 1974.

BABCOCK, WILLIAM H., wrote a rambling and sentimental historical romance, *Cian of the Chariots* (1898), which offers a tediously self-righteous warning against religious intolerance in an untraditional account of Arthur's struggle against the Saxons. [RHT]

&⁂ Babcock, William H. *Cian of the Chariots: A Romance of the Days of Arthur Emperor of Britain and His Knights of the Round Table, How They Delivered London and Overthrew the Saxons After the Downfall of Roman Britain.* Boston: Lothrop, 1898.

BADGER, JOHN D'ARCY, Canadian publisher, brought out in 1972 a sequence of fifty-six irregular sonnets, *The Arthuriad.* Each of the sonnets is accompanied by a lengthy free-verse commentary; more polemical than poetic, they offer a reinterpretation of the Arthurian and Christian myths in an argument for the universal adoption of a "radical-centrist" political humanism. [SRR]

&⁂ Badger, John d'Arcy. *The Arthuriad.* Toronto: Pendragon House, 1972.

BADON. According to Gildas, the Britons won a decisive victory over the Saxon invaders at the "siege of Mount Badon" (*obsessio Badonici montis*). This was the climax of a struggle with varying fortunes, beginning from the counterattack against the Saxon settlements launched by Ambrosius Aurelianus. Badon brought a spell of relative peace and order. In his own time, Gildas laments, the Britons have lost respect for their fathers' achievement and are fighting among themselves; but he has no doubt about the achievement. He does not name any British commander at the battle. Later, the commander is said to have been Arthur.

Badon presents three main problems: its date, its location, and Arthur's connection with it.

Gildas makes a puzzling statement about the date. It is usually understood as follows: "The year of Badon . . . was the year of my birth; as I know, one month of the forty-fourth year since then has already passed." Since he is probably writing in the 540s, he appears to be saying that Badon was fought in the late 490s or early 500s. This is certainly the likeliest meaning. But Bede seems to have read Gildas in another text, now lost, because he takes the "forty-fourth year" quite differently and reckons the period from the Saxons' first settlement in Britain, with Badon coming at the end of it. As he dates the settlement around the middle of the fifth century, the result turns out to be quite similar. Gildas's involved Latin has even been construed in a third sense, as saying the battle took place in the forty-fourth year from the British counterstroke that began the war, a reading that might shift it definitely from the last decade of the fifth century into the first decade of the sixth. On any showing, however, it belongs about the year 500. Gildas wrote when it was still within living memory, and he is unlikely to be far wrong whatever his meaning actually is. The irreconcilability of the date given for Badon in the *Annales Cambriae*, 518, is therefore a reason for treating that chronicle's Arthurian entries with reserve.

Gildas's British victory ca. 500, followed by a long lull, accords fairly well with archaeological and historical data. Generally speaking, there were no more Saxon encroachments for several decades, and some evidence for a reverse migration back to the Continent suggests that in Britain the advance was halted. There are even arguable traces of local withdrawals. The only question arises from entries in the *Anglo-Saxon Chronicle* claiming continued progress by the West Saxons in Hampshire and victories won by them, in contrast with Gildas's assertion of a respite. Archaeology, however, shows that these Saxons were few and their progress was meager, while their battles in the *Chronicle* are skirmishes only, or fictitious. Gildas may have regarded them as not worth mentioning. He may not even have heard of them.

As to Badon's whereabouts, it was in the south of Britain. The settlements of northern Angles were still unorganized and in most areas sparse. A defeat in that quarter would not have deterred the Saxon kings established in Kent and elsewhere. The word *mons*, "mountain" or "hill," has often been supposed to refer to a hill fort. Several place-names with the element *Bad-* in them do denote hill forts or locations close by. There has been speculation about a folk-hero or demigod called Badda, who was associated with hill forts and might have given his name to several. Against the year 667, the *Annales Cambriae* note a "second battle of Badon," which is unlikely to have been in the same place as the first.

Given the hill-fort assumption, historians have tried to pick out a particular one as Gildas's. Some have favored Badbury Rings in Dorset, though it is hard to see how enough Saxons could have been there early enough. Liddington Castle in Wiltshire has a village of Badbury near its foot, and excavation has shown that its earthwork defenses were refurbished at about the right time. Geoffrey of Monmouth locates the battle at Bath, where the baths, in one of the manuscripts of Nennius, are called *balnea Badonis*. One or two modern authors have agreed, pointing, for instance, to the hill fort of Solsbury just outside the town. There are other candidates.

Almost everything that is said about Badon rests on probabilities only. It need not have been a hill fort at all. Very likely it was, but nothing shows who was besieging whom, or which group or groups of Saxons took part. The proved British reoccupation of hill forts suggests that the Britons were the besieged, in which case the victory may have come through a sortie or a relief operation. Its impact would have been moral rather than material. No battle conceivable at that time could have inflicted such losses as to deprive the Saxons of the manpower and resources for further war. Badon would have been decisive as an unnerving catastrophe far from their home bases, perhaps involving the death of a king and consequent loss of leadership.

Lastly, there is the problem of Arthur's role. He is first presented as the victor by Nennius in the ninth century and next by the *Annales* in the tenth. Both references are dubious not only because of the long interval but because of apparently legendary touches that call them in question. The early Welsh have little to say about this battle—it is not in the Triads, for instance—and it seems to have carried no great weight in the making of Arthur as they imagined him. On the other hand, there is no alternative candidate as the British commander. Ambrosius would almost certainly have been too old, and probably dead. The commander would surely have been a man of some note, remembered afterward for the victory, and it may be doubted whether a *totally* unconnected Arthur could have supplanted him in tradition and effaced his name. (*See also* ARTHUR, ORIGINS OF LEGEND.) [GA]

Gildas, *De Excidio Britanniae*, ed. and trans. Michael Winterbottom under the title *The Ruin of Britain*, and Nennius, *Historia Brittonum*, ed. and trans. John Morris under the title *British History and the Welsh Annals*. In *History from the Sources*. Chichester: Phillimore, 1978, 1980, Vols. 7 and 8.

Alcock, Leslie. *Arthur's Britain*. London: Penguin, 1971.

Chambers, E.K. *Arthur of Britain*. London: Sidgwick and Jackson, 1927.

Morris, John. *The Age of Arthur*. New York: Scribner, 1973.

BADON PARCHMENTS: *see* MASEFIELD, JOHN.

BALADRO DEL SABIO MERLÍN, EL ("The Shriek of Merlin the Sage"), a
Spanish romance based upon an earlier Hispanic translation of the *Merlin*
branch of the Post-Vulgate *Roman du Graal*. It survives in two versions: a 1498
incunabulum and a 1535 imprint. Although there is strong evidence pointing to
the original translation of the *Roman du Graal* as a single work—sections of the
three branches are preserved together in a late fifteenth-century copy of a
translation attributed to one Joannes Bivas in 1313 and in Lope García de
Salazar's history of England within his *Libro de las bienandanzas e fortunas*,
compiled between 1461 and 1467—at some point the *Baladro* was separated from
the first branch. In the 1535 imprint, however, the adapter considered the
Baladro to form the first part of the *Demanda del Sancto Grial*, the third branch of
the Spanish adaptation of the *Roman du Graal*. The recent discovery of two early
fourteenth-century fragments of a Galician-Portuguese translation of the Post-
Vulgate *Merlin* makes it clear that the *Baladro* reflects a tendency by later
adapters of Arthurian romance to modify the original with material from other
sources. In this case, the author or editor of the *Baladro* incunabulum made use
of two fifteenth-century Spanish sentimental romances—the *Siervo libre de amor*,
by Juan Rodríguez del Padrón, and *Grimalte y Gradissa*, by Juan de Flores—and
prophecies derived ultimately from Geoffrey of Monmouth's *Historia Regum
Britanniae*, as well as adding preliminary and concluding remarks of his own
apparent creation. Some critics also believe that a series of *Baladro* adventures
involving Baudemagus, adventures ascribed to a mysterious *Conte del Brait*,
were the invention of the Spanish author, but the question remains unresolved.
The adapter of the 1535 imprint also made a change, appending a series of
cryptic prophecies attributed to Merlin concerning Spanish history, material
taken from an earlier text of prophecies surviving in Castilian and Catalan
manuscript copies. [HLS]

🍋 Bohigas Balaguer, Pedro, ed. *El Baladro del Sabio Merlín según el texto de la edición de Burgos de
1498*. 3 vols. Barcelona, 1957–62.
   Bonilla y San Martín, Adolfo, ed. *El Baladro del Sabio Merlín, primera parte de la Demanda del
   Sancto Grial*. In *Libros de caballerías, primera parte: Ciclo artúrico–Ciclo carolingio*. Madrid: Bailly-
   Baillière, 1907, pp. 3–162.

BALAN: *see* BALIN AND BALAN.

BALIN AND BALAN, two brothers who fought for Arthur in his war
against King Lot (see Malory's Book II). Balin (also called Balin le Sauvage and
The Knight with Two Swords) killed Garlon, and when King Pellam tried to
avenge this death Balin inflicted the Dolorous Stroke on him. Eventually, the
two brothers kill each other in battle (without recognizing each other) and are
buried in the same tomb. Merlin sets Balin's sword in the stone, from which
Galahad will eventually draw it. (*See also* DOLOROUS STROKE.) [NJL]

"**BALIN AND BALAN**": *see* TENNYSON, ALFRED LORD.

BALLAD OF ELAINE, THE: see WRIGHT, SIDNEY FOWLER.

BALLADS: *see* "AUSGLEICHUNG, DIE"; "BOY AND THE MANTLE, THE"; BROADSIDES; BROADSIDES (SPANISH); "GALIANS TÁTTUR"; "KING ARTHUR AND KING CORNWALL"; "KING ARTHUR'S DEATH"; "LEGEND OF KING ARTHUR, THE"; "MARRIAGE OF SIR GAWAIN, THE"; "SIR LANCELOT DU LAKE"; "TISTRAM OG JOMFRU ISOLT"; "TÍSTRAMS TÁTTUR"; "TISTRUM OG ISALT"; "TRISTRAMS KVÆÐI."

BALTIC REGION, ARTHURIAN CLUBS IN. For several centuries, during the later Middle Ages and beyond, an Arthurian cult flourished in a number of Baltic towns, including Danzig, Riga, Culm, and Elbing. The documents that remain from the period are not literary texts but rather charters and lists of rules for the societies (known by a variety of names, such as Artushof or Societas Arturi), which were a combination of a social or fraternal organization with a merchants' exchange. Among the activities of the clubs were annual festivities (in presumed imitation of Arthur's court), during which members dressed in chivalric costumes and held tournaments. (*See also* ROUND TABLES.) [NJL]

&. Schlauch, Margaret. "King Arthur in the Baltic Towns." *Bibliographical Bulletin of the International Arthurian Society*, 11 (1959), 75–80.

BARBOUR, JOHN: *see* SCOTTISH ARTHURIAN CHRONICLES.

BARING, MAURICE (1874–1945), displays wit and urbanity in *The Camelot Jousts*, which appeared in the London daily paper *The Morning Post* and was later published with similar pieces in *Dead Letters* (1910). In an exchange of correspondence, Arthur and Guinevere discuss arrangements for jousts at Camelot as if they were an Edwardian weekend party. The Queen is deliciously catty about Mark and Iseult, and spiteful in her pique when she realizes that Lancelot is taking undue interest in Elaine. [CNS]

&. Baring, Maurice. *Dead Letters*. London: Constable, 1910.

BATAGLIA: see CANTARI DI TRISTANO, I.

BAYERISCHE CHRONIK, DIE: *see* FUETRER, ULRICH.

BEAR OF BRITAIN, THE: *see* FRANKLAND, EDWARD.

BEARDSLEY, AUBREY: *see* DENT *MORTE D'ARTHUR.*

BEAUDOUS: *see* ROBERT DE BLOIS.

BEDE, in the *Historia Ecclesiastica Gentis Anglorum* (A.D. 731), gives an account of the Germanic invasion of Britain, taken mostly from Gildas. He refers to the battle of Badon but does not mention Arthur. He writes that the leaders of the Saxons were two brothers named Hengist and Horsa and gives genealogies of Saxon kings. Bede's work was used by later writers, such as Geoffrey of Monmouth and Layamon. [AEG]

❧ Bede. *Opera Historica*, ed. C. Plummer. London, 1896.

BÉDIER, (CHARLES MARIE) JOSEPH (1864–1938), in 1903 succeeded Gaston Paris in the Chair of French Medieval Language and Literature at the Collège de France; in 1921 he was elected to the Académie Française. In addition to seminal work on the origins of French epic poetry, Bédier edited and translated the *Roman de Tristan par Thomas* (2 vols., 1902–05). He is best known to Arthurians for his graceful reconstitution of the legend of *Tristan et Iseut*, which has been frequently reprinted since its first appearance in 1900. [WWK]

❧ Bédier, Joseph. *Le Roman de Tristan et Iseut.* Paris: Piazza, 1900.

BEDIVERE. The career of Bedivere, or Bedwyr as he is called in Welsh, has undergone five distinct developments. In early Welsh tradition, he is renowned for his valor and for his close friendship with Arthur and Kay. *Culhwch and Olwen* comments upon his skill with a spear, despite his having but one hand, and notes that he never shrank from an enterprise on which Kay was bound. Geoffrey of Monmouth preserves these two features in his portrayal of Bedivere, and he is followed by later chroniclers. Bedivere acts as Arthur's cupbearer and is later created Duke of Normandy. He and Kay accompany the King when he kills the Giant of Mont St.-Michel. He is then slain in the battle against the Romans.

Despite this early prominence, Bedivere is virtually ignored in the romances. He acts as Arthur's constable rather than butler, and like both the

King and Kay he usually remains at court while newer heroes ride forth to win renown.

This neglect is reversed in the English Stanzaic *Le Morte Arthur*, which introduces the third development in Bedivere's career. Here, Bedivere, rather than Girflet as in the Vulgate *Mort Artu*, is the surviving companion who casts Arthur's sword Excalibur into the mere after the battle of Camlann. He spends his remaining years praying by the King's tomb in the hermitage at Glastonbury. His role in the story of Arthur's death is preserved by Malory and most later authors.

Tennyson introduces the fourth development when he has Bedivere narrate "The Coming of Arthur." Other authors who use Bedivere as narrator include Edwin Arlington Robinson, George Finkel, Catherine Christian, and Roy Turner.

In modern Arthurian fiction, Bedivere has regained his early prominence, and he has even started to replace Lancelot as Guenevere's lover. Concerned to create a credible picture of the Dark Ages, yet wishing to preserve the tragic motif of the trusted friend who betrays his king, Rosemary Sutcliff makes Bedivere the Queen's lover in *Sword at Sunset*. Her lead has been followed by both Gillian Bradshaw and Mary Stewart. [RHT]

BEK, THOMAS, OF CASTELFORD, a Yorkshireman who wrote a verse chronicle of British, Scottish, and English history ca.1327; 39,674 lines survive in a single manuscript, Göttingen University Library Codex Hist. 740. Although the later part of the chronicle does not follow any known source closely, the account of Arthur follows Geoffrey of Monmouth, with some details taken from Wace, Robert of Gloucester, Pierre de Langtoft, and others. Like the later part, it shows the author's interest in Scotland and York. Only the part of the chronicle covering the coronation of Arthur through the death of Cadwallader (ll.19,715–27,466) has been edited, but Perrin gives a detailed account of the contents of the manuscript. [EDK]

🕮 Castelford, Thomas. *Thomas Castelford's Chronicle*, ed. in part Frank Behre. Göteborg: Elanders, 1940.

Perrin, M.L. *Über Thomas Castelfords Chronik von England.* Boston: Ginn, 1890.

BEL GHERARDINO, an Italian *cantare* thought to have been composed in the mid-fourteenth century, tells the story of the love of the knight Gherardino for the White Fairy. Some episodes may be based on Marie de France's *Lanval.* [SJN]

🕮 Levi, Ezio, ed. *Fiore di leggende: cantari antichi.* Bari: Laterza, 1914.

BEL INCONNU, LE: *see* RENAUT DE BEAUJEU.

BELLENDEN, JOHN: *see* SCOTTISH ARTHURIAN CHRONICLES.

BELOVED EXILE: see GODWIN, PARKE.

BENOÎT, PIERRE (1886–1962), published *Monsalvat* in 1957; in this novel he transposed the Grail quest to the France of 1944. A history professor and a student embark on the quest, which takes them to Montsalvy, to Montségur, to the monastery of Montserrat (where they recognize the enchanted setting of the *Parsifal*). The Grail, which in this novel has evil powers, causes the death of two German officers who are seeking it and leads also to the loss of the professor's daughter, wife, and companion. After suffering from a fever, the professor finds the Grail at Montsalvy and transports it to the Holy Land. This work, replete with Wagnerian and Catharist influences, succeeds better than most such efforts in providing a modern setting for the quest while remaining faithful to the spirit of its medieval predecessors. [RB]

🙙 Benoît, Pierre. *Monsalvat*. Paris: Michel, 1957.

BERGER, THOMAS, author of *Arthur Rex* (1978), the finest ironic fantasy on the Arthurian legend written this century. The story is loosely based upon Malory's version, supplemented by material from romances like *Sir Gawain and the Green Knight*. Berger has a keen eye for the ridiculousness inherent in romance conventions, which he parodies in such observations as: "Knights did perish only in battles and ladies from love." He also delights in ironic reversal for comic purposes: when Morgan la Fey discovers that her evil schemes are invariably frustrated, she reforms, convinced that "corruption were sooner brought amongst mankind by the forces of virtue."

Human imperfection does finally doom Arthur's idealistic dream of a nobler world. However, the heroic struggle of Arthur and his knights to achieve that dream, though it leads them from one comic misadventure to the next, wins our admiration. Since they do not fear to behave generously, even when it makes them ridiculous, they succeed beyond all expectations in an impossible task. This reversal of expectations, whereby apparently naïve and foolish behavior turns out to be the noblest wisdom, creates not only one of the most appreciative responses to Arthurian legend but also a profound controlling vision in the novel. [RHT]

🙙 Berger, Thomas. *Arthur Rex: A Legendary Novel*. New York: Delacorte, 1978.

Thompson, Raymond H. "Humor and Irony in Modern Arthurian Fantasy: Thomas Berger's *Arthur Rex.*" *Kansas Quarterly*, 16 (Summer 1984), 45–49.

BERNOUILLI, KARL ALBRECHT: *see TRISTAN,* MODERN GERMAN VERSIONS OF GOTTFRIED'S.

BÉROUL, author of a late twelfth-century *Tristan* romance, written in Anglo-Norman French and preserved in fragmentary form. It belongs to what is generally called the *version commune* or the *version primitive* of the Tristan legend. That is, it is presumed that this text belongs to a more primitive, noncourtly stage of the legend, whereas that of Thomas d'Angleterre integrates the work thoroughly into the current of courtly love. Béroul's text is an extensive fragment. It relates the encounter of Tristan and Isolde under the tree in which her husband, Mark, is hiding; the episode in which the dwarf spreads flour on Isolde's floor in order to detect Tristan's footprints (in the event he visits her at night); the scene in which Tristan, having been taken prisoner, asks permission to enter a chapel and pray, whereupon he leaps to freedom from a window; Mark's delivering Isolde to a colony of lepers, for their pleasure and her punishment; the lovers' life in the forest (including Mark's discovery of them and his erroneous conclusion that they are guiltless) and their eventual repentance, caused by the waning of the love potion that they had drunk long ago; and the long episode in which Isolde is tested and in which she exonerates herself by swearing an equivocal oath.

The structure of the work is cyclical. Tristan and Isolde, despite their best intentions, repeatedly fall back into their sinful ways. Mark becomes suspicious, initially refuses to believe he is being betrayed (by both of them: Isolde is his wife, and Tristan is both his vassal and his nephew), and is finally convinced. The lovers resolve to reform. After a period of abstinence on their part, the cycle repeats itself. This is a highly ironic and ambiguous text. Appearances are always deceiving: when the lovers appear most innocent, they are consistently the most guilty. When Mark thinks them innocent, he is being tricked, or else he is misinterpreting the evidence. Even the lovers' desire to reform is motivated by less than noble impulses: they have no particular desire to live a life of Christian purity and virtue, but they are willing to make the effort if that will return them to a life of luxury at the court. [NJL]

> Béroul. *Le Roman de Tristan*, ed. Ernest Muret. Paris: Champion, 1962.

BERSERKER: *see* CARLSEN, CHRIS.

BIENANDANZAS E FORTUNAS, LIBRO DE LAS: *see* SALAZAR, LOPE GARCÍA DE.

BIKET, ROBERT, author of the 580-line *Lai du cor* ("The Lai of the Horn"), composed during the second half of the twelfth century. The lai is an early setting of the Arthurian chastity test, involving a drinking horn, made by a fay, which will spill its contents on cuckolds. Arthur tries to drink from it and is thoroughly soaked, after which Guinevere explains that she is guilty of having once given a ring to a young man. Arthur forgives her, especially when the horn also empties its contents on all the other men at court except Caradoc.

The *Lai du cor* is notable for its unusual (and archaic) six-syllable line and for Robert's humorous irreverence toward Arthur. Variants of the test are found in "The Boy and the Mantle," *Caradoc, Ain Hupsches Vasnachtspill von Künig Artus, Dis Ist Frauw Tristerat Horn von Saphoien*, and *The Romance of Sir Corneus*. [NJL]

❖ Biket, Robert. *The Anglo-Norman Text of Le Lai du Cor*, ed. C.T. Erickson. Oxford: Blackwell, 1973.

BINYON, LAURENCE (1869–1943), English poet, art historian, orientalist, and Keeper of Prints and Drawings at the British Museum, is now best known for the Remembrance Day favorite "For the Fallen." He also wrote *Tristram's End* (1913), an ode; *Arthur, A Tragedy* (1923); and the unfinished *Madness of Merlin* (1947), which he described as "dialogue arranged as story rather than drama." *Tristram's End* is divided into three parts, the first and third in iambic lines of varying length and irregular rhyme, the second in eight-line stanzas that represent the alternating voices of the lovers as they recall the past. Binyon utilizes the Thomas–Gottfried tradition of the black and white sails, the lying wife, and the lovers' deathbed reunion in Brittany. The second Isoud takes the bodies to Cornwall, where Mark recognizes that they have been not traitors but victims.

Arthur, A Tragedy illustrates Binyon's ambition to restore blank-verse drama to the modern stage. It was produced at London's Old Vic in 1923. The plot, derived from Malory, presents the final events of Arthur's reign: the tournament at Astolat and Elaine's fatal love, the Mordred–Agravain entrapment of Lancelot and Guenevere, the siege of the Joyous Gard, Guenevere's return to Arthur at the pope's command, and her withdrawal to a nunnery. In a departure from the *Morte Darthur*, Arthur and Guenevere meet and are reconciled before Arthur proceeds to the last battle and Avalon.

In *The Madness of Merlin*, Binyon wanted to treat the sage independently of the Arthur story. He turned to Celtic traditions of prophetic madmen (Myrddin and Lailoken) who withdrew to the forests of the Scottish Lowlands after defeat in battle. Geoffrey of Monmouth's *Vita Merlini* (ca. 1150) was the chief source. In addition to Merlin (a Welsh prince), the characters include his wife, Gwendolen; his sister, Gwyndyth, married to King Redderech ("an example of excessive idealism"); Saint Kentigern, the bard Taliesin, and the minstrel Peredur; and a peasant, Himlian, who bears Merlin's son. Though Merlin is twice rescued from the wilderness, he refuses to be saved, thus illustrating, in Binyon's words, "the way things always turn out differently from what one expects." The mystical poetry is considerably better than average. [MAW]

❖ Binyon, Laurence. *Arthur, A Tragedy*. London: Heinemann, 1923.

——— . *The Madness of Merlin*. London: Macmillan, 1947.

BIRTH OF A LEGEND: *see* MITCHELL, MARY.

BIRTH OF ARTHUR, THE: *see* BOUGHTON, RUTLAND.

BIRTH OF GALAHAD, THE: *see* HOVEY, RICHARD.

BIRTH OF TRISTRAM, THE: *see* STAINED GLASS.

BISHOP, FARNHAM, and ARTHUR GILCHRIST BRODEUR set their highly idealized and sentimental historical romance *The Altar of the Legion* (1926) in sinking Lyonesse shortly after Arthur's death. King Owain ap Urien and the black-cloaked Irish cavalry known as his ravens (figures developed from *The Dream of Rhonabwy*) help in the heroic resistance against the Saxons. [RHT]

 ❦ Bishop, Farnham, and Arthur Gilchrist Brodeur. *The Altar of the Legion.* Boston: Little, Brown, 1926.

BIVAS, JOÃO: *see* VIVES, BROTHER JUAN.

BLACK BOOK OF CARMARTHEN: *see* CELTIC ARTHURIAN LITERATURE.

BLACKMORE, SIR RICHARD (1654–1729), composed two English verse epics based on Arthurian themes: *Prince Arthur: An Heroick Poem: In Ten Books* (1695) and *King Arthur: An Heroick Poem: In Twelve Books* (1697). As early as Michael Drayton, English writers had suggested that Arthur should be the subject of an English national epic closely modeled on classical forms, and Blackmore set out to realize this aim. In the preface to *Prince Arthur*, his first published work, Blackmore outlined the criteria of the epic form according to the categories of Le Bossu: "a feign'd or devis'd Story of an *Illustrious Action*, related in Verse, in an *Allegorical, Probable, Delightful* and *Admirable* manner, to cultivate the Mind with Instruction of Virtue." He was concerned in particular with the moral aspect of literature (he especially deplored the abuses of the Restoration stage) and wished, moreover, to show how Christian theology could be incorporated into the epic. *Prince Arthur* opens with Arthur's return to Britain to reclaim the crown after the Saxon overthrow of Uter's kingdom. The poem includes accounts of Lucifer's attempts to thwart Arthur's purpose, an analysis of the development of Christianity, a catalogue of the kings of Britain (leading up to the reign of William and Mary), and various battles. It culminates in a final single combat between Tollo and Arthur for the hand of Ethelina and the control of the kingdom. The chief historical authority for the poem is Geoffrey of Monmouth's *Historia Regum Britanniae*, which has been recast stylistically with Vergil as a model—the poem opens, for example, with a clear echo of the *Aeneid*: "I sing the *Briton* and his Righteous Arms." There are also borrowings from both Spenser and Milton. Much of the interest, however, lies in the allegorical adaptations of the source material. There are many obvious identifications of contemporaries: Arthur is an immediately recognizable portrayal of King William, Octa is James II, Ethelina is Queen Mary, the wise Pascentius is Thomas Osborne, Earl of Danby, and so forth.

Prince Arthur was highly popular, especially with King William, who—after Mary's death and a Jacobite attempt to reclaim the throne—wished to see his cause presented in the most favorable light. It is therefore not surprising that Blackmore's knighthood and the publication of *King Arthur* occurred in the same year. This second Arthuriad opens with the Gallic lords (the Huguenots) imploring Arthur to intervene against the outrages of King Clotar (Louis XIV). Although Arthur is tempted by Lucifer, and his troops become temporarily dispirited, he finally returns and decapitates Clotar, and we see the beginning of an age of peace. Apart from the political allegory, Blackmore includes in this poem discussions of many contemporary themes, such as Lockean psychology and the Newtonian cosmology. He is especially aware of Milton as a model, and although *King Arthur* was less popular than *Prince Arthur* had been Blackmore probably helped to advance Milton's reputation during the early eighteenth century.

Blackmore had strong supporters for his poetry, but he was also attacked by many of the great writers of his day, Defoe, Swift, and Pope, for example. In particular, through Pope's *Peri Bathous* the name Blackmore is often somewhat unjustly viewed by historians of literature as almost synonymous with poetaster. [JPC]

Brinkley, Roberta F. *Arthurian Legend in the Seventeenth Century*. Baltimore: Johns Hopkins Press, 1932.

Solomon, Harry M. *Sir Richard Blackmore*. Boston: Twayne, 1980.

BLAKE, WILLIAM (1757–1827), incorporates Arthurian figures and patterns into the powerful mythic narrative of his epic poem *Jerusalem, the Emanation of the Giant Albion* (composed during the first two decades of the nineteenth century). Blake's complex treatment of his Arthurian materials derives from the enigmatic view, expressed in his *Descriptive Catalogue* of 1809, that the "stories of Arthur are the acts of Albion, applied to a Prince of the fifth century, who conquered Europe, and held the Empire of the world in the dark age, which the Romans never again recovered." On the one hand, Arthur is for Blake only a particular British "Prince of the fifth century," a limited representation of the larger and more important Albion, the gigantic figure of Britain whose progress he traces in *Jerusalem*. Thus, Arthur appears at the beginning of the poem's third chapter as the "hard cold constrictive Spectre" of Albion, which is his circumscribed and (in isolation) dangerous faculty of

Reason; in Blake's personal mythology, Arthur becomes Albion's antagonist, a Druid, an empirical philosopher in the tradition of Bacon, Newton, and Locke, and a Satanic enemy and tempter of Christ. On the other hand, the undying tale of Arthur's "death, or sleep, and promise to return again" (as Blake describes it in the *Descriptive Catalogue*) provides Blake with a potent analogue for the death and resurrection of Albion, which constitute the central action of his poem. Though Blake does not attempt a British epic deriving exclusively or even primarily from the matter of Arthur, he does combine Arthurian materials with biblical and personal myths in a major prophetic work of far-reaching political significance for modern Britain. [MDC]

Blake, William. *The Poetry and Prose of William Blake*, ed. David V. Erdman. Garden City, N.Y.: Doubleday, 1965.

Ashe, Geoffrey. *Camelot and the Vision of Albion*. London: Heinemann, 1971.

Damon, S. Foster. *A Blake Dictionary*. London: Thames and Hudson, 1973.

BLANDÍN DE CORNUALLA,

BLANDÍN DE CORNUALLA, an anonymous Provençal verse romance (2,394 lines) of apparent Catalan authorship dating from the late thirteenth century or first half of the fourteenth. Inspired ostensibly by Arthurian romance, the author narrates in linear fashion, with some humor and irony, the adventures of two friends from Cornwall, the knights Blandín de Cornualla and Guiot Ardit de Miramar, ending the tale with their respective marriages to the sisters Brianda and Irlanda, whose names may betray his familiarity with the Tristan story. The romance emphasizes chivalric ideals and includes troubadour themes and imagery as well as stock romance characters and situations. [HLS]

Pacheco, Arseni, ed. *Blandín de Cornualla i altres narracions en vers dels segles XIV i XV*. Barcelona: Edicions 62, 1983.

BLANK, RICHARD

BLANK, RICHARD, a German film director who made a television movie (of approximately ninety minutes' duration) of Wolfram's *Parzival* in 1980. Using the translation by Wolfgang Mohr (1977), Blank presents the story in an anti-illusionistic manner, with references to the modern world. Blank's film thus differs both from popular fantasy movies (for example, *Excalibur* and Veith von Fürstenberg's Tristan story of 1981, *Feuer und Schwert*) and from the highly stylized Arthurian films of Robert Bresson and Eric Rohmer. [UM/WCM]

Müller, Ulrich. "Parzival 1980—auf der Bühne im Fernsehen und im Film." In *Mittelalter-Rezeption* II, ed. Jürgen Kühnel, Hans-Dieter Mück, Ursula Müller, and Ulrich Müller. Göppingen: Kümmerle, 1982.

BLEEDING LANCE

BLEEDING LANCE, a lance or spear that first appeared in Chrétien de Troyes's *Perceval*, where it was associated with the Grail in the ceremony in the Fisher King's castle. It was carried by a youth (*uns vallés*, l. 3192), and from its tip came a drop of blood. Here and in subsequent romances, it remained in direct relationship with the ritual of the Grail. This lance soon came into association with the apocryphal legend of Longinus, the blind Roman soldier whose spear pierced the side of Christ while he hung on the cross (see, e.g., the Continuations of Chrétien's *Perceval*, the Didot-*Perceval*, *Durmart le Gallois*). The romances also claim for the Lance the power of healing (e.g., *Estoire, Queste*) as well as the role of avenger (e.g., *Estoire, Merlin* Continuation), which led J.D. Bruce to ascribe to it in the Vulgate Cycle the twofold attributes of God: wrath and mercy. Originally, this was not the same weapon as that which wounded the Fisher King, but it became so identified in Wolfram's *Parzival*, in the various romances of the Vulgate Cycle, and in Malory. Though in Chrétien the blood issuing from the spear tip does not seem to flow into the Grail, as a result of Robert de Boron's equating of the Grail with the cup of the Last Supper the blood became the Blood of Christ, emblem of the Real Presence (e.g., *Perlesvaus, Queste*). Upon the death of Galaad in the *Queste* (Perceval in the Manessier Continuation), the Lance and the Grail were removed by a hand from heaven, never to reappear. [RFO'G]

West, G. D. *An Index of Proper Names in French Arthurian Prose Romances*. Toronto: University of Toronto Press, 1978, pp. 186–87.

BLIND HARRY: *see* SCOTTISH ARTHURIAN CHRONICLES.

BLIOCADRAN PROLOGUE, an 800-line prologue to the *Conte del Graal* of Chrétien de Troyes, appearing in two of its fifteen manuscripts and in the Prose *Perceval* of 1530. Date and authorship are unknown, but it was probably composed in the early thirteenth century, somewhat after the work of Robert de Boron but before the *Perlesvaus*. The poem, in seven episodes, tells the story of Perceval's father, named Bliocadran, who dies in a tournament when Perceval is born. His widow flees the court to preserve her son from knowledge of arms and chivalry.

Bliocadran is the sole survivor of twelve brothers. His wife and people beg him not to go to tournaments, since all his brothers have died in them. Yet, when Bliocadran's first child is about to be born, a messenger arrives with news of a tournament announced by the King of Wales, and Bliocadran insists on going. He is mortally wounded in the tournament and lingers two days.

Bliocadran's son had been born three days after he left for the tournament. When the child is seven months old, his mother decides to flee to the waste forest to keep her son from ever hearing about chivalry. She pretends to be going on a pilgrimage to St. Brendan of Scotland. The lady, her attendants, and all her belongings are assembled at Calfle on the coast of Wales. After reaching the waste forest, they search fifteen days for a proper site. Fourteen years later, Bliocadran's people have given the lady and her son up for lost. The mother has told her son that, when hunting in the forest, if he should see men "dressed as though they were covered with iron" (l. 757), they would be devils; he is to retreat, cross himself, and say his Credo. The next day, when he returns from hunting, his mother asks him what he found. "Diversion and pleasure" is his answer. The mother does not inquire further, and the young man says no more.

The *Bliocadran Prologue* is an elucidation of the material contained in lines 407–88 (Roach edition) of Chrétien de Troyes's *Conte del Graal*, where Perceval's mother reveals to him that his father had been a renowned knight who had been wounded, impoverished, and exiled in the waste forest under unspecified circumstances after the death of Utherpendragon. Although the *Prologue* changes some of the narrative details (there are eleven brothers in the *Prologue* who die in combat instead of two brothers, and the father dies in a tournament instead of grieving fatally over the deaths of his two older sons), it nevertheless dramatizes Chrétien's narrative theme: the fear of the havoc wrought by chivalric pursuits that caused Perceval's mother to protect her son by raising him in ignorance of the existence of chivalry.

Because the *Prologue* is an elaboration of unexplained material in Chrétien's *Perceval*, it can be considered another Perceval "continuation" or Perceval romance (Romance of Perceval's Father). (*See also* CONTINUATIONS.) [LDW]

꩜ Wolfgang, Lenora D., ed. *Bliocadran: A Prologue to the Perceval of Chrétien de Troyes.* Tübingen: Niemeyer, 1976.

Brugger, Ernst. "Bliocadran, the Father of Perceval." In *Medieval Studies in Memory of Gertrude Schoepperle Loomis*, ed. Roger Sherman Loomis. Paris: Champion, 1927, pp. 147–74.

Newstead, Helaine. "Perceval's Father and Welsh Tradition." *Romanic Review*, 36 (1945), 3–31.

Thompson, Albert Wilder. "The Text of the *Bliocadran*." *Romance Philology*, 9 (1955–56), 205–09.

BOCCACCIO, GIOVANNI (1313–1375). Although Boccaccio certainly had French romances available to him during his youth at the Angevin court of Naples, his use of Arthurian materials began only after his return to Florence, continuing then to the end of his life. The *Amorosa Visione* (1342) lists many Arthurian knights and ladies in its triumph of Fame (Canto 11), while Lancelot and Tristan reappear in the triumph of Love (Canto 29). Both categories are subsequently overturned in the triumph of Fortune, and the narrator is urged by his guide to turn from these worldly matters to the pursuit of salvation. In the *Elegia di Madonna Fiammetta* (1343–44), the heroine compares her love tragedy to Isolt's (Chapter 8) and that of other tragic heroines in order to claim pridefully that her own misery is greater than all others'. Like Dante's Francesca, Fiammetta is an example of the destructive powers of obsessive passion, who, although still alive at the end of her tale, has clearly descended into a state of damnation and despair. The lusty widow of the *Corbaccio* (1355) is satirically characterized as reading Arthurian love stories instead of prayerbooks, and as becoming sexually aroused by these readings. The book is a misogynistic tirade intended to cure a hapless lover of his erroneous love.

More complex is the use of Arthurian materials in the *Decameron* (1349–51). The book's subtitle, "Prencipe Galeotto" (Prince Galehaut), has been variously interpreted as a defense of the work's erotic contents (Boccaccio is a go-between, a friend to lovers) or as a reference to *Inferno* (Canto 5), and thereby a warning about the reader's moral responsibility for the way one reads and acts. The latter interpretation seems reinforced by Tale 10.6, in which a king falls in love with two sisters named Ginevra and Isotta (Guenevere and Isolde) but then vanquishes his own lust and has them honorably married. He thus avoids Francesca's sinful imitation of the Arthurian lovers' example and becomes explicitly a positive example of behavior to be imitated. Hollander has pointed out that Boccaccio in his preface begs his women readers not to let the plague description frighten them from reading on ("di più avanti leggere")—thus negatively evoking the last line of Francesca's speech in hell: "that day we read no farther" ("quel giorno più non vi leggemmo avante"). The use of the Lancelot story as pornography by the bawdy widow of the *Corbaccio* further supports the connection between allusions to this tale and the problem—already recognized by Dante—of authors' versus readers' responsibility for the influence of literature on behavior. It has even been suggested that "Galeotto" unmasks the dangerous seductions of fiction itself, and that the *Decameron* narrators therefore distance themselves from the historical world to emphasize the distinction between reality and fiction. There is some disagreement as to the relevance of Dante's *Inferno*, Canto 5, to Boccaccio's subtitle; but Boccaccio's continual imitation of Dante's writing makes such an allusion probable. Thus, Dante would be a formative influence on Boccaccio's own views of the Lancelot legend, making moral questions paramount. The *Amorosa Visione* seems to reinforce this concern with moral interpretation. For the *Elegia*, too, it is important that the famous Arthurian love stories are tragedies. The *Decameron* narrator claims to be finally freed from the miseries of excessive love and, alluding to Ovid's *Remedia Amores*, offers to help distract ladies from such melancholy passion. He is thus scarcely a go-between to their loves.

Besides the "Galeotto" subtitle, the *Decameron* contains very little Arthurian reference; but a few tales bear perhaps some resemblance to Arthurian materials. An indirect connection has been suggested between the story of Alatiel (2.7) and strands of a complex romance within the Old French Prose *Tristan* of the previous century. The theme of the eaten heart, occurring in a tale (4.9) derived from the Provençal *vida* of Guillem de Cabestaing, can also be found in the "Lai Guiron" sung by Ysolt in the marriage segment (Sneyd fragment, ll. 781–90) of Thomas's *Tristan*. In any case, even though the *Novellino*, an earlier collection of Italian *novelle* known to Boccaccio, had drawn directly from Arthurian legends for a number of tales, Arthurian stories were not a major or direct source for the *Decameron*.

De Casibus Virorum Illustrium (1355–62) recounts the history of King Arthur, drawn mainly from Geoffrey of Monmouth, but adds to it the twelve rules of the Round Table. Boccaccio's chapter was cited in turn by Lydgate. Boccaccio avoids any reference to fabulous adventures and prefaces the narrative by commenting that Arthur's fame makes his inclusion in this book of histories seem necessary despite serious doubts about the historical truth of the matter. Emphasizing Arthur's military career, he suggests that Arthur's pride in conquests abroad led to his destruction at home. His final moral is that only humble things endure.

In all, Boccaccio's treatment of Arthurian materials seems remarkably negative. The famous King and his loving knights offer moral examples of what to avoid, not what to imitate. Dante may well have been a powerful influence on this attitude. [JLS]

🕭 Bruce, J. Douglas. "A Boccaccio Analogue in the Old French Prose Tristan." *Romanic Review*, 1 (1910), 384–94.

Gardner, Edmund G. *The Arthurian Legend in Italian Literature*. London: Dent, 1930, pp. 228–38.

Mazzotta, Giuseppe. "The *Decameron*: The Marginality of Literature." *University of Toronto Quarterly*, 42 (Fall 1972), 68–69.

Padoan, Giorgio. "Mondo Aristocratico e Mondo Communale nell'Ideologia e nell'Arte de Giovanni Boccaccio." *Studi sul Boccaccio*, 2 (1964), 124–25.

Viscardi, Antonio. "Arthurian Influences on Italian Literature from 1200 to 1500." In *Arthurian Literature in the Middle Ages*, ed. Roger Sherman Loomis. Oxford: Clarendon, 1959, pp. 419–29.

BODMER, JOHANN JACOB (1698–1783), a Swiss-German professor of history, is known primarily for his contributions to the literary theory of his time, which resulted in the liberation of German literature from the artificial constraints of French classical models, and for his collection of medieval German manuscripts, which was a major factor in the revival of interest in medieval German literature. Ironically, his own lack of talent as a creative writer is revealed in his abridged translations of parts of Wolfram's *Parzival* (*Der Parcival*, 1753, and *Gamuret*, 1755), both based on a 1477 printing of a composite of two manuscripts and both written in inappropriate, stiff hexameters. A later ballad, "Jestute" (1781), relating the Jeschute–Orilus episode from *Parzival*, was also of little literary significance. [RWK]

🕭 Bender, Wolfgang. *J.J. Bodmer und J.J. Breitinger*. Stuttgart: Metzler, 1973.

BOEC VAN MERLINE: see MAERLANT, JACOB VAN.

BOECE, HECTOR: see SCOTTISH ARTHURIAN CHRONICLES.

BOIARDO, MATTEO MARIA(1441–1494), was associated at various periods of his life with the Este court at Ferrara, serving from 1480 to 1482 as Ercole d'Este's representative in the city of Modena and from 1487 until his death as governor of Reggio. His literary fame rests on an influential collection of love poems, the *Amorum libri tres* or *Canzoniere*, which are noteworthy examples of Petrarchan lyrics of courtly elegance, and on the most significant chivalric romance of the fifteenth century, the *Orlando Innamorato*, which, left unfinished at the poet's death, served as the starting point for the composition of Ariosto's *Orlando Furioso*, completed early in the following century. Traditionally, Boiardo has been credited with having realized in his lengthy poem (three books totaling sixty-nine cantos) a fusion of Carolingian epic tradition and the *matière de Bretagne*, creating thereby a unique Italian genre. Though in truth such a fusion occurs in works predating the *Orlando Innamorato*, Boiardo's poem, in its reflection of the culture and ideals of Italian Renaissance court life during the golden age of Este patronage, is the first masterpiece of the Italian romance genre and the earliest to manifest a sophisticated use of such narrative techniques as interlace. It is well known that Ferrara and similar northern Italian courts were fascinated by medieval epic traditions and that the Este library contained numerous Arthurian romances familiar to Boiardo and other courtiers. Boiardo's work continued and developed the fourteenth- and fifteenth-century *cantari* tradition and also served the literary and aesthetic tastes of a court audience. The framework of the poem is essentially Carolingian, recounting the struggle of the Christian forces of Charlemagne with those of the pagan Agramante. However, the focus of the romance is on the Arthurian elements, including the innumerable fantastic adventures of knights-errant, magic fountains and enchanted forests, and particularly love, which has frequently been seen as the motive force behind a highly energized series of complex episodes, commencing with that of the hero-protagonist, Orlando. A transformation of the French Roland, Orlando becomes a victim of the ineluctable forces of love, represented by Angelica, the daughter of the King of Cathay, sent to undermine the valor of the Christian armies. Boiardo borrows episodes, locales, and characters from Arthurian tradition, transforming them into a tapestry of courtly elegance and sensibility with a markedly international Gothic flavor. [RJR]

Boiardo, Matteo Maria. *Orlando Innamorato di Matteo Maria Boiardo rifatto da Francesco Berni*. Florence: Sansoni, 1971.

Franceschetti, Antonio. "*L'Orlando Innamorato* e gli ideali cavallereschi nella Ferrara del Quattrocento." In *Atti del R. Istituto Veneto di Scienze, Lettere ed Arti*. Venice: Classe di scienze morali e lettere, 1971–72, pp. 315–33.

Gardner, Edmund G. *The Arthurian Legend in Italian Literature*. London: Dent, 1930.

Rajna, Pio. *Le Fonti dell' "Orlando Furioso."* Florence: Sansoni, 1876, 1900.

BOND, NANCY, author of a fantasy for juveniles, *A String in the Harp* (1976). In this first novel, a young boy, Peter, is drawn back from the twentieth century to sixth-century Wales after discovering the tuning fork for Taliesin's harp. Though the novel focuses on his adventures in time and his struggle to return the key to Taliesin's grave and keep it from an ambitious and evil museum curator, the actual heart of the book is the boy's difficulty in coping with the death of his mother and his estrangement from his sisters and his grieving and withdrawn father. [RCS]

Bond, Nancy. *A String in the Harp*. New York: Atheneum, 1976.

BOOK ILLUSTRATION (AMERICAN). Arthurian illustration in the United States is chiefly represented by juvenile books. Americans shared the Victorian conviction that Malory's *Morte Darthur* (in abridged forms) provided models of gentlemanly behavior. The most significant promoter of "the high nobility of spirit that moved these excellent men" was "the father of American illustration," Howard Pyle (1853–1911), whose personal identification with a romantic past was expressed in *The Story of King Arthur and His Knights* (1903), *The Story of the Champions of the Round Table* (1905), *The Story of Sir Launcelot and His Companions* (1907), and *The Story of the Grail and the Passing of Arthur* (1910). The books are lavishly decorated with Beardsleyesque headpieces, tailpieces, and full-page pen-and-ink drawings featuring enigmatic ladies, neo-Gothic furnishings, and complexly patterned dress and armor.

American editions of popular British juveniles commonly featured American artists. In 1917, Pyle's most famous pupil, N.C. Wyeth (1882–1945), provided nine watercolors for Sidney Lanier's *The Boy's King Arthur* (1880), combining brilliantly costumed medieval characters with the landscapes and muscular farm horses of the Brandywine Valley. Louis Rhead (1857–1926), introducing a 1923 reprint of Knowles's *King Arthur and His Knights* (1862), deplored the artists' failure to research sixth-century social history and revealed that his own stylistic sources were the Book of Kells and Abbey's Grail decorations for the Boston Public Library. The result is medieval pastiche with Pre-Raphaelite leanings.

In the last thirty years, a conscious imitation of medieval manuscripts has characterized much illustration. Gustaf Tenggren's muscular heroes in golden armor occupy a primitive Nordic world to complement Sterne and Lindsay's *King Arthur and the Knights of the Round Table* (1962). For Keith Baines's *Sir Thomas Malory's Le Morte d'Arthur* (1963), Enrico Arno's black-and-white line drawings imitate Gothic manuscripts. Ruth Robbins's *Taliesin and King Arthur* (1970), with its two-dimensional figures, frontal positioning, and marginalia, suggests Anglo-Saxon sources. Herschel Levit in Mary MacLeod's *King Arthur* (1963) combines Romanesque forms with turquoise and crushed-strawberry colors. Virgil Burnett's sophisticated full-page drawings for Silverstein's *Sir Gawain and the Green Knight: A Comedy for Christmas* (1974), with their contorted, bare-branched trees, snakey-haired lady, and symbolic candles and toads, recall Beardsley and Rackham. In general, American artists have been less successful than the British in developing original visualizations of Arthurian romance. [MAW]

Mahoney, Bertha E., L.P. Latimer, and Beulah Folmsbee. *Illustrators of Children's Books.* Boston: Horn Book, 1947– (with supplements).

Pitz, Henry C. *Howard Pyle: Writer, Illustrator, and Founder of the Brandywine School.* New York: Potter, 1975.

BOOK ILLUSTRATION (BRITISH). An important aspect of Victorian medievalism was the revived interest in the Arthurian legends, particularly as found in Malory's *Morte Darthur* and Tennyson's *Idylls of the King*. Tennyson's works invited illustration. Woodcut designs by Dante Gabriel Rossetti, Holman Hunt, and Daniel Maclise accompanied the Arthurian compositions in Moxon's 1857 edition of *Poems*, and in 1866–67 the folio editions of four idylls, "Elaine," "Vivien," "Guinevere," and "Enid," contained thirty-six steel-engravings designed by the eminent Alsatian artist Gustave Doré. Although he fails to encapsulate the poet's moral concerns, Doré evocatively portrays a romantic wilderness of misty lakes, dense forests, pounding seas, and castle-topped crags.

From 1870 to 1940, the predominant influence on Arthurian illustration was Pre-Raphaelitism. Landscapes recreated with some botanical accuracy, neo-Gothic furnishings, bright colors, complexity of pattern and symbol, and sensuously beautiful women were the illustrator's stock in trade. The most extensive pictorial cycle in this tradition was the series of forty-eight watercolors provided by W. Russell Flint for the Medici Society's deluxe *Morte* (1910–11). What seems to determine Flint's choice of subjects is the opportunity to present ladies in various degrees of nakedness. Though he clearly found the Grail quest uncongenial, his secular scenes, with their tapestries, carved pillars, rose gardens, and swan-decorated lakes, opulently convey the ambience of courtly society.

William Morris's view of a book as a unified work of art with all the visual elements in harmony—type, illustration, border, page layout, paper, binding—resulted in the production of several profusely decorated Malorys, generally in limited editions. An immediate response to the Kelmscott books was J.M. Dent's *Morte D'Arthur* (1893–94), which contained twenty-one full-page illustrations and 585 headings, borders, initials, and ornaments by the then-unknown Aubrey Beardsley. Though a Burne-Jones influence was evident in the early chapters, Beardsley soon developed the Art Nouveau style characterized by whiplash line, abstract floral motifs, and starkly contrasted black-and-white forms. Even more original was his treatment of content, for his knights, lethargic and spiritless, are completely dominated by their mistresses and the fays. Far from glorifying chivalric romance, Beardsley satirized it, shocking Victorian sensibilities with his effeminate heroes, androgynous nudes, lecherous satyrs, and sensual angels.

While the Beardsley drawings were economically reproduced by a new photomechanical process, Charles Gere and Robert Gibbings returned to the art of wood-engraving. In the twenty-seven cuts that Gere supplied in 1913 for the Ashendene Press Malory, the Burne-Jones Kelmscott style is applied to such conventional subjects as Arthur's wedding feast, Tristram and Isolde's shipboard drink, and Arthur's departure for Avalon. The Golden Cockerel *Morte* (1936) shows that Robert Gibbings was more decorator than illustrator, for he seldom illustrates specific incidents. Such botanical forms as spearlike grass and stylized trees provide a continuum for human figures energetically engaged in the rituals of knight-errantry.

Because the Victorians saw Malory's knights as exemplars of gentlemanly behavior, abridged editions for juveniles became the most popular form of presentation. The audience justified the use of illustrations that would convey not only the sense of a historical past (occurring anywhere between the sixth and sixteenth centuries), but also an aura of magic and mystery. The most popular abridgments, like Sir James Knowles's *King Arthur and His Knights* (1862), Sidney Lanier's *The Boy's King Arthur* (1880), and Alfred W. Pollard's *The Romance of King Arthur and His Knights of the Round Table* (1917), were illustrated by various artists, including Walter Crane, Arthur Rackham, A.G. Walker, Innes Fripp, H.J. Ford, Lancelot Speed, and Walter Hodges.

Recently, a diversification of texts has extended the range of pictorial subjects. Errol Le Cain's picture book *King Arthur's Sword* (1968) uses collage and unrealistic color to present a comic fantasyland for the amusement of young readers. The eccentricities of T.H. White's *The Book of Merlyn* (1977) are enhanced by Trevor Stubley's clever black-and-white drawings of anthropomorphic animals and a dunce-capped Merlin. Translations and adaptations of medieval metrical romances have provided opportunities for mingling realism and fantasy, as in Dorothy Braby's six color engravings for Gwyn Jones's *Sir Gawain and the Green Knight* (1952), where elegance of costume and sinuosity of line are enhanced by the subtle use of pink, olive, and aquamarine. The well of Arthurian inspiration shows no signs of going dry. [MAW]

Bland, David. *A History of Book Illustration.* London: Faber and Faber, 1969.

Muir, Percy. *Victorian Illustrated Books.* London: Batsford, n.d.

BOOK OF MERLYN, THE: *see* WHITE, T. H.

BOOK OF TALIESIN: *see* CELTIC ARTHURIAN LITERATURE.

BOORMAN, JOHN, made the 1981 film *Excalibur*, an imaginative and ambitious attempt to tell the full Arthurian story from Malory. The adaptation, by Boorman and Rospo Pallenberg, does indeed include most of the sequences related by Malory, from the conception of Arthur through the love of Lancelot and Guenevere and the entire Grail quest. In the process, the film—even though it runs more than two hours—gives short shrift to a number of sequences and characters, and for some viewers the narrative pace dilutes the effect rather than intensifies it.

The only fully developed character is Merlin (played by Nicol Williamson), who thus serves as something of a central figure for the unfolding drama and who also provides some lighter moments to offset the generally somber mood of the film.

The film effectively blends fantasy and magic with realistic portrayals of martial violence. Filmed on several Irish locations, with admirable cinematography by Alex Thompson, *Excalibur* is often sumptuous and spectacular. Despite some flaws and lapses, it is an appealing and reasonably successful translation of Malory to the screen. [NJL]

BOROWSKY, MARVIN, portrays Arthur in *The Queen's Knight* (1955) as an illiterate oaf who, though brought to the throne by Mordred and Merlin as a straw-king, rallies the realm with peasant good sense. Lancelot is all that Arthur is not—a doughty warrior, a proud nobleman, and a great lover. Guinevere cannot resist him, though she comes to respect her husband. The kingdom falls because Arthur, who tries his utmost, cannot unite all that is best in it. Borowsky's novel is insightful, if somewhat clumsy in technique. [CNS]

Borowsky, Marvin. *The Queen's Knight.* New York: Random House, 1955.

BOSTON PUBLIC LIBRARY MURALS. The second-floor Delivery Room of the Boston Public Library (McKim, Mead and White, architects, 1887–95) contains a frieze depicting The Quest of the Holy Grail, by Edwin Austin Abbey (1852–1911), executed in two stages between 1890 and 1901. There are fifteen scenes of varying width based upon a great many literary sources, from Robert de Boron to Tennyson, and arranged to "suit the exigencies of pictorial treatment," with the scarlet figure of Galahad as "the brilliant recurring note" (Abbey). The narrative begins with The Vision (or Infancy of Galahad) and continues through his Vigil, The Siege Perilous, The Departure or Benediction, The Castle of the Grail and the Failure, The Loathly Damsel, The Conquest of the Seven Deadly Sins, The Key to the Castle, Delivering the Captive Virtues, Leaving Blanchefleur, Amfortas Released, Galahad Departs, The Voyage to Sarras, Sarras, and The Golden Tree and Achievement of the Grail. [JFO'G]

Baxter, Sylvester. *The Legend of the Holy Grail.* Boston: Curtis and Cameron, 1904.

BOUGHTON, RUTLAND (1878–1960), British composer, devoted much of his last forty years to a grandiose cycle of Arthurian operas. Only the earlier parts were ever produced, and they were far less successful than *The Immortal Hour,* a setting of Fiona Macleod's Celtic drama, or *The Queen of Cornwall,* based on Thomas Hardy's mummers' play. The music for the operas remains unpublished. Turning first to the theme when collaborating with the poet Reginald Buckley, who wrote the libretto for the first two parts, Boughton developed it as the expression of his conviction that Christianity was declining and would be supplanted by socialism. The five parts of the cycle are *The Birth of Arthur, The Round Table* (culminating in Arthur's proclamation of the quest of the Grail), *The Lily Maid* (about Elaine's love for Lancelot), *Galahad* (which contains Boughton's ideas about the function of the arts), and *Avalon* (with Arthur's death). [CNS]

Buckley, Reginald, and Rutland Boughton. *The Music Drama of the Future.* London: Reeves, 1911.

Hurd, Michael. *Immortal Hour: The Life and Period of Rutland Boughton.* London: Routledge and Kegan Paul, 1962.

BOURCHIER, SIR JOHN: *see ARTHUR OF LITTLE BRITAIN.*

BOWERS, GWENDOLYN, author of *Brother of Galahad* (1963), a historical romance for juveniles. Young Hugh of Alleyn travels to Camelot, where he becomes a knight and rides with Galahad. [RHT]

Bowers, Gwendolyn. *Brother to Galahad.* New York: Walck, 1963.

"BOY AND THE MANTLE, THE." The hero of this ballad preserved in the Percy Folio is Craddocke, a figure familiar to readers of the French romances as Caradoc Briebras. Craddocke's success derives from the fact that his wife, alone among the women assembled at Carlisle, has remained faithful to her husband. Only she is able to pass the test of the magic mantle. Similarly, Craddocke is the only male in Arthur's court who is able to meet the cuckold's challenge of carving the boar's head and of drinking from a magical horn. This ballad bears comparison with a number of other Arthurian works, most notably with the *Cort Mantel* and Robert Biket's *Lai du cor.* [JN]

Child, Francis James, ed. *The English and Scottish Popular Ballads.* Boston: Houghton-Mifflin, 1884, Vol. 1, pp. 257–74.

BOY APPRENTICED TO AN ENCHANTER, THE: *see* COLUM, PADRAIC.

BRADLEY, KATHERINE H.: *see* FIELD, MICHAEL.

BRADLEY, MARION ZIMMER, author of *The Mists of Avalon* (1982). Set in Romano-Celtic Britain of the late fifth century, this fantasy relates the Arthurian legend from the viewpoint of the women in the saga: Igraine, wife of Gorlois; their daughter, Morgaine; Igraine's younger sister, Morgause, later Lot's queen; Igraine's half-sister Viviane, Lady of the Lake, priestess of the Mother Goddess on the Holy Isle of Avalon, and mother of Lancelot; her descendants Niniane and Nimue; and Gwenhwyfar, Arthur's queen. Morgaine is the focal character. The central struggle in the book is between the older religions (Druids, early Christians, and worshipers of the Mother Goddess) and a more narrow-minded Christianity, with both beliefs headquartered on the Holy Isle of Avalon (Glastonbury). This continuing conflict provides the background for the rise and fall of Arthur, who, fusing the royal bloods of both pagan and Christian groups, is destined to effect peace in Britain. Bradley follows the Arthurian legend faithfully, incorporating the conception of Arthur by Uther and Igraine; the conception of Mordred (known as Gwydion) by

Arthur and his half-sister (though here Morgaine, rather than Morgause); Arthur's crowning, marriage to Gwenhwyfar, and establishing of the Companions of the Round Table; the love affair between Gwenhwyfar and Lancelot; Galahad's conception by Lancelot and Elaine; the love affair between Morgaine, married to Uriens, and Accolon; the Grail quest; Galahad's achievement of the Grail and holy death; Arthur's and Mordred's killing of each other; Lancelot's death at Glastonbury. The major departures from the legend are the close familial ties between all of the women, except the Christian Gwenhwyfar, thereby creating a pagan sorority; the pagan Grail hallows, which included Excalibur, all euhemerized into the Christian Holy Grail and Sacred Spear; and Arthur's appointing first Galahad, then Mordred as his heir. Bradley's concern with the pagan Arthurian women necessarily lessens her emphasis on the history of Arthur and depicts Christianity as a repressive, interloping religion. Yet the novel ends on a note of reconciliation of Arthurian past and present, paganism and Christianity. Given its feminist thrust, it represents an original and at times engrossing account of the Arthurian legend. [VML]

ᐒ Bradley, Marion Zimmer. *The Mists of Avalon.* New York: Knopf, 1982.

   Day, Mildred Leake. Review of *The Mists of Avalon. Avalon to Camelot,* 1 (1983), 27.

BRADLEY, WILL, author of a romantic fantasy, *Launcelot and the Ladies* (1927), in which the protagonist relives scenes from the love triangle formed by Launcelot, Guenevere, and Elaine (a fusion of the two Elaines). Given a comparable choice in his own life, he marries the younger, unattached woman. [RHT]

ᐒ Bradley, Will. *Launcelot and the Ladies.* New York and London: Harper, 1927.

BRADSHAW, GILLIAN, author of an Arthurian trilogy. The series begins with *Hawk of May* (1980), narrated by Gwalchmai (= Hawk of May, Gawain's name in Welsh). At fourteen, about to be initiated by his mother, Morgawse, into "Darkness," the boy recoils in horror, escapes, and spends three years in the Isles of the Blessed. He returns to seek service with a reluctant Arthur, from whom he learns the dark secret of Medraut's incestuous origin. In *Kingdom of Summer* (1981), which begins nine years later, Rhys ap Sion, Gwalchmai's servant, tells the story of his master's ill-fated love affair with Elidan. The central action of the story is the struggle between Morgawse, the Queen of Darkness, and Gwalchmai, the Champion of Light. In the end, Morgawse is beheaded by Agravain, and Gwalchmai finds Elidan, but he receives no forgiveness and leaves her without learning that Gwynn, a Percival-like character, is his son. *In Winter's Shadow* (1982) shifts the focus to Gwynhwyfar, whose first-person narrative of her passion for Bedwyr, her love for Arthur, her fear and hatred of Medraut, and her guilt and shame for her part in the breakup of the Family, written years later in a convent where she is abbess, is a gripping and convincing account from the Queen's perspective. Medraut, whom she had tried to poison, exposes the lovers. Bedwyr, in trying to rescue her, accidentally kills Gwynn. This inspires in Gwalchmai a passion for revenge that leaves the empire vulnerable to Medraut's usurpation and the ensuing tragedy. Bradshaw borrows material from a variety of traditional sources, and she integrates it with skill to produce a convincing, if increasingly somber, vision of the Arthurian legend. [MAG]

ᴥ Bradshaw, Gillian. *Hawk of May.* New York: Simon and Schuster, 1980.

———. *Kingdom of Summer.* New York: Simon and Schuster, 1981.

———. *In Winter's Shadow.* New York: Simon and Schuster, 1982.

BRAN (BRAN THE BLESSED), a Celtic sea-deity, or the son of one, reputed to have performed marvelous exploits. He appears (as Bendigeidfran, "Bran the Blessed") in the second branch of the *Mabinogi* and is mentioned in the Triad of Three Fortunate Concealments (where his severed head—a powerful talisman—was buried to protect Britain from invasion) and in that of Three Unfortunate Disclosures (in which Arthur dug it up).

Bran is considered by some to be the inspiration for, or the prototype of, Bron the Fisher King. The association with the latter is strengthened by Bran's death from a wound made by a poisoned spear (the Fisher King having suffered from a poisoned wound through the thigh or genitals). Bran also possessed a magic horn—a horn of plenty that produced food and drink whenever they were desired—and some advocates of the Celtic theories relate that horn to the Grail, which, in Chrétien de Troyes's *Perceval,* contains a single Mass wafer capable of sustaining life indefinitely. There is a possibility that other characters (in particular Perceval's father) may also be descended from Bran; indeed, the mystery surrounding the name and identity of Bran makes him a versatile figure, and a character of the same name has even turned up (in Susan Cooper's series The Dark Is Rising, from the 1960s and 70s) as the son of Arthur and Guinevere. [NJL]

ᴥ Newstead, Helaine. *Bran the Blessed in Arthurian Romance.* New York: Columbia University Press, 1939.

BRANWEN: *see MABINOGI.*

BRAVE GERAINT, THE: *see HUGHES, ARTHUR.*

BREIÐFJÖRÐ, SIGURÐUR (1798–1846), an Icelandic poet who gained fame as the author of over twenty-five cycles of *rímur* (narrative poems, of medieval origin, divided into groups of stanzas, each division called a *ríma.*) Among Sigurður Breiðfjörð's *rímur* are the "Rímur af Tistrani og Indiönu," published in 1831, which derive from the eighteenth-century Danish chapbook

BRENTANO, CLEMENS

En tragoedisk Historie om den ædle og tappre Tistrand. The Tistran-*rímur* consist of fourteen *rímur* with a variable number of stanzas ranging from forty-nine to eighty. The stanzas of one *ríma* follow the same metrical pattern, but the patterns vary from *ríma* to *ríma.* The stanzas are bound by end-rhyme and alliteration. [MEK]

🕮 Breiðfjörð, Sigurður. *Rímur af Tistrani og Indiönu.* Copenhagen, 1831.

BRENTANO, CLEMENS: *see* "AUSGLEICHUNG, DIE."

BRESSON, ROBERT, made the controversial 1974 film *Lancelot du Lac,* which recounts the aftermath of the unsuccessful Grail quest and Lancelot's promise to God not to continue his affair with Guenevere. He is torn between carnal and divine love and between his appetites and his obligation to Arthur. Originally entitled *Le Graal,* the film stars Luc Simon as Lancelot, Laura Duke Condominas as the Queen, and Vladimir Antolek as Artus. Bresson emphasizes the themes of fatality and predestination, and the image of death colors virtually every scene. We witness bloody battles, skeletons hanging from trees, and a thoroughly unromanticized view of chivalry and life.

In an attempt to make the film's themes applicable to other periods, Bresson intentionally creates a certain number of anachronisms (especially in terms of costumes) and systematically avoids the temptation to make a period piece. His directorial style is elliptical in the extreme; for example, the film opens with a scene of two sword blades striking each other to evoke a battle; elsewhere, he will give us a view of a warhorse's rump to suggest the power and energy of combat. His self-conscious use of such ellipsis and of eccentric camera angles and sound effects proves distracting for many viewers.

Critical reaction to the film varied widely. Bresson's supporters termed it admirable, tender, and passionate, a cinematic poem that stands as one of his most beautiful masterpieces. Others saw it as arid, sterile, and pretentious; some found it bordering on self-parody, and one condemned Bresson's technique as "aesthetic constipation." Despite severe criticism by some, the film won the 1974 International Critics' Prize, which was, however, refused. [NJL]

BRETA SǪGUR ("Sagas, or Stories, of the Britons"), the Old Norse version of Geoffrey of Monmouth's *Historia Regum Britanniae.* It is a free translation, with many additions and substitutions. Contractions and omissions are, however, much more common, particularly in the second half of the work. In both extant manuscripts, the *Breta sǫgur* follow *Trójumanna saga* (the Old Norse version of the Fall of Troy), and this probably accounts for one significant difference from Geoffrey. Geoffrey's dedication and his description of Britain are replaced by five chapters on the adventures of Aeneas. Chapter 6 then picks up Geoffrey's account of Brutus. The main storyline of the *Breta sǫgur* continues to follow that of Geoffrey's *Historia*. Within individual episodes, however, the order of events is often varied. The Old Norse translator was more interested than Geoffrey in Christianity and, for example, substitutes the standard hagiographic story of St. Ursula for Geoffrey's secular version. He also takes particular interest in English ecclesiastical history. Other changes reflect the *Breta sǫgur*'s northern orientation. For example, Hengist and Horsa are accompanied by the hero þiðrik, and the list of Scandinavian countries occupied by Arthur is expanded. Geoffrey's *Prophetiae Merlini* appear in their proper place in a verse translation known as *Merlínússpá*, made by the Icelandic monk Gunnlaugr Leifsson. The *Breta sǫgur* conclude with an account of the West Saxon kings, which is not drawn from Geoffrey. Many minor variations and omissions may derive from the Latin exemplar, and others are almost certainly misreadings of the Latin. The *Breta sǫgur* were probably written early in the thirteenth century, although a slightly later date is also possible. Although both manuscripts in which the *Breta sǫgur* are preserved are Icelandic, it is uncertain whether the work was written in Iceland or in Norway. The author of the *Breta sǫgur* is unknown, but the whole may be the work of Gunnlaugr Leifsson or one of his contemporaries. [CLB]

�763 Jónsson, Finnur, ed. *Hauksbók, udgiven efter de Arnamagnæanske håndskrifter No. 371, 544 og 675, 4° samt forskellige papirhåndskrifter.* Copenhagen: Det kongelige nordiske Oldskrift-Selskab, 1892–96, pp. 231–301.

BRIDAL OF TRIERMAIN, THE: *see* SCOTT, SIR WALTER.

BRIGHT-HELMED ONE, THE: *see* VINEY, JANE.

BRITANNIA TRIUMPHANS: *see* JONES, INIGO.

BRITO DI BRETTAGNA: *see* PUCCI, ANTONIO.

BRITTANY, "Lesser" Britain as distinct from "Great" Britain: the north-west peninsula of France, inhabited by the Bretons, people of British descent whose ancestors played a major role in Arthurian legend-making. Under the Roman Empire, it was part of the somewhat larger territory of Armorican Gaul. Colonization from Britain began during the last phase of the Empire in the West.

Welsh tradition associates the settlement with the emperor Maximus, who was proclaimed in Britain in 383 and captured Rome in 388 but was overthrown soon after. His army included numerous Britons, and according to the Welsh he allotted them lands on the Continent. Nennius (early ninth century) says: "He gave them many districts from the lake on top of Mount Jove to the city called Quentovic, as far as the Western Mass, that is the Western Ridge. They are the Armorican British, and they never came back, even to the present day." Nennius's statement spreads them out widely; by implication, it was the settlement in what is now Brittany that survived.

The story is enlarged on in the *Mabinogion* tale *The Dream of Macsen Wledig*. Here, Macsen—Maximus himself—marries the British princess Elen, and, when her brother Cynan brings a British army to Rome to aid him, he rewards Cynan's warriors for the consequent victory with a free hand in Armorica. They kill the men and marry the women, cutting out their tongues to prevent them from corrupting the British language with speech of their own. This is an onomastic legend. *Llydaw*, the Welsh name for Brittany, is made out to have been derived from *lled* 'half' and *taw* 'silent,' because only the male half of the population could speak.

Cynan or (in Breton) Conan, surnamed Meriadoc, is also depicted as the founder in the *Legend of St. Goeznovius*. Its author knows the tongue story but seems not to know the reason for it, so the point is lost. This Breton version says nothing of Maximus and treats Conan's colonization as a purely British enterprise.

There is some evidence for a British presence in Armorica at least as early as these accounts imply. But the first serious colonization took place in the late 450s, being marked historically by a reference to a "bishop of the Britons," Mansuetus, as attending a council at Tours in 461. Gildas describes the overseas movement as a flight of refugees from the Saxon ravagings, and so at first it presumably was. Yet the bulk of the emigration seems to have come from southwestern Britain, a long way from the Saxon enclaves. It is likely that some Britons went over in a more deliberate way by arrangement with Aegidius, the Roman ruler of northern Gaul, and cooperated during the next decade or so in coastal defense and other measures of control. The migrant leaders included people of wealth and education (Gildas says they took many books with them), and they apparently helped in the repulse and containment of Saxon marauders occupying the lower Loire valley. However, nothing suggests a cohesive mass settlement, transforming the character of the region, as early as this. The supposed case for it depends wholly on the assumption that a large British force that operated in Gaul ca. 468–70 was recruited in Armorica, implying a large British population already there. But the little that is recorded about this army indicates that most if not all of it came directly from Britain, and with the army eliminated as evidence not much remains.

The next step, in the later fifth century, was the beginning of an influx of "saints"—ecclesiastics, most of them Welsh, who crossed over from Britain and were active in organizing Breton communities. In the first half of the sixth century, a fresh wave of general emigration, on a larger scale, finally converted most of Armorica into "Brittany"; the names "Brittany" and "Armorica" became interchangeable. The country was nominally subject to the kings of the Franks but kept a decided character of its own. The earlier

Armorican people were absorbed. Breton developed as a language in its own right, evolved from the Celtic British speech of the imperial era, like Welsh and Cornish. Brittany had local dynasties and retained economic and cultural ties with Cornwall. Several regional rulers may have held some kind of authority on both sides of the Channel.

Brittany's traditions of Arthur were strong, but mainly oral, so that their nature is a matter of inference rather than knowledge. To judge from the *Legend of St. Goeznovius*, they were built on a genuine historical foundation. But motifs of a poetic and fanciful sort may have originated here, too. Notable is the idea of Arthur's immortality and destined return, which is often mentioned as a Breton belief by a series of authors beginning with Henry of Huntingdon (*see* RETURN, LEGENDS OF ARTHUR'S). Geoffrey of Monmouth shows a pro-Breton bias, pointing to his use of materials from that quarter, perhaps brought to England by Bretons returning to their ancestral island with the Norman conquerors, as many did. If the "ancient book in the British language" that he claims as his source had any reality, it is more likely to have come from Brittany than from Wales.

Breton stories, spread abroad by minstrels through France and beyond, probably underlie much Arthurian romance on the Continent. Arthur holds court in Brittany in Chrétien's *Cligés* and explicitly at Nantes in Wolfram's *Parzival*. Brittany figures in the Tristan legend and may have supplied some of its elements. Wace, who first mentions the Round Table, claims to have heard of it from the Bretons. He also mentions the enchanted forest of Brocéliande, in the heart of their country. He was disappointed with it himself, but it reappears in romance, and its remnants harbor Arthurian folklore to this day—as do other Breton locations. [GA]

❦ Cavendish, Richard. *King Arthur and the Grail*. London: Weidenfeld and Nicolson, 1978.
Chadwick, N.K. "The Colonization of Brittany from Celtic Britain." *Proceedings of the British Academy*, 51 (1966).
———. *Early Brittany*. Cardiff: University of Wales Press, 1969.
Fleuriot, Léon. *Les Origines de la Bretagne*. Paris: Payot, 1980.
Loomis, Roger Sherman, ed. *Arthurian Literature in the Middle Ages*. Oxford: Clarendon, 1959.

BROADSIDES were single sheets of paper that contained printing on only the front, or *recto*, side; the size of the sheet fluctuated between folio and sixteenmo. If the printing extended onto the reverse side as well, the page was called a "broadsheet"; when these sheets were folded together once, twice, or more times, they formed a small pamphlet termed a "chapbook" or "cheapbook," a forerunner of the modern paperback. Although the subject matter and style of these sheets were quite heterogeneous, ranging from verse to prose, from religious tract to bawdy tale, from bucolic poem to popular song, the broadside was particularly associated with the transmittal of a specific genre of popular literature, the ballad.

The practice of printing ballads on broadsides, first documented during the latter half of the fifteenth century, can be traced to the confluence of several causes: the decline of the professional minstrel, the invention of movable type (increasing literacy among the populace), and an insatiable demand for inexpensive reading material. Indeed, the broadside ballad may be seen as one of the first forms of popular literature produced on a mass scale. It was simple to print, it was within the reach of even the poorest as it sold for only pennies, and it could be hawked anywhere. The broadside ballad attained maximum popularity during the sixteenth and seventeenth centuries; thereafter, although it lingered on until the late nineteenth century, it was supplanted in large measure by the production of chapbooks. From the sixteenth through the eighteenth centuries, a Gothic typeface called "Black-Letter" was used; from the eighteenth century onward, the Black-Letter type was replaced with a Roman type called "White-Letter." The text was printed in four columns, and then the page was divided in half, each leaf being sold separately. Frequently, a decorative woodcut illustration preceded the text.

The broadside was an ephemeral form of literature; as such, it was destined for momentary consumption: to be read, reread, and then discarded. Consequently, the broadsides that have survived until the modern era represent only a small fraction of the thousands printed during the Renaissance and Baroque.

The history of the broadside ballad has been intertwined from the first with that of the Arthurian tradition. The earliest broadsides in England, dating from the last two decades of the fifteenth century, were the work of the presses of William Caxton, the first editor of Thomas Malory's *Le Morte Darthur*. Other famous collectors of broadside ballads, such as Sir Walter Scott and Alfred Lord Tennyson, participated in the later Arthurian Revival. Two of the earliest broadsides, from ca. 1508, treat Arthurian themes: one is a version of *Sir Eglamour*, and the other is a metrical romance of *Golagros and Gawane*. Other examples of Arthurian ballads that circulated on broadsides include "Sir Lionel," "The Boy and the Mantle," "King Arthur and King Cornwall," and "The Marriage of Sir Gawain."

Broadsides are of invaluable worth to scholars, as they attest to the ceaseless fluctuations wrought by word-of-mouth dissemination: the addition or deletion of characters, the rearrangement of existing scenes, and the insertion of new material. From the broadside, scholars can more accurately trace the evolution of cycles like the Arthurian, for these texts, reflecting the oral tradition, help to bridge the gap between the different manifestations of the material in manuscript form. [JK]

⊷ Child, Francis James, ed. *The English and Scottish Popular Ballads*. Boston: Houghton-Mifflin, 1884.

Shepherd, Leslie. *The Broadside Ballad: A Study in Origins and Meaning*. Wakefield, West Yorkshire: E.P., 1978.

BROADSIDES (SPANISH), or *pliegos sueltos* ("loose sheets") as they are termed in Spanish, derive their name from the format in which they were sold.

Analogous to their English counterparts, they consisted of a page folded in half lengthwise, each half being sold separately. Printers of broadsides in Spain also made use of a Gothic type (*letra gótica*), placed woodcut illustrations above the text, and frequently indicated the melody to which the ballad was to be sung. The practice in Spain of printing ballads on broadsides follows the same chronology as the rest of Europe, with the sixteenth and seventeenth centuries being the period of greatest production.

Spanish broadsides play a pivotal role in the history of Spanish literature, for they are a direct link with the late Middle Ages. If it were not for the printers and collectors who became interested in the oral-traditional literature circulating around them and who rescued such literature from oblivion by preserving it on broadsides, an entire literary epoch would have been lost. Even more significantly, broadsides were the raw material from which the compilers of the sixteenth- and seventeenth-century songbooks drew their versions of ballads and other songs. Such is the case with the only three ballads of Arthurian material that have survived on the Iberian peninsula: one deals with Tristan and Isolde ("Herido está don Tristán") and the other two with Lancelot ("Nunca fuera caballero" and "Tres hijuelos había el rey"). Precious relics of a much larger ballad cycle, these three poems hint at what must have been a flourishing Arthurian tradition on the Iberian peninsula. [JK]

Rodríguez-Moñino, Antonio, ed. *Diccionario de pliegos sueltos poéticos (siglo XVI)*. Madrid: Castalia, 1970.

BROCÉLIANDE. The forest of Brocéliande, identified with the forest of Paimpont in modern-day Brittany, was famous throughout the Middle Ages for its enchantments, in particular its storm-making spring, known sometimes as the fountain of Bérenton. The spring is central to Chrétien de Troyes's *Yvain* and is mentioned by Giraldus Cambrensis. Wace recounts in a famous passage of his *Roman de Rou* how he traveled personally to Brocéliande to seek the marvels about which the Bretons spoke but was unable to find any: "I saw the forest and I saw the land; I looked for marvels, but I did not find them" (*Roman de Rou*, ed. Holden, ll. 6393–95). In the sequels to the Old French *Merlin*, Brocéliande is the site of the enchanted prison in which Niniane holds Merlin captive. The forest is also mentioned in the Old French *Tournoiement Anticrist* (by Huon de Méry), in *Claris et Laris*, and in *Brun de la Montaigne*, as well as in the German romance of *Garel von dem blühenden Tal*, by Der Pleier. [WWK]

BRODEUR, ARTHUR GILCHRIST: *see* BISHOP, FARNHAM.

BROKEN STONE: see MONACO, RICHARD.

BROTHER ROBERT, active during the first half of the thirteenth century, produced in 1226 a Norwegian translation of Thomas's *Tristan* entitled *Tristrams saga.* This translation, the only complete version of the Thomas-branch of the legend, influenced the dissemination of Tristan material in Scandinavia and especially exerted influence in Iceland, where a ballad, "Tristrams kvæði," and a prose adaptation, *Saga af Tristram ok Ísodd,* were produced. Robert's name also appears in *Elis saga* (a translation of *Elie de St. Gille,* a *chanson de geste*). Scholars have associated Robert with the Norwegian translations of several Arthurian works made during King Hákon's reign (1217–63): *Ívens saga* and *Parcevals saga* (based on Chrétien de Troyes's *Yvain* and *Perceval*), *Möttuls saga* (a version of the fabliau *Le Mantel mautaillié*), and *Strengleikar* (a collection of twenty-one lais). His nationality is unknown, but his name suggests Anglo-Norman origins. Given the ties with England during Hákon's reign, Brother Robert may have been a cleric associated with Norwegian monasteries, at Lyse or Hovedoya, which maintained close ties with England. Although the scope of Robert's known translations is modest, his activity attests the importance of Hákon's interest in French romance and is crucial to the transmission of Arthurian material in Scandinavia. (*See also* TRISTRAMS SAGA OK ÍSÖNDAR.) [IJR]

Leach, Henry G. *Angevin Britain and Scandinavia.* Cambridge, Mass.: Harvard University Press, 1921.

Schach, Paul. "Some Observations on the Translations of Brother Robert." In *Les Relations littéraires franco-scandinaves au Moyen Âge: Actes du Colloque de Liège.* Paris: Société d'Edition "Les Belles Lettres," 1975, pp. 117–35.

BRUCE: see SCOTTISH ARTHURIAN CHRONICLES.

BRUT: see LAYAMON; PROSE *BRUT*; WACE.

BRUTS, **WELSH:** *see* GEOFFREY OF MONMOUTH.

BUCH DER ABENTEUER, DAS: see FUETRER, ULRICH.

BUCHANAN, GEORGE: *see* SCOTTISH ARTHURIAN CHRONICLES.

BULWER-LYTTON, EDWARD GEORGE (1803–1873), wrote two Arthurian poems, "The Fairy Bride" (1853), a brief tale of a young knight's unhappy encounter with an unearthly lover, and *King Arthur* (1848), a twelve-book epic recounting the triumph of Arthur and his Britons over a Saxon invasion. In *King Arthur,* Bulwer-Lytton creates his own narrative, rather than reshapes traditional Arthurian materials, and fashions his own personal allegory of Arthur's career as the genesis of British political freedom. He recasts Guenevere as two separate persons (Arthur's bride, Genevieve, and Lancelot's bride, Genevra), thereby eliminating the issue of Lancelot's and Guenevere's adultery, which is central to the Arthurian poems of his contemporaries Tennyson and Morris. [MDC]

Lytton, Edward George Earle Lytton Bulwer-. *King Arthur*. London: Colburn, 1848.

Bulwer-Lytton, Victor Alexander. *The Life of Edward Bulwer, First Lord Lytton*. 2 vols. London: Macmillan, 1913.

BURGHLEY NEF. Ship models made of precious materials were often used as incense boats, reliquaries, and votive offerings in the later Middle Ages. Secular pieces, known as nefs, may originally have been made as drinking vessels; they were related only in the most general form to these ecclesiastical pieces. The Burghley Nef (Victoria and Albert Museum, London) has a nautilus shell for its hull, and the poop and fo'c'sle are formed of ornamental open battlements. Fully rigged, swarming with sailors, and armed with so many guns that one cannon seems to be aimed at the main mast, this fantastic creation glides over a silver sea on the back of a silver mermaid. The nef also has cast-silver passengers, a young couple seated in front of the main mast who seem to have been playing chess but now clasp hands and gaze fondly at each other. The figures depicted can only be Tristan and Isolde on the voyage to Cornwall.

The Burghley Nef is stamped with the mark of a Parisian goldsmith, Pierre le Flamand (two banners forming a St. Andrew's cross under a crowned fleur-de-lis) and the letter mark (a crowned "Y") for the year 1482/3. [MS]

Oman, Charles. *Medieval Silver Nefs*. London: Victoria and Albert Museum, 1963.

BURMEISTER, LUDWIG PETER AUGUST: *see* LYSER, JOHANN PETER.

BURNE-JONES, EDWARD (1833–1898), a painter who featured Arthurian subjects throughout his oeuvre. It is his visual interpretation that is associated with the mid- to late Arthurian Revival. His attenuated figures, floating in a dreamlike setting, were influential; his style provided the prototype for the later Victorian painters, such as Edwin Austen Abbey and John William Waterhouse, and even more extensively for book illustrators, especially Aubrey Beardsley, Walter Crane, and Arthur Rackham.

Burne-Jones became acquainted with Arthurian subjects at Exeter College, Oxford, in 1853, when he was introduced to the poetry of Tennyson by his friend William Morris. In 1855, Morris gave him the Southey edition of *Le Morte Darthur*, a volume he had coveted but could not afford. Their mutual enthusiasm for Malory influenced Pre-Raphaelite painter Dante Gabriel Rossetti, as seen in the Oxford Union Murals project (1857), in which Burne-Jones painted *The Death of Merlin*. His interest in Tennyson revived in 1858, when he met the poet and was inspired to draw many Arthurian subjects, including *Sir Galahad* (Fogg Art Museum, Cambridge).

In the next two decades, his elongated figure style and evocative Arthurian vision gained maturity. The former is seen in the Dunlop Windows project (1862), while the latter emerged in such non-Arthurian but chivalric works as *The Merciful Knight* (1863, Birmingham City Art Gallery) and *Le Chant d'Amour* (1865, Museum of Fine Arts, Boston). The innocent dream world took on erotic connotations in *The Beguiling of Merlin* (1875–77, Lady Lever Art Gallery, Port Sunlight), in which he blended ideas from Tennyson and French romance.

In the last decades of his life, his Arthurian interest increased. A sketchbook of 1885 (British Museum, London) contains extensive notes on Arthurian heraldry, foreshadowing the decorative-arts designs of the subsequent years, including the Rottingdean Windows (1886, Victoria and Albert Museum, London) and the Stanmore Hall Tapestries (1891–94, Collection, Duke of Westminster), both illustrating the quest for the Holy Grail. In 1895, he designed scenery and costumes for J.C. Comyns Carr's drama *King Arthur* (lost, known through sketchbooks). He was to have illustrated a luxury edition of *Le Morte Darthur* for Morris's Kelmscott Press; the project was abandoned, but he did design a frontispiece and title page for each of the two volumes of Sebastian Evans's *The High History of the Holy Grail* (London: Dent, 1898). His culminating work was *Arthur in Avalon* (1880–98, Museum of Art, Ponce, Puerto Rico), an enormous project, unfinished at his death. The artist felt it to be the summation of all his ideals in art. He defined his Arthurian vision in writing to Thomas Rooke, who was on holiday in Avallon, Burgundy, in 1886: "But how is it that you are at Avalon, where I have striven to be with all my might." [DNM]

Burne-Jones, Georgiana. *Memorials of Edward Burne-Jones*. 2 vols. London: Macmillan, 1906.

BURNETT, VIRGIL: *see* BOOK ILLUSTRATION (AMERICAN).

BURNHAM, JEREMY, and TREVOR RAY, authors of *Raven* (1977), a fantasy for adolescents based upon their own screenplay for a British television series of the same name. A rebellious youth emerges as reluctant leader of a conservationist movement to save an ancient network of caves linked with Arthur's cave legend. There are suggestions that the hero is Arthur reborn and that his mentor is Merlin. [RHT]

Burnham, Jeremy, and Trevor Ray. *Raven*. London: Corgi, 1977.

CABELL, JAMES BRANCH (1879–1958), American novelist whose most famous work was *Jurgen: A Comedy of Justice* (1919). This picaresque romance recounts the adventures of Jurgen, a thirteenth-century pawnbroker in the mythical realm of Poictesme, married to a shrewish wife, Dame Lisa. Like Faust, he magically regains his youth and embarks on an amatory odyssey through time, his conquests including a pliant Guenevere, the Lady of the Lake, and Helen of Troy.

Although the Arthurian characters are peripheral, *Jurgen* follows the pattern of many twentieth-century American works on Arthur, in that it satirizes the excesses of Arthur's chivalric world, such as nonpareil-yet-adulterous ladies, jousting at the drop of a lance, and overly idealistic tenets for establishing a social order in a Christian world. Cabell ironically mocks the restrictive sexual and religious mores of his own time; the book was banned and of course became a bestseller. *Jurgen*, however, is a witty, erudite comedy, if not of justice then of human nobility battling with and being undercut by human frailty. It is in every way the best work in Cabell's eighteen-volume Biography of the Life of Manuel, and represents an original adaptation of Arthurian material. [VML]

❧ Cabell, James Branch. *Jurgen: A Comedy of Justice*. New York: McBride, 1919.

———. *The Letters of James Branch Cabell*, ed. Edward Wagenknecht. Norman: University of Oklahoma Press, 1975.

Cover, James P. *Notes on Jurgen*. New York: McBride, 1928.

CAD GODDEU: see CELTIC ARTHURIAN LITERATURE.

CADBURY–CAMELOT. Cadbury Castle, an Iron Age hill fort beside the village of South Cadbury in Somerset, has three features of Arthurian interest: first, its longstanding designation by the name *Camelot*; second, a miscellany of local folklore related to this; and third, its proved reoccupation and refortification during the period within which Arthur supposedly lived.

There was never a castle here in the medieval sense. The hill itself is the castle, being made so by its huge system of earthwork ramparts, now largely overgrown with woods, but still exposed in places. The topmost bank of the four encircles an eighteen-acre enclosure, rising to a summit plateau 500 feet above sea level. John Leland, in his *Itinerary* (1542), wrote: "At the very south end of the church of South-Cadbyri standeth Camallate, sometime a famous town or castle. . . . The people can tell nothing there but that they have heard say Arthur much resorted to Camalat."

Leland uses the name as if it were an accepted one. Arguably, he is merely speculating, prompted by the place-name *Camel* that occurs in the neighborhood. By itself, this hardly seems a sufficient explanation, and folklore may also have played a part. A version of the Arthurian cave legend probably already existed here. In its modern form, it asserts that a pair of gates concealed in the hillside swing open once a year, revealing the sleeping king. There is sixteenth-century evidence for the highest part of the hill being known as Arthur's Palace. Further legends, recorded in more recent times, may or may not be old. On Midsummer Eve or Midsummer Night or Christmas Eve (it is doubtful which, and it may be only every seven years), the ghosts of Arthur and his knights ride across the hilltop and out through the ancient gateway in the fortifications. Below, a track running toward Glastonbury is Arthur's Hunting Causeway, and on winter nights, it is said, spectral riders and horses can be heard on it. The nearby River Cam is eligible as Camlann, the scene of the battle in which Arthur fell.

After Leland, other antiquaries, such as Stukeley, take up the "Camelot" theme, and the name appears on maps, justifying its use to distinguish this Cadbury from others. Any deeper significance must depend on definitions. The Camelot of the romancers who created it is a medieval dream-city that would be futile to seek anywhere. It has, however, the special attribute of being peculiarly King Arthur's capital; no other monarch reigns there; and Cadbury could be claimed as "the real Camelot" so far as anything ever was, if it were connected in some way with the original Arthur, having (for example) been refurbished as his personal citadel. It would be the far-off reality behind the Camelot of the romancers. This is a possibility that the archaeology of the site may be held to raise.

The principal excavation was carried out during 1966–70 under the direction of Leslie Alcock. It confirmed an Iron Age settlement on the plateau, with which the defenses were associated. This survived undisturbed for some time after the Roman conquest of southern Britain. Then the hill was stormed and captured. The inference is that Cadbury was a center of resistance in some unrecorded British revolt, possibly an offshoot of Boudicca's in A.D. 60–61. The Roman period was followed by a complete gap, after which the dating evidence of imported pottery attests reoccupation.

This phase of the site—Cadbury 11, in Professor Alcock's terminology— may have begun ca. 460 or at any time over the next few decades, but not much after 500. Buildings belonging to it include a timber hall on the plateau, in the "Arthur's Palace" area, and a gate-house reminiscent of Roman auxiliary forts. However, the most striking feature is embedded in the topmost bank: a drystone wall about sixteen feet thick running around the entire perimeter, a distance of nearly three-quarters of a mile. This massive enhancement of the rampart incorporated pieces of Roman masonry and was bound together by a framework of wooden beams. Celtic, not Roman, in style, it was a fairly sophisticated structure embodying an impressive amount of labor.

At the time of its discovery, Cadbury 11 was interpreted as an army base. Since the scale and elaborateness of the refortification were archaeologically unmatched in that period, the results permitted a connection with Arthur conceived as the war-leader of Welsh tradition. Over the next few years, it was widely assumed that Cadbury's apparent uniqueness was accidental, and the excavation of other hill forts would refute it. This did not happen. Reoccupation during the same period was proved in various places, but the stone-and-timber defensive work remained without a contemporary parallel in the archaeology of England and Wales. Comparable structures were found in Scotland but were markedly smaller. In a 1982 reassessment, Alcock suggested that Cadbury was a political center rather than a military one, the seat of a king with resources of wealth and manpower unequaled—on the existing evidence—in the Britain of his time.

Considered historically, such a view raises the issue of the British high kingship that appears to have existed at least in name during much of the fifth century. It is interesting that Vortigern, a holder of this office, is portrayed by Nennius as trying to build himself a personal fortress on a hill in Wales. Moreover, he uses "timber and stones," as at Cadbury. Though the story may be fictitious, it hints that "timber and stones" were regarded as the proper materials for a high king's citadel. A project like the one ascribed to Vortigern might have been actually undertaken at Cadbury by a successor.

Whether this successor can be meaningfully equated with Arthur is a question outside the scope of archaeology. (*See* ARTHUR, ORIGINS OF LEGEND.) But the nature of Cadbury 11 makes it less likely that Leland's Camelot identification was a pure guess. Somehow, he hit on what is easily the most appropriate site throughout Britain. Even a modern archaeologist could not have picked it out on a visual appraisal alone, without excavation. As perhaps at Castle Dore and Tintagel, some kind of tradition is probable. The actual romantic name need not have been part of it, since by the sixteenth century "Camelot" was familiar as the name of Arthur's home, and Leland could simply have applied it to a place where he understood that home to have been.

A literary by-product of the work at Cadbury was the choice of this location for Camelot by novelists, such as Marion Zimmer Bradley, Catherine Christian, and Mary Stewart. [GA]

Alcock, Leslie. *"By South Cadbury Is That Camelot . . .": Excavations at Cadbury Castle 1966–70.* London: Thames and Hudson, 1972.

———. "Cadbury–Camelot: A Fifteen-Year Perspective." *Proceedings of the British Academy,* 68 (1983).

CAEN CAPITAL, a capital in the church of St.-Pierre, Caen, illustrating two scenes from Arthurian romances—Lancelot crossing the Sword Bridge and Gawain on the Perilous Bed—together with non-Arthurian material (the Capture of the Unicorn, Aristotle Ridden by Phyllis, Samson and the Lion, and the Pelican in Her Piety). In the context of these well-known symbols of Christian sacrifice (the pelican, the unicorn), strength and protection (Samson), and the power of Women (Phyllis, the Virgin), the adventures of Arthur's knights, who fight temptations and evil powers in the service of their ladies, take on moral implications that make them acceptable for inclusion as church decoration. The selection and depiction of the Arthurian scenes seem to have been inspired by early fourteenth-century Parisian ivory caskets, thus the capital can be dated at mid-fourteenth century. [MS]

Loomis, Roger Sherman, and Laura Hibbard Loomis. *Arthurian Legends in Medieval Art.* London: Oxford University Press, pp. 71–72; figs. 138–39.

CAERLEON, a small town by the River Usk in Gwent, at the southeast corner of Wales. Its name means "City" (originally "Fort") "of the Legion." As the Roman *Isca Silurum,* it combined a military establishment with a center of civilian population. It has been proposed as the "City of the Legion" that is the scene of Arthur's ninth battle in Nennius. In this context, however, Caerleon is a less probable candidate than Chester, the Roman base near the northern end of the Welsh borderlands.

Caerleon's chief importance in Arthurian literature is as the place where Geoffrey of Monmouth has Arthur hold a plenary court, after organizing the conquests made in his first Gallic campaign. Geoffrey may have chosen it simply because it was near his native Monmouth and he had seen the ruins, which in the twelfth century were still conspicuous. In fact, he mentions them (Book IV, Chapter 19). His lavish description of the court prepares the way for the romancers' concept of Camelot as a special Arthurian capital. Here also, he locates the convent to which Guinevere retires.

Today, thanks to excavation and preservation, a large part of the complex of Roman buildings has survived. The amphitheater is the finest specimen in Britain. Before it was restored to daylight, it was covered by an accumulation of earth that concealed the structure but kept the shape, a hollow oval. The resulting mound was claimed locally as the true Round Table, the idea being that the knights sat facing inward as the original spectators did.

Caerleon has a version of the cave legend. A mysterious stranger in a three-cornered hat guided a farmer to a cave where a thousand of Arthur's soldiers lay asleep, waiting till they should be needed. One detail, that their heads were resting on guns, suggests that this tale is hardly one of the earliest forms of the legend. [GA]

Geoffrey of Monmouth. *Historia Regum Britanniae*, Book IX, Chapters 12–15; Book XI, Chapter 1.

Ashe, Geoffrey. *A Guidebook to Arthurian Britain*. Wellingborough: Aquarian, 1983.

CALIBURNUS: *see* EXCALIBUR.

"CALIDORE": *see* PEACOCK, THOMAS LOVE.

CAMELOT, Arthur's principal residence and preferred castle. Although later descriptions of the castle appear to owe a good deal to Geoffrey of Monmouth's depiction of Caerleon, Camelot is not mentioned prior to Chrétien de Troyes, in whose work it occurs but once (at the beginning of *Lancelot*—and even there it is not present in all manuscripts). It was during the thirteenth century that Camelot became prominent, especially in the Vulgate Cycle of romances. From that time on, it served as the point of departure for the Grail questers, and in the *Mort Artu* Gawain expressed his desire to be buried at Camelot, which had obviously become by that time the ideological, as well as geographical, center of the Arthurian world. The ultimate ruin of Camelot, according to *Palamedes* and the Spanish *Demanda del Sancto Grial*, was the work of the aged Mark, who (hearing that Lancelot was dead) invaded Logres, destroying Joyous Gard, Lancelot's tomb, Camelot, and the Round Table.

During the thirteenth century, various writers described Camelot in considerable physical detail. The castle was surrounded by plains, with a forest and a river nearby. There was at least one church, and there was, naturally enough, a town or city around (or near) the castle.

There is nothing surprising about Camelot, at least in terms of its physical presentation: it is a beautiful city and an extraordinary castle, but it could not have been significantly different from many another city and castle. Only two facts set it apart from others: first, it eventually takes on religious as well as ideological overtones (certain knights even being baptized there); second, it is not clear where it is. Malory identifies Camelot with Winchester, but other writers are far less specific. In certain texts, it appears to be located in southern England, but few works will permit us to be any more precise than that.

Scholars continue to look for Camelot, and some believe they have found it (or its prototype) at Cadbury–Camelot. But while a good deal of energy has been expended on the search for the "actual" Camelot, it is clear that Camelot's geographical imprecision, whether conscious or not, is a stroke of genius on the part of romance authors: for Camelot, located nowhere in particular, can be anywhere; in the world of Arthurian romance, it is less a specific place than a state of mind, a source of inspiration, an idea.

Modern versions of the legend have generally maintained this lack of precision. Camelot, in effect, is the center of the Arthurian universe, and no more geographical detail is needed. On the other hand, authors almost universally update the castle itself, transforming it into a typical (if unusually opulent) castle of the High Middle Ages, complete with drawbridges, portcullises, and crenelated towers. Such a transformation is carried very nearly to its logical conclusion in the film version of *Camelot*. [NJL]

🙪 Pickford, Cedric E. "Camelot." In *Mélanges de langue et de littérature médiévales offerts à Pierre Le Gentil*. Paris: SEDES, 1973.

CAMELOT: *see* LERNER, ALAN JAY.

CAMELOT JOUSTS, THE: *see* BARING, MAURICE.

CAMERON, JULIA MARGARET (1815–1879). In the fall of 1874, Alfred Tennyson asked his close friend Julia Margaret Cameron to make photographic illustrations after his *Idylls of the King* for publication as wood-engraved frontispieces in a Henry S. King and Company Cabinet edition of his *Works* (London, 1874–76; Cameron images used in Volumes 6, 7, and 9). With Tennyson's encouragement, Cameron published her original prints in a two-volume gift book, *Illustrations to Tennyson's "Idylls of the King" and Other Poems* (London: King, 1875), and as individual prints. The earlier of the two volumes was of *Idylls* subjects; the second included other Tennyson works. The *Idylls* chapters illustrated are: "Gareth and Lynette," "Geraint and Enid," "Merlin and Vivien," "Lancelot and Elaine," "The Holy Grail," "Guinevere," and "The Passing of Arthur." The first volume of Cameron's *Illustrations* was reviewed in the London *Times* on 1 February 1875, and the photograph "The Parting of Lancelot and Guinevere" was reproduced on the cover of *Harper's Weekly* for 4 September 1877. Cameron's account of the project is given in a series of her letters, reprinted in Helmut Gernsheim's *Julia Margaret Cameron, Her Life and Photographic Work* (2nd ed. Millerton, N.Y.: Aperture, 1975). [JL]

CAMLANN (CAMLAN), in Welsh literature the scene of Arthur's last battle, in which he clashed fatally with Mordred, and most of the combatants perished on both sides. Neither Gildas nor Nennius mentions such a battle. It appears first in the tenth-century *Annales Cambriae* as "the strife of Camlann, in which Arthur and Medraut fell." The date is given as Year 93 of the chronicle, probably 539.

Nothing is said here to make Mordred a villain, or even to show that he and Arthur were opposed. Early bardic allusions are favorable to him. In the Triads, however, the enmity and tragedy are clearly emerging. Camlann is one of the three "futile battles," in which Arthur not only fought Mordred but through some unexplained lapse of judgment allowed many of his troops to join his opponent. A strong and sad tradition makes the battle a massacre with so few survivors that they are individually named. The Welsh have much more to say about Camlann than about Badon.

The name corresponds to the British *Camboglanna* 'crooked bank' (i.e., of a river), or less probably *Cambolanda* 'crooked enclosure.' There is a place called Camlan today, a valley in Merioneth with a small river flowing down it, but several rivers have the "crooked" element in their names. Geoffrey of Monmouth chooses the Camel in Cornwall. Another candidate is the Somerset Cam, which is near Cadbury–Camelot. A multiple burial is said once to have come to light in the fields below the hill. The original British form *Camboglanna* is actually found as the name of a Roman fort on Hadrian's Wall, allegedly though questionably Birdoswald, high above the River Irthing, which runs through a valley and is suitably crooked. Naturally, this fort has been favored as the site.

Wherever the battle was, it may be accepted as historical. The question is whether the involvement of Arthur is also historical. On the face of it, this is a different case from that of Badon, because bards would have wished to connect him with a victory but not with a dismal inter-British quarrel. Perhaps, then, the facts were too clear to set aside. Yet an Arthurian battle in 539 (no other source offers any alternative) seems very late; it is suspect because the same chronicle almost certainly errs about Badon; and it is further suspect in view of evidence from the Welsh saints' lives that legend did come to involve Arthur in activities extending far into the sixth century, activities that were certainly fictitious.

Nevertheless, some scholars have picked out the Camlann entry in the *Annales* as the one reliable Arthurian statement, partly because it is free from manifest legend, partly on the ground that, although it occurs in a tenth-century text, it was copied (or may plausibly be supposed to have been copied) from a contemporary record. But the form of the name tells against this argument. If it started as *Camboglanna*, it would have become *Camlann* in Welsh, but it would have passed through an intermediate form *Camglann* and taken a long time doing so. Hence, the *Annales* entry mentioning "Camlann" is not contemporary or anything like it. A copyist might have modernized the older spelling, but it cannot be proved that the older spelling was there for him to modernize.

While Arthur's involvement with Camlann could be authentic, it could also be one of many cases of his association over the centuries with battlefields and other sites up and down Britain. Geoffrey's Camel location may itself be due to this process. There was indeed a battle beside the Camel, and local legend grew to be highly circumstantial about it, indicating a field near Slaughter Bridge a mile above Camelford. The battle, however, was probably one between the Cornish and the West Saxons, fought in 823. Camlann's identification with the Birdoswald fort raises a special difficulty, because the triadic version of Arthur's quarrel with Mordred places this in Cornwall, with Arthur living at Kelliwic. Furthermore, the *Mordred/Modred* form of the name, which replaces the Welsh *Medraut* or *Medrawd*, is Cornish and implies a Cornish tradition. Geoffrey is at least looking in a plausible direction. But Birdoswald is a long way from Cornwall.

The problem is not made simpler by traces of another account of Arthur's end. In the *Prophetiae Merlini*, which Geoffrey inserts in his *Historia Regum Britanniae*, he makes the prophet foretell Arthur's career and predict a mysterious passing that seems to be in Gaul. When he came to write the actual story, Geoffrey introduced Camlann, but the denouement is still interwoven with events overseas, wholly foreign to the Welsh version, as is Geoffrey's portrayal of Mordred as Arthur's traitorous deputy. In the Vulgate Cycle and Malory, while Mordred's villainy is retained, Camlann as such disappears again. The final and fatal battle is fought near Salisbury.

Camlann probably happened; Arthur's name was connected with it by the tenth century; and, if it was discreditable, there may have been a reason for that connection that was more compelling than pure fancy. On the other hand, all would-be reconstructions of a real Camlann with a real Arthur in it fall short of conviction. Also, there are grave obstacles to the belief that he was active so late. This difficulty might be overcome by the hypothesis of a minor Arthur, who perished in the battle and was absorbed into a saga originating from an earlier leader. Another possibility is suggested by a Welsh poem about a battle fought by the West Country ruler Geraint. Though this mentions Arthur, it does not say that he was present in person, but an ambiguity in the wording has led to its being construed as saying that he was. An early bardic lament over Camlann might have introduced his name in the same way, with the same result. (*See also* ARTHUR, ORIGINS OF LEGEND.) [GA]

Alcock, Leslie. *Arthur's Britain*. London: Penguin, 1971.

Ashe, Geoffrey. *A Guidebook to Arthurian Britain*. Wellingborough: Aquarian, 1983.

Bromwich, Rachel. *Trioedd Ynys Prydein*. Cardiff: University of Wales Press, 1961.

CANDLE IN THE WIND, THE: *see* WHITE, T. H.

CANNING, VICTOR, British author of three Arthurian novels, published separately as *The Crimson Chalice* (1976), *The Circle of the Gods* (1977), and

The Immortal Wound (1978); these were later issued together as *The Crimson Chalice* (1978). The setting of the stories is Late Roman Britain in transition from the fragmented society of Roman magistrates and Celtic tribes to the unified realm of Arturo, here depicted as the son of Baradoc, a Celtic chieftain, and Gratia, a British Roman. Their story and that of Arturo's early efforts toward defeating the Saxons are given in greater detail in the first book than much of the traditional Arthurian material in the subsequent works.

Canning's Arthur-figure, Arturo, is a picaresque visionary. Outlawed by prince Geraint, the Celtic leader, and by the ambitious Ambrosius, he proceeds to steal cavalry mounts and to recruit men bored by standard military routine, in order to form an attack force against the Saxons and force an awareness of his strength upon the established leaders. Arturo views himself as a man inspired by the gods—this justification is offered throughout the novel for any act on his part.

Canning gives Arturo two wives. The first, Daria, a love-match, is murdered at Ambrosius's behest. The second, Gwennifer, corresponds to the Guenevere of legend; childless, she engages in love affairs, but this does not lead to conflict and friction, since Arturo is, here as always, treated as somehow above the obstacles and potential tragedies of the story. The Arturo of the latter portions of the novel is bland when compared with the rebellious child and young soldier. The major exceptions to this approach are the loss of Daria, which is deeply felt, and the inevitable compromise between vision and reality. The action reaches its climax in the battle of Mount Badon. By contrast, the closing pages of the story, when the aging Arthur, forewarned by a detailed dream, goes to the final encounter with Mordreth, are perfunctory.

Canning retains the general outlines of the Arthurian story, even to a kind of Grail, a silver chalice that functions more as a talisman for Arturo than as the object of a spiritual quest for his knights. On the whole, however, Canning's imaginative recreations and Arturo's faith in the "immortal wound," the cyclical existence of the chosen hero, tend to overshadow or even diminish the power of the tale. [AAR]

❧ Canning, Victor. *The Crimson Chalice*. New York: Morrow, 1978.

CANTARE DEI CANTARI, a kind of omnibus *cantare* including many ancient stories as well as material from the Roland and Arthurian cycles. Composed in Italy about 1380, it was assigned its suggestive title by its nineteenth-century editor. [SJN]

❧ Rajna, Pio, ed. "Il Cantare dei Cantari e il Sirventese del Maestro di tutte le arti." *Zeitschrift für Romanische Philologie*, 2 (1878), 220–54, 419–37.

CANTARE DI LASANCIS: *see CANTARI DI TRISTANO, I.*

CANTARI, popular narrative poems taking their generic name from a sub-stantivization of the Italian verb *cantare* 'to sing.' They were sung in the piazzas by performer-poets called *canterini, cantastorie,* or *cantambanchi* (from *cantari in banca,* singers on the platform designated for such entertainments). *Cantari* were usually composed in *ottava rima* and often divided into *giornate* (a section suitable for performance in one day, or *giorno*) of about fifty octaves. These works are difficult to date, individually or as a genre, since the manu-scripts or early printed books that transmit them to us are necessarily later transcriptions of poems possibly transmitted orally for generations. Most scholars believe, however, that performances of *cantari* were frequent in Italy from the second half of the thirteenth century until the end of the fifteenth, first in such Tuscan centers as Florence (where the *canterini* had a *banco* in the piazza of S. Martino al Vescovo), Siena, Lucca, and Pisa, and later farther north at Bologna, Venice, and especially Verona. In the fifteenth century, *cantari* became popular entertainments in the south as well, particularly at Naples. *Canterini* strove to keep the audience's attention by combining in rapid succession accounts of astonishing deeds, evocations of mysterious atmosphere, and descriptions of luxurious costume and decor. To the same end, they often in a single *cantare* sang about some characters whose celebrated names could attract an audience and about others, less well known or entirely new, whose stories could be elaborated without the constraints imposed by traditional plots. In this way, *canterini* made use of many stock figures from ancient myth and history, from the tales of Roland, and from Arthurian literature but often mentioned such figures only in passing. One of the few *cantari* by an author whose name is known to us, Antonio Pucci's mid-fourteenth-century *Gismi-rante,* is typical in this regard: the protagonist's dying father recommends, as the *cantare* opens, that he travel to Arthur's court and make himself known to Tristan and Lancelot, whose names are not mentioned again—though Arthur is alluded to several more times, as feeling affection for Gismirante, conducting a court with special customs, granting Gismirante's wish for knighthood, bid-ding him farewell, and serving as the endpoint of a journey Gismirante hopes (unsuccessfully) to make with his chosen lady. In the second *cantare* of *Gismi-rante,* Arthur and his circle are absent entirely, no doubt because they have served their purpose for Pucci, in attracting an audience. Because such hetero-geneity of source and plot was typical of the genre, it is impossible to discriminate definitively a body of *cantari* that can be labeled "Arthurian": such a well-known figure as Lancelot, for example, is likely to be introduced in many *cantari* that nonetheless do not give him a continuing or important role (just as a "guest star" might appear in one episode of a television series in need of higher ratings). Among the *cantari* most frequently studied today, however, several are notable for their Arthurian content: *Bel Gherardino, Cantare dei cantari, I Cantari di Carduino, I Cantari di Tristano, Li Chantari di Lancellotto, La Donna del Vergiù, Febusso e Breusso, Fiorio e Biancifiore, Liombruno, La Pulzella Gaia,* and *Quando Tristano e Lancielotto combattettero al petrone di Merlino.* [SJN]

❧ Balduino, A. *Cantari del Trecento.* Milan: Marzorati, 1970.

CANTARI DEL "FALSO SCUDO," I: *see CANTARI DI TRISTANO, I.*

CANTARI DI CARDUINO, I (1370s), have been dubiously attributed to Antonio Pucci (1318–1388), bell-ringer and town crier of the commune of Florence. The *primo cantare*, reminiscent of the *enfances* of Perceval, tells of the murder of Arthur's favorite knight, Dondinello, by jealous barons and the flight of his widow and infant son into the forest, where the child is raised in the fear of God and ignorance of knights and knighthood. At the age of twelve, he discovers knights hunting in the forest, and, although they pursue him as a wild man, he determines to serve their leader, Arthur. At court, Carduino impresses the knights with his rusticity and his appetite. A damsel accompanied by a dwarf interrupts the feast with a request that Arthur provide her with a champion who will liberate her city and her sister from the enchantments of an evil sorcerer. The *secondo cantare*, reminiscent of tales featuring Gawain's son or brother, recounts the adventures of Carduino and the enchanted city. On his way to the city, he is assaulted by giants and lusty ladies in a series of castles, and he encounters and kills Calvano's brother, Aguerisse, thus unwittingly avenging his father's murder. When he arrives at the enchanted city, he sees a rocky wasteland infested with dragons and other beasts. Challenged by a strange knight, Carduino defeats him in combat, finds his ring, and, breaking it, releases the city from enchantment. When he kisses the chained serpent, she is transformed into the angelically beautiful Beatrice. The quest is completed, the expected marriage is celebrated, a glorious progeny is prophesied, and all ends happily. The *Carduino* is a masterpiece of popular Italian literature. It is of great importance to literary history because it represents a variant, and possibly more authentic, version of the *enfances* of Perceval than that found in Chrétien and because it represents an important branch of the Fair Unknown/ *fier baiser* story type. It is of particular importance to students of English literature because of its resemblance to the verse romances *Sir Perceval of Galles* and *Libeaus Desconus* and to Malory's "Tale of Sir Gareth." [DLH]

Rajna, Pio, ed. *Cantari di Carduino giuntovi quello di Tristano e Lancillotto quando combattettero al petrone di Merlino.* Bologna: Romagnoli, 1873.

CANTARI DI TRISTANO, I, dating from the second half of the fourteenth century, are a group of six *ottava rima* narratives of episodes from the life of Tristan. The *Bataglia* recounts the combat of Tristano and Lancilotto at Merlin's *peron*, when Tristano had expected to meet and fight, for the honor of the queen, his rival Palamides. It is not until Tristano utters the name "Isotta" that Lancilotto and Tristano realize that they are fighting for the honor of different queens. The *Cantare di Lasancis* tells of the return to Camelot after the combat at the *peron* and Tristano's discovery that Marco has imprisoned Isotta. As he leaves for Cornwall, Lasancis arrives demanding to avenge his brother, who was killed by Lancilotto; the fragment ends before the combat begins. In *I*

Cantari del "Falso Scudo" ("The False Shield"), Tristano appears in only the first *cantare*, where he is listed as one of those defeated by the Knight with the Enchanted Shield. He does not appear in the second *cantare*, which deals briefly with Galasso (Galahad) and his defeat of the Knight with the Enchanted Shield. In *Le Ultime Imprese di Tristano* ("The Last Deeds of Tristan"), Tristano embarks on the quest of the Grail but abandons the pursuit to defend the chastity of a damsel pursued by the infamous Knight Without Pity. *La Morte di Tristano* and *La Vendetta di Lancilotto* are the best known of the *cantari*. The first tells how Marco kills Tristano with the lance of Morgan le Fay and how Isotta, overcome by the force of Tristano's last embrace, dies with him. The *Vendetta* recounts the Arthurian campaign led by Lancilotto to avenge the death of Tristano. The *cantari* as a group are important evidence of the extent of Tristano's popularity in Italy, but the narratives, although competent, are derivative and the verse is undistinguished. [DLH]

Bertoni, Giulio, ed. *Cantari di Tristano*. Modena: Società Tipografica Modenese, 1937.

Rajna, Pio, ed. *I Cantari di Carduino guintovi quello di Tristano e Lancielotto quando combattettero al petrone di Merlino*. Bologna: Romagnoli, 1873.

CAPGRAVE, JOHN (1393–1464), Augustinian friar from Norfolk whose works include saints' lives, biblical commentaries, theological treatises, the *Nova Legenda Angliae* (*see DE SANTO JOSEPH AB ARIMATHIA*), and the *De Illustribus Henricis*. He is the author of the English *Abbreuiacion of Cronicles* (1462–63), drawn primarily from the *Chronicon Pontificum et Imperatorum* of Martinus Polonus and the St. Albans chronicles of Thomas Walsingham. Capgrave gives a brief account of Arthur's conquests and of his being wounded and taken to Avalon, and he also tells of the twelfth-century discovery of Arthur's body at Glastonbury and of Edward III's interest in the Round Table. [EDK]

Capgrave, John. *The Chronicle of England (from the Creation to 1417)*, ed. F.C. Hingeston. London: Longman, 1858.

———. *John Capgrave's Abbreuiacion of Chronicles*, ed. Peter J. Lucas. London: Oxford University Press, 1983.

CARADOC, LIVRE (OR ROMAN) DE, a romance embedded in the First Continuation of Chrétien de Troyes's *Perceval*. Though it has no independent manuscript existence, it could be excerpted without damage to the narrative of either the Continuation or itself. The *Livre* appears in all three redactions of the Continuation and varies in length from some 3,300 to 5,800 lines. The biography of Caradoc consists of three parts: 1) He is born to Ysave, Arthur's niece, and to her adulterous lover, Elïavrés, a sorcerer. Despite his bastard birth, Caradoc remains the legitimate heir of his father, King Caradoc of Nantes. As a newly dubbed knight in King Arthur's court, Caradoc alone accepts the challenge of the Beheading Game, a motif made famous in English literature by *Sir Gawain and the Green Knight*. Caradoc escapes unscathed because the challenger, who turns out to be his legitimate father, relents. 2) Caradoc imprisons his mother in a tower in Nantes; he rescues a maiden, Guigner, on his way back to join Arthur; he establishes his reputation as the best knight of the court. He learns that Eliavrés has visited his mother, goes back to Nantes, and humiliates the sorcerer. The wicked couple take revenge on the hero by attaching to his arm a deadly serpent, which will slowly sap his life away in two years' time. But he is saved by Guigner and her brother. She immerses herself in a vat of milk while Caradoc sits in a tub of vinegar. As the viper leaps to the sweeter host, the brother slashes off its head, but not without cutting off the maiden's nipple, which is later restored in gold by a magic shield. 3) Caradoc passes the supreme test of the drinking horn. Only he can drink its enchanted wine without spilling a drop, because he alone in the court possesses a truly faithful lover, Guigner. A variant of the latter episode may be found in Robert Biket's *Lai du cor*. The *Livre de Caradoc* has been rarely studied and obviously merits further scholarly attention. [JLG]

Roach, William, ed. *The Continuations of the Old French "Perceval" of Chrétien de Troyes: The First Continuation*. 3 vols. (Vol. 2 with Robert H. Ivy, Jr.) Philadelphia: American Philosophical Society, 1949–52.

CARADOC OF LLANCARFAN, author of the *Vita Gildae* ("Life of St. Gildas"), a work (ca. 1140) drawing on romance literature and hagiography. This is the first known text to associate King Arthur with Glastonbury. According to the *Vita*, King Melwas of the Summer Region carried off Guinevere, and Arthur, "the tyrant," brought all the forces of Devon and Cornwall to Glastonbury to retrieve her; the abbot of Glastonbury, however, accompanied by Gildas, obtained her release. In this episode, Caradoc explains that the origin of the name "Glastonbury" is from "Isle of Glass" (and by implication that "Somerset" derives from "Summer Region"). The etymologies both carry otherworldly implications, which paved the way for the later association of Glastonbury with Avalon. [JPC]

Mommsen, Theodorus, ed. *Vita Gildae Auctore Caradoco Lancarbanensi*. In *Monumenta Germaniae Historica, Auctores Antiquissimori, 13. Chronica Minora, 3*. Berlin: Weidmann, 1898, pp. 107–10.

CARLE OFF CARLILE, THE, an early sixteenth-century balladlike poem (500 lines), preserved in the Percy Folio MS, is a later version of *Syre Gawene and the Carle of Carlyle*. The two texts are incomplete but complement each other; both derive from the same tail-rhyme romance, whose metrical pattern is still visible in *The Carle* in the regular occurrence of three-stress instead of four-stress lines. The beheading that disenchants the Carl it shares with *The Turke and Gowin*. [ESK]

Madden, Frederic, ed. *Syre Gawayne*. London: Bannatyne Club, 1839.

Kurvinen, Auvo, ed. *Sir Gawain and the Carl of Carlisle in Two Versions*. Helsinki, 1951.

CARLSEN, CHRIS, is the author of *Berserker: The Bull Chief* (1977), a sword-and-sorcery fantasy of more than usual violence. The hero is an Irish warrior who helps Arthur in his war against the Saxons but is murdered for his pains. Guenevere is transformed into a savage Irish warrior queen named Grania. [RHT]

&⁊ Carlsen, Chris. *Berserker: The Bull Chief.* London: Sphere, 1977.

CARMICHAEL, DOUGLAS, author of the novel *Pendragon* (1977), a recreation of the twelve battles that Arthur fought to consolidate his kingdom. The book incorporates both early lore and later legends into an account that eschews magic in favor of rational explanations, provides psychological motivation for familiar incidents, and makes action-packed battle scenes come alive. [MAG]

&⁊ Carmichael, Douglas. *Pendragon.* Hicksville, N.Y.: Blackwater, 1977.

CARPENTER, RHYS (1889–1980), American scholar and archaeologist, composed a dramatic poem, *The Tragedy of Etarre* (1912), based upon the story, from the fourth book of Caxton's Malory, of Pelleas's unrequited love for Etarre and of Gawain's treacherous intervention. Although written as dialogue, in blank verse, and divided into acts and scenes (with some stage directions), it is nevertheless a dramatic poem rather than a play. [SRR]

&⁊ Carpenter, Rhys. *The Tragedy of Etarre: A Poem.* New York: Sturgis and Walton, 1912.

CARR, J. COMYNS (1849–1916), was a reviver of Arthurian drama. His *King Arthur* was produced at London's Lyceum in 1895, with Henry Irving as King Arthur, Forbes Robertson as Launcelot, and Ellen Terry as Guenevere. The Prologue presents Arthur's acquisition of Excalibur at the Magic Mere while a Chorus of Lake Spirits comments prophetically. The four acts—"The Holy Grail," "The Queen's Maying," "The Black Barge," "The Passing of Arthur"—compress Malory's time scheme. Conflict is provided by Morgan and her son, Mordred. Launcelot wrestles with the demands of Elaine (whose love predates Guenevere's), Arthur, the Queen, and God. *Tristram and Iseult* (1906), a somewhat Wagnerian version, covers events enacted in Cornwall and Ireland but departs from tradition by casting Andret as Tristram's murderer. (*See also* SULLIVAN, SIR ARTHUR.) [MAW]

&⁊ Carr, J. Comyns. *King Arthur: A Drama in a Prologue and Four Acts.* London: Macmillan, 1895.
——— . *Tristram and Iseult: A Drama in Four Acts.* London: Duckworth, 1906.

CARTA ENVIADA POR HISEO LA BRUNDA A TRISTÁN; RESPUESTA DE TRISTÁN ("Iseult's Letter to Tristan; Tristan's Reply"), a highly rhetorical epistolary exchange in Spanish between Iseut of Cornwall and Tristan, the former complaining of Tristan's marriage to Iseut of the White Hands and Tristan defending his actions. The work is contained in an early sixteenth-century manuscript copy (Madrid, Biblioteca Nacional 22021). The Iseut letter is adapted from a similar but shorter and less rhetorical letter found in most redactions of the Prose *Tristan*, but Tristan's reply would seem to be the creation of the Spanish author. The letters demonstrate a tendency in late-medieval Spain to fuse Arthurian and sentimental material, with the rhetoric of the letters betraying that of the sentimental romance, a genre that began to develop in Spain in the fifteenth century and that made extensive use of letters. The Iseut letter in fact incorporates actual lines from one such romance, *Grimalte y Gradissa*, by Juan de Flores. While the letters may have been extracted from a remodeled Spanish Prose *Tristan*—curiously, *Grimalte y Gradissa* material is also found in a 1501 printing of the Spanish Prose *Tristan*—they may have been simply a rhetorical exercise. [HLS]

• Sharrer, Harvey L. "Letters in the Hispanic Prose Tristan Texts: Iseut's Complaint and Tristan's Reply." *Tristania*, 7 (1981–82), 3–20.

CASSIODORUS, ROMAN DE: see SEPT SAGES DE ROME, LES.

CASTEL RÓNCOLO: *see* RUNKELSTEIN MURALS.

CASTELFORD, THOMAS: *see* BEK, THOMAS, OF CASTELFORD.

CASTLE DOR: see QUILLER-COUCH, SIR ARTHUR.

CASTLE DORE, an earthwork fort near Fowey in Cornwall, involved in the Cornish localization of the Tristan story. Inhabited during the last three centuries B.C., it was vacant during the Roman era, but excavation has shown that from the fifth century A.D. onward the enclosure contained sizable timber buildings. These suggest a princely or royal household. The place's closeness to the old trackway across Cornwall may have given it a continuing importance, as perhaps happened also with Castle Killibury, the likeliest candidate for Kelliwic.

Several Tristan localities are to be found in this neighborhood, such as Lantyan (Béroul's *Lancien*) and the parish of St. Sampson, with its church at Golant. Just outside Fowey is the Tristan Stone, a transplanted monument that formerly stood much nearer to Castle Dore. Its inscription shows that it once marked the grave of "Drustanus, son of Cunomorus." The first name is a form of "Tristan." The second Latinizes *Kynvawr*, the name of a king who reigned in Cornwall during the first half of the sixth century. Castle Dore was doubtless a residence of his.

A ninth-century Life of St. Paul Aurelian identifies Cunomorus with Mark. This identification played a part in localizing the Tristan tale hereabouts. The claim that the localization is history rather than fancy, and that the man commemorated by the inscription is *the* Tristan, depends on the Mark= Cunomorus equation being correct. It is not widely accepted, but it has its supporters. If, as the inscription states, Tristan was the king's son and not his nephew, Iseult (whether as a real person or as a creature of imagination) would have had to be a young stepmother. Poets might have altered the relationship to make the situation more acceptable. [GA]

Ashe, Geoffrey. *A Guidebook to Arthurian Britain*. Wellingborough: Aquarian, 1983.
Bromwich, Rachel. *Trioedd Ynys Prydein*. Cardiff: University of Wales Press, 1961.
Ditmas, E.M.R. *Tristan and Iseult in Cornwall*. Gloucester: Roberts, 1969.
Radford, C.A. Ralegh. "Castle Dore." In *The Quest for Arthur's Britain*, ed. Geoffrey Ashe. London: Pall Mall, 1968.

CAVE LEGEND. According to the Welsh "Stanzas of the Graves," in the Black Book of Carmarthen, Arthur's grave is a mystery. William of Malmesbury confirms this in his *Gesta Regum Anglorum* (ca. 1125): "The grave of Arthur is nowhere beheld." Therefore, William adds, "ancient songs" prophesy his reappearance. The idea that his grave could not be found because he had none, being immortal, seems to have originated in Brittany and spread to Cornwall, and thence to Wales. Its more literary form, deriving from the Bretons, was that he was in the enchanted isle of Avalon. But a folk-belief of another kind took hold among the Welsh and in parts of England and Scotland: that he was asleep in a cave until his messianic return. Both the principal versions of his survival, the island story and the cave story, may have their ancestry in a Celtic myth reported by Plutarch, about a banished god sleeping in a cave in a western island.

There are two real caves bearing Arthur's name, in Anglesey and Herefordshire. But the typical form of the legend makes his cave an elusive place that can be found only on rare occasions. Usually, it houses more than the King—a company of slumbering knights, or a royal treasure, or both. Sometimes, indeed, Arthur himself is absent, presumably in another cave. One location, which is probably of very long standing, is Cadbury Castle in Somerset: Cadbury-Camelot. Others are Craig-y-Ddinas in Glamorgan, Alderley Edge in Cheshire, Richmond Castle in Yorkshire, Sewingshields in Northumberland, and the Eildon Hills near Melrose in Scotland. At least nine more have been recorded besides these.

The legend varies from place to place, but it commonly includes an account of someone entering the cave with unhappy results. At Craig-y-Ddinas, a Welshman is said to have been guided into it by an English wizard. He saw the King and his knights asleep in a circle, their heads pointing outward. They wore armor, and weapons lay beside them. Within the circle were a heap of gold and a heap of silver. The magician told the Welshman that Arthur was sleeping till the time when he should wake and restore justice and peace throughout Britain. Meanwhile, it was permissible for the visitor to carry off some of the treasure, but he must not disturb the knights. If one of them woke, he would ask if it was day, and then the only way to escape unscathed was to reply, "No, sleep on." Also, the treasure must on no account be squandered. The Welshman succeeded in getting out with some gold, but he did squander it and came back alone for more. The second time, he had forgotten the formula; several of the knights woke up, gave him a beating, and ejected him from the cave. For the rest of his days, he was infirm from the beating and very poor, and could never find the entrance again.

In English and Scottish versions, the intruder is tested in other ways and fails through panic or confusion. He may be confronted with magical objects, such as a sword and a horn, which he uses wrongly. At Sewingshields, Arthur actually does wake, but the victim fails to complete the ritual and he goes back to sleep. The Melrose story is told by Walter Scott. Canonbie Dick, a horse-dealer, was riding home one night with a pair of horses that he had been unable to sell. A stranger in antique clothing offered to buy them, paying with obsolete gold coins. The same thing happened several times. Dick became curious about the stranger's dwelling. The stranger—who was in fact the mysterious poet Thomas the Rhymer—warned him that he must not show fear and led him through a doorway into a vast torchlit chamber under the Eildon Hills, full of sleeping knights and horses. On a table lay a sword and a horn. Thomas told Dick that he must choose whether to draw the sword or blow the horn. Dick blew the horn and learned too late that this was wrong: it was the act of a man summoning help and therefore showed fear. With a noise like thunder, the knights began to stir, and Dick's fear became genuine enough. A violent wind swept him out of the cave, and the door closed behind him. He told his tale to some shepherds and fell dead. Naturally, no one else ever found the entrance. It is said to have been in an odd-looking rocky hillock called the Lucken Hare, where witches used to hold meetings.

Though this folklore-Arthur lay hidden from the world, he could emerge in phantasmal form and join the legendary Wild Hunt, careering among the clouds with other heroes, and occasionally descending to earth. At Cadbury, he had both a cave and a "hunting causeway." Accompanied by his knights, he became a spectral huntsman in France as well as Britain. About 1211, Gervase of Tilbury mentions this belief, together with another giving him a permanent place of concealment in Mount Etna. Doubtless, this was an importation into Sicily by Normans or by Bretons in Norman service. The Sicilian Arthur is awake at least some of the time and talks to people from outside. But the notion of an undying king or hero asleep underground spread widely through medieval Europe, attaching itself to other characters. Whether all the variants were derived from Arthur by way of his vogue in romance it is impossible to tell, because in most cases written records fail to show when or how the beliefs arose. The most famous was almost certainly imitative. This was the German legend of Emperor Frederick II slumbering inside the Kyffhäuser mountain.

After a couple of centuries, the sleeper's identity changed, and he became Frederick I, Barbarossa, as he is still.

There is a similar ambiguity at several of the Welsh locations. The person in the cave is normally supposed to be Arthur, but according to some he is Owen Lawgoch, a medieval Welsh patriot. Loomis indicates that versions of the legend were still quite widely accepted during the nineteenth century, and in fact it has survived into the twentieth. (*See also* FOLKLORE; RETURN, LEGENDS OF ARTHUR'S; TOPOGRAPHY AND LOCAL LEGENDS.) [GA]

Ashe, Geoffrey. *A Guidebook to Arthurian Britain*. Wellingborough: Aquarian, 1983.

Chambers, E.K. *Arthur of Britain*. London: Sidgwick and Jackson, 1927.

Loomis, Roger Sherman, ed. *Arthurian Literature in the Middle Ages*. Oxford: Clarendon, 1959.

Rhys, John. *Celtic Folklore*. 2 vols. Oxford: Clarendon, 1901.

CAWEIN, MADISON J. (1865–1914), author of a pioneer American adaptation of Malory material, *Accolon of Gaul* (1889), based on *Morte Darthur*, Book IV, Chapters 6–15. Written in heroic couplets with Keatsian ornamentation and Tennysonian characters (including Vivian and Dagonet), the poem depicts a young Accolon whose vow of chastity is negated by Morgane's amorous aggressiveness, as his vow of chivalric loyalty is negated by her devious plots against Arthur and Urience. [MAW]

Cawein, Madison J. *Accolon of Gaul with Other Poems*. Louisville, Ky.: Morton, 1889.

CAXTON, WILLIAM (ca. 1422–1491). Though the thirty years Caxton spent as a mercer are often eclipsed by his introduction of printing to England, the diplomacy and business sense he gained during this period are at least partially responsible for the success of his middle-age venture. After serving as Governor of the English Nation at Bruges for nine years, Caxton began a translation of the *Recuyell of the Histories of Troy*, demand for which caused him to take up printing. Having learned the trade under Johan Veldener, he opened a shop in Bruges, where he printed five other books besides the *Recuyell*. Two years later, he introduced printing to England, choosing Chaucer's *Canterbury Tales* as his first title in folio, and opened a shop at Westminster, from which he issued over 100 (extant) titles.

For a pioneer printer, Caxton had a remarkable range of tastes—or certainly a clear sense of the tastes of his readership. He published the works of the great writers of antiquity in translation (including Ovid, Vergil, and Cicero), prose romances (*Blanchard and Eglantyne, The Four Sons of Aymon*), mythical stories (*The History of Jason*), beast fables (*Reynard the Fox*, Aesop's *Fables*), religious and philosophical works (*The Curial*, Boethius's *Consolation*, *The Moral Proverbs* of Christine de Pizan), historical works (Trevisa's translation of Higden's *Polychronicon*, a *Description of Britain*), chivalric romances (*Paris and Vienne*), and also grammar books, vocabularies, statutes of the realm, indulgences, and other miscellaneous pieces. Most of all, he published the best

4 *Edward Burne-Jones, Arthur at Avalon (1880–98). Courtesy Museo de Arte de Ponce, Puerto Rico.*

5 Cadbury Castle, Somerset. Courtesy British Tourist Authority.

6 Aubrey Beardsley, "How Sir Bedivere Cast the Sword Excalibur into the Water," from the Dent Malory (1894). Courtesy Kenneth Spencer Research Library, University of Kansas.

7 Woodcut, "Kunig Artus," for a Nine Worthies series (ca. 1475), Bern, Burgerbibliothek Cod. A 45, p. 309. Courtesy Bern Burgerbibliothek.

literature England had to offer at the time, including the *Canterbury Tales, Troilus and Criseyde, Confessio Amantis, Le Morte Darthur,* and many of the minor works of Chaucer and Lydgate.

Universal as Caxton's tastes were, he showed a marked preference for chivalric literature, an interest that dates at least as far back as his association with the Duchess of Burgundy (ca. 1470) and probably farther. Before publishing *Le Morte Darthur* in 1485, he translated and printed *Godfrey of Bouillon* and *The Ordre of Chyualry* (in whose prologue and epilogue, respectively, he mentioned the stories of Arthur), and afterward *Charles the Grete, Paris and Vienne,* and *The Fayttes of Armes and Chyualry.* The works on Godfrey, Charlemagne, and Arthur were apparently planned as a series designed to honor the three Christian Worthies. It should not be surprising that the work honoring the English Worthy, Sir Thomas Malory's *Morte Darthur,* is the one for which Caxton is most remembered.

Caxton finished printing *Le Morte Darthur* on 31 July 1485; the book most likely took about ten months to print. Only one typeface was used, type 4*, probably because there are no running heads or titles. Five-line woodcut initials are used at the beginning of each of the twenty-one books, and a similar three-line series is used for chapter beginnings. Otherwise, the folio is not decorated: there are no illustrations or borders, which suggests that there was no decoration in the manuscript Caxton printed from. This book survives in two extant copies: the only complete one is housed in the Pierpont Morgan Library in New York; the other, which lacks eleven of the original leaves, is in the John Rylands University Library in Manchester. Aside from two sheets that were completely reset, there are few variant readings between the two copies.

Caxton divided Malory's text into twenty-one books and 506 chapters and added a table of rubrics, a prologue, and a colophon. The table and prologue were printed after the rest of the text was set, as the signatures indicate; this may account for the discrepancies between the table and the text itself. The basis for Caxton's layout cannot be fully determined, since his exemplar is no longer extant, but it is worth noting that nineteen of the twenty book divisions have some counterpart in the only manuscript version of Malory's work, which was in his office while the *Morte* was being printed.

Caxton's role as editor of *Le Morte Darthur* is unclear. His English is a more "standard" dialect than that of the manuscript, and his version is generally regarded as the more readable; but without his copy text we cannot ascertain how much of the revision can be assigned to Caxton. The section in which the two versions differ most is that of Arthur's War with Lucius, Caxton's Book V, which is twice as long in the manuscript as it is in the printed text. Scholarly debate on this issue has produced two conflicting arguments. Some, after comparing his text with the manuscript, have charged Caxton with revising the Roman War episode and by extension the entire work. Others, citing Caxton's statement in his prologue and his editorial habits with other texts, believe that he did in fact print "according to his copy," and that someone else—perhaps Malory himself—revised the text he printed. Even if we follow

Caxton's critics, the revision attributed to him is not an unreasonable exercise of editorial duty.

Caxton's prologue to *Le Morte Darthur* is unlike his others, notably in what he leaves out. He fails to identify a patron, though Anthony Wydville is surely the "certain gentleman" he mentions. This may be because Richard III, who had ordered Wydville's execution two years earlier, still had the crown when the *Morte* was published. He also fails to dedicate the work, perhaps because the most likely recipient of such praise would have been Edward IV. And he gives us very little information about the author, though Malory's own political connections may have prevented this. Such political risks, along with other hesitations expressed in his prologue, make us wonder that Caxton decided to publish *Le Morte Darthur* at all. Had he not, Arthurian literature from the sixteenth century to the present might well have been deprived of its major English source. [JWS]

◪ Spisak, James W. *Caxton's Malory: A New Edition of Sir Thomas Malory's Le Morte Darthur Based on the Pierpont Morgan Copy of William Caxton's Edition of 1485*. 2 vols. Berkeley and Los Angeles: University of California Press, 1983.

Blake, N.F. *William Caxton: A Bibliographical Guide*. New York and London: Garland, 1985.

Hellinga, Lotte. *Caxton in Focus*. London: British Library, 1982.

Painter, George D. *William Caxton: A Quincentennial Biography of England's First Printer*. London: Chatto and Windus, 1976.

CELTIC ARTHURIAN LITERATURE. To a degree, all of the countries that produced Arthurian literatures in the Middle Ages were once occupied by the Celts. Celtic tribes and their kingdoms were dominant from the Iberian peninsula to the Balkans, from Cisalpine Gaul to the British Isles. The Romans changed much of that, however, and by the beginning of the Christian era Celtic strengths lay chiefly in the British Isles. By the end of the Dark Ages, the Celtic regions had further shrunk to western and northern Britain, Ireland, and northwestern France (Brittany). To scholars, the term "Celtic" is essentially a linguistic one, though that implies a cultural unity as well. The two main branches of Celtic (a sister language group to Germanic, Italic, Indo-Iranian, etc., in the Indo-European family) are Goidelic and Brythonic. The former includes in its modern descendants Irish Gaelic, Scottish Gaelic, and Manx Gaelic; the latter, Welsh, Cornish, and Breton. The traditions about King Arthur arose among the Brythonic Celts, and it is therefore in that context that we speak of Celtic Arthuriana. Where then do we find Arthur in the early Celtic sources, and what is his nature?

The problem that faces the scholar here is that of dating. The earliest manuscripts written in the vernacular and mentioning Arthur are not much earlier than the middle of the thirteenth century, although in some instances (e.g., the tale of *Culhwch and Olwen*) it can be demonstrated on linguistic grounds that the material belongs to a considerably earlier period. Some of the material, such as the "Dialogue of Arthur and Gwenhwyfar," is found only in late manuscripts. Perhaps the oldest reference to Arthur in our Celtic sources is a line in the *Gododdin* to the effect that a particular hero fought bravely, "though he was no Arthur." Tradition ascribes this poem to the late sixth century, though it exists in a manuscript of the late thirteenth century, in a language that cannot be older than the ninth to tenth century. But if it is authentic and if tradition is true, then this would surely be the earliest reference to Arthur, portrayed here as a paragon of heroic virtues.

The Welsh Triads contribute an important source of early information about the native Arthur. Their editor has demonstrated that the manuscript transmission of the Triads goes back to the early twelfth century, but it is clear that this body of traditional lore in triadic form has its roots in much earlier oral tradition. It is also clear that some of the Triads are late and owe their existence to such literary texts as Geoffrey's *Historia Regum Britanniae*. In all, there are some two dozen mentions of Arthur and his court in the Triads, plus another eight Triads that form a text known as the "Twenty-four Knights of Arthur's Court." Taken together, they constitute an important body of tantalizing references to the Arthur of native Celtic tradition.

Arthur figures prominently in one poem and is mentioned in several others in the mid-thirteenth-century manuscript known as the Black Book of Carmarthen. In "The Stanzas of the Graves," a poem about the burial places of a number of heroes, it is said that the grave of Arthur is an eternal wonder—that is, no one knows where it is. Another series of stanzas speak of the hero Geraint, and one of the stanzas claims that Arthur was present with Geraint at a battle in a place called *Llongborth* (site unknown). The most important poem in the Black Book of Carmarthen is in the form of a dialogue between Arthur and Glewlwyd Gafaelfawr ("Glewlwyd of the mighty grasp"). In *Culhwch and Olwen*, Glewlwyd is Arthur's own porter; here, he is porter of a fortress to which Arthur and his men seek admission. In the ninety surviving lines of this poem, Arthur identifies his retinue for the porter, naming Cei and Bedwyr (Kay and Bedivere), Mabon son of Modron, Manawydan son of Llŷr (Lear), and other characters known from various texts that reflect Celtic mythological tradition. The poem also celebrates adventures with witches, lions, a fierce cat, dog-headed warriors, and the like.

The Book of Taliesin, a manuscript of about 1275, contains several arcane poems that mention Arthur, treating him as an eminent figure, the object of the adulation of certain sages. For example, Arthur is named toward the end of the poem known as *Cad Goddeu* ("The Battle of the Trees"), a poem in which Gwydion and Math from the fourth branch of the *Mabinogi* are named as prominent magicians. Much of this poetry is obscure, though it is clear at times that the setting is the Celtic otherworld and that some of the characters named in them belong to inherited myth. One of these poems, clearer than the others, has attracted considerable attention and has been edited and translated several times; it is known as *The Spoils of Annwfn* (Annwfn being the name for the otherworld in Welsh). This remarkable poem tells of a raid by Arthur and his men on Annwfn to acquire its spoils or treasures. Several things deserve notice here: Annwfn is depicted as a place located at sea or across water, for Arthur and his men travel there in his ship Prydwen (the name given to Arthur's shield in Geoffrey's *Historia*!). Annwfn is variously called in this poem "the fairy fort," "the fort of intoxication," and "the glassy fort." In it is the well-outfitted prison of a certain Gweir. Among its treasures is a beautifully decorated cauldron from which emanates poetic inspiration and which contains a special sword; the cauldron, it is stated, will not boil the food of a coward. Three boatloads of men went with Arthur. The fort was guarded by 600 men, and from the expedition only seven returned.

The Spoils of Annwfn is set squarely in the mainstream of Celtic tradition in Wales, and it has clear analogues in Welsh literature. It makes reference to the tale of Pwyll, the central figure of the first branch of the *Mabinogi*, and his son, Pryderi, who is also mentioned in the second, third, and fourth branches. In the second branch, *Branwen*, we hear of a raid by Bendigeidfran ("Bran the Blessed") on Ireland, nominally to avenge his sister's churlish treatment at the hands of her husband, Matholwch the Irishman. Branwen's son, Gwern, is there, too, and a pivotal role is played by a cauldron, one into which dead warriors are cast and from which they are taken revivified. When the treacherous Efnisien is thrown into it, he breaks it. The forces of Bendigeidfran defeat the Irish in a dire battle, and from it only seven escape. In the tale of *Culhwch and Olwen*, one of the tasks set by the giant is to acquire the cauldron of Di-wrnach the Irishman and the sword of Wrnach, names that would appear to be doublets. Arthur and his men set out for Ireland and finish by taking the cauldron—full of Irish treasures—by force, thanks to the magical use of another sword. The parallels between the three texts are obvious, and it has been suggested that in *Branwen* and *Culhwch and Olwen* we have a euhemerized version of the raid on the otherworld—that is, that Ireland has been substituted in those tales for the Annwfn of the Book of Taliesin poem.

The reference to the otherworld as "the glassy fortress" is significant. Giraldus Cambrensis, in his *De Principis Instructione* (1195), states that Glastonbury was the site of the legendary Avalon. In the British tongue, he wrote, it was called the glassy isle, and that is why the Saxons called it afterward *Glæstingabyrig* ("the fort of glass"). According to Welsh tradition, Merlin was imprisoned by his lover in a glass house, where he was also custodian of the thirteen treasures of the Isle of Britain—treasures, perhaps, like those that Arthur sought from "the glassy fort."

Surely, the most important text that belongs to Celtic Arthuriana is the tale of *Culhwch and Olwen*. Though it is found in manuscripts of the fourteenth century, scholars generally agree on linguistic grounds that it belongs at least to the early eleventh century in its present form. The tale is remarkable in several ways. At one level, it has been recognized as a tale type of the Giant's Daughter. A destiny is sworn upon the hero that he will wed the giant's daughter; her father imposes a series of "impossible" tasks, hoping thereby to destroy the unwanted suitor; but with supernatural assistance the hero accomplishes the tasks, the giant is slain, and the bride is won. In this instance, the supernatural aid comes from Arthur and his men, and Culhwch and his bride-to-be are forgotten for much of the story. In fact, the largest single episode in the tale is the pursuit of the giant boar Twrch Trwyth. Traditions of this boar, which date back to Nennius's *Historia Brittonum* (ca. 800), are evocative of other supernatural pigs in Celtic tradition, including some from Gaul and Ireland. The boar's human characteristics are "explained" in the story by the statement that the beast had been a king, but God turned him into a boar because of his sins. In other exploits on Culhwch's behalf, Arthur frees Mabon son of Modron (who had been imprisoned in a stronghold located in a body of water), destroys a powerful witch, and in general participates in a world very much like that of the dialogue poem with the porter and the otherworldly Annwfn. His companions include Cei and Bedwyr and a catalogue of other heroes capable of supernatural feats. His court is located at Celliwig (site unknown) in Cornwall, and though it is well provisioned it is much more primitive than the resplendent courts of later English and continental romance.

The Dream of Rhonabwy is a literary composition that belongs to the early thirteenth century. It is unique in that its geographical and historical background is indicated clearly. Also, it employs a dream-vision form not at all common in traditional Welsh literature. The story within the story, Rhonabwy's dream, is a surrealistic presentation of Arthur and his field court just before the battle of Mount Badon; the battle of Camlann has already taken place, and in that respect the story indulges in an anachronism. The strange events that transpire invite an allegorical interpretation, and a colophon confirms the fact that the story is the creation of an individual author whose penchant was for richly descriptive detail.

The poem known as the "Dialogue of Arthur and Gwenhwyfar" is probably in reality a dialogue between Gwenhwyfar and her abductor Melwas, reflecting an episode known from Caradoc's *Vita Gildae* and Chrétien de Troyes's *Lancelot*. The "Dialogue of Arthur and the Eagle," in which the Eagle identifies himself as a grandson of Uther Pendragon, is essentially a religious poem. Both poems exist in manuscripts only from the sixteenth century, though both are surely older.

Celtic traditions concerning Merlin existed independent of Arthurian connections, though that character was eventually drawn into the Arthurian orbit. The earlier Merlin is a prophet and madman, mad in the sense of frenzied or possessed. This is a state associated with the practice of divinely inspired poetry and supernatural wisdom and is one well documented in Celtic tradition. Most of the poetry attributed to this Merlin is vaticinatory and supports political themes for the most part. In Welsh tradition, Taliesin and Merlin were presumed to be the same person (archetypal poet) alive or living among men at different periods. Both are said to have lived during the time of Arthur, and to both are ascribed political prophecies.

It can be seen from this brief summary that Arthur's appearances in early Welsh literature place him firmly in the mythological traditions of the Celts. He operates largely in the supernatural community, abetted by a retinue of supernaturally gifted heroes. His opponents are giants, witches, princes of the otherworld, and men-turned-beasts. Like the Arthur of romance, his origins were obscure and his end a mystery. By the twelfth century, the Bretons were eagerly awaiting Arthur's return, and among the Welsh poets of the twelfth to fourteenth century Arthur was held up as a paragon of heroic and courtly virtues.

Finally, it should be pointed out that, while Arthur's origins are to be found among the British Celts, his name itself may not be Celtic. It is assumed that the name is one of several in the post-Roman period (after, say, A.D. 410) that derive from Latin—in this case, from Artorius; Patricius is another noteworthy example. Still, it must be remembered that the Welsh form of the name, "Arthur," is evocative of the Welsh word for "bear," *arth*, and that in Celtic tradition gods were often assimilated to certain animals—that is, they had a zoomorphic aspect. The bear was one of these, and in Gaul there were divinities with such names as *Dea Artio* 'bear goddess,' *Andarta* 'powerful bear,' *Artgenos* 'bear's son,' and *Artaios* 'bearlike.' In this connection, it is perhaps significant that our Arthur has no patronymic prior to Geoffrey of Monmouth's work and that there is no mention of Arthur at all in the early Welsh genealogies. (*See also* ARTHUR, ORIGINS OF LEGEND.) [PKF]

❧ Bromwich, Rachel. *Trioedd Ynys Prydein.* Cardiff: University of Wales Press, 1961.

Ford, Patrick K. *The Mabinogi and Other Medieval Welsh Tales.* Los Angeles, Berkeley, and London: University of California Press, 1977.

——— . "The Death of Merlin in the Chronicle of Elis Gruffydd." *Viator*, 7 (1976), 379–90.

Jackson, Kenneth. "Arthur in Early Welsh Verse." In *Arthurian Literature in the Middle Ages*, ed. Roger Sherman Loomis. Oxford: Clarendon, 1959.

——— . *The Gododdin: The Oldest Scottish Poem.* Edinburgh: Edinburgh University Press, 1969.

Jarman, A.O.H. "The Arthurian Allusions in the Black Book of Carmarthen." In *The Legend of Arthur in the Middle Ages: Studies Presented to A.H. Diverres*, ed. P.B. Grout, R.A. Lodge, C.E. Pickford, and E.K.C. Varty. London: Boydell and Brewer, 1983, pp. 99–112.

Jones, Thomas. "The Black Book of Carmarthen 'Stanzas of the Graves.' " *Proceedings of the British Academy*, 53 (1967), 97–137.

Loomis, Roger Sherman. *Wales and the Arthurian Legend.* Cardiff: University of Wales Press, 1956.

CERVANTES SAAVEDRA, MIGUEL DE (1547–1616), author of *Don Quixote* (1605, 1615). This, the first modern novel, is also the final and comical turn to the insanity of Arthurian heroes (Yvain, Lancelot, Amadís). Adventures in Part I parody the Arthurian quest of gratuitous adventure, and in Part II the hoax-enchantment of Dulcinea recreates the abduction-rescue pattern of Chrétien de Troyes's Lancelot–Guenevere story, though there is no direct influence. Cervantes's hero styles himself as knight in imitation of Amadís de Gaula and Lanzarote (Lancelot) of Castilian ballads; Sancho recalls the figure of Arthurian dwarfs. Arthurian influence is most evident in the episode of the penitent knight (Book I, Chapter 25), the enchantments in the cave and the hoax enchanter Merlin (Book II, Chapters 23 and 35), and in the themes of "dueñas y doncellas" ("dames et damoiseles") and of Arthur's return in the form of a raven (Book I, Chapter 13). [LAM]

Entwistle, William J. *The Arthurian Legend in the Literatures of the Spanish Peninsula.* London: Dent, 1925.

Murillo, L.A. *The Golden Dial.* Oxford: Dolphin, 1975.

CHANGES, THE: *see* TELEVISION SERIES.

CHANT, JOY, author of *The High Kings* (1983), which focuses on significant episodes in Arthur's career to create a dramatic narrative frame for a beautifully illustrated book. Within this frame, bards recite traditional stories of past rulers and of Arthur himself, drawn from Geoffrey of Monmouth and Welsh tradition. Each episode and its accompanying story are preceded by a short explanation of some aspect of Celtic life relevant to the stories. [RHT]

Chant, Joy. *The High Kings*, illus. George Sharp. New York: Bantam, 1983.

CHANTARI DI LANCELOTTO, LI, or *La Struzione della Tavola Ritonda*, are seven *ottava rima* narratives of late fourteenth-century Italy that recount the fall of Camelot in a manner similar to that of the English Stanzaic *Morte Arthur*, which is also derived from the Vulgate *Mort Artu*. The seven sections into which the narrative is divided seem to reflect the duration of performances by the *cantastorie*, who were accustomed to perform on Sundays and feast days from noon to three and then, after an interval, until Vespers. The *cantari* narrate the destruction of the Round Table as follows: 1) Mordarette warns Artù that he is being dishonored by his wife and Lancelotto; Artù plans a tournament at Winchester (Vincestri) to see if Lancelotto will accompany the court or remain with the Queen. Lancelotto arrives in disguise; the Fair Maid of Astolat (Sgaleotto) falls in love with him and dies of despair. 2) A ship carries her body to Camelot, where it is discovered by Chalvano (Gawain). Ginevra (Guenevere) plans a dinner party, at which a knight is poisoned and Ginevra held responsible. Lancelotto rescues her from harm, but when he visits her later in her chambers he is ambushed by Chalvano and his brothers. Although Lancelotto escapes, the Queen is taken into custody. 3) Lancelotto rescues Ginevra from the flames, but accidentally murders Chalvano's brother, Ghueriesse (Gareth), in the attempt. 4) Artù and his troops besiege Joyous Gard until, through the intervention of the pope, it is agreed that the Queen will be returned to her husband. 5) Chalvano demands vengeance for the death of his brother and is mortally wounded in the subsequent assault on Lancelotto's French domain. 6) Mordarette rebels, and the Round Table is shattered in the course of the climactic battle on Salisbury Plain. Gilfrette (rather than the traditional Lucan) is given the task of returning Excalibur to the waves. When he finally succeeds, Artù is taken onto the mysterious ship and Camelot is burned and pillaged. 7) Following the death of Lionello, Lancelotto becomes a hermit and, dying in holiness, is buried between his friend Galeotto (Galehaut) and his son, Galahad (Galeotto). In addition to their merit as an effective popular narrative of the fall of Camelot, the *Chantari di Lancelotto* provide the only evidence that the Walter Map tradition of the Arthurian legend was known in Italy. [DLH]

Griffiths, E.T., ed. *Li Chantari di Lancelotto.* Oxford: Clarendon, 1924.

CHAPBOOKS: *see* BROADSIDES.

"CHAPEL IN LYONESS, THE": *see* MORRIS, WILLIAM.

CHAPMAN, VERA, in her Three Damosels (or Arthurian) trilogy—*The Green Knight* (1975), *The King's Damosel* (1976), and *King Arthur's Daughter* (1976)—pioneered the female narration in modern Arthurian fiction. These fantasies are indebted to Malory and *Sir Gawain and the Green Knight*, but they demonstrate considerable originality. The borrowed and created narrators provide a refreshing vision of the twelfth century. Of particular note is Chapman's creation of Arthur's daughter, Ursulet ("the small bear," Princess/Queen of all England), and her slavery in *King Arthur's Daughter*; her amplification of the raped and unhappily married Lynette of Lyonesse in *The King's Damosel*; and the fell motivation for the Beheading Game in *The Green Knight*.

The tales are set generations apart, but they are unified by characters who age and reappear and by the brooding, ever-present specter of Arthur's archenemy, Morgan le Fay. The series focuses on the more magical events of the Arthurian legend (e.g., Bertilak's shape-shifting beneath Morgan's wand, Ursulet's achieving of the Holy Grail). However, the series' major accomplishment is its portrayal of strong women maturing in a chaotic, complex, and sorcerous time. [RCS]

Chapman, Vera. *The Green Knight.* London: Collings, 1975.
——— . *The King's Damosel.* London: Collings, 1976.
——— . *King Arthur's Daughter.* London: Collings, 1976.

CHASE, MARY ELLEN (1887–1973). In *Dawn in Lyonesse* (1938), the narrator's reading of the story of Tristan and Isolde gives her insight into a comparable bond between her husband and friend. [RHT]

Chase, Mary Ellen. *Dawn in Lyonesse.* New York: Macmillan, 1938.

CHASTITY TESTS: *see* "AUSGLEICHUNG, DIE"; BIKET, ROBERT; "BOY AND THE MANTLE, THE"; *CARADOC;* "DIS IST FRAUW TRISTERAT HORN VON SAPHOIEN"; HEINRICH VON DEM TÜRLIN; *LUNETEN MANTEL, DER; MANTEL, DER; MANTEL MAUTAILLIÉ,*

LE; MÖTTULS SAGA; NAUBERT, BENEDIKTE; *SAMSONS SAGA FAGRA; SIR CORNEUS, THE ROMANCE OF; SKIKKJU RÍMUR;* VAN DER VELDE, KARL FRANZ; *VASNACHTSPIL MIT DER KRON, DAS;* WERTHES, FRIEDRICH AUGUST CLEMENS.

CHAUCER, GEOFFREY (1340?–1400). In two stories from the *Canterbury Tales,* Chaucer makes use of Arthurian material. In *The Squire's Tale,* the youthful Squire tells a chivalric romance of suitably amorous aspiration. Gawain and Lancelot are cited as exemplars of courtesy and courtly behavior but seen as distant, remote, and long-gone (ll. 95–97, 287). As with *The Wife of Bath's Tale,* discussed below, Chaucer's later Arthurian allusions are oblique and wry in comparison with those of the Chaucerian *Roman de la Rose* translation (ll. 1199, 2209).

The Wife of Bath's Tale offers a short (408 lines) but complex reworking of the Loathly Lady theme. Unlike his counterparts in ballad and Middle English romance (*The Wedding of Sir Gawain and Dame Ragnell,* "The Marriage of Sir Gawain"), the protagonist is not Gawain but an unnamed Arthurian knight. Having raped a maiden, he is granted his life by the Queen if he can say what it is that all women desire. Tutored by an old hag, the knight gives the correct answer to the assembled ladies of the court but is appalled when, as her promised reward, the hag claims him in marriage. On their wedding night, she answers his objections to her low birth, poverty, and age with a sermon principally on the theme that "he is gentil that dooth gentil dedis" (l. 1170) and offers him the choice of having her ugly and faithful, or fair and sought-after. Resigning the choice to her, the knight effectively gives her the sovereignty women desire; she promises him permanent fairness and constancy.

Other Middle English Arthurian narratives (notably *Sir Gawain and the Green Knight*) use the delayed articulation of female roles to revise the ethical categories of chivalric protagonists. Here, the knight's initial act of rape provokes reconsideration of personal identity and its consequent rights and obligations in the more general terms of marriage rather than chivalry. Chaucer juxtaposes folkloric, patristic, and courtly elements in a complex redirection of romance, affecting nonchivalric identities. The Loathly Lady's entirely inner-directed account of what constitutes a person challenges the knight's sense of how far birth, possessions, and appearance make identity, but she nonetheless acknowledges his creaturely need in her permanent fairness. The tale's Arthurian setting functions to place this realistic and accommodating application of the ideology of *gentilesse* as possible nowhere but in Faery, where mutual rights, obligations, and identities can be renegotiated. Often seen as wish-fulfillment for its teller, the tale is less a romance illustrating an individual psyche than an exemplum to provoke reevaluation of the ideologies of personal and social identity in us all. [JP]

☙ Chaucer, Geoffrey. *The Works of Geoffrey Chaucer,* ed. F.N. Robinson. 2nd ed. Boston: Houghton Mifflin, 1957.

———. *The Wife of Bath's Prologue and Tale*, ed. J. Winny. Cambridge: Cambridge University Press, 1965.

Silverstein, T. "The Wife of Bath and the Rhetoric of Enchantment." *Modern Philology*, 58 (1961), 153–73.

Carruthers, M. "The Wife of Bath and the Painting of Lions." *PMLA*, 94 (1979), 209–22.

CHAUSSON, ERNEST (1855–1899), French composer, devoted much energy in his final years to *Le Roi Arthus* (Opus 23), an opera for which he wrote, following Wagner's example, both the libretto and the music. It was first performed in Brussels four years after his death. The theme is Lancelot's passion for Guinevere. Their love is betrayed by the self-seeking Mordred. After agonies of remorse, Guinevere strangles herself and Lancelot is slain in battle, but Arthus, magnanimous and idealistic, achieves immortality as he is borne away across the sea. Chausson responds creatively to Wagner's influence without losing individuality, and in its lyricism and respect for the rhythms of French speech the opera looks forward to *Pelléas et Mélisande*. [CNS]

❦ Barricelli, J.-P., and Leo Weinstein. *Ernest Chausson*. Norman: Oklahoma University Press, 1955.

CHERRYH, C.J., author of the fine science-fiction novel *Port Eternity* (1982), in which a spacecraft is marooned in another dimension, where its human occupants are threatened by aliens. The crew are "made people"—cloned from special genetic combinations, then conditioned to order for human owners. Influenced by Tennyson's *Idylls of the King*, their owner had modeled them upon Arthurian characters, such as Lancelot, Modred, and Elaine of Astolat. Their attempts to cope with the external threat on the one hand, and the internal pressure to act out their traditional roles on the other, provide penetrating insight into the problems created for us all by our conditioned attitudes. [RHT]

❦ Cherryh, C.J. *Port Eternity*. New York: DAW, 1982.

CHERTSEY ABBEY TILES, a surviving fragment of a thirteenth-century pavement, illustrate the Anglo-Norman version of the romance of *Tristan* by Thomas of Britain. The abbey, ten miles from Windsor, enjoyed royal patronage under the Plantagenets, and W.R. Lethaby has suggested that the tiles were made in 1270 for a "King's Chapel" funded by Henry III. Among the identified subjects are thirty-five scenes from *Tristan*, three of Richard Coeur de Lion, and a number of hunts and combats.

The tiles, an inch thick and nine and a half inches in diameter, were made of dark red clay stamped with a design, and the resulting impression was filled with white clay. Each composition was in a rondel, encircled by an inscription and enframed in a foliate patterned square. Other pavements of this type have

a

b

c

d

8 Four tiles from Chertsey Abbey: a) Tristram plays his harp for Mark; b) Morhaut wounds Tristram; c) Tristram teaches Ysolt to play the harp; d) Ysolt voyages to Tristram. From The Romance of Tristram and Ysolt, *by Thomas of Britain, translated by Roger Sherman Loomis. Copyright 1923 by E.P. Dutton; 1931, 1951 by Columbia University Press. Reproduced by permission of the publisher, E.P. Dutton, a division of New American Library.*

been identified, including that of the Abbey of Halesowen near Birmingham, where some of the Chertsey Abbey tile molds were reused, but the Chertsey program appears to have been the most magnificent.

In the nineteenth century, Manwaring Shurlock, a retired physician, recognized the source of the tiles as *Tristan* and published his findings in *Tiles from Chertsey Abbey* (London, 1885). The surviving narrative concentrates on Tristan's youth: his boyhood adventures, his arrival at the court of Cornwall, and his combat with Marhaus. By coincidence, or by censorious design, only three tiles depict the scenes after Tristan and Isolde drink the potion. The tiles are presently scattered; the largest collection is in the British Museum in London, with other examples in the Victoria and Albert Museum, London, and the Survey Archaeological Society Museum at Guilford. [DNM]

⁀ Lethaby, W.R. "The Romance Tiles of Chertsey Abbey." *Walpole Society Annual*, 2 (1912–13), 69–80.

Loomis, Roger Sherman. *Illustrations of Medieval Romance on Tiles of Chertsey Abbey.* Urbana: University of Illinois Press, 1916.

CHESSBOARD QUEEN, THE: *see* NEWMAN, SHARAN.

CHESTRE, THOMAS, generally conceded to be the author of *Libeaus Desconus* and *Sir Launfal. Libeaus Desconus* is a late fourteenth-century stanzaic tail-rhyme version of the Fair Unknown story. The English version includes more motifs than Renaut de Beaujeu's *Le Bel Inconnu*, and Chestre probably used several variant versions of Fair Unknown romances. Though not always highly regarded by modern critics, Chestre's text survives in one seventeenth- and five fifteenth-century manuscripts.

Lybeaus is announced by the narrator to be Gawain's son, Gyngalyn, but he himself remains ignorant of his identity in a solitary rural upbringing, in which his mother calls him Bewfiz. He is named Lybeaus Desconus by King Arthur when he requests knighthood and the next Arthurian adventure. Initially scorned by this adventure's maiden and dwarf messengers, Lybeaus nonetheless successfully undertakes an escalating series of prowess-testing encounters en route to rescuing the Lady of Synadoun from imprisonment. He defeats Sir William Salebraunche, William's three brothers, and two giants, sending them vanquished to Arthur's court. His messenger-damsel fails to win a beauty contest, but he defeats the winning lady's knight in combat and sends Arthur the prize gerfalcon. He also fights to retain the hound of Sir Otes de Lyle the huntsman, thus indicating competence for another chivalric pursuit.

Lybeaus further experiences the interrelations of knightly prowess and love in a long *recreantise* from his quest with the Ile d'Or sorceress Dame Amoure. Rebuked by his messenger-damsel, Lybeaus re-proves himself, in a long joust with the steward of Synadoun, as being worthy of hospitality, worthy of the quest, and worthy of being Gawain's kin. He then tackles the two clerks oppressing the Lady of Synadoun; after earthquakes, other deceptive appearances, and difficult combats, he prevails and with his kiss frees the Lady of Synadoun from existence as a lamia. The romance concludes with their bridal feast and Arthurian rejoicing. [JP]

Sir Launfal is a fourteenth-century lay of 1,044 lines that survives in a single manuscript (B. L. Cotton Caligula A II). It is the work of a minstrel who identifies himself at the conclusion of the piece as Thomas Chestre. Though his primary source was an English couplet version of *Sir Landeval*, Chestre recounts his lay in the stanzaic form characteristic of the English tail-rhyme romances —i.e., in twelve-line stanzas rhyming aabccbddbeeb, aabaabccbddb, or aabaabccbccb.

From *Sir Landeval*, Chestre derived the rudiments of his narrative of the magnanimous young Sir Launfal, who leaves Arthur's court in disgrace, takes a fairy mistress during his absence from Carlisle, loses his mistress as a consequence of boasting about her to Guinevere, and is ultimately reunited with his lover and vindicated by her of the false charges leveled against him by the Queen. As all students of the poem have recognized, Chestre's indebtedness to *Sir Landeval* is marked: the later poet omits few of the details found in his original and in some passages takes over whole lines and fragments of lines from his primary source. Indeed, the verbal similarities between Chestre's poem and *Sir Landeval* are such that it would appear that Chestre was working with a version of *Sir Landeval* very similar to that which survives in Bodl. Libr. MS Rawlinson C 86.

To the version of the Launfal story preserved in *Sir Landeval*, however, Chestre added a good deal of material borrowed from other sources. From the anonymous lay of *Graelent*, for example, Chestre derived the motif of Guinevere's animosity toward Launfal, most of the incidents that take place at the mayor's dwelling during Launfal's exile from Arthur's court, and the account of the disappearance of Gyfre after Launfal's fateful encounter with the amoral Guinevere. According to Roger Sherman Loomis, the tournament and Sir Valentine episodes in *Sir Launfal* are also borrowed, in this case from a source or sources no longer extant. In short, the only parts of the poem believed to be of Chestre's own invention are the episodes concerning Launfal's relations with Sir Hugh and Sir John and with his former servant, the mayor.

Interestingly, however, it is not Chestre's lack of originality but his lack of refinement that has most frequently occasioned comment by critics of *Sir Launfal*. With only a few exceptions, students of the poem have charged that the work is unsophisticated and that, given the behavior of its principal characters, its moral tone is dubious at best. Although there is an element of validity in these charges, particularly when *Sir Launfal* is compared with extant romances intended for an aristocratic audience, we ought always to bear in mind that this lay was almost certainly composed for and recited to a popular audience acquainted only through fiction with the principles of chivalric action and decorum. [JN]

CHEVALIER À L'ÉPÉE

Chestre, Thomas. *Lybeaus Desconus*, ed. Maldwyn Mills. London: Oxford University Press, 1969.

———. *Sir Launfal*, ed. A.J. Bliss. London and Edinburgh: Nelson, 1960.

CHEVALIER À L'ÉPÉE, LE ("The Knight of the Sword"), a brief (1,206-line) French Gauvain romance composed at the time of, or shortly after, Chrétien de Troyes. The work may be by the same author (who signs himself Paien de Maisières) who wrote *La Mule sans frein*. The author plays amusingly on Gauvain's traditional lack of constancy by contrasting him in this work to others far more fickle than he. [NJL]

Johnston, R.C., and D.D.R. Owen, eds. *Two Old French Gauvain Romances*. New York: Barnes and Noble, 1973.

CHEVALIER AU LION, LE: see CHRÉTIEN DE TROYES; SALA, PIERRE.

CHEVALIER AUX DEUX ÉPÉES, LE: see MÉRIADEUC.

CHEVALIER DE LA CHARRETE, LE: see CHRÉTIEN DE TROYES.

CHEVALIER DU PAPEGAU, LE ("The Knight of the Parrot"), an independent late prose romance from the fifteenth century, in which the newly crowned Arthur sets out to liberate a lady from her oppressor. The short narrative is so action-filled that it defies summary, but it is characterized by a strong use of supernatural elements, such as the Fish-Knight and the parrot that gives its name to the romance. This latter is kept in a splendid golden cage and carried on horseback; it sings songs to Arthur and advises him on his course of action. [KB]

Heuckenkamp, Ferdinand, ed. *Le Chevalier du Papegau*. Halle: Niemeyer, 1896.

CHEVALIERS DE LA TABLE RONDE, LES: see COCTEAU, JEAN.

CHEVREFUEIL: see MARIE DE FRANCE.

CHILDREN'S LITERATURE: see JUVENILE FICTION IN ENGLISH; GERMAN ARTHURIAN LITERATURE (MODERN).

CHIVALRY. Anyone who makes the attempt to define the word "chivalry" in a few paragraphs is destined to fail, simply because the term denoted differing states and obligations, depending on whether we are dealing with the early or the late Middle Ages, with political and social reality or literary inspiration, and so on. We can, however, make some generalizations. By its origins, "chivalry" denotes a purely military status (the very word *chevalier* in French suggests a mounted soldier). Yet in its literary (and social) implementation chivalry was far more than that. It could develop into an elaborate code, and it was in many cases inextricably linked up (in complex ways) with courtly love.

L'Ordene de chevalerie, an early thirteenth-century French treatise on the theory of knighthood, tells us that the knight's duties were the following: to love God and be willing to spill one's blood for Him; to possess justice and loyalty, protecting the poor and the weak; to remain clean in flesh and pure in spirit, avoiding in particular the sin of lechery; and, remembering that death is before us all, to strive for candor and flee from pride. In a more practical piece of advice, the knight is told not to witness false judgment or treason, never to deny his protection to a lady or maiden, to be abstemious, and to attend Mass daily.

Sidney Painter, writing on chivalry in medieval France, divides his subject into three categories: Feudal Chivalry, Religious Chivalry, and Courtly Love. The ideals of the first were prowess (meaning courage, strength, and skill in the use of weapons) and loyalty, with generosity and courtesy considered important corollaries. Religious chivalry added to these virtues piety, temperance, and chastity (and of course adherence to the tenets and causes of the Church and, secondarily, to the demands of the prince). Finally, courtly love wedded the adoration of the lady to the chivalric ethic, holding love to be an ennobling, even perfecting, force. Adoration, fidelity, and the acquisition of certain social graces assumed an importance approaching—and in some cases surpassing—that of military skills and devotion to political or religious causes.

As Painter's discussion suggests, medieval Arthurian literature could emphasize the knight's obligation to God, to the king and the social order, or to a lady; alternatively, writers could attempt a synthesis of two or all of these obligations. Such a synthesis was not always comfortable or effective. In earlier French romances (e.g., those of Chrétien de Troyes), the knight often fails to understand that chivalry and love are, or can be, compatible. Thus, Chrétien's heroes may err by neglecting chivalry (Erec) or by neglecting the lady for the pleasures of knighthood (Yvain). In Chrétien's *Lancelot*, however, the service of the lady is clearly paramount, and it is that service that gives meaning to the chivalric vocation. In later works (such as the Vulgate Cycle), the quest for the Grail assumes priority, as a higher conception of chivalry supplants both courtly love and the political/social functions of knighthood. Malory often sees the demands of chivalry as incompatible with those of love: the successful Grail quester must keep himself pure (whereas the earlier French poets often interpreted "purity" in a relative way). For Galahad, amorous satisfaction would interfere with his higher calling.

Whatever the particular conception of chivalry, certain virtues remained constant. Constancy itself, the singleminded devotion to a goal, was the ideal. The knight was sworn to uphold the good and overturn evil, and he was obligated to protect the poor, the weak, the downtrodden (and specifically— according to some texts—widows, maidens, and orphans). Generosity, as Chrétien reminds us, is the queen of virtues, for knights as for others. This ideal entailed various practices, from offering hospitality to bestowing gifts to freeing captives on their word. Conversely, the knight must himself be honest and trustworthy, keeping his word and his promises.

Moreover, a knight's reputation was carefully cultivated and prized, since it was considered an accurate indication of his character; but in building and nurturing that reputation he often sought adventure for its own sake, savoring the pleasure of successful martial (or amatory) encounters. While such events—or at least the martial ones—might usefully hone the knight's skills, a number of texts (most notably Chrétien's *Perceval*) offered examples of knights who sought adventure solely for the purpose of acquiring glory, without understanding that only unswerving service to an ideal or to a person could give meaning and value to chivalry.

Not surprisingly, there grew up around general chivalric precepts a code of social conduct that could become very complex and that could (and sometimes did) become little more than meaningless ritual. It was normally assumed that a knight should possess the social graces and abilities expected of the nobility (the low-born being generally excluded from chivalric ranks), and certain knights (e.g., Gawain) take obvious pleasure in demonstrating their mastery of manners, conversational skills, and techniques of seduction. Discretion and restraint were considered virtues, but these too could go awry. Chrétien's Perceval is advised, for example, not to talk excessively, and he mistakes such trivial rules for the more important precepts of chivalry. The possibility of such error, of cultivating ritual instead of performing useful service, was exploited by a number of authors, who used Gawain or other knights as examples of chivalry gone wrong. (*See also* COURTLY LOVE.) [NJL]

Raoul de Houdenc. *"Le Roman des eles": The Anonymous "Ordene de Chevalerie, "* ed. Keith Busby. Amsterdam: Benjamins, 1983.

Painter, Sidney. *French Chivalry*. Baltimore: Johns Hopkins Press, 1940.

CHRÉTIEN DE TROYES, by general agreement the greatest French writer of medieval romance. Some would consider him the inventor of the genre, although that would do a serious injustice to the authors of the romances of antiquity, composed around, and shortly after, the middle of the twelfth century. In any event, Chrétien was without a doubt instrumental both in the elaboration of the Arthurian legend and in the establishment of the ideal form for the diffusion of that legend.

We know virtually nothing of Chrétien's life, although some information can be drawn from his own references to his work. For example, in the prologue to *Cligés* he tells us that he had translated or adapted several Ovidian works (entitled in his text *Les Commandemanz d'Ovide*, *L'Art d'amors*, and *Le Mors de l'espaule*) and that he had composed a work about Isolde and King Mark; none of these works is extant. He also lists another Ovidian adaptation, the metamorphosis (or *muance*) "de la hupe et de l'aronde et del rossignol"; this text, from Ovid's Philomela story, does exist in a version that may be his. In addition, we have from Chrétien two brief lyric poems and the five Arthurian romances for which he is known today. A romance entitled *Guillaume d'Angle-terre* (a pseudo-hagiographic narrative) bears the name "Crestiiens," and scholars disagree about the identification of this author with Chrétien de Troyes. His romances are written in octosyllabic couplets, the standard narrative form of the period.

Presumably, Chrétien was from Troyes or at least had spent a good part of his active life there; both his name and certain dialectal features of his language support this contention. We do not know when he was born. Although some scholars (e.g., Luttrell) suggest that Chrétien's primary literary activity took place in the 1180s, he probably composed his romances between the late 1150s—in the *Chevalier de la charrete* he refers to Marie de Champagne as *ma dame de Chanpaigne*, indicating that her marriage to Henry the Liberal, which took place as early as 1159, predated the composition of this work—and about 1190. His final romance, *Le Conte del Graal*, was dedicated to Philip of Flanders, who died in 1191.

There are certain common threads running through Chrétien's romances, despite differences of tone, subject matter, and artistic maturity. The most obvious of these threads is the Arthurian setting and the author's literary exploration of the notion of Arthurian chivalry. Arthur and his court remain at the center of the society explored by Chrétien, but Arthur himself is never the center of a romance (indeed, in *Yvain* he becomes something of a doddering, ineffective old man, although his authority is never questioned and the respect he receives diminishes only slightly). Chrétien's emphasis is instead on the trials, errors, and ultimate triumphs of his hero, on the hero's love interests, and on the relationship (often uncomfortable until perfected through trials or pain) of that love with the social demands of chivalry. It is also possible to see the works as exploring the problem of the individual vs. the couple, the couple vs. society, or self-interest vs. the social utility of knighthood. Generalizing further, we can state that, while Chrétien's works may not include a genuine *Bildungsroman*, they do generally trace the development of characters from naïveté to sophistication and from ignorance to understanding. This is true to a significant degree even for the heroes who, like Yvain or Lancelot, are knights accomplished and respected—but nonetheless flawed—even when we first meet them.

Erec et Enide develops with clarity the potential conflicts between love and chivalry (the latter term taken to include service to others, the quest for adventure, and concern for one's reputation). Once Erec wins his bride, he neglects his public duties, causing others to grumble. Enide herself laments the rumors about him and the responsibility she may bear for those rumors. Overhearing her expression of concern, and presumably doubting her love and devotion, he commands her—without explanation—to prepare to leave with him. There follows a period of wandering, hardship, and pain. Erec imposes silence on Enide, but she repeatedly disobeys him in order to warn him of approaching danger. Ironically, it is through disobedience (indicating concern for his welfare rather than for her own) that she proves her love for him.

The period of wandering in fact constitutes a test for both of them, providing proof of her love and of his chivalric (i.e., public, active) competence, of his ability to tend to his public duties while remaining the loving husband. Readers, not surprisingly, have frequently thought him to have an odd way of expressing his love: her husband requires Enide to go without sleep and indulge his apparently petulant actions. But neither the narrator nor Enide herself appears to entertain any doubts in this regard. In exploring ways to reconcile the lover's devotion with the knight's duty, Chrétien's first romance dramatizes a problem that will concern him repeatedly while at the same time offering the first of several solutions to that problem.

Chrétien's next romance, *Cligés*, resembles his first in a number of ways but also differs from it significantly. The primary difference is in the structure: Chrétien recounts the story of Alexandre (Cligés's father) before that of the hero himself. In so doing, Chrétien appears to be making systematic reference to the Tristan story, and some critics have contended in fact that he is composing an "anti-Tristan." Yet, despite this bipartite division, the poem's general complexion, both technical and ideological, identifies it as Chrétien's composition.

The similarity of this work to *Erec et Enide* resides in the dramatization of a "before/after" duality; here, however, the contrast is not between an earlier and a later stage of a single knight's development but between the levels of courtly sophistication of two consecutive generations. The first is Alexandre's, which is non- or "proto-courtly" (in Peter Haidu's term). The work is Chrétien's most rhetorical romance, with Alexandre, among others, indulging in extensive and self-conscious interior monologues on the subject of love and his beloved. In the course of his monologues, he grapples poorly with the subject, although his lack of subtlety in no way diminishes the intensity of his love. By contrast, Cligés proves himself a comfortable inhabitant of the courtly world, dealing easily and adroitly with the rhetoric and with the sensations of love.

The romance offers more specific reminiscences of the Tristan legend (in addition to a number of explicit references to it). Cligés loves Fénice, but she is married to his uncle Alis (Isolde had of course been the wife of Tristan's uncle). Fénice loves him, also, but she insists that she will not repeat the actions of Isolde, whose body was possessed by one man while her heart belonged to another. This dilemma provides the principal ethical problem of the second part of the romance, and Fénice does indeed find a solution.

That solution involves her taking a potion that causes her to appear to be dead. Once her "death" is established, she is free to live with Cligés—Fénice, the Phoenix, survives her death—and fully indulge her love for him. Clearly, the solution is somewhat equivocal and not entirely honorable. The lovers have in fact succeeded not in solving their problem but only in evading it. On the other hand, Fénice is apparently more interested in her reputation than in her ethics, and therein she has been successful: people cannot say (as they said of Isolde) that she divided her love between two men.

Le Chevalier de la charrete ("The Knight of the Cart"), or *Lancelot*, may well be Chrétien's best-known romance. It is known, first of all, for its dedication to Marie de Champagne and, second, for its depiction and apparent glorification of adulterous love. In a quest for Guenevere, who has been abducted from the court, Lancelot has the opportunity to find her more quickly if he accepts a ride in a cart reserved ordinarily for criminals. Mindful of his status and reputation, he hesitates briefly but then steps into the cart. When he eventually arrives in Guenevere's presence, she rejects him, and we learn that it is because of his reluctance to ride in the cart. Apparently, he has offended her by putting concern for himself (i.e., for his reputation) before concern for her. The remainder of the romance is a series of trials undertaken to expiate his offense. Among his adventures, for example, is a tourney in which the Queen commands him to do "his worst," proving thereby that he is now willing to suffer for her sake the humiliation he had avoided before.

Near the end, Chrétien left off the writing of this romance, for reasons unknown to us (although the lack of evidence has not prevented some critics from speculating that he personally disapproved of the subject, imposed on him by his patroness). Godefroy de Leigny finished the romance according to a plan (he tells us) provided him by Chrétien.

There is some indication that Chrétien may have been composing *Lancelot* and *Yvain* (also known as *Le Chevalier au lion*) at the same time. Yet the two romances differ considerably. The *Lancelot* has a discursive, somewhat loose structure, whereas *Yvain* is highly composed and almost "classically" structured. Moreover, the adulterous relationship of the former is replaced by marital love in *Yvain*. The latter work is in fact closer, in inspiration and subject matter, to *Erec et Enide* than to *Lancelot*; indeed, it is from certain points of view the mirror image of *Erec et Enide*. On the other hand, all these works share (with Chrétien's other romances) a binary opposition between two stages of the hero's progress, a "before/after" opposition, with the dividing line being an offense or error committed by the hero.

Erec, as we have seen, neglects chivalry in favor of love: Yvain does the opposite. He wins Laudine's love (after killing her husband), but immediately after his marriage he yields to the persuasive powers of Gauvain, who has asked his friend to accompany him in his quest for adventure. Laudine reluctantly gives him leave for one year; he later loses her love when he fails to return within the time granted him. The remainder of the romance depicts Yvain's grief and madness and his subsequent attempts to expiate his offense. During his wandering, he is accompanied and aided by a lion whose life he had saved. (The lion, thought by some to represent Christ or grace, more likely symbolizes Yvain's own perfected ideal of service and devotion.) The adventures through which Yvain accomplishes his expiation are intricately interlaced with one another in a pattern that gives clear evidence, if evidence were needed, of Chrétien's attention not only to elaboration of theme but to structure and composition as well.

If, in terms of form and the effective elaborations of theme, *Yvain* is Chrétien's best romance, his final romance, *Perceval*, or *Le Conte del Graal*, has proved the most fascinating. Part of its fascination is doubtless due to the intriguing possibilities of its unfinished state—possibilities that were exploited in a number of Continuations and adaptations when Chrétien (whether because of death or for other reasons) left his romance without an ending. The character of Perceval himself has also appealed to audiences, as he develops from comical bumpkin to Grail knight. Yet the primary appeal of the work must be the Grail itself.

Although the word "grail" existed before Chrétien, it originally meant simply "dish"; it was Chrétien who first attached special significance to the word. (It must be pointed out in passing that it was not, in his work, the chalice of the Last Supper or the vessel in which Christ's blood was collected: those were innovations made by writers after Chrétien: *see* GRAIL; ROBERT DE BORON.) For him, it was a beautiful and mysterious vessel, whose function is initially unknown to Perceval. In fact, the very *mystery* of the Grail, rather than its specific use, is of prime importance in the work. And the Grail procession itself, in a mysterious disappearing castle, with a bleeding lance and a strange infirm host, provides a fascinating narrative core for this remarkable work.

It is entirely appropriate for the Grail to be a mystery to Perceval. Although endowed with exceptional physical gifts, he is seriously deficient in knowledge and insight. At the beginning of the work, he does not even know what knights and churches are. When he learns about knights, he immediately resolves to become one; typically, however, he confuses the possession of armor with the status of knighthood. In valuing the trappings of chivalry (equipment, reputation, and the thrill of combat) over its ethical and social concerns, he shares a failing with a number of Chrétien's other characters, from Gauvain to the early Lancelot; the distinction between Perceval and the others resides in his naïveté and in the consistent comedy of his actions.

When he decides not to inquire about the Grail procession, he is acting typically, since he had been told that a knight is careful not to talk excessively. His failure to ask that question is the critical turning point of the work (as he later learns that the question would have cured the Fisher King, the castle's inhabitant, and would have restored the fertility of his land). This error corresponds to the crisis that we have noted in Chrétien's other works, and it requires a similar expiation. In this case, however, the hero's errors are multiple, for in addition to failing to cure the Fisher King Perceval learns that his abrupt departure from home had caused the death of his own mother. Furthermore, he had along the way taken a lady, Blancheflor, as his love, and yet he repeatedly postpones his return to her, just as he had postponed the Grail question and his return to his mother.

Perceval's adventures are abruptly interrupted, and the author turns his attentions to Gauvain, who undergoes an extraordinary series of adventures in a strange realm. The suddenness of this shift has led a good many critics to conclude that the story of Gauvain was intended to be a separate romance, but that the vagaries of manuscript transmission had fused the two sequences into one. Specific structural and thematic correspondences between the two halves provide evidence, however, that they were intended to be part of the same romance, even if the opportunity for further revision might have permitted Chrétien to provide a more graceful transition.

Gauvain's adventures are interrupted in turn by a brief (300-line) but central return to Perceval. In this episode, which takes place on Good Friday, Perceval speaks with a holy hermit, rediscovers God, and hears the explanation of the Grail castle and of his own past failings. This episode alone is responsible for imbuing the work with a largely religious meaning. Afterward, the focus returns to Gauvain, and we learn no more of Perceval in the remainder of this unfinished romance.

Perceval may have been interrupted by Chrétien's death; in any case, the poet's career obviously ended at this point. Yet during that career Chrétien was largely responsible for perfecting a literary form that was to remain central to French literature from that time on. His mastery of narrative form and style, his ability to fuse humor with high seriousness, the subtlety of his psychological portraits, and the appeal of his themes established him as a consummate artist. Those who came after developed numerous varieties of romance, but they all owed a good deal to Chrétien de Troyes, and it is reasonable to conclude that they could not have accomplished what they did were it not for their illustrious precursor. [NJL]

❧ Chrétien de Troyes. *Les Romans de Chrétien de Troyes: Erec et Enide, Le Chevalier de la charrete*, and *Le Chevalier au lion (Yvain)*, ed. Mario Roques (Paris: Champion, 1952, 1958, 1960); *Cligés*, ed. Alexandre Micha (Paris: Champion, 1958); *Le Conte du Graal (Perceval)*, ed. Félix Lecoy (Paris: Champion, 1973).

Frappier, Jean. *Chrétien de Troyes*. Paris: Hatier, 1957.

Haidu, Peter. *Aesthetic Distance in Chrétien de Troyes*. Geneva: Droz, 1968.

Kelly, F. Douglas. *Chrétien de Troyes: An Analytic Bibliography*. London: Grant and Cutler, 1976.

Lacy, Norris J. *The Craft of Chrétien de Troyes*. Leiden: Brill, 1980.

Topsfield, L.T. *Chrétien de Troyes: A Study of the Arthurian Romances*. Cambridge: Cambridge University Press, 1981.

CHRÉTIEN DE TROYES, BURGUNDIAN ADAPTATIONS OF. Chré-

tien de Troyes at the court of Burgundy presents a curious problem because the prose versions of the only two of his works that were known there fail to mention his name. These are *Cligés* (Leipzig, Universitätsbibliothek 108) and *Erec et Enide* (Brussels, Bibl. Roy. 7235), both preserved in single, paper copies dating from the middle of the fifteenth century. Wendelin Foerster, who published both texts as annexes to his editions of the original poems, was of the opinion that both manuscripts were the work of the same scribe, although G. Doutrepont, in his discussion of the Burgundian *mises en prose*, considered the dialect of the two texts sufficiently different to indicate two scribes, and possibly two editors. Indeed, the techniques of the two prose versions differ, for the editor of *Erec et Enide* constantly abbreviates passages from the poem, including a number of descriptions of combats that would seemingly have been to the taste of a Burgundian audience. He sees Enide's trials as comparable to the patient Griselda's. The Prose *Cligés* has also been altered in a number of instances, sometimes abbreviated, but also with details frequently added, apparently to conform to tastes different from those of an earlier audience. In general, analyses of love and other such emotions are omitted, although a passage concerning the hero's encounter with a lovelorn maiden in a forest is introduced as motivation for his appreciating Fénice's sorrow at his absence and his decision to return to Greece from King Arthur's court. That there are no other known copies of either work, however, suggests that the prose versions did not meet with the Duke of Burgundy's approval, nor that of other book collectors at his court.

There was, however, an independent version of the first part of *Erec et Enide* included in the compilation of Arthurian material centering on *Guiron le Courtois* prepared for one Burgundian bibliophile, Louis de Bruges, Lord of Gruthuyse (B.N. fr. 363), although here Erec appears merely as one of the knights who fights against the champion of the tournament at Val Brun, where he does not meet with success, although his life is spared through Enide's intervention. [CCW]

&. Chrétien de Troyes. *Sämtliche erhaltene Werke nach allen bekannten Handschriften*, ed. Wendelin Foerster. 4 vols. Halle: Niemeyer, Vol. 1 (*Cligés*), 1884; Vol. 3 (*Erec et Enide*), 1890.

Doutrepont, Georges. *Les Mises en prose des Épopées et des Romans chevalersques du XIVe au XVIe siècle*. Brussels: Mémoires de l'Académie Royale de Belgique, Classe de Lettres, 1939, pp. 261–64.

Lathuillère, Roger. *Guiron le Courtois: Etude de la tradition manuscrite et analyse critique*. Geneva: Droz, 1966.

CHRISTIAN, CATHERINE, wrote *The Sword and the Flame* (1978; published in the United States as *The Pendragon*, 1979), a historical novel set in a Romano-Celtic Britain more pagan than Christian. Narrated by Arthur's closest companion, Bedivere, the story encompasses Arthur's youth, Lancelot and Guenevere's adultery, the Grail quest, and Medraut's treachery. Though sometimes interesting for its treatment of tradition, the novel is too often an uninspired reworking of Malory. [VML]

ஃ Christian, Catherine. *The Sword and the Flame: Variations on a Theme of Sir Thomas Malory.* London: Macmillan, 1978. (Published in the U.S. as *The Pendragon*. New York: Knopf, 1979.)

CHRONICA GENTIS SCOTORUM: see SCOTTISH ARTHURIAN CHRONICLES.

CHRONICLE OF SCOTLAND IN A PART: see SCOTTISH ARTHURIAN CHRONICLES.

CHRONICLES, ARTHUR IN. There is no mention of Arthur in the English traditions of the fifth and sixth centuries preserved in the *Anglo-Saxon Chronicle.* Its silence, however, implies nothing either way about his reality, because, while it names a few of the Britons' leaders (Vortigern, for instance), it omits those who inflicted reverses on the Saxons, such as Ambrosius. Hence, the presumably successful Arthur would have had no place in it. His first appearance in a chronicle is in the tenth-century *Annales Cambriae*, a Welsh document that associates him with the battles of Badon and Camlann, assigned to 518 and 539 or thereabout. The provenance of these entries is unknown, and the date given for Badon seems to clash with the earlier testimony of Gildas. The Camlann entry proves at least that there was a Welsh tradition of that battle before Geoffrey of Monmouth.

Henry of Huntingdon, in his *Historia Anglorum* (ca. 1129), draws mainly on Anglo-Saxon matter for this period but adds an account of Arthur in a vague retrospect of "those times" inserted between 527 and 530. It is based on Nennius's list of his battles. Henry calls him "the leader of the soldiers and kings of Britain."

Geoffrey's transformation of Arthur into a quasi-historical monarch, with a detailed and grandiose career, completely alters his status. Where medieval historiography touches on post-Roman Britain, Geoffrey's story is commonly accepted in substance. Two authors taking a skeptical or hostile view, Giraldus Cambrensis and William of Newburgh, are distinguished spokesmen for what long remains a minority opinion. Yet there is a recurrent awareness that the story presents difficulties, especially with dating. Chroniclers' use of it varies widely in fullness and credulity.

Welsh adapters and translators of Geoffrey, in the chronicles known as *Bruts*, follow him fairly closely. Among the works written in England, the most important are by Pierre de Langtoft, Robert Mannyng (Robert of Brunne or Bourn), and John Hardyng. In the hands of these authors and many others, Geoffrey's narrative is treated selectively, sometimes modified by the authors' own fancies and sometimes augmented with material from romance. In the end, the problems arising from more genuine history, which fails to confirm Geoffrey and often casts obvious suspicion on him, become too intractable. In

Polydore Vergil (1534), a definite skepticism has set in. Raphael Holinshed (1577) can still make a serious attempt to harmonize Arthur with Anglo-Saxon and other evidence, but he drifts into speculations and contradictions that leave everything in confusion.

Scotland's chroniclers, such as John of Fordun (ca. 1385), also try to follow Geoffrey. With less of the critical spirit than their English counterparts, they are subversive instead through a difference of attitude. Repelled by Geoffrey's account of war waged by Arthur against the Scots, and by the Plantagenets' adoption of him as—in effect—a king of England, Scottish chroniclers tend to alter the values of the story and make him unsympathetic. The extreme of this process is represented by Hector Boece (1527), whose Arthur is the faithless and licentious ruler of a contemptible nation.

On the Continent, Arthur is overwhelmingly a king of romance, and interest in the historical aspect is slight. Some chroniclers mention him briefly, usually echoing Geoffrey, if with reservations. A few, such as Jean des Preis, or d'Outremeuse (late fourteenth century), exploit the romances to elaborate his career in ways of their own. There are traces, however, of a historical tradition that is independent of Geoffrey or nearly so. This places Arthur's *floruit* in and around the 460s and associates him with real persons—notably Aegidius, a Roman ruler of northern Gaul—of whom Geoffrey knows nothing.

A glimpse of it can perhaps be caught in a recension of a chronicle Geoffrey may have used himself, that of Sigebert of Gembloux, who died in 1112. About 1175, a writer known as the monk of Ursicampum (Orcamp) compiled an enlarged version of Sigebert's chronicle. He introduced matter from Geoffrey but with certain questions, raising the possibility that Arthur might be the same as the British king known as Riothamus, documented in Gaul ca. 468–70. A separate hint at this equation occurs in the *Chronicles of Anjou*, where, in a passage generally derived from Geoffrey, Arthur's betrayer becomes *Morvandus*. This suggests a conflation of "Mordred" with "Arvandus," the name of an imperial prefect who did betray Riothamus. Allusions to Arthur consistent with the equation, though not offering it in plain terms, appear in Albericus Trium Fontium (1227–51), the *Salzburg Annals* (thirteenth century), Martinus Polonus (ca. 1275), Jacques de Guise (late fourteenth century), and Philippe de Vigneulles (1525). With one or two minor corrections, genuinely required in the interests of accuracy, these could all be derived from a single source giving Arthur a sixteen-year reign running from about 454 to 470. Such a reign would allow him to be the immediate successor of Vortigern, as implied by the apparently independent account—also continental—in the *Legend of St. Goeznovius*. (*See also* CHRONICLES IN ENGLISH; SCOTTISH ARTHURIAN CHRONICLES.) [GA]

Ashe, Geoffrey. *The Discovery of King Arthur.* New York: Doubleday, 1985.

Chambers, E.K. *Arthur of Britain.* London: Sidgwick and Jackson, 1927.

Fletcher, Robert Huntington. *The Arthurian Material in the Chronicles, Especially Those of Great Britain and France.* Boston: Ginn, 1906; 2nd ed. Roger Sherman Loomis. New York: Franklin, 1966.

Fleuriot, Léon. *Les Origines de la Bretagne.* Paris: Payot, 1980.

CHRONICLES, SCOTTISH: *see* SCOTTISH ARTHURIAN CHRONICLES.

CHRONICLES IN ENGLISH. The Middle English chroniclers who wrote about Arthur generally followed the story of the rise and fall of Arthur as it was presented in Geoffrey of Monmouth's *Historia Regum Britanniae*. Although most of the chroniclers knew some of the Arthurian romances and borrowed from them details and names of some characters, like Lancelot and Yvain, they generally did not make major changes in Geoffrey's account. They apparently distinguished between what they considered to be the basically true account in Geoffrey and the basically fictitious ones in romance. Although a few Latin chroniclers, like Ranulph Higden and William of Newburgh, had doubts about the truth of Geoffrey's *Historia*, they were in the minority. In fact, most of the English chroniclers, in contrast to Higden, William, and some of the Scottish chroniclers, were enthusiastic about Arthur and portrayed him not as the weak king of some of the French romances (Chrétien's *Chevalier de la charrete*, parts of the Vulgate Cycle) but as the heroic figure developed by Geoffrey. This may at first seem surprising, since Arthur was British and an enemy of the Saxons, the ancestors of the English. Admittedly, Layamon may have been more interested in drawing a parallel to the later Norman Conquest than in praising the British; but the attitude of most of the chroniclers seems to be similar to the attitude of Caxton, who in his preface to Malory's *Morte Darthur* (1485) explains that noble gentlemen told him that he should print the history of Arthur, the "noble king and conqueror," rather than that of any of the other Nine Worthies, since Arthur "was a man born within the realm, and [was] king and emperor of the same." Although Caxton's enthusiasm was undoubtedly influenced by Henry VII's claim to be a descendant of Arthur, it also followed the tradition of earlier English chroniclers who looked upon Arthur's reign as one of the great periods in the history of the land they now inhabited. (*See also* ARTHUR; BEK, THOMAS, OF CASTELFORD; CAPGRAVE, JOHN; CHRONICLES, ARTHUR IN; HARDYNG, JOHN; MANNYNG, ROBERT, OF BRUNNE; PROSE *BRUT*; ROBERT OF GLOUCESTER; SCOTTISH ARTHURIAN CHRONICLES; *SHORT METRICAL CHRONICLE*; TREVISA, JOHN.) [EDK]

Fletcher, Robert Huntington. *The Arthurian Material in the Chronicles, Especially Those of Great Britain and France.* Boston: Ginn, 1906; 2nd ed. Roger Sherman Loomis. New York: Franklin, 1966, pp. 193–98.

Göller, K.H. *König Arthur in der englischen Literatur des späten Mittelalters.* Göttingen: Vandenhoeck and Ruprecht, 1963, pp. 19–40, 57–66.

CHRONICON MONTIS SANCTI MICHAELIS IN PERICULO MARIS ("Chronicle of St. Michael's Mount"), Breton in origin and perhaps predating Geoffrey of Monmouth's *Historia*, records in its initial entry that Arthur was king of Britain in 421. The *Chronicle* is part of the remains of the library of Mont St.-Michel and is preserved in Avranches MS 213. [MLD]

🍃 Migne, J.P., ed. *Chronicon Montis Sancti Michaelis in Periculo Maris*. In *Patrologia Latina*. Paris: Migne, 1855, Vol. 202, col. 1323.

CIAN OF THE CHARIOTS: *see* BABCOCK, WILLIAM H.

CIFAR: *see* ZIFAR, LIBRO DEL CAVALLERO.

CIRCLE OF THE GODS, THE: *see* CANNING, VICTOR.

CLARE, HELEN, author of *Merlin's Magic* (1953). Merlin sends a group of modern children on a magical treasure hunt. They meet several Arthurian characters while learning that the true treasure is the human imagination. [RHT]

🍃 Clare, Helen. *Merlin's Magic*. London: Lane, 1953.

CLARIS ET LARIS, a two-part romance of over 30,000 lines that tell the story of two friends, Claris and Laris. Claris marries Lidoine after the death of her husband, the King of Gascony. Laris is carried off by a fay, Madoine, and eventually rescued by Claris. The second half of the poem concerns the affair of Laris with Marine, sister of Yvain, whose father, Urien, is besieged by King Tallas of Denmark, who in turn has designs on Marine. Claris and Laris, together with Gauvain and Yvain, vanquish Tallas, but Laris is taken prisoner. After a series of lengthy quests, Merlin helps Brandaliz find and liberate Laris.

The romance is well structured in the balance between the two parts, and the narrative seems to have been influenced by the *entrelacement* (structural interlace) of the prose romances. Begun in 1268, *Claris et Laris* is one of the last Old French verse romances, and the author draws on a wide variety of stock motifs and earlier works, such as the romances of Chrétien de Troyes, the Continuations of the *Perceval*, Wace's *Brut*, the Didot-*Perceval*, and the *Perlesvaus*. Particularly interesting is the way in which the author specifically alludes to some of these other works and incorporates them into his own composition. *Claris et Laris* is written in a lively manner and is imbued with a slightly subversive sense of humor. [KB]

🍃 Alton, Johann, ed. *Claris et Laris*. Tübingen: Bibliothek des literarischen Vereins in Stuttgart, 1884.

Klose, Martin. *Der Roman von Claris und Laris in seinen Beziehungen zur altfranzösischen Artusepik*. Halle: Niemeyer, 1916.

CLIGÉS: *see* CHRÉTIEN DE TROYES; CHRÉTIEN DE TROYES, BURGUNDIAN ADAPTATIONS OF.

CLOSS, HANNAH, author of the historical novel *Tristan* (1940), which employs impressionistic and stream-of-consciousness techniques to relate the traditional love story of Tristan and Isolde. Events are often filtered through the mind of the hero, who is dreamer and poet as well as warrior. The images thus gain an imaginative intensity that vividly evokes the lovers' passions. [RHT]

❧ Closs, Hannah. *Tristan*. London: Dakers, 1940.

CLUTCH OF CIRCUMSTANCE, THE: *see* SENIOR, DOROTHY.

COCTEAU, JEAN (1889–1963), author of the three-act play *Les Chevaliers de la Table Ronde*, written in 1937. In the play, Ginifer, a servant of Merlin, assumes the identities of various characters (Gauvain, Galaad, Guenièvre) to confound Artus, the King, and his entourage. Although Merlin initially enjoys the favor of Artus, he is an evil character who uses his servant and his own powers to enchant (*intoxiquer*) the castle. Galaad breaks the spell, but the rebirth of the castle brings about pain and travail, including the death of the Queen and her lover. The play was first performed at the Théâtre de l'Œuvre on 14 October 1937.

Cocteau also used Arthurian material in his *L'Éternel Retour* (1943). This screenplay transposes the Tristan legend into the twentieth century. The author retains the name Marc but transposes Tristan into Patrice and Iseut into Natalie (the final syllables of the new names echoing the first syllables of the originals). After rescuing Natalie from an oafish drunkard and bully named Morolt, Patrice persuades her to marry his aging uncle Marc, but the young people soon fall madly in love through the action of a potion. The "enemies" are the Frossins (the family of his deceased first wife), and particularly their dwarf son, Achille. Despite a number of innovations, Cocteau is quite faithful to the early versions of the legend in his transposition of several episodes, such as the white sail (here a scarf) announcing the return of his mistress.

In 1951, a radio adaptation of *L'Éternel Retour* was made by Georges Beaume, with music by Georges Auric. [NJL]

❧ Cocteau, Jean. *Les Chevaliers de la Table Ronde*. In *Œuvres complètes de Jean Cocteau*. Geneva: Marguerat, 1948, Vol. 6.

———. *Three Screenplays*, trans. Carol Martin-Sperry. New York: Grossman, 1972.

COHEN, MATT, Canadian author of the story *Too Bad Galahad* (1972), which ironically reverses the hero's traditional role as perfect knight by presenting him as failed schoolmaster, would-be dragonslayer swallowed by dragon, inept lover, and quester unable to identify the Grail until he is about to die. Conflated time, word play, and antiromantic views of Malorian characters and events produce a wittily irreverent modernization. [MAW]

❧ Cohen, Matt. *Too Bad Galahad*. Toronto: Coach House Press, 1972.

COLIN, PHILIPP, and CLAUS WISSE. Between 1331 and 1336, they translated and adapted two of the French continuators of Chrétien's *Perceval*, Wauchier de Denain and Manessier, into German. Helping them in the translation was a Strassburg Jew, Sampson Pine. The result of their efforts, *Der nüwe Parzefal* (36,426 lines), was inserted between Books 14 and 15 of Wolfram von Eschenbach's *Parzival*, which also was revised in many places and received a specific dialect coloring (Alsatian).

Colin and Wisse were both from Strassburg goldsmith families that are attested in Strassburg documents from 1265 and 1148, respectively. In his epilogue, Colin reports that Lady Love and Lady Generosity have chosen his patron, Ulrich von Rappoltstein, to provide for the production of this work of literature. Ulrich, a member of the high nobility, was indeed touched by Lady Generosity and paid 200 pounds for the task.

The episodic nature of the *Nüwe Parzefal* is its most striking characteristic. It is a bourgeois work by bourgeois authors, and as a result the adventurous and the fantastic are given great play. Parzefal must cede equal time and space— indeed sometimes more—to Gawan, whose adventures are narrated in great detail. In this work, both Gawan and Parzefal achieve entry into the Grail castle, and on the third occasion Parzefal is offered the crown, which he refuses in order to ride out on more adventures. The original concept of the hero as found in Wolfram's work—that only the best knight, who has conquered his own deficiencies, is worthy of the Grail—is lost. Further, the inner integrity and value of the courtly-chivalric world, which is the key element in Wolfram's *Parzival*, disappears behind the bourgeois coating of the Colin-Wisse version. *Der nüwe Parzefal* is found in the Donaueschingen Hs. 97 (D) from the fourteenth century and is presumed to be the original. A copy, likewise from the fourteenth century, is found in the Bibliotheca Casanatensis in Rome (R). [FGG]

Schorbach, Karl, ed. *Parzifal, von Claus Wisse und Philipp Colin*. Strassburg: Trübner, 1888.
Wittmann-Klemm, Dorothee. *Studien zum "Rappoltsteiner Parzifal."* Göppingen: Kümmerle, 1977.

COLUM, PADRAIC (1881–1972), Irish-American author of *The Boy Apprenticed to an Enchanter* (1920). Merlin helps the boy Eean defeat his master, an evil magician. Merlin is considered least among the three great enchanters of the world because he would rather love than be wise. However, since love and loyalty are important in this children's fantasy, Merlin does find happiness with Vivien, following her possessive incarceration of him and his subsequent promise of devotion. [HT]

Colum, Padraic. *The Boy Apprenticed to an Enchanter*. New York: Macmillan, 1920.

"COMING OF ARTHUR, THE": *see* TENNYSON, ALFRED LORD.

COMPILATIONS, ARTHURIAN: *see* GONNOT, MICHOT; RUSTICIANO DA PISA; VAILLANT, JEHAN.

CONNECTICUT YANKEE IN KING ARTHUR'S COURT, A: see TWAIN, MARK.

CONNICK, CHARLES J.: *see* PRINCETON UNIVERSITY CHAPEL WINDOWS; STAINED GLASS.

CONSCIENCE OF THE KING: see DUGGAN, ALFRED LEO.

CONSTANTINE (1), Arthur's grandfather in Geoffrey of Monmouth. A prince from the offshoot British kingdom in Armorica (given an unhistorically early foundation), he comes to Britain by invitation near the beginning of the fifth century, to organize defense against marauding barbarians. Completely successful, he is rewarded with the crown. He has three sons: Constans, who becomes a monk; Aurelius Ambrosius; and Uther, the future father of Arthur. After reigning over Britain for ten years, Constantine is assassinated by a Pict. The crafty Vortigern persuades Constans to leave his monastery and become king. Constans is a puppet in Vortigern's hands, and presently he, too, is assassinated. Suspicion falls on Vortigern. Constantine's other sons are still children, and their guardians take them to the Breton court for safety. Vortigern seizes the crown. When the princes are grown up, however, they return and depose him, so that the royal house continues, producing Arthur in the next generation.

Constantine is vaguely based on a soldier who in 407 was proclaimed emperor as Constantine III by the Roman army in Britain. He may have been British, and he did have a son Constans who was a monk and left his monastery. Taking most of the troops overseas, he achieved control of Gaul and Spain. After various campaigns and dealings, he surrendered in 411 to a general of Honorius, the legitimate western emperor, but was murdered. Constans was already dead.

Constantine III's removal of troops from Britain was a prime cause of its severance from the Empire, which occurred in 410. Left unprotected against the assaults of Saxons and other barbarians, the Britons turned against him. Honorius authorized them to arm in their own defense, with the result that they became self-governing. Geoffrey's independent fifth-century Britain is founded, to that extent at least, on historical fact. [GA]

❧ Geoffrey of Monmouth. *Historia Regum Britanniae*, Book VI, Chapters 4–8.

CONSTANTINE (2), Arthur's successor. Geoffrey of Monmouth makes him a cousin, taking the name and a few particulars from Gildas, who denounces a king so called. Gildas's Constantine ruled only in Dumnonia, now known as the West Country. His conversion into a king of all Britain is incompatible with any historical possibility. [GA]

• Geoffrey of Monmouth. *Historia Regum Britanniae*, Book XI, Chapters 2–4.

CONTE DEL GRAAL, LE: see CHRÉTIEN DE TROYES; CONTINUATIONS.

CONTINUATIONS OF CHRÉTIEN DE TROYES'S *PERCEVAL*. About 1190, probably interrupted by death, Chrétien de Troyes abandoned his *Conte del Graal (Perceval)*, which he had undertaken for Count Philip of Flanders. But even Chrétien's failure became a momentous literary event, for his unfinished *Perceval* engendered writing and debate that have endured to the present. The mystery of the Grail, the Bleeding Lance, and the respective roles of Perceval and Gauvain were heady matters in the early thirteenth century, a ripe opportunity for imitators who perhaps believed that they might participate in Chrétien's glory, like Godefroy de Leigny, who brought to a close the *Chevalier de la charrete*.

Chrétien's *Perceval* ends abruptly at line 9234 (in the Hilka text). A first continuator picked up the story at this point and added 9,500 to 19,600 lines (depending on the various manuscript traditions) but came to no conclusion. A second continuator took over the plot where the first ended, lengthened it by some 13,000 lines, but still failed to complete the task. A third continuator, Manessier, added 10,000 lines more, with, finally, a conclusion. Gerbert de Montreuil compiled an enormous Fourth Continuation of some 17,000 lines, which survives in two manuscripts, where it is inserted between the Second and Third Continuations. Gerbert managed to compose an ending, but it has been lost in the manuscript tradition. In sum, the Continuations amount to an augmentation of more than 58,000 lines. One manuscript, B.N. f. fr. 12576, contains a "total" Perceval romance, including Chrétien's, which adds up to 63,550 octosyllabic lines.

The First Continuation was once attributed to Wauchier de Denain and even to Chrétien de Troyes. When it was shown that the author was unidentifiable, many scholars during the first half of the twentieth century persisted in naming him the Pseudo-Wauchier. Whoever he was, he probably composed his sequel about 1200, certainly no earlier than 1190. Until William Roach completed his multivolume edition, the manuscript tradition remained thoroughly confused. Now, thanks to his achievement, we can discern three redactions, a Short, a Mixed, and a Long. The Short, which is very likely the earliest, betrays the disadvantage of inadequate links to its predecessor, the *Perceval* of

Chrétien. The Long Redaction, though later probably than the others, is tied closely to Chrétien, for most of the episodes left dangling by him are completed. In all redactions, Perceval is no longer the protagonist, and is in fact absent from the action except when he appears almost coincidentally in a tournament where another warrior, Caradoc, is declared the best knight. Gauvain has replaced Perceval to the extent that the First Continuation becomes, especially in the Short Redaction, almost an independent romance and is therefore often entitled the *Gauvain-Continuation*. The main events are 1) Gauvain's clash with Guiromelant, who is able nevertheless to marry Clarissant, Gauvain's sister, with King Arthur's help; 2) the siege of the castle of Brun de Branlant, during which Gauvain seduces the sister of Bran de Lis; 3) the adventures of Caradoc, an independent romance inserted with little transition, and sometimes called the *Livre* (or *Roman*) *de Caradoc*; 4) Arthur's attack on the Chastel Orguellos, which involves two duels by Gauvain; 5) Gauvain's Grail visit, including a breathtaking episode wherein Gauvain ventures into a dark chapel near the sea at the end of a long bower of trees; 6) the misadventures of Gauvain's brother Guerrehet. Though the First Continuation lacks unity, its carefully wrought episodes can capture today's reader by their artistry of suspense.

The Second Continuation is often labeled the *Perceval-Continuation*, because in it Perceval returns to the forefront. Composed shortly after the First—i.e., about 1200—it appears to be signed by a Gauchier de Donaing (l. 31,421), who has been identified as the author of hagiographical works under the patronage of Philip of Flanders and his niece Johanna. The attribution was generally considered fraudulent until G. Vial set forth a convincing case in favor of Gauchier's authorship. The continuator lacks the spark of his predecessors; he fails to distinguish personalities among his characters and relies on repetitions and common motifs (empty castles, meals, ritual exchange of names) to lend unity to his story. He relates in a simple, straightforward manner Perceval's loss of the White Stag's head, his long quest to retrieve it, and finally his return to the Grail castle, where he meets only partial success. There, he attempts to piece together his broken sword, but a hairline fissure remains, symbolizing his failure to reach perfection. The author abandons his tale at this point.

Manessier's Continuation is normally numbered third because that is its place in most manuscripts. Probably about 1230, certainly no earlier than 1211 or later than 1244, he picks up the story with Perceval in the Grail castle and brings it to an end with the hero triumphantly crowned Grail King. Alongside Perceval's adventures come those of Sagremor and Gauvain. Perceval learns many answers at the very outset, so that much suspense is destroyed. Links to predecessors include a return to the chapel of the Black Hand, the repair by Triboet of the broken sword (as predicted in Chrétien's *Perceval*), Calogrenant's death, and echoes of the adventure of the Joie de la Cour (in Chrétien's *Erec et Enide*), but new characters and themes are introduced, notably the appearance of the Devil in several disguises. After the Fisher King's death, Perceval reigns for seven years in his place, then retires to the forest to finish his life as a hermit. The narrator surmises that the Grail, the Lance, and the silver plate must have accompanied him to heaven.

At about the same time as Manessier, Gerbert attached his Fourth Continuation to the end of the Second Continuation and imagined his own ending. Because of its survival in two manuscripts as an interpolation between the Second Continuation and Manessier, it appears to be third in the series, for the redactors concealed its conclusion. To avoid confusion, it is wise to refer to the third and fourth by their authors. Gerbert names himself five times in the first third of his poem and some scholars have identified him as Gerbert de Montreuil, the author of the *Roman de la violette*. His style is far sprightlier than the Second Continuation's rather tiresome language, and the tale holds many surprises, e.g., the sudden appearance of the Gate of Heaven, an invitation to bed by a maiden, an attack by two monstrous serpents, and above all a complete Tristan episode. Gerbert often relies on proverbs to prove a point. His final episode puts Perceval back in the Grail castle, where he manages to mend the broken sword perfectly. [JLG]

᪣ Roach, William, ed. *The Continuations of the Old French "Perceval" of Chrétien de Troyes*. 5 vols. Philadelphia: University of Pennsylvania Press/American Philosophical Society, 1949–83.

Gerbert de Montreuil. *La Continuation de Perceval*, ed. Mary Williams (Vols. 1 and 2) and Marguerite Oswald (Vol. 3). 3 vols. Paris: Champion, 1922, 1925, 1975.

Busby, Keith. *Gauvain in Old French Literature*. Amsterdam: Rodopi, 1980.

Ivy, Robert H. *The Manuscript Relations of Manessier's Continuation of the Old French* Perceval. Philadelphia: University of Pennsylvania Press, 1951.

Vial, Guy. "L'auteur de la deuxième continuation du *Conte du Graal*." *Travaux de Linguistique et de Littérature*, 16 (1978), 519–30.

COOPER, EDITH E.: *see* FIELD, MICHAEL.

COOPER, SUSAN, is best known for her Dark Is Rising series, which is composed of *Over Sea, Under Stone* (1965), *The Dark Is Rising* (1973), *Greenwitch* (1974), *The Grey King* (1975), and *Silver on the Tree* (1977).

In modern-day Britain, a changing group of young protagonists seek magical truths and personhood. However, Will Stanton does serve as the series's focus, particularly in *The Dark Is Rising*. Here he discovers that he is the lastborn of the "Old Ones," a line of immortal guardians with supernatural powers. They are opposed by a well-drawn and enigmatic evil force, known as the "Dark." The Dark is rising for a last assault upon humanity, and the books describe how talismans of power are collected to aid the forces of Light: the Drew children find the Grail; Will Stanton gathers the six signs of power; then, with the aid of a strange albino boy who turns out to be Bran (the Blessed), son of King Arthur and Queen Guenevere, he goes on to win the golden harp and crystal sword. The young people are aided by Merriman (Merlin), a senior member of the Old Ones; but since they are forced to rely largely upon their own resources, they grow rapidly in maturity and under-standing. However, it is a Welsh shepherd in whom the personal goals of the series—the union of love, wisdom, and compassion—find their culmination.

The series introduces into a modern setting elements drawn from Celtic and Arthurian legends. Within this context, Will Stanton's world becomes a dual one in which the superficial and mundane are continually overlaid with true visions of a titanic and elemental psychomachia. Curiously for a juvenile series, Christianity is viewed as an inaccurate, if successful, mythos and an inadequate defense against the Dark.

Like many romances, Cooper's novels are short on characterization. De-spite their reliance on existing mythology and archetypes, however, they represent a genuinely mythopoeic effort that deserves to be numbered among the most successful of twentieth-century juvenile fantasies. [RCS]

❧ Cooper, Susan. *Over Sea, Under Stone*. London: Cape, 1965.

——— . *The Dark Is Rising*. New York: Atheneum, 1973.

——— . *Greenwitch*. New York: Atheneum, 1974.

——— . *The Grey King*. New York: Atheneum, 1975.

——— . *Silver on the Tree*. New York: Atheneum, 1977.

COR, LAI DU: see BIKET, ROBERT.

CORBACCIO, IL: see BOCCACCIO, GIOVANNI.

CORT MANTEL, LAI DU: see MANTEL MAUTAILLIÉ, LE.

COURTHOPE, WILLIAM: *see* GEOFFREY JUNIOR.

COURTLY LOVE, a term first used by Gaston Paris in an 1883 article. It may well be a misleading designation for the medieval phenomenon it is supposed to identify. A good many scholars criticize the term and propose that it be abandoned. That is unlikely to occur, owing to its familiarity and usefulness. It is often (and probably erroneously) used interchangeably with *fin' amors*, which is the proper term for a conception of love propounded by the Provençal troubadours. A question that has occupied a good many scholars is whether courtly love, in northern France especially, was a historical and cultural phenomenon or simply a literary convention. It certainly was the latter, at least, and it is in its literary manifestations that it bears on the Arthurian legend.

The danger in talking about courtly love is that one is tempted—and sometimes obliged—to deal with it as a monolithic and uniform system, a code that was firmly established and rarely questioned. Such a notion is entirely mistaken. The troubadours presented in general a system of illicit and passionate love, but though many saw love as more ennobling when not consummated, others insisted that one would have to be a fool to waste one's effort without hope of recompense. For some, that recompense could be a smile or a word; for others, it could be nothing less than sexual pleasure.

Imported into northern France, this system of love was further developed and was even codified—although perhaps not seriously. Two names that are prominent in that development are Andreas Capellanus and Chrétien de Troyes, contemporaries at the court of Marie de Champagne during the second half of the twelfth century. Andreas is the author of *De Amore*, a treatise that purports to record "courts of love" at the court. These "courts," in which a problem concerning love was proposed, discussed, and decided, are themselves the subject of much discussion. They may never have taken place, or, if they did, they may have been nothing more than literary or social exercises, a kind of cultivated parlor game. It may well be that Andreas, inspired by Ovid, intended his work as humor or parody, but that very fact would likely confirm the existence of courtly love, at least as a literary construct. Andreas even goes so far as to offer a list of the "rules of love," according to which love and marriage are incompatible; a true lover eats and sleeps very little, thinks only of his lady, and turns pale in her presence; one can love only one person (but can be loved by many); and so on.

The text that offers the best-known elaboration of the courtly love situation (and, incidentally, the one to which the term itself was first applied) is Chrétien de Troyes's *Lancelot*, or *Le Chevalier de la charrete*. In that romance, it is clear that the duty of the lover (as the lady's vassal) is to serve her faithfully, with no thought of his own welfare. Thus, Guenevere rejects him not because, in order to come to her, he rode in a cart reserved for criminals but because he hesitated momentarily before doing so; apparently, he was briefly reluctant to dishonor himself, and that concern is incompatible with a system in which all must be subordinated to the service of the lady. Later in the work, he must expiate his sin by humiliating himself repeatedly in a tourney.

As these examples suggest, there is an inherent contradiction between the demands of courtly love and those of chivalry, as the latter is developed in practice. The knight's duty is to serve (society, the court and king, or individuals in need), but in so doing he gains a reputation for valor and courage, and it is generally important for him not to compromise that reputation. Love, however, imposes higher demands than those of chivalry, at least in *Lancelot*. In other works, the tensions between a knight's duty to his lady and his duty to himself and his chivalric calling are worked out in various ways; later, that tension will be replaced by a different one: between earthly chivalry and the higher calling of the Grail quest. Yet the ideals of courtly love (the lady on a pedestal, served unstintingly by a man who derives his joy from that service) will continue to influence literature throughout the Middle Ages and well beyond.

Jean Frappier has proposed a concept of "Arthurian love," which he defines as *fin'amors* in a Breton context, or the synthesis of *fin'amors* and Celtic fairy lore. The result is an amorous enchantment, the reflection in literature of a traditional motif: the love of a fairy for a chosen mortal. Marie de France's *Lanval* develops that motif explicitly, while other works are implicitly and subtly influenced by its spirit and conventions. This Arthurian love is by no means contrary to the spirit of what we generally call "courtly love"; rather, it extends it and invests it with a particular tonality lacking in works not part of the *matière de Bretagne*. (*See also* CHIVALRY.) [NJL]

Frappier, Jean. *Amour courtois et Table Ronde*. Geneva: Droz, 1973, pp. 43–56.

Lazar, Moshé. *Amour courtois et "fin'amors" dans la littérature du XIIe siècle*. Paris: Klincksieck, 1964.

Newman, F.X., ed. *The Meaning of Courtly Love*. Albany: State University of New York Press, 1968.

COUTTS, FRANCIS (F.B. Money Coutts Nevill, fifth Baron Latymer; 1852–1923), brought out his *Romance of King Arthur* in 1907. A revision and expansion of the trilogy of lyric dramas based on Malory that had appeared in 1897, it comprises a prologue, *Uther Pendragon*, the dramas *Merlin* and *Launcelot du Lake*, and the poem of *The Death of Launcelot*. The Wardour Street diction of the romance nullifies Coutts's attempt to reinterpret the figure of Arthur. [CNS]

Coutts, Francis. *The Romance of King Arthur*. London: Lane, 1907.

CRANE, WALTER (1845–1915), English illustrator. By the 1870s, Walter Crane's reputation was established as an illustrator of inexpensive color-plate books for children. He had already shown an interest in medieval art and literature, and like his contemporary William Morris he later sought to reconcile his enthusiasm for the Middle Ages with his attraction to socialist ideals. Crane's most ambitious project of book illustration was for an edition of Spenser's *Faerie Queene*, issued in nineteen parts between 1894 and 1897 with black-and-white illustrations, a publishing venture comparable to the Dent *Morte D'Arthur* with Aubrey Beardsley's illustrations in 1893–94. Crane's only specifically Arthurian illustrated works, *King Arthur's Knights* (1911) and *The Knights of the Round Table* (1915), selected stories retold for juveniles by Henry Gilbert, appeared at the end of his career, and belong to the pictorial style of a younger generation of illustrators who were using the new, commercially successful three-color printing process. These late works retain little of the distinctive quality of Crane's best illustrations. Lionel and Lancelot, the names given to his two sons, reflect Crane's long personal attraction to Arthurian legends. [TLS]

Massé, Gertrude. *Bibliography of First Editions of Books Illustrated by Walter Crane*. London: Chelsea, 1923.

Spencer, Isobel. *Walter Crane*. London: Studio Vista, 1975.

CRIMSON CHALICE

CRIMSON CHALICE, THE: *see* CANNING, VICTOR.

CRÔNE, DIU: *see* HEINRICH VON DEM TÜRLIN.

CRONICA SIVE ANTIQUITATES GLASTONIENSIS ECCLESIE:
see JOHN OF GLASTONBURY.

**CRONIQUES ADMIRABLES DU PUISSANT ROY GARGANTUA,
LES:** *see* GARGANTUAN CHRONICLES.

CRYSTAL CAVE, THE: *see* STEWART, MARY.

CUERO, RODRIGO DE: *see* FRUCTO DE LOS TIEMPOS.

CUKWOLD'S DAUNCE, THE: *see* SIR CORNEUS, ROMANCE OF.

CULHWCH AND OLWEN, an important Welsh Arthurian text extant in
two manuscripts: a complete copy in the Red Book of Hergest, ca. 1400, and an
incomplete one in the White Book of Rhydderch, ca. 1325. On the evidence of
the orthography and certain linguistic features of the text, it has been estimated that the tale took more or less its present shape sometime shortly before
the eleventh century. It is therefore perhaps the earliest extant vernacular
prose text from Wales.

The youth Culhwch has a curse placed upon him by his stepmother that he
shall have no woman until he has Olwen, daughter of the giant Ysbaddaden. As
a result of the curse, Culhwch is filled with love and longing for the maiden.
On his father's advice, he makes for the court of Arthur, his cousin, to seek his
help. Arthur sends seven of his men to accompany Culhwch on his quest, and in
time they locate the maiden and enter into the presence of the giant. The giant
imposes a series of seemingly impossible tasks that Culhwch must accomplish
before he can wed the daughter. With the help of Arthur and his men, the tasks
are indeed accomplished, the giant is killed, and Culhwch marries Olwen.
Thus, the story is at one level a common type of folktale, the Giant's
Daughter, embellished by a number of motifs well known to folklorists: the jealous
stepmother, love for an unseen maiden, the oldest animals, the helper animals,
the impossible tasks, and so on. But in its entirety the story is much more than
this, and Culhwch and Olwen are insignificant characters in the tale, except

insofar as they precipitate its major events. The bulk of the narrative is given over to two important catalogues and to adventures of Arthur and his men.

Before we leave Culhwch, however, it is worthwhile to look briefly at the Celtic traditions to which he belongs. Pigs were sacred animals to the Celts or at least occupied a special place in their mythological traditions. One of the nicknames of the Gaulish Mercury was *Moccus* 'boar,' and votive objects in the shape of a boar have been found at various sites sacred to the Celts. In early Irish and Welsh literature, swine play an important role, sometimes as objects of the hunt, sometimes as transformed humans of special destinies. Swineherds are shapeshifters and enjoy special status, mythologically speaking. In the Welsh Triads, we meet *Henwen* 'Ancient White (or Blessed),' a sow of mythic proportions, whose travels around Wales constitute a veritable Welsh cosmogony. In the present tale, the longest sustained adventure is Arthur's fight with Twrch Trwyth, a human king turned boar. All this has significance for the opening paragraph of the tale, which recounts Culhwch's birth. His mother went mad, we are told, and abandoned civilization. She gave birth to her son in an enclosure (*cul*) for pigs (*hwch*), whereupon she regained her senses; the boy was brought to the court by the swineherd. The Celtic evidence suggests strongly that in these briefly narrated events we have embedded the kernel of a myth about the birth of the swine-god; though the key elements in the myth were preserved, they were minimized and underplayed in favor of the Arthurian matter.

When Culhwch gets to Arthur's court, he is confronted by Glewlwyd Gafaelfawr, Arthur's porter, whom we encounter in a dialogue poem in the thirteenth-century Black Book of Carmarthen. After being admitted, Culhwch comes before Arthur, identifying himself and proclaiming his relationship. Arthur welcomes him and grants him any request he may wish to make. Naturally, Culhwch requests that Arthur get Olwen for him, and he ensures his request by invoking it in the name of Arthur's entire (presumably) retinue of warriors and courtly attendants. Over 200 names are recited by Culhwch, and the list goes on for nearly six pages, in one translation. Readers do well to pay close attention to the list, for it contains references to a wealth of tradition that has not otherwise survived. A handful of names belong to characters drawn directly from early Irish saga. Some are frivolous inventions of the author/redactor: the three maidservants Drwg, Gwaeth, and Gwaethaf Oll ("Bad, Worse, and Worst of All"), or Naw son of Seithfed ("Nine son of Seventh"), and others were probably invented for purely euphonious reasons. But the core represents names of characters that surely were traditional: among them a prodigious runner, a remarkable seer, and characters that are renowned for their leaping, eating, and hearing. Some in the list are bare names; others are characterized by an epithet or even a sentence or two that suggests a much fuller underlying tradition. For example, "Teithi Hen son of Gwynnan, whose kingdom was overrun by the sea; he barely escaped and came to Arthur. From the time he came there, his knife had this peculiarity: no haft would ever remain on it. Because of that he became sick and enfeebled while he was alive, and then he died of it."

The other catalogue in *Culhwch and Olwen* is the list of some forty tasks imposed upon Culhwch by Ysbaddaden as conditions of his betrothal to Olwen. This catalogue is a more reasoned one than the list of the members of Arthur's court. The first half comprises tasks relating to the material preparations for the wedding feast and the ritual shaving of Ysbaddaden himself; the second half of the list pertains to the hunting of Twrch Trwyth, between whose ears lie the razor, comb, and shears necessary for shaving the giant. In this catalogue, we again find tantalizing references to lost branches of the tradition. There is no direct connection between the list of tasks and the rest of the story, however, for fewer than half of them are ever accomplished, and those that are are done without regard for the order in which they were imposed.

The picture of Arthur and his court portrayed in *Culhwch and Olwen* is an intriguing one. Glewlwyd Gafaelfawr identifies himself at the beginning as Arthur's porter on New Year's Day and names four assistants who discharge that office for the rest of the year. None is permitted to enter Arthur's hall unless he is the son of a true king or a craftsman. The hall is well stocked with foods and wines drunk from solid gold horns, and visitors and wayfarers receive the same fare in adjacent lodgings. Arthur is called the chief of the nobles of Britain, and his fame has spread far and wide. His porter declares or implies that he has been with Arthur in Scandinavia, Europe, India, Corsica, Greece, and in several mythical kingdoms, too. He declares further that two-thirds of his own and of Arthur's life are past. Arthur's chief lieutenant is Cei (Kay), and Bedwyr (Bedivere) appears to be second only to Cei. True to his behavior in a good many other medieval romances, Arthur does not set out on the quest himself but delegates seven of his best men, led by Cei and Bedwyr, to help Culhwch.

After the tasks have been enumerated and imposed upon Culhwch, the men return to Arthur's court, having already accomplished the last-named task. Arthur asks which of the tasks should be attempted first (ignoring the fact that one has been accomplished already), and at this point he joins the action. From here on, Arthur plays the dominant role in the story. He rescues the divine Mabon son of Modron from his watery prison, successfully hunts a wolf-bitch and her two whelps in his ship Prydwen (after he has surrounded them, God restores to them their former human shape), and makes peace between Gwyn son of Nudd (the King of the Welsh otherworld) and his immortal enemy. Following that, he attacks Ireland, overcomes its army, and carries off a special cauldron full of Irish treasures. Next, he takes up the hunting of Twrch Trwyth, the longest episode in the tale. He pursues him from Ireland to Wales, from Wales to Brittany, and thence to Cornwall. After much fierce fighting and heavy casualties on both sides, the razor and shears are snatched from Twrch Trwyth in the mouth of the Severn, and in Cornwall Arthur's men succeed in snatching the comb. Thereupon, Twrch Trwyth charges into the sea and is not heard from again. Arthur goes off to Celliwig in Cornwall to bathe and rest. In one last adventure, Arthur encounters the "pitch-black witch from the Valley of Grief in Hell's back country" and overcomes her, cutting her in half with his knife.

It can be seen clearly that, while Arthur is portrayed as a great king whose reputation is far-flung, his activities are far from those of the feudal overlord of romance. Rather he is like the hero in a wonder tale, aided by magic and accompanied by men with supernatural gifts, and his chief opponent has affinities with the divine animals of Celtic mythological tradition. Though the frame story of Culhwch's wooing of Olwen is important and generically grounded in Celtic narrative tradition, the tale is essential Arthurian and contains a wealth of information about the native Welsh Arthur and his court. [PKF]

Evans, J. Gwenogvryn, ed. *The White Book Mabinogion.* Pwllheli, 1907.

Bromwich, Rachel. *Trioedd Ynys Prydein.* Cardiff: University of Wales Press, 1961.

Edel, Doris. "The Catalogues in *Culhwch and Olwen* and Insular Celtic Learning." *Bulletin of the Board of Celtic Studies*, 30 (1983), 253–67.

Ford, Patrick K. *The Mabinogi and Other Medieval Welsh Tales.* Berkeley, Los Angeles, and London: University of California Press, 1977.

Foster, Idris, Ll. "*Culhwch and Olwen* and *Rhonabwy's Dream.*" In *Arthurian Literature in the Middle Ages*, ed. Roger Sherman Loomis. Oxford: Clarendon, 1959.

Jarman, A.O.H., and Gwilym Rees Hughes. *A Guide to Welsh Literature I.* Swansea: Davies, 1976.

MacCana, Proinsias. *Celtic Mythology.* London: Hamlyn, 1970.

CURRY, JANE, author of *The Sleepers* (1968), an exciting fantasy for younger readers, in which four children discover Arthur and his knights sleeping in an underground cavern in the Eildon Hills. With the help of Myrddin (Merlin), they foil a plot by Morgan le Fay and Medraut to destroy the Sleepers and capture the thirteen Treasures of Prydein (Britain). [RHT]

Curry, Jane. *The Sleepers.* New York: Harcourt, Brace and World, 1968.

DANE, CLEMENCE (pseudonym of Winifred Ashton; 1888–1965). *The Saviours* (1942) consists of seven poetic radio plays narrated by Merlin and structured around the figure of *Artus redivivus*, returning in Britain's hours of need as King Alfred, Robin Hood, Elizabeth and Essex, Lord Horatio Nelson, and the Unknown Warrior of World War I. The series ends with Arthur, recognized as the indomitable spirit of Britain, predicting his next return, which would coincide with the onset of World War II. [VML]

Dane, Clemence. *The Saviours*. London and Toronto: Heinemann, 1942.

DANIEL VON DEM BLÜHENDEN TAL: see STRICKER, DER.

DANTE ALIGHIERI (1265–1321) alluded to Arthurian romance no more than some half-dozen times, yet no student of medieval literature can fail to wonder about the relationship between the greatest body of medieval secular literature and the man who was arguably the greatest secular poet of the age. Dante is known for his insistence that morally and intellectually serious literature could be written in the vernacular and for his realization in the *Divine Comedy* of this notion, still controversial in the early fourteenth century. Did he see Arthurian literature as an illustrious example of what he wished vernacular literature to do, or instead as a dangerous countermodel?

An attempt to answer this perennial question must be based on a survey of Dante's allusions to Arthurian literature. Three are rather minor. In *Inferno*, Canto 5, l. 67, he pairs Tristan with Paris, to end the parade of those damned through love. He alludes to Mordred and names Arthur in a periphrasis (*Inferno*, Canto 32, ll. 61–62), affirming that two damned souls encountered deep in the infernal realm of treachery called "Caina" were even more worthy to be there than Mordred. In a different vein, in a lyric poem addressed to his "first friend," Guido Cavalcanti, Dante expresses the wish that the two of them, with their friend Lapo Gianni, might by enchantment be put together in a marvelous boat ("Guido, i' vorrei che tu e Lapo ed io/ fossimo presi per incantamento/ e messi in un vasel . . .") and that "il buono incantatore" would then send certain ladies to join in their fantastic journey; it is entirely possible that the setting Dante evokes is derived from Arthurian romance and that the "good enchanter" is Merlin.

More suggestive of Dante's view of the Arthurian corpus than these minor allusions are a key reference in the treatise on the vernacular known as the *Vulgari Eloquentia* and a cluster of allusions (in *Inferno*, *Paradiso*, and *Convivio*) to the Lancelot romance. Dante probably first grappled with the problem that his linguistic treatise tries to resolve under the influence of Brunetto Latini, the learned Florentine writer and public servant whom Dante (*Inferno*, Canto 15, ll. 82–85) mentions as having taught him much; for Brunetto, an exile in France from 1260 to about the time of Dante's birth (1265), wrote his famous encyclopedic work, the *Livre dou Tresor*, in French, affirming that language's superiority for didactic purposes to his native Tuscan. By implication, it might seem that Dante came to disagree with his "master," if the *Comedy*, in Italian, is taken to be didactic, even encyclopedic, in character—though his explicit disagreement with Brunetto in matters of language has to do not with Brunetto's championing of French but instead (*Vulgari Eloquentia*, Book 13) with his decision to write (probably another work, the didactic poem entitled *Il Tesoretto*) in a merely municipal, Florentine, dialect. In any case, Brunetto raised the question of the adequacy of the Romance vernaculars to specific literary genres, and Dante makes a preliminary attempt to answer it early in the *Vulgari Eloquentia* (Book 9, Chapter 2), stating that Italian, Provençal, and French each might be legitimately seen as the best vernacular for different reasons: Italian because it is the closest to (Latin) grammar and therefore the most logical; Provençal because it was the language of the foremost love poets, the troubadours; and French because it dominates the field of vernacular prose, both didactic and narrative. It is in this context that Dante cites (together with instances of the *matière d'antiquité*) Arthurian romance ("Arturi regis ambages pulcerrimae"). This allusion (tangentially suggesting, not surprisingly, that Dante did not know the verse texts of the Arthurian cycle, including the work of Chrétien) indicates that Dante thought Arthurian prose literature a very important achievement indeed, establishing French as a major language by revealing, together with other prose works, a narrative capacity in the *langue d'oil* comparable in quality to the rigorous grammaticality of the language of the Italian peninsula.

In this context, Dante's most famous allusion to Arthurian romance, in the Paolo and Francesca episode of *Inferno*, Canto 5, has puzzled many who have taken Dante, through the voice of Francesca, to be condemning the Lancelot romance and its author for an immorality that has led her to eternal damnation: "Galeotto fu il libro, e chi lo scrisse" ("A Galehaut was the book and the one who wrote it"). Dante, however, is here by no means condemning Arthurian literature but rather a pair of its readers: he puts Paolo and Francesca in hell, not the Lancelot author. The Paolo and Francesca episode is related to and illuminated by two other Dantesque allusions to the Lancelot cycle. In *Paradiso*, Canto 16, ll. 14–15, Dante compares Beatrice's laugh to the Lady of Malohaut's cough at the moment of Guenevere's "first mistake" ("primo fallo"); however this comparison is to be interpreted, it suggests Dante's awareness that characters within the story are alert to Guenevere's "mistake," implying that readers are not obliged to adopt the viewpoint of the sinning protagonists of the episode. More conclusive in this regard is Dante's allusion in his vernacular treatise on the nature of poetry, *Convivio*, Book IV, Chapter 28, Section 8, to Lancelot's end, as a monk repentant of the adultery that kept him from fulfilling his high mission. Dante makes clear that Paolo and Francesca miss the warning provided by the disastrous conclusion of Lancelot and Guenevere's relationship because they do not finish reading the book: "non vi leggemmo piu avanti" ("we read no farther"). He is himself fully aware that the Lancelot author provided such a warning, and his reader must be, too, if Paolo and Francesca's situation is to succeed in teaching the reader anything important. Thus, the high judgment of Arthurian literature expressed in the *Vulgari Eloquentia* is not diminished in any way by the Paolo and Francesca episode. [SJN]

Dante, Alighieri. *Opere*, ed. Michele Barbi et al. 2nd ed. Florence: Società Dantesca Italiana, 1960.

Delcorno, Daniela Branca. "Romanzi arturiani." In *Enciclopedia Dantesca*. Rome: Istituto della Enciclopedia Italiana, 1973, pp. 1028–30.

Noakes, Susan. "The Double Misreading of Paolo and Francesca." *Philological Quarterly*, 62 (1983), 221–39.

D'ARCY, MARGARETTA: *see* ARDEN, JOHN.

DÁRIO LOBONDO ALEXANDRINO: see SILVA, ANTÓNIO DA.

DARK IS RISING, THE: see COOPER, SUSAN.

DAVEY, FRANK, a contemporary Canadian poet, composed a series of free-verse lyrics, published in 1972 as *The King of Swords*, describing the end of a love affair in terms of the life and death of Arthur. The seamier side of the Arthurian myth is used as an illustration, both sexual and social, of modern times. [SRR]

⟶ Davey, Frank. *The King of Swords*. Vancouver: Talonbooks, 1972.

DAVIS, GEORGENE, author of *The Round Table* (1930), a lyric poetic drama on Arthur, set in sixth-century Britain, concentrating on the intrigue among the Round Table company, especially Guinevere, Lancelot, and Gawain. The work proves once again how difficult it is, especially with plot alterations, to transform the Arthurian legend into drama, despite the author's explicit stage directions. [VML]

⟶ Davis, Georgene. *The Round Table: A History Drawn from Unreliable Sources*. Rutland, Vt.: Tory, 1930.

DAWN IN LYONESSE: see CHASE, MARY ELLEN.

"DAY BEFORE THE TRIAL, THE": *see* SWINBURNE, ALGERNON CHARLES.

DE AMORE: see ANDREAS CAPELLANUS.

DE CASIBUS VIRORUM ILLUSTRIUM: see BOCCACCIO, GIOVANNI.

DE EXCIDIO BRITANNIAE: see GILDAS.

DE ORIGINE, MORIBUS, ET REBUS GENTIS SCOTORUM: see SCOTTISH ARTHURIAN CHRONICLES.

DE ORTU WALUUANII NEPOTIS ARTURI ("On the Rise of Gawain, Arthur's Nephew"), a Latin prose romance about the birth, boyhood, and early adventures of Gawain. Gawain, illegitimate son of Arthur's sister Anna, is trained in arms by the emperor of Rome. His early adventures are undertaken as a Roman cavalry officer and include two major quests: first, single combat against a Persian champion to raise the siege of Jerusalem; and second, military aid for Arthur of Britannia, menaced by raiders on his northern border. Arthur rewards Gawain's brilliant victory against the raiders by revealing to him his lineage and accepting him as nephew and knight. Although ascribed by John Bale to Robert of Torigni, abbot of Mont St.-Michel (1154–86), the work is variously dated from the last quarter of the twelfth century to the last quarter of the thirteenth. [MLD]

🙮 Day, Mildred Leake, ed. and trans. *The Rise of Gawain, Nephew of Arthur (De Ortu Waluuanii Nepotis Arturi).* New York and London: Garland, 1984.

DE PRINCIPIS INSTRUCTIONE: *see* GIRALDUS CAMBRENSIS.

DE SANTO JOSEPH AB ARIMATHIA, a prose work printed by Richard Pynson in 1516. It is an epitome of Joseph's life contained in Capgrave's *Nova Legenda Angliae* and John of Glastonbury's *Cronica,* stressing the Glastonbury account of Joseph's commission by St. Philip to evangelize Britain, his founding of the oratory of Our Lady at Glastonbury, and his subsequent holy life and burial at the abbey there. [VML]

🙮 Skeat, Walter W., ed. *Joseph of Arimathie.* London: Trübner, 1871.

DEAL, BABS H., ingeniously transposes Arthurian legend to the setting of United States college football in *The Grail: A Novel* (1963). It is fascinating to identify traditional characters in new roles, though the final effect is to trivialize the legend. [RHT]

🙮 Deal, Babs H. *The Grail: A Novel.* New York: McKay, 1963.

DEATH OF ARTHUR, THE: *see* OXFORD UNION MURALS.

DEATH OF ARTHUR, THE STORY OF THE HOLY GRAIL, THE: *see* PADMORE, E.S.

DEATH OF LAUNCELOT, THE: *see* COUTTS, FRANCIS.

DEATH OF MERLIN, THE: *see* OXFORD UNION MURALS.

DECAMERONE, IL: *see* BOCCACCIO, GIOVANNI.

DECORATIVE ARTS (MEDIEVAL). Arthurian themes are often found in the decorative arts of the Middle Ages. Among the most popular were stories of the great lovers, such as Tristan and Lancelot, or themes having religious overtones, such as the Grail legend. King Arthur was represented as one of the three Christian Worthies, or in the larger context of the Nine Worthies, seldom as presiding over the Round Table. And even in this relatively select group, certain subjects caught the imagination of artists and—we must suppose—of patrons as well: Sir Lancelot crossing the Sword Bridge, Sir Gawain on the Perilous Bed, Sir Ywain charging through the castle gate with his horse caught by the portcullis, Tristan and Isolde playing chess in a garden or on the voyage to Cornwall and spied on by King Mark. This "Tryst Beneath the Tree" was the single most popular Arthurian subject. From Germany to England, artists represented the jealous King Mark's deception in painting and embroidery, wood and ivory carving, metal- and enamelwork. The subject lent itself to representation in the visual arts because the complex narrative could be condensed into a single image, and the composition permitted considerable flexibility. Mark observed the lovers from the branches while the water below reflected his features. The symmetrical composition around the tree and fountain or pool, with paired figures left and right and paired faces above and below, could be adapted to the round, square, or quatrefoil frame (e.g., mirror-back or box), and when an irregular shape had to be covered (e.g., a misericord or comb) the foliage and water could spread out over the requisite surface. The story might be made explicit by the use of elegant banderoles (like comic-strip speech balloons), as it is on a boxwood comb from eastern France or Switzerland (Museum of Fine Arts, Boston).

Literary description of Arthurian subjects, although often exaggerated and fanciful, indicates the popularity and extraordinary richness of the decorative arts of the later Middle Ages. Inventories, surviving from the fourteenth and fifteenth centuries, confirm the existence of great treasures. Since objects were admired for their intrinsic value, as well as for their workmanship, they were traded, pawned, seized as booty, and used as exchange. Owners had little hesitation in melting down works of art for the precious metals they contained, and when new items were desired, old-fashioned pieces were sent to the goldsmith. Thus, of all the pieces listed in medieval inventories, only a handful have survived to the twentieth century. Fortunate indeed is the museum or the private collector who can boast of a gold cup, ivory box, or enameled knife having secular scenes. Church treasures were able to survive, either because of conservatism of taste or the sanctity surrounding the object, be it reliquary, cross, or candlestick. Decorative artworks made from humbler materials fared little better. Instead of being lost because of the value of their materials, they were discarded as worthless or destroyed accidentally. The wells and garbage pits of cities have contained treasure troves for the archaeologist and student of the decorative arts. Thus, tiles, woodwork, leather, ceramics, or ordinary textiles are as rare and precious as the more ostentatious products of the jeweler's skill.

The most glamorous of all objects in the decorative arts were the table fountains used to dispense wine, rosewater, or perfumes. One such fountain survives (Cleveland Museum of Art), and fragments of others may have been incorporated into other works. Descriptions do exist in literature and inventories; not surprisingly, the Tryst Beneath the Tree lent itself to adaptation as a fountain. The inventory made in 1353 of the belongings of John the Good of France describes a silver fountain with Tristan and Isolde beneath a vine (surely a misunderstanding of the tree). The base of a fourteenth-century French goblet (now in Milan) also represents the meeting. That most spectacular late-medieval table decoration, the Burghley Nef (Victoria and Albert Museum, London), shows the lovers as they played chess aboard the ship taking them to Cornwall. Other metalwork may not be as rich, but it does serve to remind us of the popular art of the time. Bronze pendants used for decoration and identification of horses and hounds might be gilt and enameled with figures from the romances. Tristan and Isolde represented as lovers holding the fatal goblet can be seen on a fourteenth-century Catalan pendant (Metropolitan Museum of Art, New York).

From the smallest to the largest scale, Arthurian stories appear. Walls might be painted with the romances, as evidenced by surviving murals and tapestries. Even the floors were enriched with ornamental tiles (e.g., Chertsey Abbey Tiles, British Museum). Personal possessions—ivory, bone, or boxwood boxes, combs, hair-parters, and mirror-cases—also treated the romances of Tristan, Lancelot, and Gawain. But the complete popularization of the Arthurian heroes as seen in the minor arts came in the new medium of printing. The makers of woodblocks for playing cards reduced the great King Arthur to a king in a deck of cards, and in a Provençal deck of the mid-fifteenth century the noble Lancelot, along with Ogier, Roland, and Valery, becomes one of the four knaves. (*See also* BURGHLEY NEF; CHERTSEY ABBEY TILES; EMBROIDERY; IVORY; LOUVRE TRAY; MISERICORDS; STAINED GLASS; TAPESTRY.) [MS]

❖ Hind, Arthur. *An Introduction to a History of Woodcut*. London: Constable, 1935.

Loomis, Roger Sherman, and Laura Hibbard Loomis. *Arthurian Legends in Medieval Art*. London: Oxford University Press, 1938.

Verdier, Philippe. *The International Style*. Catalogue, Walters Art Gallery, Baltimore, 1962.

DEEPING, (GEORGE) WARWICK (1877–1950), English author of three historical romances with Arthurian connections. The borrowings are only general in *The Man on the White Horse* (1934) and *The Man Who Went Back* (1940). However, even *Uther and Igraine* departs widely from tradition in its sentimental account of virtuous love between Arthur's parents. [RHT]

❖ Deeping, (George) Warwick. *Uther and Igraine*. New York: Knopf, 1928.

"DEFENCE OF GUENEVERE, THE": *see* MORRIS, WILLIAM; SWINBURNE, ALGERNON CHARLES.

DEFENCE OF GUENEVERE, AND OTHER POEMS, THE: *see* MORRIS, WILLIAM.

DELL, FLOYD (1887–1969), American author of *King Arthur's Socks* (1916). This one-act play set in Camelot, Maine, is Arthurian in name only. Gwen Robinson, wife of Professor Arthur Robinson, and Lance Jones, an artist, declare their love for each other. Gwen, unwilling to damage a comfortable marriage, darns Arthur's socks as Lance leaves to marry their friend Vivien. [AEG]

• Dell, Floyd. *King Arthur's Socks and Other Village Plays.* New York: Knopf, 1922.

DEMANDA DEL SANCTO GRIAL, LA: *see DEMANDA DO SANTO GRAAL, A.*

DEMANDA DO SANTO GRAAL, A ("The Quest of the Holy Grail"). The Portuguese *Demanda do Santo Graal* and the Spanish *Demanda del Sancto Grial* both derive from a common source: the last branch of the Post-Vulgate *Roman du Graal*, which was translated into a western Ibero-Romance language, probably Galician-Portuguese, either at the end of the thirteenth century or in the early fourteenth. At some point, the *Demanda* branch became a separate romance, surviving as such in a fifteenth-century Portuguese manuscript (Vienna, National-bibliothek 2594) and in two Castilian imprints (Toledo, 1515, and Seville, 1535). However, the title apparently came to signify the whole Arthurian story as told in the Post-Vulgate texts. The fifteenth-century copy of the Portuguese *Livro de Josep Abaramatia*, for example, refers to this text as the first part of the *Demanda do Santo Graal*, and the Castilian *Baladro del Sabio Merlín* of 1535 calls the *Baladro* the first part of the *Demanda*. The *Demandas* contain material presumed to have formed part of the now-lost sections of the French Post-Vulgate text, including the epilogue of Mark's second invasion of Arthur's kingdom. The Portuguese version reflects more accurately than the Spanish the original language of the French and is frequently cited by critics for its qualities of style, and selections from it continue to be included in contemporary Portuguese school texts. [HLS]

• Magne, Augusto, ed. *A Demanda do Santo Graal: Reprodução fac-similar e transcrição crítica do códice 2594 da Biblioteca Nacional de Viena.* 2 vols. Rio de Janeiro: Instituto Nacional do Livro, 1955. Bonilla y San Martín, Adolfo, ed. *La demanda del Sancto Grial.* In *Libros de caballerías, primera parte: Ciclo artúrico–Ciclo carolingio.* Madrid: Bailly-Baillière, 1907, pp. 163–338.

DENT *MORTE D'ARTHUR,* a two-volume edition, was published in install-ments in 1893 and 1894 by John M. Dent and illustrated by a hitherto unknown artist, Aubrey Beardsley (1872–1898). Intended to rival the luxury editions of the Kelmscott Press, it featured over 400 drawings in black-and-white, including full-page vignettes, chapter headings, and decorative borders. Varying stylistically, Beardsley's early drawings recall Burne-Jones, while the later contributions exhibit his mature aesthetic, reflecting the decadent spirit of the late Arthurian Revival and transforming the heroic characters into androgynous phantoms. [DNM]

Malory, Sir Thomas. *Morte D'arthur*. London: Dent, 1893–94.
———. *Dent Morte Darthur*. 2 vols. Woodbridge, Suffolk: Boydell and Brewer, 1985 (facsimile).

DESTROYERS, THE: *see* MACLEISH, ARCHIBALD.

"DIALOGUE OF ARTHUR AND GWENHWYFAR," a Welsh poem extant in two manuscripts, the older of which is dated to the sixteenth century. One version consists of twelve stanzas of three or four lines each, the other has ten stanzas of three lines each. The two versions are sufficiently dissimilar to show that they derive from different manuscript (or perhaps oral) sources. The argument of the poem is quite obscure, and one critic has suggested that there must have been accompanying prose passages to provide the setting for the verses. One thing does seem clear: the poem is not a dialogue between Arthur and Gwenhwyfar but rather a dialogue involving Melwas and Gwenhwyfar, and perhaps Cei (Kay). Mary Williams argued that the dialogue was part of a mystery ritual in which Melwas was the one who sought to be initiated and Gwenhwyfar played the role of the goddess whose cult it was. Cei would be involved as the initiator or hierophant. Professor Jackson, on the other hand, insists that the poem can only be understood by reference to the abduction of Guenièvre by Meleagant in Chrétien's *Lancelot* and that it relates the appearance of Melwas (Meleagant) at Arthur's court, where he challenges Arthur to entrust the Queen to one of his knights as escort. The verse dialogue, then, would be between Melwas and Gwenhwyfar, speaking of Cei's qualifications, or maybe between Melwas and Cei himself. All three names occur in the dialogue, which is characterized by boasting, and the longer version appears to end in a fight between Cei and Melwas. [PKF]

Jackson, Kenneth Hurlstone. "Arthur in Early Welsh Verse." In *Arthurian Literature in the Middle Ages*, ed. Roger Sherman Loomis. Oxford: Clarendon, 1959.
Williams, Mary. "An Early Ritual Poem in Welsh." *Speculum*, 13 (1938), 38–51.

DICKINSON, PETER, questions the values of both medieval and modern society in *The Weathermonger* (1968), a fantasy for younger readers. The book describes a Britain plunged back into medieval ways when a misguided chemist prematurely awakens Merlin. Young Geoffrey and his eleven-year-old sister race across England in a vintage Rolls Royce, pursued by irate lords and peasants, and persuade Merlin to kick morphine and resume hibernation. [CBH]

🏵 Dickinson, Peter. *The Weathermonger*. London: Gollancz, 1968.

DIDOT-*PERCEVAL*. The title of this early (ca. 1200) French prose text has been established to avoid confusion with Chrétien de Troyes's romance, with the *Quest del Saint Graal*, or even with the *Perlesvaus*. The name comes from the former owner, Ambroise Firmin-Didot, whose manuscript was the basis of the first edition by Eugène Hucher in 1875. A second manuscript, however, in the Biblioteca Estense at Modena, offers a more coherent version of the tale. Both surviving redactions probably stem from a prose reworking of Robert de Boron's lost *Perceval*, which followed chronologically his two earlier "branches": *Joseph d'Arimathie* and *Merlin*. The manuscript tradition is so entangled that it has been difficult to separate the parts. The Didot-*Perceval* contains a final section dealing with Arthur's last days, a kind of *Mort Artu*, derived indirectly from Geoffrey of Monmouth's *Historia Regum Britanniae* but offering no serious deviations from Wace's adaptation. The author remains anonymous, though Loomis has suggested that Robert himself was responsible for the flaws in the surviving text. It has also been proposed that a clumsy continuator added the Perceval story without reliance on a *Perceval* by Robert (who may never have written one). The Didot-*Perceval* clashes frequently with Robert's works, principally because of interpolations apparently based on Chrétien and the Second Continuation. The date of composition cannot be pinned down, but we can surmise that it occurred in the second or third decade of the thirteenth century, surely after the Second Continuation and before Manessier. It is, then, an early example of French prose, produced in the same epoch as Villehardouin's *Conqueste de Constantinople*.

The events are much compressed at the tale's beginning, so that the slow progression of Perceval's self-awareness is lacking. He is in this version the son of Alain le Gros, who sends him to Arthur's court. There he sits in a forbidden seat at the Round Table, which causes darkness to cover the skies, a stone to split, and a voice to sound that rebukes Arthur for allowing the seat to be occupied against Merlin's warnings and announces the presence of the Grail, which a superior knight must seek in order to reestablish order and to rid Britain of enchantments. Thus begins the Grail quest by all the knights of the Round Table. Perceval vows never to remain two nights in one lodging until he has found the Grail. His adventures include a hunt for the White Stag, the loss of his lady's hound (both themes borrowed from the Second Continuation), a battle with the Knight of the Tomb, the perilous ford, the children in the tree, visits to his hermit uncle and the Fisher King (from Chrétien), encounters with Merlin, and finally his successful questions about the Grail, which restore health to the Fisher King, cause the sundered stone to be mended, reveal all secrets of the Grail, and win for him the privilege of remaining in the Fisher

King's house. Thereafter, Arthur occupies center stage. He conquers France, campaigns against the Romans, and earns that crown also. He is betrayed and mortally wounded by Mordred, then taken away to Avalon. Merlin reports these events to Perceval and then disappears.

The bland characterization of Perceval makes him no different from any banal chivalric hero. The carefully studied naïveté that distinguishes him in Chrétien's story becomes a glaring self-confidence as he demands, almost childishly, to sit in the thirteenth chair at the Round Table. As soon as he abandons knighthood to act as guardian of the Grail, Gauvain replaces him at the pinnacle of chivalry. The atmosphere changes abruptly after Perceval's success at the Fisher King's house; it becomes less religious and more political. Arthur demonstrates his courtesy by remaining polite in the face of insults leveled against him by Roman ambassadors. He gains the allegiance of his barons by distributing among them the lands his army has conquered in France. He wins a moral triumph over those he vanquishes and in the end earns their respect by persuasion rather than force. Character study, however, interests the author much less than straightforward narration of events. [JLG]

  Roach, William, ed. *The Didot-Perceval.* Philadelphia: University of Pennsylvania Press, 1941.

DINAS EMRYS ("Ambrosius's Fort"), the Welsh name for a hill fort on the southern fringe of Snowdonia, in Nant Gwynant near Beddgelert. The Ambrosius in question is Ambrosius Aurelianus, known in Welsh as *Emrys gwledig* (*gwledig* 'prince' or 'land-holder'). Nennius identifies him with a legendary boy-prophet who outfaced King Vortigern and his magicians—reputedly, here. Vortigern wanted to build a stronghold on top of the hill. When the building materials kept disappearing through subsidence, his magicians advised a human sacrifice. However, the boy intended as the victim confounded them by revealing a subterranean pool and other strange things. He then gave his name as Ambrosius. Nennius adds *Emrys gwledig* to make it quite clear and says Vortigern handed over the place to him. This is the original Welsh view of the lad's identity. Geoffrey of Monmouth, however, makes him out to have been the young Merlin, explaining away "Ambrosius" as an alternative name. A later legend follows Geoffrey, asserting that before Merlin left the neighborhood he hid a golden, treasure-filled cauldron, which will be found only by the person for whom it is intended.

Excavation of the hill fort has uncovered various features within its earthworks. There was a Roman building, and nearby there actually was a pool. During the second half of the fifth century, a platform of ground above a swampy hollow was built on and occupied by a prosperous household, seemingly Christian. Presumably, at some unknown stage in legend-weaving, the chief occupant was said to have been Ambrosius. This localization of the name and story may have been due to a prior association with Vortigern, the other main character. A tradition recorded in the seventeenth century tells of a combat in the valley below between a giant and a warrior, Owein (Eugenius), who was a son of the Roman emperor Maximus. Since Vortigern supposedly married one of this emperor's daughters, Owein—who figures in a Triad—would have been his brother-in-law. A lost dynastic saga, only a fragment of it preserved by Nennius, may have brought King Arthur himself to these parts. [GA]

ᏅGeoffrey of Monmouth. *Historia Regum Britanniae*, Book VI, Chapters 17–19.

Nennius. *Historia Brittonum*, Chapters 40–42.

Alcock, Leslie. *Arthur's Britain*. London: Penguin, 1971.

Bromwich, Rachel. *Trioedd Ynys Prydein*. Cardiff: University of Wales Press, 1961.

Hawkes, Jacquetta. *A Guide to the Prehistoric and Roman Monuments in England and Wales*. London: Cardinal, 1973.

"DIS IST FRAUW TRISTERAT HORN VON SAPHOIEN" ("This Is Frau Tristerat of Savoy's Horn"), an anonymous fifteenth-century *Meisterlied* based on the tale first attested in Robert Biket's *Lai du cor*. A young lady bearing a magic drinking horn arrives at King Arthur's court one day. The horn has been sent by Lady Tristerat to test the fidelity of the ladies at Arthur's court. That man who is able to drink from the horn without spilling a drop has a faithful wife. First, Arthur and then the kings of mighty lands attempt to empty the horn without mishap. Only the king of Spain succeeds, and his wife, the most beautiful woman present, turns out to be the only faithful woman. [MEK]

ᏅBruns, Paul Jacob. "Zwei Erzählungen im Meistergesang." In *Beiträge zur kritischen Bearbeitung unbenutzter alter Handschriften, Drucke und Urkunden*. Braunschweig: Reichard, 1802–03, pp. 139–43.

DISCOVERY OF PRINCE ARTHUR'S TOMB BY THE INSCRIPTION ON THE LEADEN CROSS, THE: see MORTIMER, JOHN.

DITMAS, EDITH M.R., twentieth-century British historian and folklorist, in *Gareth of Orkney* (1956) retells Malory's tale for juveniles. The addition of minor characters, social history, Welsh and Cornish geography, and the events of Gareth's year as kitchen-boy, along with the rationalization of the source's supernatural elements, produces a credible historical novel. [MAW]

ᏅDitmas, E.M.R. *Gareth of Orkney*. London: Faber and Faber, 1956.

DITTAMONDO, IL: see FAZIO DEGLI UBERTI.

DIVINA COMMEDIA: see DANTE ALIGHIERI.

DOLOROUS GARD: *see* JOYOUS GARD.

DOLOROUS STROKE. In the *Suite du Merlin* and Malory, this term describes the blow dealt King Pellean (Pellam) by Balain; the blow reduces Logres to a wasteland. Thereafter, the maimed king remains ill for many years until cured by Galahad. [NJL]

DON QUIXOTE: see CERVANTES SAAVEDRA, MIGUEL DE.

DON SYLVIO VON ROSALVA: see WIELAND, CHRISTOPH MARTIN.

DONNA DEL VERGIÙ, LA, an Italian *cantare* closely related to the French *Châtelaine de Vergi*. Composed about 1330, and containing Arthurian allusions, it is atypical of the *cantare* genre because of its tragic ending. [SJN]

📖 Levi, Ezio, ed. *Fiore di leggende: cantari antichi*. Bari: Laterza, 1914.

DORÉ, GUSTAVE (1832–1883), French illustrator. Though more famous for his illustrations of Dante and the Bible, Doré also executed thirty-six wash drawings to illustrate the first four poems of Tennyson's *Idylls of the King* (1859). For each poem—"Enid," "Vivien," "Elaine," "Guinevere"—Doré provided nine illustrations, which were then copied by English steel-engravers. The illustrated poems were published separately in folio editions from 1867 to 1868 by Moxon in London and by Hachette in Paris. In 1868, the separate editions were gathered into one volume, for which Doré added a frontispiece depicting Tennyson surrounded by his Arthurian characters (and a few creatures of Doré's own invention). The illustrations were popular, especially in England, and went through several editions. Doré's engravings have been credited with a Pre-Raphaelite melancholy, perhaps because of the work done by English engravers. Doré, however, could read Tennyson only in translation, and his work is distinctly continental in flavor rather than English. Highly romantic, the engravings most typically depict dramatic moments of violence or characters in quiet contemplation amidst scenes of fantastic castles, crumbling ruins, or sublime landscapes. The drawings are uneven in quality (Doré's drawings of women are particularly weak), but the best are equal to his most famous illustrations and create a magical, otherworldly realm of Arthurian legend. [LH]

📖 *Catalogue des dessins aquarelles et estampes de Gustave Doré*. Paris: Cercle de la Librairie, 1885.

DORST, TANKRED, is one of the best-known contemporary dramatists of the Federal Republic of Germany. Critics regard his *Merlin oder das Wüste Land* ("Merlin or the Wasteland"; 1981), written in collaboration with Ursula

Ehler, as the first major dramatic work of the 1980s. The play has had several successful productions since its premiere in Düsseldorf in 1981. *Merlin*, possessing a multidimensional scope, depicts the complete story of Arthur and the Grail, from origins to decline and fall. Without abridgment, the play requires almost an entire day of staging, and fifty actors are necessary for the more than 100 scenes. Dorst's literary sources include Malory's *Le Morte Darthur*, T.H. White's *The Once and Future King*, William Rowley's *The Birth of Merlin* (in the German rendering of Ludwig Tieck), Immermann's *Merlin*, and T.S. Eliot's *The Waste Land*. Dorst strives for a kind of universal world-theater, in the tradition of Goethe's *Faust* or a great "mystery play." His *Merlin* contains a baroque profusion of images and is unique in its blending of drama, epic storytelling, and song. It relates the story of Merlin, the son of the Devil, in a grotesque manner that relies on many anachronisms with contemporary relevance. In opposition to his father's schemes, Merlin seeks to engender a better, civilized world. The collapse of this civilization is depicted, however, and, in contrast to the Anglo-Saxon Arthurian tradition, no principle of hope informs the conclusion. The "elite utopia" (Dorst) of the Round Table that Merlin creates must perish because of human inadequacy, and the ending is a cosmic catastrophe that destroys the entire world. According to critical opinion, the tenor of *Merlin* reflects the mood of Europe at the onset of the 1980s. [UM/WCM]

🙪 Dorst, Tankred, with Ursula Ehler. *Merlin oder das Wüste Land.* Frankfurt: Suhrkamp, 1981.

Krohn, Rüdiger. "Die Geschichte widerlegt die Utopie?": Zur Aktualität von Tankred Dorsts Bühnenspektakel 'Merlin oder Das Wüste Land.'" *Euphorion*, 78 (1984).

DRACO NORMANNICUS: *see* ÉTIENNE DE ROUEN.

DRAESEKE, FELIX AUGUST BERNHARD (1835–1913), one of the few German composers of nineteenth-century "medieval operas" (other than Richard Wagner) who is deserving of some note. His opera *Merlin* (1900–05), a free reworking of Immermann's play, was first performed posthumously in Gotha (1913). [UM/WCM]

🙪 Fischer, Jens Malte. "Singende Recken und blitzende Schwerter." In *Akten des DFG-Symposions zur Mittelalter-Rezeption*, ed. Peter Wapnewski. Stuttgart: Metzler, 1985.

Roeder, Erich. *Felix Draeseke: Der Lebens- und Leidensweg eines deutschen Musikers.* 2 vols. Dresden, 1932; Berlin, 1937.

DRAGON LORD, THE: *see* DRAKE, DAVID.

DRAKE, DAVID, is the author of *The Dragon Lord* (1982), a sword-and-sorcery fantasy about an Irish warrior who serves Arthur against the Saxons. Arthur and his followers, who include Lancelot, Gawain, and Merlin, exhibit the pride and sadistic violence typical of figures in the genre. [RHT]

🙪 Drake, David. *The Dragon Lord.* New York: Doherty, 1982.

DRAWING OF THE DARK, THE: see POWERS, TIM.

DRAYTON, MICHAEL (1563–1631), author of *Poly-Olbion* (1612), a poem celebrating the topography of Britain, in which Arthurian material is related to geographical details associated with Arthur. Drayton's Arthur is chiefly the Arthur of Geoffrey of Monmouth, though he may have been influenced by Camden, Holinshed, and Malory. Drayton accepts the historicity of Arthur. [AEG]

Drayton, Michael. *Works*, ed. J. William Hebel. Oxford: Oxford University Press, 1933, Vol. 4.

DREAM OF RHONABWY, THE, a thirteenth-century (?) Welsh prose tale the single medieval copy of which is found in the fourteenth-century Red Book of Hergest. The story is given a precise setting in terms of geography and date. Iorwerth, an otherwise-unattested brother of Madog ap Maredudd, prince of Powys, died 1159, became an outlaw. The prince mustered his warband to seek him throughout his land. Rhonabwy and his companions on the quest were quartered in the house of one Heilyn Goch (the Red) (apparently a historical figure), but its filthy condition and the flea-infested blankets they were given made sleep impossible. Rhonabwy retired and lay upon a yellow ox-skin, whereupon he was granted a vision of Arthurian Britain. The greater part of the tale relates this dream, which portrays the Arthurian age as an age of gigantic heroes with whom Rhonabwy's puny contemporaries are contrasted. Rhonabwy sees a succession of armies, swordbearers, servitors, and messengers, whose rich dress and equipment are colorfully described. Arthur and Owain play chess while a group of squires complain that Arthur's men are attacking Owain's ravens, followed by a second group protesting that the ravens are now killing Arthur's men, a battle that is ended when Arthur crushes the chessmen and Owain lowers his standard. Bards sing Arthur's praise in incomprehensible poetry, and his enemies ask for a fortnight's truce. The commotion of the armies arising to follow Arthur to Cornwall awakens Rhonabwy. The tale is a succession of narrative but colorful non sequiturs, and the illogical realism of a dream world with its convoluted standards of behavior is well presented. The tale is comedy of a high order and is intended to be satirical on more than one level. Its content explodes the myths of the heroic Arthurian age, as of bardic poetry, and derides the age of Madog ap Maredudd, but its narrative method seems to parody accepted conventions of interlace and digressive description. It is a consciously composed story: the scribe's colophon, noting that the tale was read, never recited, is explained by its status in the repertoire as a literary not a traditional tale, rather than by the explanation offered that the wealth of descriptive detail overtaxed the memories of storytellers. [BFR]

🍂 Richards, G.M., ed. *Breudwyt Rhonabwy*. Cardiff: University of Wales Press, 1948.

Jones, Gwyn, and Thomas Jones, trans. *The Mabinogion*. 2nd ed. London: Dent, 1974.

Jarman, A.O.H., and Gwilym Rees Hughes. *A Guide to Welsh Literature I*. Swansea: Davies, 1976.

DRUSTAN THE WANDERER: *see* TAYLOR, ANNA.

DRYDEN, JOHN (1631–1700), whose *King Arthur* (1691), a "Dramatik Opera," is little indebted to the Arthur of history or romance. The plot concerns King Arthur's battle with Oswald, the pagan leader of the Saxons, for the control of Great Britain. Both men are also contending for Emmeline, the beautiful and blind daughter of the Duke of Cornwall. Arthur emerges victorious from a complicated series of trials, influenced by Spenser and Tasso, which include adventures in an enchanted forest where Emmeline is held captive and Arthur's temptation by sirens. Arthur defeats Oswald in single combat and is united with Emmeline, whose sight Merlin has restored. The work was lavishly staged, with music by Henry Purcell. The piece, begun in 1684, was intended to be a political allegory flattering Charles II. William and Mary were on the throne when it was produced in 1691, and Dryden wrote that he was compelled to alter it greatly owing to the current political situation. [AEG]

🍂 Dryden, John. *The Dramatic Works*, ed. Montague Summers. London: Nonesuch, 1931–32, Vol. 6.

DUE TRISTANI, I, an Italian romance published in Venice in 1555. The first book is a translation or close adaptation of the Spanish *Don Tristan de Leonis*, except for a long interpolation in which Tristan and Isolde have two children (whom they name after themselves) and in which a sorceress falls in love with Tristan. This book offers the story of Tristan and Isolde's love, Mark's suspicions and periodic reconciliations with Tristan, and the lovers' death in each other's arms. Book 2 is the story of the younger Tristan and Isolde. The former is crowned King of Cornwall by Mark (who assumes that he is the son of Isolde of the White Hands) and is later knighted by Arthur and given his father's seat at the Round Table. Guinevere falls in love with him, but he evades her advances. The end of the work recounts a number of strange adventures and concludes with the marriage of Isolde to King Juan of Castile and that of Tristan to the Infanta Maria. [NJL]

🍂 *L'Opere magnanime dei due Tristani, cavalieri della Tavola Ritonda*. Venice: Tramezzino, 1555.

Gardner, Edmund G. *The Arthurian Legend in Italian Literature*. London: Dent, 1930, pp. 295–303.

DUGGAN, ALFRED LEO (1903–1964), author of historical novels both for adults and for young readers. His novel *Conscience of the King* (1951) is the picaresque autobiography of the part-Saxon Coroticus son of Eleutherius, who later assumes the name Cerdic Elesing. The elderly Cerdic recalls how he successfully manipulated and destroyed all who were obstacles to his total independence, except for Arthur at Mount Badon, his one "mistake." His constant self-justification is maintained in ironic tension with the novel's title. [AAR]

• Duggan, Alfred Leo. *Conscience of the King.* New York: Coward-McCann, 1951.

DUKE OF WAR, THE: *see* O'MEARA, WALTER.

DU MAURIER, DAPHNE: *see* QUILLER-COUCH, SIR ARTHUR.

DU MAURIER, GEORGE (1834–1896), parodied the enthusiasm for Arthurian subjects in a loose burlesque of "The Lady of Shalott": "A Legend of Camelot," published in five installments in *Punch* in March 1866. His verses mocked those of Tennyson and Morris, his flowing-tressed women and posturing men imitated those of William Holman Hunt and Dante Gabriel Rossetti, and his format satirized the Moxon Tennyson. [DNM]

• Ormond, Leonée. "A Mid-Victorian Parody: George Du Maurier's 'A Legend of Camelot.'" *Apollo*, 85 (January 1967), 54–59.

DUNLOP WINDOWS. In 1862, Bradford merchant Walter Dunlop commissioned a set of thirteen stained-glass panels for his music room in his house at Harden Grange near Bingley, Yorkshire, from the newly founded design firm Morris, Marshall and Falkner. William Morris was given full artistic freedom for the commission. He chose the tragedy of Tristram as told by Malory as the subject, and he hired only Pre-Raphaelite artists: Ford Madox Brown, Edward Burne-Jones, Arthur Hughes, Valentine Prinsep, and Dante Gabriel Rossetti. The subjects were *The Birth of Tristram* (Hughes), *The Slaying of Sir Marhaus* (Rossetti), *Sir Tristram Demands La Belle Isounde* (Prinsep), *Sir Tristram Drinks the Love Potion with La Belle Isounde* (Rossetti), *The Madness of Sir Tristram* and *The Marriage of Sir Tristram to Isounde les Blanc Mains* (both Burne-Jones), *The Lovers at Camelot* (Morris), *Sir Tristram Slaine by King Mark* (Brown), *The Tomb of Tristram and Isounde* (Burne-Jones), and *King Arthur, Sir Lancelot, Queen Guenevere, and Isounde les Blanc Mains* (all Morris).

The windows were a unified program in clear compositions and graceful, medievalized figure style. The narrative sequence was presented with outstanding clarity, each panel placed in order and linked to the next with an inscription. The Dunlop Windows, now in the City Art Gallery, Bradford, were the most successful of the Pre-Raphaelite ensembles. [DNM]

❧ Wroot, Herbert E. "Pre-Raphaelite Windows at Bradford." *International Studio*, 63 (1917), 69–73.

DURMART LE GALLOIS, a French romance of nearly 16,000 lines, dating from the second quarter of the thirteenth century. It shows knowledge of Chrétien de Troyes's *Erec, Cligés,* and *Yvain,* as well as later texts, and has a distinct moralistic tendency.

After an affair with the wife of his father's seneschal, Durmart comes to his senses and attempts to win the love of the Queen of Ireland, whom he has never met but whose beauty he has heard of. He meets her without being aware of her identity, wins a sparrowhawk for her, and then sets out to find her, rescues Guenevere from an aggressor, and wins a tournament. He refuses to join the Round Table until he has found his love. Coming unawares to Ireland, he finds the Queen besieged in Limerick by Nogant, who eventually flees (on a camel!) rather than face a combat with Durmart. The Queen and Durmart are married. At the end of the romance, Durmart founds an abbey and visits Rome, which he frees from the pagans. [KB]

❧ Gildea, Joseph, ed. *Durmart le Gallois: roman arthurien du treizième siècle.* 2 vols. Villanova, Pa.: Villanova University Press, 1965.

DUTCH ARTHURIAN LITERATURE: *see* MIDDLE DUTCH ARTHURIAN LITERATURE.

DYCE, WILLIAM: *see* QUEEN'S ROBING ROOM.

EAGLES HAVE FLOWN, THE: *see* TREECE, HENRY.

EARTHFASTS: *see* MAYNE, WILLIAM.

"EGYPTIAN MAID, THE": *see* WORDSWORTH, WILLIAM.

"EHBRECHERBRUCK, DIE": *see* SACHS, HANS.

EHLER, URSULA: *see* DORST, TANKRED.

EILHART VON OBERGE. In line 9446 of the Middle High German *Tristrant*, the author names himself as "von Hobergin her Eylhart." Despite scholarly efforts on the one hand to identify the author with a certain Eilhart attested in documents as hailing from Oberg near Braunschweig, and on the other hand to seek his home in the middle Rhine area, his identity and origins remain uncertain.

Scholars date the composition of *Tristrant* as early as 1170, but not later than 1190. The work is the oldest complete Tristan romance. Eilhart's *Tristrant* has in the past been considered an infelicitous translation of a French source, but contemporary scholarship (e.g., Buschinger) inclines to discern in the remarkable quadripartite structure of the romance the work of an adapter, rather than a translator, of a French original. Eilhart's French source, like Béroul's, was the so-called *Estoire*.

Eilhart's *Tristrant* deviates substantially from the classic and better-known tale of tragic love transmitted in Thomas's and Gottfried von Strassburg's fragmentary versions and in the thirteenth-century Norwegian translation of Thomas's *Tristan*, *Tristrams saga ok Ísöndar*. Because Mark wants Tristrant to inherit his throne, he really has no intention of getting married. When his courtiers continue to importune him regarding marriage, he hits upon what seems to be an impossible task. He has seen two swallows fight over a woman's beautiful hair and vows not to marry any woman but the one from whose head the hair has come. Tristrant is charged with the bridal quest. Since he does not realize that Isalde is the woman he seeks, he orders his helmsman to steer clear of Ireland, where he had earlier been healed of the poisoned wound that Morhold had inflicted on him. His plans to avoid Ireland, a country hostile to strangers, are thwarted, however, by a terrible storm that drives the ship onto Irish soil. When Tristrant is revived by Isalde after having slain the dragon, he recognizes in her the woman he is seeking.

The most significant discrepancy between Eilhart's version and the romance deriving from Thomas's *Tristan* pertains to the love potion. In Eilhart's work, the love philter is so powerful for a period of four years that the lovers cannot bear to be parted for even half a day. But after four years the effect of the potion begins to wane, and one day during their forest sojourn the lovers suddenly cannot bear the hardships of their existence any longer and take steps to escape. Tristrant returns Isalde to her husband after he has confessed his sin to a hermit. Although the lovers part of their own accord and Tristrant eventually marries a second Isalde, with whom he is said to be happy, they are still under the spell of a powerful if not-less-effective outside force. Tristrant continues his secret assignations with Isalde. Their relationship is not without shadow, however. In one episode, Tristrant, disguised as a leper, seeks out Isalde. She fails to recognize him and scornfully sends him away. Tristrant reacts with bitterness, and the lovers are reconciled only when Tristrant learns that Isalde has been wearing a hairshirt that she will not remove until she has been reassured of his love once more.

A number of episodes in Eilhart's romance are tinged by an uncourtly or precourtly tone. When the lovers are discovered in *flagrante delicto* by King Mark, he orders Tristrant to be broken on the wheel but Isalde to be burned. Her sentence is modified, however, at the suggestion of a leprous duke, who proposes that she be handed over to him to be raped by every member of his leprous retinue.

Tristrant contains a fair share of humorous, even farcical, elements. As a member of King Arthur's hunting party, Tristrant is able to enjoy the hospitality of King Mark's court for one night. But Mark is not above suspicion. Since Mark and Isalde, as well as Arthur and his knights, sleep in communal quarters, Mark arranges to have the floor of the hall studded with sharp projecting blades. Not unexpectedly, Tristrant makes his way to Isalde's bed and is badly cut. To cover up for one of their own, Arthur's knights accept Kay's suggestion to have a brawl, during which everyone is badly cut.

Some of the episodes in *Tristrant* have analogues in other fiction. During one of his journeys to visit Isalde, Tristrant gets involved in three contests in which he surpasses others: throwing the javelin, leaping over a ditch, and casting a stone. Although he is in disguise, his superiority in these sports identifies him. The episode is reminiscent of Gunther's and Siegfried's experiences in their quest for Brünhild. In another episode, Kehenis, the brother of Tristrant's wife, wishes to enjoy the sexual favor of Gymele, Isalde's handmaiden. Prompted by Isalde, Gymele places a magic pillow under his head, so that he quickly falls asleep. The incident is analogous to similar incidents in the so-called maidenking romances in Icelandic literature.

Tristrant adopts many disguises in order to be able to conduct his illicit relationship with Isalde. He appears as leper, as pilgrim, and as fool. In the last disguise, he manages to lead a double life at court: Mark's fool by day and Isalde's lover by night.

The ending of Eilhart's *Tristrant* diverges significantly from that in the versions deriving from Thomas's romance. When Tristrant and Isalde have died, Mark learns about the magic potion and deeply regrets his former actions. He has the lovers buried in one grave, on which he plants a rosebush (Isalde) and a grapevine (Tristrant). The two plants grow and intertwine in such a manner as to become inseparable. [MEK]

❧ Eilhart von Oberge. *Tristrant: Édition diplomatique des manuscrits et traduction en français moderne avec introduction, notes et index*, ed. and trans. Danielle Buschinger. Göppingen: Kümmerle, 1976.

———. *Tristrant: Synoptischer Druck der ergänzten Fragmente mit der gesamten Parallelüberlieferung*, ed. Hadumod Bussmann. Tübingen: Niemeyer, 1969.

———. *Eilhart von Oberge's Tristrant*, trans. J.W. Thomas. Lincoln: University of Nebraska Press, 1978.

Buschinger, Danielle. "La structure du *Tristrant* d'Eilhart von Oberg." *Études germaniques*, 27 (1972), 1–26.

Lichtenstein, Franz, ed. *Eilhart von Oberge*. Strassburg: Trübner, 1877.

"ELAINE": *see* TENNYSON, ALFRED LORD.

ELAINE OF ASTOLAT. Often identified simply as the *demoiselle d'Escalot* (e.g., in the Vulgate *Mort Artu*) or the Fair Maid of Astolat, but sometimes bearing the name Elaine or Elayne, she is the woman who falls in love with

Lancelot and dies of grief when he does not reciprocate. A barge eventually arrives at Camelot, bearing her body and a letter attributing her death to Lancelot's rejection of her. In Tennyson, she is known as the Lady of Shalott, who is required to view the world through a mirror and who dies when "she look'd down to Camelot." The character is doubled in Natsume Sosēki's *Kairo-kō: A Dirge*. The Japanese text, drawing heavily on Tennyson and presumably on Malory as well, has the Lady of Shalott die when she looks away from her mirror and directly at Lancelot; but we later meet Elaine of Astolat, whose story roughly parallels the traditional account of her love for Lancelot, her death as a result of unrequited love, and the boat bearing her body to court. [NJL]

ELAINE OF CORBENIC. Unnamed in most French texts, the mother of Galahad is called Elaine by Malory. As daughter of King Pelles, Keeper of the Grail, she is descended from Joseph of Arimathea, but in order to join the holy line to that of Lancelot she must first seduce the reluctant knight. Convinced through enchantment that she is Guenevere, Lancelot hastens to Elaine's bed, where he engenders not only the Grail Knight but also a mountain of trouble with the jealous Queen. Modern authors portray her as either naïve (Erskine and both Bradleys) or sanctimonious (Mitchison and Godwin). Godwin and Christian fuse her with Elaine of Astolat. [RHT]

ELAINE WITH THE ARMOUR OF LANCELOT: *see* HUGHES, ARTHUR.

ELIDOR: *see* GARNER, ALAN.

ELIE DE BORRON: *see PALAMEDES.*

ELIOT, T(HOMAS) S(TEARNS) (1888–1965), ventured into the Arthurian world, specifically the Grail story, in *The Waste Land*, a poem in five parts, first published in the *Criterion* (1922) and destined to be one of the most important and influential poems of the twentieth century.

For Eliot, the center of the Grail story was the Wasteland and its Fisher King, the sexually maimed king whose healing leads to his kingdom's restoration. Using the city as an objective correlative of the modern human condition, Eliot saw his environment as a wasteland, cut off from its traditions and spiritually and intellectually dead. He incorporated many of the symbols from the Grail story into his visionary poem. In the poem's final section, "What the

Thunder Said," the Chapel Perilous, where the hero of medieval legend has to spend a night, is now "only the wind's home," another symbol of the dead world that is Eliot's universe.

In "Notes on the Waste Land," Eliot writes: "Not only the title, but the plan and a good deal of the incidental symbolism of the poem were suggested by Miss Jessie L. Weston's book on the Grail legend: *From Ritual to Romance.*" He also expressed indebtedness to J.G. Frazer's *The Golden Bough.* [DS]

 Eliot, T. S. *Poems: 1909–1925.* London: Faber and Gwyer, 1925, pp. 63–92.

ELUCIDATION, THE, a 484-line prologue in one of the fifteen manuscripts of *Le Conte del Graal* of Chrétien de Troyes; in the Prose *Perceval* of 1530; and in the fourteenth-century *Der nüwe Parzefal* of Colin and Wisse.

The author says he is beginning the best of all stories, *Le Conte del Graal,* whose secret will not be revealed until the tale is told, according to the authority of maistre Blihis. The poem will tell how Logres falls into decline and how the custom of the wells is lost when the maidens who served travelers from them are ravished and their golden cups stolen, first by King Amangon. As a result, the court of the Rich Fisher can never be found again. The knights of the Round Table set out to restore the wells and protect the maidens. They find maidens with armed knights in the forest. Gawain conquers Blihos Bliheris, who goes back to Arthur's court and tells how the maidens are descendants of those ravished by Amangon, and they are forced to wander until the court of the Rich Fisher is found again. Percevaus and Gawain find the court, and it is also found seven other times in seven "branches" (*souviestemens*) of the story. The land is revived, but evil folk set up the Castel Orguellous, which Arthur subdues after a siege of four years. The last eight lines of the *Elucidation* are lines 61–68 of the *Conte del Graal,* where Chrétien promises "rimoier le mellor conte . . . Qui soit contés en cort roial" (*Elucidation,* ll. 479, 481). [LDW]

 Thompson, Albert Wilder, ed. *The Elucidation: A Prologue to the Conte del Graal.* New York: Institute of French Studies, 1931.

Hilka, Alfons, ed. *Der Percevalroman.* Halle: Niemeyer, 1932, pp. 417–29.

Bruce, James Douglas. *The Evolution of Arthurian Romance.* 2nd ed. 2 vols. Baltimore: Johns Hopkins Press, 1928, Vol. 2, pp. 85–89.

EMBROIDERY. 1) GERMAN, MEDIEVAL. Descriptions of embroidered hangings and clothing attest to the widespread use of Arthurian material as inspiration for needlework; however, little of this secular embroidery has survived. Of the German medieval embroideries dating from the fourteenth century, six depict the story of Tristan, and others, the adventures of Sir Gawain and Sir Ywain. Among the finest depictions of the Tristan story are the so-called Wienhausen embroideries, worked by nuns in the Cistercian convent of Wienhausen in Hanover. The designers seem to have had access to a lost version of the *Tristan*, for they include details found in neither Eilhart von Oberge nor Gottfried von Strassburg.

Large linen panels (the largest, 12 feet 3 inches by 7 feet 8 inches) were embroidered in colored wool in horizontal bands. In the earliest of the three Wienhausen embroideries (ca. 1310), the story is told as a continuous narrative in three bands of pictures and text alternating with four rows of arcades enclosing heraldic shields. In the two later embroideries (dated ca. 1325 and ca. 1340), the scenes are divided only by text bands and foliage or architectural elements. Other Tristan embroideries are to be found in Luneburg (fragments of white linen embroidered in white, green, and yellow illustrating the bath, the tryst, and the ship), Erfurt (a linen tablecloth 14 by 3 feet, from the Benedictine convent at Wurzburg embroidered in red and blue, ca. 1370), the Victoria and Albert Museum, London (fragments of a larger piece stitched together, related to the Erfurt embroidery in style and technique), and Regensburg (a large, 9 by 4 foot linen panel worked in bright colored wool and representing famous lovers including Tristan and Isolde's tryst by the tree). Other German embroidery designers represented the story of Sir Gawain and the lady Orgeluse as told by Wolfram von Eschenbach (Brunswick Museum, from the Benedictine convent of Kreuzkloster, related to the Wienhausen embroideries, second quarter of the fourteenth century) and the adventures of Sir Ywain, made about 1325 for the banker Johannes Malterer of Freiburg and his wife, Anna (Augustinermuseum, Freiburg in Breisgau). The Freiburg embroidery is a linen strip 16 feet by 26 inches worked in colored wool, with a border of roses enclosing a series of eleven spiked quatrefoils that frame scenes demonstrating the wiles of women. In the two Ywain scenes, the Knight of the Lion kills Ascalon and is presented to Laudine.

2) ITALIAN, MEDIEVAL. The Tristan story inspired Sicilian needleworkers to create pictorial linen quilts in which figures, setting, text, and decorative frames were worked in low relief by means of fine stitchery and cotton padding. Heraldic devices suggest that two quilts, one now in the Victoria and Albert Museum, London, and the other in the Bargello, Florence, were made for the wedding of Piero di Luigi Guicciardini and Laodamia Acciaiuoli in 1395. Depicted are scenes from Tristan's youth, his championship of King Mark and Cornwall against Ireland, and his victory over Amoroldu, the knight who treacherously wounded him. The fragment of a third quilt, the so-called Pianetti quilt, had Tristan and Isolde as a central medallion. The Italian quilts do not seem to depend on any single surviving manuscript for their iconography but rather combine incidents from the *Tavola Ritonda*, the *Cuento de Tristan de Leonis*, and the *Morte Darthur*, with additional details unique to the quilts. [MS]

Loomis, Roger Sherman, and Laura Hibbard Loomis. *Arthurian Legends in Medieval Art.* London: Oxford University Press, 1938, pp. 50–55, 67–68, 72–73, 78–79; figs. 76–86, 128, 143–44, 167 (German); pp. 63–65; figs. 117–19 (Italian).

Schuette, Marie. *Gestickte Bildteppiche und Decken des Mittelalters.* 2 vols. Leipzig, 1927, 1930.

EMERSON, RALPH WALDO (1803–1882), American essayist and poet whose interest in Arthurian legend is reflected in his journals, notebooks, and lectures. He uses Merlin to symbolize the figure of the ideal poet in five poems: "Politics," "The Harp," "Merlin I," "Merlin II," and "Merlin's Song" (1846–67). [RHT]

 ❧ Taylor, Beverly, and Elisabeth Brewer. *The Return of King Arthur: British and American Arthurian Literature Since 1800.* Woodbridge, Suffolk: Boydell and Brewer, 1983.

EMPEROR ARTHUR, THE: see TURTON, GODFREY E.

ENCHANTED CUP, THE: see ROBERTS, DOROTHY JAMES.

ENCHANTEUR POURRISSANT, L': see APOLLINAIRE, GUILLAUME.

ENFANCES GAUVAIN, LES, two fragments (712 lines) of an early thirteenth-century French manuscript that tell of the birth and early life of Gauvain. According to the first fragment, Gauvain is the child of Arthur's sister, Morcades (Morgause), and her page, Lot. The child is entrusted to Gauvain le Brun, who gives it his own name and then sets it adrift on the sea in a cask. The second fragment tells how the child is rescued by a fisherman who learns of the circumstances of his birth and brings him to Rome, where he is educated and knighted by the pope. Similar events are related in Wace's *Brut*, the *Perlesvaus*, and the *De Ortu Waluuanii*. [KB]

 ❧ Meyer, Paul. "Les Enfances Gauvain." *Romania*, 39 (1910), 1–32.

ENGLISH ARTHURIAN LITERATURE (MEDIEVAL). The Arthurian legend enjoyed great popularity in England during the Middle Ages. The story of Arthur was celebrated in chronicle and romance throughout the twelfth to the sixteenth centuries, taking its impetus both from the belief that Arthur had been King of Britain, and from a large influx of French Arthurian romances. Although the chronicle and romance traditions are distinct, English romancers, using primarily French sources, tended in many cases to imbue their stories with heroic, noncourtly elements from the chronicles, thus creating a peculiarly English type of Arthurian romance.

  The Arthurian chronicle tradition, based on Geoffrey of Monmouth's *Historia Regum Britanniae*, for the most part presented the Arthurian story as true. The chronicles tended to stress the role of Arthur as a strong and powerful king, whereas the romances, based on the French, present him more often in a passive role, remaining at court while his knights go off in search of adventure. Except for the Scottish chronicles, which were critical of Arthur for national reasons, he was seen as an English warrior-hero, and it is that aspect of his career, rather than the courtly, that is recorded in chronicle accounts. The English Arthurian chroniclers include Robert of Gloucester, Thomas Bek of Castelford, Robert Mannyng of Brunne, John Trevisa, John Capgrave, and John Hardyng. The anonymous *Arthur*, the *Short Metrical Chronicle*, and the English Prose *Brut* also survive. These chronicles, mostly in verse, span the thirteenth through the fifteenth centuries.

Layamon's *Brut*, written in the late twelfth century, is one of the earliest stories of Arthur in English. Basing his work on Wace's *Roman de Brut*, a French adaptation of Geoffrey of Monmouth's *Historia*, Layamon removes many of the courtly features found in the French author, recalling Geoffrey's more military Arthurian world. Although it was approximately another seventy-five years before true Arthurian romance began appearing in England, there were no doubt oral versions of French romances and Celtic stories available. When the romances were eventually written down, many of them took an attitude toward Arthurian romance rather more like that of Layamon than of their French originals.

The English Arthurian romances use a variety of verse forms as well as prose. Many of the shorter tail-rhyme romances are believed to have been composed for oral delivery, whereas others are clearly the products of clerkly authors. Regardless of their origins, the English romances, with a few major exceptions, are less courtly and sophisticated, but simpler and shorter than their French predecessors. Emphasis remains on dramatic action and adventure rather than on love and psychological *finesse*; nonetheless, even in the most sophisticated romances, such as *Sir Gawain and the Green Knight* and Malory's *Morte Darthur*, these very "English" qualities contribute to the overall narrative effect.

Robert W. Ackerman has usefully divided the English Arthurian romances, except for Malory, into three categories: works whose main concern is with periods or episodes in King Arthur's life; romances taken from the French Vulgate *Estoire del Saint Graal* and *Merlin*, giving the early history of the Grail; and, the largest number, those romances about individual Arthurian knights.

The first English romance about Arthur's early life and battles, and, in fact, one of the earliest English Arthurian romances, is *Arthour and Merlin*. It includes an account of Merlin's part in Uther's succession to the crown and the birth and crowning of Arthur, followed by a version of Arthur's battles against the rebellious kings. It is believed to follow closely a lost variant version of the French Vulgate Cycle; it stresses campaigns and battles over love and courtesy. The fourteenth-century Alliterative *Morte Arthure*, an account of Arthur's life and death, follows primarily the chronicle tradition, leaving out any mention of the love between Lancelot and Guenevere, and stressing honor and battles over courtly courtesy. Its style is more epic than romance. Conversely, the Stanzaic *Le Morte Arthur*, approximately contemporary with the alliterative poem, is a condensation/adaptation of the French Vulgate *Mort Artu* and thus includes the love between Lancelot and Guenevere. The final battle leading to the end of Arthur's kingdom is therefore the result of complex romance plot elements derived from the French rather than of the simple usurpation of Arthur's throne by Mordred found in the alliterative poem. Although differing greatly, both of these romances offer effective literary portrayals of the Arthurian world. Malory later used both in his version.

The early sixteenth century produced the remaining works featuring Arthur himself as hero. Two versions of the same ballad are "The Legend of King Arthur" and "King Arthur's Death." A fragmentary ballad, "King Arthur and King Cornwall," features magical adventures, and magic is also important in John Bourchier, Lord Berner's *Arthur of Little Britain*, a sixteenth-century translation of the French romance *Artus de la Petite Bretagne*.

Although the actual quest for the Grail appears in Middle English only in Malory, there are some works dealing with the early history of the Grail and Joseph of Arimathea. The popularity of this part of the Arthurian story may be due to its connections with Glastonbury. The *Joseph of Arimathie* (ca. 1375) is an early alliterative poem based on the *Estoire del Saint Graal*. The most complete English account of Joseph of Arimathea and the Grail, however, is to be found in Lovelich's *History of the Holy Grail* (ca. 1450), also an adaptation of the *Estoire*. Lovelich also produced a *Merlin* in verse, a translation of the French Vulgate *Merlin*. An anonymous prose *Merlin* (ca. 1450), another close translation of the French Vulgate, is more complete and brings the story up to the birth of Lancelot.

The majority of Middle English Arthurian romances relate the adventures of individual knights; most of them take Gawain as central figure. In England, Gawain seems to have been in fact more popular than Arthur himself. Other Arthurian knights are for the most part the subjects of only one or two works each. The Gawain romances largely fall into three groups: those containing the themes of beheading, of testing, or of the Imperious Host; those in which the main subject is the performance of vows; and those using the Loathly Lady theme.

The beheading/testing/Imperious Host group comprises poems from the early fifteenth to the early sixteenth centuries. *Syre Gawene and the Carle of Carlyle* (ca. 1400) and the later balladlike version, *The Carle off Carlile* (ca. 1500), both contain the Imperious Host and beheading themes, and *The Turke and Gowin* (ca. 1500) contains both the testing and beheading plots. *The Grene Knight* (ca. 1500), a late condensation of *Sir Gawain and the Green Knight*, of course includes both the beheading and testing themes.

Among the Gawain poems concerning the performance of vows are two alliterative poems: *The Awntyrs off Arthure at the Terne Wathelyn* (after 1375) and the Scottish *Golagros and Gawane* (late fifteenth century). In spite of its title, *The Awntyrs* is generally considered a Gawain poem since he accepts the challenge to joust and is very much the hero of the work. *The Avowing of King Arthur, Sir Gawain, Sir Kay, and Baldwin of Britain* (ca. 1425), although including the performance of vows by all the knights named in the title, is also considered a Gawain poem because it shares characters and setting with *The Awntyrs off Arthure* and *The Wedding of Sir Gawain and Dame Ragnell.*

The Loathly Lady theme is represented in *The Wedding of Sir Gawain and Dame Ragnell* (ca. 1450), "The Marriage of Gawain" (a fifteenth-century ballad), and Chaucer's *Wife of Bath's Tale* (1392–94). Although the plots are quite similar, it is generally agreed that Chaucer's source is earlier than that for the other two works.

The Jeaste of Syr Gawayne, a romance of the fifteenth century, is unrelated to other Gawain poems in English. It is primarily a seduction story, based on two passages in the First Continuation of Chrétien's *Perceval.*

Although demonstrating varying degrees of narrative sophistication, none of these poems develops the strands of the Gawain stories in English as fully as *Sir Gawain and the Green Knight.* An alliterative poem written 1370–90, it is the earliest of the Gawain poems; its author is believed to have been well educated and familiar with courtly life. The *Gawain*-poet combines the themes of beheading, temptation, and performance of vows in a poem distinguished by its tightly patterned structure and effective use of visual imagery.

The remaining romances on individual knights are for the most part adaptations of the French. *Lancelot of the Laik,* the only Middle English romance, apart from Malory, in which Lancelot plays a dominant role, is a late fifteenth-century Scottish rehandling of the first portion of the French Prose *Lancelot.* A late fragmentary ballad, "Sir Lancelot du Lake," survives; it is probably based on Malory. *Ywain and Gawain,* a romance from the first half of the fourteenth century, is in fact about Ywain rather than Gawain; it is a close adaptation of Chrétien de Troyes's *Yvain* (*Le Chevalier au lion*). The single poem on Perceval, the early fourteenth-century *Sir Perceval of Galles,* appears to be based on Chrétien's *Perceval* (*Le Conte del Graal*), although it omits the Grail theme. The late thirteenth-century poem *Sir Tristrem* is a condensed version of the French *Tristan* by Thomas d'Angleterre.

The story of Sir Launfal, a form of the Fairy Mistress story, exists in four lays that ultimately derive from Marie de France's *Lai de Lanval.* The three shorter anonymous lays, *Sir Landeval, Sir Lambewell,* and *Sir Lamwell,* are believed to stem from a lost Middle English translation of Marie's lai, while the longer *Sir Launfal,* by Thomas Chestre, is a version of *Sir Landeval* augmented with other material. Thomas Chestre is also believed to be the author of the late fourteenth-century poem *Libeaus Desconus,* a story about Gawain's son, Gyngalyn, based on the Fair Unknown motif found in Renaut de Beaujeu's *Le Bel Inconnu.*

The chastity test found in some French romances is represented in Middle English Arthurian romance by *The Romance of Sir Corneus* (1450) and the later ballad "The Boy and the Mantle." In the test, a husband's ability to drink from a horn proves that he is not a cuckold. Traditionally, the testing takes place in either the court of Arthur or that of King Mark. Another early fifteenth-century romance of adventure, *Sir Degrevant*, is only marginally Arthurian; the hero is early identified as a knight of the Round Table, but there the relationship ends.

The most complete Middle English treatment of the Arthurian story is Sir Thomas Malory's fifteenth-century prose *Morte Darthur*. Using primarily French Arthurian prose romances (Vulgate, Post-Vulgate, Prose *Tristan*), Malory begins his story with Merlin's part in the begetting of Arthur and ends with the destruction of Arthur's kingdom; he includes Tristan material and the quest for the Grail, the only such account in Middle English. Besides his French sources, Malory also drew from the Alliterative *Morte Arthure* and the Stanzaic *Le Morte Arthur*, indicating some familiarity with English Arthurian romance. No mere translator, Malory consistently adapted his material to his own conception of the Arthurian story, pruning away what he felt did not belong. The result is an abbreviated, direct, immediate account of the Arthurian story that has remained popular for many centuries and that became the source for much later Arthurian literature.

Whether tail-rhymed, alliterative, or written in prose, whether courtly or popular, English Arthurian literature retains its own character in spite of its many borrowings from other literatures, mainly French. The elaborate interlace of the French prose cycles never made its way into English romance, nor did the analyses of questions of love found in Chrétien. English romance relies instead on action, adventure, and direct speech to produce straightforward narrative about knightly conflicts and values. [SNI]

ಶ Barber, Richard W. *Arthur of Albion: An Introduction to the Arthurian Literature and Legends of England*. London: Barrie and Rockliff with Pall Mall, 1961.

[Loomis], Laura A. Hibbard. *Mediaeval Romance in England*. New York: Franklin, 1963.

Loomis, Roger Sherman, ed. *Arthurian Literature in the Middle Ages*. Oxford: Clarendon, 1959.

Mehl, Dieter. *The Middle English Romances of the Thirteenth and Fourteenth Centuries*. London: Routledge and Kegan Paul, 1969.

ENGLISH AND AMERICAN ARTHURIAN LITERATURE (MODERN). 1) FICTION. The popularity of prose fiction about the Arthurian legend is a relatively recent phenomenon in English. Even in the Middle Ages, romances in prose were heavily outnumbered by those in verse, although they tried to make up in length what they lacked in numbers. This pattern persisted into the nineteenth century, but it has been dramatically reversed in the twentieth.

As the Middle Ages gave way to the Renaissance, literary tastes changed and Arthurian legend proved to be one of the casualties. For some time, medieval romances remained popular and even spawned imitations during the late sixteenth and early seventeenth centuries. Among them were a few episodic prose romances loosely associated with Arthurian legend. Best known are *Tom a Lincolne* (1599–1607), by Richard Johnson, and *History of Tom Thumb, the Little* (1621), a prose version of the popular ballad. Such works seek merely to take advantage of the dwindling popularity of Arthurian legend by using it as unimportant background to a series of independent adventures. Typically, they depart widely from tradition.

For the rest of the seventeenth and all of the eighteenth centuries, prose fiction shared the neglect into which Arthurian legend sank, and it was not until the Romantic movement led to a revival of interest in the Middle Ages that the situation improved. The publication of medieval Arthurian romances in the early nineteenth century, especially Malory's *Le Morte Darthur*, provided the impetus for new versions, but the century belonged to poetry as far as Arthurian legend was concerned, for novels were few and insignificant, with the exception of two ironic works: Thomas Love Peacock's *The Misfortunes of Elphin* (1829) and Mark Twain's *A Connecticut Yankee in King Arthur's Court* (1889).

Poetry, along with drama, continued to dominate the early part of the twentieth century, but the number of novels grew steadily after the First World War, then markedly after the Second. This growth has been matched by a sharp decline in the number of plays and longer poems, so that, while short poems have remained popular, prose fiction is now the dominant literary form for dealing with the Arthurian legend. This fiction can be divided into five broad categories: retellings, realistic fiction, historical fiction, science fiction, and fantasy. They are distinguished by their attitude toward setting.

Retellings are either translations or modernizations of versions composed in the Middle Ages. Since most are aimed at younger readers, they tend to simplify their material to varying degrees and to remove elements that are deemed morally unsuitable (*see* JUVENILE FICTION). The setting of the sources is reproduced with little change. These stories, particularly when retold with skill by an author like Rosemary Sutcliff, serve to introduce Arthurian legend to a wide public.

Unlike fantasy, *realistic fiction* offers what is intended to be a rational explanation for the Arthurian element that it introduces into a contemporary setting. It is thus realistic in its treatment of this element as opposed to others, like character and plot. Several are mystery thrillers that borrow items with Arthurian associations in constructing their plots. Thus, in Jonathan Gash's *The Grail Tree* (1979), the best of these, murder is committed to steal an ornate silver casket that holds a cup reputed to be the Grail. More common are novels that transpose parts of the legend into a modern setting, although the borrowings may be made elaborately explicit in some cases or merely vaguely evoked in others. The love story of Tristan and Isolde has inspired both Maria Kuncewicz's *Tristan* (1974) and *Castle Dor* (1961), by Sir Arthur Quiller-Couch and Daphne du Maurier. That of Lancelot and Guenevere has been ingeniously transposed to the settings of United States college football in Babs H. Deal's *The Grail: A Novel* (1963) and gothic romance in Nicole St. John's *Guinever's Gift* (1977). The Grail quest forms the basis of John Cowper Powys's mystical novel *A Glastonbury Romance* (1933) and of Walker Percy's penetrating exploration of appearance and reality in *Lancelot* (1978).

Historical fiction, which is a much larger category, places events back in Arthur's day. This may be either during the Dark Ages (the years between the withdrawal of Roman protection at the beginning of the fifth century and the final tide of Anglo-Saxon conquest in the last half of the sixth) or else during the High Middle Ages pictured in the romances that were the literary sources for the modern versions.

Among the novels set in the Dark Ages, a few focus upon events before or after Arthur's career, as does Adam Fergusson's political satire of postcolonial experience, *Roman Go Home* (1969), or upon the lives of figures who have only brief contact with him, like Cerdic, the protagonist of Alfred Duggan's *Conscience of the King* (1951). Those in which the Arthurian element plays an important role, however, range from the harshly realistic to the sentimentally romantic. Since the former present the reality of life in a cruel age, they are usually pessimistic in mood, as in the works of Edward Frankland, John Masefield, and Henry Treece. Here, the vices of ambition, cruelty, and treachery so loudly castigated by Gildas overwhelm the impulses toward more positive goals.

Much more common have been novels that emphasize the aspirations and achievements of Arthur in order to create a more optimistic mood. Though some of these are tiresomely sentimental, many offer involving stories and challenging insights: in *Porius* (1951), John Cowper Powys probes the psychological causes of the political divisions that ruined Britain; and the Arthurian novels of Victor Canning and Mary Stewart measure the role of destiny in the rise and fall of Arthur's realm.

The complex range of traditional material has created structural problems for all the historical novelists, and only Rosemary Sutcliff has met them successfully. Her novels *The Lantern Bearers* (1959) and *Sword at Sunset* (1963) introduce us to heroes who learn the important lesson of compassion: it can be exercised only at the cost of personal suffering, but to neglect it invites even greater loss.

Although the Dark Ages have been the usual setting for historical fiction about Arthur in recent years, the High Middle Ages proved more popular prior to the 1960s. Fiction in this setting can be divided into four groups: psychological novels, sentimental romances, juvenile adventure stories, and sentimental comedies. The psychological novels focus upon character development to account for the behavior of the knights and ladies of Arthur's court. Thus, John Erskine ironically scrutinizes the idealism of Palamede in *Tristan and Isolde: Restoring Palamede* (1932), Hannah Closs recreates the rapturous passion of the lovers in *Tristan* (1940), and Jim Hunter discovers the existential dilemma of the Grail quest in *Percival and the Presence of God* (1978).

Like the medieval prose romances upon which they are modeled, the sentimental romances suffer from long and episodic plots, as well as tiresome sentimentality. At their best, as in Clemence Housman's *The Life of Sir Aglovale de Galis* (1905), they can offer penetrating insights into the gap between illusion and reality that destroyed the Round Table, but such moments seem hardly worth the tedium.

The juvenile fiction is intended to entertain and to offer both moral and historical instruction to young readers. Books like Eugenia Stone's *Page Boy for King Arthur* (1949) not only give a picture of life in a medieval castle but also warn against the perils of irresponsible conduct. They succeed only when they create a truly sympathetic hero, like E.M.R. Ditmas's *Gareth of Orkney* (1956).

The high moral tone of many Arthurian works also provoked an ironic response. In the pages of popular magazines like *Saturday Evening Post*, stories by P.G. Wodehouse, Don Marquis, and T.G. Roberts poked amiable fun at the impractical behavior of Arthurian heroes in medieval romance.

Science fiction and a related form, science fantasy, have rarely been used to treat the Arthurian legend. Andre Norton accounts for Merlin's powers as extraterrestrial technology in *Merlin's Mirror* (1975). However, apart from Mark Twain's *A Connecticut Yankee in King Arthur's Court*, which can just as easily be considered a fantasy, by far the finest Arthurian science-fiction novel is C.J. Cherryh's study of role-playing in *Port Eternity* (1982). Here, the author makes skillful use of the legend to explore the problems caused by role-playing. Minor borrowings from Arthurian legend also occur in half a dozen novels of science fantasy, a hybrid form that combines science with magic. Most interesting is the sympathetic treatment of Morgan le Fay in Poul Anderson's *Three Hearts and Three Lions* (1953).

The largest category of Arthurian fiction, especially in recent years, is *fantasy*, which is distinguished from other literary genres in that the element of the marvelous is crucial. In low fantasy, no explanation is offered for non-rational phenomena, which thus tend to be mysterious and frightening. High fantasy creates a secondary world where nonrational events are accounted for by a supernatural power that is acceptable within that world.

Few low fantasies make use of Arthurian legend, but two fine juvenile novels certainly deserve mention for the skill with which they use the supernatural as a means to develop character: William Mayne's *Earthfasts* (1966) borrows the cave legend attached to Arthur; in Nancy Bond's *A String in the Harp* (1976) the young hero finds Taliesin's harp-tuning key.

Apart from a couple of didactic fantasies, like John Cowper Powys's *Morwyn* (1937), the many Arthurian high fantasies can be readily divided into three main groups: mythopoeic, heroic, and ironic. In mythopoeic fantasy, the struggle between Good and Evil is waged directly between supernatural powers, and it usually takes place in a contemporary setting. Thus, Charles Williams relates a powerful story of spiritual conflict in a disbelieving world as competing parties search for the Holy Grail in *War in Heaven* (1930); and C.S. Lewis condemns the dehumanizing aspects of scientific progress in *That Hideous Strength* (1945).

The protagonists of these novels develop a deeper understanding of life, but only at the cost of personal loss and suffering. This pattern is adopted also in the best of the mythopoeic novels for younger readers, those by Alan Garner and Susan Cooper. The discovery of supernatural powers by the young protagonists must be paid for by a loss of innocence on the one hand and an increased burden of responsibility on the other. At the end of Garner's *The Moon of Gomrath* (1963), the hearts of both Susan and Colin are filled with yearning after they have seen and heard the Wild Hunt; and in Cooper's *The Dark Is Rising* (1973) Will Stanton's newly awakened powers as an Old One are put to a terrifying test. Where the protagonists do not discover latent supernatural powers of their own, their growth to maturity is a less intense experience, as can be seen in Andre Norton's *Steel Magic* (1965) and Jane Curry's *The Sleepers* (1968).

These fantasies introduce Arthurian legend into a modern setting through such devices as rediscovering the Grail; or wakening Merlin from the spell cast upon him by Nimue; or making Merlin, Arthur, and Morgan le Fay immortal, sometimes dwelling in Avalon, sometimes asleep in a cavern. Robert Newman and Gillian Bradshaw, however, set their mythopoeic fantasies back in Arthur's day. Newman returns to the High Middle Ages in *The Testing of Tertius* (1973), and he proceeds to teach his young protagonists that they must conquer their own subconscious fears before they can assist Merlin and Arthur in the struggle against evil. Bradshaw returns to the Dark Ages in her Arthurian trilogy (1980–82). Gwalchmai (Gawain), in the service of "Light," helps Arthur lead the struggle against the forces of "Dark" served by Morgawse. At considerable cost, they win early successes, only to watch them fade at the end, undone by human weakness and folly. Gwalchmai bitterly discovers that "even the best intentions of those devoted to Light can create Darkness."

The largest group among the fantasies is the heroic, some of which are placed in a modern setting. Peter Dickinson's *The Weathermonger* (1968) and Roger Zelazny's "The Last Defender of Camelot" (1980) achieve this by reviving Merlin from his long sleep. The modern world is linked to the past by visions in Will Bradley's *Launcelot and the Ladies* (1927), and by time travel in Meriol Trevor's didactic juvenile fantasy *Merlin's Ring* (1957).

Most of the heroic fantasies are set entirely in Arthur's day. Some, like H. Warner Munn's Arthurian novels and David Drake's *The Dragon Lord* (1982), belong to the category popularly known as sword and sorcery, and these introduce new and violent heroes into a particularly brutal Dark Age setting. Sharan Newman also makes use of the Dark Ages as the setting for her trilogy about Guinevere (1981–85), but she paints a less savage picture. Others set their stories in the High Middle Ages, notably Vera Chapman's trilogy of the Three Damosels (1975–76) and Phyllis Ann Karr's *Idylls of the Queen* (1982). The former offers a valuable female perspective on a predominantly masculine world, even if the situations often seem romantically contrived; the latter provides a sympathetic appraisal of some of the less attractive figures in Arthurian legend, as Kay painstakingly solves the mystery of who murdered Sir Patrise with a poisoned apple. Ruth Collier Sharpe also places her gothic melodrama *Tristram of Lyonesse* (1949) in Arthur's day, but she creates a disconcertingly anachronistic setting that recalls the seventeenth century.

Three authors of heroic fantasy to date have covered the complete story of Arthur's rise and fall. The best-loved version is undoubtedly T.H. White's *The Once and Future King* (1958). Like Malory, whose *Le Morte Darthur* forms the basis of his series, White creates a true mood of tragedy because he imparts a keen sense that something precious has been lost. With Arthur, there fade the bright hopes of childhood for a better, kinder world. Parke Godwin, by contrast, strikes a more positive note in *Firelord* (1980). His Arthur is one of the most attractive portraits of the King in modern fiction, balancing idealism with humorous pragmatism, compassion with heroic self-sacrifice. The development of these qualities, moreover, provides a firm structure for the novel. The sequel, *Beloved Exile* (1984), continues in a more somber mood the story of Guenevere after Arthur's death. Marion Zimmer Bradley's *The Mists of Avalon* (1982) is another of those rare Arthurian novels told from the female point of view. Morgaine is the central figure in this account of the conflict waged between tolerance and intolerance, both at a political level, where it is fought between adherents of the older religions and those who practice a dogmatic Christianity, and at a personal level, where the characters must struggle to reconcile their own conflicting impulses. The failure to resolve this conflict dooms Arthur's kingdom.

Godwin and Bradley set their novels in the Dark Ages, but like White the authors of the ironic fantasies discovered a richer potential for humor in the world of romance set in the High Middle Ages. The earliest ironic fantasies reacted against the lofty moral tone of many Victorian treatments of Arthurian legend, notably Tennyson's *Idylls of the King*. The most famous is Mark Twain's *A Connecticut Yankee in King Arthur's Court*, whose hero, Hank Morgan, journeys back in time to Arthur's day. Twain uses Hank to reveal the comedy inherent in the exaggerations of medieval romance and to criticize the ignorance and callousness of society. However, when Hank mercilessly turns the weapons created by his advanced technology against those who oppose his rule at the end of the novel, he makes it abundantly clear that the target of Twain's satire is as much society in his own day as in the Middle Ages. Indeed, the author treats Arthurian legend itself with an underlying affection that is evident in such episodes as that in which Arthur carries a child dying of smallpox down to its mother.

In Twain's work are found the three major elements of ironic fantasies about the Arthurian legend: satire of humanity's self-destructive impulses, comedy at the expense of our foolish pretensions, and a poignant affection for the aspirations of high romance. Least common is the satire, but it has gained rapidly in popularity since the publication of John Steinbeck's *The Acts of King Arthur* in 1976. Starting as a simplified retelling of Malory, this novel increasingly expands upon its source, developing notes of disillusionment not found there. The next year, 1977, saw the appearance of both *The Book of Merlyn*, T.H.

White's bitter conclusion to *The Once and Future King*, and the first part of Richard Monaco's apocalyptic Grail trilogy. They were followed in 1978 by Robert Nye's *Merlin*, where events are fittingly presided over by Satan.

More numerous have been the fantasies that combine comedy with warm affection for the legend. Several are written for younger readers, including Robert Newman's *Merlin's Mistake* (1971), which teaches its young protagonists not to take life at face value. Those for adults include James Branch Cabell's *Jurgen* (1919), John Myers Myers's *Silverlock* (1949), and Naomi Mitchison's *To the Chapel Perilous* (1955), all of which use figures from Arthurian legend to teach their protagonists some valuable, albeit unexpected, lessons about life.

More recently, Thomas Berger, in *Arthur Rex* (1978), has made delightful use of such techniques as parody and ironic reversal to probe the comedy of Arthurian romance. As he lies dying, Arthur despairs over "the triumph of perfect evil over imperfect virtue, which is to say, of tragedy over comedy. For have I not been a buffoon?" He is comforted, however, by the ghost of Gawaine, who reminds him that they did at least live their lives "with a certain gallantry." It is this gallantry, this heroic struggle to create a better world, however impractical the task given humanity's flawed nature, that distinguishes the heroes of the ironic fantasies. In the final analysis, the authors prefer their noble folly to the destructive cynicism of the real world that destroys them.

In the hands of modern authors, Arthurian tradition continues to modify and grow, and while no new heroes have won general acceptance some old ones have gained fresh prominence, notably Kay, Bedivere, Mordred, and Merlin. Women and children are also paid more attention, and they play a much more active role in events that shape Arthur's world than they did in the medieval romances. The range and popularity of prose fiction about the Arthurian legend have continued to widen throughout the twentieth century. Though no works of postmedieval fiction yet published can stand comparison with the romances of Chrétien de Troyes or Malory, nonetheless some first-rate novels have been written, and they amply repay critical attention. These achievements offer convincing evidence of the vitality of the Arthurian legend in prose fiction.

2) DRAMA. Of all the literary forms, drama has proven the least successful for Arthurian legend. The few dramatists of note who have treated the legend have produced work that is inferior by their own standards, while minor authors, despite some promising performances, have never risen above their limitations.

Arthurian drama first appeared during the Renaissance, when the surge of patriotism in England during the reign of Elizabeth I excited great interest in the chronicle play. However, though the history of Britain recounted in the chronicles provided the source for such well-known plays as *Gorboduc* (1561), by Thomas Sackville and Thomas Norton, and Shakespeare's *King Lear* (1605–06) and *Cymbeline* (1609–10), the Arthurian episodes were largely ignored. The earliest Arthurian play, *The Misfortunes of Arthur*, by Thomas Hughes, was performed before Elizabeth I in 1588. Modeled upon Seneca's *Thyestes*, it covers the events following Arthur's return from the Continent to deal with Mordred's rebellion and Guenevora's adultery. Stress is placed on the importance of loyalty to the monarch if the horrors of civil war are to be avoided, a message that was of contemporary political concern.

Only three other Arthurian dramas have survived from this period. In Ben Jonson's *The Speeches at Prince Henry's Barriers* (1610), Arthur and Merlin are among the characters who praise the achievements of the more recent English rulers, most notably James I and his son, for whom the masque was performed. Thomas Middleton's *Hengist* (also known as *The Mayor of Queenborough*) and *The Birth of Merlin*, sometimes attributed to William Rowley, were published in 1661 and 1662, respectively, but were composed perhaps forty years earlier. Both offer melodramatic versions of the invasion of the Saxons and their wars against the Britons, and like many contemporary works they emphasize such elements as lust, treachery, and intrigue. The best parts of these undistinguished plays are their humorous subplots, which are coarse but vigorous.

As the Renaissance gave way to the Augustan Age, interest in the Arthurian legend declined. John Dryden's "Dramatik Opera" *King Arthur*, with music by Henry Purcell and a variety of striking stage effects, was a briefly popular success when it was produced in 1691. The plot, however, departs drastically from tradition in its sentimentalized account of the struggle between Arthur and Oswald, leader of the Saxons, for possession of both Britain and "'Fair, Blind, Emmeline,'" daughter of the Duke of Cornwall. Henry Fielding's witty burlesque *The Tragedy of Tragedies; or The Life and Death of Tom Thumb the Great* (1730) won a more enduring popularity by parodying the very exaggerations of heroic tragedy that are so evident in Dryden's play. William Hilton's *Arthur, Monarch of the Britons, A Tragedy* (1759), on the other hand, returns to the chronicles for its account of Arthur's war against Mordred.

As the eighteenth century drew to a close and the Romantic movement began, conditions improved for a revival of interest in Arthurian legend. John Thelwall's closet drama *The Fairy of the Lake* (1801), however, looks back to Dryden's opera as the inspiration for its story, in which the Lady of the Lake assists Arthur and Guenevere against the wicked Rowenna. As the nineteenth century progressed, interest in Arthurian legend grew, but chiefly among the poets. Occasional plays, such as Reginald Heber's *Morte D'Arthur* (1841), were written and performed, but they were rarely printed and did not reach a wider audience.

The closing decades of the nineteenth century and opening decades of the twentieth witnessed an astonishing revival of Arthurian drama. First to achieve popular success was *King Arthur*, by J. Comyns Carr, produced at London's Lyceum Theatre in 1895, with Henry Irving in the title role and incidental music by Sir Arthur Sullivan. In the United States, Richard Hovey was engaged in an ambitious cycle of Arthurian plays, *Launcelot and Guenevere: A Poem in Dramas*, which appeared between 1891 and 1907. The peak year for Arthurian drama was 1923, which saw the appearance of Laurence Binyon's

Arthur, A Tragedy, John Masefield's *Tristan and Isolt*, and Thomas Hardy's *The Famous Tragedy of the Queen of Cornwall*, all three of which are marked by firm structure and dramatic power. Despite some penetrating psychological insights, the predominant mood of Arthurian plays of this era is romantic and sentimental, and this is reflected by their interest in love and its tragic consequences. The affair between Lancelot and Guenevere attracted such dramatists as Henry Newbolt, Francis Coutts, Georgene Davis, and Ernest Rhys; the passion of Tristan and Isolde found sudden popularity during the opening years of the twentieth century in the hands of Michael Field, Martha Kinross, Arthur Symons, and others; and, though the story proved less popular than the former two, Merlin's fateful infatuation with Nimue/Vivien found favor with Ethel Mumford, as well as Binyon and Coutts.

Like Tennyson, these playwrights look to medieval romance for their material. However, the plays written since the outbreak of the Second World War have signaled a concern for realism by turning back to history and chronicle. In *The Saviours* (1942), a series of radio plays by Clemence Dane that invokes the heroic spirit of resistance against desperate odds, both Merlin and Arthur play important roles; and Archibald MacLeish's *The Destroyers* (1942) uses the story of Mordred's rebellion to condemn the destruction of war. Merlin appears again in *Thor, with Angels* (1948), Christopher Fry's play about the coming of Christianity among the Saxons, and Arthur rallies Romano-British resistance against the invaders in Robert Sherriff's *The Long Sunset* (1955). Most recently, *The Island of the Mighty* (1973), by John Arden and Margaretta D'Arcy, has carried this realism still further in order to present an antiromantic picture of Arthur and his followers.

Arthurian drama has thus passed through four distinct phases. The heroic and melodramatic mood of the sixteenth and seventeenth centuries led to parody in the eighteenth; the romantic and sentimental mood of the nineteenth and early twentieth centuries has in its turn yielded to the realism and antiromanticism of the past thirty years. It is too early to decide how long this present trend will continue, but the current popularity of fantasy suggests that a new direction may well await Arthurian legend. Indeed, the success of musicals like *Camelot* (1960), by Frederick Loewe and Alan Jay Lerner, and of films like John Boorman's *Excalibur* (1981) suggests that the time is ripe for a revival of a new heroic mood in the theater. Whether Arthurian legend will at last find worthy expression as drama nevertheless remains to be seen.

3) POETRY. As the Middle Ages waned, so did interest in the Arthurian legend. During the Renaissance readers continued to enjoy medieval romances, but few authors chose them as the source for new work. Their attention had shifted from feudalism and romance to new political concerns and classical models. For a while, the Tudor attempt to reinforce their claim to the throne as descendants of Arthur stimulated interest in the chronicle account of his reign, and this was reinforced by patriotic sentiment during the reign of Elizabeth I. Yet this association with the monarchy worked against the legend when the Stuarts fell out of favor in the seventeenth century. Eighteenth-century ra-

tionalism and admiration of the classics condemned Arthur to obscurity, and it was not until the Romantic movement that conditions improved for an Arthurian revival. This culminated in the second half of the nineteenth century in the poetry of Tennyson, which firmly secured the legend's popularity, a popularity that has persisted to this day. Poetry remained the most important literary form for treatment of the Arthurian legend until the Second World War, when it yielded its preeminence to prose fiction.

Despite the popularity of medieval romances throughout most of the sixteenth century, it was not until the patriotic enthusiasm of the closing decades that a new work appeared. This was Edmund Spenser's *The Faerie Queene*, an impressive allegorical epic that was little more than half finished when the poet died in 1599. The ostensible hero is the youthful Prince Arthur, who represents the virtue of magnanimity, and he spends his time searching for Gloriana, the Faerie Queene. However, in order to develop his allegory Spenser divorces Arthur from tradition and pushes him into the background for most of the story.

A more traditional, albeit brief, account of Arthur's career, based upon the chronicles, figured in a handful of poems from the early years of the seventeenth century. Robert Chester's *Love's Martyr* (1601) traces Arthur's descent from Joseph of Arimathea. Thomas Heywood's *Troia Britanica* (1609) includes one short stanza on Arthur in its record of the kings of Britain. Arthur was added to the historical examples used to offer political lessons in the 1610 edition of *The Mirror for Magistrates*, although Vortigern and Uther were listed as early as 1578. In *Poly-Olbion* (1612), Michael Drayton gives Arthur considerable attention in his description of the legends associated with locations throughout Britain.

This largely antiquarian interest in Arthur was but a ripple in the ebbing tide. More typical of the seventeenth century was the response of John Milton, Ben Jonson, and John Dryden, all of whom abandoned plans to write an Arthurian epic in favor of other projects. Jonson and Dryden each composed a play in which Arthur appeared, but it was not until the end of the century that another Arthurian poem was published. This was Richard Blackmore's epic *Prince Arthur* (1695), and it proved so popular that two years later he published another, *King Arthur*. Since both are allegories of contemporary political events—Arthur is King William, his foes are James II and Louis XIV—they have lost most of their interest for modern readers.

The eighteenth century, with its devotion to reason, dismissed Arthurian romance with the scorn it felt for the "barb'rous" Middle Ages. A few minor poems about Merlin were written during the first half of the century, but it was not until the Romantic revival that the situation changed. At first, attention to Arthurian legend was confined to the publication of medieval romances by scholars, and of poems by obscure talents like Thomas Warton (1777), Richard Hole (1789), and John Leyden (1803). When greater writers turned to the legend, however, the results proved disappointing. William Blake incorporates Arthurian elements into his prophetic epic poem *Jerusalem, the*

Emanation of the Giant Albion, composed during the first two decades of the nineteenth century, but this can hardly be considered an Arthurian work. Walter Scott's *The Bridal of Triermain* (1813) is a slight piece, interesting primarily for its wry humor at the expense of Arthur and his court. William Wordsworth's "The Egyptian Maid" (1835) is an imaginative but sentimental allegory of the Grail legend. Two other poems from this period, John Hookham Frere's *The Monks and the Giants* (1817–18), which makes use of Arthur and his knights to poke fun at Italian chivalric romance, and Reginald Heber's *Morte D'Arthur* (1830), which deals with events surrounding Guenevere's marriage, are both incomplete. Though not without merit, neither is particularly successful.

A new generation of poets was now coming to the fore, and they were to raise Arthurian legend to its greatest heights since the Middle Ages. Foremost among them was Alfred, Lord Tennyson, whose first Arthurian poem, "The Lady of Shalott," was published in 1832. Based upon an Italian version of the tale of Elaine of Astolat, the poem is impressive for its rich imagery and its treatment of the theme of illusion and reality. It reappeared in a revised version in 1842 as part of a collection that included three more Arthurian poems: "Sir Launcelot and Queen Guinevere," which celebrates the lovers' passion; "Sir Galahad," a vigorous monologue in praise of purity; and "Morte d'Arthur," in which the circumstances of Arthur's departure for Avalon after the battle of Camlann reflect the nineteenth-century anxiety over change. These poems aroused public interest in Arthurian legend and an anticipation that the great epic treatment it deserved would at last be written. This anticipation was not to be disappointed.

Tennyson's *Idylls of the King* appeared over a number of years. The first sign of what was to come was an 1857 trial edition of only six copies of two of the idylls, *Enid and Nimuë: or, The True and the False*. Nimuë's name was then changed to Vivien, and in 1859 the two poems were published, together with poems on Elaine and Guinevere, as *The True and the False: Four Idylls of the King*. In 1869, Tennyson expanded this initial framework when he published "The Coming of Arthur," "The Holy Grail," "Pelleas and Ettarre," and "The Passing of Arthur," the last of which is an expansion of the "Morte d'Arthur." "Gareth and Lynette" and "The Last Tournament" followed in 1872, and in 1873 "Enid" was divided into two separate idylls, "The Marriage of Geraint" and "Geraint and Enid." "Balin and Balan," composed 1872–74 but not published until 1885, completed the twelve idylls.

In covering the career of Arthur from birth to death, Tennyson develops him into a symbol of "Ideal manhood closed in real man," as he explains in the epilogue, "To the Queen." The central conflict is "Sense at war with Soul," the glorious attempt to establish the ideal kingdom on earth that fails, finally, through human weakness. Although each idyll focuses upon a separate episode in the legend, they are all influenced by this controlling vision. Thus, Tennyson modifies the traditional order of the tales to emphasize the progression from early success to later failure: the triumphant war against the Romans is shifted to the beginning of Arthur's reign. The poet also modifies the traditional characters: Arthur is absolved of all blame and placed firmly at the center of the poem; by contrast, Lancelot is burdened with guilt and Tristram reduced to a scornful, world-weary cynic. The links between the tales are reinforced by the developing patterns of imagery and symbol. The significance of both the color white and the naked babe changes from innocence and hope at the beginning of the poem to cold and death at the end.

Tennyson's achievements greatly stimulated the revival of interest in Arthurian legend, which found expression in both art and literature. Much of the poetry produced is of inferior quality: the moments of genuine humor in Edward Bulwer-Lytton's *King Arthur* (1848) fail to redeem an overly ambitious and episodic narrative; despite its vigor, Robert Stephen Hawker's *Quest of the Sangraal* (1864) fades into mystical obscurity; George du Maurier's *A Legend of Camelot* (1866) is an amusing parody of absurdities in the poetry of both Tennyson and the Pre-Raphaelites, but it grows tedious once the novelty wears off; Thomas Westwood's *The Sword of Kingship* (1866), which describes Arthur's early years, and *The Quest of the Sancgreall* (1868)—like Ralph Fullarton's *Merlin* (1890), Madison Cawein's *Accolon of Gaul* (1889), and Ernest Rhys's "The Story of Balin and Balan: From the *Morte d'Arthur*" (1897)—are imitations of Tennyson, and they suffer by comparison.

The greater talents of Matthew Arnold, William Morris, and Algernon Swinburne yielded more impressive results. Arnold's *Tristram and Iseult* (1852), the first English modernization of the story, warns against the destructive power of love. At the same time, the poem stresses the value of the human imagination that finds expression in legend. True to his own dictum, Arnold ingeniously incorporates the tale of how Vivian enchants Merlin into his poem to give greater force to his twin themes. Morris wrote several Arthurian poems, the best-known of which is "The Defence of Guenevere" (1858). The Queen here offers a passionate, albeit self-incriminating, defense of her affair with Launcelot, in which may be seen a justification for following the creative impulse. Swinburne's *Tristram of Lyonnesse* (1882) recreates the lovers' intense passion, burning all the more fiercely because of the obstacles it encounters; his *The Tale of Balen* (1896) is a more conventional, if well-paced, reworking of Malory's version of the tragic tale.

Poetry on the Arthurian legend was not confined to long narrative verse. Tennyson's shorter poems inspired others to evoke a more lyrical mood, and the steady outpouring of this kind of writing has continued unabated in the twentieth century. Among the earliest to appear were three poems by Bulwer-Lytton's son, who wrote under the pseudonym of Owen Meredith. The best of these was "The Parting of Launcelot and Guenevere: A Fragment" (1855), which explores the tensions and quarrels between the lovers. These same tensions account for Lancelot's madness in John Davidson's "The Last Ballad" (1899) and Kaufmann Spiers's "The Madness of Lancelot" (1909).

A more popular motif was the passionate yearning of one lover for another, be it Lancelot for Guenevere in Swinburne's "Lancelot," an early poem that was not published until 1925; or both together in Morris's "King Arthur's Tomb" (1858), Stephen Phillips's "The Parting of Launcelot and Guinevere" (1907), and Edward Hunt's "The Parting of Lancelot and Guinevere" (1908). It is Elaine who longs for Lancelot in Edna St. Vincent Millay's "Elaine" (1921); Iseult for Tristan in "Joyeuse Garde," another early poem by Swinburne, and Sara Teasdale's "At Tintagil" (1926); and Tristan for Iseult in Lauriston Ward's "Tristan in Brittany" (1902), Frederic Manning's "Tristram" (1910), and Millay's "Tristan" (1954). This yearning is a central feature in poems that poignantly describe the deaths of Tristan (Laurence Binyon, 1901; James Ormerod, 1928; Sydney Smith, 1948) and Lancelot (Conde Benoist Pallen, 1902; Francis Coutts, 1907; Edgar Lee Masters, 1916). By contrast, John Ciardi's powerful poem "Launcelot in Hell" (1961) presents us with an unrepentant sinner who boasts with defiant scorn that he deliberately slew the cuckold monarch out of lust for Guenevere, "a mare to be mounted."

Merlin's fate also attracted attention. Its inevitability is revealed in Gordon Bottomley's dramatic poem "Merlin's Grave" (1929), when the wizard wakens from his enchanted sleep only to be beguiled again by an endlessly reborn Lady of the Lake. In M. Jourdain's "Merlin" (1910), his sleep is an escape from the ravages of time into a union with an undying Nature. In Thom Gunn's "Merlin in the Cave: He Speculates Without a Book" (1955), he is trapped in the contemplation of his own metaphysics rather than by any external power. Both Laurence Binyon's dramatic poem *The Madness of Merlin* (1947) and R.S. Thomas's "Taliesin 1952" return to earliest tradition for their account of Merlin driven mad by the sight of slaughter.

Gawain was the subject of a handful of poems, including three by Charlton Lewis (1916), Yvor Winters (1937), and David Schubert (1974), all inspired by the fourteenth-century English verse romance *Sir Gawain and the Green Knight*. His reputation for casual love affairs is criticized in two poems by Richard Hovey, "Launcelot and Gawaine" (1888) and "The Last Love of Gawaine" (1898). Rhys Carpenter is more sympathetic to him in his long dramatic work *The Tragedy of Etarre: A Poem* (1912), in which the inexperienced knight is seduced by the lady, as in French versions of the story. Gawain's susceptibility to unattached damsels is recalled in Jessie Weston's "Knights of King Arthur's Court" (1896), where he sings a song in praise of them all, in contrast to Tristan and Lancelot, who confine their devotion to their respective ladies, and to Perceval, who thinks only of the Grail quest.

The Grail quest proved a source of inspiration for others also. Alfred Graves's "The Coming of Sir Galahad and a Vision of the Grail" (1917) and the many poems collected in A.E. Waite's *The Book of the Holy Graal* (1921) glorify its mysticism; Vachel Lindsay uses it as a rallying cry against such contemporary problems as "trafficking in young girls" in "Galahad, Knight who Perished" and drinking in "King Arthur's Men Have Come Again" (1923); and Grail imagery pervades the work of David Jones (1937–74).

The moralistic and sentimental mood of such pieces inevitably prompted humorous parodies. Both Oscar Adams's *Post Laureate Idylls* (1886), which includes poems like "The Rape of the Tarts," and Edward Hamley's "Sir Tray: An Arthurian Idyl" (1873), which relates the later life of the Lady of Shalott, satirize Tennyson's *Idylls*. Don Marquis pokes fun at the lovers in "Lancelot and Guinevere" and "Tristram and Isolt" (1922); Maggie Ross comments sardonically upon the hero's reputation both as a lover and as a warrior in "Gawain the Impossible" (1971); Eugene Field narrates how a smart trader, much like Mark Twain's Connecticut Yankee, swindles Arthur and his knights in "A Proper Trewe Idyll of Camelot" (1889).

For most, however, Arthurian legend has inspired a less critical admiration. This is particularly noticeable in the lyrical poems that use a place with legendary associations to prompt philosophical meditations. Tintagel leads Binyon (1894), Roden Noel (1902), Nancy Turner (1928), and L. Sprague de Camp (1967) to ponder the *ubi sunt* theme. To Stanley James (1927), Avalon is the place "where the broken dreams are gone," while to Fred Cogswell (1966) its timeless beauty beckons us amidst this "Clock-heavy world." To Charles Dalmon, Camelot is an alluring dream (1929), though to Gustav Davidson (1922) and to Gail White (1972) it is a dream betrayed by the passion of Lancelot and Guenevere. G.K. Chesterton's "The Grave of Arthur" (1930) reflects upon the paradox of a king who may never have lived but whose legend will never die; amidst the peril of war, Francis Brett Young's "Hic Jacet Arthurus Rex Quondam Rexque Futurus . . . " (1944) celebrates his heroic defiance in the face of doom.

Among the most interesting developments in modern Arthurian poetry has been the appearance of sequences of short poems. The earliest was Ernest Rhys's *Lays of the Round Table* (1905), a collection of romantic poems based upon incidents in Malory. The early emphasis upon the suffering that love brings prepares the reader for the Grail quest and the passing of Arthur in the second part of the collection. Coutts mixes drama and verse in *The Romance of King Arthur* (1907), which consists of two plays framed by two long poems: the first deals with Arthur's birth, the second with the deaths of Launcelot and Guenevere. John Masefield's *Midsummer Night and Other Tales in Verse* (1928) imaginatively embroiders traditional material in a series of poems that move from Arthur's begetting to the hope for his return.

These three were first published in Britain, but of the six sequences that have appeared more recently four were published in Canada, the remaining two in the United States. Margaret Atwood's "Avalon Revisited" (1963) is a series of seven short poems that focus upon the role of women. In the last, "The King," she concludes that Arthur is not in Avalon, despite all the tales, "Only those queens that were His three mortal wounds." Jack Spicer's *The Holy Grail* (1964) explores the response of the chief members of Arthur's court to the Grail. John D'Arcy Badger's sequence of fifty-six sonnets, *The Arthuriad* (1972), attacks the modern vices of cruelty, fanaticism, and selfishness and calls for a return to the values of moderation that Arthur stands for. Frank Davey's *The King of Swords* (1972) describes the end of a love affair in terms of the life and death of Arthur. Mickey Byrd invokes the Merlin legend in *Merlin and Vivien: A*

Texas Sonnet Sequence (1977). Maria Jacobs sympathetically shares Mark's point of view in her cycle of sixteen poems, "Iseult, We Are Barren" (1979).

Despite the proliferation of short poems on the Arthurian legend, longer poems have continued to appear, and the compositions of T.S. Eliot, Edwin Arlington Robinson, and Charles Williams represent the greatest achievements in Arthurian literature during the first half of the twentieth century. Robinson's *Merlin* (1917), *Lancelot* (1920), and *Tristram* (1927), all set in the last days of Arthur's rule, are permeated by a sense of loss. Recognizing their own weakness and failure, the characters nonetheless attain a stoic fortitude with which to confront their doom. Eliot's *The Waste Land* (1922), one of the most important poems of the twentieth century, reveals the relevance of the Grail legend to modern experience. Charles Williams's unfinished Arthurian cycle, published in *Taliessin Through Logres* (1938) and *The Region of the Summer Stars* (1944), explores the mystical significance of the Grail story. The downfall of Arthur's kingdom results from spiritual failure: an egotistical self-love that breeds disorder.

The remaining poems have been less impressive. The favorite subject has been the love between Tristan and Isolde, retold by An Philibin (1924), Ernest Reynolds (1930), Frank Kendon (1934), Florence Pomeroy (1958), and George Saul (1969). Episodes from Malory form the basis of Rhys Carpenter's *The Tragedy of Etarre: A Poem* (1912), the three Arthurian poems of Sidney Wright (1926–30), Clyde Furst's *Merlin* (1930), and Robert Green's *The Round Table: An Arthurian Romance Epic* (1955). More innovative have been Martyn Skinner's *Merlin or the Return of Arthur* (1951) and *The Return of Arthur: A Poem of the Future* (1955), and John Heath-Stubbs's *Artorius* (1973). Skinner brings back Arthur and Merlin to support freedom and religious faith against repression and barbarism in the year A.D. 2000; Heath-Stubbs uses the Arthurian story to comment upon contemporary life.

The many literary allusions and the wry humor of Heath-Stubbs's poem make it one of the most entertaining treatments of the legend in verse. However, the range of forms with which the poet experiments throughout the poem means that it has as much in common with the sequences of short poems as it does with longer narrative verse. The present trend in Arthurian poetry is clearly toward the former, and in the hands of skilled practitioners like Atwood and Heath-Stubbs these works give ample evidence that the poetic form remains vigorous, even though it has been overshadowed by prose fiction in recent years. [RHT]

Merriman, James Douglas. *The Flower of Kings: A Study of the Arthurian Legend in England Between 1485 and 1835.* Lawrence: University Press of Kansas, 1973.

Northup, Clark S., and John J. Parry. "The Arthurian Legends: Modern Retellings of the Old Stories." *Journal of English and Germanic Philology,* 43 (1944), 173–221.

Reimer, Stephen R. "The Arthurian Legends in Contemporary English Literature, 1945–1981." *Bulletin of Bibliography,* 38 (1981), 128–38, 149.

Staines, David. "King Arthur in Victorian Fiction." In *The Worlds of Victorian Fiction,* ed. Jerome H. Buckley. Cambridge, Mass., and London: Harvard University Press, 1975, pp. 267–93.

Starr, Nathan Comfort, *King Arthur Today: The Arthurian Legend in English and American Literature, 1901–1953*. Gainesville: University of Florida Press, 1954.

Taylor, Beverly, and Elisabeth Brewer. *The Return of King Arthur: British and American Arthurian Literature Since 1800*. Woodbridge, Suffolk: Boydell and Brewer, 1983.

Thompson, Raymond H. "Arthurian Legend and Modern Fantasy." In *Survey of Modern Fantasy Literature*, ed. Frank N. Magill. Edgehill Cliffs, N.J.: Salem, 1983, Vol. 5, pp. 2299–315.

——— . *The Return from Avalon: A Study of the Arthurian Legend in Modern Fiction*. Westport, Conn.: Greenwood, 1985.

"ENID": *see* TENNYSON, ALFRED LORD.

ENID: *A LYRIC PLAY:* *see* RHYS, ERNEST.

ENID AND NIMUË: *THE TRUE AND THE FALSE:* *see* TENNYSON, ALFRED LORD.

ENTRÉE D'ESPAGNE, L', an incomplete Franco-Italian romance epic dated ca. 1300–50, by an anonymous Paduan of considerable literary skill and erudition. The elaborate *unicum* manuscript probably circulated among the courts of Mantua, Ferrara, and the prehumanistic circles of Padua. Testimony to francophilism in both language and content, it forms a 15,805-line prelude to the Oxford *Chanson de Roland*, narrating events of the Spanish campaign including the battle for Pamplona, conquest of which takes place in the sequel *Prise de Pampelune*. The poet was familiar with much extant epic and romance, as well as texts now lost; the brief Oxford allusions to Nobles are amplified to a major episode, in which the friction between Charles and Roland that is a major theme of the first 11,000 lines escalates to violent confrontation. Part II, opening with a second prologue claiming greater originality of material, reveals the influence of Arthurian texts despite the Paduan's declaration that his "gloriose cançons" is unlike "les flabes d'Artu." The Roland who abandons the French campaign is depicted as a *chevalier errant* wandering aimlessly through trackless forests. A restorative fountain in the wilderness is the site of his *planctus*, in which Roland's lamentation over loss of chivalric status recalls the exiled Tristan. The author mentions Galahad, Meliadus, and others, and he evokes the Grail quest as a model of resolute activity. Roland's questlike voyage to the Orient, initially undertaken as a vindictive act after Charles had struck him with a mailed glove, develops into an educative experience for the hero. Denying even his name during the initial *aventures*, Roland wins back his identity as heroic and courtly knight via a series of trials. Having established himself as the finest knight serving the Persian Sultan, Roland is ready to return to Spain and carry on the fight for Pamplona. Immediately prior to his reunion with the French he encounters the hermit Samson, an episode that suggests parallels between the two men in their quest for chivalric and spiritual perfection and recalls episodes from Grail texts. The Roland who rejoins Charles has a new sense of the Christian uses of knighthood transcending the *Entrée's* earlier epic and secular romance models. [NB-C]

❧ Thomas, Antoine, ed. *L'Entrée d'Espagne: chanson de geste franco-italienne, publiée d'après le manuscrit unique de Venise.* 2 vols. Paris: Champion, 1913.

EPISTOLA AD WARINUM: see HENRY OF HUNTINGDON.

EREC: see HARTMANN VON AUE.

EREC ET ENIDE: see CHRÉTIEN DE TROYES; CHRÉTIEN DE TROYES, BURGUNDIAN ADAPTATIONS OF.

EREC IN PROSE, an anonymous French text dating from the thirteenth century. Although its editor considered it to be a vestigial Erec romance, it is less an autonomous work than a narrative sequence interlaced with other prose episodes in *La Folie Lancelot.* Despite its title, the *Erec in Prose* is only distantly related to Chrétien de Troyes's romance about Erec (Enide is absent, and there are only a few narrative echoes of the earlier poem); nor is it to be confused with the fifteenth-century *L'Histoire du noble et vaillant chevalier Erec*, a prose adaptation of Chrétien's romance (*see* CHRÉTIEN DE TROYES, BURGUNDIAN ADAPTATIONS OF).

The text recounts the quest conducted by a number of knights who are seeking Lancelot; Erec is among them, and it is in this quest that he first demonstrates his abilities and establishes his reputation as a knight. Eventually, the quest is abandoned, and the second half of the work recounts a number of miscellaneous episodes (e.g., a series of battles with Gauvain) that are not part of a linear or logical sequence of events but are elaborations of a specific motif, character, or scene. [NJL]

❧ Pickford, Cedric E., ed. *Erec: roman arthurien en prose.* Geneva: Droz, 1968.

EREX SAGA, an Old Norse prose adaptation of Chrétien de Troyes's *Erec et Enide.* There is no internal indication of time or circumstance of origin, as there is for *Ívens saga*, but it seems reasonable to assume that the original translation was connected with the court of the Norwegian king Hákon Hákonarson (r. 1217–63), responsible for the translation of *Tristrams saga, Ívens saga* (probably), and several other works of like provenance. The two primary manuscripts are seventeenth-century paper; two small vellum fragments from about 1500 preserve only nine lines of text.

Erex, one of King Arthur's twelve champions, rides out unarmed one day to accompany the Queen. He is forced to suffer insults and a blow from a dwarf, the servant of an unknown knight. After obtaining his arms, Erex rides after the knight and defeats him in a joust. He thereby avenges the disgrace and coincidentally wins the hand of the fair Evida. Erex now devotes himself to his bride to such an extent that some accuse him of neglecting his knightly duties. When he hears of this, he sets out with Evida on a series of adventures to reestablish his reputation. In the course of this journey, Erex manages, among other things, to defeat eight robbers, fight an evil earl, and rescue knights and ladies from giants, a dragon, and a band of seven armed men. He concludes by defeating a single champion in a wondrous garden. Erex, fully rehabilitated, can now return to Arthur's court, where he is crowned king, since his father has died. Erex and Evida go to their kingdom, rule it well, and have two distinguished sons.

The saga thus reproduces much of the general outline of its French original, but it rearranges and condenses episodes, adds two new ones (the dragon and the seven armed men), and supplies a brief epilogue. There are changes in characterization, motivation, and the role of women. We have here a clear attempt at adaptation to an indigenous model, the sagas of the Icelanders. [FWB]

Blaisdell, Foster W., ed. *Erex saga Artuskappa.* Copenhagen: Munksgaard, 1965.

———, and Marianne E. Kalinke, trans. *Erex Saga and Ívens Saga.* Lincoln: University of Nebraska Press, 1977.

Kalinke, Marianne E. *King Arthur, North-by-Northwest.* Copenhagen: Reitzel, 1981.

ERSKINE, JOHN (1879–1951), American author of two Arthurian novels, both urbane, witty, and thoroughly modern in outlook. The first, *Galahad* (1926), is the story of Elaine, a level-headed, strong-willed girl determined to have a child by Lancelot, resourceful enough to succeed, and clever enough to bide her time until Lancelot acknowledges his son and takes him to court. There, Guinevere, who enjoys manipulating knights, turns Galahad into a priggish idealist who censures his parents when he discovers that they are not married, walks away from Guinevere when he learns that she and Lancelot are lovers, and goes off in search of the Grail. Lancelot, on his way to a tournament, meets the second Elaine and is unwittingly the cause of her death. Lancelot, later as a religious, ponders the ironies of his life. Erskine ignores the tragic and smiles gently but knowingly at the romantic aspects of the story.

In *Tristan and Isolde* (1932), he again explores what happens to an idealist who discovers the truth about the people he admires. In this case, it is Palamede, who journeys from the East to find the idealized people described by his Christian slave/tutor. What he finds in Cornwall is Isolde, for whom he cultivates a hopeless love; Brangain, whom he rescues and who loves him, but with a clear-eyed sense of herself as a real person; and a sadly disillusioning view of chivalric knighthood in the persons of Mark, Tristan, and Segurade. In the end, Palamede is baptized, wounds Tristan, brings Isolde to him, and leaves for the Holy Land, hotly pursued by Brangain in a denouement that reads like a comedy of errors. [MAG]

&. Erskine, John. *Galahad: Enough of His Life to Explain His Reputation.* New York: Grosset and Dunlap, 1926.
——— . *Tristan and Isolde: Restoring Palamede.* Indianapolis: Bobbs-Merrill, 1932.

ERWÄHLTE, DER: *see* MANN, THOMAS.

ESCANOR: *see* GIRART D'AMIENS.

ESTOIRE DE MERLIN, L': *see* VULGATE CYCLE.

ESTOIRE DEL SAINT GRAAL, L': *see* VULGATE CYCLE.

ESTORIA DE MERLÍN, LA, a fragmentary fourteenth-century Spanish translation of the French Post-Vulgate *Merlin*; it narrates the beginning portion of Merlin's life, from his birth to his dictation of Arthur's story to Blaise. [NJL]

&. Pietsch, Karl, ed. *Spanish Grail Fragments.* Chicago: University of Chicago Press, 1924, Vol. 1, pp. 57–81.

ESTORIA DEL NOBLE VASPASIANO, LA ("The History of the Noble Vespasian"), a late-medieval adaptation of a prosified version of the late twelfth- or early thirteenth-century French poem *La Venjance Nostre Seigneur* concerning the destruction of Jerusalem. Two Spanish incunabula (ca. 1491–94 and 1499), a Portuguese incunabulum (1496), and a seventeenth-century Spanish manuscript copy survive. Distinguishing these texts from extant French, Provençal, and Catalan versions of *La Venjance Nostre Seigneur* is Emperor Vespasian's allegorical vision—derived from Evalach's vision in the *Estoire del Saint Graal*, the first branch of the Vulgate Cycle—of a child entering a doorless room, a phenomenon that convinces Vespasian of the authenticity of Jesus Christ's Incarnation. An interpolated reference to Joseph of Arimathea's imprisonment would also seem to be taken from the *Estoire del Saint Graal.* [HLS]

&. Bonilla y San Martín, Adolfo, ed. *La destruición de Jerusalén.* In *Libros de caballerías, segunda parte.* Madrid: Bailly-Baillière, 1908, pp. 377–401.

Hook, David, and Penny Newman, eds. *Estoria do muy nobre Vespesiano Emperador de Roma (Lisbon, 1496)*. Exeter: University of Exeter, 1983.

ÉTERNEL RETOUR, L': see COCTEAU, JEAN.

ÉTIENNE DE ROUEN, author of *Draco Normannicus* ("The Norman Dragon"), a rhymed Latin chronicle completed ca. 1169. For 350 lines in the second book, Étienne tells about the exchange of letters between King Arthur and Henry II over the rights of sovereignty of Brittany. Arthur boasts of his battle with Lucius Hiberius and adds details not in Geoffrey of Monmouth. He has been healed by his sister Morgana, a nymph who has granted him earthly immortality in a kingdom in the southern hemisphere. Arthur retains his ultimate authority over Brittany but grants Henry feudal rights as his vassal. [MLD]

Étienne de Rouen. *Draco Normannicus*, ed. Richard Howlett. In *Chronicles of the Reigns of Stephen, Henry II, and Richard I*. London: Longman, Trübner, 1855, Vol. 2, pp. 589ff.

EUFEMIA (d. 1312), queen of Hákon Magnússon of Norway (r. 1299–1319), had translated into Swedish verse three chivalric romances. These works, composed in 1303 on the occasion of the marriage of Eufemia's daughter Ingeborg to Duke Erik of Sweden, are known collectively as the *Eufemiavisor*. Included in the collection are *Flores och Blanzeflor* (a translation of the French *Floire et Blancheflor*), *Hertig Fredrik* (a tale whose original is not extant in French or Norwegian), and *Ivan Lejonriddaren* (a translation of Chrétien de Troyes's *Yvain*). Only the last translation belongs to the corpus of Arthurian literature. *Ivan Lejonriddaren* shares some affinities with *Ívens saga*, the Norwegian version of *Yvain* translated during the reign of Hákon Hákonarson (r. 1217–63), but scholars disagree concerning the source of the Swedish translation. The popularity of this work extended into Denmark, where it was in turn translated into Danish. Eufemia's contribution lies in the dissemination of Arthurian materials and in the exportation of Norwegian literary tastes into the rest of Scandinavia. [IJR]

Leach, Henry G. *Angevin Britain and Scandinavia*. Cambridge, Mass.: Harvard University Press, 1921.

Ståhle, Carl Ivar. "Eufemiavisorna." In *Kulturhistorisk leksikon for nordisk middelalder fra vikingetid til reformationstid*. Copenhagen: Rosenkilde and Bagger, 1958–78, Vol. 4, cols. 55–57.

EUFEMIAVISOR: see EUFEMIA; *IVAN LEJONRIDDAREN*.

ÉVIÈNE: see LADY OF THE LAKE.

EXCALIBUR, Arthur's sword, called Caliburnus (Latin *chalybs* 'steel') by Geoffrey of Monmouth. Through much of the medieval French tradition (e.g., the Prose *Lancelot*), the sword belonged at one time to Gawain, but in later works it is the exclusive property of the King. In certain texts (and in popular Arthurian lore), Excalibur is also the Sword in the Stone, but such an identification is incompatible with the tradition, found, for example, in the Post-Vulgate Cycle and Malory, whereby the sword is given to Arthur (and finally taken from him) by a hand in the lake. Merlin, who brings Arthur to the Lady of the Lake to receive Excalibur, informs the King that the scabbard is worth far more than the sword itself, for the former will protect its bearer from injury. Despite this fact, it is the sword rather than its scabbard that has captured the imagination of later writers and readers.

In the Vulgate *Mort Artu*, Arthur orders Girflet to throw the sword into the enchanted lake in order that it not fall into corrupt hands. Twice Girflet disobeys, first exchanging Excalibur for his own sword, then hiding it while throwing the scabbard into the water. Twice rebuked by Arthur, he finally throws the sword into the lake, where a hand emerging from the water catches it, brandishes it, and then disappears. (*See also* ARMS AND ARMOR.) [NJL]

EXCALIBUR: see BOORMAN, JOHN; LAUBENTHAL, SANDERS ANNE.

EXCALIBUR!: see KANE, GIL, AND JOHN JAKES.

FAERIE QUEENE, THE: *see* SPENSER, EDMUND.

FAILURE OF SIR GAWAIN, THE: *see* STANMORE HALL
TAPESTRIES.

FAILURE OF SIR LANCELOT, THE: *see* STANMORE HALL
TAPESTRIES.

"FAIR ESELT, THE": *see* SAUL, GEORGE BRANDON.

FAIR UNKNOWN: *see CANTARI DI CARDUINO, I;* CHESTRE,
THOMAS; FUETRER, ULRICH; RAOUL DE HOUDENC; RENAUT
DE BEAUJEU; ROBERT DE BLOIS; *VALLET À LA COTE MAL
TAILLIÉE, LE; WIGOLEIS VOM RADE;* WIRNT VON GRAFENBERG.

"FAIRY BRIDE, THE": *see* BULWER-LYTTON, EDWARD GEORGE.

FAIRY OF THE LAKE, THE: see THELWALL, JOHN.

FALL OF PRINCES: see LYDGATE, JOHN.

FARADAY, W. BARNARD, author of *Pendragon* (1930), a rambling and sentimental historical romance about Arthur as *dux bellorum* in the struggle against the Saxons. The book is redeemed by some entertaining passages of verbal humor and by its portrayal of the keen-witted Gwendaello (Guenevere). [RHT]

ᴥ Faraday, W. Barnard. *Pendragon*. London: Methuen, 1930.

FATTI DE SPAGNA, LI, a fourteenth-century Lombard narrative of fifty-six chapters, of which 1–38 are modeled on a lost version of the *Entrée d'Espagne*, 39–46 on a continuation of the *Entrée*, and 47–56 on the *Chanson de Roland*. Its principal innovation from romance is the motivation for Ganelon's betrayal in the irresistible love offered him by Braidamante, wife of King Marsile. Although not specifically an Arthurian text, the work uses numerous motifs characteristic of the Matter of Britain. (*See also* ENTRÉE D'ESPAGNE.) [NB-C]

ᴥ Ruggieri, Ruggero M., ed. *Li Fatti de Spagna*. Modena: Società Editrice Modenese, 1951.

FAULA, LA: see TORROELLA, GUILLEM.

FAWCETT, EDGAR (1847–1904), American author of *The New King Arthur: An Opera Without Music* (1885), an entertaining parody in the style of W.S. Gilbert that sets out to improve upon Tennyson's "creditable" treatment of Arthurian legend. [RHT]

ᴥ Fawcett, Edgar. *The New King Arthur: An Opera Without Music*. New York and London: Funk and Wagnalls, 1885.

FAZIO DEGLI UBERTI (ca. 1301–1367), a Tuscan poet who makes several references to Arthurian material in *Il Dittamondo*. In this encyclopedic poem in *terza rima*, he narrates his journey through the known world under the guidance of Solinus, the famed classical geographer. During the visits to Brittany (Book IV, Chapter 22) and Great Britain (IV, 23–26), Fazio describes numerous sites by their association with Arthurian characters: for example, Tintagel is recalled as the place where the ivy plant united the tombs of Tristan and Isolde (IV, 22, ll. 100–09); London is the location of the tower that Guinevere defended against Mordred (IV, 23, ll. 52–53); Gaunes is alluded to as the scene of the death of Dorins, son of Claudas, the usurper king (IV, 22, ll. 91–92). Among the other numerous references are Camelot (laid to ruin by Mark; IV, 23, l. 58), the Castle of the Dolorous Gard (where Lancelot began his chivalric career; IV, 23, ll. 55–57), the castle of Penevric (in which Erec and Enide consoled themselves; IV, 23, ll. 61–62), and the valley where Tristan slew the giant Nabon (IV, 23, ll. 70–72). The wide variety of sources for these place-names and the legends associated with them—e.g., *Lancelot, Tristan, Mort Artu, Palamedes, Erec et Enide*—attests to the broad culture and synthesizing attitude of Fazio degli Uberti and suggests the extent of general penetration of Arthurian material into Italy by the middle of the fourteenth century. [CK]

ed Fazio degli Uberti. *Il Dittamondo e le rime*, ed. Giuseppe Corsi. 2 vols. Bari: Laterza, 1952.
Gardner, Edmund G. *The Arthurian Legend in Italian Literature*. London: Dent, 1930, pp. 222–28.

FEBUSSO E BREUSSO, an Italian *cantare* thought by Branca to be the oldest extant representative of this genre (ca. 1325–35). The work retells the cavern episode from *Palamedes*. Its narrator is an old man who recounts to the unpolished knight Breusso the famous deeds of the mighty Febusso. [SJN]

ed Branca, Vittore. *Il cantare trecentesco e il Boccaccio del Filostrato e del Teseida*. Florence: Sansoni, 1936.

FERGUS: *see* GUILLAUME LE CLERC.

FERGUUT, a Middle Dutch verse adaptation of the Old French *Fergus* by Guillaume le Clerc. The adaptation, probably written in the second half of the thirteenth century, runs to 5,604 lines. Up to the moment when Ferguut sets out to look for his beloved (l. 2202), the Middle Dutch poet follows his Old French model, after which he increasingly follows his own path. In doing this, he ignored the historical implications of the *Fergus*. The topography of the *Ferguut*, for instance, is almost completely arbitrary, in contrast with the French source. The text is extant in one manuscript, Leiden, Universiteitsbibliotheek Ltk. 191, dating from about 1350. [BB]

ed Rombauts, E., Norbert de Paepe, and Max J.M. de Haan, eds. *Ferguut*. Culemborg: Tjeenk Willink, 1976.

FERREIRA DE VASCONCELOS, JORGE, author of the *Memorial das Proezas da Segunda Távola Redonda* ("Record of the Achievements of the Second Round Table"), a sixteenth-century Portuguese romance of chivalry. It continues the story of the Round Table beyond Arthur's death, giving Sagramor, one of Arthur's younger knights, heroic prominence. The creation of a second Round Table was an apparent pretext for the description in the romance of an actual tournament, held in 1552 at Xabregas, where Prince Dom João was armed as a knight, reflecting the desires of the Portuguese court for grandeur corresponding to that of medieval myth. The work was printed in Coimbra in 1567 but may have been composed shortly after the 1552 tournament. [HLS]

• Ferreira de Vasconcelos, Jorge. *Memorial das Proezas da Segunda Tavola Redonda*. Coimbra: João de Barreyra, 1567; 2nd ed. Lisbon, 1867.

    Moisés, Massaud. *A Novela de Cavalaria no Quinhentismo Português: O Memorial das Proezas da Segunda Tavola Redonda de Jorge Ferreira de Vasconcelos*. São Paulo: Universidade de São Paulo, 1957.

FEUER UND SCHWERT—DIE LEGENDE VON TRISTAN UND ISOLDE: *see* VON FÜRSTENBERG, VEITH.

FIELD, MICHAEL, is the pseudonym of two English writers, Katharine H. Bradley (1846–1914) and Edith E. Cooper (1862–1913), whose interest in Tristan produced verse drama: "Tristan de Leonois" in *The Accuser* (1911) and *The Tragedy of Pardon* (1911). The latter's cast includes Mark, Tristan, Jovelin, his son Kahedin, the Bishop of Thames, Melot (a dwarf), Kurvenal, three Iseults, and Brangaena. The scenes range from Dublin, Tintagel, Caerleon, and the Cornish Forest to Parmenie and Arundel. Plot elements include the love elixir, the persecution of Brangaena, Iseult's trial by ordeal, the love grotto, the significant sail, the joint burial, and the Wagnerian *Liebestod* motif. [MAW]

• Field, Michael. *The Tragedy of Pardon*. London: Sidgwick and Jackson, 1911.

    ——— . "Tristan de Leonois." In *The Accuser*. London: Sidgwick and Jackson, 1911, pp. 77–149.

FIELDING, HENRY (1707–1754), enjoyed success as a comic dramatist before turning to the novel. His *Tragedy of Tragedies; or The Life and Death of Tom Thumb the Great* appeared before the London public in a number of versions. *Tom Thumb; A Tragedy*, in two acts, was first performed as an afterpiece at the Little Theatre on 24 April 1730 and ran for forty nights. The text, with alterations, was published soon after, with a preface, prologue, and epilogue guying Colley Cibber's style. On 30 November 1730, a new act, not by Fielding but possibly by Thomas Cooke, was added; it was a malicious satire on the selection of Colley Cibber as Poet Laureate, in succession to Laurence Eusdon. The play appeared in definitive three-act form on 24 March 1731. *The Battle of the Poets* was omitted, but there was additional dramatic material and a new preface, ascribed to H. Scriblerius Secundus, and an apparatus of mock-critical notes by the same author, who is, of course, Fielding. In 1733, Mrs. Eliza Haywood and William Hatchett fashioned an opera out of *Tom Thumb*, and Thomas Arne wrote the music. That year, the libretto was set again, by the Saxon composer Johann Friedrich Lampe, but the work was performed only once. In 1780, Kane O'Hara took elements from both the play and libretto for

Tom Thumb, A Burletta, which was produced repeatedly throughout the nineteenth century.

Tom Thumb portrays the misfortunes of its diminutive hero. King Arthur wishes to reward his favorite's victories by bestowing the hand of his daughter Huncamunca, but jealous Queen Dollallolla and, in the later version, Glumdalca, Queen of the Giants, thwart the plan. A satire on pedantic criticism and heroic drama, *Tom Thumb* parodies such playwrights as Dryden, Lee, Otway, Young, Theobald, and Thomson. Fielding's verve ensures that his play still amuses after many of his butts have been almost forgotten. [CNS]

🕮 Fielding, John. *Tom Thumb*. In *Burlesque Plays of the Eighteenth Century*, ed. Simon Trussler. London: Oxford University Press, 1969.
———. *The Tragedy of Tragedies*. In *Eighteenth-Century Comedy*, ed. W.D. Taylor and Simon Trussler. London: Oxford University Press, 1969.
Dudden, F. Homes. *Henry Fielding: His Life, Works and Times*. 2 vols. Oxford: Clarendon, 1952.

FIGHT WITH SIR MARHAUS, THE: *see* STAINED GLASS.

FIGURE OF ARTHUR, THE: *see* WILLIAMS, CHARLES.

FILMS. Arthurian romance was first introduced to film audiences by the American *Lancelot and Elaine* (1910), the 1919 serial *Adventures of Sir Galahad*, and especially through adaptations of Mark Twain's *A Connecticut Yankee in King Arthur's Court*. A silent version, with Harry Meyers as Sir Boss, appeared around 1920. In a 1931 update, starring Will Rogers and Maureen O'Sullivan, the tone shifted from satire to spoof, and then to romantic comedy in a 1949 musical version starring Bing Crosby.

Comedy continued in a British film called *King Arthur Was a Gentleman* (1942). Arthur Askey played a meek soldier who rescues his friends from captivity in the belief that he has King Arthur's magic sword. The focus shifted to adventure in the 1950s. *Knights of the Round Table* (1953), MGM's first widescreen film, was a colorful but empty minispectacular, with Robert Taylor as Lancelot and Ava Gardner as Guenevere. In *The Siege of the Saxons* (1954), Janette Scott played a princess who thwarts a villainous knight with the assistance of an outlaw. In *The Black Knight* (1954), Alan Ladd played a swordmaker who poses as a knight to foil the schemes of King Mark. The preoccupation with tedious adventure culminated in *Lancelot and Guinevere* (1963), produced and directed by Cornel Wilde, who also starred as Lancelot.

The year 1963 also saw the appearance of Walt Disney's *The Sword in the Stone*, directed by Wolfgang Reitherman. Based upon T.H. White's novel of the same name, this animated feature for children is considered a premier example of the studio's expertise in animation, lavish backdrops, effervescent action, and unforgettable characters. Less successful was *Camelot* (1967), a musical starring Richard Harris and Vanessa Redgrave. Based upon the Lerner and Loewe stage success, which was in its turn based upon White's *The Once and Future King*, this account of the ill-fated love between Lancelot and Guenevere emphasizes romance and idealism.

By contrast, *Monty Python and the Holy Grail* (1975), directed by Terry Gilliam and Terry Jones, and written and acted by them and the rest of the Monty Python troop, mixes spoof, satire, visual gags, non sequiturs, outrageous juxtapositions, and rollicking good humor to delight fans who know the legend well. More recently, *Excalibur* (1981), directed by John Boorman and starring Nicol Williamson as Merlin, mingles the fantasy of magic and legend with the graphic realism of scenes of violent battle and explicit sexuality. Stunning photography, strong acting, and a philosophical tone have won high praise from critics.

Arthur the King is a "made-for-television" movie presented by CBS-TV in April 1985. In this film, directed by Clive Donner, an American tourist visits Stonehenge and falls into the Cave where Merlin and Niniane have lived for a thousand years. Merlin's magic permits her to watch events unfolding at Camelot. The focus is on Guinevere's abduction and eventual rescue by Lancelot and on the love of Gawain and Ragnell. The film makes no significant contribution to either the substance or the dissemination of the Arthurian legend.

While most English-language films have been undistinguished, the French films have all been impressive. Jean Cocteau's *L'Éternel Retour* (1943), starring Jean Marais and Madeleine Sologne, is a masterly transposition of the love story of Tristan and Isolde into a twentieth-century setting.

Tristan et Iseult (1972) is a beautifully filmed nontraditional version of the story by Yvan Lagrange that uses striking visual images to evoke its mythic basis. Lagrange's use of an original film score of electronic composition, to the virtual exclusion of dialogue, creates a repetitive ritualistic effect in keeping with his artistic interpretation.

Directed by Robert Bresson, *Lancelot du Lac* (1974) won the International Critics Prize at the Cannes Film Festival for its depiction of the spiritual pall that settles over the knights at their failure to win the Grail. The photography shows the pageantry against a background of dark forests and a dying age. The film has vision, mysticism, and elegant style.

Perceval (1978), directed by Eric Rohmer, is a jewel. It turns Chrétien de Troyes's poem into a musical film with the look of an illuminated manuscript. Shot by Nestor Admendros entirely within a studio, using stylized painted sets, a chorus of medieval musicians, and a wide-eyed Fabrice Luchini as the wise fool Perceval, the film both presents and interprets Chrétien's masterpiece, making it accessible without destroying its complexity and depth.

German directors have also been drawn, although less frequently than the French, to Arthurian subjects. The Parsifal story provided inspiration for Hans Jürgen Syberberg (*Parsifal*, 1981–82) and for Richard Blank's 1980 television film based on Wolfram. Syberberg also made a Grail cycle (*Der Gral*), and

Veith von Fürstenberg filmed the story of Tristan and Isolde in *Feuer und Schwert* (1981). [MAG/RHT]

FINAL QUEST, THE: *see* MONACO, RICHARD.

FINKEL, GEORGE, author of the militaristic novel *Twilight Province* (1967). Bedwyr records the struggle against the Saxons by a small Roman settlement in the north of Britain during the sixth century, followed by the attempt to unite Romans throughout the island under Artyr as *Comes Britanniarum*. His account seeks to demythologize the story. [SRR]

&▶ Finkel, George. *Twilight Province*. Sydney: Angus and Robertson, 1967. (Published in the U.S. as *Watch Fires to the North*. New York: Viking, 1968.)

FINNEGANS WAKE: *see* JOYCE, JAMES.

FIORIO E BIANCIFIORE, an Italian *cantare* of the thirteenth or early fourteenth century, containing Arthurian allusions, thought to be the principal source of Boccaccio's *Filocolo*. [SJN]

&▶ Branca, Vittore. *Il cantare trecentesco e il Boccaccio del Filostrato e del Teseida*. Florence: Sansoni, 1936.

FIRELORD: *see* GODWIN, PARKE.

FISHER KING, the keeper of the Grail; sometimes called the Rich Fisher. Perhaps an avatar of Bran the Blessed, the Fisher King is the wounded occupant of the Grail castle in Chrétien de Troyes's *Perceval* and other works. He and his land could have been restored had Perceval asked about the Grail procession; Perceval's failure to do so necessitates the Grail quest. Eventually, Chrétien's hero learns that the Fisher King is his cousin (although in other texts he is Perceval's uncle or grandfather). Chrétien does not give him a name, but in Wolfram von Eschenbach he is called Anfortas.

In the work of Robert de Boron, the Fisher King is identified with Hebron or Bron, Joseph of Arimathea's brother-in-law, who catches the fish that is placed on the Grail table. The Didot-*Perceval* continues and concludes the story of the Fisher King, as the work's hero returns to the Grail castle, asks the Grail question, and cures the king. [NJL]

FLECHTUNGEN: DER FALL PARTZIFALL: *see* WORKSHOP MOOSACH.

FLORIANT ET FLORETE, a French romance of 8,278 lines, probably written in the third quarter of the thirteenth century. The author uses the "lost childhood" motif found elsewhere (e.g., the Prose *Lancelot* and Ulrich von Zatzikhoven's *Lanzelet*), and the marriage-crisis-resolution structure found in Chrétien de Troyes's *Erec* and *Yvain*. Floriant is the posthumous son of a king of Sicily. He is abducted by Morgan le Fay, educated, and sent to Arthur's court, where he remains only briefly, having to return to Sicily to defend his mother, who is besieged by the wicked seneschal of the Emperor of Constantinople. During the battle, in which he is assisted by Arthur, Floriant falls in love with the emperor's daughter, Florete, whom he marries after defeating the seneschal. After accusations of inactivity, Floriant sets out, as *li Biaus Sauvages* ("the Fair Savage"), in the company of Florete, proves his prowess once more, and settles down in Palermo. A white stag one day leads him to Morgan's castle, where Florete is also taken. The conclusion of the romance is lacking. [KB]

• Williams, Harry F., ed. *Floriant et Florete.* Ann Arbor: University of Michigan Press, 1947.

FOLIE LANCELOT, LA ("The Madness of Lancelot"), a French prose romance, dating from ca. 1230, that offers episodes concerning Lancelot's madness and the youthful adventures of Perceval and Galahad. The work is based on material from the Vulgate and from the Prose *Tristan*; it appears to provide narrative preparation for the *Mort Artu*. [NJL]

• Bogdanow, Fanni, ed. *La Folie Lancelot: A Hitherto Unidentified Portion of the Suite du Merlin Contained in MSS. B.N. fr. 112 and 12559.* Tübingen: Niemeyer, 1965.

FOLIE TRISTAN DE BERNE, LA ("The Madness of Tristan"), some 574 lines that relate essentially the same material as the Oxford *Folie*. Tristan's allusions to his past adventures are less rigorously organized than in Oxford, the style is less polished, and the text is more closely related to Béroul's *Tristan* than to Thomas's. Composed in the late twelfth century and preserved in a single, rather defective, manuscript, Bern Library 354, the Berne *Folie* is in a northeastern dialect of Old French. [WWK]

• Bédier, Joseph, ed. *Les Deux poèmes de la Folie Tristan.* Paris: Didot, 1907.

FOLIE TRISTAN D'OXFORD, LA, a twelfth-century Old French poem of 998 lines that recounts how Tristan, banished from King Mark's court, disguises himself as a fool in order to see Queen Iseut. At court, he amuses Mark with his wit as he makes allusions to his past with Iseut. After Mark leaves for a hunt, Iseut remains skeptical until Tristan is warmly greeted by the dog Husdent. The work is found in a single manuscript in Oxford's Bodleian Library (Douce d 6) immediately after a truncated text of Thomas's *Tristan*, to which it is closely related. [WWK]

• Bédier, Joseph, ed. *Les Deux poèmes de la Folie Tristan.* Paris: Didot, 1907.

FOLKLORE. Despite the existence of the large numbers of carefully composed literary texts that take Arthur as their subject, his legend is inextricably bound up with the conventional materials of folklore. There have been attempts to establish a folk origin for Arthurian romances themselves, in the form of pagan rituals, the memory of which was preserved in oral tradition, expanded, and finally fixed in written form. Those attempts have not been wholly persuasive, and most scholars would hesitate to go so far. It is nonetheless clear that popular beliefs very early grew up around Arthur, and the relation of folklore and literary tradition is certainly reciprocal: while folk motifs may have contributed to the legend's dissemination, many of them may in fact have been furthered, if not formed, by the King's popularity. The latter situation appears the more common, and Loomis suggested that many Arthurian themes were borrowed not from folklore but from early sagas and other texts. He concluded that, although many elements of Arthurian stories "survive in Celtic and other folktales collected within the last century, it would be a mistake to infer their origin in 'folklore' in the strict sense of that term."

Folklore related to Arthurian subjects falls into two categories: the character of Arthur himself, and themes and motifs that find their way into Arthurian works. The former is related primarily to the legends of Arthur's survival and return, beliefs that have persisted nearly to this day. A number of stories have traditionally been told about the discovery of Arthur and his knights in various circumstances (sleeping in a cave, riding in a nocturnal hunt). Some versions that present them as sleeping insist that a call for help in their presence would immediately rouse the knights and bring them forth to battle the enemies of England. A thirteenth-century text, the *Lanercost Chronicle*, records the story of a bishop who met Arthur face to face; to ensure that the bishop would be believed when recounting the meeting, Arthur magically gave him the power to produce a butterfly whenever he opened his fist. In contrast to the detail of such stories, other folk beliefs are only vague associations, as witness the link, attested in Somerset, between Arthur and birds (especially the crow or raven).

It is hardly surprising that Arthurian and other romances cast much folk material in literary form. They draw heavily on traditional motifs, many of which Loomis and others traced to sources in Celtic myth and folklore. For example, while we find in legend numerous examples of stakes supporting severed human heads, it appears that the Celtic world provides the only folk antecedent for the particular situation of Chrétien de Troyes's *Erec et Enide*, in which a final stake is reserved for the hero's head. Among other Arthurian motifs that offer folk analogues—and that may be of folk origin—we may count the revolving or disappearing castle, the beheading test, chastity tests involving horns or mantles, fairy mistresses, the storm-producing spring, and perhaps the question test found in the Perceval stories. Such motifs are less "Arthurian folklore" per se than simply traditional materials appropriated by many authors, including those of Arthurian romance. (*See also* CAVE LEGEND; CELTIC ARTHURIAN LITERATURE; GLASTONBURY; JOSEPH OF ARIMATHEA; RETURN, LEGENDS OF ARTHUR'S; TOPOGRAPHY AND LOCAL LEGENDS.) [NJL]

❧ Brown, A.L. "Camlann and the Death of Arthur." *Folklore*, 72 (1961), 612–21.

Darrah, John. *The Real Camelot: Paganism and the Arthurian Romances.* London: Thames and Hudson, 1981.

Loomis, Roger Sherman. "Arthurian Tradition and Folklore." *Folklore*, 69 (1958), 1–25.

FOUKE FITZ WARIN, composed in Shropshire after 1250, relates the story of Arthur's squire, Cahus, as it occurs in the *Perlesvaus*. Originally written in verse, it is extant only in a later prose redaction. [NJL]

❧ Brandin, Louis, ed. *Fouke Fitz Warin.* Paris: Champion, 1930.

FOUQUÉ, FRIEDRICH BARON DE LA MOTTE (1777–1843), a Prussian nobleman of Huguenot descent. First active as a military officer, he became one of the most successful authors of the German romantic movement. Fouqué's reputation had waned sufficiently during his lifetime that he was, however, unable to find a publisher for his lengthy epic *Parcival* (1831–32). It is currently being prepared for publication from his literary remains by Frank Rainer Max and Ursula Rautenberg. *Parcival* is a tripartite, educational verse-novel in which a romantic revivification of the Middle Ages is professedly combined with an impressive enthusiasm for poetic experimentation. [UM/WCM]

❧ Max, Frank Rainer, and Ursula Rautenberg. In *Mittelalter-Rezeption II: Gesammelte Vorträge des 2. Salzburger Symposions*, ed. Jürgen Kühnel, Hans-Dieter Mück, Ursula Müller, and Ulrich Müller. Göppingen: Kümmerle, 1982.

FRANKLAND, EDWARD (1884–1958), an English author who developed his "Medraut and Gwenhwyvar," a short story about Arthur marching to fight the Saxons while his wife and nephew plot betrayal, into the historical novel *The Bear of Britain* (1944). Arthur is too honorable to seize absolute power after his victory at Badon, and his achievement is squandered through the selfish ambition of others. The somber vision is inspired by Gildas's diatribe against the greed, folly, treachery, and corruption of the British rulers. [RHT]

❧ Frankland, Edward. *The Bear of Britain.* London: MacDonald, 1944.

———. "Medraut and Gwenhwyvar." In *England Growing.* London: MacDonald, 1944, pp. 15–21.

FRAPPIER, JEAN (1900–1974), professor at the University of Paris–Sorbonne (1948–69). Frappier demonstrated broad interests in the major genres of medieval literature and philology and an abiding concern with the Renaissance, but his primary legacy was the furtherance of Arthurian studies. The demand for his works on *La Mort le Roi Artu, Le Roman breton, Etude sur Yvain, Le Mythe du graal,* and *Chrétien de Troyes* required that all of these be reissued at least once. Frappier's books are an indispensable point of departure for scholarly investigations, since he excelled at compressing the discoveries and theories of his predecessors into clear perspectives. He distilled his own carefully balanced interpretations from reasoned foundations and skillful reading of the texts. On the question of origins of French Arthurian romance, he tended toward acceptance of Celtic sources but never denied the possibility of learned (ecclesiastic) or popular influences, or the role of individual creativity. A bibliography of his works to 1969 may be found in *Mélanges Frappier*, Vol. 1 (1970). [JLG]

Foulon, Charles. "Jean Frappier (1900–1974)." *Bibliographical Bulletin of the International Arthurian Society*, 27 (1979), 238–41.

Malkiel, Yakov. "Jean Frappier: Dedication and Necrology (1900–74)." *Romance Philology*, 30 (1976), 4–8.

"FRAUW TRISTERAT HORN VON SAPHOIEN": *see* "DIS IST FRAUW TRISTERAT HORN VON SAPHOIEN."

FRENCH, ALLEN, author of a historical romance for juveniles, *Sir Marrok* (1902), in which a noble knight of Uther's court, who is transformed into a werewolf by an evil enchantress, nonetheless continues to protect his vassals. This didactic story extols the virtues of gratitude and fortitude in adversity, while it warns against being deceived by appearances. [RHT]

French, Allen. *Sir Marrok: A Tale of the Days of King Arthur.* New York: Century, 1902.

FRENCH ARTHURIAN LITERATURE. If the modern Arthur is to a considerable extent the property of the English-speaking world, it is only slight exaggeration to suggest that he was, in his literary manifestations, the invention of the French Middle Ages. Conversely, the history of French narrative literature during the Middle Ages is to a large extent the history of Arthurian literature. Arthur so captured the imagination of medieval writers and publics that he and his knights became the primary source of inspiration for at least two centuries (the twelfth and thirteenth), and the popularity of Arthurian themes continued unabated well into the sixteenth.

Not long after Wace, whose *Brut* stands between chronicle and romance, France produced its first and best writer of Arthurian romance, Chrétien de Troyes. In the late twelfth century, Chrétien wrote five romances that largely set the shape and direction of Arthurian literature for some time to come. His works are *Erec et Enide*; *Cligés*; *Lancelot* (or *Le Chevalier de la charrete*), which presents the love of Lancelot and Guenevere; *Yvain* (or *Le Chevalier au lion*); and the unfinished *Perceval* (or *Le Conte del Graal*), in which Chrétien introduces the Grail into world literature.

Soon after, Robert de Boron wrote *Joseph d'Arimathie*, in which he transformed the Grail from the holy but mysterious object it is in his predecessor into a holy relic whose meaning is entirely clear: it is the vessel in which Joseph of Arimathea caught Christ's blood after the Crucifixion. Robert also composed a *Merlin* romance, and while only a fragment of it survives it is known through two forms of a prose version (a part of the Vulgate Cycle and an introduction to the *Suite du Merlin*). We also have a prose Perceval romance, known as the Didot-*Perceval*, and a *Mort Artu* that may be prosifications or adaptations of lost works by Robert.

Both because Chrétien's *Perceval* was unfinished and because of the appeal of the Grail quest as a theme, the way was now clear for poets to compose sequels to his work, in order to bring that quest to a conclusion. The quest is in theory infinitely expandable, and the authors of the Continuations were nothing if not expansive. There were four Continuations, following alternately the adventures of Perceval and those of Chrétien's other hero, Gauvain. Taken together, the Continuations added nearly 60,000 lines to Grail literature.

The late twelfth and the thirteenth centuries produced a number of independent (i.e., noncyclic) romances, such as the early *Perlesvaus*, in which Gauvain fails the Grail test, as Perceval had done, and in which the latter frees the Grail castle. But, most notably, the thirteenth century produced the vast Arthurian cycles, characterized by length and increasing complexity (e.g., multiple quests and interlaced adventures). The great thirteenth-century prose Vulgate Cycle of Arthurian romance, from the first half of the century, consists of five works: the *Estoire del Saint Graal* and *Merlin* (probably written after the other three, before which they stand in the sequence established within the cycle), the *Lancelot*, the *Queste del Saint Graal*, and the *Mort (le Roi) Artu*. The Vulgate develops further the Joseph of Arimathea connection, the love of Lancelot and Guenevere, the choice and progress of Galahad as perfect Grail knight, and the Arthurian apocalypse.

The Vulgate was followed quickly by the Post-Vulgate *Roman du Graal*, a cycle dating 1230–40 and sometimes called the "Pseudo–Robert de Boron" cycle. The Post-Vulgate is not preserved intact, but it has been largely reconstructed, partially on the basis of extant translations in Spanish and Portuguese. Although portions of it follow the Vulgate quite closely, the apparent intention of the author(s) was to deemphasize the story of Lancelot and Guenevere's adulterous love and to concentrate instead on the Grail.

While Arthur and the Grail quest were being treated at length, another theme and set of characters were proving to have great popularity. The story of Tristan, Isolde, and Mark, while originally part of a different tradition, was soon attached (however loosely) to the Arthurian world. During the twelfth century, both Béroul and Thomas d'Angleterre composed Tristan romances, although both survive only in substantial fragments. Thomas's work is thoroughly and seriously courtly in nature, while Béroul, whose poem is traditionally (and perhaps erroneously) considered "primitive," has a good deal of fun at the expense of his characters without necessarily undermining the reader's sympathy for them.

Since the Tristan story was by nature episodic (involving brief encounters, separations, reconciliations, and further separations), a number of writers offer us the account of a single episode or a restricted sequence of events. The best known is *Chevrefueil*, Marie de France's lai that recounts a meeting of the lovers in the forest. Later texts have Tristan returning to court in disguise to see Isolde (the two *Folie Tristans*), assuming the role of a minstrel (*Tristan Ménestrel*, inserted into the Fourth Continuation of *Perceval*), or imitating birdcalls to offer her a pretext for joining him outside (*Tristan Rossignol*).

In contrast to these brief texts, the lengthy thirteenth-century Prose *Tristan* (or *Tristan Léonis*) links the lovers' story to those of Lancelot and Guenevere and to the Grail history. Here, Tristan is a friend of Lancelot and an active participant in the Grail quest, and the Prose *Tristan* completes the fusion of the Tristan story with those of Arthur, his knights, and the Grail.

Although the best-known romances from the twelfth and thirteenth centuries deal with the Grail quest, a number of writers chose instead to follow other paths, and one of the popular subjects was Gauvain. Throughout Chrétien's work, he had played a significant role, as a consummate knight but usually as a foil for the hero; and in *Perceval* he has obvious defects, notably pride, impetuousness, and frivolity. Later poets seized on his flaws and composed a number of "non-Grail" romances (most of them relatively short) in which, without being an object of derision, Gauvain becomes either a somewhat comical figure or a means of charting the progressive decline of chivalry. *Gliglois* has him losing the lady he loves to a squire who serves her more humbly and devotedly. *La Mule sans frein* comically transforms him into an uncharacteristically devoted knight but has him unstintingly pursue a largely pointless quest. His flaws and in some cases those of the Arthurian chivalric system are further explored in *Le Chevalier à l'épée*, *La Vengeance Raguidel*, *Hunbaut*, *L'Atre périlleux*, *Les Enfances Gauvain*, and *Les Merveilles de Rigomer*. On the other hand, the author of *Yder* departs from this tradition and presents a Gauvain who is unreservedly deserving of praise.

Gauvain has only a minor role in Renaut de Beaujeu's *Le Bel Inconnu*, as his son Guinglain is its principal character. Guinglain, who also appears in the First Continuation, will turn up again in the sixteenth century, in Claude Platin's *Giglain*. *Beaudous*, by Robert de Blois, is another romance about a son of Gauvain.

Chrétien's *Perceval*, with its sharp division into two distinct but related stories, appears to have begun something of a trend, and from that time on a number of romances and lais were thematically or structurally bipartite. The two parts of the work often present double quests (one of them usually conducted by Gauvain; e.g., *Meraugis de Portlesguez*, *Chevalier aux deux épées*, *Hunbaut*); and some romances (e.g., *Merveilles de Rigomer*, *Claris et Laris*) multiply the quests. Other works use the bipartite structure: the lai *Tyolet* recounts Perceval's childhood and follows that with the story of Tyolet, who cuts off a stag's foot for a maiden. *Escanor*, late in the thirteenth century, devotes its first half to a love story involving Kay before turning to a sequence in which Gauvain is accused of murder.

By the end of the thirteenth century, romances were no longer being written in verse (although an exception is presented by the fourteenth-century *Meliador*, by Jehan Froissart); moreover, most romances of the late Middle Ages were increasingly lengthy and complex works that often extend the boundaries—temporal as well as geographical—of the Arthurian romance. *Perceforest*, with its staggering 531 chapters, relates, for example, that Alexander the Great establishes the work's hero as the new British king and that the civilization founded by Perceforest is eventually destroyed by Caesar. In *Ysaïe le Triste*, on the other hand, Tristan's son inhabits a post-Arthurian world where the King's chivalric system represents a decided anachronism.

Alongside those works, the late Middle Ages have also left us vast compilations of Arthurian material (e.g., the Compilations of Jean Vaillant, Michot Gonnot, Rusticiano da Pisa). The romance entitled *Palamedes* consists of two large divisions, devoted to Tristan's father (Meliadus) and to Guiron le Courtois, respectively. The two parts were sometimes separated and during the sixteenth century were published as distinct romances (each half titled after its primary character). Among other late-medieval Arthurian works should be noted the prose renditions of Chrétien de Troyes's poems (*see* CHRÉTIEN DE TROYES, BURGUNDIAN ADAPTATIONS OF), as well as an *Erec in Prose* and an *Yvain in Prose* inspired by Chrétien's characters but based only distantly, if at all, on his work.

The sixteenth century, or a good part of it, continued both the interest in Arthurian literature and the tendency toward compilations, translations, adaptations and modernizations, prosifications, and consistent expansions of those stories. Examples are *Le Chevalier doré* (a condensation of *Perceforest*), the French prose *Amadis de Gaule* (translation by Nicolas de Herberay), a *Lancelot du Lac* printed in 1533, *L'Hystoire du Saint Graal* (1516), *Le Noble Chevalier Gauvain* (1540), and *Perceval le Gallois* (1530). A number of these works went through many editions and reprintings: Frappier notes that the *Petit Artus de Bretagne* was printed fourteen times between 1493 and 1584, and a number of other romances (e.g., the Prose *Lancelot, Meliadus*, and the *Prophécies de Merlin*) saw seven or eight reprintings during the sixteenth century. In addition, a number of popular tales, involving such figures as Gargantua, appropriated the Arthurian legend as background or structure (*see* GARGANTUAN CHRONICLES).

In addition to providing material for the reading public, Arthurian texts influenced and fascinated certain Renaissance writers, among them Rabelais. Even though Rabelais did not write an Arthurian romance, that influence is apparent in certain of his techniques and also in his specific references to Giglan, Gauvain, the Grail, Gallehault, Lancelot, Merlin, Perceforest, and Artus de Bretaigne. Other writers from the period, though not composing Arthurian works, give us an indication of the esteem in which Arthuriana was held. Ronsard, in the preface to the *Franciade*, suggested that Lancelot, Tristan, Gauvain, and Artus should serve as themes for France's national epics, and du Bellay, in his *Deffense et Illustration de la langue françoyse*, speaks of "ces beaux vieulx romans Françoys, comme un *Lancelot*, un *Tristan*, ou autres." As these examples suggest, Arthurian texts were considered to be important more as national history or linguistic material than as literary creations. Nonetheless, they were valued by a good many writers of the time.

But tastes were changing, and Montaigne reflected that change when he included *Lancelot du Lac* in a class he called *tel fatras de livres* ("such jumbles of books"), which served only to amuse children; he insisted that he did not know even their titles, much less the works themselves. Although interest in Arthur never disappeared entirely from France, it diminished radically toward the end of the sixteenth century, and from that time forward the attitude of the French toward Arthurian subjects may seem at times to border on indifference. Such interest waned in England as well (until revived during the nineteenth century), but far less than in France. Even allowing for numerous texts not mentioned here, the number of postmedieval French renderings of Arthurian works or themes amounts to an extremely small percentage of those available in English; that disparity will become particularly striking during the nineteenth and twentieth centuries. Reasons for such a difference in national appeal are not immediately apparent. It will not suffice to suggest that there were other heroes in competition with Arthur, for either they themselves have stirred French imaginations less than he, or (as in the case of Napoleon) they have fascinated readers and writers of a particular and often quite limited period.

A partial explanation may be simply that the French rejection, during the sixteenth and seventeenth centuries, of virtually everything presumed to be "medieval" caused Arthur to fall from favor. (It should be noted, however, that this rejection was only "official," and popular tastes often ignored official opinion; see below.) Moreover, there is the possibility that the very condition of Arthurian literature at that time fostered such a development, for the tales had by then been reworked, expanded, fused, divided, and further expanded to such a point that many of them had lost a good deal of their coherence and vigor; they virtually self-destructed. This phenomenon was not inevitable, but there lacked one important element to retard or prevent it: a writer with the vision and talent necessary to capture the spirit of the legend, fix its form, and present it in a way that could capture the imagination of future ages. France had indeed had such writers during the twelfth and thirteenth centuries, with Chrétien de Troyes and the author(s) of the Vulgate, but no one with comparable ability was writing Arthurian literature two centuries later. As Jean Frappier has noted: "It was our misfortune not to have had a Thomas Malory at the end of the Middle Ages." In regard to the more recent past, he might also have noted the absence of a Tennyson.

Whatever the cause, the seventeenth century saw a clear diminution of interest in the Arthurian romances from the past. The importance and interest of Arthurian works were championed during the period by Jehan Chapelain in his *La Lecture des vieux Romans* and by Marc Vulson, Sieur de la Colombière, in *Le Vray Théatre d'Honneur et de Chevalerie, ou le miroir héroïque de la noblesse* (1648). Vulson dedicated his work to Mazarin and intended it as a book of instruction for the young Louis XIV. The work gives lessons of nobility and chivalric

procedures by recounting certain events of the Arthurian story. Arthur, Guenevere, Morgan, and a number of the knights of the Round Table are presented
briefly.

The seventeenth century gave us a number of original Arthurian works in
which, as had often been the case during the Middle Ages, writers appeared to
have been drawn far more to other characters than to Arthur himself. Merlin,
for example, became a popular figure in seventeenth-century French theater
and ballet. The influence of Cervantes is apparent in such works, some of
which adopt or adapt his title. In 1640, Guérin de Bouscal entitled his play
(with ballet) *Don Quichot de la Manche*, a work that contributed (as did most of
these Merlin pieces) to the decline of the sorcerer's reputation. Mlle Béjart
reworked Bouscal's text, and her piece, entitled *Don Quichot ou les Enchante-
ments de Merlin*, was presented by Molière's troupe in 1660. The year 1671 saw
the composition of Rosidor's *Les Amours de Merlin*, a comedy in one act, and the
Comédie Française in 1687 presented *Merlin peintre* (probably written by Thuel-
lerie). In 1690, Dancourt presented *Merlin déserteur*, whose author he may also
be; in the same year, Jacques Siret (known as Raisin l'aîné) wrote *Merlin
Gascon*. Dating also from the mid-seventeenth century (ca. 1643), but not so
specifically dealing with Merlin, is *Le Libraire du Pont-Neuf ou les romans*, a ballet
featuring "les Chevaliers de la Table-Ronde."

The following century saw a number of popularizations of Arthurian
legend, of generally unremarkable quality. The Marquis de Paulmy d'Argen-
son made a number of romances known through summaries he published in
Mélanges tirés d'une grande bibliothèque. La Curne de Sainte-Palaye was among the
more successful disseminators of the Arthurian material, insisting in a series of
papers that it was a valuable source of historical information. Not unexpectedly, authors who prepared adaptations or original compositions generally
altered the tone and themes of their predecessors to make them correspond to
contemporary tastes. For example, Le Comte de la Vergue de Tressan, in
Extraits de romans de chevalerie, transformed the story of Tristan and Isolde from a
tale of passion and tragedy into simple pastoral. The Bibliothèque universelle
des romans (1775–89), in which Tressan's work appeared, published versions
of numerous medieval works, including some of Chrétien de Troyes's romances.

A number of important nineteenth-century writers were inspired by Arthurian themes or motifs (e.g., the Symbolist poets Maeterlinck, Laforgue, and
especially Verlaine; *see* SYMBOLIST ARTHURIAN MATERIAL). However, many of the
notable reworkings of Arthurian subjects throughout the century came from
writers who today are far less known. For example, in 1812 the Baron Creuzé
de Lesser presented a modern French verse rendering of *Les Chevaliers de la Table
Ronde*, a work that holds considerable interest. M.F. Marchangy's lengthy prose
composition *La Gaule poétique* (1813–17) attained great popularity during its day
(but it largely neglects Arthur in favor of Charlemagne).

A number of French writers used the Arthurian legend for eccentric
personal or political ends. A prominent example during the nineteenth century

is Edgar Quinet, who in his 1860 *Merlin l'Enchanteur* exploited Arthuriana to provide a vehicle for his attacks on Louis-Napoleon.

Throughout this period (as indeed since the sixteenth century), the interest in Arthurian literature in France was fostered as much by the popularizing efforts of scholars and editors as by the original work of poets, novelists, and dramatists. La Villemarqué, in 1842, published *Les Romans de la Table Ronde et les contes des anciens Bretons*, and from 1868 to 1877 Paulin Paris prepared five volumes of *Les Romans de la Table Ronde*, translated into modern French. Though Paris's work influenced modern notions of the Middle Ages and its literature, it appears to have enjoyed little popular success. The situation is radically different with Joseph Bédier. At the turn of the century, Bédier presented what has now established itself as the "standard" version of the Tristan story (*Le Roman de Tristan et Iseut*); that work has now gone through hundreds of editions and has been translated into a number of languages.

Though the appeal of Arthur for the twentieth century has been far weaker in France than in England or the United States, the legend has continued to attract attention. Jacques Boulenger published a four-volume modernized adaptation of *Les Romans de la Table Ronde* in 1922, and there have been various other semipopular renderings of Arthurian texts. A certain number of major authors—among them Jean Cocteau and Guillaume Apollinaire—have felt the attraction of Arthurian themes. Cocteau used Arthurian material successfully in drama and film (notably in *L'Éternel Retour*); Apollinaire, in *L'Enchanteur pourrissant*, was powerfully drawn to the presumably demonic aspects of Merlin. Julien Gracq recast both the Parsifal legend (in *Au Château d'Argol*) and the story of Perceval and the Fisher King (in his *Le Roi Pêcheur*). Certain of these works (e.g., Cocteau's) were "updated" and placed in contemporary settings, and the most striking example of such translation may well be provided by Pierre Benoît's *Montsalvat*, in which the Grail quest occurs in occupied France. All these texts (and a few others; *see* GUÉNON, RENÉ; LANGLAIS, XAVIER DE) present some interest, but in most cases they are highly idiosyncratic works, and none of the twentieth-century French settings of the legend appears to have made a genuine and enduring contribution to the Arthurian corpus. (*See also* FRENCH CHIVALRIC ROMANCES, EIGHTEENTH AND NINETEENTH CENTURIES; FRENCH EPIC, NINETEENTH CENTURY; SECOND EMPIRE; SYMBOLIST ARTHURIAN MATERIAL.) [NJL]

Barber, Richard. *King Arthur in Legend and History*. London: Sphere, 1973.

Brinkley, Roberta F. *Arthurian Legend in the Seventeenth Century*. Baltimore: Johns Hopkins Press, 1932.

Frappier, Jean. *Amour courtois et Table Ronde*. Geneva: Droz, 1973.

———, and Reinhold R. Grimm, eds. *Le Roman jusqu'à la fin du XIIIe siècle*. Heidelberg: Winter, 1978.

Loomis, Roger Sherman, ed. *Arthurian Literature in the Middle Ages*. Oxford: Clarendon, 1959.

Pickford, Cedric E. "The Maturity of the Arthurian Prose Romances." *Bibliographical Bulletin of the International Arthurian Society*, 34 (1982), 197–206.

Reid, Margaret Jane. *The Arthurian Legend: Comparison of Treatment in Modern and Mediaeval Literature; A Study in the Literary Value of Myth and Legend*. Edinburgh: Oliver and Boyd, 1938.

FRENCH CHIVALRIC ROMANCES, EIGHTEENTH AND NINE-TEENTH CENTURIES, were primarily extracts and adaptations of the prose Vulgate Cycle of medieval Arthurian literature.

The eighteenth century was characterized by the stirrings of an interest in the Middle Ages, but attitudes toward the period were ambivalent. Voltaire saw chivalry as a "counterweight to the general savagery of the customs" of the Middle Ages (*Essai sur les moeurs*). Scholars and historiographers of the Enlightenment began to study medieval historical and literary texts as a means of understanding that culture. One of the most influential of these scholars was La Curne de Sainte-Palaye (1697–1781), a member and director of the Académie des Inscriptions, a center for historical and archaeological research. A student of Old French and Old Provençal, as well as a collector and collator of manuscripts, Sainte-Palaye in 1743 gave a paper before the Académie, "Mémoire concernant la lecture des anciens romans de chevalerie." He justified the utility of reading chivalric romances because they conveyed information concerning medieval history, genealogy, geography, feudal duties, and customs. This paper served as an introduction to five other papers between 1746 and 1753: "Mémoires sur l'ancienne chevalerie considérée comme un établissement politique et militaire," published first by the Académie and then separately in 1759, 1781, and 1826 (in an edition by Charles Nodier). This work was enormously influential in exciting interest in chivalry in western Europe. Voltaire's remark, cited above, reflects this interest. The "Mémoires" were translated into English in 1784 and into German from 1789 to 1791. If for Sainte-Palaye chivalry was a coherent system created by the early monarchy, the real importance of his work was its appeal to a changing sensibility in France and western Europe. Chivalry and chivalric romances were of interest, not for scholarly reasons first of all, but because the popular imagination was increasingly attracted to primitivism, the gothic, sentimentalism, and sensibility.

The appetite and habits of the general reading public reveal these new tastes. Such romances as the seventeenth-century *L'Astrée* and translations of Ariosto, Boiardo, and Tasso continued to be popular. Readers liked popular versions of late-medieval or pseudo-medieval romances, often connecting chivalry with gallantry. The manuscript source of a particular romance did not matter to the general public, although some old texts began to appear in print. Late-medieval Arthurian material, *Amadis of Gaul*, and adaptations of *chansons de geste* all constituted "romances."

Arthur himself never captured the hearts of the reading public in the way that Charlemagne did. Nevertheless, there was a considerable vogue in the later eighteenth and in the nineteenth centuries for extracts and adaptations of Arthurian material, primarily from the prose Vulgate Cycle; these emphasized the storyline in a simple style. Chapbooks, sold by *colporteurs* in the provinces, were available in the provinces in the Bibliothèque bleue series, which included *Artus de Bretagne*, *Lancelot du Lac*, and *La Reine Genièvre*. The wealthier subscribed to the Bibliothèque universelle des romans (1775–89), edited by the Marquis de Palmy and later by J.F. Bastide; the Comte de Tressan also served on the editorial committee. The library of Palmy included fourteenth- and fifteenth-century manuscripts and early books that were used for the extracts published in the Bibliothèque; Sainte-Palaye also furnished material from his library. Palmy published extracts of the *Lancelot du Lac*, *Histoire du Saint Gréal*, *Roman du Roi Artus*, *Roman de Merlin*, and *Perceval le Gallois*. From the library of Sainte-Palaye, the Bibliothèque published versions of the *romans* of Chrétien de Troyes, including the *Aventures du chevalier Eric et de la belle Enide*, *Chevalier au lion*, and *Chevalier à la charette*. The Comte de Tressan claimed that "all the old romances of the Round Table, drawn by the Bretons from the old and fabulous chronicles of Melkin and Tézelin, were written in Latin by Rusticien de Puise" and were translated during the reign of Philippe Auguste ("Discours Préliminaire sur les romans français").

The popularity of these versions of Arthurian romances, along with the Tristan and Amadis stories, continued in the nineteenth century, even after *colportage* was outlawed early in the Second Empire. The Nouvelle Bibliothèque bleue (edited by le Roux de Lincy) appeared in 1842 and the Bibliothèque bleue, edited by Delvau, reprinted thirty chapbooks in three volumes (1859–60); Delvau included the stories *Lancelot du Lac* and *La Reine Genièvre*.

Interest in Breton material was aroused when poetic and prose versions of folk material began to appear. La Villemarqué, for example, published his *Contes populaires des anciens Bretons, précédés d'un Essai sur l'origine des épopées chevaleresques de la Table ronde* in 1842, and by 1860 a third, enlarged, edition had appeared with the title *Les Romans de la Table ronde et les contes des anciens Bretons*.

Paulin Paris recognized this continuous popular interest in the Arthurian romance, but, representing the emergence of modern medieval scholarship, he wished to base his version on medieval texts. His prose version of this material appeared in five volumes between 1868 and 1877 as *Les Romans de la table ronde mis en nouveau language*. Paris claimed to be the only person of his time to have read all the romances "of the cycle of Arthur." His version begins with Merlin and Arthur and ends with the adventures of "Mordret." Paris gave precedence over the romances of Chrétien to the "primordial" Arthurian cycle, which he ordered as follows: *Joseph d'Arimathie et Merlin* (Robert de Boron); *Continuations du Merlin* (*Le Livre d'Artus, Gauvain, Perceval*); *Lancelot du Lac; La Mort d'Artus; Tristan, Le Saint-Graal, La Quête du Saint-Graal, les dernières parties du Lancelot* (Gautier Map). Paris's version, while more satisfying than the popular versions that preceded it, still owes its essential narrative form to the Vulgate Cycle. [PAW]

❺ Estève, Edmond, "Le Moyen Âge dans la littérature du XVIIIe siècle." *Revue de l'Université de Bruxelles*, 29 (1923–24), 353–82.

Gossman, Lionel. *Medievalism and the Ideologies of the Enlightenment: The World and Work of La Curne de Sainte-Palaye*. Baltimore: Johns Hopkins Press, 1969.

FRENCH EPIC, NINETEENTH CENTURY. Writers of the nineteenth century were driven by the desire to write epics, a carryover of the classical notion that the epic was the "highest" genre. If we enlarge the definition of the epic to include works in both prose and poetry of national or universal scope, a continuous epic tradition can be traced in nineteenth-century France. During the Empire and Restoration, numerous epics on historical and heroic themes in the classical tradition were written, of which several concerned Charlemagne (e.g., d'Arlincourt's *Charlemagne ou la Caroléide*, 1810; and Millevoye's *Charlemagne*, 1812). Arthurian material received scant attention because of the political and national concerns of the period. An exception is Auguste François Creuzé de Lesser's poem of twenty cantos of decasyllables *Les Chevaliers de la Table Ronde* (1811), later called *La Table Ronde*. It was followed by *Amadis de Gaule* (1813) and *Roland* (1815). By 1839, *La Table Ronde* had appeared in its sixth edition, this time in a volume with the other two poems, *La Chevalerie, ou les histoires du moyen âge . . . Poèmes sur les trois grandes familles de la chevalerie romanesque*. Creuzé de Lesser described the chivalric stories as a "second mythology after that of the Greeks." Lancelot and Tristan are "the most brilliant heroes of the Round Table," while Guinevere and Yseult are "veritable Helens." In sythesizing the Arthurian material, Creuzé de Lesser claimed that the search for the Holy Grail was the unifying element of the poem. Actually, this epic and the two that followed it were a reproduction in verse form of the popular versions of chivalric romances sold to the public in chapbooks in the late eighteenth century. *La Table Ronde* begins with the history of Arthur and Merlin, follows the stories of Lancelot and Tristan, includes the story of Perceval and the Grail (the Fisher King is in Fingal's Cave!), and concludes with the death of Arthur and the disappearance of the Grail.

La Gaule poétique, by M.F. Marchangy (1813–17), was a series of prose narratives in eight volumes of the history of France as related to poetry, the arts, and "eloquence." Although not strictly an epic, *La Gaule poétique* deserves mention because of its great popularity. Marchangy gives much attention to Charlemagne but almost ignores Arthur. The section "On Chivalry" owes much to eighteenth-century sources, particularly La Curne de Sainte-Palaye. There, Marchangy mentions Arthur in connection with the heraldic arms of three knights of the Round Table: "Romance writers, in their fabulous stories, attribute the origin of this order to the King Arthur of Brittany who perhaps never existed."

In the so-called "humanitarian epics" that emerged from the new social and political consciousness of the century, the Arthurian legend figures in only one work, Edgar Quinet's *Merlin l'Enchanteur* (1860), a prolix prose epic in twenty-four books. In the preface, Quinet claims that his subject is "the legend of the human soul up to death, and beyond death." Trying to reconcile all legends into a single one, Quinet chose the figure of Merlin, "the soul of French tradition." Quinet's narrative has nothing to do with the Arthurian literary tradition. His Merlin stands for the French spirit and for Quinet himself, who spent years in exile because of his opposition to the Second

Empire of Louis-Napoleon. Contemporaries admired Quinet's book as a daring political allegory attacking Napoleon III. Merlin enchants Gaul, blesses the origins of the French nation (Arthur's chosen kingdom), and erects a Round Table of stone. He leaves the kingdom, performing exploits throughout Europe (which stand for the accomplishments of the French nation), only to return to find Arthur's kingdom in decline. Merlin then loses his power to enchant and withdraws into a kind of entombment representative of Quinet's own exile and the loss of French freedom. Eventually, the Satan of the poem is pardoned and Arthur and his kingdom are restored in spirit.

This nineteenth-century Arthurian epic material represents an obscure and curious footnote to the story of the role of Arthurian legend in French culture. [PAW]

Dakyns, Janine R. *The Middle Ages in French Literature, 1850–1900.* London: Oxford University Press, 1973.

Hunt, Herbert J. *The Epic in Nineteenth-Century France.* Oxford: Blackwell, 1941.

FRERE, JOHN H. (1769–1846), an English civil servant and author (writing under the pseudonym Whistlecraft) whose unfinished Arthurian burlesque in *ottava rima*, *The Monks and the Giants* (1817–18), was intended to "put a coat of varnish" on the story of King Arthur. Aside from Arthurian characters (a courteous Gawain, a restless and inventive Tristram, a Launcelot who is the best of British knights "except perhaps Lord Wellington in Spain") and traditional motifs (Christmas feast, loathly lady, distressed damsels), the material is largely original. In Cantos I and II, the knights' attack on the giants' stronghold succeeds not because of prowess but because the enemy has used stones from their protective wall to bombard the attackers. Cantos III and IV deal with an earlier event, the severance of good relations between the giants and the neighboring monks, "poor proficients in divinity," whose constant bell-ringing has "rous'd their irrational gigantic anger." Frere's object is to ridicule, by means of puns, slang, plebeian diction, pointless digression, and the citing of pseudo-authorities, the style of Italian chivalric romance. A second motive may be to criticize allegorically the British campaigns against Napoleon in Spain, events that had led to Frere's censure and removal from office. In writing *ottava rima* burlesque, Frere angled in the same waters as Byron; in Waller's words: "Byron caught the big fish, but Frere had shown him where to cast his line." [MAW]

Frere, John Hookham. *The Monks and the Giants*, ed. R.D. Waller. Manchester: Manchester University Press, 1926.

FROISSART, JEHAN (ca. 1333–ca. 1400), author of *Meliador*, an attempt to rejuvenate verse romance in the fourteenth century. An early version, composed between 1365 and 1369, was reworked between 1383 and 1388. Only fragments remain of the first version, but the revision is nearly complete in the 30,499 octosyllabic lines of B.N. f. fr. 12557.

The poem tells of a series of five tournaments arranged by Floree for the hand of her cousin Hermondine of Scotland. Knights come to England from all of western Europe to vie for Hermondine, but it is soon evident that she is destined for Meliador of Cornwall. Meliador's sister, Phenonee, is the second "prize" of the series of tournaments, and she is won by Agamanor of Normandy.

The poem is set in the early years of the kingdom of King Arthur, before the adventures of Gawain, Lancelot, Perceval, and Galahad. A direct link to Arthur's legend is afforded by the introduction of Agravain and Sagremore late in the romance, as well as by situating the final tournament at Camelot. The poem breaks off, however, before this tournament can be completed, but not before Agravain is able to woo and win Floree, the organizer of the tournaments.

Meliador is lengthy and repetitious but intricately interlaced and carefully organized. Like *Perceforest* from the same period, it presents new heroes and new adventures, and is not simply a reworking of previous romances. [WWK]

ဆ Froissart, Jean. *Meliador*, ed. A. Longnon. 3 vols. Paris: Didot, 1895–99.

Dembowski, Peter F. *Jean Froissart and His "Meliador": Context, Craft, and Sense.* Lexington, Ky.: French Forum, 1983.

FROM RITUAL TO ROMANCE: *see* WESTON, JESSIE L.

FRUCTO DE LOS TIEMPOS ("Fruit of the Times"), a Spanish compilation of British history, including a summary of the Arthurian legend, was written in 1509 in behalf of Catherine of Aragon by her tutor, Rodrigo de Cuero. Bearing the full title *Historia de Inglaterra llamada Fructo de los tiempos* and followed by a *Relación de Ynglaterra, Gales, Escocia e Yrlanda*, the work is a generally literal translation of the St. Albans Chronicle as first printed in 1497 by Wynkyn de Worde with the title *Cronycles of Englonde with the Fruyte of Tymes*, to which a *Descrypcyon of Englonde* was added in the 1502 printing, the latter corresponding to Cuero's appended *Relación*. Two manuscripts of the Spanish text survive: Real Biblioteca de El Escorial X.ii.20, an apparent autograph copy of which only the *Relación* section has been edited; and Salamanca, Biblioteca Universitaria 1850, the latter preserving a portion of the Arthurian story now missing in MS X.ii.20. [HLS]

ဆ Malfatti, C.V., ed. *The Descrypcyon of Englonde, An Addition to St. Albans Chronicle First Printed by Wynkyn de Worde, London 1502, Facsimile of British Museum G 5997; Transcription of the Abridged Spanish Translation Relacion de Ynglaterra, Gales, Escocia e Yrlanda por Rodrigo de Cuero, Londres 1509, Escorial MSS. X-II-20.* Barcelona: Sociedad Alianza de Artes Gráficas, 1973.

FRY, CHRISTOPHER, the British verse-playwright, was the author of *Thor, with Angels* for performance in Canterbury Cathedral in 1948. Merlin is the seer who paid for his immortality with his soul. He foretells, and is part of, the reawakening Christian spirit in England under Ethelred. He hints at Joseph's coming to England with the Grail and mentions the miracle at Glastonbury. [HT]

Fry, Christopher. *Thor, with Angels*. London: Oxford University Press, 1949.

FUETRER, ULRICH, German painter and poet generally believed to have been born in the Bavarian town of Landshut in the early fifteenth century. This assumption is given credibility through Fuetrer's statement in his *Bayerische Chronik* that his father lost several thousand *guldin* during the Landshut rebellion of 1410. Fuetrer himself is first mentioned in Munich municipal receipts from 1453 in his capacity as a painter. From 1482 to 1496, he appears in the Munich municipal tax records as owning a house. It is assumed that he died before October 1496, since his wife, who was then listed as the house's owner, was put in the pillory and subsequently banished from Munich.

As a painter, Fuetrer was more a craftsman than an independent artist. In 1465, he painted the Andreaskapelle of the monastery in Tegernsee. From 1476 to 1478, he worked on the interior decoration of the old City Hall in Munich, and from 1486 to 1495 he was active at the court of Duke Albrecht IV. From this latter period, his decoration of Schloss Grünwald is particularly noteworthy. Fuetrer was a highly regarded member of his guild and held the honorary office of one of the "Four."

Both as a painter and as a writer, Fuetrer must be regarded more as a skilled and conscientious adapter and reviser than as an independent poet of genius. All of his works were composed in connection with the Wittelsbach court in Munich, and all are dedicated to Duke Albrecht IV. Fuetrer probably gained access to the court through the mediation of Jakob Püterich von Reichertshausen (d. 1469); there he managed to cultivate a select circle of friends and patrons who provided him with solid support and aided him in gaining and maintaining the esteem of the ducal court. It is worthy of note that, although Fuetrer spent approximately the last decade of his life at the court as an occasional painter (1486–95), he was more highly regarded for his poetic talents, in spite of the fact that he had completed most of his literary works before this time. His works include *Prosaroman von Lanzelot* (ca. 1467), *Das Buch der Abenteuer I* (1473–78), *Die Bayerische Chronik* (1478–81), *Das Buch der Abenteuer II* (finished before 1484), and *Der strophische Lanzelot* (begun before 1484 and finished in 1487).

Fuetrer's *Prosaroman von Lanzelot* is an abridgment of the *Prosa-Lancelot* text found in the *P* manuscript and the *k* fragment. Aside from a few minor interpolations, Fuetrer's work remains true to the original.

In the first book of *Das Buch der Abenteuer* ("The Book of Adventures") Fuetrer uses *Der jüngere Titurel* of Albrecht von Scharfenberg as the framework within which he recounts the tales of Wolfram von Eschenbach's *Parzival*, Heinrich von dem Türlin's *Crône*, and *Lohengrin* as one continuous story. In addition, he works in a Trojan War narrative and the history of Merlin as more or less independent episodes. In the second book (so named by Fuetrer) are seven independent tales without a definite framework: *Floreis und Wigoleis, Seifrid de Ardemont, Meleranz, Iban, Persibein, Poytislier,* and *Flordimar.*

All of the stories in both books are adaptations of older works, although for some of Fuetrer's narratives it is at present impossible to determine which older texts or poets served as models. Fuetrer ascribes two, *Merlin* and *Seifrid de Ardemont,* to Albrecht von Scharfenberg, whose *oeuvre,* however, has not been transmitted.

In spite of the fact that Fuetrer worked from models, his achievement should not be belittled. He was extraordinarily well-read and he succeeded in blending the various Arthurian and Grail works into a cohesive whole. As one critic has put it, it seems as if Fuetrer read all available texts and then made a "card-index" of the characters, motifs, and adventures, which he then re-arranged into one continuous story. Since Fuetrer leaves out all digressive episodes that may have appeared in the original and that would not further the flow of the narrative, it is almost impossible to determine with any certainty which text was used for any specific part of his own work. The *Buch der Abenteuer* contains 5,644 *Titurel* strophes of seven lines apiece. It is Fuetrer's most important achievement as a writer and offers insight into the reception of medieval literature during the late Middle Ages and early Renaissance.

In the *Strophische Lanzelot,* Fuetrer revises his original *Prosaroman von Lanzelot* in order to bring the Lanzelot tale into harmony with the events described in his *Buch der Abenteuer.* Only a few of the 5,700 *Titurel* strophes have been published.

Fuetrer is one of the more fascinating personalities of the late medieval/ early humanistic period, and through his poetic efforts one gains an appreciation of the literary interest of the Wittelsbach court at the beginning of the "modern" era. The time was doubtless gone when an audience could identify with the exploits of the Arthurian heroes, when the listeners or readers might be able to recognize lessons in tales that would have application to their own lives. Nonetheless, the stories of the Arthurian knights exercised a definite attraction on the courtly audiences toward the end of the fifteenth century, and they viewed this literature as part of their cultural heritage and therefore worthy of preservation, even if in a form and style more commensurate with their own tastes and outlook. [FGG]

Fuetrer, Ulrich. *Poytislier aus dem Buch der Abenteuer von Ulrich Fuetrer,* ed. Friederike Weber. Tübingen: Niemeyer, 1960.

——— . *Persibein; Aus dem Buch der Abenteuer,* ed. Renate Munz. Tübingen: Niemeyer, 1964.

——— . *Wigoleis,* ed. Heribert A. Hilgers. Tübingen: Niemeyer, 1975.

FULLARTON, R(ALPH) MACLEOD, in *Merlin: A Dramatic Poem* (1890), applies Tennysonian morality—Sense at War with Soul—to the Merlin-Vivien material. Merlin, an Arthurian knight, possesses a magical ring that puts to sleep "Whomso the wearer will/So long the wearer please." Vivien's acquisition of the ring gives her power to overcome her enemies, including Merlin, whom she marries. Surprisingly, Morgan is a beneficent character who uses her crucifix to waken the hero from the first magic sleep but fails to save him from the rocky death that Merlin accepts as God's will. [MAW]

🍂 Fullarton, R. Macleod. *Merlin: A Dramatic Poem*. Edinburgh and London: Blackwood, 1890.

FUSELI, HENRY (1741–1825). Johann or Hans-Heinrich Füssli or Fuessli, known as Henry Fuseli after he moved to England, was born in Zurich. A member of the Royal Academy and famous for his illustrations for the works of Shakespeare and Milton, Fuseli also created paintings and drawings inspired by themes from Spenser's *The Faerie Queene*. Some of these Arthurian illustrations were engraved by P. Tomkins for Macklin's *Poet's Gallery* (e.g., *The Dream of Prince Arthur*, 1788). [MS]

GABONS SAGA OK VIGOLES, or *Saga af Viegoleis með Gullhiólit* ("Saga of Viegoleis with the Golden Wheel"), is the title given to two different Icelandic translations of the Danish chapbook *Her Viegoleis med Guld Hiulet*, which was first published in 1656. The Danish chapbook is in turn a translation of the fifteenth-century German prose redaction of Wirnt von Grafenberg's *Wigalois*. Shortly after the publication of the Danish chapbook in 1656, Magnús Jónsson í Vigur (b. 1637) translated the work into Icelandic, probably between the years 1656 and 1683. His translation is preserved in two late seventeenth-century manuscripts.

A different, anonymous, translation of the Danish chapbook is extant in only one eighteenth-century manuscript. Since the Danish chapbook was printed several times during the first half of the eighteenth century, the source of the second Icelandic translation was presumably one of the eighteenth-century editions. [MEK]

Nyerup, Rasmus. *Almindelig Morskabslæsning i Danmark og Norge igjiennem Aarhundreder.* Copenhagen: Seidelin, 1816, pp. 125–33.

Seelow, Hubert. "Die isländischen Übersetzungen der deutschen Volksbücher." Habilitations-Schrift, Ludwig-Maximilians-Universität München, 1984.

GAHERET: *see* GARETH.

GAIMAR, GEFFREI, author of an Anglo-Norman adaptation, now lost, of Geoffrey of Monmouth's *Historia Regum Britanniae*. To his adaptation, done in the 1140s, he appended a history of England through the reign of William Rufus; the sequel refers to his version of the *Historia*, but the latter has been replaced in the manuscripts by that of Wace. [NJL]

GALAHAD (GALAAD), the son of Lancelot and the perfect Grail knight. In the Vulgate Cycle, Lancelot (whose baptismal name was also Galahad) fathers the future hero while lying with Pelles's daughter but—under the influence of a potion—thinking her to be Guinevere. Galahad's story is told primarily in the *Queste del Saint Graal*, where, having been knighted, he arrives at Arthur's court (following various predictions, signs, and marvelous events) and passes the test of the Perilous Seat and that of the Sword in the Stone. He is thus recognized as the future hero of the Grail quest. Later, he will heal the wounded king and will die in ecstasy after seeing directly the mystery of the Grail.

Galahad was the preordained hero of the quest, and we are told that he remained virgin throughout his life, thereby compensating for his impure conception. Moreover, his physical beauty and his prowess are as evident as his moral perfection. Although details vary from text to text, his character and his role remain constant; Malory, for example, retains the French account virtually unaltered. In both, and in later tradition, Galahad is "the culmination," as Jean Frappier noted, "of the effort to fuse chivalry with religion." [NJL]

Lot-Borodine, Myrrha. "Christ-Chevalier: Galaad." In *De l'amour profane à l'amour sacré: Études de psychologie sentimentale au Moyen Âge*. Paris: Nizet, 1961.

GALAHAD: *see* BOUGHTON, RUTLAND; ERSKINE, JOHN; HAUPTMANN, GERHART.

GALAHAD, KNIGHT ERRANT: *see* SOUTHWORTH, MARY E.

"GALIANS TÁTTUR," a Faroese ballad consisting of 119 stanzas of four lines each, was recorded in 1781–82 by Jens Christian Svabo. The events narrated in the ballad take place in the days of King Artan and tell about Ívint the Strong, a close relative of King Artan, and his son Galian. The ballad appears to be based on an imperfect recollection of Arthurian matter. After a reference to King Artan's habit of not eating until some adventure has occurred, the ballad relates how the knights set out one day on a hunt. Ívint does not return to court but spends the night with a rich widow, whom he takes forcibly. She takes vengeance by giving him a magic potion that is to leave him sick for fifteen years. After nine months, she gives birth to a son named Galian. When he is grown, he sets off with the magic potion to find Ívint and cures him. The ballad ends with the reconciliation of Ívint and Galian's mother. [MEK]

🙞 Djurhuus, N., ed. "Galians táttur. "In *Færøya kvæði: Corpus Carminum Færoensium*. Copenhagen: Akademisk Forlag, 1968, Vol. 5, pp. 223–29.

Matras, Christian, ed. "Gealïans Kveaï." In *Svabos færøske visehaandskrifter*. Copenhagen: Samfund til Udgivelse af gammel nordisk Litteratur, 1937, pp. 369–82.

GAMES. Like other figures from legend, Arthurian characters have been adapted for role-playing games, such as *Dungeons & Dragons*. Arthur and his best-known knights (e.g., Lancelot and Tristan) are used as warriors at the highest levels of play, while Merlin and Morgan le Fay are prominent among the magic-users. They have also provided the inspiration for board games, both general, as in Parker Brothers' battle game *Camelot*, and specific, as in *King Arthur's Knights*, designed by Greg Stafford, where the object is to prove oneself worthy of membership in the Round Table through a series of encounters, adventures, and quests. To fit the rules of these games, the Arthurian characters have been unavoidably simplified. Even so, the games remain complex, and none has won popular success, apart from *Dungeons & Dragons*.

From fantasy role games have recently developed solo fantasy gamebooks, which are often illustrated. The reader chooses among several courses of action at vital stages of the adventure, then turns to the appropriate section to discover the consequences. Among those that borrow Arthurian elements are J.H. Brennan's *Grailquest: The Castle of Darkness* (1984), where Merlin sends the reader off to rescue Guenevere from an enchanted fortress, though the perils encountered are the monsters and traps typical of role games rather than Arthurian tradition. [RHT]

🙞 Brennan, J.H. *Grailquest, Book One: The Castle of Darkness*. London: Fontana/Armada, 1984.

Fawcett, Bill, ed. *Wizards*. Chicago: Mayfair Games, 1983.

GAMURET: see BODMER, JOHANN JACOB.

GARCÍA DE SALAZAR, LOPE: *see* SALAZAR, LOPE GARCÍA DE.

GAREL VON DEM BLÜHENDEN TAL: see PLEIER, DER.

GARETH, or Gareth of Orkney, also known in Malory as Beaumains (because of his "large-handedness" or generosity). He and Gaheret are brothers in some texts, fused into a single character in others. Gareth is Gawain's favorite brother. Arriving at court (in Malory's Book VII), Beaumains is mocked by Kay but welcomed, and eventually knighted, by Lancelot. He falls in love with

Lyones and suffers—because their love is thwarted by her sister—until Arthur gives him to her in marriage. In the Vulgate *Mort Artu* and in Malory, Gareth dies at the hand of Lancelot, who does not recognize him in the melee surrounding Guenevere's rescue by her lover. His death, which saddens Lancelot and angers Gawain, precipitates the final tragedy, or (as the *Mort Artu* calls it) the war that will have no end. It has been suggested that there may have been a French romance (now lost) concerning Beaumains; in any event, the striking resemblance of Malory's tale to the situation of *Fergus* and perhaps to that of Chrétien de Troyes's Laudine convinced R.S. Loomis (in *Arthurian Tradition and Chrétien de Troyes*) that those various narrative sequences shared a common and doubtless oral origin. [NJL]

"GARETH AND LYNETTE": *see* TENNYSON, ALFRED LORD.

GARETH OF ORKNEY: *see* DITMAS, EDITH M.R.

GARGANTUAN CHRONICLES. During the early sixteenth century, a number of tales, first oral and then written, grew up in France about the mythical giant Gargantua, best known today as one of Rabelais's heroes. The works are designated collectively as Gargantuan Chronicles, and while they are without exception less inspired than Rabelais's work, they retain some interest both as possible inspirations for his books and for the Arthurian content of several of them. Worthy of particular note are the 1532 *Les Grandes et Inestimables Cronicques du grant et enorme geant Gargantua* ("The Great and Inestimable Chronicles of the Huge and Enormous Giant Gargantua," referred to by Rabelais in his Prologue to *Pantagruel*) and *Les Croniques admirables du puissant roy Gargantua* ("The Admirable Chronicles of the Powerful King Gargantua"), which probably dates from 1534. The latter text, published by one of its editors as *The Tale of Gargantua and King Arthur*, was at one time attributed to Rabelais himself but is generally accepted as the work of one François Girault, who left his name in an acrostic near the end of the text. His work served as the source for a translation (now lost) into Elizabethan English.

The two works, and certain other texts about Gargantua, tell much the same story, with variations in detail and length (the 1532 text presenting little more than an outline of the events developed in some detail in Girault's version). According to these texts, Merlin created Gargantua's parents (Grandgosier and Gallemelle) from whale bones and from Lancelot's blood and the clippings of Guenevere's fingernails. When Gargantua was still a youth, Merlin took him to England, where he joined the company of Arthur's knights. He served Arthur for 200 years, defeating giants and entire armies; eventually, he was taken away to a faerie otherworld by Melusine (or, in some versions of the story, by Morgain). Arthur remains for the most part a colorless figure, whose most obvious trait is incompetence. Merlin is a more prominent character, but he serves primarily as a catalyst for the action and as an intermediary between Arthur and Gargantua. The focus, as in Rabelais, remains on the fabulous and often comical exploits of Gargantua. A number of events in the stories occur as well in Rabelais's work, but the latter contented himself with referring frequently to Arthurian characters and motifs, without writing a genuinely Arthurian story. [NJL]

Françon, Marcel, ed. *Les Cronicques admirables du puissant roy Gargantua*. Rochecorbon: Gay, 1956.

Girault, François. *The Tale of Gargantua and King Arthur*, ed. Huntington Brown. Cambridge, Mass.: Harvard University Press, 1932.

GARNER, ALAN, an English writer best known in Arthurian circles for his Alderley books, *The Weirdstone of Brisingamen* (1960) and *The Moon of Gomrath* (1963). Garner does not name the king who sleeps with his warriors in a cavern, but the Alderley Edge legend upon which the story is based and other hints identify him as Arthur (*see* CAVE LEGEND). Two modern children discover the cave and learn of the critical role played by the magical Weirdstone in the stasis. Their struggle to help the immortal and grandfatherly (if powerful) Cadellin (Merlin) to preserve it from the forces of evil, led by the Morrigan (Morgan le Fay), causes a growth in maturity that brings loss as well as gain. Of particular note are Garner's vivid settings (drawn in large part from his native Alderley in Cheshire) and his powerful recreations of the forces unleashed by the "Old Magic," especially the Wild Hunt. Garner skillfully manages to balance the human and the supernatural in these books, so that neither predominates.

While not specifically Arthurian, two other Garner fantasies of interest are the tragic *Elidor* (1965), which uses the Wasteland and Fisher King motifs, and *The Owl Service* (1967), which draws heavily upon the Welsh *Mabinogi*. [RCS]

Garner, Alan. *The Weirdstone of Brisingamen: A Tale of Alderley*. London: Collins, 1960; rev. ed. Harmondsworth: Penguin, 1963.

———. *The Moon of Gomrath*. London: Collins, 1963.

GAURIEL VON MUNTABEL: see KONRAD VON STOFFELN.

GAWAIN (WALWANUS, GAUVAIN, GAWEIN, GWALCHMEI, WALEWEIN), son of King Lot of Lothian and Orkney and Morgause (or Anna), Arthur's sister or half-sister. Gawain appears to have northern, possibly Scottish, origins, but it is impossible to trace him back to a historical model, however shadowy. Unlike Kay and Bedivere, who have early associations with Arthur in Celtic tradition, Gawain belongs to a later stratum of the Arthurian story, and the Welsh name Gwalchmei is first regarded as the equivalent of

Gawain in translations of Geoffrey of Monmouth's *Historia Regum Britanniae* and the Welsh romances. An early mention of Walwanus is to be found in William of Malmesbury's *Gesta Regum Anglorum*, but he first appears in a role of any importance in Geoffrey of Monmouth. However, occurrences of the name Walwanus (and variants) in charters suggest the popularity of stories about him in the eleventh century on the Continent.

In Geoffrey of Monmouth, Gawain is a valiant warrior who aids his lord and king in various campaigns. The uncle–nephew (sister's son) relationship is of particular importance in creating an intimate bond between the two that enables Gawain to function as counselor and putative heir to the throne. In Wace's adaptation of Geoffrey, Gawain has already assumed a courtly aspect and praises the virtues of love and chivalry rather than war. It is Chrétien de Troyes, however, who first allots a major role to Gawain in his romances. Gawain functions as a friend of the hero and as a model whom young knights aspire to emulate. Often, the hero of the romance becomes involved in an undecided combat with Gawain, in Chrétien's later romances the implication being that the hero is the moral victor. Chrétien seems to take a more critical attitude toward Gawain and the way of life he represents as his career progresses, and particularly in *Lancelot* and *Perceval* he is unfavorably contrasted with the hero and made the butt of some burlesque humor. Chrétien seems particularly concerned with Gawain's blind adherence to custom and frivolous attachment to the opposite sex. Even though *Perceval* is unfinished, it seems clear that Gawain is bound to fail where Perceval will succeed.

Both the burlesque and more serious strains are taken up in later Old French romances, the burlesque aspect being prevalent in the post-Chrétien verse romances (e.g., *Le Chevalier à l'épée* and *La Vengeance Raguidel*) and the serious criticism coming to the fore in the Grail romances, especially in the Vulgate *Queste*, where Gawain is depicted as a hardened and unrepentant sinner. In the Prose *Tristan*, he is an out-and-out murderous villain, no respecter of persons or property. As of this point (ca. 1230), authors wishing to depict Gawain therefore had various choices open to them: they could portray him as a real hero, as a somewhat comic figure, or as a true villain. Later French literature shows him in all of these roles.

Outside France, all authors of Arthurian romances were familiar with the French tradition, and it is interesting to note that the portrayal of Gawain varies geographically. In Germany, he remains by and large the same figure as in France, although Wolfram von Eschenbach in his *Parzival* is less harsh on him than Chrétien in *Perceval*; he becomes the hero proper of a lengthy Grail romance, *Diu Krône*, by Heinrich von dem Türlin. Gawain seems to have enjoyed considerable popularity in the Low Countries, where a special form of the name, Walewein, developed very early; the portrayal of him in Middle Dutch literature (with the exception of some texts directly dependent on French models) is almost uniformly positive, and he is named *der avonturen vader* ("the father of adventures"). Why the portrayal of Gawain in some Germanic literatures should be so positive is difficult to say, but the case of Middle

English is at least partly explicable. There is in Middle English a marked reluctance to take over any of the negative features of the French Gawain, and Middle English romance in many ways restores Gawain to a position of respect and dignity. The author of *Sir Gawain and the Green Knight*, for example, shows a Gawain who is almost but not quite perfect. Other texts, such as *Syre Gawene and the Carle of Carlyle*, portray an unimpeachably courteous and valiant knight, or at least one whose actions are not criticized. One possible explanation for this is that English authors and audiences regarded Gawain as a British hero and that it was considered unseemly to show such a figure in a poor light. A similar tendency is visible in the restoration in English literature of the French Arthur from a weak and indecisive monarch to a great warrior-king. Malory departs from this pattern of favorable treatment of Gawain in Middle English, however, when he follows his sources by presenting Arthur's nephew in an unflattering role. His lead was followed by Tennyson and most postmedieval writers, though some recent novels, by authors like Gillian Bradshaw, have shown him to better advantage once again.

Curiously, French literature, where Gawain occurs more often than anywhere else, rarely shows him in the role of a real hero, setting out on a quest he is destined to achieve, or falling properly in love. This occurs, however, in some of the transformations mentioned above, and it is this flexible, nonhero status in Old French literature (but with heroic potential) that rendered the figure of Gawain so serviceable. Authors could use Gawain as part of a design transformed to their own needs, where he might turn out to be a hero or an adjunct, courteous or not, and so on. But on the whole, despite lapses into frivolous love affairs, the figure of Gawain remains by and large admirable, with the exception of the Vulgate *Queste* and the Prose *Tristan*. A wicked Gawain of this kind is after all less useful to authors, for a debased and debauched knight makes neither a good foil for the hero of a romance nor a good hero himself. [KB]

Busby, Keith. *Gauvain in Old French Literature*. Amsterdam: Rodopi, 1980.

Whiting, B.J. "Gawain: His Reputation, His Courtesy, and His Appearance in Chaucer's *Squire's Tale*." *Medieval Studies*, 9 (1947), 189–234.

GAWAN: see STUCKEN, EDUARD.

GEBURT DES MERLIN ODER DAS KIND HAT SEINEN VATER GEFUNDEN, DIE: see TIECK, LUDWIG.

GEHRKES, ALBERT: *see TRISTAN*, MODERN GERMAN VERSIONS OF GOTTFRIED'S.

GEIGER, ALBERT: *see TRISTAN,* MODERN GERMAN
VERSIONS OF GOTTFRIED'S.

GEITARLAUF: see STRENGLEIKAR.

GEOFFREY JUNIOR (pseudonym of William John Courthope; 1842–1917),
author of *The Marvellous History of King Arthur in Avalon* (1904), a pseudo-
chronicle in archaic diction. This account of Arthur and his knights, beguiled
into forgetful pleasure in Avalon by Morgan le Fay, is a political allegory
attacking abuse of the parliamentary system in Britain. [RHT]

  ◆ [Courthope, William John]. *The Marvellous History of King Arthur in Avalon and the Lifting of
    Lyonnesse: A Chronicle of the Round Table Communicated by Geoffrey of Monmouth,* Ed. with
    Introduction and Notes by Geoffrey Junior. London: Murray, 1904.

GEOFFREY OF MONMOUTH, author of the *Historia Regum Britanniae*
("History of the Kings of Britain"), the twelfth-century Latin work that made
Arthur a quasi-historical monarch with an "official" biography. It is one of the
most important books of the Middle Ages. Besides planting highly erroneous
notions of British history, it supplied a basis and framework for Arthurian
romance and exerted an influence extending through Spenser, Shakespeare,
and many others. *The Faerie Queene* includes compressed verse paraphrases of
large portions of it.

Presumably born at Monmouth in southeast Wales, Geoffrey may have
been Welsh. However, he shows an interest in Brittany and a pro-Breton bias
that suggest that his family came from across the Channel, as numerous
Bretons did in the wake of the Norman Conquest. His father's name is said to
have been Arthur. From 1129 to 1151, Geoffrey was a minor cleric and
seemingly a teacher at Oxford, where schools already existed though the
university did not. Charters relating to church properties reveal that he was
acquainted with Walter, archdeacon of the diocese, whose name figures in his
scanty account of his sources. After 1151, Geoffrey was in London and was
consecrated bishop of the Welsh see of St. Asaph. This appointment tells in
favor of his being of Breton stock, since under the Anglo-Norman monarchy
Welshmen were not usually made bishops of Welsh sees. Owing to the turbu-
lence of the country, it is unlikely that he ever took up residence. He died in
1154 or 1155.

His first published work was a series of *Prophetiae Merlini* ("Prophecies of
Merlin"). He gave this to the world in the 1130s, while he was still busy with
the *Historia,* and later incorporated it into the larger work, as supposedly uttered
by Merlin. Hence, the *Historia* is now the context in which to find it. The germ
of the *Prophetiae* is a Welsh tradition that Merlin (or rather Myrddin—the

familiar form of the name is Geoffrey's) foretold the overthrow of the Saxons and the destruction of their usurped realm of England, in a Celtic resurgence. Most of the text, however, is Geoffrey's invention. Its oracular imagery refers to Arthur as "the Boar of Cornwall" and gives a few recognizable allusions to real events, but in the main it is hopelessly obscure except in its foreshadowing of a restored Celtic Britain. Nevertheless, there were medieval commentators who professed to expound these "Prophecies," and they were still well enough known in the sixteenth century for Rabelais to gibe at them.

The *Historia Regum Britanniae* was completed about 1136. The best of the many copies is the Cambridge University Library MS 1706, though it needs supplementing from one or two others. There are slight indications that no extant copy reproduces the original and that the *Historia* as now known is a revision datable to the 1140s. An appreciably different "Variant Version" remains puzzling. Geoffrey seems to have attempted more than one dedication. He addresses himself to Robert, Earl of Gloucester, and also to Waleran, Count of Mellent.

His most obvious aim is to glorify the Britons of old, ancestors of the Welsh and Bretons. He bewails their disunion and degeneration, which led to the loss of most of their territory to the English; but through the prophetic Merlin he holds out hope to their descendants. A second obvious aim is to please the Normans, by whom the English have in turn been conquered. Geoffrey seeks to show not only that their island realm has an august pedigree but that their lands on the Continent once belonged to Britain, so that there are precedents for Norman claims on both sides of the Channel. Deeper issues may well be raised by the portrayals of Merlin and of Arthur himself, the inspired prophet and the messianic ruler. To these, a key should perhaps be sought in Judeo-Christian apocalyptic literature and a transfer of themes from the biblical Chosen People to the Britons—an idea for which Gildas supplied a hint.

After a conventionalized description of Britain, the *Historia* opens in the age of classical epic. Geoffrey recalls Vergil's account of Aeneas, who, after the fall of Troy, is said to have led a party of Trojans to Italy, these being the ancestors of the Romans. Vergil introduces Aeneas's son Ascanius, and Geoffrey makes out that Ascanius's grandson Brutus led a further migration. He freed several thousand Trojans from slavery in Greece and took them to the island of Albion, which was promptly renamed "Britain" after himself. Basically, this is a Welsh legend found in Nennius, but Geoffrey vastly expands it. Albion, he says, was uninhabited except for a few giants, mostly in Cornwall. The Trojan settlers—now "Britons"—eliminated the giants and created a kingdom, with a capital on the Thames called New Troy, subsequently London.

From Brutus, Geoffrey goes on to a long series of further kings. They include Leir, the original King Lear, with his three daughters. Most of the kings are imaginary, though in some cases Geoffrey has taken names from Welsh princely genealogies that actually apply to a much later period. Two of the most important of his kings are the brothers Belinus and Brennius. Belinus is a euhemerized Celtic god; Brennius is a Gallic king who sacked Rome in 390

B.C. and is here (slightly misspelled) converted into a Briton. Toward the time of the Roman conquest, Geoffrey begins to adopt characters from Welsh stories preserved in the *Mabinogion*.

With the advent of Julius Caesar, he is somewhat constrained by authentic history. Yet he avoids admitting that Britain was ever conquered by Rome. Oddly at first sight, this archpatriot never mentions the heroic leaders of anti-Roman resistance, Caratacus and Boudicca. The reason is that he does not need them, because he denies the conquest itself. By agreement with the emperors, Britain survives as a tributary state within the imperial system, and its kings continue under a Roman overlordship that is only intermittently felt. Geoffrey ingeniously portrays some of the emperors, Constantine the Great for instance, as Britons or demi-Britons or Britons-by-marriage, and simply includes them in his line of kings.

He makes much of the legendary origin of Brittany, reputedly settled by Britons as a result of the activities of the pretender Maximus. Brittany, in the narrative, quickly becomes a kingdom in its own right. Meanwhile, the insular Britons are overrun by Picts, Scots, and other barbarians, and after one rescue expedition the Romans abandon them to their fate. Through the diplomacy of the archbishop of London, a Breton prince, Constantine, comes over to organize the island's defense and is made king. He has three sons—Constans, Aurelius Ambrosius, and Uther, the last being the destined father of Arthur.

Constantine is assassinated, and the sinister Vortigern disposes of Constans also and takes over the sovereignty. The two younger princes find haven in Brittany. Vortigern invites the heathen Saxons, led by Hengist, to settle in Britain as auxiliary troops. The alliance is cemented by his marriage to Hengist's daughter. Hengist contrives a massacre of the British nobles at a conference, and the Saxons ravage the country. Vortigern, hated and rejected by most of his people, flees to Snowdonia and tries to build a fortress there. The foundations keep crumbling away. Vortigern's magicians tell him he must find a boy without a father, kill him, and sprinkle his blood upon the stones. Here, Geoffrey is following an older Welsh tale in Nennius, but the outcome is different. A lad is found whose mother conceived by an incubus, and he is brought to the building site. His name is Merlin: thus the enchanter makes his debut on the stage of major literature. He reveals what the magicians did not know, that the foundations collapse because they are over a pool. Moreover, the pool has two dragons in it, a red one and a white one. When brought out into the light of day, the dragons fight; they represent the Britons and Saxons. Merlin utters his prophecies, portending doom for Vortigern and warning him that the rightful princes Aurelius and Uther are on the point of returning to Britain.

He speaks truly. They overthrow and slay the usurper and curb the Saxons, though inconclusively. Aurelius's reign is short. Uther, called Pendragon, succeeds him and begets Arthur with the aid of Merlin's magic. Geoffrey's narrative now rises toward its climactic phase, a glorious rebirth after catastrophe. Arthur becomes king while still in his teens. He routs the Saxons, not quite expelling them from Britain but reducing them to subjection. His decisive victory is at Bath (Geoffrey's interpretation of Badon), where he wields a sword called Caliburn forged in the Isle of Avalon. Then he crushes the Picts and Scots in the north and, having "restored Britain to its earlier dignity," marries Guenevere. But the restoration is only a beginning. He invades and conquers Ireland and, as an afterthought, Iceland.

Arthur now reigns in peace and prosperity for twelve years. He creates an order of knighthood that accepts men of note from all nations. His fame spreads widely, and, aware of the awe that he inspires, he conceives the notion of conquering Europe. He starts with Norway and Denmark, and then invades Gaul, still tenuously held by the Roman Empire. Vanquishing its governor, Frollo, in single combat, he reorganizes the Roman territories under his own rule, employing his cupbearer, Bedivere, and his seneschal, Kay.

In a second spell of peace, Arthur holds court magnificently at the former Roman city of Caerleon-upon-Usk. Geoffrey's description of Arthurian Caerleon is the major literary step toward the Camelot of romance. An embassy arrives from the Roman ruler Lucius demanding tribute and the restitution of conquered lands. Lucius is here styled Procurator of the Republic, though later he is once or twice called an emperor. The ambiguity of his status hints at a hazy consciousness on Geoffrey's part of the nullity of the last western emperors. By contrast, Lucius's eastern colleague, Leo, is an "emperor" unequivocally.

Arthur rejects the Roman demands and takes an army over to Gaul, where he defeats Lucius and penetrates Burgundy, but before he can pursue his more grandiose visions he is recalled to Britain by a revolt. His treacherous nephew Mordred, left in charge as his deputy, has seized the crown and made a deal with the Saxons. Arthur crushes the rebellion beside the River Camel in Cornwall but is mortally wounded and "carried off to the Isle of Avalon for his wounds to be attended to." Thus, cryptically, his reign ends. Geoffrey leaves the door open for the folk-belief in the King's immortality, but he never affirms it. The rest of the *Historia* gives a distorted though not totally fanciful account of the Britons' eventual collapse and the Saxon triumph, closing the line of kings with Cadwallader in the seventh century. After him, the remaining Britons maintain their independence in Wales only and are called Welsh.

There is no doubt that Geoffrey is a writer of fiction and can never be relied on for facts. Yet there is equally no doubt that he makes use of older materials, both genuine history and preexisting legend. Besides Roman historians, he draws upon Gildas, Nennius, Bede, and probably the *Annales Cambriae*, as well as Welsh genealogical and hagiographic matter. But the main problem with his sources is a statement he makes in a dedicatory preface: that the *Historia* is translated from "a certain very ancient book written in the British language," which was given him by Archdeacon Walter. No trace of the book exists today, and Geoffrey's claim is quite inadmissible as it stands, if only because the *Historia* contains many things (such as a reference to Normans in Arthur's army) that could not have been in an "ancient" source. The claim is therefore usually dismissed as a pure fabrication, like similar claims by other medieval authors.

Geoffrey, however, is very positive about this book in the British language. Mentioning three contemporary historians—Caradoc of Llancarfan, William of Malmesbury, and Henry of Huntingdon—he advises them to leave the kings of the Britons alone, because he has the book and they do not. He alleges further that Walter brought it *ex Britannia*. In Geoffrey's time, "the British language" might mean either Welsh or Breton, which had a common ancestor in the Late British tongue of the fifth century and had not diverged very widely from each other. But *Britannia* suggests Brittany rather than Wales.

Geoffrey makes one specific assertion about the book's contents, that it gave him material on the downfall of Arthur. In his Arthur story, it is noteworthy that known Welsh sources cannot account for more than about one-fifth of the total and that Geoffrey presents an Arthur who is not really like the warrior-prince of the Welsh and has a downfall quite at variance with the Welsh tradition of Mordred or "Medraut." In dealing with the recognized villain, Vortigern, he merely enlarges on what the Welsh have to say; in dealing with the hero, Arthur, he might be expected to do the same but instead does something significantly different. Half the story is taken up with the Gallic warfare. Judged purely by allocation of space, Geoffrey's Arthur is more a Gallic conqueror than anything else. The emphasis, and the denouement, have no real Welsh antecedents. A theory that Geoffrey makes Arthur campaign on the Continent in imitation of Maximus, or the Norman kings, may carry some weight but fails to take the full measure of the problem. Arguably, he did have a lost source, perhaps a Breton chronicle or narrative poem portraying Arthur in a role unknown to the Welsh. Such a text could not have been "ancient" in the sense of being as early as the fifth or sixth century, because Late British and its immediate derivatives were not written languages. But it might have been a Breton redaction of a truly ancient Latin original.

That possibility is linked with Geoffrey's chronological scheme. It cannot be made entirely coherent, but he arranges the family relationships, and other matters, so as to put most of Arthur's reign in the third quarter of the fifth century. Though he brings in some characters who are undoubtedly later, such anachronisms do not call the main structure in question. In particular, he says three times that Arthur's Gallic warfare occurred during the emperorship of Leo, evidently Leo I, who was eastern emperor from 457 to 474. For Arthur's passing, directly afterward, he gives the date 542, and this is so completely at odds with almost everything else that it is likely to have arisen from a mistake or corruption.

Now it has been shown that recognized processes of error could have derived 542 from 470, a date within Leo's reign, which precisely fits certain historical events that Geoffrey seems to have had in mind at this point. The error would imply a primary source using the chronology of Victorius of Aquitaine, counting the years from Christ's Passion. This was employed during the late fifth century but on the Continent was superseded by the *Anno Domini* method during the sixth. In other words, Geoffrey's dating of the Gallic warfare and Arthur's demise can be harmonized, and fixed within Leo's reign, on the hypothesis of source material that used Victorius's system and was therefore early. The Breton *Legend of St. Goeznovius*, and some chronicle references to Arthur, point to a similar tradition about his *floruit*. (*See* ARTHUR, ORIGINS OF LEGEND; CHRONICLES, ARTHUR IN; *GOEZNOVIUS, LEGEND OF ST.*; RIOTHAMUS.)

Geoffrey's third work was the *Vita Merlini* ("Life of Merlin"), a long poem in hexameters (ca. 1150). When he wrote the *Historia*, he had picked up the name of the northern bard Myrddin and applied it, modified and Latinized, to the young prophet who confounded Vortigern's magicians. He then learned more about this bard, including the fact that he lived much later. According to the Welsh, Myrddin was driven out of his mind at a battle in Cumbria in 575 and roamed through the northern forests uttering prophetic ravings. In his poem, Geoffrey uses the story after his own fashion, with a certain fudging of dates. The poem introduces another bard, Taliesin, who is made to say that after Arthur's last battle he accompanied the wounded king to the paradisal "island of apples," Avalon. Here, the enchantress Morgen reigned as chief of nine sisters, and she undertook to heal Arthur's wounds if he remained on the island. Morgen, who in romance becomes the sinister Morgan le Fay, is here a euhemerized Celtic goddess and entirely benign. There is still no commitment as to her royal patient's eventual fate.

To revert to the *Historia*: though Geoffrey established the "official" account of Arthur, together with some of the characters and motifs, his work was by no means the only creative force behind Arthurian romance. But the romances largely presupposed it and acquired conviction and verisimilitude by fitting more or less into the purportedly factual frame that it provided. Wace, in his French verse adaptation (entitled the *Roman de Brut* after Brutus), refers to Arthurian tales already current and explains that these adventures took place during the long peace following the King's first cycle of warfare. Besides Wace's version, there are several Welsh chronicles based on Geoffrey and also known by Brutus's name. The Welsh *Bruts* are more strictly quasi-historical and less relevant to romance. [GA]

❧ Geoffrey of Monmouth. *History of the Kings of Britain*, trans. Lewis Thorpe. London: Penguin, 1966.
———. *Vita Merlini*, ed. and trans. J.J. Parry. Urbana: University of Illinois Press, 1925.
Ashe, Geoffrey. "A Certain Very Ancient Book." *Speculum*, 56 (1981), 301–23.
Chambers, E.K. *Arthur of Britain*. London: Sidgwick and Jackson, 1927.
Hoffman, Donald L. "The Third British Empire." *Interpretations* (Memphis State University), 15 (1984), 1–10.
Kendrick, T.D. *British Antiquity*. London: Methuen, 1950.
Parry, John J., and Robert A. Caldwell. "Geoffrey of Monmouth." In *Arthurian Literature in the Middle Ages*, ed. Roger Sherman Loomis. Oxford: Clarendon, 1959, pp. 72–93.
Piggott, Stuart. "The Sources of Geoffrey of Monmouth." *Antiquity*, 15 (1941).
Tatlock, J.S.P. *The Legendary History of Britain*. Berkeley: University of California Press, 1950.

GERAINT AND ENID, probably written in the thirteenth century, one of the "three Welsh romances." (*Owain* and *Peredur* are the others.) *Geraint* is the closest of the three to the corresponding romance by Chrétien de Troyes, in this case *Erec et Enide*, though the hero's name is that of a late sixth- or early seventh-century king of Dumnonia (southwest Britain), rather than the Breton hero referred to in French. Geraint, one of Arthur's knights, wins Enid's hand after successfully competing for the prize of a sparrowhawk in a tournament. After their marriage, the couple are recalled to Geraint's patrimony because of the feebleness of his father the king, but the young husband neglects his duties as ruler and knight because of his overriding affection for his wife. One morning, she inadvertently reveals the courtiers' criticism of their prince to Geraint, who mistakenly (and inexplicably) takes her words to mean that she is unfaithful to him. He orders her roughly to ride out with him, but through a series of trials she eventually convinces him of her constancy and care for him. On the return journey to their court, Geraint in a final adventure overcomes the knight of the hedge of mist and destroys its enchantment. Though the first part of the story is clearly set in southwest Wales, and Geraint's country is realistically placed in the southwest peninsula, the rest of the romance has no geographical location, and Geraint's later adventures with his wife are poorly motivated. The first part is a taut, well-constructed narrative, the second more rambling. Stylistically, the narrative shows many of the rhetorical devices of Middle Welsh storytelling and pays such an attention to legal details and traditional nomenclature that, whatever its immediate origins may be, Chrétien's romance or its source, the story has been successfully put into a Welsh mold. [BFR]

≥ Jones, Gwyn, and Thomas Jones, trans. *The Mabinogion.* 2nd ed. London: Dent, 1974.

Jarman, A.O.H., and Gwilym Rees Hughes. *A Guide to Welsh Literature I.* Swansea: Davies, 1976.

GERBERT DE MONTREUIL: *see* CONTINUATIONS.

GERMAN ARTHURIAN LITERATURE (MEDIEVAL). Arthurian legends began to be adapted in Germany in the last decades of the twelfth century. We can only guess how transmission took place. We have reason to believe that influential princely patrons became acquainted with Old French Arthurian poems through their relationship with courts in France or during the Crusades. They themselves procured the manuscripts and had them adapted or translated into German. A well-known example is the landgrave Hermann of Thuringia, who provided the original versions for Herbort's *Lied von Troje* and Wolfram von Eschenbach's *Willehalm.* In only one case are we told how the original of an Arthurian story came to Germany, to be transposed there into a Middle High German verse romance. At the end of his *Lanzelet,* Ulrich von

Zatzikhoven mentions a French book written by an Anglo-Norman. It had belonged to Hugo de Morville, one of the hostages given in 1194 to the German emperor Henry VI by King Richard the Lionhearted.

We must assume that Old French Arthurian poems were also transmitted orally, as testified by Wirnt von Grafenberg in his *Wigalois*, where he affirms that a page had told him the story. Very often, however, the indications of sources in German Arthurian romances are fictitious. This is the case with the authorities cited by Heinrich von dem Türlin and by Der Pleier; and the philological controversy over Wolfram's Provençal "Kyot," whom he quotes as an authority for the final parts of his *Parzival*, is still not settled. In addition to the literary sources that constitute the major part of the Arthurian tradition in Germany, we must take into account a nonliterary stream of Arthurian narrative that had preserved a precourtly image of King Arthur, transmitted, presumably, by Breton minstrels, who traveled widely throughout Europe.

The classical German Arthurian romance follows Chrétien de Troyes closely with regard to content, substance, and structure; the Arthurian epics of the thirteenth and fourteenth centuries develop more and more into an amalgamation of all kinds of European narrative traditions. The sources used are not limited to the Old French Arthurian romances, lais, and fabliaux but also integrate elements of the antique and Byzantine romance, French and German heroic epic, fairy tales, and legends of every provenance, including historical and pseudo-historical documents. At an early stage, legends had been absorbed in French as well as in German romance, such as the Arthurian and the Tristan legends (especially by Eilhart von Oberge and Heinrich von dem Türlin, but not Gottfried von Strassburg) and the Knight of the Swan legend (Wolfram). In tracing the evolution of German Arthurian romance, we must give special consideration to the interdependence, filiations, and continuations of these works.

The variety of literary and nonliterary sources also accounts for the varying concepts of King Arthur's role and function in German Arthurian literature. Although certain fundamental characteristics remain relatively constant, the concept of King Arthur and his court undergoes considerable modification and stands for different models of social values and ethics.

The two founders of courtly Arthurian romance in Germany are Hartmann von Aue and Wolfram von Eschenbach. The first German Arthurian romance is Hartmann's *Erec*, probably composed about 1180 or later, followed by *Iwein* about twenty years afterward. Both are adaptations of Chrétien's verse romances. *Iwein* closely follows Chrétien, but the adaptation of *Erec* contains a number of significant modifications that have led to the speculation that Hartmann also used a source close to the *Mabinogi* tale *Geraint*, or to the Old Norse *Erex saga*. There are, however, no cogent reasons to doubt that Hartmann translated Chrétien's *Erec* in substance if not always in wording. The same applies to Wolfram's *Parzival* (1200–10). Yet if we can speak of Hartmann as the congenial imitator of Chrétien, we must consider Wolfram, despite his dependence on Chrétien, as the recreator of the *Perceval*.

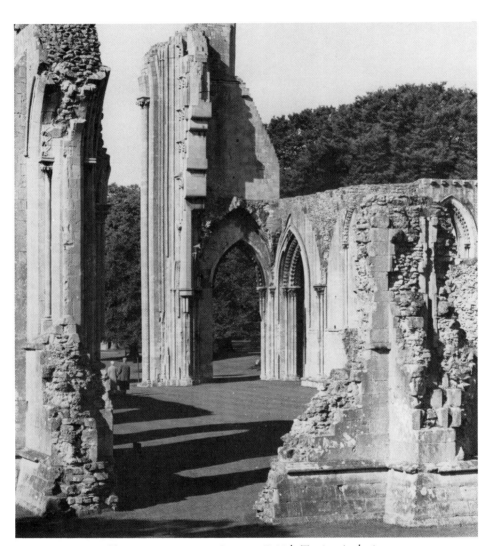

9   *Glastonbury Abbey ruins, Somerset. Courtesy British Tourist Authority.*

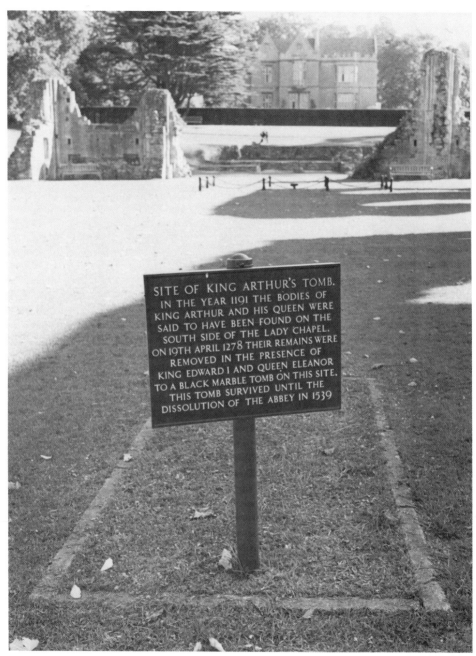

SITE OF KING ARTHUR'S TOMB.
IN THE YEAR 1191 THE BODIES OF
KING ARTHUR AND HIS QUEEN WERE
SAID TO HAVE BEEN FOUND ON THE
SOUTH SIDE OF THE LADY CHAPEL.
ON 19TH APRIL 1278 THEIR REMAINS WERE
REMOVED IN THE PRESENCE OF
KING EDWARD I AND QUEEN ELEANOR
TO A BLACK MARBLE TOMB ON THIS SITE.
THIS TOMB SURVIVED UNTIL THE
DISSOLUTION OF THE ABBEY IN 1539

10 *Marker of Arthur's grave, Glastonbury Abbey. Courtesy British Tourist Authority.*

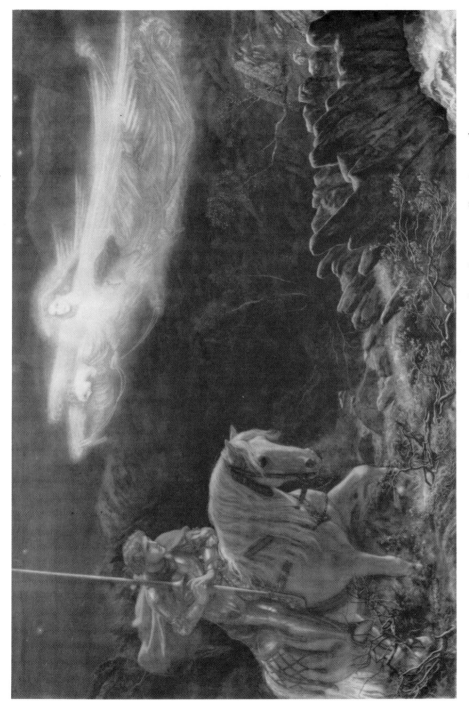

11 Arthur Hughes, Sir Galahad (1870). Courtesy Merseyside County Council, Walker Art Gallery, Liverpool.

12 William Holman Hunt, The Lady of Shalott *(1886–1905). Courtesy Wadsworth Atheneum, Hartford, Ella Gallup Sumner and Mary Catlin Sumner Collection.*

The third classical author, Gottfried von Strassburg, created in his *Tristan* a romance that was to have a profound effect on the development of the Tristan-matter in Germany, but that stands outside the pale of Arthurian literature in respect to personages, structure, and motivation. Unlike Hartmann and Wolfram, Gottfried did not affect the development of Arthurian romance in Germany. (*See* GOTTFRIED VON STRASSBURG; *TRISTAN*, MODERN GERMAN VERSIONS OF GOTTFRIED'S.)

The German adapters differ from Chrétien in their representation of King Arthur and his court. Chrétien's concept of Arthur's kingship and court reflects a social and political situation different from that of late twelfth-century Germany. Hartmann adopts the canon of courtly and princely attributes but harmonizes and idealizes them, eliminating conflict and controversy as well as references to the political reality of French vassalage. Hartmann's Arthurian romances must be seen in the light of the self-perception and self-assertion of the *Ministeriales* (lesser nobility). Hence, Arthur is conceived as paterfamilias; the relationship between the Arthurian knight and the sovereign is determined by the social and moral values of service and merit. Arthur's sovereignty is not contested. However, it does not manifest itself as a political demonstration of royal power but as a model of morality and humanity. Hatmann's *Erec* and *Iwein* may thus be read as a royal *speculum virtutum* ("mirror of virtues"), even if in the latter there is a critical distancing: Arthur's court, as the paradigm of morality and courtly joy, and of the protective and integrating forces of the Arthurian world, is occasionally called into question.

In his *Parzival*, Wolfram also portrays an intact Arthurian world, and in Arthur himself the exemplary sovereign. He discards the symptoms of decline noticeable in Chrétien's *Perceval*. Unlike Hartmann's Arthur, Wolfram's King is not an abstract idealization of moral and courtly values; placed in a realistic framework of kindred relations, with their inherent conflicts and adversities, he reflects the situation of medieval society in Germany. Wolfram places Arthur's kingdom among other principalities, with cleavages existing between allies and enemies. Wolfram's King Arthur is an idealistic projection like Hartmann's, but Wolfram stresses the cardinal virtues of the feudal lord, and among these loyalty holds the highest rank. Arthur is the incarnation of the prince of peace who in a world of antagonistic forces displays political prudence and judiciousness, a sense of justice and placability, to maintain order. This concept of Arthur was presumably intended as a corrective for the political chaos of Wolfram's own times.

Beside the courtly Arthurian epic modeled on Chrétien evolves the so-called romance of entertainment. The earliest German representatives of this genre are Ulrich von Zatzikhoven's *Lanzelet* (1195–1200) and Wirnt von Grafenberg's *Wigalois* (1210–15). The *Lanzelet* represents the more primitive type of Arthurian romance, in which the integration of an archaic narrative substratum, mostly Celtic in origin, and chivalrous courtly ethics is intended but not attained. These elements are only loosely connected, despite efforts to unite them in a homogeneous whole. On the one hand, Arthur and his circle act as dynamic agents of fabulous and fantastic adventures; on the other hand, they represent the center of chivalrous and courtly ethics and so remain static figures. Influences of a precourtly Arthurian tradition prevail in the episodes of Ginover's abduction and liberation by Arthur and his knights, which go back to an earlier Celtic version of the abduction story. Here, the King Arthur of Celtic legends is still perceptible, a mythical and heroic figure as he must have survived in the stories of Breton minstrels. Arthur is presented as the princely host, endowed with all courtly virtues, and his court the hub of joyful festivities, where for the first time the tests of virtue and chastity play a dominant role. These episodes belong to the popular genre of facetious and burlesque literature that enjoyed great popularity among the lesser writers of Arthurian romance. In his double function as leader of his knights and protagonist of adventurous actions on the one hand, and as the exemplary representative of courtly society on the other, the King Arthur of the *Lanzelet* thus combines traits of an archaic stage of Arthurian kingship and traits of the courtly ideal of sovereignty as established by Chrétien and Hartmann. The discrepancy between the two images of King Arthur is evident.

Although Wirnt's *Wigalois* belongs to the same type of Arthurian adventure story, this romance, in contrast to the *Lanzelet*, is characterized by religious overtones. King Arthur and his court serve only as a traditional setting for the initial adventure of the hero. They remain a literary relic with no function of their own and have little to do with the action. King Arthur is vested with a number of conventional attributes but is not developed into a consistent portrait. Wirnt's ideal of the sovereign is not represented by Arthur's kingship, nor are his moral values embodied in a courtly and chivalrous Arthurian world, but in a Christian king-craft grounded in medieval moral theology, and above all in the principles of faith and piety. This king-craft is not realized in a mythical and legendary kingship of the Holy Grail; its vocation is not eschatological but concrete and earthly: the establishment of peace and justice, the fight against haughtiness, violence, faithlessness, and idolatry. The representative of this ideal sovereign is not Arthur but Wigalois. A number of components contribute to the dissociation from the traditional structure of courtly Arthurian romance. First, the relationship between father (Gawein) and son (Wigalois) is much more emphasized than the relationship between the hero and Arthur. Second, Wigalois makes his appearance at Arthur's court already as the accomplished, perfect hero, equal to Arthur, thus eliminating one of the most important structural elements of Arthurian romance—the protagonist's striving for chivalric and moral stature in order to gain the recognition and honors of Arthurian society. Wigalois's liberation of Korentin is initially undertaken in the name of the Arthurian court, but in the course of events the connections with the court are disrupted. Wigalois's greatest deed of chivalry does not culminate in the recognition of Arthur's circle. The prevalent Christian purport of the Korentin adventure, as well as the religious tendency of the work as a whole, did not fit into an Arthurian world in its established literary typology.

Heinrich von dem Türlin's *Diu Crône* (composed about 1230) is an extraordinary compilation of motifs and episodes derived from almost every known Arthurian and Grail romance, from Old French lais and fabliaux, and from fairy tales and legends. This most voluminous Arthurian verse romance (30,041 lines) apart from the *Jüngerer Titurel* is like a gigantic sponge, absorbing all sorts of fabulous material. In the tradition of a *vita*, the romance starts with Arthur's birth and childhood but soon breaks off for lack of subject matter (Heinrich did not know Geoffrey's *Historia* or Wace's *Brut*). This portrait of an ideal Arthur, illustrating a young king favored by fortune, gives place in the Gazosein episode to a representation of King Arthur like that encountered in popular epics and jocular poetry. It was Heinrich's intent to make his King Arthur the ideal sovereign, embodying the ideal of courtly, chivalric, and princely life. The earlier approach, though, is treated conventionally, leading to a loss of substance of courtly and ethical values. These values no longer stand for the individual efforts and aspirations toward a higher state of accomplishment; courtly existence, as represented by Heinrich, is deprived of all vitality. The second approach falls to the level of rustic and grotesque comedy. The incompatibility of these two devices—of royal and courtly representation on the one hand and of the knight-errant on the other—turns the romance of King Arthur into the romance of Gawein. Nevertheless, a remarkable change in the perception of Arthur's kingship can be observed: Heinrich's attempt to reactivate the role of the king is probably a reflection of the new ideal of the *rex et miles*, which led to kingship taking on knightly forms of life.

The same tendency is recognizable in Der Stricker's *Daniel von dem blühenden Tal* (1220–30) but is realized in a quite different manner. It is the non-Arthurian elements that stamp this romance with its special characteristics and account for its exceptional position among German Arthurian epics. These elements have their origin in the heroic epic and explain the hybridity of *Daniel*'s substance and form. To mention just a few: courtly love, the moving force of courtly Arthurian romance, is of no importance at all. Furthermore, the lengthy descriptions of single and mass combats, shaped by the model of the *Song of Roland*, in which Arthur takes the field as commander-in-chief and dreaded, awe-inspiring fighter, are contrary to the classical Arthurian romance. This reversion to the precourtly ideal of kingship demonstrates Der Stricker's rejection of the narrative and symbolic structure of the Arthurian world in its traditional form. Instead of the traditional courtly values, we find political cleverness and energy; instead of moral exemplariness, pragmatism. Even if the quest for adventure and the individual chivalric actions of the protagonist are maintained, they are dominated by the idea of common welfare and social ethics, at the base of which are unconditional feudal faith and allegiance. The reevocation of these ideals, though not absent in classical Arthurian romance, exalts the precourtly ideal of vassalage seen in the heroic epic. In King Arthur, Der Stricker portrays another Charlemagne.

The reaction to this uncourtly romance was not long in coming. Der Pleier's *Garel von dem blühenden Tal* (1250–80), as the title indicates, was intended as an anti-*Daniel*, or corrective model in the tradition of classical Arthurian romance. Just as in Der Pleier's *Meleranz* and *Tandareis*, Arthur and his court symbolize a courtly and chivalrous world, the embodiment of decency, propriety, and courtesy—but it is a world of appearances. Der Pleier's concern is the preservation and transmission of courtly values, which in the process of imitation are, however, reduced to conventionality. Behind the façade of courtly existence, the cultural and ethical ideal of medieval nobility has been diluted to mere etiquette. In this respect, the Arthurian romances of Der Pleier are guides to courtly rules of manners and chivalrous behavior, as exemplified by Arthur and his circle. Der Pleier looks backward in order to reestablish the ideal values of the past and to set them against the decay and corruption of his own times.

Konrad von Stoffeln's *Gauriel von Muntabel* (ca. 1300) serves a similar purpose. King Arthur and his court, a paradigm of an intact world where courtly manners and chivalrous deeds are still valid, are stereotyped to a scenery of feasts, socialities, and pastimes. The figures walk about gracefully and courteously, as in a rococo park, Arthur and the Queen among them. Although Konrad maintains the narrative scheme of classical Arthurian romance, the underlying principle is not enhancement to attain a higher status but simply cumulation and seriality.

The *Wigamur*, written about 1250 by an unknown author, is an example of the treatment of Arthurian subject matter on the level of jocular poetry, where comic and burlesque elements prevail. The *raison d'être* of Arthurian knighthood consists of jousting and tilting, in addition to the extensively described pleasures of the table. The original significance of the Round Table is no longer comprehended. King Arthur, no longer the immobile center around which others move, appears as the leader of his knights on the scene of action. The Arthurian episodes here have no distinguishing quality, nor do they have a symbolic meaning. King Arthur and his knights are perceived largely as wanderers.

Albrecht von Scharfenberg's *Jüngerer Titurel* (ca. 1272) marks both the culmination and the point of disintegration of German Arthurian verse romance. Albrecht was long considered merely the continuator of Wolfram. This is certainly true with respect to the adaptation and integration of his main sources, the *Parzival* and the *Titurel* fragments, the most incidental motifs and episodes of which Albrecht exploits and reassembles to form new narrative complexes. But the moving force of Albrecht's work is its eschatological vision of the world: his concern is religious and moral instruction. While in the Arthurian romances of Heinrich von dem Türlin and of Der Pleier the Arthurian world occupies a central position, deriving its justification from the supremacy of courtly and chivalric existence, in the *Jüngerer Titurel* this supremacy is given to the transcendental order of eternal life, the sole guiding principle of existence. This perception consequently leads to the devaluation of courtly ethics and the dissolution of the Arthurian order. Though the ideal projection of the Arthurian world is ahistorical, symbolizing the reign of the just law in its stability and finality, Albrecht reintroduces historical dimensions: the fixation of Arthur's reign to the sixth century A.D.; the references to Troy, Alexander, Rome, Charlemagne, and other Christian kings and martyrs; the allusion to the conflict between Hohenstaufen and Guelph; the genealogy of the Grail kings. Albrecht's concept of history is eschatological and typological, not chronological; events and personalities, whether real or fictitious, are not seen in their temporality but in their relation to the eternal. Albrecht writes the history of the Grail through analogy to the Scriptures. In the hierarchy of kingdoms, Arthur's occupies the lowest rank, surpassed by the oriental kingdoms in wealth and magnificence and by the Grail kingdom in spirituality. In the *Jüngerer Titurel*, individual chivalric action, guaranteeing peace and order, proves ineffectual. The most valorous and noble representatives of chivalry perish; combat and belligerency take on a worldwide dimension, reflecting a permanent human condition. King Arthur excels on the battlefield, but his victories do not restore peace. The Round Table breaks up, and Arthur's attempts to reconcile the antagonistic forces bear no fruit. In the final sequences of the romance, Arthur and his court completely disappear; Arthur himself is last mentioned as a founder of monasteries. Like Robert de Boron's *Grail* romance, the *Queste*, and the *Mort Artu* of the Vulgate Cycle, Albrecht turns away from the Arthurian world and its courtly and chivalric ethics. The order of the future is projected into the theocratic realm of Prester John, who personifies the two great forces of the medieval world, kingship and priesthood. But this realm, the prefiguration of Paradise, lies in the Orient, not in the Occident. [KRG]

Bindschedler, Maria. "Die Dichtung um König Artus und seine Ritter." *Deutsche Vierteljahresschrift für Literaturwissenschaft und Geistesgeschichte*, 31 (1957), 84–100.

Brogsitter, Karl Otto. *Artusepik*. Stuttgart: Metzler, 1965; 2nd ed. 1971.

Emmel, Hildegard. *Formprobleme des Artusromans und der Graldichtung: Die Bedeutung des Artuskreises für das Gefüge des Romans im 12. und 13. Jahrhundert in Frankreich, Deutschland und den Niederlanden*. Berne: Francke, 1951.

Gürttler, Karin R. *"Künec Artûs der guote": Das Artusbild der höfischen Epik des 12. und 13. Jahrhunderts*. Bonn: Bouvier Verlag Herbert Grundmann, 1976.

GERMAN ARTHURIAN LITERATURE (MODERN). 1) INTRODUC-

TION. The appearance of Arthurian themes in postmedieval German literature must be seen as an offshoot of a more general revival of interest in German medieval culture, beginning in the mid-eighteenth century. The medieval tradition had little appeal for the German writers of the seventeenth and early eighteenth centuries. They were more concerned with providing German literature with a poetics that would elevate it to the level of the French Classicists, whom they viewed as their literary and theoretical models. This century-and-a-half hiatus was broken by the influence of the theories of the Swiss-German professor Johann Jacob Bodmer. Reacting against the artificiality of the French Classicists, he attempted to understand the internal process of poetic creation itself, which he studied in the literature of various cultures, including medieval Germany. Despite the importance of Bodmer's more general literary theories, however, his poetic translations of medieval works lacked literary quality and were perhaps too premature to have an impact.

It was the German Romantic movement at the turn of the nineteenth century that was responsible for the tremendous revival of medieval culture as a source for creative literature. Faced with religious and political fragmentation and the threat of Napoleonic occupation, many German Romantics developed an idealistic interest in the Catholicism and perceived political unity of the medieval period. This interest in their own past, coupled with a concern for poetic spontaneity, led them to research, collect, and imitate the sagas, fairy tales, and folksongs of the past and to write numerous works set in the Middle Ages. In fact, the Romantics can be seen as providing the impetus for the great wave of historical fiction and drama that swept Germany in the nineteenth century.

Yet, although Romantics, such as the famous Schlegel brothers, expressed great interest in Arthurian literature, they produced little of it. Understandably, German writers would be more likely to exploit their own mythical, historical, and literary past, especially their "national epic," the *Nibelungenlied*, rather than the Matter of Britain. Though there was an almost unbroken stream of adaptations of the *Nibelungen* material from 1803 on, adaptation of Arthurian materials in the Romantic Age was at best sporadic and not very original. Here, and among the Preromantics, it was generally limited to poetic allusions to Merlin the prophet, often independent of specific Arthurian associations, or else consisted of translations of French versions of Arthurian stories, the prime source being Count Tressan's *Bibliothèque universelle des romans* (1775–89), or else attempted to translate or rework parts of Wolfram von Eschenbach's *Parzival* or Gottfried von Strassburg's *Tristan*.

With few exceptions, German Arthurian literature of the nineteenth and twentieth centuries was based on Wolfram and Gottfried. Production of postmedieval German Arthuriana could thus not expand until critical editions of Wolfram's and Gottfried's works, by such editors and translators as Eberhard von Groote (*Tristan*, 1821), Friedrich von der Hagen (*Tristan*, 1823), Karl Lachmann (*Parzival*, 1833), San Marte (*Parzival*, 1836), Karl Simrock (*Parzival* and *Titurel*, 1842), and Hermann Kurz (*Tristan*, 1844), made this material accessible to a wider public as a potential source for creative writers. Christoph Heinrich Myller's earlier publication of Bodmer's medieval *Parzival* and *Tristan* manuscripts (1784–85) had little impact because they lacked the critical apparatus that would have made these difficult works understandable. This was not as true of the *Nibelungenlied*, the style and language of which were much more straightforward.

In quantitative terms, the greatest interest in Arthurian literature (again limited primarily to the Tristan and Parzival material) occurred in the late nineteenth and early twentieth centuries. This can be traced directly to two factors: first, the success of Richard Wagner's operas *Tristan und Isolde* (1859), *Parsifal* (1877–82), and, to a lesser extent, *Lohengrin* (1847), all of them depending heavily on translations of Wolfram and Gottfried; second, the Neoromantic development in German literature at the turn of the twentieth century, which shared with the Romantic movement of the preceding century a degree of nationalism, nostalgic idealism, and religious fervor. This development, or literary echoes of it, extended into the 1920s.

The political and social atmosphere of the National Socialist era did not favor the production of Arthurian literature, which was never extensive under the best of circumstances, and the literature of the postwar years exhibits a concern for more pressing contemporary issues. From the 1970s on, however, interest in German medieval history and literature is revealed by an increased publication of new editions and translations of medieval works; critical writings on them; literary, film, and stage adaptations; and even novels about the lives of Wolfram and Gottfried. This renewed interest reflects the desire of each of the two modern German states, particularly the German Democratic Republic, to establish its own cultural identity with a continuous tradition.

The receptivity of the Federal Republic of Germany to English and American literature, television programming, films, and technology is also having an effect on the reception of Arthurian themes into German literature. English and American novels, cartoons, video games, and films based on Arthurian literature or rich in Arthurian motifs are finding their way to the German public. Although the recent films by Richard Blank (*Parzival*, 1980, based on Wolfram), Klaus Lindemann (*Tristans Klage* ["Tristan's Lament"], produced for television in 1976, broadcast in 1979), Veith von Fürstenberg (*Feuer und Schwert* ["Fire and Sword"], 1981–82, based on Gottfried), and Jürgen Syberberg (*Parsifal*, 1982–84, based on Wagner) are still embedded in the somewhat narrow German Arthurian tradition, American films consistently command about fifty percent of the West German film market. The exponential increase in the exposure of the German public to English and American developments in Arthuriana is impressive. It is too early, however, to assess or predict the full impact of this phenomenon.

2) FICTION. Except for Johann Jacob Bodmer's verse renderings of parts of Wolfram's *Parzival*; the epic *Tristan* fragments by Schlegel, Rückert, and Immermann; and the mixture of verse and prose narrative in the translations by Felix von Hofstaeter (1741–1814) of Ulrich von Zatzikhoven's *Lanzelet* and of Ulrich Fuetrer's *Lanzelet*, *Froner Gral*, and *Theurer Merlin*, all found in his *Altdeutsche Gedichte aus den Zeiten der Tafelrunde* ("Old German Poems from the Times of the Round Table," 1811), the occurrence of German Arthuriana in narrative form is relatively infrequent before the appearance of Wagner's *Parsifal*, and it largely relies upon contemporary foreign versions of medieval material.

In 1804, Friedrich Schlegel published a *Geschichte des Zauberers Merlin* ("Story of Merlin the Magician"), a translation by Schlegel's wife, Dorothea, of the medieval French *Roman de Merlin*. Schlegel criticized his fellow Romantics for resorting to the newer, often abridged, versions of such medieval materials in Count Tressan's Bibliothèque universelle des romans (1775–89), which served as a source for Christoph Martin Wieland's blank-verse narrative *Geron der Adelige* ("The Noble Geron," 1777), and probably also for his brief prose summary of Merlin's life, *Merlin der Zauberer* ("Merlin the Magician," 1777). In the verse narrative *Die Päpstin Johanna* ("Pope Johanna," 1813, prose version published posthumously, 1848), by the Romantic poet and novelist Achim von Arnim (1781–1831), Merlin is alluded to because of the symbolism of his birth from the union of a demon and a fairy (or demon and human). He thus embodies the conflict between Good and Evil with which Johanna is faced when the Devil uses deception to achieve her election as pope. Ludwig Tieck's tale of the *Leben und Thaten des kleinen Thomas, genannt Däumchen* ("Life and Times of Little Tom Thumb," 1811, in his collection *Phantasus*), with Tom's birth prophesied by the magician Merlin, sets a combination of the English and German versions of the fairy tale against an Arthurian background. Another magician, Klinschor, owner of the Castle of Wonders in the Gawain adventure in Wolfram's *Parzival*, is reduced to the figure of a mentor-poet in the legend of the *Minnesinger* competition at the Wartburg, adapted by Friedrich von Hardenberg (known as Novalis, 1772–1801) for his idealistic Romantic novel fragment, *Heinrich von Ofterdingen* (1802). Despite their interest in Arthurian literature, the German Romantics preferred historical or quasi-historical characters and settings for their own works. Though the subjects of Benedikte Naubert's writings were typically Romantic in this sense, her depiction of the Arthurian Middle Ages as immoral and ephemeral was not.

The German interest in Arthuriana during the later nineteenth and early twentieth centuries shifted its focus to the medieval literary tradition of Wolfram's *Parzival* and Gottfried's *Tristan*, with Neoromantic developments stimulated especially by Wagner's *Parsifal* and *Tristan und Isolde*. However, whereas the Parzival material is dealt with in prose and poetry as well as dramatic works, the Tristan story occurs almost exclusively in dramatic adaptations.

The Merlin material, although still adapted occasionally, appeared more often in drama than fiction. The narrative *Merlins Wanderungen* ("Merlin's Travels," 1887), by Rudolf von Gottschall (1823–1909), takes up the conflict of values that Merlin represents as a result of his combined demonic-human origin. Lienhard's novella *Merlin der Königsbarde* ("Merlin, Bard of the King," 1900), which is typical of the Neoromantic idealism of his other works, makes Merlin a folk-hero. Paul Heyse (1830–1914) uses the title *Merlin* as a metaphor for the modern Merlin–Niniane love relationship, which his novel (1892) depicts. In Gerhart Hauptmann's mystical novel fragment *Der neue Christophorus* ("The New St. Christopher"), the first chapter of which was published in 1932 as *Merlins Geburt* ("Merlin's Birth"), a boy born of a demon and an earth spirit serves a religious apprenticeship under Father Christophorus, who perceives in him the new savior of humankind.

Metaphorical titles were also used to evoke associations with the Grail in novels with an otherwise non-Arthurian modern setting. This is the case with *Die Abendburg* ("The Evening Castle," 1909), by Bruno Wille (1860–1928), and

Montsalvasch (1912), by Erwin Guido Kolbenheyer (1878–1962). In other novels by Kolbenheyer, particularly *Amor Dei* (1908) and *Meister Johannes Pausewang* (1910), it is clear that the author has again been influenced by the Grail motifs of quest and idealism, which is also the case with the novel *Wiltfeber, der ewige Deutsch* ("Wiltfeber, the Wandering German," 1912), by Hermann Burte (1879–1960). In the 1908 novel *Zwölf aus der Steiermark* ("Twelve from Styria"), by Rudolph Hans Bartsch (1873–1952), the medieval parallel is all too obvious and borders on the ridiculous when twelve idealistic poets band together to form a vegetarian order. On the other hand, the title of the historical novel *Parzival* (1878), by Albert Emil Brachvogel (1824–1878), is misleading, since the work deals with the decline of the Knights Templar around 1300, with only occasional mention of the Grail theme.

A number of mediocre works produced in the Neoromantic enthusiasm of the turn of the century can be grouped together as more or less free adaptations of Wolfram's *Parzival*, with some Wagnerian influence: *Parzival* (an edition for the German household with pictures and facsimiles, 1888), by Emil Engelmann (1837–1900); *Parzival, ein Abenteuerroman* ("Parzival, An Adventure Novel," 1911), by Will Vesper (1882–1962); *Der Liebesgral* ("The Love Grail," 1913), a free rendering of only the Schionatulander and Gahmuret stories in novel form by Georg Terramare (1889–1948); *Lohengrin* (1913) and *Parsival* (1914), both longer prose narratives by Gerhart Hauptmann; and *Flammen über die Welt: Die Sagen Parzival, Tristan, Merlin* ("Flames over the World: The Parzival, Tristan, and Merlin Legends," 1926), one of a trilogy of shorter narrative volumes on historical, mythological, and literary figures by Siegfried von der Trenck (1882–1951). The best of these reworkings of Wolfram's text are the 1898 version *Die Sage von Parzival und dem Gral* ("The Legend of Parzival and the Grail"), by Wilhelm Hertz (1835–1902), and *Parzival der Gralsucher* ("Parzival, Seeker of the Grail," 1922), by Hans von Wolzogen (1855–1934). Finally, the three fairy tales (1892–94) of Houstan Stewart Chamberlain (1855–1927), *Weihnachtsmärchen*, *Ostermärchen*, and *Pfingstmärchen* (Christmas, Easter, and Pentecost Tales), derive directly from Wagner's *Parsifal*. The first two present the insights gained by Parsifal during periods of introspection on Christmas Eve and the eve preceding the Good Friday on which he regains the Grail, i.e., between Acts II and III of Wagner's opera. The third tale depicts Parsifal's death and is meant to span the gap between Wagner's *Parsifal* and *Lohengrin*.

The German interest in Arthuriana was curtailed during the National Socialist era and the period of social disruption immediately following World War II. Only Thomas Mann's novel *Der Erwählte* ("The Holy Sinner," 1951), based on the medieval Gregorius legend of Hartmann von Aue and written during Mann's self-imposed exile in America, is rich in Arthurian allusions.

Emphasis on the German cultural heritage by both the East and West German states since the 1970s has led to an increase in editions, translations, and adaptations of German medieval Arthurian works. Although it is difficult to draw the line between free translation or adaptation and creative writing, adapters of medieval romances in the German Democratic Republic are often accused of making ideological changes to render their versions more "socialistically" relevant. Günter de Bruyn's *Tristan und Isolde* (1975) and Werner Heiduczek's *Seltsame Abenteuer des Parzival* ("Unusual Adventures of Parzival," 1974) are examples of two such East German prose works. Lily Hohenstein's *Die Nächte in St. Wendelin: Der Lebensroman Wolframs von Eschenbach* ("Nights in St. Wendelin: The Life of Wolfram von Eschenbach," 1969) and Bruno Gloger's *Dieterich: Vermutungen um Gottfried von Strassburg* ("Dieterich: Assumptions About Gottfried von Strassburg," 1976), are biographical novels and, in a sense, literary-historical fiction.

In the Federal Republic of Germany, there is a similar awakening of interest in the rewriting of medieval German epics, for example, Ruth Schirmer's *Tristan* (1969). However, the importance of English and American cultural and literary phenomena has added a dimension lacking in the modern Arthurian fiction of the German Democratic Republic. Successful German translations of popular Arthurian adaptations by English and American writers, such as T.H. White, Mark Twain, Mary Stewart, Richard Monaco, and Marion Zimmer Bradley, have all appeared in the late 1970s or early 1980s. This has led to an increased familiarity with a broader Arthurian tradition among the German readership. The appearance of works centered on Arthur and Merlin, such as Maria Christiane Benning's *Merlin der Zauberer und König Artus* ("Merlin the Magician and King Arthur," 1980), Ulla Leippe's *Artussagen neu erzählt* ("The Legends of Arthur Retold," 1978—one of a series of children's books), Walter Schneider's television script *König Arthur* (1974), and Kurt Vethake's *König Arthur* (1975), a radio play for children, all indicate a broadening of the German Arthurian horizon.

3) DRAMA. The dramatization of Arthurian material in German literature was the domain of late nineteenth- and early twentieth-century writers, primarily under the influence of Richard Wagner's operas; earlier writers preferred to adapt the material to epic or poetic forms. The Postromantic, or *Biedermeier*, author August von Platen (1796–1835) planned to dramatize the Merlin and Tristan materials (1827–28) but did not proceed beyond sketches. Friedrich de la Motte Fouqué's *Parcival* remained unpublished, and *Die Geburt des Merlin oder Das Kind hat seinen Vater gefunden* (1829), by the Romantic Ludwig Tieck, is merely an excellent translation of William Rowley's Elizabethan drama *The Birth of Merlin or The Child Hath Found Its Father* (1662). Two obscure late Romantic *Tristan* tragedies (1854 and 1858) by Friedrich Roeber (1819–1901) and Joseph Weilen (1828–1889) are of minimal significance.

Only one Arthurian drama stood out as an exception to this reluctance to dramatize, Immermann's *Merlin: Eine Mythe* (1832), a philosophical Postromantic work that was meant to be read and that has in fact never been successfully performed. Merlin, the son of Satan and intended Antichrist, rebels against his father and presumptuously tries to save humankind by making Arthur rather than Titurel the King of the Grail. However, Merlin, seduced and robbed of his powers by Niniane, fails Arthur in his search for the Grail. Arthur and his knights perish, and Merlin dies dedicating himself to God rather than submitting to Satan. This pessimistic blend of romanticism and rationalism, which combines multiple Merlin traditions from a variety of sources, including Schlegel's translation of the Merlin story and Tieck's translation of Rowley's drama, deals basically with the inevitable incompatibility of the divine and worldly, or demonic, sides of human nature.

The Neoromanticism at the turn of the twentieth century, accompanied by the interest in medieval German Arthurian works generated by Wagner's operas, led to a surge of literary production based primarily on Gottfried's *Tristan* and Wolfram's *Parzival*, and on Wagner's adaptations of them. Almost all of the Tristan adaptations were in dramatic form, not only because of the strong influence of Wagner but also because writers saw in the inevitable tragic outcome of the Tristan and Isolde love affair a potential for adaptation as tragic drama. Whether this perception was incorrect or the literary ability to realize it too limited, these *Tristan* dramas were never successful.

The Parzival material was adapted to all genres, not least among them drama. A number of Grail plays were little more than dramatic trivializations: August Reissmann's *Das Gralspiel: Parsifal der reine Tor oder die Ritter von Salvator* ("The Grail Play: Parsifal the Ultimate Fool or The Knights of Salvator," 1883), a parody of Wagner; Wilhelm Henzen's *Parzival, ein Mysterium* ("Parzival, A Mystery Play," 1889); Paul Matzdorf's *Parsival, ein Jugendlichenspiel* ("Parsival, A Play for Children, 1915); Emanuel von Bodman's *Der Gral* (written 1915, published 1925); Friedrich Johann Pesendorfer's *Rosmunda, die Gralskönigin, eucharistisches Schauspiel für die Mädchenbühne* ("Rosmunda, the Grail Queen, Eucharistic Stage Play for Girls," 1916); Hans Rhyn's *Parzival und Kondwiramur* (1924); Gustav Renner's *Merlin* (1912). This last play, despite its title, explores the problems of striving and guilt normally associated with Parzival.

Wagner's impact is underscored both by the appearance of new Arthurian operas (for example, Goldmark's *Merlin*, 1886, with considerable contributions from Immermann's earlier play, and Felix Draeseke's *Merlin*, 1913) and also by the addition of musical elements to Parzival dramas in an attempt to enhance their effect. *Titurel* (1891), by Karl Schäfer (1849–1915), fluctuates between opera and drama and offers a depiction of the Sigune–Schionatulander love story as a prelude to the Grail legend. *Der heilige Gral* ("The Holy Grail," 1912), by Richard von Kralik, is a prelude to the story as adapted by Wagner and deals with Amfortas's loss of the Holy Lance. A choir of angels imitates Wagner's chorus. Although Kralik also wrote a *Merlin* drama (1913) emphasizing the Niniane (Viviane) episode, it was his attraction to the religious-mystical idealism of the Grail quest that most typified his Neoromantic work. The idealism of Friedrich Lienhard was more heroic than mystical; it is reflected in his numerous medieval themes, including his drama *König Arthur* (1900). This depicts the tragedy of Arthur, who tolerates Guinevere's adultery with Lancelot in order to preserve the integrity of his ideal of the Round Table.

By far the most prolific author of Arthurian literature at this time was Eduard Stucken, whose Grail cycle, or dramatic epos as it has been called, consists of seven plays: *Gawan* (1902), *Lanval* (1903), *Lanzelot* (1909), *Merlins Geburt* ("Merlin's Birth," 1912), *Tristram und Ysolt* (1916), *Das verlorene Ich* ("The Lost Self," 1922), *Der Zauberer Merlin* ("Merlin the Magician," 1924). In this protracted frenzy of Neoromantic *Jugendstil* creativity, Stucken juggled plots and characters in order to transform the Grail quest into the central thread connecting Arthurian themes based on the most diverse sources, including Immermann's *Merlin: Eine Mythe*. Finally, two additional dramas were connected only indirectly to the Arthurian tradition. Rudolf König's *Der Gral, eine Dichtertragödie aus dem deutschen Mittelalter* ("The Grail, A German Medieval Tragedy of Poets," 1914) deals with the genesis of the medieval Claus Wisse–Philipp Colin *Der nüwe Parzefal*, which extends Wolfram's work by 37,000 lines. Gerhart Hauptmann's drama fragment *Galahad* (1908–14) uses the title metaphorically to evoke the play's theme, the struggle of youthful innocence against temptation.

Interest in German Arthurian literature faded with the decline of Neoromanticism. National Socialist idealism was not oriented toward Arthuriana, and literature of the immediate postwar years reflected disillusionment rather than idealism. Arthurian interest did not revive until the 1970s, when each of the two German states emphasized the German cultural heritage as the basis for its new individual national identity. Although a revival of German medieval literature has led to new versions of the Parzival and Tristan materials, these have not generally been in dramatic form. Two West German adaptations of Wolfram's *Parzival* are Nathalie Harder's puppet play (1979–82) and a play by the experimental Munich theatrical company Werkhaus Moosach called *Flechtungen: Der Fall Partzifall* ("Weavings: The Partzifall Case," 1978), which interweaves incidents in the lives of two types of social outcast, an institutionalized psychiatric patient and the Parzival character of Wolfram's work.

Tankred Dorst has made a more important contribution to modern German Arthuriana in his monumental drama *Merlin oder das Wüste Land* ("Merlin or the Wasteland," 1981). Written in colloquial German with generous amounts of irony, humor, and absurdity, which do much to demythologize even the most mythological parts of the tradition, the play is a pessimistic allegory presenting the whole rise and decline of King Arthur and his knights, and Merlin with them. Conceived for an international theater festival in Hamburg, Dorst's *Merlin* is particularly significant as an indication of the recent developments in German Arthurian adaptation. It reflects not only a readiness on the part of West German writers to incorporate modern English and American Arthurian motifs and allusions but also the growing spirit of internationalism in West German literature and culture in general.

4) POETRY. Verse epics or narratives, such as Bodmer's *Der Parcival* (1753) and *Gamuret* (1755), Wieland's *Geron der Adelige* (1777), the *Lanzelot und Ginevra* (1860) of Wilhelm Hertz (1835–1902), and the *Tristan* fragments by Schlegel, Rückert, and Immermann, are ambitious undertakings of varying success. It is sometimes difficult to distinguish creative poetry from translation in verse. The same can be said of Hofstaeter's *Altdeutsche Gedichte aus den Zeiten der*

Tafelrunde (see above), which contains translations of Zatzikhoven's *Lanzelet* and Fuetrer's *Lanzelet, Froner Gral*, and *Theurer Merlin*. Lyric poetry, on the other hand, tends to draw on individual incidents and characters to create a mood. The character Merlin is the first to predominate in postmedieval German lyric poetry, with Parzival becoming more prevalent beginning with the post-Wagnerian Neoromanticism at the turn of the twentieth century. The principal exceptions to this generalization are Bodmer's poetically poor ballad "Jestute" (1781), and two poems in *Des Knaben Wunderhorn: Alte deutsche Lieder* ("The Youth's Magic Horn: Old German Songs," 1806–08), an extensive collection of German lyric folk poetry by Achim von Arnim (1781–1831) and Clemens Brentano (1778–1842). The title poem of this collection, "Das Wunderhorn," is a variation on the chastity-horn theme from the medieval French *Lai du cor*, by Robert Biket. A second Arthurian poem, "Die Ausgleichung" ("The Adjustment"), combines this theme with an adaptation of the related *Mantel mautaillié*.

In poems based on the Merlin material, further Arthurian associations are either lacking or minor. For his second "Kophtisches Lied" ("Coptic Song," 1787), the great Classicist Goethe borrowed the role of the oracular Merlin, prophesying from his grave, from Ariosto's *Orlando Furioso*. Goethe may also have had the old magician Merlin in mind when writing his ballad "Der Zauberlehrling" ("The Sorcerer's Apprentice," 1797). Merlin's grotto-grave in the forest of Brocéliande figures again in Wieland's long elegiac poem *Merlins weissagende Stimme aus seiner Gruft* ("Merlin's Prophetic Voice from His Grave," 1810), in which the prophet bemoans the loss of the golden age of Arthurian chivalry and, by implication, the passing of the German Classical Age of Weimar.

The theme of Merlin's forest entombment or confinement by Niniane (or Viviane), or his voluntary isolation in nature, provided a convenient formula for the Romantic poets. In Immermann's philosophical poem "Merlins Grab" ("Merlin's Grave," 1818), Merlin represents the spirit of nature as a source of enlightenment and consolation for those who are openminded enough to accept his advice. In his later poem "Merlin im tiefen Grabe" ("Merlin in the Deep Grave," 1833), written as a second epilogue to his 1832 drama *Merlin: Eine Mythe*, an older and disillusioned Immermann laments the human inability to escape the confinement within modern society and so to benefit from the rejuvenating force of nature. Nikolaus Lenau, on the other hand, depicts only the positive aspect of Merlin's association with nature in the course of his description of Merlin reveling in the physical and spiritual enjoyment of a tempest in the fifth of his *Waldlieder* ("Forest Songs," 1843).

The Swabian Romantic Ludwig Uhland offers a poetic rendition of the basically non-Arthurian story of "Merlin der Wilde" ("Merlin the Wild Man," 1829), taken from a summary of Geoffrey's *Vita Merlini*. Merlin, depressed at the death of his three brothers, prefers to contemplate the mysteries of nature, from which he derives strength and prophetic insight, rather than remain at the court of his brother-in-law, King Roderick. The poem is dedicated to Uhland's friend and fellow poet Karl Mayer (1786–1870), whom he praises as a "modern Merlin." In a poem sent to Uhland out of gratitude for this compliment, Mayer humbly rejects the comparison and applies it to Uhland instead. Wolfgang Müller von Königswinter (1816–1873) uses the same basic story in his *Merlin der Zauberer* ("Merlin the Magician," 1857), but in this version it is not Merlin as the man of nature who is emphasized. Here he is Niniane's lover, and he uses his wisdom to resolve the conflict that arises from his revelation of the love affair of Guinevere, the king's daughter.

The poetic depiction of the Merlin–Niniane relationship is, however, not usually this positive. In the third of his *Katharina* poems (1835), Heinrich Heine compares the lover to Merlin, the suitor entranced by his mistress. The lover's mistress, however, may be interpreted as anything from political freedom to abstract beauty or nature. "In der Winternacht" ("In the Winter Night," 1840–50), by Gottfried Kinkel (1815–1882), presents this same stereotype, but here lacking any deeper significance. Finally, two poems by the later Romantic Alexander Kaufmann (1817–1893), "Unter den Reben" ("Among the Grapevines," 1852) and "Merlin und Niniane" (1852), present love, embodied in Niniane, and thought, embodied in Merlin, as two sides of the human spirit that are not compatible when pursued without compromise.

Except for Bodmer's ballad "Jestute," mentioned previously, and Goethe's uncompleted poetic narrative *Die Geheimnisse* ("The Secrets," 1784), in which the depiction of an isolated brotherhood of priests offers striking parallels to the Grail community of the Parzival story, without any direct reference to it, the Parzival material is largely neglected in German poetry until the end of the nineteenth century, when its potential for mystical interpretation is drawn on by writers of various antinaturalist movements, but primarily those of Neoromanticism.

"Neoromanticism" is often used loosely to encompass several related trends, such as mysticism, impressionism, and *Jugendstil*, among others, not all of which necessarily occur in the works of all Neoromantic poets and not all of which are characteristics only of Neoromanticism. In Karl Vollmöller's cycle of poems *Parcival* (1897–1900), the coherence of the Parzival story and its relationship to medieval sources are lost in an aestheticism of bombastic metaphor and *Jugendstil* nature descriptions. This is also true, but to a considerably lesser extent, of Albrecht Schaeffer's verse novel *Parzival* (1922), which omits most of the Arthur and Gawain material, and confuses the roles of other characters, but does include Merlin as a secondary figure. *Das Nordlicht* ("The Northern Light," 1910), a lyric poem of epic dimensions (some 30,000 lines) by Theodor Däubler (1876–1934), lies somewhere between Neoromanticism and Expressionism and also suffers from an overabundance of cryptic imagery. The persona of this poem is transformed into various historical and mythological figures (including Parzival), whose striving represents humanity's upward struggle toward a mystical union with the light of salvation.

The Neoromantic prose, drama, and poetry of Friedrich Lienhard are more straightforward and give expression to an idealism tinged with chauvinism. His poem "Parzival und der Büsser" ("Parzival and the Penitent"), contained in his collection of poetry *Lichtland* ("Land of Light," 1912), shows two equally valid paths to salvation, the penitent's self-denial and Parzival's knightly battle in his search for the Grail castle. A similar idealism is expressed in *Der Stern des Bundes* ("The Star of the Order," 1914), a cycle of 100 untitled poems by Stefan George (1868–1933). George, although generally considered a Neoclassicist, was nevertheless influenced by the Grail literature at the turn of the century. He uses the term *templeis*, Wolfram's designation for a Knight of the Grail, to refer to members of an elite group that must be established in order to achieve the spiritual rebirth of humanity. A religious-philosophical movement among Catholic writers in Vienna is reflected in the works of Richard von Kralik, whose poetic chronicle *Die Gralsage* ("The Legend of the Grail," 1907), over-ambitiously attempts to compress almost all German medieval Grail and Round Table traditions, with additions from some French sources, into one connected verse epic.

A break with Neoromanticism can be seen in the works of Ernst Stadler (1883–1914), an early Expressionist whose poems in *Der Aufbruch* ("The Start," or, in a political sense, "The Awakening," 1914) express the importance of action and challenge. This volume contains "Parzival vor der Gralsburg" ("Parzival Before the Grail Castle"), in which a voice from the castle admonishes Parzival to turn back and convert his quest for the Grail into productive activity for humankind and to earn his reward through suffering for this cause.

As already mentioned, Arthurian literature ceased to be of importance in the years before, during, and immediately after World War II, when writers focused on issues of more pressing relevance. With the revival of interest in medieval literature beginning in the 1970s, and with the German readiness to accept English and American cultural trends, it is possible that such references may expand to include more than the limited Arthurian tradition of earlier German literature. The poetry of H.C. Artmann, an avid fan of all Arthuriana as early as the 1950s, may represent a step in this direction. However, modern poetry like that of Artmann, with its departure from traditional forms, is often based on free association of words, ideas, and symbols, and it relies on the reader's familiarity with the elements that make up these associations. The poems of Artmann that draw on a wide spectrum of Arthurian references, for example, are unlikely to be appreciated by readers who are unfamiliar with the allusions. It is as yet uncertain to what extent a broader conception of the Arthurian tradition will develop among German poets and whether Artmann's predilection for Arthurian allusion in poetry is an anomaly or the reflection of things to come.

5) CHILDREN'S LITERATURE. The adaptation of Arthurian legend for children's literature in Germany is a relatively recent phenomenon. In the late nineteenth and early twentieth centuries, interest in Arthuriana was rekindled by the Neoromantic movement and the success of Richard Wagner's operas. However, it focused upon the specifically German tradition represented by Gottfried von Strassburg's *Tristan* and Wolfram von Eschenbach's *Parzival*.

Moreover, since adulterous love stories were considered inappropriate reading for young people, the former was ignored, while the few adaptations for children of the latter omitted most of the Gawain sections. The results, by authors like Richard Weitbrecht (1887), Emil Engelmann (1888), and Gustav Bornhak (1910), were unmemorable.

After World War II, interest in Arthurian legend took a somewhat different turn in each of the two modern German states, both of which looked to their past as part of an attempt to reestablish a sense of cultural continuity and integrity. In the German Democratic Republic, modern Arthuriana, like Werner Heiduczek's *Seltsame Abenteuer des Parzival* (1974), mentioned above, follows the more limited German tradition, though it is not a common source for children's literature.

Although it shares this concern for German tradition, as can be seen in Nathalie Harder's puppet play *Parzival* (1979–82), the Federal Republic is also receptive to English and American cultural influences. These influences have resulted in translations not only from non-German medieval Arthurian tradition, in books like Ulla Leippe's *Artussagen neu erzählt* (1978) and radio plays like Kurt Vethake's *König Arthur* (1975), but also from modern fiction in English. Most have appeared in the past decade; they include translations of Susan Cooper's *The Dark Is Rising*, as *Wintersonnenwende* (1977, 1980, 1983), and Rosemary Sutcliff's *The Lantern Bearers*, as *Drachenschiffe drohen am Horizont* (1962, 1965, 1977), as well as her imaginative modernizations of earlier material.

Although the list is short compared with the total amount of children's literature that has been translated, it is beginning to grow rapidly in terms of both new translations and repeat editions. It reflects West German receptivity toward a more international Arthurian tradition and toward English and American literature in general. [RWK]

Frenzel, Elisabeth. *Stoffe der Weltliteratur: Ein Lexikon Dichtungsgeschichtlicher Längsschnitte.* 6th ed. Stuttgart: Kröner, 1983.

Golther, Wolfgang. *Parzival und der Gral in der Dichtung des Mittelalters und der Neuzeit.* Stuttgart: Metzler, 1925.

Hermand, Jost. "Gralsmotive um die Jahrhundertwende." *Deutsche Vierteljahresschrift*, 36 (1962), 521–43.

Müller, Ulrich. "Das Nachleben der mittelalterlichen Stoffe." In *Epische Stoffe des mittelalters*, ed. V. Mertens and Ulrich Müller. Stuttgart: Kröner, 1984, pp. 435–59.

——— . "Parzival 1980—auf der Bühne, im Fernsehen und im Film." In *Mittelalter-Rezeption II*, ed. Jürgen Kühnel, Hans-Dieter Mück, Ursula Müller, and Ulrich Müller. Göppingen: Kümmerle, 1982.

——— . "Das Suchen nach dem gestrigen Tag: ARTus und ARTmann oder die Okulation des Mittelalters durch H.C. Artmann." In *Pose, Possen und Poesie: Zum Werke Hans Carl Artmanns*, ed. Josef Donnenberg. Stuttgart: Akademischer Verlag, 1981, pp. 19–34.

Weiss, Adelaide Marie. *Merlin in German Literature.* Washington, D.C.: Catholic University of America Press, 1933.

GERON DER ADELIGE: *see* WIELAND, CHRISTOPH MARTIN.

GESCHICHTE DES ZAUBERERS MERLIN: *see* SCHLEGEL, FRIEDRICH.

GESTA REGUM ANGLORUM: *see* WILLIAM OF MALMESBURY.

GESTA REGUM BRITANNIAE ("Deeds of the Kings of Britain"), a mid-thirteenth-century chronicle, perhaps by William of Rennes, that is a Latin hexameter adaptation of Geoffrey of Monmouth's *Historia*, perhaps influenced by later accounts. Arthur is the greatest of all heroes for the author, who mentions the belief that he is not dead. Merlin uses magic songs to accomplish his wonders, such as changing the shape of Uther, who had to stay three nights with Igraine to beget Arthur. [AEG]

🙢 Michel, Francisque, ed. *Gesta Regum Britanniae*. Bordeaux: Gonnouilhow, 1862.

GIGLAIN: *see* RENAUT DE BEAUJEU.

GILBERT, HENRY: *see* CRANE, WALTER.

GILDAS, author of *De Excidio Britanniae* ("On the Ruin of Britain"), the only early work covering the phase of British history to which Arthur is commonly assigned. A statement in the text seems to place Gildas's birth somewhere about the year 500. Reputedly, he was the son of a chief in the Clyde area. Like several other Britons of future fame, he attended the school in Wales founded by St. Illtud. His style shows that either he studied elsewhere in addition, or the curriculum was broader and more Roman than might be expected. He became a monk and, according to William of Malmesbury, spent some time in the Glastonbury community; a passage in *De Excidio* may at least suggest an acquaintance with it. He is said to have gone to Brittany and founded the monastery at Rhuys. The *Annales Cambriae* put his death in or about 572.

He probably wrote *De Excidio* in the 540s—certainly not much before or after. It is a long diatribe in convoluted but far from contemptible Latin, addressed to British princes and clerics and especially to five regional kings whom he denounces individually. "Ruin" in the title refers to the disruption and destruction caused by the Saxon occupation of parts of Britain that began in the fifth century. Hence, the title is sometimes given in a longer form, with the word "conquest," *De Excidio et Conquestu Britanniae*. Gildas's theme is that the Britons brought the disaster on themselves by their sins, and national repentance is overdue. This message helped to inspire a large-scale monastic movement. It is chiefly because of his influence that Gildas has the title of saint, despite his uncharitable outlook.

Known as "the Wise" (meaning "learned"), he is a source of history but not primarily a historian. His retrospect of Roman and post-Roman Britain simply supplies him with topics for moralizing. Much of the history is grossly distorted. Though he speaks of Latin as "our language," and of Britons as "citizens," he has almost lost sight of Britain's Romanization under the Empire and regards most of its people as merely conquered and more or less contemptible. When he reaches the fifth century, he is still blundering badly, but while his post-Roman story indicates a sequence and chronology of events that cannot be wholly accepted, it is right as to the general trend and probably somewhat nearer truth than falsehood.

He says that a British governing council, together with a *superbus tyrannus* or "preeminent ruler" (in this context the conventional translation "proud tyrant" is misleading), invited Saxons from across the North Sea to settle in Britain as auxiliary troops. The *superbus tyrannus* is usually taken to be the man elsewhere called Vortigern; their identity is assumed by Bede, whose account of this period is largely a shorter paraphrase of *De Excidio*. Gildas explains that the Saxons were hired to fight the "peoples of the north," meaning principally the Picts. The arrangement crumbled when many more arrived and growing demands for supplies could not be met. The Saxons revolted and ravaged Britain, raiding across to the western sea. One effect was a British emigration (identifiable as a move to Armorica in northwest Gaul, which launched Brittany). At last, the Saxons retired within their authorized settlements. Then came a British recovery, both military and moral. Its organizer was Ambrosius Aurelianus, one of the few persons of whom Gildas approves. Decades of fluctuating warfare came to a victorious climax at the siege of Mount Badon, which Gildas seems to date to the year of his own birth, about 500. It brought a spell of comparative peace and order. But he laments that in his own time the Britons are backsliding and fighting among themselves, and the outlook is ominous.

Gildas's allusion to Badon is a well-known crux. Welsh tradition ascribes this triumph to Arthur and to no one else. But Gildas does not name the commander or refer plainly to Arthur at all. A reader might infer that there was no such person, or that he was a minor chief later exaggerated by legend. Either conclusion could be right, but the substance and style of *De Excidio* make both unsafe. Gildas only records historical facts as material for his sermon. If he did not think Arthur relevant to it, he would have seen no cause to mention him. He is oddly reluctant to name names in general, before his own contemporaries. Throughout the fifth century, Ambrosius is the only Briton he does name. If an explanation for his Arthurian silence is needed, it could lie in clerical rancor, since Arthur may have been "bad" by his standards; or Arthur may have flourished after his time, or substantially before it, beyond living memory. There are too many unknowns. The only safe statement is that Gildas is evidence for the war-effort with which Arthur is associated, but not for Arthur personally.

A medieval theory, sometimes echoed by modern scholarship, distinguished two Gildases—the author and the saint. Hagiography, however, treats them as the same person, and that assumption may be allowed to stand. A Breton "Life" composed in the ninth century has nothing of Arthurian interest, but another by a Welshman, Caradoc of Llancarfan, is important. He wrote it about 1130. He says Gildas had a brother, Hueil, a brigand and rebel but a popular hero, whom Arthur put to death. Gildas, grief-stricken, became Arthur's enemy, but eventually they were reconciled. Later, Melwas, King of Somerset, abducted Arthur's wife, "Guennuvar," and kept her at Glastonbury when Gildas was there. Arthur came to rescue her with troops from Devon and Cornwall, but the watery terrain hampered his movements. Gildas and the abbot mediated, the kings made peace, and the lady was restored.

Caradoc's two Arthur episodes are akin to those in other saints' lives. They present him unsympathetically as a foil for the saint, who forgives and helps him. However, this "Life" has several points of interest for the formation of legend. First, because of it, Gildas's omission of Arthur from *De Excidio* paradoxically became part of the story: Gildas, according to Giraldus Cambrensis, did write about him, but destroyed what he had written because of the killing of Hueil. Second, the Queen's abduction reappears in romance, with Melwas becoming Meleagant, and Lancelot replacing her husband as rescuer. Third, this is the earliest proved connection of Arthur with Glastonbury. Finally, Welsh storytellers embroider the Hueil episode, one result being that the stone on which Arthur beheaded him can still be seen in the marketplace at Ruthin.

Excavated remains of buildings on Glastonbury Tor are datable to roughly this period, and have been held to give credibility to Melwas—perhaps, if they are remains of a stronghold, but their interpretation is doubtful. [GA]

🙋 Gildas. *De Excidio Britanniae*, ed. and trans. Michael Winterbottom under the title *The Ruin of Britain*. In *History from the Sources*. Chichester: Phillimore, 1978, Vol. 7.

Alcock, Leslie. *Arthur's Britain*. London: Penguin, 1971.

Lapidge, Michael, and David Dumville, eds. *Gildas: New Approaches*. Woodbridge, Suffolk: Boydell and Brewer, 1984.

Loomis, Roger Sherman, ed. *Arthurian Literature in the Middle Ages*. Oxford: Clarendon, 1959.

"GINEVRA VERRÄT SICH IM SCHLAF UND DER KÖNIG ANTWORTET IHR MIT EINEM GEDICHT": *see* ARTMANN, HANS CARL.

GIRALDUS CAMBRENSIS (ca. 1146–1222/3). In nine, or about half, of his numerous works, Gerald of Wales made passing references to either Arthur or his contemporary, Merlin Ambrosius. Concerning Arthur, Gerald says little, only noting that according to British traditions Irish kings paid tribute to Arthur and that Roman ambassadors came to his court at Caerleon, where also Dubricius, archbishop of Caerleon, ceded the metropolitan see to the king's uncle, St. David, bishop of Menevia, subsequently known as St. David's. In addition, in *De Principis Instructione* (ca. 1193) and *Speculum Ecclesiae* (ca. 1215), Gerald recorded the 1191 discovery of the bodies of Arthur and Guenevere at Glastonbury and their reburial in the abbey there.

When treating British—that is, Welsh—traditions, Gerald appears to be of two minds. He believed in prophecies and included several by Merlin Ambrosius as well as many others from Celtic sources. But Gerald did not trust Geoffrey of Monmouth and twice revealed reservations concerning Geoffrey's version of history. [KGM]

&❧ Gerald of Wales. *Giraldi Cambrensis Opera*, ed. J.S. Brewer et al. 8 vols. London: Longman, 1861–91.

GIRART D'AMIENS, who also wrote *Méliacin*, is the author of *Escanor*, a romance of nearly 26,000 lines dated to ca. 1280. It may have been presented in 1279 to Eleanor of Castile. One of the two main plots concerns Kay, who falls in love during a tournament with Andrivete, daughter of Canor of Northumberland. Kay, however, returns to court without confessing his love, and Andrivete narrowly escapes being married for political motives by her uncle to someone of inferior social status. In the other plot, Gauvain is accused by Escanor le Beau of the murder of a cousin. Gauvain hesitates to defend himself against the accusation, and Gifflet's brother Galantivet defeats the accuser. In the meantime, Escanor le Grand, uncle of Escanor le Beau, captures Gifflet when he is unable to take Gauvain. Gauvain finally defeats Escanor le Beau and the two are reconciled.

Although much of the narrative is formed by stock motifs, the author does depart from convention in his portrayal of Kay as a timid lover and Gauvain as somewhat of a coward. An aura of religiosity pervades the end of the romance. Much of the plot hinges on necromancy and the supernatural, and the influence of the prose romances, especially the Prose *Tristan*, is particularly strong. Composed during the same period, *Escanor* has much in common in terms of narrative structure and treatment of subject matter with the romance of *Claris et Laris*. [KB]

&❧ Girart d'Amiens. *Escanor*, ed. Heinrich Michelant. Tübingen: Bibliothek des literarischen Vereins in Stuttgart, 1886.

GIRAULT, FRANÇOIS: *see* GARGANTUAN CHRONICLES.

GIRONE IL CORTESE, an Italian translation of the 1501 (?) French edition of *Gyron le Courtois*, a portion of the *Compilation* of Rusticiano da Pisa (Rusticien de Pise). In its focus on Girone, the Italian text has all but detached its hero from the traditional cycles of Arthur and Tristan to present an extended account of a nearly independent knight-errant. While there are lengthy digressions from the central storyline, the heart of the narrative is the chivalric friendship between Girone and Danain, and the strain placed on that friendship when Danain, leaving to pursue his vendetta against the Brothers of the Savage Land, leaves his wife, the Lady of Malehaut (Maloanco), in the custody of his friend, Girone, who promptly falls in love with her. The narrative includes a history of Girone's family, the House of Bruni, beginning with the dramatic entrance of the last knight of the Tavola Vecchia, the 120-year-old Branor Bruni, into Arthur's court, where he overcomes Tristan, Lancelot, and Arthur himself. The romance then concentrates on the adventures of Girone and Danain. In the longest sequence of interpolated adventures, Breunis Senza Pietà is tricked by a lady he loves and is trapped in a cave where he discovers richly appointed chambers, the effigies of a knight and a lady, and an ancient knight. This knight turns out to be Girone's grandfather, and he relates the adventures of the House of Bruni to Breunis, who mends his ways after hearing of these marvels of chivalry. The narrative returns to Girone, whose adventures at the Perilous Pass reunite him with Danain and the Good Knight Without Fear, who goes on to endure a series of adventures in the Vale of Servitude that do not conclude until the *Meliadus*, the second volume of the *Compilation*. After an encounter with Hellin the Red, the vile scion of an incestuous union, Girone and Danain part at a crossroad, Danain taking the path to the Tower of False Pleasure and Girone the path to the Tower of Wrath, in which he and his wife are both imprisoned. Girone's wife gives birth to a son, Galinans, who is fostered in evil ways by the lord of the Tower, and the last chapter of the *Girone* abandons the titular hero to tell of the death of his wicked son at the hands of Palamides. Despite its peculiarly unsatisfactory ending, the result of its position as merely a portion of the *Compilation, Girone il Cortese* is a reasonably lively romance, more coherent than its source and possessing a quality that raises it above the level of mere translation. It is also, of course, a belated translation into his native language of the earliest Arthurian romance composed by an Italian. [DLH]

Tassi, Francesco, ed. *Girone il Cortese; romanzo cavalleresco di Rustico o Rusticiano da Pisa.* Florence: Società Tipografica, 1855.

Gardner, Edmund G. *The Arthurian Legend in Italian Literature.* London: Dent, 1930.

GISMIRANTE: *see* PUCCI, ANTONIO.

GLASTONBURY. A small town in Somerset with a ruined abbey, Glastonbury has an immensely long history and is the focus of much legend and speculation. It has several Arthurian connections: as the scene of the first known version of the abduction of Guenevere; as the site of Arthur's reputed grave; as a place associated in some way with the Grail; and as the retreat to which Lancelot and others retire as hermits.

Glastonbury lies in and around a cluster of hills, of which the highest is the Tor, a curious whaleback formation visible a long way off. The country round about, as far as the Bristol Channel, is low and level. In the last centuries B.C. and the early Christian era, much of it was swampy and much was under water. From most angles, the hill-cluster would then have had the appearance of an island, though it was not completely so. In the neighborhood, till about the period of the Roman conquest, two Celtic lake-villages stood on ground artificially built up above the water-line. These were centers of the La Tène culture. Artifacts testify to developed crafts and wide-ranging trade. The land was eventually drained and the sea excluded, but the image of the hill-cluster's insularity persisted and was the reason for two controversial names applied to it: *Ynys-witrin*—i.e., the Isle of Glass—and *Avalon*.

Some etymologists believe that the oldest name was *Glastonia*, derived from a Celtic word meaning "blue-green," or more specifically "woad," the plant from which blue-green dye was made: this was a place where woad grew. *Glastonbury* is the Anglo-Saxon *Glaestingabyrig*, supposedly the result of the Saxons' coining the word *Glaestingas* for the dwellers in Glastonia and then adding *byrig*, meaning a town or inhabited spot. By a further complication, *Glast* or *Glasteing* is sometimes given as a personal name, that of the founder of the settlement.

Ynys-witrin, the Glass Island, is a Celtic form, quoted in early records as predating the Saxon occupation of this area in the seventh century. Its claim to priority has been disputed, on the ground of its being due to a misapprehension that the syllable *Glas* was literally "glass": an error implying the English language, in however early a shape, and therefore subsequent to the Saxons' advent. This is by no means certain. Amid so much confusion, the sole certainty is that the etymological roots lie deep.

As for *Avalon*, it became attached to Glastonbury because of Arthur. The place was asserted to have been his last earthly destination after his fatal wounding, the true Avalon. This claim cannot be documented before the announcement of the discovery of his grave in 1191. But the magical name seems to have owed its acceptability here to a far older otherworldly aura, which was a legacy of pre-Christian beliefs and practices.

In the Celtic scheme of things, Glastonbury's hill-on-island topography was intensely numinous. Moreover, the Tor is encircled by a system of paths or terraces, heavily weathered but still traceable over long distances. They may in part be strip lynchets, created by medieval agriculture, but a case exists for the view that the system is basically a kind of labyrinth, a great ritual work assignable to the same era as other ritual works, such as Stonehenge and Silbury. Also, there are recurrent, perhaps related, allusions to a folk-belief that the Tor is hollow, a point of entry to the underworld or otherworld that figures in the Welsh poem *The Spoils of Annwfn*. Collen, a wandering Welsh saint, is said to have actually entered the hill and tried to exorcize the underworld king Gwyn-ap-Nudd. A tower that now surmounts the hill is all that remains of a church dedicated to St. Michael, built in the fourteenth century to replace a previous church that collapsed in an earthquake. The dedication to the angelic conqueror of infernal powers may hint at a belief that these powers were present and active—an excusable suspicion after the earthquake, since in Britain the destruction of buildings from that cause is practically unknown.

Whatever its pagan past, Glastonbury was arguably the home of the first British Christian community, the first at any rate that held together and survived. It undoubtedly has a continuity without parallel in England. A Celtic-type settlement of British monks was already in being when the Saxons arrived, in a year chronicled as 658. By then, the conquerors were Christians themselves, and the community continued without a break, under the lavish patronage of the kings of Wessex. Saxon and Irish monks presently joined it. Under St. Dunstan in the tenth century, Glastonbury became a major Benedictine abbey, and during the Middle Ages it was the greatest in England, or an equal-first with Westminster. But as to how the original community had come to be there, neither documentation nor archaeology can provide a firm answer, and imagination has flourished freely.

William of Malmesbury, writing ca. 1130, gives a transcript from an alleged charter dated 601 in which a king made the monastery a grant of land. Opinions are divided as to its authenticity. An apparent allusion by Gildas, if accepted, would push back the monastery's existence sixty years further, and it is likely that there were hermits much earlier than that. A small community may have taken shape on and around the Tor before the monastic settlement of the abbey site. Excavations in 1964–66 uncovered foundations of buildings on the summit that were not later than the sixth century and could have belonged to the fifth, though their nature and use remain uncertain. A spring below the Tor, now called Chalice Well and possibly sacred before Christianity, would have given a reliable water supply.

However, the fact at the center of all the early tradition is that within the abbey precinct, on the spot now occupied by the Lady Chapel, a church once stood that was so ancient that there was no trustworthy record of its foundation. William of Malmesbury gives a long account of it. A wattle building with reinforcements of timber and lead, it was known simply as the *vetusta ecclesia*, or Old Church. The dedication was to the Virgin Mary, from which it would appear that the original builders were under devotional influences hard to parallel so early in Britain. It was around the immensely venerated Old Church that the Christian legends of Glastonbury grew. William notes a current belief that it was built in the first century by disciples of Christ himself. He speaks cautiously and names no names. But by a process of interpolation in William's book, and the concoction of spurious charters, the abbey improved its early history and eventually put a name to the disciples' leader: Joseph of Arimathea.

Other legend-making had already made a deep mark in William's time, thanks probably to Irishmen who had formerly conducted the monastic school. St. Patrick, for instance, was said to have come to Glastonbury and even to have been buried there. Gildas was also claimed as a resident, perhaps more credibly, and it is in Caradoc's "Life" of him that Arthur makes an early appearance. Writing, like William, about 1130, Caradoc tells how King Mel-was of the Summer Land (Somerset) carried off Guenevere and kept her in a stronghold at Glastonbury. Arthur came to rescue her with troops from Devon and Cornwall, but the watery terrain hindered his army's movements. Gildas and the abbot mediated, the kings made peace in the "temple of holy Mary"— that is, the Old Church—and the lady was restored. Traces of this tale can be picked out in Chrétien de Troyes.

A linkage of Glastonbury with Arthur was established, therefore, before Geoffrey of Monmouth. Geoffrey himself ignored the place; his Isle of Avalon is not here, probably not anywhere. But in 1190–91, the monks gave the connection a more sensational form by exhuming Arthur's remains in their own cemetery and publicizing the find. Though accounts of this event vary somewhat, Giraldus Cambrensis reports it in careful detail soon afterward, and the main story is sufficiently clear.

The location of Arthur's grave had long been a mystery, here and elsewhere, as William of Malmesbury attests. But a Welsh or Breton bard divulged the secret to Henry II: Arthur was buried in Glastonbury Abbey's graveyard, between two "pyramids" or memorial pillars. Henry passed the news on. In 1190 or early 1191, the abbot ordered an excavation. Seven feet

13 Leaden Cross, found in Arthur's grave, Glastonbury Abbey, from William Camden's Britannia *(1607). Courtesy Kenneth Spencer Research Library, University of Kansas.*

down, the diggers struck a stone slab, and found underneath it a cross made of lead with the inscription Hic Iacet Sepultus Inclitus Rex Arturius in Insula Avalonia, "Here lies buried the renowned King Arthur in the Isle of Avalon." Nine feet farther down, they unearthed the coffin, a hollowed-out log. Inside were the bones of a tall man, who had apparently been killed by a blow on the head, because the skull was fractured. Some smaller bones, with a lock of hair that crumbled when touched, were interpreted as Guenevere's. The bones were deposited in two chests and transferred, in 1278, to a marble tomb before the high altar in the main abbey church. There they lay till the sixteenth-century rifling and vandalism that followed the dissolution of the monasteries.

Historians generally dismiss the grave as a fabrication and a publicity stunt. In 1184, most of the abbey, including the Old Church, had burned down. Money was needed for rebuilding, and, while Henry II had supplied it and encouraged others to do so, his successor, Richard I, did not. Besides the assumed usefulness of the grave for fund-raising, a political motive has also been discerned. Proof that Arthur was dead, and would never return as a Celtic champion, was calculated to weaken Welsh morale in resisting the English.

Both motives are credible, yet despite the confidence with which they are often affirmed, both are modern speculations devoid of documentary basis. No evidence exists that the monks did try to raise money by exploiting the grave or that it was ever employed as a weapon against the Welsh. In 1958, the archaeologist Ralegh Radford showed that the story had curious points of plausibility in the light of the graveyard's known history. Five years later, he completed an excavation south of the Lady Chapel proving that the monks had indeed dug where they said and had reached a layer of early burials.

The charge of complete falsehood being thus exploded, the question is not whether they found a grave but whose grave they found. This turns on the inscribed cross. It has disappeared, but William Camden gives a facsimile of one side of it in his *Britannia* (1607). If, as Giraldus claims, there was a mention of Guenevere, it was presumably on the other. The wording, particularly the epithet *inclitus*, might suggest that the inscription is based on Geoffrey and therefore a twelfth-century forgery. On the other hand, the style and irregularity of the lettering can be held to indicate an earlier date, conceivably much earlier. Furthermore, the standard twelfth-century Latinization of "Arthur" was not "Arturius," as on the cross, but "Arturus," as in Geoffrey. Up to 1191, "Arturius" can only be paralleled in Adamnan's seventh-century *Life of St. Columba*, where the person referred to is Prince Arthur of Argyll. In other words, it occurs only as a very early form.

To a certain extent, the hypothesis of a fraud is self-destructive. If Arthur's grave carried so much weight as to be worth elaborately faking, Welshmen or others might have been expected to challenge the claim and perhaps to exhibit rival graves. This seems never to have happened. Folklore and fancy have offered several Camelots, several caves where Arthur lies sleeping, and so forth. For practical purposes, the King has only the one grave. Whether or not an original Arthur-figure actually *was* buried at Glastonbury (or reburied under unknown circumstances after interment elsewhere), a Welsh or Breton tradition may have said he was and become too firmly established to retract once it leaked out to Henry II. In that case, the grave with its identification, if fraudulent, could have been in the same class as some of the forged charters that Glastonbury was especially apt at producing. Such documents are not exactly fakes in the modern sense; they are attempts to give substance and color to beliefs that were held quite sincerely and sometimes even, in principle, correctly.

Glastonbury's known connection with the Christianized Grail begins soon after the exhumation. In Robert de Boron's *Joseph d'Arimathie*, the Grail has to be conveyed to the far west, to the Vales of Avaron. By "Avaron," Robert certainly intends "Avalon," and it is equally plain that his allusion is to the low-lying country of central Somerset; mythology or Geoffrey might have supplied an "Isle" of Avalon, but not "Vales." The author of *Perlesvaus* (early thirteenth century) professes to have adapted a Latin text at a religious house in the Isle of Avalon where (he says) Arthur and Guenevere now lie. He, also, manifestly means Glastonbury. Neither of these romances shows whether the authors really had anything more in mind than some vague tale of Christians coming to the place in the apostolic era, the kind of tale that William of Malmesbury had already noted and been doubtful about. As for Joseph of Arimathea himself, though romance brings him to Britain, it never states explicitly that he came to Glastonbury.

That idea is first documented in an interpolated text of William, composed at the abbey toward the mid-thirteenth century. The writer of the relevant passage describes Joseph's arrival in A.D. 63, at the head of a party of twelve, and the building of the Old Church. His story is not a mere borrowing from Grail romance—indeed it is incompatible with it—and the relation between Joseph's two roles, as Grail-bearer and as founder of Christian Glastonbury, is obscure. The fourteenth-century chronicler John of Glastonbury does slightly interweave them, and he also quotes a bizarre "prophecy" ascribed to a British bard called Melkin, which may preserve fragments of a separate legend. However, the precise statement that Joseph brought the Grail to Glastonbury does not seem to have been made, at least in any work of note, before Tennyson.

The *Perlesvaus* author's claim to have done research on the spot has been contested, because, it is urged, his description of Avalon's monastic site in the reign of Arthur does not fit the abbey. That is true, but it does fit the approach to Glastonbury Tor by way of an old road. The author knows the area, and is using a tradition of early Christian settlement on the higher ground. As observed, this may have a historical basis. A variant emerges at the end of Malory's work, where, after Arthur has gone, Lancelot and other survivors retire from the world to live as hermits in a retreat between two wooded hills "beside" Glastonbury. Malory's description would apply to the space between the Tor and Chalice Hill, which is adjacent to it.

Henry VIII dissolved the abbey in 1539, and the last abbot, Richard Whiting, was convicted on trumped-up charges and hanged on the Tor. Held briefly by the crown, the property passed into private hands. Over the next centuries, a series of owners used the buildings as a quarry for salable stone, till very little was left. The Church of England acquired the site in 1908, and the ruined remnants are carefully preserved.

Glastonbury has continued to show its capacity for myth-making and spellbinding. The parent specimen of its famous Holy Thorn, a local tree that blossoms approximately at Christmas, is reputed to have sprung from Joseph of Arimathea's staff—but the miracle is first spoken of only as late as 1716. Glastonbury's real historic potency—as a religious center, as a fountainhead of Arthurian legend, and in political and cultural ways not considered here—has proved to be by no means a thing of the past. Besides a revival of pilgrimage, the modern town has witnessed a striking influx of mystics, theorists, and spiritual seekers. These have further enlarged its mythology. A notion about a visit by Christ himself (of unknown provenance, but hardly ancient) has won wide support. Chalice Well, the spring near the Tor's foot, is the holy place of a fellowship with beliefs of its own. A popular theory asserts that huge zodiacal figures are traced in the surrounding landscape and that their symbolism supplies keys to Arthurian stories, notably *Perlesvaus*. This idea, though quasi-archaeological, has not commended itself to archaeologists. [GA]

William of Malmesbury. *De Antiquitate Glastoniensis Ecclesiae*, in Scott, below.

Ashe, Geoffrey. *Avalonian Quest*. London: Methuen, 1982.

Carley, James P. "Glastonbury and the Grail Legend." *Avalon to Camelot*, 1 (Spring 1984), 4–8.

Lagorio, Valerie. "The Evolving Legend of St. Joseph of Glastonbury." *Speculum*, 46 (1971), 209–31.

Radford, C.A. Ralegh."Glastonbury Abbey." In *The Quest for Arthur's Britain*, ed. Geoffrey Ashe. London: Pall Mall, 1968.

Rahtz, Philip. "Glastonbury Tor." In *The Quest for Arthur's Britain*, ed. Geoffrey Ashe. London: Pall Mall, 1968.

Robinson, Joseph Armitage. *Two Glastonbury Legends*. Cambridge: Cambridge University Press, 1926.

Scott, John. *The Early History of Glastonbury*. Woodbridge, Suffolk: Boydell and Brewer, 1981.

Treharne, R.F. *The Glastonbury Legends*. London: Cresset, 1967.

GLASTONBURY ROMANCE, A: see POWYS, JOHN COWPER.

GLIGLOIS, an anonymous French Gauvain romance composed in verse (ca. 3,000 lines) during the first half of the thirteenth century. The romance is available only in an edition prepared by Livingston from earlier notes, the unique manuscript of the work having been destroyed in the Turin fire of 1904. The hero, Gliglois, is contrasted with Gauvain. Both of them love the same woman, Beauté, but Gauvain does nothing to win her (apparently relying on his reputation and his traditional appeal to women), while his squire, Gliglois, serves her faithfully and patiently, thus gaining her love. The originality of this work lies in its removing fame and status as preconditions to success in love. The *Gliglois* was composed by an author of limited talent, but it is a competent romance, a straightforward, clear, and realistic narrative. [NJL]

❧ Livingston, Charles H., ed. *Gliglois: A French Arthurian Romance of the Thirteenth Century.* Cambridge, Mass.: Harvard University Press, 1932.

GLOAG, JOHN, author of *Artorius Rex* (1977), which concerns a Romano-Celtic Arthur of Britain, his wars, victories, loves, sorrows, triumphs, and tragedies, as written by one Caius Geladius (putatively Sir Kay) at the request of the emperor Justinian. Artorius (Arthur) ends as an impotent king, deserted by a sluttish Gwinfreda (Guenevere), his aged companions, and Merlin. [VML]

❧ Gloag, John. *Artorius Rex.* New York: St. Martin, 1977.

GLORIOUS MYSTERY, THE: *see* MACHEN, ARTHUR.

GODEFROY DE LEIGNY: *see* CHRÉTIEN DE TROYES.

GODODDIN, Y: *see* ARTHUR, ORIGINS OF LEGEND; CELTIC ARTHURIAN LITERATURE.

GOD'S GRAIL: *see* ROSSETTI, DANTE GABRIEL.

GODWIN, PARKE, American-born author of an Arthurian triptych, consisting of *Firelord* (1980), *Beloved Exile* (1984), and *The Last Rainbow* (1985). *Firelord* is notable in that it presents the story of Arthur against the background of a complex society made up of the remnants of Roman culture in Britain, the various settled Celtic tribes, and the remaining survivors of the nomadic Pictish tribes. Godwin's Arthur, though brought up by the Romano-Celtic family of Uther, is here depicted as part Pict. He is also a visionary—Merlin appears as an aspect of Arthur's own character, and Arthur's encounter with his Pictish side has the quality, at least in its beginning and ending, of a dreamlike otherworld experience.

Godwin's strengths lie not only in his effectively realized society but in the various characters of the novel, especially Guenevere. She is Arthur's equal in strength of character and in her classical training, and it is the clash of their strengths combined with the frustrations of their love-relationship that leads to their tragic discord. In Guenevere more so than in Arthur can be found the clearest evidence of the all-but-impossible struggle to forge unity from disparate elements of society.

Beloved Exile continues the story of Guenevere after Arthur's death at the hands of Modred, son of Arthur's Pictish wife, Morgana. Guenevere attempts to retain control of the fragmenting society her husband has forged. She is forced to work with those of Arthur's allies whom her conflict with Arthur has alienated and, just as Arthur had to come to terms with his Pictish side by living for a time with Morgana and her family, Guenevere, in an extended period of Saxon captivity, comes to value the positive qualities of a culture greatly different from her own. Godwin's deliberately romantic departure from the conventions of the Arthurian legend are effective in that they permit the author to establish a parallel between Arthur and Guenevere—the "alien" experience that humanizes each. Both novels are characterized by a vigorous, humorously ironic narrative tone.

The Last Rainbow moves back in time to the life of St. Patrick before his mission to Ireland. He fails dismally in his initial attempt to convert the Picts to his own self-righteous and narrow-minded concept of Christianity. From them, however, he slowly and painfully learns the lessons of compassion and forgiveness that are to prove essential to his success in Ireland. Among the characters is a young Ambrosius Aurelianus, campaigning against hostile tribes north of Hadrian's Wall.

Godwin's novels are representative of the characteristic trends of Arthurian novels of the 1970s and 1980s in their concern with anthropological and archaeological fidelity, combined with modern narrative techniques and concerns. [AAR/RHT]

Godwin, Parke. *Firelord*. New York: Doubleday, 1980.
———. *Beloved Exile*. New York: Bantam, 1984.
———. *The Last Rainbow*. New York: Bantam, 1985.

GOETHE, JOHANN WOLFGANG (1749–1832), a prolific writer in all genres, is known to world literature primarily as the greatest German Classicist and as the author of *Faust*. Like most Classicists, Goethe was not particularly interested in Arthurian literature, although he does express agreement with Friedrich Schlegel's positive evaluation of Wolfram's *Parzival*. In fact, the name "Merlin" is the only direct reference that Goethe makes to any Arthurian character in his own poetic works. In his second "Kophtisches Lied" ("Coptic Song," 1787), he employs the image of Merlin the prophet borrowed from Ariosto's *Orlando Furioso*. Goethe's oracular Merlin, lying in his grave, gives advice to wise men only, since it is futile to offer wisdom to fools. A less specific image of Merlin as the old magician may be reflected in his famous ballad "Der Zauberlehrling" ("The Sorcerer's Apprentice," 1797). In addition, in his poetic narrative fragment *Die Geheimnisse* ("The Secrets," 1784) it is difficult to ignore the parallelism between Wolfram's Grail community and Goethe's depiction of a contemplative order of twelve knight-priests whose old leader Humanus (Titurel?) will be replaced by a younger wandering "templar" (Parzival?). [RWK]

❖ Goethe, Johann Wolfgang. *Werke*, ed. Erich Trunz. Hamburg: Christian Wegner, 1948–60, Vols. 1 and 2.

Golther, Wolfgang. "Goethe's 'Geheimnisse.'" In *Parzival und der Gral*. Stuttgart: Metzler, 1925, pp. 286–88.

Weiss, Adelaide Marie. "Goethe." In *Merlin in German Literature*. Washington, D.C.: Catholic University of America Press, 1933, pp. 69–72.

GOEZNOVIUS, LEGEND OF ST. "Goeznovius" is a late Latinization of *Goueznou*, the name of a saint of Brittany. Its Welsh equivalent is *Gwyddno*. Goueznou was born in Wales but was one of many ecclesiastics who helped to create a Lesser Britain in Armorican Gaul. Contradictory datings put him in the sixth or seventh century, the former being more likely. In any case, he has no personal connection with Arthur. The relevance of the *Legenda Sancti Goeznovii* lies in the prologue. This contains the only early historical narrative in which Arthur is mentioned plainly, with no obviously dubious or fantastic touches.

Undoubtedly written in Brittany, *Goeznovius* is one of several historical works cited in the fourteenth-century *Chronique de Saint Brieuc*. The substance of it survives in a fifteenth-century manuscript formerly at Nantes Cathedral. According to an introductory sentence, its author is a cleric named William and its date is 1019. Passages of narrative prose alternate with liturgical verse. The prologue takes up the first two prose sections, setting the stage for the saint's career. Referring to an "Ystoria Britanica," the author sketches the Britons' first colonization of Armorica. He puts it before the fifth century, like Nennius and Geoffrey of Monmouth. Part of what he says is legend, but he gives local information that carries some weight. The next prose section traces the fifth-century events leading to the migration of British saints overseas. This has rhetorical phrases but nothing manifestly fictitious.

It tells how Vortigern, as usurping ruler of Britain, brought into the country Saxon auxiliaries, who inflicted great suffering on the Britons. "Presently" (*postmodum*, suggesting sooner-rather-than-later), they were largely cleared from the island and reduced to subordination by "the great Arthur, king of the Britons." Arthur's victories extended to Gaul. Then, he was "summoned from human activity," a phrase that might refer to death or an uncertain end but need not endorse the folk-belief in his immortality. Thereafter, the way was open for the Saxons to go again into the island. Their renewed depredations went on "through the times of many kings, Saxons and Britons, striving back and forth." Numerous holy men were martyred; others migrated to Brittany.

This prologue was long neglected as an Arthurian source because of its dismissal by J.S.P. Tatlock, who claimed that its date, 1019, was spurious, that it was later than Geoffrey of Monmouth, and that it was simply a précis of his

Historia Regum Britanniae. Eventually, Fleuriot reopened the question and defended 1019 as correct. However, *Goeznovius* cannot be derived from the *Historia* whatever its date. It tells a story different from Geoffrey's: glaringly different, in its account of the beginnings of Brittany; and just as surely, if not quite so glaringly, in its account of Arthur and his aftermath. It contains matter that occurs in other contexts but not in Geoffrey, proving the use of a prior tradition independent of him. More important, within its concise limits it gives a sounder summary of fifth-century British affairs than any other comparable document. Even if its author did read the *Historia*, he could not have distilled such an account from it without some other, more factual, source enabling him to select and emend.

While Arthur himself is the unknown factor, the credibility of the setting in which the text places him justifies attention to its Arthurian testimony. Here, he succeeds Vortigern directly, without Geoffrey's two intervening reigns. On this showing, his battles in Britain would belong to the anarchic period of the Saxon revolt. The Saxons' withdrawal into a limited area, probably around 460, is attested by Gildas. Arthur's incursion into Gaul can be reasonably related to British activities overseas, and to a campaign of Romans and Franks against the Saxons in the Loire valley, in which there is evidence for British participation. This happened toward the close of the 460s. Saxon landings in Britain at new points—"going again into the island"—are confirmed by the *Anglo-Saxon Chronicle*, which assigns them to the period from 477 on, consistently with Arthur's having left the scene by then, as *Goeznovius* indicates. The breakup of Britain into small warring kingdoms, and the beginning of the saints' migration, are also in accord with the apparent course of events in the late fifth century.

Goeznovius therefore tells a story that fits history quite well and is nowhere in outright conflict with known facts. The story makes Arthur prominent in the 460s, and perhaps a little before and after. This agrees with Geoffrey's single but repeated chronological fix for him, putting his Gallic warfare in the reign of the eastern emperor Leo I (457–74). It cannot be merely derived from that, because the date is indicated in a different way, by implication and circumstance without names. The concurrence is one of several facts suggesting that both Geoffrey and the *Goeznovius* author are thinking of the "king of the Britons" who is documented in Gaul ca. 468–70 as Riothamus and for some shared and older reason are calling him Arthur.

Goeznovius implies continental sources of information. The Breton monastery of Rhuys may have contributed. Gildas was its reputed founder; the community possessed copies of his work and may be supposed to have had historical interests. Early in the tenth century, the monks fled from the Norse to Berry in central France. Ebbon, the seigneur of Déols, took them under his protection till the danger was past and they could return. Déols was the scene of the final battle in Riothamus's continental campaign. A local tradition or record of that battle, and the events leading up to it, could have gone back to Brittany with the monks and helped to form the conception of Arthur. [GA]

GOLAGROS AND GAWANE

🔖 Ashe, Geoffrey, "A Certain Very Ancient Book." *Speculum*, 56 (1981), 301–23.

Chambers, E.K. *Arthur of Britain*. London: Sidgwick and Jackson, 1927.

Fleuriot, Léon. *Les Origines de la Bretagne*. Paris: Payot, 1980.

Tatlock, J.S.P. "The Dates of the Arthurian Saints' Legends." *Speculum*, 14 (1939), 345–65.

GOLAGROS AND GAWANE, a Middle Scots poem of 1,362 lines, written toward the end of the fifteenth century. No manuscript has been preserved; the poem's survival is due to the activities of the first Scottish printers, Walter Chepman and Androw Myllar, who printed it in 1508. Only one copy is now known to exist. The stanza structure is the same as that of *The Awntyrs off Arthure at the Terne Wathelyn*, except that it lacks the linking features.

The story is based on two originally unrelated episodes of the First Continuation of Chrétien de Troyes's *Conte del Graal*. In the first part, Kay the "crabbit" is, as so often, made the foil of Gawain the "gracious." When Arthur and his knights at the end of a day come upon a beautiful city, Kay offers to go and buy victuals there. He soon returns with no more than a thrashing for his boorish behavior, so that Gawain has to put things right again. In the second and longer part, Arthur tries to defeat a knight, Golagros, who had up till then held his lands as an independent lord. At the suggestion of Sir Spynagros, who replaces the Brandelis of the French text, Arthur sends three envoys, but they return empty-handed, in spite of the sugar-coated courtesy of their request. After a siege and a series of combats, Golagros is brought to submission by Gawain, who once more proves his perfect knighthood by agreeing to go through a mock defeat to allow Golagros to save face. In the original, he had done so to preserve the life of Golagros's *amie*, and this change, and the tone of the dialogue between Gawain and Golagros, confirm that the poem's main concern is with knightly honor and prowess. In Golagros, these are rewarded when Arthur releases him from his allegiance. [ESK]

🔖 *The Knightly Tale of Golagros and Gawane*. Edinburgh: Chepman and Myllar, 1508.

Madden, Frederic, ed. *Syr Gawayne*. London: Bannatyne Club, 1839.

GOLDMARK, KARL (1830–1915), an Austrian composer who had great success with the opera *Die Königin von Saba* (1875). His Arthurian opera *Merlin* (première in Vienna, 1886; revised version in Frankfurt, 1904) is based on Immermann's play of the same name. Jens Malte Fischer compared it favorably with other "medieval" operas, such as *Le Roi Artus* (1903), by Ernest Chausson. [UM/WCM]

🔖 Fischer, Jens Malte. "Singende Recken und blitzende Schwerter." In *Akten des DFG-Symposions zur Mittelalter-Rezeption*, ed. Peter Wapnewski. Stuttgart: Metzler, 1985.

GONNOT, MICHOT, the copyist for five manuscripts in the library of Jacques d'Armagnac. Moreover, he was probably the compiler who oversaw the disposition of one of them, the present Paris B.N. fr. 112, which was completed in 1470. The manuscript—which is incomplete, the first and fifth "books" having disappeared—claims to bring together in a new Arthurian *summa* material drawn mostly from thirteenth-century Arthurian romances in French prose. [C-AVC]

Pickford, Cedric E. *L'Évolution du roman arthurien en prose vers la fin du moyen âge d'après le ms. 112 du fonds français de la Bibl. Nationale.* Paris: Nizet, 1960.

"GOOD KNIGHT IN PRISON, A": *see* MORRIS, WILLIAM.

GOTTFRIED VON STRASSBURG, author of the classical version of the romance of Tristan and Isolde. An unfinished poem of some 19,500 lines in Middle High German rhymed couplets, it is a complex and difficult work composed in the first decade of the thirteenth century. A drastically reduced synopsis follows.

Tristan is conceived on the deathbed of his father, Rivalin. His mother, who revives her dying lover by the fulfillment of their mutual desire, dies herself in giving birth to the child she had conceived. Tristan, so named because of the tragic circumstances of his birth, is kidnapped from his foster parents, becomes the favorite of King Mark of Cornwall, and eventually leads a wooing expedition to win Princess Isolde of Ireland as the bride of King Mark. But on the ship from Ireland to Cornwall, Tristan and Isolde by mistake drink the magic potion intended for Mark and Isolde, and it seals their eternal love. Their life consists of deflecting the attempts of Mark and his courtiers to expose the love affair. At one point, they are banished from the court by Mark and lead an idyllic life in a secret forest glade, living in a lovers' temple. But they return to court and eventually are discovered in bed together by Mark himself. Tristan must leave and begins a life of wandering and longing for his beloved. Gottfried's version breaks off when Tristan is about to marry a woman named Isolde of the White Hands, but we learn from the preserved fragments of Gottfried's source, Thomas d'Angleterre, that the two marry, though the marriage remains unconsummated. Tristan eventually dies from a poisoned wound, and shortly before his death he sends for Isolde the Fair of Ireland, his true love. The ship sent for her is to hoist white sails if she is aboard, black if not. She comes to her dying lover with a cure, but the jealous Isolde of the White Hands lies to Tristan and tells him that the approaching ship has black sails. He dies of grief, and upon her arrival, the true Isolde clasps the body of her dead lover and breathes her last.

The story of Tristan and Isolde had an odd fate in the Middle Ages. It was well known and popular, but no single complete version from the Continent in the twelfth and thirteenth centuries has been preserved. All the extant versions are fragments. There is an Old French *Roman de Tristan*, by the Norman-French poet Béroul, hard to date but probably from the last third of the twelfth century. The German poet Eilhart von Oberge composed a Tristan romance around 1170, bringing the story to a conclusion but omitting several episodes that—as they are present in Béroul—may go back to a lost original. These "precourtly" versions have in common a fairly roughcut concept of love. The love potion and the fatal passion of the protagonists are seen as a regrettable tragic fate that breaks over the lovers against their will; the love potion wears off after four years. It was left to a certain Thomas d'Angleterre to reshape the conception of love into the sublime glorification of passion that we have in Gottfried's version. Thomas, an Anglo-Norman, wrote his poem for someone at the court of Henry II of England, probably around 1170, though the dating varies between 1155 and 1190. His patroness may have been none other than Eleanor of Aquitaine, wife of Henry and ardent devotee of courtly literature. Gottfried mentions Thomas as the true master of the tale. Thomas understood courtly ideals and courtly love much better than Eilhart or Béroul, and he transformed the legend of Tristan and Isolde into the story of passion alienating individuals from society and raising them above it in their struggle to defend their relationship from detection. Gottfried adapted Thomas's version, and he turned the legend into the vehicle of a dark and tragic, lofty and transcendent view of love. But he did a great deal more with it.

Arthurian romance, set in the landscape of Celtic fairy tale and drawing on the half-legend, half-myth of an ancient King Arthur of the Britons, presents itself to the modern reader as a fusion of Celtic and English traditions. For some time, Arthurian scholarship was dominated by the quest for the sources and analogues of twelfth- and thirteenth-century romance in Celtic materials. This point of departure is understandable, though a firm textual basis for it never existed. It is the approach to the *body* of the Arthurian materials. But their heart and soul—sensibilities, ethical values, mores of the heroes and heroines—are to be sought not in prehistoric Britain but in the courts and cathedral schools of the twelfth century. The sublime dream vision of the Arthurian knight questing for love, adventure, and identity in fairy-tale forests was dreamed by worldly, humanistic clerics who sought to educate and entertain the lay nobles and court society with paragons of chivalric conduct. "Courtly" ideals and the figure of the courtly-chivalric knight are creations of this class of men. So was King Arthur, and so were the romances of his knights. Some of these authors, Chrétien de Troyes prominent among them, were influenced by the humanist thinking of the twelfth-century schools and were exposed to the fertile climate of ideas that arose in the so-called "renaissance of the twelfth century." There is a strong element of classical revival in the ethical ideals of Arthurian romance, and it is no coincidence that the earliest romances were medieval recastings of the epics of antiquity—the war of Troy and the wanderings of Aeneas, for example. These intellectual obligations are especially evident in Gottfried. He stands out clearly among his contemporaries as a man of learning, a virtuoso poet, and a connoisseur of court life. As a stylist, he is the most important master of the German language before Goethe. His view of humanity, his mastery of classical poetic forms, the amalgamation of these with Christian forms, and his depiction of the ideal courtier anticipate ideals and poetic practices of the Renaissance in the fifteenth and sixteenth centuries. It is apparent that he was educated in the humanist cathedral schools. He is a master of classical literature; his poem is replete with classical and mythological allusion. He inclines more to allegory than any contemporary vernacular poet, and particularly in his use of this technique we can see his obligations to twelfth-century humanism.

What we know of Gottfried von Strassburg, beyond his title *Meister* and his association with Strassburg, we glean from his work. We know nothing about his biography, but a great deal about his thinking, his tastes, his attitudes toward love, woman, education, music, poetry, courts, and kings. A remarkable and important passage in his *Tristan* is the part that modern scholars call the "literary excursus." It interrupts and in a subtle way continues and comments on the ceremony of young Tristan's knighting. Faced with the task of describing the knightly splendor of the investiture, the preparation of the clothes for Tristan and the thirty pages knighted with him, he is reminded of the many poets who have gone before him and tailored, trimmed, and dyed the clothes of knighthood with their words. He praises Heinrich von Veldeke as the originator of courtly language in German, Hartmann von Aue for his clarity and transparence, a certain Blicker von Steinach for the soaring flight of his words and ideas (in an epic poem now lost). But an unnamed poet comes in for a drubbing. This "comrade of the hare" skips about on the "field of words" and lays claim to the laurel wreath, which Gottfried had set on the head of Hartmann. This poet writes in an obscure and uncourtly way, projecting the illusion of profundity in the way that carnival conjurers turn lead to gold and dust to pearls to dupe children. His target is undoubtedly Wolfram von Eschenbach. In this passage, Gottfried reveals himself as something of a literary critic, and his survey of poets might be called the earliest piece of literary criticism in the vernacular literature of the Middle Ages. He appears to set himself up as a judge of poetry and arbiter of taste, one of those who have the right to bestow the laurel wreath on their contemporaries. The ceremony of crowning poets with the laurel wreath originated in classical antiquity. It was not practiced in the Middle Ages prior to the fourteenth century, so far as is known, and Gottfried's use of it appears to be metaphorical. But even as a metaphor his bestowing of the laurel wreath on Hartmann shows us something important about Gottfried's self-awareness and about his perception of the contemporary literary scene. He sees his contemporaries as successors of the great poets of antiquity, and to underscore this indebtedness he ascribes to each of the poets he praises a classical or pagan source of inspiration: Veldeke has his wisdom from the well of Pegasus, from which all inspiration derives; Blicker's words and meanings are washed and dyed in the fountain of the fairies; Hartmann wears the laurel wreath, symbol of Apollo's favor. The same is true of the two lyric poets he names: Reinmar von Hagenau sings with the tongue of Orpheus, and the love songs of Walther von der Vogelweide are inspired by the goddess of love, Venus. Toward the end of the excursus, Gottfried places himself in the same line of descent in his invocation of the Muses and Apollo, the most artful and elaborate example of that form that any medieval poet produced, and that includes Alain of Lille and Dante. Having conjured up all his illustrious contemporaries, he finds himself speechless before the example of their eloquence, and he seeks the aid of the nine Muses sitting on their thrones on Mount Helicon and of their leader, Apollo. If they will send him a single drop of their abundant inspiration, it will restore his flagging powers and burnish his words like pure gold. But then he calls on certain beings "up there in their heavenly choirs" to grant him the inspiration of "True Helicon, the highest throne." This inspiration will render his words transparent like an exquisite jewel. It is an example of the double invocation, common in the traditions of Christian humanism: the inspiring spirits of pagan antiquity are to combine their powers with those of the Christian tradition, here referred to in the classicizing epithet "True Helicon." It is a form that we encounter in Alain of Lille's *Anticlaudianus*, in Dante's *Divine Comedy*, in Petrarch's *Africa*, and in a great many works from the Renaissance of the fifteenth and sixteenth centuries. It implies a humanist poetic program synthesizing classical and Christian inspiration, though setting the former subordinate to the latter. Here, as in a number of other places, we see clearly Gottfried's obligations to the traditions of Christian humanism.

These are also evident in one of the most remarkable and original passages that Gottfried added to the tale received from Thomas d'Angleterre, the allegory of the cave of lovers. In Thomas, the lovers abandon the court of King Mark and spend a period of time living in isolation in a distant forest. It is an idyllic scene, which Thomas modeled on the forest idyll in the *Legend of St. Giles*. But Gottfried outbids his source. He takes over the concept of an idyllic life in the forest (in Béroul and Eilhart it was nasty and brutish), and adds the lovers' temple, ingeniously wrought in prehistoric times by giants who used it for their secret amorous rendezvous. This "cave of lovers," set in a beautiful landscape (*locus amoenus*), is described in great detail. After some talk about the lovers' life there (they sing, read sad tales of tragic love, and nourish themselves by gazing into each others' eyes), he returns to the lovers' temple and begs the indulgence of his readers to hear the real significance of its architecture. He proceeds to explain the parts of the cave allegorically: the smoothness of the walls stands for love's simplicity, their height is aspiration, the green of the floor stands for constancy; the crystal bed represents the purity and transparency of love. The exegesis continues at length. Scholarly debate about the sources of the cave allegory has shown that Gottfried in part borrowed techniques of allegory at home in the Christian tradition of cathedral allegory and applied them to an adulterous love affair. The problematic nature of such a borrowing has not escaped readers, and it raises the important and difficult question of Gottfried's relation to Christianity. One reader has made of him a heretic, or sympathizer with heresy, who attempts by sacrilegious borrowings to reduce Christian forms of thought and expression to a shambles, using them to exalt a dubious love relationship. Another reader accepts this spiritualizing of love as thoroughly in harmony with Christian sensibilities. A third has denied that the cave allegory has any relation to the Christian tradition but is derivable from the epithalamial tradition of late antiquity and secular love allegories. Yet another denies this view and claims that the cave allegory is quite consistent with worldly, humanistic forms of Christian thought, in fact serves as a good example of the program mapped out in the invocation, the cooperation of the pagan and the Christian traditions. In any case, it is certain that Gottfried in his cave allegory and elsewhere in his work introduced to the romance a spiritualized conception of human passion, set parallel to religious devotion.

There are other passages that underscore Gottfried's problematic relationship to Christianity. In his prologue, he offers the story to the readers as "bread to the living"; through the story, the lovers "live on though they are dead." The eucharistic overtones are distinct, and they would seem to imply an analogy between the lovers and Christ, between the reading of their tale and the taking of the sacramental bread. Most puzzling and troublesome is an apparent attack on Christ's pliant nature that Gottfried added to the story after the famous scene of Isolde's ordeal by the hot iron. The queen is forced to prove her innocence before a court by carrying a glowing iron. When the day and place are set, Isolde arranges for Tristan to happen by disguised as a pilgrim. She asks that the "pilgrim" carry her from her ship to the place of the ordeal so that she will not be profaned before this numinous event by the touch of worldly men. The disguised Tristan carries her, but slips and tumbles to the ground, landing on top of her. She then proceeds to take the oath of innocence, swearing that no man has ever lain with her except her husband, and of course that pilgrim, whom all have just seen lying in her lap. She carries the iron and is not burned. Gottfried's comment: "Then and there it was made perfectly clear and manifest to all that Christ for all his virtue shifts like a sleeve in the wind. . . . He is at the service of all whether their affairs are upright or deceitful." It may be, as some readers have suggested, that Gottfried did not like ordeals, and his words suggest, "This is the kind of creature that men turn Christ into by foolish institutions like the ordeal." But since he earlier depicted the battle between Tristan and Morold uncritically as a trial by combat in which God renders judgment, this explanation is not compelling. However we read the passage, it is hard to escape the conclusion that it is based on some highly unmedieval suspension of the reverence appropriate to the name of Christ. This and other ambiguous uses of Christian symbolism and thought urge on us the conclusion that Gottfried's relationship to Christianity is troubled and unorthodox. Regarding the modern attempts to explain this relationship, it is best to say it remains unexplained.

In origin, the story of Tristan and Isolde is a love story. But it is worth noting that they do not fall in love until around Gottfried's line 12,000—that is, approximately halfway through the entire work (assuming that the finished work would have reached around 24,000 lines). Up to that point, the story is concerned with the tale of Tristan's parents (ca. 1,800 lines) and of Tristan's youth, education, entry into court, battles, intrigues, and the courting of Isolde for King Mark (ca. 10,000 lines). The figure of the young Tristan is on center stage in the first and longest part of the romance, and this is understandable. Thomas and Gottfried have created a hero who is quite untypical in Arthurian romance. He is highly educated, he makes his way by his wit, charm, beauty of appearance and manners, and talents in hunting, music, and foreign languages. The knight of Arthurian romance finds his destiny alone in the forest of adventure, facing adversaries natural and supernatural, whom he overcomes by his strength, knightly prowess, and constancy. By contrast, in *Tristan* intellectual and personal qualities are in the foreground. We wait long until Tristan fights on horseback, and in Gottfried's entire romance occurs not a single tourney, that most popular event of the typical Arthurian romance. Young Tristan is not first and foremost a knight, but rather a courtier and artist. He is kidnapped from his foster parents by Norwegian merchants, who admire his talents in chess and language, his bearing and presence, and imagine that they can turn a profit by selling this child prodigy. Released and washed up on the shore of Cornwall, he impresses the king's hunting party by a dazzling mastery of hunting customs and the French terms for them. At court, the king marvels at his abilities in music, which Tristan highlights by a calculated show of modesty, a well-known courtier's strategy of winning favor. After these and other shows of skill, he wins the love of King Mark (who, unbeknownst to both, is his uncle), becomes his private minstrel and master huntsman, and stands at the pinnacle of favor. Tristan's early successes at court are the result not of chivalric prowess, the least important of his abilities, but rather of what Baldesar Castiglione would call *cortegiania* 'courtiership.' The Tristan romance in the version of Thomas/Gottfried introduced a new character into Arthurian romance: the courtier-knight. The court is the main theater of events; its intrigues account for a good part of the action; the mentality of the courtier accounts for the motivations of the characters. Also, the central event of the plot is one of the favorite motifs of court literature (and court life): the clandestine love affair concealed through deception and trickery. The institution of the ruler's court has had an influence on western literature and art that is easy to underestimate. The courtly version of the Tristan romance is one good example of this influence, and it would not be inaccurate to call Gottfried's version a "courtier romance."

Until now, we have considered the literary-philosophical unity into which Gottfried transformed the tale he had received. But now we want to approach it from another angle: the rediscovery of its earliest form by reference to Celtic analogues. This approach is fraught with the danger of hypothesizing on thin evidence, a danger that did not prevent an earlier generation of scholars from attempting reconstructions as interesting as they are unverifiable. Apart from the risk of inaccuracy, another danger is the illusion created by this approach that the preserved versions of the romance are fragmented bits of a lost unity, not autonomous works of art arising out of a vital and genial attempt of a single poet to come to terms with his own world and time.

Stepping cautiously into the earlier stages of the romance, then, we can say with some certainty that the names of the main characters are traceable to Britain of the sixth or seventh century. In the Irish chronicles of the Picts, we find from the eighth century a *Talorcan filius Drostan* and a *Drest filius Talorcan*. *Drostan*, or *Drest*, appears to be a name common among Pictish chieftains, though it occurs also among the Celts of Britain. The name appears in Welsh Triads (which date in their written form from the thirteenth century or later but preserve earlier material) as *Drystan*, or *Trystan, son of Tallwch*. The same sources tell us that Drystan was the lover of Essylt, the wife of his uncle March. The Triads postdate the French and German romances and must be suspected of French influence, but the name *Tallwch* is not suspect. It is fully the equivalent in sound of the *Talorc* of the chronicles. Yet the love relationship between Drystan and Essylt, wife of King March, cannot be located in Celtic sources that predate the twelfth- or thirteenth-century romances, however strong the probability of a Celtic tradition may be.

Historians of Celtic literature tell us that the original core of the Tristan legend was a tradition that Drust rescued a princess from her fate as a tribute for a foreign oppressor; that she recognized her deliverer as he lay in a bath and thwarted the attempt of a false claimant to rob Drust of his due glory. This nucleus is preserved in the tenth-century version of the Irish saga *The Wooing of Emer*. We can gain some understanding of the genesis of the love story by reference to another Irish tale, the elopement of Diarmaid and Grainne, believed to have existed as early as the ninth century. Grainne, wife of the Irish chieftain Finn, is taken with a passion for her husband's nephew, the hero Diarmaid. He rejects her, but she forces him by a magic spell to become her lover. They flee to the forest, are pursued by Finn, and suffer hardship and deprivation in their flight. The question whether the story of Tristan and Isolde is in its origins Celtic is perhaps superfluous. There are also Persian and Hellenistic elements in the versions from the twelfth and thirteenth centuries. But from the comparison with Celtic analogues we can learn a great deal about the transformation that the love motif experienced. Earlier versions seem to have depicted the Isolde figure as a witch who ruthlessly imposes her will on a reluctant lover. The love of the two is dangerous and demonic. In these early versions, the social order, the loyalty of hero to chieftain and of nephew to uncle, are unquestioned values. In the version of Eilhart, the love potion is still seen as a curse imposed on the hero and heroine by a catastrophic chance from which they are eventually released. This crude conception of love shows us by contrast the refinements of the Thomas/Gottfried version. Here, the love potion imposes a relationship on Tristan and Isolde for which their own psyches destined them. The love is affirmed even in its most negative aspects: the disruption of the social order, the betrayal of friendship and blood relationship. Gottfried has imbued an illicit love with a pathos, a sense of the elevation of the lovers through the destructive bond that unites them. How differently society and its highest representative, King Mark, are depicted in the romance: Mark is a weakling and a coarse, sensual, shortsighted man, who, as Gottfried states openly, gets what is coming to him. His court consists of cowards, villains, and low intriguers. The whole thrust of the romance and the lovers' efforts is to thwart society's attempts to expose the love relationship. It is cultivated as a high ideal, and even the tragedy is seen as elevating and exalting. In the courtly version of the Tristan romance, loyalty to king, uncle, and society is the questioned value, not the passion of "noble hearts." (*See also* TRISTAN, MODERN GERMAN VERSIONS OF GOTTFRIED'S.) [CSJ]

ᴥ Gottfried von Strassburg. *Tristan*, ed. Reinhold Bechstein, re-ed. Peter Ganz. Wiesbaden: Brockhaus, 1978.

——— . *Tristan . . . with the Surviving Fragments of the Tristan of Thomas*, trans. A.T. Hatto. Baltimore and Harmondsworth: Penguin, 1974.

Batts, Michael. *Gottfried von Strassburg*. New York: Twayne, 1971.

Jackson, W.T.H. *The Anatomy of Love: The Tristan of Gottfried von Strassburg*. New York and London: Columbia University Press, 1971.

Jaeger, C. Stephen. *Medieval Humanism in Gottfried von Strassburg's Tristan und Isolde*. Heidelberg: Winter, 1977.

GRAAL, ROMAN DU: see POST-VULGATE CYCLE.

GRACQ, JULIEN (pseudonym of Louis Poirier; 1910–   ). From an early age, Gracq admired Wagnerian drama, and in 1939 his *Au Château d'Argol* offered a "demonic version" of *Parsifal*. The figure of the hero seems to pale before the theme of Amfortas's wound; for example, the blood from the wound flows into the Grail, profaning the myth by reversing the holy liquid from the direction it took in the First Continuation of Chrétien de Troyes.

Gracq's four-act play *Le Roi Pêcheur* was presented in 1949. (A preface to the printed edition of 1945 recommends and endorses the adaptation of medieval myths.) As the title suggests, the playwright transfers emphasis from Perceval (who does not appear until the second act) to the Grail King. The young hero assumes a solar character (borrowed from Gauvain), and his silver armor contrasts with the black clothing of Amfortas. The work is inspired as much by Wolfram von Eschenbach as by Wagner's *Parsifal*. It reestablishes the duality of Gornemant and Trévrizent, whom Wagner confused. Amfortas remains the Fisher King, since his wound (the result of his seduction by Kundry) prevents his hunting. The Grail is by now all but forgotten, and its guardians are languishing. But Kundry, now converted, resists Clingsor's order once again to seduce the young hero, and she comes to his aid instead.

Departing from Wagner's version (but following the tradition established by Chrétien de Troyes), Perceval does not ask about the Grail procession, and an exuberant vegetation—a rather surrealistic inversion of the "Wasteland"—progressively suffocates the glacial Manor, cursed by the Wound.

At a time when Anouilh, Sartre, Giraudoux, and Cocteau were grafting modern psychology onto Greek myths, Gracq was making a similar effort in regard to medieval myth. Amfortas becomes a scheming old king, trying by whatever subterfuge to hold onto his power. But this demystification and humanization of legendary characters, while accenting their realism, weakens the supernatural element, in spite of Gracq's usual mythic sense.

The work is somewhat static, since the main characters (e.g., Kundry and Perceval) evolve little or not at all during the drama, but the language, on the other hand, is magnificent. The critics were brutal, unjustly so, toward the work, and it has only rarely been revived. [RB]

• Gracq, Julien *Au Château d'Argol*. Paris: Corti, 1939.

————. *Le Roi Pêcheur*. Paris: Corti, 1945.

Baudry, Robert. "Julien Gracq et la légende du Graal." In *Actes du Colloque International sur Julien Gracq*. Angers: Presses de l'Université d'Angers, 1981.

Dandrea, Claude. "Le Roi Pêcheur et la légende du Graal." In *Actes du Colloque International sur Julien Gracq*. Angers: Presses de l'Université d'Angers, 1981.

McLendon, Will L. "Thèmes wagnériens dans les romans de Julien Gracq." *French Review*, 41 (1968), 539–48.

GRAELENT, an anonymous Breton lai of 756 lines, of the early thirteenth century, not actually Arthurian, but notable for its utilization of basically the same story as Marie de France's *Lanval*. The existence of *Graelent* suggests that the Arthurian setting of *Lanval* is not original but a later accretion. [KB]

• Tobin, Prudence Mary O'Hara, ed. *Les Lais anonymes des XIIe et XIIIe siècles: édition critique de quelques lais bretons*. Geneva: Droz, 1976.

Weingartner, Russell, ed. and trans. *Graelent and Guingamor: Two Breton Lays*. New York and London: Garland, 1984.

GRAIL (GRAAL). We must distinguish at the outset between the French word *graal* (which became *grail* in English) and the thing or things it came to designate in medieval literature.

The word itself is not shrouded in mystery. It is one of the numerous reflexes of medieval Latin *gradale*, a word that meant "by degree," "in stages," applied to a dish or platter that was brought to the table at various stages or servings during a meal. In the early thirteenth century, Helinand of Froidmont wrote: "Gradalis autem sive gradale gallice dicitur scutella lata et aliquantulum profunda in qua pretiosae dapes cum suo jure divitibus solent apponi gradatim, . . . et dicitur vulgari nomine *graalz*" (". . . a wide and somewhat deep dish in which expensive meats are customarily placed for the rich, . . . and it is commonly called a 'grail'") (Migne, *Patrologia Latina*, Vol. 212, col. 814). As a common noun, it figures in inventories of precious plate as early as 1010 as *gradales duas de argento*, and *grassalete argentei* from an inventory dated 1294. Even in some early literary texts, the word is found with the simple meaning of dish or plate, without any of the overtones of sacredness or splendor it came to acquire: "Sire, dist il, Deus te gart de tot mal! Ersoir mangai o toi a ton grääl" ("Sir, said he, may God protect you from all harm! Yesterday evening, I ate with you from your grail") (*Roman d'Alexandre*).

Although not perhaps in widespread usage, the word *graal* was undeniably common enough in Old French and designated some sort of dish or serving vessel.

The prodigious fortune of the word was due directly to Chrétien de Troyes. In his *Conte del Graal*, the youth Perceval, seated on a couch next to the Fisher King, beholds a magnificent procession that, at each course of the repast, emerges from a chamber at one end of the hall, passes before the table, and disappears into another chamber. The first to appear is a young boy holding a bleeding lance; he is followed by two youths with candelabra. Finally

Un graal entre ses deus mains	3220
Une damoisele tenoit,	
Qui avec les vallés venoit,	
Bele et gente et bien acesmee. . . .	
Li graaus, qui aloit devant,	3232
De fin or esmeré estoit;	
Prescïeuses pierres avoit	
El graal de maintes manieres,	
Des plus riches et des plus chieres	3236
Qui en mer ne en terre soient;	
Totes autres pierres passoient	
Celes del graal sanz dotance.	

("A beautiful and comely maiden who accompanied the youths held a grail in her hands. . . . The grail, borne ahead of the procession, was worked with fine gold, and there were in the grail many precious stones, the finest and most costly in the world; surely the stones in the grail surpassed all others.") That Chrétien designated the vessel *un graal* is proof that he regarded the word as a common noun, a platter or dish of costly workmanship. In a later passage, we learn that the *graal* does not contain a pike, a salmon, or a lamprey (suggesting a rather large serving platter not unlike that described by Helinand), rather

D'une sole oiste le sert on,	
Que l'en en cel graal li porte;	
Sa vie sostient et conforte,	6424
Tant sainte chose est li graals.	
Et il, qui est esperitax	
Qu'a se vie plus ne covient	
Fors l'oiste qui el graal vient.	6428

("He [the old king] is provided with a single Mass wafer, which is brought to him in the grail; and it sustains his life, such a holy thing is the grail. And he is so spiritual that he needs nothing more than the wafer contained in the grail.") Noteworthy are the spiritual overtones absent in the first appearance of the *graal*. Here, the ancient king is sustained over the years by the single Mass wafer contained in the vessel.

But even though we know much about the *graal* at this stage, we remain in complete ignorance where Chrétien derived the elements of his mysterious procession, or for that matter why a grail was conceived as the centerpiece of this splendid ritual. In all likelihood, Chrétien drew on some ancient myth of food-producing vessels, perhaps but not necessarily of Celtic origin, of the type catalogued by Stith Thompson (D 1472.1.19 to D 1472.1.33): cauldrons of plenty, cornucopias, etc., and applied the name of an ornate platter to the vessel, thereby with one stroke providing the foundation for the myth of the Grail, or Holy Grail.

The story would have doubtless remained there, a mysterious procession with at its center a jewel-encrusted and luminous vessel that had the power to produce food, if it had not been for an author who wrote some ten or fifteen years after Chrétien left his *Perceval* unfinished. Robert de Boron recognized the possibilities of the *graal* as he read about it in Chrétien. Whereas the latter left the reader wondering what precisely the *graal* was and what function it had in the narrative, Robert was most specific. It was the vessel of the Last Supper used by Joseph of Arimathea to catch Christ's blood after the Deposition and was later placed at the center of an altarlike table where a sort of "service" was held. Finally, it was transported to Arthurian Britain by Joseph's family to become henceforth the Holy Grail (*Le Saint Graal*). Robert transformed Chrétien's enigmatic vessel, *un graal*, into *le Graal*, a type of Christian chalice and symbol of Christ's real presence. The transition from a vessel producing food for the body to the vessel of the Christian cult, the chalice, which produces nourishment for the soul, was an obvious one in an age imbued with Christian typology.

In the many works in which this precious vessel appears, the Grail or Holy Grail assumes many forms and functions, although in all cases it retains its basic power as a food provider or is associated with food consumption at table. In Chrétien, it seems clearly a platter that sustains the old king in the second chamber. In Robert, it is a cup used at table that assumed later characteristics of the Mass chalice and whose service broke the famine. In Wolfram von Eschenbach's *Parzival*, it is a "thing" called a Grail, a stone or *lapsit exillis* that produces an abundance of the most savory foods. In the First Continuation of the *Perceval*, the Rich Grail, floating about the hall, provides food and drink to all in attendance. Manessier, in his Continuation, depicts the Grail carried by a maiden as in Chrétien. The Welsh *Peredur* presents the gruesome spectacle of a great salver carried by two maidens in which a man's head is found swimming in blood. In the *Perlesvaus*, the Grail is, as in Robert's poem, the vessel used by Joseph to collect the blood of Christ, but it causes rejuvenation and is carried in a ceremony before Gauvain, who perceives in it visions of a chalice, then the form of a child (signifying the real body of Christ), and finally the Crucifixion. In the Prose *Lancelot*, the Grail assumes the shape of a chalice. In the *Queste del*

Saint Graal, as in Malory, it becomes synonymous with the beatific vision and is an object of a quest by Bors, Perceval, and the pure knight Galahad. When the quest is achieved, a hand descends from heaven and removes the Grail forever from its earthly, sinful abode. What is most astonishing is that, in the midst of this wealth of story and Christian legend, the official Church kept complete silence, never approving or condemning its many and shifting fictions.

The appeal of the Holy Grail is not limited to the Middle Ages. With the fascination for medieval literature and culture manifested in the nineteenth century, the Grail once again became associated with the arduous yearnings after mystical experience. Tennyson, Wagner, T.S. Eliot, T.H. White, and Charles Williams all wrote about the struggle between the forces of Good and Evil centering on the possession of the most sacred of vessels, the Holy Grail. (*See also* SCHOLARSHIP, MODERN ARTHURIAN.) [RFO'G]

Loomis, Roger Sherman. *The Grail: From Celtic Myth to Christian Symbol.* Cardiff: University of Wales Press, 1963.

Marx, Jean. *Nouvelles recherches sur la littérature arthurienne.* Paris: Klincksieck, 1965.

Nitze, William A., and Harry F. Williams. *Arthurian Names in the Perceval of Chrétien de Troyes.* Berkeley: University of California Press, 1955, pp. 275–78.

O'Gorman, Richard. "Ecclesiastical Tradition and the Holy Grail." *Australian Journal of French Studies*, 6 (1969), 3–8.

GRAIL, THE: *see* DEAL, BABS H.

GRAIL WAR, THE: *see* MONACO, RICHARD.

GRAL, DER: *see* KRALIK, RICHARD VON; SYBERBERG, HANS JÜRGEN.

GRAL, EIN DRAMATISCHES EPOS, DER: *see* STUCKEN, EDUARD.

GRALSAGE, DIE: *see* KRALIK, RICHARD VON.

GRAN RE MELIADUS, IL ("The Great King Meliadus"), an Italian translation (1558–59) of the French *Meliadus de Leonnoys.* Set in the early years of Arthur's reign, it describes the love of Meliadus for the Queen of Scotland, recounts the former's exploits, and presents the illustrious youth of Tristan (who is three years old when the story opens). The events of this work are entwined with those of *Girone il Cortese*, as the French texts from which they derive had once been parts of the same work (*see* PALAMEDES). [NJL]

Gardner, Edmund G. *The Arthurian Legend in Italian Literature.* London: Dent, 1930, pp. 47–63.

GRANDES ET INESTIMABLES CRONICQUES DU GRANT ET ENORME GEANT GARGANTUA, LES: *see* GARGANTUAN CHRONICLES.

GRAS, MOSSÈN, author of the *Tragèdia de Lançalot*, a Catalan incunabulum version of the *Mort Artu*. From the nine surviving leaves, it is evident that Gras condensed the initial episodes of the *Mort Artu* and gave a sentimental treatment to the love triangle of Lancelot, Guenevere, and the Maid of Ascalot, using rhetoric commonly found in Hispanic sentimental romances of the fifteenth century. [HLS]

᪲ Gras, Mossèn. *Tragèdia de Lançalot*, ed. Martí de Riquer. Barcelona: Quaderns Crema, 1984.

"GRAVE OF KING ARTHUR, THE": *see* WARTON, THOMAS.

GREAT CAPTAINS, THE: *see* TREECE, HENRY.

GREAT RETURN, THE: *see* MACHEN, ARTHUR.

GREEN, ROGER LANCELYN: *see* JUVENILE FICTION IN ENGLISH.

GREEN KNIGHT, THE: *see* CHAPMAN, VERA.

GREEN MAN, THE: *see* TREECE, HENRY.

GREENWITCH: *see* COOPER, SUSAN.

GRENE KNIGHT, THE, a late (ca. 1500) tail-rhyme version of that pearl of English Arthurian romances, *Sir Gawain and the Green Knight*. The *Grene Knight* is a perfect example of the disastrous effect that the combination of popular demand and lack of poetic skill and feeling could produce. In spite of its abbreviated form (516 lines), the poem shows no trace of the concentration of its famous ancestor, in which every detail matters; the poem spoils what tension is left by revealing everything beforehand, without, however, explaining anything. Thus, we are told who the Green Knight is (a Sir Bredbeddle), and why he travels to Arthur's court (to lure away Sir Gawain, who is loved by his wife), but not why he should be transformed into a *green* knight, especially as his arrival at court causes no consternation. Lack of competence at times has hilarious results, as when the Green Knight politely sets "his head vp on againe" before shaking hands in parting with the King. The rest of the story is in the same vein: Gawain is tempted only once by the Lady, but with three kisses, while the Green Knight is hunting hinds, boars, foxes, etc.; these winnings they share instead of exchanging them. The Lady gives Gawain a white "lace"; it duly saves his neck, and the next day the two knights return to Arthur's court together. The story explains, the poet says, why the Knights of the Bath wear a white "lace" until they have performed a deed of valor (which seems to agree with contemporary practice). Some peculiar details: Morgan is called Aggteb, the Green Knight lives at Castle Hutton in the West Country, and Arthur resides at Carlisle in the unidentified Castle of Flatting, in the Forest of Delamore (i.e., Delamere Forest, Cheshire). [ESK]

Madden, Frederic, ed. *Syr Gawayne.* London: Bannatyne Club, 1839.

GREY KING, THE: *see* COOPER, SUSAN.

GRINALDA DE FLORES: *see* SILVA, ANTÓNIO DA.

GUENEVERE (GUINEVERE, GUENIÈVRE, GWENHWYFAR, GUENHUMARE, GINEVRA), the wife of King Arthur and mistress of Lancelot du Lac.

Geoffrey of Monmouth's *Historia* (ca. 1135) identifies Guenevere as a noble Roman whom Arthur married for her surpassing beauty and whom his nephew, Mordred, also married after usurping his uncle's throne. Guenevere's guilt and fear of Arthur's wrath in both Wace's *Brut* (ca. 1155) and Layamon's *Brut* (ca. 1200) could indicate that she was a willing accomplice in Mordred's treachery, but Hardyng's *Chronicle* (ca. 1457) probably reflects the reality of any early medieval queen caught in her circumstances when it says that she was forced to wed the traitor. The Alliterative *Morte Arthure* (ca. 1400) is unique in concluding that Guenevere is the mother of Mordred's two sons. All the English chronicles comment on the misfortune of her barrenness as Arthur's wife; however, Welsh tradition maintained that she bore him sons. The Welsh also preserved the tradition of her infidelity, blaming her to such an extent that in some parts of the country, as recently as the end of the last century, it was regarded as an insult to a girl's moral character to call her Guenevere.

Lanval, a late twelfth-century romance in which Marie de France characterizes Arthur's queen as a seductress, may reflect this Welsh tradition, since Ulrich von Zatzikhoven's *Lanzelet* (1195) does not corroborate Marie's judgment of the Queen's character. At the same time, even though it is allegedly based upon a French (*welschez*) book, the German romance exhibits no awareness of a liaison between Guenevere and Lancelot. This seems to have been the invention of another Marie, Countess of Champagne. Chrétien de Troyes claims to have received from her both the *matière* and the *sen* of his *Chevalier de la charrete* (ca. 1178). The title refers to Lancelot, who loves and serves his lady, the beautiful and haughty Queen, with a fervor akin to religious adoration and protests that he owes all his knightly worth to her love. Approximately fifty years later, the anonymous author(s) of the French prose romances of Arthur now known as the Vulgate Cycle decided to incorporate Chrétien's love story. They glorify the love affair in the early part of the *Lancelot*, where the Lady of the Lake assures the young Queen that she is not wrong to love the best knight in the world. Later, however, they condemn their love as the cause of Lancelot's failure in the *Queste del Saint Graal* and as one of the causes of the fall of the Round Table in the *Mort Artu*.

Sir Thomas Malory conflates the romance and chronicle traditions in his *Morte Darthur* (1469–70), with the result that his portrait of Guenevere is richer and more subtle than that of any of his sources. She is the epic Queen of history and chronicle, bounteous of her gifts to the knights of the Round Table, and she is also the tragic heroine of romance, deserving of our pity for having been given in marriage to a man she must respect but cannot love, and fated to love a man she cannot marry. Malory praises Guenevere as a "trew lover" and gives her an exceptionally "good ende" by suggesting that she and Lancelot are finally united in spirit after each has renounced the vanities of this world for the "perfeccion" of the religious life.

Modern English versions of Guenevere's life and love all derive ultimately from Malory and at the same time reflect the different values and intentions of their authors. Alfred, Lord Tennyson, portrays Guenevere in his *Idylls of the King* (1859) as a fallen woman who grovels on her knees before a Victorian husband godlike in forgiveness. T.H. White domesticates the love in his *Once and Future King* (1939–40), portraying Guenevere as just plain "Jenny" to her "Lance" and imagining that Arthur benevolently overlooks their affair until his kinsmen force him to take action. Thomas Berger suggests in *Arthur Rex* (1978) that Guenevere seduced Lancelot in order to prove her power and in so doing, perhaps inadvertently, calls attention to the real powerlessness of women, even of queens, in medieval society. A more sympathetic handling of this theme appears in Sharan Newman's *Guinevere* (1981) and *The Chessboard Queen* (1983), the first two volumes of a projected trilogy retelling the Arthurian legend from Guenevere's point of view. By contrast, a few novels, like Parke Godwin's *Firelord* (1980) and *Beloved Exile* (1984), portray Guenevere as the inheritor of a matriarchal tradition and a powerful ruler in her own right. [BK]

❧ DiPasquale, Pasquale, Jr. "Malory's Guinevere: Epic Queen, Romance Heroine and Tragic Mistress." *Bucknell Review*, 16 (1968), 86–102.

Weston, Jessie L. *The Legend of Sir Lancelot du Lac*. London: Nutt, 1901.

GUÉNON, RENÉ (1886–1951), in *Le Roi du Monde* (1925), interpreted the Grail legend in light of his belief in a Revelation prior to all religions and available to all humanity. According to Guénon, the angels shaped the Grail from an emerald that fell from the forehead of Lucifer at the time of his fall. The Grail was entrusted to Adam until he was dismissed from Eden; it was later recovered by Seth, the representative of order and stability. Between Seth and Christ, the Druids may have been the Grail guardians. The work goes on to make the Grail the cup of the Last Supper and to connect it with Joseph of Arimathea, with Nicodemus (who helped transport it to Britain), and with the establishment of the Round Table by Arthur and Merlin. Constructed by Arthur, according to Merlin's plans, the Table was to receive the Grail once it was achieved. The essential role of the knights of the Round Table seems to be the Grail quest; the Grail doubtless represents both the Book (*grad(u)ale*), i.e., tradition, and the Vase (*grasale*), the primordial state recovered by the one who achieves this supreme degree of knowledge. The Grail, the "Book of Life," is often associated with the Lance, the symbol of the "Axis of the World." The blood flowing from the Lance corrresponds to the dew emanating from the "Tree of Life," the vital principle intimately related to blood. Montsalvat, the "Mont du Salut" that holds the Grail, represents the sacred isle, the polar mountain, the Land of Immortality (identical with the earthly paradise), in the "Center of the World." [RB]

🕿 Guénon, René. *Le Roi du Monde.* Paris: Gallimard, 1925.

———. "L'Ésotérisme du Graal." In *Lumières du Graal.* Paris: Cahiers du Sud, 1951, pp. 37–49.

GUILLAUME LE CLERC. Not to be confused with the author of the *Bestiaire*, this Guillaume wrote *Fergus*, a romance sometimes named *Fergus et Galienne*, written between 1200 and 1233, possibly at the request of Alan of Galloway to celebrate his marriage in 1209. Scotland is the setting, scholars believe, and a Scottish lord, a son-in-law of Henry I of England, may have been a historical model for the hero, at least in name. The action begins in a forest near Glasgow, but the plot is hardly more than a rearrangement of Chrétien de Troyes's *Perceval*, *Yvain*, and *Erec*, with echoes of his *Lancelot* and perhaps even *Cligés*. Fergus earns fame as the *Chevalier au bel escu* ("Knight of the Fair Shield"), a hint that the author may have also imitated Renaut de Beaujeu's *Bel Inconnu*. The romance was translated into Dutch in the fourteenth century. [JLG]

🕿 Guillaume le Clerc. *The Romance of Fergus*, ed. Wilson Frescoln. Philadelphia: Allen, 1983.

———. *Ferguut*, ed. E. Rombauts, N. de Paepe, and M.J.M. de Haan. Culemborg: Tjeenk Willink, 1976.

"GUINEVERE": *see* TENNYSON, ALFRED LORD.

GUINEVERE: see HILL, GRAHAM; NEWMAN, SHARAN.

GUINEVERE EVERMORE: see NEWMAN, SHARAN.

GUINEVER'S GIFT: see ST. JOHN, NICOLE.

GUIRON LE COURTOIS: see PALAMEDES.

GUNNLAUGR LEIFSSON (d. 1218 or 19), an Icelandic monk of the Benedictine monastery of þingeyrar and the author of several hagiographic works. He translated Geoffrey of Monmouth's *Prophetiae Merlini* into Icelandic verse as *Merlínússpá* and may have had a hand in *Breta sǫgur*, the Old Norse translation of Geoffrey's *Historia.*

Merlínússpá is preserved in only one of the Icelandic manuscripts of the *Breta sǫgur*, although the other surviving manuscript refers to it. *Merlínússpá* was translated around 1200, and both manuscripts give the author as Gunnlaugr Leifsson. Gunnlaugr turned Geoffrey's Latin prose into Old Norse poetry. His understanding of the tradition of vatic poetry that Geoffrey was imitating is clearly indicated by his choice of the Eddic verse form *fornyrðislag* ("old story meter"). *Fornyrðislag* is also the meter of the *Vǫluspá* ("Sibyl's Prophecy"), a Scandinavian prophetic poem composed probably no later than the tenth century. Gunnlaugr's *Merlínússpá* in fact contains several specific verbal echoes of *Vǫluspá* and other Eddic poetry.

Merlínússpá is divided into two sections that appear to have been transposed in the manuscript. Part 1 has a few verses of introduction and then translates the middle of Geoffrey's *Prophetiae.* The last few verses of Part 1 are a drastic condensation of the end of the *Prophetiae.* Part 2 opens with an extended introduction about Vortigern, Merlin, and the two dragons. It then translates the *Prophetiae* up to the point at which Part 1 begins. With the exception of those passages that he eliminates, Gunnlaugr's translation is close and careful. Many of his changes are minor ones dictated by the poetic form in which he was working. Gunnlaugr's more substantial changes seem intended to make the poem clearer. In particular, he expands passages and changes words to make explicit references to Arthur and to other events that occur later in Geoffrey's *Historia.* Such familiarity with the *Historia Regum Britanniae* as a whole makes it extremely unlikely that Gunnlaugr was working from a separate "Libellus Merlini." [CLB]

❧ Jónsson, Finnur, ed. *Hauksbók, udgiven efter de Arnamagnæanske håndskrifter No. 371, 544 og 675, 4° samt forskellige papirhåndskrifter.* Copenhagen: Det kongelige nordiske Oldskrift-Selskab, 1892–96, pp. 271–83.

GUNS OF AVALON, THE: see ZELAZNY, ROGER.

GWENEVERE: A LYRIC PLAY: see RHYS, ERNEST.

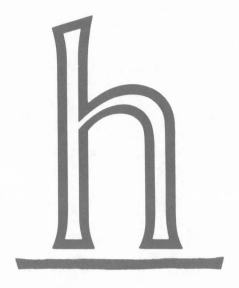

HÁKON HÁKONARSON, King of Norway (r. 1217–63), encouraged the translation of French literature of his time. Ultimately, his efforts established a body of translated works that was accessible not only in Norway but also in the rest of Scandinavia. The earliest work commissioned by Hákon is *Tristrams saga*, a translation of Thomas's *Tristan*. Written in 1226, this translation represents the only complete version of the Thomas-branch of the Tristan legend. According to its preface, *Tristrams saga* was translated by "Brother Robert." His name occurs in association with *Elis saga*, a translation of *Elie de St. Gille*, a *chanson de geste*, also made at Hákon's behest. The remaining translations that originated in Hákon's court are anonymous and include works that specifically contain Arthurian material: *Ívens saga*, a version of Chrétien de Troyes's *Yvain*; *Möttuls saga*, a rendering of the fabliau *Le Mantel mautaillié*; and *Strengleikar*, a significant compilation of the lais of Marie de France. It is also possible that two additional translations of Arthurian material—*Parcevals saga* and *Erex saga*, based on Chrétien's *Perceval* and *Erec et Enide*—were also translated during this period. The extant manuscripts of these two translations do not mention Hákon's patronage. The literary activity at Hákon's court was influenced by close ties to Angevin England, which provided King Hákon with model and material. The translations share a common style characterized by rhetorical embellishments, rhythmic prose, and artistic elaboration. Hákon's patronage occupies an important position in the spread of Arthurian literature in the

North. Many of these translations reached Iceland, where they were recopied or, as in the case of *Tristrams saga*, adapted. A similar influence is present in Sweden, where *Ivan Lejonriddaren*, a translation of *Yvain*, was probably related to *Ívens saga*. These contributions position Hákon at the center of the international movement of Arthurian literature in Scandinavia. [IJR]

Leach, Henry G. *Angevin Britain and Scandinavia.* Cambridge, Mass.: Harvard University Press, 1921.

HAMILTON, LORD ERNEST (1858–1939), the author of *Launcelot: A Romance of the Court of King Arthur* (1926), echoes Malory so assiduously as to give the effect of parody. In this version, Pelles is a converted Norseman, Launcelot is Elaine's husband, and Guenevere is a lecherous, deceitful liar who lures the hero to Vortigern's tower under false pretense, seduces him, and plans to murder Elaine. The complexities of the situation baffle the hero, but then, as the author tells us, "Sir Launcelot was a man of simple mind." [MAW]

Hamilton, Lord Ernest. *Launcelot: A Romance of the Court of King Arthur.* London: Methuen, 1926.

HARDER, NATHALIE, a contemporary German artist who adapted the *Parzival* of Wolfram von Eschenbach for the puppet theater (1976–79). Titled *Recht mitten durch: Eine Miniature aus dem Mittelalter nach Wolfram von Eschenbach—ein Traum aus dem Mittelalter*, the dreamlike piece is performed in two and a half hours with over fifty marionettes. For interpretive models, Harder looks to Eric Rohmer's film *Perceval le Gallois* (1978) and C.G. Jung's depth-psychology. The play has been performed successfully in Berlin and elsewhere. [UM/WCM]

HARDIESSES DE PLUSIEURS ROYS ET EMPEREURS: *see* SALA, PIERRE.

HARDT, ERNST, whose five-act drama *Tantris der Narr* ("Tristram the Jester," 1909) won for its author a leading place among German dramatists and poets. The play recounts Iseult's lament after Tristram has been ordered from Mark's court and marries Iseult of Brittany, Mark's condemnation of her to a leper's life, her two rescues by a disguised Tristram, and finally Tristram's death. This is a dramatic and moving treatment of the legend. [VML]

Hardt, Ernst. *Tantris der Narr.* Leipzig: Insel, 1909.
———. *Tristram the Jester*, trans. John Heard, Jr. Boston: Gorham, 1913.
Heard, John, Jr. "The Marriage of Tristram." *Poet-Lore*, 48 (1942), 72–83.

HARDY, THOMAS (1840–1928), author of *Queen of Cornwall* (1923). In this "new version of an old story arranged as a play for mummers in one act," Tristram, deceived by the white-handed Iseult, appears disguised at Mark's court, where he is killed by Mark. Iseult of Ireland kills her husband and then jumps to her death from a cliff. [AEG]

🕮 Hardy, Thomas. *The Famous Tragedy of the Queen of Cornwall at Tintagel in Lyonnesse*. London and New York: Macmillan, 1923.

HARDYNG, JOHN (1378–ca. 1465), wrote two versions of his verse chronicle of Britain and England that covers the period from the legendary settling of Britain to the mid-fifteenth century. The first version (19,000 lines), found in only one manuscript (Lansdowne 204) and so far unedited, was completed by 1457 for presentation to Henry VI. A second version (12,600 lines) was prepared for Richard, Duke of York (d. 1460); this version was revised for Edward IV and was in its final form by 1464. This shorter version survives in eleven manuscripts, and Richard Grafton printed two editions of it, along with his own prose continuation, in 1543. Although Hardyng's political sympathies are Lancastrian in the first version and Yorkist in the second, an important political message in both versions was that England should conquer Scotland. Undoubtedly, much of his reason for writing the chronicle was to answer Scottish nationalist historians like John of Fordun who claimed that Scotland was historically independent of England. Although Hardyng's rhyme-royal stanzas are usually dismissed as doggerel, his chronicle has been valued for some of the information it gives about events in fifteenth-century England. His use of the Arthurian legend is also of interest, for he draws upon material, such as the Joseph of Arimathea legend and Galahad's Grail quest, that other English chroniclers usually ignored. And few writers could speak more enthusiastically about the glories of Arthur's reign. The chronicle was a minor source for both Malory's *Morte Darthur* and Spenser's *Faerie Queene*. Besides contributing to Spenser's knowledge of the legendary history of Britain and giving Malory a number of details, such as Arthur's coronation as Roman emperor, Hardyng, writing in the tradition of what Gransden calls chivalric historiography, could have influenced both Spenser and Malory's conceptions of Arthurian chivalry. [EDK]

🕮 Hardyng, John. *The Chronicle of John Hardyng*, ed. Henry Ellis. London: Rivington, 1812.

Göller, K.H. *König Arthur in der englischen Literatur des späten Mittelalters*. Göttingen: Vandenhoeck and Ruprecht, 1963, pp. 34–38.

Gransden, Antonia. *Historical Writing in England. Vol. 2: c1307 to the Early Sixteenth Century*. Ithaca, N.Y.: Cornell University Press, 1982, pp. 274–87.

Kennedy, E.D. "Malory and His English Sources." In *Aspects of Malory*, ed. Toshiyuki Takamiya and Derek Brewer. Woodbridge, Suffolk: Boydell and Brewer, 1981, pp. 27–55.

Lagorio, Valerie M. "The Evolving Legend of St. Joseph of Glastonbury." *Speculum*, 46 (1971), 209–31.

"HARP, THE": *see* EMERSON, RALPH WALDO.

HARTMANN VON AUE. Not much is known about Hartmann as a person. He calls himself *Hartman von Ouwe* or *ein Ouwaere* and *Dienestman . . . z'Ouwe*; he was therefore a *Ministerialis*, a member of the still unfree but rising new nobility, and he came from an *Ouwe* ("land on the water"). Which *Ouwe* or *Aue* is meant is not clear. Reichenau (on the Lake of Constance), Weissenau (near Ravensburg), and Au (near Freiburg) have all been suggested. This last Au becomes the preferred solution, if the powerful dukes of Zähringen were indeed Hartmann's literary patrons. Hartmann proudly mentions several times that he is a learned author (*doctus poeta*), a fervent reader of books. He probably received his training in a monastery school, but again we do not know where; if Gregorius's education (see below) is partly autobiographical, the Reichenau monastery would be a possibility. There is general agreement, however, that Hartmann was born and raised in the upper Rhine region.

Hartmann's literary output encompasses several genres. He is a many-sided epic writer as well as a lyric poet or *Minnesinger*. His works consist of two Arthurian romances, *Erec* and *Iwein*; a hagiographical legend, *Gregorius*; a miracle story, *Der arme Heinrich* ("Poor Henry"); and a dialogue between the body and the heart on love, *Büchlein*, or *Klage* ("Complaint"). As a German troubadour, he produced eighteen love songs, among them three Crusade songs. The so-called *Zweites Büchlein* is not by Hartmann.

An ambitious courtly poet aiming at a wider audience, Hartmann appears to have striven continuously to improve his language and style. He does so not only in the area of general refinement (rhythmical flow and lucidity) but also by avoiding vocabulary and rhyme words that would work less well in dialects other than his own Swabian or Alemannic. On the basis of such refinements and adaptations, a generally convincing sequence of Hartmann's epic works has been established: *Klage, Erec, Gregorius, Armer Heinrich, Iwein*. His songs cannot be assigned to specific times, not even his Crusade songs, because Hartmann can have participated (if he did at all) in either the Crusade of 1189/90 or that of 1197. From evidence of Hartmann's literary relations, especially with Wolfram von Eschenbach and Gottfried von Strassburg, we can infer that Hartmann was still alive around 1210 and that his *Iwein* was finished by 1205. He probably started his literary career around 1180, and he may well have been born around 1155 or even five to ten years earlier.

As a *Dienestman* ("vassal"), Hartmann must have depended upon noble lords or ladies, and also as a writer and poet, with respect to his literary working conditions and labors: commission and sponsorship, manuscripts of French and other sources, time for writing, writing materials (especially parchment), and scribes. Again, we can only guess who were Hartmann's patrons. The court of the ruling Staufer dynasty might have sponsored Hartmann's songs, particularly his Crusade songs, because it had done so before in the case of Friedrich von Hausen. Since nothing is known about the Staufers' interest in other genres in the vernacular, we have to look for other courts with regard to Hartmann's epic works. A plausible case has recently been made for the dynasty of the dukes of Zähringen. They had large holdings of land in the southern parts of Germany, in Switzerland, and in the eastern parts of France; and they also had a residence in Freiburg (Black Forest). They could have employed a man like Hartmann in many ways. But any other dynasty, or even (for *Gregorius*) a monastery with good French connections, could have been a Maecenas to one or more of Hartmann's works.

Erec is a free adaptation of the first Arthurian romance, *Erec et Enide*, by Chrétien de Troyes. It consists of somewhat more than 10,000 short lines in rhymed couplets (the beginning, about 100 lines, is missing, and there are some further lacunae). According to Chrétien, King Arthur goes on his customary spring hunt together with his knights; he who catches the White Stag may kiss the most beautiful young lady at court. (Here Hartmann's work begins.) Young and inexperienced, Erec, son of King Lac of Karnant, does not take part. Riding out with Queen Ginover, he receives a whiplash from a dwarf who belongs to a knight named Iders. Erec decides, unarmed as he is, to follow Iders. He chances upon old and impoverished Count Koralus, the father of beautiful but equally poor Enite. From him, Erec learns about a sparrowhawk contest in which Iders will claim the prize for his lady. Erec requests and receives arms as well as Enite from her father. He then claims the sparrowhawk for Enite, takes it, and conquers Iders. With Enite, he returns to Arthur's court, and the King, having captured the White Stag himself, bestows the kiss on Enite. The couple are married at court with great pomp.

Erec and Enite ride to Karnant, where King Lac designates them as future king and queen of his lands. But they indulge only in the sexual joys of marriage; Erec neglects his knightly duties, and the courtly community loudly voices its disapproval. One morning, Enite repeats these reproaches in bed, believing that Erec is still asleep. He questions her, learns about the criticism at court, and at once goes on a journey with her, forbidding her to speak with him.

Two series of encounters follow. During the first, Erec twice meets a group of highway robbers, then a count who covets Enite, finally the dwarf-king Guivreiz. Enite warns him every time, and Erec is able to conquer all of his adversaries, but in his fight with Guivreiz he is wounded. He is brought to Arthur's camp and his wound is treated, but the couple leave the next morning. During the second series of encounters, Erec first frees a knight from two giants, but his wound breaks open and, apparently dead, he tumbles from his horse. Enite laments her "dead" husband; in this predicament, she is chanced upon by Count Oringles de Limors, who also covets her and forces her to marry him. At the wedding party, her cries of protest awaken Erec, who kills the count with his own sword and flees with Enite. He now recognizes his wife's perfect faithfulness and asks her to forgive him for her harsh treatment during the journey. In a second encounter with King Guivreiz, a still-weak

Erec is conquered for the first time. The king brings the couple to his castle, Penefrec; here Erec, through the good care of Enite herself and Guivreiz's sisters, is entirely cured. Thus, the couple's marital problems come to an end and a happy solution.

Erec's last and crowning adventure is the battle of *Joie de la curt* ("Joy of the Court"). Young Mabonagrin lives with his lover in isolation from courtly society, in a miraculous garden that he cannot leave unless conquered in a knightly duel. Erec gladly takes on the challenge, even after learning that eighty predecessors have been killed to date. But he is victorious and liberates also the eighty widows of the slain knights. The Joy of the Court is restored. Erec returns to Arthur's court, where the King himself restores the mourning widows to joy. Upon hearing that his father had died, Erec and Enite return to Karnant. They are crowned king and queen, and a grand courtly celebration takes place. The couple now lead an exemplary life—as lovers, as marriage partners, and as rulers.

This romance presents a fictional "mirror of princes"; mature rulership requires a mature royal couple, and the narrative depicts the growth of Erec and Enite toward this ideal, in concordance with societal, moral, and religious values. The story makes its points against the background of young love and its perils, emphasizing a passive, even masochistic component in Enite and a strongly sadistic character in Erec and several other male figures. Hartmann tells his tale in a semiallegorical way: all of the couple's encounters mirror Erec's or Enite's inner development; the antagonists represent the courtly alter egos of the protagonists. It is thus no accident that Erec has to conquer robbers and greedy noblemen on his road toward mature kingship; and the final adventure in the garden reflects the couple's liberation from a selfish state of isolation from society and its values. Since the story is clearly told and well structured and integrated, the symbolic and semiallegorical inner meaning becomes transparent through the characters themselves, their actions, and the overall composition, with its "double course" and its crowning last adventure. In view of Erec's and Enite's inexperience, and of the "happy end," the question of guilt appears less important and deserves to be deemphasized. It is more appropriate to read most early Arthurian romances as "comedies" and as representatives of a worldly *felix culpa* ideology.

Iwein is a much closer adaptation of another Arthurian romance by Chrétien de Troyes, *Yvain*. Hartmann's work consists of 8,166 short lines in rhymed couplets. At Pentecost, Kalogrenant tells a group of other knights at Arthur's court about a hapless adventure of ten years before, his defeat by King Askalon, lord of a magic well. His nephew Iwein decides to avenge his uncle. He departs secretly, before Arthur and his knights, who also want to visit the well, can leave. Arriving at the well, Iwein fights and conquers Askalon, but in pursuing the deadly wounded knight into the castle he is trapped between the portcullis and the gate. Lunete, the maidservant of the now-widowed Queen Laudine, prevents him from being killed by means of a magic ring that makes him invisible. Iwein observes the mourning Laudine and falls in love with her, and Lunete manages to talk her lady into marrying Iwein. Soon thereafter, Arthur and his knights visit the couple and rejoice at Iwein's new status, but at Gawein's prompting the new husband negotiates a leave of absence, swearing to come back within a year, and returns to Arthur's court. Because of uninterrupted knightly activity with Gawein, Iwein forgets the deadline. Lunete appears at court and publicly condemns him for his *Untriuwe* ("breach of faith"). Iwein experiences a crisis and goes mad. He lives in the woods like an animal but is found by the Lady of Narison, who cures him with an ointment from "Feimorgan." Grateful, he frees her from her oppressor, Count Aliers, but refuses to marry her. He then happens upon a fight between a dragon and a lion; he helps the lion, and they become friends.

As in *Erec*, two series of adventures occur. Iwein finds Lunete held captive and condemned to death. She had been accused of high treason because of her complicity with Iwein but had been unable to find a champion against her accusers. After defeating the giant Harpin, Iwein, with the lion's help, conquers Lunete's accusers, thus winning her case. Laudine sees the "knight with the lion" but does not recognize Iwein.

In the second series of adventures, Iwein pledges to help the younger daughter of the deceased Count of the Black Thorn against her older sister, who claims the whole inheritance for herself and who has won Gawein as her champion. But before Iwein can carry out his promise, he has to free 300 female weavers from their oppressor. He does so with the help of the lion by defeating two giants. In the ensuing fight with Gawein, the two friends at first do not recognize each other, but at last they do, and each concedes the victory to the other. King Arthur himself decides the case against the older daughter, obliging her to share the inheritance with her sister.

Iwein has now fully expiated his lack of faithfulness toward Laudine and, indirectly, toward society by fulfilling his knightly duties "on time" and in the service of his fellow men. The scene is now set for a reconciliation with Laudine. He returns to the well, and Lunete again brings the two together. Laudine accepts Iwein back; the narrator states his expectation that the couple will lead a happy life together from that point on.

The *Iwein* story, too, is a mirror of princes, but the emphasis is different from that in *Erec*: since Laudine is the queen and has her own land, Iwein appears as the young and inexperienced prince consort, who fails by not understanding his duties. At the first opportunity, he falls back into the carefree existence at court. By missing the deadline, he demonstrates his lack of concern as the new lord of the well and as co-ruler. Iwein therefore not only will have to free himself from Arthur's court but he also has to make amends for his serious *Untriuwe* as a "time violation" (first adventure series) and to show in deeds his knightly willingness to help his fellow men in trouble (second series). Again, the inner meaning becomes quite transparent through the overall composition and the single actions and deeds (or the lack thereof).

Hartmann narrates his story in a detached and often ironic way, even serious scenes appearing in a humorous light, especially those involving Lunete or the lion. But this light touch also makes for a high degree of elusiveness. What is the meaning, for example, of Iwein's close relationship with Gawein, which the narrator seems to view as positive though it causes Iwein's *Untriuwe*? What is the exact role and meaning of the lion—Iwein's noble alter ego? Symbol of *Triuwe*? symbol of rulership? image of Christ? In particular, the male/female relationships in this work deserve more study.

In general, Hartmann manifests an optimistic view of the courtly world. Human beings are perfectible, not subjected to fate. By rational insight into their own selves, under the guidance of a benign Providence and enlightened by God's grace, they attain a higher position in secular or religious life. This balance between the human and the divine is Hartmann's hallmark and constitutes the essence of his idea of *Maze*, or harmony with God. Such a view has connections with Staufic ideologies and basic thoughts and feelings of the Gothic period in Europe. [PWT]

ॐ Hartmann von Aue. *Erec*, ed. Albert Leitzmann; 5th ed. Ludwig Wolff. Tübingen: Niemeyer, 1972.

――― . *Erec*, trans. J.W. Thomas. Lincoln: University of Nebraska Press, 1982.

――― . *Iwein: Eine Erzählung*, ed. G.F. Benecke and Karl Lachmann; 7th ed. Ludwig Wolff. Berlin: de Gruyter, 1968.

――― . *Iwein*, ed. and trans. Patrick M. McConeghy. New York and London: Garland, 1984.

Neubuhr, Elfriede. *Bibliographie zu Hartmann von Aue*. Berlin: Schmidt, 1977.

Wapnewski, Peter. *Hartmann von Aue*. Stuttgart: Metzler, 1962; 7th ed. 1979.

HAUPTMANN, GERHART (1862–1946), Nobel Prize winner (1912) and one of the most important German poets and dramatists of the twentieth century, often used medieval subject matter. Written for his twelve-year-old son, Benvenuto, *Parsival* (1914) and *Lohengrin* (1913) freely adapt the stories of Wolfram von Eschenbach, Robert de Boron, and Richard Wagner. These prose narratives, which center on Parsival, the seeker after God, and the world of the Grail, are characterized by a pseudo-adolescent sentimentality. From 1917 to 1944, Hauptmann worked on an unfinished novel, *Der neue Christophorus* (originally to be called *Merlin*). This fragment, heavy with myth and mysticism, concerns an "earthman," a new Merlin, conceived in death by an ancient "superman" and born in a coffin. He is to be initiated into the great esotericism of the German nationality and of humanity by Pater Christophorus. The work stands clearly in the German Merlin tradition as set down by Immermann. Hauptmann also left unfinished the drama *Galahad* (1908–14). [UM/WCM]

ॐ Hauptmann, Gerhart. *Lohengrin*. Berlin: Ullstein, 1913.

――― . *Parsival*. Berlin: Ullstein, 1914.

HAWK OF MAY: see BRADSHAW, GILLIAN.

HAWKER, ROBERT STEPHEN (1803–1875), published his mystical poem *The Quest of the Sangraal* in 1864. Though based upon Malory, it reduces the number of Grail questers to four: Lancelot, Tristram, Perceval, and Galahad. Three more parts were planned but never completed. [RHT]

   Hawker, Robert Stephen. *The Quest of the Sangraal: Chant the First.* Exeter: Printed for the author, 1864.

HEATH-STUBBS, JOHN, a contemporary English poet, composed a version of the tales of Arthur, published in 1973. *Artorius* owes as much to classical Greek literature and to Northrop Frye's theory of literary genres as to Malory. The twelve parts, each corresponding to a sign of the zodiac, are grouped into four sections corresponding to the seasons; within each of these four sections, one part is in epic verse, the other two in genres ranging from Aristophanic comedy to Pindaric ode to Sophoclean tragedy. The complete cycle recounts the life of Arthur from the spring of his victory on Mount Badon to the winter of his last battle and passing to Avalon. It is offered, according to the Invocation, as a paradigm of the life of man: " . . . his season's progress/ From spring's heyday to high summer and harvest,/ And lastly to the laggard lagoon of old age/ Where his son supplants him and the cycle returns." [SRR]

   Heath-Stubbs, John. *Artorius: A Heroic Poem in Four Books and Eight Episodes.* London: Enitharmon, 1973.

HEBER, REGINALD (1783–1826), bishop and hymnologist, wrote two Arthurian fragments. *Morte D'Arthur* (1812), an intended epic in Spenserians, presents a victorious Arthur married to Ganora (Guenevere), supposedly a villager, who longs for her forester-lover Cadual (Lancelot in disguise). Morgue and her son Mordred provide plot complications. *The Masque of Gwendolen* (1816) combines Merlin, Titania, and the Loathly Lady. Heber's moralistic treatment prefigures Tennyson. [MAW]

   Merriman, John Douglas. *The Flower of Kings: A Study of the Arthurian Legend in England Between 1485 and 1835.* Lawrence: University Press of Kansas, 1973.

HEILIGE GRAL, DER: *see* KRALIK, RICHARD VON.

HEINE, HEINRICH (1797–1856), one of the great lyric poets of later German Romanticism and at the same time, through his irony and scathing satire, one of its strongest critics. In the third of his nine *Katharina* poems (1835), Heine alludes to the entrancement of the lover in the traditional Merlin–Niniane story. However, Heine's reference may be to an incapacitating fixation not only for a mistress but for any abstract ideal, such as beauty, nature, or political freedom. [RWK]

❧ Heine, Heinrich. *Werke und Briefe*, ed. Hans Kaufmann. Berlin: Aufbau, 1962, Vol. 1.
Spencer, Hanna. *Heinrich Heine*. Boston: Twayne, 1982.
Weiss, Adelaide Marie. "Heinrich Heine." In *Merlin in German Literature*. Washington, D.C.: Catholic University of America Press, 1933, pp. 126–28.

HEINRICH VON DEM TÜRLIN, German poet of the first half of the thirteenth century. Heinrich was perhaps a descendant of the distinguished family of freedmen recorded under the name of *von/vor/pey dem Turlin/Turleine* (*de Portula*) in the ducal town of St. Veit on Glan/Carinthia. He may also be identical with one Heinrich von dem Turlein, a witness recorded on a deed, dated 1229, of Count Albert I of Gorce and Tyrol. Heinrich mentions his name on four occasions in his *Crône*, first in the acrostic ll. 182–216; and Rudolf von Ems praises him in his *Alexander* (ll. 3219–28). There is no testimony as to where Heinrich lived and worked, although various conjectures have been advanced, such as the court of Duke Bernhard of Carinthia, or the court of Duke Frederic II in Vienna; and there is no evidence as to his social status (commoner or *Ministerialis*) or occupation (chancery or military service). The only indication Heinrich himself provides in the *Crône* (ll. 2973–82) leads to the assumption that his native country lay somewhere in the southeastern part of the Empire, which is corroborated by the Bavarian-Austrian linguistic characteristics of the *Crône*. He must have received an excellent education; he read Latin and French and had an astounding knowledge of German and French literature.

Heinrich has been linked with the anonymous *Der Mantel*, a fragment of 994 lines, and he is the author of the voluminous Arthurian romance *Diu Crône* ("The Crown," 30,041 lines). The *Mantel* fragment, an adaptation of the Old French fabliau *Le Mantel mautaillié*, relates a chastity and fidelity test at Arthur's court. Variants of this motif occur twice in the *Crône*, with the goblet and glove tests. The fragment must have been composed before the *Crône*, as proven by Heinrich's self-quotation (*Crône*, ll. 23,502–05).

"Allr Âventiure Krône" is the title given by Rudolf von Ems (*Alexander*, l. 3219) to Heinrich's Arthurian romance, inspired by the lines 29,916–21 and 29,966–90 in *Diu Crône*, where Heinrich compares his work to a crown adorned with precious stones.

The hero of the countless adventures, which are grouped into four sequences of different length and framed by five great feasts at Arthur's court, is Gawein, despite Heinrich's announced intention to write the story of King Arthur (ll. 164–74). The main episodes of the first part of the romance are Ginover's abduction by Gasozein, the single combat between Arthur and Gasozein (which never takes place), and Ginover's liberation by Gawein. These episodes constitute the first sequence, interlaced by the Sgoidamur-Amurfina sequence of the magic bridle and Gawein's captivity at Amurfina's castle. The double wedding of the couples Gawein–Amurfina and Gasozein–Sgoidamur at Arthur's court in Karidol concludes the first part (ll. 13,860–934). The second part has two main sequences: the quest for the Grail, with

Gawein's first visit to the Grail castle, and the Vrou Saelde (Dame Fortune) and Fimbeus–Giramphiel sequence, with the acquisition of Fimbeus's magic girdle, Gawein's visit at Ordohorht, the allegorical castle of Vrou Saelde, and the bestowal of the ring of fortune. The climax is reached with Gawein's successful Salie adventure (inspired by the Gawein books of the *Parzival*), his invitation to Arthur followed by another great feast at Arthur's court, and the delivery of the ring of fortune to Arthur (ll. 21,819–22,989). The anticlimax, initiated by the appearance of the knight on the ibex and by the glove test, leads to the loss of the magic stone of Fimbeus's girdle and the ring of fortune. Gawein, Keii, Lanzelet, and Calocreant then depart from Karidol and after another series of fabulous adventures recover the magic objects and restore them to Arthur. The Grail sequence finds its conclusion with the deliverance of the Grail company and its eternal rest in the realm of the dead. A feast of joy at Karidol celebrates the reunion of the four Arthurian knights (ll. 29,744–910).

It is impossible to enumerate all the adventures Gawein encounters as knight-errant. Many of them, traditionally assigned to other heroes of the Round Table, like Parzival, Iwein, and Lanzelet, are now attributed to Gawein to enhance his status and prestige as the outstanding representative and defender of the Arthurian world. They are occasionally interspersed by critical comments, for instance in the episode of the deliverance of the Grail castle, where Heinrich stresses the exemplariness of his protagonist compared with Parzival's failure. Thus, Gawein is the model of all chivalric virtues, the favorite of Dame Fortune, successful in all his endeavors like the hero of the fairy tale who undergoes no evolution or crisis.

The mostly negative criticism that *Diu Crône* has received is not quite justified; recent studies have led to a reevaluation. Heinrich's merit resides in his inventiveness and his ability to combine a variety of subject matters and motifs of Arthurian and non-Arthurian provenance into a coherent plot, even if a great number of episodes are to be considered padding, introduced for their elements of fantasy rather than for their significance within the narrative structure of the romance.

Heinrich's sources range from Chrétien de Troyes's *Perceval* and *Lancelot*, Old French lais and fabliaux (such as *La Mule sans frein, Le Chevalier à l'epée*, the *Lai du cor*), and the Continuations of the *Perceval* to the German Arthurian romances of Ulrich von Zatzikhoven, Hartmann von Aue, and Wolfram von Eschenbach and to German heroic epics and other sources, not all of which have been traced. Heinrich's narrative technique varies from courtly stylization to realistic descriptions, including comic and burlesque elements. The most remarkable feature of the *Crône* is its tendency to desymbolize and demystify (particularly apparent in the Grail episodes) in favor of rationalization, realistic imagery, and allegorization. (*See also* MANTEL, DER.) [KRG]

🙋 Heinrich von dem Türlin. *Diu Crône*, ed. G.H.F. Scholl. Stuttgart, 1852.

Cormeau, Christoph. *"Wigalois" und "Diu Crône": Zwei Kapitel zur Gattungsgeschichte des nachklassischen Aventiureromans*. Munich: Artemis, 1977.

Heller, Edmund Kurt. "A Vindication of Heinrich von dem Türlin, Based on a Survey of His Sources." *Modern Language Quarterly*, 3 (1942), 67–82.

Kratz, Bernd. "Zur Kompositionstechnik Heinrichs von dem Türlin." *Amsterdamer Beiträge zur älteren Germanistik*, 5 (1973), 141–53.

HEINRICH VON FREIBERG, author of a continuation of Gottfried von Strassburg's incomplete *Tristan.* Composed at the behest of Reimund von Lichtenburg, Heinrich's *Tristan* is dated ca. 1285–90. Unlike Ulrich von Türheim, the earlier continuator of Gottfried's *Tristan*, Heinrich von Freiberg masters the language of courtly romance and approximates the style of his revered master, Gottfried. The sources for Heinrich's continuation are Eilhart von Oberge's *Tristrant* and Ulrich von Türheim's *Tristan.* Heinrich's continuation opens with a prologue (84 lines) in which he contrasts Gottfried's artistic mastery with his own deficiency. The tale proper commences with Tristan's betrothal and marriage to Îsôt Blanschemanîs (Isolde of the White Hands). Tristan explains his failure to consummate the marriage as the result of an oath to the Virgin Mary to live chastely for one year. Heinrich draws on and incorporates Eilhart's hunting episode, in which Tristan and Arthur's knights are severely wounded by a trap that King Mark has set in his hall. Heinrich borrows Eilhart's motif of the intertwining rose and vine, but like Ulrich before him he reverses the plants: Mark plants the rose over Tristan's body and the vine over Îsôt's. [MEK]

☙ Heinrich von Freiberg. *Tristan*, ed. Reinhold Bechstein. Leipzig: Brockhaus, 1877.

Buschinger, Danielle. "À propos du *Tristan* de Heinrich von Freiberg." *Études germaniques*, 33 (1978), 53–64.

HENRY OF HUNTINGDON (d. ca. 1154) based his account of the Arthurian period in his *Historia Anglorum* primarily on Nennius, Bede, and the *Anglo-Saxon Chronicle.* He lists the twelve battles of Arthur, inserting the list between the *Chronicle* entries for 527 and 530. He suggests, moreover, that the sites are now unknown. In his letter to Warinus (ca. 1139), Henry describes Arthur's last battle in detail and also says that the Bretons deny his death and still await his return. Many of the later chroniclers supplemented Geoffrey of Monmouth's dry account of this battle with details from Henry's more spirited version. [JPC]

Henry is also the author of the *Epistola ad Warinum* (ca. 1139). Henry writes to Guerin, mentioning that Robert of Torigni, then librarian at Bec, has shown him a book by Geoffrey of Monmouth on the history of the kings of Britain. He summarizes the book, including some details about the final battle and death of Arthur that are not in surviving texts of the *Historia Regum Britanniae.* Robert of Torigni and later chroniclers included Henry's summary of Geoffrey in their works. [MLD]

❧ Henry of Huntingdon. *Epistola ad Warinum.* In *Chronicles of the Reigns of Stephen, Henry II, and Richard I,* ed. Richard Howlett. London: Longman, Trübner, 1885.

———. *Henrici Archidiaconi Huntendunensis Historia Anglorum,* ed. Thomas Arnold. London: Longman, 1879.

HER VIEGOLEIS MED GULD HIULET ("Viegoleis with the Golden Wheel"), the oldest extant edition of the Danish chapbook *Her Viegoleis med Guld Hiulet.* It dates from the year 1656 and is a translation of an anonymous 1472 German prose redaction of Wirnt von Grafenberg's *Wigalois.* The German chapbook exists in two branches, the younger of which is characterized by a rather modern language, and it is presumably this younger version that is the source of the Danish chapbook. The Danish translator had command of neither his own language nor of German. The Danish chapbook was translated into Icelandic and is known as *Gabons saga ok Vigoles.* [MEK]

❧ Jacobsen, J.P., Jørgen Olrik, and R. Paulli, eds. *En smuck lystig Historie/Om den berømmelige Ridder oc Heldt Her Viegoleis med Guld Hiulet.* In *Danske Folkebøger fra 16. og 17. Aarhundrede.* Copenhagen: Det danske Sprog- og Litteraturselskab, 1921, Vol. 4.

HERALDRY. Heraldry—that is, the use of a shield device and a helmet crest to identify a knight in battle and tournament—was traditionally one of the distinctive features that set a knight apart from other members of medieval society. The custom originated in the twelfth century, when the newly introduced visored helmet made the face of its wearer unrecognizable. Though in classical antiquity and the Dark Ages individual warriors could be known by their personal shield emblems, true heraldry is different insofar as shield devices and helmet crests are hereditary within a family and carry legal status, on seals for instance, beyond mere marks of recognition. They were also displayed on banners, horse trappings, and the surcoats covering the knights' armor; from the latter use, it became customary to call them "coats-of-arms."

By the time the great Arthurian epics were composed, heraldry had become so firmly established as an integral part of knightly culture that neither the authors nor their audience could imagine the knights of the Round Table without proper heraldic bearings.

The "historical Arthur" lived in the preheraldic Dark Ages, and his famous dragon banner is definitely derived from the battle standard of Late Roman auxiliary cavalry. But his dragon helmet crest, which according to Geoffrey of Monmouth's *Historia* (ca. 1135) he had inherited from his father, Uther Pendragon, is an example of how true heraldry came into being.

King Arthur's shield device seems to have been first a cross and/or an icon of the Virgin Mary, as reported in the *Annales Cambriae* and in Nennius's *Historia Brittonum* (ca. A.D. 800). Though he is said to have carried these "on his shoulders," this might result from a confusion of Welsh *ysqwyt* 'shield' and *ysqwyd* 'shoulder' in the translation into Latin from a hypothetical Welsh source. From the fourteenth century on, however, the shield charges attributed to King Arthur are three crowns, probably meant to indicate his superiority over ordinary kings. In the fifteenth century, after the idea had taken hold that these three crowns stood for his three realms of North Wales, South Wales, and Logres, their number was increased up to thirteen, to represent all the kingdoms allegedly conquered by him. The color of Arthur's shield is usually red, though in French sources it is blue, corresponding to the French royal arms.

Some authors of Arthurian epics were experts in heraldry—Chrétien de Troyes seems to have been a herald himself, and Wolfram von Eschenbach and Hartmann von Aue were knights—and went to considerable lengths to describe their heroes' armorial bearings. There is occasional disagreement among competing authors and also with the illustrators of the manuscripts about the charges borne by their favorite heroes, in much the same way that the authors of the Grail romances disagree about the exact nature of the Grail, but these arms by themselves conform to the accepted rules of heraldry, though they might become marked as something out of the ordinary by frequent application of the unusual tinctures *vert* (green) and *purpure* (purple).

(It will be useful to define a few of the more common heraldic terms: *Or* [French] = "gold" or yellow; *Argent* [French] = "silver" or white; *Gules* [Persian *gûl* 'a rose'] = red; *Azure* [Arabic *az'raq* 'sky'] = blue; *Sable* [the Siberian mink] = black; *Vert* [French] = green; *Purpure* = purple.)

Shortly after the middle of the fifteenth century, a roll of arms, *Les Noms, Armes, et Blasons des Chevalliers et Compaignons de la Table Ronde*, was compiled as an appendix to the famous *Livre des tournoys*, by King René d'Anjou (ca. 1455), which gave detailed instructions how a tournament should be held "according to the rules set up at the time of King Uterpendragon and King Artus and his Knights of the Round Table." Of this Arthurian roll of arms, the three most important copies in this country are in Cambridge (Harvard University Library, Hofer 1), in New York City (Pierpont Morgan Library 16), and in Baltimore (Walters Art Gallery). Among these, the Harvard roll is the earliest, ca. 1470, but it lists the shields and names of only 150 knights, while the Morgan copy (ca. 1500), gives names and shields of 175 knights together with brief descriptions of their achievements and their appearances, such as the color of their eyes and hair; the Walters roll (ca. 1510) is the most comprehensive, adding the knights' crests, shield supporters, and "reasons" (mottoes). The author of this Arthurian roll of arms is thought to have been Jacques d'Armagnac, Duke of Nemours, who was married to a niece of King René's. Interestingly enough, many of the arms of the lesser knights, which had to be filled in because they would not be recorded in the romances, were borrowed from a contemporary (ca. 1440) handbook of heraldry, *Le Traitié du Blazon d'Armes*, by Clément Prinsault, dedicated by its author to Jacques "filz de monseigneur le duc de Nemours."

Some of these arms are directly related to motifs in the tales, such as the arms of Yvain, "le Chevalier au Lion," who bears: *Azure, a lion Or*, and those of

14 Arthurian heraldry.

(Left) *King Arthur's full arms, late version French style:* Azure, thirteen crowns Or; *crest:* a dragon Or issuant from a crown; *mantlings:* party azure and Or, lined ermine; *supporters:* two white greyhounds collared gules; *motto:* PENDRAGON. *The greyhounds are probably borrowed from the arms of the contemporary king of England, Henry VII.* (right) *King Arthur's arms, late version English (Tudor) style:* Quarterly, 1 and 4 Vert, a cross argent, in the cantel the Virgin and Child Or, 2 and 3 Gules, three crowns in pale Or.

The two versions of Sir Kay's arms: a) Sable, a chief argent. *b)* Azure, two keys argent.

The arms of Bauiers le Forcenné and of Sagramours le Desrée: c) Gyronny of sable and Or *(originally Sagramours's)*. *d)* Sable, two stars Or, on a canton argent a star sable.

e) Yvain "le Chevalier au Lion": Azure, a lion Or. *f) Lancelot du Lac:* Argent, three bends gules.

g) *King Arthur's shield: standard version, early fifteenth century. Three golden crowns in either red (English) or blue (French tradition) field. h) Gawain's "shield for Peace":* Gules, a pentangle Or.

"Canting" arms: i) Tristram of Lyonesse: Vert, a lion Or. *j) Brumor de la Fontaine:* Quarterly Or and sable, a fountain argent over all. *k) Brandelis de Vaulxsur:* Gules, three swords (*brands*) erect argent, hilts azure.

The earlier arms of the princes of Orkney: l) Gawain: Argent, a canton gules. *m) Gareth:* Argent, a canton gules, semé with eagles Or. *n) Mordred:* Gules, a canton argent.

The later arms of the princes of Orkney: o) Gawain: Purpure, a double-headed eagle Or. *p) Gareth:* Purpure, a double-headed eagle Or, over all a bendlet gules. *q) Mordred:* Purpure, a double-headed eagle Or, a chief argent.

Lancelot: *Argent, three bends gules*, referring to his having the strength of three ordinary men. Others are "canting arms," representing a wordplay on the knight's name, such as Tristram de Lyonesse's: *Vert, a lion Or*, Sir Brumor de la Fontaine's: *Quarterly Or and sable, a fountain argent over all*, or Sir Brandelis des Vaulxsur's: *Gules, three swords* (brands) *erect argent*. On occasion, a scribal error can change a charge, such as Sir Kay's: *Sable, a chief argent*, which he bears in the early French romance *Durmart le Gallois* (ca. 1220) to indicate his position as seneschal and "head" of Arthur's household, into *two keys argent*, in the armorial roll. This makes sense, too, but is the result of reading *clefs* 'keys' instead of *chef* 'chief.' Sometimes, an entirely new character is created by such a mistake. For instance, in the Arthurian roll is listed Bauiers le Forcenné, who owes his existence to a misunderstanding of the description of the banner *(baniers)* of Sagramours le Desrée in the Second Continuation of *Perceval*: "Aprés recoisi Sagremor/ Qui baniers de noir et d'or/ Portoit, ce sanbloit, gironees. . . ." Interestingly, it is the spurious Sir Bauiers who retains the arms gyronny, while Sagramours's shield is changed to: *Sable, two stars Or, on a canton argent a star sable*. In some cases, heraldry is used for comic relief. In Wolfram's *Parzival*, King Hardiess of Gaskon bears the forepart of a griffin in his shield, while his retainers bear the griffin's hindquarters!

Owing to the complexity of traditions in Arthurian epics, the arms even of champions of the first magnitude can differ fundamentally from author to author. For instance, Chrétien does not mention Gawain's arms at all, though he gives detailed descriptions of the blazons of a number of minor knights. Wolfram, who makes it a special point that for his *Parzival* he did not follow Chrétien, but a rival authority, "Kyot the Provençal," has Gawain wearing a surcoat with two *gampilûns* of sable in appliqué work. This is a variant of the single *gampilûn* borne by his cousin, Ilinot, Arthur's son. The *gampilûn* has escaped zoological classification so far; most likely, it is a Germanic phonetic rendering of the dragonlike heraldic *gamelyon*, whose name was later reassigned to the now more familiar chameleon!

In the thirteenth-century French romances *Durmart*, *Escanor*, and the Second Continuation of *Perceval*, Gawain's arms are: *Argent, a canton gules*, with related blazons for his brothers. These are probably "canting arms" in French, derived from the name of their father, King Loth of Orkney, because *lot* means "section," and a canton can be considered to be a section of a shield.

According to Geoffrey of Monmouth, Gawain was educated in Rome and was given his arms (not described) by Pope Sulpicius (alas, a pope unknown to all other historians); in the *Perlesvaus*, Gawain received from Pope Gregory the Great the shield of Judas Maccabeus: *Gules, an eagle Or*. In "official" fifteenth-century tradition, as represented by the roll of arms attributed to Jacques d'Armagnac, Gawain bears: *Purpure, a double-headed eagle Or*, a device derived from both the shield of Judas Maccabeus and the emblem of the Holy Roman Empire. Again, his brothers share the same arms with appropriate differences.

Gawain's most famous armorial bearings, however, are those assigned to him in *Sir Gawain and the Green Knight* (ca. 1365): *Gules, a pentangle Or*, the "Seal of Solomon, that the English call 'the endless knot.'" The *Gawain*-poet's elaborate explanation that this "devys" is a symbol of Gawain's being perfect in his five senses, in the dexterity of his five fingers, in his reverence of the five wounds of Christ, in his love for the Queen of Heaven and her five joys, and in his five virtues makes it clear that the pentangle is a strictly personal badge and not his inherited family coat-of-arms. When in the fourteenth century tournament armor developed away from battle armor, it became fashionable for knights to have garnitures of two shields, a "shield for War," of the traditional triangular shape bearing the family arms, and a "shield for Peace," a squarish targe with a cutout for couching the lance, displaying the personal badge for use in tournaments and other peaceful pursuits. Therefore, when Gawain went on his quest for the Green Chapel, he quite properly took along his "shield for Peace." The reason the *Gawain*-poet chose the pentangle as Gawain's "devys" might have been that he saw a "canting" reference to Gawain's home country, Orkney, in *Or-knit*, the golden knot.

Though the heraldry of the Arthurian roll of arms was accepted as authentic and perpetuated in handbooks of heraldry up to the nineteenth century, nothing of it—with exception of the shield of Sir Galahad—was incorporated into *Le Morte Darthur*. Surprisingly, Sir Thomas Malory's monumental work contains only a handful of heraldic descriptions. For this reason, modern retellers of the tale, such as Lord Tennyson and T.H. White, and particularly illustrators like Howard Pyle, N.C. Wyeth, Robert Ball, and Hal Foster, have had to rely on their own imagination. It is heartening to see, though, that the designer of "King Arthur's Merry-go-round" in Disneyland *did* research the "authentic" shields of the knights of the Round Table from the roll of arms of Jacques d'Armagnac! (*See also* ARMS AND ARMOR; ROUND TABLES; TOURNAMENT BOOKS.) [HN]

Brault, Gerard J. *Early Blazon: Heraldic Terminology in the Twelfth and Thirteenth Centuries with Special Reference to Arthurian Literature.* London: Oxford University Press, 1972.

Crompton, N.J.R. "Mediaeval Symbolic Heraldry." *The Coat of Arms,* 8, 60 (October 1964), 166–68.

de Blangy, Alphonse. *La Forme des tournois au temps du roy Uter et du roy Artus, suivie de l'Armorial des chevaliers de la Table Ronde.* Caen, 1897.

Nickel, Helmut. "Arthurian Heraldry." *Avalon to Camelot,* 1 (1984), 11–12.

Pastoureau, Michel. *Armorial des chevaliers de la Table Ronde.* Paris: Léopard d'Or, 1983.

Sandoz, Edouard. "Tourneys in the Arthurian Tradition." *Speculum,* 19 (1944), 389–420.

Scott-Giles, C.W. "Some Arthurian Coats of Arms." *The Coat of Arms,* 8, 64 (October 1965), 332–39, and 9, 65 (January 1966), 30–35.

Timpson, George F. "Heraldry in Wolfram's Parzival." *The Coat of Arms,* 4, 31 (July 1957), 278–81.

HERDER, JOHANN GOTTFRIED VON

HERDER, JOHANN GOTTFRIED VON (1744–1803). In his *Volkslieder, Erster Theil*, published in Leipzig, 1778, Johann Gottfried von Herder included "Der Knabe mit dem Mantel: Ein Rittermährchen." This is a German translation of the medieval English ballad "The Boy and the Mantle," which ultimately derives from *Le Mantel mautaillié*. It seems plausible that the modern German writers who adapted the mantle tale—Benedikte Naubert, F.A.C. Werthes, and Karl Franz van der Velde—were familiar with Herder's German translation. [MEK]

🙪 Herder, Johann Gottfried von. "Der Knabe mit dem Mantel: Ein Rittermährchen." In *Herders Poetische Werke*, ed. Carl Redlich. Berlin: Weidmann, 1885, Vol. I, pp. 244–50.

HERE BEGYNNETH THE LYFE OF JOSEPH OF ARMATHIA WITH A PRAYSING TO JOSEPH (printed by Richard Pynson, 1520) is a poetic tribute to Joseph, his apostolic missions in the Holy Land, the city of Sarras, France, and England, his founding of Glastonbury Abbey and burial there, and an extensive list of posthumous miracles. *A Praysing to Joseph* extols him as Glastonbury's great healer, obviously promoting the abbey's pilgrimage interests. [VML]

🙪 Skeat, Walter W., ed. *Joseph of Arimathie*. London: Trübner, 1871.

"HERIDO ESTÁ DON TRISTÁN": *see TRISTAN* IN SPANISH AND PORTUGUESE.

HIGDEN, RANULPH (d. 1363/4), a Benedictine monk from Cheshire, wrote the *Polychronicon*, a Latin universal chronicle that was the most popular source of world history in England until the publication of Raleigh's *History of the World* in the seventeenth century. There are 118 manuscripts. It was translated into English by John Trevisa in 1387 and by an anonymous translator in the fifteenth century. Higden based his Arthurian section primarily upon Henry of Huntingdon and William of Malmesbury. Unlike many English chroniclers, he questioned the reliability of Geoffrey of Monmouth, wondering why none of the continental chroniclers mention Arthur's conquest of thirty kingdoms. [EDK]

🙪 Higden, Ranulf. *Polychronicon Ranulphi Higden*, ed. C. Babington and J.R. Lumby. 9 vols. London: Longman, 1865–86, Vol. 5, pp. 328–38.
　Taylor, John. *The Universal Chronicle of Ranulf Higden*. Oxford: Clarendon, 1966.

HILDEBRANDT, RITA and TIM, are wife and husband who have combined to produce an illustrated science-fiction novel, *Merlin and the Dragons of Atlantis* (1983), set millennia in the past. Both the dragons and Merlin's skills are the products of highly developed sciences in Atlantis and Lemuria, lost when they are engulfed. Tim's illustrations are interesting; Rita's story is not. [RHT]

🙪 Hildebrandt, Rita and Tim. *Merlin and the Dragons of Atlantis*. Indianapolis and New York: Bobbs-Merrill, 1983.

HILL, GRAHAM, author of the play *Guinevere*. Performed at the Court Theatre in London on 13 October 1906, the play is a melodramatic account of the love between Launcelot and Guinevere and its tragic consequences. [RHT]

🕏 Hill, Graham. *Guinevere: A Tragedy in Three Acts*. London: Mathews, 1906.

HILTON, WILLIAM (fl. 1740), an obscure English poet whose *Poetical Works* (1775–76) included *Arthur, Monarch of the Britons, a Tragedy* (1759). The drama utilized the account of Arthur's downfall found in Geoffrey of Monmouth's *Historia*. Arthur's dying assertion, "Britons must be free," illustrates a patriotic intention appropriate to the conflicts of the Seven Years' War then being waged. [MAW]

🕏 Merriman, James Douglas. *The Flower of Kings: A Study of the Arthurian Legend in England Between 1485 and 1835*. Lawrence: University Press of Kansas, 1973.

HISTORIA ANGLORUM: see HENRY OF HUNTINGDON.

HISTORIA BRITTONUM: see NENNIUS.

HISTORIA ECCLESIASTICA GENTIS ANGLORUM: see BEDE.

HISTORIA MAJORIS BRITANNIAE: see SCOTTISH ARTHURIAN CHRONICLES.

HISTORIA MERIADOCI, Latin prose, dated variously from the last quarter of the twelfth century to the last quarter of the thirteenth. Attributed by John Bale to Robert of Torigni, abbot of Mont St.-Michel, 1154–86, it is probably by the same author as *De Ortu Waluuanii*. Meriadoc and his sister Orwen are the children of Caradoc, king of Wales during King Uther's time. Caradoc is murdered by his brother Griffin and the children kidnapped. But the children are secretly protected, and Sir Kay raises Meriadoc. Two principal quests follow: first, Meriadoc with Arthur's help obtains revenge on Griffin, and second, Meriadoc goes into the service of the emperor of Germany in his war against Gundebald, who has abducted the emperor's daughter. Meriadoc rescues the princess and after war and betrayal finally wins her hand. [MLD]

🕏 Bruce, J.D., ed. *Historia Meriadoci and De Ortu Waluuanii*. Göttingen: Vandenhoeck and Ruprecht, 1913.

HISTORIA REGUM BRITANNIAE: see GEOFFREY OF MONMOUTH.

HISTORIA RERUM ANGLICARUM: *see* WILLIAM OF NEWBURGH.

HISTORIE VAN DEN GRALE: *see* MAERLANT, JACOB VAN.

HISTORIE VAN MERLIJN. In 1926, W. Nijhoff discovered two quires in the Royal Library at Brussels, eight pages in all, of a Dutch chapbook, the *Historie van Merlijn* (now with the signature Oude Druk V.H. 27526 A). They were found wrongly bound in a copy of the *Cronijcke van Vlaenderen int corte van 621–1532.* This work was printed by Symon Cock at Antwerp in 1539. The *Historie van Merlijn* was also printed by Symon Cock between 1534 and 1544. The chapbook is an adaptation of an English one, *A Lytel Treatyse of þe Byrth and Prophecye of Marlyn.* This is a version of the Middle English *Arthour and Merlin* and was printed in London in 1510. [BB]

🕮 Kronenberg, M.E., ed. "Een onbekend volksboek van Merlijn (c. 1540)." *Tijdschrift voor Nederlandsche Taal- en Letterkunde*, 48 (1929), 18–34.

HISTORY OF THE HOLY GRAIL, THE: *see* LOVELICH, HENRY.

HOËL. Several kings or lords of Britain or Brittany (usually clearly identified as the latter), or of Breton cities, are given this name in a number of Arthurian texts: Geoffrey of Monmouth's *Historia Regum Britanniae* (as *Hoelus*), Wace's *Brut*, Marie de France's *Guigemar* (as *Hoïlas*), the Vulgate *Suite du Merlin*, and Renaut de Beaujeu's *Le Bel Inconnu.* According to the Tristan tradition, King Hoël of Brittany is the father of Iseut White-Hands and Kahedin; this is probably true as well in the lost parts of Thomas's *Tristan*, and in the Prose *Tristan* and those romances influenced by it. In the chronicles, Hoël is usually a cousin of Arthur. [C-AVC]

HOLE, RICHARD (1746–1803), Anglican clergyman and archetypal Pre-Romantic, wrote *Arthur, or the Northern Enchantment in Seven Books* (1789). Conflict ensues between Arthur (aided by Merlin, the father of Arthur's beloved Inogen) and Hengist the Saxon (aided by the Fatal Sisters). Disguise, shape-shifting, monsters, and magic castles are romantic motifs, but the heroic couplets and epic conventions produce a classical effect. [MAW]

🕮 Merriman, James Douglas. *The Flower of Kings: A Study of the Arthurian Legend in England Between 1485 and 1835.* Lawrence: University Press of Kansas, 1973.

HOLINSHED, RAPHAEL: *see* CHRONICLES, ARTHUR IN.

HOLLOW HILLS, THE: see STEWART, MARY.

HOLMES, URBAN TIGNER, JR. (1900–1972). For most of his career a professor at the University of North Carolina, Holmes's most significant contribution to Arthurian studies was his controversial Judeo-Christian interpretation of the Grail. He argued that Chrétien de Troyes was perhaps a converted Jew and intended the *Conte del Graal* to portray the good that would result from the Jews' conversion. (*See also* SCHOLARSHIP, MODERN ARTHURIAN.) [WWK]

∂ᴥ Holmes, Urban T., Jr., and M. Amelia Klenke. *Chrétien, Troyes, and the Grail.* Chapel Hill: University of North Carolina Press, 1959.

"HOLY GRAIL, THE": *see* TENNYSON, ALFRED LORD.

HOLY GRAIL, THE: see SPICER, JACK.

HOLY GRAIL AND OTHER POEMS, THE: see TENNYSON, ALFRED LORD.

HOUSMAN, CLEMENCE, author of the thoughtful, though rambling, historical romance *The Life of Sir Aglovale de Galis* (1905). Housman (sister of A.E. Housman) expands imaginatively upon Malory's account to examine the ill-starred career of Aglovale, son of King Pellinore and brother of Lamorak and Percivale. Unlike other knights, Aglovale refuses to deny his failures, even when they bring him dishonor and shame. He thus serves to comment upon the hypocrisy of a court whose concern with the appearance of justice rather than its reality ultimately proves its downfall. [RHT]

∂ᴥ Housman, Clemence. *The Life of Sir Aglovale de Galis.* London: Methuen, 1905; rev. ed. London: Cape, 1954.

HOVEY, RICHARD (1864–1900), Professor of English Literature at Barnard College, introduced Arthurian drama to America in a series of verse-plays intended to retell the whole story under the title *Launcelot and Guenevere: A Poem in Dramas.* Completed were two masques, *The Quest of Merlin* (1891) and *Taliesin*, and two five-act closet dramas, *The Marriage of Guenevere* and *The Birth of Galahad* (1898). The pageantic *Quest of Merlin* is exuberantly eclectic in its combination of characters from Teutonic mythology (the Norns, Valkyries, and Gnomes), classical mythology (Pan, Bacchus, Aphrodite, Naiads, Satyrs), Celtic mythology via Shakespeare (Mab, Puck, Oberon, Titania, and fairies as well as the fées Nimue and Argente), and Christian mythology (angels, associated by their presence in Avalon). The scenario includes the drunkenness of Merlin, which Maynadier describes as "not only disagreeable—for Merlin does not get drunk pleasantly—but purposeless." The purpose of Merlin's quest is to ascertain from the supernatural powers the prospects for Arthur's forthcoming marriage.

In *The Marriage of Guenevere*, the marriage is effected and the plots of Morgause (whose lover is Peredur, Guenevere's brother) are thwarted by Arthur's refusal to think ill of his queen and chief knight. Hovey ameliorates criticism of the lovers' conduct by providing Arthur with several paramours— "Ay, he has been a gay dog in his day"—and sending him off to war before the marriage is consummated. Since Launcelot is her first lover, Guenevere feels justified in calling him "husband." In *The Birth of Galahad*, to avoid charging Launcelot with infidelity in the matter of Elaine of Corbenic, Hovey presents Galahad as the son of Launcelot and Guenevere, though he is passed off as the child of the recently widowed Ylen. That Hovey rejected the Victorian attitude to adultery is suggested by the angel's words to Percival in *Taliesin*: "Better the rose of love out of the dung-hill of the world's adulteries/ Than the maid icicle that keeps itself from stain of earth where no life is." [MAW]

&. Hovey, Richard. *Launcelot and Guenevere: A Poem in Dramas*. 5 vols. Boston: Small, Maynard, 1898–1907.

HOW SIR GALAHAD, SIR BORS AND SIR PERCIVAL SAW THE SANGRAEL: *see* OXFORD UNION MURALS; ROSSETTI, DANTE GABRIEL.

HOW SIR GALAHAD, SIR BORS AND SIR PERCIVAL WERE FED WITH THE GRAEL; BUT SIR PERCIVAL'S SISTER DIED BY THE WAY: *see* ROSSETTI, DANTE GABRIEL.

HUGHES, ARTHUR (1830–1915), English painter and illustrator, began his association with the Pre-Raphaelites and Arthurian subjects in 1857, when Dante Gabriel Rossetti invited him to take part in the Oxford Union Murals project. William Holman Hunt called Hughes's own design for *The Death of Arthur* superior to the others. Hughes also contributed *The Birth of Tristram* to the Dunlop Windows (1862).

During the 1860s and 1870s, Hughes expanded his repertoire, using Tennyson as his exclusive source. Works include *The Brave Geraint* (1862, Private Collection), *Elaine with the Armour of Lancelot* (undated, Private Collection), *Sir Galahad* (1870, Walker Art Gallery, Liverpool), and *The Lady of Shalott* (1873, Private Collection). He also painted inventions upon themes from Tennyson, as in *The Rift in the Lute* (1862, City Gallery, Carlisle), which was based on

Vivien's song in *Merlin and Vivien*. Hughes's work is distinguished by a graceful draughtsmanship and a vivid palette. More than his contemporaries, Hughes was able to instill lyricism into his vision of Tennyson's Arthuriad. [DNM]

◆ Gibson, Robin. "Arthur Hughes: Arthurian and Related Subjects of the Early 1860s." *Burlington Magazine*, 112 (July 1970), 451–56.

HUGHES, THOMAS, with collaborators, wrote *The Misfortunes of Arthur* for performance by members of Gray's Inn before Elizabeth I at Greenwich in 1587. Senecan in rhetoric and dramatic technique, the tragedy has dumb shows devised by Francis Bacon. Based on Geoffrey of Monmouth, it depicts Arthur's fatal revenge on Mordred, who has seduced Guenevora. [CNS]

◆ Hughes, Thomas. *The Misfortunes of Arthur*, ed. H.G. Grumbone. Berlin: Felber, 1900.

HUNBAUT, an early thirteenth-century French romance of 3,818 lines that breaks off incomplete. It tells of Gauvain's mission on Arthur's behalf to the Roi des Isles in the company of Hunbaut. The two of them demand that the king submit to Arthur and then leave in great haste. They become separated and accomplish a number of exploits, liberating various people from their oppressors.

Hunbaut is actually a Gauvain romance and is particularly interesting when compared with other Gauvain romances that contain similar episodes, such as those of the imperious host and the damsel who keeps an image of the hero so that she may recognize him when he comes her way. More particularly, the poem contains a version of the Beheading Test also found in the First Continuation of the *Perceval*, Paien de Maisières's *La Mule sans frein*, the *Perlesvaus*, and *Sir Gawain and the Green Knight*. Hunbaut functions as a kind of moralizing contrast to Gauvain, who is constantly getting into scrapes as a result of unconsidered and unreasonable behavior. [KB]

◆ Winters, Margaret, ed. *Hunbaut*. Leiden: Brill, 1984.

"HUNT, THE": *see* JONES, DAVID.

HUNTER, JIM, British author of the historical novel *Percival and the Presence of God* (1978), which recounts Percival's search for Arthur and his adventures along the way, including that of the Fisher King and the Grail. The story, narrated by Percival, describes his youthful sense of divine direction, his failure either to achieve the Grail or to find Arthur, and his subsequent doubts about his heroic destiny and significance. The novel is thus the projection of an essentially twentieth-century consciousness upon the medieval character, done both skillfully and successfully. [SRR]

◆ Hunter, Jim. *Percival and the Presence of God*. London: Faber and Faber, 1978.

HUPSCHES VASNACHTSPILL UND SAGT VON KÜNIG ARTUS, AIN
("A Shrovetide Play of King Arthur"). The full title of the anonymous
fifteenth-century Shrovetide play is *Ain hupsches vasnachtspill und sagt von künig
Artus, wie er siben fursten mit iren weyben zuo seinem hoff geladen het und wie si durch ain
horn geschendet worden gar hupsch zuo hören* ("A Shrovetide Play About King
Arthur, How He Invited Seven Kings with Their Wives to His Court and How
They Were Embarrassed by a Horn"). The play, which derives ultimately
from Robert Biket's *Lai du cor*, opens with Arthur's decision to invite seven
mighty kings to a great feast where rich and poor will be wined and dined.
King Arthur refuses, however, to invite his sister, the Queen of Zipper, who
has offended him. To avenge the slight, she sends to Arthur's court a magic
drinking horn from which all men are to drink. They learn that only a man
with a faithful wife can drink from the horn without spilling a drop. The play
augments the tale known from the *Lai du cor* with a scene in which a knight
falsely accuses another of having committed adultery with Guinevere. Trial-
by-combat clears the accused knight's name and the accuser is banished from
court. [MEK]

Keller, Adelbert von, ed. "Ain hupsches vasnachtspill und sagt von künig Artus." In
Fastnachtspiele aus dem fünfzehnten Jahrhundert: Nachlese. Stuttgart: Litterarischer Verein,
1858, Vol. 146, pp. 183–215.

HUTH MERLIN: *see SUITE DU MERLIN.*

IDYLLS OF THE KING: *see* TENNYSON, ALFRED LORD.

IDYLLS OF THE QUEEN, THE: *see* KARR, PHYLLIS ANN.

IGERNE (YGUERNE, IGRAYNE), the wife of the Duke of Tintagel, who was much desired by King Uther Pendragon but would not consent to lie with him. Merlin arranges for Uther to come to her in the guise of the duke, her husband, and he begets upon her the future King Arthur. That very night, the duke is killed, and Uther arranges soon afterward to wed Igerne. For his services, Merlin had demanded a boon: he requests and is granted the child to raise. [WWK]

ILL-MADE KNIGHT, THE: *see* WHITE, T. H.

ILLUMINATED MANUSCRIPTS, ARTHURIAN: *see* MANUSCRIPTS, ARTHURIAN ILLUMINATED.

IMMERMANN, KARL LEBERECHT (1796–1840), wrote dramatic works and novels containing stylistic features of classicism, romanticism, and the new realism. Twice, he used Arthurian subject matter, first in his ambitious play *Merlin* (1832) and again in the posthumously published fragment *Tristan und Isolde: Ein Gedicht in Romanzen* (1841). The latter is the most comprehensive Tristan poem of the nineteenth century. For Immermann, Merlin is the son of Satan, who paradoxically wants to save the world. The play, which was intended to vie with Goethe's *Faust*, concludes, however, with failure and ruin, not salvation. Tankred Dorst's play *Merlin* (1981) takes inspiration from Immermann. [UM/WCM]

Immermann, Karl. *Merlin*. Leipzig: Klemm, 1832.

———. *Tristan und Isolde: Ein Gedicht in Romanzen*. Leipzig: Reclam, [1841].

Moenkemeyer, Heinz. "Immermanns 'Merlin': Die Tragödie des selbsternannten Erlösers." In *Schiller-Jahrbuch*. Stuttgart: Kröner, Vol. 5, 1961.

IMMORTAL WOUND, THE: *see* CANNING, VICTOR.

IN PARENTHESIS: *see* JONES, DAVID.

IN WINTER'S SHADOW: *see* BRADSHAW, GILLIAN.

INTERNATIONAL ARTHURIAN SOCIETY (founded 1949) comprises some 1,000 individual members and 300 institutional subscribers over the globe, but mainly concentrated in western Europe and North America. Its goal is to further Arthurian studies by enabling scholars and enthusiasts to meet and learn of each others' activities. It is organized into national branches, some of which meet annually, and a triennial international congress, which is the ultimate governing body. To facilitate contact and to provide information, it publishes an annual *Bibliographical Bulletin*, which contains a critical bibliography of all printed studies of the preceding year, an up-to-date checklist of reviews of works previously noted in the *Bulletin*, reports of scholarly activities, short research articles, a list of publications received at the Centre de Documentation Arthurienne (Paris), summaries of papers read at the triennial international congresses, and a list of members, with addresses.

The founding of the society is generally attributed to Eugène Vinaver, though credit must also be given to Jean Frappier and Roger Sherman Loomis for its growth after the Second World War. Vinaver himself attributed the conception to a physician, Dr. Hambly Rowe, who suggested in the late 1920s that Arthurian scholars should meet in Cornwall. The First International Congress was in fact held in Truro, Cornwall, in 1930, and at that time was sponsored by the embryonic Arthurian Society of Oxford, which Vinaver had initiated in 1928. The latter was rechristened the Society for the Study of Medieval Languages and Literature, and its publication, *Arthuriana* (1929–30), was renamed *Medium Aevum*. The Second International Congress, planned for 1932, was not realized until 1948, at Quimper, where the members launched the *Bulletin Bibliographique de la Société Internationale Arthurienne*. [JLG]

⊷ Thorpe, Lewis, et al. "The First Arthurian Congress, Truro, 23–30 August 1930." *Bibliographical Bulletin of the International Arthurian Society*, 25 (1973), 179–96.

IRELAND, SAMUEL (1777–1835), English manuscript-forger. His Arthurian "Shakespeare" play *Vortigern* was produced by Sheridan in 1796 but proved too feeble and transparently bogus to survive. He confessed the fabrication. [GA]

ISEULT ON THE SHIP: *see* MORRIS, WILLIAM.

ISLAND OF THE MIGHTY, THE: *see* ARDEN, JOHN, AND MARGARETTA D'ARCY.

ISOLDE: *see* TRISTAN AND ISOLDE.

ISOLDE OF THE WHITE HANDS (ISEUT [YSEUT] AUX BLANCHES MAINS), sometimes known as Isolde of the Fair Hands or Isolde of Brittany. Tristan, separated from the woman he loves, marries Isolde of the White Hands because she shares his beloved's name. Their marriage remains unconsummated, and he confesses that it is because he loves another woman. Eventually, as Tristan is waiting for Isolde to arrive and heal him, his wife causes his death by informing him, untruthfully, that Isolde is not aboard the approaching ship. (*See also* TRISTAN AND ISOLDE.) [NJL]

ISOLDE WEISSHAND: *see* LUCKA, EMIL.

ITALIAN ARTHURIAN LITERATURE. Although rarely serving as the locale for the adventures of Arthur and the knights of the Round Table, Italy certainly bears literary and artistic witness to their passage. Perhaps the only indication we possess of Arthur's "physical" presence in Italy is the legend of his residence in Mount Etna (Mongibello), and it is this fabulous tale that the anonymous poet of the "Detto del gatto lupesco" evokes in a playful and comic manner. In this poem, the jongleur, who identifies himself as a "wolflike cat," meets two knights in an inn and learns of their quest for Arthur:

> Cavalieri siamo di Bretagna,
> ke vegnamo de la montagna
> ke·ll'omo apella Mongibello.
> Assai vi semo stati ad ostello
> per apparare ed invenire
> la veritade di nostro sire
> lo re Artù, k'avemo perduto
> e non sapemo ke·ssia venuto.
> Or ne torniamo in nostra terra,
> ne lo reame d'Inghilterra. [ll. 25–34]

("We are knights of Brittany who come from the mountain called Mongibello. We have stayed here in the inn a long time to learn and discover the truth about our lord, King Arthur, whom we have lost, and we don't know what's happened to him. Now we are returning to our country, to the kingdom of England.")

The fascination that the *matière de Bretagne* exerted on the Italian popular imagination may be documented in at least two ways. In the twelfth and thirteenth centuries, many names of Arthurian provenance began to appear among the populace (Arturius, Galvanus, Merlinus, Tristaynus), a fact that attests both to the diffusion and to the popularity of these legends in Italy. In this same period, there were carved above the portals of some cathedrals (Modena, Bari) and depicted in the mosaic pavement of others (Otranto) knights in combat, castles and besieged towers, and other figures and events from the Arthurian cycle.

In Italian literature, the principal players in the Arthurian drama assumed a new, double life: a "symbolic" existence as emblematic figures in superficial allusions, and a "real" literary life as principal characters in a sustained narrative or sequence of episodes. On the one hand, lyric poets used these figures as standards of comparison against which they measured elements of their own experience: beauty, prowess, wisdom, and the like. On the other hand, other authors mined the rich (mainly French) Arthurian treasure trove and composed a number of prose romances, *novelle,* and *cantari,* thus creating a large and distinct body of Italian Arthurian literature.

The story of Tristan and Isolde is the most popular of the Arthurian legends in Italy, the most widely cited, and the subject of the greatest number of versions. We may therefore determine the impact of the *matière de Bretagne* on Italian literature by examining the various manifestations of this single tale. Henricus of Settimello (late twelfth century) was the first author to mention Tristan in Italy. In his *Elegia de diversitate fortunae et philosophiae consolatione* ("Elegy on the Contradiction of Fortune and the Consolation of Philosophy"), he stressed the grief associated with this famous lover in the following paronomastic verse: "Quis ille/ Tristanus qui me tristia plura tulit?" ("Who is that Tristan who bore more sorrows than I?")

The Italian lyric tradition began at the court of the emperor Frederick II of Hohenstaufen in Sicily, and these vernacular poets followed the example of their Provençal forebears in their use of the Tristan legend as a source of comparisons. There, they found standards against which to measure elements of their own experience: the unsurpassed strength and courage of Tristan, the supreme beauty of Isolde, and the powerful nature and indestructible force of their love. In the following verses from his *discordo*, Giacomo da Lentini declares his own love to be much stronger than Tristan's: "Tristano a Isolda/ non amau sì forte." ("Tristan did not love Isolde so strongly"; "Dal core mi vene," l. 35.) Re Giovanni alludes to Isolde's beauty in "Donna, audite como" (ll. 58–60):"E Tristan se ne godia/ de lo bel viso rosato/ ch'Isaotta blond'avia." ("And Tristan took great pleasure in the lovely rosy face that blond-haired Isolde had.")

In the thirteenth and early fourteenth centuries, the Italian lyric evolved both linguistically and thematically at the hands of innovative poets, such as Guittone d'Arezzo, Guido Guinizelli, Guido Cavalcanti, and Dante Alighieri. In this period of gradual transformation, the allusions to the legend of Tristan and Isolde, although less frequent, remained essentially the same. Bonagiunta da Lucca, in the *ballata* "Donna vostra belleza" (ll. 31–33), refers to the intensity of Tristan and Isolde's passion: "Ed eo . . ./'nnamorato son di vue/ assai più che non fue—Tristan d'Isolda." ("And I love you, even more than Tristan loved Isolde.")

In the sonnet "Lo disioso core e la speranza" (ll. 5–8), the Florentine poet Chiaro Davanzati refers to the beauty of his lady as being greater than that of Isolde: "di voi non veggio simiglianza/né pari di bieltà sì graziosa:/ch'Isotta né Tisbïa per sembianza,/nesuna in gioia fue sì poderosa." ("I do not know anyone similar or equal to you in pleasing beauty: for neither Isolde nor Thisbe in appearance was so great in bestowing happiness.")

In a ballad on Fortune ("Se la Fortuna o 'l mondo," ll. 53–56), written in the first quarter of the Trecento, Frate Stoppa de' Bostichi first alludes to the prowess of Tristan and the other knights of the Round Table: "Tristano e Lancialotto/sono iti, benchè ancor lor fama vale./Gli altri di Camelotto/per la Fortuna feciono altrettale." ("Tristan and Lancelot have gone away, but their fame still endures. The other knights of Camelot fared the same because of Fortune.") In a subsequent strophe (ll. 79–80), he incorporates the *ubi sunt* motif in reference to the beauty of Isolde and others: "Dov'è la gran bellezza/di Ginevra, d'Isotta, e d'Ansalone?" ("Where is the great beauty of Guinevere, Isolde, and Absalom?")

There are fewer and fewer of these superficial allusions to Arthurian figures in the lyric poetry of the fourteenth century: the reason for this perhaps lies in the compilation and diffusion of numerous major and well-developed prose romances during this period. The increased familiarity with the legend and its resulting "commonness" may have vitiated the exotic quality that these allusions once possessed. Or else the disfavor into which these allusions fell may simply reflect changing attitudes toward the nature and aesthetics of poetry and indicate, in particular, the desire to avoid empty phrases and artificial conventions.

Only infrequently in the thirteenth century do we come across an allusion that seems to indicate a more specific knowledge of the Tristan legend. For example, in the *canzone* "Madonna mia, a voi mando" (ll. 41–48) Giacomo da Lentini speaks of having made a wax image of his lady, whom he compares to Isolde: "In gran dilettanza era,/madonna, in quello giorno/quando vi formai in cera/le belleze d'intorno./Più bella mi parete/ca Isolda la bronda;/amorosa, gioconda,/flor de le donne sete." ("In great delight I was that day, my lady, when I formed your beautiful image in wax. You seem to me more beautiful than Isolde; loving, joyful, you are the flower of women.") The inspiration of this allusion probably comes from the well-known "Salle aux Images" episode (Bédier's term) in Thomas's *Tristan*.

Despite this and a few other examples that suggest a knowledge of the early metrical romances, the prose version of the Tristan legend was the most widely known in Italy and furnished the basis for virtually all of the Italian redactions of the story. The several extant late thirteenth- and early fourteenth-century prose romances range from essentially literal translations of the Old French *Roman de Tristan* to liberal adaptations and compilations of diverse source materials. The earliest of the Italian Tristan romances is the *Tristano Riccardiano*, which presents freely selected portions from its Old French source, as well as numerous "new" elements and episodes. The most original of the prose romances, the *Tavola Ritonda*, combines in a harmonious whole episodes from various sources (*Roman de Tristan, Palamedes, Tristano Riccardiano, Mort Artu*) and a wealth of new elements and adventures, all of which give it a certain artistic autonomy and individuality. An episode in the Tristan legend, drawn primarily from Béroul—the lovers' moonlight meeting at the fountain in the garden, where Mark is hiding in a pine tree—provides the subject for one (No. 65) of the short stories in *Il Novellino*.

Originally part of the oral tradition, the *cantari* paraphrase specific episodes from the prose romances (both Old French and Italian) and are noteworthy as examples of the art of the jongleur. Three *cantari* treat the Tristan legend: *La Morte di Tristano, QuandoTristano e Lancielotto combattettero al petrone di Merlino,* and *La vendetta che fe messer Lanzelloto de la morte di miser Tristano.*

Other Arthurian figures were generally incorporated in Italian literature in the same manner as Tristan and Isolde: either as superficial references and allusions in lyric poetry or as the subject of major prose romances, *novelle*, and *cantari*. In the sonnet "Ben aggia ormai la fede e l'amor meo" (ll. 10–12), Guittone d'Arezzo refers to the well-known prowess of Lancelot: "Siccome a Lanzelotto omo simiglia/un prode cavaler, simil se face/a lei di fera donna a maraviglia." ("Just as one compares a valiant knight to Lancelot, so does one liken a wonderfully proud lady to her.")

In a sonnet addressed to the Compiuta Donzella di Firenza, Maestro Torrigiano compares her favorably to Guinevere (ll. 1–4): "Esser donzella di trovare dotta/sì grande meraviglia par a 'ntendre,/ca, se Ginevra fosse od Isaotta,/ver' lor di lei se ne poria contendre." ("The existence of a young woman so gifted in writing poetry seems such a marvelous thing to hear that, if Guinevere or Isolde were still alive, one could argue for her superiority over them.")

In the following verses (ll. 1–4), Chiaro Davanzati praises the outstanding beauty of his lady, who surpasses even Morgan le Fay: "Ringrazzo amore de l'aventurosa/gioia e de l'allegrezza che m'à data,/che mi donò a servir la più amorosa/che non fue Tisbia o Morgana la fata." ("I thank Love for the wondrous joy and happiness that he has given me, for he gave me to serve the most lovely one, even more so than Thisbe or Morgan le Fay.")

Allusions of this sort are common in lyric poetry, and the list could be extended to include, among others, Arthur, Merlin, Ywain, and Erec.

Dependent in large part on their Old French forerunners, the Italian prose romances treat the entire range of Arthurian material and the different generations of characters in that corpus. Basing his account on the *Roman de Tristan* and the *Palamedes*, Rusticiano (or Rustichello) da Pisa (late thirteenth century) compiled the earliest Arthurian romance in Italy, the *Meliadus*, which, written in French, is extant only in fragmentary form. Its two major portions were translated early on into Italian as *Girone il Cortese* and *Il gran re Meliadus*. Merlin is the subject of two fourteenth-century romances, both of which derive from Old French sources: the *Storia di Merlino*, by the Florentine chronicler Paolino Pieri, and the later *Vita di Merlino con le sue profezie*. These numerous *volgarizzamenti* and redactions hold an important place in the history of early Italian literature, for they contributed in a major way to the establishment and expansion of Italy's heretofore relatively small literary patrimony in the vernacular.

Arthurian material is also present in the *novella* (short story) tradition. Several stories in *Il Novellino*, for example, have as their principal characters Meliadus, Lancelot, the Maid of Scalot, and Merlin. A story concerning Merlin is also included in the collection of tales called *Libro dei Sette Savi di Roma*, and another about Galehaut is found in the *Conti dei Antichi Cavalieri*.

The *cantari* display a much broader range in Arthurian subject matter, for they draw upon both the prose romances and the Breton lais. In addition to Tristan and Lancelot, the *cantari* feature a host of protagonists, and a survey of a few titles will give an idea of their diversity: *Pulzella Gaia, Bel Gherardino, Liombruno, Carduino, Febusso e Breusso*—all anonymous—and Antonio Pucci's *Gismirante* and *Brito di Brettagna*. The *Cantare dei cantari* allows the reader to look at the repertoire of the jongleur and to observe the literary tastes of the society he serves. In this anonymous *cantare*, the poet lists all the subjects he is able to sing about, and nine full stanzas (of fifty-nine) are devoted to Arthurian material.

Dante Alighieri was familiar with the *matière de Bretagne* and mentions the "Arturi regis ambages pulcerrimae" in *De Vulgari Eloquentia* (I,x,2) as evidence of the preeminence of the French language in vernacular prose. While not using Arthurian figures in stock allusions as preceding generations of poets had done, Dante does incorporate certain episodes from the prose romances into the literary and moral structure of the *Divina Commedia*. Most famous in this regard is his presentation of the sinful passion of Paolo and Francesca, which is played out against and defined by the episode in the Old French Prose *Lancelot*, in which Lancelot and Guinevere kiss for the first time under the guidance of the Lady of Malehaut.

In the early fourteenth-century allegorical poem *L'Intelligenza*, the poet (possibly Dino Compagni) celebrates his lady ("Intelligenza") and describes her palace. Included as integral parts of the decoration of this palace are several Arthurian figures and their stories—Tristan and Isolde, Guinevere, Merlin, and others. In his mid-fourteenth-century encyclopedic poem in *terza rima Il Dittamondo*, Fazio degli Uberti imagines himself traveling through the known world guided by the classical geographer Solinus. In his journey, he sees and comments in some detail on several places of Arthurian interest in Brittany and Great Britain.

Giovanni Boccaccio includes a chapter on Arthur in *De Casibus Virorum Illustrium* and uses Arthurian motives and allusions in the *Decameron* (the subtitle of which is "Prencipe Galeotto"), *Amorosa Visione, Corbaccio,* and *Elegia di Madonna Fiammetta*.

In the *Trionfo d'Amore* (Book III, ll. 79–82), Francesco Petrarca speaks in a disdainful and disparaging manner of the Arthurian knights and ladies, who appear in the procession of those subjugated by Love: "Ecco quei che le carte empion di sogni,/Lancilotto, Tristano e gli altri erranti,/ove conven che 'l vulgo errante agogni./Vedi Ginevra, Isolda e l'altre amanti." ("Here are those who fill the pages of books with dreams—Lancelot, Tristan, and the other knights-errant—dreams that lead the common folk astray through desire. See Guinevere, Isolde, and other lovers.")

The final chapter in this survey of the presence of the *matière de Bretagne* in Italy concerns the conflation of the Arthurian and the Carolingian cycles. As early as the fourteenth century, the poet of the Franco-Italian epic *L'Entrée d'Espagne* endows Roland with the amorous and chivalric sensibility of a knight of the Round Table. Similarly, in the *cantare* cycles concerned with the exploits of Roland—*La Spagna* and *Li fatti di Spagna*—we find many of the marvelous trappings and adventures common to the Arthurian tradition. Andrea da Barberino imbues his late fourteenth-century narratives concerning the matter of France—*Aspramonte, Storie Nerbonesi, Reali di Francia*—with a distinctly Arthurian spirit. Such will be the case as well with Matteo Maria Boiardo, whose *Orlando Innamorato* captures (even in its title) much of the spirit of Arthurian romance and sets the stage for Ludovico Ariosto's *Orlando Furioso*, which is replete with courtly knights and ladies and wondrous adventures. [CK]

Arese, Felice, ed. *Prose di romanzi: Il romanzo cortese in Italia nei secoli XIII e XIV.* Turin: UTET, 1950.

Branca, Daniela. *I romanzi italiani di Tristano e la Tavola Ritonda.* Florence: Olschki, 1968.

———. "Tavola rotonda: La materia arturiana e tristaniana: Tradizione e fortuna." In *Dizionario critico della letteratura italiana*. Turin: UTET, 1973, Vol. 3, pp. 471–76.

Ferrante, Joan M. *The Conflict of Love and Honor: The Medieval Tristan Legend in France, Germany and Italy*. The Hague: Mouton, 1973.

Gardner, Edmund G. *The Arthurian Legend in Italian Literature*. London: Dent, 1930.

Graf, Arturo. "Appunti per la storia del ciclo brettone in Italia." *Giornale storico della letteratura italiana*, 5 (1885), 80–130.

Kleinhenz, Christopher. "Tristan in Italy: The Death or Rebirth of a Legend." *Studies in Medieval Culture*, 5 (1975), 145–58.

Viscardi, Antonio. "Arthurian Influences on Italian Literature from 1220 to 1500." In *Arthurian Literature in the Middle Ages*, ed. Roger Sherman Loomis. Oxford: Clarendon, 1959, pp. 419–29.

IVAN LEJONRIDDAREN (or *Herr Ivan*) is a Swedish adaptation of Chrétien de Troyes's *Yvain*. It is one of three works known collectively as *Eufemiavisor*, after Queen Eufemia, wife of King Hákon Magnússon of Norway (r. 1299–1319), who commissioned the work. *Ivan Lejonriddaren* is dated 1303 and is preserved in four fifteenth-century Swedish manuscripts and two Danish manuscripts. Unlike the Norwegian prose translation of *Yvain*—i.e., *Ívens saga*—*Ivan Lejonriddaren* is in verse, in rhymed couplets known as *Knittelvers*. Certain textual similarities between *Ivan Lejonriddaren* and *Ívens saga* suggest that the anonymous translator, who is thought to have been a Swede at the Norwegian court, made use of both the Norwegian saga and Chrétien's *Yvain*. *Ivan Lejonriddaren* is a fairly accurate, albeit somewhat reduced, rendering of Chrétien's romance. It has the distinction of being the only medieval Swedish Arthurian romance and the only verse translation of an Arthurian romance in the North. [MEK]

Noreen, Erik, ed. *Herr Ivan*. Uppsala: Svenska Fornskrift-Sällskapet, 1930–32; 2nd ed. 1956.

Hunt, Tony. "Herr Ivan Lejonriddaren." *Mediaeval Scandinavia*, 8 (1975), 168–86.

Ronge, Hans. "Ivan Lejonriddaren." In *Kulturhistorisk leksikon for nordisk middelalder, VII*. Copenhagen: Rosenkilde and Bagger, 1962, cols. 525–27.

ÍVENS SAGA, an Old Norse prose translation of Chrétien de Troyes's *Yvain*. A statement in the text indicates that it was commissioned by the Norwegian king Hákon Hákonarson (r. 1217–63). There are three primary manuscripts, two fifteenth-century vellums (both defective) and one seventeenth-century paper. The latter is considerably shortened and modified but nevertheless preserves some readings, lacking in the vellums, which must be original on comparison with the French.

Íven, one of King Arthur's knights, slays the guardian of a magic fountain to avenge Kalebrant, his kinsman, who had earlier been disgraced by the knight. Íven falls in love with the guardian's widow and after a reconciliation marries her. Íven is aided in this by Luneta, the lady's confidante, whom Íven had once befriended at Arthur's court. When Arthur and his men later arrive,

Íven successfully defends the spring. After the subsequent feasting, Valven (Gawain) persuades Íven that he must accompany them and preserve his reputation as a champion. His lady gives Íven leave but sets a term of a year. When Íven forgets to return, a maiden appears with a message from his lady that banishes him. In a fit of madness, Íven wanders off into the forest but is later cured with a magic ointment by another lady. He defeats an earl who is attacking this lady's lands; he then rescues a lion from a dragon, and the lion becomes his constant companion. Among his numerous adventures is an episode in which Íven rescues Luneta from being burned at the stake. Finally, a duel between Íven and Valven, each unrecognized by the other, ends in a draw, and Íven is joyfully reintroduced into Arthur's court. However, he must still be reconciled with his lady, a task that Luneta accomplishes with the aid of a ruse.

Although this saga is more a translation and less an adaptation than *Erex saga*, there are still a number of changes, presumably intentional, vis-à-vis its French original. Alliteration is used as an effective stylistic device, particularly in dramatic scenes. [FWB]

◈ Blaisdell, Foster W., ed. *Ívens saga*. Copenhagen: Reitzel, 1979.

———, and Marianne E. Kalinke, trans. *Erex Saga and Ívens Saga*. Lincoln: University of Nebraska Press, 1977.

Kalinke, Marianne E. *King Arthur, North-by-Northwest*. Copenhagen: Reitzel, 1981.

IVORY. Among the earliest ivories with Arthurian scenes are the small boxes, or caskets, intended to hold a lady's prized personal possessions. Products of the Cologne school in the thirteenth century, they are often decorated with scenes from the romance of Tristan. Figures of a man with a harp and woman with a goblet are identifiable as Tristan and Isolde.

The finest Arthurian ivories were the product of the Parisian workshops especially during the second quarter of the fourteenth century. A flourishing trade in luxury objects, such as ivory boxes, combs, mirror cases, and hair-parters, required workshop methods of production, using set iconography and formulaic compositions; nevertheless, the many surviving objects of high quality attest to the skill of the Parisian craftsmen. Ivory jewel boxes were carved with scenes intended to appeal to the taste of noble ladies. Some of the subjects could be given a moralizing interpretation, but most represent the famous lovers of history, the attack on the Castle of Love, or the fountain of youth. Tristan and Isolde meeting by the well (the so-called Tryst Beneath the Tree), Sir Lancelot Crossing the Sword Bridge, and Sir Gawain on the Perilous Bed are the most popular Arthurian scenes, although Galahad receiving the keys to the Castle of Maidens also appears. Excellent examples of these ivory caskets may be seen in the Metropolitan Museum in New York, the Walters Gallery in Baltimore, the Victoria and Albert Museum and the British Museum in London, the Bargello in Florence, and Cracow Cathedral in Poland. The caskets differ only slightly. The Perceval Casket in the Louvre is unusual in its depiction of the youth of Perceval, and was probably based on the *Conte del*

Graal. The figures of SS. Christopher, Martin, George, and Eustace decorate the lid of the Louvre Casket.

Ivory mirror-backs (Cluny Museum, Paris; the Vatican Museum) were carved with the same repertoire of scenes as the caskets. Since the subject had to be composed within a roundel or quatrefoil (the square of the mirror-back originally was filled out by hunched monsters or foliage at the corners), symmetrical compositions with Tristan and Isolde spied on by King Mark or playing chess were popular. A hair-parter in Turin also has Tristan and Isolde and the face of King Mark, in a very compressed composition, and another in the Metropolitan Museum has the lovers with their little dog.

These Parisian ivories have usually been interpreted as a celebration of love and youth, with scenes from the romances considered appropriate as gifts for young ladies. Frederick Baekeland, in a psychological study of the iconography, however, has pointed out the underlying conflict and sexual tension expressed in the selection and juxtaposition of scenes, in the theme of youth and age, and the issues of sexual choice and surrender. [MS]

Baekeland, Frederick. "Two Kinds of Symbolism in a Gothic Ivory Casket." *Psychoanalytic Study of Society*, 6 (n.d.).

Koechlin, Raymond. *Les Ivoires gothiques français.* 2 vols. Paris: Picard, 1924, pp. 43–44.

Loomis, Roger Sherman, and Laura Hibbard Loomis. *Arthurian Legends in Medieval Art.* London: Oxford University Press, 1938, pp. 55–54, 66–67, 70–71, 73–74, 76.

IWEIN: see HARTMANN VON AUE.

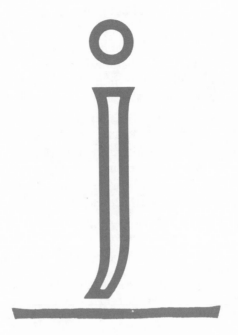

JAKES, JOHN: *see* KANE, GIL.

JANUALS LJÓÐ: see STRENGLEIKAR.

JAUFRÉ, the only surviving Provençal Arthurian romance. A work of some 11,000 lines, it may be the product of two authors, both of them anonymous. *Jaufré* has been variously dated from about 1180 to as late as 1225.

The hero is probably the same person as Chrétien de Troyes's Girflet. Most scholars who have studied *Jaufré* have noted that its author(s) had an intimate knowledge of the works of Chrétien de Troyes; their conclusions have been based on groupings of names, reflections of motifs and episodes, and some rhetorical and stylistic similarities. In a few cases (e.g., Rita Lejeune), those who propose the earliest possible dating have suggested that it might have been Chrétien who used the *Jaufré* text as inspiration, rather than the opposite.

The hero of the work sets out to avenge injuries or affronts done to Melian and Arthur by Taulat. In the process, he falls in love with Brunissen, the mistress of the castle of Monbrun. These parallel narrative lines are filled out by a number of miscellaneous episodes. The author has a taste for fantasy and comedy, and it is possible to see his work as a parody of chivalric romance.

The character attained some popularity beyond the bounds of this text, specifically in the Spanish prose *Tablante de Ricamonte y de Jofre hijo del conte Donason.* [NJL]

  Brunel, Clovis, ed. *Jaufré: Roman arthurien en ancien provençal.* 2 vols. Paris: Picard, 1943.
    Rémy, Paul. "Jaufré." In *Arthurian Literature in the Middle Ages,* ed. Roger Sherman Loomis. Oxford: Clarendon, 1959, pp. 400–05.

JEALOUSY OF SIR PALOMEDES, THE: *see* OXFORD UNION MURALS.

JEASTE OF SYR GAWAYNE, THE. Like *Golagros and Gawane,* the *Jeaste* (541 lines, but the opening is lacking) is a late fifteenth-century adaptation of events related in the First Continuation of Chrétien de Troyes's *Conte del Graal,* with a Gawain who is more humane and who magnanimously spares the lives of the father and two brothers of the girl with whom he has made love. The poem ends with the truce between the third brother, Brandles, and Gawain, who has to walk back to the court as his horse has apparently been killed. The dated manuscript (1564) contains six illustrations. [ESK]

  Madden, Frederic, ed. *Syr Gawayne.* London: Bannatyne Club, 1839.

JERUSALEM, THE EMANATION OF THE GIANT ALBION: *see* BLAKE, WILLIAM.

"JESTUTE": *see* BODMER, JOHANN JACOB.

JOHN OF FORDUN: *see* CHRONICLES, ARTHUR IN.

JOHN OF GLASTONBURY. In the mid-fourteenth century, John Seen, a monk of Glastonbury Abbey, composed his *Cronica sive Antiquitates Glastoniensis Ecclesie* ("Chronicle or the Antiquities of the Church of Glastonbury"), a comprehensive history of his monastery from earliest times to his own day. In his chronicle, John included a detailed account of the 1190–91 discovery of King Arthur's body in the abbey cemetery and several Arthurian genealogies. More important, he quoted fragments from the hitherto unknown prophecy of Melkin the Bard, in which the Grail of French romance tradition reappeared in a metamorphosed form as two cruets containing the blood and sweat of Jesus. [JPC]

  John of Glastonbury. *The Chronicle of Glastonbury Abbey: An Edition, Translation and Study of John of Glastonbury's "Cronica sive Antiquitates Glastoniensis Ecclesie,"* ed. James P. Carley, trans. David Townsend. Woodbridge, Suffolk: Boydell and Brewer, 1984.

JOHNSON, BARBARA FERRY, is the American author of *Lionors* (1975), an uninspired sentimental historical romance based loosely upon Malory. It tells the story of the Earl of Sanam's daughter, who bore Arthur a child (in this instance a blind daughter). [RHT]

  Johnson, Barbara Ferry. *Lionors.* New York: Avon, 1975.

JOHNSON, RICHARD (1573–1659), recounts in the euphuistical romance *Tom a Lincolne* (1607) the adventures of the natural son of Arthur and Angellica, the Earl of London's daughter. He bestows the bell Great Tom on Lincoln in memory of Antonio, who fostered him after he was exposed in infancy. Marrying Prester John's daughter is the height of his brief good fortune. [CNS]

  Johnson, Richard. *Tom a Lincolne.* In *A Collection of Early Prose Romances,* ed. William J. Thoms. 3 vols. London: Pickering, 1858, Vol. 2, pp. 219–361.

JOHNSTON, NORMA: *see* ST. JOHN, NICOLE.

JONES, DAVID (1895–1974), partly construed the poet's task as the embodiment of "the mythus and deposits" constituting his or her own cultural matrix. Because no other tradition is "equally the common property of all the inhabitants of Britain," the myth of Arthur is central to Jones's writings. Most overtly Arthurian is "The Hunt" (1965) based on *Culhwch and Olwen,* while "The Sleeping Lord" (1967), *The Anathemata* (1952), and *In Parenthesis* (1937) are enriched by frequent allusion to Arthurian material. His sources are primarily Malory and the *Mabinogi.* [PD]

  Jones, David. "The Myth of Arthur." In *Epoch and Artist.* London: Faber and Faber, 1959, pp. 212–59.

JONES, INIGO (1573–1652), English architect best remembered for his introduction of Renaissance architectural theory into Jacobean England. Jones devised costumes and scenery for masques presented at the Stuart court during the years 1604–40. Many of the fifty-seven masques contained chivalric allusions, but only two, *Prince Henry's Barriers* (written by Ben Jonson, presented on 6 January 1610 in honor of the prince's first bearing of arms) and *Britannia Triumphans* (written by William Lawes, presented on 17 January 1638 as the King's Twelfth Night Masque), have specific Arthurian reference, with Merlin appearing as a major character. Jones's taste for the Renaissance classical aesthetic is revealed in the few surviving drawings of these works, such as the designs for *Prince Henry's Barriers* (Collection, Duke of Devonshire), which include a costume for Merlin and the setting for Act I, "The Fallen House of Chivalry." (*See also* Pageant Design [British].) [DNM]

Harris, John. "Jones, Inigo." In *Macmillan Encyclopedia of Architects*. New York: Free Press, 1982, Vol. 2, pp. 504–13.

Orgel, Stephen, and Roy Strong. *Inigo Jones: The Theatre of the Stuart Court*. 2 vols. London: Sotheby Parke Bernet, 1973.

Stong, Roy. *Festival Designs by Inigo Jones*. Catalogue, International Exhibitions Foundation, 1967–68.

JONSON, BEN: *see* ENGLISH AND AMERICAN ARTHURIAN LITERATURE (MODERN); JONES, INIGO.

JÓNSSON Í VIGUR, MAGNÚS: *see* *GABONS SAGA OK VIGOLES.*

JOSEP ABARAMATIA, LIVRO DE, a sixteenth-century copy of a lost Portuguese translation made in the late thirteenth or early fourteenth century of the first branch of the Post-Vulgate *Roman du Graal*. It survives also in fragmentary form in Castilian fragments (Salamanca, Biblioteca Universitaria 1877, and in Lope García de Salazar's *Libro de las bienandanzas e fortunas*). The Portuguese text (Lisbon, Torre do Tombo 643) is important for the reconstruction of the original French romance, since no French manuscript survives of the first part. However, some details, such as a reference to Wace, may indicate that the Portuguese version is not strictly a literal translation. [HLS]

Carter, Henry Hare, ed. *The Portuguese Book of Joseph of Arimathea*. Chapel Hill: University of North Carolina Press, 1967.

Castro, Ivo. "Sobre a Data da Introdução na Península Ibérica do Ciclo Arturiano da Post-Vulgata." *Boletim de Filologia* [Lisbon], 68 (1984), 81–98.

JOSEP ABARIMATIA, LIBRO DE, fourteenth-century fragments of a Castilian translation of the *Estoire del Saint Graal*, from the French Post-Vulgate; the narrative follows that of the Portuguese *Livro de Josep Abaramatia* but is missing the beginning and end. [NJL]

Pietsch, Karl, ed. *Spanish Grail Fragments*. Chicago: University of Chicago Press, 1924, Vol. 1, pp. 3–54.

JOSEPH D'ARIMATHIE: *see* ROBERT DE BORON.

JOSEPH OF ARIMATHEA. All four Gospels relate how Joseph, a rich man from Arimathea, obtained the body of Christ after the Crucifixion and laid it in the tomb. He is briefly sketched as a prominent Jew who had kept his discipleship a secret. In the apocryphal *Acts of Pilate* (part of a pseudo-Gospel ascribed to Nicodemus), he is said to have been imprisoned, and delivered by the risen Lord. When the Grail takes on its Christian form, and its provenance is explained in Robert de Boron's *Joseph* and the *Estoire del Saint Graal,* these hints are expanded. According to the romances, Joseph acquired the Grail and hid it in his house. When he was imprisoned, Christ appeared to him, gave him the Grail, and taught him its mysteries. It miraculously sustained him for more than forty years, till he was released by the emperor Vespasian, and set off with many companions on the adventures that brought the Grail to Britain.

Joseph is also named as the founder of Christian Glastonbury. The precise relation between his two legendary roles is open to debate. No major author explicitly combines them before Tennyson. In the formative medieval phase, they are not wholly separate, but the links remain conjectural. While the romances show awareness of Glastonbury, none incontestably brings Joseph there. The earliest known text that does is an edition of the *De Antiquitate Glastoniensis Ecclesiae* of William of Malmesbury. Produced at Glastonbury Abbey ca. 1247, this edition declares that in A.D. 63, when the apostle Philip was in Gaul, he sent twelve missionaries to Britain under Joseph's leadership. A "barbarian king" granted them land at Glastonbury as a place to live. In honor of the Virgin Mary, they built the celebrated Old Church.

However, William's original treatise, written toward 1130, says virtually nothing of this. He notes a belief that the Old Church was built by disciples of Christ, but does not commit himself to the story or give any names. The account of Joseph in the thirteenth-century recension is interpolated. It is commonly supposed that the interpolator annexed him from Grail romance, probably from the *Estoire del Saint Graal,* thus providing the community with a bogus founder who was both biblical and Arthurian and safeguarding its claim to an early beginning.

This view may be correct, but the issue is by no means as simple as it is often made out to be. As between the Grail cycle and the corpus of Glastonbury legend, the flow is not all in one direction. Robert de Boron, writing before the close of the twelfth century, knows a story of early Christians making their way to Somerset. One or two romance passages seem to show awareness of conditions at Glastonbury long before the authors' time. If these carry any weight, they must reflect abbey tradition. The abbey's date for Joseph's arrival, A.D. 63, is incompatible with the Grail version and argues another source, rather than a borrowing. John of Glastonbury's fourteenth-century *Cronica* does adapt incidents from romances, but it also includes a strange oracular text, the "Prophecy of Melkin," which mentions Joseph in terms implying—again—some other source than Grail matter.

The fundamental problem is "Why Joseph?" He is a most unlikely choice either as Grail-bearer or as missionary to Britain. Christian legend credited the island with much more impressive visitors, among them St. Paul and even St. Peter. Yet the cautious, little-traveled, and (one would think) elderly Joseph was preferred to them as hero. The usual opinion is that his role as possessor of the Grail was prior. He came to be associated with Britain because the Grail was; as its possessor, he had to be the person responsible for getting it there. The question is why he should have had the Grail, since he was certainly not present at the Last Supper. One theory is that the connection arose from ecclesiastical symbolism. At Mass, the priest laying the paten on the chalice was said by some commentators to represent Joseph closing the tomb with a stone. This would give him a link with the chalice, and hence with the Grail as prototype of all chalices. But the symbolism was not very familiar, and it may be questioned whether there is any proved instance of a motif like this creating a literal legend. Loomis's suggestion that the Grail–Joseph linkage was due to a kind of wordplay (*cors* in Old French meaning both "horn" and "body"—in this case a pagan horn of plenty and the body of Christ) failed to carry conviction.

In the absence of a clear reason for the Grail's evoking the figure of Joseph, it is reasonable to try the alternative: that he was connected with Britain first, as an early Christian who went there or as an associate of Christians who did. On this showing, he became the Grail-bearer when the Grail was given its Christian meaning and an apostolic figure had to be found who could account for its journey westward. A hagiographic tradition, strong enough to give Joseph a preferred status over St. Paul and the rest, might underlie both romance and the Glastonbury story. The simplest hypothesis, of course, is the naïve one: that the legend is (in substance) true and he did come. It cannot be disproved! But a notion about his British presence could have begun with some such thing as a misunderstood inscription. The French legend of Lazarus coming to Marseilles, with his sisters Mary and Martha, was inspired by the memorial of a bishop of the same name who died there in the fifth century. An antiquarian fancy along these lines might have taken shape in Wales, as other legends of early missions did, and drifted into England and thence to France, in common with the rest of the Celtic lore that the Arthurian literary growth drew in. It may be noteworthy that Joseph is linked with Philip in an eighth-century Georgian manuscript telling how they built a church at Lydda dedicated to Mary. If this is relevant at all, its relevance is not to the romances but to the Glastonbury story, as possibly a transplanted version.

That story underwent developments. In John's *Cronica*, Joseph was made out to have been a direct ancestor of Arthur and to have brought to Britain not the Grail but two "cruets" containing drops of the blood and sweat of Christ. Later, he became involved in the Marseilles legend, having supposedly come to Gaul with Lazarus and his companions and then journeyed on to Britain. Also, by a misreading of the dates in the abbey's account of him, his British advent was pushed back to A.D. 31. The shift was prompted by a wish to establish seniority for the Church in England, on the ground that Joseph arrived before any Christians reached France or Spain.

Other legends are almost certainly post-Reformation. At Glastonbury, Joseph is said to have driven his staff into the ground; it became the original Holy Thorn tree, blossoming at Christmas, as its descendants still do. He is also said to have been Mary's uncle and to have brought Jesus on a visit to Britain as a boy. Defenders of the literal truth of this tale, and of others about his British career, urge the possibility that he was engaged in the tin trade. [GA]

Ashe, Geoffrey. *Avalonian Quest*. London: Methuen, 1982.

Lagorio, Valerie. "The Evolving Legend of St. Joseph of Glastonbury." *Speculum*, 46 (1971), 209–31.

Loomis, Roger Sherman. *The Grail: From Celtic Myth to Christian Symbol*. Cardiff: University of Wales Press, 1963.

Scott, John. *The Early History of Glastonbury*. Woodbridge, Suffolk: Boydell and Brewer, 1981.

Treharne, R.F. *The Glastonbury Legends*. London: Cresset, 1967.

JOSEPH OF ARIMATHIE (ca. 1350), a semialliterative Middle English fragment of 709 lines (extant only in MS Vernon), is drawn from the Vulgate *Estoire del Saint Graal*. An encomium to Joseph as an apostolic evangelist, the poem accords well with the devotional works, hagiographic writings, and other homiletic romances that comprise the manuscript. The *Joseph* is a greatly abridged adaptation of its Old French source. The author concentrates on Joseph's post-Crucifixion adventures, as he, carrying the sacred container of Christ's Precious Blood, leads his family and followers westward, and en route converts the rulers and people of the city of Sarras. The English adaptation differs from its source in two major ways. First, it treats the Holy Grail not as a wonder-working talisman linked with Arthur's reign but rather as a reliquary of the Precious Blood, with which the legendary Joseph of Arimathea was associated. Second, it consistently deemphasizes the part played by Josephe, Joseph's fictional son. Although there is no reference to England or Glastonbury, apart from one fleeting reference to the "Auenturus of Bruytayne" (11. 231–32), the portrait of Joseph agrees with Glastonbury's spurious claim to him as founder of its abbey and protoevangelist of Britain. [VML]

Skeat, Walter W., ed. *Joseph of Arimathie*. London: Trübner, 1871.

Lawton, David A., ed. *Joseph of Arimathea: A Critical Edition*. New York and London: Garland, 1983.

Lagorio, Valerie M. "The *Joseph of Arimathie*: English Hagiography in Transition." *Medievalia et Humanistica*, n.s., 6 (1975), 91–101.

JOYCE, JAMES (1882–1941), includes the love story of Tristan and Isolde among the many legends and allusions in his great complex novel *Finnegans Wake*. The legend serves to transfer the incestuous longings for his own daughter, that exist in the unconscious mind of the central character, Earwicker, into a more acceptable fantasy. [RHT]

Joyce, James. *Finnegans Wake*. London: Faber and Faber, 1939.

"JOYEUSE GARDE": *see* SWINBURNE, ALGERNON CHARLES.

JOYOUS GARD (JOYEUSE GARDE), Lancelot's castle, formerly called Dolorous Gard because of a sinister enchantment. Lancelot captures it and breaks the spell. Inside, he finds a tomb with his own name on it and knows this to be his destined home and eventual resting place. Arthur and Guenevere visit the castle as his guests, and "Joyous Gard" becomes its new name. When Guenevere is brought to Carlisle for execution, Lancelot rescues her and takes her to Joyous Gard; but the tragic strife that results causes it to revert to its "dolorous" name. After Lancelot's death, his body is taken there for burial.

Joyous Gard is supposedly in northern England. The Vulgate Cycle places it near the Humber, but the English preference is to put it on the site of a known castle in Northumberland. Malory offers a choice: "Some men say it was Alnwick and some men say it was Bamburgh." The Bamburgh identification may not be wholly fanciful. The present castle beside the North Sea occupies the site of a much earlier fort. Toward the middle of the sixth century, the chieftain of the Angles who had settled here, Ida, asserted his independence by taking possession and raising a stockade. Furthermore, the place was a fort of the Britons even before Ida. Its original name, preserved with various spellings in copies of Nennius, was *Din Guayrdi*. In other words, it had a name sounding rather like "Gard." Apparently, this item of topography passed through Wales to the romancers, and was reinterpreted to give Lancelot a plausible home.

If this is so, it shows that information concerning pre–Anglo-Saxon places, effaced in England by the conquest, could survive among the Britons' descendants and be rediscovered, even repatriated. That process may explain the medieval emergence of Amesbury as an "Arthurian" town (*see* AMBROSIUS AURELIANUS) and underlie some of the associations of Glastonbury. [GA]

Morris, John. *The Age of Arthur*. New York: Scribner, 1973.

JÜNGERE TITUREL, DER: see ALBRECHT VON SCHARFENBERG.

JUVENILE FICTION IN ENGLISH. Arthurian fiction and illustration specifically intended for young readers originated in the Victorian age, when the knight regained his medieval significance as an ideal figure. The chief source was Malory's *Morte Darthur*, presented in abridgments and adaptations that modernized the language (in varying degrees) but obscured the adultery of the courtly lovers and the Catholic significance of the Grail quest. As in Caxton's preface, a didactic motivation was claimed, with emphasis on the "gentlemanly" qualities of Arthur and his knights. Sidney Lanier, whose *The Boy's King Arthur* (1880) was frequently reprinted, asserted of Launcelot's "majestic manhood" that "larger behavior is not shown us anywhere in English literature." In his adaptations, *The Story of King Arthur and His Knights* (1903), *The Story of the Champions of the Round Table* (1905), *The Story of Sir*

Launcelot and His Companions (1907), and *The Story of the Grail and the Passing of Arthur* (1910), Howard Pyle also emphasized moral values. Not only did the knights afford perfect examples of courage and humility, but Arthur himself was "the most honorable, gentle knight who ever lived in all the world."

While Malory is the chief source, adapters have also used Geoffrey of Monmouth's *Historia*, the Welsh *Mabinogion* (translated by Charlotte Guest in 1838–49), and Middle English romances, such as *Sir Gawain and the Green Knight*; for the Tristan story, the Old French metrical version is sometimes preferred. Development is straightforward, with emphasis on story rather than on setting or character. Minor characters are omitted and major characters, such as the two Elaines and the various fées, may be fused. Retellings that remain reasonably faithful to Malory while accommodating their sources include Roger Lancelyn Green's *King Arthur and His Knights of the Round Table* (1953) and Rosemary Sutcliff's fine series.

Aside from recounting traditional material, modern Arthurian fiction for juveniles has taken two directions—the historical novel and the fantasy. Historical novelists like Henry Treece in *The Eagles Have Flown* (1970) or Rosemary Sutcliff in *The Lantern Bearers* (1959) generally localize the action in that period of the Dark Ages when a historical Arthur would have lived. Relying on Gildas, Bede, Nennius, and Geoffrey of Monmouth to provide characters and events, and on such historians and archaeologists as R.G. Collingwood, John Morris, and Leslie Alcock for social history, they depict the chaotic time between the withdrawal of the Roman legions from Britain in the fifth century and the establishment of Saxon kingdoms in the sixth. Artos the Bear is essentially a battle-leader, "a ruthless and possibly half-barbaric Celt" in Treece's conception, "the shining point of the arrowhead" and "one whom men would feel that they were following into the light," in Sutcliff's.

Writers of Arthurian fantasy have two paramount preoccupations—Celtic mythology and time shift. The former provides supernatural characters (e.g., Merlin, Morgan le Fay–Morrigan, the Lady of the Lake, the "Old Ones"), magical artifacts (e.g., Excalibur, the Treasures of the Tuatha De Danaan), and, most important, an otherworld consisting of a *locus amoenus* (Avalon) or a hollow hill. The hollow-hill motif associated with the legend of Arthur's sleep until the time of his return (*see* CAVE LEGEND) appears in William Mayne's *Earthfasts* (1969) and Alan Garner's *The Weirdstone of Brisingamen* (1960). Andre Norton creates an eclectic Avalon that contains Excalibur, Merlin's ring, and Huon's silver horn in *Steel Magic* (1967) and unicorns and flying saucers in *Here Abide Monsters* (1974).

Time shift may involve transition between this world and the otherworld or between the present and the past. In *Earthfasts*, the removal of the otherworld's time mechanism—a candle in Arthur's cavern beneath Garebridge Castle, Yorkshire—brings into present time a drummer boy who had disappeared in 1742, a boggart, giants, and King Arthur with his knights. Peter Dickinson's *The Weathermonger* (1968) describes the return of the Dark Ages to England because Merlin, discovered in his cavern and kept high on morphine, "was muddled and wanted everything to be just as he was used to it." Penelope Lively uses memory, both individual and collective, to bridge present and past in *The Whispering Knights* (1971), where three modern children meet Morgan le Fay. Susan Cooper's The Dark Is Rising series presents movement in both directions, with Merriman (Merlin) as the transitional agent. The hero, Will Stanton, moves into the past to observe the building of a Roman fortress, the battle of Badon, and a Victorian Christmas party, while the Grail resurfaces in modern Cornwall and Guenevere brings Arthur's son Bran to grow up in contemporary Wales.

Common elements in Arthurian fantasy are a young protagonist assisted by siblings or friends, a quest to acquire magical artifacts, a supernatural guide, a confrontation between Good and Evil in which the child plays a crucial role, and a good deal of folklore associated with the "Old Ones." The supreme example of the genre, T.H. White's *The Sword in the Stone*, successfully combines comic fantasy, medieval social history, and moral purpose, as the young Arthur is taught the proper use of power by means of formal lessons, forest adventures, and transformations that illustrate Merlin's precept, "Education is experience and the essence of experience is self-reliance." The continuing use of the Arthurian legends in children's literature suggests that Arthur's cry "Resurgam" is as relevant now as it ever was in the past. (*See also* GERMAN ARTHURIAN LITERATURE [MODERN].) [MAW]

᠍*Children's Literature in Education.* New York and London: APS, 1970–

Thompson, Raymond H. *The Return from Avalon: A Study of the Arthurian Legend in Modern Fiction.* Westport, Conn.: Greenwood, 1985.

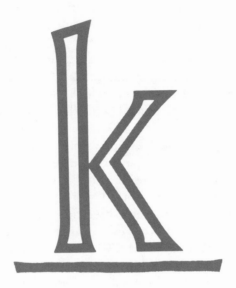

KAIRO-KŌ: A DIRGE: *see* SOSĒKI, NATSUME.

KAISER, GEORG (1878–1945), the most significant dramatist of the German Expressionist movement. However, his transitional drama *König Hahnrei* ("King Cuckold," 1910, first staged 1913)—influenced by Gottfried von Strassburg and Wagner but based primarily on Joseph Bédier—is an unsuccessful mixture of Neoromantic psychologizing and expressionistic language and setting. Mark obtains vicarious pleasure from his voyeuristic and yet repressed awareness of Tristan's and Isolde's affair, whereas the lovers' attraction for each other derives from its illicit nature. Mark eliminates anyone who threatens the stability of this perverse romantic triangle. [RWK]

Kaiser, Georg. *Werke*, ed. Walther Huder. Frankfurt: Propyläen, 1971, Vol. 1.
Batts, Michael. "Tristan and Isolde in Modern Literature." *Seminar*, 5 (1969), 79–91.
Schüler, Ernst. *Georg Kaiser*. New York: Twayne, 1971.

KANE, GIL, and JOHN JAKES, authors of *Excalibur!* (1980), a fast-moving adventure story in which Guinevere and Lancelot are lovers before her marriage to Arthur but not after, Nimue is Morgan disguised, Galahad discovers

15 *Dante Gabriel Rossetti, "The Palace of Art," from the Moxon Tennyson (1857).*
Courtesy Kenneth Spencer Research Library, University of Kansas.

> *"Or mythic Uther's deeply-wounded son*
> *In some fair space of sloping greens*
> *Lay, dozing in the vale of Avalon,*
> *And watch'd by weeping queens."*

16 Daniel Maclise, "Arthur Obtains the Sword Excalibur," from the Moxon
Tennyson (1857). Courtesy Kenneth Spencer Research Library, University of Kansas.

17 *John Hamilton Mortimer, "The Discovery of Prince Arthur's Tomb by the Inscription on the Leaden Cross." Pen and ink with watercolor after his painting (ca. 1767). Courtesy National Galleries of Scotland.*

18 *Dante Gabriel Rossetti,* Sir Tristram and La Belle Yseult Drinking the Love Potion. *Watercolor (1867). Courtesy the Trustees, Cecil Higgins Art Gallery, Bedford, England.*

that England is the Grail, and Modred poisons Arthur and fights him with Saxon troops. [MAG]

🐟 Kane, Gil, and John Jakes. *Excalibur!* New York: Dell, 1980.

KARR, PHYLLIS ANN, American author of *The Idylls of the Queen* (1982), which turns a short episode in Malory (Caxton's Book XVIII, Chapters 1–8) into a murder mystery. Narrated by Sir Kay, the novel tells of the death of Sir Patrise by poisoned apple and of Kay's attempts to discover the truth of the matter in order to clear Guenevere of suspicion. [SRR]

🐟 Karr, Phyllis Ann. *The Idylls of the Queen.* New York: Ace, 1982.

KATHARINA: see HEINE, HEINRICH.

KAY (CEI, KEU, KEI, CAYOUS), Arthur's seneschal, a ubiquitous, but never a major, character in Arthurian romance. He is neither clown, coward, nor traitor, but a scoffer, scapegoat, troublemaker, and foil who contrasts with the protagonist, such as Gawain, Lancelot, or Yvain. Chrétien de Troyes invented situations that were to become typical in later narrative. In the *Chevalier au lion*, Keu unfairly insults Calogrenant for rising at Queen Guenièvre's unexpected arrival, and in the *Chevalier de la charrete* he beguiles Arthur into granting him the honor of pursuing the Queen's kidnapper, at which task he meets immediate and humiliating defeat. Such events are mimicked by imitators, like Paien de Maisières's *La Mule sans frein* and the anonymous *L'Atre périlleux*. Because of his behavior, he is often linked with the *gab*, an Old French word whose primary meaning was "mockery." Keu himself is a *gabeor* in the Didot-*Perceval*, and in the First Continuation of the *Perceval* he is mocked by Arthur's knights.

Chrétien's characterization depicts Keu as strangely favored by Arthur, an attitude that is very likely traceable to Celtic sources. In *Culhwch and Olwen*, Cei is an exceptional hero of mythological origins. He rides the salmon and can breathe under water for nine days and nights. He is capable of transforming himself into a giant. He is shrewd but cruel, a victorious warrior and an advocate of courtly etiquette. In *The Dream of Rhonabwy*, Cei is considered the most handsome rider in Arthur's army. Elsewhere, he appears as a hardy drinker and an angry warrior. Such traits, admirable in an epic hero like Roland, were inappropriate in the polite courtly society of twelfth-century France. Thus, scholars have assumed that Chrétien was reflecting a new social attitude while at the same time representing through Arthur the old respect for Cei, which Welsh poets maintained throughout the Middle Ages.

The German adapters follow Chrétien's lead, though Hartmann von Aue underscores Keu's maliciousness and Wolfram makes him an exemplary expression of conventional courtly order. Later French imitators, especially those who merely adopted the Arthurian framework, turned Keu into a likable character (*Durmart le Gallois*) or even a bashful lover (Girart d'Amiens's *Escanor*), but in the English romances Sir Kay retains his mocking spirit (Malory's "Tale of Gareth"; *The Avowing of King Arthur, Sir Gawain, Sir Kay, and Baldwin of Britain*). In the short Dutch *Walewein ende Keye*, he slanders Gawain and is proved a scornful liar. In sum, he underwent a blending of traditions: the revered hero, the epic warrior, the wicked seneschal, and even kitchen humorist, by a fusion of his name with Old French *keu* 'cook.' [JLG]

Dean, Christopher. "Sir Kay in Medieval English Romances: An Alternative Tradition." *English Studies in Canada*, 9 (1983), 125–35.

Gallais, Pierre. "Le Sénéchal Keu et les romanciers français du XIIe et du XIIIe siècles." Diss., Poitiers, 1967.

Haupt, Jürgen. *Der Truchsess Keie im Artusroman*. Berlin: Schmidt, 1971.

Herman, H.J. "Sir Kay: A Study of the Character of the Seneschal of King Arthur's Court." Diss., Pennsylvania, 1960.

KEITH, CHESTER, described his *Queen's Knight* (1920) as "neither a mere romance of adventure nor a historical novel" but a prose epic. Keith's treatment of the familiar Lancelot–Guenevere material reflects his belief that "there is only one gift a man may not give to his dearest friend—and that is the woman he loves for if he does that he breaks the thread of fate." [MAW]

Keith, Chester. *Queen's Knight*. London: Allen and Unwin, 1920.

KELLIWIC (CELLIWIG). A Welsh Triad lists the "Three Tribal Thrones of the Island of Britain," at places where Arthur used to hold court. The northern one, it says, was at Pen Rhionydd, possibly near Stranraer in Galloway. The Welsh one was at St. David's. The Cornish one was at Kelliwic or Celliwig. This last name preserves a tradition reaching back beyond medieval fancy. Kelliwic in Cornwall is mentioned as an Arthurian residence before any recorded ideas about Caerleon or Camelot. It figures not only in the Triads but in the Welsh tale *Culhwch and Olwen*. Patriotism would surely have located Arthur in Wales if it could. Kelliwic attests a belief that he had a home—perhaps even his principal home—outside; a belief too firmly rooted to challenge.

Kelliwic means "woodland." The best candidate is probably Castle Killibury or Kelly Rounds, a pre-Roman Iron Age hill fort near Wadebridge. Post-Roman reoccupation, as at Castle Dore, might have led to its acquiring a certain importance through proximity to the trade route from sea to sea. There are other claimants, notably Callington. In no case is there any known evidence for Arthur's literal presence. Kelliwic, however identified, is simply an attempt to give local exactitude to his deep-rooted association with the West Country. At least, it has not been proved to be more.

The Triads summarize a story making it the scene of aggression by Mordred. He and his men raided it and "consumed all," and he dragged Guenevere from her chair and struck her (or worse). A reprisal by Arthur was a major step toward the catastrophe of Camlann. Here, Arthur and Mordred sound like feuding equals. The conception of Mordred as deputy ruler and traitor seems to have originated with Geoffrey of Monmouth, who combined the Welsh tradition with a separate "treachery" theme. Though he still put the catastrophe in Cornwall, he dropped Kelliwic. [GA]

Ashe, Geoffrey. *A Guidebook to Arthurian Britain*. Wellingborough: Aquarian, 1983.

Bromwich, Rachel. *Trioedd Ynys Prydein*. Cardiff: University of Wales Press, 1961.

Loomis, Roger Sherman, ed. *Arthurian Literature in the Middle Ages*. Oxford: Clarendon, 1959.

KENDON, FRANK, composed *Tristram* (1934), a generally pedestrian narrative poem in nine sections, connected by songs sung by Tristram. Opening with the journey of the lovers from Ireland, it concludes with their death in Brittany. [RHT]

Kendon, Frank. *Tristram*. London: Dent, 1934.

KENT, WILLIAM (1685–1748), English architect and designer, began his career as a painter but soon, under the patronage of Lord Burlington, turned to architecture and landscape design. As a member of the intellectual circle around Queen Caroline, wife of George II, Kent was called on to design gardens and buildings in the grounds of Richmond Palace, where in 1735 he created one of his most popular, or notorious, works—Merlin's Cave. This "cave above ground" (as it was satirized in Bolingbroke's journal *The Craftsman*) was a decorative garden pavilion, Palladian in overall design with central block and lower flanking wings, but having a Gothic entrance and thatched roofs. Inside, in Gothic niches, wax figures represented Merlin and his secretary, Queen Elizabeth and her nurse, Elizabeth of York (queen of Henry VII), and Minerva. Edmund Curll published a description of the cave in 1736, and Swift made it the subject of satirical epigrams. Nevertheless, Merlin's Cave caught the public fancy; taverns were named after it, and the owners of a coffeehouse set up a model for the entertainment of the customers. Dryden's opera *King Arthur* was revived as *Merlin or the British Enchanter*, and Covent Garden used Kent's interior design as a set for *The Royal Chace*. Capability Brown destroyed Merlin's Cave when he redesigned the gardens later in the century.

Kent's work as an illustrator is less well known, but included illustrations for Spenser's *Faerie Queene*, done in 1751. [MS]

Allen, B. Sprague. *Tides in English Taste (1619–1800)*. Cambridge, Mass.: Harvard University Press, 1937, Vol. 2, pp. 135–38.

Jourdain, Margaret. *The Work of William Kent*. London: Country Life, 1948, pp. 24, 48, 73 (ill. for *The Faerie Queene*, figs. 12 and 13).

KING ARTHUR: see BULWER-LYTTON, EDWARD GEORGE; CARR, J. COMYNS; DRYDEN, JOHN.

KING ARTHUR: AN HEROICK POEM: see BLACKMORE, SIR RICHARD.

"KING ARTHUR AND KING CORNWALL," a fragmentary ballad preserved in the Percy Folio. It bears comparison with the Old French *Pèlerinage de Charlemagne*. While engaged in a search for a Round Table that, according to the shrewish Guinevere, is infinitely superior to that which he already possesses, Arthur happens upon the castle of King Cornwall. Cornwall is a magician who exercises mastery over Arthur and his knights until they are successful in conjuring a seven-headed fiend and in procuring a magical wand, steed, horn, and sword—the instruments of Cornwall's power. [JN]

Child, Francis James, ed. *The English and Scottish Popular Ballads*. Boston: Houghton-Mifflin, 1884, Vol. 1, pp. 274–88.

KING ARTHUR OBTAINS THE SWORD EXCALIBUR FROM THE LADY OF THE LAKE: see OXFORD UNION MURALS.

KING ARTHUR'S DAUGHTER: see CHAPMAN, VERA.

"KING ARTHUR'S DEATH." Although its sources are the Stanzaic *Le Morte Arthur* and Malory, this sixteenth-century continuation of the ballad known as "The Legend of King Arthur" affords us an interesting variation on the familiar theme of Arthur's passing. After the battle against Mordred, Lukin (as opposed to Bedivere) disposes of Excalibur and returns to the spot where he had left the dying Arthur, only to discover that the King has vanished. Notwithstanding Lukin's speculation at the conclusion of the ballad, that Arthur may be on the barge seen leaving the shore, the actual whereabouts and fate of the King remain shrouded in mystery. [JN]

Hales, John W., and Frederick J. Furnivall, eds. *Bishop Percy's Folio Manuscript*. London: Trübner, 1867–68, Vol. 1, pp. 501–07.

KING ARTHUR'S SOCKS: see DELL, FLOYD.

"KING ARTHUR'S TOMB": *see* MORRIS, WILLIAM.

KING ARTHUR'S TOMB: see ROSSETTI, DANTE GABRIEL.

KING OF SWORDS, THE: see DAVEY, FRANK.

KING OF THE LORDLESS COUNTRY: see TURNER, ROY.

KING OF THE WORLD'S EDGE: see MUNN, H. WARNER.

"KING O'MEARA AND QUEEN GUINEVERE": see MARQUIS, DON.

"KING RYENCE'S CHALLENGE": see PERCY, THOMAS.

KINGDOM OF SUMMER: see BRADSHAW, GILLIAN.

KING'S DAMSEL, THE: see CHAPMAN, VERA.

KINROSS, MARTHA, author of *Tristram and Isoult* (1913). This three-act play in blank verse opens at a tournament in Camelot, continues in Tintagel (where a treacherous Mark tries to kill both lovers), and concludes with the lovers' death in Brittany. Although melodramatic, it gives greater emphasis to the woman's point of view than usual. [RHT]

&❧ Kinross, Martha. *Tristram and Isoult.* London: Macmillan, 1913.

KINSMEN OF THE GRAIL: see ROBERTS, DOROTHY JAMES.

"KNABE MIT DEM MANTEL, DER": see HERDER, JOHANN GOTTFRIED VON.

KNIGHTS OF THE TABLE SUMMONED TO THE QUEST BY A STRANGE DAMSEL, THE: see STANMORE HALL TAPESTRIES.

KÖNIG HAHNREI: see KAISER, GEORG.

KÖNIGIN VON SABA, DIE: see GOLDMARK, KARL.

KONRAD VON STOFFELN, author of *Gauriel von Muntabel*, a verse romance (4,100 lines) written in southwestern Germany probably in the later thirteenth century. The poem is preserved in two fifteenth-century manuscripts and an earlier fragment. The texts of the full manuscripts differ substantially in length. In the longer, the work is attributed to Konrad von Stoffeln, who has not been identified but may have belonged to the noble Hohenstoffeln family.

Gauriel is rejected by his wife because he vaunts her beauty. (Apparently she is a supernatural being whose marriage to him was not to be revealed.) Before leaving him, she makes him hideously ugly so that other women will not be interested in him. After six months of suffering, he sets out to find her, accompanied by a ram he has trained to fight, and soon receives a letter from her in which she promises forgiveness and restoration of his beauty if he will bring three great heroes of Arthur's court captive to her kingdom, Fluratrone. Gauriel pitches his tent at the edge of a forest within Arthur's sight. When a damsel is sent to inquire his business, he detains her and vows to hold her prisoner until a knight defeats him. This sets in motion a long series of single combats in which Gauriel defeats many knights of the Round Table and kills some, finally triumphing over Walban, Gawan, and Iwein. With these heroes, and joined by Erec (who had been away from court on an adventure), Gauriel proceeds to Fluratrone, overcomes monstrous interdictors, and is reconciled with his wife.

Two weeks later, he decides that he must spend a year at the Round Table to make up for his detention of the damsel. Arthur gives a great feast of welcome for the five worthies. One day, Gauriel, Erec, and Pliamin hear that a daughter of the Count of Asterian has been kidnapped. They track her down, Gauriel defeats the kidnapper, and all return to Arthur's court, where Gauriel's wife joins him for the final festivities.

The narrative seems remarkably weak in proportion, motivation, and integration of episodes. Borrowings from the romances of Hartmann von Aue abound (e.g., the animal companion and the year's absence, from *Iwein*); Hartmann's literary language and style are evidently the author's model. Critics have not found a theme or central idea in the romance, and some have judged it harshly. One might suspect parody or persiflage in the figure of Arthur's knight Pontifier, so grim that he never laughs except at burning churches or fatal head-wounds, and in the four-way fight between Iwein, Gauriel, the former's lion, and the latter's ram, but the tedious bulk of the narrative does not support such suspicions. [SLW]

Konrad von Stoffeln. *Gauriel von Muntabel*, ed. Ferdinand Khull. Graz: Leuschner and Lubensky, 1885.

Schultz, James A. *The Shape of the Round Table: Structures of Middle High German Romance.* Toronto: University of Toronto Press, 1983.

"KOPHTISCHES LIED": *see* GOETHE, JOHANN WOLFGANG.

KRALIK, RICHARD VON (1852–1934), a minor Catholic Neoromantic writer and editor of the Viennese religious-philosophical journal *Der Gral* (1905–37). Author of idealistic religious ballads, epics, and dramas, he reacted against the extreme aestheticism of some of his German literary contemporaries. Apart from his drama *Merlin* (1913), dealing primarily with the Niniane (here Viviane) episode, his Arthurian works are typical of the wave of *Parzival* adaptations brought on by Wagner's opera. His three-act musical drama *Der heilige Gral* ("The Holy Grail," 1912) makes use of a choir of angels as a superficial imitation of the chorus in Wagner's *Parsifal*. His poetic chronicle *Die Gralsage* ("The Legend of the Grail," 1907), on the other hand, is an attempt to compress all of the German and some French Grail traditions into one verse epic. [RWK]

ꝃ Kralik, Richard von. *Die Gralsage.* Ravensburg: Alber, 1907.

———. *Der heilige Gral.* Trier: Petrus, 1912.

———. *Gral und Romantik,* ed. Moriz Enzinger. Graz and Vienna: Stiasny, 1963.

Hermand, Jost. "Gralsmotive um die Jahrhundertwende." *Deutsche Vierteljahresschrift,* 36 (1962), 521–43.

KUBIE, WILHELM (pseudonym of Willy Ortmann; 1890–1948), an Austrian writer who based several novels on historical and literary themes. In *Mummenschanz auf Tintagel* (1937, 1946), he relates Arthurian subject matter from the standpoint of the knight Bedivir, whose soul dwells in various beings and objects over the millennia. Bedivir tells the story of Tristan and Isolde from his point of view as a friend of Mark. The poetic material is treated here in a farcical manner (*Mummenschanz* = "masquerade"). The ideals of the Round Table do not coincide with reality, and the majority of the "Arthurian" knights take the part of Modred. The Arthurian realm goes to ruin in a kind of fraternal war. [SSch/WCM]

ꝃ Kubie, Wilhelm. *Mummenschanz auf Tintagel.* Cologne and Leipzig: Schaffrath, 1937; rev. ed. Linz and Vienna: Österreichischer Verlag für Belletristik und Wissenschaft, 1946.

KUNCEWICZ, MARIA, author of the 1974 novel *Tristan,* an intricate and often self-conscious transposition of the Tristan story into the period following World War II, in Cornwall and later on Long Island. The novel (originally published in Polish, 1967) exploits many of the specific events of the legend: the potion, Mark's overhearing the lovers' conversation, betrayal by bloodstains on the bed, marriage to a woman resembling the object of one's love, and so on. The Tristan legend provides not only a parallel to, but also (by the characters' fascination with it) an influence on, the modern story. [NJL]

ꝃ Kuncewicz, Maria. *Tristan: A Novel.* New York: Braziller, 1974.

KURZE MANTEL

KURZE MANTEL, DER: *see* NAUBERT, BENEDIKTE.

KYOT: *see* WOLFRAM VON ESCHENBACH.

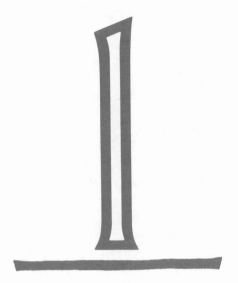

LABYRNTHO AFFECTUOSO: _see_ SILVA, ANTÓNIO DA.

LADY OF KING ARTHUR'S COURT, A: _see_ STERLING, SARA.

"LADY OF SHALOTT, THE": _see_ TENNYSON, ALFRED LORD.

LADY OF SHALOTT, THE: _see_ HUGHES, ARTHUR.

LADY OF THE LAKE, a name designating several different women, although the distinction among them is frequently blurred. In addition to being known as the Lady of the Lake, or the Dame du Lac, she most often bears such names as Viviane, Éviène, or Niviene; elsewhere, she is Nimuë or (in Wordsworth) Nina. Readers of Malory will recognize her as the being who gives Excalibur to Arthur and later receives it back from him, and some works also identify her as the lady responsible for Lancelot's upbringing. In Malory, the Vulgate Cycle, and various other settings of the legend (e.g., Apollinaire), she enchants Merlin with spells he had taught her. Some texts in fact tell us that she not only enchants him but also kills him. In the *Vita di Merlino*, for example, the Lady of the Lake serves as a scribe for Merlin, recording his prophecies, after which she tricks him into lying in a tomb; then, by a charm she had learned from him, she closes the lid and seals the wizard's doom (although the author assures us that Merlin's spirit will not die). [NJL]

LAFORGUE, JULES: *see* SYMBOLIST ARTHURIAN MATERIAL.

LAIS DE BRETANHA, a set of five anonymous Galician-Portuguese troubadour lyrics with prose headings that link the compositions to the Prose *Tristan* and the Prose *Lancelot* of the Vulgate Cycle. The texts probably date from the late thirteenth or early fourteenth century, the period when the French cyclical romances were translated into Galician-Portuguese. However, the poems, while recalling the use of lais in some French prose-romance manuscripts, show greater affinity with the themes and structure of medieval French and Galician-Portuguese lyric traditions than with Arthurian narrative as such. The lais are preserved in independent manuscript copies, at the beginning of the *Cancioneiro da Biblioteca Nacional* of Lisbon and in Vatican Lat. 7182. [HLS]

Pellegrini, Silvio, ed. "I lais portoghesi del codice vaticano lat. 7182." *Archivum Romanicum,* 12 (1928), 303–17.

D'Heur, Jean-Marie. "Les Lais arthuriens anonymes français et leur tradition galaïco-portugais." *Bibliographical Bulletin of the International Arthurian Society,* 24 (1972), 210.

Sh[arrer], H[arvey]. "BRETÃO, Ciclo." In *Grande Dicionário da Literatura Portuguesa e de Teoria Literária.* Lisbon: Iniciativas Editoriais, n.d., Vol. II, p. 148.

LANÇAROTE DE LAGO, a largely unedited Spanish translation of the *Lancelot* branch of the Vulgate Cycle, surviving in a sixteenth-century manuscript (Madrid, Biblioteca Nacional 9611). From linguistic evidence, the text would seem to have been rendered first into a northwestern Hispanic language, possibly Galician-Portuguese, in the late thirteenth or early fourteenth century. The surviving sections, which correspond in part to an unedited long version of the French romance, narrate Lancelot's adventures following his departure from Arthur's court after having taken a seat at the Round Table and end with a search for Tristan, the latter involving a short series of adventures extraneous to the Prose *Lancelot* but linking the Spanish version to a lost Tristan romance. Two traditional Spanish ballads are thought to have derived from the Prose *Lancelot* but not the Spanish text as it survives: "Nunca fuera caballero de damas tan bien servido" and "Tres hijuelos había el rey." The first, quoted by Cervantes in *Don Quixote*, tells of how Lancelot served Guenevere by decapitating a haughty gallant. The second reveals much affinity with the story of the "Cerf au pied blanc" as preserved in the *Lai de Tyolet* and the Dutch *Roman van Lancelot.* [HLS]

Bohigas Balaguer, Pedro. "El *Lanzarote* español del manuscrito 9611 de la Biblioteca Nacional." *Revista de Filología Española*, 10 (1924), 282–97.

Sharrer, Harvey L. *A Critical Bibliography of Hispanic Arthurian Material, I: Texts: The Prose Romance Cycles.* London: Grant and Cutler, 1977, item Aa3.

LANÇAROTE DO LAGO: *see* SILVA, ANTÓNIO DA.

"LANCE": *see* NABOKOV, VLADIMIR.

LANCELOET EN HET HERT MET DE WITTE VOET

LANCELOET EN HET HERT MET DE WITTE VOET ("Lancelot and the Deer with the White Foot"), a Middle Dutch verse romance (ca. 850 lines) that has been transmitted exclusively in the *Lancelot-Compilatie*. Central to the story is the task set by a damsel to bring her the "white foot" of a deer that is guarded by lions. Lanceloet succeeds in his attempt but is cheated by a knight who leaves him severely wounded and who claims the damsel with the aid of the white foot. Walewein saves Lanceloet and defeats the impostor. The Middle Dutch text is related to the French *Lai de Tyolet* but is not based on it. The version transmitted in the *Lancelot-Compilatie* is greatly abridged. The original Middle Dutch text may date from the first half of the thirteenth century. [BB]

Draak, Maartje, ed. *Lanceloet en het hert met de witte voet.* Culemborg: Tjeenk Willink, 1979.

LANCELOT (LANCELOT DU LAC, LAUNCELOT, LANZELET, LANCILOTTO, LANSELOET)

LANCELOT (LANCELOT DU LAC, LAUNCELOT, LANZELET, LANCILOTTO, LANSELOET), the favored lover of Queen Guenevere. Lancelot is the central hero of three medieval romances—Chrétien de Troyes's *Le Chevalier de la charrete* (third quarter of the twelfth century), Ulrich von Zatzikhoven's *Lanzelet* (ca. 1194–1204), and the Prose *Lancelot* (ca.1225)—and plays a prominent role in several others, most notably in Malory's *Le Morte Darthur.* Adaptations of the Vulgate *Lancelot* spread his fame into Italy, Portugal, Scotland, and the Netherlands.

In Chrétien's *Chevalier de la charrete*, Guenevere has been carried off to the land of Gorre by Meleagant, the wicked son of the good king Bademagu. After Sir Kay competes unsuccessfully for her and is captured and led away into Gorre with the Queen, both Gawain and Lancelot set off to rescue her. On his way, Lancelot encounters a dwarf driving a cart who agrees to aid him in his search if he will climb into the cart. Lancelot hesitates momentarily, for to mount into a cart was considered a sign of shame, but after two steps his love for the Queen overcomes his pride as a knight. Gawain soon happens upon them but refuses to join Lancelot in the cart. After overcoming several temptations designed to delay him in his quest or divert him altogether, Lancelot crosses over the treacherous Sword Bridge into Gorre, while Gawain chooses the easier, yet still dangerous Underwater Bridge. When he finally encounters the Queen, Lancelot is rebuffed without explanation; only much later does he learn that she is angry because of the two steps in which he let his knightly pride dominate his love for her. Guenevere eventually relents, and Lancelot spends a night of pleasure with her. He frees the captives but is himself captured by Meleagant's men. Finally released from his tower prison, Lancelot returns to Arthur's court to slay Meleagant.

Chrétien gives no background information about his hero, other than that his name is Lancelot del Lac and that he had once been given a magic ring by a fairy who had raised him as a child (ll. 2335–50). Lancelot's cognomen may have led to his association with Niniane, the Dame du Lac, in the thirteenth-century Prose *Lancelot*, and Ulrich shows some familiarity with this motif when he has the young Lancelot carried off by a mermaid and raised in a kingdom of women until the age of fifteen. In Ulrich's *Lanzelet*, the young hero, ignorant of his name and royal birth, sets out to win a place at Arthur's court. Three times he approaches castles and slays the lord in combat, and three times he inspires the lord's daughter or niece with burning passion. The first two, after a brief dalliance, economically disappear from the story; but the third, Yblis, the daughter of Iweret of Dodone, remains his wife. By defeating Iweret in an adventure reminiscent of Yvain's at the fountain, Lanzelet avenges his foster mother for an unspecified wrong and is rewarded by being told his name and his royal kinship. He next hears that Valerin of the Tangled Wood has claimed Guenevere (much like Meleagant in Chrétien's *Charrete*) and rides rapidly to Arthur's court to defend the Queen in combat. He defeats Valerin but does not kill him, and soon Valerin proves false to his word and abducts the Queen. Lanzelet participates with the other knights of the Round Table in her rescue, which is effected with the aid of a magician. Ulrich's poem is a hodgepodge of marvelous adventures; it shares with Chrétien's the abduction theme and Lancelot's championing of the Queen, but it has no cart, no Sword Bridge, and no hint of an adulterous affair between Lancelot and Guenevere. Furthermore, there are countless adventures that have no parallels in the French poem.

Chrétien tells us at the beginning of his romance that his patroness, Marie de Champagne, had given him the material for this story, and there is no reason to doubt him on this point. Neither the character of Lancelot nor his affair with Guenevere predates *Le Chevalier de la charrete*. Where Marie got the theme, however, is much more problematic. The story of the abduction of the Queen may well be related to a Celtic abduction motif, the *aithed*, a version of which is depicted on the tympanum at Modena. Similarities between the *Charrete*, the *Lanzelet*, and the Prose *Lancelot* suggest a common source that, like the abduction motif, might ultimately have been Celtic. Ulrich's immediate source, however, was a poem written in the Anglo-Norman dialect of Old French. Ulrich clearly did not know the central theme of Chrétien's romance, the passion of Lancelot and Guenevere, so he could not have meant Chrétien's poem in his repeated references to his source. It seems likely that Marie heard a narrative much like the one later imitated by Ulrich and suggested to Chrétien that it be modified to celebrate the newly popular concept of courtly love by making Lancelot the Queen's lover.

In the thirteenth-century Prose *Lancelot*, the hero continues as the champion and lover of the Queen. As in Ulrich's poem, he is carried off after the death of his father, King Ban of Benoyc, to be raised by the Lady of the Lake, who is here identified as the fairy Niniane. He is soon joined by his orphaned cousins, Lionel and Bohort, and at the age of eighteen is taken by the fairy to be knighted at Arthur's court. There she tells him that he is of royal parentage and bestows upon him the magic ring first mentioned by Chrétien; but she does not tell him his name. At court, he meets and is enraptured by Guenevere, who bestows upon him his sword of knighthood. This bestowal symbolically divides his loyalty between Arthur and the Queen, and much of the action of the romance, as well as the eventual destruction of Arthur's kingdom in the *Mort Artu*, can be traced back to this double allegiance.

After a series of adventures, the young knight, still ignorant of his name, reaches the castle of Dolorous Gard, which he captures with help from the Lady of the Lake. There in a magic cemetery, he finds his name inscribed inside the lid of the tomb in which he will one day lie. Hundreds of pages of adventures ensue, during which Lancelot is continually referred to as "the best knight in the world." But after his adultery with the Queen, his perfection begins to tarnish, and he is shocked to learn that because of his sins he will not himself be able to fulfill the quest of the Holy Grail. This adventure will be achieved by Lancelot's son, Galahad, whom he begets on the daughter of the Grail King Pelles, with the connivance of Pelles himself, who provides a potion that makes him believe he is lying with Guenevere.

In the *Queste del Saint Graal*, a sequel to the Prose *Lancelot*, Lancelot comes to recognize his guilt and does penance for it. He is rewarded by being able to reach the Grail castle and participate in its mysteries but is denied the supreme vision, which is reserved for his son Galahad and for his companions Perceval and Bohort.

In the *Mort Artu*, the last of the Old French Vulgate romances, Lancelot relapses and recommences his affair with Guenevere. This ultimately leads to a break with Arthur and to the war that destroys his kingdom.

Much of the material from the Vulgate Cycle was reworked by Malory in the fifteenth century for his *Le Morte Darthur*, and again Lancelot is constantly at the center of the action. Thus, from its first appearance in Chrétien's *Charrete* until Malory's day, Lancelot's affair with Guenevere remained at the center of the Arthurian legend, with the curious exception of Ulrich's *Lanzelet*. In terms of secular chivalry, Lancelot was without peer, but when knighthood became impregnated with Christian ideals in the thirteenth century his adulterous relationship led not only to his own downfall, but also to the destruction of Arthur's kingdom. In postmedieval literature, Lancelot is often presented as a somber and intense figure, plagued by guilt at the betrayal of the man who is both his king and his friend, yet unable to escape his passion for Guenevere. [WWK]

❧ Chrétien de Troyes. *Lancelot, or The Knight of the Cart* (*Le Chevalier de la charrete*), ed. and trans. William W. Kibler. New York and London: Garland, 1981.

Malory, Sir Thomas. *Works*, ed. Eugène Vinaver; 2nd ed. Oxford: Oxford University Press, 1977.

Ulrich von Zatzikhoven. *Lanzelet*, trans. K.G.T. Webster, rev. Roger Sherman Loomis. New York: Columbia University Press, 1951.

Weston, Jessie L. *The Legend of Sir Lancelot du Lac*. London: Nutt, 1901.

"LANCELOT": *see* SWINBURNE, ALGERNON CHARLES.

LANCELOT: see CHRÉTIEN DE TROYES; PERCY, WALKER; ROBINSON, EDWIN ARLINGTON; VANSITTART, PETER; VULGATE CYCLE.

LANCELOT, ROMAN VAN. The Vulgate *Lancelot* was not only adapted into Middle Dutch (*Lantsloot vander Haghedochte*) but also translated at least twice. In fragments from about 1350 preserved in Rotterdam (Gemeentebibliotheek, Hs. 96 A 7), a faithful prose translation has been transmitted. A verse translation has also been preserved, extant in the *Lancelot-Compilatie* and in fragments found in Brussels (Royal Library II, 115-3) and also in The Hague (Royal Library 75 H 58). The Brussels fragment contains a text that belonged to the lost first part of the *Lancelot-Compilatie*. A third Middle Dutch translation may have existed. This conjecture is based on a Ripuarian copy of before 1476, which according to the colophon is based on a Middle Dutch model. This codex is preserved in Cologne (Bibliothek des historischen Archiv, Codex W. f.^{0} 46 Blankenheim). [BB]

  Draak, Maartje. *De Middelnederlandse vertalingen van de Proza-Lancelot*. Amsterdam: Koninklijke Akademie der Wetenschappen, 1954.

"LANCELOT AND GUINEVERE": *see* MARQUIS, DON.

LANCELOT AND THE LADIES: see BRADLEY, WILL.

LANCELOT DO LAC, the earliest Old French prose version of the Lancelot story, probably composed between 1215 and 1220. This version, known variously as Sommer III (for its first editor), the *Marche de Gaule* (for its opening words), or the "Galehaut section," was soon incorporated into the vast Vulgate Cycle. Thirteen manuscripts conclude this section, after Lancelot and Galehaut's journey to Sorelois and the False Guinevere episode, with the death of Galehaut. In most of the manuscripts, however, the Sorelois and False Guinevere episodes contain allusions and scenes that prepare the way for Galahad's quest for the Grail, and the death of Galehaut is surrounded by episodes leading up to the prose reworking of Chrétien de Troyes's *Le Chevalier de la charrete*. The *Lancelot do Lac* presents the text of the best of the noncyclic manuscripts (Paris, B.N. fr. 768). In this version, there is no preparation for the Vulgate *Queste* or for the condemnation of illicit love in the *Mort Artu* section; everything culminates in the death of Galehaut. It is likely that the shorter noncyclic version was composed first, then incorporated into the Vulgate Cycle, rather than the longer version having been shortened and disentangled from its links to the rest of the cycle. [WWK]

Kennedy, Elspeth, ed. *Lancelot do Lac: The Non-Cyclic Old French Prose Romance*. 2 vols. Oxford: Clarendon, 1980.

LANCELOT DU LAC: *see* BRESSON, ROBERT.

LANCELOT IN THE QUEEN'S CHAMBER: *see* OXFORD UNION MURALS; ROSSETTI, DANTE GABRIEL.

LANCELOT, MY BROTHER: *see* ROBERTS, DOROTHY JAMES.

LANCELOT OF THE LAIK, a late fifteenth-century Middle Scots adaptation of the story of Galehot's war against Arthur in the first major division of the French Vulgate *Lancelot*. It is an incomplete fragment of 3,484 lines, written in Chaucerian five-stress couplets by an unknown author and surviving in a single manuscript (Cambridge University Library Kk. 1.5). Although the author generally follows his French source, making only minor alterations in details and sequence of events, he makes two major changes. First, he adds an introduction (ll. 1–333), indebted to the conventions of courtly literature, in which a lovesick narrator explains that he will omit Lancelot's early adventures and tell instead of the wars between Arthur and "Galiot," of Lancelot's defense of Arthur and role in establishing peace, and of Venus's rewarding Lancelot by enabling him to win his lady's love. Although the announced subject is "love ore armys," the text ends before the end of the war between Arthur and Galiot and before love becomes important to the story. The introduction, however, enables one to see the author's original plan for the romance. Second, the author expands considerably the section of the Vulgate *Lancelot* in which a wise man rebukes Arthur for his weakness and ineptness and tells him how to be a good and just ruler (ll. 1307–2128). Although scholars have not found much literary merit in *Lancelot of the Laik*, they have been interested in this political section of the romance because its negative portrait of Arthur has affinities with portraits of Arthur in some other Scottish works (*see* SCOTTISH ARTHURIAN CHRONICLES) and because changes from the source suggest that the political advice was intended as an admonition to James III of

Scotland. Because much of the advice is general and similar to what can be found in other works of *speculum regis* literature, there is some doubt about its applicability to James; but many scholars have felt that this work, like Blind Harry's *Wallace*, was intended for him and that the political passage was the *raison d'être* for the romance. [EDK]

෨ Skeat, Walter W., ed. *Lancelot of the Laik.* London: Trübner, 1865.

Gray, Margaret M., ed. *Lancelot of the Laik.* Edinburgh: Blackwood, 1912.

Alexander, Flora. "Late Medieval Scottish Attitudes to the Figure of King Arthur: A Reassessment." *Anglia*, 93 (1975), 17–34.

Göller, K.H. *König Arthur in der englischen Literatur des späten Mittelalters.* Göttingen: Vandenhoeck and Ruprecht, 1963, pp. 137–42.

Lyall, R.J. "Politics and Poetry in Fifteenth and Sixteenth Century Scotland." *Scottish Literary Journal*, 3 (1976), 5–29.

Vogel, Bertram. "Secular Politics and the Date of *Lancelot of the Laik.*" *Studies in Philology*, 40 (1943), 1–13.

LANCELOT UND GINEVRA: see SCHIRMER-IMHOFF, RUTH.

LANCELOT-COMPILATIE. In the Royal Library at the Hague, under the signature Hs. 129 A 10, a codex is preserved from the beginning of the fourteenth century that is unique in two respects. First, the manuscript contains no fewer than ten Middle Dutch Arthurian romances (and for that reason has been called the "flagship of the Middle Dutch Arthurian fleet"). Second, the manuscript derives its unique status from the traces of use it contains. Decades after the codex was produced, someone, usually referred to as the corrector, furnished the text with comments. He corrected copyists' mistakes and tried to purge the text of Flemish dialectal peculiarities. Apart from this, he introduced changes to make the story more comprehensible to a listening audience and provided the lines of verse with directions for reading (signs in the margin) to aid recitation.

The nucleus of the *Lancelot-Compilatie*, as the collection of texts is called, is a verse translation of the Old French Prose *Lancelot*, the *Queste del Saint Graal*, and the *Mort Artu*. The translation of this trilogy is so large that it was too cumbersome for a single codex, and the text has been divided into two bindings. However, the first part of the *Lancelot-Compilatie* has been lost. The part that has been preserved (Hs. 129 A 10) begins two-thirds of the way into the translation of the Prose *Lancelot*.

In between the translations of the parts of the French cycle, seven Arthurian romances have been interpolated. Two romances were inserted before the translation of the *Queste del Saint Graal*: *Perchevael* and *Moriaen*. Another five romances were inserted between the second and third parts of the trilogy: *De Wrake van Ragisel, Van den Riddere metter mouwen, Walewein ende Keye, Lanceloet en het hert met de witte voet*, and *Torec*.

In the translation of the *Mort Artu*, one section has been replaced by a fragment of Jacob van Maerlant's *Spiegel Historiael*. The latter is an adaptation of the *Speculum Historiale* of Vincent of Beauvais, on which Maerlant was working in the years 1283–88.

On the final page of the codex, there is a notice that records Lodewijk van Velthem as the owner. In later times, the manuscript may have been part of the library of John IV, Count of Nassau (1410–1475). It certainly belonged to Frederik Hendrik (1584–1647) and to William IV (1711–1751). [BB]

Jonckbloet, W.J.A., ed. *Roman van Lancelot (XIIIe eeuw)*. 2 vols. The Hague, 1846–49.

Gerritsen, W.P., and Frits P. van Oostrom. "Les Adaptateurs néerlandais du 'Lancelot (-Graal)' aux prises avec le procédé narratif des romans arthuriens en prose." In *Mélanges de langue et littérature françaises du Moyen Âge et de la Renaissance offerts à Charles Foulon*. Rennes: Université de Haute Bretagne, 1980, Vol. 2, pp. 105–14.

LANCELOT'S VISION OF THE SANGRAEL: see OXFORD UNION MURALS; ROSSETTI, DANTE GABRIEL.

LANCILLOTTO DEL LAGO, an Italian translation (published in 1558–59) of the French *Lancelot du Lac* printed in 1533. It presents versions of the *Lancelot* proper, the *Queste*, and the *Mort Artu*. [NJL]

Gardner, Edmund G. *The Arthurian Legend in Italian Literature*. London: Dent, 1930, p. 307.

"LANETHEN MANTEL," a fifteenth-century German *Meisterlied* ultimately deriving from *Le Mantel mautaillié*, presumably via the thirteenth-century Middle High German metrical version *Der Mantel*. In the ballad, the impetus for the mantle chastity test is vengeance: Laneth, the bearer of the garment and Arthur's niece, has been falsely accused of illicit intimacies by Guinevere. A dwarf counsels her as to how she can avenge the insult and gives her the mantle for that purpose. All the ladies but one—a young woman married to an old man—fail the mantle test. Guinevere curses the Devil for her failure, and King Arthur becomes furious with his niece for thus embarrassing Guinevere. Laneth admits that the deed was motivated by hurt and anger and that she was determined to clear her good name. [MEK]

Bruns, Paul Jakob. "Zwei Erzählungen im Meistergesang." In *Beiträge zur kritischen Bearbeitung unbenutzter alter Handschriften, Drucke und Urkunden*. Braunschweig: Reichard, 1802, pp. 143–47.

LANGLAIS, XAVIER DE (1906–1975), author of *Le Roman du Roi Arthur*, a modern retelling of the Arthurian story, with the addition of some details from the *Mabinogi* and from a Breton story of Merlin. Langlais invented certain

details and episodes, in an attempt, he says, to restore the Arthurian story to its presumed original unity. He also composed a Breton version of the same work and a Breton *Tristan hag Izold*, published in 1958. [NJL]

&. Langlais, Xavier de. *Le Roman du Roi Arthur.* 15th ed. 5 vols. Paris: Edition d'Art H. Piazza, 1965.

LANGTOFT, PETER: *see* PIERRE DE LANGTOFT.

LANIER, SIDNEY: *see* BOOK ILLUSTRATION (AMERICAN); JUVENILE FICTION IN ENGLISH.

LANTERN BEARERS, THE: *see* SUTCLIFF, ROSEMARY.

LANTSLOOT VANDER HAGHEDOCHTE ("Lancelot of the Cave"), a Middle Dutch verse adaptation of the Prose *Lancelot* that originally must have comprised over 100,000 lines. However, the text, dating from the second half of the thirteenth century, has been transmitted incomplete. Thirty-five fragments from one codex of about 1350 have been preserved. The fragments together comprise some 6,070 lines.

Lantsloot vander Haghedochte occupies a unique place among the medieval translations and adaptations of the Prose *Lancelot*, because of its freedom: the poet closely follows the main outline of the story, but within this he often goes his own way. The adaptation is characterized by three tendencies. The poet continually tries to motivate the story and to make it imaginable. Apart from this, he deviates from the "realism" of the Prose *Lancelot* by using vague spatial indications, by blurring time, and by getting rid of "historical" elements. Moreover, he tries to stylize the portraits of his main characters as much as possible according to the courtly ideal (removing familiar forms of address, idealizing the knightly combat, etc.).

It appears from these tendencies that the Middle Dutch adapter was somebody with conservative ideas. He partially reversed the modernism of the Prose *Lancelot* and tried to find links again with Arthurian romance in the style of Chrétien de Troyes. [BB]

&. Van Oostrom, Frits P. *Lantsloot vander Haghedochte: Onderzoekingen over een Middelnederlandse bewerking van de "Lancelot en prose."* Amsterdam and New York: Koninklijke Nederlandse Akademie der Wetenschappen, 1981.

LANVAL: *see* MARIE DE FRANCE; STUCKEN, EDUARD.

LANZELET: *see* ULRICH VON ZATZIKHOVEN.

LANZELOT: see STUCKEN, EDUARD.

LAPRADE, VICTOR DE: *see* SECOND EMPIRE.

"LAST DEFENDER OF CAMELOT, THE": *see* ZELAZNY, ROGER.

LAST ENCHANTMENT, THE: see STEWART, MARY.

LAST RAINBOW, THE: see GODWIN, PARKE.

"LAST TOURNAMENT, THE": *see* TENNYSON, ALFRED LORD.

LAUBENTHAL, SANDERS ANNE, author of *Excalibur,* a skillful and dramatic blending of the modern and the old. Modern characters fulfill Arthurian quests (most specifically for the Grail) as they search for Excalibur, brought to the New World by Prince Medoc and now hidden in Mobile, Alabama. They are opposed by Morgan le Fay and Morgause. [RCS]
꙳ Laubenthal, Sanders Anne. *Excalibur.* New York: Ballantine, 1973.

LAUNCELOT: A ROMANCE OF THE COURT OF KING ARTHUR: see HAMILTON, LORD ERNEST.

LAUNCELOT AND GUENEVERE: A POEM IN DRAMAS: see HOVEY, RICHARD.

LAUNCELOT DU LAKE: see COUTTS, FRANCIS.

LAURENT DE PREMIERFAIT: *see* LYDGATE, JOHN.

LAURIN, ROMAN DE: see SEPT SAGES DE ROME, LES.

LAWES, WILLIAM: *see* JONES, INIGO.

LAYAMON, author of the *Brut*, an adaptation of Wace's French *Roman de Brut* into English alliterative verse (32,241 half-lines). One of the major works of the early Middle English period, it marks the first occurrence of the Arthurian story in English. The author, a priest at Arley Regis in Worcestershire, wrote this chronicle covering the period from Brutus to Cadwalader (A.D. 689) sometime between 1189 and the early thirteenth century. The chronicle is dated on the basis of a reference in the prologue to Eleanor, "who was Henry [II]'s queen"; it is thus assumed that it was written after the death of Henry II in 1189 and possibly after the death of Queen Eleanor in 1204. Although Layamon mentions in his prologue two sources in addition to Wace (Bede and a book he associates with "St. Albin" and Augustine of Canterbury), his chronicle is based primarily upon Wace. He used Bede's *Historia Ecclesiastica Gentis Anglorum* for at least one episode. The third source remains a mystery. Some assume that it was Alfred's translation of Bede; others, a book Layamon had seen that had contained selections by Augustine and Albin of Canterbury (or even Alcuin of York); others, that the book never existed, that Layamon, displaying what Stanley has called "doubtful erudition," thought Albin, Abbot of St. Augustine's, Canterbury (708–732), or Alcuin of York (731–804), and Augustine of Canterbury (597) were contemporaries and like many other medieval writers created what he thought sounded like a plausible source.

The chronicle survives in two manuscripts, B.L. Cotton Caligula A. ix and B.L. Cotton Otho C. xiii, both written between 1250 and 1350. The Caligula manuscript appears to be closer to Layamon's text, with language more archaic than that of other West Midland texts of the second half of the thirteenth century. Although some of the apparent archaisms may represent dialectal peculiarities of Worcestershire in the later thirteenth century, this manuscript indicates that Layamon, while adapting a French source, generally avoided French words, preferring English words and poetic compounds, some of which go back to the Old English period, some of which appear to be coinages designed to give his diction what Stanley calls "antique colouring." The scribe of the Otho text apparently attempted to modernize Layamon by eliminating many of the archaisms and replacing many of Layamon's English words with ones derived from French. Writing in an alliterative style and using epic formulas and a predominantly English vocabulary, Layamon was imitating native meters for an English audience at a time when most nonreligious writing was being done in Anglo-Norman or Latin. But although he was writing alliterative verse and at times manages to reproduce the Anglo-Saxon type of half-line, he also uses some rhyme and assonance, his alliteration is irregularly placed and sometimes absent, and he appears to have made little effort to produce consistently the formulas, vocabulary, and rhythm of the alliterative verse of the Old English period. In fact, the later alliterative poetry of the fourteenth century, found in works like *Sir Gawain and the Green Knight* and the Alliterative *Morte Arthure*, seems in some ways closer to classical Anglo-Saxon verse (in, for example, the absence of rhyme and assonance in the alliterative line). Layamon's lines are sometimes said to be derived from

Anglo-Saxon popular poetry that is represented by some of the poems in the *Anglo-Saxon Chronicle* and that may have developed from oral poetry; they are sometimes said to have affinities with the prose of Aelfric. In any event, he was trying to write in what was primarily a pre-Conquest style.

Layamon follows the main events of Wace's account of Arthur's rise to power and conquest of Europe, but his chronicle is more than a translation. While one thinks of Wace's adaptation of Geoffrey of Monmouth as a move toward courtly romance, one thinks of Layamon's adaptation of Wace as a move back to a more heroic age. He cuts out much in Wace that was typical of courtly literature (interest in love and chivalry, for example) and adds details that depict a much rougher, more brutal society. In Wace, for example, Arthur and his men besiege Winchester; in Layamon, they burn the town and slay both old and young. Details—such as Arthur's order, after a knight started a brawl at court, to cut off the noses of the women related to him; Arthur's dream of cutting Guenevere to pieces; and Gawain's threat, after hearing that Guenevere had sided with Modred, to have her torn apart by horses—suggest that ideals of chivalry had not had much effect upon Layamon. He expands Wace by adding concrete details that make the narrative more vivid (Arthur turns red and white when he learns that he has become king; Arthur receives fifteen wounds at his last battle, into the smallest of which one could thrust two gloves), by adding many similes that allude to nature, particularly animals, by developing descriptions of battle more fully, and by giving the characters more direct speech and thus making his episodes more dramatic (the compassion Uther Pendragon shows to the poor men asking for alms outside his castle; Arthur's nightmare that foreshadows the destruction of his kingdom just before he receives the news of Modred's rebellion). Some details that Layamon adds to his account, such as the name of Modred's son and the accounts of the elves blessing Arthur at his birth or of Arthur's being taken to Argente (Morgan) in Avalon, may come from oral Celtic traditions about Arthur.

In his attempt to write English alliterative verse and his preference for words of English rather than French origin, Layamon was undoubtedly writing for an English audience that had some nostalgia for pre-Conquest England; but his apparent sympathy for the British and his lack of sympathy for the invading Saxons, the ancestors of the English, have puzzled some modern readers. Like later English chroniclers, he may simply have felt enthusiasm for Arthur as a great hero who lived in what was to become England. He would also have seen a parallel between the Norman conquest of the English and the English conquest of the British and may have been presenting a sympathetic portrait of a people forced to defend their homeland against invaders, a situation that twelfth-century Englishmen could be expected to understand. Another possibility, which Stanley has pointed out, is that by accepting the anti-English attitude of his Anglo-Norman source Layamon was presenting to the English the moral cause for the Norman Conquest. Layamon would have known, at least through Bede, Gildas's warning that God had punished the British for their sins; and late in the Anglo-Saxon period Wulfstan, in his *Sermo Lupi ad*

Anglos, had warned the English that God would similarly punish them. Layamon, in incorporating the anti-English attitude from his source, may have been thinking of the warning that God would punish the English just as he had punished the British, and the priest of Arley Regis may thus have been trying to present in his chronicle a moral explanation for the Norman Conquest. [EDK]

🔊 Layamon. *Brut*, ed. and trans. Frederic Madden. 3 vols. London: Society of Antiquaries, 1847.
——— . *Brut*, ed. G.L. Brook and R.F. Leslie. London: Oxford University Press, 1963, 1978.
Wace and Layamon. *Arthurian Chronicles*, trans. Eugene Mason. London: Dent, 1912.
Everett, Dorothy. "Layamon and the Earliest Middle English Alliterative Verse." In *Essays on Middle English Literature*, ed. Patricia Kean. Oxford: Clarendon, 1955, pp. 23–45.
Stanley, E.G. "Layamon's Antiquarian Sentiments." *Medium Aevum*, 38 (1969), 23–37.

LAYS OF THE ROUND TABLE AND OTHER LYRIC ROMANCES: *see* RHYS, ERNEST.

LEAF BURNERS AND OTHER POEMS, THE: *see* RHYS, ERNEST.

LEARNED AND TRUE ASSERTION OF . . . PRINCE ARTHURE, KING OF GREAT BRITTAINE, A: *see* LELAND, JOHN.

LEBEN UND THATEN DES KLEINEN THOMAS, GENANNT DÄUMCHEN: *see* TIECK, LUDWIG.

LEE, THOMAS HERBERT, in *The Marriage of Iseult: A Tragedy in Two Scenes* (1909), compresses the plot of the love story in order to intensify the tragedy, but the attempt is frustrated by inept and melodramatic writing. [RHT]

🔊 Lee, Thomas Herbert. *The Marriage of Iseult and Other Plays*. London: Mathews, 1909.

"LEGEND OF CAMELOT, A": *see* DU MAURIER, GEORGE.

"LEGEND OF KING ARTHUR, THE." Although it has come to be recognized as a ballad in its own right, this poem of 96 lines constitutes the first part of a longer ballad in the Percy Folio entitled "King Arthur's Death." The "Legend" takes the form of a first-person narrative in which Arthur reviews the major events of his life, recalls his many military triumphs, and laments the unhappy consequences of his last great battle against Mordred. [JN]

🔊 Hales, John W., and Frederick J. Furnivall, eds. *Bishop Percy's Folio Manuscript*. London: Trübner, 1867–68, Vol. 1, pp. 497–501.

LEGEND OF KING ARTHUR, THE: *see* TELEVISION SERIES.

LEGENDA SANCTI GOEZNOVII: *see* GOEZNOVIUS, LEGEND OF ST.

LELAND, JOHN (ca. 1503–1552), English antiquary. During the third and fourth decades of the sixteenth century, Leland traveled throughout England and Wales, examining library collections and also making detailed notes concerning architecture and landscape. A strong patriot, he was a firm up-holder of Geoffrey of Monmouth's vision of the English past and defended, in particular, the historicity of King Arthur, whose name, he observed, was linked with many sites. Leland was the first known modern commentator to identify the legendary Camelot with South Cadbury and he saw (and noted the inscription on) the famous leaden cross commemorating King Arthur at Glastonbury Abbey. From his notes, he composed, in 1544, his encyclopedic *Assertio Inclytissimi Arturii Regis Britanniae* (translated by Richard Robinson in 1582 as *A Learned and True Assertion of . . . Prince Arthure, King of Great Brittaine*). This text is a compilation of almost all the literary and archaeological evidence available in Tudor England on what would now be called the historical Arthur. [JPC]

• Mead, W.E., ed. *The Famous Historie of Chinon of England by Christopher Middleton.* London, 1925.

    Carley, James P. "Polydore Vergil and John Leland on King Arthur: The Battle of the Books." *Interpretations* (Memphis State University), 15 (1984), 86–100.

LENAU, NIKOLAUS (1802–1850), author of a nine-part lyric poem cycle, *Waldlieder* (1843–44). Merlin the Magician is the focal point of Part V, the pivotal and longest (64-line) segment. An initiate, in harmony with the "eternal laws" of existence, Merlin is for Lenau the ultimate poet-priest-magician. In nature and the inner realm, Merlin attains the spiritual power, unity, insight, solace, and release that the despairing Lenau so ardently seeks. [RGD]

• Lenau, Nikolaus. *Sämtliche Werke und Briefe,* ed. Walter Dietze. 2 vols. Frankfurt: Insel, 1971.

LE NOIR, PHILIPPE: *see* APOLLINAIRE, GUILLAUME.

LEO I, Roman emperor in the East, reigning at Constantinople from 457 to 474. He supplies the only chronological fix for Arthur—that is, the only clear synchronization with known history outside Britain—that is given by any of the sources up to the time of Geoffrey of Monmouth.

    Describing Arthur's expeditions to Gaul, Geoffrey portrays that country as still belonging to the Empire, or at least claimed by it. However, the nature of the imperial power is ill defined. In the first expedition, Gaul is ruled by the tribune Frollo "in the name of emperor Leo." In the second, there is an equivocal western emperor, Lucius. But Lucius has a colleague whose imperial status is definite, who is not in Rome but somewhere beyond, and whom Arthur never confronts; and this "real" emperor is still named as Leo, twice. In all three places, he can only be Leo I. Leo II was a child who succeeded him and died almost at once, and there was not another Leo for centuries. Even the allegiance of Frollo could have a factual basis. During the 460s, an interregnum occurred when Leo had no western colleague and was sole emperor.

The naming of Leo, three times, is wholly gratuitous, since he plays no part in the story. Geoffrey's general methods would suggest that when he wrote of Arthur's Gallic warfare his imagination was working (however wildly) on records putting British activities in Gaul in Leo's reign. He has a comparable chronological fix for Vortigern, making his major Saxon dealings coincide with the British mission of Germanus and Lupus, two Gallic bishops whose careers—including their visit to Britain in 429—are attested by continental records. In that instance, Geoffrey is undoubtedly drawing on older writings, and he is likely to be doing the same when he mentions Leo. This is one reason why interest attaches to the Gallic expedition, in Leo's reign, of the British king known as Riothamus. [GA]

৯ Geoffrey of Monmouth. *Historia Regum Britanniae,* Book IX, Chapter 11; Book X, Chapter 6; Book XI, Chapter 1.

LERNER, ALAN JAY, wrote the libretto for *Camelot*, basing it freely on T.H. White's *The Once and Future King*. The music was by Frederick Loewe. First produced on Broadway in 1960, it was quite successful, though over-shadowed by *My Fair Lady*. After a cheery opening depicting a dim-witted Arthur's marriage to Guenevere, the tone becomes more somber: Lancelot's principles and passions conflict, though the knight remains a glittering figure. Mordred is the villain of the piece but reaps no benefit. The musical is a curious mixture of comedy and chivalric sentiment, though the glorification of "one brief shining moment" of splendor struck a chord immediately after the death of John F. Kennedy. A film version of *Camelot* appeared in 1967. [CNS]

৯ Lerner, Alan Jay. *Camelot: Book and Lyrics*. London: Chappell, 1960.
Laufe, Abe. *Broadway's Greatest Musicals*. New York: Funk and Wagnalls, 1969.

LESLIE, JOHN: *see* SCOTTISH ARTHURIAN CHRONICLES.

LEWIS, C(LIVE) S(TAPLES) (1898–1963), author of *That Hideous Strength* (1945). In this conclusion to his Space Trilogy, Lewis uses traditional Grail characters and the idealistic essence of the legend to make his apocalyptic point. Edgestow, seat of Bracton College and a typical English country village, is being taken over by NICE (National Institute of Coordinated Experiments), an amalgam of sadistic, fascist technocrats dedicated to the principle of dehumanization and the establishment of an elite corps that would effect and then dominate a new world order. NICE plans to enlist the diabolic services of Merlin, who lies slumbering in nearby Bracton Wood. Opposing NICE is a small band of people headed by Elwin Ransom, who is called both the Pendragon and Mr. Fisher King, and who has a painful, unhealable foot wound, the objective correlative of the NICE wasteland. Ransom and his group are the first to make contact with Merlin, who then spearheads the plan that turns NICE headquarters into a self-destructing Tower of Babel. Edgestow perishes in an apocalyptic holocaust, leaving Ransom's faithful remnant to restore civilization to their world. Ransom explains that England is two countries— Arthur's Logres and self-serving Britain, with a succession of Pendragons to uphold Logres throughout the ages. Thus, Lewis combines the belief in *Artus redivivus* with the Arthurian tradition of the Fisher King line of Grail guardians. Further, every nation is similarly dichotomized and haunted by its evil element, which must be constantly fought and overcome.

Although Lewis's *That Hideous Strength* is unabashedly reactionary with regard to scientific progress, empiricism, and atheism, his investing of human worth and hope in the Pendragon and Logres is in the mainstream of Arthurian moral realism. Moreover, his work, written in troubled modern times, strikes the dual apocalyptic theme of warning the world against encroaching disaster while affirming faith in a beneficent, providential Christian God. Lewis was also the editor of *Arthurian Torso*, a volume comprising Charles Williams's *Figure of Arthur* and Lewis's own *Williams and the Arthuriad*, a commentary on Williams's Arthurian cycle. [VML]

&▲ Lewis, C.S. *That Hideous Strength: A Modern Fairy Tale for Grown-ups*. London: Lane, 1945.
Williams, Charles, and C. S. Lewis. *Arthurian Torso*. London: Oxford University Press, 1952.
Holmer, Paul. *C.S. Lewis: The Shape of His Faith and Thought*. New York: Harper and Row, 1976.
Moorman, Charles. *The Precincts of Felicity: The Augustinian City of the Oxford Christians*. Gainesville: University of Florida Press, 1966.

LEYDEN, JOHN (1775–1811), Scottish physician and poet whose *Scenes of Infancy* (1803) recalls, with Ossianic overtones, a Border childhood. Arthurian allusions include the Caledonian Merlin prophesying Camlann, Arthur's battles in the Cheviot Hills, and the legend of Arthur and his knights sleeping in the Eildon Hills until the horn's blast signals "proud Arthur's march from Fairyland." [MAW]

&▲ Leyden, John. *Scenes of Infancy Descriptive of Teviotdale*. Edinburgh: Ballantyne, 1803.

LIBEAUS DESCONUS: *see* CHESTRE, THOMAS.

LIBER DE COMPOSITIONE CASTRI AMBAZIAE, Latin prose, ca. 1140. The founding legend of the House of Anjou contains a section on King Arthur, focusing on his war with Rome as an ally of Clodius. Lucius, the Roman general, is consul under the emperor Honorius. Sir Kay becomes the lord of Ambaziae. [MLD]

Marchegay, Paul Alexandre, and André Salmon, eds. *Chroniques des comtes d'Anjou.* Paris: Société de l'Histoire de France, 1856–71.

LIENHARD, FRIEDRICH (1865–1929), a versatile and prolific German journalist and writer who often employed medieval themes. In his "Parsifal und der Büsser" (1912), a poem of twelve stanzas, Lienhard depicts the protagonist as a heroic victor who changes the world. The author interprets the Grail as a symbol of German "inwardness." This orientation represents a misunderstanding of Richard Wagner. Lienhard is also the author of the play *König Arthur* (1900) and the novella *Merlin der Königsbarde* (1900). [UM/WCM]

Lienhard, Friedrich. "Parsifal und der Büsser." In *Lichtland: Neue Gedichte.* Stuttgart: Greiner and Pfeiffer, 1912.

LIFE AND DEATH OF ARTHUR: see PRINCETON UNIVERSITY CHAPEL WINDOWS.

LIFE OF SIR AGLOVALE DE GALIS, THE: see HOUSMAN, CLEMENCE.

LIGHT BEYOND THE FOREST, THE: see SUTCLIFF, ROSEMARY.

LILY MAID, THE: see BOUGHTON, RUTLAND.

LINDSAY, PHILIP (1906–1958), tells of Lancelot's tragic passion for Guinevere in *The Little Wench* (1935). With a wealth of medieval detail and references to many Arthurian tales, the long novel shows that love was "the poison that ate into the very heart of chivalry." Arthur remains a shadowy but charismatic figure in the background. [CNS]

Lindsay, Philip. *The Little Wench.* London: Nicholson and Watson, 1935.

LIOMBRUNO, an Italian *cantare* of the last third of the fourteenth century. It contains Arthurian allusions and is more permeated with fantasy—fairies, magic rings, enchanted cloaks—than other extant *cantari*. [SJN]

&. Levi, Ezio, ed. *Fiore di leggende: cantari antichi*. Bari: Laterza, 1914.

LIONORS: *see* JOHNSON, BARBARA FERRY.

LITTLE WENCH, THE: *see* LINDSAY, PHILIP.

LIVELY, PENELOPE, combines details of modern life with Arthurian mystery in *The Whispering Knights* (1971), a children's tale. Three youngsters learn a lesson about responsibility when they reenact the witches' spell from *Macbeth* and conjure up Morgan le Fay. She threatens to despoil their Cotswold valley with a motor road, but her malevolence is defeated by the Whispering Knights, twenty-nine ancient standing stones outside the village. [CNS]

&. Lively, Penelope. *The Whispering Knights*. London: Heinemann, 1971.

LIVRE D'ARTUS, LE, an independent prose continuation of Robert de Boron's *Merlin* contained only in B.N. fr. 337. (Other continuations are the Vulgate *Merlin* and the *Suite du Merlin*.) The *Livre d'Artus* begins with the Vulgate *Merlin* continuation but soon branches off into a long series of battles, single combats, enchantments, love affairs, and the like, largely inspired by the Vulgate Cycle itself. Its principal hero is Gawain, and several of its episodes have significant analogues in Chrétien de Troyes's *Erec et Enide*. [WWK]

&. Sommer, H. Oskar, ed. *The Vulgate Version of the Arthurian Romances*. 8 vols. Washington, D.C.: Carnegie Institution, 1908–16, Vol. 7.

LOEHR, MAJA: *see TRISTAN*, MODERN GERMAN VERSIONS OF GOTTFRIED'S.

LOEWE, FREDERICK: *see* LERNER, ALAN JAY.

LOGRES, the setting of Chrétien de Troyes's *Chevalier de la charrete* and *Perceval*, as well as of much of the Vulgate Cycle. Logres is probably to be identified as England, but it is primarily a poetic creation, the sometimes vague locus of adventure and romance. [NJL]

LOHENGRIN (LOHERANGRIN). In Wolfram von Eschenbach's *Parzival,* Lohengrin makes his appearance (very briefly) as the son of Parzival and Condwiramurs. His background and identity are cloaked in mystery, and his wife (the Princess of Brabant) is forbidden to ask of such matters; when she does, his fate is sealed, and he is borne away by a swan. In Wagner's opera *Lohengrin,* the hero explains, before his disappearance, that the Grail gives its guardians magical powers that can be maintained only so long as their identity is unknown. [NJL]

LOHENGRIN: see HAUPTMANN, GERHART; WAGNER, RICHARD.

LOHENGRIN, FILS DE PARSIFAL: see SYMBOLIST ARTHURIAN MATERIAL.

LONG SUNSET, THE: see SHERRIFF, ROBERT CEDRIC.

LOOMIS, ROGER SHERMAN (1887–1966), one of the most prolific and important scholars ever to be attracted to the Arthurian legend. Born in Japan and educated at Williams College, Harvard, and Oxford, he taught briefly at the University of Illinois and spent the remainder of his academic career at Columbia, with the exception of a year at Oxford.

Author or editor of more than twenty books and 100 articles, he is known principally as the foremost proponent of theories concerning the influence of Celtic legend and literature on Arthurian romance. From his 1927 book *Celtic Myth and Arthurian Romance* until his death, he refined his positions, adding or discarding facts and modifying interpretations, but remaining an ardent—he said "pugnacious"—champion of Celtic theories. His books and ideas provoked controversy (often heated), both because a good many scholars thought the ideas themselves radical or even fanciful and because Loomis sometimes pushed them to limits that even he eventually considered "rash." Among the formulation of his theories might be noted in particular *Arthurian Tradition and Chrétien de Troyes* (1949) and *The Grail: From Celtic Myth to Christian Symbol* (1963).

Whatever their views of Celtic theories, all Arthurian scholars are indebted to Loomis for his editing the monumental—and still standard—*Arthurian Literature in the Middle Ages: A Collaborative History* (1959). In addition, he authored (with Laura Hibbard Loomis) *Arthurian Legends in Medieval Art* (1938), which also remains the standard work on its subject. He moreover published on Chaucer (*A Mirror of Chaucer's World,* 1965), on medieval and Tudor drama, on folklore, and on other subjects. Along with Eugène Vinaver and Jean Frappier, Loomis was instrumental in the founding of the International Arthurian Society. [NJL].

ᨠ Loomis, Roger Sherman. *Studies in Medieval Literature: A Memorial Collection of Essays.* With a Foreword by Albert C. Baugh and a Bibliography of Loomis by Ruth Roberts. New York: Franklin, 1970.

LOT, king of Orkney and Lothian, husband of Morgause (or Anna)—Arthur's sister (or half-sister), and father of Gawain, Gaheris, Gareth, and Agravain. He is a rebellious vassal in Arthur's early reign but later becomes a staunch ally. He appears in all major versions of the Arthurian story from Geoffrey of Monmouth through the French prose romances and their derivations, including Malory. [KB]

LOUVRE TRAY. Arthurian heroes are among the devotees of Venus decorating a presentation tray once in the Arconati-Visconti Collection and now in the Louvre. The tray is one of the popular type known as *desco da parto*, on which gifts were brought to women after the birth of a child, a custom in fourteenth- and fifteenth-century northern Italy and Tuscany.

Six heroes—from left to right Achilles, Tristan, Lancelot, Samson, Paris, and Troilus, identified by the French form of their names—kneel in a lush meadow. All wear fashionable dress of about 1400. Lancelot and Tristan are represented as young lovers, while Achilles and Samson are older bearded knights. All turn and gesture toward Venus, who appears in a mandorla, flanked by winged bird-footed erotes, one of whom carries the bow and arrow of Cupid. Venus is represented as a nude, winged female wearing a crown on her long, flowing blonde hair. Beams of golden light stream from her to the heads of the knights. Such frankly sensual depiction of the theme of Venus's power, in a parody of Pentecostal iconography, heralds the Renaissance. [MS]

LOVELICH, HENRY, author of *The History of the Holy Grail* (ca. 1450). This octosyllabic couplet poem, a slavish translation of the Vulgate *Estoire del Saint Graal,* is the most complete English account of the early history of Joseph of Arimathea and the Holy Grail. Lacking the first eleven chapters, the extant work continues for forty chapters, recounting Joseph's service to the crucified Christ, his conversion, his apostolic mission as a latter-day Moses traveling westward with the ark of the Holy Grail, leading the Chosen People to the Promised Land of Britain, the conversion of Sarras, the evangelization of Britain, and the establishment of the line of Grail guardians that will extend to King Arthur's reign. Like the author of the *Joseph of Arimathie,* Lovelich consistently emphasizes the importance of Joseph over that of his fictional son, Josephe, and in Chapter 54, his most important departure from his source, he reports the burial of Joseph, Apostle of Britain, at Glastonbury Abbey.

Lovelich has also given us *Merlin* (ca. 1450), a verse translation of the Vulgate *Estoire de Merlin.* Unlike *Arthour and Merlin,* this work and the anonymous English Prose *Merlin* (ca. 1450–60) stress Merlin's role as the prophet of the Holy Grail, thereby allying him and Arthur with the vessel and its redemptive purpose. This alliance rests on four important links: 1) the Grail book, dictated by Merlin to the hermit Blaise; 2) the trinity of tables (the table of the Last Supper, the Grail table, and the Round Table; 3) the Arimathean lineage, whereby Percival, Galahad, and others are identified as "kin of Joseph of Arimathea," an honored epithet; and 4) the Grail quest. Although a comparison of the English metrical and prose versions reveals a close agreement, Henry Wheatley feels that their differences indicate that the two translators worked independently upon different French manuscripts. Lovelich's account ends at line 27,582 with Arthur's victory over Claudas, while the Prose *Merlin* continues until the births of Lancelot, Lionel, and Bors, and tells of the forthcoming quest of the Grail, which will test—and mark the dissolution of—Arthur's Round Table. [VML]

Lovelich, Henry. *The History of the Holy Grail* (Parts 1–4), ed. Frederick J. Furnivall. 4 vols. London: Trübner, 1874, 1875, 1877, 1878.

———. *Merlin* (Parts 1–3), ed. Ernst A. Kock. 3 vols. London: Oxford University Press, 1904, 1913, 1930.

Wheatley, Henry B., ed. *Merlin, or The Early History of King Arthur* (Parts 1–4). 4 vols. London: Kegan Paul, Trench, Trübner, 1865, 1866, 1869, 1899.

Ackerman, R.W. "English Rimed and Prose Romances." In *Arthurian Literature in the Middle Ages,* ed. Roger Sherman Loomis. Oxford: Clarendon, 1959, pp. 485–89.

Eckhardt, Caroline D., ed. *The Prophetia Merlini of Geoffrey of Monmouth: A Fifteenth-Century English Commentary.* Cambridge, Mass.: Medieval Academy of America, 1982, pp. 3–10.

Lagorio, Valerie M. "The Glastonbury Legends and the English Arthurian Grail Romances." *Neuphilologische Mitteilungen,* 4/79 (1978), 359–66.

LUCIFER: *see* STUCKEN, EDUARD.

LUCIUS. In Geoffrey of Monmouth's *Historia*, Arthur's second and greater Gallic war is provoked by a demand for tribute from the Roman ruler Lucius Hiberius. Geoffrey hesitates over his status. He introduces him as Procurator of the Republic. "Procurator" was a title given to deputies of the emperor in minor provinces. It suggests something less than supreme authority, and that impression is reinforced by the fact that the Senate has power to give Lucius orders. Later, Geoffrey calls him an emperor; but he associates him with another, who is not in Rome, who is inactive throughout, yet whose imperial dignity is unquestioned.

In Wace and subsequent romance, Lucius becomes, simply, an emperor. However, his original ambiguity points to an awareness on Geoffrey's part of the realities of the period A.D. 455–76. During that time, the Empire was breaking up in the West, and the western emperors were evanescent figures with little real power. Their eastern colleagues were still dominant, securely enthroned. Geoffrey confirms this reading of his ideas by calling Lucius's co-emperor Leo. He is clearly thinking of Leo I, who reigned at Constantinople throughout most of this period.

Where he found Lucius is not so clear. No such emperor ever existed. A sustainable conjecture is that he took him from the *Chronicle* of Sigebert of Gembloux (d. 1112). Noting the late western emperor Glycerius, Sigebert gives this unfamiliar name as *Lucerius* and allots the reign, inaccurately, to the years 469–70. Thus, he gives Leo I a western colleague with a name that Geoffrey could have garbled, quite characteristically, into *Lucius.* Also, he makes him emperor at the time of the Gallic campaign of the British king styled Riothamus—a fact in accord with the view that Geoffrey had this in mind when composing his tale of Arthur in Gaul. [GA]

Geoffrey of Monmouth. *Historia Regum Britanniae,* Book IX, Chapter 15, through Book X, Chapter 13.

LUCKA, EMIL (1877–1941), German writer of novels, dramas, and essays. In 1908 or 1909 appeared a "story of olden times," *Isolde Weisshand.* The tale begins after the discovery of the lovers' adultery, when Tristan is forced to leave Mark's court. He marries Isolde of the White Hands after she cures him of a wound with skills she learned from Merlin. He leaves her, however, after the wedding night and goes off in search of Isolde the Fair ("Isolde Blondhaar"). While at sea, he happens upon a ship meant to bring Isolde the Fair to her final resting place. Together they disappear into the ocean fog. [SSch/WCM]

Lucka, Emil. *Isolde Weisshand.* Berlin: Fischer, [1909?].

Schwarz, Alexander. *Sprechaktgeschichte: Studien zu den Liebeserklärungen in mittelalterlichen und modernen Tristandichtungen.* Göppingen: Kümmerle, 1984.

LUDWIG, EMIL: *see TRISTAN,* MODERN GERMAN VERSIONS OF GOTTFRIED'S.

LUNETEN MANTEL, DER, an anonymous fifteenth-century Shrovetide play that derives ultimately from *Le Mantel mautaillié,* presumably via the thirteenth-century Middle High German version *Der Mantel.* A lady named Lunet sends a magic mantle to Arthur's court; it will be given to the woman whom it best fits—that is, a faithful woman. By shrinking and tearing as one woman after another tries on the magic garment, the mantle reveals the rampant infidelity of Arthur's court. The tone of the play is coarse, and the exposed women glibly rationalize their infidelity by pointing out the sexual inadequacies of their husbands. Not only Guinevere and the wives of mighty kings, but even the wife of the court jester, fail the test. The day is finally saved by the youngest queen present, wife of the king of Spain, the oldest monarch among those assembled. The play concludes with praise for pure wives. [MEK]

Der Luneten Mantel. In *Fastnachtspiele aus dem fünfzehnten Jahrhundert.* Zweiter Theil. Stuttgart: Litterarischer Verein, 1853, pp. 664–78.

LYDGATE, JOHN (1370–1451), English poet. Drawing upon Laurent de Premierfait's French translation of Boccaccio's *De Casibus Virorum Illustrium,* Lydgate presents in *Fall of Princes* an account of Arthur's war against the Roman consul Lucius that Boccaccio had adapted from some Arthurian chronicle. Lydgate, however, eliminates most of Arthur's flaws that appear in his source and adds details that make Arthur into a greater king. Although many of Lydgate's other monarchs in *Fall of Princes* fall because of "vicious living," Arthur's tragedy is due to envious Fortune and to Mordred, who treacherously rebelled against him. [EDK]

≈ Lydgate, John. *Lydgate's Fall of Princes* (Part 3), ed. Henry Bergen. London: Oxford University Press, 1924, pp. 898–914. (The chapters on Arthur in Boccaccio and Laurent de Premierfait appear in Part 4, 1927, pp. 327–36.)

Göller, K.H. *König Arthur in der englischen Literatur des späten Mittelalters.* Göttingen: Vandenhoeck and Ruprecht, 1963, pp. 131–36.

LYFE OF JOSEPH OF ARMATHY, THE, a prose translation (printed by Wynkyn de Worde) of Joseph's *vita* in Capgrave's *Nova Legenda Angliae.* It recounts Joseph's activities following Christ's Crucifixion, his journey westward to the Promised Land of Britain, along with his fictional son Josephes, his imprisonment by the King of North Wales, and subsequent rescue. There is no mention of Joseph's Glastonbury connection. [VML]

≈ Skeat, W. W., ed. *Joseph of Arimathie.* London: Trübner, 1871.

Horstmann, Carl, ed. *Nova Legenda Angliae.* Oxford: Clarendon, 1901, Vol. 2, pp. 78–82.

Lagorio, Valerie M. "The Evolving Legend of St. Joseph of Glastonbury." *Speculum,* 46 (1971), 209–31.

LYONESSE, a country of romance. In the best-known versions of the story of Tristan, he is the son of its king. It may originally have been Leonais in Brittany, or Lothian (Old French *Loenois)* in Scotland. However, it eventually becomes part of Cornwall. As such, it is more or less equated with a region known to Cornish folklore as Lethowstow. According to legend, this is now under the sea. It formerly filled the present Mount's Bay, and stretched far west around Land's End and beyond, joining the Isles of Scilly to the mainland and to each other. Mostly low-lying, it contained a number of towns and 140 churches. At some indefinite date, the ocean swept in, and it has been submerged ever since.

This extension of Cornwall resembles other minor "Atlantises." Wales has its Lost Cantref (district) under Cardigan Bay, and Brittany its drowned city of Ker-Is. Lyonesse is not completely devoid of factual foundation. Part of Mount's Bay was above water and inhabited as late as the second millennium B.C. In the Scillies, remains of huts and walls below the high-water mark suggest that there was land linking some of the islands in the early Christian era. The fourth-century emperor Maximus banished a heretic to the *Sylina Insula*—the *isle* of Scilly. At that time, enough of the islands may have been connected to give the impression of a single main piece of land, rather than an archipelago.

In the realm of Arthur, Lyonesse is somewhat marginal. It includes a district, Surluse, that is ruled by Galahalt, and he is described as lord of the Loingtaines, or Faraway, Isles, suggesting a confused notion of the Scillies. Today, one of them is called Great Arthur, and an islet is Little Arthur. Tennyson makes Lyonesse the scene of the King's last battle; Excalibur is cast away at Loe Bar, a ridge dividing Loe Pool from open water, where the coast east of Mount's Bay runs down to the promontory of the Lizard. [GA]

ꝗ Ashe, Geoffrey. *A Guidebook to Arthurian Britain*. Wellingborough: Aquarian, 1983.

LYSER, JOHANN PETER (pseudonym of Ludwig Peter August Burmeister; 1804–1870), German poet, folklorist, translator, graphic artist, and musician. Burmeister is responsible for one of the most curious transmutations of the Arthurian mantle tale, the oldest literary attestation of which is *Le Mantel mautaillié*. In Lyser's collection of folk and fairy tales *Abendländische Tausend und eine Nacht* (1838), there appears as the story of the 600th through 605th nights a tale entitled "Lenora" after its eponymous heroine.

In Lyser's version of the mantle tale, the heroine is falsely accused of a liaison with a black knight. The charge is brought by Guinevere and her ladies out of spite that Adolar, one of the most eligible young knights at Arthur's court, should spurn them for Lenora. The heroine's name is cleared when the chastity-testing mantle is brought to Arthur's court and she alone succeeds in the trial by mantle.

Lyser himself informs us in a note to the tale that he knew both Benedikte Naubert's *Der kurze Mantel* and Werthes's *Das Pfauenfest*. In addition, Lyser also drew on an oral version, which he does not, however, identify. [MEK]

ꝗ Lyser, Johann Peter. *Abendländische Tausend und eine Nacht, oder die schönsten Mährchen und Sagen aller europäischen Völker*. Meissen: Goedsche, 1838, Vol. 8, pp. 249–54; Vol. 9, pp. 3–16.

LYTEL TREATYSE OF ÞE BYRTH AND PROPHECYE OF MARLYN, A: *see* ARTHOUR AND MERLIN; HISTORIE VAN MERLIJN.

MABINOGI (MABINOGION). The four branches of the *Mabinogi* represent the finest flowering of the Welsh genius in the Middle Ages. Although the branches—the tales of *Pwyll, Branwen, Manawydan,* and *Math*—are only loosely connected, they are, as the metaphor suggests, sprung from the common root of inherited Celtic tradition. Sometime around the middle of the eleventh century, a single writer of considerable ability gave shape to this material in approximately the form we have it now, although the two surviving complete versions are found in manuscripts of a later period, the White Book of Rhydderch (ca. 1325) and the Red Book of Hergest (ca. 1400). The term *mabinogi* has been subjected to close scrutiny a number of times, and for years it was understood to be built on the word *mab* 'son' and to be roughly equivalent in meaning to French *enfance,* and therefore to be a story of boyhood deeds or of youth in general. In fact, the word is used to translate Latin *infantia* in a fourteenth-century gospel of the boyhood of Jesus. The most recent explanation of *mabinogi* is that it is a word that originally meant a collection of material relating to the British-Celtic god *Maponos* 'divine youth.'

This last explanation fits in well with the fact that the *Mabinogi* is heavily informed by inherited Celtic mythological traditions, and it is these traditions that scholars have long sought to unravel in their discussions of the four branches. In the first branch, for example, we find reflections of the horse-goddess *Epona*, a Celtic divinity worshiped virtually throughout Gaul and, adopted by Roman cavalry units, in Rome. In the many surviving depictions of Epona, we find her seated on a horse or between horses, surrounded by birds, holding a bag or cornucopia (symbols of bounteous sustenance). Her Latin nickname was *Regina*, and in the *Mabinogi* she appears as Rhiannon ("great queen, queen goddess"), riding slowly past the magical mound on which Pwyll and his retainers sit. Yet, however slowly she rides, the fastest horse in the realm cannot catch her. Later in the story, after she has been accused of destroying her son, she is driven from the court and compelled to act like a horse, carrying visitors to the court on her back. Besides her abundant equine associations, Rhiannon, like Epona, possesses a bag into which endless quantities of food can be put, and there is reference to the birds of Rhiannon in the second branch. Scholars are in agreement that her antecedents lie in Celtic traditions about the great mother goddess Epona. The fourth branch introduces us to another well-known Celtic goddess, Dôn. In Irish, she is known as Danu, mother of the mythological tribe the Túatha Dé Danann. She is tutelary goddesss of the River Donau and a host of other rivers on the Continent.

And yet the stories themselves are not, superficially, concerned with myth. While we have no information about the author/redactor, the circumstances reponsible for his undertaking the work, the conditions under which the stories were told or read, or the audience, it seems clear from the way in which the stories develop that the primary interest lay in their entertainment value. Whether or not she is Epona and whether or not the audience was aware of that, Rhiannon is depicted as a strong-willed woman capable of taking charge of her own destiny. She leaves her own kingdom because her people are trying to marry her to a suitor she does not want. She tells Pwyll that she wants him for a husband—and the sooner the better. Later, when he has botched the wedding feast and is in danger of losing her, she berates him for his foolishness and then patiently explains to him how he can rectify the situation. Even her punishment is undertaken with her own complicity and by her leave. Her character is strongly contrasted with that of Pwyll, who is indecisive and passive. In the third branch, her husband is Manawydan, and here too there is stark contrast between the assertive Rhiannon and her passive mate. Branwen, in the second branch, presents a different type of woman, one whose family makes decisions for her and who accepts her fate unquestioningly.

While myth may not function in an explicit way in the tales, magic and enchantment certainly do. The mound at Arberth is explicitly a place to which one goes to behold wonders. Bendigeidfran (Bran the Blessed) is so big that he can cross the Irish sea by wading and, lying across a river, be a bridge over which his army can pass. In the third branch, the kingdom of Dyfed becomes a wasteland—buildings, animals, people, all save the four principals of the story disappear. In the fourth branch, a virgin gives birth to twins while stepping across a magic wand, the brothers Gwydion and Gilfaethwy are turned into animals who mate with each other and bear offspring, a wife for Lleu is made from flowers, and so on. Although these acts of magic are integral to the stories, they are presented in a completely unselfconscious way in the narra-

347

tives. Pwyll does not seem surprised when he unexpectedly encounters Arawn, king of Annwfn (the otherworld), even though Pwyll is hunting in his own kingdom. Gwydion and Gilfaethwy clearly object to being turned into animals and try to escape Math's punishment, but they get through the three years in animal form without much more apparent discomfort than if they had been away at boarding school—and without raising the eyebrows of any of the other characters. In the four branches, then, wonder, magic, and marvels are taken for granted. The storyteller's principal concern is with the characters and their relationships to one another as they move through the story. Indeed, some of the most memorable scenes in the *Mabinogi* are those involving human relationships: the pillow talk between Arawn and his wife when he returns to her after being away for a year; the scene in which Manawydan reassures the bereft Cigfa; Gwydion's grief and search for his nephew; and the scene in which Gronw and Blodeuedd fall in love at first sight, then plot their adulterous affair.

The geographical detail in the tales is for the most part authentic. The first and third branches are set in Dyfed in southwest Wales; the second is set at Harlech in mid-north Wales and in Ireland; the fourth branch is set mainly in north Wales. In the third branch, Manawydan and Pryderi travel into England to practice their crafts. It is not so easy, however, to determine the temporal setting of the tales. The characters swear by God, and there is a bishop and a priest in the third branch, but the tales are clearly pre- or at least non-Christian. The one possibly historical character named in the four branches is Caswallawn, the Welsh form of the name Cassivellaunos, who led his people in battle against Caesar in Britain in 54 B.C.; otherwise, the time frame is almost entirely obscure.

For students of Arthurian literature, the second branch holds perhaps the greatest interest. The name Bendigeidfran is a Welsh compound that means "Blessed Bran," and this figure has generally been taken to be the prototype of Bron, the Fisher King of the Grail romances. To be sure, the epithet "blessed" conjures up notions of Christian sanctity, and that is probably why this Bran was credited with introducing Christianity into Britain. (In a Welsh Triad of the "Three Saintly Lineages of the Isle of Britain," one of its early editors substituted the name of Bran the Blessed for Joseph of Arimathea.) *Bendigeid* is a clear borrowing from Latin *benedictus* and was no doubt substituted for an earlier native word that meant "blessed" in non-Christian contexts. Welsh *gwen* (masculine *gwyn;* in compounds, without initial *g-*) is just such a word, and it has special otherworldly and mythological connotations. In particular, it is found in many of the words for things associated with Arthur in Welsh tradition: Ehang*wen,* his dwelling; Pryd*wen,* his ship (or shield); *Gwen*hwyfar, his wife; Carn*wennan* (with diminutive suffix), his knife; *Gwenn,* the mantle that renders him invisible. Interestingly enough, the resulting form with Bran would be Branwen, the name given to Bendigeidfran's sister in the second branch. Bran's depiction in the second branch establishes him clearly as an otherworldly type. He is said to be the son of Llŷr (Lear), the sea-god (Irish

Ler), and his ability to cross water without the aid of a ship reinforces that connection. The word *bran* in Welsh means "crow, raven" and is often used as an epithet for a warrior. Indeed, in Irish mythological tradition the scald-crow is the preeminent form assumed by the warrior-goddess.

The four branches of the *Mabinogi* constitute important reflexes of inherited Celtic tradition in the Middle Ages. Although Arthur does not appear in these tales, some of the *Mabinogi* characters—e.g., Pryderi, Pwyll, Gwydion, and Math—appear with Arthur in other branches of the tradition (*see* CELTIC ARTHURIAN LITERATURE), and the tales depict a world in which the native Welsh Arthur would be very much at home. [PKF]

Evans, J. Gwenogvryn, ed. *The White Book Mabinogion.* Pwllheli, 1907.

Ford, Patrick K., trans. *The Mabinogi and Other Medieval Welsh Tales.* Berkeley, Los Angeles, and London: University of California Press, 1977.

Bromwich, Rachel. *Trioedd Ynys Prydein.* Cardiff: University of Wales Press, 1961.

Ford, Patrick K. "On the Significance of Some Arthurian Names in Welsh." *Bulletin of the Board of Celtic Studies,* 30 (1983), 268–73.

Hamp, Eric P. "Mabinogi." *Transactions of the Honourable Society of Cymmrodorion,* 1974–75, 243–49.

Jarman, A.O.H., and Gwilym Rees Hughes. *A Guide to Welsh Literature I.* Swansea: Davies, 1976.

MacCana, Proinsias. *The Mabinogi.* Cardiff: University of Wales Press, 1977.

Williams, Ifor, ed. *Pedeir Keinc y Mabinogi.* Cardiff: University of Wales Press, 1930.

MACHEN, ARTHUR (LLEWELLYN JONES) (1863–1947), Welsh novelist, journalist, translator, essayist, actor, and mystic, regarded the Grail legends as "the glorified version of early Celtic Sacramental Legends." The Arthurian knights represented Welsh saints, the "desolate enchantment of Britain" the Celtic church's defeat by the Roman, and the Grail a persistent source of glory and power, knowledge of which was transmitted by the "Secret School." These ideas were expressed in critical articles (e.g., *Academy*, [1907]), in *The Glorious Mystery* (1924), and in two novels, *The Great Return* (1915) and *The Secret Glory* (1922). Machen uses the theory of perichoresis to explain the reappearance of the Grail in modern times, an idea adopted by Charles Williams and C.S. Lewis. In *The Great Return*, a reporter investigates strange occurrences in the Welsh village of Llantrisant—an unnaturally bright light and the smell of incense in the church, the ringing of the wonderful bell of Teilo Sant, and miraculous cures. (One reviewer complained that even if there were a Grail that could return, Machen lacked good taste in making it appear to common farmers and village grocers.)

The Secret Glory combines savage criticism of the English public school with an allegorical representation of the Grail quest. The hero, Ambrose Meyrick, is so persecuted by masters and fellow students that, having established his supremacy in studies and sports, he runs away to London with a housemaid. There he leads a free but increasingly renunciatory life. An epilogue describes his journey to Asia with the Grail, which he had seen as a boy in the possession of a Welsh farmer, Cradock, and of which he has now become the Keeper.

Having completed "the most glorious Quest and Adventure of the Sangraal" by withdrawing the vessel from the materialistic world, he is crucified by Turks.

Machen also wrote a short story, "Guinevere and Lancelot," based on Malory (*Notes and Queries*, 1926). [MAW]

Machen, Arthur. *The Great Return*. Westminister: Faith, 1915.

———. *The Secret Glory*. London: Secker, 1922.

———. *The Glorious Mystery*. Chicago: Covici-McGee, 1924.

Sweetser, Wesley D. *Arthur Machen*. New York: Twayne, 1964.

MACLEISH, ARCHIBALD (FLEMING), American author of *The Destroyers* (1942), a deterministic poetic drama about the rebellion in Roman Britain, with Arthur as the principal protagonist, aided by his Armorican kinsman Howell, and Medrawt as the main antagonist as well as Ginevra's lover. The play is concerned with treason but even more with the futility and mindless carnage of war, emphasized in the closing speeches of Ginevra and Merlin. [VML]

Macleish, Archibald Fleming. *The Destroyers*. New York: Day, 1942.

MADNESS OF MERLIN, THE: *see* BINYON, LAURENCE.

MAERLANT, JACOB VAN, a Middle Dutch poet about whom we know little. He came from Flanders and was born before 1235; he probably died shortly after 1288. Of the many works he has to his name, the best-known are *Alexanders Geesten* (ca. 1260), an adaptation of the Latin *Alexandreis* of Gautier de Châtillon; the *History van Troyen* (ca. 1263), an adaptation of the *Roman de Troie* of Benoît de Sainte-Maure; *Der Naturen Bloeme* (ca. 1270), an adaptation of Thomas of Cantimpré's *De Naturis Rerum*; and the *Spiegel Historiael* (1283–88), an adaptation of Vincent of Beauvais's *Speculum Historiale*.

Jacob van Maerlant's first Arthurian romance was probably the *Torec*. This romance, of about 3,850 lines, has been transmitted exclusively in the *Lancelot-Compilatie*. The story, which contains numerous fairy-tale elements, deals with Torec's quest for the precious diadem stolen from his grandmother. He succeeds in securing the object and marries Miraude after fulfilling her condition: defeating all the knights of the Round Table in a tournament.

In his *History van Troyen*, Maerlant mentions the romance *Toerecke* as his work. This makes it probable that the text in the *Lancelot-Compilatie* is an adaptation of a Middle Dutch romance written by Maerlant sometime before 1263. He translated or adapted an Old French romance that has not survived (*Torrez chevalier au cercle d'or*).

About 1261, Maerlant was engaged in two more Arthurian romances. Commissioned by Count Adelbrecht van Voorne, he adapted the Old French prose versions of Robert de Boron's *Joseph d'Arimathie* and *Merlin*, under the titles *Historie van den Grale* and the *Boec van Merline*. In the former, he took great liberties in his adaptation; time and again, he made a stand against the way the Old French poet treated his material. He often permitted himself to make radical changes in order to reconcile the story with the Bible. Maerlant's romance has been preserved exclusively in a Middle Low German *Umschreibung* (rendering) from the Middle Dutch, in a codex dating from about 1425. That codex (Burgsteinfurt, Fürst zu Bentheimsche Schlossbibliothek, B 37) also contains his *Boec van Merline* and Lodewijk van Velthem's *Merlijn-Continuatie*. The *Historie van den Grale* is preserved incomplete, two pages having been torn from the manuscript during the nineteenth century; the text now comprises 1,600 lines.

In adapting the *Merlin*, Maerlant remained quite faithful to the original but allowed himself one important variation. This concerns an interpolation of about 900 lines, the so-called *Processus Satanae* ("Satan's Lawsuit"). Of the *Boec van Merline*, only 336 Middle Dutch lines have been preserved (Münster, Hauptstaatsarchiv, Dep. Landsberg-Velen), in addition to which a complete Middle Low German *Umschreibung* from the Middle Dutch is extant in the codex noted above; it comprises about 8,470 lines.

In the years 1283–88, Maerlant worked on his *Spiegel Historiael*, commissioned by the Count of Holland, Floris V. It is an adaptation of Vincent of Beauvais's *Speculum Historiale*. In 1288, Maerlant had to stop working for reasons of health. (The work was continued by Lodewijk van Velthem.) In Vincent, the history of Britain, from the arrival of Brutus up to the disappearance of Arthur, is described only briefly. Maerlant extended the description to some 1,500 lines (spread over Books 1, 5, and 6 of Part III), basing the material on Geoffrey of Monmouth's *Historia Regum Britanniae*. He explicitly distanced himself from the "fiction" of Arthurian romances in Old French (and transposed into Middle Dutch). Maerlant refused to include in his description fictional characters, such as Lancelot and Perchevael, whom, after all, he did not find in Geoffrey. [BB]

❧ Maerlant, Jacob van. *Historie van den Grale und Boek van Merline*, ed. Timothy Sodman. Köln: Bhohlau, 1980.

———. *Torec*, ed. M. Hogenhout and J. Hogenhout. Abcoude (Netherlands), 1978.

———. *Spiegel Historiael*, ed. M. de Vries and E. Verwijs. 3 vols. Leiden: Brill, 1863.

Gerritsen, W.P. "Jacob van Maerlant and Geoffrey of Monmouth." In *An Arthurian Tapestry: Essays in Memory of Lewis Thorpe*, ed. Kenneth Varty. Glasgow: French Department of the University, 1981, pp. 368–88.

Knuvelder, G. P. M. *Handboek tot de geschiedenis der Nederlandse letterkunde*. 5th ed. 's-Hertogenbosch: Malmberg, 1970, Vol. 1, pp. 207–18.

MAETERLINCK, MAURICE: *see* SYMBOLIST ARTHURIAN MATERIAL.

MAJOR, JOHN: *see* SCOTTISH ARTHURIAN CHRONICLES.

MALORY, SIR THOMAS. Everything that we know with certainty about the author of *Le Morte Darthur* is found in his book. He was called Thomas Malory, he was a knight and a prisoner, and he finished his work during the ninth year of King Edward IV's reign (4 March 1469 to 3 March 1470). He loved hunting, tournaments, and chivalry, had read widely in Arthurian romance, and had access to a splendid collection of such romances while he was writing. He shows few signs of having read anything non-Arthurian. His English was that of the Midlands, with some more northerly elements perhaps deliberately adopted from Arthurian poems because he felt them suitable to the stories he was telling. He could read and write French and was proud of it, but his French was far from perfect. He once describes with particular sympathy how a prison illness made one of his characters suicidally depressed, which suggests that he himself may have suffered something similar. A passage near the end of the book reproaching the English for their ingratitude to good kings suggests, since it was presumably written under the Yorkist Edward IV, that he sympathized with the ousted Lancastrian king Henry VI.

The most important of these factors for identifying the author are his name and rank. Of the six Thomas Malorys known to have been alive at about the right time, four are so obscure that they could hardly have become knights. One of them, Thomas Malory of Hutton Conyers in Yorkshire, has been suggested as the author; but as late as 1471 he was certainly not a knight. Of the two men of higher rank, Thomas Malory of Papworth St. Agnes in Huntingdonshire was not a knight at all: he is called esquire in official and personal documents throughout his life and after his death.

That leaves Sir Thomas Malory of Newbold Revel in Warwickshire, who was certainly a knight and a prisoner, although his recorded imprisonments are at the wrong time. He was born about 1416, succeeded his father in the family estates, and at first lived as a respectable country landowner, representing his county in Parliament in 1445. In 1450, however, he was said to have begun a spectacular career of crime, starting with the attempted murder of a local magnate and proceeding to rape, theft, extortion, cattle-rustling, sacrilegious robbery, deer-stealing, and miscellaneous vandalism. The accusations were probably politically motivated, but that does not mean they were groundless. By 1452, he was in prison in London, where he spent eight years waiting for a trial that never took place. The Yorkist leaders began to take an interest in him, and the Lancastrian authorities, presumably in consequence, showed themselves unusually determined to keep him locked up. When the Yorkists seized power in 1460, they apparently freed him; and in 1462 he followed them on a winter campaign in the north. In the mid-1460s, he again looks briefly like a respectable country landowner, but in 1468 and again in 1470 he was excluded by name from general pardons offered by King Edward. It has been suggested that he was implicated in a Lancastrian plot discovered in June 1468. Some of those involved were certainly imprisoned, and we may imagine the *Morte Darthur* being written then. The prisoners were freed by a Lancastrian invasion in October 1470, a revolution that must have brought Sir Thomas prosperity. When he died on 14 March 1471, he was expensively buried in the fashionable church of Greyfriars, Newgate.

Besides *Le Morte Darthur*, Malory may have written another English Arthurian romance, *The Wedding of Sir Gawain and Dame Ragnell*, a reworking of the traditional folktale of What Women Most Desire. There are some notable similarities between the two works in language and handling of material. The similarities are particularly striking at the end of *The Wedding*, where its author, in terms much like those that Malory uses at the end of various sections of the *Morte Darthur*, reveals that he is in prison and prays for his release. Even if *The Wedding* is by Malory, it cannot be seen as an achievement of the same order as the *Morte Darthur*—its near-doggerel versification alone would prevent that. It is easy, however, to see it as an early effort from the same author, valuable not only for itself but for the light it can throw on his development.

The *Morte Darthur* was more ambitious than *The Wedding of Sir Gawain* in almost every respect, as well as much more successful. There are two versions, one printed and one in manuscript. The former, produced by William Caxton at Westminster in 1485, survives in a perfect copy in the Pierpont Morgan Library in New York, a copy lacking eleven leaves in the John Rylands Library in Manchester, and perhaps a single leaf in Lincoln Cathedral (which has been missing for some years). Until the mid-twentieth century, this was the only known version. Editions derived directly or indirectly from it established *The Morte Darthur* as an English literary classic in the sixteenth century and reestablished it as one in the nineteenth.

The manuscript, discovered at Winchester College in 1934, is now in the British Library in London. It has lost its first and last quires and suffered minor damage elsewhere, but that did not prevent it being used as the basis for an outstanding edition by Eugène Vinaver, published in 1947, which immediately became the standard modern *Morte Darthur*. Vinaver established that neither of the surviving versions of the *Morte* derives from the other: rather, each is at least two copying stages removed from a common original. Caxton must therefore have printed from another manuscript, now lost. Nevertheless, the surviving manuscript has "offsets" of printer's ink from one type font that Caxton had begun using in 1480 and another that he had stopped using in 1483, and a parchment strip used to repair the manuscript is waste from his printing shop datable to 1489. It must therefore have been in his hands from at least 1483 until at least 1489. There has been much speculation about how Caxton obtained his manuscripts, and how the surviving one got to Winchester.

Many of the differences between the two versions of *Le Morte Darthur* are scribal errors in which one is (often obviously) wrong and the other right; but others are the result of deliberate change. One change was advertised—Caxton said in his preface that he had divided his edition into twenty-one books containing 507 chapters—but there were others, notably a drastic rewriting of the Roman-war section that was cut to half its length and restyled to match the other sections. Small changes elsewhere tended to make the Caxton version a little clearer and more modern in idiom than the manuscript version, and slightly less vivid. Vinaver assumed that Caxton had made all these changes, to make the *Morte* more attractive to potential customers. It was therefore an editor's duty to recover the unrevised *Morte* as far as possible from the manuscript version, as representing Malory's work uncontaminated by Caxton. Recently, however, it has been suggested that only Malory had the time, temperament, knowledge, and resources to revise the Roman-war story as it had been revised in Caxton's text. This raised the question of who was responsible for the other changes. It was plainly possible that both Malory and Caxton made changes and that scholarly scrutiny, however close, might often not be able to decide who had changed what. At present, these issues have not been resolved. There is therefore no scholarly consensus about the principles on which editions of the *Morte Darthur* should be produced, or (of course) on how well the available editions match up against those principles.

The discovery of the Malory manuscript focused critics' attention on the unity of *Le Morte Darthur*. The manuscript showed that Malory had organized his work into sections called either books or tales. It is now usual to call them tales, so avoiding confusion with Caxton's books, and to recognize eight of them, although Malory actually divides the fifth into two. The tales are much longer than Caxton's books, and can be seen as more self-sufficient. Each is based on a single major source and ends with an *explicit*, a short statement by the author as narrator closing the tale, and sometimes adding more information about it or the next one or himself. Some critics felt that Malory had written eight independent stories, whose *explicits* emphasized their separateness. These critics pointed to discrepancies between tales to strengthen their argument: Sir Carados, for instance, is killed in the third tale but appears in a tournament in the fourth; and Sir Tristram is mentioned as adult in all the first four tales, yet the fifth begins with the story of his birth.

Malory called his work *The Whole Book of King Arthur and of His Noble Knights of the Round Table*. (The title *Le Morte Darthur*, although now established too firmly to be challenged, came into being when Caxton mistook the title of the last tale for the title of the whole.) The phrase "whole book" shows that Malory thought of what he had written as a comprehensive and authoritative collection of Arthurian stories. The comprehensiveness lay in including everything important, not literally everything. As narrator, Malory often speaks of stories that he has not included, a feature of the *Morte Darthur* that helps to give it a kind of solidity, as part of a greater quasi-historical whole. As author, he did in fact select material from a mass of stories in different books for his tales and arranged those tales in a sequence that made a coherent account of the rise, flourishing, and fall of King Arthur and his knights.

The first tale, taken from the French Prose *Merlin*, tells how Arthur became undisputed king of Britain. Malory turned a long book about Merlin into a short book about Arthur by beginning his story at the point at which Arthur's parents meet. From then on, the tale follows its source closely, telling of Arthur's mysterious conception and secret upbringing, of his proving himself king by drawing the sword from the stone and defeating his rebellious barons in war, begetting Mordred in unknowing incest, marrying Guenivere, and obtaining Excalibur and the Round Table, and of the early adventures of the first knights of the Round Table. It ends with Lancelot and Tristram coming to court.

The second tale, taken from the English Alliterative *Morte Arthure*, tells of foreign conquest. Malory, among other things, cut his source's tragic ending, saved from death several characters needed for later tales, and increased Lancelot's part to that of Arthur's most promising young knight. The Roman emperor Lucius demands tribute from Arthur, who, enthusiastically supported by his barons, defies him, invades France, defeats and kills Lucius, and is crowned emperor in Rome. He establishes good government there, and he and his knights return triumphantly to Britain.

The third tale consists of several episodes, mostly taken from the French Prose *Lancelot* of the Vulgate Cycle, set in a frame of Malory's making, which places the story at the end of the Roman war. However, where the main theme of the *Lancelot* was Lancelot's adulterous affair with Guenivere, the theme of this tale is his chivalry. He is said to be in love with Guenivere and undertakes his quests for her, but we never see them together, and what we hear suggests a strong, chaste, and still-distant passion. What we see is Lancelot's supreme knightly ability in one testing situation after another, bringing about justice, gaining friends and followers, and coming to be accepted as the best knight in the world—a phrase that is to echo throughout the *Morte Darthur*.

The fourth tale is taken from a lost English poem, based on a Younger Brother folktale. Its hero, Gareth, is Gawain's brother, and much of Gawain's part in the source has plainly been transferred to Lancelot, to suit their characters and the parts they are to play later. The tale is set at a time when the Round Table is at its most flourishing, and Lancelot is Arthur's friend and the greatest man in his kingdom. It tells how Gareth, by asking the King for the traditional three boons, acquires knighthood, a quest, a bride, lands, vassals, reputation, and Lancelot's friendship. That friendship displays the chivalrous natures of both men and does so all the more strikingly because it cuts across the clan loyalties of rival great families, which are emerging as an important feature of Arthur's world.

The fifth tale, which is based on the French Prose *Tristan*, is the only one not placed in time in relation to its predecessor. However, since it opens with the birth and upbringing of Tristram, who has been spoken of as adult in all the previous tales, it is natural to take the opening episode as a kind of flashback. The tale takes up almost a third of the whole *Morte Darthur*. At the beginning, Tristram, Isolde, and Mark quickly settle into the relationships that tradition had established for them. The body of the tale shows a world filled with interlaced adventures, quests, tournaments, and strange encounters. The major and minor characters of Arthurian society appear from time to time, their individual and group relationships to each other hardly changing throughout. Nor is there much, in plot development or any other way, to create an awareness of time passing. The result is to create quintessentially here what we find less perfectly in the other tales, the timeless world of romance. The absence of a real conclusion increases the effect. Malory's source had had one, a Grail story that would have been incompatible with his next tale. He did not reproduce it; but at the end a Grail episode interpolated into the *Tristan* from the Prose *Lancelot* provides a lead-in to the next tale. That episode shows that Lancelot and Guenivere's affair has almost certainly been consummated.

The world that is at its zenith in the fifth tale begins its decline in the sixth, a Grail story closely following the action of the French *Queste del Saint Graal*. The Grail appears at Arthur's court, and his knights swear to pursue it. The three best find it, but only one of them returns. The others fail and are disgraced, and some of them do not return either. Lancelot, drawn by his love for God, but unable to root out his love for Guenivere, stumbles on on the heels of the three successful knights, constantly warned that he is no longer the best knight in the world, and is granted a partial vision of the Grail.

The seventh tale consists of five episodes, two mainly from the French *Mort Artu* with some help from the English Stanzaic *Le Morte Arthur*, two from hints from other French romances, and one apparently of Malory's own invention. It opens at the end of the Grail quest, and shows Arthur's court in a kind of Indian summer before its destruction. Superficially, all is well, but Lancelot and Guenivere have begun their affair again, and each of the five episodes shows them narrowly escaping discovery.

The last tale, drawn again from the *Mort Artu* and Stanzaic *Le Morte Arthur*, shows Lancelot and Guenivere at last discovered. Their enemies trap them in compromising circumstances, and she is condemned to death. He rescues her but in doing so accidentally kills Gareth, thus earning Gawain's bitter enmity. Gawain drives Arthur to pursue Lancelot even to his own lands in France; Mordred, left as regent, attempts to seize the crown and Guenivere. Arthur returns and fights Mordred in a battle in which nearly everyone on both sides is killed. Arthur himself kills his son, who "mortally" wounds him, and he is taken away to the Vale of Avalon to be healed of his wounds. (The mortal/healing paradox goes back to Geoffrey of Monmouth.) Lancelot and Guenivere enter the religious life and undertake such penances that each dies a good death, and Lancelot's kinsmen go to the Holy Land and die fighting on Crusade.

Malory clearly had reason for believing that he had created a "whole book" on the level of plot. An exemplary study by R.H. Wilson showed that he had done the same with characterization, reconciling disparate sources and adding touches of his own. Much the same could be said of the story's ideas and ideals, of the imaginary world in which the action takes place, and of the style. In these matters, too, there are anomalies like that involving Sir Carados: Sir Bors's character in the Grail quest, for instance, is not compatible with his actions in the two final tales, and the style of parts of the Roman-war story, at least in the manuscript version, is distractingly different from that elsewhere. Such things, however, do not matter, because they are dwarfed by the massive coherence, immediacy, and symbolic power of the *Morte Darthur* as a whole, and because Malory as narrator does not claim the authorial omniscience and omnipotence of a nineteenth-century novelist—at times even telling us that he does not know this or that. Malory as author may not have known it, but his occasional small faults as narrator act as a final grace-note in presentation: by diminishing him, they make the story greater. Knowingly or unknowingly, his whole mode of presentation makes his story stand free of him as the greatest creation in English of a romance world, a world that was not but might have been, parallel to ours and inviting comparison with it. [PJCF]

Malory, Sir Thomas. *The Works*, ed. Eugène Vinaver. 2nd ed. 3 vols. Oxford: Clarendon, 1967; rev. 1973.

Bennett, J.A.W., ed. *Essays on Malory*. Oxford: Clarendon, 1963.

Field, P.J.C. *The Last Years of Sir Thomas Malory*. Manchester: John Rylands University Library, 1983.

Life, Page West. *Sir Thomas Malory and the "Morte Darthur": A Survey of Scholarship and Annotated Bibliography*. Charlottesville: University Press of Virginia, 1980.

Lumiansky, R.M., ed. *Malory's Originality*. Baltimore: Johns Hopkins Press, 1964.

Takamiya, Toshiyuki, and Derek Brewer, eds. *Aspects of Malory*. Woodbridge, Suffolk: Boydell and Brewer, 1981.

MAN ON THE WHITE HORSE, THE: *see* DEEPING, WARWICK.

MAN WHO WENT BACK, THE: *see* DEEPING, WARWICK.

MANAWYDAN: *see MABINOGI.*

MANESSIER: *see* CONTINUATIONS.

MANN, THOMAS (1875–1955), perhaps the greatest twentieth-century German writer, is known primarily for such sociopolitical masterpieces as *Der Zauberberg* ("The Magic Mountain," 1924) and *Dr. Faustus* (1947). Research for *Dr. Faustus* led him to write his somewhat lighter novel *Der Erwählte* ("The Holy Sinner," 1951), which is an adaptation of Hartmann von Aue's Gregorius legend. Although this work is basically not Arthurian in substance, Mann indulges his penchant for irony by enriching the medieval world of his hero with nomenclature from Wolfram von Eschenbach's *Parzival* and to a lesser extent from Gottfried von Strassburg's *Tristan*. Some two dozen proper names and other allusions provide the knowledgeable reader with instant, generally humorous, characterizations and the potential for multilevel interpretation. The title of Mann's novella *Tristan* (1903), on the other hand, is merely a reference to the symbolic function of Wagner's music in the story and in the lives of the characters it depicts. (*See also* TRISTAN, MODERN GERMAN VERSIONS OF GOTTFRIED'S.) [RWK]

ᨘ Mann, Thomas. *Der Erwählte*. Frankfurt: Fischer, 1951.

    Weigand, Herman. "Thomas Mann's *Gregorius*." *Germanic Review*, 27 (1952), 10–30, 83–95.

MANNYNG, ROBERT, OF BRUNNE, Lincolnshire author of *Handlyng Synne* (1303) and the *Story of England* (1338). The latter is an English verse chronicle based primarily upon the French chronicles of Wace and Pierre de Langtoft. Although Mannyng professes admiration for the French prose works about Arthur and mentions a few characters from romance, such as Blase and Yvain, his account of Arthur generally follows Wace's *Brut*. Mannyng feels that Arthur was the greatest Christian king and regrets that little has been written about him in English. [EDK]

ᨘ Mannyng, Robert. *The Story of England of Robert Mannyng of Brunne*, ed. Frederick J. Furnivall. 2 vols. London: Eyre and Spottiswoode, 1887.

    Fletcher, Robert Huntington. *The Arthurian Material in the Chronicles, Especially Those of Great Britain and France*. Boston: Ginn, 1906; 2nd ed. Roger Sherman Loomis. New York: Franklin, 1966.

    Göller, K. H. *König Arthur in der englischen Literatur des späten Mittelalters*. Göttingen: Vandenhoeck and Ruprecht, 1963, pp. 28–31.

MANTEL, DER, the Middle High German metrical version of *Le Mantel mautaillié*. A fragment of nearly 1,000 lines, the text breaks off approximately halfway through the tale, after Enite has tried on the mantle. The introduction of Erec and Enite into the mantle tale is an innovation vis-à-vis the French source. The work has been ascribed to Heinrich von dem Türlin, primarily because of the advocacy of Otto Warnatsch, who argued that *Der Mantel* was written by Heinrich as the introductory episode to a larger composition that was to be devoted to the exploits of Lancelot. Bernd Kratz has argued convincingly, however, that Heinrich's authorship is dubious at best. Unlike *Le Mantel mautaillié*, *Der Mantel* has a long prologue (ll. 1–109) devoted to praising King Arthur. The German version enlarges upon the French source; there is an abundance of rhetorical ornamentation, dialogue, descriptive detail, and authorial commentary. [MEK]

ᨘ Warnatsch, Otto. *Der Mantel, Bruchstück eines Lanzeletromans des Heinrich von dem Türlin, nebst einer Abhandlung über die Sage vom Trinkhorn und Mantel und die Quelle der Krône*, ed. Karl Weinhold. Breslau: Koebner, 1883.

    Kratz, Bernd. "Die Ambraser *Mantel*-Erzählung und ihr Autor." *Euphorion*, 71 (1977), 1–17.

MANTEL MAUTAILLIÉ, LE (or *Lai du cort mantel*), an anonymous twelfth-century Old French version of the same chastity-test story that forms the basis of Robert Biket's *Lai du cor*, an episode from the First Continuation of Chrétien's *Perceval*, and other tales. The hero, as in Biket's version, is also called Caradoc, and the setting is likewise Arthurian. The main difference is that instead of a drinking horn the supernatural object is a cloak that shrinks or stretches so as to fit those ladies who have been unfaithful. [KB]

☙ Bennett, Philipe, ed. *Mantel et Cor: Deux Lais du 12e siècle.* Exeter: University of Exeter, 1975.

MANUSCRIPTS, ARTHURIAN ILLUMINATED. 1) INTRODUCTION. Illuminated manuscripts of Arthurian legends were among the most popular and the most profusely illustrated vernacular texts of the Middle Ages. They survive today in enormous numbers, particularly the lengthy Vulgate Cycle in prose, of which over 180 manuscripts survive, rivaled only by the *Roman de la rose.* Many other Arthurian manuscripts have not survived but are known from inventories, like those of the dukes of Berry and Burgundy, the counts of Flanders and Hainaut, and even lesser nobles or ecclesiastics. The exploits of the knights of the Round Table were commemorated also in stone, tiles, and textiles, or on painted walls, some of these showing scenes now lost to the illuminated-manuscript tradition.

The beginnings of Arthurian illumination are difficult to chart. Many of the earliest surviving manuscripts are unillustrated, and the earliest illustrations date from long after the beginnings of the literary traditions they depict. Hardly any Arthurian illumination survives from the twelfth century, the period of the *Mabinogi,* Geoffrey of Monmouth, Wace, Chrétien de Troyes, Marie de France, and Layamon. A small historiated initial showing King Arthur in combat with the giant of Mont St.-Michel in the Douai Manuscript of Geoffrey of Monmouth's *Historia Regum Britanniae* is all that survives (Loomis, fig. 340), while the Modena archivolt and the Otranto mosaic (dated 1165) show that, in other media, artistic interest in the Matter of Britain had already spread to the Mediterranean.

The traditional explanation for the lack of early illustrated manuscripts is that Arthurian subject matter had to await the emergence of the lay craftsman in the thirteenth century. The Loomises, in their otherwise superb and unsurpassed survey of Arthurian art, write that "monks alone in that century [twelfth] were masters of beautiful bookmaking" (p. 89). It is now acknowledged that much, even most, of the fine book illumination of the twelfth century was the work of lay craftmen, such as Master Hugo, painter of the Bury Bible and creator of other works of art for the abbey of Bury Saint Edmunds. But the major *patrons* of fine books were mainly wealthy ecclesiastics and their communities. Clearly, in such a context, books in the vernacular—history, law, medicine, epic, and poetry—took second place to the splendid Psalters and Bibles commissioned by wealthy abbots and bishops. Certain non-liturgical texts that were often illustrated, like the twelfth-century bestiaries, could no doubt be justified on the grounds that their text had a spiritual interpretation. What seems to change in the thirteenth century is that many more laypeople commissioned, purchased, and owned books, which they had read to them or, increasingly, read themselves. The fashion among noble patrons for splendidly illustrated books extended from devotional books to those read for instruction or entertainment. From the early thirteenth century, the wealthy, especially women, owned beautiful Psalters for use in private prayer, a preference that shifted at the end of the century to the illustrated Book of Hours, which remained in vogue until the end of the Middle Ages. Vernacular illustrations were produced in the same ateliers.

Against this background, it is not surprising that the earliest surviving Arthurian romance with illustrations (Rennes 255) was made in the early 1220s at a French court workshop that specialized in Psalters and also made moralized Bibles; it may have belonged to a member of the royal family. What is curious is that it contains parts of the Vulgate Cycle—the *Estoire*, the *Merlin*, and the beginning of the *Lancelot*—prose versions of the Grail and Lancelot stories rather than their earlier versions in verse, by distinguished literary figures like Chrétien de Troyes. Relatively little Chrétien illustration survives; it all dates from the second third of the thirteenth century and later, and it is not of the highest quality. The Rennes manuscript contains a sequence of illuminations in the form of historiated initials interspersed at intervals in the text, a format that continued into the late Middle Ages alongside the more elaborate decorative schemes worked out later in the thirteenth and fourteenth centuries.

Paris did not maintain its reputation as the most important center for the production of Arthurian illumination. Most of the Parisian manuscripts of the Vulgate have a single miniature at the beginning of each branch, and in general the quality of these books ranks far below the best products of Parisian ateliers in the time of St. Louis (1234–70), when illuminators seem mainly to have been called upon for high-class liturgical or devotional books, or university texts. A notable exception is the *Roman de la poire* (Paris, B.N. fr. 2186), which includes a splendid sequence of full-page miniatures, unmatched elsewhere, of famous lovers, including the Arthurian heroes and heroines Tristan and Isolde and Cligés and Fénice alongside Paris and Helen and Pyramus and Thisbe.

In Germany, the full-page format is favored in the two earliest surviving Arthurian illuminated manuscripts, Wolfram von Eschenbach's *Parzival* and Gottfried von Strassburg's *Tristan*, both now in the Bayerische Staatsbibliothek in Munich (cgm 19 and cgm 51, respectively). One of the scribes in the *Parzival* also wrote the *Tristan*, but the illuminations in each are by different artists and probably of different dates; both are sets of subdivided miniatures (two registers in *Tristan*, three in *Parzival*) that were inserted into their respective manuscripts after the texts were completed. The lack of comparative material makes it difficult to date or localize these manuscripts with any certainty. They have been variously dated between the second quarter and the end of the thirteenth century, and Strassburg has been suggested as their provenance.

In France, the center of vernacular book production in general and Arthurian illumination in particular shifted by the last quarter of the thirteenth century to the northeast, to Picardie, Artois, and Flanders, as well as Hainaut, which, although in the Empire, was part of the ecclesiastical Province of Reims and artistically closer to France and Flanders than to Germany. These regions were especially prolific in book production during the last quarter of the

19–44 *Illuminations from Arthurian manuscripts.*

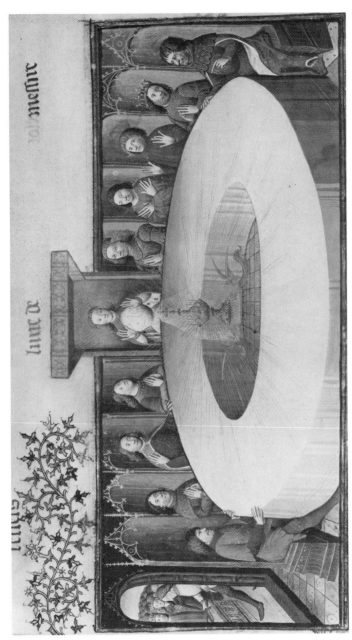

19 *Galahad and the Perilous Seat (Bibliothèque Nationale fr. 120, Cycle de Lancelot, fol. 524v; fifteenth century).*

20 *Combat of Lancelot and Gawain* (*Bibliothèque Nationale fr. 120*, Cycle de Lancelot, *fol. 590v; fifteenth century*).

21 Knighting of Galahad/Galahad and the Sword in the Stone/Tourney (Bibliothèque Nationale fr. 99, Tristan, fol. 561r; dated 1463).

22 *Lancelot Rescues Guenevere* (*Bibliothèque Nationale fr. 342, fol. 186; dated 1274*).

23–31 From John Rylands
University Library fr. 1,
Vulgate Cycle (ca. 1315–25).
Courtesy John Rylands
University Library.

23 Fire Consumes an Occupant
of the Perilous Seat (fol. 109v).

24 Arthur Convokes the
Grail Questers (fol. 114v).

25 A Knight (Avalin) Who
Wants to Kill Gawain Gives
Poisoned Fruit to Guenevere, but
She Offers It to Another Knight
(fol. 223r).

26 Tournament Called by Arthur After Death of Gaheriet (fol. 224v).

27 After Entrusting Guenevere to Mordred, Arthur Assaults Lancelot (fol. 240v).

28 Arthur Besieging Gaunes (fol. 244v).

29 Arthur and Knights, En Route to Punish Mordred, Arriving at Castle of Dover (fol. 253v).

30 Body of Gawain Placed on Bier While a Lady Grieves over Him and a Knight Attacks the Lord of the Palace (fol. 254r).

31 Arthur Tarries at the Castle of Dover After Sending the Body of Gawain to Camelot, and Before Going to Fight Mordred (fol. 255r).

32–37 From Pierpont Morgan Library 805–06, Lancelot Proper *(ca. 1315).*
Courtesy Pierpont Morgan Library.

32 Guenevere and the Lady of Malohaut with Attendants/Lancelot with Squire/
Combat of Lancelot and Galehot's Knights (MS 805, fol. 60).

33 Galehot and First Kiss of Lancelot and Guenevere/Seneschal Conversing with
Lady of Malohaut and Laura of Carduel (MS 805, fol. 67).

34 Combat of Lancelot and Gawain/Combat of Hector des Mares and the King of
the Hundred Knights (MS 805, fol. 105).

35 Lancelot in Horsecart, Followed by Gawain and Squires (MS 806, fol. 158).

36 Lancelot Lifting the Tombstone of Galahad, King of Wales (MS 806, fol. 161v).

*37 Lancelot Crossing the Sword Bridge/Guenevere with King Baudemagus/
Baudemagus Meeting Lancelot (MS 806, fol. 166).*

38–44 *From Princeton University Library, Garrett 125,* Yvain (*late thirteenth century*).
Courtesy Princeton University Library.

38 Kay Reproaches Calogrenant for Having Risen in the Presence of Guenevere (fol. 40r).

39 Marriage of Yvain and Laudine (fol. 52r).

40 *Yvain Delivers the Lion from the Venomous Grasp of the Dragon (fol. 37r).*

41 *Yvain, Aided by His Lion, Battles Harpin de la Montagne (fol. 56v).*

42 *Yvain Rescues Lunete from Three Knights (fol. 58v).*

43 Yvain Defeats the
Two Demons
(fol. 26v).

44 Combat of Yvain
and Gawain
(fol. 38r).

thirteenth and the first quarter of the fourteenth century. Workshops produced multiple copies of Arthurian manuscripts; the surviving examples are copiously illustrated, usually with small miniatures in one text column but sometimes with historiated initials instead or as well. Complete copies of the Vulgate are Bonn 526, written in Amiens in 1286, and Paris, B.N. fr. 110, products of the same illuminator's shop, located probably in Cambrai; and London, B.L. Add. 10292–94, made after 1316 in the same shop as Oxford, Bodl. Douce 215/ Manchester, John Rylands University Library fr. 1/New York, H.P. Kraus, Catalogue 165, no. 3, and London, B.L. Royal 14 E III, probably in St. Omer or Thérouanne, or possibly in Ghent. Other important Arthurian manuscripts of the fourteenth century are in New York (Pierpont Morgan Library 805–07) and Paris (Bibliothèque de l'Arsenal 5218), the latter written, illuminated, and bound by Pierart dou Tielt in Tournai. Both of these manuscripts include long miniatures that spread across the entire text, as well as historiated initials. Pierart dou Tielt is the only illuminator among the group whose work is signed. In the rest of these manuscripts, there is evidence that the task of illuminating these long romances was one that depended on intermediaries of various kinds, usually in the form of written marginal notes or symbols to guide the illuminators, and suggesting—as do the division of hands within the illumination, or the slight variations within a single style—that the artistic atelier was a complex organization in which a great deal of collaboration took place on different levels: among artists, scribes, rubricators, minor decorators, and note writers. What is lacking so far is the documentary evidence to follow each stage of the process in detail.

From the fourteenth century, too, many more vernacular manuscripts survive. The French Arthurian texts were copied and illustrated in Italy, alongside Italian versions of the stories, and German versions with illustrations survive in considerable numbers. It is surprising to note the general absence of fine Arthurian manuscripts in England, although there is evidence of French or Flemish-made Arthurian books in English fourteenth-century libraries. On the Continent in the late Middle Ages, Arthurian manuscripts were owned by some of the best-known book collectors of the period, like Gian Galeazzo Visconti or Jean, Duke of Berry, and his grandson Jacques d'Armagnac, owners of the complete Vulgate Cycle (Paris, B.N. fr. 117–20), and Engelbert II, Count of Nassau and Vianden, owner of the *Guiron le Courtois* (Oxford, Bodl. Douce 383). These manuscripts are characterized by the general interest in realistic representation that is one of the hallmarks of the period, with spatial depth and scenic landscapes, although the selection of subjects and their position in the text changes little from the cycles worked out in the thirteenth century. The importance of the change in stylistic fashions is well exemplified by the overpainting of many of the scenes in Jean de Berry's Vulgate to suit the taste of Jacques d'Armagnac. Fortunately for the history of medieval painting, such adaptations are rare: the up-to-date patron simply preferred to commission a new copy, and the treasured images of the past remain intact. [MAS]

2) BRITISH MANUSCRIPTS. Although Arthurian romances purport to

tell the history of Britain, the number of illuminated Arthurian manuscripts made by English artists is small. Of course, the English nobility imported manuscripts from France, and then in the fifteenth century from Flanders; however, some native artists also illustrated their history. Among the finest are the thirteenth-century *Prophetiae Merlini*, 1250–70, with illustrations of Merlin and Vortigern (B.L. Cotton, Claudius B VII), and Pierre de Langtoft's *Chronicle* ending in the year 1307 (B.L. Royal 20 A II) illustrating the early kings of Britain. In the *Chronicle*, in tinted drawings, the artist depicted Vortigern burning in his tower and Arthur as an imposing king. Arthur carries a shield on which are represented the Virgin and Child, as described by Geoffrey of Monmouth, rather than the later device of three gold crowns. The crowns of thirty kingdoms won by Arthur are ranged below his feet.

Many English manuscripts are notable for their historical interest rather than for intrinsic aesthetic value. Wace's *Brut* (B.L. Edgerton 3028) depicts Merlin transporting Stonehenge from Ireland to Salisbury Plain, the first illustration of that famous site. Of poor aesthetic quality but of great iconographical and literary interest are the illustrations to *Sir Gawain and the Green Knight* (B.L. Cotton Nero A X), ca. 1390–1400. Depicted in crude drawings and smudgy colors are four scenes: 1) Gawain holds an axe, Arthur and Guenevere sit at the table, and the Green Knight on horseback holds up his severed head; 2) Gawain in bed is tempted by his host's wife; 3) Gawain fulfills his vow by meeting the Green Knight at the Green Chapel; and 4) Gawain back in Camelot kneels before Arthur and the Queen.

King Arthur may also appear in incidental fashion, for example, in the Wheel of Fortune, a popular medieval moralizing device. Although Arthur sits at the top of the wheel, crowned as king, the turn of the wheel topples even the most powerful ruler to the ground again. Arthur and the Wheel of Fortune appear in the *Annales Cambriae* of ca. 1316 (B.L. Add. 10294). In the same manuscript are to be found the beautiful paintings of Sir Bedivere by the lake as the hand reaches up to grasp Excalibur, and the dramatic end of the fellowship of the Round Table at the battle of Camlann. [MS]

3) DUTCH MANUSCRIPTS. The history of Dutch manuscript illumination is inextricably bound to that of its more powerful neighbors, Germany and Flanders. By the fourteenth century, however, it is possible to speak of a Dutch, as opposed to Franco-Flemish or German, school of painting. Only two of the many Arthurian manuscripts made in Holland were illustrated: *Ferguut* (Leiden, Rijks-Univ. 191) and *Walewein* (Leiden, Rijks-Univ. Letterkr. 195). The *Ferguut*, a manuscript of ca. 1300, has only one illumination, an initial "D" enclosing a picture of the hero. The romance of *Walewein*, dated 1350 by the scribe, has a full-page, brilliantly colored illustration of Walewein and the magic chessboard, inserted in a parchment different from the rest of the manuscript. The scarcity of Arthurian illuminated manuscripts in Holland may be accounted for by the lack of wealthy nobles dedicated to a courtly ethic and the patronage of the arts and to the early emergence of towns, where practical men of affairs preferred history to romances. However, since King Arthur was

considered a historical figure, his life as told by Geoffrey of Monmouth was included in histories, such as the early fourteenth-century copy of Jacob van Maerlant's work *Spiegel Historiael* (The Hague, Royal Library XX). In this manuscript, Arthurian scenes occupy four of the sixty-eight illuminations. In the finest (f. 163v)—a composite scene of Mordred's death and the mortally wounded Arthur carried from the field in a cart—is a vigorous and moving depiction of the tragic end of the fellowship of the Round Table.

Many Dutch artists found employment in the court of Burgundy. The famous painter Guillaume (Willem) Vrelant, who was active in Bruges from 1454 until his death in 1481/82, was Dutch. A member of the guild of St. John and a friend of the transplanted German Hans Memling, he headed a large workshop that produced both religious and secular works, including illuminations for the *Chroniques de Hainaut* (1468). [MS]

4) FLEMISH MANUSCRIPTS. Flanders, the southern Netherlands, played a role in Arthurian manuscript production well before the glorious days of Burgundian ducal patronage in the fifteenth century. Chrétien de Troyes dedicated his *Conte del Graal* to Philip d'Alsace, Count of Flanders, and the *Historia Regum Britanniae* (ca. 1180) and *Prophetiae Merlini* were copied and illuminated there. A twelfth-century copy of the *Historia* contains a handsome illumination of Arthur fighting the Giant of Mont St.-Michel (Paris, Douai 880 f. 66). The adventures of the knights of the Round Table were so well known in Flanders that by the end of the thirteenth century the poet Jacob van Maerlant reported that more people read the romances than the Bible. Accounts and inventories also indicate that the Arthurian romances were as popular with the Flemish aristocracy as they were with their French relations.

Maastricht, in eastern Belgium, was the early center of manuscript production, but its style is closely associated with French work. In the thirteenth and early fourteenth centuries, the Ile de France remained the center of manuscript illumination, and the books mentioned in the inventories were in all likelihood imported from Paris.

By the middle of the fourteenth century, a distinctly Flemish school appears. The *Queste del Saint Graal* (Paris, Bibliothèque de l'Arsenal 5218) was signed and dated 15 August 1351 and was illuminated by the scribe Pierart dou Tielt, who worked in Tournai. Although most of the paintings are conventional scenes of jousts and feasts, one represents the mystery of the Grail as it was revealed to Arthur's knights by angels and Bishop Josephe (f. 88). The Bleeding Lance and the Grail with the Christ child rest on a long table lit by candles. Pierart enriches the page with foliage and grotesques, including, at the bottom of the Grail page, monkey, pig, and goat musicians, and a dancing bear.

A copy of Robert de Boron's *Roman du Graal* and *Merlin*, by Johan de Loles of Hainaut (dated July 1357), includes still-visible instructions for the painter (Yale University Library). Vivid narratives and splendid borders become important characteristics of later Flemish manuscript illumination.

In 1384, Margaret, wife of Philip the Bold, inherited Flanders from her father, and thus Flanders and Burgundy were united to form a single political unit. The power and prosperity of the later Burgundian dukes Philip the Good and Charles the Bold ensured a continuous patronage of the arts. Bruges, Ghent, and Brussels, as well as Dijon, became art centers, and the Flemish cities had thriving manuscript workshops. Philip the Good built up the greatest personal library in Europe, reputed to contain nearly 900 books. The duke ordered copies, translations, and new prose editions of Arthurian romances, including the Vulgate Cycle, *Tristan, Guiron le Courtois, Erec et Enide, Cligés*, and *Perceforest*. Taste was changing, however, and in the fifteenth century history, in the form of epics and chronicles, replaced romance as the most popular form of secular literature. Chronicles, such as the *Chroniques de Hainaut*, were produced in luxurious editions (Brussels, Bibl. Roy. 9243); Volume II of the *Chroniques* contained Geoffrey's *Historia*, for Arthur was believed to have ruled Hainaut. The scribe Jacotin de Bos completed the history on 8 December 1449, and Guillaume Vrelant illuminated it in 1468. Seven of the sixty illustrations were dedicated to King Arthur. Of special interest is the wedding of Arthur and Guenevere, in which figures are depicted in contemporary costumes and are set in a meticulously rendered church interior. In other illuminations, cities and castles, extensive landscapes, and genre details (an old woman warming her feet at a fire, armorers at work before a battle) suggest the interest in realism and close observation that characterize Flemish art through the ages.

The marriage of Margaret of York, sister of Edward IV, and Charles the Bold in 1468 sealed a new Burgundian–English alliance, an alliance that enhanced trade and cultural relations between the two powers. Bruges and Ghent, already centers of manuscript production, now provided books for the English market. The *St. Albans Chronicle* (Lambeth Pal. Lib. 6), written in English and illuminated ca. 1470, includes nine Arthurian miniatures. The lively narratives characteristic of Flemish painting are placed in a deep landscape; and the realism of the spatial setting, denied in turn by the microscopic realism of the floral borders, is a prime contribution of Flemish fifteenth-century painters to the history of art.

Among the luxury manuscripts produced by Flemish painters for the Burgundian court, of interest to Arthurian scholars is the *Guiron le Courtois* (Oxford, Bodl. Douce 383) originally made for a knight of the Golden Fleece and later vandalized; seventeen folios survive. The arms are those of Engelbert of Nassau, a lieutenant of Charles the Bold and a patron of two other important manuscripts—the *Roman de la rose* and a Book of Hours. Stylistically, *Guiron* is related to the Vienna Statutes of the Golden Fleece (Vienna, Ö.N.B. 2606) as well as the *Roman de la rose* (B.L. Harley 4425). The *Guiron* was translated by Vasque de Lucene, who came from Portugal after the marriage of Philip the Good and Isabel of Portugal. The manuscript is dated 1480–1500. The painter is a master of spacious landscape and architectural setting; and his figures act in a real space. Observable details, such as the serving hatch in the palace, contrast with elegant figures. In the borders, fanciful acanthus scrolls and centaurs balance realistic strawberries and butterflies. The subtle color scheme is enhanced with discreet use of gold highlights. [MS]

5) FRENCH MANUSCRIPTS. Despite the rich twelfth-century production of French Arthurian romances and lais (Béroul, Thomas d'Angleterre, Chrétien de Troyes, Marie de France, etc.), that period apparently saw few manuscript copies of Arthurian (or other) works. It was only during the following century that the establishment of courtly culture in France encouraged the production of vernacular texts for a romance-loving upper-class audience. It is likely that half the Arthurian prose romances were decorated with historiated initials, rectangular miniatures, and marginalia. Initially, the prose Vulgate Cycle, consisting of *Estoire del Saint Graal, Merlin, Lancelot, Queste del Saint Graal*, and *La Mort Artu*, provided the most popular subjects for secular workshops in northern France, the source of much notable Arthurian illumination. Many early manuscripts are folios with texts clearly written on vellum, rubrics indicating pictorial subjects, and miniatures occupying the width of a column. The bright colors range from gold, pink, and vermilion to blue, mauve, and light green. Since the workshops also produced Bibles and Psalters, the influence of pattern books is evident in repetitive battle scenes (based on illustrations for the biblical book of Kings), feasts (Marriage of Cana and Last Supper types), and the iconography of the Grail quest, which includes Adam and Eve, the Crucifixion, and the Harrowing of Hell. Subjects are often suggested by genre rather than by specific textual description.

The high point of Arthurian illumination is represented by a group of northern French manuscripts (ca. 1300–20): Yale University Library 229; Paris, B.N. fr. 95; Manchester, John Rylands Library fr. 1, 2; London, B.L. Royal 14 E III and Add. 10292–94; New York, Pierpont Morgan Library 805–07. The elegant ease of courtly society is conveyed by pictures of ladies holding lapdogs, knights playing chess or hunting, lovers naked in bed, and nobles picnicking by a fountain. Knight-errantry is visualized through jousts, tournaments, and forest encounters with damsels, evil knights, and monsters. A courtly ambience is also evoked by gold-leaf backgrounds, golden crosses, crowns, swords, goblets, and architecturally elaborate Gothic castles and monasteries with pink or blue walls and lapis-lazuli roofs. Pink, blue, mauve, and orange horses, castle-destroying flames from heaven, and demons from hell convey the wonders of Celtic magic and Christian mystery; a life remote from the real world is also suggested by the characters' unaging faces, marked, in Loomis's words, by "an incredible youthfulness, a bland sweetness, a slightly astonished expression." Despite the frequent use of conventional scenes, the superiority of these manuscripts depends partly on careful matching of image and text in climactic scenes, e.g., the sword tests, Lancelot's crossing of the Sword Bridge, the Grail questers' approach to the Ship of Solomon, the arrival of Elaine's corpse, and Bedivere's restoration of Excalibur. The symbol-studded miniatures contain no images irrelevant to the action.

After the Hundred Years' War, which inhibited book production, workshops responded to the demand of wealthy collectors for luxury editions reflecting the flamboyant, materialistic late-medieval world. Under the influence of Italian painting, composed landscapes and interiors revealing a new-found knowledge of perspective replaced architectural frames, patterned backgrounds, and frontal images. Heraldic splendors emphasized the pageantic aspect of life.

Throughout this period and well into the fifteenth century, illuminators and miniaturists continued to perfect their art, often romanticizing their subjects but also introducing greater realism into their depictions of places, people, and objects. In certain manuscripts of this period, the artists carefully reproduce contemporary dress—the men's plumed acorn hats, long velvet gowns slashed to reveal shirts, and ridiculously abbreviated doublets; the women's low-cut dresses, golden chains, and steeple headdresses. Physiognomy is equally realistic—a grey-haired, scraggy-bearded Arthur, bored and cynical courtiers, ladies exchanging sly looks as Tristan arrives at court.

The period following the Hundred Years' War saw the formation of great libraries, such as the royal library of Charles V and Charles VI. A number of illuminators from the late Middle Ages were well known and highly respected artists; among the best were Jean Fouquet (d. ca. 1481) and Michel Colombe, one of the last of the great French illuminators. But before the century ended, the painter was displaced by the woodblock cutter as the scribe was by the typesetter. Technological change made the illuminator superfluous, and although the art of illumination continued to be cultivated well into the sixteenth century, the quality of that art was declining dramatically. The great masterpieces of the genre had already been created. [MAW]

6) GERMAN MANUSCRIPTS. German nobility in the Middle Ages adopted Arthurian romances with an enthusiasm that would be repeated in the Romantic revival of the nineteenth century. Unfortunately, however, only two illuminated manuscripts have survived from the period before 1300, a *Tristan* and a *Parzival*, both mid-thirteenth century and both now in Munich. In both, the paintings are on separate leaves inserted into the manuscripts. In *Tristan* (Munich, cgm 51), fifteen leaves painted on both sides and containing eighty-four miniatures illustrate the story of Tristan's parents and the hero's exploits at the court of King Mark. The last leaves lack the finesse of the first, and the painting is clearly the work of several hands.

Even in the fourteenth and fifteenth centuries, no truly great artist worked on an Arthurian manuscript in Germany. German artists tended to use stock scenes based on religious iconography; for example, most feasting scenes resemble the Last Supper, and even the Round Table may be represented as a long rectangle. Nevertheless, German artists tend to be energetic storytellers, even when their figures are crude and their settings minimal. The drawing is often hard and angular, with bold outlines; brilliant color, abundant ornament, and twisting banners bearing texts all add to the decorative, folk-art–like quality.

In the later years of the fourteenth century, a German romance, the *Wigalois* of Wirnt von Grafenberg, was produced for Duke Albrecht von Braunschweig-Genburhagan (r. 1361–84) (Leiden, Rijks-Univ. 537). It is signed, dated 1372, and illuminated by the scribe Jan von Brunswik, a Cistercian monk from Amelungsborn (he includes a self-portrait on the last page). In forty-seven miniatures, Jan illustrates the text of *Wigalois* with such specificity and brilliant color that Loomis related the miniatures to the Wienhausen and Brunswick embroideries. The very characteristics he notes—decorative architecture, stars and dots, four-petaled flowers of the ground and borders—also resemble fourteenth-century German and Austrian enamels.

By the fifteenth century, a truly national character emerges in German manuscript painting, a style related, in its angularity and emphasis on linear effects, to woodcuts. At this time, printers began to challenge the scribes for the attention of patrons. Just as Flanders now dominated the luxury-manuscript trade, southern German workshops turned out popular editions in large numbers. Such manuscripts as those found in the University of Heidelberg library (the earliest a *Lanzelet*, dated by the scribe to 1420, Bibl. Palzgerm. 371) are close to folk art. Simply colored drawings suffice as illustrations for books that give the impression of being produced hastily for the trade. Surviving records of the workshop of Diebolt Lauber in the Alsatian city of Hagenau confirm this impression. Lauber was both scribe and painter, but he also had at least sixteen workers under him. It is not surprising that painters sought easy effects; the fancy dress, including plumed hats, can only strike today's viewer as amusing.

Switzerland had its manuscript shops, too. A fifteenth-century *Parzival* in Berne (Bergerbibliothek Codex AA91), inscribed 1467 by Johann Steinhein de Constanica, was first owned by Jorg Friburger of Berne. Even the paper has a Berne watermark. Twenty-eight drawings done in an archaic style are colored with washes to give the effect of hand-colored woodcuts. Gawain on the Perilous Bed and Gawain picking the forbidden fruit are especially fine. Nevertheless, an overview of the period suggests that the most creative artists were being attracted to the new medium of printing. [MS]

7) ITALIAN MANUSCRIPTS. Elaborately illustrated Italian manuscripts attest the popularity of Arthurian material in many centers in fourteenth-century Italy. By the late thirteenth century, cycles of Arthurian images appear in three distinct formats. Historiated initials containing one or two characters and occasional horses, bits of architecture, or a ship are the principal decorative features of several manuscripts from Bologna (Chantilly, MS 1111, *Mort Artu*, 1288; Oxford, Bodl. Douce 178, *Estoire del Saint Graal, Merlin*). Despite their modest format, the great number of episodes represented and the handsome color schemes (dominated by oranges, blues, and browns) make these sequences quite impressive.

Framed miniatures set into a column of text occasionally appear in Bolognese and in late thirteenth-century Venetian manuscripts (Venice, Marciana fr. App. XXIX [243], *Merlin*), but this type of scene is never as important in Italy as in France.

More distinctly Italian is the unframed miniature that fills the entire lower margin of a given folio and spreads upward into the side margins and between the columns of text. This arrangement is found throughout the group of sixteen Arthurian manuscripts recently attributed to artists working at the Angevin court in Naples between 1290 and 1320. Throughout these French texts, innovative Italian artists have executed rough but lively drawings in pen-and-ink with some touches of color. The tournament, battle, and banquet scenes follow repetitious formulas apparently developed to enhance speed of production. Representative examples with dozens of drawings are a *Tristan* and a *Lancelot*, both now in Paris (B.N. fr. 760; fr. 16998).

Most luxurious of all the Italian Arthurian manuscripts are those decorated for the Visconti courts at Pavia and Milan. The earliest of these is a *Tristan* dating to 1320–40 (Paris, B.N. fr. 755). In the lower margins of most of its 161 folios are painted complex scenes with elegantly attired figures set in exquisitely detailed palace interiors or outside of crenelated castles. The compositions borrow from French models, such as the illustrated Vulgate Cycle known to have been in the Pavia library (Paris, B.N. fr. 130), but the figure types and rendering of space reflect the innovations of Giotto. The colors are predominantly pale greens, blues, pinks, and white punctuated with deep reds or solid black. Gold crowns, utensils, and areas of background enhance the sumptuous effect.

The Lombard love of naturalistic detail and of fully developed settings reaches a peak in two Visconti manuscripts executed about 1380, a *Guiron le Courtois* and a volume containing the *Queste del Saint Graal* and the *Mort Artu*, also both in Paris (B.N. nouv. acq. fr. 5243; fr. 343). In the wide lower margins, knights conversing or playing chess sit in porticoes of buildings whose upper stories are glimpsed in the side and center margins. Castle towers are set obliquely to the picture plane, and their projecting balconies are filled with gossiping ladies. Tents in broad landscapes frame battle and jousting scenes. And a truly circular Round Table is depicted for the Pentecost feast, modeled on Pietro Lorenzetti's innovative Last Supper fresco of the 1320s in Assisi. Delicate tans and greys are used for the architecture, horses, and armor; contrasted with these subdued colors are the bright reds, greens, and blues of the patterned fabrics worn by knights and ladies alike. Life in the courts of Trecento Italy is here given its most vividly realistic rendering.

A coda to the story of Italian Arthurian manuscripts is found in the 289 wonderfully charming drawings of *La Tavola Ritonda* of 1446 by the Lombard artist Bonifazio Bembo (Florence, B.N. Pal. 556). Vivaciously curving pen lines delineate scenes in which ladies wear flowing robes and elaborately high coiffures, while Lancelot and Tristan don the fabulous hats and feathery cloaks of the late International Gothic style. This famous cycle reveals the persistence of the Arthurian romances in an artistic culture otherwise already far down the path of Renaissance classicism. [LA]

8) SPANISH MANUSCRIPTS. Arthurian romances were popular in Spain. King Pedro IV of Aragon, for example, acquired several Arthurian books between 1339 and 1356. Spanish authors, such as Joanot Martorell (*Tirant lo Blanc*) and Guillem Torroella (*La Faula*), contributed to Arthurian literature and describe painted chambers and palace halls decorated with Arthurian

subjects. However, little visual evidence of this rich art survives. A thirteenth-century French Prose *Tristan* (Paris, B.N. fr. 750) signed and dated 1278 by the scribe Petrus de Tiergevilla, was illustrated by a Spaniard, who painted a golden three-towered castle (the arms of Castile) on Sir Kay's shield. The composition of the historiated initials is distinctive, for each letter encloses a series of events, represented in two or three registers, rather than the usual single scene. A typical illuminated manuscript of the second half of the fourteenth century, a Castilian *Guiron (Tristan)*, contains a miniature showing the knight Branor le Brun and the women whom he assisted.

These fourteenth-century painters worked in the style of the great northern French illuminators; by the beginning of the fifteenth century, however, they fall first under the influence of the Italian Renaissance miniaturists and then under the domination of Flemish shops. The *Chronicle of the Knight Cifar* (Paris, B.N. Esp. 36), a fifteenth-century Castilian manuscript, is richly illuminated with borders of fantastic spiky foliage filled with birds and putti. Some 250 paintings, including many scenes of civic and military life, provide a rich source of information about costume, armor, architecture, and customs. Though the interior scenes are rendered with an adequate knowledge of linear perspective, the landscapes lack the sophisticated understanding of spatial relationships found in the great Flemish models. On the first folio are the arms of Castile and Leon supported by angels, a reminder that the Spanish monarchy patronized scribes and illuminators. Queen Isabel herself built up a great library in Toledo, and her accounts record many payments to scribes and painters. [MS]

9) SOME OUTSTANDING MANUSCRIPTS. *Bonn, Universitätsbibliothek, HS 526: Cycle de Lancelot* (northern France, 1286). Parchment, 477 ff. 465 x 320 mm. Text in 3 columns, 56–60 lines. 340 illustrations, mainly miniatures in one text column, and a few historiated initials. Rubrics in red above miniatures. Some marginal guides to the illuminator. The writing of this manuscript was completed in Amiens by Arnulfus de Kayo on 28 August 1286, according to a colophon at the end of the volume. The wording "qui est ambianis" suggests that Arnulfus did not usually work in Amiens, and the stylistic associations of the illumination are with manuscripts whose calendars suggest associations with other important centers, like Arras, Thérouanne, St. Omer, and particularly Cambrai. Especially close stylistically to the illustrations in this manuscript are those in the *Bestiary* formerly in the library of Sion College, now in the J. Paul Getty Museum (Malibu, Ludwig XV, 5), written in 1277; those in St. Omer 5, the second volume of a two-volume Bible; and those in Cambrai 99, a Breviary of Marquette. Less closely related stylistically, but probably also products of the same workshop are another complete Vulgate Cycle (Paris, B.N. fr. 110); a Prose *Tristan* and a fragmentary *Lancelot* (London, B.L. Add. 5474); and a *Cycle de Guillaume* (Boulogne-sur-Mer 192), written in 1295 and perhaps the same manuscript as the "livre de gestes" mentioned by Guillaume de Hainaut, Bishop of Cambrai, in his will in 1296: he says that one of the monks of St. Sépulchre, Cambrai, had had it made for him.

London, British Library, MS Additional 10292–94: Cycle de Lancelot (Flanders, after 1316). Three volumes: Add. 10292, 216 ff. 405 x 300 mm, 238 miniatures; Add. 10293, 383 ff. 405 x 300 mm, 346 miniatures; Add. 10294, 96 ff. 405 x 300 mm, 73 miniatures. Text in 3 columns, 50 lines. Miniatures in one text column, borders for the opening pages of the branches, except for *Mort Artu*, which lacks the beginning. Rubrics in red above miniatures; many marginal notes (rarely legible) in leadpoint for the rubricator and possibly also for the illuminator. Two contemporary illuminators divided the work, although they never worked in the same quire. The date 1316 is written into the miniature in Add. 10292, f. 55v, on the tombs of Nabor and le sire de Karabel, which are being sculpted. The activity of this workshop seems to have spanned the period ca. 1300–50 or later. Two other Prose *Lancelots* were produced: London, B.L. Royal 14 E III (incomplete: *Estoire, Queste, Mort Artu*), and Manchester, John Rylands University Library fr. 1, other parts of which are Oxford, Bodl. Douce 215, and New York, H.P. Kraus, Catalogue 165, no. 3. The cycles of all three manuscripts are closely related, and the first illuminator of Add. 10292–94 either worked himself on all three sets or had assistants whose style was almost identical. He also worked on the frontispiece in the Psalter of Tournai (St. Omer 270), added in 1323 when Gilbert de Sainte-Aldegonde gave the manuscript to the Charterhouse at Longuenesse near St. Omer. Also closely related, but probably earlier, are a Psalter (London, B.L. Stowe 17) and a fragmentary Book of Hours (London, B.L. Add. 28784). The second illuminator did not collaborate on the other *Lancelots*, but his work appears again in the Hours of Thérouanne or St. Omer (New York, Pierpont Morgan Library M 754, and London, B.L. Add. 36684), dated after 1318 because of the inclusion of an indulgence of that year, and in part of the Vincent of Beauvais *Speculum Historiale* (Boulogne-sur-Mer 130), a direct copy of an earlier manuscript with the same text and picture cycle (Boulogne-sur-Mer 131), made in 1297 for Eustache Gomer de Lille, abbot of the Benedictine monastery of Saint Bertin at St. Omer. The associations of the workshop with St. Omer are striking, but the workshop also has close stylistic links with Ghent, and perhaps Cambrai.

Munich, Bayerische Staatsbibliothek, cgm 19: Wolfram von Eschenbach, Parzival, Titurel, Tagelieder; and Three Exemplars (Germany, ?Strassburg, second quarter or second third of the thirteenth century). Parchment, 75 ff. 295 x 210 mm. Text in 3 columns, 70–72 lines. Illustrations on both sides of two single inserted leaves, each divided into three registers, illustrating scenes from Books XII–XV of *Parzival*. The illustrations are probably fragments of a more extensive narrative sequence, of which the rest is now lost. The texts are written by seven anonymous scribes, to the first of whom has also been attributed the script of the Munich manuscript of Gottfried von Strassburg's *Tristan* (cgm 51). Though neither manuscript contains direct evidence of date or localization, both are assumed to have been written in Strassburg and have been associated with the writing-shop of the notary Meister Hesse, whose activity in Strassburg is documented between 1228 and 1236, and who is praised in the text of Rudolf von Ems's *Wilhelm von Orlens*. The Munich manuscript of *Wilhelm von Orlens* (cgm 63) has also been attributed to Strassburg, although the script is different and probably later than that of the *Parzival* or the *Tristan*. In the absence of any signed work by Meister Hesse, most scholars are now reluctant to accept him as the scribe of the *Parzival* or the *Tristan*; there is also some hesitation about the dates of all three manuscripts, owing to the lack of comparative dated material. The same problems apply to the illuminations in the books, which in the case of the *Parzival* and the *Tristan* are on separate leaves and need not have been planned with the writing of the texts. They are certainly by quite different artists and are somewhat mediocre in quality and condition, which makes the question of attribution still more vexed.

New York, H.P. Kraus, Catalogue 165, No. 3; Oxford, Bodleian Library, MS Douce 215; Manchester, John Rylands University Library, MS French 1: Vulgate Cycle Flanders, ca. 1315–25). Parchment, Kraus i, 118 ff.; ii, 233 ff.; iii, 104 ff.; each 405 x 290 mm. Oxford 45 ff. 411 x 292 mm. Manchester i, 129 ff.; ii, 128 ff.; each 411 x 292 mm. Text in 2 columns, 44 lines. 109 miniatures in the Kraus volumes, 6 in the Oxford volume, 74 miniatures and a historiated initial in the Manchester volumes. Rubrics. Many marginal notes (particularly legible in the Kraus volumes) for the rubricator and the illuminator. Illuminations by two contemporary artists, with marginal miniatures added by a fourteenth-century artist. The first artist is the same as, or is very closely related to, the first painter in two other Prose *Lancelot* manuscripts (London, B.L. Add. 10292–94, and London, B.L. Royal 14 E III). This painter worked on all of the volumes. The second painter appears only in a few miniatures in the Oxford and Manchester volumes, but his work is important as it can also be traced in a number of other manuscripts, particularly a group of Psalters and Books of Hours associated with Ghent and Cambrai, including MSS Oxford, Bodl. Douce 5–6, a Psalter made for the abbey of St. Peter, Blandin, Ghent; Cambridge, Trinity College B.11.22, a Franciscan Book of Hours; a Franciscan Psalter, Copenhagen, Royal Library GKS 3384 8°; and a Psalter Hours with a calendar and litany of Cambrai, Baltimore, Walters Art Gallery 82. Since the stylistic associations of the first artists are primarily with books made for St. Omer or Thérouanne, this manuscript is important in extending the parameters of the group, perhaps suggesting close collaboration between two ateliers, or perhaps the existence of several styles within a single large atelier. In either case, the location of the atelier or ateliers cannot yet be resolved with certainty.

New York, Pierpont Morgan Library, MS 805: Lancelot Proper (northern France, ca. 1315). Parchment, 266 ff. 346 x 254 mm. Text in 3 columns, 48 lines, now bound in two volumes, ff.1–142v, ff.143–266. 39 miniatures in 3 text columns, 136 historiated initials. 6 notes for the illuminator in the margins. The illuminations are by two main artists, with perhaps a third collaborator for f.l. On the whole, one of the main artists painted the large miniatures and the other the historiated initials, but where there is a historiated initial on the same leaf as a miniature, it is painted by the same hand as the miniature. Both artists are anonymous, and nothing is known about the patron of the manuscript, but the artists both reappear in other manuscripts. The artist of the miniatures also painted a detached leaf in the Österreichisches Museum für angewandte Kunst (Vienna), a medical treatise by Roger of Salerno (London, B.L. Sloane 1977), and a *Vie de Sainte Benoîte* (Berlin, Dahlem Museum, Kupferstichkabinett Hs. 78.B.16), all of which contain full-page miniatures. Some idea of the date and provenance of the group is provided by the colophon of the Berlin manuscript, which was made in 1312 for Helouis d'Escoufflans, a nun at the abbey of Sainte Benoîte d'Origny (diocese of Laon). The artist of the historiated initials reappears in Paris, B.N. fr. 789, which contains three versions of the Alexander legend and the *Istoire de Judas Machabee*, and other manuscripts associated with Amiens.

Oxford, Bodleian Library, MS Douce 383(21958): *Guiron le Courtois* (Flanders, ca. 1500). Parchment, 18 ff. 450 x 325 mm. Text in 2 columns, 38 lines. Rubrics. 5 large miniatures with borders. This fragmentary manuscript contains the arms of Engelbert II of Nassau and of the Order of the Golden Fleece. Its impressive miniatures have been variously attributed to painters associated with the patronage of Engelbert, particularly the *Roman de la rose*, London, B.L. Harley 4425. Other products of the same workshop include the Statutes of the Order of the Golden Fleece (Vienna, Ö.N.B. 2606), a number of prayer books, and another *Guiron* manuscript (Paris, B.N. fr. 358–63).

Paris, Bibliothèque de l'Arsenal, MS 5218: *La Quest del Saint Graal* (Tournai, 1351). Parchment, 106 ff. 285 x 196 mm. Ff. 1–91v contain the *Quest del Saint Graal* with three illuminations, one of which, painted in two columns, illustrates the mysteries of the Grail. Written, illuminated, and bound by Pierart dou Tielt, in 1351, as indicated in a colophon. Pierart is documented as being responsible for the upkeep of the library at the Benedictine abbey of St. Martin at Tournai during the abbacy of Gilles le Muisit; and this manuscript includes a chronicle of the abbey. Also attributed to Pierart dou Tielt are an added miniature in a twelfth-century Gospel Book of the use of St. Martin's, Tournai (Washington, D.C., Library of Congress, De Ricci 127); *Pamphile et Galathee* (Brussels, B.R. 4783); a Book of Hours (Brussels, B.R. IV 453); and parts of the *Roman d'Alexandre* (Oxford, Bodl. 264).

Paris, Bibliothèque Nationale, MS Français 117–20: *Cycle de Lancelot* (Paris, ca. 1400). Parchment, 602 ff. in all, numbered continuously: Vol. 1., 154 ff. 494 x 341 mm, 3 miniatures; Vol. 2, 155–308 ff., 526 x 344 mm, 50 miniatures; Vol. 3 526 x 344 mm, 50 miniatures; Vol. 4 526 x 344 mm, 17 miniatures. Rubrics. Text in 2 columns, 65 lines, miniatures generally in one text column, a few in 2 columns, opening miniatures in four parts. These volumes comprise one of ten extant sets of manuscripts that contain the entire Vulgate Cycle. This set was purchased in 1405 by Jean, duc de Berry, for 300 *escus d'or* from the book-dealer Regnault du Montet (about whom it is also known that he sold a *Tristan* in England, and was tried for treason). This set of *Lancelot* volumes contains the arms and signature of Jean, duc de Berry, and appears in his inventories.

Subsequently, it passed to Jean's grandson Jacques d'Armagnac, at which time substantial alterations were made to many of the miniatures. The illuminator of ca. 1400, named by Millard Meiss the Master of Berry's Cleres Femmes, also worked on a number of other manuscripts owned by Jean de Berry: Boccaccio's *Cleres et nobles femmes* (Paris, B.N. fr. 598), from which the illuminator takes his name, a manuscript given to Jean de Berry in 1404 by Jean de la Barre; a Livy (Geneva, Bibliothèque Publique fr. 77); and a *Bible Historiale* (Paris, B.Ars. 5057–58). The anonymous illuminator who repainted parts of B.N. fr. 120 reappears in the *Lancelot* (Paris, B.N. fr. 112), where he collaborated with the illuminator Evrard d'Espingues, who also illustrated the *Tristan* (Chantilly, Musée Condé 404). B.N. fr. 112 was written in 1470 in Tournai by Micheau Gantelet, and also belonged to Jacques d'Armagnac.

Paris, Bibliothèque Nationale, MS Français 2186: Roman de la poire (Paris, ca. 1250). Parchment, 83 ff. 205 x 135 mm. Text in one column, 20 lines. 9 full-page miniatures, many containing two scenes in roundels or quatrefoils, 18 historiated initials. Among the prefatory full-page miniatures in this manuscript are representations of famous lovers from literature, including some of the earliest French representations of Tristan and Isolde, as well as Cligés and Fénice, Pyramus and Thisbe, Paris and Helen. Other couples in the full-page sequence are less certainly identified, but they also include the hero and heroine of the *Roman de la poire*, who appear again in the historiated initials illustrating the text. They are shown as a noble couple, both wearing heraldic garments emblazoned with the arms of France charged with *a cross or lozengy gules*. These arms are probably fictitious, as they cannot be traced in the contemporary heraldic sources, but the use of France differenced may indicate that the manuscript was made for a royal patron. The painting is of extremely high quality and the anonymous artist has been associated with a large Parisian workshop named the "Bari atelier" after a gradual now at San Nicola, Bari, which is a copy of a book made for use at the French royal *capella*.

Rennes, Bibliothèque Municipale, MS 255(148): Estoire, Merlin, Lancelot (ending incomplete) (Paris, ca. 1220–30). Parchment, 276 ff. 440 x 310 mm. Text in 3 columns, 45 lines. 57 historiated initials. This is the earliest illustrated surviving Vulgate Cycle manuscript. It can be approximately dated and localized on the basis of its codicological and stylistic affinities with a group of Psalters made in Paris for ladies of the French royal household early in the 1220s: Manchester, John Rylands University Library lat. 22; Leningrad, Saltykov-Schtschedrin State Public Library lat. Q.v.I, 67; Paris, B.N. n.a. lat. 1392, and other manuscripts, including the moralized Bibles in Vienna (Ö.N.B. Codex 1179) and Toledo Cathedral Library. The decade of the 1220s is very close to the likely date of composition of the first parts of the Vulgate Cycle, and although the manuscript contains no firm evidence of patronage it is likely that this manuscript, and possibly even its texts, were also royal commission. [MAS]

ɜ Branner, Robert. *Manuscript Painting in Paris During the Reign of Saint Louis: A Study of Styles.* Berkeley: University of California Press, 1977.

Loomis, Roger Sherman, and Laura Hibbard Loomis. *Arthurian Legends in Medieval Art.* London: Oxford University Press, 1938.

Meiss, Millard. *French Painting in the Time of Jean de Berry.* 2 vols. London: Phaidon, 1967.

Stones, M.A. "The Earliest Illustrated Prose *Lancelot* Manuscript?" *Reading Medieval Studies*, 3 (1977), 3–44.

MAP, WALTER (ca. 1140–ca. 1210), compiled *De Nugis Curialium* ("Courtiers' Trifles") in the last quarter of the twelfth century at the urging of a friend, who requested that Walter "put down in writing sayings and doings hitherto unrecorded or anything conspicuously remarkable." Born in Hereford, Walter had a childlike fascination with the superstitious, the incredible, and the marvelous. He relates with particular relish tales of his neighbors, the Welsh. His work is a series of anecdotes taken from his own observations and experiences, from stories he has read or heard, and from contemporary and ancient history. Although none is specifically Arthurian, certain of his tales contain motifs and themes that have analogues in contemporary Arthurian literature. The fragments, gathered after Walter's death and arranged in a loosely thematic format, are preserved in a single manuscript (Oxford, Bodley 851) of the late fourteenth century. The Vulgate Cycle of Arthurian romance is attributed, in the text itself, to Walter, but the attribution has long been recognized as false. [WWK]

‏ Map, Walter. *De Nugis Curialium (Courtiers' Trifles)*, ed. and trans. M.R. James, rev. C.N.L. Brooke and R.A.B. Mynors. Oxford: Clarendon, 1983.

MARCHE DE GAULE: see LANCELOT DO LAC.

MARIE DE FRANCE, a twelfth-century French poet who may have been a resident of England. She composed a version of the St. Patrick legend (*L'Espurgatoire Saint Patrice*), a collection of fables (*Ysopet*), and the lais for which she is best known. Her contribution to Arthurian literature was made in two lais: *Chevrefueil* and *Lanval.* The former is a 118-line poem recounting a brief and passionate encounter between Tristan and Isolde in a forest. *Lanval* (646 lines) deals with an "otherworld" adventure of the hero, who leaves Arthur's court after being treated unjustly; he then finds love with a fairy being who swears him to secrecy. Later, Guenevere makes advances to him, and in his own defense he is forced to reveal his love. Despite this violation of his oath, his lady arrives at the last moment to save him from punishment. Marie's accomplishment in these lais (as in her others) resides in a combination of economical narrative with effective analysis of emotion, and in a combination of the ideal with worldly realities. [NJL]

‏ Marie de France. *Lais*, ed. Alfred Ewert. Oxford: Blackwell, 1960.

Mickel, Emanuel J., Jr. *Marie de France.* New York: Twayne, 1974.

MARK (MARC, MARCO), King of Cornwall, is the deceived husband in the triangle with Isolde of Ireland and his sister's son, Tristan. Early versions of the legend treat Mark with sympathy: he is an essentially noble figure placed in an impossible position by the two people whom he loves best. However, his role as the deceived husband and tales like the one that he had horse's ears made him an object of ridicule, and as sympathy for the lovers grew, so Mark's character deteriorated. It reached a nadir in the French Prose *Tristan* (early thirteenth century), where he emerges as a despicable and cowardly villain, who finally murders his nephew. It is a reputation he has retained in most modern literature. (*See also* CASTLE DORE; TRISTAN AND ISOLDE.) [RHT]

❧ Weismann-Wiedemann, Friederike. "From Victim to Villain: King Mark." In *The Expansion and Transformation of Courtly Literature.* Athens: University of Georgia Press, 1980, pp. 49–68.

MARQUES, ROMAN DE: *see* **SEPT SAGES DE ROME, LES.**

MARQUIS, DON(ALD ROBERT PERRY) (1878–1937), American humorist, wrote three Arthurian burlesque pieces. The first two are short poems: "Tristram and Isolt" tells how Mark traps the lovers; "Lancelot and Guinevere" comments irreverently upon how their affair brought the lovers not happiness but guilt. This idea is expanded in the stage-Irish short story "King O'Meara and Queen Guinevere," which pokes fun at people who take life too seriously. [RHT]

❧ Marquis, Don. "King O'Meara and Queen Guinevere." *Saturday Evening Post*, 202, 37 (15 March 1930), 6–7 ff.; 38 (22 March), 22–23 ff.

——— . *Sonnets to a Red-Haired Lady (By a Gentleman with a Blue Beard) and Famous Love Affairs.* Garden City, N.Y.: Doubleday, Page, 1922.

MARRIAGE OF GUENEVERE, THE: *see* HOVEY, RICHARD.

MARRIAGE OF ISEULT: A TRAGEDY IN TWO SCENES, THE: *see* LEE, THOMAS HERBERT.

"MARRIAGE OF SIR GAWAIN, THE," a ballad version of the Loathly Lady story, of uncertain relation to *The Wedding of Sir Gawain* and extant (with lacunae) only in the Percy Folio of 1660, though possibly of the fifteenth century. Arthur and "gentle" Gawain share the functions of answering the challenger and marrying the Lady (his sister). Family and feasting are particular concerns here. [JP]

❧ Hales, John W., and Frederick J. Furnivall, eds. *Bishop Percy's Folio Manuscript: Ballads and Romances.* London: Trübner, 1867–69, Vol. 1, p. 103.

MARSHALL, EDISON, author of *The Pagan King* (1959), a lively if at times contrived historical novel in which Arthur learns about illusion and reality. Vivain's friendship masks bitter enmity; the hostile Vortigern is his father; his half-brother and rival, Modred, proves a generous foe. Arthur finally resigns his kingship to wander as a bard, transforming historical fact into glorious legend. [RHT]

☙ Marshall, Edison. *The Pagan King.* Garden City, N.Y.: Doubleday, 1959.

MARTIN, FRANK (1890–1974), Swiss composer of *Le Vin herbé* ("The Potion"), an oratorio relating the love of Tristan and Isolde as presented in Joseph Bédier's version of the story. The oratorio, completed in 1940, uses a choir of twelve and a small string orchestra, plus piano; the music is reminiscent of early polyphony. [NJL]

MARTÍNEZ, FERRÁN: *see ZIFAR, LIBRO DEL CABALLERO.*

MARVELLOUS HISTORY OF KING ARTHUR IN AVALON, THE: *see* GEOFFREY JUNIOR.

MASEFIELD, JOHN (1878–1967), Poet Laureate of England from 1930 until his death. Known especially for his poems about sailing and the sea, he published several works of poetry, one novel, and a play based on Arthurian legend. The influence of Yeats and the Celtic revival is evident in his use of material from the Welsh Triads (Tristan as one of the Noble Swineherds of Britain, and the character Gwenivach, Gwenivere's sister and rival), and in his recasting of *The Spoils of Annwfn* as "The Sailing of Hell Race."

The largest body of Masefield's Arthurian poetry is to be found in the collection *Midsummer Night and Other Tales in Verse* (1928), which includes such poems as "The Begetting of Arthur," a highly romantic account of Uther's elopement with Ygern and his murder by henchmen of her father, Merchyon of Cornwall, or "The Taking of Morgause," the story of her abduction by the pirate King Lot of Orkney. Most of the poetry is encumbered with too-pat rhyme schemes and balladlike rhythms that undercut the seriousness of its content. There are, however, poems of some power, such as "Midsummer Night," in which the narrator enters a "hollow hill" to hear Arthur and others describe their roles in the downfall of the Round Table. "The Breaking of the Links" succeeds because of the drama of the subject matter, the trial of Gwenivere; in this poem, the rhyming is more free and less obtrusive. Masefield's Arthurian poetry deals largely with conventional episodes that he recasts with situations or characters of his own invention, e.g., Arthur's divine helpers, who resemble both the *sidhe* and the classical deities.

One distinctive element in Masefield's Arthuriana is his fascination with the story of Tristan and Isolt. Evident both in the poem "The Love-Gift " and in his play *Tristan and Isolt* (1927) is his sympathy for King Mark. This play was Masefield's last, not particularly impressive, venture in the genre. To such conventional elements as the young Tristan's freeing Cornwall from tyranny, the love potion, the substitution of Brangwen for Isolt on the wedding night, and the banishment of the lovers, Masefield adds new elements that include the lovers' public avowal of their love, explicit emphasis on Tristan's political irresponsibility, and Isolt's revulsion against their love affair. This leads to her brutal repudiation of the half-mad Tristan and thus to his death, although unknown to her Mark has been killed in battle. Isolt then stabs herself over Tristan's corpse.

The strength of the drama lies in Mark's torment and in the pathos of Brangwen's unvoiced and unrequited love for him. The structure of the drama is weakened by an overlong comic episode involving Tristan's substituting for Mark's swineherd. In contrast, the poem "Tristan's Singing," in the 1931 collection *Minnie Maylow's Story and Other Tales and Scenes*, is, with its focused lyricism, a better example of Masefield's skill.

Badon Parchments (1947) is a short, slow-paced epistolary novel of the events leading up to Arthur's defeat of the Saxon forces at Badon Hill. Arthur appears only at the beginning and at the end of the novel, which is primarily a report by John of Cos, emissary of the Byzantine emperor, on the feuding and pusillanimous behavior of British nobles. The story of Arthur was one of especial significance to an England torn and permanently changed by two wars—the vacillating and deceitful ministers of *Badon Parchments* are evidence of Masefield's concern.

The Arthurian works by Masefield are not a major element of his canon, although they are of some interest in their use of Celtic elements. They exemplify convention leavened with moderate invention. [AAR]

Masefield, John. *Badon Parchments*. London: Heinemann, 1947.
———. *Midsummer Night and Other Tales in Verse*. London: Heinemann, 1928.
———. *Tristan and Isolt: A Play in Verse*. London: Heinemann; New York: Macmillan, 1927.
Sternlicht, Sanford. *John Masefield*. Boston: Twayne, 1977.

MASQUE OF GWENDOLYN, THE: *see* HEBER, REGINALD.

MASQUE OF THE GRAIL, THE: *see* RHYS, ERNEST.

MATH: *see* MABINOGI.

MATIÈRE DE BRETAGNE (MATTER OF BRITAIN), the traditional des-

ignation of literary material deriving from Britain (in the broadest sense, including Brittany) and of presumed Celtic ancestry. The term, which is a convenient and accepted label if something of a misleading oversimplification, comes from lines written by the French poet Jean Bodel in *Les Saisnes* (late twelfth century). Bodel divides acceptable literary material into the Matter of France (the epics or *chansons de geste*), of Rome (the romances of antiquity), and of Britain (the Breton lais and romances). The usual, but not exclusive, subject of much of the Matter of Britain is Arthur. [NJL].

"MAYING OF QUEEN GUENEVERE, THE": *see* MORRIS, WILLIAM.

MAYNE, WILLIAM, English author of *Earthfasts* (1966), a serious fantasy for younger readers in which an eighteenth-century drummer boy intrudes into the cave where Arthur rests. This causes an irruption into twentieth-century England of legendary phenomena whose impact demonstrates the value of an open mind. The schoolboy Keith returns a surprisingly menacing Arthur to his rest, but the drummer boy must remain in the modern world. [CBH]

ᴥ Mayne, William. *Earthfasts.* London: Hamilton, 1966.

MEDIEVALISM. John Ruskin apparently coined the word *medievalism* in 1853 to distinguish one of three periods of architecture: classicism, medievalism, modernism. The term rapidly came to be employed not only for the study of the Middle Ages, which had been going on since the sixteenth century, but in particular for the use of medieval inspiration or models for almost every aspect of modern life.

The Matter of Britain has always been at the heart of medievalism in the English-speaking countries and often elsewhere, even though the two have not always advanced in step. There were always reasons for studying the Middle Ages. In the sixteenth and seventeenth centuries, the pamphlet wars of the Reformation involved elaborate study of medieval religious history and institutions. In France and the Netherlands, this was to lead to the vast series of medieval texts and documents edited by the Maurist and Bollandist Fathers (the latter continuing today) and hence to the development of the ancillary sciences of history, in particular diplomatic, paleography, and chronology; in sixteenth-century England, the assertion of the historic independence of the English church from Rome led to the recovery and study of Anglo-Saxon. At the same time, the Matter of Britain enjoyed unprecedented influence as an important element of Tudor and Stuart policy, both foreign and domestic. This, however, was the pseudo-historical Arthur of Geoffrey of Monmouth, not the Arthur of the romantic cycle.

Already assailed by the critical historical temper (one of the more fortunate products of Renaissance humanism), this Arthur was involved in the downfall of the Stuart monarchy, and the romantic Arthur was involved in turn. In the seventeenth century, English legal medievalism was the main basis of parliamentary opposition to the Stuarts. "Magna Carta," in Coke's memorable reminder to the 1628 Parliament, "is such a fellow he will have no sovereign." Thus, medievalism and Arthurianism were for a time apparently opposed. In these centuries, only Spenser managed to handle Arthurian material effectively, in *The Faerie Queene*, and this work already had an air of antiquarianism, of revival: Malory and the Middle Ages were beginning to be something in the past. Spenser's epic, in C.S. Lewis's words, typifies in some ways "the great literature of the fifteen eighties and nineties . . . which humanism . . . would have prevented if it could."

While medievalism grew, however, the great legend—rejected by Milton as an epic subject, rendered absurd by Blackmore, redeemed from neglect only by Dryden and Purcell's *King Arthur, the British Worthy* (1691)—survived into the eighteenth century in little more than local antiquities and country ballads. The Medieval Revival of that century involved a study of the romance, but this was antiquarian rather than popular. It might be thought that the society that produced Ossian and Rowley could have handled Arthur, but, except satirically, the Romantics found the Matter unmanageable, even when they cared to attempt it. "As to Arthur, you could not by any means make a poem on him national to Englishmen. What have we to do with him?" asked Coleridge.

By the end of the eighteenth century, everything was ready for the great outburst of historical study that was to characterize the nineteenth century. Vast collections of documents had been assembled and edited, principally in France; Voltaire, Vico, and Herder had devised philosophies of approach to the past; Scott would show how history might be told ("Scott taught Europe to write history," said Thierry); the Middle Ages, if not respectable, were at least fashionable. The greater part of nineteenth-century historical writing was to be medieval, increasingly as it became recognized what society owed to medieval institutions, to parliament rather than senate, jury rather than tribune, and to medieval "representation" rather than Greek "democracy."

Scholarship apart, there were powerful social impulses to medievalism. In *Le Génie du Christianisme* (1802), Chateaubriand undertook to show that medieval literature and art were superior to pagan by reason of their Christianity. The argument was useful to Protestant and Catholic alike, and as employed by A.W. Pugin and John Ruskin it was to have a wide-ranging effect in England and America. Political motives to medievalism were even stronger than religious. In eighteenth-century France, it had been necessary to invent "feudalism" in order that the Revolution might overthrow it, but the loss of political direction following the downfall of Napoleon could only be reconciled with national pride by recalling what Michelet called "the epic of the people" in its largely medieval entirety. In Germany, the demand for political and economic unity was to be supported by recalling the cultural heritage of the medieval German empire, while the English preferred to attribute their power and prosperity to the slow maturing of their medieval institutions rather than to industrialization.

The Arthurian recovery was signaled by the republication of Malory after almost 200 years: the two editions of 1816 and Southey's of 1817 were the first since 1634. Meanwhile, medievalism had become not only respectable but necessary. The Oxford Movement in religion, the Arthurian Revival in art, the Gothic Revival in architecture, and the Young England movement in politics illustrate a dominance that was to last through the 1860s and yield ground only slowly until 1914. The first of Tennyson's Arthurian poems, "The Lady of Shalott," came in 1832; myth was restored and the pseudo-historical Arthur now troubled only historians. Tennyson spoke for his age: his high moral treatment of the legend inspired not only the Pre-Raphaelite poets and artists and their successors on the one hand, but on the other the new, or reformed, public schools of England, which were satisfying the demand for an enlarged middle class of professional men, administrators, and soldiers. This public-school ethos proved equally assimilable in the United States, as shown by the popularity of a native work, Sidney Lanier's *The Boy's King Arthur* (1880).

Around the turn of the century, the fortunes of both medievalism and Arthurianism changed significantly: both were enlarged by new studies, such as anthropology, and new social interests, such as occultism. J. Comyns Carr's *King Arthur* (1895), with designs by Burne-Jones and music by Sir Arthur Sullivan, both summed up Victorian Arthurianism and heralded a wave of drama and poetry that, expanding to include prose fiction in the thirties, continues unabated: the poetry reached a peak with large-scale treatments by Edwin Arlington Robinson, T.S. Eliot, Charles Williams, and David Jones.

The First World War dealt a serious blow to the public ethos of chivalry and the dominance of medievalism as a social force: after 1914, Europe no longer looked to the past for models. Medievalism remained strong in particular contexts, such as Thomist philosophy in Roman Catholic circles, Gothic Revival architecture in the Bauhaus, and economic medievalism (which had powerfully influenced Karl Marx and William Morris earlier) in the English Labour movement. Meanwhile, medieval, including Arthurian, scholarship was being steadily consolidated and institutionalized: the Medieval Academy of America was founded in 1925, the International Arthurian Society, in 1949.

Even greater changes occurred after the Second World War. By about 1960, it became apparent that the great age of collection (in all the arts), textual establishment, and editing was virtually over, and that medieval art and literature were now available for critical appreciation and popular enjoyment, as shown by the current popularity of medieval music, dance, and drama ensembles. In Arthurian studies, the most dramatic change has been the emergence of a third Arthur, the Arthur of history. Finally, medievalism in general, and certainly Arthurian subcreation, have benefited immeasurably from the readmission of fantasy to the canons of literary acceptance in the last fifteen years. (*See also* ARTHURIAN REVIVAL.) [LJW]

🙠 Chandler, Alice. *A Dream of Order: The Medieval Ideal in Nineteenth-Century English Literature.* Lincoln: University of Nebraska Press, 1970.

Clark, Kenneth. *The Gothic Revival.* London: Constable, 1928; rev. ed. 1962.

Ferguson, Wallace K. *The Renaissance in Historical Thought.* Boston: Houghton Mifflin, 1948.

Fraser, John. *America and the Patterns of Chivalry.* Cambridge and New York: Cambridge University Press, 1982.

Girouard, Mark. *The Return to Camelot: Chivalry and the English Gentleman.* New Haven, Conn.: Yale University Press, 1981.

Kenney, Alice P., and Leslie J. Workman. "Ruins, Romance, and Reality: Medievalism in Anglo-American Imagination and Taste 1750–1840." *Winterthur Portfolio,* 10 (1975), 131–62.

Merriman, James D. *The Flower of Kings: A Study of the Arthurian Legend in England Between 1485 and 1835.* Lawrence: University Press of Kansas, 1973.

MELECH ARTUS ("King Arthur"), a fragmentary Hebrew prose text, dating from 1279, extant in a Vatican manuscript. The work, a condensed *Morte d'Arthur*, is based ultimately on the Vulgate *Merlin* and *Mort Artu*, but was probably translated from an Italian or French intermediary (doubtless a prose text in which the episodes were already abridged). Following a brief prologue, the Hebrew text recounts the birth of "Artusen," so-called because he was born through the "art" of Merlin, to whom he was to be delivered for upbringing. Suddenly, with only a paragraph of transition, Arthur is King, and the Round Table has lost forty-two of its finest knights in the Grail quest. After the election of their replacements, the story turns to the Winchester tourney, which Lancelot attends incognito, wearing on his helmet the sleeve of the Maiden of "Askalot." As he is distinguishing himself in battle and earning the admiration of all, the text breaks off in mid-sentence. [NJL]

🙠 Leviant, Curt, ed. and trans. *King Artus: A Hebrew Arthurian Romance of 1279.* Assen: van Gorcum; New York: Ktav, 1969.

MELERANZ: *see* PLEIER, DER.

MELIADOR: *see* FROISSART, JEHAN.

MELIADUS: *see* PALAMEDES.

"MELIAGRANCE AND GUENEVERE": *see* ORMEROD, JAMES.

MEMORIAL DAS PROEZAS DA SEGUNDA TÁVOLA REDONDA: *see* FERREIRA DE VASCONCELOS, JORGE.

MENA, FERNANDO DE: *see PERSEFORES, HISTORIA DEL NOBLE REY.*

MERAUGIS DE PORTLESGUEZ: *see* RAOUL DE HOUDENC.

MÉRIADEUC (or *Le Chevalier aux deux épées*), a French romance of 12,352 lines probably composed in the second quarter of the thirteenth century. The Knight of the Two Swords is so called because he won a second weapon at Arthur's court after unfastening a sheath about the waist of Lore of Caradigan. Lore wishes to marry the anonymous knight, who has since disappeared. The sword had in fact come from the corpse of the hero's father, Bleheri, killed in his war against Brien de la Gastine. After the hero comes by chance to his mother's castle, and discovers his identity and the nature of his father's death (Brien had tricked Gauvain into helping him and Gauvain had unwittingly slain Bleheri), he avenges him, is reconciled with Gauvain, and marries Lore. A subplot tells how Gauvain searches for Mériadeuc and eventually fights incognito with him, defeats the traitor Brien des Illes, and consummates his relationship with a girl he had championed earlier.

This poem is a quintessential Gauvain romance, containing motifs and episodes found elsewhere, all woven into a well-structured and well-written whole. [KB]

Foerster, Wendelin, ed. *Li Chevaliers as deus Espees.* Halle: Niemeyer, 1877.

MERLIJN-CONTINUATIE: *see* VELTHEM, LODEWIJK VAN.

MERLIN (MYRDDIN), prophet and magician, was born of the fertile imagination of Geoffrey of Monmouth in his *Historia Regum Britanniae* (ca. 1135), with some inspiration from local traditions and the chronicler Nennius. Geoffrey had him engendered in a nun, a daughter of the King of Demetia, by a beautiful incubus. He is born in the city of Carmarthen, and his name comes from the Welsh form of the toponym, *Caermyrddin* 'Myrddin's Town,' with *l* being substituted for *d* to avoid the unpleasant Latin form *Merdinus*.

In Geoffrey's *Vita Merlini* and in Welsh texts, Merlin/Myrddin is a prophet living in sixth-century north Britain, with evident pan-Celtic loyalties. In medieval Wales, numerous mantic poems were ascribed to his authorship; although none of the extant Welsh texts predate Geoffrey, it is generally held that they are the elaboration of a much earlier folkloric Wildman in the Woods theme, widespread through the British Isles. An early legend, reflected in such texts as the *Afallennau* (from the Black Book of Carmarthen), has Myrddin reduced to misery and madness, living in the Caledonian Forest. Since the battle of Arfderydd, Myrddin has endured this suffering, thinking himself hunted by Rhydderch, lamenting his fate, and remembering a happier past. Geoffrey incorporated a list of Merlin's prophecies into his *Historia* and devoted another work entirely to Merlin, the *Vita Merlini* (ca. 1150). Thanks largely to Geoffrey's authority, Merlin was accepted throughout western Christendom as a great seer.

Merlin first appears in the vernacular around the year 1200 in the Old French verse *Merlin*, by Robert de Boron, a continuation of his *Joseph d'Arimathie*. Only a fragment of Robert's poem remains, but there are two prose redactions, in the Vulgate Cycle and in the so-called *Suite du Merlin*, or *Huth Merlin*. Robert's *Merlin* is heavily indebted to Geoffrey, but Robert's religious conception of his material causes Merlin to take on an important redemptive and prophetic role. *Merlin* opens with an assembly of devils plotting to bring about the ruin of humankind by creating a prophet to rival Christ who would be half-human, half-devil. One of their number drives a wealthy man to despair and cohabits with one of his daughters in her sleep. However, she tells her confessor Blaise and is signed with the cross so that, when her son is born, he has a hairy body and preternatural knowledge but not his father's will to evil. Because of his father, he knows the past; and God, because of his mother's goodness, allows him to foretell the future. At baptism, the infant is named Merlin. He soon shows his special powers by saving his mother from a sentence of death; and before he is three years old he dictates to his mother's confessor the story of Joseph of Arimathea and the transferral of the Holy Grail to Britain and tells of his own supernatural conception.

The setting is now fifth-century Britain, where King Constant has just died, leaving three sons, Moine, Pendragon, and Uter. The first is murdered and his place usurped by his seneschal, Vertigier, who eventually allies himself with the Saxons. Pendragon and Uter flee abroad. Vertigier attempts to build an impregnable tower, but three times it collapses. On the advice of his astronomers, he sends for a "fatherless child," whose blood is to be mixed with the mortar. Merlin is produced and explains that the tower is unstable because it is set on the back of two dragons, who move around under its weight. He explains that the two dragons symbolize King Constant's sons and Vertigier, and that Vertigier will be killed in a great struggle between them. And indeed, three months later Pendragon and Uter land at Winchester, and Vertigier perishes in the flames of his own tower. Pendragon now reigns and with the help of Merlin persuades the Saxons to leave Britain. But they soon return and Pendragon is slain, as Merlin has predicted, in a great battle at Salisbury. His brother defeats the enemy and assumes the throne, taking the name Uterpendragon. On Merlin's advice, he has the Round Table constructed, an exact replica of the Grail table fashioned by Joseph of Arimathea, which in turn was a replica of the table of the Last Supper. During a great Christmas celebration at Carduel, Uter falls in love with the virtuous Ygerne, wife of his vassal the Duke of Tintagel. Merlin casts a spell that causes her to believe that Uter is her husband, and through this deception Arthur is conceived in the castle of Tintagel. The duke is killed that same night, and Uter soon weds Ygerne, who confides to him how she had been victimized. On Merlin's advice, Uter does not reveal to her that he is the father and instead has Merlin give the child to foster parents unaware of his royal descent. After Uter's death, the young Arthur proves himself the rightful heir by pulling the sword from the stone.

In the prose Didot-*Perceval*, which is likewise thought to have been based on a poem by Robert, Merlin assists Perceval in his adventures at the Grail castle. After Perceval assumes his place as the Grail King and fills the Siege Perilous at Arthur's Round Table, Merlin retires to the woods near the Grail castle in company with his mother's confessor, Blaise, who will write down for posterity the adventures of the Round Table and the Grail.

In Robert's conception, Merlin, rescued from the devils by the holiness of his mother, plays a redemptive role as mediator between earthly chivalry and the heavenly plan of salvation: he oversees the conception and early education of Arthur, creates the symbolism of the Round Table, and prepares Perceval for the Grail quest.

Robert's *Merlin* was given two continuations, designed to link Arthur's early years to the *Lancelot–Graal* story: the "historical" one of the Vulgate and the "romantic" one of the *Huth Merlin*. Both tell of the early years of Arthur's reign and his wars against rebellious vassals, but the *Huth* continuation emphasizes such familiar episodes as the birth of Mordred, the revelation of Arthur's parentage by Merlin, his combat with Pellinor, the obtaining of Excalibur from the lake, the tragic tale of Balain, the installation of the Round Table at Arthur's court, the enchantment of Merlin by Viviane, Morgain's plots to destroy Arthur, as well as many other adventures. Merlin's role as prophet is still important, but there is increased exploitation of his skills as a necromancer. In the French *Lancelot–Graal*, where Perceval's quest is superseded by that of Galahad, Merlin's role is reduced to a minimum: he does not appear in person, but is remembered as the prophet of the Grail.

In England, the legend of Merlin was well known through Geoffrey of Monmouth, his French translator Wace, the French prose romances, and English adaptations of the French material. Robert Mannyng included a translation of Wace's *Brut* as the first part of his *Story of England* (1338), where the legends of Merlin occupy some 7,000 lines. Besides Malory's well-known adaptations, there are three other English tales involving Merlin: *Arthour and Merlin* (about 10,000 lines; composed in Kent in the second half of the thirteenth century); Lovelich's nearly 30,000-line translation of only half of the Vulgate *Merlin*; and the English Prose *Merlin* of about 1450, which is a fairly literal translation of the Vulgate *Merlin*.

In all these romances, both English and French, Merlin is constantly at the center of the action, predicting events and using his magical powers to control history. He is puckish and benevolent and constantly makes use of his shapeshifting powers to aid and befuddle. He is the creator of the Round Table, and its prophet. Robert and his continuators judiciously mingle Merlin's prophetic and magical powers to create what is certainly the most colorful and one of the most ubiquitous characters in Arthurian romance.

In many minor works of the late Middle Ages, the Renaissance, and into the eighteenth century, Merlin plays an episodic role as a *deus ex machina* whose magical powers move along or resolve plot complications. In this late period, and particularly after the Romantic period in the nineteenth century, Merlin's original function as prophet is entirely lost and he becomes uniquely Merlin the Magician/Wizard. [WWK]

Loomis, Roger Sherman, ed. *Arthurian Literature in the Middle Ages*. Oxford: Clarendon, 1959, Chapters 3, 8, 19, 23, 24, and 37.

Markale, Jean. *Merlin l'enchanteur, ou l'eternelle quête magique*. Paris: Retz, 1981.

Zumthor, Paul. *Merlin le prophète*. Lausanne: Payot, 1943.

MERLIN: *see* COUTTS, FRANCIS; DRAESEKE, FELIX AUGUST BERNHARD; GOLDMARK, KARL; IMMERMANN, KARL LEBERECHT; KRALIK, RICHARD VON; LOVELICH, HENRY; NYE, ROBERT; ROBERT DE BORON; ROBINSON, EDWIN ARLINGTON; VULGATE CYCLE.

"MERLIN" I AND II: *see* EMERSON, RALPH WALDO.

MERLIN: *A DRAMATIC POEM:* *see* FULLARTON, R. MACLEOD.

MERLIN AND THE DRAGONS OF ATLANTIS: *see* HILDEBRANDT, RITA AND TIM.

"MERLIN AND THE GLEAM": *see* TENNYSON, ALFRED LORD.

"MERLIN AND VIVIAN": *see* MUMFORD, ETHEL WATTS.

MERLIN DER WILDE: *see* UHLAND, LUDWIG.

MERLIN DER ZAUBERER: *see* WIELAND, CHRISTOPH MARTIN.

MERLIN L'ENCHANTEUR: *see* SECOND EMPIRE.

MERLIN MERLOT: *see* VILAIN QUI DEVINT RICHE ET PUIS PAUVRE, LE.

MERLIN ODER DAS WÜSTE LAND

MERLIN ODER DAS WÜSTE LAND: see DORST, TANKRED.

MERLIN OR, THE RETURN OF ARTHUR: see SKINNER, MARTYN.

MERLIN'S CAVE: see KENT, WILLIAM.

MERLINS GEBURT: see STUCKEN, EDUARD.

MERLIN'S GODSON: see MUNN, H. WARNER.

MERLIN'S MAGIC: see CLARE, HELEN.

MERLIN'S MIRROR: see NORTON, ANDRE.

MERLIN'S MISTAKE: see NEWMAN, ROBERT.

MERLIN'S RING: see MUNN, H. WARNER; TREVOR, MERIOL.

"MERLIN'S SONG": see EMERSON, RALPH WALDO.

MERLINS WEISSAGENDE STIMME AUS SEINER GRUFT: see WIELAND, CHRISTOPH MARTIN.

MERLÍNÚSSPÁ: see GUNNLAUGR LEIFSSON.

MERVEILLES DE RIGOMER, LES, an incomplete French verse romance of 17,271 lines written in the second half of the thirteenth century by an author who calls himself Jehan. At the request of Dionise, mistress of the Castle of Rigomer, Lancelot sets out to free it from enchantment but is rendered powerless, by a magic lance and ring, and becomes a servant. Gauvain sets out to free Lancelot, is himself imprisoned but freed by his mistress Lorie, before freeing Lancelot and the Castle of Rigomer. He refuses to marry Dionise and returns to court. A second plot involves Arthur's restoring to the heiress of Quintefuele her heritage. The poem breaks off without a conclusion.

As well as knowing Chrétien de Troyes and the Prose *Lancelot*, the author excels at inventing supernatural creatures, such as talking birds, flame-breathing panthers and other savage cats, a man-eating falcon. *Les Merveilles de Rigomer* is one of the last Old French Arthurian romances to have been written in verse. [KB]

• Foerster, Wendelin, and H. Breuer, eds. *Les Merveilles de Rigomer*. 2 vols. Dresden: Gesellschaft für romanische Literatur, 1908–15.

MIDDLE DUTCH ARTHURIAN LITERATURE.

Arthurian material must have been popular in the Netherlands very early. This is proved by Flemish proper names (e.g., Iwain and Walewainus) that appear in charters from the beginning of the twelfth century. Later on, it was not only in Flanders that Arthurian romances were in vogue. From manuscript transmissions beginning in the second half of the thirteenth century, it appears that Arthurian romances were also written, copied, recited, and read in Brabant, Limburg, and Holland.

The manuscript transmission of Middle Dutch Arthurian literature is a peculiar business. Four complete manuscripts have been transmitted, as well as fragments of eighteen codices. A remarkable fact is that two of those manuscripts contain nearly all of the Middle Dutch Arthurian romances. Manuscript 's-Gravenhage, K.B. Hs. 129 A 10 (known under the collective term *Lancelot-Compilatie*), contains no fewer than ten romances; and in the codex Burgersteinfurt, Fürst zu Bentheimsche Schlossbibliothek, B 37, three romances have been preserved (the *Historie van den Grale*, the *Boec van Merline*, and the *Merlijn-Continuatie*).

According to current scholarship, few of these can be regarded as faithful translations from the Old French. Of the oldest Old French verse romances, only Chrétien de Troyes's *Perceval* was transposed literally into Middle Dutch, as appears from the Liège *Perchevael* fragments, which date to the thirteenth century. In addition, the Vulgate *Lancelot–Queste–Mort* was translated twice. A faithful verse translation is preserved in the *Lancelot-Compilatie*, and the so-called Rotterdam fragments contain an extremely literal prose translation of the Prose *Lancelot*. The *Suite du Merlin*, too, was translated. In 1326, Lodewijk van Velthem completed his verse translation, the *Merlijn-Continuatie*.

A large number of Middle Dutch Arthurian romances are adaptations from the Old French. The oldest are adaptations of the *Vengeance Raguidel* (under the title *Wrake van Ragisel*) and of Thomas's *Roman de Tristan*, both in fragments dating from the thirteenth century. The *Fergus* was also adapted into Middle Dutch, probably in the second half of the thirteenth century. The text, under the title *Ferguut*, has been transmitted in a codex dated ca. 1350. The Old French Prose *Lancelot* was not only translated twice but also adapted once. This verse adaptation, *Lantsloot vander Haghedochte*, has been transmitted in fragmentary form. Some 6,000 lines are extant from a splendid manuscript that must have once contained over 100,000. Finally, mention should be made of the adaptations by Jacob van Maerlant, who about 1261 transposed prose versions of Robert de Boron's *Joseph d'Arimathie* and *Merlin* into Middle Dutch (*Historie van den Grale* and *Boec van Merline*).

One Arthurian romance occupies an exceptional position in regard to the question of whether the work is a translation or an adaptation. The *Torec*, attributed to Jacob van Maerlant, goes back to an Old French Arthurian romance (*Torrez chevalier au cercle d'or*), but the source has not survived.

Five romances do not seem to go back to an Old French source. Four of these have been preserved in the *Lancelot-Compilatie*: *Lanceloet en het hert met de witte voet*, *Moriaen*, *Van den Riddere metter mouwen*, and *Walewein ende Keye*. These were written mainly in the second part of the thirteenth century. From the same period dates one of the high points of Middle Dutch Arthurian romance: the *Roman van Walewein*, by Penninc, who did not manage to finish his work. Pieter Vostaert completed the romance, which comprises about 11,200 lines. The well-considered structure of the work is based on Aarne-Thompson Tale Type 550 (cf. Grimm's *Der Goldene Vogel*).

In the *Lancelot-Compilatie*, versions of a number of Arthurian romances have been transmitted that occupy an exceptional position. These are adaptations of Middle Dutch Arthurian romances. Responsible for these versions is the compiler of the *Lancelot-Compilatie*, who inserted abbreviated versions of the *Perchevael*, the *Riddere metter mouwen*, and the *Wrake van Ragisel* in his composite codex (of the other romances found in the *Lancelot-Compilatie*, the *Moriaen* was inserted unchanged, *Lanceloet en het hert met de witte voet* was probably abbreviated, and of the *Torec* and *Walewein ende Keye* no fragments have survived).

After the fourteenth century, the popularity of Arthurian romances appears to have waned. This may be deduced from the lack of manuscript transmissions after that date and the scant dispersion of the material in chapbooks. Only one chapbook, the *Historie van Merlijn* (ca. 1540), has been partly preserved. [BB]

🕮 Berteloot, A. "Artus in den Niederlanden: ein Überblick." In *Studia Belgica: Aufsätze zur Literatur- und Kulturgeschichte Belgiens*, ed. Hans-Joachim Lope. Berne, 1980, pp. 17–28.

Besamusca, Bart. *Repertorium van de Middnederlandse Arturepiek: Een beknopte beschrijving van de handschriftelijke en gedrukte overlevering*. Utrecht, 1985.

Gerritsen, W.P. "Artus IV. Mittelniederländische Literatur." In *Lexikon des Mittelalters*. Munich: Artemis, 1980, Vol. 1, cols. 1085–87.

Sparnaay, Hendricus. "The Dutch Romances." In *Arthurian Literature in the Middle Ages*, ed. Roger Sherman Loomis. Oxford: Clarendon, 1959, pp. 443–61.

MIDDLETON, THOMAS: *see* ENGLISH AND AMERICAN ARTHURIAN LITERATURE (MODERN).

MIDSUMMER NIGHT AND OTHER TALES IN VERSE:
see MASEFIELD, JOHN.

MIRABILIA: see NENNIUS.

MISERICORDS, hinged seats in the choir stalls of medieval churches that when tipped up offer shelflike support for the person who must stand during a lengthy service (their name implies "indulgence"). The brackets under these hidden seats are often carved, displaying figures and scenes inspired by fables, romances, or incidents of daily life. Popular Arthurian subjects include Tristan and Isolde under the spreading branches of the tree in which King Mark is concealed (Chester and Lincoln Cathedrals, fourteenth century) and Ywain plunging through the turreted castle gate as the portcullis bisects his horse (Chester, Lincoln, Boston, Enville, late fourteenth century; New College, Oxford, late fifteenth century). [MS]

Anderson, M.D. *Misericords*. Harmondsworth: Penguin, 1954.
———. *The Choir Stalls of Lincoln Minster*. Lincoln, 1951.
Bond, Francis. *Woodcarvings in English Churches, Misericords*. London and New York: Clarendon, 1910, Part 2, Sec. 7.
Loomis, Roger Sherman, and Laura Hibbard Loomis. *Arthurian Legends in Medieval Art*. London: Oxford University Press, 1938, pp. 68, 79; figs. 131–32, 168–70.

MISFORTUNES OF ARTHUR, THE: see HUGHES, THOMAS.

MISFORTUNES OF ELPHIN, THE: see PEACOCK, THOMAS LOVE.

MISTS OF AVALON, THE: see BRADLEY, MARION ZIMMER.

MITCHELL, MARY, in *Birth of a Legend* (1956), tells the story of Lohengrin, the son of Perceval. The mysterious arrival of the Swan Knight to defend a maiden in trial-by-combat arouses suspicions in minds unprepared to accept a miracle with simple faith when their own interests are affected. [RHT]

Mitchell, Mary. *Birth of a Legend*. London: Methuen, 1956.

MITCHISON, NAOMI, contemporary English author of a thoughtful, ironic fantasy, *To the Chapel Perilous* (1955), which creates humor by introducing the press into the Arthurian world, then sending reporters with modern professional standards to investigate conflicting claims about the Holy Grail: is it cauldron of plenty, stone, spear, dish, or cup? Truth turns out to be more complex than we expect. [RHT]

☙ Mitchison, Naomi. *To the Chapel Perilous*. London: Allen and Unwin, 1955.

MODENA ARCHIVOLT. Possibly the earliest representation of an Arthurian theme in monumental sculpture appears on the Cathedral of Modena in northern Italy. On the north portal, known as the Porta della Pescheria, the archivolt and lintel are carved in high relief with secular scenes: archivolt figures are identifiable as Arthurian from the inscriptions; the lintel has decorative sculpture including birds, animals, and a man riding a sea-horse.

The action depicted on the archivolt centers on a moated, stone castle having a shield hung on the wall and timber towers as outworks. A woman (Winlogee) is held prisoner by a man (Mardoc). On the left, three mounted knights (Artus de Bretania, Isdernus, and an unnamed knight) charge with lances set; the tower is defended by a thug with a pick-axe. On the right, two knights (Carrado and Galvagin) attack each other with lances, while two more knights (Galvariun and Che) gallop along with their lances at rest over their shoulders. The sculptor, known as the Arthur Master, works with more energy than finesse, but he faithfully records the details of military architecture and knightly equipment. His artistic source and the date of his work have been the subject of long and often heated debate.

Scholars of Arthurian literature and the history of Italian Romanesque art have argued over the sculpture of Modena Cathedral. The cathedral, begun in 1099, is universally considered to be one of the masterpieces of Romanesque art, and its sculpture—especially the work of Wiligelmo on the west façade—is some of the earliest and finest work in Italy. If an early date is also accepted for the sculpture of the north portal, then the sculpture would antedate the earliest written Arthurian romance. Arthurian legends could have come to Italy even before they were brought by Crusaders and the Norman conquerors of southern Italy. Archaeological and art-historical evidence and analysis, however, suggest a date in the second quarter of the twelfth century, no earlier than 1120. Loomis never ceased arguing for a date at the beginning of the century; however, in recent work Stiennon dated the sculpture between 1120 and 1140.

With few exceptions, scholars have agreed on the Arthurian interpretation of the sculpture. The story is that of Carrado of the Dolorous Tower. Winlogee (Guenevere), while riding with the knight Isdernus in the forest, is abducted by a giant, Carrado, who takes her to the Dolorous Tower and turns her over to Mardoc. Artus de Bretania, Galvagin (Gawain), Galvariun, and Che, joined by Isdernus, set out to rescue her. They approach the castle by the two wooden gates, but Burmalt holds off one party with his club, while Carrado and Galvagin fight at the other gate. According to one story, Galvagin was given Carrado's magical sword in order to kill him and enter the castle. Once in the castle, he found the shields of vanquished knights hanging on the walls; finally, he was able to restore the Queen to Arthur. Loomis has made a convincing case for the Breton origin of the names engraved on the arch and identified Winlogee as Guenevere, Mardoc as Mordred, and Carrado as Curoi. He argued that the story comes from the Vulgate *Lancelot*, although the names Winlogee and Mardoc do not appear in the French romance, and Galvagin (Gawain) replaces Lancelot as the hero. He argued further that in an early version of the story of Guenevere's abduction Gawain rather than Lancelot was the rescuer. Other scholars have suggested that the sculpture illustrates the romance of Yder rather than Gawain or Lancelot, and also suggest that Arthur himself rescued Guenevere, with the help of his knights. Lejeune also regards the sculpture on the tower at Modena as Arthurian in inspiration. [MS]

Hutchings, Gweneth. "Isdernus of the Modena Archivolt." *Medium Aevum*, 1 (1932), 204–05.

———. "Gawain and the Abduction of Guinevere." *Medium Aevum*, 4 (1935), 61–66.

Loomis, Roger Sherman. "Modena, Bari, and Hades." *Art Bulletin*, 2 (1923–24), 71–74.

———. "The Date, Source, and Subject of the Arthurian Sculpture at Modena." In *Medieval Studies in Memory of Gertrude Schoepperle Loomis*. Paris: Champion, 1927, pp. 209–28.

Stiennon, Jacques, and Rita Lejeune. "La Légende arthurienne dans la sculpture de la cathédrale de Modène." *Cahiers de Civilisation Médiévale*, 6 (1963), 281–96.

MONACO, RICHARD, writer of fiction, poetry, and films. His Grail trilogy, loosely based on Wolfram von Eschenbach's *Parzival*, is unequaled in Arthurian literature for its depiction of violence both graphic and senseless. *Parsival* (1977) interlaces the story of the naïve prince's awakening from innocence to bitter experience, and his (much altered) Grail-castle adventures, with the search for him by a new character, the faithful servant Broaditch. *The Grail War* (1979) both rationalizes and despiritualizes the Grail quest. Broaditch's last quest and that of Parsival, for his son, Lohengrin, are interwoven in *The Final Quest* (1980).

The novels are all antiromances of the most extreme sort, with many scenes of murder and mayhem, rape and cannibalism, among other atrocities. As in the originals by Chrétien and Wolfram, Gawain's adventures are counterpointed with Parsival's, but neither emerges as admirable; the contrast between the best worldly and the best spiritual knight disappears, as Parsival continually rejects his mission as Grail savior, first in extreme knightly brutality and then in his turning to family life for comfort from the horror of a harsh, feudal, plaguey, hungry, and war-torn world—a true wasteland. Gawain, even more than his medieval counterpart, is a womanizer and an unchivalrous warrior. Opposed to both Gawain and Parsival is Clinschor, his role greatly expanded from Wolfram into that of a frightening representative of the powers of darkness seeking to gain the Grail. Another new character, John of Bligh, emblemizes the forces behind medieval peasant revolts and crazed cults. Throughout, the Grail appears as a nebulous, perhaps nonexistent, source of wealth and power, of which Parsival is (wrongly) thought to have the secret. In the bittersweet ending, he discovers its light within himself, but his problems—including a mistress as well as a disillusioned wife—seem insoluble.

Monaco has begun another fantasy series that again treats Arthurian legend in a highly unorthodox way. Events are set anachronistically in the strife-torn years before Augustus established imperial rule in Rome. *Runes* (1984) deals with the adventures of Arthur's parents, here the son of Spartacus the Gladiator and a British slave. *Broken Stone* (1985) continues their story and introduces the young Arturus (Arthur) to his half-sister Morga (Morgan le Fay). The forces of Good (Avalon) are engaged in a supernatural struggle against those of Evil, and the latter seem to have all the advantages as they scheme to reunite the three stones of the Black Grail. However, they are frustrated finally by their own ambition and treachery. [MF/RHT]

Monaco, Richard. *Parsival or A Knight's Tale*. New York: Macmillan, 1977.
——— . *The Grail War*. New York: Pocket Books, 1979.
——— . *The Final Quest*. New York: Putnam, 1980.
——— . *Runes*. New York: Ace, 1984.
——— . *Broken Stone*. New York: Ace, 1985.

MONSALVAT: *see* BENOÎT, PIERRE.

MONTALVO, GARCÍ RODRÍGUEZ DE, author of *Amadís de Gaula* (1508), a chivalric romance in prose, the major contribution in Spanish to Arthurian literature. Montalvo, a Castilian nobleman of whom little is known, restyled and shortened the primitive fourteenth-century version (also in Castilian) consisting of three books, adding a fourth. His non-Arthurian *Sergas de Esplandián* (1510) is the fifth book or sequel. Books I and II of the primitive *Amadís* were composed ca. 1340, probably in Castile, by a single author who adapted Arthurian motifs and characters from French sources (principally the Vulgate, or Pseudo-Boron, Cycle and the Prose *Tristan*) to create a new, unified story. The pseudo-historical narrative takes place not long after Christ and before the time of Arthur, whose reign is foretold. The central plot coincides with the legends of Lancelot and Tristan, in that the love between the hero and the daughter (not the wife) of his king compels them to conceal their secret passion. They must undergo separation, tests of fidelity and jealousy, penitential exile, and love-madness. The originality of the primitive *Amadís* stems from its transposition of adulterous and "courtly" love into the "true" fidelity of Amadís to Oriana. He is himself son of an illicit marriage between royal parents, separated from them at birth and destined to gain fame and kingdoms through his skill and bravery. His career, aided by Urganda the enchantress (based on Morgan le Fay), follows a schema traditional in myth and folklore. Oriana is daughter of Lisuarte, King of Britain. They become lovers from childhood; but separated by his enigmatic ancestry, career-in-arms, and, in Montalvo's redaction, her father's political aims, they are obliged to conceal their "secret" marriage and the birth of their son from her father for almost the entire length of the story. Book III of the primitive version introduced materials from Hispanic versions of the *matière de Rome*, telling of Amadís's death at the hands of his young son and Oriana's suicide. Montalvo suppressed this outcome and in Book IV depicts Amadís as a moral and military leader and father figure. Recent study has moved from debate on sources and authorship to analysis of style, structure, and theme and evaluation of Montalvo's originality. He preserved the archaic charm of the Arthurian materials in Books I and II, including magical and supernatural forces, while interpolating his views on love and morality. The fame of *Amadís de Gaula*—as a model of chivalric conduct and courtly speech, as a portrait of medieval pageantry and ritual, or as an inventive and stately interlacing on a grand scale, the first in modern prose fiction—is owed to his craft. [LAM]

Montalvo, Garcí Rodríguez de. *Amadís de Gaula*, ed. E.B. Place. 4 vols. Madrid: CSIC, 1959–69.

———. *Amadís of Gaula*, trans. E.B. Place and H.C. Behn. 2 vols. Lexington: University of Kentucky Press, 1974, 1975.

Pierce, Frank. *Amadís de Gaula.* New York: Twayne, 1976.

MONTY PYTHON AND THE HOLY GRAIL (1975) is a film by the comedians known collectively as Monty Python: John Cleese, Graham Chapman, Terry Gilliam, Eric Idle, Terry Jones, and Michael Palin. Gilliam and Jones directed it. The Arthurian element (the Grail quest) serves as a skeletal pretext for extended humorous sketches, such as the Black Knight who continues to fight after Arthur hacks him to bits and the attack by a killer rabbit. Characters include Arthur, Launcelot, Galahad, Bedivere, Gawain, and others, and the filmmakers show an acquaintance with many Arthurian conventions, even though there are few reflections of actual traditional motifs or narrative sequences. The film makes extensive use of slapstick physical comedy, exaggerations, anachronisms, verbal humor, and parody of film conventions (i.e., voice-over, sound effects); it is a masterpiece of comic absurdity, if not a lasting contribution to Arthuriana. [NJL]

Monty Python and the Holy Grail (Book), designed by Derek Birdsall, photographs by Drew Mara. London: Methuen, 1977 (includes first draft and last version of screenplay).

MOON OF GOMRATH, THE: *see* GARNER, ALAN.

MOORE, GEORGE (1852–1933), contrasts decadence with naïveté in *Peronnik the Fool* (1924). An illiterate cowherd attuned to nature, Peronnik journeys with the crippled Sir Gilles de Lacenaire to Grey Castle and, overcoming temptation, wrests the fateful Bowl and Spear from the sorceress Redemonde. The drought breaks in Peronnik's home village, Saint-Jean-de-Braie, but he is not allowed to remain; as a knight, he must go forth to seek further adventure. [CNS]

> Moore, George. *Peronnik the Fool.* New York: Boni and Liveright, 1924.

MOOSACH: *see* WORKSHOP MOOSACH.

MORDRED (MODRED, MEDRAUT), Arthur's nephew. Early Welsh tradition is generally favorable to Mordred, whose name (as *Medraut*) appears almost as early as does that of Arthur. The *Annales Cambriae* record that in 539 both fell in the battle of Camlann but do not make clear whether they were friends or foes. Though opponents in *The Dream of Rhonabwy*, both seek to avoid a conflict caused by others. This tale may have been influenced by Geoffrey of Monmouth, who first identifies Mordred as the son of Arthur's sister Anna, and thus brother of Gawain. Camlann becomes the climax of his attempt to seize both his uncle's kingdom and wife. Since most medieval writers condemn this revolt, they portray Mordred as a villain and traitor.

The Vulgate *Mort Artu* takes the treachery a step further by making Mordred the issue of Arthur's incest with his half-sister Morgause, though the couple are unaware of their relationship at the time. Guenevere, who is in love with Lancelot, is still the object of Mordred's passion, but she rejects him with horror. At Camlann, Arthur kills Mordred, but he receives his mortal wound in the process. In the *Suite du Merlin*, Arthur unsuccessfully arranges for his infant son to be exposed in a boat.

The incest motif is preserved in romances based upon the *Mort Artu*, including Malory's, but Mordred remains no more than Arthur's nephew elsewhere. The Alliterative *Morte Arthure* offers a sympathetic portrait of Mordred as a figure who suffers genuine remorse for his deeds. Some Scottish chronicles even support Mordred as the true heir to the throne usurped by the illegitimate Arthur.

Since the Middle Ages, the incest motif has been retained (Rosemary Sutcliff) or rejected (Tennyson), depending upon the vision of the author. Mordred's mother is usually Morgause, occasionally Morgan le Fay. Mordred is regularly evil, but a few authors do portray him as a human being trapped by a fate he seeks to avoid (Edward Frankland, Henry Treece, Phyllis Karr, Mary Stewart). [RHT]

> Bruce, J.D. "Mordred's Incestuous Birth." In *Medieval Studies in Memory of Gertrude Schoepperle Loomis,* ed. Roger Sherman Loomis. Paris: Champion, 1927, pp. 197–208.
> Varin, Amy. "Mordred, King Arthur's Son." *Folklore,* 90 (1979), 167–77.

***MORDRED: A TRAGEDY: see* NEWBOLT, SIR HENRY.**

MORGAN LE FAY (MORGAIN, MORGANA). Descended from the Celtic deities Morrigan, Macha, and Modron (a divine mother), Morgan first appears in Geoffrey of Monmouth's *Vita Merlini* as foremost among nine sisters on the Isle of Avalon, to which Arthur journeys to be healed of his mortal wound. Chrétien de Troyes notes not only her healing powers but also her relationship as Arthur's sister. In the French verse romances, Morgan remains a powerful and generally benevolent fay, but in the prose romances her reputation declines.

In the Vulgate Cycle, Morgan is still on good terms with her brother, whom she carries off in a boat after the battle of Camlann. However, after her affair with Guiomar is broken up by his cousin, Guenevere, she grows to hate the Queen, and constantly seeks either to seduce Lancelot from her side or to expose their affair. In the Prose *Tristan*, she sends to Arthur's court a magic drinking horn from which no unfaithful lady can drink without spilling. In the Post-Vulgate Cycle, Morgan, here the wife of King Urien and mother of Yvain, becomes Arthur's enemy after he executes one of her lovers, and she incites another lover, Accolon, to kill the King with his own sword.

From a fay untouched by time, Morgan degenerates into a mortal who must conceal her age through magic arts; her once-prized favors are condemned as promiscuity in romances that favor the devotion of courtly lovers; the famed healer now schemes to destroy others, almost invariably with humiliating results. This is how Morgan is pictured by Malory, but she was paid little attention in English literature (a notable exception being *Sir Gawain and the Green Knight*) until rediscovered by modern fantasy writers. Juvenile fiction by authors like Jane Curry and Penelope Lively portrays her as an evil enchantress from the past who threatens a new generation of heroes; but adult fiction by authors like Parke Godwin and Marion Zimmer Bradley, both of whom make her the mother of Mordred, offers a sympathetic portrait of this fascinatingly ambiguous figure. (*See also* AVALON.) [RHT]

Bogdanow, Fanni. "Morgain's Role in the Thirteenth-Century French Prose Romances of the Arthurian Cycle." *Medium Aevum*, 38 (1969), 123–33.

Paton, Lucy Allen. *Studies in the Fairy Mythology of Arthurian Romance.* 2nd ed. Roger Sherman Loomis. New York: Franklin, 1960.

MORIAEN, a Middle Dutch work from the second half of the thirteenth century. The main character is a Moorish knight in search of his father. Walewein and Lancelot also play important parts; at the request of Arthur, they go in search of Perchevael. Both quests are brought to a successful conclusion, and the romance ends with the marriage of Acglovael, Moriaen's father, to the Moorish queen.

The text has been transmitted in two ways. A version included in the *Lancelot-Compilatie* numbers 4,720 lines. A fragment in the Royal Library at Brussels (MS IV 1059), dating from the first half of the fourteenth century, contains 176 lines, which agree almost word for word with the corresponding lines in the *Lancelot-Compilatie*. [BB]

ᴥ Paardekooper-van Buuren, Haaneke, and Maurits Gysseling, eds. *Moriaen*. Zutphen: Thieme, 1971.

Weston, Jessie L., trans. *Morien: A Metrical Romance Rendered into English from the Middle Dutch*. London: Nutt, 1901.

MORRIS, WILLIAM (1834–1896), English poet, novelist, designer, and socialist. 1) MORRIS AS POET. Morris recreates episodes from Sir Thomas Malory's *Morte Darthur* in the four Arthurian poems that open his first and most highly praised book of verse, *The Defence of Guenevere, and Other Poems* (1858). This group contains two pairs of poems: "The Defence of Guenevere" and "King Arthur's Tomb" treat the adulterous love of Launcelot and Guenevere; the much shorter "Sir Galahad, A Christmas Mystery" and "The Chapel in Lyoness" treat the quest for the Holy Grail.

"The Defence of Guenevere" begins abruptly as Arthur's queen, threatened with burning at the stake for her adultery, attempts to counter the accusations of infidelity brought against her by Gauwaine. In her monologue, Guenevere defends her difficult choice of Launcelot's passionate attentiveness over "Arthur's great name and his little love." She recalls the first arrival of Launcelot at Arthur's court, her subsequent joyful sexual encounters with him, and the "bitter day in *la Fausse Garde*" when the stealthy Mellyagraunce discovered the wounded Launcelot's blood on her bed. Despite the self-incriminating nature of her recollections, which tend more toward her condemnation than toward her exoneration, Guenevere appears to evoke pity in Gauwaine by the passion of her defense. Nevertheless, Gauwaine ultimately turns away from Guenevere, leaving her to her execution, which is forestalled only by the sudden arrival, at the very end of the poem, of her rescuer, Launcelot. In "King Arthur's Tomb," set after the death of Arthur, Guenevere's stance toward Launcelot and Arthur has markedly changed. At the beginning of the poem, a weary, confused, and morally uncertain Launcelot rides to meet Guenevere at Glastonbury, and there they reminisce about their unlawful yet exhilarating love. Upon his arrival, he falls asleep, exhausted and unsuspecting, on Arthur's tomb. Guenevere, preparing herself privately to receive her former lover, offers an impassioned prayer, in which her attention wavers between love of Christ and love of Launcelot. The last meeting of Launcelot and Guenevere (whose setting derives partly from Dante Gabriel Rossetti's 1855 watercolor of *Arthur's Tomb*) reveals frustrated passion, remorse, and misunderstanding. While Guenevere cannot conceal her abiding love for the still-attentive Launcelot, she rebukes him for being untrue to Arthur, whom she now acknowledges as her rightful lord and as "the greatest king/ that ever lived." The third poem of Morris's Arthurian group begins with Galahad's monologue, in which he recounts his arrival at a chapel, his dejection at the prospect of the solitary and endless search for the Grail, his awesome vision of Christ, who has assured him that he will receive, for his purity, a heavenly love surpassing earthly love, and his visitation by two angels and four saints, who promise to bring the Grail to him while he sleeps. The poem continues with dramatic dialogue, in which an angel directs Galahad, now awake, to seek his father, Launcelot, and informs him of the imminent arrival of Bors, Percival, and Percival's sister, the only three persons other than Galahad himself who are sufficiently pure to see the Grail. The poem ends as Bors tells Galahad of the destruction and disarray of the other knights who have sought the Grail in vain. In the final poem of the group, Galahad renders spiritual aid to the dying and tormented knight Ozana.

The poems of Morris's Arthurian group succeed, through retrospection and allusion, in suggesting within a restricted compass the larger patterns of the Arthurian legend. They manage to combine their modern poetic concerns (the minutely accurate yet symbolic presentation of physical phenomena sought by Morris and his Pre-Raphaelite friends, and the tracing of mental processes and psychic states developed by Robert Browning in the dramatic monologue) with profound respect for their traditional source. Morris shares with his friend Rossetti (to whom the 1858 volume is dedicated), and with his more famous contemporary Tennyson, a deep affection for Malory's narrative. Far more than Tennyson, Morris restrains himself in his Arthurian poems from tracing a moral or parabolic significance for the Victorian era in the grand Arthurian themes of earthly love and spiritual aspiration.

For Morris's other poems on Arthurian themes, see "Near Avalon" and "A Good Knight in Prison" from the *Defence* volume, as well as the fragments "The Maying of Queen Guenevere," "St. Agnes' Convent," and "Palomydes' Quest." [MDC]

2) MORRIS AS ARTIST. Morris introduced Edward Burne-Jones to the Arthurian poetry of Tennyson while they were classmates at Exeter College, Oxford, in 1853. Together, they read Malory's *Le Morte Darthur* in 1855, and in 1857 Morris read the saga aloud to Burne-Jones and Dante Gabriel Rossetti as they painted in the latter's studio.

Morris's renditions of the legend in painting and drawing include only studies for unfinished works, such as *Iseult on the Ship* (1858) and the finished watercolor *Queen Guenevere* (1858, Tate Gallery, London). He painted one mural and the ceiling in the Oxford Union Murals project (1857), and he directed the Dunlop Windows project (1862), for which he designed five of the panels. His firms Morris and Company and Merton Abbey Tapestry Works sponsored many Arthurian projects, and he planned an edition of *Le Morte Darthur*, to be illustrated by Burne-Jones and published by the Kelmscott Press, but the project was abandoned at his death.

Morris's major contribution to the history of Arthurian art was his influence upon other artists. His poetry suggested an alternative source, his decorative-art projects joined Pre-Raphaelite designs with Arthurian themes, and his continual choice of Malory over Tennyson was crucial for the Pre-Raphaelite interpretation of the Arthurian legend. [DNM]

• Morris, William. *The Defence of Guenevere, and Other Poems.* London: Bell and Daldy, 1858.

Henderson, Philip. *William Morris: His Life, Work and Friends.* London: Thames and Hudson, 1967.

Raymond, Meredith B. "The Arthurian Group in *The Defence of Guenevere and Other Poems.*" *Victorian Poetry,* 4 (1966), 213–18.

Silver, Carole. *The Romance of William Morris.* Athens: Ohio University Press, 1982.

MORT ARTU, LA: see VULGATE CYCLE.

MORTE ARTHUR, LE: see STANZAIC *LE MORTE ARTHUR.*

MORTE ARTHURE: see ALLITERATIVE *MORTE ARTHURE.*

"MORTE D'ARTHUR": *see* TENNYSON, ALFRED LORD.

MORTE D'ARTHUR: see HEBER, REGINALD.

MORTE DARTHUR, LE: see MALORY, SIR THOMAS.

MORTE DI TRISTANO, LA: see CANTARI DI TRISTANO, I.

MORTIMER, JOHN (ca. 1741–1779), British history painter, was the only artist to paint the subject *The Discovery of Prince Arthur's Tomb by the Inscription on the Leaden Cross* (ca. 1767); his source was John Speed's *The History of Great Britaine . . .* (1611). The painting is lost and known only through drawings (National Gallery of Scotland, Edinburgh, and Victoria and Albert Museum, London) and an engraving by J. Ogborne (1797). Mortimer also designed illustrations for John Bell's *The Faerie Queene* (1778) and painted subjects from Spenser, *Sir Arthegal the Knight of Justice* (1778) and *A Head of Despaire* (1779). [DNM]

• Sunderland, John. "Mortimer, Pine and Some Political Aspects of English History Painting." *Burlington Magazine,* 116 (June 1974), 317–26.

MORWYN: see POWYS, JOHN COWPER.

MOTTE-FOUQUÉ, FRIEDRICH: *see* FOUQUÉ, FRIEDRICH BARON DE LA MOTTE.

MÖTTULS SAGA, an Old Norse prose translation of the French fabliau *Le Mantel mautaillié.* A statement in the text indicates that the work was undertaken at the behest of the Norwegian king Hákon Hákonarson (r. 1217–63). A single vellum leaf from about 1300 contains the beginning of the text. A vellum from about 1400 preserves the text in fragmentary form: one leaf from approximately the middle and a leaf and a half from the end. Two copies of the latter manuscript, both seventeenth-century paper, have the full text.

King Arthur is preparing for a feast at Pentecost at which knights and ladies from all over will be his guests. He refuses to begin, however, until some great event has been related or taken place (a trait also mentioned in *Parcevals saga*). A young man comes rushing in; he is in possession of a lovely mantle. Each of the ladies present, starting with the Queen, must try on this mantle, which will fit only a lady who has been faithful to her husband or beloved. All of the ladies, including the Queen, fail the test, much to the surprise and chagrin of the men. Finally, a maiden is discovered who had remained in an upper room because she was slightly indisposed. She comes down, the mantle fits perfectly, and the feasting begins. Afterward, she and her knight take leave of Arthur. The tale ends on the note that good women should always be welcomed and praised.

Comparison of the vellums (and the seventeenth-century copies) with the French demonstrates that the original translation must have been fuller and closer to the French than any of the individual preserved texts; i.e., all show condensation. However, the tale as it now stands evinces a skillful use of amplification and various stylistic features, such as alliteration. Notable is an explicit authorial presence, unlike anything in the other Old Norse Arthurian works. An extended opening encomium of Arthur coupled with the tale's content produces a clever parody of the Arthurian scene. [FWB]

Cederschiöld, Gustaf, and F.-A. Wulff, eds. *Versions nordiques du fabliau français "Le mantel mautaillié."* Lund: Gleerup, 1877.

Kalinke, Marianne E. *King Arthur, North-by-Northwest.* Copenhagen: Reitzel, 1981.

MOXON TENNYSON, a collection of Alfred Tennyson's early writings published as *Poems* (London: Moxon, 1857), illustrated by artists chosen by the poet, with the assistance of publisher Edward Moxon. The artists, both traditional Academic figures and Pre-Raphaelite painters, were given specific subjects, and their finished drawings were translated to wood blocks by the Dalziel Brothers. In this volume, Tennyson's Arthurian poetry was first published with illustrations.

Of the fifty-five subjects, only six were Arthurian. Academician Daniel Maclise designed "Arthur Obtains Excalibur" and "Arthur in the Death Barge" for "Morte d'Arthur." William Holman Hunt and Dante Gabriel Rossetti each submitted a design for "The Lady of Shalott," and Rossetti also interpreted "Sir Galahad" and "The Palace of Art." Rossetti unjustifiably complained that he had been given the unwanted subjects and that the Dalziel

Brothers butchered his designs, but the Moxon Tennyson established his public image as an Arthurian artist. Although not a financial success, the Moxon Tennyson influenced book illustration into the early twentieth century. [DNM]

⊷ Layard, George Somes. *Tennyson and His Pre-Raphaelite Illustrators: A Book About a Book*. London: Paternoster Row, 1894.

MR. MERLIN: see TELEVISION SERIES.

MULE SANS FREIN, LA: see PAIEN DE MAISIÈRES.

MUMFORD, ETHEL WATTS, author of "Merlin and Vivian" (1907), verse lyrics for a short music drama that tells how Vivian learned Merlin's spells and imprisoned him forever. [AEG]

⊷ Hadley, Henry. *Merlin and Vivian*. Op. 52. New York: Schirmer, 1907.

MUMMENSCHANZ AUF TINTAGEL: see KUBIE, WILHELM.

MUNN, H. WARNER, author of the fantasy trilogy *King of the World's Edge* (1939), *The Ship from Atlantis* (1967) (both bound together in 1976 as *Merlin's Godson*), and *Merlin's Ring* (1974). The books trace the journey of Ventidius Varro, a centurion in Arthur's army, and Myrdhinn (Merlin) in Arthur's ship Prydwen after the battle of Camlann; their struggle to establish a kingdom in the New World; and the return and subsequent adventures of Varro's son Gwalchmai over the centuries and across continents. [MAG]

⊷ Munn, H. Warner. *Merlin's Ring*. New York: Ballantine, 1974.
——— . *Merlin's Godson*. New York: Ballantine, 1976.

MURALS (MEDIEVAL). Literary references to mural paintings with Arthurian subjects abound; however, few secular paintings remain from the Middle Ages. Secular painting is especially vulnerable: domestic architecture is remodeled regularly in accord with changes in fashion; castles or royal residences are damaged or destroyed in times of war or civil unrest. Thus, those few surviving secular murals are often in isolated provincial centers and do not represent the work of the leading artists of the day or (with a few exceptions, such as Runkelstein) the taste of major patrons. Furthermore, many paintings have suffered from ill-advised restoration or repainting. Arthurian murals must often be studied second-hand, in early photos or watercolor reproductions.

The most famous Arthurian murals in literature are surely those painted by Sir Lancelot himself on the walls of the chamber in which he was imprisoned by Morgan le Fay. Here, he recalled his love for Queen Guenevere, and later, when Morgan entertained King Arthur in the room, the murals revealed the deception practiced on the King. Again, in the romance of *Perlesvaus*, Sir Gawain learned of his illegitimacy from the paintings on chapel walls. Throughout medieval literature, descriptions of palaces include lists of the subjects of wall paintings: the castle hall in Boccaccio's *Amorosa Visione*, Martorell's description of the decoration of the palace at Constantinople in *Tirant lo Blanc*, or Guillem Torroella's description, in *La Faula*, of mural paintings in Morgan le Fay's palace. Chaucer, too, included Tristan and Isolde in his mural of ill-fated lovers, and the Alsatian poet Altswert described the Palace of Venus as decorated with paintings of Arthur and his knights. These simple lists of subjects lack any reference to composition or style. They do suggest, however, the popularity of Arthurian material, especially of the great lovers, Tristan and Isolde and Lancelot and Guenevere.

Typical of the surviving Arthurian mural complexes are the great tower of the chateau of St.-Floret near Issoire in the Auvergne in France, mid-fourteenth century; the ceiling of the Palazzo Chiaramonte in Palermo, Sicily, from the 1370s; the Summer House of Schloss Runkelstein (Castel Roncolo), two kilometers north of Bolzano in the Tyrol, ca. 1400; and the great hall of the castle of La Manta near Turin, ca. 1430.

The St.-Floret paintings have been dated to the fourteenth century on the basis of the will drawn up for Athon de St.-Floret in 1364, as well as on the type of armor represented in the painting. Today, the paintings can be studied best in watercolor copies made at the beginning of the twentieth century, for they are not well preserved and are located high on the walls. Best preserved are the stories of the knights Branor le Brun and Tristan, on the north and south walls, respectively. Texts accompanying the paintings indicate that the painters' sources were the Prose *Tristan* and the *Meliadus*. In one of the best-preserved scenes, Isolde pretends to see a strange fish in the fountain in order to call Tristan's attention to the reflection of King Mark.

Tristan and Isolde also appear on the ceiling of the Palazzo Chiaramonte in Palermo; however, the figures on the beams are at such a great distance that they are barely visible. The owners of the Palazzo were a Norman family who established themselves in Sicily in the twelfth century. The palace built by Manfredi I between 1307 and 1321 was refurbished by Manfredi III, the powerful ruler of Palermo. The painted ceiling was part of his commission, and an inscription records the names of three Sicilian painters who executed the ceiling between 1377 and 1380.

King Arthur appears in his role as one of the Nine Worthies in the great hall of the fourteenth-century castle of La Manta in the Piedmont south of Turin. The owners, Valerano and Clemensia Provana, commissioned the paintings about 1430. Valerano's father, Tommaso, had composed a poem, *Le Chevalier errant*, in which he described the Palace of Fortuna as having a hall with the seats of the Nine Worthies. The poem may have suggested the theme for the decoration of the actual castle hall. At La Manta, the painters represented the Worthies as life-sized armed figures standing amid flowers and trees. King Arthur, on his blue shield and surcoat, bears the three gold crowns identified in the inscription as Britain, Scotland, and England.

Other examples of mural painting may be studied conveniently in reproductions published by Loomis, for many of them are recorded in watercolors and drawings. They include the story of Ywain, in a thirteenth-century house in Schmalkalden in Thuringia; Percival, in a house in Lübeck (ca. 1330, recorded in watercolor before its destruction) and a house in Constance (drawing preserved); and the three Christian Worthies, in the castle in Sion, Switzerland. (*See also* PISANO, ANTONIO; RUNKELSTEIN MURALS.) [MS]

Loomis, Roger Sherman, and Laura Hibbard Loomis. *Arthurian Legends in Medieval Art.* London: Oxford University Press, 1938, figs. 92–105 (St.-Floret), 106–16 (Palermo), 60–75, 171–201 (Schloss Runkelstein), 14 (La Manta), 159–66 (Schmalkalden), 150–54 (Lübeck), 149 (Constance), 17 (Sion).

Nickel, Heinrich L. *Mittelalterliche Wandmalerei.* Leipzig, 1979, pp. 280–83 (Schmalkalden).

MYSTICAL VISION OF CHRIST: *see* PRINCETON UNIVERSITY CHAPEL WINDOWS.

NABOKOV, VLADIMIR (1899–1977), author of the 1952 story "Lance." Set sometime in the future, the story presents Lancelot Boke's experiences as a member of "the first interplanetary expedition" and reflects Nabokov's preoccupation with time. Evoking Lanceloz del Lac, the *Chevalier de la charrete*, and the Sword Bridge leading to the otherworld, the story implicitly relates space exploration to chivalric adventure, and the author notes that "the future is but the obsolete in reverse." [NJL]

ε♣ Nabokov, Vladimir. "Lance." In *Nabokov's Dozen*. New York: Doubleday, 1958.

NAUBERT, BENEDIKTE (1756–1819). Not until two years before her death, with the publication of her novel *Rosalba*, did Benedikte Naubert divulge her name. More than eighty original works and translations were published anonymously by her. In the years 1789–93, she published a volume of tales entitled *Neue Volksmährchen der Deutschen*. In this collection is a novel entitled *Der kurze Mantel*, a recreation of the tale about the chastity-testing mantle, the oldest literary version of which is the late twelfth- or early thirteenth-century *Le Mantel mautaillié*. The primary sources for Naubert's novel, however, were presumably a sixteenth-century prose version of the fabliau, *Le manteau mal taillié*, and the English ballad "The Boy and the Mantle." Naubert also drew on the folktale of Frau Hulda, or Frau Holle, a good fay who punishes the lazy but

403

rewards the diligent, especially those who occupy themselves with spinning. In general, the novel contains all the essential elements of the mantle story. There is one significant change, however: the magic mantle is not woven by supernatural creatures but unwittingly by the heroine herself, although this is not divulged until the very end of the novel, when the mantle has attested the heroine's chaste way of life.

Naubert's work is characterized by pronounced criticism of the Arthurian world, which she depicts as being controlled by lascivious and cunning women. The novel expresses disdain for court society and glorifies proletarian virtues.

Der kurze Mantel was not only translated into English (by George Soane in *Specimens of German Romance*, London, 1826) but also inspired a *Singspiel* by Friedrich August Clemens Werthes, an opera libretto by Karl Franz van der Velde, and a short prose version by Johann Peter Lyser. [MEK]

Naubert, Benedikte. *Der kurze Mantel. Und: Ottilie. Zwei Volksmährchen.* Vienna: Armbruster, 1819.

Soane, G. *Specimens of German Romance: Selected and Translated from Various Authors.* London, 1826.

"NEAR AVALON": *see* MORRIS, WILLIAM.

NENNIUS, a monk of Bangor in north Wales, commonly named as compiler of a *Historia Brittonum* ("History of the Britons"), which was used by Geoffrey of Monmouth and has figured largely in attempts to reconstruct a historical Arthur. The principal version is a copy in an early twelfth-century hand, one of a medley of items in the British Library manuscript Harley 3859. Copied with it in that context are the *Annales Cambriae* and a collection of Welsh genealogies. There are other manuscripts of the *Historia* alone. Formerly, it was sometimes ascribed to Gildas, but its Latin is cruder than his, and the apparent date of composition is much later—near the beginning of the ninth century. While the ascription to Nennius is itself uncertain, his name may be used for convenience.

On his own admission, he is artless. He has "made one heap of all he has found" rummaging among old documents. This gives him a kind of credibility. At least, he has genuinely "found," not invented; he hardly seems capable of invention. However, while most of his materials are prior to the ninth century, they are so full of legends, errors, inconsistencies, and matter that was probably oral rather than written that they seldom inspire much trust.

Early sections offer various notions about the first peopling of the British Isles. These include a fantasy elaborated by Geoffrey, tracing the origin of the Britons to a party of migrating Trojans. Britain's Roman phase is covered by a confused narrative of the few emperors who were specially concerned with the island. One is Maximus, proclaimed in Britain in 383. The *Historia* mentions the tradition that British soldiers whom he led overseas remained on the Continent and founded Brittany.

Nennius portrays the Britons as becoming independent by killing the Roman *duces* ("commanders"). In the fifth century, he gives an account of Vortigern, his hiring of Saxon auxiliaries, and their mutinous attack on their British employers, which forms the basis of Geoffrey's account of the same disaster. After a digression about St. Patrick, Nennius prefaces his chapter on Arthur with the words: "In that time the Saxons strengthened in multitude and grew in Britain." It is not clear when "that time" is meant to be, except that it is still in the fifth century; a reference to the death of the Saxon chief Hengist is a parenthesis and useless for dating. Nennius goes on to enumerate twelve victories won by Arthur over the Saxons and perhaps allies of theirs. "Arthur fought against them in those days with the kings of the Britons, but he himself was leader of battles [*dux bellorum*]." The first battle is said to have been fought at the mouth of the River Glein; the next four by another river, Dubglas, in the district Linnuis; the sixth by another river, Bassas; the seventh in the Caledonian Wood; the eighth in Fort Guinnion; the ninth in the City of the Legion; the tenth by the River Tribruit; the eleventh on the "hill that is called Agned"; and the twelfth on Mount Badon, where Arthur personally slew 960 of the enemy in a single charge.

This list is thought to be based on a lost Welsh poem in Arthur's praise. Such a poem need not have been contemporary or anything like it, so the implications for history are uncertain. Most of the place-names are obscure, a fact that makes deliberate fabrication less likely. The Glein could be the Glen in the south of Lincolnshire. Linnuis is probably Lindsey, the northern portion of the same county. Most nearly certain are the Caledonian Wood, which was in southern Scotland, and the City of the Legion, which, to judge from the *Annales Cambriae*, means Chester. Badon is the major success mentioned by Gildas, at which the Britons' leader is here said to have been Arthur.

Nennius gives him a military paramountcy among the Britons. Nothing shows whether this is political as well. Clues to the dating of his battles are hard to reconcile. The Caledonian Wood seems to imply that he fought Picts, and Bede names them as allies of the auxiliaries in their revolt, but not later. Chester seems to imply enemy raiding right across the country, and Gildas mentions this as occurring in the revolt, but not later. Hence, both the identifiable battle sites point to that phase. The revolt may have been a long-drawn and sporadic ordeal rather than a brief cataclysm, but it cannot be stretched far outside the period 440–60. Badon, however, was fought round about 500. Arguably, Arthur's singlehanded exploit proves his association with Badon to be a product of legend. Nennius's "kings of the Britons" are no help: the plural does not imply Britain's political breakup toward the close of the fifth century, because he speaks of regional rulers under a high king at an earlier stage. Nor can the list be simplified by rejecting some of the battles on the ground that a single leader could not have ranged so widely. Well-attested campaigns in later times show that he could. This does not prove that the battles are all authentic or indeed that any of them are, only that picking and choosing is unsafe.

After the Arthur section come chapters of mainly northern history and genealogy, some of it fairly acceptable. Notes that follow give a date, 425, for Vortigern's rise to power, and another, 428, for the first authorized Saxon settlement. These are expressed in Roman style, with the names of the consuls for the year, and supply Nennius's best chronological fixes.

An appendix of *Mirabilia* ("Marvels") may be a little later than the rest of the book, but not much. Among the marvels are two local legends showing that such tales were already attaching themselves to Arthur in the ninth century. One concerns a stone marked with a paw-print of his dog Cabal. It lies on a heap, and if anybody takes it away, it returns to the heap. This is in the "region of Buelt" in south-central Wales. The other marvel is a tomb near Licat Amr—Gamber Head, a spring in Herefordshire—said to contain the body of Arthur's son Amr, whom he killed himself in some unrecorded tragedy. The "marvelous" feature is that it changes in size. [GA]

Nennius. *Historia Brittonum*, ed. and trans. John Morris under the title *British History and the Welsh Annals*. In *History from the Sources*. Chichester: Phillimore, 1980, Vol. 8.

Alcock, Leslie. *Arthur's Britain*. London: Penguin, 1971.

Jackson, Kenneth Hurlstone. "The Arthur of History." In *Arthurian Literature in the Middle Ages*, ed. Roger Sherman Loomis. Oxford: Clarendon, 1959.

NEUE CHRISTOPHORUS, DER: *see* HAUPTMANN, GERHART.

NEUE VOLKSMÄHRCHEN DER DEUTSCHEN: *see* NAUBERT, BENEDIKTE.

NEW KING ARTHUR: AN OPERA WITHOUT MUSIC, THE: *see* FAWCETT, EDGAR.

NEW PARSIFAL, THE: *see* TREVELYAN, ROBERT CALVERLY.

NEWBOLT, SIR HENRY (1862–1938), whose poetic drama *Mordred: A Tragedy* (1895) modifies Malory's account of the fall of the Round Table. It is distinguished by its sympathetic portrayal of the main characters, including Mordred, all of whom struggle to maintain right conduct as they see it. Though never staged, the play develops both plot and character relationships effectively. [RHT]

Newbolt, Sir Henry. *Mordred: A Tragedy*. London: Unwin, 1895.

NEWMAN, ROBERT, author of *Merlin's Mistake* (1970), in which Brian, a sixteen-year-old squire; Tertius, a boy whom Merlin has mistakenly gifted with future knowledge; and young Lianor, disguised as a crone, join forces as their separate quests lead them to Nimue's castle and Merlin. This fantasy for adolescents makes humorous use of Arthurian conventions to teach lessons about appearance and reality. However, in the sequel, *The Testing of Tertius* (1973), the tone becomes more complex and serious, as the young people face Nimue and the evil wizard Urlik to rescue Merlin and Blaise and to keep Arthur and Britain safe. [JW]

꙳ Newman, Robert. *Merlin's Mistake*. New York: Atheneum, 1970.

——— . *The Testing of Tertius*. New York: Atheneum, 1973.

NEWMAN, SHARAN, author of an Arthurian trilogy: *Guinevere* (1981), *The Chessboard Queen* (1984), and *Guinevere Evermore* (1985). Newman emphasizes Guinevere's upbringing in one of the last fully Roman households and the difficulty with which she adjusts to the sweeping and radical social changes inherent in Arthur's reign. Newman incorporates traditional Arthurian episodes with new material, most of which deals with the interweaving of a fantastic otherworld and its creatures, especially a unicorn, with Guinevere's own world. [AAR]

꙳Newman, Sharan. *Guinevere*. New York: St. Martin, 1981.

——— . *The Chessboard Queen*. New York: St. Martin, 1984.

——— . *Guinevere Evermore*. New York: St. Martin, 1985.

NÍELS JÓNSSON (1782–1857), an Icelandic writer whose *œuvre* is extant mostly in manuscript. Like his better-known countryman Sigurður Breiðfjörð, Níels Jónsson was inspired by the Danish chapbook *En tragoedisk Historie om den aedle og tappre Tistrand* ("A Tragic Tale of the Noble and Courageous Tistrand") to compose *rímur*, or cantos, about Tistrand and Indiana, entitled *Rijmur af þeim Tistrani Hrobjartar Hertogasyni af Borgund og Indíaunu Drottníngu Mógols Dóttur af Indíalandi* ("Verses About Tistran Hrobjart, Son of the Duke of Burgundy, and Queen Indiana, Daughter of the Ruler of India"). The work, which consists of seventeen *rímur*, has been published only in part. The author's revised version (ca. 1850) of the *rímur* written in 1844 is preserved in his own manuscript (Lbs 982 8vo) in the National Library, Reykjavik. [MEK]

꙳ Níels Jónsson. *Tistrans rímur og Indíönu*. In *Sýnisbók íslenzkra rímna: Specimens of Icelandic Rímur*, sel. William A. Craigie. Reykjavik: Leiftur, 1952, Vol. 3, pp. 195–98.

NINE WORTHIES, or *les neuf preux*, a group of historical personages who were considered to be particularly worthy of admiration or veneration. First formulated during the early fourteenth century, in Jacques de Longuyon's *Les Voeux du paon*, the list comprises three pagans (Hector, Caesar, Alexander), three

Christians (Arthur, Charlemagne, Godefroy de Bouillon), and three Jews (Joshua, David, Judas Maccabeus). The notion of the Nine Worthies quickly gained popularity and provided material for numerous poets, such as Guillaume de Machaut and Eustache Deschamps. Predictably, the Worthies were soon joined (as the result of Deschamps's inventiveness) by Nine Female Worthies but then also, less predictably, by a tenth male: Bertrand du Guesclin, the great Breton warrior. Once integrated into the Nine Worthies group, Arthur served (e.g., in vernacular history writing) along with others as an example of glory, valor, and splendor, although it was most often his image as warrior that engaged the interest of authors and artists. The entire group served as the frequent subject for artistic endeavors other than poetry: the best-known example is the Nine Worthies Tapestry now in the Metropolitan Museum (Cloisters), New York. Other examples include a series of mural paintings in the castle of La Manta, Piedmont (early fifteenth century); a series of three windows in the Lüneberg Rathaus; frescoes at Sion, Switzerland; woodcuts in the Hôtel de Ville of Metz (mid-fifteenth century); tapestries in the château of Langeais (Loire Valley, sixteenth century); and a number of manuscript miniatures. [NJL]

🖎 Tyson, Diana B. "King Arthur as a Literary Device in the Fourteenth Century." *Bibliographical Bulletin of the International Arthurian Society*, 33 (1981), 237–57.

NIVIENE: *see* LADY OF THE LAKE.

NOMS, ARMES, ET BLASONS DES CHEVALLIERS ET COMPAIGNONS DE LA TABLE RONDE, LES: see HERALDRY.

NORTON, ANDRE (pseudonym of Alice Mary Norton), author of *Merlin's Mirror* (1975), which retells the story of Merlin and Arthur as science fiction. As elsewhere in her writing, Norton focuses on the alienated and powerful outcast. Merlin is the product of cross-breeding with alien beings, and his powers are attributed to extrasensory perception. The work is concerned primarily with human ambivalence and emotional dilemmas. In her juvenile fantasy *Steel Magic* (1965), three children enter Avalon, where they recover the talismans of power stolen from Merlin, Arthur, and Huon of the Horn. [RCS]

🖎 Norton, Andre. *Merlin's Mirror*. New York: DAW, 1975.
———. *Steel Magic*. Cleveland: World, 1965 (later title: *Grey Magic*, 1967).
Schlobin, Roger C. *Andre Norton: A Primary and Secondary Bibliography*. Boston: Hall, 1980.
Yoke, Carl B. *Roger Zelazny and Andre Norton: Proponents of Individualism*. Columbus: State Library of Ohio, 1979.

NOVELLINO, IL (or *Cento Novelle Antiche*), is a collection of short tales written by an anonymous Florentine around 1300. Materials are drawn from classical mythology, the Bible, medieval legends, miracle stories and saints' lives, and historical anecdotes both ancient and medieval. Five tales focus on Arthurian matters. In No. 26, Merlin, appearing as an isolated seer, rebukes a woman for encouraging her husband's sinful usury in order to buy herself a dress. In No. 45, Lancelot fights with the Saxon knight Alibano, who, on discovering the identity of his foe, laments, "Your name undoes me more than your prowess." In No. 63, King Meliadus frees his own enemy, who, without recognizing Meliadus, has defended the king's superiority over himself. In No. 65, Tristan and Isotta, perceiving that King Mark is watching their tryst from a pine-tree, deceitfully convince him of their innocence. No. 82 describes the death of the Lady of Scalot. There is also a reference in No. 28 to the story of Lancelot's riding on the cart of shame. [JLS]

• *Il Novellino: Le ciento nouelle antike.* Bologna: Benedetti, 1525.

 D'Ancona, Alessandro. "Del Novellino e delle sue fonti." *Studi di critica e storia letteraria*, 2 (1912), 2–163.

 Gardner, Edmund G. *The Arthurian Legend in Italian Literature.* London: Dent, 1930, pp. 88–94.

 Viscardi, Antonio. "Arthurian Influences on Italian Literature from 1200 to 1500." In *Arthurian Literature in the Middle Ages*, ed. Roger Sherman Loomis. Oxford: Clarendon, 1959, pp. 419–29.

"NUNCA FUERA CABALLERO DE DAMAS TAN BIEN SERVIDO": *see LANÇAROTE DE LAGO.*

NÜWE PARZEFAL, DER: see COLIN, PHILIPP, AND CLAUS WISSE.

NYE, ROBERT, author of *Merlin* (1979), a bawdy, farcical *tour de force* in four books (Black, White, Red, and Gold). Narrated by Merlin from the crystal cave, the book recounts his own and Arthur's conception, birth, and Grail quest in surrealistic, phantasmagoric vignettes, transformed by the alchemy of language into a psychology of sexual fantasy. [MAG]

• Nye, Robert. *Merlin.* New York: Putnam, 1979.

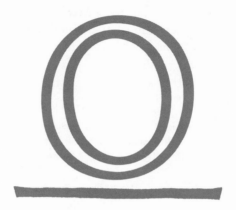

OBERON: *see* WIELAND, CHRISTOPH MARTIN.

O'MEARA, WALTER, author of the historical novel *The Duke of War* (1966), in which events surrounding Arthur's victory at Badon are chronicled by a young Romano-British girl. Since her villa is used as Arthur's campaign headquarters, she is well placed to observe his domestic, as well as his military and political, problems. [RHT]

    🙐 O'Meara, Walter. *The Duke of War*. New York: Harcourt, Brace and World, 1966.

ONCE AND FUTURE KING, THE: *see* WHITE, T.H.

OPERA: *see* BOUGHTON, RUTLAND; CHAUSSON, ERNEST; DRAESEKE, FELIX AUGUST BERNHARD; GOLDMARK, KARL; PURCELL, HENRY; VAN DER VELDE, CARL FRANZ; WAGNER, RICHARD.

ORIGINAL CHRONICLE OF SCOTLAND: *see* SCOTTISH ARTHURIAN CHRONICLES.

ORLANDO FURIOSO: *see* ARIOSTO, LUDOVICO.

ORLANDO INNAMORATO: *see* BOIARDO, MATTEO MARIA.

ORMEROD, JAMES (1883–1947), author of three Arthurian poems. "Tristram's Tomb," a ballad, describes how "Iseult of Ireland now hath wed/ Sir Tristram in Death's orat'ry," their union symbolized by the embracing brier rose. "Meliagrance and Guenevere," a blank-verse drama in two scenes, relates the consequences of Guenevere's maying. "St. Joseph of Arimathea," a closet drama in blank verse, gives Joseph's account of the Crucifixion, Easter morning, Pentecost, and the eventual transference of the Grail to Glastonbury. [MAW]

&❧ Ormerod, James. *Tristram's Tomb and Other Poems.* London: Mathews and Marrot, 1928.

ORTMANN, WILLY: *see* KUBIE, WILHELM.

ORTU WALUUANII, DE: *see* DE ORTU WALUUANII.

OTRANTO MOSAIC. King Arthur, identified by the inscription *Rex Arturus*, is represented as wearing a crown, holding a scepter or club, riding on a goatlike animal, and confronting a giant cat (possibly the Capalus, or giant cat of Lausanne) among the Old Testament figures in the floor mosaic in the nave of the Norman cathedral of Otranto, Italy. The mosaic was made in 1165 by the priest Pantaleone, at the request of the Archbishop Jonathan. In a section of the mosaic depicting the history of humanity beginning with Adam and Eve, King Arthur appears with Cain and Abel and has been interpreted as an allegory on the fall and subsequent impurity of mankind. The goat-riding figure may also represent Arthur as a supernatural or fairy king, part of the legend of the immortal Arthur who dwelt in a magical subterranean kingdom entered through a cave (or Mount Etna) in Sicily. [MS]

&❧ Gianfreda, G. *Il mosaico pavimentale della Basilica Cattedrale di Otranto.* 2nd ed. Casamari, 1965.
   Loomis, Roger Sherman, and Laura Hibbard Loomis. *Arthurian Legends in Medieval Art.* London: Oxford University Press, 1938, p. 36; figs. 9, 9a.
   Petrucci, Alfredo. *Cattedrali di Puglia.* Rome: Bestetti, 1960, pp. 97–98.

OVER SEA, UNDER STONE: *see* COOPER, SUSAN.

OWAIN (or *The Lady of the Fountain*), probably dating to the thirteenth century, is one of three Middle Welsh prose tales commonly referred to as "the three romances," the others being *Geraint and Enid* and *Peredur*. All three have some as-yet-undefined relationship with romances by Chrétien de Troyes—*Yvain*, *Erec et Enide*, and *Perceval*. It has been claimed that the Welsh tales derive directly (either by formal translation or by retelling from memory) from the French; another view is that both Welsh and French texts stem from a common Old French source that was itself based on Welsh or Breton materials. Other critics see the three Welsh tales as having a single author who used dynastic themes reflecting sovereignty myths for patriotic purposes and whose work underlies Chrétien's poems, though the Welsh stories in their extant forms reveal French influence. In fact, the three Welsh stories differ in the extent of their resemblance to the French, and they are best examined separately. It should be emphasized that none can be shown to be a word-for-word translation and that stylistically all are excellent examples of traditional Middle Welsh prose writing. *Owain* is the story of the defeat by one of Arthur's knights of the Knight of the Fountain and his subsequent marriage to the widow, the Lady of the Fountain. His return to Arthur's court leads to his forgetting his wife, but the realization of his neglect causes him to lose his reason. He is restored to health, overcomes adversaries with the help of a lion, and regains his position as knight and husband. The theme of the "romance" appears to be Owain's path to critical self-awareness and maturity. Such a theme, together with the courtly setting, places this story in a different category from most other Middle Welsh tales and suggests strongly that it is an attempt to adapt chivalric romance to the conventions of the native Welsh narrative tradition. [BFR]

ᶿ Thomson, R.L., ed. *Owain*. Dublin: Dublin Institute for Advanced Studies, 1970.

Jones, Gwyn, and Thomas Jones, trans. *The Mabinogion*. 2nd ed. London: Dent, 1974.

Jarman, A.O.H., and Gwilym Rees Hughes. *A Guide to Welsh Literature I*. Swansea: Davies, 1976.

OWEN, FRANCIS, in *Tristan and Isolde: A Romance* (1964), retells the story for younger readers with comment upon historical and geographical details and with an untraditionally happy ending: the lovers live out their lives with Lancelot and Guenevere in Joyeuse Garde after the deaths of both Mark and Arthur. [RHT]

ᶿ Owen, Francis. *Tristan and Isolde: A Romance*. Ilfracombe, Devon: Stockwell, 1964.

OWL SERVICE, THE: see GARNER, ALAN.

OXFORD UNION MURALS. In 1857, Dante Gabriel Rossetti was asked by the Oxford Union Committee to design a program of ten murals in the Debating Hall of the new Union Building. Rossetti saw the project as an opportunity to provide an alternative to the frescoes in the Queen's Robing

Room. In accordance with John Ruskin's teachings, Rossetti and his staff—Edward Burne-Jones, Arthur Hughes, John Hungerford Pollen, William Morris, Valentine Prinsep, and Rodham Spencer Stanhope—all in sympathy with Pre-Raphaelite ideas, took only materials and lodging for payment.

The design of the building was inappropriate for murals; the second floor walkway, the designated area, was punctuated with large windows, and the excessive illumination forced the artists to whitewash them to see to paint.

Rossetti chose the following subjects from Malory: *King Arthur Obtains the Sword Excalibur from the Lady of the Lake* (Pollen), *The Jealousy of Sir Palomedes* (Morris), *Sir Pelleas Leaving Lady Ettarde* (Prinsep), *Sir Gawain Meets Three Ladies at the Well* (Stanhope), *The Death of Merlin* (Burne-Jones), *The Death of Arthur* (Hughes), *Lancelot's Vision of the Sangrael*, *Lancelot in the Queen's Chamber*, and *How Sir Galahad, Sir Bors and Sir Percival Saw the Sangrael* (all Rossetti). The work began in August 1857, but by November Rossetti left, and the others, excepting Burne-Jones, followed. Only Morris had finished his mural, and painted the ceiling, and Burne-Jones completed his by the following spring. In June 1859, the Union Society hired William and Breton Riviere to finish the work.

Technically, the murals were a disaster. The excessive illumination made viewing impossible, and by 1870 they had deteriorated on the damp, absorbent walls, which had not been treated. The Society asked Morris and Rossetti to advise about restoration; Morris suggested wallpaper, Rossetti, whitewash. Despite a restoration supervised by Professor E.W. Tristram in 1936, the present state is lamentable. They can be seen only poorly from the infrared photographs taken by John Renton in 1975. They are significant, however, for the murals linked the Pre-Raphaelites with Arthurian subject matter and attest their preference for Malory over Tennyson, and for romantic over heroic subjects. [DNM]

❧ Christian, John. *Oxford Union Murals*. Chicago: University of Chicago Press, 1981.

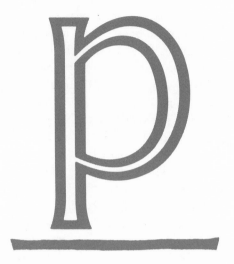

PADMORE, E.S., author of *The Death of Arthur, The Story of the Holy Grail* (1936), a play that covers events from Arthur's marriage to his death. Mordred, a cynical malcontent, seeks to destroy the spiritually minded Arthur by revealing the sin that surrounds him. Though disillusioned, the King retains something of his mystical vision. [RHT]

🖝 Padmore, E.S. *The Death of Arthur, The Story of the Holy Grail.* London: Jenkins, 1936.

PAGAN KING, THE: *see* MARSHALL, EDISON.

PAGEANT DESIGN (BRITISH). During the Elizabethan and Jacobean periods (sixteenth and early seventeenth centuries), the cult of chivalry surrounding the monarchs led to renewed interest in the etiquette and mythology of King Arthur and his knights of the Round Table. When Queen Elizabeth visited Leicester at Kenilworth, for example, she was received with a pageant in which Morgan le Fay welcomed her as Arthur's heir. Spectacles produced for the entertainment of the court—tilts, tournaments, barriers, pageants of every kind—adopted the imagery of Arthurian romances. Sir Henry Lee (1533–1611), the Master of the Armory and Queen Elizabeth's personal champion, began a great series of pageants by challenging all comers on the Queen's

Accession Day, 17 November 1558. He created a drama at the entry of each contestant to enhance the spectacle in the tiltyard. In the pageant held at Woodstock in 1575, the Faerie Queene made her first appearance. When George Clifford, third Earl of Cumberland, succeeded as champion in 1580, he appeared in the Accession Day pageant as the Knight of Pendragon Castle, and arrived for the tilt on a sham-castle surrounded by Arthurian figures (see Nicholas Hilliard's portrait of the earl in costume for the event). The Accession Day tilts (changed to 24 March after James I's accession in 1603) continued to be held until 1621.

Arthurian imagery inspired the pageants known as the barriers, that is, mock tournaments held in settings made up of mock fortifications. In 1610, for his first public appearance in arms, Prince Henry chose an Arthurian theme. He took the name of Meliadus, Lord of the Isles, and with six companions challenged all comers. As surveyor to the prince, Inigo Jones designed and staged the event, and Prince Henry's barrier was performed in the Banqueting House at Whitehall on Twefth Night. As the pageant began, the Lady of the Lake was "discovered" in mourning near Merlin's Tomb, bewailing the fall of the House of Chivalry. The scene shifted to a neo-Gothic setting, St. George's portico, where King Arthur appeared and presented the prince with a shield. The prince and his six companions set out to revive knighthood in England, and the tourney began.

The Arthurian imagery chosen by Prince Henry was appropriate, for he was a descendant of King Arthur, or so his father, James I, claimed. For James's triumphal entry into London in 1604, triumphal arches and two seventy-foot pyramids illustrating this claim were erected at the entrance of the Strand. In effect, James was claiming "Arthur's seat," and thus fulfilled Merlin's prophecy of the union of the two kingdoms England and Scotland. Anne of Denmark, queen of James I and a patron of the arts, also commissioned works with Arthurian themes. She introduced the court masque and commissioned Ben Jonson and Inigo Jones to create spectacular entertainments for the court. In the Christmas masque in 1610/11, Prince Henry took the role of Oberon, son of King Arthur and ruler of the fairy kingdom. The untimely death of the prince in 1612 and his mother in 1619 ended the attempt to combine a neomedieval ideal of chivalry with the new art of the continental Baroque. [MS]

ǝ Orgel, Stephen, and Roy Strong. *Inigo Jones: The Theatre of the Stuart Court.* 2 vols. London: Sotheby Parke Bernet, 1973.

Strong, Roy. *Festival Designs by Inigo Jones.* Catalogue, International Exhibitions Foundation, 1967–68.

———. *Artists of the Tudor Court.* Catalogue, Victoria and Albert Museum, London, 1983.

PAIEN DE MAISIÈRES (perhaps a pseudonym parodying the name Chrétien de Troyes), the author of *La Mule sans frein* ("The Mule Without a Bridle"), a brief French romance of 1,136 lines, dating from the time of Chrétien's works or shortly after. The "hero," Gauvain, is more precisely an antihero, as he undertakes (with uncharacteristically single-minded devotion) a quest to recover a bridle. In the process, he undergoes a number of comical trials and remains unaware of far more momentous events unfolding around him. The work is preserved in the same manuscript as *Le Chevalier à l'épée*, which may be by the same author. [NJL]

Johnston, R.C., and D.D.R. Owen, eds. *Two Old French Gauvain Romances*. New York: Barnes and Noble, 1973.

PALAMEDES, a French prose romance of the thirteenth century, predating the cyclic version of the Prose *Tristan*. The work, which is anonymous (although attributed in the prologue to Elie, or Hélie, de Borron), is preserved as part of the *Compilation* of Rusticiano da Pisa and, in fragmentary form, in several manuscripts. The full title of the work (according to some manuscripts) identifies its heroes as Palamedes, Meliadus (the father of Tristan), and Guiron le Courtois. The last two of them play prominent roles, respectively, in the two halves of the romance; in fact, the two parts of the work could be—and often were—considered to be independent texts, and the titles *Meliadus* and *Guiron* (or *Gyron*) *le Courtois* were attached to them.

Palamedes offers stories of an older Arthurian generation, involving the fathers of such figures as Palamedes, Arthur, Tristan, and Erec. The convoluted narrative recounts (among other adventures) the abduction of the Queen of Scotland by Meliadus, who is then attacked by the King of Scotland but aided by Guiron. The latter's lady is abducted but then rescued, and they both are then captured; although he is later freed, she dies in childbirth. The second book continues these series of abductions, battles, and seemingly random adventures. In spite of the apparent formlessness of the work, it achieved remarkable popularity. [NJL]

Gyron le Courtoys. Paris: Antoine Vérard, 1501; repr. with intro. by Cedric E. Pickford. London: Scolar, 1980.
Meliadus de Leonnoys. Paris: Galliot du Pré, 1528.

"PALOMYDES' QUEST": *see* MORRIS, WILLIAM.

PARCEVALS SAGA, an Old Norse prose translation of Chrétien de Troyes's unfinished *Perceval* (or of roughly the first 6,500 lines; the remainder is preserved separately as *Valvens þáttr*). There is no internal indication of circumstance of origin, but it is assumed that the translation was connected with the court of the Norwegian king Hákon Hákonarson (r. 1217–63), responsible for the translation of *Tristrams saga* and (probably) *Ívens saga*. The primary manuscripts are a vellum from about 1400 (one lacuna of one leaf) and a vellum fragment from about 1350. Some ten lines of the latter correspond to lines now lost in the former.

Parceval, son of a champion (now deceased) and a captured princess, has been raised in the wilderness. When he is twelve, he meets five knights in the forest, asks one if he is God, learns that King Arthur dispenses the splendid arms, and determines to find this king. His mother gives him a quantity of good advice and sorrowfully parts with him. After meeting a woman alone in a tent and taking from her a kiss and a ring, Parceval proceeds to Arthur's court, where the Red Knight has taken the King's gold goblet, insulted the Queen, and challenged Arthur for his kingdom. Parceval asks Arthur to make him a knight, but Kæi (Kay) tells him to take the arms from the Red Knight. He does so. He then meets Gormanz, who teaches him the use of arms and gives him more good advice. Parceval next rescues Blankiflur and her castle from a besieging army but must move on to find his mother (he later learns she died). There follows the episode at the Grail castle, with suffering king and Bleeding Lance. Following Gormanz's advice, Parceval does not ask about any of this. After several more encounters, Parceval is brought back to Arthur's court by Valven (Gawain). The story then follows Valven on a series of adventures but returns to Parceval for the Good Friday encounter. Parceval confesses to a hermit, his mother's brother, who tells him about the Grail and admonishes him to go to church. In an abrupt conclusion, Parceval returns to Blankiflur, marries her, and is always victorious in combat.

The overlapping lines in the two vellums suggest that the original translation was much closer to the French source than either preserved text now is; both show condensation. The saga contains some interesting stylistic effects for emphasis, such as alliteration, assonance, and rhyme, especially at the end of some chapters. [FWB]

ॐ Kölbing, Eugen, ed. *Riddarasögur*. Strassburg: Trübner, 1872.

Kalinke, Marianne E. *King Arthur, North-by-Northwest*. Copenhagen: Reitzel, 1981.

PARCIVAL: *see* FOUQUÉ, FRIEDRICH BARON DE LA MOTTE; VOLLMÖLLER, KARL GUSTAV.

PARCIVAL, DER: *see* BODMER, JOHANN JACOB.

PARLEMENT OF THE THRE AGES, THE, a fourteenth-century alliterative dream-vision debate (665 lines) written in the North Midlands of England ca. 1350–90. A young hunter dreams that he overhears a debate among three men: thirty-year-old Youth, sixty-year-old Middle Age, and one-hundred-year-old Old Age. The latter, lecturing the others on the transience of earthly things, describes Arthur among the Nine Worthies, giving a brief summary of his career and death (ll. 462–512) that draws upon both chronicles and the French Vulgate Cycle and includes some details that appear to be original with the author. Gawain, for example, throws Arthur's sword into the lake, and not Girflet (Vulgate *Mort Artu*) or Bedivere (Stanzaic *Le Morte Arthur*). [EDK]

• Offord, M.Y., ed. *The Parlement of the Thre Ages*. London: Oxford University Press, 1959.
  Gardner, John, trans. *The Alliterative Morte Arthure, The Owl and the Nightingale, and Five Other Middle English Poems*. Carbondale: Southern Illinois University Press, 1971.

PARSAFORESTO, an Italian translation (printed in 1556–58) of the French *Perceforest*. Like its French original, *Parsaforesto* links up Arthurian history with that of Alexander the Great, who installs Arthur's ancestor Parsaforesto as King of Britain. [NJL]

• *La dilettevole historia del valorosissimo Parsaforesto re della Gran Brettagna, con i gran fatti del valente Gadiffero re di Scotia, vero essempio di Cavalleria*. 6 vols. Venice: Tramezzino, 1556–58.

PARSIFAL: *see* SYBERBERG, HANS JÜRGEN; WAGNER, RICHARD.

"PARSIFAL UND DER BÜSSER": *see* LIENHARD, FRIEDRICH.

PARSIVAL: *see* HAUPTMANN, GERHART; MONACO, RICHARD.

"PARTING OF LAUNCELOT AND GUINEVERE": *see* PHILLIPS, STEPHEN.

PARZIVAL: *see* BLANK, RICHARD; SCHAEFFER, ALBRECHT; VESPER, WILL; WOLFRAM VON ESCHENBACH.

"PASSING OF ARTHUR, THE": *see* TENNYSON, ALFRED LORD.

PEACOCK, THOMAS LOVE (1785–1866), an employee of the East India Company for thirty-seven years, devoted his leisure to writing poetry and novels and cultivating literary friendships. Arthurian interest was first revealed in "Calidore" (ca. 1816), a poetic fragment in which Arthur and Merlin send the protagonist from a classical otherworld to Wales in search of a wife and a disputatious philosopher. "The Round Table; or, King Arthur's Feast" (1817) describes Merlin's attempt to entertain his bored monarch by summoning to their otherworld castle all subsequent British rulers. Peacock's major contribution was a satirical-historical romance, *The Misfortunes of Elphin* (1829), set in sixth-century Wales.

Peacock's interest in history and legend increased after his marriage to Jane

Gryffydh, who made accessible to him materials then unavailable in English translations, such as *The Myvyrian Archaiology of Wales*, the *Mabinogion*, and the *Hanes Taliesin*. The flooding of Gwaelod through Prince Seithenyn's neglect, the mysterious birth and heroic life of the bard Taliesin, and Gwenhyvar's kidnapping by Melvas as told in Caradoc's *Vita Gildae* are combined through the device of an Arthurian court in Caerleon. Bardic songs and Triad materials are also used. Taliesin, the protagonist who links the main characters, effects the rescue of his future father-in-law, Elphin, and of Gwenhyvar. Opportunities for satire arise from ironic comparisons between nineteenth-century England and sixth-century Wales (when people, lacking polluted water and air, paper money, steam engines and poorhouses, were "lost in the grossness of beef and ale") and from allegorical identifications of Seithenyn's rotten dam with the English constitution, and the "plump, succulent" monastery at Avallon with the Established Church, for example. Comic invention reaches a peak in the characterization of Seithenyn, a gargantuan drunkard who proclaims, "Wine is my medicine; and my quantity is a little more." Peacock was reportedly proud of the fact that Welsh archaeologists treated *The Misfortunes* as a valuable addition to Welsh history. [MAW]

&. Peacock, Thomas Love. *The Misfortunes of Elphin*. London: Hookham, 1829.

———. *Nightmare Abbey, The Misfortunes of Elphin, Crotchet Castle*, ed. Charles B. Dodson. New York: Holt, Rinehart, and Winston, 1971.

Felton, Felix. *Thomas Love Peacock*. London: Allen and Unwin, 1973.

"PELLEAS AND ETTARRE": *see* TENNYSON, ALFRED LORD.

PELYARMENUS, ROMAN DE: see SEPT SAGES DE ROME, LES.

PENDRAGON, a title Geoffrey of Monmouth applies to Uther, the father of King Arthur. When there appears a star with a single ray ending in a fireball shaped like a dragon, Merlin associates the star and the dragon with Uther. Having later become king, Uther has two gold dragons made, one for the cathedral of Winchester, the other to take into battle. Geoffrey tells us that thenceforth he is called Uther Pendragon, which in the British tongue means "dragon's head" and which recognizes both his symbol and his sovereignty as chieftain or king. (In fact, the word apparently means "head dragon"—"foremost leader.") In *Arthour and Merlin*, Pendragon is the name of Arthur's brother.

There is a Pendragon Castle in Cumbria, Westmorland, which dates from the twelfth century and is now in ruins; it is sometimes contended, on the basis of the name, that this is the site of an earlier fortification belonging to Uther. [NJL]

&. Ashe, Geoffrey. *A Guidebook to Arthurian Britain*. Wellingborough: Aquarian, 1980, pp. 166-67.

PENDRAGON: *see* CARMICHAEL, DOUGLAS; FARADAY, W. BARNARD.

PENDRAGON CASTLE: *see* PENDRAGON.

PENNINC and PIETER VOSTAERT, Middle Dutch authors of the *Roman van Walewein*; they are known exclusively for this work. They are assumed to have been Flemings who wrote their poem in the second half of the thirteenth century. Penninc, the more important of the two, began the romance but stopped after some 7,800 lines. Pieter Vostaert completed the work, which numbers about 11,200 lines and is one of the undisputed high points among Middle Dutch Arthurian romances.

The story deals with Walewein's quest for the Floating Chessboard, which Arthur is determined to acquire. Walewein must fulfill a number of tasks that arise one from the other (King Wonder, for instance, agrees to part with the Floating Chessboard only if Walewein captures the miraculous Sword with the Two Rings for him). This main action is regularly interrupted by sudden challenges to adventure. Walewein always accepts the challenge, completes the adventure, and then resumes the quest for the chessboard. He is assisted on his journey by a speaking fox, Roges, who regains his human shape once Walewein has accomplished his tasks. Eventually, Walewein returns to Arthur with the chessboard and with Roges, as well as his beloved Ysabele.

The *Roman van Walewein* is a fairy tale rewritten into an Arthurian romance, a variant of Aarne-Thompson 550, to which belong Grimm's *Der Goldene Vogel* and the story known in Russia as *Of Iwan Tsarewitsj, the Firebird, and the Grey Wolf*.

The *Roman van Walewein* has been transmitted to us complete in a codex dating from 1350 (Leiden, Universiteits Bibliotheek ltk. 195). The inserted leaf before the beginning of the text contains the well-known miniature depicting Walewein on horseback pursuing the Floating Chessboard. In addition, fragments are preserved at Ghent (Universiteits Bibliotheek 1629) from the second half of the fourteenth century, containing 388 lines of the *Roman van Walewein*. [BB]

Van Es, G.A., ed. *De jeeste van Walewein en het schaakbord van Penninc en Pieter Vostaert*. 2 vols. Zwolle: Tjeenk Willink, 1957.

Draak, A. Maartje E. *Onderzoekingen over de "Roman van Walewein."* Haarlem, 1936; 2nd ed. Groningen: Bouma, 1975.

PERCEFOREST, an immense Old French prose romance of the mid-fourteenth century that links the Alexander materials with the world of King Arthur. It is divided into 531 chapters in six books and, if edited, would fill some 6,000 or 7,000 pages. However, it has (except for Part I) found no modern editor and exists complete in only one manuscript (Paris, Bibliothèque de l'Arsenal 3483–94), compiled in 1459–60 for Philip the Good, Duke of Burgundy. There are three other partial manuscripts and two sixteenth-century printed editions. The author was probably attached to the monastery of St. Landelin at Crespin in Hainaut.

Unlike many prose romances of its time, *Perceforest* is not an adaptation of an earlier verse romance but presents entirely new materials. After a brief geographical excursus on the island of Britain, the anonymous author traces its history from the legendary Brutus, following Geoffrey of Monmouth. The romance proper begins with Chapter 17 of Book I, and is marked by inventiveness, exuberant style, and complex interlacing. The first three books tell of England before Caesar's conquest. The author links England to the glories of Alexander the Great, who comes to Britain to establish its new king, Perceforest. Through the efforts of Alexander and Perceforest, the island is brought from chaos and superstition to culture and chivalry.

In Book IV, Caesar conquers Britain and destroys the courtly civilization that had been so painstakingly established by Perceforest. This tragedy is overcome, however, as civilization is gradually restored in Books V and VI. In Chapter 12 of Book V, the author traces the ancestry of King Lot of Orkney. He goes on to recount the arrival of Joseph of Arimathea on the island, and there are many allusions to the Arthurian Grail materials. Book VI tells of the Christianization of Britain, both before and after the Danish and Saxon invasions. The final chapter of this final book tells of the adoration of the Holy Grail and recounts the episode of the *roi mehaingne* ("maimed king"), a close imitation of the *Queste del Saint Graal*. [WWK]

ಶ Taylor, Jane H.M., ed. *Le Roman de Perceforest*. Geneva: Droz, 1979 (Part I).

Flutre, L.F. "Études sur *Le Roman de Perceforêt*." *Romania*, 70 (1948–49), 474–522; 71 (1950), 374–92, 482–508; 74 (1953), 44–102; 88 (1967), 475–508; 89 (1968), 355–86; 90 (1969), 341–70; 91 (1970), 189–226.

Lods, Jeanne. *Le Roman de Perceforest: origines, composition, caractères, valeur et influence*. Geneva: Droz, 1951.

PERCEVAL (PARSIFAL, PARZIVAL, PERCHEVAEL, PRESSI-VALLE),

introduced in the *Conte del Graal*, by Chrétien de Troyes, makes a rapid, if painful, transition from bumpkin to Grail hero. His mother has kept him ignorant of chivalry (which she blamed for his father's death); once he learns of the existence of knights, however, he disregards his mother's grief and leaves for Arthur's court. He receives some basic chivalric instruction from Gornemanz, and soon he embarks on his first adventures. As a guest in a strange castle, he is witness to the Grail procession, but having been advised to talk little, he does not inquire about what he sees. Later, he learns that his question would have cured the infirm Fisher King. He sets out to expiate his sin, but the unfinished state of Chrétien's romance prevents him from completing his quest. Throughout the work, Perceval shows himself to be extraordinarily precocious in the acquisition of chivalric skills but decidedly deficient in terms of responsibility and understanding.

In the Continuations of Chrétien's *Conte del Graal*, Perceval meets first with partial success (in the Second Continuation) and is then crowned Grail King (in the Third). In the Didot-*Perceval*, the young man has the same brashness he had demonstrated in Chrétien, but the charm and naïveté that had characterized him earlier are lacking. Despite the modification of his character, this romance and others (e.g., the Prose *Joseph* and *Merlin*) trace his success in bringing the quest to a conclusion and curing the Fisher King.

Perceval was initially a popular figure, giving rise to a number of other works, for example, the *Parzival* of Wolfram von Eschenbach and the Middle Dutch *Perchevael* (a literal translation of Chrétien's work). However, with the Vulgate, authors began to focus on other heroes, and perhaps because Perceval was tainted by sin (with Blanchefleur, as well as in the Grail castle), Galahad replaced him as the perfect Grail knight.

In Wagner's opera, Parsifal is the Pure Fool, whose role as the Grail knight is long unrecognized either by the young man himself or by those around him. His destiny in Wagner requires absolute purity, including sexual abstinence, a condition not imposed on him in most earlier traditions.

Various modern treatments of Perceval have shown him either rejecting his messianic role (e.g., Richard Monaco) or failing to achieve his goal and expressing serious doubts about himself (e.g., Jim Hunter.) In a number of instances, writers (notably T.S. Eliot) have been drawn less to Perceval himself than to the theme of the Wasteland. [NJL]

🐾 Owen, D.D.R. "The Development of the Perceval Story." *Romania*, 80 (1959), 473–92.

Weston, Jessie L. *The Legend of Sir Perceval*: *Studies upon Its Origin, Development and Position in the Arthurian Cycle*. 2 vols. London: Nutt, 1906, 1909.

PERCEVAL: *see* CHRÉTIEN DE TROYES; CONTINUATIONS.

PERCEVAL AND THE PRESENCE OF GOD: *see* HUNTER, JIM.

PERCEVAL LE GALLOIS: *see* ROHMER, ERIC.

PERCHEVAEL, a Middle Dutch translation of Chrétien de Troyes's *Perceval* (*Le Conte del Graal*) originating in the first half of the thirteenth century. Of this translation, some 1,150 lines have been preserved, the majority in fragments dating from the last quarter of the thirteenth century (Liège, University Library 1333). The other fragments are kept in Brussels (Royal Library II 115–

2), Prague (Museum of National Literature 392/zl), and Düsseldorf (Landes- und Stadtbibliothek F. 23).

A much-abridged version of this translation is included in the *Lancelot-Compilatie*, followed by an adaptation of the first part of the anonymous Old French First Continuation of Chrétien's romance. The *Perchevael* in the *Lancelot-Compilatie* comprises almost 6,000 lines. [BB]

ঙ Gysseling, Maurits, ed. *Corpus van Middelnederlandse teksten (tot en met het jaar 1300)*, II, 1. The Hague: Nijhoff, 1980, pp. 501–19.

Jonckbloet, W.J.A., ed. *Roman van Lancelot*. 2 vols. The Hague: van Stockum, 1846–49, pp. 247–84.

Fuehrer, M.R. *A Study of the Relation of the Dutch Lancelot and the Flemish Perchevael Fragments to the Manuscripts of Chrétien's "Conte del Graal."* Diss., Washington, 1939.

PERCY, THOMAS (1729–1811), an antiquarian bishop whose historically significant *Reliques of Ancient English Poetry* (1765) included six Arthurian ballads. "Sir Lancelot du Lake" (124 lines) recounts Lancelot's battle with Tarquin (Malory, Book VI, Chapters 7–9). "The Boy and the Mantle" (196 lines) describes chastity tests at Arthur's court. "The Marriage of Sir Gawain" (160 lines) retells the Middle English romance *The Wedding of Sir Gawain and Dame Ragnell*. In "King Ryence's Challenge" (42 lines), sung before Queen Elizabeth at Kenilworth in 1575, the Welsh king demands Arthur's beard to decorate his mantle. "King Arthur's Death" (184 lines) closely follows Malory's account from Gawain's dream to the King's departure. "The Legend of King Arthur" (96 lines) reproduces Geoffrey of Monmouth's account of Arthur's genealogy and wars. [MAW]

ঙ Percy, Thomas. *Reliques of Ancient English Poetry Consisting of Old Heroic Ballads, Songs and Other Pieces of Our Earlier Poets*. 3 vols. London: Dodsley, 1765.

PERCY, WALKER, author of *Lancelot* (1978), which transposes the Grail quest into the contemporary world of filmmaking. The predicament of the narrator-hero, Lancelot Lamar, who has watched his early promise and idealism fade after an unhappy marriage, reflects the spiritual wasteland that is modern America. He seeks escape in alcohol, just as others do in the illusion provided by Hollywood. Viewing himself as the "Knight of the Unholy Grail," Lancelot sets out to expose the corruption that lies behind the glittering façade. This he achieves by recording on videotape the sexual promiscuity of both his wife and daughter. Since he is so deeply corrupted by the very sins that he condemns, however, he too is destroyed in the final cataclysm. This is a symbolic novel, and the Arthurian borrowings, which include the figures of Merlin and Percival, deepen the significance of the symbols. The powerful vision of spiritual desolation in the modern world gives fresh meaning to the myth of the Grail quest. [RHT]

ঙ Percy, Walker. *Lancelot*. New York: Farrar, Straus and Giroux, 1978.

PEREDUR, one of "the three Welsh romances" probably dating from the thirteenth century. (The others are *Geraint and Enid* and *Owain*.) Peredur is brought up by his mother, in the company of females and far from chivalrous society, in an attempt to protect him from the dangers of knightly pursuits and tournaments, which have killed his father and brothers. The appearance of three knights kindles the boy's imagination, and he makes his way to Arthur's court to be dubbed. His rustic appearance and naïveté create welcome relief at court. Setting out to avenge Cei's insult to a dwarf, Peredur undergoes a series of adventures that bring out his innate chivalry; but his education is continued at the courts of two of his uncles. The first uncle, who is lame, advises him never to enquire about the significance of what he sees. At the court of the other, he sees being carried in procession a bleeding lance and a head upon a salver. More adventures follow, including a period spent at the court of the witches of Caerloyw, who instruct him in arms, before he returns at last to Arthur's court. Peredur embarks upon another round of adventures culminating in a period of fourteen years when he ruled with "the empress of great Constantinople," an episode that contains many clear remnants of a sovereignty myth. The story returns abruptly to Arthur's court, where Peredur is berated by a loathly damsel for failing to ask the meaning of the marvels he saw at his uncle's castle, for that question would have restored the king to health and the land to prosperity. After many adventures, it is revealed that the witches of Caerloyw had beheaded Peredur's cousin and lamed his uncle and that Peredur has been fated to avenge them. In spite of the story's obvious resemblances to Chrétien de Troyes's *Perceval*, the differences are nevertheless striking. The order of events is changed, the head upon the salver replaces the Grail, and the episodes culminating in the fourteen years' sojourn with the empress are not found in the French version. Independent references show that Peredur was a figure well established in Welsh tradition, and it is possible that *Peredur* is a retelling in Welsh of material found in, or used by, Chrétien, combined with independent folklore and dynastic traditions about the hero. The Grail and its attendant mysteries are represented in Welsh by the head, and the tale becomes one of vengeance for the slaying of a kinsman. [BFR]

Goetnick, Glenys, ed. *Historia Peredur vab Efrawc*. Cardiff: University of Wales Press, 1976.

Jones, Gwyn, and Thomas Jones, trans. *The Mabinogion*. 2nd ed. London: Dent, 1974.

Jarman, A.O.H., and Gwilym Rees Hughes. *A Guide to Welsh Literature I*. Swansea: Davies, 1976.

PERILOUS SEAT (SIEGE PERILOUS, SIÈGE PÉRILLEUX), a vacant seat at the Round Table, to be occupied eventually by the knight destined to accomplish the Grail quest. In the Didot-*Perceval*, Perceval sits there, causing darkness and the splitting of a stone, whereupon a voice rebukes Arthur for permitting this act. As the *Queste del Saint Graal* informs us, Galahad is the knight for whom the seat is reserved. (*See also* ROUND TABLE.) [NJL]

PERLESVAUS, an early Old French Grail romance in prose, dating from the beginning of the thirteenth century. It is extant in three manuscripts, two fragments, and an early printing. The name of the hero, Perlesvaus, is a variant of Perceval, explained as *perd-les-vaux* ("to lose the vales") of Kamaalot, his heritage.

The plot is too lengthy and complex to summarize, but it involves a pilgrimage by Arthur to Cornwall to repent of his inactivity and the lengthy adventures of Gauvain (who sees the Grail and Lance but fails to ask the question), of Lancelot (including one of the Beheading Test analogues of *Sir Gawain and the Green Knight*), and of Perceval (who avenges his mother and frees the Grail castle from the King of Castle Mortal). The end of the romance concerns a political intrigue, in which Brien des Illes is the central villain, and the story of Perceval's retirement from the world.

The *Perlesvaus* follows Robert de Boron's *Joseph* in that the Arthurian story, and in particular the quest for the Grail, is interpreted in a religious spirit. Here, the spirit is militant and is dominated by the opposition of the New Law and the Old Law, of Christians and heathens. The religious spirit is mixed with a large dose of the supernatural and savage bloodshed, which gives the whole romance a wild and anarchic feeling. Symbolism and allegory are also prevalent. In some ways, the *Perlesvaus* is unconventional: it contains, for example, the only full-length account of Arthur and Guenevere's legitimate son, Loholt, whose death causes the Queen to die of grief, thereby modifying Lancelot's subsequent behavior considerably.

The author seems to have known Chrétien de Troyes's *Perceval*, its early Continuations, and the work of Robert de Boron, but the romance certainly predates the Vulgate *Queste del Saint Graal*. In its turn, it seems to have influenced the *Mériadeuc* (in the prominent role given to Brien des Illes) and *Fouke Fitz Warin* (in which a whole episode from the *Perlesvaus* was rewritten in verse). There are grounds for associating the romance with Glastonbury Abbey and the British Isles in general. A Middle Welsh adaptation exists under the title *Y Seint Greal*. [KB]

⚜ Nitze, William A., and T.A. Jenkins, eds. *Le Haut Livre du Graal: Perlesvaus.* 2 vols. Chicago: Chicago University Press, 1932–37.

PERONNIK THE FOOL: *see* MOORE, GEORGE.

PERROS RELIEF, an early-medieval granite relief on a pier in the Romanesque church of St. Efflam in Perros-Guirec on the north coast of Brittany. It illustrates two male figures, one holding a crozier and one nude, spraddled, and displaying large sexual organs. The scene is traditionally considered to represent Arthur and the Irish saint Efflam of Brittany. The saint vanquished a dragon through prayer after Arthur failed to kill the monster in a day-long battle. [MS]

ᴥ Renouard, Michel. *Art roman en Bretagne*. Rennes: Ouest-France, 1978.

PERSEFORES, HISTORIA DEL NOBLE REY, a late sixteenth-century Spanish translation by Fernando de Mena of the first two parts of the four-teenth-century French Alexander and Arthurian romance *Perceforest*, surviving in an unedited manuscript (Madrid, Biblioteca de Palacio 266–67) bearing the title *La antigua y moral historia del noble rey Persefores y del esforçado Gadifer su hermano, reyes de Inglaterra y Escoçia*. The Mena translation, based perhaps on a manuscript copy and a 1531 imprint of the French in the library of Philip II, tends to abbreviate the French text but at the same time reveals the translator's interest in presenting an accurate and smooth rendering of the original. Although never printed, the *Persefores* forms part of the great vogue of sub-Arthurian chivalric romances in sixteenth-century Spain and Portugal and may have been intended as a mirror of princes and chivalry. [HLS]

ᴥ Michael, Ian. "The Spanish *Perceforest*: A Recent Discovery." In *Studies in Medieval Literature and Languages in Memory of Frederick Whitehead*, ed. W. Rothwell, W.R.J. Barron, David Blamires, and Lewis Thorpe. Manchester: Manchester University Press, 1973, pp. 209–18.

PFAUENFEST, DAS: *see* WERTHES, FRIEDRICH AUGUST CLEMENS.

PHILLIPS, STEPHEN (1868–1915), best known for romantic dramas like *Paolo and Francesca* (1900), included his blank-verse "Parting of Launcelot and Guinevere" in his *New Poems* of 1908. He paints a Pre-Raphaelite scene in Tennysonian language to evoke the suppressed sexuality of the knight's last meeting with the Queen in the nunnery to which she had retired. [CNS]

ᴥ Phillips, Stephen. *New Poems*. London: Bodley Head, 1908.

PIERI, PAOLINO (fl. 1300–05). A Florentine writer best known for the *Cronica delle cose d'Italia*, Paolino is also author of *La Storia de Merlino*, a prose text recounting Merlin's youth and recording his prophecies. [NJL]

ᴥ Pieri, Paolino. *Storia di Merlino*, ed. Ireneo Sanesi. Bergamo: Istituto Italiano d'Arti Grafiche, 1898.

PIERRE DE LANGTOFT (d. ca. 1307) was the author of a *Chronicle* written in Anglo-Norman alexandrines, probably in England. Condensing material from Geoffrey of Monmouth in order to treat the history of England up to the death of Edward I, Pierre condemns Guenevere and praises Arthur as the greatest of kings. [NJL]

&. Pierre de Langtoft. *The Chronicle of Pierre de Langtoft*, ed. Thomas Wright. 2 vols. London: Longmans, Green, 1866–68.

PISANO, ANTONIO (known as Pisanello; ca. 1395–1455). Only a single series of large-scale paintings depicting an Arthurian romance has survived from early Renaissance Italy: the recently discovered mural cycle in the Sala del Pisanello of the Ducal Palace in Mantua. Commissioned in the late 1440s by the ruler of Mantua, Marchese Lodovico Gonzaga, the frescoes were begun—but left unfinished—by Pisanello, one of the most famous artists of his day. *Sinopie* (drawings on the first layer of plaster) were discovered on three walls of the Sala (or hall), which measures 17.40 by 9.60 meters, but only one wall reached the point of being partially painted. On the basis of French inscriptions in the *sinopie*, the iconography can be identified as an episode taken from the Prose *Lancelot*. The story chosen by the Gonzaga tells of the hero Bohort's visit to King Brangoire's castle, his participation in a tournament and a banquet, and his love intrigue with King Brangoire's daughter, which results in the conception of Helain Le Blanc.

Inventories of the princely libraries of the Courts of Milan, Ferrara, and Mantua reveal that north Italian princes were avid readers of Arthurian romance during the fourteenth and fifteenth centuries, often preferring the texts in the original language. In the 1407 inventory of the Gonzaga library, for instance, sixty-seven volumes out of a total of 392 codices were in French, of which seventeen were Arthurian prose romances.

Although only the scenes showing the tournament and some of the knights' vows at the banquet have survived in the Sala del Pisanello, suggestive parallels can be drawn between Pisanello's pictorial design for the mural cycle and the narrative techniques, especially that of *entrelacement* or interlacing, of the Vulgate *Lancelot*. Whether deliberately or fortuitously, the thirteenth-century French romance and the fifteenth-century Italian frescoes convey related aesthetic values. [JW-M]

&. Woods-Marsden, Joanna. *Art and Life at a Renaissance Court: Pisanello's Arthurian Cycle in Mantua*. Princeton, N.J.: Princeton University Press, in press.

PLATIN, CLAUDE: *see* RENAUT DE BEAUJEU.

PLEIER, DER, author of three lengthy Arthurian romances: *Garel von dem blühenden Tal* ("Garel of the Flowering Valley"), 21,310 short lines in rhymed couplets (the beginning, ca. 100 lines, is missing); *Tandareis und Flordibel* (18,339 short lines mostly in rhymed couplets); and *Meleranz* (12,834 short lines in rhymed couplets). Little is known about the author. He wrote between 1240 and 1270; his rhymes point to Austria, perhaps to the Salzburg area. His pen name probably means "(glass) blower" and perhaps refers metaphorically to his writing technique of using old materials, melting them up, and fusing them into "new" works.

In *Garel*, Ekunaver of Kanadic provokes Arthur and his court by sending his messenger, the giant Karabin, who announces, after a year's term, a campaign of revenge. Arthur accepts this declaration of war. Garel, one of his young knights, follows Karabin in order to explore Ekunaver's lands. On his journey, he becomes involved in several adventures; defeats many knights and princes and helps others, obliging all of them to provide him with troops; and finally frees Queen Laudamie of Anferre from her oppressor, the monstrous Vulganus, and marries her. With his old and new troops, he is able to conquer Ekunaver before Arthur arrives at the battlefield. The hostile parties arrange a reconciliation, there follows a splendid celebration at Arthur's court, several marriages are concluded, and on the battlefield Ekunaver and Garel have a monastery built.

The *Garel* story was meant as a reaction to *Daniel von dem blühenden Tal*, by Der Stricker (ca. 1230). Daniel is an overly cunning and ruthless hero, an antihero in the view of Der Pleier, who raises his own protagonist again to the level of high knightly and courtly ideals.

Tandareis und Flordibel tells how the youthful prince Tandareis of Tandernas and Flordibel, an oriental princess, fall in love at Arthur's court. They cannot admit this publicly, however, because Arthur had assured her that he would kill anybody who wanted to come into the possession of her love. The couple flee to Tandernas. Arthur besieges the castle, and several fights take place. But Gawan is able to bring about a reconciliation between Arthur and the couple under the condition that Flordibel entrusts herself to Arthur's wife, Queen Jenover; Tandareis must journey to foreign countries in order to establish himself as a real knight.

In two series of adventures, Tandareis defeats robbers and giants and frees imprisoned knights and ladies, among them the oppressed queen Albiun. Arthur keeps hearing about the young knight's victories and tries to get him back to court, but his attempts fail. He then decides to organize a tournament once a month for a whole year. Tandareis appears three times incognito and wins, every time in a different guise. He is recognized but refuses to return to court. Arthur tries other ways to get him back and finally succeeds. The King and Tandareis come to a lasting reconciliation, the couple is reunited, and after some more complications (other ladies claim Tandareis!) the wedding takes place at Arthur's court, where at a splendid celebration several other couples are also married. Tandareis and Flordibel return to his kingdom, where the coronation feast is celebrated at Pentecost.

Meleranz relates how a prince of France decides to go to Arthur's court at the age of twelve. On his way there, Meleranz encounters the young queen Tydomie of Kameric under a lime-tree. They fall in love, but Meleranz rides on to court. Two years later, he is dubbed a knight; on this occasion, he receives from Tydomie belt, wreath, and clasp, clear signs of her lasting love, and he resolves to return to the place under the lime-tree. On the way back, he gets involved in three interconnected adventures. He is victorious in all three but learns that Tydomie is in danger of being married to King Libers by her uncle Malloas. Meleranz defeats both of them. During a splendid celebration, attended by King Arthur as well as the King of France, the wedding takes place; the narrator predicts that the marriage will be happy and blessed with two sons and one daughter.

Although Der Pleier claims French narratives as sources for his works, none has been found. His achievement appears to consist in recombining narrative plots and motifs found in "classical" Arthurian works by Hartmann von Aue, Wolfram von Eschenbach, Wirnt von Grafenberg, Gottfried von Strassburg, and Der Stricker into new stories that are well constructed and pleasantly narrated. The author also takes most characters from earlier German romances; in doing so, he draws heavily upon the genealogies of Arthur's family and other dynasties that are to be found in Wolfram's *Parzival* and *Titurel*, developing the characters and filling in narrative lacunae. There are strong restorative trends in these works, and a decidedly nostalgic flavor. Der Pleier must have appealed to a reading public well versed in Arthurian fiction. He consciously and adroitly establishes a comprehensive but specific narrative world, and the reading or listening pleasure of his public probably consisted mainly in recognizing and enjoying the old in the new as well as the new in the old. Although Der Pleier is not an original writer, he is a fascinating figure particularly because of his revival of Arthurian literature in German lands after several generations of neglect. [PWT]

Pleier, Der. *Garel von dem blüenden Tal*, ed. Wolfgang Herles. Vienna: Halosar, 1981.

——— . *Tandareis und Flordibel: Ein höfischer Roman*, ed. Ferdinand Khull. Graz: Styria, 1885.

——— . *Meleranz*, ed. Karl Bartsch. Hildesheim: Olms, 1974.

Kern, Peter. *Die Artusromane des Pleier: Untersuchungen über den Zusammenhang von Dichtung und literarischer Situation*. Berlin: Schmidt, 1981.

Riordan, John Lancaster. "A Vindication of the Pleier." *Journal of English and Germanic Philology*, 47 (1948), 29–43.

"POLITICS": *see* EMERSON, RALPH WALDO.

POLYCHRONICON: *see* HIGDEN, RANULPH.

POLY-OLBION: *see* DRAYTON, MICHAEL.

POMEROY, FLORENCE M., English poet, brought out her *Tristan and Iseult: An Epic Poem in Twelve Books* in 1958. This blank-verse narrative follows the details of the "complete" story of the two lovers as it is found in Bédier, and it is presented in a deliberately archaic diction composed of extended quasi-Homeric simile and recondite vocabulary. [AAR]

Pomeroy, Florence M. *Tristan and Iseult: An Epic Poem in Twelve Books*. Oxford: Lane, 1958.

PORIUS: see POWYS, JOHN COWPER.

PORT ETERNITY: see CHERRYH, C.J.

PORTUGUESE ARTHURIAN LITERATURE: *see* SPANISH AND
PORTUGUESE ARTHURIAN LITERATURE.

POST-VULGATE CYCLE (or the *Post-Vulgate Romance of the Grail*, or *Roman
du Graal*), a rehandling of the Vulgate Cycle of Arthurian prose romances
composed between 1230 and 1240 by an anonymous writer but attributed to
"Robert de Borron." (Hence, this work was once known as the "pseudo–
Robert de Boron" cycle.) The author's aim was to create out of the several
branches of the Vulgate a more homogeneous unity, one that would center on
Arthur and the Grail rather than on the love of Lancelot and Guenevere.

The Post-Vulgate has not been preserved in its complete form; it has had to
be reconstructed from scattered French fragments that have only gradually
come to light and from certain Portuguese and Spanish translations. Like the
Vulgate, the Post-Vulgate probably began with a history of the Grail in pre-
Arthurian times (the *Estoire del Saint Graal*). To judge from the Galician-
Portuguese *Livro de Josep Abarimatia* and the Castilian *Josep*, the Post-Vulgate
Estoire del Saint Graal did not differ substantially from the Vulgate version. This
was followed, as in the Vulgate, by the prose rendering of Robert de Boron's
Merlin. The Vulgate *Merlin* continuation, however, is replaced by a brief
account of Arthur's early wars against the rebel kings and the Saxons (adapted
from the Vulgate) together with a new series of adventures, including such
episodes as Arthur's begetting of Mordred, the revelation of Arthur's parentage, his combat with Pellinor, the obtaining of Escalibor from a hand in the
lake, the wars against Rion and Lot, the tragic tale of Balain, the story of
Merlin and Niviene, and the adventures of Gauvain, Yvain, and Le Morholt.
The Post-Vulgate *Suite du Merlin* was rendered into Castilian (*El Baladro del Sabio
Merlin*, Burgos, 1498; Seville 1535), Galician-Portuguese, and English (Malory's
"Tale of King Arthur"); it is known in French in the main from two fourteenth-century manuscripts: the so-called Huth Manuscript (Add. 38117, British Library, London), which like the *Baladro* lacks the account of Arthur's wars
against the rebel kings, and the manuscript Add. 7071 of Cambridge University
Library, identified by Eugène Vinaver in 1945. Both the Huth and Cambridge
manuscripts are incomplete at the end. The conclusion to the adventures of
Gauvain, Yvain, and Le Morholt—missing in both but appearing in Malory—
was discovered in 1895 by Eduard Wechssler in a fifteenth-century compilation
of Arthurian prose romances.

No branch corresponding to the Vulgate *Lancelot* formed part of the Post-
Vulgate. Referring to the contents of his *livre*, the Post-Vulgate author admits

having excluded *la grant hystore de Lanscelot*, as it would have made "the middle portion three times as big as the other two." To supply a transition to the last part of his "book" (versions of the *Queste del Saint Graal* and the *Mort Artu*), he adapted a few relevant incidents from the Agravain section of the Vulgate *Lancelot* and from the First Version of the Prose *Tristan* and combined them with his own inventions. This section of the *Suite*, which largely bridges the gap between adventures of Gauvain, Yvain, and Le Morholt, is found in B.N. fr. 112 and in a late thirteenth-century codex, B.N. fr. 12599.

Versions of the *Queste del Saint Graal* and *Mort Artu* that complete the *Roman du Graal* (based on the Vulgate but completely remodeled so as to link up with the earlier portions of the narrative) have been preserved in almost-complete form in Galician-Portuguese (*A Demanda do Santo Graal*) and partially in Castilian (*La Demanda del Sancto Grial*). But of the French original only fragments of varying lengths have survived, some of which are found in certain manuscripts of the Second Version of the Prose *Tristan* and other later compilations.

In the Vulgate Cycle, the combination of such incompatible themes as that of the Grail and Lancelot's love for Guenevere produced an inevitable clash of ideologies. This *double esprit* and the *joie de vivre* so characteristic of the early parts of the *Lancelot* proper are absent from the Post-Vulgate. *Fin'amors* is condemned unequivocally throughout the narrative. The author treats it from a severely ascetic and tragic angle. Influenced no doubt by the mystical theology of St. Bernard of Clairvaux—for whom all faults, even those perpetrated unknowingly, are imputable sins—the Post-Vulgate conceives of Arthur's kingdom as the *roiaume aventureux*, the land in which the monarch and many of his knights are doomed to commit, unwittingly, outrages that the whole country will have to expiate. The two main tragedies to befall the Arthurian world— the adventures of the Grail inaugurated by Balain's Dolorous Stroke and the destruction of the realm brought about by Arthur's incestuous son Mordred— are both interpreted as divine punishment for sins committed inadvertently, through pure mischance.

Structurally, too, the Post-Vulgate is more closely knit than the Vulgate. The author, who conceived his Arthuriad as a whole, was anxious not only to reinterpret Arthurian history but to motivate the various peripeties better than his predecessors had done. He achieved this, like most thirteenth-century prose writers, not psychologically but structurally, supplying the material antecedents of the events to be elucidated. Long narrative sequences begun in the early portions of the *Romance*, notably the *Suite du Merlin*, foreshadow themes in the *Queste* and *Mort Artu*. The sections dovetail to form an indestructible whole.

All this enables us to comprehend the significance of the tripartite division of the *Romance*. The sections cut across those of the Vulgate Cycle: the first part, for example, ends not with the *Estoire del Saint Graal* but in the midst of one of Balain's adventures. But if we regard the Post-Vulgate as a single "book," the story of Arthur's kingdom—which is also *La Haute Escriture del Saint Graal*, the title significantly given by the author to the *whole* romance—it falls logically into three parts, corresponding to the three phases in the history of the kingdom. First comes the story of Logres before the beginning of the Grail adventures; this ends at the point where Balain sets out on the quest during which he will strike the Dolorous Stroke. The second part shows us Logres suffering for Balain's act. The last part, beginning with the news of the coming of the Good Knight who will achieve the adventures of the Grail, includes not only the *Quèste* but also an account of Arthur's death. [FB]

Bogdanow, Fanni. *The Romance of the Grail: A Study of the Structure and Genesis of a Thirteenth-Century Arthurian Prose Romance.* Manchester: University of Manchester Press, 1966.

———— . "The *Suite du Merlin* and the Post-Vulgate *Roman du Graal.*" In *Arthurian Literature in the Middle Ages,* ed. Roger Sherman Loomis. Oxford: Clarendon, 1959, pp. 325–35.

POVEST O TRIŠTANU I IŽOTI, a sixteenth-century Russian/Serbo-Croatian prose version of the Tristan story. The work is based on the French Prose *Tristan* but adds a number of episodes not found in the French. [NJL]

Veselovski, A.N., ed. *Trischan i Izhotta: Istorii Romana i Povesti.* Petrograd, 1888.

POWERS, TIM, author of *The Drawing of the Dark* (1979), a fantasy that transforms the Turkish siege of Vienna in the sixteenth century into part of the struggle between Good and Evil. The former is led by the Fisher King and Merlin, who brings back from Avalon the spirit of King Arthur, temporarily resurrected as an Irish soldier of fortune. The process of his self-discovery is marked by both thoughtfulness and humor. [RHT]

Powers, Tim. *The Drawing of the Dark.* New York: Ballantine, 1979.

POWYS, JOHN COWPER (1872–1963), English-born author of three Arthurian novels, *A Glastonbury Romance* (1932), *Morwyn* (1937), and *Porius* (1951). Powys's books are concerned as much with metaphysical issues as with event and character; this is quickly established in *A Glastonbury Romance*, Powys's best-known work, which deals with the lives of a family in and around Glastonbury. In the midst of their mundane concerns with business, with inheritances, and especially with love in all of its varieties, they find that they must deal with the powerful ambience of the legendary ruins and with those who seek to exploit the human desire to partake in or perform the miracles associated with the Holy Well of Glastonbury.

A Glastonbury Romance is Arthurian not simply in its Glastonbury setting and its invocation of the magic associated with the Grail but also in the constant permutations of the Arthurian roles among its characters, from the betrayed "ruler" and women who resemble Celtic fays to the eventually mad scholar seeking the truth behind the mysterious "esplumoir Merlin." Powys interweaves the events of this novel with tortuous passages exploring love and, more frequently, sexual freedom. In this, the book, as does *Morwyn*, bears some resemblance to the work of D.H. Lawrence. One of the strengths of the novel is the author's clear-sighted depiction of human frailties even in the midst of his various advocacies. This immense, flawed novel is nevertheless influential in modern Arthurian fiction, most notably in its references to the Great Goddess and the remnants of her influence and religion.

Morwyn, the least successful of Powys's three Arthurian novels, impinges on the Arthurian legend only in that Taliesin and Merlin put in appearances. A fantastic journey through hell experienced by the middle-aged narrator, his dog, and the object of his passion, the young female Morwyn, the novel is a thinly disguised diatribe against the dual oppressors science and religion, both of which, in the narrator's view, torture for the sake of truth.

The action of *Porius* takes place during one week of A.D. 499. Porius, the son of a Romano-Celtic family, decides to join Arthur's cause. His rites of passage are extended: he must free himself from the domination of his parents and of the remnants of the old religion represented by his three aunts, while accepting the burdens laid on him by the mad sorcerer Myrddin Wyllt. His personal struggle is complicated by the conflicts of his village, as an increasingly intolerant Christian community attempts to suppress participation in the rites of the Goddess or of Mithras. Arthur makes one brief appearance (although not to Porius). Taliesin appears as an inspired bard and cook, and Medraut is depicted as already forming treacherous alliances with the Saxons and Arthur's Celtic enemies. *Porius* contains more humor than Powys's other Arthurian fiction: Porius, a young giant of a man, resembles the classic fairy-tale hero, and his dilemmas are viewed with a certain amusement.

The difficulties and infelicities of Powys's prose style will keep his works from the status of great fiction, but they must be reckoned with in any study of twentieth-century Arthurian literature. [AAR]

&. Powys, John Cowper. *A Glastonbury Romance*. New York: Simon and Schuster, 1932.
——— . *Morwyn: or, The Vengeance of God*. London: Cassell, 1937.
——— . *Porius: A Romance of the Dark Ages*. London: Macdonald, 1951.

PRAYSING TO JOSEPH, A: *see* HERE BEGYNNETH THE LYFE OF JOSEPH OF ARMATHIA.

PRECHTL, ROBERT: *see* TRISTAN, MODERN GERMAN VERSIONS OF GOTTFRIED'S.

PRE-RAPHAELITES. One of the stated aims of the original Pre-Raphaelite Brotherhood, founded in 1848, was "to have genuine ideas to express." As early as 1849, they turned to the Arthurian poetry of Tennyson for these ideas, as seen in the unfinished *Mort d'Arthur* (Tate Gallery, London) by F.G. Stephens (1828–1907). In 1850, William Holman Hunt (1827–1910) drew a subject from *The Lady of Shalott* (National Gallery of Victoria, Melbourne), and at the same time Hunt and Stephens became acquainted with the fresco project in the Queen's Robing Room, through a renewed association with Hunt's former drawing instructor William Dyce. Among the other Pre-Raphaelites, Elizabeth Siddal (?1831–1862) painted Arthurian themes.

After the Brotherhood was dissolved in 1853, Dante Gabriel Rossetti undertook responsibility to perpetuate the Pre-Raphaelite ideals of reform in painting, and he turned to Arthurian themes of his own invention in 1854, painting *King Arthur's Tomb* (Private Collection), a subject with no discernible source in the literature. Arthurian subjects were linked to the Pre-Raphaelite movement, first through the Moxon Tennyson (1857) and then through an exclusively Pre-Raphaelite endeavor, the Oxford Union Murals (1857), Rossetti's response to the Queen's Robing Room. The latter project solidified the connection between Pre-Raphaelitism and Arthurian subjects, drew Edward Burne-Jones and William Morris among others into the movement, and broke the Pre-Raphaelite link with Tennyson, forging one instead with Malory, a bond that endured to the end of the Arthurian Revival.

Arthurian subjects remained a standard of Pre-Raphaelite painting. Group projects continued, as in the Dunlop Windows (1862). The preferred narrative, in contrast to the Academic tradition, was of forbidden love. Artists associated with the movement, Arthur Hughes, Frederick Sandys (1832–1904), and Frederic Shields (1833–1911), explored and invented themes outside the literature while maintaining the Pre-Raphaelite aesthetic of slender figures, jewel-toned palette, and meticulous detail. Former associates continued to interpret Arthurian subjects: Hunt painted *The Lady of Shalott* (1886–1905, Wadsworth Athenaeum, Hartford) and Thomas Woolner sculpted marbles of *Guinevere* and *Elaine* (1870s, both unlocated). The Pre-Raphaelite love of evocative subject matter and highly naturalistic detail became a ubiquitous feature of the late Arthurian Revival, influencing the styles of Academic painters James Archer, John Lyston Byam Shaw, Joseph Noël Paton, George Frederick Watts, and John William Waterhouse. The Pre-Raphaelites left an indelible mark on the course of the Arthurian Revival, expanding both the corpus and the iconography and offering an alternative interpretation to the heroic and moral subjects preferred by the government and the Royal Academicians. [DNM]

Fredeman, William E. *Pre-Raphaelitism: A Bibliocritical Study*. Cambridge, Mass.: Harvard University Press, 1965.

PRESBYS HIPPOTES, HO ("The Old Knight"), a brief Greek verse text, dating from around 1300 and perhaps taken from the *Compilation* of Rusticiano da Pisa. The title refers to an old man whom Palamedes, Gawain, Lancelot, and Tristan are unable to defeat. [NJL]

Breillat, Pierre. "La Table Ronde en Orient: Le poème grec du *Vieux Chevalier*." *Mélanges d'Archéologie et d'Histoire Publiés par l'École Française de Rome*, 55 (1938), 308–40.

PRIESTLEY, J(OHN) B(OYNTON) (1894–1985), lightheartedly interweaves Arthurian magic with satire of modern advertising techniques and reflections on the nature of time in *The Thirty-First of June* (1961). Melicent, princess of Peradore, a kingdom owing allegiance to Arthur, gazes into an enchanted mirror and falls for Sam, a painter who works for an advertising agency in London. [CNS]

🎕 Priestley, J.B. *The Thirty-First of June*. London: Heinemann, 1961.

PRINCE ARTHUR: AN HEROICK POEM: *see* BLACKMORE, SIR RICHARD.

PRINCE HENRY'S BARRIERS: *see* JONES, INIGO.

PRINCETON UNIVERSITY CHAPEL WINDOWS. The Milbank Choir of the Chapel (Cram and Ferguson, architects, 1925–28) includes windows depicting the four Christian epics of Bunyan, Milton, Dante, and Malory executed by the Boston stained-glass artist Charles J. Connick (1875–1945). *Le Mort d'Arthur* is found in the central bay of the north wall, where scenes organized thematically rather than narratively are grouped into three tiers (bottom to top): *Life and Death of Arthur*, *Aspirations of Chivalry*, and *The Quest of the Holy Grail*, with *The Mystical Vision of Christ* surmounting all. Thirty-six individual panels contain "portraits" (e.g., Malory, Modred, Percival) as well as key events (*Modred Kills Arthur*, *Galahad Achieves the Grail*). [JFO'G]

🎕 Stillwell, Richard. *The Chapel of Princeton University*. Princeton, N.J.: Princeton University Press, 1971.

PROCESSUS SATANAE: *see* MAERLANT, JACOB VAN.

PROPHÉCIES DE MERLIN, LES, attributed to Maistre Richart d'Irlande and composed in the 1270s. Ostensibly translated from Latin, the work is unrelated to Geoffrey of Monmouth's *Prophetiae Merlini*. Although various Arthurian characters are introduced, the text consists essentially of conversations between Merlin and several scribes. In the course of these conversations, Merlin makes a number of prophecies that are in fact references to political events of the twelfth and thirteenth centuries. The author criticizes religious abuses and exhorts readers to be properly obedient to the Church. [NJL]

🎕 Paton, Lucy Allen, ed. *Les Prophécies de Merlin*. 2 vols. New York: Heath, 1926.

PROPHETIAE MERLINI: *see* GEOFFREY OF MONMOUTH.

PROSA-LANCELOT, a German prose version (ca. 1250) of the Vulgate *Lancelot* that exists in one complete manuscript (Pal. germ. 147 [*P*] in Heidelberg, ca. 1430) and in three important fragments. The narrative may have been by more than one translator. The *Prosa-Lancelot* is divided into three parts that deal with Lancelot's life and death: Galahad, the Grail quest, and the death of Arthur. It offers a compendium of characters and locales found in traditional Arthurian literature up to the time of its composition, as well as new personalities, such as Lancelot's cousins Lionel and Bohort; his half-brother, Hestor/ Hector; King Claudas, a renegade Arthurian knight who is the mortal enemy of Lancelot's father, Ban, and the rival of King Arthur; Lancelot's friend Galahot; and his son, Galaad, destined to replace Perceval in the Arthurian tradition as the Grail hero.

Also of interest in the *Prosa-Lancelot* is the conception of chivalry, which is viewed within the framework of the history of salvation. The chivalric way of life is legitimized by the Lady of the Lake as a *militia christiana*, a prefiguration of the new type of fulfilled spiritual knighthood that finds its culmination in the figure of Galaad. Thus, the Arthurian chivalric order is viewed as a necessary and valuable, if less perfect, prerequisite for the new order of knighthood. [FGG]

Kluge, Reinhold, ed. *Lancelot.* 3 vols. Berlin: Akademie, 1948, 1963, 1972.

PROSAROMAN VON LANZELOT: *see* FUETRER, ULRICH.

PROSE BRUT, the title scholars give to a group of Anglo-Norman, English, and Latin prose chronicles, written in the late thirteenth, fourteenth, and fifteenth centuries, that cover the history of Britain. They include the familiar story of Arthur's rise to power, his conquest of the Romans, and his fall through the treachery of Mordred.

The earliest of these chronicles is the Anglo-Norman *Brut*, of which at least two redactions were written; it survives in at least forty-seven manuscripts. It appears to have been originally compiled from several sources shortly after 1272, but most manuscripts include continuations to 1333. It has never been edited.

The English *Brut* was translated from the Anglo-Norman *Brut* a little before 1400, but continuations carry events in some manuscripts past the mid-fifteenth century. The survival of approximately 170 manuscripts indicates that it was one of the most popular works written in English in the Middle Ages. Caxton and others printed editions of a version of it in the fifteenth and sixteenth centuries, and it was an important source for English chronicles of the sixteenth century. Although Brie's edition of 1906 and 1908 made a version of the *Brut* accessible to modern readers, several English versions of this chronicle have never been published, and it is not yet clear how they are all related. The amount of Arthurian material in the different versions ranges from a short paragraph in some to the long account found in many manuscripts and edited by Brie. Here, Arthur appears as the ideal king who attracts knights to his Round Table from many foreign lands and as a champion of Christianity fighting the pagan Romans. He is "wel bilouede of al men," "the most worthi lord of renoun that was in al the worlde," a model for future kings to follow.

The Latin *Brut* is found in at least fifteen manuscripts, and like the Anglo-Norman version it has never been edited. Scholars have argued that it was translated from either the Anglo-Norman (Brie) or the English *Brut* (Kingsford). If either of these hypotheses is true, the Latin *Brut* represents the unusual situation in which a vernacular work was translated into Latin instead of vice versa. [EDK]

&a Brie, Friedrich, ed. *Geschichte und Quellen der mittelenglischen Prosachronik The Brute of England oder The Chronicles of England.* Marburg: Elwert, 1905.

———, ed. *The Brut or the Chronicles of England.* London: Oxford University Press, 1906, 1908.

Fletcher, Robert Huntington. *The Arthurian Material in the Chronicles, Especially Those of Great Britain and France.* Boston: Ginn, 1906; 2nd ed. Roger Sherman Loomis. New York: Franklin, 1966, pp. 214–20.

Kingsford, C.L. *English Historical Literature in the Fifteenth Century.* Oxford: Clarendon, 1913, pp. 113–39.

Matheson, Lister M. "Historical Prose." In *Middle English Prose: A Critical Guide to Major Authors and Genres,* ed. A.S.G. Edwards. New Brunswick, N.J.: Rutgers University Press, 1984, pp. 210–14.

Meyer, Paul. "De quelques chroniques anglo-normandes qui ont porté le nom de *Brut.*" *Bulletin de la Société des anciens textes français,* 1878, 104–45.

Starke, Fritz-Joachim. *Populäre englische Chroniken des 15. Jahrhunderts.* Berlin: Junker and Dünnhaupt, 1935, pp. 90–135.

PROSE *EREC*: *see EREC IN PROSE.*

PROSE *LANCELOT*: *see* VULGATE CYCLE.

PROSE *MERLIN* (1), an Old French transcription made early in the thirteenth century from a verse *Merlin* attributed to Robert de Boron (only 504 lines of which survive). The surviving forty-six manuscripts of the Prose *Merlin* divide themselves into two distinct groups, depending on whether it was inserted into the *Joseph–Merlin–Perceval* prose trilogy or into the cyclic *Lancelot–Graal.* The romance relates how Merlin, the child of a virgin and an incubus, became King Arthur's counselor thanks to his knowledge of "things past and yet to come"; he prepared for the splendor of Arthur's reign, notably by the establishment of the Round Table. [C-AVC]

&a Micha, Alexandre, ed. *Merlin, roman en prose du XIIIe siècle.* Paris and Geneva: Droz, 1979.

———. *Étude sur le "Merlin" de Robert de Boron, roman du XIIIe siècle.* Paris and Geneva: Droz, 1980.

PROSE *MERLIN* (2), a mid-fifteenth-century English translation of the *Estoire de Merlin* portion of the thirteenth-century French Vulgate Arthurian cycle, extant only in Cambridge University Library MS Ff 3 11 (a fragment of a related manuscript survives in Bodleian MS Rawlinson Misc. olim 1262, later 1370). The French source-manuscript of the Prose *Merlin* was like, but not identical to, that used by Lovelich in his contemporary verse translation of *Merlin*. The Cambridge manuscript breaks off shortly after Gawain receives the imprisoned Merlin's last message, but it lacks only a little of the Vulgate *Merlin*'s ending. There is no particular reason to think the translator intended a whole cycle in the manner of Malory's *Morte Darthur*. The *Estoire de Merlin*, also reworked in the romance *Arthour and Merlin*, seems itself to have been of interest in England.

The Prose *Merlin* covers Merlin's history from his demonic conception to his final imprisonment by Nimiane. Merlin's activities as strategist, counselor, and politico-military tactician for the Arthurian regime are paramount. Several apparently digressive anecdotes, such as his appearances in Rome as a white hart and laughing wild-man, reinforce this role: in non-Arthurian contexts, he remains "Merlin of Nothumbirlande, the maister counseller of kynge Arthur of Breteyne," whose powers are harnessed to the quasi-eschatological task of establishing the Arthurian reign, not used for personal dominance.

Merlin's foresight is crucial in Arthur's complex series of wars against rebel British kings, invading Saxons, and the Romans. In the numerous accounts of melées, battles, and single combats (e.g., Bohors and Amaunt's moving combat "body for body"), the translator often draws on native alliterative and doublet traditions without abandoning the practice of anglicizing French words into English lexis (cf. Malory's "play" for "wound"). Though he follows the structure and theme of his French original closely, he permits himself more radical assimilations and innovations stylistically: the *matière* is fully "translated." His profound respect for this legendary British history ensures that the translator keeps carefully all his source's authenticating references to textual transmission but does not obtrude his own role at all. [JP]

᳚ Wheatley, Henry B., ed. *Merlin, or The Early History of King Arthur: A Prose Romance.* 2 vols. London: Kegan Paul, Trench, Trübner, 1865, 1899.

PROSE *TRISTAN*, a lengthy French romance that has been transmitted in two basic versions, dating from the second and third quarters of the thirteenth century. Many manuscripts are extant as well as printed editions based on the latest manuscript version. Both attributions, of the first version to Luces de Gat (Gaut, Galt) and of the second to Hélie de Borron, are almost certainly false.

The Prose *Tristan* is the first great Arthurian prose romance written after the Vulgate Cycle and is profoundly influenced in almost all aspects by it. The authors of this romance were the first to "Arthurianize" properly the story of Tristan and Iseut, a process barely begun in Béroul and Thomas. Tristan is an Arthurian knight and member of the Round Table, King Mark becomes a villain, and the moral issues of the adulterous love affair are greatly simplified insofar as they survive at all. The chivalric values and problems presented in the Prose *Tristan* are simple, much more so than in Chrétien's romances or in the Vulgate Cycle.

The romance begins with the story of Tristan's ancestors and birth, a common tendency of literature of the period being to elaborate on the prehistory of a popular hero. After the murder of Tristan's father, Meliadus, the young knight is taken to the court of King Pharamont of Gaul by his tutor, Governal, and then on to the court of Mark. Here, the narrative more or less rejoins the story told in the poems, and the author seems to have known both the Béroul-Eilhart and Thomas-Gottfried versions. After his marriage to Iseut of the White Hands, Tristan returns to Cornwall and his first love before Mark banishes him from Cornwall for good. After proving himself as a knight, he is made a member of the Round Table and occupies the seat left vacant by Le Morholt, whom he had killed. Some versions of the Prose *Tristan* include a traditional version of the hero's death, while others have Mark kill him treacherously with a poisoned lance as he is singing a lay for Iseut.

Into this basic framework are woven innumerable adventures of Tristan, Palamedes, and many Arthurian heroes; and frequently whole episodes from other romances, in particular the Vulgate *Queste* and *Mort Artu*, are interpolated. The whole shows a tendency toward creating a *summa arthuriana*.

It is the life of the knight-errant and his quest for adventure that dominate the Prose *Tristan*, resulting in long descriptions of tournaments and jousts. Any other departure from the norm of Arthurian romance and from the Tristan story can also generally be explained in the same way. This is not to say that the characters do not express noble and idealistic sentiments but rather that they do not enter into the typically courtly form of analysis. Palamedes, for example, an invention of the Prose *Tristan*, is desperately in love with Iseut but unfailingly loyal to Tristan. Despite his unrequited love, Palamedes never conducts inner dialogues with himself about the hopelessness of his position. Paradoxically, perhaps, Dinadan, another invention of the Prose *Tristan*, constantly calls into question the most fundamental concepts of the Arthurian world: he enters into a discussion about the point of jousting with a knight who has just challenged him; he condemns love as folly, since it tortures its servants and even causes their death. Yet Dinadan is a valiant knight and a passionate friend of Tristan, whose death leaves him dazed and wondering about the purpose of life.

Perhaps because of the way in which the various versions of the Prose *Tristan* came into being (often by accretion and interpolation), the narrative structure has been seen as wanting in some respects. Although partly based on the idea of *entrelacement* so successfully employed in the Vulgate Cycle, the narrative does not employ the device successfully or consistently. Episodes often have no real relationship with what precedes or follows, and no conclusions can be drawn about the placement of a particular episode and its consequences for the interpretation of the whole. This is no doubt also related to the expectations of the audience of the prose romances of the time, who probably read the romances by episode and did not bother to look back and forth for links to other parts of the romance. It is easy to see how a less demanding public of this kind can tempt an author to pile episode upon episode.

The popularity of the Prose *Tristan* was enormous: more than fifty manuscripts survive in Old French, as well as innumerable fragments; a printed version is among the earliest French printed books. It was imitated in the Italian *Tavola Ritonda* and in Spanish, Danish, Russian, and Polish, not to mention the adaptation by Malory. In France, later romances, such as the *Palamedes* (otherwise known as *Meliadus* and *Guiron le Courtois*), the Compilations of Rusticiano da Pisa, Jehan Vaillant, and Michot Gonnot, and the *Prophécies de Merlin*, derive from the Prose *Tristan*. As yet, there is no complete edition of this important text, the complex manuscript tradition being largely responsible. [KB]

ra Baumgartner, Emmanuèle. *Le Tristan en prose: Essai d'interprétation*. Geneva: Droz, 1975.

Löseth, Eilhert. *Le Roman en prose de Tristan*. Paris: Champion, 1891.

PROSE *YVAIN*: *see* YVAIN IN PROSE.

PSEUDO-MAP CYCLE: *see* VULGATE CYCLE.

PSEUDO-ROBERT DE BORON CYCLE: *see* POST-VULGATE CYCLE.

PSEUDO-WAUCHIER: *see* CONTINUATIONS.

PUCCI, ANTONIO (ca. 1310–1388), a popular Florentine poet whose lyrics are interesting for their glimpses of everyday life in fourteenth-century Florence. He wrote two *cantari* based on Arthurian themes: *Gismirante* and *Brito di Brettagna*. The first *cantare*, in two parts, recounts the adventures of Gismirante, the son of a former knight of the Round Table who, on his deathbed in Rome, sends him to Arthur's court to become a knight. Once there, Gismirante wins the admiration and affection of the entire court. After seven years, the opportunity comes for Gismirante to prove his mettle: the absence of tales of new adventure has caused the court to abstain from eating. Gismirante saves the court from starvation with the help of a fairy, who tells him about the most beautiful woman in the world and gives him a single strand of her golden hair. Enamored of this princess and undaunted by the attendant difficulties in courting her, he sets out to win her as his bride. The remainder of the *cantare* recounts his numerous adventures before and after winning the princess and includes a number of marvelous and folkloristic elements. He saves three beasts—a griffin, an eagle, and a hawk—all of which return to assist him at crucial junctures; he receives a magic horse from another fairy; the princess possesses a magic wand that can alter a river's flow. One long episode concerns a giant ("un uomo selvaggio") who abducts the princess and holds her and forty-three other ladies captive in an enchanted castle. To defeat the giant, Gismirante must discover the secret place where his heart is hidden. The giant's heart is guarded by a "Chinese box" arrangement of animals, consisting successively of a wild boar, a hare, and a swallow. The *cantare* concludes with the marriage of Gismirante and the princess at Arthur's court.

In *Brito di Brettagna*, Pucci bases his story on that found in the *De Amore* of Andreas Capellanus (Book II, Chapter 8) and employs a similarly striking array of motifs (a vaunt, single combats, the quest) and marvelous elements (a magic horse, a sumptuous banquet in the field), all of which derive from Arthurian literature. Brito's lady promises to grant him her love if he will bring her three items from King Arthur's castle: a sparrowhawk, two hunting dogs, and the scroll containing the rules of love. He learns from a fairy that to obtain these things he must declare that his lady is more beautiful than that of any other king and demonstrate the validity of this "vaunt" by winning in single combat. Further, to gain access to Arthur's court, he must first win the hawk's glove, which is guarded at the bridge of gold by two giants. After the successful conclusion of his quest, Brito returns to his lady. [CK]

Sapegno, Natalino, ed. *Poeti minori del Trecento.* Milan and Naples: Ricciardi, 1952, pp. 869–81.

Gardner, Edmund G. *The Arthurian Legend in Italian Literature.* London: Dent, 1930, pp. 247–52.

Levi, Ezio. "I cantari leggendari del popolo italiano nei secoli XIV e XV." *Giornale storico della letteratura italiana,* Supp. 16 (1914), 92–113.

PULZELLA GAIA, LA ("The Merry Maiden"), an Italian *cantare* of the third quarter of the fourteenth century, concerns the tribulations of Morgana's daughter. It presents Morgana, however, only in passing; at the end of the first *cantare*, she speaks in the accents of a woman of the people. [SJN]

Levi, Ezio, ed. *Fiore de leggende: cantari antichi.* Bari: Laterza, 1914.

PURCELL, HENRY (1658–1695), composed the music for John Dryden's *King Arthur*, first performed in 1691. The collaboration resulted in an outstanding example of so-called Restoration semiopera. Dryden provided, together with a heroic theme, a text offering many opportunities for instrumental and choral ensembles, solo singing, dance, and spectacular effects to musical accompaniment. Purcell rose to the challenge of creating music for situations as diverse as Druidical rites, rural jollification, and a scene celebrating the Order of the Garter, during which the soprano sings the air "Fairest Isle." Owing much to the traditional masque and to familiar English musical forms,

PWYLL

Purcell also looks to the Continent for inspiration. Though the music is very highly rated, complete performances of *King Arthur* are now rare. [CNS]

🦋 Moore, R.E. *Henry Purcell and the Restoration Theatre*. London: Heinemann, 1961.

PWYLL: see MABINOGI.

PYLE, HOWARD: *see* BOOK ILLUSTRATION (AMERICAN); JUVENILE FICTION IN ENGLISH.

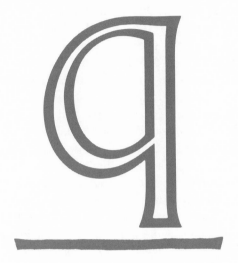

**QUANDO TRISTANO E LANCIELOTTO COMBATTETTERO AL PE-
TRONE DI MERLINO** ("When Tristan and Lancelot Fought at the Tomb of
Merlin"), an Italian *cantare* believed to represent a fairly late (fifteenth-
century) stage in the development of the tradition. [SJN]

Branca, Daniela Delcorno. "I cantari di Tristano." *Lettere italiane*, 23 (1971), 289–305.

QUEEN GUENEVERE: *see* MORRIS, WILLIAM.

QUEEN OF AIR AND DARKNESS, THE: *see* WHITE, T.H.

QUEEN OF CORNWALL: *see* HARDY, THOMAS.

QUEEN YSEULT: *see* SWINBURNE, ALGERNON CHARLES.

QUEEN'S KNIGHT: *see* KEITH, CHESTER.

QUEEN'S KNIGHT, THE: *see* BOROWSKY, MARVIN.

QUEEN'S ROBING ROOM. The new palace at Westminster, begun in 1836, was extensively decorated in fresco painting. The Fine Arts Commission, comprising government officials and leaders of the art world, oversaw the vast undertaking, which was intended to depict the glories of British history and culture in an allegorical mode. Of all the rooms in the palace, the Queen's Robing Room, where the monarch prepared for her appearance in the House of Lords, was seen to have the greatest symbolic significance and therefore posed a special iconographical problem. The solution was found when the painter William Dyce (1806–1864) observed to the president of the Commission, Prince Albert, that Malory's *Le Morte Darthur* was a British equivalent for the German national epic the *Nibelungenlied*. Albert admired the allegorical interpretation of the *Nibelungenlied* in King Ludwig of Bavaria's Munich Residenz and in 1848 suggested that Dyce design and execute in the Robing Room an ensemble of frescoes based on the Arthurian legend, a subject absent from the repertoire of British painters since the Middle Ages.

Dyce investigated the literature and came to the conclusion that he would "consider the companions of the Round Table as personifications of certain moral qualities which make up the ancient idea of Chivalric greatness." His first design, however, *Piety: The Knights of the Round Table Departing on the Quest for the Holy Grail* (1849, National Gallery of Scotland, Edinburgh) was rejected by the Commission. A higher moral tone, free from mystical associations, was demanded, and Dyce quickly learned to edit the legend. The completed frescoes show the King and his champions as exemplars of Victorian moral virtue. The subjects were *Religion: The Vision of Sir Galahad and His Company* (1851), *Generosity: King Arthur Unhorsed, Spared by Sir Lancelot* (1852), *Courtesy: Sir Tristram Harping to La Belle Isolde* (1852), *Mercy: Sir Gawaine Swearing to Be Merciful and Never Be Against Ladies* (1854), and *Hospitality: The Admission of Sir Tristram to the Fellowship of the Round Table*, which was near completion at the artist's death in 1864 and finished according to his design by C.W. Cope. The remaining designs, *Courage: The Combat Between King Arthur and the Five Northern Kings* and *Fidelity: Sir Lancelot Rescuing Queen Guenevere from King Meliagaunce*, were abandoned, and drawings do not survive. The ensemble was completed in 1868 with the addition of eighteen bas-relief oak panels at the dado, depicting narrative scenes from Arthur's history and the quest for the Grail, carved by H.H. Armstead (1828–1875).

The frescoes in the Robing Room constitute the first and most significant monument of the Arthurian Revival. As the first Victorian artist to address Arthurian themes, Dyce set the prototype. His massive, sculpturesque figures, based on those in German history painting, and simple yet theatrical settings became a standard convention. The physical identities he formulated—a broad-chested, bearded, middle-aged king; heroic, dark Lancelot; a tawny-haired Gawaine; a long-haired, mustachioed, brunette Tristram; and a fair, athletic Galahad—endured until the end of the century. Above all, his moral interpretation, guided by the censorious scrutiny of the Prince and the Commission, gave Arthurian imagery a didactic iconology, and his expurgated Arthuriad foreshadowed the tone of Tennyson's *Idylls of the King*. [DNM]

🙠 Boase, T.S.R. "The Decoration of the New Palace at Westminster." *Journal of the Warburg and Courtauld Institutes*, 17 (1954), 319–58.

Mancoff, Debra N. *The Arthurian Revival in Victorian Painting*. 2 vols. Ann Arbor, Mich.: University Microfilms International, 1982, Vol. 1, pp. 284–369.

QUEST OF MERLIN, THE: *see* HOVEY, RICHARD.

QUEST OF THE HOLY GRAIL, THE: *see* PRINCETON UNIVERSITY CHAPEL WINDOWS.

QUEST OF THE SANCGREALL, THE: *see* WESTWOOD, THOMAS.

QUEST OF THE SANGREAL, THE: *see* HAWKER, ROBERT STEPHEN.

QUESTE DEL SAINT GRAAL, LA: *see* VULGATE CYCLE.

QUESTING BEAST, a strange beast or monster that reappears frequently in French, Spanish, and Italian romance. Malory describes it as "the strongeste beste that ever he [Arthur] saw or herde of." From the beast's belly, there came a noise like the barking, or questing, of "thirty coupyl houndes." The beast is pursued in Malory's Book I by Pellinor, in French romance and the rest of Malory by Palamede, and in Spanish and Italian texts by Perceval. [NJL]

QUILLER-COUCH, SIR ARTHUR (1863–1944), author of *Castle Dor* (1962), which was completed from his notes by Daphne du Maurier. The story of Tristan and Isolde is transposed into nineteenth-century Cornwall, in the vicinity of Castle Dore, Mark's reputed fortress. Most of the traditional motifs and characters, including the love potion and the spying dwarf, are woven into a fascinating plot involving a Breton fisherman, an elderly innkeeper, and his headstrong young wife. The connection between past and present is made explicit through the researches of a local physician, yet despite his knowledge he fails "to stay a senseless repetition of one of the saddest love stories in the world." The triumph of fate over human will powerfully evokes the spirit of the original legend. [RHT]

🕭 Quiller-Couch, Arthur, and Daphne du Maurier. *Castle Dor*. London: Dent, 1962.

QUINET, EDGAR: *see* FRENCH EPIC, NINETEENTH CENTURY; SECOND EMPIRE.

RAOUL DE HOUDENC, author of *Meraugis de Portlesguez*, possibly of *La Vengeance Raguidel*, and a number of shorter allegorical and didactic pieces. Active in the first quarter of the thirteenth century, Raoul de Houdenc is probably to be identified with Radulfus de Hosdenc, a knight, of Hodenc-en-Bray in the Beauvaisis.

Meraugis de Portlesguez, a verse romance of 5,938 lines, is concerned with the rivalry of two friends, Meraugis de Portlesguez and Gorvain Cadrut, for the love of the beautiful Lidoine. One of the main issues is whether Meraugis (who loves Lidoine for her *courtoisie*) or Gorvain (who loves her for her beauty) has the better claim to her love. When Guenièvre and her damsels find in favor of Meraugis, Lidoine sends him off to prove himself worthy of her, while Gorvain leaves in high dudgeon, complaining of the lack of justice to be found at Arthur's court. Gauvain in the meantime sets out to seek the *Espee as Estranges Renges* ("Sword of the Strange Hangings") and becomes involved in many adventures, some of them burlesque and comic. In one such, he defeats the guardian of an island and becomes the new guardian until such time as he is himself defeated; he then fights with Meraugis before recognizing him and devising a plan by means of which they can escape from the island (it involves Meraugis dressing up in women's clothes).

Raoul is one of Chrétien's most successful followers, and his achievement lies in a clearly thought-out treatment of some complex emotional problems arising from the initial situation, a carefully structured plot, and a deft touch of comedy. He also has a penchant for dialogue and inner dialogue and was clearly influenced by dialectic and logic. His shorter didactic poems, in particular *Le Roman des Eles*, are concerned with issues similar to those at the heart of the romance and may assist in interpreting it. Raoul was a gifted and productive poet who was admired in the Middle Ages, as witnessed by the praise allotted to him by Huon de Mery in his *Tournoiement de l'Antéchrist* (thirteenth century), where he is mentioned in the same breath as Chrétien as one of the masters of French poetry. [KB]

Raoul de Houdenc. *Meraugis de Portlesguez*, ed. Mathias Friedwagner. Halle: Niemeyer, 1897.
——. *"Le Roman des Eles": The Anonymous "Ordene de Chevalerie,"* ed. Keith Busby. Amsterdam: Benjamins, 1983.
Kundert-Forrer, Verena. *Raoul de Houdenc: Ein französischer Erzähler aus dem XIIIe Jahrhundert.* Zurich: Juris, 1960.

RAVEN: *see* BURNHAM, JEREMY; TELEVISION SERIES.

RAY, TREVOR: *see* BURNHAM, JEREMY.

READ ALL ABOUT IT!: *see* TELEVISION SERIES.

RECHT MITTEN DURCH: EINE MINIATURE AUS DEM MITTELALTER NACH WOLFRAM VON ESCHENBACH: *see* HARDER, NATHALIE.

RED BOOK OF HERGEST: *see MABINOGI.*

REGION OF THE SUMMER STARS, THE: *see* WILLIAMS, CHARLES.

RELIQUES OF ANCIENT ENGLISH POETRY: *see* PERCY, THOMAS.

RENAUT DE BEAUJEU, author of *Le Bel Inconnu* ("The Fair Unknown"), a verse romance of 6,266 lines written ca. 1185–90. The poem relates the story of Gauvain's son, Guinglain, who is assigned the task of liberating the daughter of the King of Wales, transformed into a serpent by two enchanters. Although young and inexperienced, Guinglain goes to Sinaudon, conquers the two enchanters (Mabon and Evrain), releases Esmeree from the spell, and marries her. As with most romances of this type, the basic plot (also present in the Italian *Carduino*, the Middle High German *Wigalois*, and the Middle English adaptation of Renaut, Chestre's *Libeaus Desconus*) is enhanced by motifs to be found elsewhere: sparrowhawk contest, seduction by a fairy, prevention of the rape of a damsel. Also interesting is the theme of the *Fier Baiser* by means of which Guinglain releases Esmeree from the enchantment. This, like much else in Arthurian romance, is of Celtic origin, and is related more or less distantly to the various versions of the Loathly Lady story (as found in Chaucer's *The Wife of Bath's Tale*).

Le Bel Inconnu is one of the earliest post-Chrétien verse romances and still shows unmistakable signs of Chrétien's influence, in particular of *Erec et Enide*. Renaut de Beaujeu has given his romance a clear and logical structure, a quest for love that is threatened by the complication of the encounter with the fairy before being brought to a happy conclusion. The poet adds a personal touch when he says that he is writing his romance for one to whom he has given his own heart. Despite its chronological proximity to Chrétien, it is difficult to argue that Renaut is concerned with the same issues as his predecessor. There is no question of the conflict between love and chivalry, for example, so central to Chrétien's first four romances, or of religion, so central to the meaning of *Perceval*.

The story of Gauvain's son is also related elsewhere, particularly in the First Continuation of Chrétien's *Perceval* (where he is called Lionel and not Guinglain), and there are grounds for believing that the story may originally have been associated with Gauvain himself and that Guinglain may be seen as a double of his father. In the early sixteenth century, Claude Platin wrote a prose *Giglain*, in which he combined the story of Guinglain with that of Jaufré, hero of a Provençal romance. [KB]

ɚ Renaut de Beaujeu. *Le Bel Inconnu*, ed. G. Perrie Williams. Paris: Champion, 1929.

RERUM SCOTICARUM HISTORIA: see SCOTTISH ARTHURIAN CHRONICLES.

RETURN, LEGENDS OF ARTHUR'S. The possibility of Arthur's return has figured significantly in his story since William of Malmesbury (1125), Henry of Huntingdon (1129), and Wace (1155) repeated the "Breton hope" apparently popular in folk tradition. Although most medieval chroniclers refuted the claim, it enjoyed such a firm hold in the popular imagination that, according to Hermann of Tournai (1146), violence erupted at an 1113 religious gathering when a churchman declared that Arthur was actually dead. Malory cautiously recorded the legend of the *Rex quondam Rexque futurus* (using the Latin inscription he found in the mid-fourteenth-century Alliterative *Morte Arthure*), remarking that "men say that he shall come again. . . . I will not say it shall be so, but rather I will say, here in this world he changed his life."

Despite popular credence in the myth of the return, medieval romances almost never recorded its fulfillment. In Étienne de Rouen's Latin poem *Draco Normannicus* (1168), Arthur writes a letter warning Henry II to leave Brittany alone, for he has returned from Avalon to marshall troops against Henry's intrusions. And the thirteenth-century German verse *Manuel und Amande* maintains that after his apparent death Arthur returned to reign another twenty-five years. Otherwise, romances treated the return as a promise for the future. Medieval and Renaissance writers occasionally depicted Arthur awaiting his return in Avalon (or in less traditional locations, such as Sicily or the island of Brasil), surrounded by former companions or by fairy ladies, and perhaps restored annually by the Grail, but these descriptions by and large appeared in the essentially non-Arthurian accounts of such figures as Loquifer, the Bâtarde de Bouillon, and Ogier the Dane, who visited Arthur's magic isle in their travels.

In his poem "The Grave of King Arthur" (1777), Thomas Warton memorialized the traditional debate over whether Arthur would return. But depiction of that second coming awaited nineteenth- and twentieth-century British and American writers, who in most instances have described the return or survival of his associates more often than of the King himself. Walter Scott's *Bridal of Triermain* (1813) recounts the awakening of Arthur's daughter in Plantagenet England. Thomas Love Peacock, who in "The Round Table; or King Arthur's Feast" (1817) described Arthur's boredom in Avalon, in "Calidore" (1816) depicted the King, impatient to return, dispatching a young knight to nineteenth-century England to assess whether the time was right. The most significant version of the myth in the nineteenth century is that of Alfred Tennyson, who treated Arthur's promised return in two imaginative ways: "The Epic" (1842), the modern frame for his earliest tale of the death of Arthur (the "Morte d'Arthur"), depicts the King returning in the narrator's dream as "a modern gentleman/ Of stateliest port," thereby suggesting that the medieval ideals of the Round Table could be maintained in the nineteenth century, though necessarily in modern forms. The expanded version of "The Passing of Arthur" (1869) that concludes the *Idylls of the King* implies that Arthur's departure from this world is actually a return to his proper home, where he is welcomed "beyond the limit of the world" like "a king returning from his wars."

In the twentieth century, John Masefield remained closer to medieval tradition in the title poem of *Midsummer Night and Other Tales in Verse* (1928), which relates how on midsummer night the King and his knights awaken, again turning to stone at the end of the hour, and ends with the hope of Arthur's return. The mythic possibility of this return seized the popular imagination with new force during World War II, when newspaper editorials announced that England's need had never been greater and writers of the period used the material to dramatize the threat of totalitarianism. The myth furnished the collective title *The Once and Future King* (1958) for books that T.H. White had published separately, beginning in 1939. The novel concludes with Arthur imagining his return to establish a brighter world. Adapting the prophecy to a modern setting, C.S. Lewis's novel *That Hideous Strength* (1945) shows Merlin awakening to help destroy an organization that aims to recondition the human race. Arthur himself never returns; however, various Arthurian figures appear throughout the work, and finally both Merlin and Mr. Fisher King, who heads the resistance against the evil organization, like Arthur go to another sphere. Martyn Skinner used the myth similarly in two satiric epics. In *Merlin; or, the Return of Arthur* (1951), Merlin recalls Arthur from Avalon, first taking him to hell to view a documentary film about the sickening realities of the modern world; *The Return of Arthur: A Poem of the Future* (1955) brings Arthur to England about the year 2000 to overthrow a totalitarian regime.

Recent science-fiction writers have employed the mythic return to depict a cosmic conflict between Good and Evil. In *Merlin's Mirror* (1975), Andre Norton, while focusing on Merlin in his medieval setting, adapts the story of Arthur's survival through the device of time travel, showing the wounded King being put in a life-suspension chamber to await the arrival of space travelers with advanced medical arts. Other writers follow the more common pattern of showing Arthur's companions rather than the King himself returning to the modern world: Morgan le Fay, Launcelot, and Merlin reappear in locations ranging from Cornwall to San Francisco and Mobile, Alabama. This concentration on Arthurian characters other than the King emphasizes that the most significant "return" of Arthur has been not in particular accounts of his second coming but in the revitalization of the entire body of Arthurian material after its relative dormancy between the Middle Ages and the nineteenth century. (For the legend of Arthur's Return in folklore, *see* Cave Legend; Folklore; Topography and Local Legends.) [BT]

Loomis, Roger Sherman. "The Legend of Arthur's Survival." In *Arthurian Literature in the Middle Ages*. Oxford: Clarendon, 1959.

RETURN OF ARTHUR, THE: *see* SKINNER, MARTYN.

REYNOLDS, ERNEST RANDOLF, English scholar and sometime actor, was awarded, in 1930, the Kirke White Prize of Nottingham University for his poem *Tristram and Iseult*. The sixty-five eight-line stanzas are divided into a prelude and three parts, each describing, in images of flowers and gems, a particular scene from the story. In his preface, Reynolds calls it "pictorial poetry" and acknowledges an indebtedness to Wagner. [SRR]

Reynolds, Ernest Randolf. *Tristram and Iseult*. Nottingham: Clough, 1930.

RHEAD, LOUIS: *see* BOOK ILLUSTRATION (AMERICAN).

RHYS, ERNEST (1859–1946), English editor, poet, dramatist. Rhys was one of the most productive of the many authors from the turn of the century who were inspired by the Arthurian legend. His long poem "The Story of Balin and Balan: From the *Morte d'Arthur*" is collected in *The Garden of Romance* (1897). His next collection, *Welsh Ballads and Other Poems* (1898), contains five short Arthurian poems inspired by Welsh tradition, one of which deals with a version of the widespread cave legend. *Lays of the Round Table and Other Lyric Romances* (1905) contains twenty-four short Arthurian poems, and *The Leaf Burners and Other Poems* (1918), three: based upon Malory, they ponder the mysteries of love, the Grail, and death.

Rhys's three Arthurian plays were all written for music composed by Vincent Thomas. *Gwenevere: A Lyric Play*, which was first performed in 1905 at the Coronet Theatre, London, is based upon Malory's account of the Queen's life. It was followed in 1908 by *Enid: A Lyric Play* and *The Masque of the Grail*, both performed at the Court Theatre. The former is derived from the Welsh tale of Geraint, but it compresses the plot and combines the hero's enemies in one figure, Earl Dwrm; the latter mingles Welsh and French tradition in a short play about Galahad, confronted by the choice of seeking glory or staying home to care for the sick Pelleas. Rhys's treatment of Arthurian legend is romantic and mystical, though he demonstrates more talent than most of his contemporaries, particularly in the creation of a lyrical and pensive mood well suited to the music. [RHT]

ꙮ Rhys, Ernest. *The Garden of Romance*. London: Kegan Paul, Trench, Trübner, 1897.
————. *Lays of the Round Table and Other Lyric Romances*. London: Dent, 1905.
————. *The Leaf Burners and Other Poems*. London: Dent, 1918.
————. *Welsh Ballads and Other Poems*. London: Nutt, 1898.
Starr, Nathan Comfort. *King Arthur Today: The Arthurian Legend in English and American Literature 1901–1953*. Gainesville: University of Florida Press, 1954.

RICHART D'IRLANDE: *see* PROPHÉCIES DE MERLIN, LES.

RIDDARASÖGUR: see SCANDINAVIAN ARTHURIAN LITERATURE.

RIDDERE METTER MOUWEN, DIE ("The Knight with the Sleeve"), an original Middle Dutch verse romance probably written in the second half of the thirteenth century. The main character is Miraudijs, who is called the Knight with the Sleeve after Clarette has given him a white sleeve at the beginning of the story as a token of attachment. After many tribulations, the knight gains the hand of his beloved, finds his lost father, and is witness to the marriage of his parents.

The text has been transmitted to us in two ways. A complete version of 4,020 lines has been preserved as part of the *Lancelot-Compilatie*. In addition, the Royal Library at Brussels possesses a fragment (MS IV 818) dating ca. 1360–70. It contains 320 lines of a more original and much more elaborate version. The compiler of the *Lancelot-Compilatie* abridged the text to one-third. This makes it probable that the *Riddere metter mouwen* originally numbered some 13,500 lines. [BB]

De Kruyter, C.W., ed. *Die Riddere metter mouwen*. Leiden: New Rhine, 1975.
De Haan, Max J.M., L. Jongen, B.C. Damsteegt, M.J. Van der Wal, and A. Neesen, eds. *Roman van den Riddere metter mouwen*. Utrecht: HES, 1983.

RIDING OF LANCELOT, THE: *see* WRIGHT, SIDNEY FOWLER.

RIFT IN THE LUTE, THE: *see* HUGHES, ARTHUR.

RIJMUR AF ÞEIM TISTRANI . . . : *see* NÍELS JÓNSSON.

RÍMUR: *see* SCANDINAVIAN ARTHURIAN LITERATURE.

RIOTHAMUS. *Riothamus* is the style given in continental documents to a fifth-century "king of the Britons," whose career seemingly underlies parts of the account of Arthur in Geoffrey of Monmouth. It Latinizes a title or honorific in the British language—that is, the parent tongue from which Welsh, Cornish, and Breton evolved.

The known context is the disintegrating Roman Gaul of the late 460s. The north was dominated by Syagrius, a man of imperial loyalty ruling a fragment of the Empire. Within his sphere of influence were Franks who cooperated with him, and lately arrived Britons in Armorica, the pioneer Bretons. Southward were the Burgundians, with rulers of their own but friendly to Rome. Hostile Saxons, however, were settled along the lower Loire, and a serious threat came from the southwest, where the Visigothic king Euric was powerful on both sides of the Pyrenees and had ambitious designs.

In 467, the eastern emperor Leo I appointed Anthemius, a Byzantine noble, as his western colleague. A pressing need was to check Euric. Britain had been out of the Empire for decades, but Anthemius, possibly encouraged by a pro-Roman trend among its rulers, negotiated a British alliance. The "king of the Britons," Riothamus, came to Gaul in 468 "by the way of Ocean" with 12,000 ship-borne troops (thus the sixth-century historian Jordanes). The Britons were temporarily stationed north of the Loire and may have assisted in a campaign against the Saxons near Angers. But Gaul's imperial prefect, Arvandus, was acting treacherously. He wrote to Euric urging him not to come to terms with the "Greek emperor," meaning Anthemius, but to crush "the Britons posted north of the Loire" and carve up Gaul with the Burgundians. Arvandus was detected and brought to justice, but the Empire's hollowness in Gaul was exposed.

Meanwhile, Riothamus moved into Berry and occupied Bourges. Probably in this phase, the Gallo-Roman author Sidonius—formerly city prefect of Rome, now bishop of Clermont, or shortly to become so—wrote to him on behalf of a landowner whose slaves the Britons were enticing away, doubtless to employ them as bearers or mercenaries. Riothamus advanced to Déols near Châteauroux. There Euric pounced on him with an overwhelming force, "before the Romans [presumably the troops of Syagrius] could join him." The Britons were defeated and Euric drove them from Bourges. Riothamus escaped with a remnant of his army into the nearby territory of the friendly Burgundians, in late 469 or early 470.

Some historians have minimized him as simply a chief of Bretons—i.e., settlers in Armorica—but at that time the Armorican settlement was too sparse. The scattered colonies could not have fielded an army with any prospect of checking Euric; and Arvandus's proposal to him would have made little sense, since he would have achieved nothing by overrunning them. Jordanes's testimony that the Britons came "by the way of Ocean" seems decisive. An army from Britain would have done so, the Armorican settlers would not, since they were on the Continent already and had been for years. A king of the Britons might have gathered recruits from them and counted them as still his subjects. In the judgment of James Campbell (1982), Riothamus is credible as "a British ruler having authority on both sides of the Channel." That he was prepared in 468 to take soldiers out of Britain, and stay overseas for at least a year, helps in dating Ambrosius Aurelianus. Action against the Saxons in the island, under Ambrosius's leadership, had apparently convinced its rulers that they were contained and neutralized.

The Latin form *Riothamus*, used with slight variants in continental texts, corresponds to the British *Rigotamos*. *Rig*, with the added *o* in a compound, meant "king"; *tamos* was a superlative suffix. As a noun, this word would mean "king-most" or "supreme king" (cf. the modern word *generalissimo*). As an adjective, it would mean "most kingly," "supremely royal." It appears later as a proper name, becoming *Riatham* in Breton and *Rhiadaf* in Welsh. But in the fifth-century setting—in Sidonius's letter, for instance—it looks like a designation for a ruler whose name was something else. Cognate in sense with *Vortigern* and *Vortimer*, and applied to a king of the Britons, it suggests that he was one of the high kings of the period—recasting the style, perhaps, to dissociate himself from discredited predecessors. To judge from the cross-Channel context, he probably held territory in the southwest, but at that time, when the Britons' unity under Rome was still remembered, he might have claimed paramountcy over a much wider area. At any rate, it is hard to believe that his parents happened to give him a name that turned out to be so apt for the office he held as an adult.

As a noun, "supreme king," *Riothamus* would be a title. Similarly, "Genghis Khan," meaning "very mighty ruler," is the accepted designation of a Mongol chieftain whose name was Temujin. As an adjective, "supremely royal," *Riothamus* would be an honorific. Again, the first Roman emperor, whose name was Octavian, adopted the epithet *Augustus*, meaning "majestic," with an overtone of sacredness; after which every emperor was Augustus, "His Majesty." Plutarch records a Greek word, *Basileutatos*, exactly equivalent to *Riothamus*, which was definitely not a name but a term of honor bestowed on Minos of Crete.

That this king of the Britons would have had a separate name—and could have had another one even if *Riothamus* was his name—has inspired attempts to give him substance in Britain by identifying him with someone else. Fleuriot makes him out to be Ambrosius. One of several objections is that Gildas, the single real authority, describes Ambrosius as a general only. But Fleuriot acknowledges that the story of Riothamus, whoever he was, has gone into the making of the story of Arthur. Geoffrey of Monmouth portrays Arthur campaigning in Gaul and makes him contemporary with persons living in Riothamus's time, notably Leo I. Nor is he the only author who does so. (For the traces of an identification or semi-identification, *see* ARTHUR, ORIGINS OF LEGEND.)

A Riothamus appears in Breton genealogies who may be the King, correctly or incorrectly dated. But there were certainly other men so called in the sixth century. [GA]

❧ Gregory of Tours. *History of the Franks*, Book II, Chapter 18.

Jordanes. *Gothic History*, Chapter 45.

Sidonius Apollinaris. *Letters*, Book I, 7, Book III, 9.

Ashe, Geoffrey. "A Certain Very Ancient Book," *Speculum*, 56 (1981), 301–23.

———. *The Discovery of King Arthur*. New York: Doubleday, 1985.

Campbell, James, ed. *The Anglo-Saxons*. Ithaca, N.Y.: Cornell University Press, 1982.

Fleuriot, Léon. *Les Origines de la Bretagne*. Paris: Payot, 1980.

Jackson, Kenneth Hurlstone. *Language and History in Early Britain*. Edinburgh: Edinburgh University Press, 1953.

RITTER WIDUWILT, a fourteenth-century Yiddish work, preserved in its original verse form in three manuscripts and known also through two eighteenth-century prose versions. The text relates (often humorously) the story of Wigalois, omitting or condensing some episodes known from earlier texts. Although Cormeau has argued that the Yiddish work is based on Wirnt von Grafenberg's *Wigalois*, others have held that it derives instead from an oral tradition. [NJL]

❧ Landau, Leo, ed. *Arthurian Legends, or the Hebrew-German Rhymed Version of the Legend of King Arthur*. Leipzig: Avenarius, 1912.

Cormeau, Christoph. "Die jiddische Tradition von Wirnts *Wigalois*: Bemerkungen zum Fortleben einer Fable unter veranderten Bedingungen." *Zeitschrift für Literaturwissenschaft und Linguistik*, 8 (1978), 28–44.

ROAD TO CAMLANN, THE: *see* SUTCLIFF, ROSEMARY.

ROBERT DE BLOIS. During the second half of the thirteenth century, Robert de Blois, who is best known for such didactic works as *Enseignements as Princes*, composed *Beaudous*, a verse romance about Gawain's son, the Fair Unknown. The hero's mother conceals his name from him so that he may win renown for his own achievements, not just because of his lineage. This he accomplishes during a series of adventures that culminate when he gains a kingdom and the love of its princess. To lure him back to his court, Arthur holds a three-day tournament, but Beaudous changes his shield on successive days to hide his identity. He defeats Arthur's finest knights, including Perceval, Kay, Lancelot, Cligés, Yvain, and Erec, before an inconclusive encounter with Gawain. The poem concludes with a recognition scene, followed by the double wedding and coronation of father and son, for Gawain belatedly decides to marry Beaudous's mother when he succeeds his father as king.

The romance follows the traditional pattern of the Fair Unknown story, retold by Renaut de Beaujeu and others, and the account of the tournament owes much to the works of Chrétien de Troyes, particularly *Cligés*. Because it suffers by comparison with these romances, *Beaudous* has been too readily dismissed and ignored by critics. However, it possesses a charm of its own, and its picture of knighthood interestingly reflects the author's didactic concerns. Moreover, Robert does introduce some untraditional features, notably Gawain's marriage and his succession to his father's throne (in Ireland, not Orkney). That he should choose to marry his lady only after their son is old enough to join in a double ceremony reveals the rich ironic potential in the situation, but it is not developed. [RHT]

🕭 Robert de Blois. *Sämmtliche Werke: I. Beaudous*, ed. Jacob Ulrich. Berlin: Mayer, 1889.

Lamarque, Gisèle Andrée, ed. "*Le Roman de Biaudeaus*: A Critical Edition." Diss., North Carolina, 1968.

ROBERT DE BORON, a Burgundian poet who composed the first cycle of Grail romances. About this author we know only what he himself has revealed in his work, his name and the name of his noble patron: "Meistres Robers dist, de Bouron,/ Se il voloit dire par non" (l. 3156); "A ce tens que je la retreis/ O mon seigneur Gautier en peis,/ Qui de Mont Belyal estoit . . ." (l. 3490). This Gautier has been identified as Gautier de Montbéliard, Lord of Montfaucon, who took the cross and set out on the Fourth Crusade in 1202, never to return to his homeland. He died in 1212. About eighteen kilometers from Montbéliard, there is the village of Boron, presumably Robert's place of origin. The most logical conclusion, supported by the majority of critics, is that Robert, a cleric from Boron in the Franche-Comté, was the author of the works that bear his name and that he was in the service of or somehow close to the Lord of Montbéliard, to whom he recounted (*retreis*) his romance before Gautier's departure (*en peis* 'at peace,' or 'at rest'), in any case before his involvement in the events of the Fourth Crusade.

Robert is the author of a trilogy written in French octosyllabic verse, the *Joseph d'Arimathie* (so-called by scholars, although it was edited under the title *Le Roman de l'Estoire dou Graal*), the *Merlin*, and in all probability a *Perceval*, generally known as the Didot-*Perceval*. Of the original cycle, only the *Joseph* and the initial 504 lines of the *Merlin* survive in their original verse form, but a prose adaptation of the three romances was made by an anonymous redactor shortly after its composition. It was this prose version that ultimately gave rise to the vast cycle of Arthurian prose romances known as the Vulgate Cycle. (*See* PROSE *MERLIN* [1]; DIDOT-*PERCEVAL*.)

The *Joseph* has been variously dated. We must consider that Robert had completed most or all of the romance prior to 1202, the date of Gautier's departure for the Holy Land. The early limit is somewhat more difficult to establish, though it is widely thought that the Vales of Avalon mentioned in the romance are to be identified with the area around Glastonbury in Somerset, where the bones of Arthur and his queen were presumably discovered in 1191. The years 1191–1202 thus limit considerably the period of composition and support the conclusion that Robert's *Joseph* postdated Chrétien de Troyes's *Perceval* and that he derived certain crucial details from the work of the Champenois poet.

After a prologue relating the Fall of Man and leading up to the Passion, Robert tells how the vessel of the Last Supper was given by Pilate to the obscure disciple Joseph of Arimathea, who in turn used it to collect the blood of the crucified Christ after the Deposition. Joseph is imprisoned by the Jews, but the risen Christ visits him and delivers the twice-hallowed vessel into his possession and reveals to him the secrets bound up with it. After the passage of many years, the emperor Vespasian, cured of the foulest disease by Veronica's cloth, arrives in Judea to avenge the death of Christ. Vespasian discovers Joseph alive in prison, miraculously sustained by the precious vessel, and is converted to Christianity by his words.

Suddenly, the narrative takes an unusual turn. Joseph's sister, Enygeus, and her husband, Hebron (or its shortened form Bron), appear as if from nowhere and in the company of some followers leave Judea with Joseph and go into exile in some "distant land." After an initial success, their crops fail, owing to the sin of lechery, of which some of the company were guilty. To separate the innocent from the guilty, Joseph is directed by the Holy Spirit to set up, in memory of the table of the Last Supper, a second table where will be celebrated the service of the Grail (but not so-named until later). Bron is sent to catch a fish that will occupy a place at the table close to the vessel. When all is ready, the followers are bidden to seek a place at the table, but mysteriously only those who are untainted with the sin of lust can approach the table, and their hearts are filled with ineffable delight. (Here, the Grail is named and is derived in typical medieval fashion from the verb *agreer* 'to delight.') One of the banished sinners, Moysés by name, attempts to take a place at the table against the dire warning of Joseph and is swallowed up in the earth. Twelve sons are born to Enygeus and Bron, of which eleven marry and adopt the earthly life. The twelfth is named Alain; he will take charge of his brothers and lead them toward distant lands in the West, preaching the name of Christ. A future offspring of this Alain, the "third man" (Perceval?), will be the ultimate keeper of the Grail. Another follower of Joseph, Petrus, is also to travel to the West, to the Vales of Avalon, and there await the coming of Alain's son. Finally, Bron, henceforth to be called the Rich Fisher, will take possession of the holy vessel and follow the others to the West to wait for the third man to whom the vessel will be entrusted. All of this comes to pass and the significance of the Holy Trinity is fulfilled. Joseph returns to Arimathea to end his days.

Robert is a sorry poet, often confusing in detail and on occasion even guilty of self-contradiction. But what he lacks in graceful expression and elegant poetic turn of phrase is made up for by a magnificent vision of universal history centered on the Holy Grail. He was the first to identify the vessel of the Last Supper with the mysterious *graal* of Chrétien's *Perceval* and describe how this sacred vessel was used by Joseph of Arimathea to collect the blood of Christ. It was this bold vision that bridged the gap between sacred history and the world of Arthurian Britain (the Round Table was the "third table," in keeping with Trinitarian symbolism) and gave the impulse to the thorough Christianization of the Grail myth. [RFO'G]

Robert de Boron. *Le Roman de l'Estoire dou Graal*, ed. William Nitze. Paris: Champion, 1927.

——— . *Merlin, roman du XIIIe siècle*, ed. Alexandre Micha. Geneva: Droz, 1980.

Roach, William, ed. *The Didot-Perceval*. Philadelphia: University of Pennsylvania Press, 1941.

Nitze, William. "Messire Robert de Boron: Enquiry and Summary." *Speculum*, 28 (1953), 279–96.

O'Gorman, Richard. "The Prose Version of Robert de Boron's *Joseph d'Arimathie.*" *Romance Philology*, 23 (1970), 449–61.

——— . "La Tradition manuscrite du *Joseph d'Arimathie* en prose de Robert de Boron." *Revue d'Historie des Textes*, 1 (1971), 145–81.

ROBERT OF GLOUCESTER. The two versions of the late thirteenth-century verse chronicle attributed to Robert of Gloucester appear to have been the work of at least three people. Both versions, the longer (ca. 12,000 lines, surviving in seven manuscripts and a fragment) and the shorter (ca. 10,000 lines, eight manuscripts), incorporate an earlier anonymous English chronicle from Brutus to the death of Henry I (1135). Sometime after 1270, Robert of Gloucester appears to have written the continuation of this earlier chronicle to 1270 that is found in the longer version; and this longer version was revised, possibly by someone other than Robert, near the end of the thirteenth century. Someone else appears to have written the shorter version, which adds to the earlier anonymous chronicle to 1135 some details from Layamon's chronicle and a continuation to the accession of Edward I (1272). Nothing much is known about the Robert of Gloucester to whom the whole work was once attributed. Some have suggested that he was a monk of St. Peter's, Gloucester, but

Gransden notes that Robert may have been a secular clerk, since the chronicle seems in some ways to belong to the secular tradition of historiography and since none of the manuscripts appears to have originated in a monastic library. The Arthurian story belongs to the earlier, anonymous, part of the chronicle; it is the second chronicle, after Layamon, to tell the story of Arthur in English. Presenting, like most chroniclers, a heroic picture of Arthur, the author follows Geoffrey of Monmouth closely, with some details added from Henry of Huntingdon and some that suggest knowledge of Arthurian romance. (Merlin, for example, is described as an enchanter; Gawain is the "flour of corteysye.") In the part of the chronicle that Robert of Gloucester actually seems to have written, there is a reference to the discovery of Arthur's bones at Glastonbury during the reign of King Richard. [EDK]

Robert of Gloucester. *The Metrical Chronicle of Robert of Gloucester*, ed. W.A. Wright. 2 vols. London: Eyre and Spottiswoode, 1887.

Fletcher, Robert Huntington. *The Arthurian Material in the Chronicles, Especially Those of Great Britain and France*. Boston: Ginn, 1906; 2nd ed. Roger Sherman Loomis. New York: Franklin, 1966, pp. 193–98.

Gransden, Antonia. *Historical Writing in England c550–c1307*. Ithaca, N.Y.: Cornell University Press, 1974, pp. 432–38.

Hudson, Anne. "Tradition and Innovation in Some Middle English Manuscripts." *RES*, n.s., 17 (1966), 359–72.

ROBERT OF TORIGNI: *see DE ORTU WALUUANII; HISTORIA MERIADOCI.*

ROBERTS, DOROTHY JAMES, author of three historical novels based upon Malory. *The Enchanted Cup* (1953) recreates the ill-fated love of Tristram and Isoud. *Launcelot, My Brother* (1954) is the account by Bors (here Launcelot's brother rather than cousin) of Launcelot's love for Guinevere and the destruction of the Round Table. *Kinsmen of the Grail* (1963) focuses upon the Grail quests of Perceval and Gawin, a quest for what all search for but few find: the meaning of life. All three novels are written with clarity and emotional insight, particularly the last, which brings a fresh, modern perception into both theme and the psychology of character. [MAG]

Roberts, Dorothy James. *The Enchanted Cup*. New York: Appleton-Century-Crofts, 1953.

——— . *Launcelot, My Brother*. New York: Appleton-Century-Crofts, 1954.

——— . *Kinsmen of the Grail*. Boston: Little, Brown, 1963.

ROBERTS, THEODORE GOODRICH, Canadian author of three Arthurian novelettes and nine short stories in *Blue Book Magazine* (1947–52). Inspired by Malory, these romantic comedies laugh gently at the foibles of chivalry. The short stories deal with the adventures of Dinadan, an impractical romantic who hides behind the pose of cynicism. [RHT]

🙠 Thompson, Raymond H. *The Return from Avalon: A Study of the Arthurian Legend in Modern Fiction.* Westport, Conn.: Greenwood, 1985.

ROBINSON, EDWIN ARLINGTON (1869–1935), American-born poet, composed three Arthurian works: *Merlin* (1917), *Lancelot* (1920), and *Tristram* (1927). All three poems are lengthy blank-verse narratives set in the last days of Arthur's realm, and all are characterized by an ambience of fatality. The events described do not depart much from those given in Malory, except in *Tristram*. The style of the poems is primarily that of extended meditation and self-analysis, with some scenes of dramatic interaction. In terms of style, the dialogues can only with difficulty be considered as mimetic. They are, rather, dialectical argument recast as speech.

Merlin begins with the meditations of Dagonet, the "fool" knighted by Arthur, who muses on speculations by other knights about the fate of the realm, but Merlin is the central focus of the poem. Despite his passion for Vivian, the sage cannot submit to a life of ease and blandishment, depicted in an extended and elaborate flashback, and must return to Arthur even if he can do nothing. The poem ends with Merlin exacting an oath of fealty from the despairing Dagonet as they go to join the King.

Lancelot centers on the catastrophe set in motion by the love affair of Lancelot and Guenevere. The poem could easily be entitled "Lancelot and Gawaine," since it is the tragedy of friendship betrayed that informs the greater portion of the work. Dramatic dialogue predominates as Gawaine tries and fails to warn Lancelot; as Gawaine's brothers plot; as Lancelot and Guenevere struggle with the dissolution of their affair and of their world; and, most movingly, as Arthur is torn between love and law, in a scene that shows him skirting the edges of madness on the day of Guenevere's scheduled execution. The poem is flawed by occasional passages of overwrought pseudo-Shakespearian diction, but this is swept aside when characters speak with simple feeling, as Arthur does in the passage just mentioned, or as Gawaine does when he learns of his brothers' deaths at Lancelot's hands. Lancelot and Guenevere part at her convent, but Robinson chooses to depict Lancelot as an eternal wanderer, a departure from the symmetry of the traditional ending of their story.

Of Robinson's three Arthurian poems, *Tristram* is the most unified in lyric focus and original in its approach to the material of legend; the lovers' language in both *Lancelot* and *Merlin* becomes in *Tristram* as much philosophy as passion. The poem begins and ends in pathos as Isolt of the White Hands waits in Brittany for Tristram's arrival, watching the sea, and watching still after his death. This Isolt is preserved from mawkishness by the poet's insistence on her clear-sighted appraisal of her hopes despite her passion for Tristram.

The lyric focus of the poem is loss. For risking one last rendezvous, Tristram is banished on the night of Mark's wedding with Isolt of Ireland. Mark loses his nephew and retainer, and he never possesses the love of Isolt.

Isolt, who remains in the background for much of the poem, is slowly destroyed by Tristram's absence. Like Isolt of Brittany, she sees clearly, more so than Tristram, that the affair can end only in death; in a reversal of the conventional details of the legend, it is Tristram who comes to her deathbed, with Mark's consent, there to be slain treacherously by the jealous Andred.

Robinson reduces the multiple episodes of lovers' meetings and deceptions of Mark to the wedding-night encounter and the extended idyll at Joyous Garde after Tristram is summoned from Brittany to Arthur's court. He thus emphasizes the deprivation that robs Tristram of any joy in his marriage and drains life itself from Isolt of Ireland, so that when she is abducted by Mark's men from Joyous Garde she yields slowly to death. Relief from the intensity of the characters' emotion is provided by Morgan le Fay, sometime rescuer of Tristram and an ironic observer of the affair's progress. On the other hand, Morgan is implicated in the lovers' final catastrophe by Mark, who suspects her of further inflaming Andred's insane jealousy of the lovers. These three characters, Mark, Andred, and Morgan, who establish essentially negative relationships, are thus set in opposition to the three lovers.

As one might expect in poems written in a relatively brief timespan and having common subject matters, there are specific mutual correspondences, especially among the minor characters, such as Gawaine and Bedivere. Gawaine, lighthearted and in love with life, is troubled by the events around him, but he is incapable of real engagement until personal tragedy strikes. Bedivere is a mixture of resignation and hope. He is Arthur's oldest and most clear-sighted knight, if one discounts the wise folly of Dagonet, yet he is the one who can envision a new world beyond the downfall of Arthur's kingdom.

Further correspondences among the poems can be found in the pervasive motif of the passage of time and the emblematic imagery of the colors of hair, eyes, and complexion for female characters. All three poems are characterized by vivid contrasts in the use of inner and outer spaces—rooms, castles, gardens, and forests, and, in *Tristram*, the sea; the contrasts are generally ironic, since the characters in the poems are all prisoners of their circumstances.

The structural complexity of *Merlin* is not repeated in the other two poems. *Lancelot* is structured according to the events of the legend, and Robinson does not use the additional framing furnished by the character of Dagonet in *Merlin* or of Isolt of the White Hands in *Tristram*. The dramatic action of *Lancelot* flows consistently from the weaknesses of the characters rather than from their strengths; it is only final renunciations that do not go awry. Published over a ten-year period, Robinson's three Arthurian poems show not so much a progression in poetic technique as a varied experimentation in the presentation of traditional material. [AAR]

&❧ Robinson, Edwin Arlington. *Merlin*. New York: Macmillan, 1917.

——— . *Lancelot: A Poem*. New York: Seltzer, 1920.

——— . *Tristram*. New York: Macmillan, 1927.

Winters, Yvor. *Edwin Arlington Robinson*. New York: New Directions, 1971.

ROEBER, FRIEDRICH: *see TRISTAN*, MODERN GERMAN
VERSIONS OF GOTTFRIED'S.

ROHMER, ERIC, the director of *Perceval le Gallois* (1978), a faithful setting of
the text of Chrétien de Troyes's last work. This eccentric and beautiful film
(with Fabrice Luchini as Perceval) begins with Perceval's encounter with
knights in his mother's forest and presents all the major scenes of the original—
Gornemant, Blancheflor, the Grail castle and Fisher King, the Hermit episode—up to the early adventures of Gauvain.

Much of the text is a modernized, but somewhat archaic, rendering of
Chrétien's own. The characters not only speak the words ascribed to them but
they also speak of themselves in the third person (as when Blancheflor says of
herself, "she weeps," and then does so). This kind of narration is contributed
also by singers and various nameless characters, whose function is to provide
transitions and announce action. Rohmer systematically shuns realism, a characteristic most evident in his use of scenery composed of stylized, painted trees
and buildings. The effect is visually similar to that of a medieval miniature, and
theatrically more like a pageant or a morality play than a drama.

The film departs strikingly from Chrétien's work only in the addition of a
sequence in Latin, depicting the stations of the Cross and Christ's agony in
crucifixion. [NJL]

ROI ARTUS, ROMAN DE: *see* RUSTICIANO DA PISA.

ROI DU MONDE, LE: *see* GUÉNON, RENÉ.

ROI PÊCHEUR, LE: *see* GRACQ, JULIEN.

ROMAN DE TRISTAN ET ISEUT, LE: *see* BÉDIER, JOSEPH.

ROMAN DU GRAAL, LE: *see* POST-VULGATE CYCLE;
ROBERT DE BORON.

ROMAN DU ROI ARTHUR, LE: *see* LANGLAIS, XAVIER DE.

ROMAN VON TRISTAN UND ISOLDE, DER: *see* SCHIRMER-
IMHOFF, RUTH.

ROMANCE OF KING ARTHUR, THE: *see* COUTTS, FRANCIS.

ROSALBA: *see* NAUBERT, BENEDIKTE.

ROSSETTI, DANTE GABRIEL (1828–1882), became interested in chivalric stories in his youth. His first Arthurian subject, *King Arthur's Tomb* (1854, Private Collection), was his own invention. After designing three subjects for the Moxon Tennyson (1857), he organized the Oxford Union Murals project, using Malory as his text. Of his own contribution, *Lancelot's Vision of the Sangrael* and *Lancelot in the Queen's Chamber* are known only through drawings, and *How Sir Galahad, Sir Bors and Sir Percival Saw the Sangrael* was not begun. He also participated in the Dunlop Windows project.

His later Arthurian subjects were refinements of earlier designs, such as *How Sir Galahad, Sir Bors and Sir Percival Were Fed with the Grael;* but *Sir Percival's Sister Died by the Way* (1864, Birmingham City Galleries) and *Sir Tristram and La Belle Yseult Drink the Love Potion* (1867, Cecil Higgins Art Gallery, Bedford). By the end of the 1860s, Rossetti was concerned with writing his own Arthuriad, *God's Graal,* which was never finished; by the 1870s, Arthurian subjects vanished from his work. Rossetti's influence was crucial in the Arthurian Revival. He urged other artists, notably Edward Burne-Jones, Arthur Hughes, and William Morris, to undertake Arthurian subjects; his own style was associated with the romantic facet of Arthurian painting, and he added erotic and mystic subjects to the Victorian repertoire. [DNM]

🕮 Surtees, Virginia. *The Paintings and Drawings of Dante Gabriel Rossetti (1828 to 1882): A Catalogue Raisonné.* 2 vols. Oxford: Clarendon, 1971.

ROUND TABLE. King Arthur's celebrated Round Table is first mentioned by Wace in 1155 in his *Roman de Brut.* In lines 9747–58, he ascribes the origin of the table to Arthur's desire to prevent quarrels of precedence among his barons and to promote a sense of equality: "On account of his noble barons, each of whom thought himself the best and none of whom accounted himself the worst, Arthur made the Round Table, of which the Britons tell many fabulous tales. There sat his vassals, all noble and all equal; they sat equally at table and were equally served. No one of them could boast of sitting higher than his peer."

Layamon, in his adaptation of Wace's *Brut* in the early thirteenth century, expanded his source by creating a fierce quarrel over precedence at a Yuletide feast, with many dead and wounded. A Cornish carpenter, hearing of this fight, created a great Round Table that could seat 1,600 and more men, yet was easily portable. Both Wace and Layamon refer to Breton storytellers as the source for this Round Table, and in spite of the hesitations of some scholars there is no compelling reason to doubt them on this point. An ancient Celtic custom had warriors sit in circles around their king or the bravest warrior, and certain specific details recounted in Celtic stories (the number of warriors, the quarrel of precedence) recur in Wace and Layamon.

By a later tradition, recounted in prose texts of the thirteenth century, the origin of the Round Table is ascribed to Merlin. In the prose redaction of Robert de Boron's *Merlin* (ca. 1200), Merlin recalls in a celebrated passage Christ's table of the Last Supper and Joseph of Arimathea's Grail table, each of which had twelve places and one empty seat, in memory of Judas's betrayal. At Uther Pendragon's request, Merlin has a third table constructed to seat fifty knights. He tells Uther that one seat must remain empty and will be filled only after Uther's death by the knight who will achieve the Grail quest. In the Didot-*Perceval*, a continuation of Robert's *Merlin*, the number of places is again thirteen, with one still empty "por le senefiance del liu u Judas sist." Since Merlin had left this place empty at Uther's table, Arthur does not dare fill it now. However, Perceval, after defeating the knights of the Round Table in a tournament, demands Arthur's permission to occupy the empty seat. This provokes an earthquake and occasions the "enchantments of Britain," which will not end until one of the knights then at table will surpass all others in chivalry, reach the abode of the rich Fisher King, and ask concerning the Grail.

In the opening pages of the *Queste del Saint Graal* (the principal source of Malory's "Tale of the Sankgreal"), Galahad is led forward to occupy this seat, now known as the Siege Perilous. He goes on to achieve the adventure of the Sword in the Stone and assists at the great evening meal at Camelot at which all at the Round Table are fed miraculously from the Holy Grail. (*See also* PERILOUS SEAT; ROUND TABLES; WINCHESTER.) [WWK]

Loomis, Roger Sherman. *Arthurian Tradition and Chrétien de Troyes*. New York: Columbia University Press, 1949, pp. 61–70.

Tatlock, J.S.P. *The Legendary History of Britain*. Berkeley: University of California Press, 1950, pp. 471–77.

ROUND TABLE, THE: *see* BOUGHTON, RUTLAND; DAVIS, GEORGENE.

"ROUND TABLE, OR KING ARTHUR'S FEAST, THE":
see PEACOCK, THOMAS LOVE.

ROUND TABLES, festive events involving jousting and dancing in imitation of Arthur and his knights. The first known Round Table took place in Cyprus in 1223, to celebrate a knighting, and such pageants remained popular throughout much of Europe during the remainder of the Middle Ages. In many cases, the participating knights assumed the names and arms of Arthur's knights, and René d'Anjou even built an "Arthurian" castle for a Round Table he held in 1446. (*See also* BALTIC REGION, ARTHURIAN CLUBS IN; PAGEANT DESIGN [BRITISH]); ROUND TABLE; TOURNAMENT BOOKS.) [NJL]

Scherer, Margaret R. *About the Round Table*. New York: Metropolitan Museum of Art, 1945, pp. 24–26.

ROWLEY, WILLIAM: *see* ENGLISH AND AMERICAN ARTHURIAN LITERATURE (MODERN); SHAKESPEARE, WILLIAM; TIECK, LUDWIG.

RUNE: see MONACO, RICHARD.

RUNKELSTEIN MURALS. Schloss Runkelstein (properly, Castel Róncolo, for it now lies in Italy) guards the southern approaches to the Brenner Pass just north of the Italian city of Bolzano in the southern Tyrol. The thirteenth-century castle was purchased in 1385 by the bankers and patrons of the arts Nikolas and Franz Vintler. Before his death in 1413, Nikolas Vintler added a summer house and decorated the castle with paintings. In 1500, the emperor Maximilian acquired the castle and between 1503 and 1511 ordered the restoration of the paintings. In the nineteenth century, the castle was restored again and given to the town of Bolzano by the emperor Franz Joseph.

The Summer House where the Arthurian paintings are to be found was an open structure with gallery and loggia. In the gallery are paintings of the Nine Worthies including King Arthur, knights seated at the Round Table, three pairs of lovers including Tristan and Isolde, and giants and giantesses. The romance of Tristan, following the version of Gottfried von Strassburg, rendered in grisaille, is found in the so-called Ladies' Chamber. Additional grisailles (with touches of green and red) in the loggia illustrate the adventures of Wigalois as told by the Austrian poet Wirnt von Grafenberg. Although badly damaged and defaced, the latter subject can be identified by the repeated inscription "Vigelas"; furthermore, an inventory of 1493 lists a "Vigelas sal."

The thirteenth-century romance *Garel von dem blühenden Tal*, by the Austrian author Der Pleier, also found a place among the paintings in the Summer House, in the room known as the "Library." Ten of twenty-two paintings survive, from about 1400; although also repainted in the sixteenth century and restored in the nineteenth, they are in slightly better condition than those of Wigalois, and the artist's attention to details lends a note of human interest to the fantasy of the romance. For example, in the representation of Garel at Arthur's Round Table the table stands in a meadow under a leafy tree where musicians entertain the King and his knights. Above, a pennant bearing Arthur's emblem of three crowns flutters from a long trumpet, and one hungry knight reaches for food from the central platter. [MS]

Loomis, Roger Sherman, and Laura Hibbard Loomis. *Arthurian Legends in Medieval Art.* London: Oxford University Press, 1938, pp. 60–75, 79–84; figs. 60–75, 171–83, 184–201.

RUSTICIANO DA PISA, or Rusticien de Pise, has a double claim to the attention of posterity. As a prisoner in Genoa in 1298, he wrote an account in French of the adventures of his fellow prisoner, Marco Polo. Earlier in his career, he had composed a vast Arthurian *mélange* known as the *Roman de Roi*

Artus or the *Compilation*) that, although written in French, is the first Arthurian romance by an Italian. This *Compilation*, apparently derived from a book that had been in the possession of Edward I of England when he journeyed through Italy on his way to the Crusade in the Holy Land in 1272, is preserved as a large interpolation in manuscripts of *Palamedes*. In the sixteenth century, the *Compilation* was divided into two volumes and printed as the *Gyron le Courtois* (Verard, 1501?) and the *Meliadus de Leonnoys* (Janot, 1528, 1532). The rambling *Meliadus* contains the adventures of Tristan's father; the *Gyron*, less connected to the adventures of Tristan and the knights of the Round Table, celebrates the House of Bruns and its most notable representative, Gyron. The *Compilation* influenced a Greek poem of ca. 1300 (*Ho Presbys Hippotes*), the Spanish *Tristán de Leonís*, and most subsequent prose versions of *Tristan* in Italian. [DLH]

❧ Gardner, Edmund G. *The Arthurian Legend in Italian Literature.* London: Dent, 1930.

   Löseth, Eilert. *Le Roman en prose de Tristan.* Paris: Champion, 1891.

SACHS, HANS (1494–1576), the most prolific sixteenth-century German dramatist and *Meistersinger*. Sachs is known to the non-German world primarily through Richard Wagner's opera *Die Meistersinger von Nürnberg*. The celebrated shoemaker of Nürnberg composed approximately 4,400 *Meisterlieder* and close to 130 dramas in his lifetime, not to mention his Shrovetide plays. In his most productive period, Sachs produced up to 450 titles per year. In the years 1545–53, he composed one drama and seven *Meisterlieder* inspired by the *matière de Bretagne*.

Sachs's first Arthurian composition is the *Meisterlied* "Die Ehbrecherbruck" ("The Adulterers' Bridge"), dated 17 March 1545. The poem relates how a suspicious King Arthur had a magic bridge built that would not carry unfaithful persons and would announce their infidelity by the sounding of a bell. At a great feast, the King and Queen lead a procession across the bridge. The knights and ladies fall off to right and left, but Arthur's wife safely crosses the bridge. Sachs concludes by observing that many a person would not be able to cross the bridge today.

The drama *Tragedia von der strengen Lieb, Herr Tristrant mit der schönen Königin Isalden* ("Tragedy of the Strong Love of Sir Tristrant and the Beautiful Queen Isalde"), dated 7 February 1553, is based on the chapbook *Ein wunderbarliche vnd fast lustige Historij von Herr Tristrant vnd der schönen Isalden* ("A Marvelous and Almost Happy Tale of Sir Tristrant and the Beautiful Isalde"), first published in 1484. The drama is composed in seven acts and commences and concludes with didactic considerations (*see* TRISTAN, MODERN GERMAN VERSIONS OF GOTT-FRIED'S).

Sachs's Arthurian *Meisterlieder* that are devoted to the Tristan matter commemorate specific events in the life of the lovers: the spying episode in the orchard, the lovers' sojourn in the woods, Tristrant's battle with Morhold, the slaying of the dragon, Tristrant disguised as a fool, and Tristrant's death. The first five *Meisterlieder* were composed in December 1551, the last in March 1553, shortly after Sachs had written the drama. [MEK]

🙠 Sachs, Hans. "Tragedia mit 23 personen, von der strengen lieb herr Tristrant mit der schönen königin Isalden, unnd hat 7 actus." In *Hans Sachs*, ed. Adelbert von Keller. Tübingen: Litterarischer Verein, 1879, Vol. 12, pp. 142–86.

Könneker, Barbara. *Hans Sachs*. Stuttgart: Metzler, 1971.

Sobel, Eli. *The Tristan Romance in the Meisterlieder of Hans Sachs*. Berkeley: University of California Press, 1963.

SAGA AF TRISTRAM OK ÍSODD, a shortened retelling from Iceland of the Tristan story, dated to the fourteenth century. Some episodes have been drastically changed or deleted, while others have been added. In this saga, Mark is called Mórodd. His sister's knight is killed in a joust, and she falls in love with his slayer, Kalegras. She sends for him and they remain in bed for three years. She gives birth to Tristram but dies of grief when Kalegras is killed. After being kidnapped by African warriors and sold as a slave, Tristram arrives at the court of Mórodd. The saga deviates from other versions in that it states that a piece of sword lodges in Tristram's head. In Ireland, he is cured by Ísodd, and the queen offers Tristram her daughter as a reward for killing the dragon. He demurs and says that his uncle is a more suitable husband. During the voyage to England, Tristram and Ísodd drink from a horn, but it is not stated that this is a love potion. Indeed, it is made clear that Ísodd is already quite fond of Tristram. The remainder of the text abounds in further deviations. From his union with the other Ísodd, here called Ísodd the Dark, Tristram has a son who becomes king of England. The author mentions that there is a great saga about his children.

Opinions about this saga are varied: it was once thought to be based on an unknown source, while others saw it as an inaccurate and clumsy retelling of Brother Robert's version. More recently, Paul Schach has suggested that it may have been a satire, because so many events in the story have been reversed, often with humorous effect. The Icelandic fairy tales and Scandinavian ballads about Tristan show greater similarity to this version than to Robert's. [MCH]

🙠 Brynjúlfsson, Gísli, ed. *Saga af Tristram ok Ísodd i Grundtexten med oversættelse*. In *Annaler for nordisk Oldkyndighed og Historie*, 1851, pp. 3–160.

Hill, Joyce, trans. "The Icelandic Saga of Tristan and Isolt (Saga af Tristram ok Ísodd)." In *The Tristan Legend: Texts from Northern and Eastern Europe in Modern English Translation*. Leeds: University of Leeds, Graduate Centre for Medieval Studies, 1977, pp. 6–28.

Schach, Paul. "The Saga af Tristram ok Ísodd: Summary or Satire?" *Modern Language Quarterly*, 21 (1960), pp. 336–52.

SAGA AF VIEGOLEIS MEÐ GULLHIÓLIT: see GABONS SAGA OK VIGOLES.

SAGAN AF TISTRAN OK INDIÖNU: see TISTRANS SAGA OK INDIÖNU.

"ST. AGNES' CONVENT": *see* MORRIS, WILLIAM.

ST. GOEZNOVIUS: *see GOEZNOVIUS, LEGEND OF ST.*

ST. JOHN, NICOLE (pseudonym of Norma Johnston), author of *Guinever's Gift* (1977), a gothic romance that transposes the Arthur-Guenevere-Lancelot triangle to a contemporary setting. [RHT]

☙ St. John, Nicole. *Guinever's Gift*. New York: Random House, 1977.

"ST. JOSEPH OF ARIMATHEA": *see* ORMEROD, JAMES.

SAINTE-PALAYE, LA CURNE DE: *see* FRENCH ARTHURIAN LITERATURE; FRENCH CHIVALRIC ROMANCES, EIGHTEENTH AND NINETEENTH CENTURIES.

SAINTS' LIVES, ARTHUR IN. Like other Celtic lands, Wales in the so-called Dark Ages has innumerable saints, not all of them generally recognized. Their written "Lives" are seldom early or factual enough to carry much documentary weight. Traditions were handed down and embroidered for centuries, often in a community founded by the saint, before an official Life was compiled. The resulting texts usually contain a small amount of authentic matter embedded in a mass of fiction, miracles, and would-be edification. The monastery of Llancarfan in Glamorgan was a major hagiographic center, and five of the Llancarfan Lives, all in Latin, introduce Arthur. That of St. Cadoc, the monastery's own founder, is ascribed to Lifris, who taught there in the late eleventh century. That of Gildas is the work of Caradoc in the twelfth. Arthur also appears in Lives of SS. Illtud, Carannog, and Padarn, written during the same period.

Llancarfan's account of Cadoc begins by telling how he was born. His mother eloped with a local ruler in southern Wales, and Arthur, together with his knights Cai and Bedwyr (Kay and Bedivere), prevented her father from reclaiming her. She married her lover, and Cadoc was their firstborn. Long after, when Cadoc was abbot of Llancarfan, he gave sanctuary for seven years to a man who had killed three of Arthur's soldiers. Arthur at last found out where he was and came to complain. Supported by David and other saints, Cadoc confronted the angry leader across the River Usk and defended his right to grant long-term sanctuary. Arthur demanded 100 cows as compensation, making awkward conditions. When Cadoc supplied them, they became bundles of fern. Arthur, nonplussed, withdrew his objections.

The Life of Illtud says briefly that he was Arthur's cousin and served him as a soldier before turning to the religious life. That of Carannog tells of the saint going to Somerset, where Arthur ruled at Dunster as co-prince with Cato (who figures in Geoffrey of Monmouth's *Historia* as Cador). Arthur had stolen Carannog's portable altar. The saint banished a giant serpent that Arthur had been pursuing without success, and the altar was restored to him. In the Life of Padarn, the saint is in his monastery near Aberystwyth when "a certain tyrant named Arthur," from foreign parts, tries to rob him of a fine tunic. Padarn says, "Let the earth swallow him up," and it does. Arthur has to beg forgiveness before he can extricate himself. (For the more important *Vita Gildae*, or Life of Gildas, *see* GILDAS.)

These stories disclose a discrepancy in Welsh clerical views of Arthur. Whereas Nennius and the *Annales Cambriae* make him a Christian champion, winning battles by celestial aid, most of the Llancarfan matter presents him unfavorably. He is not an outright heathen; much less is he (as some have imagined) a demon in disguise, since a demon would not have repented as he does in the stories; but he is a most unsatisfactory son of the Church and a troubler of the saints. This portrayal is more likely to reflect convention than fact. Arthur is cast in the role of the Recalcitrant King, a stock character in this class of literature, who is brought in so that the saint can teach him a lesson through supernatural powers or superior virtue. His rapacity may be an echo of clashes between abbots and warrior chiefs, requisitioning monastic goods to supply their forces, but nothing can safely be inferred about a real Arthur's real behavior.

Arthur's status in the saints' lives has the same ambiguity as in Welsh tradition generally. Sometimes he is the leader of a war-band, sometimes he is a regional despot, twice he is called King of Britain. His kingship has an air of limitation and uncertain legitimacy. Doubt also overhangs the indications of place and time. While he is spoken of as having a residence at Dunster, and as being a foreigner at Aberystwyth, the stories spread so widely that they fail to define any convincing home territory. As for the chronology, it stretches him out too far. St. Carannog supposedly is a grandson of the Welsh patriarchal hero Cunedda, who belongs early in the fifth century, so that Carannog belongs in that century, too, and so, by implication, does Arthur. A young St. Illtud in Arthur's service likewise implies the fifth century. Gildas, however, was not even born till about 500, and Cadoc's abbacy cannot have begun much before the middle of the sixth century, while David's presence beside him could point to an even later date.

Clearly, some of the hagiographers have shifted Arthur in time so as to work him in. But is he a fifth-century figure wrongly associated with saints who lived long afterward, or is he a sixth-century figure, contemporary with Cadoc and wrongly made to flourish much earlier by writers on other saints? While the saints' lives give no certain answer, those of Gildas and Cadoc, in putting him very late, also betray what looks like a fundamental unsoundness by making him an anachronism. Both credit him, at some stage of his career, with a national kingship however questionable. He could have had this after a fashion in the fifth century but not in the time of the two saints, after Britain's breakup into small kingdoms. The passages where the title occurs allow him to be a fifth-century high king ignorantly or irresponsibly transplanted. They rule him out as an authentic contemporary of Gildas or Cadoc. Of course, his sovereignty may be a purely legendary accretion; the value of this clue can be assessed only in the context of other evidence.

Brittany has a Life of St. Efflam with an episode like the Carannog tale, in which the saint overcomes a monster that has proved too much for Arthur. The Arthurian passage in the *Goeznovius* narrative, also of Breton provenance, is a text of a different type and not part of the hagiographic legend itself. [GA]

Chambers, E.K. *Arthur of Britain*. London: Sidgwick and Jackson, 1927.

Loomis, Roger Sherman, ed. *Arthurian Literature in the Middle Ages*. Oxford: Clarendon, 1959.

Morris, John. *The Age of Arthur*. New York: Scribner, 1973.

SALA, PIERRE, author of nine French works from the late fifteenth and early sixteenth centuries. Three of his compositions are Arthurian. The first is a modernized verse redaction of *Le Chevalier au lion*; Sala omitted certain of the episodes from Chrétien de Troyes's original and condensed others. His *Hardiesses de plusieurs roys et empereurs* includes several Arthurian episodes from the Vulgate *Merlin* and the *Prophécies de Merlin*. Finally, between 1525 and 1529, Sala wrote a prose *Tristan* that is considered to be his masterpiece. [NJL]

Sala, Pierre. *Tristan en prose*, ed. Lynette Muir. Geneva: Droz, 1958.

Frappier, Jean. *Amour courtois et Table Ronde*. Geneva: Droz, 1973, pp. 273–74.

SALA DEL PISANELLO: *see* PISANO, ANTONIO.

SALAZAR, LOPE GARCÍA DE, author of *Libro de las bienandanzas e fortunas* ("The Book of Prosperity and Fortune"), a late fifteenth-century Spanish universal history containing a largely legendary summary of the history of England, from its founding by Brutus of Troy to the reign of Edward III. The principal sources for the legendary material are a variant version of the fourteenth-century Spanish pseudo-historical romance *Sumas de historia troyana*, by Leomarte, and the three branches of the Post-Vulgate *Roman du Graal*. Salazar makes free use of his sources, most notably the substitution of seamen's accounts of the mythical North Atlantic island of Brasil for the story of Arthur's passing to the Isle of Avalon. Salazar also interpolates material from the *Roman du Graal* and the Prose *Tristan* in his narration of French and Flemish history. Within his history of the reign of the Spanish king Pedro the Cruel, taken from the fourteenth-century chronicle of the king's rule by Pero López de Ayala, Salazar includes verbatim the text of a prophecy attributed to Merlin. [HLS]

ೋ Salazar, Lope García de. *The Legendary History of Britain in Lope García de Salazar's "Libro de las bienandanzas e fortunas,"* ed. Harvey L. Sharrer. Philadelphia: University of Pennsylvania Press, 1979.

SAMSONS SAGA FAGRA ("Saga of Samson the Fair"), a fourteenth-century Icelandic work that has been repeatedly linked to the *matière de Bretagne* because the hero is the son of one King Arthur of England. This is not the famous ruler of legend, however. The saga relates the adventures encountered by Samson in his search for his beloved Valentina, daughter of King Garlant of Ireland, and a maid-in-waiting at Arthur's court. The saga's sole link to the Arthurian matter is the appearance of the chastity-testing mantle—this is actually a blind motif—which has been borrowed from *Möttuls saga*. The author of *Samsons saga* supplements the information provided by *Möttuls saga* with matter concerning the origin of the mantle, its magic properties, and its subsequent appearance at the legendary Arthur's court. The author adds that there is a tale about the last, called *Skickiu saga*, and this is an alternate title for *Möttuls saga*. [MEK]

ೋ Wilson, John, ed. *Samsons saga fagra*. Copenhagen: Samfund til Udgivelse af gammel nordisk Litteratur, 1953.

Simek, Rudolf, trans. *Die Saga vom Mantel und die Saga vom schönen Samson. Möttuls saga und Samsons saga fagra*. Vienna: Braumüller, 1982.

SAPIENTES: *see SETTE SAVI DI ROMA.*

SAUL, GEORGE BRANDON, American scholar and poet of the mid-twentieth century, who wrote a dramatic poem in 700 blank-verse lines, "The Fair Eselt." Divided into a large number of short scenes that are held together through the narration of a "Master of Revels," it recounts the story of Tristan and Eselt, replacing the magical elements of the traditional tale with psychological explanations and ending with a moral about passion in the modern world. [SRR]

ೋ Saul, George Brandon. "The Fair Eselt." In *Hound and Unicorn: Collected Verse—Lyrical, Narrative, and Dramatic*. Philadelphia: Walton, 1969, pp. 217–53.

SAVIOURS, THE: *see* DANE, CLEMENCE.

SCANDINAVIAN ARTHURIAN LITERATURE. In the introduction to *Tristrams saga ok Ísöndar*, the Norwegian translation of Thomas's *Tristan*, we hear that 1,226 years after the birth of Christ the story of Tristram was written down in Norwegian by a certain Brother Robert at the request of King Hákon Hákonarson—or Hákon IV—king of Norway from 1217 to 1263. To judge by authorial commentary in other *riddarasögur*, or chivalric sagas, the name given to Old Norse–Icelandic translations of continental literature, Hákon also commissioned the translation of twenty-one Breton lais, known in Norwegian as *Strengleikar*—among them the Arthurian *Januals ljóð* (= *Lanval*) and *Geitarlauf* (= *Chevrefueil*), as well as *Ívens saga*, which derives from Chrétien de Troyes's *Yvain*, and *Möttuls saga*, a translation of the anonymous *Lai du cort mantel* or *Le Mantel mautaillié*. Two other works of Chrétien de Troyes are presumed to have been translated during Hákon's reign—although the works themselves are silent regarding royal patronage: *Erex saga* (= *Erec et Enide*) and *Parcevals saga* with *Valvens þáttr* (= *Perceval*). The earliest Arthurian fiction in Scandinavia thus consists of four romances and three lais.

Two reasons have been adduced for Hákon's program of translation, which also included non-Arthurian works, such as *Elis saga*, a translation of *Elie de St. Gille*, a *chanson de geste*: edification and entertainment. Earlier scholarship interpreted the Norwegian translations as didactic documents intended to instruct the Norwegian nobility in the ideals and duties of chivalry. This interpretation of the function of the Norwegian translations ignores the fact, however, that *Tristrams saga* glorifies adultery, that the portrayal of King Arthur is not entirely positive in the sagas, and that Arthur's court is depicted in a negative light both in *Januals ljóð* and especially in *Möttuls saga*. Internal testimony suggests that the primary function of the translations was entertainment. In the prologue to *Möttuls saga*, we are told that this tale about a curious and amusing incident at Arthur's court was translated at Hákon's request to provide entertainment and amusement. A similar statement is found in *Elis saga*. The prologue of the *Strengleikar* reiterates that the lais are meant as entertainment. If one considers the fact that Arthurian literature has continued to be a source of amusement and pleasure in our own day, then it is unlikely that Hákon's Norwegian court was not more entertained than edified by the latest fiction from France.

Although the four romances and three lais named above became known in Scandinavia in Norwegian translation, only *Geitarlauf* and *Januals ljóð* are extant in a Norwegian manuscript (from ca. 1270). The other works are known to us only in Icelandic manuscripts, the oldest of which is a single leaf of *Möttuls saga* from ca. 1300, the youngest—but the oldest complete redaction of *Erex saga*—a manuscript from the middle of the seventeenth century.

In addition to the romances and lais, Geoffrey of Monmouth's *Historia*

Regum Britanniae—a major portion of which is devoted to King Arthur—also became known in the North through *Breta sögur* and *Merlínússpá*. The *Breta sögur*, extant only in Icelandic manuscripts, are an early thirteenth-century translation of the *Historia*. Both Norway and Iceland have been proposed as transmitters of the *Historia*, but proof for either thesis is wanting. *Merlínússpá* ("The Prophecy of Merlin"), however, is the work of an Icelander: it is a metrical version of Merlin's prophecies in Book VII of the *Historia*, composed around 1200 by Gunnlaugr Leifsson (d. 1218 or 1219), a monk at the Benedictine monastery of Þingeyrar.

The one Arthurian work that is associated with neither Norway nor Iceland in the Middle Ages is *Ivan Lejonriddaren*, or *Herr Ivan*, a Swedish translation of Chrétien de Troyes's *Yvain*. *Ivan Lejonriddaren*, which dates to 1303, is one of three works (the other two being *Hertig Fredrik av Normandie* and *Flores och Blanzeflor*) that are collectively known as *Eufemiavisor*, after Queen Eufemia, the German wife of King Hákon Magnússon of Norway (r. 1299–1319), who instigated the translation of these works on the occasion of her daughter's engagement and marriage to Duke Erik of Sweden.

Ivan Lejonriddaren is unique not only because it is the sole translation of an Arthurian work into Swedish but also because it is written in rhymed couplets. All the other works belonging to the *matière de Bretagne* are translations into prose. Although there are stylistic differences from work to work, the prose of the Old Norse–Icelandic *riddarasögur* is on the whole highly rhythmical and rhetorical, characterized by synonymous and antithetical collocations as well as alliteration. Occasionally, one finds rhyming couplets in passages where the author wishes to emphasize the content. The prose of *Parcevals saga* in particular is interspersed with short rhyming verses that are usually at the end of a chapter. The couplets may be the work of the translator but may also be by a later redactor. The prose of the translated sagas is thus quite unlike the laconic and elliptic prose known from the indigenous Sagas of Icelanders.

Although the Old Norse–Icelandic Arthurian literature was presumably written during a relatively short period—during the reign of Hákon IV—the Arthurian sagas display considerable diversity in the extent to which they reproduce their sources. The three lais are relatively faithful translations, but the longer romances are considerably shorter than their French counterparts. Passages devoted to psychological analysis and interior monologue are, if not completely missing, greatly reduced. Earlier scholarship had ascribed the reduction of text in the *riddarasögur* to a lack of understanding and a distaste for extensive reflections and sentimental discourses on the nature of love. Recent manuscript evidence, however, enables us to postulate relatively faithful Norwegian translations that were condensed and modified by Icelandic redactors during centuries of manuscript transmission.

Erex saga is the most extreme example of the modification of the content and style of a thirteenth-century Norwegian translation that presumably reproduced Chrétien's *Erec et Enide* in most of its details. The seventeenth-century versions in which the saga is extant reflect a work that is the result of a systematic and intentional revision of the structure of the tale. By interpolating two new adventures—encounters with a flying dragon and with seven armed men—an anonymous Icelandic redactor produced a work that is structurally distinct from the French romance, a work that must be considered a recreation of the tale.

Although the Arthurian *riddarasögur* may be said to transmit the substance of the French romances and lais from which they derive, there are certain additions and modifications in the sagas vis-à-vis their sources that suggest a process of acculturation. Most of the discrepancies between the *riddarasögur* and the French originals are the work of one or more Icelandic redactors rather than the Norwegian translator. In *Ívens saga* and *Erex saga*, for example, the position of women is somewhat different from that in the French romance. After Íven has rescued 300 enslaved maidens, the lord of the castle offers the hero his daughter as reward, but Íven replies sanctimoniously that he would never bargain for a woman in such a manner, that the daughter is a free agent. In *Erex saga*, the hero falls in love with Evida (Enide) at first sight and immediately proposes. The father is pleased but informs Erex that Evida must make the decision herself. A similar deference to woman occurs in the Earl Placidus (Count of Limors) episode. Unlike the French count, who marries Enide over her objections, the Scandinavian earl heeds his courtiers' admonitions—that it is contrary to God's law to marry Evida unless she herself assents—and so does not marry her. *Ívens saga* is extant in two redactions, and in the younger version one observes a systematic revision of the saga. The mistress of the spring is portrayed as a decisive and aggressive individual who reserves the right to make independent decisions and is not subject to the desires of her courtiers.

In a work like *Möttuls saga*, which is extant in manuscripts dating from ca. 1300 through the middle of the nineteenth century, we can observe the process of modification and interpolation that the sparse manuscript evidence from *Erex saga* only allows us to postulate. Like its French source, *Möttuls saga* is a hilarious account of a chastity test conducted at King Arthur's court by means of a magic mantle. One by one, beginning with Guenevere, the ladies of the illustrious knights must submit to the trial. The peculiar manner in which the mantle does not fit permits Kay to interpret the exact nature of the sexual transgression. The serial nature of the plot encouraged interpolation and thus, at the same time that relatively accurate copies of a medieval manuscript of the saga were produced in the seventeenth and eighteenth centuries, there are also deviating redactions in which new female characters and further mantle tests are introduced. In the French lai and in the Norwegian translation, the chastity test is entirely unmotivated, but two early nineteenth-century manuscripts of the saga provide fuller information about the origin of the mantle and the motivation of the woman who sent it to King Arthur's court.

Most scholars consider *Tristrams saga ok Ísöndar* the first work translated at Hákon's court, but it is also possible that the *matière de Bretagne* was introduced into Norway by way of *Möttuls saga*. The evidence for such a hypothesis is the saga's prologue, which is independent of the French lai; it is an encomium of Arthur and the most extended portrait of the monarch in Scandinavian literature. Had the Norwegian court been ignorant of the Arthurian tradition when *Möttuls saga* was translated, a portrayal of Arthur and his court would have been necessary if Hákon's retainers were to appreciate fully the farcical nature of the plot.

Icelanders not only transcribed the thirteenth-century Norwegian translations through some six centuries but were also inspired to produce original Arthurian literature. Of the works belonging to the *matière de Bretagne*, the Norwegian *Tristrams saga* had the greatest impact on Icelandic literature. In Icelandic romances as well as Sagas of Icelanders, the several motifs from the saga recur, such as the embedded sword-fragment, the voyage for healing, and the ambiguous oath. Analogues to the Hall of Statues episode proliferate. The contribution of the other Arthurian romances to Icelandic literature is more modest. The grateful-lion motif from *Ívens saga* recurs in six indigenous Icelandic romances and in a post-Reformation folktale. The chastity-testing mantle from *Möttuls saga* appears in the indigenous romance *Samsons saga fagra*. In this saga, the mantle can be used to reveal not only infidelity but also laziness and theft. The conclusion of *Samsons saga* relates how the mantle came to Arthur's court and refers the reader to *Möttuls saga* for information concerning the mantle test.

The Norwegian *Tristrams saga* also inspired one of the most curious of Icelandic romances, the fourteenth-century *Saga af Tristram ok Ísodd*, which Henry Goddard Leach dismissed as a "boorish account of Tristram's noble passion," but which in recent times has been interpreted as a parody of the Norwegian *Tristrams saga*. The Icelandic *Tristram* appears to be a parody not only of the Tristram romance but also of Arthurian romance in general through the exaggeration and humorous use of such motifs as Erec's *recreantise* and Perceval's drops-of-blood episode.

The French metrical romances and lais were turned into prose in Norway. Subsequently, the prose sagas generated not only prose imitations but also metrical narratives, known as *rímur*, a popular genre in Iceland in the late Middle Ages and even as late as the nineteenth century. Of the medieval Arthurian *riddarasögur*, only *Möttuls saga* generated a *rímur*-version, entitled *Skikkju rímur* ("mantle verses"). The *Skikkju rímur* contain three *rímur*, or cantos. The individual stanzas of each *ríma* are bound by end-rhyme and alliteration. Although *Möttuls saga* is the primary source of the *Skikkju rímur*, the author was also familiar with other romances, such as *Erex saga*, from which he borrowed not only Erex and his beloved but also the wedding guests. The *Skikkju rímur* alone explain how the Round Table came into being and contain additional mantle tests. The interpolated material in the *rímur* was in turn the source of the interpolations in two of the eighteenth-century manuscripts of *Möttuls saga*.

At the end of the Middle Ages, the Tristan matter found its way into Icelandic, Danish, and Faroese ballads. The Icelandic "Tristrams kvæði," dating probably from the fifteenth century, relates the tale from the wounding of Tristan to his death. In Denmark, several versions of the ballad of "Tistram og Jomfru Isolt" are known, the oldest believed to date from the fifteenth century. Unlike the Icelandic ballad, the Danish versions depart drastically from the classical Tristan tale, and only one version, in which Tistram and Isolt are brother and sister, has a tragic conclusion. One ballad, entitled "Tistrum og Isalt," and known through manuscripts of the sixteenth and seventeenth centuries, celebrates a nocturnal lovers' tryst under a linden-tree. The most unusual of the Scandinavian Tristan ballads is the Faroese "Tístrams táttur," in which Tístram refuses to marry the daughter of the French king, is hanged, and is then avenged by his beloved Ísin, who subsequently dies of a broken heart.

Another Faroese ballad, "Galians táttur," is devoted to Ívint and his son Galian. Although the ballad is set at King Arthur's court and appears to be a reflex of *Ívens saga*, the relationship to the Arthurian matter is tenuous.

During the Middle Ages, the *matière de Bretagne* was imported into Norway from France. The Norwegian translations were transmitted in Icelandic manuscripts and inspired original compositions. In the seventeenth century and later, there occurred a second wave of foreign importations into Scandinavia. This time, the literature came from Germany, was translated in Denmark, and was subsequently translated from Danish into Icelandic.

In 1656, the Danish chapbook *Her Viegoleis med Guld Hiulet* was published. The Danish prose romance derives from an anonymous fifteenth-century German prose redaction of the medieval romance *Wigalois*, by Wirnt von Grafenberg. In the same century that the German chapbook was translated into Danish, the Danish chapbook was translated into Icelandic and entitled *Gabons saga ok Vigoles*.

As already mentioned, the thirteenth-century Norwegian *Tristrams saga ok Ísöndar* had considerable impact on indigenous Icelandic literature, more so than the other translated Arthurian romances. The same phenomenon occurs in modern times with the eighteenth-century Danish chapbook *En tragoedisk Historie om den ædle og tappre Tistrand*, which inspired the composition of two Icelandic *rímur* cycles in the nineteenth century. Unlike the Norwegian *Tristrams saga*, which may be considered a fairly accurate rendering of Thomas's *Tristan*, the Danish chapbook is a drastic revision of its source, the fifteenth-century German chapbook *Ein wunderbarliche vnd fast lustige Historij von Herr Tristrant vnd der schönen Isalden*. Although most of the characteristic motifs and situations of the Tristan matter are found in the Danish chapbook, the romance has been rewritten in such a manner as to remove what might be offensive to eighteenth-century sensibilities. Instead of an adulterous relationship, we are told about a case of platonic love. Tistrand and Indiana—as Isolt is called in the chapbook—have children by Innanda and King Alfonsus, respectively. The strongest expression of love that Tistrand is permitted is a chaste kiss on Indiana's hand.

Not only was the Danish chapbook translated into Icelandic in the nineteenth century (*Tistrans saga ok Indiönu*) but it also inspired the composition of two *rímur* cycles, those by Sigurður Breiðfjörð (1831) and Níels Jónsson (1844–50). [MEK]

🙚 Kalinke, Marianne E. *King Arthur, North-by-Northwest*. Copenhagen: Reitzel, 1981.

Leach, Henry Goddard. *Angevin Britain and Scandinavia*. Cambridge, Mass.: Harvard University Press, 1921.

Mitchell, P.M. "Scandinavian Literature." In *Arthurian Literature in the Middle Ages*, ed. Roger Sherman Loomis. Oxford: Clarendon, 1959, pp. 462–71.

Schlauch, Margaret. *Romance in Iceland*. Princeton, N.J.: Princeton University Press, 1934.

SCENES FROM THE MORTE D'ARTHUR: *see* WRIGHT, SIDNEY FOWLER.

SCENES OF INFANCY: *see* LEYDEN, JOHN.

SCHAEFFER, ALBRECHT (1885–1950), prolific German author from the circle of Stefan George. He lived in exile in the United States from 1939 to 1950 but returned home shortly before his death. Using Wolfram von Eschenbach, Robert de Boron, and Richard Wagner as sources, he composed *Parzival* (1922), a popular epic poem of over 20,000 lines. This "story of the spirit" (*Seelengeschichte*) is characterized by polished and picturesque language and a plethora of images, motifs, and allusions. Schaeffer only briefly considers the Arthurian court and the death of Arthur. [UM/WCM]

🙚 Schaeffer, Albrecht. *Parzival*. Leipzig: Insel, 1922.

Schulze, Ursula. "Ideologisierung durch Strukturverlust." In *Akten des DFG-Symposions zur Mittelalter-Rezeption*, ed. Peter Wapnewski. Stuttgart: Metzler, 1985.

SCHIRMER-IMHOFF, RUTH, contemporary German author among whose works are a Tristan novel (1969) and a "romance of love at the Arthurian court," *Lancelot und Ginevra* (1961). She treats Arthurian subject matter from the parentage of Merlin to the fall of Arthur's realm, using as source (according to her own testimony) the Old French Vulgate Cycle. Both novels are successful poetic adaptations of traditional material. [SSch/WCM]

🙚 Schirmer-Imhoff, Ruth. *Lancelot und Ginevra, ein Liebesroman am Artushof*. Zurich: Manesse, 1961.

——— . *Der Roman von Tristan und Isolde*. Zurich: Manesse, 1969.

SCHLEGEL, AUGUST WILHELM: *see* SCHLEGEL, FRIEDRICH.

SCHLEGEL, FRIEDRICH (1772–1829), **and AUGUST WILHELM SCHLEGEL** (1767–1845), through their literary journal *Athenäum*, were the fathers and leading theoreticians of German Romanticism. The enthusiasm of these two brothers for medieval culture led ultimately to the promotion of the German tradition of medieval literature throughout the nineteenth century. Unfortunately, their creative contributions to Arthurian literature are more limited. The *Geschichte des Zauberers Merlin* ("Story of Merlin the Magician"), published by Friedrich in 1804, is merely a translation by his wife, Dorothea, of the medieval French *Roman de Merlin*. August Wilhelm Schlegel promoted German Arthurian works in his many popular lectures and even began a verse translation of Gottfried's *Tristan*, which he planned to complete from French sources. He abandoned this undertaking after the first canto of ninety-one stanzas (published in 1811), which takes Tristan up to his kidnapping by Norwegian merchants. [RWK]

Schlegel, August Wilhelm. *Sämtliche Werke*, ed. E. Böcking. Leipzig, 1846, Vol. 1.

Schlegel, Friedrich. *Sammlung von Memóiren und romantischen Dichtungen des Mittelalters aus altfranzösischen und deutschen Quellen*, ed. L. Dieckmann. Paderborn, Munich, and Vienna: Schöningh, 1980.

Eichner, Hans. *Friedrich Schlegel*. New York: Twayne, 1970.

Golther, Wolfgang. *Tristan und Isolde in den Dichtungen des Mittelalters und der neuen Zeit*. Leipzig: Hirzel, 1907, pp. 261–68.

SCHNEEGANS, LUDWIG: *see TRISTAN*, MODERN GERMAN VERSIONS OF GOTTFRIED'S.

SCHOLARSHIP, MODERN ARTHURIAN. 1) INTRODUCTION. Many of the major issues that have occupied twentieth-century scholars were studied no less attentively in the nineteenth century. We have more information now; and new approaches, techniques, and interpretations are characteristic of modern scholarship. But, as this survey will show, in producing texts, in studying the Grail's origins, in searching for the historic Arthur, and in many other areas of Arthurian studies, the nineteenth century provided the background against which the work of the twentieth century should be viewed.

One measure of the flourishing of Arthurian scholarship in this century can be seen in attempts to cover the field. James Douglas Bruce's impressive two-volume study *The Evolution of Arthurian Romance* (1922, 2nd ed. 1928) addressed virtually every aspect of Arthurian literature before 1300, provided résumés of many works, and surveyed much of previous scholarship. By the 1950s, a new "survey of the field" was needed, but it was impossible that the work could be undertaken by one person. Thus, *Arthurian Literature in the Middle Ages* (1959), edited by Roger Sherman Loomis, was a collaborative effort by a number of scholars prominent in specialized areas. In more recent years, scholars have generally concentrated on single authors, single works, or even limited aspects of a particular author or work; but we also have essays that survey scholarship and outline problems yet to be solved.

Bibliography has become an increasingly complex but necessary adjunct to Arthurian studies. Bruce compiled an extensive and authoritative bibliography of Arthurian studies and editions, and it was supplemented by A. Hilka in 1928. Eugène Vinaver, with H.J.B. Gray and then with F.M. Williams, produced one-year bibliographies in *Arthuriana* in 1929 and 1930. John J. Parry, later with Margaret Schlauch, produced cumulative bibliographies for 1922–29, 1930–35, and 1936–39; beginning with Volume 1 of *Modern Language Quarterly* (1940), Parry issued yearly bibliographies until 1955, when Paul A. Brown continued the work up to 1962. Meanwhile, the International Arthurian Society began in 1949 to publish a yearly bibliography in its *Bulletin Bibliographique*. A measure of the proliferation of twentieth-century Arthurian studies can be seen in the *Bulletin*'s increased length over the years. It lists editions, books, and articles dealing only with Arthurian material produced before 1500. Therefore, none of the growing body of work on, for example, the Arthurian creations of Victorian poets is included. Nevertheless, the 226 entries in the 1949 bibliography had nearly tripled by 1981 to 618 entries and 552 the following year. Reflecting the international scope of modern Arthurian studies, entries typically come from the United States, Canada, Great Britain, France, Germany, the Low Countries, Scandinavia, Spain, Italy, and, since 1975, from Japan.

The need to collate this bibliographic material has been recognized for some years, and an *Arthurian Bibliography* has recently been published (Vol. 1, Pickford and Last, 1981; Vol. 2, Pickford, Last, and Barker, 1983; Vol. 3, Last, 1985), a list of nearly 10,000 entries compiled from these previous bibliographies. Volume 1 of another large bibliographic project was published in 1984; it is the first of two volumes of more than 400 pages each, edited by Edmund Reiss, Louise Horner Reiss, and Beverly Taylor. This first volume of *Arthurian Legend and Literature: An Annotated Bibliography* includes Arthurian material of the Middle Ages and selected studies of that material; and Volume 2 covers Arthurian poetry and fiction from the Renaissance to the present and the growing body of commentary on this latter field.

But so large is the amount of material to be listed or described that bibliographies of individual works and authors have also been found necessary or helpful. Malory studies provide a good example. Vinaver's first edition of the Winchester manuscript (1947) listed only ninety-one books and articles on Malory, whereas his 1967 list of critical works, with some omissions, numbered 177. A mere fourteen years later, Toshiyuki Takamiya and Derek Brewer brought the 1967 bibliography up to date by the addition of 133 new items (*Aspects of Malory*, 1981). Much of this bibliographic material, as well as a number of nineteenth-century periodical and review articles and brief commentary on Malory from earlier centuries, has been collected in a book-length work by Page West Life, *Sir Thomas Malory and the "Morte Darthur": A Survey of Scholarship and Annotated Bibliography* (1980). Other bibliographies issued recently include those on the *Morte Arthure* (Michael Foley, *Chaucer Review*, Vol. 14), the *Gawain*-poet (Malcolm Andrew, 1980), Wolfram (Joachim Bumke, reissued 1970), and Chrétien (F.D. Kelly, 1976). And still, these modern bibliographical listings do not include literary histories and other general studies, such as Bernhard Ten Brink's *History of English Literature* (in German 1877–93; in English

1883–96) or Albert Baugh's *Literary History of England* (2nd ed. 1967), which address many Arthurian works and problems.

Another area of Arthurian scholarship that has received increased attention of late is the study of the Arthurian legend itself—not in its historic development but in the ways Arthurian romance (in various forms) has been perceived and drawn upon in particular periods and societies since its birth. Early studies in this area include Mungo MacCallum's *Tennyson's Idylls of the King and Arthurian Story* (1894) and Howard Maynardier's *The Arthur of the English Poets* (1907). Contributions by Ronald Crane (1919), William Edward Mead (1925), Roberta F. Brinkley (1932), Charles Bowie Millican (1932), and Nathan Edelman (1946) all deal with the reception and treatment of Arthurian romance in the sixteenth and seventeenth centuries. There are also studies on the treatment of Arthurian characters in later literature; Maurice Halperin's study (1931) of Tristan and Isolde in the nineteenth and twentieth centuries is an example, as is Nathan Comfort Starr's survey of twentieth-century Arthurian works, *King Arthur Today* (1954). More general studies include Alice Chandler's *A Dream of Order* (1970), Geoffrey Ashe's *Camelot and the Vision of Albion* (1971) and other works, and Richard Barber's *King Arthur in Legend and History* (1973). James Douglas Merriman's *The Flower of Kings* (1973) studies the Arthurian legend in England from 1485 to 1835, and *The Return of Arthur* (1983), by Beverly Taylor and Elisabeth Brewer, considers nineteenth- and twentieth-century Arthurian literature. Raymond H. Thompson's *The Return from Avalon: A Study of the Arthurian Legend in Modern Fiction* was published in 1985. These books, while concerned mainly with literary treatments of the Arthurian legend, also provide some discussion of the scholarly treatment as well. Cedric Pickford discussed *Changing Attitudes Towards Medieval French Literature*, much of it Arthurian romance, in a 1966 publication and, more recently, examined "the way in which critics and readers . . . after the Middle Ages reacted to and enjoyed (or otherwise)" the French prose romances (*Bulletin Bibliographique*, 1982). Stephen Knight's *Arthurian Literature and Society* (1983) addresses the ways in which individual romances, such as *Culhwch and Olwen*, Chrétien's *Le Chevalier au lion*, Malory's *Morte Darthur*, and Tennyson's *Idylls of the King*, represented and commented upon dominant elements of the societies from which they arose.

As this brief survey of bibliographies and general works has suggested, the field of Arthurian studies is vast indeed. No single essay can attempt to give more than general outlines even in particular areas; therefore, the remainder of this entry deals briefly with some major points in three areas of Arthurian scholarship; publication of texts, Grail studies, and the historical Arthur.

2) TEXTS. The development of Arthurian scholarship has been in large part determined by the accessibility of appropriate texts. An essential contribution of the nineteenth century was the publication, from manuscript or from early printed editions, of most of the poems and prose romances associated with Arthur and his knights.

Reflecting the growth of various antiquarian interests in late eighteenth-century England, for example, Bishop Percy's *Reliques of Ancient English Poetry*

(1765), including six Arthurian ballads, was enormously popular; before the end of the eighteenth century, similar collections by Pinkerton and Ritson appeared containing Gawain and Lancelot poems, and two translations into English of Le Grand d'Aussy's modern *French Fabliaux, or contes du XIIe et du XIIIe siècles* (1779–81) which included Arthurian lais of Marie de France. The growing influence of Romanticism, with its interest in the medieval past and its rejection of many Neoclassical standards for literature, no doubt contributed to an enhanced market for the longer Arthurian works that were published after the turn of the century. In addition, Thomas Warton's ambitious *History of English Poetry* (1774–81) had featured some discussion of the origins of Arthurian romance as well as consideration, with some summary, of individual French romances. More scholarly was Joseph Ritson's "Dissertation on Romance and Chivalry," the preface to his *Ancient Engleish Metrical Romanceës* (1802), a carefully edited collection that included *Ywaine and Gawin* and *Lybeaus Disconnus*. George Ellis's *Specimens of Early English Metrical Romances* (1805) also had a "Historical Introduction on the Rise and Progress of Romantic Composition in France and England"; Ellis furnished brief extracts pieced together by his own prose paraphrases of such Arthurian poems as *Arthour and Merlin* and the Stanzaic *Le Morte Arthur*.

French Arthurian material, too, became more accessible in England in the early nineteenth century. John Colin Dunlop's *History of Fiction* (1814) provided English prose summaries of several long French romances, mainly from the Vulgate Cycle but including also romances of Perceval and Tristan. Robert Southey's introduction to an 1817 edition of Malory's *Morte Darthur* also summarized or commented upon the French romances "from which the Morte Arthur has been compiled." Drawn mainly from French printed editions of the fifteenth and sixteenth centuries, which Southey was able to borrow from the libraries of friends and collectors like Richard Heber and David Laing, his summaries and descriptions included the Vulgate *Merlin*, *Lancelot*, the Prose *Tristan*, and a Prose *Perceval*.

Besides these collections and summaries, longer romances, both French and English, were published in increasing volume through the century. Sir Walter Scott's *Sir Tristrem* (1804), from the Auchinleck Manuscript, also included an "elegant precis" by George Ellis of what are now known as the Douce fragments of Thomas's twelfth-century *Tristan*. Two inexpensive (and poorly edited) editions of Malory, the first since 1634, appeared in 1816, followed by a more elaborate edition with Southey's introduction in 1817. By 1900, there would be seven more complete editions of Malory and numerous abridgments and adaptations.

Beginning in 1812 with the Roxburghe Club, the founding of book clubs and literary and publishing societies both reflected and encouraged an interest in the publication of older literature. These groups sponsored variously the publication of several Arthurian editions, including the Stanzaic *Morte* (1819), *Arthour and Merlin* (1838), and Sir Frederic Madden's Gawayne collection in which *Sir Gawain and the Green Knight* was first printed (1839). The Society of

45 *Woodcut,* King Arthur and His Knights, *from* Tristan of Leonnoys (Tristan, Chevalier de la Table Ronde). *Paris: Antoine Verard, 1506.*

Antiquaries made possible Madden's edition of Layamon's *Brut* (1847), which remained the standard edition until 1963. In addition, Lady Charlotte Guest's translations from the *Mabinogion* began appearing in 1838, and in 1847 the first edition of the Alliterative *Morte Arthure* was published. The introductions to many of these editions, especially those of Madden, reflect the progress and the problems of Arthurian scholarship at about mid-century. Madden drew upon the work of French scholars like Gervais de la Rue, Francisque Michel, and Paulin Paris.

Publication of romances continued with Frederick J. Furnivall's edition of Lovelich's *History of the Holy Grail* (1861–63), the French Vulgate *Queste* (1864), and another Stanzaic *Morte* (1864). Furnivall founded the Early English Text Society in 1864, and among its early publications were a fragmentary English poem, *Arthur* (1864), and the text of the English Prose *Merlin* (1865–69). The introduction planned for the Prose *Merlin* was delayed for a number of years, initially because of the discovery in 1869 of the *Huth Merlin*, or *Suite du Merlin*, which would be edited and published by Jacob Ulrich and Gaston Paris in 1886.

Other EETS publications in the Arthurian field were Skeat's edition of four short Joseph of Arimathea romances (1871) and Leon Kellner's *Caxton's Blanchardyn and Eglantine* (1890). Skeat's introductory material drew on the work of Paulin Paris, Henry Morley *(English Writers)*, F.G. Bergmann *(The San Greäl*, in French 1842; in English 1870), and the Flemish scholar W.J.A. Jonckbloet. Meanwhile, H. Oskar Sommer had been publishing a three-volume scholarly edition of Malory (1889–91) that included copious source comparisons. Sommer also produced the first complete edition of the French Vulgate romances (1908–16).

The developing pattern of publication was somewhat similar, if less extensive, in France. In the late eighteenth century, summaries of the romances began to be published out of the great collections. The Comte de Tressan wrote modernized summaries of old romances, including a *Tristan de Leonis* praised by Sir Walter Scott as "an elegant and beautiful abridgement" *(Sir Tristrem)*. Dunlop's English summaries, mentioned above, were also translated into French and German and reprinted. Paulin Paris had described several medieval Arthurian texts in *Les Manuscrits françois de la Bibliothèque du Roi* (1836–48) and had himself produced a modernized version of the Vulgate Cycle under the title *Les Romans de la Table Ronde mis en nouveau langage* (1868–77). Among early editors, Francisque Michel published an incomplete version of the Thomas *Tristan* fragments along with Béroul (1835–39; Bédier's edition of Thomas would not appear until 1903); Michel also edited *Le Roman du Saint Graal* (1841), which contained Robert's *Joseph d'Arimathie* and *Merlin*. Hersart de la Villemarqué had published a popular collection of old Breton ballads, *Barzaz Breiz*, some of them containing Merlin material, in 1839; not until 1868 was it revealed that la Villemarqué had treated his materials with the same freedom that Bishop Percy had used, altering and adding passages to his originals.

In 1849, Jonckbloet edited the Dutch *Roman van Lancelot* with an appendix consisting of his edition of Chrétien's *Lancelot*. Potvin, whose edition of Chrétien's *Perceval* (1866–71) included an edition of the *Perlesvaus*, and Foerster brought out editions of all Chrétien's romances by the century's end. In 1875, Gaston Paris and Paul Meyer founded the Société des Anciens Textes Français, under whose auspices Paris and Ulrich published the *Huth Merlin*. In his introduction to this edition and in the pages of the periodical *Romania*, founded in 1872, Paris made important contributions to Arthurian scholarship. The Prose *Tristan* was not substantially edited until the twentieth century (R.L. Curtis, 1963, 1976; edition in progress), but Eilert Löseth provided a useful summary in 1891.

In Germany, too, the nineteenth century saw the publication of editions of the Arthurian romances of Eilhart, Gottfried, Hartmann, and Wolfram. An edition of Gottfried's *Tristan* had appeared as early as 1785 and was followed by several editions in the 1800s. The German *Lanzelet* appeared in 1845, and Albert Schulz published in German selections from the Red Book of Hergest (1842), several Merlin romances and fragments (*Die Sagen von Merlin*, 1853), and Geoffrey of Monmouth (1854). Notable also were Bartsch's edition of Wolfram (1875–77) and Kolbing's edition of the Scandinavian *Tristrams Saga ok Ísöndar* (1878). The persistence and thoroughness of nineteenth-century German editors are suggested if perhaps exaggerated by Furnivall in a statement of the aims of the newly formed EETS in 1864. He is quoted by H.B. Wheatley as saying that none of the Society's early participants should rest "till Englishmen shall be able to say of their early literature what the Germans can now say with pride of theirs—'every word of it is printed, and every word of it is glossed.'"

Most of the texts here mentioned were published out of manuscript or early printed editions for the first time in the nineteenth century, and scholarship owes a debt to the energetic and dedicated editors of the period. However, some of the work was undertaken in haste, with more enthusiasm than care, in a time when linguistic studies were not far advanced. In addition, many early nineteenth-century editions were out of print and again difficult of access by the mid-twentieth century. Consequently, almost every major Arthurian work here mentioned has been edited anew, as a number of fine scholarly editions have appeared during the last thirty or so years. These new editions have in turn stimulated fresh examinations and assessments of the works themselves. And the discovery of new material, through rare now, does occur. Obvious examples are Malory's Winchester manuscript, discovered in 1934, and a second manuscript of the *Suite du Merlin* found in 1945. Fragments of romances have been found quite recently—as separate leaves or as incorporations into other works; findings of this sort have been reported, for example, by Fanni Bogdanow (*Bulletin Bibliographique*, 1976) and Ceridwen Lloyd Morgan (*Bulletin Bibliographique*, 1979).

3) GRAIL STUDIES. The Holy Grail has fascinated generations of scholars. However, considerations of the origins of this vessel are enmeshed in a complex of related problems. The study of Celtic origins has brought to light Irish and Welsh analogues but also numerous theories about the transmission of Celtic material to French romance. Attempts to trace the origin of Grail

stories have led to necessary study of the chronology and relationships of the works of Robert de Boron, Chrétien and his continuators, and Wolfram, as well as the Vulgate Cycle, the Welsh *Peredur*, the *Perlesvaus*, and the Post-Vulgate *Roman du Graal*. The study of these relationships has in turn produced conflicting opinions on the nature and process of romance composition, opinions that affect dating and that are used to support or attack various theories about whether the Grail's entry into Arthurian romance better represented a Celtic survival or a Christian impulse.

In the nineteenth century, the debate over the origin of the Grail in Christian or Celtic sources was complicated by two factors: the chronology of existing romances was faulty, and the authenticity of Celtic material, especially the Welsh, was held in question.

Sir Frederic Madden's contribution to Arthurian studies was considerable, but his remarks about chronology, like those of his distinguished French colleague Paulin Paris, contained inaccuracies that would be uncritically repeated for decades. Chief among these was the notion that French prose romances preceded metrical ones, that Chrétien's works, for example, appeared to have been drawn from the prose romances. Madden dated Chrétien's works closely enough (1170–95), but because he and other scholars believed the Vulgate Cycle to have been composed mainly by Robert de Boron and Walter Map—because of numerous manuscript attributions to these authors—they necessarily dated these romances too early, to the reign of Henry II (d. 1189), at whose court Map was known to have served. These problems along with the question of a Latin original, sometimes also attributed to Map, for the *Estoire del Saint Graal* made it difficult for such early researchers at Madden, Paris, de la Rue, Michel, and Bergmann to come to a clear understanding of the Grail's first entry into Arthurian romance (now generally accepted as having occurred in Chrétien's *Perceval*) and its subsequent development therein. By 1883, however, with the publication of Gaston Paris's "Le Conte de la Charrette" (*Romania*, Vol. 12), the notion that prose romances had provided Chrétien's sources was put to rest, as Paris showed that Chrétien's poem was undoubtedly the direct source of the corresponding episodes in the Prose *Lancelot*.

The authenticity of early Welsh material, especially that pertaining to Arthur, had been defended by Sharon Turner as early as 1803, and much early material was made available in the *Myvyrian Archaiology of Wales* (1801–07), edited by Owen Jones, Edward Williams, and William Owen Pughe. Pughe's *Cambrian Biography* (1805) made additional Welsh material readily available, as did the later publication of the *Mabinogion*. But beginning with Pughe, there developed a tendency to see the Celtic material as the repository (in somewhat altered form) of esoteric ancient doctrines and rituals and to view it as useful primarily for elucidating these doctrines and religious practices. The work of Edward Davies (1804 and 1809) on Druidical lore in the Welsh material extended this attitude with unsubstantiated claims and was exceeded by the bizarre theories about pagan Druidism of the Arthurian period put forth by Algernon Herbert (*Britannia After the Romans*, 1836, 1841); Herbert also declared that the "Alcoran of Arthurian Romance" was the "Book of the Saint Greal," which he said was later translated into Latin perhaps by Map and then into French, but had been composed in Welsh in the year 717. These excesses in England led to an opposite extreme in the debunking work of D.W. Nash. In *Taliesin* (1858), and in related essays published or cited by Furnivall in the introductory matter of his Arthurian editions of the 1860s, Nash insisted that surviving Welsh materials could not be dated before the twelfth and thirteenth centuries and implied that therefore the material in them could be no older. He found much influence from Geoffrey and from later romances and said that there was nothing in the "genuine remains of Irish or Welsh 'story' which can be taken as the germ of the [Grail] legend." Matthew Arnold's lectures "On the Study of Celtic Literature" (1865–66, published 1867) restored some balance and no doubt some respectability to the study of Celtic literature partly through his suggestions that Nash's work of demolishment, though useful, had gone too far, that the nature of the Celtic genius as expressed in its literature lay in the evocation of "an older, pagan, mythological world." This older world and its survival in folktale and romance would be most fruitfully explored by Alfred Nutt in his *Studies on the Legend of the Holy Grail* (1888), a landmark in Grail studies.

While finding it neither "necessary, or even advisable" to incorporate what the *Encyclopædia Britannica* (1878) and "some other English 'authorities' say about the Grail legends," Nutt included a "Sketch of the Literature Connected with the Grail Cycle" that surveyed the contributions, theories, and Grail-romance editions of a number of continental scholars and a few English ones. The reader is directed to this chapter for an admirable summary of the views of such scholars as la Villemarqué (who early argued for the Celtic origin of the Grail legend), Albert Schulz (Christian), Simrock, Rochat, Paulin Paris, Potvin, Hucher, Zarncke, Birch-Hirschfeld (at length), E. Martin, and W. Hertz. Nutt disagreed with Birch-Hirschfeld's conclusion (*Die Sage vom Gral*, 1877) that the Grail was Christian in origin but considered his work "at present the only basis for sound criticism." In other related areas, Birch-Hirschfeld had been among the first to question Walter Map's supposed authorship of the *Queste*, thus helping to clear the way for more accurate chronology, and also expressed the then-unpopular view that Wolfram's only major source for *Parzival* was Chrétien and that the Provençal "Kyot" was an invention of Wolfram's to justify his departures from Chrétien's version of the Grail story.

Nutt's hypothesis was that the story surrounding the Grail had its origin in Celtic myth and in stories of the Great Fool type. The Grail itself, he believed, was in its earliest form the Celtic cauldron of knowledge and regeneration, and the visit to the Grail castle was originally a visit to the Celtic otherworld. However, Nutt agreed that once the vessel became connected to Joseph and thus to Christ, it became in subsequent romances a Christian symbol, although he noted that these later romances retained many of the archaic features that mark them as Celtic in ultimate origin.

Besides this hypothesis, Nutt's most important specific contributions were three: he emphasized the importance of little-utilized Irish analogues; he identified much of the confused material of the various romances as originating in two formulas, a feud quest and an unspelling quest; and he insisted that the incidents found in the Grail romances were "not variants of one, and that an orderly and logical original."

This single-source theory, which Nutt wished to dispel, had grown out of nineteenth-century theories about the process by which the romances had been composed, theories that lasted into the twentieth century and accounted in part for the postulation of so many "lost sources." The idea was that many shorter works, such as Chrétien's poems, as well as longer works, such as the *Suite du Merlin*, that seemed to consist of fragments of narrative clumsily stitched together, represented in degenerated form pieces of earlier, more complete, and more coherent romances. Ferdinand Lot had introduced the term *entrelacement* in his study of the Prose *Lancelot* (1918) to explain the process by which later romances were composed of intertwining segments, and Eugène Vinaver's work developed this theory to undermine the long-held notion that behind virtually every romance was a more perfect version (see *The Rise of Romance*, 1970, as well as Fanni Bogdanow's summary of work in this area, her introduction to the *Romance of the Grail*, 1966). But Nutt's assertion that there never existed "a Grail legend, a definite fixed sequence of incidents," of which Chrétien and others had produced more or less corrupt versions, did much to clear the way for the work of later proponents of the Celtic origin of the Grail. No longer looking for whole originals, John Rhys, A.C.L. Brown, Laura Paton, Helaine Newstead, and R.S. Loomis found numerous analogues from Celtic myth to explain incidents and objects of the Grail legend and other Arthurian romances.

Meanwhile, the theory of Christian origin had found many champions in the nineteenth century. Some nineteenth-century editors and authors (Furnivall, Henry Morley, and Ernest Rhys are examples) made much of the way in which the quest of the Holy Grail added a high spiritual quality to the stories of Arthur and his knights, perhaps to provide an antidote to their uneasiness about the immoralities that occurred elsewhere in, for instance, Malory's *Morte Darthur*. This concept of the elevating spiritual role of the Grail accounted in part for a reluctance to see in its origins barbaric crudities, such as witches' cauldrons and bleeding heads on platters. Robert's *Joseph d'Arimathie* and the Vulgate *Estoire del Saint Graal* were more acceptable as providing the original background for later developments. But more serious scholars continued to support the Christian-origin theory on the grounds of problems with the transmission (and transformation) of the Celtic elements and the absence of a coherent Celtic original. These latter were among the objections raised by J.D. Bruce in his summary of three theories of origin (*Evolution of Arthurian Romance*, 1928). Bruce, then, favored a Christian origin over Celtic. Other notable scholars who minimized the Celtic content of Grail and other Arthurian romances include Wendelin Foerster, Joseph Bédier, Edmond Faral, and Albert Pauphilet. Pauphilet, for example, recognized the ultimately Celtic *origin* of the material but was more concerned with the spirit of Cistercian piety that pervaded the Vulgate *Queste* (*Études sur la Queste del Saint Graal*, 1921).

Bruce also discussed a third theory, which, although it had been suggested by Simrock as early as 1842, had been fully launched, perhaps with the influence of Frazer's *Golden Bough*, in the decades following Nutt's work. This was the ritual theory—that the concept of the Grail, the elements in the Grail procession, and the Maimed King sprang from the (consciously or unconsciously preserved) rituals of vegetation cults like those dedicated to the worship of Osiris or Adonis. Two major proponents of this theory were W. A. Nitze and Jessie L. Weston, and although the intelligence and lucidity of Weston's presentations have been regarded with respect, the ritual theory has failed to find favor except insofar as vegetation myth is seen to form some of the background of the Celtic material.

Bruce's work is invaluable as a survey of earlier scholarship, but to assess what aspects of his own work and the work he discusses have held up and what have been superseded by later findings, one must turn to *Arthurian Literature in the Middle Ages*. Here, essays by Roger Sherman Loomis support the Celtic origins of the Grail stories, and essays by other scholars—Kenneth Hurlstone Jackson, I.L. Foster, Rachel Bromwich, Helaine Newstead, and Jean Frappier, for example—establish and show the use of Celtic sources by later romancers. (Frappier, while he acknowledged Celtic sources for Chrétien's Grail romance, emphasized that Chrétien's handling of his sources was individual and deliberate.) In several other books and articles, Loomis developed and supported his view of the Celtic origins of the Grail and other Arthurian stories. Loomis's work has seemed to establish beyond question that Chrétien's *Perceval*, and much of the Grail material of later romances, grew out of Irish saga, passed on to the Welsh, and combined with other narratives that were transmitted orally to the French and Anglo-Normans, at which time the platter or cauldron acquired Christian attributes that were rapidly extended to other elements of the story.

These findings have not been challenged in the main in more recent years, although questions of the precise form and manner in which the Celtic "Grail" material reached Chrétien and others have been raised. The theory of oral transmission from Wales through the Bretons and thus to the French had been suggested by Sharon Turner in 1799 and supported by George Ellis in 1805, although it is more often associated today with Heinrich Zimmer's studies of the 1890s. D.D.R. Owen's *The Evolution of the Grail Legend* (1968) explores five possible avenues of transmission, favoring the route "from the Welsh to the Bretons and thence to the Anglo-Normans." Owen has also postulated, as background to Chrétien's *Perceval* and some later romances, the development of a story of the Fair Unknown type with elements drawn from other Celtic sources, a story necessarily altered in particular thematic aspects for an Anglo-Norman audience and thus passed to Chrétien.

Not all scholars have accepted without question the comparative literary methods used to establish sources for Chrétien's works. One recent attack has come from Claude Luttrell in *The Creation of the First Arthurian Romance* (1974). Luttrell challenges Celtic analogues to *Perceval* suggested by Loomis and criticizes Owen's hypothetical source story for that romance, contending that "originals have been assumed which are in fact ghosts conjured up from Chrétien's works." Tony Hunt, pointing out some strengths and weaknesses of this book's argument (*Bulletin Bibliographique*, 1978), notes that Luttrell "has compelled Chrétien scholars to re-examine their assumptions." But perhaps more typical of post-Loomis work is a recent report of research in progress by Jean-Claude Lozachmeur and Shigemi Sasaki (*Bulletin Bibliographique*, 1982), which draws on Loomis's views of the origin and development of the Grail story—with a few modifications—to develop a theory of the two archetypes (Vengeance and Magic; cf. Nutt above), adding the probable derivation of the latter from the former to explain some of the obscurities of Chrétien's Grail story and other Grail romances.

This is not to say that other theories of the Grail's origin have not been proposed, nor that its meaning in Chrétien or Wolfram has not been explored. Noting the problems that have arisen from confusion of *Perceval*'s sources with its actual twelfth-century meaning, Urban T. Holmes and M. Amelia Klenke argued in *Chrétien, Troyes, and the Grail* (1959) that Chrétien, perhaps a converted Jew, intended his *Perceval* to represent the possible great good that would come from the conversion of the Jews to Christianity. In this Judeo-Christian interpretation, the Grail castle symbolizes the Temple of Solomon in Jerusalem, and the objects of the Grail procession are drawn from medieval iconography of the Church Triumphant as presented in the Synagoga (old-law)/Ecclesia (new-law) motif in medieval art.

Henry and Renee Kahane in collaboration with Angelina Pietrangeli proposed another origin of the Grail material in *The Krater and the Grail: Hermetic Sources of the Parzival* (1965). According to this theory, the word *grail* derives from the Greco-Latin *crater* and is related to the Krater of Hermetism, a sort of gnostic, non-Christian philosophy that arose probably in the second or third century A.D. Several Hermetic treatises were preserved in the *corpus hermeticum*, and from them, in this view, "Kyot," Wolfram, and possibly Chrétien culled various myths and motifs to make a kind of *Urparzival*. Another fascinating theory of the origin of the Grail has been presented in articles by C. Scott Littleton and Ann C. Thomas (*Journal of American Folklore*, 1978, 1979). "The Sarmatian Connection" notes the existence of a magical cup, the Amonga, with qualities like those of the Grail, in the epic traditions of the Sarmatians, warrior tribes of the Caucasus. The cup never runs dry and can be possessed only by those free of fault or demonstrating great courage. According to these reports, some 5,000 Sarmatian auxiliaries, posted to Britain in the second century to serve under Lucius Artorius Castus, established there a colony whose traditions featured mounted warriors, a dragon banner, and the stories of the cup and also of a mortally wounded king brought to the shore of a sea into which he bids his companions throw his sword; they hide the sword and lie, he tells them to go again, and when the sword is thrown in, the sea turns blood-colored and turbulent.

4) THE HISTORICAL ARTHUR. In his introduction to an edition of Malory's *Morte Darthur* (1868), Edward Strachey said that "most recent critics are disposed to prefer Gibbon's belief to Milton's skepticism as to the actual existence of Arthur," and the same may be said of present-day critics. In his *History of Britain*, Milton had said Arthur's existence has been doubted heretofore, "and may again with good reason." Gibbon based his "belief" on Nennius's account of Arthur's twelve battles, although he added, without naming a source, that "the declining age of the hero was imbittered by popular ingratitude and domestic misfortunes." He traced additions to the legend made by Geoffrey and others through the long prose romances and said that, through an unjust reversal of public opinion toward these obvious exercises in imagination, his own age questioned the very existence of Arthur.

Writing some twenty years after Gibbon's first edition, Sharon Turner took a similar approach, saying that to deny Arthur's actual existence simply because of later embellishments is an objectionable extreme. Unlike Gibbon, Turner was familiar with much early Welsh material and used it in his account: ". . . this victory [Badon] only checked the progress of Cerdic and does not appear to have produced any further success. . . . Arthur was, therefore, not the warrior of irresistible strength. . . . This state of moderate greatness suits the character, in which the Welsh bards exhibit Arthur. They commemorate him; but it is not with that excelling glory, with which he has been surrounded by subsequent tradition" (*History of the Anglo-Saxons*).

Although he had apparently read the Welsh materials about Arthur that Turner had used, Joseph Ritson distrusted their authenticity and believed Geoffrey of Monmouth's work to have influenced some of the Welsh accounts of Arthur. As displayed in *The Life of King Arthur* (1825), published twenty-two years after Ritson's death, his knowledge of the early Arthurian material is impressive, as is his rigorous skepticism about much of it. He called Gildas "querulous," recognized the ambiguities in Gildas's "forty-four years" passage (which could provide either of two dates for the battle of Badon Hill), derided Geoffrey's "miraculous history," and claimed that the monks of Glastonbury "filled their monastery with forgery and falsehood." But he acknowledged that the Britons had popular stories about Arthur before Geoffrey, such as the tradition that Arthur did not die. Exactly what Ritson believed to be true and authentic about Arthur is harder to determine from this book, but in the preface to *Ancient Romanceës* (1803) he had declared it "manifest from authentick history" that Arthur was a brave warrior and probably a petty king.

British historians of the following decades offered even more cautious views about Arthur's existence, and the distrust of Celtic material posed problems here as in Grail studies. Sir Francis Palgrave found British history before the introduction of Christianity to the Anglo-Saxons to be derived from "the most obscure and unsatisfactory evidence." Noting the tradition that

Gildas is supposed to have thrown the real history of Arthur into the sea, Palgrave adds that "the same misfortune appears to have fallen on all the British annals of the next three centuries" (*Rise and Progress of the English Commonwealth*, 1832). In *History of the Anglo-Saxons* (1831), although he mentions such figures as Ambrosius Aurelianus and Vortigern, Hengist and Horsa, with some skepticism, Palgrave moves through an account of the English conquest without mentioning the name Arthur.

A popular *History of the Anglo-Saxons* by the poet and novelist Thomas Miller (1848) went through five editions; Miller, acknowledging Sharon Turner as his guide, found no record of Arthur's deeds besides the "slight mention" in Gildas and Nennius and what tradition has preserved in the "lays of Welsh bards." His account of Arthur's battles does not lend an air of clear authenticity: "His twelve battles have a glorious indistinctness,—they sink behind the other in the sunset. . . ."

Some eighty years later, in a work first published in 1926, G.M. Trevelyan was still cautious. He mentions a "half mythical King Arthur" leading Celts against the heathen, but notes the lack of "authentic chronicles of the Saxon Conquest. . . . The most important page in our national annals is a blank. The chief names of this missing period of history—Hengist, Vortigern, Cerdic, Arthur—may be those of real or of imaginary men" (*History of England*). However, R.G. Collingwood, in *Roman Britain* (1924, rev. ed. 1932) and in *Roman Britain and the English Settlements* (1936), was more positive in postulating the existence of a Romanized Celt named Artorius, whose "mobile field army" harried the Saxons in various parts of Britain, or that at the very least the "legend" stood for a "fact"—that "isolated and crippled as she was, Britain preserved for a time her Roman character and went down fighting."

In the meantime, the nature of the written record was being examined anew. R.H. Fletcher's *Arthurian Material in the Chronicles* (1906) provided a detailed chronological discussion of Arthurian material from Gildas through fifteenth- and sixteenth-century chronicles. Fletcher allowed that Nennius's account suggested the existence of a "bold warrior and an energetic general" who "sustained the falling fortunes of his country" but advised caution, given the possibility that even Nennius's "modest eulogy" was based not on fact but on "the persistent stories of ancient Celtic myth or the patriotic figments of the ardent Celtic imagination." E.K. Chambers's *Arthur of Britain* first appeared in 1927 and is still useful as the source of early Latin texts concerning Arthur. Newer editions of Geoffrey and the Welsh Triads and poems especially have made some of Chambers's comments outdated, but his presentation of the evidence is careful, and the 1964 reissue contains a valuable supplementary bibliography by Brynley F. Roberts.

This added material points out later studies in several areas covered by both Fletcher and Chambers. J.S.P. Tatlock's *Legendary History of Britain* (1950), for example, was openly skeptical about the historic value of most Welsh material and saints' lives; Tatlock, sounding at times like a latter-day Ritson, believed *Culhwch and Olwen*'s presentation of Arthur to have been influenced by Geoffrey of Monmouth's work, and he stated that the "earliest indication that Arthur was known to either tradition or history" is in the composite work attributed to Nennius. However, more recent publications have taken a different view. Particular attention should be called to essays by Jackson, A.O.H. Jarman, Foster, and Bromwich in *Arthurian Literature in the Middle Ages*. These essays and other more recent works have argued for the authenticity of early Arthurian Welsh material and made more probable the existence of a person named Arthur. Jackson answered the question "Did Arthur exist?" by saying, "The only honest answer is, 'We do not know, but he may well have existed.' The nature of the evidence is such that proof is impossible." Jackson found no evidence of historic value in Nennius's *Mirabilia*, in Welsh saints' lives, or in Geoffrey, but he did give an ingenious explanation of Gildas's failure to mention Arthur by name. He cited lines about Arthur from the early Welsh *Gododdin* but noted the possibility of interpolation. Jackson cited as evidence for a real Arthur the fact that several persons in Celtic Britain were named Arthur in the late sixth and early seventh centuries. In addition, he discussed possible sites for some of the battles named by Nennius; he concurred in the suggestion first made by H.M. Chadwick and Nora K. Chadwick (*The Growth of Literature*, 1932) that Nennius's list of twelve Arthurian battles had its origin in an early Welsh battle-listing poem. Rachel Bromwich, among others, has further suggested that Nennius's list contained battles not originally Arthur's at all.

Discussion of these battle sites is often linked with questions of Arthur's original sphere of activity, northern or southern Britain. J.S. Stuart Glennie, in an essay attached to the EETS Prose *Merlin* (1869), had argued at length that Arthur was originally a hero of the north—that is, of southern Scotland and the Border Country. W.F. Skene and D.W. Nash also leaned toward northern claims over southern ones. More recently, Bromwich (*Studia Celtica*, 1975–76, and elsewhere) has put forth cogent arguments supporting the view that "the earliest traditions of Arthur belonged to the *corpus* of north British material which was preserved and developed in Strathclyde and from there transmitted to North Wales" during the ninth century or earlier. Nora Chadwick, too, calling the evidence for a historical Arthur "highly unsatisfactory," referred to a "growing body of opinion" that views early traditions about Arthur as the model of a hero-warrior as originating in north Britain (*Celtic Britain*, 1963).

However, Jackson, in the essay in *Arthurian Literature in the Middle Ages*, and probably a majority of nineteenth- and twentieth-century explorers of this topic, have supported a southern locale—Somerset, Cornwall, or Wales—as Arthur's probable center of activity. When *ALMA* appeared in 1959, efforts that would lead to the excavation of South Cadbury hill were just getting underway. As Edward Strachey, among others, had pointed out in the nineteenth century, the hill had been identified as Camelot by John Leland, the Tudor antiquary, in 1542, and the nearby River Cam provides one of the conjectural sites for the battle of Camlann. Archaeological work at Cadbury in the 1960s revealed, among several layers showing some 4,000 years of periodic occupation of the site, evidence of British refortification on a large scale around the year 500. Details of the excavation and similar work from such sites as Glastonbury and Castle Dore are attractively illustrated in *The Quest for Arthur's Britain* (1968). In this book, Geoffrey Ashe and Leslie Alcock conclude that the British rampart of around 500 was built "to defend the home or headquarters of a great British chieftain." His name cannot be established, but the evidence points to the real existence of a military leader, in a place traditionally associated with Arthur, in the right period, "a person big enough for the legends to have gathered round him." *Arthur's Britain* (1971), by Alcock, is a detailed historical and archaeological study of the period 367–634. Alcock reviews and evaluates many of the problems of dating associated with Nennius, the Easter annals, Gildas, and the *Anglo-Saxon Chronicle*, provides a historical background to the period, and discusses archaeological findings to conclude that there is "acceptable historical evidence that Arthur was a genuine historical figure," who led Celts against the English during the late fifth and early sixth centuries, achieving a major victory at Mount Badon in about 490; Alcock points out, though, that this victory did not materially affect the character of the English settlement of Britain. If this sounds as though nothing much has changed since Sharon Turner made similar statements, the difference lies in the fact that the Latin and Welsh Arthurian material has been studied and tested in ways not available to early historians, and archaeology has provided evidence unknown to them so that the existence of a historical Arthur seems today less a matter of belief or faith than of nearly substantiated fact.

Even Geoffrey of Monmouth's spurious historicity is being, in part, rehabilitated. Recent studies by Geoffrey Ashe and others suggest that there may have been a germ of historical truth in Geoffrey's account of Arthur's continental victories. Chambers had published an extract from the Latin "Life" of the Breton St. Goueznou (Goeznovius), possibly written in 1019, which speaks of Arthur as having won many victories in Gaul as well as in Britain. Ashe (*Speculum*, Vol. 56, 1981) has recalled attention to this passage and suggested a link and a source for Geoffrey's account of Arthur on the Continent in the fifth-century Riothamus, who took a British army to Gaul. [MJP]

SCOTICHRONICON: *see* SCOTTISH ARTHURIAN CHRONICLES.

SCOTORUM HISTORIAE: *see* SCOTTISH ARTHURIAN CHRONICLES.

SCOTT, SIR WALTER (1771–1832), wrote only one work of Arthurian inspiration, the verse tale *The Bridal of Triermain*. This is surprising, for his edition of *Sir Tristrem*, first published in 1804, was well received, and he revealed an interest in Malory in the introduction and notes to *Marmion* (1808). Composed during the period of his major successes in verse narrative, just after *Rokeby* and immediately before *The Lord of the Isles*, *The Bridal of Triermain* is a curious work, one that Scott himself did not take with complete seriousness. He was secretive about writing it and had it published anonymously, taking an unholy delight when the critics were uncertain how to judge it.

"Lyulph's Tale," the Arthurian episode of *The Bridal of Triermain*, is one of two romances that Arthur, a nineteenth-century young gentleman, relates to his beloved, Lucy; the other is an account of the twelfth-century Roland de Vaux's search for a Sleeping Beauty. For "Lyulph's Tale," Scott invents a traditional Arthurian story, adding some irreverence and a spice of satire. Arthur comes to a magic castle where he falls in love with Guendolen. After tarrying for three months, he feels obliged to return to Camelot, but he promises that, should a daughter be born and later come to court, she should marry the knight who proves most valiant in a tourney. A decade and a half later, Gyneth presents herself, and Arthur must fulfil his vow. Her charms are so great that the knights are enthralled, and the tourney becomes a bloodbath. The fighting is stopped only when Merlin imposes peace after a young man is slain, and the magician sentences Gyneth to a centuries-long slumber. She is not awakened until Sir Roland de Vaux discovers her. This amalgam of Arthurian romance and a Sleeping Beauty tale formed the basis of two stage works, J.L. Ellerton's operetta *The Bridal of Triermain* (1831) and Isaac Pocock's "chivalric entertainment" *King Arthur and the Knights of the Round Table* (1834). [CNS]

Scott, Sir Walter. "The Bridal of Triermain." In *Poetical Works*. London: Longman, 1813.
Johnson, Edgar. *Sir Walter Scott*. 2 vols. London: Hamilton, 1973.

SCOTTISH ARTHURIAN CHRONICLES. References to Arthur in Scottish Arthurian chronicles can be positive or negative; and it is easy to account for the chroniclers' reactions by considering both the ultimate source of their information, Geoffrey of Monmouth's *Historia Regum Britanniae*, and the feelings of Scottish nationalism that developed in the late Middle Ages and that found expression in the chronicles. In Geoffrey of Monmouth, the Picts and the Scots are Arthur's enemies; Arthur conquers Scotland; and Arthur's kingdom is eventually destroyed by the traitorous Scot Mordred. Yet Geoffrey's account is not completely biased against the Scots, for Arthur has in it some important Scottish allies: Loth of Lodensia, Gawain, and King Auguselus.

As one might expect, when the Scots began to write their own chronicles, their reactions to this material were mixed, and by the late fifteenth and sixteenth centuries the use of it, by some chroniclers at least, was colored by feelings of nationalism and by their antagonism toward the English, who had accepted the British Arthurian history as a part of their own nation's past glory. Some, like Barbour, Andrew of Wyntoun, and Blind Harry, accept Arthur's reputation uncritically and refer to him with admiration as a great

British king; their allusions to him, however, are brief, and they make little effort to tell much of the Arthurian story. Others accept the fact that Arthur was a great king, but they are also skeptical or critical. John Leslie, for example, in his brief account of Arthur, doubts the stories of Arthur's foreign conquests. John of Fordun and John Major give more detailed accounts than any of the above; and although they admire Arthur they point out that he was illegitimate and that the true heirs to the throne were Mordred and Gawain, who were passed over because they were too young. This view that Scots, not Arthur, should have ruled Britain, popularized by John of Fordun's fourteenth-century chronicle, became the basis for bitter attacks on Arthur in the fifteenth-century *Chronicle of Scotland in a Part* and in the sixteenth-century chronicles of Boece, Bellenden, Stewart, and Buchanan.

John Barbour (ca. 1316–1396), archdeacon of Aberdeen, wrote the *Bruce*, the great epic-chronicle of medieval Scotland. Although Barbour appealed to the patriotism of the Scots, unlike some later Scottish writers he admires Arthur and refers to him as a valorous king who was slain treacherously by Mordred, his sister's son; the Arthurian story, like those of Troy, Alexander, and Julius Caesar, is for Barbour an exemplum about treason.

John of Fordun, one of the most influential medieval Scottish chroniclers, wrote the Latin *Chronica Gentis Scotorum* (ca. 1385), sometimes called the *Scotichronicon*, a title more properly applied to Walter Bower's popular continuation of the work (1447). Apparently attempting to do for Scottish history what Geoffrey of Monmouth had done for British, John drew upon earlier short chronicles and legends that gave the Scots a distinguished past and that offered evidence that Scotland was historically independent of England. Although he presents Arthur as an admirable king ("beloved by almost all men"), the author asserts that the British throne was not lawfully his because he was conceived out of wedlock. The true heirs were Gawain and Mordred, the sons of Arthur's sister Anna and the Scottish consul Lot. Arthur became king by necessity because of the threat from the Saxons and the youth of Gawain and Mordred. Mordred later rebelled because of Arthur's weak claim to the throne. John of Fordun's treatment of Arthur was the basis for the more hostile presentations in the later chronicles of Boece, Stewart, and Bellenden.

Andrew of Wyntoun's *Original Chronicle of Scotland* (ca. 1420), a Scottish vernacular chronicle in verse, begins with the Creation, emphasizes general world history in Books I–V, and focuses on Scottish and British history in Books VI–IX. The account of Arthur is a brief summary of the war against Lucius (Book V, Chapter 13.). Unlike some Scottish chroniclers, Andrew speaks favorably of Arthur, who was slain by "Mordred the traitor." He says that his source for the Arthurian story was the "Gestis Historiall" of "Huchone of the Auld Ryall."

The *Chronicle of Scotland in a Part* (*The Scottis Originale*) is an anonymous short chronicle in Middle Scots (ca. 1460) that presents Arthur as a tyrant, a "huris sone" who was made king by the "devilry of Merlin," while the true heirs, Mordred and Gawain, were passed over because they were Scottish; therefore,

Mordred, "in his rychtwyse querele," slew Arthur. It is an extreme development of the version of the Arthurian story presented by John of Fordun.

Blind Harry wrote the *Wallace* (ca. 1476–78), the Scottish verse epic-chronicle in twelve books inspired by Barbour's *Bruce*, as a thinly veiled attack on the pro-English policies of James III. Harry, once thought to have been an uneducated blind minstrel, was apparently a literate writer who drew upon written sources. Although the work is biased against the English, Harry admired the "gud king Arthour," compares his hero, Wallace, to him, and, in a passage echoing Barbour's Arthurian allusion, says that Arthur, like Ector, Alexander, and Julius Caesar, was destroyed through cowardice.

John Major (b. 1469/70) was a Scottish historian, influenced by French humanism, who wrote the *Historia Majoris Britanniae* (1521). He bases his Arthurian account upon Geoffrey of Monmouth and John of Fordun. Major presents John's story that Arthur was illegitimate and that the true heirs to the throne were Gawain and Mordred, the sons of Loth and Anna, who here is the sister of Aurelius (not Arthur). But they were too young and Arthur was chosen king. Major expresses genuine admiration for Arthur, noting that he was noble, handsome, and chivalrous; that he conquered many foreign lands; and that he was one of the Nine Worthies. He is skeptical about magic elements in the Arthurian story and doubts that Arthur will return, although he mentions that, when Arthur was buried at Glastonbury, people sang, "Hic jacet Arthurus Rex magnus Rex futurus."

Hector Boece, first principal of the University of Aberdeen, wrote the influential Latin chronicle *Scotorum Historiae* (1527), later translated into Middle Scots prose by John Bellenden (1531) and Middle Scots verse by William Stewart (1535). Boece's story of Arthur diverges markedly from earlier accounts and carries to an extreme the sentiments against Arthur that were implicit in John of Fordun's chronicle. From John, it incorporates Arthur's illegitimacy and weak claim to the throne but adds several new elements: Arthur's conquests are limited to Britain; Arthur recognizes Mordred as his successor but is persuaded to break the treaty, thus causing hostilities to be renewed; Guenevere is taken prisoner and held by the Picts for the rest of her life. J.B. Black describes the chronicle as a "wild welter that recalls the grotesque pages of Geoffrey of Monmouth."

John Bellenden, at the request of James V of Scotland, translated Boece's *Scotorum Historiae* into Middle Scots prose in 1531. He shortened the Arthurian section somewhat but maintained Boece's bias against Arthur. He noted that Gawain fought on Arthur's side "against his native people."

Also at the request of James V, William Stewart translated Boece's history into 61,000 lines of Scottish verse in 1535. He adds considerably to Boece's Arthurian account, calling Arthur the most unfortunate of all British kings, one punished by God for being "faithless and untrue" to King Mordred.

John Leslie published his *De Origine, Moribus, et Rebus Gentis Scotorum* at Rome in 1578; it was translated into Scottish in 1596 by Father James Dalrymple. Like Boece, Bellenden, and Stewart, he limits Arthur's conquests to Britain, but he praises Arthur as noble, courageous, and honorable. He mentions Arthur's Round Table, which Leslie himself had seen, and notes that Arthur had twenty-four knights.

Although considered a Scottish humanist, George Buchanan followed Hector Boece fairly closely in the account of Arthur that he presented in his *Rerum Scoticarum Historia* (1582); changes from the source tend to make Arthur's character worse than it is in Boece. He also finds the account of Arthur's conception a fiction invented by Merlin and Uther to lessen Igerne's shame, and he has Guenevere help Mordred plan Arthur's downfall. [EDK]

&. Andrew of Wyntoun. *The Original Chronicle of Andrew of Wyntoun*, ed. F.J. Amours. 6 vols. Edinburgh: Blackwood, 1903–14.

Barbour, John. *Barbour's Bruce*, ed. M.P. McDiarmid and J.A.C. Stevenson. 2 vols. Edinburgh: Blackwood, 1980, 1981.

Bellenden, John, trans. *The Chronicle of Scotland Compiled by Hector Boece*, ed. R.W. Chambers, E.C. Batho, and H.W. Husbands. 2 vols. Edinburgh: Blackwood, 1938, 1941.

Blind Harry. *Harry's Wallace*, ed. M.P. McDiarmid. 2 vols. Edinburgh: Blackwood, 1968–69.

Boece, Hector. *Scotorum Historiae*. Paris: Ascensius, 1527.

Buchanan, George. *Rerum Scoticarum Historia*. Edinburgh: Arbuthnet, 1582.

——— . *The History of Scotland*, trans. John Watkins. London: Fisher, Jackson, 1827.

Scott, W., D. Laing, and T. Thomson, eds. "The Chronicle of Scotland in a Part." *Bannatyne Miscellany*. Edinburgh: Bannatyne Club, 1855.

"The Scottis Originale." In *The Asloan Manuscript*, ed. William A. Craigie. Edinburgh: Blackwood, 1923, pp. 185–96.

Johannis de Fordun. *Chronica Gentis Scotorum*, ed. W.F. Skene. Edinburgh: Edmonston and Douglas, 1871.

——— . *John of Fordun's Chronicle of the Scottish Nation*, trans. F.J.H. Skene, ed. W.F. Skene. Edinburgh: Edmonston and Douglas, 1872.

Leslie, John. *Historie of Scotland*, trans. James Dalrymple, ed. E.G. Cody and William Murison. 2 vols. Edinburgh: Blackwood, 1888, 1895.

Major, John. *Historia Majoris Britanniae tam Angliae quam Scotiae*. Paris: Ascensius, 1521.

——— . *A History of Greater Britain as Well England as Scotland*, trans. A. Constable. Edinburgh: University of Edinburgh Press, 1892.

Stewart, William, trans. *The Buik of the Cronicles of Scotland or a Metrical Version of the History of Hector Boece*, ed. W. Turnbull. 3 vols. London: Longman, 1858.

Alexander, Flora. "Late Medieval Scottish Attitudes to the Figure of King Arthur: A Reassessment." *Anglia*, 93 (1975), 17–34.

Black, J.B. "Boece's *Scotorum Historiae*." In *University of Aberdeen: Quatercentenary of the Death of Hector Boece*. Aberdeen: University of Aberdeen Press, 1937, pp. 30–53.

Brie, Friedrich. *Die Nationale Literatur Schottlands*. Halle: Niemeyer, 1937, pp. 317–53.

Fletcher, Robert Huntington. *The Arthurian Material in the Chronicles, Especially Those of Great Britain and France*. Boston: Ginn, 1906; 2nd ed. Roger Sherman Loomis. New York: Franklin, 1966, pp. 245–48.

Göller, K.H. "König Arthur in den schottischen Chroniken." *Anglia*, 80 (1962), 390–404.

SECOND EMPIRE, FRENCH ARTHURIAN MATERIAL DURING.

During the Second Empire, the Middle Ages were the subject of perpetual controversy. Critical and creative writers in France saw in them the image of an idealized or sinister past, a detested present, or a longed-for future. For Ultramontane Catholics, the Middle Ages represented a lost paradise. Republicans, scornful of attempts on the part of Louis-Napoleon's regime to present itself as an age of chivalry revived, loathed them as a malignant presence in the land. Liberal Catholics (and some republicans) strove to dissociate certain favored enclaves in medieval literature and society from imperial contamination and set them up as an antidote to it, a source of refreshment and consolation. One such enclave was Arthurian legend and romance, popularized by T.H. de la Villemarqué (*Les Romans de la Table Ronde et les contes des anciens Bretons,* 1842; 3rd ed. 1860; *La Légende celtique en Irlande, en Cambrie, et en Bretagne,* 1859; and *Myrdhinn ou l'enchanteur Merlin,* 1862) and Paulin Paris (*Romans de la Table Ronde mis en nouveau langage,* 1868–77). Some critics denounced the Arthurian matter as immoral and expressed distaste for its un-Christian dwarfs and fairies, its cult of Woman, and its glorification of adulterous love, but republicans, such as the Celtophile Henri Martin (*Histoire de France,* 4th ed. 1858), extolled its Gallic, dissident, and "prerevolutionary" character and the "democratic" nature of the Round Table.

The essay *La Poésie des races celtiques* (1854), by the Breton intellectual historian Ernest Renan (1823–1892), had an important influence on other writers, including Matthew Arnold. Renan (a covert opponent of the Empire in his writings on the Middle Ages) praises the originality and refinement of the Celtic genius, as well as its thirst for the infinite, attachment to lost causes, and unorthodox, non-Roman spirit. When Arthurian legend spread to the Continent, these qualities brought about a profound modification in European sensibility. The mood of the essay is elegiac, a lament for the passing of a doomed world, which is set against the immorality and vulgar materialism of modern bourgeois society. The Round Table was nobly egalitarian; the central role accorded to women was a civilizing factor. Unaware that Lady Charlotte Guest's version of the *Mabinogion* was expurgated, Renan denies that the Arthurian legend in its primitive Welsh or Breton form was immoral and accuses later French imitators of it, such as Chrétien de Troyes, of coarsening and sensualizing its refined ideal of love. Renan also frowned on the re-use of this material by modern creative writers of his own day: the poetry of past ages, in his opinion, could be evoked only by critics and historians. However, Edgar Quinet (1803–1875), who was best known for his earlier poetic drama *Ahasvérus* (1833), exploited Arthurian legend in *Merlin l'Enchanteur* (1860).

This prolix utopian fantasy in two volumes, sensational in its own day as an attack, launched from exile, on the Empire, is now read mainly by Quinet specialists, who detect in it some "extraordinary moments." Influenced by Henri Martin, who had glorified Merlin as a "political prophet," Quinet identifies with his hero throughout and uses him as a mouthpiece to denounce Louis-Napoleon (who features as the pagan villain Hengist). Viviane, Quinet's second wife, furnished the second edition with explanatory notes. Merlin reconciles the nations of the world at the Round Table, the ideal federation of future republics. His servant Jacques Bonhomme, who joins a traveling circus, enticed by the bright clothes offered to him, represents the common people of France seduced by the tawdry glitter of the Empire. Political and social life under the Empire are censured through the vehicle of King Arthur's sleep (the eclipse of the Republic) and Merlin's entombment (Quinet's exile and France under imperial rule). In the end, Arthur awakens (each time he has turned over in his sleep, an enslaved nation has thrown off the shackles of oppression); Merlin emerges from his tomb; Jacques sees the error of his ways; and the nations of Europe are roused from their slumber one after the other. Tyrannical governments are overthrown everywhere, while Merlin converses with his brother Jonathan the Yankee across the ocean (by electric cable, according to Viviane Quinet's gloss). Quinet was obliged, his wife says, to "follow the guiding thread of legend," but the reader receives little inkling of this, despite the occasional surface archaism and echo of Béroul's *Tristan*.

Another, much shorter, Arthurian fantasy, *La Tour d'Ivoire* (1865), was produced by Quinet's friend and fellow opponent of the Empire, the poet Victor de Laprade (1812–1883). This insipid verse narrative tells of a knight in quest of the Grail who braves a series of temptations to find ideal Love in the shape of a noble and ethereal lady in an ivory tower awaiting him at the end of his quest. His adventures along the way in the perilous forest form a sequence of oblique allusions to the immorality and materialism of the Empire. Both *Merlin l'Enchanteur* and *La Tour d'Ivoire* were praised by critics as modern Arthurian ventures immeasurably superior to their medieval predecessors. [JRD]

Crossley, Ceri. *Edgar Quinet (1803–1875): A Study in Romantic Thought*. Lexington, Ky.: French Forum, 1983.

Dakyns, Janine R. *The Middle Ages in French Literature, 1851–1900*. Oxford: Oxford University Press, 1973.

Wardman, H.W. *Ernest Renan: A Critical Biography*. London: Athlone, 1964.

SECRET GLORY, THE: *see* MACHEN, ARTHUR.

SEINT GREAL, Y: *see* PERLESVAUS.

SENIOR, DOROTHY, author of *The Clutch of Circumstance* (1908), a sentimental historical romance inspired by Malory. Set in Arthur's day, it includes nontraditional figures like Cormac, King of Leinster. [RHT]

Senior, Dorothy. *The Clutch of Circumstance: or The Gates of Dawn*. London: Black, 1908.

SEPT SAGES DE ROME, LES, a series of seven Old French prose romances taking as its point of departure the widely diffused Indo-European legend of the Seven Sages, a combination, essentially, of the story of Potiphar's Wife with the storytelling device of Scheherazade in the *Thousand and One Nights*. The Seven Sages legend is a frame-story, into which are interpolated a series of tales and countertales told, on the one hand, by the wicked empress, condemned to death for having attempted the seduction of her princely stepson, to avert her execution, and, on the other, by each of the seven sages, preceptors of the innocent prince, to seal and hasten her doom.

One of the Old French prose versions of this legend, the *Roman des Sept Sages de Rome*, gave rise to a continuation, the *Roman de Marques de Rome*, in which a short version of the second part of the *Cligés* story of Chrétien de Troyes is incorporated as an exemplum. The influence of the works of Chrétien de Troyes and the Matter of Britain becomes particularly marked in its sequel, the *Roman de Laurin*, which unlike its two predecessors in the cycle is not a *roman à tiroir*, or frame-story with interpolated tales, but a *roman d'aventures* into which Chrétien's Matter of Britain is introduced, transforming it into a predominantly Arthurian romance. The Matter of Britain was apparently introduced into the cycle of the Seven Sages of Rome by the author of *Laurin* after he had exhausted the themes, chiefly misogynous, that he had inherited from the Seven Sages legend and from the *Marques de Rome*. That he turned to the tales of King Arthur and his knights to pad his story attests to their popularity and freshness in France a century after Chrétien de Troyes, especially in the new prose form in which we find them in the Vulgate Cycle. It points up, too, not only the change in narrative structure but also a change in spirit in the cycle, substituting an interest in chivalric action for the earlier attraction of folk wisdom, encompassed in the interpolated tales and exempla, that characterized the Seven Sages material.

The Arthurian element in the *Roman de Laurin* is explicit. The hero, Laurin, Emperor of Constantinople and son of Marques, the seneschal of Rome, decides to seek adventure at the court of Arthur. Arriving in Great Britain and traveling under the name of Alyenor, he rescues Baudemagus, knight of Arthur's Round Table, from a band of robber knights. Together, they liberate fifteen beautiful damsels whom the knights had held as concubines. En route, Laurin is rendered unconscious by the waters of a magic fountain, while Baudemagus joins a group of beautiful young damsels in a sumptuous repast around a table in a meadow. Baudemagus meets a girl on a palfrey, who alternately sings and weeps and who is maltreated by a hunchbacked knight who defeats Baudemagus in battle. After three days, Laurin awakens, meets the lady of the meadow and avenges Baudemagus's defeat, in the process liberating four more members of the Round Table: Gyglain, Orenyaus, Pinel le Roux, and Mordred.

Laurin learns from Gyglain that the famous knight Gawain, Gyglain's father, has disappeared. One day at Whitsun, when Arthur was holding court at Windsor, a white horse and a white dog visited the palace. The dog summoned Gawain from the dinner table, the knight mounted the horse, and, led by the dog, he rode away, never to be seen again.

The journey to Arthur's court is resumed, the party coming upon a mysterious castle that appears to recede as they advance. At sunset, they meet a weeping maiden on a white mule, seeking the Knight of the White Shield.

Laurin is attacked by an overwhelming force and is imprisoned. Baudemagus, Mordred, and the other knights of the Round Table meet and joust with the Knight of the White Shield, rumored to have killed Gawain. The White Knight is recognized as Gawain himself by Baudemagus, but his identity is kept secret from the others.

The knights go on to Winchester, where they are welcomed by King Arthur, Perceval, and others, and Baudemagus relates his adventures to Lancelot, Kay, and their companions. Laurin arrives in Winchester, meets such celebrities as Yvain, Erec, Perceval, and Lancelot, and wins the day in the Winchester tourney. The White Knight appears at court with a girl on a white palfrey. The damsel defies Arthur to criticize the knight's killing of Gawain and then leaves scornfully. The seneschal Kay fails to bring back the damsel and the White Knight, and Laurin is dispatched to search for them. A magical thunderstorm bursts upon him. He meets Maligne, a female knight, and subsequently Proserpyne, the damsel on the white palfrey, and her champion, the White Knight, with whom he breaks several lances, and persuades them to return with him to Arthur's court.

Back in Winchester, Laurin, as Arthur's champion, meets the White Knight in single combat and forces him to reveal himself to the assembled court as Gawain. After a celebration, the entire court moves on to Camelot to meet Queen Guinevere. She welcomes Gawain warmly but is annoyed with Lancelot for not winning the tourney at Winchester. Later, the knights of the Round Table, to whose numbers have been added Laurin and his companions, are sent by Arthur to help Marques in Aragon, where they gain a notable victory.

The *Roman de Cassidorus*, which follows the *Laurin* in the cycle of the Seven Sages, is, like the later works in the cycle, less obviously Arthurian, although much of its narrative depends heavily on the Matter of Britain. Differing totally in this respect from *Laurin*, it represents a reversion within the cycle to the frame-story type of narrative, and therefore contains not only a running narrative constituting essentially a complicated romance of chivalry but also two series of interpolated tales or exempla in which allusions to Arthurian names and places are often found: one recounts the story of a sodomite king of Logres; in another, a version of the tale of the Loathly Damsel, the maltreated maiden makes her appearance at the court of Uther at Windsor Castle. The principal Arthurian feature of *Cassidorus*, however, occurs not incidentally in the interpolated stories but as a major episode of the frame-story itself, namely in an adaptation of the Knight of the Lion story from Chrétien's *Yvain*, in which Helcana, the wife of Cassidorus, has the role of Yvain (cf. the female-knight theme in *Laurin*, above).

The Knight of the Lion motif reappears in the *Roman de Pelyarmenus*, sequel to the *Cassidorus* and the *Roman de Helcanus*, but in this romance the role of Yvain falls to the emperor Cassidorus himself. In the immediately preceding romance, Helcanus, the son of Cassidorus, repairs to Britain to seek his father and like Laurin before him meets the Arthurian heroes of that legendary place.

In the final romance of the cycle, the *Roman de Kanor*, sequel to *Pelyarmenus*, the motif of Chrétien's *Chevalier de la charrete* provides the dominant Arthurian theme. [JPal]

Keller, Heinrich Adelbert von, ed. *Li Romans des Sept Sages*. Tübingen, 1836.

Alton, Johann, ed. *Le Roman de Marques de Rome*. Tübingen, 1889.

Thorpe, Lewis, ed. *Le Roman de Laurin*. Cambridge: Bowes and Bowes, 1950.

Palermo, Joseph, ed. *Le Roman de Cassidorus*. 2 vols. Paris: Picard, 1963, 1964.

Niedzielski, Henri, ed. *Le Roman de Helcanus*. Geneva: Droz, 1966.

Brodtkorb, Lorna Bullwinkle, ed. *Le Roman de Pelyarmenus*. Ann Arbor, Mich.: University Microfilms, 1965.

McMunn, Meradith Tilbury, ed. *Le Roman de Kanor*. 2 vols. Ann Arbor, Mich.: University Microfilms, 1978.

Runte, Hans, J. Keith Wikeley, and Anthony J. Farrell. *The* Seven Sages of Rome *and the* Book of Sindbād: *An Analytical Bibliography*. New York and London: Garland, 1984.

SETTE SAVI DI ROMA, the Italian version of the Seven Sages of Rome cycle. There are nine extant redactions of this *roman à tiroir* (frame-story with interpolated tales). In the frame-story, a Potiphar's Wife analogue, a wicked stepmother attempts by means of exempla to persuade her imperial husband to execute his son for allegedly attempting to rape her; seven wise men alternate with her in telling exempla to sway their master the other way. The penalty for false accusation being capital, this is also a *Halsgeschichte*, like the frame of the *Thousand and One Nights*. Each of the Italian versions includes the story known as *Sapientes*, in which Merlin plays a major role. *Sapientes*, which is one of the tales told by the emperor's wife, is in fact strikingly similar to the Vortigern's Tower episode of the Merlin narrative cycle: a king—of England in the most popular version, the 1542 *Erasto* (in two earlier redactions he is named Herod)—who is overreliant on the counsel of seven sages, is powerless to leave the city without losing the faculty of sight, just as Vortigern is powerless to erect a fortress. Eventually, the king learns that a certain Merlin may be able to solve his predicament. In the *Libro dei sette savj di Roma*, as in the *Vita di Merlino*, the messengers sent out to find Merlin come across him playing with other children, one of whom taunts him with his lack of a father. Merlin accepts the royal summons and on his arrival instructs the monarch to uncover the source of his infirmity by digging—which reveals not two dragons, as in the Merlin legend, but seven cauldrons, which can be extinguished (thereby restoring the king's strength) only when each of the seven sages has been decapitated. Though Geoffrey of Monmouth's *Historia Regum Britanniae* is the most probable ultimate source of *Sapientes*, the latter in its turn influenced later versions of the story of Merlin, such as Paolino Pieri's *Storia di Merlino*. [JKW]

Gardner, Edmund G. *The Arthurian Legend in Italian Literature*. London: Dent, 1930.

Krappe, A.H. "Studies on the *Seven Sages of Rome: Sapientes.*" *Archivum Romanicum*, 8 (1924), 398–407.

Runte, Hans, J. Keith Wikeley, and Anthony J. Farrell. *The* Seven Sages of Rome *and the* Book of Sindbād: *An Analytical Bibliography*. New York and London: Garland, 1984.

Wikeley, J.K. "Italian Versions of the *Seven Sages of Rome*." Thesis, Alberta, 1983.

SEVEN SAGES OF ROME, THE: see *SEPT SAGES DE ROME, LES; SETTE SAVI DI ROMA.*

SHAKESPEARE, WILLIAM (1564–1616). In *The Fairy Mythology of Shakespeare*, Alfred Nutt points out that Shakespeare derived the idea of a fairy realm from the medieval romance, particularly that of the Arthurian legend. In his fairy realm, Shakespeare reproduced the external trappings of a medieval court, and Shakespeare's ladies are similar to those of the faroff island of Avalon. Shakespeare also inherited certain philosophical concepts that emphasized a hierarchical structure in society, particularly as it relates to nobility. For instance, in Malory's *Morte Darthur* this idea is illustrated in Book I (young Arthur and the sword), Book III (the account of Torre, supposedly a son of a cowherd but actually son of King Pellinor), and Book VII (the account of Sir Gareth).

In *Cymbeline*, the king's sons, Guiderius and Arviragus, brought up in the mountains of Wales, show the strengths of nobility despite their ignorance of their lineage.

In more specific ways, the Arthurian influence on Shakespeare is seen in two references to the Merlin legend. In *1 Henry IV*, Act III, scene i, Hotspur says: "He angers me with telling me of the moldwarp and the ant, of the dreamer Merlin and his prophecies. . . . " In *King Lear*, Act III, scene ii, the fool declares: "This prophecy Merlin shall make." These references to Merlin as a prophet probably came from Geoffrey of Monmouth, Layamon, or Caxton. Shakespeare's knowledge of Arthur and Merlin was commonly accepted in the seventeenth and eighteenth centuries: the title page of the play *The Birth of Merlin* indicates William Shakespeare and William Rowley as the authors. The scholar C.F. Tucker Brooke lists the play as one of the apocryphal works attributed to Shakespeare, but recent criticism has attempted to show Shakespeare's presence in the play. *Merlin* was first published in 1662 by Thomas Johnson for Francis Kirkman and Henry Marsh. The play was obviously written much earlier, though the date is uncertain. (*See also* IRELAND, SAMUEL.) [JPM]

Berkeley, David, and Donald Edison. "The Theme of *Henry IV, Part 1.*" *Shakespeare Quarterly*, 19 (1969), 25–31.

Dominik, Mark. *William Shakespeare and The Birth of Merlin.* New York: Philosophical Library, 1985.

Hawkes, Terence. "The Fool's Prophecy in *King Lear.*" *Notes and Queries*, 205 (1960), 330–32.

Nutt, Alfred. *The Fairy Mythology of Shakespeare.* London: Nutt, 1900.

Smith, Roland M. "*King Lear* and the Merlin Tradition." *Modern Language Quarterly*, 7 (1946), 153–74.

SHARPE, RUTH COLLIER, author of *Tristram of Lyonesse* (1949), the only complete treatment of the Tristan legend in modern fantasy. The story, placed in a disconcertingly anachronistic setting that recalls the eighteenth century, is transformed into a tediously long and sentimental gothic melodrama with a convoluted plot and a happy ending. [RHT]

46 *Cloisters tapestry, King Arthur, for a Nine Worthies series (ca. 1400).*
All rights reserved, Metropolitan Museum of Art; Munsey Fund, 1932.

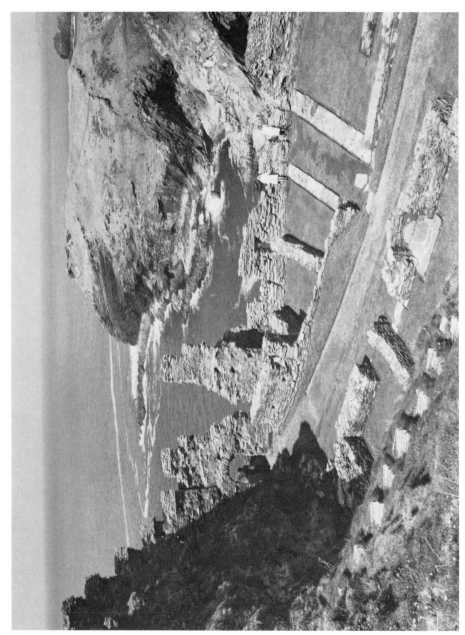

47 Tintagel. Courtesy British Tourist Authority.

48 *The Round Table, Castle Hall, Winchester (thirteenth century?). Courtesy British Tourist Authority.*

49 Archivolt, Modena Cathedral (early twelfth century). From left to right: Isdernus, Artus de Bretania, Burmaltus, Winlogee, Mardoc, Carrado, Galvagin, Galvariun, Che. Photograph by Norris J. Lacy.

📌 Sharpe, Ruth Collier. *Tristram of Lyonesse: The Story of an Immortal Love*. New York: Greenberg, 1949.

SHERRIFF, ROBERT CEDRIC, a British screenwriter in the 1930s and later an amateur archaeologist, composed a play, entitled *The Long Sunset* (1955), about a Roman family in Britain in A.D. 410, when the Legions were withdrawing to the Continent. Arthur is called upon to help establish a new system of defense for this family and their neighbors. [SRR]

📌 Sherriff, Robert Cedric. *The Long Sunset*. London: Elek, 1955.

SHIP FROM ATLANTIS, THE: *see* MUNN, H. WARNER.

SHORT METRICAL CHRONICLE, THE, written, ca. 1307, in English four-stress couplets, was probably intended to teach history through recitation or memorization. Although it was originally only 900 lines long, later redactors added to it, with one of the five known recensions consisting of 2,400 lines. While one manuscript (B.L. Add. 19677) devotes only a few lines to Arthur, others (Auchinleck, Royal) draw upon the chronicle account of Arthur's war against Lucius and add Yvain (Royal) and Lancelot (Auchinleck) from romance. Auchinleck develops with some originality the story of Lancelot and Guenevere, having Lancelot build Guenevere a castle at Nottingham and offer to defend her honor at Glastonbury. [EDK]

📌 Zettl, Ewald, ed. *An Anonymous Short Metrical Chronicle*. London: Oxford University Press, 1935.

Fletcher, Robert Huntington. *The Arthurian Material in the Chronicles, Especially Those of Great Britain and France*. Boston: Ginn, 1906; 2nd ed. Roger Sherman Loomis. New York: Franklin, 1966, pp. 198–99.

SHORTHOUSE, J.H. (1834–1903), in *Sir Percival* (1886), transposes the Grail quest to a contemporary Victorian setting in order to launch a sanctimonious attack upon women committed to socialism. [RHT]

📌 Shorthouse, J.H. *Sir Percival: A Story of the Past and of the Present*. London and New York: Macmillan, 1886.

SIEGE PERILOUS: *see* PERILOUS SEAT.

SILVA, ANTÓNIO DA, MESTRE DE GRAMÁTICA, an obscure eighteenth-century Portuguese author of popular chapbooks who borrowed heavily from Arthurian and other romances—ostensibly Spanish prose versions—to create new short chivalric tales for the contemporary Lisbon public. In four of his chapbooks—*Lançarote do Lago* (1746), *Grinalda de Flores* (1747), *Labyrntho Affectuoso* (1750), and *Dário Lobondo Alexandrino* (1750), to use shortened titles—we find situations, adventures, stock characters, and even whole passages taken from the Prose *Tristan*, the *Tablante de Ricamonte*, possibly the Post-Vulgate *Roman du Graal*, and, in the case of *Lançarote do Lago*, from Cervantes's novel *Don Quixote*. These Silva texts, like other chapbook romances of medieval origin that continued to be printed into the twentieth century in Spain, Portugal, among the Portuguese in New England, and in Brazil, where chapbook literature continues to flourish, exemplify the perennial attraction of the medieval chivalric myth, despite Cervantes's death knell to the romance of chivalry in his satiric treatment of the genre in *Don Quixote*. [HLS]

• Sharrer, Harvey L. "Two Eighteenth-Century Chapbook Romances of Chivalry by António da Silva, Mestre de Gramática: *Lançarote do Lago* and *Dário Lobondo Alexandrino*." *Hispanic Review*, 46 (1978), 137–46.

——— . "Eighteenth-Century Chapbook Adaptations of the *Historia de Flores y Blancaflor* by António da Silva, Mestre de Gramática." *Hispanic Review*, 52 (1984), 59–74.

SILVER ON THE TREE: *see* COOPER, SUSAN.

SIR CORNEUS, ROMANCE OF, a brief fifteenth-century English verse account of the traditional chastity test involving a drinking horn that spills its contents on drinkers whose wives are unfaithful. Arthur and others are shown to be cuckolds, but, apparently undisturbed by the revelation, they join in a happy dance. The work, also known as *The Cukwold's Daunce*, shares its theme with Robert Biket's *Lai du cor*, among other works. [NJL]

• Hartshorne, Charles Henry, ed. *Ancient Metrical Tales*. London: Pickering, 1829, pp. 206–29.

"SIR GALAHAD": *see* TENNYSON, ALFRED LORD.

SIR GALAHAD: *see* HUGHES, ARTHUR; STAINED GLASS.

"SIR GALAHAD, A CHRISTMAS MYSTERY": *see* MORRIS, WILLIAM.

SIR GAWAIN AND THE GREEN KNIGHT, by common consent the finest Middle English Arthurian romance, is preserved in a single manuscript, B.L. Cotton Nero A x Art. 3, which dates from about the year 1400. Written in alliterative stanzas of irregular length, each followed by a rhymed "bob-and-wheel," the poem itself is usually dated from the last quarter of the fourteenth century, but there is no precise evidence for this except the language, which may be (but probably is not) removed considerably from the author's original. The dialect of the sole extant copy, which may also be the author's dialect, is generally Northwest Midland; it has recently been localized more precisely as that of a small area in southeastern Cheshire or northeastern Staffordshire. About the author nothing is known except what may be deduced from the poem. It is widely assumed—based on the evidence of similarity of dialect, moral concerns, and literary techniques, as well as some verbal similarities— that the other three poems in the manuscript, *Pearl, Cleanness*, and *Patience*, are by the author of this romance, but the case is far from proved. Specific identifications of the author, usually based on the supposed anagrams and numerological codes, with members of Northwest Midland families, are even less securely based, though both John de Massey and Hugh de Massey have been seriously proposed. Above the beginning of the poem on fol. 91r of the manuscript appears "Hugo de" in a fifteenth-century hand, but whom it refers to is not clear.

The poet promises his audience "an outtrage awenture of Arthurez wonderez" (l. 29), and the poem lives up to this description. Fitt I tells how, at the splendid New Year's Day feast at Camelot, Arthur, in accordance with his custom, refuses to eat until he has heard or seen a marvel or until some incident has enlivened the proceedings. Scarcely has the first course been served than "þer hales in at þe halle dor an aghlich mayster" (l. 136), handsome and elegantly dressed but bigger than an earthly man, colored green and wearing green garments, and riding on a big green horse. In one hand, he bears a holly branch and in the other a green axe, "hoge and vnmete" (l. 208). Though he explains that the holly branch is a symbol of peace and that he has come to Camelot only for "a Crystemas gomen" (l. 283), his behavior is provocatively aggressive and contemptuous and the contest he proposes is dangerous: he will allow one of Arthur's knights to strike him a single blow with the axe, if in a year's time, should he survive, he is permitted to return the blow. Though Arthur, offended at the Green Knight's disparagement of his court, is angered into undertaking the contest himself, his council persuades him to give it to Gawain, who duly beheads the man. But the Green Knight recovers his head, remounts his horse, and reminds Gawain of his promise to receive a return blow at the Green Chapel a year hence. He leaves the axe as a memento.

In Fitt II, Gawain prepares to meet his commitment. On 2 November, after Arthur's feast of All Saints, Gawain sets out on his quest, dressed in the finest armor available and bearing on his shield the device of the pentangle to symbolize his human perfection. He journeys through Wales and the northwest of England "in peryl and payne and plytes ful harde" (l. 733), seeking but failing to find the Green Chapel. He spends Christmas at a splendid castle he chances upon; he is entertained lavishly by the lord, his beautiful wife, and a mysterious old lady dressed in black. His host tells him that the place he seeks "is not two myle henne" (l. 1078) and invites Gawain to spend the last three days of the year at the castle. He further proposes an exchange-of-winnings game whereby whatever he gains while hunting is to be Gawain's and whatever Gawain gains while taking his ease in the castle is to become his host's.

Fitt III is taken up with this game. His host presents Gawain on three successive days with venison, a boar, and a fox skin; in return, Gawain gives him the kisses (though he refuses to reveal where he got them) that he had received from the host's wife, who on each of the three mornings had attempted to seduce him in his bedroom. He does not give up, however, a green girdle that she gives him as a talisman to protect his life.

At the beginning of Fitt IV, on New Year's Day, Gawain sets out for the Green Chapel accompanied by a guide his host has provided. Before he leaves Gawain, the guide seeks to dissuade him from keeping his appointment by describing his adversary's terrifying deeds. But Gawain persists, and though the Green Chapel turns out to be "nobot an olde caue/Or a creuisse of an olde cragge" (ll. 2182–83) the Green Knight appears dressed as before, with another axe. His first two blows are feints, to unnerve Gawain, but the third cuts his neck slightly. Gawain, having survived the blow, rejoices, but his spirits are dashed when the Green Knight explains to him that the three blows were related to his performance in the exchange-of-winnings game: by keeping the green girdle when he should have given it up, Gawain "lakked a lyttel" (l. 2366), and the blow is a fittingly slight punishment for that moral lapse. For the Green Knight reveals himself as none other than Gawain's host at the castle, Sir Bertilak de Hautdesert, who had himself set his wife to tempt Gawain. He also reveals that the old lady in black was Morgan le Fay, the enchantress, who had set up the whole adventure to test "þe grete renoun of þe Rounde Table" (l. 2458) and to frighten Guinevere. Gawain returns to Camelot wearing the green girdle as a sign of his blameworthiness, but the rest of Arthur's court adopt similar garments in his honor.

On one occasion, the author says that he had "herde" the story he tells (l. 31), but most scholars have assumed that he used written sources like the "boke of romaunce" (l. 2521) he refers to elsewhere. The "beheading game" first appears in the Middle Irish *Fled Bricrend* (ca. 1100), where Cuchulainn one day beheads a giant challenger and then next day makes himself ready to receive the return blow: but the axe is merely drawn down thrice with its edge reversed on Cuchulainn's neck. In another variant of the story from the same source, three heroes in turn behead the challenger before Cuchulainn, but only Cuchulainn is brave enough to reappear for the return blow. Similar tests of courage and honor appear in Arthurian literature, but none is exactly as in *Sir Gawain and the Green Knight*. In *Le Livre de Caradoc*, part of the anonymous First Continuation of Chrétien's *Perceval*, the challenger interrupts Arthur's feast on horseback, and the period between blows is a year. But the feast is at Pentecost; the hero is Caradoc; the weapon is a sword; there is no journey and there are no feinted blows; and the adversary turns out to be Caradoc's father. In the *Perlesvaus*, Lancelot beheads a knight and in a year's time is faced by his brother, who appears sharpening an axe (cf. ll. 2199–207). After a feinted blow, from which he flinches, Lancelot is spared when a lady appeals for his life. The incident causes the enchantment on a waste city to be lifted. In Paien de Maisières's *La Mule sans frein*, Gawain is the hero involved: but the incident takes place one day in a strange castle and involves as adversary a *vilain*, who on the following day lifts his axe but does not strike the return blow. In the Middle High German *Diu Crône*, by Heinrich von dem Türlin, appears a similar version of the story: but here the adversary is the enchanter Gansgouter, who lifts his axe twice but does not strike Gawain. In *Hunbaut*, there is no return blow, for Gawain prevents the *vilain* challenger from recovering his head after the first contest.

Parallels to the Lady's temptation of Gawain are plentiful in romance, though they are not very exact. In *Yder*, a queen, at her husband's instigation, makes explicit advances to the hero, but he rebuffs her in a grotesquely comic and physical way. In the Prose *Lancelot*, Morgan le Fay incites her maid to seduce the hero while he is in bed, but he resists. In *Hunbaut*, his host makes Gawain kiss his daughter but is offended when he does so more than once. In *Le Chevalier à l'epée*, an imperious host causes Gawain to sleep with his daughter, but a magic sword wounds him every time he makes advances to her. No extant romance, however, makes the outcome of the beheading game depend upon the hero's moral behavior in relation to temptations, and it may well be that the author of *Sir Gawain and the Green Knight* put together for himself the elements he had encountered in several romances. He certainly appears to have been widely read in this genre: he almost certainly derived the character of Bertilak, for example, from the enemy of the Round Table who appears in the continuation of the French *Merlin*, from which he probably took also the general concept of the youthfulness of Arthur and his court (ll. 85–89).

The materials of the poem are therefore disparate. And the poet frequently turns aside from his story to dwell upon details in long, formal, technical descriptions of a sort characteristic both of romance and of Alliterative Revival poetry: there are accounts of a banquet (ll. 107–29), the Green Knight and his horse (ll. 136–220), the turning of the seasons (ll. 500–35), the arming of the hero (ll. 567–668), a provincial castle (ll. 763–802), and an old lady and a young lady (ll. 943–69), and three highly specialized and exact descriptions of a deer hunt (ll. 1133–77, 1319–71), a boar hunt (ll. 1414–67, 1561–1618), and a fox hunt (ll. 1690–1730, 1894–1921). But the narrative impetus, despite these pauses, is maintained.

Certain narrative procedures emphasize the symmetry and shapeliness of the work. Significance is pointed up by means of parallels and contrasts. The most obvious is the highly wrought parallel between the three hunts that enclose the Lady's three temptations of Gawain, and the three blows of the Green Knight's axe (ll. 2345-57). But parallels are implied also between Arthur's court and Bertilak's, between Gawain's journey from Camelot and his journey back, and between the two memorials of the encounter with the Green Knight—the axe left at Camelot (ll. 476–80) and the green girdle (ll. 2513-21)—symbols respectively of success and partial failure. Among the most striking contrasts that the poet makes are those between the privations of the harsh winter landscapes through which the hero travels and the welcoming warmth and opulence of the courts at which he is entertained, between the noisy movement and dangerous physicality of the hunting field and the quiet, static moral drama played out in Gawain's bedroom at Hautdesert, and preeminently between the pentangle symbolizing Gawain's moral excellence and the compromising green girdle, what he calls the "syngne of my surfet" (l. 2433). But a circular movement encloses the poem, emphasized by the fact that the opening line, "Siþen þe sege and þe assaut watz sesed at Troye," is virtually repeated in line 2525, the last line of the poem apart from the final five-line "bob-and-wheel." Critics have seen significance in this arrangement of fives and have linked it with the five sets of five virtues associated with the pentangle (ll. 619–65). Significance has also been seen in the fact that the poem (like *Pearl*) has 101 stanzas—a number interpreted as indicating a flawed perfection.

The poet, therefore, has a sure grasp of form but also a gift for the dramatic incident or image, an instinct for suspense, and a finely judged sense of high comedy, seen at its best in those sections in which the Lady attempts to seduce the embarrassed Gawain, whose reluctance is somewhat disabled because she plays on his reputation as a seducer of women (ll. 1290–1301). Above and beyond this, however, the poet is a moralist: that is perhaps why somebody attached "Hony soyt qui mal pence"—the motto of the Order of the Garter—to the poem at an early stage on fol 124v. But the poem is not only celebratory: the author wishes to test his embodiment of human perfection to his limits.

It is difficult to describe and assess the nature and extent of Gawain's moral faultiness, and there has been much scholarly debate on the matter. Some, pointing to the statement that Morgan le Fay organized the Green Knight's challenge to test the renown of the Round Table, argue that the poem centrally concerns itself with fame and reputation and that the humbling of Gawain's pride is the main issue: "þe loke of þis luf-lace schal leþe my hert" (l. 2438). Some give emphasis to Bertilak's explanation of Gawain's action in terms of his love for his life (l. 2368) and link that with Gawain's own strictures on his "cowarddyse" (ll. 2374, 2508). Some point to Gawain's admitted "couetyse," in its various broad and narrow senses, as his most important fault (ll. 2374, 2508). Occasionally, the part that the "wyles of wymmen" (l. 2415) had in his downfall has been stressed. Alternatively, his undoing is caused by what he calls "þe faut and þe fayntyse of þe flesche crabbed" (l. 2435), particularly the sin of sloth. Most scholars, however, prefer to see the hero's fault in more general terms as a failing in courtesy, or as an example of "vnleute" (l. 2499), or "vntrawþe" (l. 2509).

That there is a problem over the seriousness of Gawain's fault is clear, for the poem suggests various ways of looking at it. On the one hand, there is the relieved, perhaps approving, but certainly accommodating laughter of the Arthurian court (ll. 2513–21), and on the other the shamefaced, obsessive self-condemnation of Gawain (ll. 2374–88, 2505–12). Bertilak's criticism, which is perhaps meant to be taken as authoritative, is relatively mild: the hero may have shortcomings, but "As perle be þe quite pese is of prys more/So is Gawayn, in god fayth, bi oþer gay kny3tez" (ll. 2364–65). The poet's assessment of chivalric behavior may not be tolerant, but it is understanding and compassionate. [VJS]

ƨ❧ Tolkien, J.R.R., and E.V. Gordon, eds. *Sir Gawain and the Green Knight*; 2nd ed. Norman Davis. Oxford: Clarendon, 1967.

Andrew, Malcolm. *The Gawain-Poet: An Annotated Bibliography*. New York and London: Garland, 1979.

Benson, Larry D. *Art and Tradition in Sir Gawain and the Green Knight*. New Brunswick, N.J.: Rutgers University Press, 1965.

Brewer, Elisabeth, trans. *From Cuchulainn to Gawain: Sources and Analogues of Sir Gawain and the Green Knight*. Cambridge: Brewer, 1973.

Burrow, J.A. *A Reading of Sir Gawain and the Green Knight*. London: Routledge and Kegan Paul, 1965.

Howard, Donald R., and C.K. Zacher, eds. *Critical Studies of Sir Gawain and the Green Knight*. Notre Dame, Ind.: University of Notre Dame Press, 1968.

SIR GAWAIN MEETS THREE LADIES AT THE WELL: *see* OXFORD UNION MURALS.

SIR LAMBEWELL, a sixteenth-century lay of 316 rhyming couplets that, like *Sir Landeval* and *Sir Lamwell*, is thought to be derived from a Middle English translation (now lost) of Marie de France's *Lanval*. Although close in subject to *Sir Landeval*, *Sir Lambewell* contains a number of original passages in which its author seeks to lend added emphasis to two motifs that are of central importance in both works—the sanctity of Lambewell's oath to his mistress and her status among women as the fairest of the fair. *Sir Lambewell* survives in the Percy Folio. [JN]

ƨ❧ Hales, John W., and Frederick J. Furnivall, eds. *Bishop Percy's Folio Manuscript*. London: Trübner, 1867–68.

SIR LAMWELL, a sixteenth-century lay that survives in three fragments. The first, ninety lines in length, is preserved in Cambridge University Library Kk V.30; it betrays a strong Scottish influence in its diction and spellings. In subject, the Cambridge text corresponds closely to the opening ninety lines of the second *Lamwell* fragment, a sixteenth-century (?) printed text of eight damaged leaves and 420 lines (Bodl. Lib. Malone 941). Except for a passage of about fifty lines, which correspond more closely in style and content to the third fragment (Bodl. Lib. Douce fragments e. 40), the Malone *Lamwell* affords us a relatively faithful rendition of the Launfal story as recorded in lines 1–420 of *Sir Lambewell*. [JN]

ƨ❧ Furnivall, Frederick J., ed. *Captain Cox, His Ballads and Books; or Robert Laneham's Letter*. London: Taylor, 1871.

Hales, John W., and Frederick J. Furnivall, eds. *Bishop Percy's Folio Manuscript.* London: Trübner, 1867–68.

"SIR LANCELOT DU LAKE," a fragmentary ballad preserved in the Percy Folio that has its origins in the Tarquin episode of Malory's *Morte Darthur.* Lancelot sets out from Arthur's court to prove his valor, encounters a maiden, and engages Tarquin in fierce single combat. The conclusion and missing central portion of this late Elizabethan ballad survive in a seventeenth-century printed version. [JN]

❧ Hales, John W., and Frederick J. Furnivall, eds. *Bishop Percy's Folio Manuscript.* London: Trübner, 1867–68.

SIR LANDEVAL, a lay of 535 lines in short couplets dating from the first half of the fourteenth century. It is thought to have its origins in the same Middle English translation (now lost) of Marie de France's *Lanval* as do *Sir Lambewell* and *Sir Lamwell.* Preserved in Bodl. Lib. Rawlinson C 86, *Sir Landeval* is close in subject to the French *Lanval* and to Thomas Chestre's *Sir Launfal;* indeed, Chestre's immediate and primary source would appear to have been a version of *Sir Landeval* not very different from that which survives in the Rawlinson Manuscript. [JN]

❧ Bliss, A.J., ed. *Sir Launfal.* London and Edinburgh: Nelson, 1960.

"SIR LAUNCELOT AND QUEEN GUINEVERE: A FRAGMENT": *see* TENNYSON, ALFRED LORD.

SIR LAUNFAL: *see* CHESTRE, THOMAS.

SIR MARROK: *see* FRENCH, ALLEN.

SIR PELLEAS LEAVING LADY ETTARDE: *see* OXFORD UNION MURALS.

SIR PERCEVAL OF GALLES, an anonymous short English romance of 2,288 lines, composed ca. 1300–40 and extant only in the Thornton Manuscript (Lincoln Cathedral A. 5. 2, fol. 161r–76r). It has many striking resemblances to Chrétien de Troyes's *Perceval* or *Le Conte del Graal* but omits the central Grail theme altogether. The poem opens with a history of Perceval's parents, including an account of the father's murder by the Red Knight. Young Perceval is raised by his mother in the forest of Wales, and after he meets the three knights (identified as Gawain, Ewain, and Kay) he sets out for Arthur's court. He encounters the sleeping Maiden of the Hall, with whom he exchanges rings. At King Arthur's court, he comes into contact with the Red Knight and kills him with his dart. He then kills the Red Knight's mother, meets his own uncle, and learns of the plight of the damsel Lufamour (who replaces Blancheflor in this poem). He goes to Lufamour's castle in Maidenhead (where he is joined by Arthur, Gawain, Ewain, and Kay), defeats the besieging Sultan in combat, beheads him, and then marries Lufamour. Next, he remembers his mother and vows to return to the forest. When he encounters the Wretched Maiden for a second time, he discovers that it was the exchange of rings that rendered him invulnerable. He also learns of his mother's sorrow over his supposed death. He is then reunited with his mother (at the same well where the poem began), takes her home to Lufamour, and finally ends his days in the Holy Land.

Early scholars interpreted *Sir Perceval of Galles* as a debased rendition of a now-lost primitive source for Chrétien's poem and suggested that the author did not himself know the French *Perceval*. More recently, however, it has been argued that *Sir Perceval of Galles* is a deliberate adaptation of Chrétien; the author has consciously tightened the plot, defined family relationships, increased the *enfances* aspect of the story, and clarified the revenge motif. Sir Perceval's final reconciliation with his mother, moreover, thematically replaces the Grail episodes. The poem is organized around one individual and has a principle of almost circular coordination, with key episodes and even phrases balancing one another. It is in many ways typical of English tail-rhyme romances but is more sophisticated than most. As a comic parody, too, it anticipates Chaucer's *Sir Thopas*, for which it may indeed have been a model. [JPC]

Campion, J., and F. Holthausen, eds. *Sir Perceval of Galles*. Heidelberg: Winter, 1913.

Rodriguez, Marcia. "*Sir Perceval of Gales*: A Critical Edition." Diss., Toronto, 1976.

Fowler, David C. "*Le Conte du Graal* and *Sir Perceval of Galles*." *Comparative Literature Studies*, 12 (1975), 5–20.

SIR PERCIVAL: *see* SHORTHOUSE, J.H.

SIR TRISTRAM AND LA BELLE YSEULT DRINK THE LOVE POTION: *see* ROSSETTI, DANTE GABRIEL.

SIR TRISTREM, a Middle English romance of 3,344 lines, dating probably from the end of the thirteenth century, and found only in the Auchinleck Manuscript, 1330–40. The dialect was originally identified as northern, showing modifications by a southern scribe, and subsequently as essentially Southeast Midland. The early attribution of the poem to Thomas of Erceldoune or

Thomas of Kendale is now considered unreliable. The poem follows closely, though in condensed form, the fragmentary Old French *Tristan* by the Angevin poet Thomas.

Tristrem, son of Duke Roland of Ermonie and Blanchefleur, sister of King Mark of England, is brought up in ignorance of his parentage. At fifteen, he comes by chance to Mark's court, where he charms all by his courtly accomplishments and knowledge of hunting. Discovering that Mark is his uncle, he serves him by defeating Moraunt, brother of the Queen of Ireland, and later by bringing back her daughter, Ysonde, as bride for Mark. On the voyage, however, Tristrem and Ysonde drink the potion intended for the royal couple and fall irrevocably in love. At court, they continue their affair by a series of stratagems designed to lull Mark's mounting suspicions. Finally, Tristrem flees to Brittany, where he marries Ysonde of the White Hands but does not consummate the marriage. With her brother Ganhardin, he returns to England to see Queen Ysonde and there is wounded. The folio containing the poem's conclusion is missing.

The poem uses a distinctive eleven-line stanza form, of eight three-stress lines followed by a one-stress "bob" and two more three-stress lines, rhyming abababbcbc. Alliteration also enhances the meter and frequently links the bob to the preceding line. This complex form poses difficulties that the poet cannot always overcome. His tags and metrical fillers, along with the ballad techniques of telescoped action, unattributed dialogue, and anticipation of events, result in a narrative that despite moments of genuine vigor is often obscure and hard to follow. [DBM]

🙠 *The Auchinleck Manuscript: National Library of Scotland, Advocates MS. 19.2.1.* Introduction by Derek Pearsall and I.C. Cunningham. London: Scolar, 1977.

Kölbing, Eugen, ed. *Sir Tristrem.* In *Die nordische und die englische Version der Tristan-Sage.* Heilbronn: Henninger, 1882, Vol. 2.

McNeill, George P., ed. *Sir Tristrem.* Edinburgh: Blackwood, 1886.

Pickford, Cedric E. "*Sir Tristrem*, Sir Walter Scott and Thomas." In *Studies in Medieval Literature and Languages in Memory of Frederick Whitehead*, ed. W. Rothwell, W.R.J. Barron, David Blamires, and Lewis Thorpe. Manchester: Manchester University Press, 1973.

Rumble, T.C. "The Middle English *Sir Tristrem*: Towards a Reappraisal." *Comparative Literature*, 11 (1959), 221–28.

SKIKKJU RÍMUR ("Mantle Verses") are a fourteenth-century Icelandic metrical version of *Möttuls saga*, the thirteenth-century Norwegian translation of *Le Mantel mautaillié*. The *Skikkju rímur* consist of three *rímur*, or cantos, with a variable number of stanzas, each stanza consisting of four lines connected to each other both by alliteration and end-rhyme. The *rímur* relate how a chastity-testing mantle is sent to Arthur's court. The magic garment exposes all women but one as unfaithful wives or lovers. The anonymous author of the *Skikkju rímur* augments and modifies the narrative as told in *Möttuls saga* by having the wives of visiting monarchs also submit to the mantle test. The interpolated guests are borrowed from the wedding scene in *Erex saga*. The author of the

Skikkju rímur also provides more detailed information concerning the origin of the magic mantle; his source presumably was *Samsons saga*. [MEK]

ᐁ Jónsson, Finnur, ed. *Skikkju rímur.* In *Rimnasafn: Samling af de ældste islandske rimer.* Copenhagen: Samfund til Udgivelse af gammel nordisk Litteratur, 1913–22, pp. 327–56.

SKINNER, MARTYN, English poet and farmer, prided himself on having won prizes in both professions. Between 1950 and 1966, he wrote, and published in several parts, a comic epic of 14,000 lines in rhyme-royal stanzas and in the manner of Byron's *Don Juan*. Consisting of *Merlin; or, The Return of Arthur* (1951) and *The Return of Arthur* (1955, 1959; these three parts collected and concluded in 1966), the epic recounts Arthur's return to England in the 1990s to save Europe from a Marxist technocracy. [SRR]

ᐁ Skinner, Martyn. *Merlin; or, The Return of Arthur: A Satiric Epic.* London: Muller, 1951.
———. *The Return of Arthur: A Poem of the Future.* London: Chapman and Hall, 1966.

SLEEPERS, THE: *see* CURRY, JANE.

"SLEEPING LORD, THE": JONES, DAVID.

SLIP, THE: *see* STANMORE HALL TAPESTRIES.

SMITH, JOHN MOYR (fl. 1872–89), a designer of transfer-printed ceramic tiles for English firms, notably Mintons China Works, for which he provided twelve illustrations of scenes from Tennyson's *Idylls of the King* for a set of six-inch square tiles, ca. 1875. [TLS]

ᐁ Austwick, Jill, and Brian Austwick. *The Decorated Tile: An Illustrated History of English Tile-making and Design.* New York: Scribner, 1981.

SOSĒKI, NATSUME (1867–1916), author of *Kairo-kō: A Dirge* (1905), the only major prose resetting of Arthurian themes in Japanese. Inspired by both Malory and Tennyson (and probably by *The Faerie Queene* as well), it consists of a brief introduction and five sections. "The Dream" relates a meeting between Lancelot and Guenevere, her recounting a dream in which the two are bound together by a coiled snake, and Lancelot's departure for a tourney. In "The Mirror," the Lady of Shalott, to continue living, must look at the world only through a mirror. When Lancelot passes, she turns and gazes directly at him; before dying, she puts a curse of death on him. In "The Sleeve," Elaine of Astolat prevails on Lancelot to wear her sleeve on his shield at the tourney. In "The Transgression," Guenevere learns of Lancelot's apparent love for (or dalliance with) Elaine, and Mordred and others denounce the Queen for her sin with Lancelot. "The Boat" tells how Elaine, grieving for the wounded and absent Lancelot, dies; her body is placed in a boat and borne to Camelot, along with a letter proclaiming her love. This elegant and lyrical work is a striking blend of Western material (both medieval and Victorian) with Japanese and Chinese textures. [NJL]

⁊ Sosēki, Natsume. *Kairo-kō: A Dirge*, trans. Toshiyuki Takamiya and Andrew Armour. In *Arthurian Literature II*, ed. Richard Barber. Cambridge: Boydell and Brewer, 1983.

SOUTHWORTH, MARY E., a prolific compiler of American cookbooks, also wrote a novel, *Galahad, Knight Errant* (1907). Dismissing the analysis of symbolism, which "destroys the exquisite beauty," she identifies the Grail as a golden cup set with a stone from Lucifer's crown. In forty-two pages, she combines Malory's version with the *Parzival* of Wolfram von Eschenbach (Amfortas, the questions, Loathly Maiden, Castle of Maidens, and Blanch-fleur). Galahad shows that "it is possible to have the strength to overcome the bad and the grace to remain unsullied." [MAW]

⁊ Southworth, Mary E. *Galahad, Knight Errant*. Boston: Gorham, 1907.

SPAGNA, LA, a late fourteenth-century Italian text of the Carolingian expedition to Spain familiar from the *Chanson de Roland*. There are two principal versions: the "maggiore," consisting of forty *canti*, and the "minore," in thirty-four *canti*. Termed a *summa* of this material, the poem begins with preparations for departure; recounts the reconquest of numerous cities, Ganelon's treason, and the tragedy at Roncevaux; and closes with the execution of Ganelon. Like other Franco-Italian and Italian narratives based on French epic, *La Spagna* emphasizes the theme of the Maganzi traitor family and diminishes Charles's mythic stature and unquestioned authority. Innovations suggest the influence of romance: Paris is the royal capital, to which Charles returns to recover both his throne and his queen on the wings of a friendly devil, and where *cortesia* reigns in an ambiance of luxury and refinement. The poet also stresses *cortesia* in the Charles–Roland relationship, at least until Roland's departure for the Orient, where the amorous princess Dionés contributes to Arthurian tonality. Additional Arthurian associations include a number of traditional motifs, including quests, giants, and enchantments. *La Spagna* enjoyed wide diffusion in Italy and exercised direct influence on Pucci, Boiardo, and Ariosto. [NB-C]

⁊ Catalano, Michele, ed. *La Spagna: poema cavalleresco del secolo XIV*. 3 vols. Bologna, 1939.

SPANISH AND PORTUGUESE ARTHURIAN LITERATURE. The Arthurian legend reached medieval Spain and Portugal mainly by way of France. Although remote in time and space, it had a larger impact upon the culture and society of the Iberian peninsula than is generally recognized. Allusions to the Matter of Britain are found in the early literatures of the various linguistic and political divisions of the peninsula and date as far back as 1170. Arthurian material in Wace's *Roman de Brut* was translated in the thirteenth century as part of a now-lost Navarrese version of the *Liber Regum*, and a well-known episode concerning Merlin and Uther Pendragon from Geoffrey of Monmouth's *Historia Regum Britanniae* was used to illustrate the doctrine of transubstantiation in a fifteenth-century Spanish vernacular sermon, but there is no evidence that the verse romances of Thomas, Béroul, or Chrétien de Troyes were rendered into any of the Ibero-Romance languages. Rather, it was translations of the widely popular thirteenth-century French prose romances— the Vulgate Cycle, the Prose *Tristan*, and the Post-Vulgate *Roman du Graal*—that became, with their emphasis on heroic adventure, the primary vehicle for the transmission of the legend in the peninsula. From the early fourteenth century to the mid-sixteenth, these translations and their later reworkings—extant in twenty-six manuscript and printed texts, some merely fragments—lexically enriched the Ibero-Romance languages, provided inspiration to poets and prose writers, and played an important role in influencing social customs and individual attitudes and morals, especially among the aristocracy.

Catalonia was particularly receptive to the Arthurian legend and showed considerable originality in its literary treatment of the subject. Of apparent Catalan authorship are *Jaufré*, a verse romance much influenced by works of Chrétien, and *Blandín de Cornualha*, a verse narrative that reveals the impact of the prose-romance cycles in its Cornish setting and emphasis on action over the love theme. A Spanish prose adaptation of the *Jaufré*, the *Tablante de Ricamonte* (first printed in 1513), was known to Cervantes; it continued to be printed down to the late nineteenth century and has even survived in Tagalog translation. *La Faula*, a verse narrative by the Mallorcan poet Guillem de Torroella, makes use of a variety of Arthurian sources in recounting the poet's imaginary voyage on a whale to a distant island and his encounter there with Morgan le Fay and King Arthur. Allusions and references to Arthurian names and places abound in Catalan and Valencian poetry, historiography, and romance from the late twelfth century to the end of the Middle Ages—for example, in troubadour lyrics of Guerau de Cabrera, Guillem de Berguedà, Ramon Vidal de Besalú, and Guillem de Cervera; the chronicles of Bernat Desclot and Ramon Muntaner; the lyric poetry of Jaume March, Andreu Febrer, Arnau March, Ausiàs March, Joan Rocafort, and Bernat Hug de Rocabertí; such miscellaneous works as Bernat Serradell's *Testament*, Ramon Perellos's *Viatge al Purgatori de Sant Patrici*, and Jaume Roig's *Spill*; and the romances *Curial e Güelfa* and *Tirant lo Blanc*. And, in addition to the surviving Vulgate and Prose *Tristan* texts, the translation and circulation of the cyclical romances, as well as the importation of *Meliadus, Palamedes, Guiron le Courtois*, and the *Prophécies de Merlin*, are attested to in numerous Catalan and Aragonese documents and letters. From such sources, we also learn of tapestries of the Nine Worthies (one presumably being Arthur) and the knights of the Round Table, and the depiction of the story of *Jaufré* in wall paintings at Saragossa. The neo-Arthurian prose romance *Perceforest* may have been known to the anonymous Catalan author of the poem *Frayre de Joy e Sor de Plaser* (the first two parts of the *Perceforest* were eventually translated into Spanish in the mid-sixteenth century by Fernando de Mena). The prose romances came under attack, however, from the Dominican friar Antoni Canals (ca. 1352–1415), who condemned the reading of the *Lancelot* and the *Tristan* in his epistle *De Modo Bene Vivendi* (wrongly attributed to St. Bernard).

In the western part of the peninsula, the Matter of Britain also took early root. Arturus was a name used in Salamanca in 1200, and in Portugal we find the name Merlinus in 1190 and Galvam in 1208. On the model of Provençal troubadours, poets writing in Galician-Portuguese in the thirteenth and fourteenth centuries often allude to Arthurian subjects, taking their material primarily from the cyclical prose romances; e.g., Martin Soares, Alfonso X, Gonçal' Eannes do Vinhal, Estevão da Guarda, Fernand' Esguio, and the anonymous poet of the five *Lais de Bretanha*. The Post-Vulgate *Roman du Graal*, which must be reconstructed to some extent from the surviving Hispanic texts, was translated into a western Ibero-Romance language by Brother Juan Vives (or João Bivas) ca. 1313–14. Versions of all three branches of the cycle survive in Galician-Portuguese and Portuguese—the *Livro de Josep Abaramatia*, copied ca. 1543–44, early fourteenth-century fragments of the *Merlin* discovered in bindings at the Biblioteca de Catalunya, and the *Demanda do Santo Graal*, copied in the fifteenth century—as well as in Spanish, but the evidence points to a Leonese or Galician-Portuguese origin. The fourteenth-century *Livro de Linhagens*, or *Nobiliário*, of Dom Pedro, Count of Barcelos, contains a reworking of the Wace material in the Navarrese *Liber Regum*, incorporating details from a version of the *Roman du Graal*. Similar material is also found in the Spanish *Crónica de 1404* and Martín de Larraya's fifteenth-century copy of the *Libro de las generaciones*. The Prose *Tristan* and the Vulgate *Lancelot* were apparently translated in the northwest at about the same time as the *Roman du Graal*, but only a short Galician-Portuguese manuscript fragment of the *Tristan* survives. Elements of Arthurian romances linked to Cistercian authorship (e.g., the Vulgate *Queste*) have been traced in a tale in the fifteenth-century Portuguese exempla collection *Horto do Esposo*. References to Arthurian characters in Fernão Lopes's chronicles of the reign of João I (1385–1433) make it clear that the prose romances were widely read at the Portuguese court. We know that the library of Dom Duarte, João's son by Philippa of Lancaster, contained a *Livro de Tristam*, a *Merlim*, and a *Livro de Galaaz* (probably the *Demanda*). The *Perceforest* may also have been known to the fifteenth-century Portuguese chronicler Gomes Eanes de Zurara. And late-medieval and early sixteenth-century courtly lyrics gathered by Garcia de Resende in his *Cancioneiro geral* (1516) include a number of allusions to Arthurian characters.

In northern and central Spain, we find early references to Arthur's fatal battle with Mordred in annals attached to a manuscript of the Navarro-Aragonese *Fuero general de Navarra* (ca. 1196–1212) and in the Castilian *Anales toledanos primeros* (1217). The earliest surviving Spanish romance of chivalry, the *Libro del caballero Zifar* (ca. 1300), contains several Arthurian references, to the story of Yván (probably Yvain) and to Arthur's fight with the Cath Palug (an apparent borrowing from the Vulgate *Merlin*). The library of Carlos III of Navarre (1361–1425) included a now-lost Navarrese translation of the Vulgate *Lancelot* as well as a copy in French. A long version of the *Lancelot* was translated from a northwestern dialect into Castilian by 1414 but is extant only in a partial mid-sixteenth-century copy, with an appended set of chapters linking the Lancelot story to that of Tristan. Two medieval Spanish ballads concerning Lancelot survive: "Nunca fuera caballero de damas tan bien servido" (cited by Cervantes in *Don Quixote*) and "Tres hijuelos había el rey" (still surviving in modern oral tradition). The widely influential neo-Arthurian romance *Amadís de Gaula*, probably composed in the first half of the fourteenth century, was modeled in large part on the plot and style of the Prose *Lancelot* and also the Prose *Tristan*. The language of the original text is much disputed, some claiming Galician or Portuguese priority, others Spanish or even Catalan, but French now seems unlikely. The three branches of the *Roman du Graal* are preserved in two manuscript versions from the late fifteenth century (one shows marked Leonese features and the other, by the Vizcayan chronicler Lope García de Salazar, is heavily condensed and reworked, especially in the account of King Arthur's passing to the island of Brasil) and the last two branches in several printed versions, titled the *Baladro del Sabio Merlín* (Burgos, 1498; Seville, 1535) and the *Demanda del sancto Grial* (Toledo, 1515; Seville, 1535). The 1535 imprint of the *Baladro* interpolates a set of cryptic prophecies attributed to Merlin concerning late-medieval Spanish history, derived from an earlier text preserved in Catalan and Spanish manuscripts. Merlin texts are known to have formed part of the libraries of the Count of Benavente and Queen Isabella, the latter also possessing a Spanish version of the *Demanda*. Elements from the early Grail history as found in the Vulgate or Post-Vulgate *Estoire del Saint Graal* are included in Spanish and Portuguese incunabula adaptations of the French prose romance *Destruction de Jerusalem*, titled *La estoria del noble Vespasiano* (Toledo, ca. 1490; Seville, 1499) and *Estória do mui nobre Vespasiano, emperador de Roma* (Lisbon, 1496). The Prose *Tristan* may have been translated into Aragonese and Spanish through a Catalan intermediary, although the theory of an Italian origin has not been totally disproven. A mixed Castilian/Aragonese version, the *Cuento de Tristán de Leonís*, seems generally closer to the surviving Catalan fragments than the other extant Spanish Tristan texts. The Prose *Tristan* would seem to have inspired the medieval Spanish ballad "Herido está don Tristán," which comes down to us in several fragmentary versions; and elements from the romance were interpolated by García de Salazar in his *Libro de las bienandanzas e fortunas*. Arthurian allusions are common in Spanish texts of the late Middle Ages and early sixteenth century and constitute another reflection of the continuing vogue of the prose romances, especially among the aristocracy; e.g., Juan Ruiz's *Libro de buen amor*, Rodrigo Yáñez's *Poema de Alfonso XI*, Pero López de Ayala's *Crónica de don Pedro I* (in his *Rimado de Palacio*, Ayala also disparages the

Amadís and the *Lancelot* as time-wasting works read when he was young), Fernán Pérez de Guzmán's *Mar de historias*, the *Libro del conocimiento de todos los reinos*, Alfonso Martínez de Toledo's *Corbacho* (or *Arcipreste de Talavera*), Gutierre Díez de Games's *Victorial* (or *Crónica de don Pero Niño*), Juan de Flores's *Triunfo de amor*, and numerous poems by court and church poets from the late fourteenth and fifteenth centuries, such as Pero Ferrús, Alfonso Álvarez de Villasandino, Fray Migir, Juan Alfonso de Baena, Juan de Dueñas, Fray Gauberte del Monge, Francisco Imperial, the Marquis of Santillana, Diego Martínez, Ruy Paes de Ribera, Alfonso de Córdoba, and Juan del Encina. Authors of several sentimental romances of the fifteenth century were influenced by Arthurian material: Juan Rodríguez del Padrón reworked elements from the Prose *Tristan* and the tale of King Arthur's passing in his *Siervo libre de amor*; and Diego de San Pedro, in his *Cárcel de amor*, made use of the episode of Lancelot's rescue of Guenevere from the stake in the *Mort Artu*. In turn, excerpts from Juan de Flores's sentimental romance *Grimalte y Gradissa* are found in the *Libro del esforçado cavallero don Tristán de Leonís*, a Spanish version of the Prose *Tristan* printed in 1501 and also surviving in editions dated 1520 and 1528 as well as a 1534 reworking with sequel, the *Corónica del buen cavallero don Tristán de Leonís y del rey don Tristán de Leonís, el joven su hijo*, later translated into Italian. A sixteenth-century manuscript copy of an epistolary exchange between Isolde and Tristan contains additional material from *Grimalte y Gradissa*; and the extant incunabulum fragment of Mossèn Gras's *Tragèdia de Lançalot*, a Catalan reworking of the Vulgate *Mort Artu*, also reveals rhetoric associated with sentimental romances.

Throughout Christian Spain and Portugal, Arthurian literature served as an exemplar for aristocratic society, prompting the mimicry of Arthurian tourneys and jousts, even molding the behavior of individuals. In Muntaner's *Crónica*, we learn of "round tables" (i.e., jousting, feasting, and dancing) held at Barcelona, Saragossa, Calatayud, and Gascony in the thirteenth century. The nature of such activities is described at length and contrasted with Arthur's Round Table in *La gran conquista de Ultramar*. Alfonso the Magnanimous of Aragon is said to have used the arms of Tristan on his shield in a tourney held at Barcelona. In the *Libro de la montería*, attributed to Alfonso XI of Castile and León, a Galician noble is chided for hunting a giant called the "Dragón Negro de la Lana Encantada" instead of proper beasts of venery. In the *Crónica do Condestabre de Portugal Nun' Alvares Pereira* and in the first part of Fernão Lopes's *Crónica del Rei Dom João I*, we read that Dom Nuno Alvares Pereira, Constable of Portugal, was an avid reader of the Galahad story and that he emulated the model of celibacy exemplified by Galahad. In the second part of Lopes's *Crónica*, historical personages are mocked through comparisons of their deeds with those of Tristan, Lancelot, Kay, Galahad, and Arthur. In 1434, an extraordinary imitation of chivalric adventure took place in the province of León, described for us by a witness, Pero Rodríguez de Lena, in the *Libro del passo honroso*: with the permission of Juan II of Castile, a young knight named Suero de Quiñones held control of a bridge over the River Órbigo as a tribute to his lady-love. In a series of tourneys, Suero and nine companions faced sixty-eight

Spanish and foreign knights; Suero and all but one of his friends were wounded; among the challengers one was killed and many others injured.

In the late Middle Ages, the practice of giving Arthurian names to children and even to animals also reflects the popularity of the romances. Alfonso X's brother Enrique had two falcons named Lanzarote and Galván. Lanzarote was also given as a Spanish baptismal name in 1344. Juan I of Aragon read contemporary Merlin prophecies as a youth and called one of his hounds Merlin. In García de Salazar's *Bienandanzas e fortunas*, we find various individuals in Spain's northern provinces bearing the names Tristán, Galaz, Persival, and Florestán (Amadís's half-brother); and in Fernando de Rojas's *Tragicomedia de Calisto y Melibea*, there is a fictional servant by the name of Tristán. Zurara's *Crónica da tomada de Ceuta* and *Crónica da Guiné* and Resende's *Cancioneiro geral* also reveal the use of the names Tristão, Lançarote, and Lionel in fifteenth-century Portugal.

Although the Arthurian legend appealed primarily to the nobility and clergy, by the end of the Middle Ages, particularly as a result of the advent of printing, the legend also had an impact upon the middle class. Though some medieval and Renaissance writers condemned the chivalric romances as frivolous, the Arthurian texts were widely read for more than 300 years, either in the original or in translation. The vogue for Arthurian romance also gave rise to Spain's most influential romance of chivalry, the *Amadís de Gaula*, reworked by Garci Rodríguez de Montalvo and printed in 1508. This and other Hispanic romances, such as *Tirant lo Blanc* and *Palmerín de Inglaterra*, caused an important rebirth of the romance of chivalry throughout Europe in the sixteenth century. [HLS]

ᴥ Entwistle, William J. *The Arthurian Legend in the Literatures of the Spanish Peninsula*. London: Dent, 1925.

Malkiel, María Rosa Lida de. "Arthurian Literature in Spain and Portugal." In *Arthurian Literature in the Middle Ages*, ed. Roger Sherman Loomis. Oxford: Clarendon, 1959.

Sharrer, Harvey L. *A Critical Bibliography of Hispanic Arthurian Material*. Vol. 1, *Texts: The Prose Romance Cycles*. London: Grant and Cutler, 1977.

SPECULUM ECCLESIAE: *see* GIRALDUS CAMBRENSIS.

SPENSER, EDMUND (1552–1599), began work sometime during the 1570s on his romantic epic *The Faerie Queene*, of which he completed slightly more than half before his death in 1599. Arthur is the hero of this allegorical poem; he is intended to be at once a model of the ideal nobleman and a representation of the Aristotelian virtue of magnanimity (or "magnificence" as Spenser terms it), the virtue that is the sum of all the rest. The epic is set in motion when Uther Pendragon is attacked by Octa, son of Hengist, and his kinsman Eosa. Arthur is still a prince. Having seen Gloriana, the Faerie Queene, in a dream vision, Arthur has fallen in love with her. As he searches for her, he encounters trials through which he demonstrates his virtue and prowess. Had Spenser lived to complete his poem, presumably Arthur would have been united with Gloriana (i.e., magnanimity would have been joined with glory) in a climactic embodiment of Spenser's theme that the return of the house of Arthur (the Tudors) restores the glory of England. In developing this theme, however, Spenser makes scant use of the traditional Arthurian story. Arthur and Merlin are the only characters who figure importantly, and Arthur himself has none of his usual adventures (indeed, his very quest for Gloriana is based on Chaucer's anti-Arthurian *Tale of Sir Thopas*); only one of Arthur's knights, Tristram, even has a role, and that an insignificant one. To compliment both Elizabeth I and the Order of the Garter, Spenser substitutes the Order of Maidenhead, who are Gloriana's knights, for the Round Table. By the very nature of his role in *The Faerie Queene*, Spenser's Arthur has to be essentially invincible; in part because of his infallibility, he is neither the most important nor the most memorable of Spenser's knights. *The Faerie Queene* is a great poem, but not a great Arthurian poem. [LRG]

⊷ Spenser, Edmund. *The Faerie Queene*. In *Poetical Works,* ed. J.C. Smith and E. de Selincourt. London: Oxford University Press, 1912.

Millican, Charles Bowie. *Spenser and the Table Round*. Cambridge, Mass.: Harvard University Press, 1932.

SPICER, JACK, American poet of the mid-twentieth century who published among his last works a series of forty-nine free-verse lyrics under the title of *The Holy Grail* (1964). The work is evenly divided into seven books, each of which recounts the response of one of the principal Arthurian characters to the Grail; under this guise, through a reinterpretation of the Grail's significance and through an almost "metaphysical" and often humorous juxtaposition of medieval and modern images, Spicer raises questions about poetry in the modern world. [SRR]

⊷ Spicer, Jack. *The Holy Grail*. San Francisco: White Rabbit, 1964.

SPIEGEL HISTORIAEL: *see* MAERLANT, JACOB VAN.

SPOILS OF ANNWFN, THE (PREIDDEU ANNWFN), a short Welsh poem (dating ca. 900) in the Book of Taliesin. A somewhat enigmatic text, it describes an expedition by Arthur and his followers to a city (which doubtless represents the Celtic otherworld) where he obtains a magic cauldron. (*See also* CELTIC ARTHURIAN LITERATURE.) [NJL]

⊷ Evans, J. Gwenogvryn, ed. *Poems from the Book of Taliesin*. Llanbedrog: Tramvan, 1915, pp. 26–41.

SQUIRE'S TALE, THE: *see* CHAUCER, GEOFFREY.

STAINED GLASS. 1) MEDIEVAL. Representations of King Arthur in stained glass are unknown before the fifteenth century. In spite of the popularity of sculptured "galleries of kings" on church façades of the twelfth and thirteenth centuries, there appear to be few counterparts in stained glass of that period. Apart from the glazed series of imperial figures at Strasbourg Cathedral (ca. 1200) and representations of the first thirty-six kings of France at Reims Cathedral (thirteenth century), the subject of kingship in stained glass was limited to the ancestors of Christ in biblical genealogies (Matthew 1:1–17, Luke 3:23–38).

In England, by the fifteenth century, there was a conscious attempt to link King Arthur with the English royal line (e.g., the Tudor king Henry VII claimed descent from Arthur and named his eldest son Arthur in 1486). Several stained-glass programs are known to include depictions of King Arthur along-side other secular kings and ecclesiastics (e.g., east window of York Minster, 1405–08; north window in antechapel originally in library of All Souls College, Oxford, 1441–47; St. Mary's Hall, Coventry, 1450–1500). Another factor that may have contributed to the growth in popularity of King Arthur in the fifteenth century, particularly by the last quarter of the century, was Caxton's publication of Malory's *Morte Darthur*. [NK]

2) MODERN. The revival of Arthurian subjects in modern stained glass corresponded to the renewed interest in secular medieval themes by the Pre-Raphaelites. In 1861, William Morris, in partnership with Edward Burne-Jones, Dante Gabriel Rossetti, Ford Madox Brown, and others, founded the London decorating firm of Morris, Marhall, Faulkner & Co. In the same year, the firm produced a *King and Queen*, most probably Arthur and Guenevere, now in the Victoria and Albert Museum, London. A series of designs for the story of Tristan and Isolde followed in 1862. The Bradford City Art Gallery possesses two panels in this series, the *Fight with Sir Marhaus* and *Tristram Leaving the King of Ireland*. Cartoons for the *Birth of Tristram* and *Tristram's Madness* are in the possession of the Birmingham City Art Gallery. In Kirkby Lonsdale are panels of Lancelot and Elaine dating around 1870–82. In 1886, Burne-Jones designed four panels for the firm, showing episodes of Lancelot, Gawain, Galahad, and the Holy Grail (now in the Victoria and Albert Museum). Burne-Jones also designed tapestries on this theme at about this time.

Louis Comfort Tiffany's windows also include Arthurian themes, often based on well-known paintings. *Sir Galahad*, in the 1902 Ogden Cryder Memorial window in St. Andrew's Dune Church, Southampton, N.Y., was copied from Frederick Watts's painting *Sir Galahad* (1862), now in the Fogg Art Museum, Cambridge, Mass. A drawing of Sir Galahad sustained by the Holy Grail while in prison was illustrated in the Tiffany studio's promotional booklet *Tributes to Honor*. One of Tiffany's better-known windows is the 1917 three-panel composition of the *Red Cross Knight* (after Spenser's *Faerie Queene*) in the National Headquarters of the American Red Cross, Washington, D.C.

In England, a number of Arts and Crafts designers continued Arthurian themes, for example Veronica Whall, with her series in "King Arthur's Hall" at Tintagel, Cornwall, in 1933. Another set was made by Arnold Robinson, a pupil of Christopher Whall, Veronica's father, about 1914. The windows are now in the possession of Robinson's son, Geoffrey, director of Joseph Bell & Son, Bristol. A cartoon for one of these windows was illustrated in the catalogue *The Pre-Raphaelite Era* (Delaware Art Museum, 1976, No. 6–7), wrongly attributed to Louis Davis. In 1901, Dorothy C. Smyth designed a panel showing Isolde holding the love potion, set near the main entrance of Mackintosh's Glasgow School of Art. In this same tradition, the Boston stained-glass artist Charles J. Connick produced a large series of panels on the Grail legend in 1922 for an alcove in Princeton University's Proctor Hall, and the *Morte Darthur* window in the Epic Series for the university's chapel. Other American firms produced Arthurian windows: notably J. Gordon Guthrie (a Galahad window) and Willet Stained Glass Studios (a Quest for the Grail, in the Fort Lincoln Cemetery, Washington, D.C., and a Parsifal, after Wagner's opera, in the Allegheny Cemetery, Pittsburgh). [VCR]

Caviness, Madeline Harrison. *Stained Glass Before 1540: An Annotated Bibliography*. Boston: Hall, 1983.

Cormack, Peter (William Morris Gallery, London), and Helene Weis (Willet Studios, Philadelphia). Unpublished research.

Duncan, Alastair. *Tiffany Windows*. New York: Simon and Schuster, 1980.

Loomis, Roger Sherman, and Laura Hibbard Loomis. *Arthurian Legends in Medieval Art*. London: Oxford University Press, 1938.

Nelson, Philip. *Ancient Painted Glass in England 1170–1500*. London: Methuen, 1913.

Sewter, A. Charles. *The Stained Glass of William Morris and His Circle*. New Haven, Conn., 1973.

STANMORE HALL TAPESTRIES. In 1891, Australian mining millionaire W.K. D'Arcy commissioned a six-panel tapestry ensemble for the dining room of his Uxbridge estate, Stanmore Hall, from Morris and Company. Burne-Jones designed the cartoon, illustrating the quest for the Holy Grail, and the panels were made by another of Morris's firms, the Merton Abbey Tapestry Works. The ensemble, completed in 1894, included *The Knights of the Table Summoned to the Quest by a Strange Damsel*, *The Arming and Departure of the Knights*, *The Failure of Sir Lancelot*, *The Failure of Sir Gawain*, *The Achievement of Sir Galahad Accompanied by Sir Percival and Sir Bors*, and *The Slip*. A verdure panel of a thick forest, festooned with shields, was designed to cover the dado. The tapestries, now in the collection of the Duke of Westminster, were copied twice: for Laurence Hodson (1895–96, Birmingham City Galleries) and for D'Arcy's partner George McCulloch (1898–99, Private Collection). [DNM]

Marillier, H.C. *History of the Merton Abbey Tapestry Works*. London: Constable, 1927.

STANZAIC *LE MORTE ARTHUR,* an English verse romance of 3,969 lines, generally believed to have been written in the fourteenth century. The poet has been identified as coming from the northern border of the West Midlands. The poem survives in only one manuscript, B.L. Harley 2252, in which it occupies ff. 86–133. These folios can be dated between 1460 and 1480, though the manuscript was not compiled till the early sixteenth century. The poem was copied by two scribes, probably from the East Midlands and the southern border of the East Midlands, respectively. A leaf has been lost from the manuscript between ff. 102 and 103, which probably contained an account of the funeral ceremonies of the Maid of Ascolat.

The romance is written throughout in eight-line stanzas of four-stress lines. There are ten short stanzas; the irregularity may be attributed to scribal error, since nine of them are in the hand of the second scribe. The rhyme-scheme is abababab, and the prevailing rhythm iambic, though variations on both rhyme-scheme and rhythm occur. The poet also makes considerable use of alliteration; it appears in forty-two percent of the lines. Some lines have as many as four alliterated syllables, though two or three are more common. The alliteration is not merely decorative: it frequently coincides with the stress register, indicating the rhythm, and, although some alliterative phrases function merely as metrical fillers, many others carry the emphasis or meaning of the lines. The blend of initial alliteration, stress, internal alliteration, assonance, and end-rhyme creates a distinctive sound texture. Detractors of the poem have termed it "minstrel-like" because of the limited rhymes and frequent use of stock phrases and metrical fillers; supporters of the poem point to its balladlike simplicity, economy, and power. Economical changes of scene or speaker at stanza-breaks, an emphasis on dialogue, and an absence of motivational explanation help to move the narrative swiftly, giving it an objective quality in which character and action speak for themselves.

The action of the poem falls into two unequal parts. Four years after the quest of the Grail, Arthur calls a tournament at Winchester. Lancelot attends in disguise, is wounded by his brother Ector, and inspires the love of the Maid of Ascolat; he refuses her courteously but agrees to wear her sleeve at the tournament, and he leaves his armor with her at Ascolat afterward. This action causes Gawayn to believe that Lancelot is the Maid's lover, and Gaynor (Guenevere), the Queen, to rebuke him for his infidelity to her and drive him away. Thus, when she is unjustly accused by Sir Mador of murdering his brother with a poisoned apple, she has no champion to defend her. By law, she must be burned, but Lancelot arrives in time to defeat Mador and restore harmony at court.

The second part of the poem puts Gaynor in deadlier peril, as the result of an ambush of the two lovers in the Queen's chamber by Aggrawayne and his fellows. Lancelot survives the ambush and rescues Gaynor from burning, but in the fighting at the fire Gawayn's brothers Gaheries and Gaheriet are killed. Gawayn swears revenge on Lancelot and pursues it implacably, even after the pope has persuaded Arthur to be reconciled with the Queen. Gawayn and Arthur besiege Lancelot and his kinsmen even in his own country, Benwicke, till they are forced by the news from England to return. Mordred, Arthur's nephew and son, who had been left as regent in England, has usurped the crown and attempted to marry the Queen, who escaped to the Tower of London.

In the ensuing battles between Arthur's army and Mordred's, Gawayn is killed. An attempt at a truce is made as the two suspicious hosts face each other on Salisbury Plain, but an adder appears from a bush, a sword is drawn to kill it, and the battle is joined. Mordred is killed and Arthur fatally wounded; though a ship full of weeping ladies carries him away to the vale of Avalon, his tomb is found the next day by the faithful Bedwere at the hermitage founded by the former Archbishop of Canterbury. Later, Lancelot, searching for Gaynor, finds that she has taken the veil; after a poignant farewell, he becomes a hermit, living out his last seven years with his kinsmen at the archbishop's hermitage, which subsequently becomes the Abbey of Glastonbury.

The stanzaic poem is based on the French *Mort Artu*. The poet has considerably condensed his source, omitting such episodes as Arthur's visit to Morgan's castle (where he sees Lancelot's paintings), his defeat of the Roman emperor in Burgundy, and the seizure of power after Arthur's death by Mordred's sons, who are subsequently defeated by Lancelot. He has also provided many original touches, such as the adder in the bush and the farewell scene between the lovers. (Only one late French manuscript contains a brief account of such a meeting, and it is probably an interpolation.) The greater emphasis on dialogue and action and the omission of the explicit philosophizing on Fortune that characterizes the French romance produce a narrative in which tragedy results from a complex interweaving of character and accident rather than from the power of Fate. Gaynor's imperiousness, Lancelot's chivalry, and Gawayn's intransigence affect the plot as powerfully as chance details, such as Gaheriet's failure to wear armor at Gaynor's execution and the adder on Salisbury Plain.

The Stanzaic *Le Morte Arthur* is one of the primary sources of the final two tales of Sir Thomas Malory's *Le Morte Darthur*, "The Tale of Lancelot and Guinevere" and "The Morte Arthur Saunz Guerdon" (Caxton's Books XVIII–XXI). Malory rearranges the episodes of the first part of the poem and adds original episodes in his seventh tale, but his eighth tale is directly dependent on the stanzaic poem, with frequent verbal reminiscences. [DBM]

Bruce, J.D., ed. *Le Morte Arthur: A Romance in Stanzas of Eight Lines.* London: Oxford University Press, 1903.

Hissiger, P.F., ed. *Le Morte Arthur: A Critical Edition.* The Hague: Mouton, 1975.

Schmidt, A.V.C., and Nicolas Jacobs, eds. *Medieval English Romances, Part Two.* London: Hodder and Stoughton, 1980.

Knopp, Sherron E. "Artistic Design in the *Stanzaic Morte Arthur.*" *Journal of English Literary History,* 45 (1978), 563–82.

Wertime, Richard A. "The Theme and Structure of the Stanzaic *Morte Arthur.*" *PMLA,* 87 (1972), 1075–82.

"STANZAS OF THE GRAVES, THE": *see* ARTHUR, ORIGINS OF LEGEND; CELTIC ARTHURIAN LITERATURE.

STEEL MAGIC: *see* NORTON, ANDRE.

STEINBECK, JOHN (1902–1968), American Nobel laureate, evinced a career-long interest in matters Arthurian, and especially in Malory. As early as *Tortilla Flat* (1935), he attempted to impose a Malorian pattern upon the story of his twentieth-century *paisano* losers; but its author's preface and his chapter titles *à la* Caxton do nothing to make Danny's Monterey house like the Round Table or his friends like its knights. Critics, sometimes with hints from Steinbeck, have also seen Arthurian motifs in other works, such as *Of Mice and Men* (1937) and *Cannery Row* (1945). Yet none of these emerges as an appropriate modern analogue for the *Morte Darthur*: their antiheroes and antiheroic plots prove a recalcitrant fit. A much more ambitious attempt at modernizing Malory is the posthumously published "translation" *The Acts of King Arthur and His Noble Knights* (1977). Moving with increasing freedom of invention through the Winchester version, Steinbeck retells its Tales I and III (Vinaver ed.). Reduced to about one-fifth of its original, this is truly "more Acts than Morte," as Steinbeck said. Only minor changes, mostly to suit its author's conception of modern taste, appear in the early parts. Rather more originality emerges in the triple quest of "Gawain, Ewain and Marhalt," with lively dialogue and the kind of incidental humor at which Steinbeck excelled. Most expanded of the Malorian stories is the "Lancelot," where the tutelage of Lionel becomes more explicit than in the original, and Lancelot and Guinevere discover their love more explicitly than in Malory. Thematic differences between the more literal and the more imaginative parts of the work make a jarring contrast, and the latter, more original tales are occasionally marred by Steinbeck's recurrent tendency toward sentimentality. [MF]

Steinbeck, John. *The Acts of King Arthur and His Noble Knights, from the Winchester MSS of Thomas Malory and Other Sources*, ed. Chase Horton. New York: Farrar, Straus and Giroux, 1976.

Hayashi, Tetsumaro, ed. *Steinbeck and the Arthurian Theme*. Muncie, Ind.: Ball State University Press, 1975.

STEPHEN OF ROUEN: *see* ÉTIENNE DE ROUEN.

STERLING, SARA, author of *A Lady of King Arthur's Court* (1909). Subtitled "A Romance of the Holy Grail," this insubstantial novel chronicles the happy outcome of the love of Dieudonnée and Anguish, Prince of Ireland, who after much suffering achieves a vision of the Grail. [AEG]

Sterling, Sara. *A Lady of King Arthur's Court*. London: Chatto and Windus, 1909.

STEWART, MARY, novelist and sometime lecturer in English literature, has written four Arthurian novels, three focusing on Merlin and one on Mordred. In *The Crystal Cave* (1970), she depicts Merlin as bastard son of Ambrosius Aurelianus (in Nennius, his cognate character) by a Welsh princess. Tutored by the sage Galapas in the cave that he eventually himself inhabits, Merlin seeks and discovers his father, whom he serves as seer until the former's death. Performing a like function for his uncle, Uther Pendragon, he moves the monoliths of Stonehenge from Ireland and presides at the conception of Arthur, as in traditional story.

The Hollow Hills (1973) is largely an untraditional account of Merlin's mostly long-distance supervision of Arthur's *enfances*, his search for the sword of Macsen Wledig (whose Celtic legend Stewart conflates with the conventional motif of the Sword in the Stone), and his abetment of Arthur's winning the throne. The climax of the book, Morgause's (here deliberate) seduction of the young monarch and her conception of Mordred, is an important foreshadowing for Stewart's later novels.

In *The Last Enchantment* (1979), Stewart continues to recount Merlin's supervision of Arthur's reign. In an interesting conjunction, she lays the blame for Merlin's traditional madness (as in the Welsh Myrddin poems) upon his poisoning by Morgause. The latter continues as chief villain, while Merlin's love for Nimue (who succeeds him as physician and seer to Arthur) is presented as idyllic and nondestructive; his disappearance is self-willed and not permanent. Guinevere's lover—a flexible role usually filled since Chrétien by Lancelot—is played by Bedivere.

In *The Wicked Day* (1984), Stewart turns her attention to Mordred, here a sympathetic character who is the unwilling instrument in the debacle of his battle with Arthur. His mother, Morgause, is the decisive agent of revenge in what has always been a family feud. But no one can forestall the wicked day, which—as traditionally—is precipitated by an Edenic snake.

Stewart uses various sources—Geoffrey of Monmouth, Celtic myth, Chrétien, and Malory among others—plus her own imagination to recreate the Arthurian story. Her plots are absorbing examples of their kind—the popular romance—and her characters' psychology is mostly convincing. In her use of Merlin's and Mordred's *enfances*, she restores to twentieth-century readers one of the most popular medieval Arthurian modes of explaining subsequent plot and character. While self-conscious narrators, especially in the Merlin trilogy, and occasional self-pity in the Mordred novel, somewhat vitiate her literary achievement, Stewart's use of early British history and her rationalization of the marvelous in Arthurian legend remain artful. [MF]

Stewart, Mary. *The Crystal Cave.* London: Hodder and Stoughton, 1970.
——— . *The Hollow Hills.* London: Hodder and Stoughton, 1973.
——— . *The Last Enchantment.* London: Hodder and Stoughton, 1979.
——— . *The Wicked Day.* London: Hodder and Stoughton, 1984.

STEWART, WILLIAM: *see* SCOTTISH ARTHURIAN CHRONICLES.

STONEHENGE. Geoffrey of Monmouth calls this monument on Salisbury Plain the Giants' Ring—*Chorea Gigantum*, suggesting a circular dance. He says that the stones composing it were brought from Africa to Ireland by giants and arranged in a circle on "Mount Killaraus." Rituals were performed there, and the stones had healing properties. When Aurelius Ambrosius wanted to create a worthy memorial for 460 nobles massacred by Hengist's Saxons, Merlin proposed transplanting the Giants' Ring to Britain. An expedition headed by Uther, with Merlin as adviser, crossed to Ireland. The Britons failed to shift the stones, so Merlin employed his arts to dismantle them. They were shipped to Britain, and he arranged them in the same formation around the nobles' mass grave. Aurelius, Uther, and Arthur's successor, Constantine, were also buried there.

In a folkloric version of this tale, Merlin enlists the help of the Devil, who steals the stones from an old Irishwoman, ties them into a bundle, and flies over to Salisbury Plain.

So far as Geoffrey's giants have any reality, they are the pre-Celtic megalith-builders, imagined as huge because of the size of the stones. In the case of Stonehenge, the architectural design and implied skill could readily have suggested that ordinary mortals would have needed magical aid. Actually, the monument was built on its present site, in stages, long before Merlin. But a smaller circle inside the larger one has provoked speculation relating to him. Archaeologists long believed that the stones composing it could not have been quarried anywhere nearer than the Prescelly Mountains in southwest Wales. If they were, they would doubtless have been floated up the Bristol Channel on rafts, and Geoffrey's account of sea-borne stones from the west could preserve a factual tradition. Geologists, however, dispute the necessity of such a far-away origin. [GA]

 Geoffrey of Monmouth. *Historia Regum Britanniae*, Book VIII, Chapters 10–13.

 Grinsell, L.V. *Legendary History and Folklore of Stonehenge*. St. Peterport: Toucan, 1975.

STORIA DEL SANT GRASAL, a Catalan work, surviving in a munuscript dated 1380, offering a faithful translation of the Vulgate *Queste del Saint Graal*, from Galahad's arrival at court to the completion of the Grail quest. [NJL]

 Crescini, Vincenzo, and Venanzio Todesco, eds. *La versione catalana della Inchiesta del San Gral.* Barcelona: Institut d'Estudis Catalans, 1917.

STORIA DI MERLINO, LA: *see* PIERI, PAOLINO.

"STORY OF BALIN AND BALAN: FROM THE *MORTE D'ARTHUR,* THE": *see* RHYS, ERNEST.

STORY OF ENGLAND: *see* MANNYNG, ROBERT.

STRENGLEIKAR ("Stringed Instruments") is the name given to a collection of twenty-one lais and a prologue translated into Norwegian from French sources during Hákon Hákonarson's reign (1217–63). Preserved in codex De la Gardie 4–7 (Uppsala University Library) and in one other fragment, this compilation contains eleven lais attributed to Marie de France, six anonymous lais found in other collections, and four lais not attested in other sources. These translations represent the third major collection of lais in existence and belong to the literary activity associated with the Norwegian court during the first half of the thirteenth century. The *Strengleikar* collection is possibly the work of a cleric connected with Hákon's court. Some scholars have suggested that Brother Robert, the translator of *Tristrams saga*, may have participated in the translation of the lais.

The fidelity of the translation in relation to the Old French varies considerably. Some tales have extensive omissions and abridgment, while others display a complete and careful rendering of the French. In each case, the translator has transformed the verse lais into Norwegian prose often characterized by an ornate style that encourages rhetorical embellishments, rhythmic prose, and artistic elaboration.

Of the lais collected in *Strengleikar*, only *Geitarlauf* and *Januals ljóð* have Arthurian subjects. The first, a translation of Marie de France's *Chevrefueil*, recounts the meeting of Tristram and Ísönd in the forest. The tale centers on a message inscribed by Tristram in a piece of hazelwood. In a striking deviation from the French, the Norwegian version clarifies the exact content of Tristram's communication. Otherwise the translation follows closely the original with few omissions. Like other translations written at Hákon's behest, *Geitarlauf* displays stylistic embellishments, especially alliteration, as well as textual amplification. Because of a missing leaf in the manuscript, *Januals ljóð*, which translates Marie de France's *Lanval*, begins with line 157 of the French. Approximately three-quarters of the remaining 490 lines are translated. This abridgment does not alter the overall plot. The Norse version still recounts quite faithfully the adventures of Janual (Lanval), a knight from Arthur's court who is befriended by a fairy mistress and who finally escapes with her to Avalon. Like *Geitarlauf*, *Januals ljóð* exhibits stylistic embellishments (alliteration, repetition) as well as marked amplification (and at times reduction) of the text.

These translations reveal a sophisticated art that adapted the original sources into the language of the North. The compositions in the *Strengleikar* are unique and preserve a tradition that even in Europe was limited. That they reached Norway attests the interest in French and especially Arthurian literature favored by Hákon's court. [IJR]

ॐ Cook, Robert, and Mattias Tveitane, eds. *Strengleikar: An Old Norse Translation of Twenty-one Old French Lais.* Oslo: Kjeldeskriftfondet, 1979.

Leach, Henry G. *Angevin Britain and Scandinavia.* Cambridge, Mass.: Harvard University Press, 1921.

Meissner, Rudolf. *Die Strengleikar: Ein Beitrag zur Geschichte der altnordischen Prosalitteratur.* Halle: Niemeyer, 1902.

STRICKER, DER, flourished in the first half of the thirteenth century. He was a commoner, as his name indicates, probably from Franconia, who later lived and worked in Austria. He had a solid knowledge of practical theology and German literature. Rudolf von Ems mentions him in his *Alexander* and *Willehalm von Orlens* and appreciates his talents as narrator.

Der Stricker is among the early representatives of the genres of didactic poetry and exempla; he deals with religious themes and practical morality but also with courtly love and praise of women (*Frauenehre*). He excels in his popular stories and anecdotes on everyday situations, where comical and burlesque elements prevail, his best-known story being the *Pfaffe Amîs* ("Priest Amîs").

Among his epic works are *Karl*, an adaptation of Konrad's *Song of Roland* to the literary taste and style of his time, and the Arthurian romance *Daniel von dem blühenden Tal* (8,482 lines), for which no direct source is known. The romance relates the adventures of the young knight Daniel, who, attracted by the fame of Arthur's court, offers his services to Arthur. He sets out on a series of combats against the forces of Evil, which he successfully overcomes not only by his intrepidity but also by cunning. The setting is the world of fairy tale and legend, inhabited by supernatural creatures and outfitted with magic objects. Correspondences can be established with ancient Greek myths (the myths of Polyphemus and of the Gorgon), with Christian legends (the legend of Silvester), with Arthurian romances (*Jaufré*, the Prose *Lancelot*, and especially Hartmann's Arthurian romances), and with the *Song of Roland* and the *Song of Alexander*. Unlike other courtly Arthurian romances, *Daniel* is characterized by the spirit of heroic epic; King Arthur personally and actively engages in hostilities, the precourtly ideal of vassalage plays an important role, and specifically courtly values are not developed. Later in the thirteenth century, *Daniel* inspired another Arthurian verse romance, *Garel von dem blühenden Tal*, by Der Pleier. [KRG]

* Stricker, Der. *Daniel von dem blühenden Tal*, ed. Gustav Rosenhagen. Breslau: Koebner, 1894.

De Boor, Helmut. "Der Daniel des Stricker und der Garel des Pleier." *Beiträge zur Geschichte der deutschen Sprache und Literatur*, 79 (1957), 67–84.

Rosenhagen, Gustav. *Untersuchungen über Daniel vom blühenden Tal vom Stricker*. Kiel: Schardt, 1890.

STRING IN THE HARP, A: *see* BOND, NANCY.

STROPHISCHE-LANZELOT, DER: *see* FUETRER, ULRICH.

STUCKEN, EDUARD (1865–1936), a widely traveled and versatile German author. Between 1901 and 1924, he wrote eight plays, which he arranged according to the story of Arthur and collected under the title *Der Gral, ein dramatisches Epos: Gawan* (1901), *Lanval* (1903), *Lanzelot* (1909), *Merlins Geburt*

(1913; later title: *Lucifer*), *Tristram und Ysolt* (1916), *Das verlorene Ich* (1922; later title: *Uter Pendragon*),*Vortigern* (1924), and *Zauberer Merlin* (1924). These dramatic works, which combine religious mysticism and *Jugendstil*, were for the most part performed and enjoyed success on important stages of Europe. Most famous were *Gawan, Lanval,* and *Lanzelot.* They were highly praised for their hypnotic effect but are now largely forgotten. [UM/WCM]

Stucken, Eduard. *Der Gral, ein dramatisches Epos.* Berlin: Reiss, 1924.

Carlson, Ingeborg L. *Eduard Stucken: Ein Dichter und seine Zeit.* Berlin: Haude and Spener, 1978.

Poletti, Elena, and Ursula Schulze. In *Mittelalter-Rezeption II*, ed. Jürgen Kühnel, Hans-Dieter Mück, Ursula Müller, and Ulrich Müller. Göppingen: Kümmerle, 1982.

SUITE DU MERLIN, a thirteenth-century continuation of the prose redaction of Robert de Boron's *Merlin.* The *Suite* has been preserved in two fourteenth-century manuscripts, both incomplete: B.L. Add. 38117 (often referred to as the *Huth Merlin*) and Cambridge University Library Add. 7071. The publication of the former in 1886 was an important step toward the rehabilitation of the Arthurian prose romances. The Cambridge manuscript, discovered in 1945 by Eugène Vinaver, is far more complete, but it remains unpublished. This *Suite* forms the basis for Malory's "Tale of King Arthur" (Caxton's Books I–IV). It tells of the early years of Arthur's reign; his victories over neighboring kings; the circumstances of Mordred's birth; the obtaining of Excalibur from the lake; the tragic life of Balain; the quests undertaken by Gawain, Torre, and Pellinor; Merlin's enchantment by Niniane; and the adventures that Gawain shares with Yvain and the Morholt. [WWK]

Paris, Gaston, and J. Ulrich, eds. *Merlin.* 2 vols. Paris: Didot, 1886.

SULLIVAN, SIR ARTHUR (1842–1900), of Gilbert and Sullivan fame, never had the opportunity of writing the Arthurian opera he dreamt of, but he did compose the incidental music for J. Comyns Carr's *King Arthur.* It was rated a considerable success when first performed at the Lyceum Theatre in London in 1894, with scenery and costumes by Edward Burne-Jones. [CNS]

SULPICIUS. According to Geoffrey of Monmouth, Gawain's father sent him to Rome as a boy to serve in the household of Pope Sulpicius, who dubbed him a knight. Sulpicius is also mentioned in the Latin romance *De Ortu Waluuanii,* but the allusion derives from Geoffrey and does not imply any separate tradition.

No such pope ever existed. Tatlock and others have explained Sulpicius as a product of Geoffrey's waywardness or imperfect memory. He picked up the name of a real pope, Simplicius, and modified it. Simplicius succeeded to the papacy in 468 and held office till 483. Geoffrey's apparent reference to him is unhistorical, but it hints that background reading may have led him to passages in chronicles where Simplicius figured. This is in keeping with his evident awareness of the reign of the eastern emperor Leo I, six years of which (468–74) overlapped Simplicius's pontificate.

Within the overlap lies the Gallic campaign of the British king called Riothamus. Use by Geoffrey of known sources mentioning this campaign could have supplied him with the pope's name as well as the emperor's. Sulpicius, or Simplicius, may thus be held to strengthen the likelihood that he did use them, or other documents of similar content. [GA]

SUMARIO DE HISTORIA DE LOS REYES DE BRETAÑA ("Summary of the History of the Kings of Britain"), a lost thirteenth-century Navarrese work derived from Wace's *Brut*. It survives with modifications in a Portuguese genealogical register and in two Hispanic universal chronicles: the *Livro Velho* or "Old Book" section of the Portuguese *Livro de Linhagens* (also called *Nobiliário*), compiled in the fourteenth century by Dom Pedro, Conde de Barcelos; the Spanish *Crónica de 1404*, or *Crónica general de 1404*, originally written in Portuguese; and Martín de Larraya's late fifteenth- or early sixteenth-century copy of the Navarrese *Libro de las generaciones*. Some details in the *Livro de Linhagens* account were probably based upon the *Mort Artu* of the Vulgate Cycle; additions in the *Crónica general de 1404* were in all likelihood taken from the Post-Vulgate *Roman du Graal*. [HLS]

ᴥ Catalán, Diego, and María Soledad de Andrés, eds. *Edición crítica del texto español de la Crónica de 1344 que ordenó el Conde de Barcelos don Pedro Alfonso*. Madrid: Gredos & Universidad de Madrid, Seminario Menéndez Pidal, 1971, Vol. I, pp. lvii, lix–lx, 239, 274–90.

Catalán Menéndez Pidal, Diego. *De Alfonso X al Conde de Barcelos: cuatro estudios sobre el nacimiento de la historiograffa romance en Castilla y Portugal*. Madrid: Gredos & Universidad de Madrid, Seminario Menéndez Pidal, 1962, pp. 360–401.

SURVIVAL, LEGENDS OF ARTHUR'S: *see* RETURN, LEGENDS OF ARTHUR'S.

SUTCLIFF, ROSEMARY, English novelist, has written six books based on Arthurian themes, four of them for younger readers. All of them are evocative, insightful, and readable. *Sword at Sunset* (1963) is the longest and most sophisticated. It retells Arthur's story in the first person—a daring conception, since he must die at the end. His remembrance begins with Ambrosius giving the young Artos the sword of Maximus; continues with his seduction by Ygerna, his half-sister, whose issue, Medraut, will destroy him; moves on to the buying of horses on the Continent, where he meets and takes into service Bedwyr, the Harper, who becomes his friend and his wife's lover. Guenhumara, a chieftain's daughter who nurses his wounds after a battle, is given to him in marriage with a dowry of 100 men. The novel captures the loneliness and hardship of her life as the wife of Arthur, delivering her child among the Ancient People of the Hills, blaming her husband when the child later dies, turning to Bedwyr in her loneliness, being betrayed by Medraut. Though the story departs significantly from that of Malory, Sutcliff retains the twin themes of incest, with its consequent retribution, and the breaking of the brotherhood, through the illicit love between the Queen and the King's best friend.

The Lantern Bearers (1959), set in the pre-Arthurian period, describes the struggle of Vortigern and Ambrosius, as seen through the eyes of Aquila, a young Romano-British Decurion who defects when the troops are recalled to Rome. Captured by Saxons, he spends three years as a thrall in Juteland, but when his master emigrates to his homeland Aquila escapes and joins Ambrosius in the struggle against the invaders. He finds personal peace, however, only after he learns to forgive his enemies.

The other four books are retellings of the legend. *Tristan and Iseult* (1971) tries to return to the Celtic original as far as possible. It omits the love potion and the role of Brangain and ends with the stories of the black and white sails and the hazel and honeysuckle growing over the lovers' single grave. A condensation of this book is included in *The Sword and the Circle* (1981), which follows Malory "in the main" for its account of the early years of Arthur's kingdom but also draws upon other sources. Sutcliff here succeeds admirably in the difficult task of combining a well-known collection of legends in a unified and absorbing tale. Two other of Sutcliff's books follow Malory more closely. *The Light Beyond the Forest* (1979) is a simplifed but never condescending account of the Grail quest. Though Sutcliff pays equal attention to chivalric adventure and Christian allegory, she preserves a sense of Celtic mystery and unexplained happenings. *The Road to Camlann* (1981) concludes with the tragic story of the fall of Arthur and the Round Table. [MAG]

Sutcliff, Rosemary. *The Lantern Bearers*. London: Oxford University Press, 1959.

———. *The Light Beyond the Forest: Quest for the Holy Grail*. London: Bodley Head, 1979.

———. *The Road to Camlann*. London: Bodley Head, 1981.

———. *The Sword and the Circle: King Arthur and the Knights of the Round Table*. London: Bodley Head, 1981.

———. *Sword at Sunset*. London: Hodder and Stoughton, 1963.

———. *Tristan and Iseult*. London: Bodley Head, 1971.

Thompson, Raymond H. *The Return from Avalon: A Study of Modern Arthurian Fiction*. Westport, Conn.: Greenwood, 1985.

SVABO, JENS CHRISTIAN: *see GALIANS TÁTTUR.*

SWINBURNE, ALGERNON CHARLES (1837–1909), turned to the Arthurian legends early in his career, not because of any special interest in the material, but because of the Pre-Raphaelite fascination with the Arthurian stories and in particular the Arthurian poetry of William Morris. Swinburne's Arthurian poetry falls naturally into three divisions: the early poetry of the late 1850s, written under the direct influence of Morris; *Tristram of Lyonesse* (1882); and *The Tale of Balen* (1896).

There are four early Arthurian poems: *Queen Yseult*, a long unfinished poem in six cantos, based on the romance of *Sir Tristrem* and following the career of Tristram from his birth until his marriage to Yseult in Brittany; "Joyeuse Garde" (78 lines), a possible continuation of *Queen Yseult*, which depicts the love of Tristram and Yseult; "The Day Before the Trial" (44 lines), a soliloquy by King Arthur on the day before his wife's trial, suggested by Morris's "The Defence of Guenevere"; and "Lancelot" (327 lines), a version of Lancelot's quest for the Grail, similar to Morris's portrait of Galahad in "Sir Galahad: A Christmas Mystery" and taking the form of a dialogue between Lancelot and an angel.

Swinburne's major Arthurian creation is *Tristram of Lyonesse*. Divided into a prelude and nine sections, it focuses on Tristram's love, his subsequent sufferings, his marriage, and his tragic death. Angered by Tennyson's recreation of the Arthurian world and in particular his treatment of the Tristram story, Swinburne makes the fatal passion the poem's center. Selecting the lyrical moments of the medieval romance, he fashions his own account of the fatal grandeur of human love. Arguably the finest and most famous treatment of the Tristram legend in the English language, the poem is a celebration of sexual love realized in all its beauty and tragedy.

Late in his career, Swinburne returned to the Arthurian world to write *The Tale of Balen*, which closely follows Malory's version of the Balin story. Divided into seven sections, the poem is a further exploration of fate's power in human affairs, but it lacks the lyrical intensity and power of his more original recreation of the Tristram story.

Swinburne's Arthurian poetry, initially a consequence of his interest in Pre-Raphaelite poetry, reflects his permanent fascination with the implications of the Tristram story. *Tristram of Lyonesse* is that exceptional vehicle that allows a writer to depict the medieval world in a poetic celebration of his own understanding of the human condition. [DS]

Swinburne, Algernon Charles. *Tristram of Lyonesse*. London: Chatto and Windus, 1882.
——— . *The Tale of Balen*. London: Chatto and Windus, 1896.
——— . *The Complete Works of Algernon Charles Swinburne*, ed. Edmund Gosse and T.J. Wise. 20 vols. London: Heinemann, 1925–27.
McSweeney, Kerry. "The Structure of Swinburne's 'Tristram of Lyonesse.'" *Queen's Quarterly*, 75 (1968), 690–702.
Staines, David. "Swinburne's Arthurian World." *Studia Neophilologica*, 50 (1978), 53–70.

SWORD AND THE CIRCLE, THE: *see* SUTCLIFF, ROSEMARY.

SWORD AT SUNSET: *see* SUTCLIFF, ROSEMARY.

SWORD IN THE STONE. According to traditional accounts, Arthur's royalty is revealed when, as a young man, he is able to withdraw a sword from a stone or from an anvil placed on a block of stone. This motif, absent from Geoffrey of Monmouth, apparently originated with Robert de Boron, in his *Merlin* romance. That work exists only in a fragment, but scholars are agreed that it survives in two prose redactions (the *Suite du Merlin* and the Merlin portion of the Vulgate Cycle). In Robert's work (and also in Malory), the sword is embedded in an anvil, but some later writers omitted the anvil, and the sword and stone have become standard elements of Arthur's early history. Robert had partially explained the significance of the objects—the sword represents justice; the stone doubtless symbolizes Christ—thereby establishing Arthur as defender of the faith and as king by divine right. This special relationship of Arthur to God is not so strongly emphasized by later writers, and the symbolism of sword and stone is similarly deemphasized; the withdrawal of the sword (a test often arranged by Merlin) becomes a means not of divine selection of a king but of his revelation. In most accounts, the sword is first given to Kay, whose possible claim to the kingship is disproved when he is unable to repeat the sword's removal.

In the Vulgate and thereafter, the test of the Sword in the Stone also serves to reveal Galahad as the preordained Grail knight. Malory, for example, tells us how Merlin inserted Balin's sword into a marble stone, where it remained until Galahad was able to remove it. [NJL]

𝕬 Micha, Alexandre. "L'Épreuve de l'épée." *Romania*, 70 (1948–49), 37–50.

Morris, Rosemary. *The Character of King Arthur in Medieval Literature.* Cambridge: Boydell and Brewer, 1982, pp. 36–49.

SWORD IN THE STONE, THE: *see* WHITE, T.H.

SWORD OF KINGSHIP: A LEGEND OF THE MORT D'ARTHUR, THE: *see* WESTWOOD, THOMAS.

SYBERBERG, HANS JÜRGEN, contemporary film director and member of the "New German Cinema." In his famous version of Richard Wagner's *Parsifal* (1981–82), he includes episodes from medieval sources—for example, the scene with the three drops of blood in the snow and, with the aid of puppets, the story of Parsifal's forebears. Six of Syberberg's films make up the cycle he calls *Der Gral: Ludwig* (1972), *Theodor Hirneis* (1972), *Karl May* (1974), *Winifred Wagner* (1975), *Hitler* (1977), and *Parsifal.* The reference to the Grail in the title is meant to suggest that these films offer a connected representation of German-European history and ideology. [UM/WCM]

𝕬 Syberberg, Hans Jürgen. *Parsifal: Ein Filmessay.* Munich: Heyne, 1982.

SYMBOLIST ARTHURIAN MATERIAL. French Symbolist poets of the 1880s and 1890s cultivated states of soul that they often chose to portray in a medieval guise. Their Middle Ages were nebulous and subjective in reaction against Parnassian precision and impersonality. Poems and plays were steeped in an atmosphere of immemorial time that can often loosely be called Arthurian: magic forests and towers, melancholy knights, palely loitering ladies, bedraggled banners, and defaced escutcheons. Their sources were scarcely ever directly medieval, though medieval studies had gathered momentum after the Franco-Prussian War, and from 1880 onward medieval literature was taught in secondary schools. The Symbolist Middle Ages derived from recent, and for the most part non-French, versions of the period: Tennyson, Poe, the Pre-Raphaelites, Wagner. Ludwig of Bavaria's Arthurian fantasies enthralled these poets, who preferred to see the past through the eyes of a modern mediator. Maurice Maeterlinck's Arthurian names were, he claimed, taken from Malory, but they were really adaptations or compounds of those in the *Idylls of the King*. An important precursor of the Symbolists was Paul Verlaine (1844–1896), who produced some fine poems, including the first two of the collection *Sagesse* (1881), in which medieval imagery is a vehicle for personal emotion. The moral climate in which the poet lived during his two years' imprisonment (1873–75) for wounding Rimbaud is translated into an Arthurian landscape that hauntingly dramatizes Verlaine's inner strife and remorse. His prison is transmuted into a magic castle in which he forges a new soul for himself. Tennyson's *Idylls* were an important source of inspiration for these poems. Another interesting work in which Arthurian material was used as a vehicle for complex modern sentiment is Jules Laforgue's *moralité légendaire* in prose, *Lohengrin, fils de Parsifal* (1886), a satire on contemporary love and marriage. Lohengrin arrives on his swan to rescue and marry Elsa, a disgraced Vestal Virgin. A burlesque honeymoon ensues, ending in Lohengrin's escape from the marriage bed when his pillow turns into the swan and carries him into outer space. There are undertones of astringent self-mockery in Verlaine's intense confessional seriousness; Laforgue fuses comic inventions with stinging irony; but most French poets around this time were thoroughgoing idealists rather than ironists, and for them Arthurian material was conducive to an atmosphere of soulful melancholy. It was fashionable to give literary magazines names like *Le Saint-Graal* (1892) and *Durendal* (1894). [JRD]

Verlaine, Paul. *Sagesse*, ed. V.P. Underwood. London: Zwemmer, 1944.

Bowden, M.M. *Tennyson in France*. Manchester: Manchester University Press, 1930.

Dakyns, Janine R. *The Middle Ages in French Literature, 1851–1900*. Oxford: Oxford University Press, 1973.

Ramsey, Warren. *Jules Laforgue and the Ironic Inheritance*. New York: Oxford University Press, 1953.

SYMONS, ARTHUR (1865–1945), English author of *Tristan and Iseult* (1917). In this poetic drama, Tristan and Iseult, who are not lovers, drink the love potion by mistake. Surprised by Mark, Tristan is repentant, Iseult defiant. Tristan marries Iseult of Brittany, is stabbed, and Iseult of Ireland dies beside him. Mark says that, had he known all, he would have surrendered Iseult. [AEG]

Symons, Arthur. *Tristan and Iseult.* London: Heinemann, 1917.

SYRE GAWENE AND THE CARLE OF CARLYLE, a short English romance (ca. 1400) that exists in two versions; both of them are incomplete, but since the texts overlap and complement one another the entire poem can be reconstructed. The longer and certainly less inferior poem is the one discussed here (the other being *The Carle off Carlile*). It lacks the beheading scene, which reshapes the Carl both physically and spiritually into a normal human being and is therefore crucial to our understanding of the plot. Yet there is no gap in the manuscript, which points to an incomplete exemplar. The poem itself is a test of courtesy and its related virtues of valor and obedience. During a hunt, Bishop Baldwin, Kay, and Gawain get lost and have to ask for shelter from the ill-famed Carl of Carlyle. Kay boasts that he will teach him a lesson but soon changes his mind when he sees the four pets (a bull, a boar, a lion, and a bear) and giantlike stature of his host. The Carl says that he can offer them only a carl's courtesy, which is supposedly a rough variant of the sophisticated courtesy of Arthur's court. In the same way, the poem is a crude imitation of the courtly romance, and yet neither the Carl nor the poem is entirely without merit. There is a humorous sneer at the clergy when the Bishop, threatened by the Carl, exclaims: "Don't, I'm a man of holy orders!"—he will not fight but did not hesitate to go hunting. Kay shows himself similarly ill-bred. Only Gawain passes the tests of courtesy and obedience toward his host and is rewarded with his daughter. Remarkable features are the obedience shown the Carl first by his pet animals and later by his wife, whom he presses to go to bed with Gawain but stops at the last moment, and his daughter, who is summoned to sleep with Gawain instead. Although the names of the main characters are identical, the poem bears no relationship to *The Avowing of King Arthur.* [ESK]

Madden, Frederic, ed. *Syr Gawayne.* London: Bannatyne Club, 1839.
　Kurvinen, Auvo, ed. *Sir Gawain and the Carl of Carlisle in Two Versions.* Helsinki, 1951.

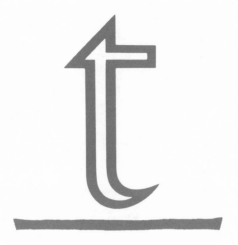

TABLANTE DE RICAMONTE, the short title of a Spanish prose romance adapted probably from a lost late-medieval French prosification of the thirteenth-century Provençal poem *Jaufré*. The earliest known Spanish version was printed at Toledo in 1513: *La coronica de los nobles caualleros Tablante de Ricamonte y de Jofre hijo del conde Donason*. Notably absent is the *Jaufré* poet's use of irony and humor. In the Spanish version, the hero Jofre's adventures as a newly armed knight from Arthur's court are given serious treatment, reflecting it would seem the late-medieval interest in resurrecting chivalric ideals of the past. The text underwent numerous reprintings across the years, surviving as a popular chapbook down to the late nineteenth century. The chapbook version was translated into Tagalog verse, and episodes from it were also adapted by an eighteenth-century Portuguese chapbook author, António da Silva. [HLS]

 Bonilla y San Martín, Adolfo, ed. *Cronica de los muy notables caualleros Tablante de Ricamonte y de Jofre hijo del Conde Don Ason* [Estella, 1564]. In *Libros de caballerías, primera parte*. Madrid: Bailly-Baillière, 1907, pp. 457–99.

TABLANTE DE RICAMONTE SAMPO NANG MAGASAUANG SI JOFRE AT NI BRUNIESEN ("Tablante de Ricamonte Together with the couple Jofre and Bruniesen"), a nineteenth-century Tagalog translation and condensation of the Spanish *Tablante de Ricamonte*, itself an adaptation of the Jaufré story. (*See also* SPANISH AND PORTUGUESE ARTHURIAN LITERATURE.) [NJL]

  ❧ Fansler, Dean S. "Metrical Romances in the Philippines." *Journal of American Folklore*, 29 (1916), 217–22.

TALE OF BALEN, THE: see SWINBURNE, ALGERNON CHARLES.

TALIESIN. Although there is doubt about his historicity, Taliesin is believed to be a sixth-century poet, and he is listed in the Triads as one of the three chief Christian bards of the Isle of Britain. Twelve of his poems survive, including three panegyrics to Urien's son Owein. He also figures as a character in early Welsh poetry, such as *The Spoils of Annwfn*, which is collected in the Book of Taliesin, and this establishes his traditional role as both poet and seer with otherworld associations. He is sometimes identified with Merlin as a manifestation of the archetypal poet reincarnated in various eras. Taliesin was ignored outside of Welsh tradition until rediscovered by modern writers, most notably Charles Williams. [RHT]

  ❧ *The Poems of Taliesin*, ed. J.E. Caerwyn Williams and Ifor Williams. Dublin: Dublin Institute for Advanced Study, 1968.

    Guest, Charlotte, trans. "Taliesin." In *The Mabinogion*. 1849; London: Dent, 1906.

TALIESIN: see HOVEY, RICHARD.

TALIESSIN THROUGH LOGRES: see WILLIAMS, CHARLES.

TANDAREIS UND FLORDIBEL: see PLEIER, DER.

TANTRIS DER NARR: see HARDT, ERNST.

TAPESTRY. Prized for their intrinsic value, workmanship, and unique ability to turn cold, barren halls into sumptuous, warm chambers, suites of tapestries were sought by the nobility to enhance their owners' comfort and prestige. These splendid hangings—like paintings made of colored wool and linen with silk, gold, and silver threads—were given and received as diplomatic gifts, taken as booty and spoils of war, and considered excellent investments. In Spain, in 1356 and 1368, Queen Leonor, wife of Pedro IV of Aragon, acquired tapestries with the stories of King Arthur and the knights of the Round Table. In England, "cloth of arras," that is, tapestry, is often listed in inventories. The English apparently preferred the stories of Lancelot and Perceval, although King Arthur was included as a figure in tapestries of the Nine Worthies. The fifteenth-century inventories of King Charles VI of France list 150 tapestries, several with Arthurian subjects: a quest for the Grail, the Nine Worthies, and the story of Ywain. Charles's wife, Queen Isabelle of Bavaria, owned a Perceval and a large Holy Grail tapestry, and his uncles, the royal dukes, also collected tapestries. Louis of Anjou owned seventy-six tapestries, including the Nine Worthies, the Three Christian Worthies, two with stories of Lancelot, and several with Tristan. The bibliophile Jean de Berry had a Nine Worthies tapestry worked with gold and silver thread. Philip the Bold, Duke of Burgundy, who had a taste for sumptuous materials and magnificent scale, owned a King Arthur tapestry so large that he had it divided into four pieces for storage. His inventory also lists tapestries illustrating the jousts of Lancelot and the story of Perceval. He sent his largest Perceval tapestry (sixty-four feet wide) as a diplomatic gift to the Duke of York, uncle of the King of England.

The finest surviving tapestry of King Arthur is from a suite of the Nine Worthies, now in the Metropolitan Museum, The Cloisters Collections, New York. King Arthur is seated in an elaborate Gothic niche surrounded by tracery and figures of bishops and cardinals. Arthur wears over his armor a tabardlike garment and he carries a banner; both tabard and banner are decorated with the three golden crowns symbolizing the kingdoms of North Wales, South Wales, Logres. The style and technique of weaving resemble that of the well-known Angers Apocalypse; thus this tapestry may be the work of Nicolas Bataille, and a date of about 1385 has been suggested. The tapestry may have been made for Jean de Berry (1340–1416), although it is not listed in the inventory made at the time of the duke's death. The entire set must have been very impressive; even this fragment measures fourteen feet by nearly ten feet.

By the end of the fifteenth century, wealthy burghers also could afford the luxury of tapestry; Mathias Eberle of Basel, for example, owned a tapestry of the Three Christian Worthies (now in the Historical Museum at Basel). In it, Arthur is represented as an elegant, fashionably dressed youth holding a banner displaying the three crowns. [MS]

❧ Goebel, Heinrich. *Wandteppiche*. 2 vols. Leipzig, 1923, 1928.

Loomis, Roger Sherman, and Laura Hibbard Loomis. *Arthurian Legends in Medieval Art*. London: Oxford University Press, 1938, pp. 27–30, 38–40; figs. 12, 15.

Salet, Francis, and Geneviève Souchal. *Masterpieces of Tapestry*. Paris: Éditions des Musées Nationaux, 1973, pp. 34–38.

TAVOLA RITONDA, LA ("The Round Table"), an elaborate conflation of several Arthurian tales, achieved its finished form in the second quarter of the fourteenth century, although it may have been based on the book that Piero, Count of Savoy (d. 1268), brought to England as a gift for King Edward and that subsequently passed into the hands of Gaddo de' Lanfranchi and then on to Rusticiano da Pisa, himself a compiler of Arthurian stories. In its eclectic use of sources, the *Tavola* draws indirectly on Thomas's *Tristan*, the ancestor of the *Tristano Riccardiano*, as well as the *Palamedes*, the Prose *Tristan*, the Vulgate *Queste del Saint Graal*, popular Italian traditions, and other sources that have not yet been identified. The *Tavola* preserves the Italian concern to distinguish between the Old Table presided over by Uther Pendragon and the New Table guided by Arthur, but it deals only briefly with the adventures of Uther's reign in order to focus on the achievements of the Arthurian knights Lancilotto (Lancelot) and Tristano. The narrative contribution of the *Tavola* lies in its ambitious fusion of disparate accounts to compile a complete history of the New Table focusing on Tristano and including an original narration of the vengeance that Arthur exacts from Mark for his murder of Tristan. The thematic contribution of the *Tavola* lies in its reinvestment of the Tristan legend with the passion of the earlier verse redactions, considerably reduced in the French Prose *Tristan*. [DLH]

Polidori, Filippo-Luigi, ed. *La Tavola Ritonda o l'istoria di Tristano*. Bologna: Romagnoli, 1864–65.

Gardner, Edmund G. *The Arthurian Legend in Italian Literature*. London: Dent, 1930.

TAYLOR, ANNA, British author of the historical novel *Drustan the Wanderer* (1971). Drustan (Tristan) tells the story of his love for Essylt (Isolde). This tale of blind passion and ill fate in a world itself torn asunder by political and religious strife draws upon earlier romances rather than Malory, and it uses the findings of recent historical and archaeological research to recreate the historical setting. [SRR]

Taylor, Anna. *Drustan the Wanderer: A Novel Based on the Legend of Tristan and Isolde*. London: Longmans, 1971.

TELEVISION SERIES on the Arthurian legend have usually been prepared for younger viewers. An early example is *The Adventures of Sir Lancelot*, produced in the mid-1950s by Sapphire Film Productions for the Incorporated Television Programme Company in Britain. Lancelot, played by William Russell, performs a number of untraditional deeds of knight-errantry, such as leading a band of shepherds against some robber knights who have been preying upon them. Greater realism was achieved in another British series, *Arthur of the Britons*. The twenty-four episodes, which were shown on HTV in the early 1970s, reveal the harshness of life in the Dark Ages.

The Legend of King Arthur, which was shown on BBC-TV in the late 1970s, follows the traditional story more closely, from the conception of Arthur to the last meeting of Lancelot and Guinevere after the battle of Camlann. The series stars Andrew Burt as Arthur, Felicity Dean as Guinevere, and David Robb as Lancelot, but it is Morgan le Fay, played by Maureen O'Brien, who provides the main link between the twelve episodes with her thirst for revenge against Arthur. Shortened to eight episodes to focus more strongly upon the role of Lancelot, the series was scheduled to be shown on PBS in North America.

The Arthurian legend also figures in stories placed in a modern setting. In *Raven*, a series that appeared in the mid-1970s on ATV in Britain, with screenplay by Jeremy Burnham and Trevor Ray, a conservationist movement saves an ancient network of caves that is linked with Arthur's cave legend. It is strongly implied, moreover, that their leader is none other than Arthur reborn, and that the cranky archaeologist who helps him is Merlin. Merlin appears again briefly in a TV Ontario series from the late 1970s, *Read All About It!*, this time so that he can use his magic to transport some children to another world. Merlin's power also lies behind the upheavals that take place in *The Changes*, a popular series in the 1970s that was developed for BBC-TV from Peter Dickinson's trilogy. More recently, viewers in North America saw an undistinguished and short-lived situation comedy called *Mr. Merlin*. Merlin, now a garage-owner, raises a few laughs in his efforts to teach his apprentice, a typical California teenager, the responsibilities involved in using magic. (*See also* FILMS.) [RHT/MAG]

Davies, Andrew. *The Legend of King Arthur*. London: Fontana/Armada, 1979.

Thompson, Raymond H. *The Return from Avalon: A Study of the Arthurian Legend in Modern Fiction*. Westport, Conn.: Greenwood, 1985.

TENGGREN, GUSTAF: *see* BOOK ILLUSTRATION (AMERICAN).

TENNYSON, ALFRED LORD (1809–1892), father of the Arthurian renaissance in Victorian England, who spent much of his life recreating the legends in his poetry.

By the early nineteenth century, the Arthurian legends had become a literary anachronism. Tennyson's poetry brought about a rebirth of interest in the material and eventually placed it on a new plateau of respect and significance for writers and artists of the later nineteenth century.

The past always exerted a powerful attraction for Tennyson, functioning as a mirror that might indicate the moral condition of the present. By nature nostalgic, Tennyson sought in the past not a retreat from the plight of his time but a barometer of the moral temper of Victorian England. And throughout his life, the Arthurian legends were his most powerful inspiration.

"The vision of Arthur as I have drawn him," he wrote, "had come upon me when, little more than a boy, I first lighted upon Malory." In the figure of Arthur, Tennyson found a character whose life would stand as an example for Victorian readers of the need for an idealistic spiritual vision. Although Malory always remained Tennyson's major source of knowledge of the legends, the poet also studied all available histories and commentaries that might clarify his understanding of the medieval world. In his twenties, he was already searching for a proper avenue into a poetic recreation of the legends. His early Arthurian efforts reveal a thorough knowledge of medieval texts, a commitment to a recreation of the story of Camelot, and a constant experimentation with varying degrees of source fidelity, from faithful adaptation to almost complete originality. His early attempts to depict the King and his realm are an important preparation for his final commitment to an Arthurian epic, *Idylls of the King*, which would occupy much of his attention from the 1850s until his death.

Outlines and sketches of possible Arthurian works show the variety of Tennyson's early plans. A prose sketch from about 1833 emphasizes the splendor and beauty of Camelot, qualities that would appeal to the young disciple of John Keats; another sketch concerns itself with an allegorical interpretation of the legends; there is also a draft of a five-act play.

Tennyson's first published Arthurian poem, "The Lady of Shalott," written by May 1832, is based on a medieval Italian novelette, *Donna di Scalotta*. This version of a maiden's hapless love for Lancelot provides the Arthurian setting for a study of the artist and the dangers of personal isolation from the world. At this time, Tennyson seemed ignorant of Malory's story of Elaine: "I doubt whether I should ever have put it in that shape if I had been then aware of the Maid of Astolat in Mort Arthur."

Tennyson had already employed an Arthurian setting in "Sir Launcelot and Queen Guinevere: A Fragment," which was "partly if not wholly written in 1830." The five extant stanzas, the opening of a projected poem, focus on the beauty of nature and the beauty of Guinevere: the blossoming springtime becomes a backdrop for the youthful and innocent Guinevere and Lancelot. The poem is an attempt to create a highly visualized story involving central figures from the Arthurian world.

"Sir Galahad," written by September 1834, employs an Arthurian figure as a vehicle for exploring the virtue of chastity. In this reflective lyric, Galahad is a pure knight, the paragon of virtue, whose love of the divine motivates all his actions. The essential character of Galahad, derived from Malory, Tennyson presents in terms of the virtue—chastity—that makes him the outstanding knight. Yet Galahad's introspection, his exuberant joy bordering on arrogance, his ceaseless desire for activity and movement, are all qualities that make him a distinctly Victorian figure, a precursor of the Galahad of the Pre-Raphaelites.

The last of Tennyson's early Arthurian poems, "Morte d'Arthur," completed by October 1834, is the poet's most faithful recreation of Malory's structure and language. The poem is a careful expansion of Malory's account of the final moments in King Arthur's life. Taking an essentially dramatic moment, Tennyson retells the episode with a degree of embellishment that does not violate, but rather enriches, the source. Written shortly after the death of Tennyson's best friend and mentor, Arthur Henry Hallam, the poem chronicles the death of another Arthur, the mythic King who here is presented with the same idealization as is Hallam himself in *In Memoriam* (1850).

In the four early poems, Tennyson focuses on the three major concerns of the Arthurian world that will dominate his ultimate achievement in the *Idylls of the King*. In "Sir Launcelot and Queen Guinevere," he studies the nascent love of the knight and his queen. In "Sir Galahad," the chastity of the knight is a prelude to a brief description of the Holy Grail, which will vex the poet's imagination and retard his Arthurian epic for many years. In the "Morte d'Arthur," Tennyson turns to Arthur as ideal ruler, the symbolic embodiment of the perfection of the old order. Out of these three themes will come a focal point that will provide the poet with a coherent structure for his final treatment of Camelot.

With the publication of the widely acclaimed *In Memoriam* in 1850, and with the poet's acceptance that same year of the Laureateship, the Arthurian world beckoned Tennyson even more strongly than before. In 1852, he published two socially hortatory poems, "The Third of February, 1852" and "Hands All Round," under the pseudonym "Merlin."

Tennyson's first new Arthurian poem takes as its plot the seduction by Nimuë (Vivien) of Merlin, drawn from Southey's translation of the *Roman de Merlin*, which had appeared in the introduction to his 1817 edition of Malory. "Vivien" is a detailed narrative account of the corrosive power of lust and the destructive nature of wanton sensuality. An antidote to the negative horror of Vivien, "Enid," Tennyson's next Arthurian poem, is a similar portrait of a female character, but one who is the embodiment of truth. The story of Enid's patient submission to her jealous husband Geraint, drawn from Lady Charlotte Guest's *Mabinogion*, forms a much longer narrative than the more focused "Vivien."

Printed together in a trial edition in 1857, *Enid and Nimuë: The True and the False*, the two poems comprise a separate work in their own right, but they also exist, more powerfully, as part of an incomplete context suggested by the framework that Tennyson adds to the story of Enid. The plot from the *Mabinogion* offered an excellent contrast to the completed study of Vivien, yet it also gave Tennyson an opportunity to expand his brief study of an ideal order that Arthur was intent on establishing. In "Enid," this order is not fully organized, yet the sin of adultery already exists at its center; in "Vivien," the destruction of Merlin is only part of a wider decay operating throughout Camelot.

Even before the publication of the trial edition, Tennyson was contemplating a successor to the two Arthurian poems. The successor was "Guinevere," the portrait of a complex woman at war with her own being, one who partakes of both Enid's ennobling goodness and Vivien's destructive sensuality. In "Guinevere," a dramatic rendition of the final meeting of Arthur and his queen (a scene the poet himself invented), Arthur is an almost divine force trying to lead humanity to the highest realization of its capability; Guinevere is a passionate and intelligent woman, conscious of human complexity and ultimately aware of the necessity for a proper response to the demands of an ideal vision.

"Elaine," Tennyson's next Arthurian poem, allowed a return to the story of the Lady of Shalott, seen now through the light of Malory's version. Vividly depicting Elaine as the victim of her unreciprocated love, the poem shows the destructive power of Guinevere's sin as it begins to influence innocent human beings. Tennyson retells Elaine's story in the light of the particular world already presented in "Vivien," "Enid," and "Guinevere." This quartet of poems about women became the foundation of Tennyson's long-anticipated Arthurian epic. The original title of the quartet, *The True and the False*, was changed to *Idylls of the King*; the phrase on the title page, "Flos Regum Arthurus" ("Arthur, Flower of Kings"), taken from Joseph of Exeter, emphasizes the importance of King Arthur to the world of these four idylls, which were published together in a single volume in 1859.

To complete his developing Arthurian epic, Tennyson knew that he had to compose a version of the Grail quest, yet he feared the task: "I doubt whether such a subject could be handled in these days, without incurring a charge of irreverence. It would be too much like playing with sacred things. The old writers *believed* in the Sangreal." He shied away from the topic until 1867, when he found a suitable approach: he would use one of the questers, specifically a failed quester, to narrate the story. "The Holy Grail" follows the *Queste del Saint Graal* by making Percivale a soiled contrast to the perfect Galahad. Inspired by Malory, Tennyson goes on to create his own portrayals of six questers: the perfect Sir Galahad and Percivale's faultless sister, the slightly deficient Percivale, the sinful Lancelot, the selfless Bors, and the despicable Gawain. In Tennyson, the quest accelerates the decay of the Round Table, functioning as an external force that harms a world already wounded by the Queen's adultery. By implying that the absence of the Grail is dependent upon Guinevere's sin, Tennyson subtly links the external force of destruction with the sin at the center of the realm.

After completing "The Holy Grail," Tennyson created a frame for his Arthurian work. In the early "Morte d'Arthur," he found his natural conclusion. His next new poem was to comprise the beginning. "The Coming of Arthur" is an account of Arthur's birth that employs Malory's version but sets it within a context of conflicting stories and rumors that undercut its credibility. The resulting confusion emphasizes the poem's focus—not Arthur's origin, but how others come to accept him. A new order automatically raises suspicions about its origin and validity.

The next idyll, "Pelleas and Ettarre," is the direct continuation of "The Holy Grail," and it depicts the younger generation of knights who have come to fill the void created by the Grail quest. Drawn from a brief incident in Malory, Tennyson's poem makes Pelleas the embodiment of the confusion and despair that confront the idealistic man looking upon the decay of Camelot.

With a few lines added to the beginning and end, the "Morte d'Arthur became "The Passing of Arthur" and allowed another quartet of Arthurian poems to be made ready for publication. Titled *The Holy Grail and Other Poems*, the volume appeared in December 1869; the following month, the collected edition of the eight *Idylls of the King* was published.

Two more idylls were added to the series in the 1870s: "The Last Tournament" and "Gareth and Lynette," both natural outgrowths of "Pelleas and Ettarre." "The Last Tournament," a somber study of the autumn of the Round Table, continues the tragic movement of the Pelleas idyll by focusing on Camelot's disintegration; the society that drove Pelleas to madness must now endure the consequence of that madness—the transformation of Pelleas into the evil Red Knight of the North. The idyll also includes Tennyson's version of the Tristram story, ending with Tristram's brutal murder by Mark. Malory's Tristram, second only to Lancelot as an ideal knight, here becomes a cynical realist dedicated to the practice of free love, an example of the beast to which man has returned.

"Gareth and Lynette," the happiest idyll, is a direct contrast to "Pelleas and Ettarre." Its springtime setting and the growth of its young characters into noble adulthood are taken directly from Malory; they display the perfection that once belonged to Arthur's realm. The poem offers the only fully developed study of Camelot as Arthur envisioned it, and it dramatizes the power of such an ennobling world on a young knight who is similar to Pelleas. At this time, however, Camelot allows the youthful Gareth to realize his ideal vision.

The two new idylls were published together in 1872 and incorporated into an edition of the *Idylls* in January 1873. Tennyson also made small additions to strengthen the humanity of the King and to maintain narrative clarity and consistency with the new idylls. This edition also divided the original "Enid" into two parts, marking a definite step toward the final creation of an epic poem in twelve books. Also added was the epilogue, "To the Queen."

Believing that some introduction to his account of Merlin and Vivien was necessary, Tennyson turned to Malory's story of "Balin, or the Knight of the Two Swords" for the twelfth member of the sequence. "Balin and Balan," published in 1885 and incorporated into the whole series in an 1886 edition, is a study of the destructive power of self-denial. Balin chooses self-denial as the seemingly proper road to self-improvement; Malory's Pellam becomes a heathen king whose conversion to Christianity is a flight into self-denying asceticism. Malory's presentation of an unestablished realm and the natural chaos of a disordered world has become the barometer of the early decay of the established realm.

Idylls of the King reshapes the medieval accounts of Arthur's career into a vehicle for the poet's own vision of an idealistic philosophy significant to his generation. "The general decay of faith/Right through the world" finds a remedy and a hope in Arthur; the decaying Camelot serves as an indictment of Victorian England. Tennyson's recreation of the Arthurian world is an attempt to reform his generation by showing the effects of sensuality, materialism, and spiritual blindness.

Tennyson's interest in the Arthurian world and his own epic did not abate with the completion of the *Idylls*. In "Merlin and the Gleam," written in 1889, Tennyson composed his "literary history," choosing Merlin to represent the poet in pursuit of his vocation. At the same time, he was also contemplating a great stage drama on the legend of Tristram of Lyonesse, since he had been obliged to cut down the story for its inclusion in the *Idylls*. The project, however, remained unrealized.

The second half of the nineteenth century saw an unprecedented interest in the world of Camelot, and the Arthurian painting and literature of the period reveal Tennyson's pervasive influence. The Pre-Raphaelite Brotherhood took Tennyson's Sir Galahad as their standard-bearer. For the 1857 edition of Tennyson's *Poems*, Dante Gabriel Rossetti contributed five illustrations, three of them Arthurian, representing his first extended treatment of this material. Rossetti's associates, Edward Burne-Jones, Holman Hunt, Daniel Maclise, and John Everett Millais, also entered the Arthurian world under Tennyson's guidance; their Arthurian paintings are either illustrations of Tennyson's poems or depictions of incidents originating in Tennyson's Arthurian world.

Poets were also conscious of Tennyson's influence. Matthew Arnold, disapproving of Tennyson's medieval characters, created his own version of the Tristram story in his only foray into the Arthurian world. William Morris, who shared Arnold's dislike of Tennyson's Arthurian poetry, composed a series of Arthurian poems. However, his plan to create an Arthurian cycle may have been dimmed by the popularity of the *Idylls*, for it never materialized. So too, Swinburne, whose method of handling the legends is both a direct criticism of Tennyson's method and an acknowledgment of his influence.

A final testimony to Tennyson's importance is the sudden emergence in the later nineteenth century of scholarly commitment to medieval Arthurian texts, including Malory. Moreover, in 1862, James Knowles compiled *The Story of King Arthur and His Knights of the Round Table*, the first modernization of Malory and a volume destined to pass through seven editions before 1900. The book is dedicated to Tennyson: "This attempt at a popular version of the Arthur legends is by his permission dedicated, as a tribute of the sincerest and warmest respect." Five more modernizations appeared before the end of the century, and each noted Tennyson's role in the steadily growing interest in King Arthur. [DS]

❧ Tennyson, Alfred Lord. *Idylls of the King*, ed. J.M. Gray. New Haven: Yale University Press, 1983.

————. *The Poems of Tennyson*, ed. Christopher Ricks. London: Longmans, 1969.

Buckley, Jerome H. *Tennyson: The Growth of a Poet*. Cambridge, Mass.: Harvard University Press, 1960.

Rosenberg, John D. *The Fall of Camelot: A Study of Tennyson's Idylls of the King*. Cambridge, Mass.: Belknap, 1973.

Staines, David. *Tennyson's Camelot: The Idylls of the King and Its Medieval Sources*. Waterloo, Ontario: Wilfrid Laurier University Press, 1983.

Tennyson, Hallam Lord. *Alfred Lord Tennyson: A Memoir*. 2 vols. New York: Macmillan, 1897.

TESTING OF TERTIUS, THE: *see* NEWMAN, ROBERT.

THAT HIDEOUS STRENGTH: *see* LEWIS, C.S.

THELWALL, JOHN (1764–1834), English lecturer and pamphleteer, contributed a closet drama, *The Fairy of the Lake* (1801), to the Gothic Revival.

Drydenesque in its combination of mythology, legendary history (Hengist, Rowenna, Vortigern), magic spells, stagey songs, and spectacles, the work reveals the Lady of the Lake as the *dea ex machina* who rescues Guenevere from Vortigern's incestuous designs and Rowenna's necromancy to unite her with an ineffectual Arthur. [MAW]

✒ Merriman, James Douglas. *The Flower of Kings: A Study of the Arthurian Legend in England Between 1485 and 1835.* Lawrence: University Press of Kansas, 1973.

THIRTY-FIRST OF JUNE, THE: *see* PRIESTLEY, J.B.

THOMAS D'ANGLETERRE.

The legend of Tristan was recorded twice in Old French verse of the twelfth century: once by Béroul and once by a certain Thomas. This latter retelling has been variously dated from ca. 1150 to 1200, but most critics today place it around 1175. Thomas composed his work in England, possibly for the court circle of Henry II and his queen, Eleanor of Aquitaine.

Thomas's *Tristan* is extant in only eight fragments from five different manuscripts. There is some overlapping, but in all the fragments come to about one-sixth of what the whole is estimated to have been. The Cambridge fragment (52 lines) recounts the discovery of the lovers in the orchard by Mark, who has been brought there by a dwarf, and Tristan's tearful farewell to Iseut. The Sneyd fragment (888 lines) tells of Tristan's marriage to Iseut of the White Hands in an attempt to forget his love for the queen. It is characterized by two lengthy interior monologues: one as Tristan determines to marry her; a second when he regrets his action and determines to do penance by never consummating his marriage. The fragment ends with Iseut the Blond's grief when Cariados tells her of Tristan's marriage.

The Turin fragments (now lost; 256 lines and 3 lines) begin with Tristan in the Chamber of Images, where he laments his sad fate and uncertainties before statues of Iseut and Brangain. They tell also of Iseut's unwilling submission to Mark and of Iseut of the White Hands's admission to her brother Kaherdin that her marriage has not been consummated. The first Strasbourg fragment (68 lines; destroyed by fire in 1870) tells of Kaherdin's wonder as he first beholds Iseut the Blond.

The final three fragments (Douce, 1,815 lines; Sneyd, 839 lines; Strasbourg, 151 lines—destroyed) narrate the end of the poem, including Brangain and Iseut's quarrels, Tristan's return disguised as a leper, Tristan le Nain, Tristan wounded, the ship with the white sail, and the death of the lovers.

Thomas's version is characterized throughout by his courtly concern for the depiction of the birth, growth, and sufferings of love. These are developed in lengthy monologues that reveal the psychological states of the principal characters: hope, fear, hesitation, passion. For Thomas, the potion is an eternal *symbol* of the value and intensity of Tristan and Iseut's love. This love is predicated on the individual merits of the lovers and is a product of their own free will. They take full responsibility for their love, and it becomes their only morality, their only law. [WWK]

   Thomas. *Les Fragments du Roman de Tristan, poème du XIIe siècle*, ed. Bartina H. Wind. Geneva: Droz, 1960.

THOR, WITH ANGELS: *see* FRY, CHRISTOPHER.

TIECK, LUDWIG (1773–1853), is generally classed as an early German Romantic because of his close association with the founders of the movement. However, he was a prolific writer in all genres and active during all stages of the Romantic period. He was particularly interested in the Middle Ages and also in English literature. In his *Leben und Thaten des kleinen Thomas, genannt Däumchen* ("Life and Times of Little Tom Thumb," 1811), the dwarf Thomas, whose birth was prophesied by Merlin from his grave, uses Merlin's seven-league boots to aid Arthur in his war against the Saxons. Tieck's excellent translation of William Rowley's 1662 Elizabethan drama *The Birth of Merlin or The Child Hath Found Its Father* (*Die Geburt des Merlin oder Das Kind hat seinen Vater gefunden*, 1829), had an influence on later German works, such as Immermann's *Merlin: Eine Mythe* (1832). [RWK]

   Tieck, Ludwig. *Schriften.* Berlin: Reimer, 1828, Vol. 5.
     Weiss, Adelaide Marie. "Ludwig Tieck." In *Merlin in German Literature.* Washington, D.C.: Catholic University of America Press, 1933, pp. 81–94.

TIFFANY, LOUIS COMFORT: *see* STAINED GLASS.

TINTAGEL, a place on the north Cornish coast, the scene of the begetting of Arthur according to Geoffrey of Monmouth and subsequent romancers. The conventional reading of the story makes it his birthplace, too, though Geoffrey gives no actual warrant for this. King Uther, he says, had an ungovernable desire for Ygerna, the wife of Duke Gorlois of Cornwall. The consequent quarrel between the king and the duke led to a local war. Gorlois put his wife in Tintagel Castle, supposedly out of Uther's reach. But the king made his way to her, magically disguised as her husband. Thus Arthur was conceived. Since Gorlois had just been killed, Uther was able to revert to his true shape and make Ygerna his queen.

    Tintagel village is at the head of a ravine that runs downhill to a cove. The locale that Geoffrey has in mind is a huge rocky promontory above the cove, with ruins of a castle. It is almost an island, being connected with the mainland only by a ridge. The ridge has crumbled, so that today a visitor to the ruins and the rest of the promontory has to cross by a footbridge and climb a long flight of steps. In past times, when the ridge was much higher, the crossing from the adjacent hill on the mainland was correspondingly easier, but the path would have been so narrow that a small force could have kept Uther out if he had approached in a normal manner.

Geoffrey's most obvious motive in his choice of this place was therefore topographical. However, a further question arises. The castle was started not earlier than 1141 by Reginald, Earl of Cornwall. But Geoffrey had completed his *Historia* about 1136. When he wrote, the headland was bare, without visible traces of any relevant buildings. To invent an important stronghold on an empty spot, with no previous associations, would have been out of keeping with his habitual practice. The *Historia* as we have it may be a second edition, and he could have added Tintagel after the castle was begun—perhaps to please a half-brother of Reginald's, Earl Robert of Gloucester, from whom he hoped for favor. But this is guesswork, and archaeology offers another explanation.

Dotted about the promontory are the remains of a number of stone buildings quite different from the castle, which were excavated during the 1930s by C.A. Ralegh Radford. In and around these structures, Radford discovered what has sometimes been called Tintagel pottery. He identified fragments of high-quality vessels, some of them of a type used for expensive goods, such as wine and oil. They were not of British make; they had been imported from the Mediterranean region, probably the eastern part, and could be dated to the later fifth century or the sixth. Thus, they provided—for the first time in Britain—an archaeological means of proving occupation in a broadly "Arthurian" span of time. Foreign ware of this kind, classifiable into types, has since come to light in many other places. Where it occurs, it suggests the presence of a wealthy household, importing costly commodities from remote lands.

At Tintagel, Radford interpreted the scattered complex of buildings as a monastery. More recent study, in the light of work on other sites, makes it likelier that the pottery came from a fifth-century ruler's fortress that he never recognized. The inference is that Geoffrey knew an authentic tradition, probably not of actual persons but of the place's occupation in the right period and suitability for his story. Something of the sort may be implied also by his putting Arthur's origin in Cornwall at all, when we might expect him to prefer Wales. For whatever reason, he sensed that Cornwall was correct.

Rock formations around the headland have been given fanciful names, such as Arthur's Chair, and Arthur's Cups and Saucers. A Cornish folk-belief that he turned into a bird has a local version: usually, he is said to have become a raven (a tale known to Cervantes), but a variant makes him a red-legged chough, such as may occasionally be seen perching on Tintagel's cliffs. Further legends aver that the castle was built by giants, that it was painted in a checker pattern of green and blue, and that it vanished on two days of the year. In the neighborhood, folklorists have reported a megalith called Arthur's Quoit and a pond from which the Round Table rises if watched for on the right night.

Other characters are involved with Tintagel besides Arthur. In the Tristan romances, Tintagel Castle belongs to King Mark. Starting from the cove at the foot of the headland, a natural tunnel runs right through its base, and this is Merlin's Cave. The enchanter's ghost reputedly haunts it. When the tide is rising, the sea works its way slowly through the cave, making impressive and eerie sounds.

Tennyson, wishing to get rid of Uther's misconduct but keep Tintagel, invented a legend of his own in which Arthur, as an infant, is mysteriously washed ashore in the cove and taken up from the water by Merlin. In another story, perhaps as recent as Tennyson's, Arthur's life not only begins but ends here. Mortally wounded at Slaughter Bridge on the River Camel, he is said to have been brought to Tintagel and to have died in the castle. His body was conveyed to Glastonbury for burial. The sea moaned and the wind sighed around the promontory till he was laid in his grave. [GA]

Padel, O.J. "Tintagel: An Alternative View." In *A Provisional List of Imported Pottery in Post-Roman Western Britain and Ireland*, ed. Charles Thomas. Redruth: Institute of Cornish Studies, 1981.

Radford, C.A. Ralegh. "Tintagel." In *The Quest for Arthur's Britain*, ed. Geoffrey Ashe. London: Pall Mall, 1968.

"TISTRAM OG JOMFRU ISOLT," a Danish ballad extant in three redactions. The oldest of these probably dates from the fifteenth century. In the oldest version, Tistram decides to woo the emperor's daughter, Isolt. The latter falls in love with him despite her mother's opposition, and during the emperor's absence from the country the two elope, return to Tistram's country, and presumably live happily ever after. The second version is similar to the first except that the mother attempts to poison the lovers, only to be forced to drink the poison herself. Only the third version of the ballad is tragic: Tistram and Isolt are brother and sister, children of the King of Denmark. The mother does not love Isolt and sends her out of the country to be fostered by the Empress of Rome. Without knowing that she is his sister, Tistram woos Isolt as in the other versions. When the empress tells them that they are siblings, Isolt refuses to believe her. The lovers attempt to elope but Isolt is imprisoned in a tower. When Tistram manages to join her there, the empress poisons them. [MEK]

Olrik, Axel, ed. "Tistram og Jomfru Isolt." In *Danmarks gamle Folkeviser*. Copenhagen: Gyldendal, 1919, Vol. 3, pp. 37–46.

Bradley, S.A.J. "The Danish Ballads of Tristan and Isolt." In *The Tristan Legend: Texts from Northern and Eastern Europe in Modern English Translation*, ed. Joyce Hill. Leeds: University of Leeds, Graduate Centre for Medieval Studies, 1977, pp. 144–55.

Schach, Paul. "Tristan and Isolde in Scandinavian Ballad and Folktale." *Scandinavian Studies*, 36 (1964), 281–97.

"TÍSTRAMS TÁTTUR," a Faroese ballad belonging to the Tristan matter but showing no affinity to any of the other Scandinavian versions. The ballad is extant only in a version recorded by V.U. Hammershaimb in 1848 from a seventy-seven-year-old Faroese woman. The ballad, thirty-seven stanzas of four lines each, relates how Tístram's parents separated him from his beloved Ísin by sending him to France, where he was to marry the daughter of the French king. He refuses and is hanged. Upon hearing the news, Ísin herself sails to France and sets the countryside ablaze. To the French king, who asks why she is burning him to death, she replies that she is avenging the fact that Tístram has been taken from her. She removes Tístram from the gallows and then dies of a broken heart. [MEK]

Djurhuus, N., ed. "Tistrams táttur." In *Føroya kvæði. Corpus Færoensium*. Copenhagen: Akademisk Forlag, 1968, Vol. 5, pp. 283–85.

Lockwood, W.B. "The Faroese Ballad of Tristan." In *The Tristan Legend: Texts from Northern and Eastern Europe in Modern English Translation*, ed. Joyce Hill. Leeds: University of Leeds, Graduate Centre for Medieval Studies, 1977, pp. 156–58.

Schach, Paul. "Tristan and Isolde in Scandinavian Ballad and Folktale." *Scandinavian Studies*, 36 (1964), 281–97.

TISTRANS SAGA OK INDIÖNU (or *Sagan af Tistran ok Indiönu*), an Icelandic translation of the eighteenth-century Danish chapbook *En tragoedisk Historie om den ædle og tappre Tistrand*. The saga is extant in three manuscripts from the eighteenth and nineteenth centuries that are preserved in the National Library, Reykjavik. [MEK]

"TISTRUM OG ISALT," a Danish ballad preserved in nine manuscripts that date from the sixteenth and seventeenth centuries. The ballad tells of a tryst between Sir Tistrum and Lady Isalt. Tistrum sends a page to arrange for a secret nocturnal meeting. A handmaiden accompanies Isalt to the meeting-place, and Tistrum and Isalt spend the night under a linden-tree. At daybreak, the handmaiden admonishes the lovers that they must part. Isalt's angry husband, King Magnus, awaits the women, but the handmaiden succeeds in having him believe that they had aided a woman in childbirth. [MEK]

Brynjúlfsson, Gísli, ed. *Saga af Tristram og Ísönd samt Möttuls saga*. Copenhagen: Det kongelige nordiske Oldskrift-Selskab, 1878, pp. 339–42.

Bradley, S.A.J. "The Danish Ballads of Tristan and Isolt." In *The Tristan Legend: Texts from Northern and Eastern Europe in Modern English Translation*, ed. Joyce Hill. Leeds: University of Leeds, Graduate Centre for Medieval Studies, 1977, pp. 144–55.

Schach, Paul. "Tristan and Isolde in Scandinavian Ballad and Folktale." *Scandinavian Studies*, 36 (1964), 281–97.

TITUREL: *see* WOLFRAM VON ESCHENBACH.

TO THE CHAPEL PERILOUS: *see* MITCHISON, NAOMI.

TOM A LINCOLNE: see JOHNSON, RICHARD.

TOM THUMB; A TRAGEDY: see FIELDING, HENRY.

TOO BAD GALAHAD: see COHEN, MATT.

TOPOGRAPHY AND LOCAL LEGENDS. Places associated with Arthur fall into two groups. Only a few, though probably a significant few, belong to both. The first group comprises those where attempts have been made to establish his historical presence. The second comprises those where his name appears, or where local folklore or legend has something to say about him. Other Arthurian characters occasionally appear in the same way. In the first group, the number of places counted depends on the number of speculations judged worth considering; but within the bounds of serious scholarship, this group is not large. The second can be defined more objectively. It embraces about 160 locations in Britain, plus a few more in Brittany.

Several places in the first group correspond, conjecturally, to battle sites listed in Nennius's *Historia Brittonum.* This text supplies "the mouth of the River Glein," "the River Dubglas in the district Linnuis," "the River Bassas," the "Forest of Celidon" or "Caledonian Wood," "Fort Guinnion," "the City of the Legion," "the River Tribruit," "the hill that is called Agned," and "Mount Badon"—a total of ten names, plus an eleventh, "Breguoin," which appears instead of "Agned" in some manuscripts. The problem in finding locations that these names may be thought to represent is that several seem to have been effaced when Anglo-Saxon settlement imposed a different language, while even the rest are, in varying degrees, questionable.

Philological scrutiny has yielded some credible equations. *Glein* means "clear" or "pure," and there are rivers still called Glen in southern Lincolnshire and Northumberland. Both flow into larger rivers and have no "mouth" on the sea, but the word could be used for a confluence. *Dubglas,* meaning "blue-black" or "the black stream," has a cluster of variants—such as Douglas, Dulas, Dawlish, Divelish—and is not helpful. But *Linnuis* probably derives from *Lindenses,* the dwellers in or around *Lindum,* and points to what is now Lindsey, the northern portion of Lincolnshire. In conjunction with *Glein,* it could suggest that Arthur came to this part of the country to oppose Anglo-Saxon encroachments via the Wash and Humber.

Bassas and *Guinnion* are baffling, but the Caledonian Wood and the City of the Legion are the nearest to being sure. The former spread over the southern uplands of Scotland, and the latter, in this context, is almost certainly Chester. *Agned,* according to Geoffrey of Monmouth, is Edinburgh, but he is no longer taken seriously. One guess is that the name may come from a record of British activities in Gaul after the first migration to Armorica, and that *Agned* is a scribally contracted and garbled version of *Andegavum*, Angers. There Saxon settlers in the Loire valley were defeated about 469 by an imperial force that may have included Britons. The alternative *Breguoin* is believed to denote *Bremenium*, the Roman fort of High Rochester in Northumberland, but a poetic allusion to a battle there in the late sixth century hints that its connection with Arthur is anachronistic and therefore spurious (which may also be the case with any of the others, though nothing comparable suggests it).

As for *Badon*, the major victory, it has been detected in several areas. The surviving place-name Badbury is often invoked. On this basis, two former Iron Age hill forts, Badbury Rings in Dorset and Liddington Castle in Wiltshire, which has a village called Badbury close by, have both been favored; the latter perhaps more plausibly. However, Geoffrey's identification of Badon with Bath is approved by some historians, who have stresssed the potentialities of hill forts neighboring it, such as Little Solsbury.

Two further Arthurian places have been looked for with an eye to historical fact. These are Camlann (or Camlan) and Camelot. *Camlann* probably means "crooked bank" and refers to a winding river, beside which Arthur could have fought against Mordred in his last battle. A present-day Camlan in Merioneth has attracted little attention. Geoffrey chooses the River Camel in Cornwall, not an absurd idea but usually dismissed as a mistake. The Somerset Cam has some support. Much has been made of the Roman fort *Camboglanna* on Hadrian's Wall, because this name would have evolved into *Camlann* in Welsh, but the early legend of Arthur and Mordred implies a Cornish tradition and has no trace of a northern origin. Camlann remains elusive. As for Camelot, fanciful identifications with Winchester, Caerwent, and Camelford rest on the misconception that the Camelot of romance was a real city. The only original reality here would have been some sort of Arthurian headquarters, from which the notion of the King's having a personal capital might have been derived. In that sense, the claim of the Somerset hill fort Cadbury Castle carries unrivaled weight.

Places proposed as Kelliwic, Arthur's Cornish home, may be allotted to this group, though even the likeliest of them cannot be given much credence as the residence of a real Arthur. The most favored site is Castle Killibury or Kelly Rounds, a hill fort near Wadebridge. Five other candidates include Callington, across Bodmin Moor, and Callywith, nearer to Bodmin.

Finally, one major Arthurian place raises no problem as to what or where it was, because it still exists under its old name. This is Glastonbury. The question is whether the connection with Arthur has anything in it, allowing Glastonbury's inclusion among places where he may literally have been. Important here is the claim of the monks at Glastonbury Abbey to have found his grave. While most scholars assume that this was fraudulent, some have argued for a prior tradition and even for a bare chance of genuineness.

If we turn to what may loosely be called Arthur's folklore map, this had demonstrably begun to take shape by the ninth century. An appendix to Nennius listing various *Mirabilia*, or Marvels of Britain, mentions two that involve him. The first is in Buelt in central Wales, where Builth Wells preserves the name. This is a stone marked with a dog's paw-print, made by Arthur's dog Cabal during the hunting of the boar Twrch Trwyth, an adventure told at length in *Culhwch and Olwen*. It lies on top of a heap and cannot be removed, because, after a day and a night, it always reappears on the heap. Not far from Rhayader is a hill called Corngafallt, Cabal's Cairn, but it is uncertain whether this is the place intended. The second "marvel" is in Ercing, a district that stretched across Herefordshire. Near the spring Licat Amr, the writer says, is the burial mound of Arthur's son Amr. Arthur killed him there and buried him. The mound changes in size, being anything from six feet long to fifteen at different times. *Licat* means "eye" and also the source of a river, the place from which water flows. The spring is Gamber Head, the source of the Gamber; the mound may have been Wormelow Tump, which no longer exists and therefore cannot be measured.

Two other scraps of local lore are on record before Geoffrey of Monmouth. Hermann of Tournai describes a journey through Devon and Cornwall in 1113, during which the travelers were informed that they were in Arthur's country and were shown Arthur's Chair and Arthur's Oven, probably rock formations or prehistoric stone structures. Arthur's Chair cannot now be identified; Arthur's Oven may have become King's Oven on Dartmoor.

Numerous features of the landscape have acquired names like these. As a rule, it is quite impossible to tell when. Some are natural objects. Some are megaliths, dating from long before any imaginable Arthur. Largest of all is a mountain, Ben Arthur in Argyllshire. Britain has at least six stones known as Arthur's Stone and eleven more known as Arthur's Quoit, most of them in Wales. Four hills show a vaguely saddlelike configuration—a double top with a dip between—that has inspired the name Arthur's Seat, the one beside Edinburgh being the most famous. Cornwall has Arthur's Bed, a large stone lying flat with a hollow in its upper surface; Arthur's Hall, perhaps a misunderstood medieval reservoir; and Arthur's Hunting Lodge, the hill fort Castle-an-Dinas. Earthworks and other formations are "Round Tables," to the number of five at least, a curious instance being at the center of King's Knot below Stirling Castle, once a formal garden of the Royal Stuarts.

The legend of Arthur and his knights lying asleep in a cave has at least fifteen locations. Cadbury Castle is one of them. Others are in Wales, Cheshire, Yorkshire, Northumberland, and Scotland. (*See* CAVE LEGEND.) Normally, the cave is an enchanted underground chamber that is entered only under peculiar circumstances and can never be found otherwise. In addition, two real caves bear Arthur's name, one near Monmouth, one in Anglesey.

At Tintagel, the scene of Arthur's conception and presumably birth, and at Glastonbury, linked with him in several ways, local legends have been created by known literature, such as Geoffrey's *Historia* and the Grail romances. A literary theme that has given other places an Arthurian aspect is the casting-away of Excalibur. This is said to have happened at Pomparles Bridge just outside Glastonbury, where there would then have been an expanse of water;

but it is also said to have happened at Llyn Llydaw in Snowdonia, at Bosherston in Dyfed, and at Dozmary Pool on Bodmin Moor and Loe Pool near Helston, both in Cornwall.

Guenevere, Lancelot, Kay, Mark, and Tristan are also encountered here and there, but, next to Arthur himself, Merlin is the character who figures most frequently and widely. Besides various spots around Carmarthen, his reputed birthplace, he is mentioned at Drumelzier in Peebles and Marlborough in Wiltshire, having been buried in both; at Tintagel, where his ghost haunts Merlin's Cave under the castle headland; and at other Cornish locations. Also, he is in a magic retreat on the Welsh island of Bardsey, keeping the Thirteen Treasures of Britain and a seat on which he will enthrone Arthur when the King returns.

Since only four sites of this type can be proved before Geoffrey—Nennius's pair and Hermann's pair—it is plausible to conclude that literature rather than genuine folklore accounts for most of them, as it does at Tintagel. Of those that clearly reflect romance, some may be surprisingly recent in their Arthurian guise. Dozmary Pool, for instance, has real folkloric associations, but they are not with Arthur. They are with Jan Tregeagle, a figure of popular legend whose ghost roams the moor. The Excalibur story may have been imposed on this atmospheric tarn in the course of the Arthurian vogue started by Tennyson. Even when a place's Arthurian character is spelled out in a medieval text, the lack of any tradition older than that may be fairly obvious. Thus, Guildford is alleged to be Astolat, the home of the lily maid Elaine, and Malory says so. But his only apparent reason is that his plot requires Astolat to be a halting place on the road from London to Camelot. Since he locates Camelot at Winchester, a glance at the map shows Guildford to be a natural choice. There is no need to postulate any prior folk-belief.

Yet explanations of this kind actually have only a rather limited scope. Considering how long the romance-image of "King Arthur and the Knights of the Round Table" has been the familiar one, it is remarkable how little it has stamped itself on the landscape. Most of the Arthurian sites are in places that the romances never mention, often obscure and out of the way. The assorted Stones, Quoits, and so forth are things of immemorial age having nothing to link them with an idealized medieval court. Legends attached to them are apt to portray an Arthur who sounds like some timeless titan or demigod in a barbaric fairyland.

Whereas in his literary guise he fights giants, his topographic lore sometimes makes him a giant himself. Seated on King's Crags in Northumberland, he tossed a huge boulder at Guenevere on Queen's Crags—which are half a mile away. It bounced off her comb and now lies on the ground between, showing the toothmarks. On another occasion, walking through Carmarthenshire, he felt a pebble in his shoe and threw it aside, and it flew seven miles, landing on top of a heap of stones in the Gower peninsula. That pebble is still there, the capstone of what is actually a megalithic burial chamber, and it weighs twenty-five tons. Tales like this, whatever their true age, owe nothing to medieval romance. They are rooted in the soil of Celtic imagination, *Culhwch and Olwen* country, with its superhuman denizens who can run along treetops, drink whole seas dry, and hear the stirring of an ant at a fifty-mile range.

The central contrast appears in the two main versions of Arthur's survival. Romance puts him in the isle of Avalon. Geoffrey introduces this literary motif in his *Vita Merlini*. Describing the western "island of apples," he shows acquaintance with Celtic myth, and probably with popular Breton ideas. Even so, the island retreat never commended itself to the folklore of Wales. There and elsewhere in Britain, Arthur lives on as the sleeper in the secret cavern, with attendant knights around him. In this case, we have two expressions of the same theme, and it is not the one known to romance that inspires local legends.

There is a further consideration. Taken together, the two versions, island and cave, amount to evidence for a common source long before Geoffrey—indeed, before Arthur himself, whose legend here seems to have annexed a senior one. In A.D. 82, an official named Demetrius, on a visit to Roman Britain, noted one of the few myths of the British Celts ever to be recorded in plain terms. His report, or some of it, is transmitted by Plutarch. The Britons told of a god lying asleep in a cave on an island, a warm and pleasant place "in the general direction of sunset," with attendant spirits around him. Unfortunately, Plutarch follows the practice of his time by giving not the god's Celtic name but the name of a classical deity with whom he can supposedly be equated. Plutarch's chosen equivalent is Cronus, Zeus's father and predecessor in sovereignty, who presided over a golden age but went into exile on his son's rise to power. It is likely that both versions of Arthur's immortality derive ultimately from this British Cronus, the departed ruler who slept in a cave on a paradisal western isle. Certainly, it emerges that Arthur's cave legend has a remote Celtic antecedent, which supplied the mold, at whatever stage this particular hero was fitted into it.

To appraise the list of sites as a whole, in relation to the map, is to bring out a further point. For eight centuries, romance has depicted Arthur as king of all Britain, yet very little indeed of the topographic lore has developed in those areas where Anglo-Saxon dominance has been fullest. Arthur, it has been remarked, is more widespread than anybody except the Devil; so perhaps he is, but he is not everywhere. Preponderantly, the place-names and local legends belong to the West Country, Wales, Cumbria, southern Scotland—to the Celtic fringe, where Celtic people, descendants of Arthur's people, maintained a measure of identity longest, and in some cases still do. They occur in Brittany also, the overseas extension of the same fringe. In most of England, on the other hand, they are scanty. Arthur's folkloric presence belongs almost wholly to regions where he might have been active and where descendants of the Britons did create a saga of him before medieval romance began. The inference is that the saga, not the romance, was the main foundation for local lore and that, however late some of this may be, it has generally depended on deep and authentic popular roots. Nothing necessarily follows, of course, about folk-memory of historical fact, though in a few instances (as at Cadbury) archaeology supplies grounds for suspecting it. (*See also* FOLKLORE; RETURN, LEGENDS OF ARTHUR'S.) [GA]

Alcock, Leslie. *Arthur's Britain*. London: Penguin, 1971.
Ashe, Geoffrey. *A Guidebook to Arthurian Britain*. Wellingborough: Aquarian, 1983.
Chambers, E.K. *Arthur of Britain*. London: Sidgwick and Jackson, 1927.
Rhys, John. *Celtic Folklore*. 2 vols. Oxford: Clarendon, 1901.
Snell, F.J. *King Arthur's Country*. London: Dent, 1926.

TOREC: see MAERLANT, JACOB VAN.

TORROELLA, GUILLEM, the fourteenth-century Mallorcan author of *La Faula* ("The Tale"), one of the most original Hispanic adaptations of a French Arthurian text. Composed in verse (1,269 lines) and written in Catalan with some dialogue in French, *La Faula* narrates the purportedly autobiographic vision of the poet involving his fantastic voyage on a whale to the Enchanted Island—identified by modern critics with Sicily—where King Arthur and his sister Morgana wait for Arthur's messianic return to Britain. The poet describes in detail Arthur's palace, where he sees paintings depicting deeds of leading knights of the Round Table and then observes an infirm but young-looking Arthur lamenting the decline of chivalry. Arthur informs the poet of how Morgana brought him to the island after the battle of Salisbury Plain, how every year the Holy Grail provides him with youth-giving nourishment, and how figures depicted on his sword Excalibur provide a moral lesson for kings. Arthur charges the poet with recounting this lesson to the world together with all else he has seen. Torroella skillfully combines material from the *Mort Artu* branch of the Vulgate Cycle with topics and narrative devices found in other French courtly romances. His style is noteworthy for its use of *amplificatio* in the description of objects, animals, and places. [HLS]

Torroella, Guillem. *La Faula*, ed. Pere Bohigas and Jaume Vidal Alcover. Tarragona: Tàrraco, 1984.

TOUR DE L'IVOIRE, LA: see SECOND EMPIRE.

TOURNAMENT BOOKS. Tournaments originated as training exercises for deadly warfare; the early tournaments, known as Round Tables, were immensely popular exercises of both military and carousing skills. By the time tournaments became fashionable court entertainments, however, the mounted knights had lost their effectiveness on the battlefield. Henry V of England's victory over the French at Agincourt in 1415 completed the rout. Tournaments continued, and in fact reached new popularity, in the nostalgic revival of a romantic chivalry in the fifteenth century under such enthusiasts as King René I of Naples and Anjou and the Tudor monarchs in England (who came to power in 1485). King René wrote the finest book of tournament ceremonial (Paris, B.N. fr. 2692), 1460–65, in which he described and illustrated every detail of the pageant.

Heralds, whose function of announcing and identifying the participants had expanded into that of judges, scorekeepers, and ultimately genealogists who recorded and authenticated coats-of-arms, also had their tournament rolls. The military roll of arms, known as *Sir Thomas Holmes' Book*, 1448, illustrated with pairs of jousting knights, recorded arms of knights of the shires. The ceremonial extended into literature; King Arthur and his knights also had their personal coats-of-arms, recorded in such manuscripts as the *Names and Blazons of the Knights of the Round Table* (Pierpont Morgan Library, MS 16). Specific events might also be recorded; *The Great Tournament Role of Westminster* depicts the tournament held in honor of the birth of a son to Henry VIII and Catherine of Aragon 12–13 February 1510/11. The procession at the entrance, the king tilting, and the exit of the participants are depicted in a continuous narrative.

Tournaments continued to be popular under Elizabeth and James I. The Queen's Champions organized spectacular Accession Day Tilts, which were pageants designed around allegorical themes often based on the stories of the knights of the Round Table. (*See also* ARMS AND ARMOR; HERALDRY; ROUND TABLES.) [MS]

ᴥ Anglo, S. *The Great Tournament Role of Westminster.* Oxford, 1968.

Brault, Gerard J. *Early Blazon: Heraldic Terminology in the 12th and 13th Centuries with Special Reference to Arthurian Literature.* London: Oxford University Press, 1972.

Marks, Richard, and Ann Payne. *British Heraldry from Its Origins to ca. 1800.* London: British Museum, 1978.

TRAGÈDIA DE LANÇALOT: *see* GRAS, MOSSÈN.

TRAGEDIE VON DER STRENGEN LIEB, HERR TRISTRANT MIT DER SCHÖNEN KÖNIGIN ISALDEN: *see* SACHS, HANS.

TRAGEDY OF ETARRE, THE: *see* CARPENTER, RHYS.

TRAGEDY OF PARDON, THE: *see* FIELD, MICHAEL.

TRAGEDY OF TRAGEDIES: *see* FIELDING, HENRY.

**TRAGOEDISK HISTORIE OM DEN ÆDLE OG TAPPRE TIS-
TRAND, EN.** The full title of the eighteenth-century Danish chapbook about
Tristan and Isolt is *En tragoedisk Historie om den ædle og tappre Tistrand, Hertugens
Søn af Burgundien, og den skiønne Indiana, den store Mogul Kejserens Daatter af Indien*
("A Tragic Story of the Noble and Courageous Tistrand, Son of the Duke of
Burgundy, and Indiana, the Daughter of the Ruler of India"). According to the
title page, the novel had been translated from German into Danish, but the
Danish version is unlike any earlier Tristan novel known in German. Since a
number of German chapbooks were translated into Danish during the seventeenth and eighteenth centuries, the source presumably was the fifteenth-
century German chapbook *Ein wunderbarliche vnd fast lustige Historij von Herr
Tristrant vnd der schönen Isalden.* The earliest extant edition of the Danish
chapbook is that published in Christiania, now Oslo, in 1775. During the next
twenty-five years, there were three further editions issued in Copenhagen
(1785, 1792, and 1800). These four editions may be found in the Royal Library
in Copenhagen.

Although the Danish *Tistrand* retains most of the significant motifs and
episodes of the medieval Tristan matter, such as the fight with the dragon, the
love potion, the sword between the lovers, and the marriage to the second
Isolt, the author of the chapbook has rewritten the romance with an eye not
only to removing all that might offend eighteenth-century sensibilities but also
to presenting Isolt as a being governed by reason and the lovers as saintly
figures.

The source for the unusual names in the Danish *Tistrand* is not known. The
protagonists are Tistrand of Burgundy and Indiana of India. Tistrand marries
Innanda, whose appearance and name remind him of his beloved Indiana.
Tistrand's uncle and Indiana's husband is King Alfonsus of Spain, and Indiana's
handmaiden is called Galmeye. An otherwise-unknown figure in the Tristan
romances plays a major role in the chapbook: Roderich, Tistrand's mother's
brother's son, who envies Tistrand's favored position with both King Alfonsus
and Indiana and who plots at one time or another to kill Tistrand, Alfonsus,
and Indiana. In the Danish chapbook, Tistrand kills not Indiana's uncle but
rather her beloved, Kunchin, son of the Emperor of China.

The plot commences with Tistrand's decision to visit his uncle in Spain and
to prove himself worthy of being his heir. King Kunchin attacks the Spanish
realm but is killed by Tistrand. A splinter of Tistrand's sword lodges in the
body of Kunchin, which is taken to Indiana, Kunchin's beloved. Tistrand has
received a wound from Kunchin's poisoned sword, and no physician is able to
cure him. When he learns about Indiana's wondrous healing powers, he decides
to seek her out. She does not realize his identity and heals him.

When Tistrand triumphantly returns to Spain, Roderich makes an unsuccessful attempt upon his life. Fearing for his own safety, Tistrand suggests that
his uncle should marry, and then Tistrand himself goes to seek the hand of
Indiana for his uncle. Upon arriving in India, Tistrand encounters a poisonous

dragon and kills it but is overcome by the fumes from the dragon's tongue, which he has cut out as proof of his deed. He is found and revived by Indiana but also recognized as Kunchin's killer when she sees Tistrand's sword. Indiana listens to reason, however, and does not kill Tistrand, as she desires, but instead agrees to marry Tistrand's uncle.

On their voyage to Spain, Tistrand and Indiana unwittingly imbibe the love potion intended for Alfonsus and Indiana and fall in love. Theirs is not a sexual union, however; Tistrand must be satisfied to kiss Indiana's hand. Once in Spain, Tistrand continues to sleep in the king's bedroom, although a screen separates him from the royal couple. On two occasions, Tistrand steals out of bed in order to kiss the sleeping Indiana's hand. Each time, he withdraws in haste for fear that Indiana might awaken and be displeased. On the second occasion, Roderich has strewn sand to entrap Tistrand, but the latter jumps to—not into—Indiana's bed. The exertion of the jump causes his nose to bleed as he bends over Indiana's hand for the kiss. As he turns to leave her bedside, he is seized by Roderich as if it were in *flagrante delicto*. Tistrand and Indiana are sentenced to hanging and burning, respectively. On the way to his execution, Tistrand is rescued by his men, while Indiana is saved from burning only to be delivered to a worse fate: she is handed over to a leprous heathen king. Tistrand and his men succeed in freeing her, however.

Since the lovers cannot return to court, they make their abode in the woods. Although Tistrand pleads with Indiana to let him sleep with her, she refuses and maintains that despite the death sentence she is still Alfonsus's wife. Finally, she relents to the extent that Tistrand may share her resting place, but only if a sword separates them physically: the sword in the chapbook—unlike the sword in the medieval romances—retains its true symbolic value. While hunting, King Alfonsus comes upon the lovers as they sleep in this manner and has them recalled to court, where they receive full pardon. The lovers undergo a trial by ordeal and are vindicated.

Once the lovers have been fully rehabilitated, Tistrand takes leave to visit his parents. In France, he marries Innanda, whose beauty and name remind him of Indiana. After Tristrand's departure from Spain, Roderich makes several attempts on the lives of Alfonsus, Indiana, and their unborn child but is finally caught and sentenced to be drawn and quartered. He prefers to take his own life.

Although the marriage between Tistrand and Innanda is consummated and they have children, Tistrand cannot forget Indiana and daily admires and kisses a likeness of her. Innanda comes upon the scene one day and henceforth regards her husband coolly. During a subsequent secret meeting with Indiana, Tistrand tells her about the incident with the likeness. Indiana is pragmatic and advises Tistrand to throw the likeness away in order to save .the marriage. She comforts him with the thought that their respective children will be able to marry each other even though Tistrand and Indiana could not.

Accompanying Innanda's brother on a bridal quest to England, Tistrand is wounded by a poisoned arrow as they abduct the bride. He sends for Indiana to heal him and asks that a red sail be raised if she returns with his men but a black sail if she is not on board. Both Indiana and her husband, Tistrand's uncle, rush to save Tistrand, but Innanda betrays her husband by announcing that the sail is black. Tistrand dies in despair. Upon learning of Tistrand's death, Indiana informs Innanda that she had not come to take Tistrand away from her but rather to give him back to her by healing him.

Now that Tistrand is dead, Indiana herself can no longer live. Before expiring, Indiana exacts from her husband the promise that her children by Alfonsus and Tistrand's by Innanda be united in marriage and that she be buried in one coffin with Tistrand. Only after the lovers are dead does Galmeye, Indiana's handmaiden, reveal the source of the lovers' irresistible attraction to each other, that is, the love potion. Tistrand's uncle is shaken and says that he would have granted wife and kingdom to Tistrand had he known the true situation.

The bodies of Tistrand and Indiana are laid out on a royal bed, and a lily grows from each breast and intertwines with the other. The lovers receive a royal burial in the monastery of St. Diogenes and Pope Cleo canonizes them. As a sign of their eternal love, the French coat-of-arms carries the fleur-de-lis.

The several editions of the Danish *Tistrand og Indiana* attest the popularity of the romance in eighteenth-century Denmark and Norway. The chapbook was also known in Iceland in the nineteenth century. A translation, *Tistrans saga ok Indiönu*, exists in several manuscripts, and the two nineteenth-century authors Sigurður Breiðfjörð and Níels Jónsson wrote *rímur* about Tístran and Indíana.

The version of the Tristan romance that became known in modern Scandinavia through the Danish chapbook lacked the very elements that are the essence of the medieval romance, that is, adultery and willful deception. The chapbook tells a tale of platonic love; Tistrand and Indiana belong more to the realm of hagiography than romance. [MEK]

⧫ *En tragoedisk Historie om den ædle og tappre Tistrand, Hertugens Søn af Burgundien, og den skiønne Indiana, den store Mogul Kejserens Daatter af Indien. Nu nyligen af Tydsk paa Dansk oversat.* Christiania, 1775.

Nyerup, Rasmus. *Almindelig Morskabslæsning i Danmark og Norge igjennem Aarhundreder.* Copenhagen: Seidelin, 1816, pp. 118–19.

———. "Almuens Morskabslæsning." *Iris og Hebe*, October–December 1796, 192–210.

TRAITIÉ DU BLAZON D'ARMES: *see* HERALDRY.

TREECE, HENRY (1912–1966), British apocalyptic poet, historian, and novelist, wrote three historical novels using Arthurian material. Believing that the Age of Migration provided one of the "crossroads of history," when "individuals of opposing sides meet and learn from one another, merge and come to terms," he brings his protagonists in contact with an unromantic, fifth-century Arthur, "a ruthless and possibly half-barbaric Celt, who had adopted Roman manners and military methods." The Bear's missing eye, teeth, and fingers, his tattooed cheeks and lame leg, indicate a violent life. In the juvenile novel *The Eagles Have Flown* (1954), two boys—Festus, a Romanized Celt, and Wulf, a Jute—provide the narrative view of Arthur's battles, a theme expanded in the adult novel *The Great Captains* (1956). Camlann and Camelot are identified with Colchester. In *The Green Man* (1966), Amleth (Hamlet), motivated by visions and lust for vengeance, travels from Jutland to Geatland, Arthur's Britain, and Pictish Caledonia, where he encounters three aggressive societies. The large cast of characters includes Gwenhwyvar, Ygerne, Kei, Bedwyr, Gavin, Medreut, a Pictish queen descended from Clytemnestra, and Beowulf, the hero's nemesis. Treece rationalizes some mythic elements (e.g., the Sword in the Stone is Caliburn deliberately buried in an oak-bole; the Round Table is Arthur's shield around which the Welsh kings unhierarchically sit) but retains Merlin's prophetic powers and the Green Man's fertility rites. He demonstrates his view that an author should "tell his real readers about real life" by emphasizing the terror and violence of battle, murder, rape, mutilation, cannibalism, and unbridled cruelty. His Arthurian world is derived from the chronicles of Gildas and Nennius, the architecture and artifacts of Roman Britain, archaeological research, and his own observation of British landscape and seascape. Whether or not it is real, it is certainly brutal. [MAW]

꙾ Treece, Henry. *The Eagles Have Flown*. London: Allen and Unwin, 1954.

———— . *The Great Captains*. London: Bodley Head, 1956.

———— . *The Green Man*. New York: Putnam, 1966.

Anon. "Henry Treece: Lament for a Maker." In *Only Connect*, ed. Sheila Egoff, G.T. Stubbs, and L.F. Ashley. Toronto: Oxford University Press, 1969.

Fisher, Margery. *Henry Treece*. London: Bodley Head, 1969.

"TRES HIJUELOS HABÍA EL REY: *see LANÇAROTE DE LAGO*.

TREVELYAN, ROBERT CALVERLY (1872–1951), makes intellectual mockery of Wagnerian pretension in his verse "operatic fable" *The New Parsifal* (1914). After an introduction poking fun at the self-importance of both Wagner and the Lord Chamberlain (the British dramatic censor), we see Klingsor transported to Circe's Isle. The potency of the Grail is questioned, British professors appear, and the unlikely new Parsifal arrives in an airplane. [CNS]

꙾ Trevelyan, R.C. *The New Parsifal*. London: Chiswick, 1914.

TREVISA, JOHN (ca. 1342–1402), during the 1360s and 70s lived at Oxford, where he may have helped translate the Lollard Bible. After becoming Vicar of Berkeley (ca. 1380), he translated into English Higden's *Polychronicon* (1387),

Aegidius Romanus's *De Regimine Principum*, and Bartholomaeus Anglicus's *De Proprietatibus Rerum* (1398). His translation of the Arthurian section of the *Polychronicon* includes a lively protest against Higden's doubts about the truth of the Arthurian stories, doubts based largely on the silence about Arthur in foreign chronicles. The Gospel of John contains much, Trevisa reminds us, omitted by Mark, Luke, and Matthew; similarly, Geoffrey of Monmouth's account contains much about which others were ignorant. [EDK]

&▪ Trevisa, John. *Polychronicon Ranulphi Higden*, ed. C. Babington and J.R. Lumby. 9 vols. London: Longman, 1865–86, esp. Vol. 5, pp. 328–38.

Taylor, John. *The Universal Chronicle of Ranulf Higden.* Oxford: Clarendon, 1966, pp. 134–42.

Fowler, D.C. "New Light on John Trevisa." *Traditio*, 18 (1962), 289–317.

———."John Trevisa: Scholar and Translator." *Transactions of the Bristol and Gloucestershire Archaeological Society,* 89 (1970), 99–108.

TREVOR, MERIOL, author of *Merlin's Ring* (1957), a didactic juvenile fantasy about a boy transported briefly, through the power of Merlin's ring, back to the months preceding Arthur's victory at Badon. After witnessing the political scheming among the Britons, he learns the dangers of ambition, spite, and greed. [RHT]

&▪ Trevor, Meriol. *Merlin's Ring.* London: Collins, 1957.

TRIADS, summaries of Welsh bardic lore, grouped in sets of three. The series known as the "Triads of the Island of Britain" relates to a semilegendary heroic age when the Britons were still predominant—or, at least, had not entirely succumbed to the Saxons—and records the names and exploits of the principal heroes, together with several villains. More than a dozen of these Triads introduce Arthur, and most of the characters who are mentioned belong, like him, to a period stretching from the Roman twilight into the seventh century. However, the heroic age is vague and blends with the pre-Roman, so that Julius Caesar's opponent Cassivellanus also appears, as does the euhemerized god Beli, supposedly his father. Among the post-Roman characters, some are historical or have real originals. Others are doubtful or fictitious.

The triadic form in general may reflect Celtic ideas about the mystique of the number three. But in the "Island of Britain" series, the Triad is a mnemonic device. Bards arranged their topics in threes under headings that applied in common, so that any member of the Triad would bring the others to mind. By way of illustration, a modern storyteller who told stories from Shakespeare might link *Othello, Cymbeline,* and *The Winter's Tale* by means of a Triad like this:

> Three Jealous Islanders:
> Othello in Cyprus,
> and Posthumus in Britain,
> and Leontes in Sicily.

The tale of Othello would be a reminder of the plays with Posthumus and Leontes in them, supplying encores. Some of the Welsh Triads are brief like this example, others amplify. Many are late, influenced by Geoffrey of Monmouth or Arthurian romance, and quite a number are outright forgeries. The most valuable are in manuscripts of the thirteenth, fourteenth, and fifteenth centuries, which despite their date contain matter far older than Geoffrey. In a few instances, Nennius or the *Mabinogion* may preserve a story complete. Usually, however, the story is lost and only the triadic summary survives.

Arthur's elevation above other characters is shown not only by the frequency of his appearances but by the fact that several Triads have been enlarged into tetrads to bring him in. Thus, the Triad of the "Three Exalted Prisoners" lists them as Llyr, Mabon, and Gwair. It then adds that there was a prisoner still more exalted, namely Arthur, and notes three places of confinement from which his cousin Goreu released him.

Traditions such as this suggest guerrilla warfare or solitary adventuring rather than kingship. Most of the Triads that say anything of consequence about Arthur, and are free from Geoffrey's influence, do tend to have a primitive air. He is seldom portrayed as a mighty war-leader against the Saxons. In fact, the battle of Badon is never mentioned. The battle of Camlann is: it is one of the "Three Futile Battles," the outcome of a conflict between Arthur and Mordred, which sounds more like a feud of barbaric equals than a case of treason. According to another Triad, the "Three Unrestrained Ravagings," Mordred came to Arthur's court at Kelliwic in Cornwall, where his men consumed all the food and drink, and their leader struck Guenevere. Arthur retaliated with a similar raid on Mordred's court.

The triadic Arthur is apt to be unexpected. For instance:

> Three Frivolous Bards of the Island of Britain:
> Arthur,
> and Cadwallawn son of Cadfan,
> and Rahawd son of Morgant.

In *Culhwch and Olwen*, Arthur justifies the description in some degree by making up a short verse, at which Cai takes offense. Another Triad makes Arthur guilty of one of the "Three Wicked Uncoverings" or "Unfortunate Disclosures"—the digging up of the head of Bran, buried on Tower Hill in London as a talisman against foreign dangers. Arthur removed it, on the ground that the Britons should rely on the military effort under his leadership. The magic was gone and in due course the Saxons conquered. In another Triad, he is one of the "Red Ravagers." Wherever he walked, neither grass nor plants would spring up for seven years.

Tristan, as "Drystan," also appears in several Triads. The most remarkable makes him one of the "Three Powerful Swineherds." Strictly speaking, he was a deputy swineherd. He looked after Mark's pigs while their usual guardian took a message to Iseult for him. Arthur tried to raid the herd but failed to get a single pig, whether by force, deception, or stealth.

Guenevere, as "Gwenhwyfar," occurs a few times apart from her husband. She is added to the Triad of the "Three Faithless Wives" as "one more faithless than those three." A puzzling Triad lists Arthur's "Three Great Queens" and says they were all called Gwenhwyfar. This may be a case of multiple personality such as is found here and there in Celtic legend, being derived, it seems, from ancient representations of deities (notably the Great Mother) in triple form. There may be a connection with the True and False Guineveres in the Vulgate Cycle. [GA]

ે Bromwich, Rachel. *Trioedd Ynys Prydein.* Cardiff: University of Wales Press, 1961.

——— . "The Welsh Triads." In *Arthurian Literature in the Middle Ages*, ed. Roger Sherman Loomis. Oxford: Clarendon, 1959, pp. 44–51.

TRISTAN: *see* TRISTAN AND ISOLDE.

TRISTAN: see BÉROUL; CLOSS, HANNAH; GOTTFRIED VON STRASSBURG; HEINRICH VON FREIBURG; KUNCEWICZ, MARIA; MANN, THOMAS; THOMAS D'ANGLETERRE.

TRISTAN. Only one fragment has been preserved of the Middle Dutch adaptation of the *Tristan* of Thomas (Vienna, Österreichische Nationalbibliothek, Series Nova 3968). The fragment numbers 158 lines and dates from the middle of the thirteenth century. The text has been transmitted in a Low Frankish dialect. The adaptation originated at the end of the twelfth century or the beginning of the thirteenth. [BB]

ે Smet, G., and Maurits Gysseling, eds. "Die niederfrankischen Tristan-Bruchstüke, Cod. Vind. ser. Nova 3968." *Studia Germanica Gandensia*, 9 (1967), 197–234.

TRISTÁN: see TRISTAN IN SPANISH AND PORTUGUESE.

TRISTAN, **MODERN GERMAN VERSIONS OF GOTTFRIED'S.** The relationship of the Tristan story to the Arthurian corpus is a tenuous one, and in Germany at least the development proceeded largely unaffected by the *matière de Bretagne.* Perhaps because the story became the basis for one of the most brilliant literary achievements of German medieval literature, or perhaps because the story in its German form appealed so strongly to something in the German character, it has remained a constant source of material for German writers. The number of literary recreations, excluding editions and translations, is consequently so large that no attempt can be made here to survey or even list them. Emphasis will therefore be placed on a few periods at which interest seems to be peculiarly intense.

Gottfried von Strassburg makes it clear at the beginning of his *Tristan* that he has been careful to seek out the "genuine" source; Eilhart von Oberge's version is not acceptable to him. Gottfried's source is Thomas d'Angleterre, whose work he seems to use freely, although comparison is not easy, given the fragmentary nature of the Thomas manuscripts and the lack of an ending to Gottfried's work. The essential feature of the story as related by Gottfried is the positive attitude toward the love relationship. The effect of the love potion is absolute, permanent, and fully accepted by the lovers. The poem depicts the emotional relationship as a supreme experience but one that conflicts with contemporary social and religious norms. The story is not placed in relation to the Arthurian world.

When Gottfried's work was completed by later writers—Ulrich von Türheim in 1235 and Heinrich von Freiberg in 1290—these poets turned to Eilhart as a source and to a tradition in which the love relationship was brought about by a force, the potion, that was not permanent (usually limited to four years) and was seen rather as an unfortunate aberration than as a positive experience. This became the dominant tradition through the following centuries, as the story was told and retold in prose, sometimes with the inclusion of figures from the Arthurian world (already in Heinrich von Freiberg's version, Tristan spends some time at Arthur's court). In the chapbooks that appear every ten to twenty years from 1484 to 1664, the basic elements of the story remain much the same: parentage, battle with Morold, cure, wooing mission, love potion, intrigues, banishment, marriage to Isolde Weisshand, visits to Isolde, second poisoned wound, black/white sail, death. Only once, approximately in the middle of this period, is the story taken up by a major poet, and his attitude toward the material may be taken as representative of the prose works in general.

Hans Sachs treated the story in two ways. In 1553, he completed a seven-act tragedy on the topic (*Tragedia von der strengen Lieb, Herr Tristrant mit der schönen Königin Isalden*) and wrote also the last of a series of seven fairly short *Meisterlieder*. His source is the chapbook published in Worms in 1550. He adheres closely to the substance of it. Each poem treats only one aspect of the story, but the drama takes the lovers through the usual sequence of events. The seven "acts" are little more than scenes in which 1) Tristan kills Morold; 2) Tristan obtains a cure for his wound, returns to Ireland, and kills the dragon; 3) Tristan wins Isolde for Marke and shares the love potion with her; 4) the lovers engage in intrigues but successfully deceive the king; 5) they are caught, condemned to death, escape to the forest, and are finally separated; 6) Tristan visits Isolde in fool's clothing; 7) Tristan is wounded and dies, Isolde arrives too late and dies also. The work closes with a speech by the "Herold" in which the audience is encouraged to take heed of the fate of the lovers and to resist love's blandishments in favor of honorable marriage. The chapbook of 1484 had ended with a similar warning against worldly love.

The development of an interest in Germany's literary past and the Romantic revival of the Middle Ages in particular are the prime factors in the rediscovery and further development of the Tristan story at the end of the eighteenth and beginning of the nineteenth century. There were editions and translations both of Gottfried's work and of the chapbooks. Academic reaction was for the most part hostile to the content of the story while grudgingly admitting the poetic qualities of Gottfried's version. One might have expected the Romantic poets to take up the story with enthusiasm; that they did not is symptomatic of their essentially conservative stance in moral matters (the most scathing condemnation of Gottfried ever written is from Eichendorff's pen). Typical of the Romantics, too, is the existence of so many fragmentary attempts to treat the material. A.W. Schlegel, Friedrich Rückert, and many others left fragments of translations and poetic or dramatic versions, of which only that by Immermann is at all extensive.

August von Platen planned the earliest Tristan drama in the 1820s; a complete but brief plan seems to have been drawn up in June of 1827 (*Sämtliche Werke*, ed. Max Koch and Erich Petzet. Leipzig: Hesse, 1910, Vol. 10, 373–82). However, nothing further came of this plan, which envisaged five acts, beginning with the situation after Isolde's arrival in Cornwall. The meeting between Tristan and Isolde is betrayed to Marke by Auctrat, who wounds Tristan with a poisoned arrow, since banishment is in his view not a sufficient punishment. It is also Auctrat who tells Tristan of the black sail; there is no second Isolde.

The first part of a dramatic version by Friedrich Roeber was published in 1840, but it is not clear from the subsequent edition of this version together with a revised version in 1898, whether or not the whole had been completed at the earlier date (*Tristan und Isolde. Eine Tragödie. In zwei nach Inhalt und Form verschiedenen Bearbeitungen*. Leipzig: Baedeker, 1898). The dates are given here as 1838 and 1898. Roeber's concern is with the morality of the action, and he therefore has Brangane as a regular substitute for Isolde in the first version, while in the second the marriage (and the moral dilemma) is continually postponed. Brangane is in any case in love with Marke, and her feeling is reciprocated in the later version. It is Roeber's view that tragedy can be convincing only if the tragic characters are morally sound.

Karl Immermann, too, was perplexed by the problem of morality, but he takes a different approach in his dramatic poem *Tristan und Isolde*, which remained unfinished at his death in 1840 and which has been both fulsomely praised and condemned as extraordinarily bad (Düsseldorf: Schaub, 1841). It is certainly of very uneven quality, lacking in concentration, and would, if completed, have been inordinately long. The most interesting aspect is Immermann's attempt to change the function of the ordeal. Isolde demands the ordeal without any plan for falsifying the oath, and she even rejects Tristan's offer of rescue by force. She survives the ordeal, because she knows in her heart that she wishes to be pure and is acting only under the influence of the potion. The passing of the test she sees as a sign of grace, and this enables her to regain the moral strength to refrain from sin, even though her love for Tristan does not die; she insists on the separation.

A number of plays on the Tristan material appeared in the latter half of the nineteenth century, most of them in blank verse and all of them designated either as tragedies or as *Trauerspiele*. Josef Weilen's play *Tristan* appeared in 1860 (Breslau: Max), presumably too early to be influenced by Wagner, whose opera had been published in 1859 but was not performed until 1865; there are, however, clear signs of the influence of Immermann—for example, in the figure of Ritter John and in the lovers' intention to commit suicide by throwing themselves from the ship. Tristan is betrayed to Marke before the lovers have any assignation, but after his departure Isolde refuses to marry Marke and falls into a decline. When Tristan returns in the guise of a pilgrim, he claims to be able to cure Isolde, but, when she is brought before him, the true story of their innocent and compulsive love is told, at which point Tristan gives Isolde to Marke and kills himself. Isolde dies of grief. The tenor of the work as a whole is pessimistic rather than genuinely tragic. "Das Höchste Recht auf Erden ist die Liebe" (p. 122), but love cannot thrive in society as it is.

A better work is Ludwig Schneegans's *Tristan* (Leipzig: Wigand, 1865), for here the plot has been purged of medievalisms and subplots. Tristan and Isolde fall in love on the voyage (without a love potion), and their attempt to suppress their feelings and renounce their love on the day that Isolde marries Marke is thwarted only because their parting is betrayed to the king. He banishes them on the spot but later, when he finds them in the cave, literally drags Isolde from Tristan, who flees and attempts to find solace with the second Isolde. The main issue in this work is the right to love. Marke is guilty of marrying Isolde without love, and Tristan and Isolde are "guilty" of attempting renunciation.

Albert Gehrkes's *Isolde* (Berlin: Heimann, 1869) avoids many of the problems posed by the medieval plot, for Tristan and Isolde are openly in love before Tristan is revealed as the killer of Morhold (in this work Isolde's father). There is nevertheless a potion, but Isolde is told by its guardian, the Marshall, that it is a "hate potion," for it is his hope that she will drink it with him in order to be freed from his importunate love. In Cornwall, prior to the marriage ceremony, the Marshall assassinates Tristan but is then deceived by Isolde, who puts poison rather than the love/hate potion into the wine, thus avenging the death of both her father and Tristan.

Bessel's short work *Tristan und Isolde* (Kiel: Lipsius and Tischer, 1895) also simplifies the plot considerably. Here, Tristan and Isolde are in love before Marke sends Tristan to woo for him, and the love potion is deliberately administered and the lovers told of this by Brangane, who wants them to declare themselves. Immediately after the marriage, however, the lovers are caught with the usual ruse. Tristan is condemned to death and Isolde is forced to swear loyalty to Marke in order to save Tristan (which naturally causes doubts in his mind about her loyalty). In the final scene, she forgets to hoist the white flag and Tristan stabs himself; they exchange last words before Tristan dies and Isolde stabs herself. The emphasis in this work is firmly on the innocence of the lovers, caught in an impossible situation. When Marke learns the truth, he sets out to save them but comes too late.

The first decades of the twentieth century produced a large number of editions, translations, and reworkings of the Tristan story, many of them based on Gottfried, and most of them again in dramatic form. Of the prose versions, the best known is probably the novella by Thomas Mann (1903), but this work, set in the modern context of a sanatorium, is better seen as a satire on Wagner and his relationship with the Wesendonks. In 1923, Mann also drafted the plot for a film version, based primarily on Gottfried, a project that was never carried out. The only major change that he makes in his plot summary is to substitute for the earlier episodes a situation in which Tristan and Isolde know of each other by repute and are attracted to each other prior to their meeting. Their love develops during the wooing mission, and the potion only has the effect of releasing them from the restrictive bonds of duty. Mann planned, rather surprisingly, to retain most of the subsequent episodes of intrigue.

Other prose works, such as Emil Lucka's *Isolde Weisshand* (Berlin: Fischer, 1909) and Will Vesper's *Tristan und Isolde* (Munich: Langewiesche-Brandt, 1911), are much inferior to the dramatic works. There is a stronger tendency to embroider on the original in the prose, but neither here nor in the stage works is there more than the occasional attempt to modernize the medieval situation entirely. One such exception is *Tristans Ehe*, by Karl Albrecht Bernouilli (Leipzig: Reclam, 1926; an earlier version perhaps in 1916). In this work, Marke is an American millionaire, and there are modern equivalents of traditional episodes, including a dwarf, a miniature dog, and "Tristan" as a clown. The action revolves around Isolde's unbalanced state of mind after "Tristan's" disappearance and the efforts made by the psychiatrist to cure her. In the final scenes, he seems to have succeeded, for, despite a near-riot in the mental asylum, the two couples—"Marke" and "Isolde" and "Tristan" and the second "Isolde"—are reunited!

Returning to more traditional paths, Albert Geiger's play is entitled *Tristan* (Karlsruhe: Bielefeld, 1906) but consists of two parts, "Blanscheflur" and "Isolde." The first part follows the Gottfried plot fairly closely, except that Riwalin dies immediately after taking Blanscheflur to his bed and she is then rejected by her brother Marke (as much, it would seem, on Riwalin's account as on hers). Tristan's mother lives to bring him up, and it is an altercation over an apparent love affair and her fear that Tristan is displaying inherited tendencies that bring about her death. The Tantris–Tristan plot and the garden scene are distinctly Wagnerian. In the strange final scene, Tristan is dying of a wound received while saving his beleaguered and plague-stricken country from the enemy; he is found in an inn by Isolde, who has been wandering the world in search of him. She, too, is dying—in her case from the plague.

In contrast with Geiger's work, Emil Ludwig's play *Tristan und Isolde* (Berlin: Oesterfeld, 1909) begins, like Wagner's opera, with the shipboard scene, although with a genuine love potion. Thereafter, though, the plot is much more in line with Eilhart: the lovers are caught and condemned to death; Tristan escapes from the chapel and frees Isolde from the lepers. Marke finds them in the forest and exchanges swords. At this point, there is a voluntary separation, during which Tristan meets and marries the second Isolde. In the guise of a fool, he receives the death wound on a visit to Isolde. The ending is the traditional one.

Ernst Hardt's *Tantris der Narr* (Leipzig: Insel, 1907) explores in detail the love-hate relationship in which the main characters are enmeshed. This drama is restricted to a single episode, based on Tristan's visit to Isolde in the guise of a fool. The crisis is precipitated by a report that Tristan has been seen but has fled on being challenged in the name of Isolde. This angers Isolde, who feels doubly betrayed, because Tristan has denied her and yet rendered her life forfeit (under the terms of the ambiguous oath) by his presence. Marke condemns her but has his doubts; Denovalin, in love with Isolde, wavers between the desire to protect or destroy her. Finally, Isolde herself is unable to recognize Tristan in the fool, even when he shows detailed knowledge of her past. Only Tristan's dog, Husdent, recognizes him, and with the dog Tristan leaves the palace as Isolde realizes her error too late. In part because Hardt concentrates on a single episode, this is one of the most successful of modern recreations.

In Georg Kaiser's play *König Hahnrei* (Berlin: Fischer, 1913), the medieval situation is retained, but it has no real significance. The central figure here is the king, and the entire plot revolves around his sexual problems. He is almost senile and experiences vicarious pleasure through his knowledge of the relationship between the lovers. He therefore does his best to conceal, not to discover, their secret and is disturbed only by feelings of jealousy with regard to Isolde's fondness for her much younger brother. The king's overt encouragement of their passion has the effect eventually of destroying it. Urged to embrace, they feel only revulsion and are united in death when the king's spear transfixes them both as they stand passively before him.

Like many plays, Eduard Stucken's *Tristram und Yseult* (Berlin: Reiss, 1916) begins with the Tantris–Tristan plot and the shipboard scene. In this case, Tristan and Isolde think they are taking poison and declare their love as the ship arrives in Cornwall. The marriage is put off for a while and Tristan and Isolde are able to escape to the forest. Here, the lovers are found by Marke's men, and Isolde is forced to return to Marke in order to save Tristan's life. She is again forced to deny Tristan when he comes in the guise of a pilgrim, since his presence is known to the king. In the conclusion, Isolde comes to Tristan and the misunderstanding is clarified, but Isolde does not die of grief; she is strangled by the dying Tristan!

Maja Loehr's *Tristans Tod* (Vienna: Heller, 1919) has little to recommend it beyond the economy of action. The emphasis is on the two Isoldes, the first of whom believes herself betrayed by Tristan's subsequent marriage and therefore is more generous to Marke, while the second Isolde feels herself equally betrayed by the discovery of the real reason for Tristan's coldness after the marriage ceremony. In the final scene, after the usual betrayal and remorse, Tristan stabs himself and Isolde takes poison.

The dramatic *Trilogie der Leidenschaft: Ysot, Marke, Tristan* (Munich: Musarion, 1922), by Robert Prechtl (pseudonym of Robert Friedländer), has little action despite its length, for most of the plot is narrated in the course of the dialogue. Thus, the first part begins with the report of the death of Morolt, Ysot's brother, and the arrival almost simultaneously of Tristan to woo on behalf of Marke. Ysot's hatred gradually turns to love, which is openly expressed when Tristan is willing to accept poison from her hands, as he in turn loves her and prefers death to dishonor. The second part revolves entirely around the false oath. Tristan and Ysot genuinely desire to renounce their relationship at the moment of taking the ordeal. After successfully undergoing the ordeal, they separate voluntarily, but Ysot subsequently makes it plain to Marke that love between them is impossible. The third and last part is restricted to the death of Tristan, who is waiting for both Ysots. Here, there is a strange variation, as it is the lover of Kaedin, maddened by his death, who tells Tristan of the black sail and then kills herself. The two Ysots are reconciled at Tristan's deathbed, not knowing at the end whether it is one or both of them or love itself that is the object of Tristan's desire. Throughout the work, there is an emphasis on the demonic, destructive nature of love, underlined by a brief love scene between two of Tristan's youthful followers in his sickroom.

Another lengthy work is Joseph-Hurter Ammann's *Tristan und Isolde* (Zurich: Amaltha, 1928). The first part ends with the love potion, while the second begins with Tristan's arrival in Karke to aid Kaherdin, thereby avoiding all difficulties with regard to the episodes of deception. The work is marred by many extraneous and at times tedious passages of "medievalizing" detail, such as the scenes with the doctors who disagree about the possible cure for Tristan.

Recreators of the story of Tristan and Isolde face two basic problems, the one technical and the other intellectual. On the one hand, they must modify the medieval aspects of the story sufficiently to make the material palatable to a modern public, and on the other hand they must find a critical point around which to build the plot. The first problem clearly can impinge on the second. In the works that have been cited here, the major elements that have been redefined by the authors are the love potion, the ordeal, and the death of the lovers. The potion is generally no longer the source of their love; this develops by itself. The death of the lovers seems at times unnecessarily complicated, as authors strive to avoid what is apparently the unacceptable idea of Tristan's death by mischance and Isolde's death from a broken heart. Yet the idea of suicide—i.e., the death of the lovers at their own hand—may flow from the authors' desire to strengthen the tragic quality of their end.

The ordeal is the element that most closely relates to the general line of modern dramatic interpretations, which can be largely summed up in one word: renunciation. By this is not meant the "if only I had known" type of renunciation indulged in by Marke, who is willing to renounce his claim to

Isolde (too late). It is rather the lovers' own attitude toward their love that is the specifically modern feature. As morally sound individuals (to use Roeber's term), they recognize the impossibility of their situation and the need to renounce any thought of union. They part or plan to part voluntarily, and they can survive the ordeal because they are willing to renounce. Only rarely is there any suggestion that their love is a positive force, something that might take precedence over worldly considerations, something that should be rejoiced in rather than suppressed.

The exploration of this theme produces little genuine tension, as the plot movement is based essentially on misunderstandings, accidents, and so forth. The only element that appears to be successful in generating the kind of dramatic tension that holds the public's interest is the relationship between Tristan and Isolde after separation. In a sense, the medieval situation of Marke, wavering between belief and disbelief, is transferred to the lovers, who are led by circumstances to waver between trust and mistrust, to doubt the steadfastness of each other's love. This aspect plays a role in many of the works and it is the sole topic in Hardt's work, probably the most successful of the modern dramatic versions.

In the last few decades, literary versions have been few and far between. The cause may lie in the radically changed attitude to myth and legend. These stories are no longer retold in modified form but completely recreated in a modern idiom and frequently in an "alien" form. Thus, there have been versions of the Tristan story in music, ballet, or film where only the essence is preserved; characters, situations, and medium are all transposed to our era. It is difficult to consider such transpositions as modern versions of a given medieval text, and, while a work like Nossack's *Spätestens im November* (Berlin: Suhrkamp, 1955) may be based on the Tristan story and may take that concept to its (for our age) ultimate conclusion, consideration of this and similar works belongs rather in the realm of motif research and not in the pages of an Arthurian encyclopedia. This and other works suggest, however, that the story of Tristan and Isolde is still very much alive. [MSB]

TRISTAN ALS MÖNCH ("Tristan as Monk"), a brief German romance (2,705 lines) from the first half of the thirteenth century and originating in the South Franconian/Alemannic dialect area. It has been transmitted in two manuscripts: *R*, Hs. Nr. 14697 in the Bibliothèque Royale de Belgique (Brussels); and *S*, Cod. ms. germ. 12 in the Staats- und Universitätsbibliothek Hamburg (missing since World War II). *S* is a copy of a lost manuscript from Strassburg, S^+. *R* contains, in addition to *Tristan als Mönch*, the *Tristan* of Gottfried von Strassburg and the conclusion of the *Tristan* continuation of Ulrich von Türheim. Both manuscripts date from the fifteenth century.

The source is uncertain, although it is probably to be found in French. The work belongs to the "disguise" category of *Tristan* narratives and is quite similar to *Tristan Ménestrel*, by Gerbert de Montreuil, in which Tristan disguises himself as a minstrel in order to meet again with Isolde. Nowhere else, however, does Tristan take on the disguise of a monk.

The connection with the Arthurian matter is tangential. Arthur has invited Tristan and Isolde of the White Hands to a festival at Caridol. Tristan dreams of Isolde and desires to see her once again. He changes identity with a dead knight and enters a monastery and assumes the name of "Brother Wit." The dead knight, whom everyone assumes to be Tristan, ostensibly wished to be buried in Cornwall and the funeral procession, accompanied by Brother Wit in his capacity as chaplain, journeys to Cornwall, and all connection with Arthur ceases. In Cornwall, Tristan reveals himself to Isolde, who, in order to bring Tristan to her in privacy, feigns sickness. Tristan disguises himself as a physician, and he and Isolde enjoy the intimacy of one another's company. Isolde is "cured," and Tristan takes his leave with the profuse thanks of King Mark. [FGG]

&. Bushey, Betty C., ed. *Tristan als Mönch*. Göppingen: Kümmerle, 1974.

Jungreithmayr, Anna. "*Tristan als Mönch*: Ansätze zu einem Textverständnis." *Sprach–Text–Geschichte*. Göppingen: Kümmerle, 1980, pp. 409–40.

TRISTAN AND ISEULT: see SUTCLIFF, ROSEMARY.

TRISTAN AND ISEULT: AN EPIC POEM IN TWELVE BOOKS: see POMEROY, FLORENCE M.

TRISTAN (TRISTRAN, TRISTRAM, TRISTREM) AND ISOLDE (ISOLT, ISEUT, YSEUT).

The legend of Tristan and Isolde was one of the most popular love stories of the Middle Ages and was widespread throughout Europe. With the coming of the Renaissance, it shared the obscurity into which Arthurian legend lapsed until its revival in the nineteenth century. This interest culminated in the early decades of the twentieth century, but it has since declined again.

As the story spread, details were altered and added, but its basics may be summarized as follows. The love between Tristan and Isolde is anticipated by that between the hero's parents, Rivalin, King of Lyonesse, and Blancheflor, sister to Mark, King of Cornwall (or Meliadus and Elizabeth, as they are named in the prose romances). They marry, but she dies in childbirth, and her son's name commemorates this loss. The boy is raised by a tutor, Governal, who becomes his faithful companion. Together, they travel to Cornwall to seek adventure, though in some versions Tristan is kidnapped and put ashore there.

Concealing his identity, he distinguishes himself for his skill in both harping and hunting before he undertakes his first major feat, the combat with Morholt. Morholt is the brother-in-law and champion of Anguish, King of

Ireland, who demands tribute from Cornwall; he is slain by his youthful opponent after a long struggle. Tristan's wounds refuse to heal, however, because Morholt's weapons were poisoned. In despair, he has himself set in an open boat, which drifts to Ireland, though in later accounts he goes there deliberately in search of Isolde, Anguish's only daughter, who has special healing skills. Concealing his identity under the name of Tantris, he makes a slow recovery. In some accounts, Isolde's love for Tristan begins to develop while she learns harping from him during his convalescence. Later, Anguish offers his daughter's hand in marriage to the knight who can slay a dragon that is ravaging the land. Tristan, who has returned seeking her as a bride for his uncle, King Mark, slays the dragon and cuts out its tongue but is overcome by its poisonous fumes. When the king's steward produces the dragon's head and claims the reward, Isolde finds Tristan and nurses him back to health again. Though angry when she discovers that he slew her uncle, Morholt, she spares his life so that he can refute the claim of the steward, whom she detests. In prose versions, Tristan wins her for Mark by defending her father in trial-by-combat.

On the voyage back to Cornwall, Tristan and Isolde accidentally drink the love potion intended for the bridal couple, and thereafter cannot escape their love. To disguise her loss of virginity, Isolde persuades her faithful maid, Brangwain, to take her place in Mark's bed on the wedding night, but fearing betrayal she arranges her murder, though she later repents and spares her. This is the first of many deceptions that the lovers practice, including the Tryst Beneath the Tree; but the plotting of courtiers who envy Tristan finally traps the lovers, usually by marks of blood in flour scattered around Isolde's bed.

In some versions, the lovers are condemned to death, but Tristan escapes and rescues Isolde from a group of lepers to whom she was given as punishment; in others, she tricks Mark by swearing a false oath in an ordeal by hot iron, but is later banished with Tristan. They seek refuge in the forest, but Isolde eventually returns to Mark, while Tristan goes into exile.

In the course of his wanderings, he meets and marries Isolde of Brittany, also known as Isolde of the White Hands. Since Tristan cannot forget his love for Isolde of Ireland, however, the marriage remains unconsummated. In the prose romances, Tristan is murdered by the treacherous Mark, but in the verse romances he receives a poisoned wound while aiding his brother-in-law and friend, Kaherdin. He summons Isolde of Ireland to heal him, but when his jealous wife reports that the ship has black sails, not the white that were the signal that her rival is coming, he dies in despair. Isolde of Ireland dies from grief, and the lovers are buried side by side. From his grave there grows a vine, from hers a rose; they meet and intertwine.

The traditions out of which this story developed have prompted much conjecture. While some have sought its historical roots near Castle Dore in Cornwall, others have argued for north Britain, since the hero's name in Welsh tradition, Drystan son of Tallwch, is Pictish in origin. The Celtic basis of the legend has been long recognized, but features were also borrowed from classical, Germanic, and oriental sources, such as the Persian *Wîs and Râmîn*.

Some scholars believe that the legend passed through Brittany to France, where an archetypal *Ur-Tristan* was composed about 1150. This was closely followed by verse romances of the so-called common version, most notably the German *Tristant* of Eilhart von Oberge (ca. 1170) and the Anglo-Norman *Roman de Tristan* by Béroul (late twelfth century). This version of the legend emphasizes dramatic action and elemental passion.

The archetype was refined and rationalized by the Anglo-Norman Thomas d'Angleterre (ca. 1170). His poem was the source for Gottfried von Strassburg's *Tristan* (ca. 1210), as well as for several Scandinavian accounts, including Brother Robert's Norse saga (1226), and for the English verse *Sir Tristrem* (late thirteenth century). Works in this group comprise the "courtly version."

There also developed a prose tradition, in which Tristan becomes a knight of the Round Table, second in valor only to Lancelot, and encounters many chivalric adventures typical of the prose romances. This starts in the second quarter of the thirteenth century with the French Prose *Tristan*, which exists in first and second (or enlarged) versions. The romance proved so popular that it largely superseded the poetical versions. It was added to, adapted into other languages (particularly Italian and Spanish), and eventually condensed by Sir Thomas Malory as part of *Le Morte Darthur* (1485).

Gottfried's poem remained influential in postmedieval treatments of the Tristan legend in German, culminating in Wagner's opera *Tristan und Isolde* (1865). In other languages, the prose version dominated. Prose Tristan romances were popular in the sixteenth century, though they had little impact on literature. Once they passed out of fashion, the love story attracted little attention until the nineteenth-century revival of interest in Arthurian legend. Alfred Lord Tennyson uses Tristan to illustrate the moral decline of Arthur's followers in "The Last Tournament" (1871), but both Matthew Arnold's *Tristram and Iseult* (1852) and Algernon Swinburne's *Tristram of Lyonesse* (1882) are more sympathetic to the lovers. The legend reached the height of its postmedieval popularity in the largely romantic poems and plays composed in the opening decades of the twentieth century by writers like Arthur Symons and Edwin Arlington Robinson. Since then, interest has waned.

The lovers may be presented as heroic figures caught in the grip of an implacable fate or as unscrupulous and self-centered adulterers. Tristan may be an artist-figure whose heightened sensitivity causes him acute anguish or a valiant knight serving his lady with splendid deeds; Isolde may be a lonely Irish exile seeking tenderness in a hostile court or a proud queen, graciously rewarding her devoted lover. Yet, whether victims or villains, true-hearted or tricksters, they remain for most people the symbol of a tragic love. (*See also* CASTLE DORE; GOTTFRIED VON STRASSBURG; ISOLDE OF THE WHITE HANDS; MARK.) [RHT]

Ferrante, Joan M. *The Conflict of Love and Honor: The Medieval Tristan Legend in France, Germany and Italy*. The Hague and Paris: Mouton, 1973.

TRISTAN AND ISOLDE

[Loomis], Gertrude Schoepperle. *Tristan and Isolt: A Study of the Sources of the Romance.* Frankfurt and London, 1913; 2nd ed. Roger Sherman Loomis. New York: Franklin, 1959.

Newstead, Helaine. "The Origin and Growth of the Tristan Legend." In *Arthurian Literature in the Middle Ages,* ed. Roger Sherman Loomis. Oxford: Clarendon, 1959, pp. 122–33.

TRISTAN AND ISOLDE: *see* ANSPACHER, LOUIS K.

TRISTAN AND ISOLDE: A ROMANCE: *see* OWEN, FRANCIS.

TRISTAN AND ISOLDE: RESTORING PALAMEDE: *see* ERSKINE, JOHN.

TRISTAN AND ISOLT: *see* MASEFIELD, JOHN.

TRISTÁN DE LEONÍS, EL CUENTO DE: *see TRISTAN* IN SPANISH AND PORTUGUESE.

TRISTÁN DE LEONÍS Y SU HIJO, DON: *see TRISTAN* IN SPANISH AND PORTUGUESE.

TRISTAN EN PROSE: *see* SALA, PIERRE.

TRISTAN HAG IZOLD: *see* LANGLAIS, XAVIER DE.

TRISTAN IN PROSE: *see* PROSE *TRISTAN.*

TRISTAN IN SPANISH AND PORTUGUESE. The narrative offered by the French Prose *Tristan* and by some Tristan material from the Post-Vulgate was known in medieval Spain and Portugal through several adaptations and translations; it is generally held, however, that in the main the Hispanic Tristan texts were derived from the French texts by way of intermediaries that may have been French, Provençal, or Italian. The earliest Hispanic works are from the fourteenth century and exist only in fragmentary form, in Catalan (*Tristany de Leonis*) and Galician-Portuguese. A fuller Aragonese text, *El Cuento de Tristán de Leonís*, dates from the late fourteenth or early fifteenth century. Tristan's death is described in a fifteenth-century Spanish ballad "Herido Está Don Tristán." Finally, there is a sixteenth-century Castilian *Don Tristán de Leonís y su Hijo*, which appends to the story of Tristan and Isolde that of the lovers' two children; it was this story that served as a basis for the Italian *I Due Tristani*. The Spanish Tristan texts generally play down the love story, emphasizing instead the ideals of heroism and chivalry (but *see* CARTA ENVIADA POR HISEO). [NJL]

Bonilla y San Martín, Adolfo, ed. *Libro del esforçado cauallero don Tristan de Leonis y de sus grandes fechos en armas.* Madrid: Sucesores de Hernando, 1912.

Coronica del buen cauallero don Tristan de Leonis y del rey don Tristan de Leonis, el joven su hijo. Seville: Domenico de Robertis, 1534.

Pensado Tomé, José L., ed. *Fragmento de un "Livro de Tristán" galaico-portugués.* Santiago de Compostela: Consejo Superior de Investigaciones Cientificas, 1962.

TRISTAN MÉNESTREL: see FRENCH ARTHURIAN LITERATURE.

TRISTAN ROSSIGNOL: see FRENCH ARTHURIAN LITERATURE.

TRISTAN STONE, a monolith, some seven feet tall, located near Fowey in Cornwall. A Latin inscription on the stone (which probably dates from the sixth century) indicates that this is the grave-marker of one Drustanus, son of Cunomorus. The name *Drustanus* is the equivalent of Tristan, and the stone is taken in popular lore as the gravestone for Isolde's lover. If Cunomorus (or Cynvawr) is Mark—as he was reputed to be in an early chronicle—the poets made a significant change in identifying him as Tristan's uncle, rather than his father. In any event, we have no proof that the Tristan named on the stone corresponds to the Tristan of romance. (*See also* CASTLE DORE.) [NJL]

Ashe, Geoffrey. *A Guidebook to Arthurian Britain.* Wellingborough: Aquarian, 1983, pp. 105–07.

TRISTAN UND ISOLDE: see IMMERMANN, KARL LEBERECHT; VESPER, WILL; WAGNER, RICHARD.

TRISTANO PANCIATICCHIANO, described by Gardner as an "Arthurian medley," is an eclectic romance of the early fourteenth century based on the same "unorthodox" French redaction as the *Tristano Riccardiano* until Tristano departs for Little Britain; thereupon, it turns to a source much like the one Malory used for his version of the Tristan, except that, owing either to an authorial decision or to a lacuna in the original, all of the adventures in the Forest Perilous are eliminated; when Tristano leaves Little Britain, he arrives in Cornwall without delay. The five sections of the "medley" recount with relative brevity the Grail quest, the birth of Tristano and his life until Isotta receives the false report of his death, a portion of *Mort Artu*, the adventures of

Tristano leading up to the Tournament at Lonezep (Verzeppe) and the adventures of Palamides in the Red City, and the death of Tristano and Isotta (which Parodi has edited to provide a conclusion to the incomplete *Tristano Riccardiano*). The *Panciaticchiano* account of the death of Tristano is remarkable for the detail and sentiment of its treatment of the dual demise of the lovers and the spectacular tomb, richer than that of Galeotto (Galehaut), prepared for them by Marco. The lovers are interred richly but, apparently, permanently, since the text provides no hint of the symbolic vines rooted in the hearts of the lovers. [DLH]

Parodi, E.G., ed. *Il Tristano Riccardiano*. Bologna: Romagnoli, 1896.

Gardner, Edmund G. *The Arthurian Legend in Italian Literature*. London: Dent, 1930.

TRISTANO RICCARDIANO, composed after Rusticiano's *Compilation* (later than 1272) but before 1300, is the earliest Arthurian romance in Italian. Considered a "magnificent fragment" by Gardner, it is a derivative of the French archetype of the Hispanic Tristans. The narrative begins with an account of the three sons of Filicie (Meliadaus, the brother rather than the brother-in-law of Marco, the second son of Filicie, and the third son, Pernam). Marco treacherously murders Pernam and is condemned by Meliadus, who in his own kingdom marries Eliabel, who gives birth to Tristano in a forest, where she has gone to seek her husband, who has been led away by an enchantress. She dies in childbirth, and the life of Tristano follows its usual course, with a few variations in the order of incidents and the names of characters. Although the prose tradition is generally held to develop an interest in Tristan's chivalry at the expense of his love, the *Tristano Riccardiano* seems to exaggerate this tendency. Nearly half of the romance as it is preserved concerns Tristano's marriage and his adventures in Little Britain. While the desire to see Isotta once again motivates his decision to return to Cornwall, it is his adventures in the desert of Nerlantes and his rescue of Arthur from enchantment that claim the author's attention. It is a bibliographical accident that the concluding pages of the *Tristano Riccardiano* have been lost, but it is true to the spirit of this redaction that the hero is last seen in an (original) encounter with Pressivalle lo Gallese at the Fountain of Adventure and never actually completes his journey to the perpetually anticipating Isotta. [DLH]

Parodi, E.G., ed. *Il Tristano Riccardiano*. Bologna: Romagnoli, 1896.

Gardner, Edmund G. *The Arthurian Legend in Italian Literature*. London: Dent, 1930.

TRISTANO VENETO. Preserved in a late fifteenth-century manuscript in Vienna (Pal. 3325), the *Tristano Veneto* is a faithful fourteenth-century translation in Venetian dialect of the Old French Prose *Tristan*, which also follows the versions of certain episodes found in the *Tristano Riccardiano* and in the *Compilation* of Rusticiano da Pisa. Although interesting for its combination of various redactions, the *Tristano Veneto* has been studied primarily for its importance to research in Italian dialectology and linguistics. [CK]

🐦 Arese, Felice, ed. *Prose di romanzi: Il romanzo cortese in Italia nei secoli XIII e XIV*. Turin: UTET, 1950, pp. 261–75.

Parodi, E.G., ed. "Dal *Tristano Veneto*." In *Nozze Cian—Sappa-Flandinet*. Bergamo, 1894, pp. 105–29.

Gardner, Edmund G. *The Arthurian Legend in Italian Literature*. London: Dent, 1930.

"TRISTAN'S SINGING": *see* MASEFIELD, JOHN.

TRISTANY DE LEONIS: *see* *TRISTAN* IN SPANISH AND PORTUGUESE.

TRISTRAM: *see* KENDON, FRANK; ROBINSON, EDWIN ARLINGTON.

TRISTRAM AND ISEULT: *see* ARNOLD, MATTHEW; CARR, J. COMYNS; REYNOLDS, ERNEST RANDOLF.

"TRISTRAM AND ISOLT": *see* MARQUIS, DON.

TRISTRAM AND ISOULT: *see* KINROSS, MARTHA.

TRISTRAM LEAVING THE KING OF IRELAND: *see* STAINED GLASS.

TRISTRAM OF LYONESSE: *see* SHARPE, RUTH COLLIER; SWINBURNE, ALGERNON CHARLES.

"TRISTRAM OG ÍSÓL BJARTA." The Tristan matter was known in Iceland primarily through the Norwegian translation of Thomas's *Tristan* (*Tristrams saga ok Ísöndar*) and a parodistic Icelandic version of the same (*Saga af Tristram ok Ísodd*). There exist also several versions of a folktale about the lovers that has only a tenuous affinity to the classic medieval romance. Five versions of the folktale—each with a different title—have been published: "Sagan af Fertram og Ísól bjarta," "Sagan af Tístram og Ísól björtu," "Tristram og Ísól bjarta," "Sagan af Tristram og Ísoddu," and "Sagan af Helgu kóngsdöttur." The folktales have a number of distinguishing motifs that place them in the category of the Wicked Stepmother tale. The infant Tristram (or Ísól) floats in a chest onto the shores of a foreign kingdom; the royal couple already have a child (Tristram or Ísól) and adopt the foundling; Tristram and Ísól are reared together; the queen dies and the king marries again; the wicked stepmother throws Ísól into a ditch in the woods intending for her to die; the stepmother's own daughter impersonates Ísól and is to marry Tristram; she is pregnant by a thrall and to avoid detection on the nuptial night she exchanges roles with a peasant girl who is the real Ísól; Tristram learns of the impersonation and the true identity of the peasant girl. The folktales end on a happy note with the wedding of Tristram and Ísól. [MEK]

➥ Árnason, Jón. *Íslenzkar þjóðsögur og ævintýri*. 2nd ed. Árni Böðvarsson and Bjarni Vilhjálmsson. Reykjavik: Bókaútgáfan þjóðsaga, 1954, 1956, Vol. 2, pp. 308–17; Vol. 4, pp. 486–95.

Schach, Paul. "Tristan and Isolde in Scandinavian Ballad and Folktale." *Scandinavian Studies*, 36 (1964), 281–97.

Sveinsson, Einar Ól. *Verzeichnis isländischer Märchenvarianten mit einer einleitenden Untersuchung.* Helsinki: Suomalainen Tiedeakatemia, Academia Scientiarum Fennica, 1929, pp. 126–30.

TRISTRAM UND YSOLT: *see* STUCKEN, EDUARD.

TRISTRAM'S END: *see* BINYON, LAURENCE.

"TRISTRAMS KVÆÐI," an Icelandic ballad of uncertain date, but most probably from the fifteenth century. The ballad is extant in four redactions of unequal length, the longest of which contains thirty-two stanzas. The stanzas are a variant of the quatrain with only two stresses in the second and fourth lines. "Tristrams kvæði" derives ultimately from *Tristrams saga ok Ísöndar*, the early thirteenth-century Norwegian translation of Thomas's *Tristan*. Certain correspondences between "Tristrams kvæði" and the younger Icelandic *Saga af Tristram ok Ísodd*, which also derives from the Norwegian translation and is dated around 1400, suggest that the ballad either postdates the Icelandic saga and borrowed from it or that the ballad antedates the saga, in which case the saga author was influenced by the ballad, which would then be older than any other extant Icelandic ballad.

"Tristrams kvæði" focuses on the events from the wounding of Tristram to his death. The female antagonists are contrasted through the use of the epithets "fair" and "dark" (Ísodd bjarta, Ísodd svarta). Three of the four redactions are punctuated by the ominous refrain "Þeim var ekki skapað nema að skilja" ("for them it was fated only to part"), whereas one redaction contains the more optimistic refrain "Og er sá sæll, sem sofna náir henni" ("he is blissful who is lucky enough to fall asleep beside her"), which presumably alludes to the eventual union of Tristram and Ísodd in death. Despite their being buried on either side of the church, their union is represented symbolically by the intertwining branches of the two trees that grow from their graves. [MEK]

Helgason, Jón, ed. *Íslenzk fornkvæði. Islandske folkeviser.* Copenhagen: Munksgaard, 1962, 1963, 1965, Vol. 1, pp. 137–43; Vol. 3, pp. 198–201; Vol. 4, pp. 221–26; Vol. 5, pp. 22–25.

Hill, Joyce. "The Icelandic Ballad of Tristan." In *The Tristan Legend: Texts from Northern and Eastern Europe in Modern English Translation.* Leeds: University of Leeds, Graduate Centre for Medieval Studies, 1977, pp. 29–38.

Ólason, Vésteinn. *The Traditional Ballads of Iceland: Historical Studies.* Reykjavik: Stofnun Árna Magnússonar, 1982, pp. 213–20.

Schach, Paul. "Tristan and Isolde in Scandinavian Ballad and Folktale." *Scandinavian Studies,* 36 (1964), 281–97.

TRISTRAM'S MADNESS: *see* STAINED GLASS.

TRISTRAMS SAGA OK ÍSÖNDAR is of great importance not only for students of Icelandic and Norwegian literature but also for those who want to understand the history of the Tristan material in Europe, because the saga is the sole complete representative of the Thomas d'Angleterre branch of the romance. The preface of the saga states that Brother Robert translated it in 1226 at the instigation of King Hákon Hákonarson (r. 1217–63). On the basis of this date, many scholars assume that it was the first French romance to be translated into a Scandinavian language. Because there was no tradition of longer verse narrative in Norwegian vernacular literature, the translation of Thomas's romance into Norwegian required the development of a suitable prose style. The result is the so-called "court style," which takes many features from earlier religious literature. Its characteristics are shared by many of the translated romances, and include frequent use of the present participle, alliteration, and amplification.

Comparison of Thomas's and Gottfried's incomplete versions shows that Robert neither leaves out episodes nor changes their order. However, the intense psychological interest and introspective passages in Thomas are shortened dramatically; the scene in which Tristan contemplates marriage covers 368 lines of verse in Thomas's version, but only eight lines of prose in *Tristrams saga.* It is assumed that Robert consciously deleted material that would have been unpalatable to an audience unfamiliar with romantic literature. Certain changes in Robert's text tend to make the characters more sympathetic. For example, the unseemly accusations that Isolt and Brengvein fling at each other (ll. 1–344 in the Douce fragment of Thomas) are greatly reduced in the saga. There are several brief additions in the saga, including a short prayer that Ísönd piously utters before her death.

Although *Tristrams saga ok Ísöndar* was translated for a Norwegian king, all existing manuscripts are from Iceland, which attests the popularity of the saga in that country. There are numerous borrowings from the Tristan material, including the *Saga of Tristram ok Ísodd*, several ballads, and episodes in native romances and family sagas. [MCH]

  Kölbing, Eugen, ed. *Tristrams saga ok Ísöndar. Mit einer literaturhistorischen Einleitung.* Heilbronn: Gebrüder Henninger, 1878.

  Schach, Paul, trans. *The Saga of Tristram and Ísönd.* Lincoln: University of Nebraska Press, 1973.

  ———. "The Style and Structure of Tristrams saga." In *Scandinavian Studies: Essays Presented to Dr. Henry Goddard Leach on the Occasion of His Eighty-fifth Birthday,* ed. Carl F. Bayerschmidt and Erik J. Friis. Seattle: University of Washington Press for the American-Scandinavian Foundation, 1965, pp. 63–86.

"TRISTRAM'S TOMB": *see* ORMEROD, JAMES.

TRISTRANT: *see* EILHART VON OBERGE.

TRISTRANT UND ISALDE, a German prose version of Eilhart von Oberge's *Tristrant.* The oldest extant incunabulum of this chapbook was printed in Augsburg in 1484. The text was reprinted fifteen times between 1484 and 1664, and there exist seven modern printings or editions, the most recent dating from 1966. In general, the anonymous author of the chapbook is faithful to his medieval source, but there are explanatory or didactic intercalations, and occasionally Eilhart's vivid vocabulary and imagery are toned down. The author of the chapbook also tended to substitute indigenous German vocabulary for French loan words and modern equivalents for words perceived to be outdated. [MEK]

  Brandstetter, Alois, ed. *Tristrant und Isalde: Prosaroman.* Tübingen: Niemeyer, 1966.

  ———. *Prosa Auflösung: Studien zur Rezeption der höfischen Epik im frühneuhochdeutschen Prosaroman.* Frankfurt: Athenäum, 1971.

  Melzer, Helmut. *Trivialisierungstendenzen im Volksbuch: Ein Vergleich der Volksbücher "Tristrant und Isalde," "Wigoleis" und "Wilhelm von Österreich" mit den mittelhochdeutschen Epen.* Hildesheim: Olms, 1972.

TURKE AND GOWIN, THE (ca. 1500), has been preserved, together with three other Gawain stories (*The Carle off Carlile, The Grene Knight,* and *The Marriage of Sir Gawain*), in the Percy Folio (ca. 1660), a collection of (near) contemporary verse and late and much-debased versions of medieval romances. The poem as we have it numbers 335 lines, but about half of it is lost because halves of pages were torn out and used to light the fire by the maids of a one-time owner. Some guesswork is necessary for the interpretation of the text. It combines the challenge and beheading plot of *Sir Gawain and the Green Knight* with that of a series of three tests in the land of giants. The character of the Turk is as dualistic as the plot, for at Arthur's court he behaves like the traditional fierce challenger, whereas he metamorphoses into the helpful fairy once Gawain has to face the contests with the giants of the King of Man. In the end, the two plots come together when Gawain by decapitating the Turk lifts the spell on the enchanted Sir Gromer, who is subsequently made King of Man (this ending is similar to that of *The Carle off Carlile*). The only parallel to the testing episode is in the Old French *Pèlerinage de Charlemagne* (twelfth century), which agrees in the presence of a spherical object (a brass tennis ball and a *pelotte*), in the cauldron of molten lead, in the vanishing garment, and in the assisting figure. As it is unlikely that the *Pèlerinage* served as a direct source for *The Turke*, both the Charlemagne and the Arthurian romances may go back to a story, now lost, about a king who pays a visit to the court of a rival, situated in the otherworld. [ESK]

ᶔ Madden, Frederic, ed. *Syr Gawayne*. London: Bannatyne Club, 1839.

TURNER, ROY, author of *King of the Lordless Country* (1971). This historical romance is an involving, if improbable, account of Arthur's rise to power, culminating in his victory at Badon. Bedwyr relates how he and Arthur are recruited into the Circle, a band of warriors led by Gwenhwyfar and dedicated to noble ideals. [RHT]

ᶔ Turner, Roy. *King of the Lordless Country*. London: Dobson, 1971.

TURTON, GODFREY E., contemporary English lexicographer and author of *The Emperor Arthur* (1967), a historical novel narrated by Pelleas as a nostalgic retrospective. The characters are Romanized Celts, and the story employs a pronounced pagan-Christian opposition: even the Grail quest is depicted as a Church-fomented plot. The traditional story of Pelleas and Ettard is woven in among the series of conspiracies that form most of the action. [AAR]

ᶔ Turton, Godfrey E. *The Emperor Arthur*. New York: Doubleday, 1967.

TWAIN, MARK (pseudonym of Samuel Langhorne Clemens; 1835–1910), apparently first encountered Arthurian legend when some member of his household purchased Sidney Lanier's *The Boy's King Arthur* in 1880, and he at least dipped into Malory in 1884 during a reading tour with George C. Cable. He started work in earnest on what was to become *A Connecticut Yankee in King Arthur's Court* in the winter of 1884/5, but he put it aside before finishing it in a creative burst in time for publication on 10 December 1889. The attractive illustrations were the work of Daniel Beard, who collaborated closely with the author. Initial sales were disappointing, but the novel soon established itself and has retained its popularity. It has been made into a film three times and turned into a musical comedy by Richard Rodgers and Lorenz Hart.

The novel is a characteristic Twainian amalgam of fantasy and fun, observation and satire, that both amuses and provokes reflection as it confronts the customs of olden times with the brash values of the New World. Hank Morgan travels back in time to the days of King Arthur, and he uses his technological expertise to gain power. He humorously exposes the follies and ignorance of medieval society and the exaggerations of the world of romance. However, we gradually discover that his own values are no better. Despite his professed concern for the rights of the individual, Hank is prepared to further his own interests with a callous disregard for human life and dignity. When he uses electric wire and gatling machine guns to slaughter his enemies in their thousands, he reveals that technological progress has not changed humanity's destructive nature.

Yet despite the satire against the ignorance and cruelty of both medieval and modern society, and the comedy aimed at the exaggerations of the world of romance, there remain in the novel an underlying admiration and an affection for Arthurian legend itself, witnessed in the generosity and heroism of Lancelot and Arthur. [CNS/RHT]

అ Twain, Mark. *A Connecticut Yankee in King Arthur's Court.* New York: Webster, 1889.

"TWENTY-FOUR KNIGHTS OF ARTHUR'S COURT": *see* CELTIC ARTHURIAN LITERATURE.

TWILIGHT PROVINCE: see FINKEL, GEORGE.

TYOLET, an anonymous Old French lai from the end of the twelfth century that imitates, in the first part, the story of Perceval's childhood from Chrétien's romance, with supernatural additions characteristic of the lai. In the second part, probably the original lai, Tyolet succeeds in cutting off the white foot of a stag for the daughter of the King of Logres—this where others had failed. He is, however, attacked by lions and left for dead. Gauvain finds Tyolet and foils a false knight who claimed that he had achieved that white-foot quest. Tyolet marries the princess.

The white-foot episode occurs elsewhere, notably in the Second Continuation of the *Perceval*, the Didot-*Perceval*, the Welsh *Peredur*, and the Middle Dutch *Lanseloet en het hert met de witte voet.* The author of *Tyolet* seems to have known Marie de France's *Lanval.* [KB]

అ Tobin, Prudence Mary O'Hara, ed. *Les Lais anonymes bretons.* Geneva: Droz, 1976.

UBERTI, FAZIO DEGLI: *see* FAZIO DEGLI UBERTI.

UHLAND, LUDWIG (1787–1862), a popular German poet of the so-called "Swabian" school of later Romanticism. He is known for his interest in folk literature and for the lyricism of his own folk ballads, many of which were set to music by such composers as Schubert, Schumann, Liszt, and Brahms. The important role of nature in his poetry is reflected in his poem *Merlin der Wilde* ("Merlin the Wild Man," 1829, published 1831), which relates the essentially non-Arthurian tradition of Merlin from Geoffrey's *Vita Merlini*. A depressed Merlin, King of Demetia, wishes to return to his forest retreat but is detained by King Roderick, his twin sister's husband. Merlin exchanges a prophecy about the infidelity of his sister for permission to leave. She discredits the prophecy, but Merlin is still allowed to return to his beloved forest, the source of his strength and insight. [RWK]

Uhland, Ludwig. *Werke*, ed. Hans-Rüdiger Schwab. Frankfurt: Insel, 1983, Vol. 1.
Weiss, Adelaide Marie. "Ludwig Uhland." In *Merlin in German Literature*. Washington, D.C.: Catholic University of America Press, 1933, pp. 94–104.

ULRICH VON TÜRHEIM. In line 26 of his *Tristan*, written around 1235, Ulrich von Türheim informs us that a certain "Kuonrât der schenke von

Wintersteten" asked him to write a conclusion to Gottfried von Strassburg's unfinished *Tristan*. In the prologue to his continuation, Ulrich praises Gottfried's literary art and laments the fact that the great master had been snatched from life so prematurely. Ulrich's *Tristan*, a work of some 3,700 lines, picks up the tale with Tristan's decision to marry the other Ŷsôt. Ulrich's continuation is greatly indebted to Eilhart von Oberge's *Tristrant*, from which he borrows, for example, the magic-pillow episode and Tristan's sojourn as fool at Mark's court. Compared with the work of the more gifted Heinrich von Freiberg, who also wrote a continuation of Gottfried's *Tristan*, Ulrich's effort is pedestrian and uninspired. [MEK]

�763 Ulrich von Türheim. *Tristan*, ed. Thomas Kerth. Tübingen: Niemeyer, 1979.

Kerth, Thomas. "The Denouement of the Tristan-*Minne*: Türheim's Dilemma." *Neophilologus*, 65 (1981), 79–93.

ULRICH VON ZATZIKHOVEN, identified by many scholars with the "capellanus Uolricus de Cecinchoven plebanus Loumeissae," a cleric named as a witness on a document of 1214 from Lommis near Zezikon (= Zatzikhoven) in Switzerland. He is known to have composed only one work, the Middle High German *Lanzelet*. Ulrich claims that his source was "ein welschez buoch" that had been brought to Germany by Huc (Hugo) von Morville, one of the nobles who remained as hostage at the court of the emperor Henry VI after Richard the Lion-Hearted returned to England in 1194. One assumes therefore that *Lanzelet* was composed sometime after 1194, but not later than 1205, and that it is based on a lost French or, more likely, Anglo-Norman source.

Like most Arthurian romances, *Lanzelet* (ca. 9,400 lines of verse) is composed of a series of more or less independent episodes, which in this case fall into three occasionally overlapping categories. The work begins when Lanzelet's father is overthrown by his vassals and the infant hero is abducted by a water-fay queen; he grows up in her magical kingdom, ignorant of his name and ancestry; he will learn these, he is told, only when he defeats Iweret, the best knight alive. After a series of unrelated adventures, Lanzelet does kill Iweret, thereby winning the hand of his daughter, Iblis, and the kingdom of Dodone; soon after, a messenger appears and reveals Lanzelet's name. Falling at the center of the work, these episodes are by far its most elaborate. In the last two episodes, after a second series of unrelated adventures, Lanzelet finally claims his father's throne and then returns with Iblis to take possession of Dodone. Thus, the beginning, middle, and end of the work constitute a single group of episodes distinguished by a single constellation of interwoven themes: exile and return; loss and recovery of identity; winning Iblis and her kingdom.

The second category of episodes comprises those in which Lanzelet defeats a knight, each time winning a kingdom and a bride. In his first adult adventure, Lanzelet kills Galagandreiz and wins his nameless daughter; in the next episode he defeats Linier and wins his niece, Ade; after a few intervening adventures comes the central episode, in which Lanzelet wins Iblis by killing Iweret. One observes in this series an increase in courtliness both of the combats (Galagan-dreiz: knife-throwing; Linier: fighting giants, a lion, and Linier; Iweret: single combat) and of the women won (Galagandreiz's daughter offered her love to two other guests before coming to Lanzelet; Ade helps Lanzelet out of charity; the love of Iblis is elaborated with all the familiar topoi of romance love). Surprisingly, however, Lanzelet's conquests do not end with Iblis. A few episodes after winning her, Lanzelet sets out and "wins" the Lady of Pluris, who keeps him for a year as her captive lover.

The third category of episodes traces Lanzelet's increasing integration into the world of Arthur's court. After Lanzelet's first adventure, word of his prowess reaches Arthur; after the second, Walwein (Gawain) is dispatched to locate the new hero. In the third episode, Lanzelet fights Walwein until they are interrupted, and then he distinguishes himself at a tournament before Arthur's court. In these episodes, Arthur seeks Lanzelet; in the second half of the romance, however, after Lanzelet has overcome Iweret and learned, along with his name, that he is Arthur's nephew, the relation is reversed: now Lanzelet seeks Arthur, in whose behalf he performs a series of adventures. On arriving at court, Lanzelet discovers that Valerin has claimed the Queen, but Lanzelet defends her successfully in judicial combat. On returning from his captivity at Pluris, Lanzelet discovers that Valerin has abducted the Queen, and he is active in her rescue. This pattern of increasing involvement with the world of Arthur culminates in the last two episodes of the work, where it finally unites with the other two episode series (regaining identity; winning wife): Arthur accompanies Lanzelet and Iblis as they celebrate their coronation first in his father's kingdom, then in hers.

Ulrich's *Lanzelet* is the first German representative of the European Lance-lot tradition, with which it shares a number of features: infant abduction by a water fay; childhood in a magical kingdom; suppression of identity; champion of Guenevere. Yet it differs from this tradition in ways that are even more striking. Most remarkably, there is not even a hint of what the tradition is best known for, the adulterous love of Lancelot and Guenevere. Further, even though Lanzelet defends the Queen, he never actually rescues her. Finally, questions of kingship and succession play an uncharacteristically large role (revolt against Lanzelet's tyrannical father; defeat of the violent Galagandreiz; the lengthy portrayal of Lanzelet's accession and kingly virtues).

Lanzelet is the second of the German Arthurian romances, falling chrono-logically after Hartmann von Aue's *Erec* but before his *Iwein* and Wolfram von Eschenbach's *Parzival*; like them, it is composed in the four-stress rhymed couplets characteristic of Middle High German courtly narrative. Ulrich's work has often been taken to task for the ways in which it differs from those of Hartmann and Wolfram: its hero is regarded as flawless throughout; its narrator lacks the literary self-consciousness of his more celebrated contem-poraries; as a consequence the work does not seem to question the common-places of romance ideology and literary convention, as do those of Hartmann and Wolfram. Yet in all these ways, *Lanzelet* agrees with the rest of the lesser-known Middle High German Arthurian romances—among which, because of its balanced proportions, the variety of its episodes, and its easy, slightly ironic tone, it has always been a favorite.

Although Ulrich was not as well known as Hartmann or Wolfram, he was not forgotten by later authors: Heinrich von dem Türlin incorporated elements from *Lanzelet* into *Diu Crône*, and Ulrich was twice praised by Rudolf von Ems (*Alexander*, l. 3199; *Willehalm*, l. 2197). Two complete manuscripts of *Lanzelet* survive (W, thirteenth century; P, 1420) as well as fragments of three others (B, early thirteenth century; G and S, fourteenth century). [JAS]

&. Ulrich von Zatzikhoven. *Lanzelet: Eine Erzählung*, ed. K.A. Hahn. Frankfurt: Brönner, 1845.

———— . *Lanzelet: A Romance of Lancelot*, trans. Kenneth G.T. Webster. New York: Columbia University Press, 1951.

Pérennec, René. "Artusroman und Familie: *das welsche buoch von Lanzelete*." *Acta Germanica*, 11 (1979), 1–51.

Schultz, James A. "'Lanzelet': A Flawless Hero in a Symmetrical World." *Beiträge zur Geschichte der deutschen Sprache und Literatur* (Tübingen), 102 (1980), 160–88.

ULTIME IMPRESE E MORTE DI TRISTANO, LE ("The Last Deeds and Death of Tristan"), an Italian *cantare* that condenses many episodes from Arthurian romance. (*See also* CANTARI DI TRISTANO.) [SJN]

&. Branca, Daniela Delcorno. "I cantari di Tristano." *Lettere italiane*, 23 (1971), 289–305.

UTER PENDRAGON: *see* STUCKEN, EDUARD.

UTHER AND IGRAINE: *see* DEEPING, WARWICK.

UTHER PENDRAGON, Arthur's father in Geoffrey of Monmouth. After a youth spent in Breton exile with his elder brother, Aurelius Ambrosius, he returns to Britain with him to dethrone Vortigern. Aurelius, as king, sends Uther and Merlin to Ireland to bring back the Giants' Ring, otherwise Stonehenge. When Aurelius is poisoned, a celestial portent appears. Merlin interprets this as forecasting the glories of Uther and his unborn offspring. Its main feature is a luminous dragon, whence Uther's sobriquet "Pendragon." Geoffrey explains it as meaning "a dragon's head"; more probably it means "head dragon," which may be interpreted as "foremost leader."

Uther becomes king. He holds court in London and is smitten with desire for Ygerna, the wife of Gorlois, Duke of Cornwall. Observing his advances, Gorlois leaves without permission and immures his wife in Tintagel Castle, approachable only by a narrow isthmus, easily guarded. Taking his conduct as an insult, Uther leads an army to ravage the ducal lands. Merlin magically turns him into a replica of Gorlois, enabling him to enter Tintagel and reach

Ygerna, who supposes him to be her husband. Thus, Arthur is begotten. Since the real Gorlois has fallen in battle, Uther can resume his true shape and marry the lady. The remainder of his life is troubled by ill health and aggressive Saxons. After about sixteen years, he dies—like Aurelius, by Saxon poison—and is buried beside him at Stonehenge.

An early Welsh poem mentions "Uthr Pendragon." However, there is no proof that he was a real person. Pendragon Castle in Cumbria allegedly stands on the site of an older fort that Uther built, but the story cannot be traced back far. *Uthr* in Welsh means "terrible, awe-inspiring." The connection with Arthur could perhaps be a mere mistake, since the poetic phrase "Arthur the terrible" might have been misconstrued as "Arthur son of Uthr." [GA]

ε◆ Geoffrey of Monmouth. *Historia Regum Britanniae*, Book VI, Chapters 5, 8; Book VIII, Chapters 1, 11, 14–24.

UTHER PENDRAGON: *see* COUTTS, FRANCIS.

VAILLANT DE POITIERS, JEHAN LE, completed an Arthurian compilation, probably about 1391, which he claims to have written at the behest of Jean de Bourbon (d. 1410). The entire work is an ambitious project but evinces little coherence. It begins with a version of the *Histoire des Géants*, followed by an abbreviated version of the *Brut*; thereupon succeed endless tales from the times of Uterpendragon and Arthur, tales inspired by and interpolated from previous Arthurian romances. [C-AVC]

   Lathuillère, Roger. *Guiron le courtois: Étude de la tradition manuscrite et analyse critique.* Geneva: Droz, 1966.

Pickford, Cedric E. *L'Évolution du roman arthurien en prose vers la fin du moyen âge d'après le ms. 112 du fonds français de la Bibl. Nationale.* Paris: Nizet, 1960.

VALLET À LA COTE MAL TAILLIÉE, LE, a brief French fragment (from the thirteenth century) concerning a young man whose desire to serve at Arthur's court is championed by Gawain. [NJL]

   Meyer, Paul, and Gaston Paris. "Fragment du *Vallet a la Cote Mal Taillie.*" *Romania,* 26 (1897), 276–80.

VALVENS ÞÁTTR, a continuation of *Parcevals saga,* the Old Norse prose translation of Chrétien de Troyes's unfinished *Perceval* (from line 6514 to the end). Because this part deals exclusively with Valven (Gawain), it was—at some now indeterminable point—separated from *Parcevals saga* and treated as an individual work. The primary manuscripts are a vellum from about 1400 (the same one for *Parcevals saga*) and a single vellum leaf from perhaps fifty years earlier, which contains the beginning, corresponding roughly to the first page of the former.

Valven leaves the castle where he had been staying and comes upon a seriously wounded knight and a sorrowing girl under a large oak. He rouses the knight, who tells him that another knight is stationed on the road ahead and kills all who come past. Valven promises to return. He helps a lovely but arrogant girl, who says she will follow him—but to his disgrace. Valven returns to the injured knight and heals him through his knowledge of herbs, whereupon the ingrate steals Valven's horse. They meet again later, fight, and Valven recovers his steed. In an enchanted castle, he survives a shower of crossbow bolts and the attack of a giant lion, thereby freeing the castle from its spell. In a series of adventures, Valven defeats another knight, meets his own sister (whose existence he has been unaware of), and returns to his arrogant female companion. Her nature has now changed completely—for the better. Valven sends a man to King Arthur to announce that he may be present at an impending duel, and the tale comes to an abrupt end.

The fragmentary nature of the work is clear, but of course the French original was itself incomplete. Notable is the absence of the stylistic features that characterize *Parcevals saga*. [FWB]

❧ Kölbing, Eugen, ed. *Riddarasögur*. Strassburg: Trübner, 1872.

Kalinke, Marianne E. *King Arthur, North-by-Northwest*. Copenhagen: Reitzel, 1981.

VAN DEN RIDDERE METTER MOUWEN: *see RIDDERE METTER MOUWEN.*

VAN DER VELDE, CARL FRANZ (1749–1824), who has been called the German Walter Scott because of his many historical novels, was inspired by Benedikte Naubert's *Der kurze Mantel* to produce in the years 1816–17 an opera libretto entitled *Der Zaubermantel*. Like Naubert's modern adaptation of *Le Mantel mautaillié*, van der Velde's libretto expresses a disdain for the aristocracy and glorifies the virtues of the working man. The weaknesses of Arthur and his knights are made manifest in the libretto. King Arthur worries about his gout and cannot get along without a midday siesta. Impotent in the face of Guinevere's wiles and machinations, Arthur is cast in the role of the long-suffering husband.

Although van der Velde hoped that Karl Maria von Weber might be interested in his libretto, *Der Zaubermantel* failed to find a composer. [MEK]

❧ van der Velde, C.F. *Der Zaubermantel. Oper in drei Akten. Die böhmischen Amazonen. Romantisches Gemälde in zwei Akten*. Dresden: Arnoldische Buchhandlung, 1827.

VANSITTART, PETER, offers in the novel *Lancelot* (1978) an antiromantic picture of the decline of Roman Britain and the ensuing material and moral chaos. In laconic prose, Lancelot, sensitive, solitary, and aging, recalls first his youth in a villa, then his period of service under Ambrosius Aurelianus, during which he met the whore Gwenhever. Artorius emerges toward the end as an enigmatic, half-barbaric figure. [CNS]

🕮 Vansittart, Peter. *Lancelot*. London: Owen, 1978.

VASNACHTSPIL MIT DER KRON, DAS ("The Shrovetide Play with the Crown"), an anonymous fifteenth-century Shrovetide play, contains a variant version of the Arthurian chastity test transmitted in the *Lai du cor* and *Le Mantel mautaillié*. A wondrous crown, sent to King Arthur by the King of Abian, is to be tried on by all men present. It will be given to the king or lord whom it best fits. One king after another tries on the crown only to have horns grow out of his head to indicate that he has enjoyed illicit love. In each case, the wronged wife berates her husband and receives feeble excuses. The game is short-lived, and the play ends with a decision to return the crown to its sender. [MEK]

🕮 *Das vasnachtspil mit der kron*. In *Fastnachtspiele aus dem fünfzehnten Jahrhundert. Zweiter Theil*. Stuttgart: Litterarischer Verein, 1853, pp. 654–63.

VELTHEM, LODEWIJK VAN, a Middle Dutch poet about whom little is known. He came from Brabant, and he lived and worked in the second half of the thirteenth century and the first half of the fourteenth. Velthem became known mainly as the executor of Jacob van Maerlant's literary testament. His continuation of Maerlant's *Spiegel Historiael* (1283–88), which treats the period 1248–1316, was intended for the Count of Holland, Gerard van Voorne, son of Adelbrecht van Voorne. One of the many events that he describes concerns a Round Table organized by King Edward I of England, a festive performance in which the participants appeared as Arthurian knights (*Spiegel Historiael* V, Book 2, Chapters 15–20).

Velthem continued two other works by Jacob van Maerlant, the *Historie van den Grale* and the *Boec van Merline*: in 1326, he completed his *Merlijn-Continuatie*, an adaptation of the *Suite du Merlin*. His verse romance was intended as a sequel to the work by Maerlant, who had transposed Old French prose versions of Robert de Boron's *Joseph d'Arimathie* and *Merlin* into Middle Dutch verse around 1261.

In Middle Dutch, Velthem's adaptation has been transmitted in fragmentary form. Some 1,650 lines have been preserved, in fragments from the second half of the fourteenth century (Leiden, U.B. ltk. 1107; Maastricht, Rijksarchief 167 III 10; and Münster Hauptstaatsarchiv, Dep. Landsberg-Velen). In addition, a complete version of Velthem's work is preserved in a Middle Low German *Umschreibung* (rendering) from the Middle Dutch, in a codex from about 1425 (Burgersteinfurt, Fürst zu Bentheimsche Schlossbibliothek B 37).

This manuscript which has always been in the possession of the counts of Bentheim, also contains Middle Low German *Umschreibungen* of Maerlant's *Historie van den Grale* and *Boec van Merline*. Velthem's work comprises almost 26,000 lines.

Even this does not exhaust Velthem's concerns with Arthurian romance. A notice on the last leaf of the *Lancelot-Compilatie* indicates that he was the owner of this codex. The questions of whether he was also responsible for the composition of the compilation, and of whether he perhaps even transposed the Old French *Lancelot–Queste–Mort* into Middle Dutch, have not yet been answered. [BB]

De Pauw, Napoleon, ed. *Middelnederlandsche gedichten en fragmenten*. Ghent, 1903, Vol. 2, pp. 66–72.

Sodmann, Timothy. "Die münsterschen Fragmente von Lodewijks van Velthem *Boec van coninc Artur*." *Niederdeutsches Wort*, 23 (1983), 39–81.

Stallaert, K.F., ed. "De Merlijn van Jacob van Maerlant." *Nederlandsch Museum*, 1 (1880), 51–63.

Te Winkel, Jan. *De Ontwikkeling der Nederlandsche Letterkunde*. Haarlem, 1922–27, Vol. 1, pp. 490–500.

VENDETTA CHE FE MESSER LANZELLOTO DE LA MORTE DI MISER TRISTANO, LA ("Lancelot's Revenge for the Death of Sir Tristan"), an Italian *cantare*, the plot of which departs somewhat from the main body of Tristan literature in recounting Lancelot's revenge. Variants of this *cantare* appear in several codices that contain *Le Ultime imprese e morte di Tristano*. [SJN]

Branca, Daniela Delcorno. "I cantari di Tristano." *Lettere italiane*, 23 (1971), 289–305.

VENGEANCE RAGUIDEL, LA, a verse romance of 6,182 lines, dating from the first quarter of the thirteenth century, written by a certain Raoul, possibly to be identified with Raoul de Houdenc. The story centers on Gauvain's quest to avenge the death of Raguidel, whose body arrives at Arthur's court on a boat. With the aid of Yder, the quest is eventually achieved and the murderer, Guengasoain, brought to justice. Within the framework of this quest, many other adventures are related, often in a humorous and burlesque style: the Pucele du Gaut Destroit, infatuated with Gauvain, who plans to guillotine him when he scorns her love, or the faithless Ydain, who deserts Gauvain for another knight, and is then given to the hunchback Druidain.

The influence of Chrétien is clear, in particular of *Erec, Yvain*, and *Perceval*, and Raoul draws on the usual selection of stock motifs and adventures. *La Vengeance Raguidel* was adapted into Middle Dutch as *Die Wrake van Ragisel*. [KB]

Friedwagner, Mathias, ed. *La Vengeance Raguidel*. Halle: Niemeyer, 1909.

VERA HISTORIA DE MORTE ARTHURI, Latin prose, the only extant copy of which dates from the early fourteenth century. This version of

Arthur's final battle and death describes his wound from a poisoned spear, his funeral rites, and the mysterious disappearance of the King's body from the bier during a thick mist. [MLD]

> Lapidge, Michael, ed. "An Edition of the *Vera Historia de Morte Arthuri.*" *Arthurian Literature*, 1 (1981), 19–93.

VERGIL, POLYDORE. Trained in the new humanist tradition, the Italian Polydore Vergil came to England in 1502 and remained there until 1553. During this time, he wrote his *Anglica Historia*, of which the earliest manuscript copy can be dated to 1512–13. In the early parts of this work, Vergil set about to debunk Geoffrey of Monmouth; in particular, he attacked Geoffrey's accounts of Brutus and Arthur. Brutus is dismissed altogether and Arthur emerges with considerably diminished stature. What Vergil is willing to grant as factual concerning Arthur (after discrediting the "anilibus fabellis" of medieval writers) is even less than the earlier skeptic William of Malmesbury had accepted: Arthur ruled after Uther and would have perhaps reunited Britain for a time if he had lived longer. Contemporary patriotic reaction against Vergil was often vitriolic, and ultimately he was pilloried by the Arthurians as "that most rascall dogge knave in the worlde." [JPC]

> Carley, James P. "Polydore Vergil and John Leland on King Arthur: The Battle of the Books." *Interpretations* (Memphis State University), 15 (1984), 86–100.
>
> Hay, Denys. *Polydore Vergil.* Oxford: Clarendon, 1952.

VERLAINE, PAUL: *see* SYMBOLIST ARTHURIAN MATERIAL.

VERLORENE ICH, DAS: *see* STUCKEN, EDUARD.

VESPER, WILL (1882–1962), a German author with strong nationalistic (later Nazi) tendencies. He adapted traditional material in *Parzival* and *Tristan und Isolde*, both published in 1911 as part of the popular series Bücher der Rose. Vesper trivializes his medieval antecedents. Parzival appears, for example, as a prefascist conqueror and savior-figure. [UM/WCM]

> Vesper, Will. *Parzival.* Ebenhausen bei München: Langewiesche-Brandt, [ca. 1911].
>
> ———. *Tristan und Isolde.* Ebenhausen bei München: Langewiesche-Brandt, 1911.
>
> Schulze, Ursula. "Ideologisierung durch Strukturverlust." In *Akten des DFG-Symposions zur Mittelalter-Rezeption*, ed. Peter Wapnewski. Stuttgart: Metzler, 1985.

VILAIN QUI DEVINT RICHE ET PUIS PAUVRE, LE ("The Man Who Became Rich and Then Poor Again"), also known as *Merlin Merlot*, is an anonymous French tale from the thirteenth century. It recounts the story of a poor man whose wish to be wealthy and powerful is granted by Merlin. The man's initial gratitude and respect for Merlin are gradually replaced by casual indifference and then scorn, at which point the magician threatens to restore his original poverty. He ignores the threat, and soon his children die, and his neighbor steals all his money. [NJL]

VIN HERBÉ, LE: *see* MARTIN, FRANK.

VINAVER, EUGÈNE (1899–1979), an eminent Arthurian scholar and one of the founding members of the International Arthurian Society. Among his invaluable contributions to Arthurian scholarship is his work on the Prose *Tristan* and its relation to Malory, as well as his definitive edition of Malory's *Morte Darthur, The Works of Sir Thomas Malory*. This edition grew out of his identification of the Malory manuscript discovered at Winchester by W.F. Oakeshott in 1934. In his later years, Professor Vinaver enhanced understanding of and appreciation for Arthurian romance in books and articles that identify and describe medieval aesthetic principles. In these works, especially *À la recherche d'une poétique médiévale* (1970) and *The Rise of Romance* (1971), he illuminates formal principles, such as interlace, analogy, and repetition, underlying much medieval romance. [SNI]

VINCENT DE BEAUVAIS: *see* MAERLANT, JACOB VAN.

VINEY, JAYNE, author of a historical novel, *The Bright-Helmed One* (1975), which follows Arthur's career by focusing, successively, upon the fortunes of one of his warriors, of his half-Jutish wife Winifrith (Guenevere), and of Cai. The result is a disjointed exploration of the theme of loyalty and betrayal. [RHT]

&c. Viney, Jayne. *The Bright-Helmed One*. London: Hale, 1975.

VISUAL ARTS, ARTHURIAN LEGEND IN. Any attempt to construct a comprehensive history of the Arthurian legend in the visual arts will prove to be an elusive endeavor. Surveying the known examples of Arthurian imagery, diverse in age, geographic origin, and media, we can discern only a single thread of continuity: Arthurian art was dependent upon Arthurian literature; each surge of development in the written tradition was followed by a manifestation in the arts. This symbiotic relationship has characterized Arthurian imagery from its emergence in the twelfth century to its zenith during the late Middle Ages, from its decline during the Renaissance to its revival in Victorian England. There exists even today a vestigial interest in the arts.

Just as its narrative subjects have been drawn from literature, the aesthetic conventions of Arthurian art have reflected contemporary taste. No single stylistic mode can be exclusively labeled Arthurian. As the legend was recast for each succeeding audience, the visual vocabulary was translated to satisfy the current canon. In its dependency upon literary tradition, and in its chameleonlike adaptability, Arthurian imagery defies broad generalizations. Although comprehensive surveys exist (e.g., Scherer's), the survey approach simply addresses an assemblage of images with little insight into the art-historical problems of style and iconography. The sheer diversity of this corpus is best understood as a series of separate phases, each with an individual aesthetic, iconography, and iconology.

The true breadth and variety of Arthurian iconography in the medieval era are cloaked in uncertainty. Sacred themes supplanted the profane during the Middle Ages, and, as Roger Sherman Loomis has pointedly observed (*Arthurian Legends in Medieval Art*, pp. 3–4), the inferiority of secular objects, as well as their rarity, has diminished the attention given to them. It is true that no lay patron rivaled the munificence of the Church in its commission of luxurious objects, embellished with sacred themes. It was not until the fourteenth century that the laity emerged as a substantial force in art patronage, but at no time did the splendor and extravagance of secular works vie with the finest of the sacred.

The perishability of some of the media—textiles, delicate wood and ivory carvings, single-leaf woodcuts—presents another obstacle and constitutes a major loss. Metal objects were often melted for re-use; fresco disappeared beneath coats of whitewash. Private collections suffered the ravages of time to a far greater extent than ecclesiastical collections; the riches of the laity often vanished during civil unrest and social reversal, while the treasures of the Church enjoyed the security of the vaults of the cathedrals and monasteries. What has survived has been selected on the basis of coincidence and circumstance.

Arthurian objects have often survived only in a state of partial preservation. A late Flemish luxury manuscript of *Guiron le Courtois* (ca. 1480; Oxford, Bodl. Lib. Douce 383) retains only seventeen folios of what was believed to have been a lavishly illustrated work (Loomis, pp. 128–30). The "Frauenlob" murals in Constance and the Parzival murals in Lübeck are known only from postmedieval copies, the former through black-and-white copies made in 1860, shortly after their discovery, the latter (destroyed in 1929) through watercolor drawings by Wilhelm Boht, now in the St. Annen Museum, Lübeck (see Loomis, pp. 37, 75–76). The depiction of Arthur in the stained-glass ensemble in St. Mary's Hall in Coventry was heavily restored twice, in 1783 and in 1893, and its original appearance is obliterated (see *Walpole Society Annual*, 19 [1931], 103ff.). The modification of objects, combined with questions of identification, impedes the compilation of a comprehensive catalogue. Loomis has rightly observed (pp. 6–7): "Omniscience alone can determine how many illustrations of the Round Table legend remain to be discovered under a coat of whitewash or in some provincial museum or in an art dealer's shop, and only Fortunatus' purse and at least a lifetime of patience would serve to discover and reproduce every miniature from an Arthurian MS, every woodcut from incunabula, and every illustration of Arthur among the Nine Worthies."

Written records do suggest that the surviving objects represent only a small fraction of the whole tradition. For large-scale interior decorative programs that have vanished, such as "Arthur's Hall" and "Guenevere's Chamber" at Dover Castle (ca. 1250), a manuscript's tinted drawing is often the sole evidence (for the example of Dover Castle, see Loomis, p. 138). Inventories of vast private collections, now dispersed, suggest the popularity of Arthurian iconography. The collection of Louis, Duke of Anjou, documented during the years 1364–65, contained tapestries depicting the Nine Worthies and scenes from the romances of Lancelot as well as gilt-and-enameled cups decorated with subjects from the legend of Tristan. Commission orders—such as a request for roof tiles sent by Pedro IV of Aragon to his counselor Johan Ximenez of Huesca, discussing a chamber in Aljaferia painted with the history of Jaufré— allude to vanished programs.

Literary descriptions, although unreliable as documentation of lost works, were likely based on actual types and bear witness to the demand for elegant secular objects. Vivid descriptions of complex painted and sculpted programs suggest the compositional ideas and the techniques that were employed. In Thomas d'Angleterre's *Tristan*, the grieving lover builds a "Hall of Images" populated with lifelike statues of Queen Ysolt and her entourage. The Vulgate *Lancelot* describes an intricate painting, complete with incriminating inscriptions, executed by Lancelot when he was held captive by Morgan le Fay. Arthur's discovery of the telltale picture is illustrated in a manuscript of the *Lancelot* (ca. 1470; B.N. fr. 112, Vol. II, fol. 193), an illumination that indicates the size and disposition of figures in such an ensemble. Another popular type, a procession in which Arthur, his champions, and their ladies ride in a cavalcade, is described in detail by Boccaccio in *Amorosa Visione*, Cantos XI and XXIX.

On the basis of surviving monuments, it appears that the history of Arthurian art begins in the twelfth century. Arthurian iconography seems to have appeared almost at random, and the literary inspiration for the early subjects remains a topic for speculation. The crude Perros relief, carved on a nave pier in the church of St. Efflam in Brittany (ca. 1100), was more likely based on a local saint's legend than a strict Arthurian source. Arthurian iconography emerges as an independent motif in an archivolt sculpture on the Porta della Pescheria, the north portal of Modena cathedral (1100–40). Loomis (p. 75) has hypothesized that the source was oral tradition, for Arthur's adventures were probably disseminated by Breton troubadours passing through Italy en route to the Holy Land. The remaining history of Arthurian art in the twelfth century is fragmentary, and few other monuments have been identified.

The impetus for a continuous development came with the burgeoning of the romance tradition at the end of the twelfth century. The visual arts responded, but in an evolution subsequent, not parallel, to the literature. From the thirteenth through the fifteenth centuries, Arthurian imagery enjoyed generous patronage and pan-European popularity. The influence of courtly society was clearly manifest in the arts. Subjects became focused and distinct, and the execution and visual conventions attained an unprecedented refinement, typical of the arts commissioned by courtly patrons.

Both the material remains and the documentation reveal that Arthurian subjects appeared in all forms of the visual arts, and the prevailing demand was for objects for private rather than public appreciation. Manuscripts, wall paintings, carved and enameled works, and tapestries and other textiles were adorned with Arthurian motifs. Yet the appearance of such objects in public art, particularly in the sacred realm, was not unknown and accounts for most of the sculpture and stained glass in the tradition.

The repertoire of subjects grew in direct response to the growth of the literature. Furthermore, this repertoire was shared by all the visual arts; subjects were used freely in all media. For example, in the fourteenth and fifteenth centuries, the iconography of the Nine Worthies appeared in manuscript illumination, sculpture, stained glass, and tapestry with equal regularity. A romance subject, such as the Tryst Beneath the Tree from the Tristan legend was favored for toilette articles—jewel caskets, mirror-backs, combs—but also appeared on architectural elements, such as corbels, and in furniture carving, such as misericords. It is through the study of the development of the media, rather than that of a single motif, that we can demonstrate the intricate breadth of the whole.

The proliferation of Arthurian subject matter in manuscript illumination was a natural consequence of the development of the romance. Loomis does note, however, that patronage for such manuscripts arose nearly a century later, suggesting (pp. 37–39) that in the twelfth century Arthurian romances were read aloud and the texts were unadorned. He credits the growth of an illuminated tradition to the expansion of courtly culture in the thirteenth century, as well as the simultaneous establishment of lay scriptoria (there were, for example, seventeen lay illuminators working in Paris by 1292).

Illuminated manuscripts combined text with various forms of decoration, from modest borders and tinted drawings to lavish historical initials and, in the finest luxury manuscripts, full-page miniatures. The manuscript tradition flourished in France, Flanders, and Italy and to a lesser extent in England, Germany, Holland, and Spain. In each case, the style reflected national taste. France was the uncontested leader in the production of both sacred and secular illuminated manuscripts in the Gothic era. During the thirteenth and fourteenth centuries, the Vulgate *Lancelot* and *Queste del Saint Graal* provided the most popular subjects. The fifteenth century was graced by luxury manuscripts, enriched with full-page, narrative illustrations, such as two manuscripts in the Bibliothèque Nationale, a *Lancelot* (ca. 1405; fr. 117–20), once owned by Jean, duc de Berry, and the *Estoire–Merlin–Lancelot* (ca. 1466; fr. 96). At the same time, the tournament book was introduced as a heraldic guide to the arms of Arthur's champions. By the end of the century, named artists, such as

Evarard d'Espingues and Jean Colombe, appear, suggesting an association of illuminators with specialized subject matter.

The early Flemish illuminators turned to historical works, like Geoffrey of Monmouth's *Historia Regum Britanniae* (ca. 1180; Douai, MS 880), practicing a plain, blunt aesthetic, but by the fourteenth century they emulated the French models; such works as the *Queste del Saint Graal* (ca. 1350; Bibliothèque de l'Arsenal 5218) attained a refinement that was maintained through subsequent decades. Guilame Vrelant was an important figure in the mid-fifteenth century, as Flanders shed the cloak of medieval anonymity. Illuminators from Italy displayed a distinctive style, incorporating the classicizing, natural concept of the figure. Lombard manuscripts (ca. 1295–1325), the earliest pictorial transcriptions of the Arthurian story, were crude, but by the mid-fourteenth century such works as the Prose *Tristan* in the Bibliothèque Nationale (ca. 1320–40; fr. 755) and the *Meliadus* (fourteenth century; B.L. Add. 12228), featuring French texts, equaled Flemish achievements. The Italian tradition waned earlier than others, fading out of fashion by the mid-fifteenth century.

In England, the clear preference was for historical works that associated Arthur with other monarchs, such as the *Flores Historium*, illustrated by Matthew Paris (ca. 1230–50; Manchester, Chetham's Library 6712), and Pierre de Langtoft's *Chronicle* in the British Library (ca. 1207; Royal 20 A II). The indigenous romance tradition, which did not emerge until the late medieval era, did not attain French or Flemish standards. In Germany, subjects reveal a national bias, with manuscripts of *Parzival* and *Tristan* reigning supreme from the mid-thirteenth through the fifteenth centuries. In Holland, the tradition was weaker, and such manuscripts as the *Spiegel Historiael* (ca. 1325; The Hague, MS XX) were often concerned only in part with Arthurian iconography. Spain developed a hybrid tradition, wherein Norman scribes worked with Spanish illuminators, as in the Prose *Tristan* (ca. 1278; B.N. fr. 750).

Courtly taste had a strong influence upon decorative arts. Delicate ivory jewel caskets, combs, and mirror-backs were carved with Arthurian motifs for female patrons. In the thirteenth century, the Cologne School was prominent, only to be surpassed by the Parisian School in the fourteenth century. Romance subjects were preferred: the ill-starred love of Tristan and Isolde, the lives of Perceval and Galahad, the adventures of Lancelot. Scenes from Arthurian romance were often combined or contrasted with other vignettes to present a commentary on love.

Arthurian motifs were widely used in interior decoration. Pavements, such as those in Otranto Cathedral (ca. 1165) and Chertsey Abbey (ca. 1270), depicted single subjects and full narratives. Fresco and mural painting was practiced throughout Europe, as evidenced in the Great Tower of the St.-Floret Chateau in the Auvergne (ca. 1350), the Summer House in the Castle Runkelstein in the Tyrol (ca. 1400), the Great Hall of the Castle of La Manta of Saluzzo (ca. 1430), and the Hall of the Round Table in the Palazzo Ducale in Mantua, painted by Pisanello (before 1455). Ensembles often combined sources, illustrating romance subjects and the Nine Worthies in a single program. Arthur figured prominently in the art of tapestry as well; the Nine Worthies was a favored motif, as in the Parisian King Arthur Tapestry (fourteenth century; Metropolitan Museum of Art, New York). Other textiles of less monumental scale, such as embroidered hangings and bed quilts, were enhanced with romance subjects.

Sculpture is rare among surviving objects and its tradition is adumbrated. Appearances seem random and oddly located, as the capital carved with Lancelot crossing the Sword Bridge at St. Pierre in Caen (ca. 1350) or the fourteenth-century misericord carvings in the cathedrals at Lincoln and Chester. A life-sized painted stone sculpture of King Arthur as one of the Nine Worthies has been identified in the Hall of the Hanseatic League in the Rathaus in Cologne (ca. 1325).

The diversity of subject matter, the persistent use of contemporary detail, and the variety of media prevented the amalgamation of a single, distinctive style. Artists did not formulate individual physical types: Arthur appeared sometimes bearded, sometimes clean-shaven, with or without a crown, and the absence of heraldry or previous knowledge of the subject impeded comprehension. It was the literature and the courtly taste of the patron that provided the tenuous continuity of the development of medieval Arthurian imagery.

The association of Arthurian imagery with an elite audience ended with the advent of printing in the mid-fifteenth century. The combination of printed text with woodcut illustrations in an inexpensive and easily reproduced format popularized the legend. Single-leaf woodcuts could grace the wall of a modest home, and the rising merchant, who would find the price of an illuminated manuscript prohibitive, could afford a printed volume, illustrated with woodcuts. We see this development throughout Europe: in the shops of Jean Dupré in Paris and of Anton Sorg in Augsburg and in the Spanish broadside tradition. Outstanding among the illustrated editions was the *Morte Darthur* printed in 1498 by Wynkyn de Worde, heir to William Caxton's London enterprise.

The succeeding century, with its shift in cultural ideals, saw the first decline in Arthurian interest. During the Renaissance, Arthurian subjects waned in the popular realm but were occasionally employed by monarchs, particularly in England, as political propaganda. The Winchester Round Table, likely crafted for a tournament in the fourteenth century, was given a fresh coat of paint by Henry VII in 1485 and changed to Tudor colors and devices. Henry VIII (who repainted the table again in 1522) carried banners lauding Arthur as a world conqueror when he met Francis I at the Field of Cloth of Gold in 1520. In Germany, Emperor Maximilian turned to Arthurian monarchical iconography in his commission of the bronze statue of the King at Innsbruck from the workshop of Peter Vischer the Elder in 1513.

The passing of the sixteenth century marked the full decline of Arthurian imagery. Aside from a rare Arthurian costume in Queen Elizabeth's Accession Day Tilts and Prince Henry's revival of the monarchical symbol in his commission of *Prince Henry's Barriers* (1610), by Ben Jonson with designs by Inigo Jones, the subjects vanished from the artist's repertoire. Throughout the remainder of the seventeenth century and the first half of the eighteenth, interest in Arthur languished. The literature declined, but the art disappeared.

In the eighteenth century, particularly in England, a new interest in medieval heritage arose. As early as the 1720s, garden follies, such as Merlin's Cave in Richmond, by William Kent, were built to evoke a romanticized vision of the past. The Gothic Revival pursued "ancient" literature with unprecedented zeal, but it was *The Faerie Queene* of Edmund Spenser that inspired the artists. Illustrated editions of *The Faerie Queene* served to increase public interest. In the last quarter of the eighteenth century, paintings based on Spenser's poem, especially those of Henry Fuseli and John Hamilton Mortimer, were featured at Thomas Macklin's Poets Gallery in London (1788–1800). In every case, only the subjects were Elizabethan, for in style these paintings reflected the classicizing standards espoused by the Royal Academy of Art.

The Gothic Revival in literature brought Malory's *Le Morte Darthur* out of almost 200 years of obscurity, with three new editions in the early nineteenth century. A similar interest among artists did not arise until the Victorian era, and no Arthurian work of art based on a source other than *The Faerie Queene* predates the year 1849. The legend came to be regarded as a paradigm of modern behavior, the result of popular medievalism, which redefined chivalry as a modern behavioral code, and the reinterpretation of the legend by contemporary poets for their own audience, so that Arthurian iconography was introduced into Victorian painting as a new national allegory. In 1848, the government commissioned William Dyce to paint an ensemble of frescoes for the Queen's Robing Room in the new palace at Westminster, illustrating the virtues of national character as exemplified in the Arthurian legend. Dyce edited all incidents of sin and pessimism out of the legend. This expurgated version, the first Victorian Arthuriad in the visual arts, foreshadowed the interpretive mode of Tennyson's *Idylls of the King*, and it began a revival that would endure until the end of the century.

During the 1850s and the 1860s, every sector of the Victorian art world embraced Arthurian subject matter. Three sources provided the inspiration: Tennyson's poetry, Malory's *Le Morte Darthur*, and Dyce's frescoes. The Pre-Raphaelite artists, most prominently Edward Burne-Jones, William Morris, and Dante Gabriel Rossetti, explored the potential of the new subject, in painting, as in the Oxford Union Murals (1857), and in decorative arts, such as the Dunlop Windows (1862) and the Stanmore Hall Tapestries (1891–94). Academic artists, such as James Archer, Joseph Noël Paton, Thomas Woolner, and John William Waterhouse, addressed similar themes, but with greater moral content. The most popular subjects were Sir Galahad, Elaine, Tristan and Isolde, Lancelot and Guenevere, the Lady of Shalott, and the Death of King Arthur, but subjects were limited only by the artist's familiarity with the literature. Book illustration also flourished; notable among the many illustrated editions were the Moxon Tennyson (1857) and the *Idylls of the King* illustrated by Gustave Doré (1868) and by Julia Margaret Cameron (1874). Parodies appeared as well, as in the work of George du Maurier.

The Arthurian Revival waned with the century, as a new generation rejected chivalric idealism and the canon of aestheticism drained the heroic figures of their power. Aubrey Beardsley's drawings for the Dent *Morte D'arthur* typify the late decadent phase. The Arthurian Revival differed from the medieval manifestation of the legend in several ways. Primarily, it was brought into being as a royal, sanctioned allegory with a clear, moral iconology. Also, the visual arts in the Victorian era developed in parallel rather than subsequent to the literature. Further, artists developed definite prototypes, assigned physical characteristics to characters, and formulated a clear iconography. The Victorian era borrowed only the superficial trappings from the medieval achievements; in interpretation, form, and influence, the revival marked a distinct new phase of development.

A minor interest in Arthurian imagery was manifest outside of England in the nineteenth century. In France, the subject matter was restricted to the decorative arts, as in the work of Victor Adam. In Germany, interest was revived through the works of Wagner, which inspired stage design by Heinrich Döll and the elaborate palace decorations at Neuschwanstein and Schlossberg commissioned by Ludwig II of Bavaria (1860–80). It was also through Wagnerian influence that the Belgian Symbolists, such as Paul Delville, turned to Arthurian themes. In America, the model was English, as evidenced in Edwin Austen Abbey's murals for the Boston Public Library (1895). Only England, however, enjoyed a full-scale revival of the legend in the arts.

Vestiges of the revival continued into the twentieth century in England and America. It remained a minor theme in British painting until World War I. In both countries, book illustration, particularly for the juvenile audience, became the dominant expression. British illustrators included Walter Crane, Edmund Dulac, and Arthur Rackham, while Howard Pyle and N.C. Wyeth developed an independent American tradition. Arthur and his champions also appeared in British public-school decoration and, in rare instances, in American institutions, such as the Princeton Chapel Windows design by Charles Connick (1931).

By the 1940s, Arthurian subjects had fallen into neglect. The self-expressive trend in European and American painting disdained literary subjects, and the nonrepresentational vocabulary of the modern painter expressed formal rather than narrative ideas. From the 1960s to the present, cinema has been the major medium for exploration of Arthurian subjects. The films of John Boorman, Robert Bresson, and Eric Rohmer provide personal visions of the legendary world. It is too early in the development to assess cinema's position in the history of Arthurian art; it may be a response to the current wealth of new fiction, a new force in the arts, or a brand of escapist entertainment.

The history of Arthurian art is riddled with discontinuity. Its origins have yet to be discovered, while its current manifestations await evaluation. Two major phases can be recognized, but these phases were distinct in their style, their interpretation, and their motivation. They shared only the legendary subject matter, and ultimately it is the literature that lends structure to the study of the Arthurian art. (*See also* DECORATIVE ARTS [MEDIEVAL].) [DNM]

𝕝 Loomis, Roger Sherman, and Laura Hibbard Loomis. *Arthurian Legends in Medieval Art.* London: Oxford University Press, 1938.

Mancoff, Debra N. *The Arthurian Revival in Victorian Painting.* 2 vols. Ann Arbor, Mich.: University Microfilms International, 1982.

Scherer, Margaret R. *About the Round Table.* New York: Metropolitan Museum of Art, 1945.

VITA DI MERLINO CON LE SUE PROFETIE ("The Life of Merlin, with His Prophecies"), also known as *Historia di Merlino*; a free Italian translation of the prose version of Robert de Boron's *Merlin.* The work offers a number of departures from the French text and includes some "prophecies" that appear to refer to recent Italian events. [NJL]

𝕝 *La Historia di Merlino.* Venice: Tramezzino, 1480.

VITA MERLINI: *see* GEOFFREY OF MONMOUTH.

VIVES, BROTHER JUAN (or João Bivas), the early fourteenth-century Spanish translator of the French Post-Vulgate Cycle. His translation is known through Spanish and Portuguese redactions and fragments, such as *Estoria de Merlín, Livro de Josep Abaramatia, Libro de Josep Abarimatia, Baladro del sabio Merlín, Lançarote,* and *Demanda del Sancto Grial.* [NJL]

𝕝 Entwistle, William J. *The Arthurian Legend in the Literatures of the Spanish Peninsula.* London: Dent, 1925, pp. 172ff.

VIVIANE: *see* LADY OF THE LAKE.

"VIVIEN": *see* TENNYSON, ALFRED LORD.

VOLKSLIEDER: *see* HERDER, JOHANN GOTTFRIED VON.

VOLLMÖLLER, KARL GUSTAV (1878–1948), a film pioneer, engineer, businessman, and Neoromantic poet from the circle of Stefan George who worked on Hollywood films until his death. Vollmöller's early creation, the poem cycle *Parcival* (1897–1900; published in 1902), is considered to be the most "modern" treatment of the subject, one reason being its imagistic language.

The poem by Wolfram von Eschenbach, here framed in the diction of the *Jugendstil*, is made to mirror the modern period. [UM/WCM]

ᴥ Vollmöller, Karl Gustav. *Parcival*. Milan: Treves, 1902.
  Schulze, Ursula. "Ideologisierung durch Strukturverlust." In *Akten des DFG-Symposions zur Mittelalter-Rezeption*, ed. Peter Wapnewski. Stuttgart: Metzler, 1985.

VON ARNIM, ACHIM: *see* "AUSGLEICHUNG, DIE."

VON FÜRSTENBERG, VEITH, contemporary film director and member of the "New German Cinema," shot the first German fantasy film, *Feuer und Schwert—Die Legende von Tristan und Isolde*, in Ireland ("Fire and Sword . . . ," 1981); it was not a commercial success. In part, von Fürstenberg gives the medieval subject matter a new interpretation. Isolde, for example, offers the love potion to Tristan with premeditation. The film is distinguished by its poetic images, but it inclines to an apathy that does not do justice to the material. It neither attains the forceful imagery of Boorman's *Excalibur* (which was filmed at exactly the same time, also in Ireland), nor does it exhibit the extreme, but convincing, stylization of Rohmer's *Perceval le Gallois*. [UM/WCM]

VORTIGERN, a fifth-century British ruler, blamed by the Welsh for the Saxons' settlement in Britain, and thus for their eventual takeover of what is now England. Vortigern's friendship with them is the cause of the troubles that Arthur temporarily ends.

"Vortigern" in Welsh is *Gwrtheyrn*, and the king figures in the Triads as Gwrtheyrn the Thin. Despite his bad reputation, one or two places in Wales are named after him, such as Nant Gwrtheyrn by Caernarvon Bay. Nennius's *Historia Brittonum* makes him reign during a vague forty-year period after the end of Roman rule. When the Saxon brothers Hengist and Horsa land with three ships, Vortigern allows them to live in the isle of Thanet and to bring more of their heathen compatriots from the Continent. He promises to maintain them if they will fight the Picts and Scots who are harassing Britain. They do so but also exploit Vortigern's failings to seize more territory. Hengist gives him his daughter as a wife, in exchange for Kent. Later, he tricks Vortigern into arranging a conference at which the British nobles are massacred; Hengist then imprisons him and extorts further lands.

Nennius names Ambrosius as Vortigern's chief British rival. This is Ambrosius Aurelianus. However, the narrative adds little to what is known of him. He appears in a legendary tale: Vortigern tries to build a fortress among the Welsh mountains, but supernatural happenings halt the work. The king's magicians say that he must find a boy with no father, kill him, and sprinkle his blood on the building site. A boy whose mother claims to have conceived without intercourse is brought to the spot. He challenges the magicians to tell what is under the foundations. When they cannot, he reveals a pool with two serpents—one red, one white—that fight each other. The boy interprets them as representing the Britons and Saxons. His name turns out to be Ambrosius (in Welsh, *Emrys*—the place is still called Dinas Emrys). Vortigern, shaken, gives him authority over western Britain.

With all this, Nennius interweaves legends of St. Germanus, who visited Britain twice to oppose the Pelagian heresy, a doctrine of British origin. The first visit was in 429 with another bishop, Lupus; the second was about 446. However, Nennius's Germanus episodes, like his tale of Ambrosius, are too fanciful to be much use in linking Vortigern with history. The saint and the king clash, but with no reason given, apart from scandal about Vortigern living in incest with his daughter. Nennius offers several versions of his end. The most credible is that he wandered from place to place amid general hate, "until his heart broke and he died without honor."

Geoffrey of Monmouth adopts and expands most of this, prefacing it with a story making Vortigern an unscrupulous usurper and closing with his death when the rightful princes return. (*See* AURELIUS AMBROSIUS; CONSTANTINE [1].) In Geoffrey's version, the prophetic youth becomes Merlin. Vortigern's Saxon settlers remain in Britain, and the glories of Arthur are founded on a campaign that subdues them for many years.

Despite the fantasy, Vortigern did exist. He appears in sources unaffected by Welsh legend. Gildas speaks of a *superbus tyrannus*, or "preeminent ruler," who, in concert with a council, brought in the Saxons, and while he leaves this man anonymous, the English historian Bede in 731 calls him Vortigern. Also, the *Anglo-Saxon Chronicle* refers to Vortigern as the Britons' king at the time of a battle in Kent.

Nennius gives a genealogy suggesting a Gloucestershire background for him and makes him an ancestor of a Welsh royal house. He is mentioned on a ninth-century monument near Llangollen in north Wales, the Pillar of Eliseg. According to this, St. Germanus gave a blessing to one of his sons (an incident known to Nennius), and Vortigern's wife, who bore this son, was a daughter of Maximus, an emperor proclaimed in Britain. After Maximus's downfall in 388, his young daughters became imperial wards. An eventual marriage of one of them to a British noble could have been part of a treaty transferring authority to him, which he might then have exploited to achieve sovereign power. A title that Geoffrey alleges Vortigern held seems to give an oblique hint at the Maximus connection.

Appended to the *Historia Brittonum* is a note dating Vortigern's supremacy from 425. Geoffrey says his surrender of Kent occurred at the time of Germanus's first visit, in 429, and this is at least compatible. As to his status when he reigned, the meaning of "Vortigern" itself is a clue. Though found later as a name, it is probably a title here, or, at any rate, a designation. In the British language, it would have meant "over-chief" or "over-king." Taken in conjunction with other royal designations, "Vortimer" and "Riothamus," it indicates that the Britons (like their Celtic kinsfolk in Ireland) had high kings—kings with paramountcy at least in theory over a number of regional rulers—and the man called Vortigern was one, his personal name being unrecorded. It is noteworthy that Nennius names a ruler of Kent whom Vortigern sets aside by superior authority in his deal with Hengist. Gildas's phrase *superbus tyrannus* would be a Latin rendering of the "high king" dignity, the word *tyrannus* in the Latin of the time implying not so much tyranny as doubtful legitimacy. The high kingship seemingly remained unstable and ill-defined, never evolving a standard form of the title, and faded out as Britain disintegrated.

Historians have suggested that Vortigern was a nationalist, sponsoring the Pelagian heresy as a British version of Christianity, this being the truth behind Germanus's conflict with him. The idea is speculative. But the advent of the Saxons (a term comprising the Saxons proper and their associates the Angles and Jutes, all destined to blend as "English") is a fact of history. A few were already in Britain early in the fifth century, possibly as squatters. Larger groups came later, apparently as "federates"—barbarians allotted land and maintenance in return for military service. This was Late Roman practice; in Britain, the federates got out of hand, and many more of their kinsfolk arrived in their wake, without permission. Bede puts the first authorized settlement around the middle of the fifth century. This dating reflects a confusion in Gildas, and archaeology proves it to be too late. The notes appended to Nennius make the process begin in 428, Vortigern's fourth year. The real extent of his personal responsibility is uncertain. [GA]

🐾 Nennius. *Historia Brittonum*, Chapters 31, 36–49, 66.

Geoffrey of Monmouth. *Historia Regum Britanniae*, Book VI, Chapter 6, through Book VIII, Chapter 2.

Alcock, Leslie. *Arthur's Britain*. London: Penguin, 1971.

Bromwich, Rachel. *Trioedd Ynys Prydein*. Cardiff: University of Wales Press, 1961.

Chadwick, N.K., ed. *Studies in Early British History*. Cambridge: Cambridge University Press, 1954.

Dumville, David. "Sub-Roman Britain: History and Legend." *History*, 62 (1977).

VORTIGERN: *see* IRELAND, SAMUEL; STUCKEN, EDUARD.

VORTIMER, in Nennius's *Historia Brittonum*, Vortigern's eldest son, who breaks with him and makes war on the Saxons he has settled in Kent. Vortimer fights them four times and drives them out but dies soon after. They return with Vortigern's acquiescence and resume their depredations. Geoffrey of Monmouth expands the story, saying that the Britons, angry at Vortigern's pro-Saxon stance, deposed him and made Vortimer king instead. When he won the Kentish victory, his Saxon stepmother poisoned him, and Vortigern was back in power.

As a figure of history, Vortimer eludes definition. If he existed at all, he probably did die before Vortigern, because there is no hint of a succession. Morris, one of the few modern historians to take him seriously, equates three of his battles with three recorded in the *Anglo-Saxon Chronicle* and dated 455, 457, and 465. Since Vortigern is unlikely to have lived beyond the mid-450s, this attempt to pin Vortimer down involves pulling back the *Chronicle* dates ten years or more. Geoffrey puts his campaign earlier still—contemporary with the mission of Germanus and Lupus in 429. This, however, is a product of his dynastic fictions. In 429, any Saxons settled in Britain as auxiliary troops would still have been few and controllable.

When he writes of Vortimer, Nennius employs the Welsh spelling *Guorthemir*. This has variants of its own, but the fifth-century original from which it derives is a British form *Vortamorix*, which, like *Vortigern*, would probably have been a title or designation. The syllable *vor* meant "over"; *tamo-* was a superlative suffix; *rix* meant "king." As *Vortigern* is the "over-king," so *Vortimer* is the "over-most" or "highest" king. Its etymological closeness to "Riothamus" or *Rigotamos*, the designation of a king who was certainly real, may be thought to favor Vortimer's own reality. Whether or not he was actually Vortigern's son, he may have put up a rival claim to authority, adopting a distinctive and grander form of the royal style. [GA]

Nennius. *Historia Brittonum*, Chapters 43–44.

Geoffrey of Monmouth. *Historia Regum Britanniae*, Book VI, Chapters 13–14.

Bromwich, Rachel. *Trioedd Ynys Prydein*. Cardiff: University of Wales Press, 1961.

Morris, John. *The Age of Arthur*. New York: Scribner, 1973.

VOSTAERT, PIETER: *see* PENNINC.

VULGATE CYCLE (also called the Lancelot-Grail Cycle or the Pseudo-Map Cycle), is one of the major literary monuments that mark the shift from verse to prose in the writing of Arthurian romance. In the twelfth century, when Chrétien de Troyes was composing his now-classic chivalric tales in verse, prose was reserved largely for translations of Latin works (commentaries or paraphrases of sacred texts and sermons in particular). In the thirteenth century, prose became the medium of vernacular chronicles (those by Robert de Clari and Villehardouin followed later by Joinville's *Histoire de Saint Louis*). When authors begin to cast the Arthurian material into prose around 1210, the scope of these tales becomes simultaneously more historical and more religious: the focus shifts from the courtly knight to the Grail quester, and the material is organized into cycles of tales that attempt to recount the entire history of the Grail from its origin in the Passion of Christ to the successful accomplishment of the quest by the chosen hero. The earliest example of this tendency is found in the *Roman du Graal*, a prose trilogy that is attributed to Robert de Boron and that recounts the biblical history of the Grail vessel (*Joseph d'Arimathie*), its arrival in Great Britain along with the discovery of the future King Arthur (*Merlin*), the quest for the Holy Grail, and the subsequent demise of Arthur's world (*Perceval*).

The Vulgate Cycle (ca. 1215–35) offers a more elaborate version of this literary scenario, expanding the Prose *Perceval* into two separate tales: the *Queste del Saint Graal* and the *Mort* (*le roi*) *Artu*, and adding a lengthy rendition of the *Lancelot* story to make a total of five roughly sequential narratives. The *Lancelot propre* (or *Lancelot en prose*), the *Queste*, and the *Mort Artu* were written first, and supplemented by the *Estoire del Saint Graal* and the *Estoire de Merlin* (or Vulgate *Merlin*), although the latter two are designed to head the sequence in terms of narrative chronology.

Though the cycle is anonymous, it contains elaborate scenarios of fictive authorship. The *Queste* and *Mort Artu* are attributed to Walter Map, a scribe at the court of Henry II who died before the composition of the texts he is supposed to have written. The *Estoire* and the *Merlin* bear the name of Robert de Boron, purported author of the *Roman du Graal* and its predecessor in verse. Emphasis is placed particularly in the *Queste* on genealogies of narrative transmission. The tale is said to have passed from the oral deposition of knights who recount their adventures at King Arthur's court, to a scribal copy of this narrative, to a Latin version later translated into French. The *Merlin* results ostensibly from Merlin's dictation to his scribe Blaise, who combines accounts of the Arthurian past with those of Christ's miracles. The *Estoire* claims to issue directly from the mouth of God and from a book that Christ (the divine author) gave the vernacular "author" to copy.

Appeal is thus made to two distinct traditions of authority: the Divine Book has its secular counterpart in King Henry's written records, and the all-powerful voice of God has its vernacular rival—the oral tales of King Arthur's knights. This conflation of written and oral modes is played out in the very pages we read, since the tales committed to writing are recounted to us by the textualized and highly ambiguous voice of *li contes*. This fictive voice usurps the traditional role of author and narrator by speaking, becoming silent, ending one narrative segment to begin another. Scholars have argued for both single and multiple authorship of the cycle—the most convincing theory postulates an original "architect" whose plan for the *Lancelot*, *Queste*, and *Mort Artu* was carried out by a series of authors—but the historical authors of the Vulgate Cycle remain well concealed behind the voice of *li contes* and the fabricated attributions of authorship accompanying it.

An elaborate matrix of cross-references involving prophecy and family lineage serves to thematize the conjunction of sacred and secular modes that is cultivated throughout the cycle. The *Lancelot* announces at its beginning that Lancelot was given the baptismal name of Galahad, thus forging a crucial link between the archetypal knight-lover and the chosen hero of the *Queste del Saint Graal*. At the end of the *Lancelot*, we learn that Lancelot is in fact Galahad's father, having engendered the Grail hero during a visit with King Pelles's daughter at Corbenic, although the son far surpasses the more courtly Lancelot in spiritual achievement. Galahad represents the ideal conjunction of religious and chivalric modes, and of past and future epochs. Descending from David and Joseph of Arimathea on his father's side, and from the Grail kings on his mother's, he is the embodiment of biblical history destined to cure the ills of the troubled Arthurian world.

The belated prologue to the Vulgate Cycle supplied by the *Estoire* recasts this father/son scenario in yet a more religious vein. A highly Christianized version of Robert de Boron's *Joseph*, this tale adds to the story of the Grail keeper, Joseph of Arimathea, the narrative of his son, Josephe, whose purity and chastity qualify him to become the first Christian bishop. Joseph catches Christ's blood in the Holy Vessel after the Crucifixion, miraculously survives forty-three years in prison, and, when liberated, transports the sacred object to Sarras (the imaginary land of the Saracens). It is, however, Josephe who has a privileged vision of Christ while contemplating the Grail and becomes the spiritual leader of the Christians. The evangelization of the East and West ensues in highly stylized accounts of conversion: Mordred, Nascien, and Celidoine are instructed in succession to journey to a desert isle where each falls prey to a bewitching temptress until a *prudhomme* offers spiritual guidance and release. A final voyage leads the faithful to Great Britain, where the Grail, sign of the covenant between God and his chosen people, performs a series of miracles. When Josephe dies, he confers the Grail on Alain, the first Fisher King, who places it in Corbenic Castle, where its guardians await the arrival of the *Bon Chevalier*. Without drawing directly on biblical apocrypha, this romance invents episodes that imitate the apocryphal tradition, mixing them with incidents modeled after Breton saints' lives, the *Tristan*, and Old French romances to provide an elaborate "preview" of the tales to come.

In the *Estoire de Merlin*, the most chronicle-like of the Vulgate stories, Merlin as prophet and enchanter becomes the nexus where chivalric and sacred threads of the narrative cross. With a knowledge of the past (inherited from his incubus father) and a divine gift of foresight, Merlin confounds onlookers with his ability to explain mysterious events and predict the future. After using his magic to disguise King Uther as the Duke of Tintagel so that the king can lie with Igerne, the duke's wife, and engender Arthur, Merlin establishes the future king's authority—by having him pull the sword from the stone—and assures his military supremacy—by inventing ingenious combat strategies. Chivalry here dons a supernatural dimension, however, as the Round Table, originally characterized as a meetingplace of Arthur's most valiant knights, becomes an exact replica of the Grail table—itself fashioned after the table of the Last Supper. The principal heroes of this tale are Arthur and Gawain, who with Merlin's help score repeated victories against Arthur's rebellious barons. Their military successes are developed in detail in a narrative *suite* (the *Suite-Vulgate* or historical *suite*) that links the *Merlin* proper to the *Lancelot*. It is also in this portion of the tale that we learn of Arthur's marriage to Guenevere, Merlin's love of Viviane, and the birth of Lancelot.

The *Lancelot*, which alone accounts for half of the Vulgate Cycle, details the adventures of its most popular if flawed chivalric hero. Drawing on the scenario recounted in Chrétien de Troyes's *Chevalier de la charrete*, and on the *enfances* provided by a lost Anglo-Norman tale (predecessor of the German *Lanzelet* by Ulrich von Zatzikhoven, ca. 1200), the Vulgate *Lancelot* enlarges the legendary biography of its hero by adding a long series of highly stylized adventures. Lancelot's role as outlined by the Lady of the Lake, a fairy mentor who holds her power from Merlin and the Devil, is essentially secular: to combine earthly chivalry with charitable acts, defending the Church and protecting the weak. Lacking specific instruction in chastity or spirituality, Lancelot falls in love with Guenevere and, to prove his worth, undertakes a series of exploits that form the bulk of the tale. Although these episodes are highly repetitive, they fall into three major patterns—imprisonment and release, deception and perception, wounding and healing—patterns that characterize both the captive state of Logres awaiting the chosen hero, and the captive nature of the romance text, which, while claiming to possess the authority of Scripture, indulges wholeheartedly in the verbal trap of secular narrative. In addition to being arranged in patterns, the disparate adventures of the many knights are carefully knit together in the *Lancelot* through a technique of *entrelacement*, the interweaving of narrative segments within a remarkably consistent chronology.

A lengthy segment of the tale is devoted to Galehaut, who is the go-between for Lancelot and Guenevere during a period when their love is threatened by the False Guenevere and Morgain, and when Arthur himself is seduced by the enchantress Camille. Gauvain and Hector become principal chivalric heroes in this segment, only to be eclipsed by Lancelot in the "Conte de la charrete" portion of this tale. Lancelot's activities deviate significantly from those recounted in the cemetery scene of Chrétien's *Charrete*: the tombstone that previously named Lancelot as the future liberator of Gorre is here replaced by two tombstones. The hero's failure at the second one, attributed to his lust for Guenevere, predicts his subsequent exclusion from the Grail quest. As Lancelot's behavior becomes demonstrably more flawed, his cousin Bohort emerges as one of the elect who will join Perceval and Galahad on the final quest of the Grail.

The *Queste* begins with a description of Galahad's uncanny powers as chosen hero and ends with his privileged viewing of the mysterious Grail vessel. The bulk of the tale is concerned, however, with attempts of less-successful knights: Lionel, Hector, and Gauvain, who form the elite of earthly questers, and Perceval and Bohort, who are chosen but less accomplished than Galahad. Drawing on Chrétien's *Conte del Graal* and its First and Second Continuations, this text combines mythic elements from the Matter of Britain—the Perilous Seat, the Sword in the Stone, the abolition of evil customs—with more Christianized motifs. The Bleeding Lance and Broken Sword, found in Robert de Boron's unfinished Grail trilogy and in the Didot-*Perceval*, become the lance of Longinus and King David's sword. The Grail itself is the vessel from which Christ ate the paschal lamb with his disciples.

To substantiate the text's authority and give the illusion that it advances didactic truth, the exploits, visions, and dreams recounted in the course of this tale are routinely interpreted by resident hermits who offer to tell the *senefiance* and *vérité* of what we read. This unusual method of composition has led scholars to read the *Queste* allegorically: as a spiritual treatise promulgated by the Cistercian order of monks who used the romance mode for purely didactic purpose. Such an undertaking, however, raises the complex problem of transcribing the ineffable into language. If the ethereal Grail exists, as we are told, beyond the realm of mortal speech, how can one possibly represent it in a romance text? The problematic rapport between Lancelot and Galahad as representatives of the secular and sacred worlds is here reproduced in another form, as the secular strives to achieve what lies clearly beyond its grasp.

The *Mort Artu* provides a *suite* for the *Queste* and a conclusion to the entire cycle. The final holocaust on Salisbury Plain, in which Arthur and his bastard son Mordred kill each other, is preceded by an inexorable succession of narrative events set in motion by the renewed love affair between Lancelot and Guenevere and complicated by incidents of misunderstanding and misinterpretation. These two narrative strains are established early in the tale when Lancelot, who comes to the Winchester tournament in disguise, is accused of adultery with the Queen and suspected of loving the Dame d'Escalot. When the Queen is charged subsequently with poisoning a knight at Arthur's court, Lancelot comes to her defense and accidentally kills Gauvain's brother, Gaheriet, inciting Arthur and his nephew to declare war against Lancelot and his family. When departing for battle, Arthur entrusts his kingdom to Mordred, who usurps the royal power, prompting the King's return and the mortal combat between father and son. Before dying, Arthur orders his squire Girflet to throw the famed sword Excalibur into the lake, where a disembodied hand catches it. A boat bearing Morgain and her enchanted attendants then carries Arthur out to sea. Continuing some narrative incidents established in the *Lancelot propre*, this tale also builds on the adultery scenario of the Tristan legends and develops the military schema laid out in Geoffrey of Monmouth's *Historia Regum Britanniae* and *Vita Merlini* and the end of the Didot-*Perceval*. But the *Mort Artu* is distinguished from these predecessors and all other volumes of the Vulgate Cycle by the dramatic alignment of events in an inexorable chain of cause and effect proceeding relentlessly from a harmless chivalric tournament to a bloody cataclysmic battle.

Despite its emphasis on chronological sequence, however, this chronicle of Arthur's last days does not come to a definitive close. The text's apparent grounding in linear time and secular history is undermined in the final pages by a timeless openendedness reminiscent of scriptural narrative. Arthur, though dead and buried, is expected to return miraculously at a later date, effecting a human resurrection in line with the Second Coming. And the Arthurian narrative, having come to an apocalyptic end, will similarly be continued in subsequent romance texts. [EJB]

VULGATE CYCLE

🙠 Sommer, H. Oskar, ed. *The Vulgate Version of the Arthurian Romances*. 8 vols. Washington, D.C.: Carnegie Institution, 1908–16.

Micha, Alexandre, ed. *Lancelot: roman en prose du XIIIe siècle*. 7 vols. Geneva: Droz, 1978–80.

———, ed. *Merlin: roman du XIIIe siècle*. Geneva: Droz, 1979.

Pauphilet, Albert, ed. *La Queste del Saint Graal*. Paris: Champion, 1923.

Frappier, Jean, ed. *La Mort le roi Artu: roman du XIIIe siècle*. Geneva: Droz, 1954; 3rd ed. 1959.

Hucher, Eugène, ed. *Le Saint-Graal*. 3 vols. Le Mans: Monnoyer, 1875–78.

Burns, E. Jane. *Arthurian Fictions: Re-reading the Vulgate Cycle*. Columbus: Ohio State University Press, 1985.

Leupin, Alexandre. *Le Graal et la littérature*. Lausanne: L'Âge d'Homme, 1982.

WACE. Almost all we know of Wace's life comes from autobiographical passages in his last work, the *Roman de Rou*. He was born on the Norman isle of Jersey early in the twelfth century (1110?). As a child, he was educated at Caen in Normandy and later in the Ile de France. After many years, he returned to Caen and took up a literary career. His earliest works, like Chrétien de Troyes's, were translations from Latin to *romanz* (Old French). Only three are extant: *The Life of St. Margaret*, *The Life of St. Nicholas*, and *The Conception of Our Lady*. His most important work, whose popularity is attested by some twenty-four manuscripts and fragments, was his *Roman de Brut*, which, he tells us at the end, he completed in 1155. This work, which was dedicated to Eleanor of Aquitaine, probably attracted the attention of her husband, Henry II Plantagenet, for whom he began in 1160 his *Roman de Rou*, a verse history of the dukes of Normandy. Around 1175, however, he was supplanted in this task, at Henry's insistence, by a certain Master Beneeit.

Wace's *Brut* is a key text in Arthurian studies, for it is among the earliest works to introduce Celtic matter into French. His principal source is Geoffrey of Monmouth's *Historia Regum Britanniae*, whose Latin prose chronicle is expanded to about 15,000 French octosyllabic lines. Wace omits the names of some minor characters, abbreviates purely religious history, and deletes some brutal passages, such as Arthur's torturing of the Picts and Scots. But his additions are of particular interest for the study of Arthurian romance: he is the first to mention the Round Table; he alludes to Breton storytellers and the existence around 1150 of an oral tradition concerning Arthur; he adds topical details based most likely on personal travels in southwestern England; he comments on the "Breton Hope" of Arthur's messianic return from the Isle of Avalon. Also important in this regard is a passage in the *Roman de Rou* concerning the forest of Brocéliande.

Wace is noted for his skill in description and lively style. He had great influence on subsequent French authors of Arthurian materials: on Chrétien de Troyes and Marie de France, as well as on the anonymous authors of the Vulgate *Merlin*, the *Mort Artu*, the Didot-*Perceval*, and the *Livre d'Artus*. [WWK]

&. Wace. *Le Roman de Brut*, ed. I. Arnold. 2 vols. Paris: SATF, 1938–40.

———. *Le Roman de Rou de Wace*, ed. A.J. Holden. 3 vols. Paris: SATF, 1970–73.

WAGNER, RICHARD (1813–1883). The mention of Wagner in an Arthurian context immediately calls to mind two of his greatest operas, *Tristan und Isolde* and *Parsifal*. Yet his fascination with such subjects is suggested as early as 1850, in his marginally Arthurian opera *Lohengrin*, which presents the story of King Parsifal's son. The Holy Grail theme occurs at various points through the opera, but its significance is explained only in the third (and final) act, when the hero's "narrative" offers details of Monsalvat, the castle where the Grail is guarded by a group of holy knights. Those knights have magical powers, so long as their identity is not known. Lohengrin reveals his ancestry and the fact that he has been sent by the Grail.

Wagner's first contact with Arthurian legend had probably been in Dresden, where he studied medieval literature. He no doubt studied Gottfried von Strassburg's *Tristan* and may have been familiar with the earlier works of Thomas, Béroul, and Eilhart von Oberge. Wagner mentions Wolfram von Eschenbach's *Parzifal* in his correspondence, and it is likely that he also knew Chrétien de Troyes's *Perceval*. The Tristan and Parzifal stories must have impressed the composer deeply, for he returned to the medieval texts and used them as the basis for two of his greatest operas (presented in 1865 and 1882). However, he uses his music-drama as a showcase for philosophical ideas that had for some time been taking form in his mind. His philosophy necessitated several important changes in the legends, as did the demands of a musical presentation. Wagner's dramas, although based on the medieval texts, are new and personal creations.

In the interest of dramatic simplicity, Wagner had to condense the plot of Gottfried's *Tristan*. The action of the opera is very simple, being reduced to three main dramatic situations corresponding to the three acts of the opera. The battles and adventures that occupy the first part of Gottfried's romance and establish Tristan's chivalric reputation are reduced to a few lines in the first act of the opera. Gottfried's vivid accounts of hunting scenes are practically eliminated from the text of the opera and are merely alluded to musically with hunting-horn sounds in the second act. Wagner reduces the group of conspirators against Tristan to one person, Melot, and completely does away with the second Isolde (Isolde of the White Hands). By limiting the number of characters, Wagner is able to rivet the spectator's attention on the tragic couple and thus intensify the drama.

Both Gottfried and Wagner emphasize the change in the two main characters after the drinking of the love potion. In Gottfried's version, the gentle Isolde is willing to sacrifice Brangaene's virginity to hide her own guilt. Later on, she actually commands two of her squires to kill the innocent Brangaene, a task they are unable to perform. After the potion, Isolde's reason and her sense of justice are overshadowed by her all-consuming passion. Wagner underlines this change by emphasizing the music in the last two acts. In the first act, the music had served to highlight the text. This is consistent with Wagner's essay on the synthesis of the arts published in 1851, *Oper und Drama*, where he preaches a complete union of word and tone. The music and text would be fused to form an indivisible unit he called "die Versmelodie" ("melodic verse"). The melodic line is dependent on the words to which it is united; the music then helps to extend the emotional content of the words into the more expressive sphere of music. This is the central exposition of Wagner's "Gesamtkunstwerk." The text is enhanced by the music, but the words of the drama are still prominent. We are still in a rational, conceptual world. With the drinking of the love potion, we enter a new world, a world dominated by music. The voice is often lost under the weight of the orchestra. Wagner sometimes extends vowel sounds to such an extent that the concept is lost. The emotion, the passion, is all-important. The wonderful second-act love duet contains many passages of free canonic imitation. The lovers sing at the same time, but the one sings words the other has already finished. Naturally, the words are difficult to understand; the conceptual gives way to the passion of the moment.

This shift of emphasis from the textual to the musical, so appropriate in the Tristan drama, is probably due in part to Wagner's reading of the German philosopher Arthur Schopenhauer. Schopenhauer held music to be a superior art, being independent of the world as representation in that it does not derive its material from phenomena and is thus closer to the metaphysical will itself. Music after *Tristan und Isolde* plays a more important and a more independent role than in the earlier operas. The leitmotifs are less strictly associated with a particular text or with a particular object.

Wagner's interest in Schopenhauer may also have influenced some of the changes he made in the text. In Gottfried's version, the lovers drink the love potion by mistake, thinking it to be wine. Isolde truly hates Tristan, and there is no love until after the potion has been mistakenly drunk. In Wagner, Isolde reveals that her supposed hatred is in fact love. Knowing that she can never find happiness in this world, she decides to drink the death potion and to avenge herself of Tristan's rejection by having him drink of it also. Tristan also expresses a death wish and gladly downs the potion. Having drunk what they believe to be a death potion, they are free to confess their love: Isolde free of her shame and Tristan free of his duty to King Mark. Rather than causing their love, the potion in Wagner's opera simply permits the lovers to voice their love.

The lovers engage in a Schopenhauerian dialogue in the love duet of the second act. The idea of love is inexorably tied to the idea of death. They embrace and cry out, "löse von/ der Welt mich los!" ("separate me from the world!"), and later, "So stürben wir,/ um ungetrennt,/ ewig einig" ("so we would die, to be united, forever one"). They express a desire to lose themselves in the infinite (Schopenhauer's universal will): " . . . in ungemess'nen Räumen / übersel'ges Träumen. / Du Isolde, / Tristan ich, / nicht mehr Tristan, / nicht Isolde" (" . . . in boundless spaces, blissful dreams; you Isolde, I Tristan; no longer Tristan, nor Isolde").

The "night and day," "dark and light," symbolism is important throughout the opera. The day seems to represent the world and worldly reality; the night, death or an escape from that reality. The light of day is the lover's enemy. In the opera, Tristan and Isolde can meet only at night. The lovers must remain separated until the light of Brangaene's torch is extinguished. When the lovers are discovered in the garden, Tristan turns to Isolde and asks: "Wohin nun Tristan scheidet,/ willst du, Isold', ihm folgen?/ Dem Land, das Tristan meint,/ der Sonne Licht nicht scheint" ("Will you, Isolde, follow Tristan where he is going? To the land, Tristan means, where the sun's light does not shine"; Act II, scene iii). With Isolde's promise to follow, Tristan drops his guard and, inviting death, is mortally wounded. The symbolism continues in the third act. Tristan regains consciousness and tells Kurvenal that he has been in the endless realm of "earthly night." But he cannot find peace because "accursed day" still shines on Isolde. The lovers will never find rest until they both find the peace of eternal night and are united in death. Gottfried's ending, where Tristan, betrayed by his wife, dies of despair before Isolde arrives, was rejected by Wagner. The lovers must die in each other's arms. Isolde must keep her promise and follow Tristan to the land where "sunlight has no gleams." When Isolde arrives, Tristan rips off his bandages, once again attempting suicide, this time successfully. Isolde follows him after assuring the audience that Tristan lives again "calmly happy," having at last found release.

In Gottfried's version, Tristan and Isolde consummate their love immediately after drinking the potion. In a later episode, they do so eight times in as many days, and Gottfried insists that this pair of lovers "did not play the prude." Wagner allows the lovers very little time together and never permits total union until the final union in death; nevertheless, the music of the opera is intensely sensual. There are three moments of highest passion depicted in the orchestra, but each time the lovers are foiled. They have only a few minutes together to confess their love after drinking the potion before they land in Cornwall. The sailors interrupt their bliss by announcing the world of reality and ending their dream: "Heil dem König!/ Kornwall Heil!" The music of the love duet in the second act modulates to an ever-higher key as the passion of the lovers rises. But Brangaene interrupts them twice with her eerie and significant warning, "Habet Acht!/ Habet Acht!/ Schon weicht dem Tag die Nacht" ("Be careful! Be careful! Already the night is yielding to the day"). The lovers continue their song but are finally interrupted by the sudden entrance of Kurvenal, King Mark, and the traitor Melot, announced in the orchestra by a tremendous dissonance. The music is exquisitely sensual in the final scene, when Isolde sings the famous "Liebestod." Isolde ends the opera alone, for Tristan has already died in the previous scene, but the union of their spirits is imminent.

Both Gottfried and Wagner depict society and the official marriage of Isolde and King Mark as an obstacle to Tristan's and Isolde's true love. In the opera, as in many medieval romances and in most troubadour poetry, the lovers find love outside of marriage. Yet Wagner seems to suggest not only that love and marriage are incompatible but that love and any sort of tangible or temporal satisfaction are incompatible. The lovers believe that the only true fulfillment is in death.

The two lovers' yearning for death and their dissatisfaction and uneasiness in this world are expressed eloquently in the music, which modulates unceasingly from bar to bar, all but abolishing any sense of tonal center. Wagner increases the tension over long periods of time, denying the resolution to the listener, who finds release only when the lovers die. The B-major chord at the end of the "Liebestod," awaited since the love duet of the second act, floats upward into infinity, and the listener can exhale at last after forty-five minutes.

Wagner's music reveals the intent of the spoken word, and the listener is immediately aware if the speaker is sincere, sarcastic, or lying. The orchestra is constantly commenting upon the action, and the music adds its power to the dialogue. Although Wagner's libretto is not great poetry, the combination of music and drama produces a powerful effect.

The music plays perhaps a greater role in Wagner's last opera, *Parsifal*, than in any of the preceding. Whereas in *Tristan* the words are sometimes unintelligible owing to prolonged separation of syllables or simultaneous singing of different vocal lines, *Parsifal* goes a step farther and quite often has no spoken dialogue at all. It is interesting to note that although *Parsifal* is one of his longest operas in presentation time, the libretto is the shortest. Gestures and music are accorded great importance. This can be partially explained by the fact that *Parsifal* is an opera of Christian ritual. In the scenes that portray, for instance, the partaking of communion by the knights, Kundry's baptism, or the anointing of Parsifal, the gesture is all-important. Music intensifies the action and translates the character's reaction to the event.

The music also reveals truths that may or may not be evident to the characters on stage. Parsifal's role as the Pure Fool who will redeem the Grail Brotherhood is revealed to the audience before any of the characters, including Parsifal, is aware of the fact. This is accomplished by means of the famous Wagnerian leitmotif. The distinctive Pure Fool motive, characterized by a descending diminished fifth, rising major sixth, and descending perfect fifth, is prepared by Gurnemanz ("ihm hilft nur eines, nur der Eine") and is finally introduced by Amfortas, who explains that only "der reine Thor" can heal him. The complete motive ("Durch Mitleid wissend, der reine Thor, harre sein', den ich erkor") is sung by Gurnemanz, who explains to four squires the promise issued from the Grail. The squires immediately repeat the motive in four-part harmony. This rendition of the motive directly precedes news of Parsifal's shooting of the swan and his entrance on stage. Parsifal is thus associated with the Pure Fool theme by juxtaposition. He is present at the Hall of the Grail when young boys, invisible above the stage, again sing the complete motive in four-part harmony. But no one recognizes Parsifal as the promised one, and Gurnemanz chases Parsifal from the hall proclaiming him "nothing but a fool." The orchestra, however, insists on the true identity of Parsifal by quietly playing the Pure Fool motive, which is now clearly associated in the listener's mind with the Grail's promise. To insist further upon the fact, a solo voice sings the words "Durch Mitleid wissend, der reine Thor" ("Knowing, through pity, the purest fool") just after Parsifal's departure.

The opera as a whole is highly chromatic. The harmony is forever changing and, as in *Tristan*, provides few satisfying cadences. Half and deceptive cadences predominate, lending the work a sense of restlessness. The few passages of extended diatonicism offer a welcome contrast; they are most often related to the Grail, to the Grail Brotherhood, or to Parsifal. "The Good," then, is represented by the relative stability of the diatonic passages, which in turn suggests the peace offered to the servants of the Holy Grail. The Grail theme itself has not a single accidental, staying completely within one key. This theme, besides being reassuringly diatonic and familiar in a sea of chromaticism, would no doubt have been recognized by Wagner's contemporaries as the Dresden Amen. Mendelssohn had already capitalized on the theme's religious connotations in his Reformation Symphony, and Wagner most probably also counted on its associations to add to the solemn atmosphere of his opera.

Amfortas's first-act speech to the Grail Brotherhood effectively translates his suffering; its chromaticism is all the more effective owing to the diatonic harmony established as the Grail Knights proceed to the communion tables immediately before Amfortas speaks. The purity and peace of the diatonic and relatively stable harmonic structure of the music associated with the knights is supported by a regular and stately rhythm. Amfortas's music, on the other hand, is characterized by an irregular rhythm whose frequent rests and off-beat accents betray his agitation. Amfortas's physical and mental suffering are recounted in the text, as is his feeling of isolation. But it is the music that renders the passage so moving.

One of the most distinctive and poignant musical motives of Amfortas's monologue is the triplet figure in the orchestra, the last note of which is suspended into the following chord and then resolved upward, the dissonance of the suspension emphasizing Amfortas's yearning. This figure helps link Amfortas musically to Kundry and Parsifal, whose destinies are so closely intertwined with his own. The figure recurs as Kundry bemoans her servitude to Klingsor, and as Parsifal, after Kundry's kiss, realizes the cause of Amfortas's suffering.

As he did in *Tristan*, Wagner condenses the medieval legend to fit his dramatic ends. He once again organizes the story around three main dramatic situations that correspond to the three acts of the opera. Wagner's immediate source was Wolfram von Eschenbach, whom he had already incorporated as a character in his *Tannhäuser*. He greatly reduces the number of characters, completely eliminating Gawain, who rivals Parzival himself in importance in Wolfram's romance and who plays an important role in Chrétien's account, as well. Wagner concentrates the action on only four main characters: Kundry, Klingsor, Amfortas, and Parsifal (Wagner changed the spelling in the belief that two Arabic words, *Fal parsi*, meant "pure fool"). A fifth major character, Gurnemanz, serves as a kind of narrator, filling in information as necessary.

Wagner's characters are sometimes more complex than their counterparts in Wolfram's romance. The opera's Kundry is much more developed than Wolfram's Cundrie, a sorceress. Kundry, who in some respects resembles the Loathly Damsel of other Arthurian tales, is a woman of strong contradictions. She desires to do good and makes great sacrifices to help the Brotherhood of the Grail. But at the same time, owing to Klingsor's magic powers, she is an agent of evil and has even occasioned the downfall of the leader of the Grail Brotherhood. Klingsor refers to Kundry as Gundryggia, a wandering spirit of Nordic mythology, and as Ahasuerus, the man who laughed in the face of Christ and who became the Wandering Jew. The link between the two is, of course, their restlessness and search for peace.

Amfortas is also characterized by his restlessness and yearning. Wagner's Amfortas, like Wolfram's Anfortas, is plagued by a wound that will not heal. But Wagner changes more than the spelling of the name. Whereas Anfortas was wounded in the genitals (as was the *Roi Pêcheur* in Chrétien's tale), Amfortas of the opera is wounded in the side. The medieval rendition of the legend is consistent with fertility myths of earlier cultures in which the king's fertility is intimately linked with the land's productivity. Wagner aligns his Amfortas with Christian tradition, having him wounded by the same spear that pierced Christ's side. Amfortas, unlike his counterpart in the medieval romance, suffers mentally as well as physically. The keeper of the Holy Grail has betrayed the Brotherhood through his weakness and now must continue to serve, his wound an all-too-obvious mark of his sin. His guilt is compounded in the third act, when the Grail Brotherhood degenerates and his father, Titurel, dies because of Amfortas's reluctance to reveal the Grail. Amfortas's wound and its consequences seem designed to accentuate his failure by the suggested comparison with Christ. The sinful Amfortas is wounded in the same place and by the same spear as the blameless Christ. And whereas Christ, the Son of God, is sacrificed to save humankind, Amfortas sacrifices his father and the Brotherhood rather than endure the pain of revealing the Grail.

Parsifal puts an end to Kundry's and Amfortas's restlessness and yearning, just as the diatonicism associated with the young hero finally gains dominance over the chromaticism of the opera. In the third act, Parsifal returns to transform discord into harmony, giving Kundry a kiss of pure love in return for her lecherous one of the second act, and returning the holy spear to the Grail Brotherhood, making Amfortas whole.

The act that enables Parsifal to "redeem" the others is his renunciation of Kundry's advances. Total sexual abstinence is certainly not required in Wolfram's rendition, nor is it necessarily part of Christian tradition. This aspect of Wagner's opera may be due to Schopenhauer's idea of total renunciation.

In the years between *Tristan* and *Parsifal*, Wagner's focus shifts from the individual couple to universal compassion. In *Parsifal*, the disdain for the material world extends to the body itself as an objectification of the will. Individual or sexual love is replaced by the broader and nobler love of humankind. He turns from eros to agape, or, in the context of *Parsifal*, to *Mitleid*.

Wagner is quite justly best known as a composer, and it is certainly the music, more than anything else, that infuses his operas with their magic. He has, however, made an important contribution to opera history by the care he takes with all elements of his music–drama. In both *Tristan und Isolde* and *Parsifal*, Wagner combines a powerful medieval legend and a talent for music and drama to create a new work of art that is at the same time personal in its uniqueness and universal in its application. [FLT]

Beckett, Lucy. *Richard Wagner: Parsifal*. Cambridge: Cambridge University Press, 1981.

Newman, Ernest. *The Wagner Operas*. New York: Knopf, 1949.

Stein, Jack M. *Richard Wagner and the Synthesis of the Arts*. Westport, Conn.: Greenwood, 1973.

WALDLIEDER: *see* LENAU, NIKOLAUS.

WALEWEIN, ROMAN VAN: *see* PENNINC AND PIETER VOSTAERT.

WALEWEIN ENDE KEYE, a Middle Dutch verse romance, dating to the thirteenth century, that comprises some 3,660 lines. It has been transmitted exclusively in the *Lancelot-Compilatie*. Keye accuses Walewein of bragging, after which Walewein angrily leaves the court and performs so many heroic deeds that he disproves Keye's accusation. The humiliated Keye is eventually removed from the court. [BB]

Jonckbloet, W.J.A., ed. *Roman van Lancelot*. 2 vols. The Hague: van Stockum, 1846–49, Vol. 2, pp. 126–51.

WALLACE: *see* SCOTTISH ARTHURIAN CHRONICLES.

WAR IN HEAVEN: *see* WILLIAMS, CHARLES.

WARTON, THOMAS (1728–1790), Oxford professor and critic, encouraged the Gothic Revival with *Observations on the Faerie Queene of Spenser* (1754), which defended chivalry as a civilizer of "savage and ignorant people" and discussed Spenser's use of Malory. His *History of English Poetry* (1774–81) included Arthurian romance. "The Grave of King Arthur" (1777), an ode in octosyllabic couplets, countered the tradition of *Rex Quondam, Rexque Futurus* with the claim of a Glastonbury burial. [MAW]

Johnston, Arthur. *Enchanted Ground: The Study of Medieval Romance in the Eighteenth Century.* London: Athlone, 1964.

WASTE LAND, THE: *see* ELIOT, T.S.

WASTELAND, a motif, of probable Celtic origin, that relates the fertility of the land to the condition of its king or leader. In Chrétien de Troyes's *Perceval*, the land lies barren so long as the Fisher King's wound (in the genitals) remains uncured; had Perceval asked about the Grail, he would have cured the king. Texts gradually place more emphasis on the king's wound than on the restoration of the wasteland, and in some works, such as the *Queste*, there is no mention of a wasteland related to the infirmity of the king. Other romances (e.g., *Perlesvaus*) suggest that the king's condition and the troubles of the land (whether barrenness or, more often, a perpetual state of war and crime) are the *result* of the hero's failure, rather than a condition that preceded it.

Modern literature has seen some strikingly original settings of the wasteland motif. One of the more curious is that of Julien Gracq, who in *Le Roi Pêcheur* inverts it to show the manor being strangled by a lush vegetation wildly out of control. The best-known modern treatment is of course in T.S. Eliot's *The Waste Land*, in which the poet, inspired by Jessie L. Weston's book *From Ritual to Romance*, appropriates the wasteland as a metaphor applicable to the city, the modern world, and the human condition. [NJL]

WATCH FIRES TO THE NORTH: *see* FINKEL, GEORGE.

WAUCHIER DE DENAIN: *see* CONTINUATIONS.

WEATHERMONGER, THE: *see* DICKINSON, PETER.

WEDDING OF SIR GAWAIN AND DAME RAGNELL, THE, a tail-rhyme version in 855 lines of the Loathly Lady story, extant in the early sixteenth-century Rawlinson Manuscript, though probably written in the fifteenth century. Dame Ragnell and Arthur's challenger, Sir Gromer Somer Joure, are siblings, but the emphasis is less on family relations than on courtly shame and honor, here treated via a comedy of manners.

The court is horrified when Gawain, according to his promise, marries Dame Ragnell, who had saved Arthur's life. Guinevere begs for a quiet wedding; the court anxiously investigates the nuptial chamber the next morning to see if Gawain has survived. Dame Ragnell's ugliness is twice elaborately described and her monstrous appetite dwelt on. Her insistence on a public wedding, as well as her inversion of the beauty topos, answers the court's inversion of *curtesye*, whereby gratitude for her rescue of Arthur is given only after she becomes beautiful.

The author is versed in romance convention: Arthur finds adventure initially by pursuing a deer, Gawain has an attack of postnuptial *recreantise*, and so forth. Gawain is a pleasantly youthful romance figure; he loyally and optimistically helps Arthur by collecting a whole book of answers to the question of what women most desire, and he readily assents to the wedding. But his experience deepens, for his openness and courtesy permit Dame Ragnell's transformation and his own recognition that the question of whether she shall be beautiful publicly by day or privately by night is too hard for him. He gives her sovereignty, she publicly gives him obedience. A son, Gyngalyn, is conceived, and after five years Dame Ragnell dies, much mourned by Gawain.

Similarly, the romance itself deepens and extends its initial ethical vocabulary. A narratorial explicit invokes God as "veray kynge ryalle," yielding body and soul to him in hope of redemption from prison. The anonymous author, though no Chaucer, develops interesting problems and implications from the source matter. This is a better late-medieval romance than is usually allowed. [JP]

Sands, D.B., ed. *Middle English Romances*. New York: Holt, Rinehart and Winston, 1966.

Sumner, L., ed. *The Weddynge of Sir Gawen and Dame Ragnell*. Northampton, Mass.: Smith College, 1924.

WEILEN, JOSEF: *see TRISTAN*, MODERN GERMAN VERSIONS OF GOTTFRIED'S.

WEIRDSTONE OF BRISINGAMEN, THE: *see* GARNER, ALAN.

WELSH ARTHURIAN LITERATURE: *see* CELTIC ARTHURIAN LITERATURE.

WELSH BALLADS AND OTHER POEMS: *see* RHYS, ERNEST.

WELSH *BRUTS: see* GEOFFREY OF MONMOUTH.

WERTHES, FRIEDRICH AUGUST CLEMENS (1748–1817), was well known for his many dramas that were performed at the Vienna Hofburgtheater. He collaborated with the celebrated composer Johann Rudolf Zumsteeg to produce a *Singspiel* entitled *Das Pfauenfest* ("The Peacock Feast"), which was premiered at the Stuttgart Hoftheater on 24 February 1801.

Das Pfauenfest is a dramatization—with musical interludes—of the Arthurian mantle tale that derives ultimately from the medieval French fabliau *Le Mantel mautaillié*. Werthes's source, however, was Benedikte Naubert's *Der kurze Mantel*. Although the *Singspiel* was well received at the court of Duke Friedrich I of Württemberg, it has fallen into oblivion. [MEK]

&❧ Werthes, F.A.C. *Das Pfauenfest: Ein Singspiel in zwey Akten*, with music by J.R. Zumsteeg. Leipzig: Breitkopf und Härtel, n.d.

WESTON, JESSIE LAIDLEY (1850–1928), an indefatigable translator of Arthurian romances from Old French, Middle English, Middle High German, and Dutch. Weston also published monographs on Gawain (1897), Lancelot (1901), and Perceval (1906–09). She is known especially for her study of the origins and development of the Grail legend, *From Ritual to Romance* (1920), which was a major influence on T.S. Eliot's *The Waste Land*. [WWK]

WESTWOOD, THOMAS (1814?–1888), one of Tennyson's first imitators, published privately *The Sword of Kingship: A Legend of the Mort D'Arthur* (1866), a rendering in blank verse of Malory's opening chapters (Book I, Chapters 3–7), with emendations to avoid offending Victorian sensibilities and additions to present Arthur as a Christ-type. *The Quest of the Sancgreall* (1868) mingles vague quests, magic artifacts, and sexual temptations, but, true to the medieval source, identifies the Grail as the Catholic Eucharistic vessel. [MAW]

&❧ Westwood, Thomas. *The Sword of Kingship: A Legend of the Mort D'Arthur*. London: Whittingham and Wilkins, 1866.
———— . *The Quest of the Sancgreall, The Sword of Kingship, and Other Poems*. London: Smith, 1868.
Reid, Margaret J.C. *The Arthurian Legend: Comparison of Treatment in Modern and Mediaeval Literature*. Edinburgh and London: Oliver and Boyd, 1938.

WHISPERING KNIGHTS, THE: *see* LIVELY, PENELOPE.

WHISTLECRAFT: *see* FRERE, JOHN H.

WHITE, T(ERENCE) H(ANBURY) (1905–1964), sometime public school-teacher and freelance writer of short stories, poems, journalism—and five novels based on the Arthurian legend. First published separately, *The Sword in the Stone* (1938), *The Witch in the Wood*—later retitled *The Queen of Air and Darkness* (1939), and *The Ill-Made Knight* (1940) eventually appeared with *The Candle in the Wind* as a tetralogy: *The Once and Future King* (1958). A later work, *The Book of Merlyn*, intended originally by White to be part of his *magnum opus* and duplicating some of its incidents, was published in 1977. White's main medieval source is Malory's *Morte Darthur*, and his novels contain some of the best modern commentary on their original.

The Sword in the Stone, eventually made into a Walt Disney film, treats Arthur's *enfances*, always vague in medieval versions of his story. Here, Merlin trains the future monarch (in counterpoint to his conventional knightly grooming), leading him through shape-shifting transformations that mimic Darwinian evolution. As fish, ant, wild goose, and badger, Arthur learns that Might should work for Right and that the best rule is the freest. Essentially a comedy, the book ends with a delightful version of the Sword in the Stone episode and a coronation attended by all those who have participated in his education, both men and beasts.

Comedy mixed with tragedy appears in the second novel, *The Queen of Air and Darkness*. Interwoven narrations include Arthur's early wars against the rebel kings; the comic adventures of Pellinore, Grummore, and Palomides; and the tragic education (or neglect of education) of Gawain and his brethren by their mother, Morgause of Orkney. Tragic, too, is the book's climax, Morgause's deliberate seduction of her half-brother, Arthur, which will lead to Mordred's birth.

This movement from the comedy of the first book to the mixed genre of the second yields to more serious concerns in *The Ill-Made Knight*, which features a physically ugly Lancelot. His perception of himself as monkeylike colors both his complementary feeling of sinfulness and the ever-growing and mutual attraction he feels to the beautiful Guenevere. A notable addition to Malory's account is Lancelot's prizing of his virginity, which he loses to the Grail Princess Elaine before his adultery with Guenevere, whom he had previously loved unwillingly and virtuously. Such familiar episodes as the Roman War, Lancelot's madness, and his initial rescue of the Queen from the stake are also reworked. In White, the Grail quest is unimportant—Lancelot's relation to God is direct. It is told in retrospect as its participants return to Arthur's court (thus from a *Mort Artu*/Stanzaic *Morte Arthur* viewpoint). White further alters conventional Arthurian characterization: Gawain is almost parodically braid Scots in his speech; Elaine of Astolat gets fat; and Lancelot, Guenevere, and Arthur demonstrably age.

The final book is *The Candle in the Wind*. It treats the clan feuds of the house of Pellinore and Lot, the discovery of Lancelot and Guenevere's adulterous relationship, Arthur's revelation of Mordred's parentage (here rather like that in the *Mort Artu*), and Guenevere's further rescues by her lover. New is

Arthur's unsuccessful replacement of knight-errantry with common law as a novel attempt to harness Right to Might. After a moving account of the Lancelot–Gawain feud, the tetralogy ends *in medias res* before the battle of Salisbury, as Arthur commands his young page—no less than Thomas Malory—to withdraw to safety in order to tell his king's story. (This latter episode, along with much in the last two novels, inspired the Broadway musical *Camelot*, which, however, is an oversimplification and—in spite of its lovely songs—lessening of White's work.)

In the posthumous *Book of Merlyn*, some material White included in his tetralogy is repeated. The enchanter appears one last time before Arthur in his tent at Salisbury. His invocation of their former teacher/student relationship leads to his taking Arthur, once again, back to the animals of the first book, this time to learn about the abolition of war. Didactically and rather unconvincingly presented, the book's theme is humanity's patent inferiority to the animals. So incongruent is this idea with White's earlier books that his publisher's refusal to issue it with them is thoroughly understandable.

T.H. White's achievement in *The Once and Future King*, if not in his *Merlyn*, is undoubtedly the finest in twentieth-century Arthurian prose. Setting aside the rampant misanthropy of the *Merlyn*, one may say of his corpus that it is inventive, perceptive, and above all newly creative of its medieval materials. Its narrator is detached, omniscient, and implicative of an authorial presence much like that of the historical White (as is true of Malory's narrator, and this is perhaps one of their meeting points). The story moves, with relative ease, from an anachronistic, quasi–children's book through stages of comedy and tragedy, to the final catastrophe. Like the Brontës, White has "domesticated" romance, especially in the wonderful Lancelot/Guenevere/Arthur scenes of *The Candle in the Wind*. He draws upon a wide and scholarly range of knowledge in medieval history, beast lore (he also translated a twelfth-century bestiary), practical naturalism, and all periods of literature to make a new and often enchanting Arthuriad.

Much in his books is both political and autobiographical. White's concern with communism and fascism and his tortured unwillingness to fight in World War II emerge everywhere, as does his concomitant guilt. Additionally, his own miserable childhood, his lifelong loneliness, and his sexual ambiguity, together with his love of animals, are transmuted into this compellingly readable narrative. If White's personal quest to "find an antidote to war" results, in his work, only in the failure of Arthur's belated discovery of law, that is as much the burden of the Arthurian matter he chose as of his own valiant effort to reorder it as a parable for his time. [MF]

White, T.H. *The Once and Future King*. London: Collins, 1958.

———. *The Book of Merlyn*, ed. Sylvia Townsend Warner. Austin: University of Texas Press, 1977.

Warner, Sylvia Townsend. *T.H. White: A Biography*. London: Chatto and Windus, 1967.

WHITE BOOK OF RHYDDERCH: *see MABINOGI.*

WHOLE BOOK OF KING ARTHUR AND OF HIS NOBLE KNIGHTS OF THE ROUND TABLE, THE: see MALORY, SIR THOMAS.

WICKED DAY, THE: see STEWART, MARY.

WIELAND, CHRISTOPH MARTIN (1733–1813), one of the principal writers of the eighteenth-century German Rococo and Enlightenment. Wieland was familiar with the available Arthurian stories from foreign sources, particularly the summaries in Count Tressan's *Bibliothèque universelle des romans* (1775–89). His brief prose summary of Merlin's life, *Merlin der Zauberer* ("Merlin the Magician," 1777), is probably taken from Tressan, as is his *Geron der Adelige* ("The Noble Geron," 1777), which is essentially a translation, in blank verse, of the medieval French *Guiron le Courtois*. His first acquaintance with the prophet and magician Merlin, to whom he merely alludes in his *Don Quixote* imitation *Don Sylvio von Rosalva* (1764) and his verse tale *Oberon* (1780), came from Ariosto's *Orlando Furioso*, on which *Oberon* is based. In Wieland's long elegiac poem *Merlins weissagende Stimme aus seiner Gruft* ("Merlin's Prophetic Voice from His Grave," 1810), Merlin, after 1,000 years in his grave, laments the loss of the golden age of Arthurian chivalry long ago. This reflects the older Wieland's despair at the passing of the German Classical age of Weimar. Still, the mood of despair is broken at the end of the poem when Merlin prophesies great things for the yet-unborn son of the fairy Viviane, and, by implication, for Germany. [RWK]

&❧ Wieland, Christoph Martin. *Werke*, ed. Fritz Martini and Hans Werner Seiffert. Munich: Hanser, 1966.
McCarthy, John A. *Christoph Martin Wieland*. Boston: Twayne, 1979.
Weiss, Adelaide Marie. "Wieland." In *Merlin in German Literature*. Washington, D.C.: Catholic University of America Press, 1933, pp. 55–69.

WIFE OF BATH'S TALE, THE: see CHAUCER, GEOFFREY.

WIGALOIS: see WIRNT VON GRAFENBERG.

WIGAMUR, a German romance of somewhat over 6,000 lines, is poorly preserved. One fifteenth-century manuscript (W) transmits the whole tale but with many lacunae; two fragmentary manuscripts from ca. 1300–50 (M, S) supply some material missing from W but cover only a third of the story. The text in W is replete with flaws suggesting scribal indifference. The romance is generally dated to the mid-thirteenth century, but without firm evidence.

Wigamur, son of King Paldriot of Lendrie, is abducted by a "wild-woman" named Lesbia, who raises him in a cave. A semihuman sea monster then carries him off to an underwater realm, training him in certain manly skills and later sending him ashore. Wigamur finds a warhorse in the ruins of a sacked castle. On it, he defeats the knight Glakotelesfloyer, then returns to the castle and discovers the maiden Pioles. She is affianced to the King of Nordein, who is away at a tournament. Wigamur passes two chaste nights with her, then gives her over, apparently for protection, to a dwarf at a nearby castle. Received by Arthur's uncle, Yttra, Wigamur completes his chivalric education. He intervenes in a fight between an eagle and a vulture; the grateful eagle accompanies him thereafter, so he is known as the Knight with the Eagle. He champions a damsel in a property dispute before Arthur but declines her hand and lands because he holds himself unworthy and is ignorant of his parentage.

Wigamur accompanies Arthur to aid Queen Ysope, besieged by the heathen king Marroch. He then discovers his identity by nearly championing King Atroclas against Paldriot, his father, and marries Atroclas's daughter, Dulceflur. After defeating Lypondrigan at a tournament held by Queen Dinifogar, the hero reunites Pioles with her fiancé; he again defeats Lypondrigan, who had abducted Dulceflur, and presumably retires with his wife to Lendrie.

This story has many parallels in German Arthurian romances (e.g., the animal companion in Hartmann von Aue's *Iwein* and Konrad von Stoffeln's *Gauriel von Muntabel*; exotic names in Wolfram von Eschenbach's *Parzival*). Wigamur is a naïve but modest and chaste hero, perhaps a deliberate counterpart to the protagonist of *Lanzelet*, by Ulrich von Zatzikhoven. Though no philosophical or aesthetic subtlety has been discovered in the romance, it has a number of vivid and engaging sequences beside many commonplace descriptions and enumerations. Its poor transmission and the lack of a critical edition are obstacles to evaluation and appreciation. [SLW]

Kraus, Carl von. *Mittelhochdeutsches Übungsbuch*. 2nd ed. Heidelberg: Winter, 1926, pp. 108–67. (Fragments M, S, and parallels in W.)

von der Hagen, F.H., and J.G. Büsching, eds. *Wigamur*. In *Deutsche Gedichte des Mittelalters*. Berlin, 1808, Vol. 1, Part 4. (Manuscript W.)

Blamires, David. "The Sources and Literary Structure of *Wigamur*." In *Studies in Medieval Literature and Languages in Memory of Frederick Whitehead*, ed. W. Rothwell, W.R.J. Barron, David Blamires, and Lewis Thorpe. Manchester: Manchester University Press, 1973, pp. 27–46.

WIGOLEIS VOM RADE, a condensed prose version of Wirnt von Grafenberg's Arthurian romance *Wigalois*, composed ca. 1200–15. The oldest incunabulum of the chapbook was printed by Johann Schönsperger in 1493 in Augsburg. This text is based upon a prose redaction in manuscript—now lost—from the years 1472–83. The chapbook was translated into Danish (*see* HER VIEGOLEIS MED GULD HIULET) and from Danish into Icelandic (*see* GABONS SAGA OK VIGOLES). [MEK]

Brandstetter, Alois. *Prosa Auflösung: Studien zur Rezeption der höfischen Epik im frühneuhochdeutschen Prosaroman*. Frankfurt: Athenäum, 1971.

WILLIAM OF MALMESBURY (ca. 1095–1143). In 1125, William, a monk in the abbey of Malmesbury, wrote two of his most important works, one of which was the *Gesta Regum Anglorum*. William mentions Arthur twice in it. First, Arthur aided Ambrosius Aurelianus in holding back the barbarians—that is, the Saxons, whom William wrongly calls Angles. At the siege of Mount Badon, Arthur, with the image of the Virgin Mary on his armor, singlehandedly defeated 900 of the enemy. Second, while the tomb of Walwen, Arthur's nephew, had been found during the reign of William I, Arthur's tomb still remained undiscovered in 1125, as William related in the *Gesta Regum*. Noting that the British had created fables about Arthur, William was of the opinion that because of his achievements he deserved to be commemorated not in fiction but in authentic history. [KGM]

ᴥ William of Malmesbury. *Gesta Regum Anglorum*. In *Willelmi Malmesbiriensis Monachi de Gestis Regum Anglorum Libri Quinque*, ed. William Stubbs. 2 vols. London: Eyre and Spottiswoode, 1887–89.

WILLIAM OF NEWBURGH (1135/6–ca. 1198). Between 1196 and 1198, William wrote his *Historia Rerum Anglicarum* at the request of Ernald, abbot of Rievaulx. Although the *Historia* begins with William of Normandy's conquest of England, its preface is devoted to the place of Arthur and Merlin in history. Using the historical works of Gildas and especially Bede, William subjected Geoffrey of Monmouth's history of Arthur and Merlin to harsh but careful criticism. He pointed out that Bede had never mentioned Arthur and that Geoffrey told of activities that should have made Arthur famous and known to other writers—who in fact know nothing of him. For these and other reasons, William concluded that Geoffrey's Arthur and Merlin were fictional creations of the British. [KGM]

ᴥ William of Newburgh. *Historia Rerum Anglicarum*. In *Chronicles of the Reigns of Stephen, Henry II, and Richard I*, ed. Richard Howlett. London: Longman, Trübner, 1885, Vol. 1.

WILLIAM OF RENNES: *see GESTA REGUM BRITANNIAE.*

WILLIAMS, CHARLES (1886–1945), among modern English poets, the foremost reshaper and recreator of Arthurian mythology. Williams's Arthuriad is composed of two cycles of poems, *Taliessin Through Logres* (1938) and *The Region of the Summer Stars* (1944). At his death, he left an unfinished prose work on *The Figure of Arthur*, which was edited by his friend C.S. Lewis and published with Lewis's own commentary on the poems in *Arthurian Torso* (1948). Williams's first published novel, *War in Heaven* (1930), depicts a modern reappearance of the Holy Grail.

The individual poems in the Arthurian cycle are complex both in structure and interrelationships, but the overall structure is clear. *Taliessin Through Logres* portrays the establishment, growth, and fall of the realm of Arthur. In a sense, it shows the progress through the earthly kingdom. The poems of *The Region of the Summer Stars* (the "third heaven" of poets and lovers) take up the same themes, but from a perspective *sub specie aeternitatis*.

Williams's original contribution to Arthurian legend lies in his development of the myths of King Arthur and the Grail, their gradual coalescence, and the further history of the Grail. Other elements, such as the story of Lancelot and Guinevere, are represented only in passing. From the outset, the empire of King Arthur is concerned with the Grail quest, which Williams treats as being mystic, unchivalric, and ascetic. The union of the legendary kingdom and the Grail is a highly complex symbol of the fusion of Empire and Christendom, and thus of Christ's Second Coming.

The cycle begins with the coronation of the King. Even at this early point, the reader is haunted by premonitions of disaster. Merlin does not take part in the coronation ceremonies. Instead, he sits in the steeple of St. Stephen's and meditates on the inevitable downfall of the realm. He foresees the Dolorous Blow, the wounding of the Grail-keeper with the Sacred Lance. Man wounds himself, and this is an image of Original Sin, of the Fall. The result is the destruction of order and the spread of anarchy. Balin kills his brother, Balan, without recognizing him. The Fall and the first murder destroy the innocence of the kingdom; the disease of disorder spreads throughout the land.

Even Arthur is affected. In the early versions of the Matter of Britain, Mordred was nephew to the King, but in later versions he became the son conceived in incest. This crime was usually recounted by medieval authors without explicit comment, even though they recognized that the result was the traitor Mordred, the destroyer of the Arthurian world. In Williams's Taliessin cycle, however, incest has become a symbol of egotistic self-love, which Williams calls "Gomorrha," and Arthur has thus become an antagonist of the Grail, which he betrays through his egotism, as well as his lack of *caritas* and *largesse*.

Arthur is an unmoved mover, the passive center of his kingdom. Another must act in his stead, and as in Malory this is Lancelot, beloved by both King and Queen. He serves as the poet's example for the Way of Affirmation, just as the nun Dindrane, who sacrifices her blood for a leper, is an example of the Negative Way of the soul's quest for the Eternal. ("This also is thou; neither is this thou.") Guinevere is marginal for Williams: he feels no sympathy for her. And so she can only sit, wait, and love. Galahad, the purest of knights, cannot be born from her. His mother must stem from the family of the Grail kings; his father must belong to the leaders of secular knighthood. Originally, Williams considered making Arthur the father of Galahad but gave up the plan because the fate of the Round Table had to be determined through the King. With Galahad's conception, Merlin's task is fulfilled; he disappears into the mystic darkness whence he came. In the person of Galahad, the symbols of stone and shell are united: the geometric and the vital, Byzantium and Brocéliande. Williams calls this process the finding of identity. Galahad is an image of the

New Man, exemplary incarnation of the union of Arthur's world and the Grail.

The poem on Galahad closes with Taliessin's vision of the ascent of the soul to the inner heaven. Like Dante, Williams regards the planetary spheres as levels of holiness and as grades of spiritual development. The first planet is Mercury, the god of opposition and of change, an image of competition among the planetary houses. Venus is the sphere of orientation and decision, that is, "of preference." Jupiter, with its two moons, refers to irony and defeated irony, which does not take umbrage at the unavoidable vicissitudes of this world but smiles at the apparent absurdity of things. Saturn is the planet of loneliness and meditation, promise and symbol of a future Golden Age. Logres, Arthur's kingdom, has so far reached only the sphere of Jupiter. There, Galahad and Lancelot live side by side, the unrest of the human heart and the misery of existence. But the path of the future is already clearly recognizable. The enormous forces of Brocéliande have created Galahad but have exhausted themselves in the effort. Logres becomes Britain. Carbonek and Camelot are farther apart than ever before.

Like Galahad, who has already seen the Holy Grail in Camelot, Perceval and Bors are the Elect of the Grail. They are living flesh and blood but at the same time incarnations of typical attitudes toward life. Perceval is the pure lover, full of spiritual questions and problems; Bors is the ordinary mortal, married and the father of children, a person striving toward perfection but entangled in the needs and problems of everyday life. Galahad, however, is of a different make. He is not a "christlike figure" but a symbol of the divine spark in human beings, that is, the human "capacity for Christ." In Carbonek, after Galahad has healed the wounded king, he sees a vision of Christ in the Holy Grail. As instructed, he travels to Sarras, where he disappears from sight. This marks the final separation of the Arthurian world and the Grail. Arthur's thoughts center more and more on his own power, which results in his loss of *caritas* and *largesse*. He begins war with Lancelot; Mordred betrays the King; father and son kill one another.

The poem "Prayers of the Pope" ends the cycle. As a kind of refrain, we hear the desperate cry: "Send not, send not the rich empty away." The realm has been split into warring factions. The pope feels the schism within himself, the return of chaos and thus of spiritual death. The vision of the development of humankind toward the Epiphany has dissolved. A magnificent opportunity has remained unused.

But Williams does not dismiss us without hope. Taliessin's household will remain and the work will go on. Above all, there is the hope of Brocéliande. The roots of the forest grip the tentacles of Po'l'u; the forces of death are held in check and bound fast by the Mother of Making.

The constellation of characters, symbols, and images in Williams's Arthuriad is mapped out in a universe of the poet's own creation. Logres stands for both the genuine realm of Britain and the mythic world of Arthur. The visionary city of Byzantium, like London, is the navel of the empire, the legendary New Jerusalem, and the emperor who reigns there is a symbol of God-in-action, the Divine Mover, or even Fate. The vision recedes; Logres is, on the surface of things, lost. But Brocéliande, the realm of forest and sea, points the way to hope. It stands for the untapped resources of the subconscious, the future path of the soul on its quest. In apparent defeat, humiliation, and even death rests the seed of salvation. The poems leave us with the certainty of the ultimate good. The rites of passage lead on.

Williams has widened the dimensions of the Arthurian story, reminding us of Milton and his representation of the Fall. Heaven and earth are united in a new mythic empire, which is not the less real because it never existed. Indeed, the poet has always in mind the spiritual reality behind the façade of material appearances. His Arthuriad is not a stylized portrait of a utopian *phantastikon* but a universally valid representation of the modern human situation.

The same tenor of thought underlies the plays and novels of the author, as well as his essays on literature and on Christianity. In many aspects, it is related to views shared by his old Oxford companions, C.S. Lewis and J.R.R. Tolkien, particularly in a tendency toward elements of fantasy and the supernatural. Certain themes re-echo: the primacy of the transcendental, the nature of love as a mirror of the Divine and as a mystical perception of the whole human relationship, the painful way of the soul in quest of perfection, and the image of the City as an image of the Church.

Williams returns the Holy Grail to a modern setting in his novel *War in Heaven* (1930), in which the struggle between Good and Evil for possession of the Grail takes place on both the physical and spiritual levels. The inadequacy of human reason to comprehend the reality of the mystical world again leaves humankind spiritually impoverished.

It can only be regretted that the work of Charles Williams, and in particular his poetry, has not yet found the appreciation it deserves. Williams recognized the potential of the Arthurian myth better than his predecessors, and he has expressed what others have only vaguely anticipated. [KHG]

Williams, Charles. *Taliessin Through Logres*. London: Oxford University Press, 1938.
——— . *The Region of the Summer Stars*. London: Oxford University Press, 1944.
——— . *The Figure of Arthur*. In *Arthurian Torso*, by Charles Williams and C.S. Lewis. London: Oxford University Press, 1948.
——— . "On the Arthurian Myth." In Williams's *The Image of the City and Other Essays*, ed. Anne Ridler. London: Oxford University Press, 1958.
Cavaliero, Glen. *Charles Williams: Poet of Theology*. London: Macmillan, 1983.
Göller, Karl Heinz. "From Logres to Carbonek: The Arthuriad of Charles Williams." *Arthurian Literature*, 1 (1981), 121–73.
Lewis, C.S. *Williams and the Arthuriad*. In *Arthurian Torso*, by Charles Williams and C.S. Lewis. London: Oxford University Press, 1948.

WILLIAMS AND THE ARTHURIAD: *see* LEWIS, C.S.

WINCHESTER, cathedral city in Hampshire, formerly the Roman *Venta Belgarum*. Its chief Arthurian significance lies in its identification with Camelot, which is asserted by Malory.

In the post-Roman decline of urban Britain, *Venta Belgarum* probably survived better than most towns. It may have passed with no complete break into the small domain of Cerdic, the putative founder of the West Saxon dynasty, from which English royalty is descended. With its new name, Winchester was the capital of Wessex under Alfred the Great. For many years afterward, it rivaled London as a place for coronations and royal entombments.

A vague tradition of Winchester's age and dignity explains its importance in the imagined Britain of Arthur. Geoffrey of Monmouth introduces it several times. In his *Historia*, Constans, the eldest son of Arthur's grandfather Constantine, is educated here for the monastic life. Hengist captures the city; Merlin mentions it in the *Prophetiae*; Aurelius Ambrosius restores it after the Saxon devastation, and dies here. Arthur himself fights Mordred at Winchester, and after his passing one of Mordred's sons seizes the place and holds it till he, too, is defeated and slain.

Malory's Winchester=Camelot equation became known to many readers through Caxton's edition, published in 1485 (though the preface shows, curiously enough, that Caxton rejected it himself). One result was that Henry VII, who tried to exploit the Arthurian mystique, had his heir-apparent baptized in the cathedral and named Arthur. The intention was that he should reign as Arthur II and, in the eyes of his subjects, fulfill the prophecy of the King's return. Unfortunately for the plan, he died young. Royal interest in Winchester may have had something to do with its college's possession of a Malory manuscript antedating the Caxton edition. This was rediscovered in 1934.

At some point during the Middle Ages, the city's association with Arthur led to its acquiring the most famous relic of him. Caxton, in his preface, says the Round Table is at Winchester. It is not; but a Round Table imitative of it is still on view in the great hall of the castle. This is what Caxton supposed to be the original, as did Hardyng thirty-five years earlier.

Strictly speaking, it is a table-top only, since the legs—twelve of them, to judge from the mortise holes—are gone. It is made of oak, and is eighteen feet across and two and three-quarter inches thick. The weight is about a ton and a quarter. Today, it is fixed to the wall high above the floor and is painted in twenty-four segments, green and white, allotted to knights whose names appear around the rim. They would have been rather crowded, shoulder to shoulder, and all the more so because there is also a place for Arthur himself with a picture of a king. At the center is a rose.

The paintwork is easier to date than the table. Henry VIII had it done in 1522 for a state visit by the emperor Charles V. The pictured king is Henry himself, with the beard that he had recently grown, and the rose is a Tudor rose. The whole design was repainted in the eighteenth century without change. As for the table itself, one conjecture is that it was made for Edward III in 1344, when he formed a project for reviving the Arthurian knighthood (he gave up the notion and founded the Order of the Garter instead). In 1976–77, the table was moved out from the wall and subjected to a series of tests. Indications in the method of carpentry, and tree-ring patterns in the wood, appeared to support the Edward III theory, but carbon-dating suggested a slightly earlier time.

It now seems likely that this massive piece of furniture was made for a type of aristocratic festival known as a Round Table. Quite a number were held during the Middle Ages, in England and overseas. Nobles played Arthurian roles, danced, banqueted, and competed in jousts. The apparent age of the Winchester table would fit it into the reign of Henry III or that of Edward I. Henry was born at Winchester and might have presented the table to his birthplace, if he had it made for himself. During at least part of his reign, he disapproved of Round Tables and tried to ban them, but he may not have been entirely consistent, and several were held while he was king if not under his auspices. Edward I, however, is more promising. An Arthurian enthusiast, he favored such functions and attended at least five, organizing a lavish one himself in 1299 to celebrate his second marriage. The Winchester table could have been made for that occasion. [GA]

Geoffrey of Monmouth. *Historia Regum Britanniae*, Book VI, Chapters 5, 16; Book VII, Chapter 4; Book VIII, Chapters 9, 14; Book XI, Chapters 2, 3.

Malory, Sir Thomas. *Le Morte Darthur*, Book XVIII, Chapter 10.

Ashe, Geoffrey. *A Guidebook to Arthurian Britain*. Wellingborough: Aquarian, 1983.

Loomis, Roger Sherman. "Arthurian Influence on Sport and Spectacle." In *Arthurian Literature in the Middle Ages*. Oxford: Clarendon, 1959.

WINCHESTER ROUND TABLE: *see* WINCHESTER.

WIRNT VON GRAFENBERG, author of *Wigalois*, a romance of about 11,700 lines written ca. 1200–15. Wirnt, who names himself twice (ll. 141, 10,576), is the central figure of a didactic poem by Konrad von Würzburg written ca. 1250 ("Der Welt Lohn"), but little is known of his life. *Wigalois* reveals his familiarity with great romances of Hohenstaufen culture—e.g., *Erec* and *Iwein*, by Hartmann von Aue, and *Parzival* (at least the first six books), by Wolfram von Eschenbach. Many scholars believe that he belonged to an influential family seated near Grafenberg (Bavaria). Thus, he appears integral to the florescence of Arthurian literature in German between 1180 and 1220. It is likely that Wirnt's story derives from French sources, written or oral, though no direct relationships have been found. The early part of *Wigalois* is much like Renaut de Beaujeu's romance *Le Bel Inconnu* (ca. 1200). Allusions to *Wigalois* are found in German literature from about 1220 on; nearly forty complete or fragmentary manuscripts preserve it; a large series of fourteenth-century murals in a Tyrolian castle depicts episodes from it; and a prose redaction was published in 1493 and often thereafter. *Wigalois* belongs among the more popular German castings of Arthurian lore.

In the story, an unknown knight comes to Arthur's court and offers the Queen a beautiful girdle, vowing to challenge Arthur's knights the next day should she choose not to keep it. The girdle has marvelous powers, but the Queen returns it, and with its help the stranger defeats all opponents, Gawein being the last. With Gawein as prisoner, he returns to his fabulous country: there Gawein marries his niece, Florie, but after some blissful months leaves her to visit Arthur. Lacking the girdle, Gawein cannot find his way back to Florie; she bears a son, Wigalois, who excels in manly virtue and, at the age of twenty, goes in search of his father.

He comes to Arthur's court, seats himself on a stone that rejects all but the most excellent, and is accordingly welcomed. Gawein becomes his mentor (neither perceives their relationship). When a damsel comes to Arthur seeking a champion for a dread adventure, Wigalois gains the commission—much to her distress, for she doubts the prowess of this young and unknown knight. Traveling with her, Wigalois triumphs in combat with four separate knights and a pair of giants and thus wins her confidence. At her mistress's castle, Roimunt, he learns that, ten years before, the heathen Roaz had assassinated King Lar and usurped his country, Korntin. The legitimate heiress, Larie, dwells at Roimunt and is to marry the hero who liberates her land. Wigalois and Larie fall in love. He finds his way into Korntin by following a strange beast; this is transformed into the spirit of King Lar, who tells Wigalois that Gawein is his father and equips him to fight a dragon. Though he kills the dragon, he is gravely injured and robbed of his armor. Restored to strength by the widow of one of the dragon's victims, he is nearly killed by a monstrous forest-woman, slays a powerful dwarf, and so reaches Glois, the fortress of Roaz. The bridge into Glois is blocked by a turning water-wheel studded with swords and axes. God answers the hero's prayer and brings the wheel to a stop. Entering the city, Wigalois kills a centaur and two guards, then fights all night with Roaz, finally killing him. The wife of Roaz, Japhite, dies of grief.

In Korntin, the hero marries Larie in the presence of several Arthurian knights, including Gawein, whose relationship to him is joyfully acknowledged. A messenger reports that King Amire of Libia has been slain by Lion of Namur—this for love of Queen Liamere, second cousin to Larie. Wigalois and Gawein mount a punitive expedition; after much fighting, Gawein kills Lion. Father and son travel to Arthur's court, Gawein learning on the way that Florie has died; then Wigalois and Larie return to Korntin, where she bears a son of whom amazing adventures are told.

Stylistically facile, though not distinguished, *Wigalois* is carefully constructed. The hero's adventures are framed by stories of his father; his great mission (the liberation of Korntin) proceeds through stages of escalating peril; the final conflict at Namur confirms his manhood and cements the bond with his father. An atmosphere of the sinister and supernatural grows ever stronger as he approaches the devilish Roaz at Glois; his success depends not only on his courage and hardihood but also on God's direct intervention. The victory of Christian over heathen (e.g., Gawein over Lion) is an important motif. Numerous details associate Wigalois's adventures with Christian tradition, notably with elements in the Revelation of John (discussed by Wirnt, ll. 10,272–305), suggesting that the author's many pious excurses express an important part of his character. Unlike the heroes of Hartmann and Wolfram, Wigalois is not a gravely flawed knight achieving reconciliation with God and man through selfless adventure. He seems instead to embody the knight in full harmony with Fortune (hence his emblem, the wheel). Wirnt wants his audience to reflect on the excellence and final happiness of one whose behavior so reflects God's will that life withholds nothing from him. The relative disfavor of *Wigalois* among modern readers may arise in this unproblematic essence, for the poem is very interesting in story, composition, atmosphere, and authorial presence. [SLW]

◆ Wirnt von Grafenberg. *Wigalois, der Ritter mit dem Rade*, ed. J.M.N. Kapteyn. Bonn: Klopp, 1926.

——— . *Wigalois, the Knight of Fortune's Wheel*, trans. J.W. Thomas. Lincoln and London: University of Nebraska Press, 1977.

Cormeau, Christoph. *"Wigalois" und "Diu Crône": Zwei Kapitel zur Gattungsgeschichte des nachklassischen Aventiureromans.* Zurich and Munich: Artemis, 1977.

WISSE, CLAUS: *see* COLIN, PHILIPP.

WITCH IN THE WOOD, THE: *see* WHITE, T.H.

WOLFRAM VON ESCHENBACH, the greatest German epic poet of the high Middle Ages, that period of extraordinary literary and artistic achievement around the year 1200. He was recognized as such by some of his contemporaries, and his reputation has remained alive throughout the centuries. To be sure, he was no innovator like Hartmann von Aue, who with his classical style introduced Arthurian literature to Germany, nor was he a consummate master of language and love like Gottfried von Strassburg. On the contrary, Wolfram's style is anything but polished. It is obscure and complex, frequently with the immediacy of conversation, but his works show an intense grappling with the problems of human existence that sets him apart from his contemporaries. In recent years, appreciation of Wolfram's genius has spread beyond German-speaking areas, so that he is now recognized as one of the great poets of world literature.

Wolfram's works include his monumental *Parzival*, which is a reworking, expansion, and completion of Chrétien de Troyes's *Le Conte del Graal*; his unfinished *Willehalm*, a tragic romance based on the Old French *chanson de geste Aliscans*; two fragments commonly known by the title *Titurel*, but actually dealing with the love of young Schionatulander and Sigune, two of the characters in *Parzival*; and nine lyric poems, mostly dawn songs (possibly the first in German), attributed to Wolfram in the various collections of *Minnesang*.

The chronology of Wolfram's works is not completely clear. One thing is certain: his *Parzival* preceded his *Willehalm*, because Wolfram mentions the former in the prologue to the latter. Most scholars believe that his lyric poems came before *Parzival* and that the *Titurel* fragments, written in strophic form, were composed either immediately before or during the work on *Willehalm*. One historical event, the destruction of vineyards during the siege of Erfurt in 1203–04, is mentioned in Book VII of *Parzival*, so that the beginning of work on *Parzival* is believed to lie between 1200 and 1210. In *Willehalm*, there is a mocking reference to the coronation of Otto IV in October 1209, and in the same year a new siege weapon, the tribocco mentioned in *Willehalm*, was supposedly introduced into Germany. Wolfram names Landgrave Hermann of Thuringia as the provider of the Old French source for his *Willehalm* and appears to refer to him as deceased in the last book. Hermann died on 25 April 1217, so that *Willehalm* was probably begun after about 1212 and left unfinished sometime after 1217, maybe as late as the 1220s.

Despite the fact that Wolfram, or at least the first-person narrator of his works, makes numerous references to himself and his circumstances, very little concrete biographical knowledge is actually available. Eschenbach is probably the old Middle Franconian city of Ober-Eschenbach southeast of Ansbach, today Wolframs-Eschenbach in Bavaria. Mention is made of Wolfram's grave there in the Frauenkirche as late as the middle of the fifteenth century and the early seventeenth century, and a von Eschenbach family is known there from 1268 to the second half of the fourteenth century. Wolfram was probably not of the nobility, but rather a poor man, dependent on patronage from the powerful and wealthy for his livelihood. He does call himself a soldier on one occasion, but that is no reason to assume that he was even a *Ministerialis*. He spent at least some time at the court of Hermann of Thuringia, who undoubtedly commissioned *Willehalm*, and the Count of Wertheim may have been an early patron. Geographical references in his works indicate that he traveled about, even as far as Styria.

Wolfram claims to be illiterate (*Parzival*, Chapter 115, ll. 27–30), yet he also is proud of his wealth of knowledge and is eager to display it. He is acquainted, for example, with lists of precious stones and the Arabic names of planets that are both probably derived from written sources. Nevertheless, he surely did not enjoy a traditional clerical education, for he shows no knowledge of the Latin school authors. He did know some French, but certainly not very well, because he probably misunderstood his French sources on occasion. Scholars have continued to speculate on Wolfram's literacy and how he actually composed, but perhaps it is significant that Wolfram always says: "as I heard tell" or "the story says"; he never says: "as I read" or "as it is written." He is well acquainted with the German literature of his day: Heinrich von Veldeke, Hartmann von Aue, Walter von der Vogelweide, and Neidhart von Reuental are all mentioned. He knew the German *Alexander, Rolandslied, Kaiserchronik*, Eilhart von Oberge's *Tristrant*, the *Nibelungenlied*, and other heroic sagas, and apparently engaged in a literary feud with Gottfried von Strassburg.

His professed analphabetism could well be part of his reaction to the obviously learned Hartmann and Gottfried, for Wolfram does not hesitate to heap scorn on those who keep referring to their literary sources. He relies instead on his own divinely inspired creative sense (*Willehalm*, Chapter 2, ll. 16–22) for his artistic achievements. Nevertheless, Wolfram is acutely aware of the importance of sources and repeatedly refers to his *Aventiure* or to the *Maere* that he is retelling.

Wolfram's best-known work is his *Parzival*, an Arthurian epic of some 25,000 lines, written in rhymed couplets. His chief source is undeniably Chrétien de Troyes's *Perceval*, or *Le Conte del Graal*, but Wolfram's version differs from Chrétien's in many respects. Two differences are immediately apparent. First, Chrétien's *Perceval* remains fragmentary, having been left unfinished after 9,234 lines (there are, of course, numerous Continuations, which Wolfram probably did not know, with the possible exception of the First Continuation and the so-called *Bliocadran Prologue*), whereas Wolfram has brought his story to a satisfactory conclusion. Second, Wolfram has expanded his *Parzival* by the addition of two books that describe the adventures of Parzival's father, Gahmuret, in the East and his ultimate marriage to Herzeloyde, who later gives birth to Parzival after Gahmuret's death. Also, Wolfram's concept of the Grail and the Grail society is quite different from Chrétien's. Wolfram's Grail family goes beyond the courtly family of King Arthur to function as a divinely ordained instrument in the affairs of the world. Parzival is related to the Arthurian family through his father and to the Grail family through his mother. Wolfram is keenly aware of family relationships and has almost all characters of any importance related to one another in some way. Furthermore, Wolfram gives names to characters nameless in Chrétien, and changes some others. Nevertheless, the general sequence of events is preserved by Wolfram in the parts that correspond to Chrétien's work, although some episodes are shortened or expanded.

In an epilogue to *Parzival*, Wolfram finds fault with Chrétien for not having done justice to the story, indicating clearly that he must have been acquainted with Chrétien's version. Earlier, however, he had mentioned a certain "Kyot" as his source. According to Wolfram, Kyot was a Provençal who had provided the true story of the Grail, a story written in Arabic that he had found discarded in Toledo. That manuscript contained a report about the Grail and the Grail family by an astronomer named Flegetanis, who was part Jewish and who had read about the Grail in the stars. Kyot, the Christian, had to learn Arabic in order to read what Flegetanis had written. Thereupon, he searched through Latin chronicles to find the story of the Grail family, which he finally located in Anjou. This is patently a fantastic fabrication to impress the gullible and to delight the cognoscenti in Wolfram's audience.

Along with his invention of Kyot, Wolfram exhibits a very different concept of the Grail from the one found in Chrétien. What was there a dish or bowl has become a stone, named enigmatically *lapsit exillis*, quite possibly an intentionally distorted "Latin" term, although there have been many attempts at explanation, none of which has been completely convincing. It was to this stone that God had banished the angels who had remained neutral in the struggle between God and Lucifer. Later, a human family was entrusted with the protection of the Grail and lived from the food and drink that it miraculously provided. The Grail could be carried only by a virgin and had the power to keep anyone who came into its presence from dying for the next week. Wolfram's Grail is practically inaccessible, being guarded by an order of knights in a castle that cannot be found by those who seek it. Children are named to the Grail by means of an inscription that appears on the stone. They grow up there as knights and ladies to be sent out later to occupy thrones that lack rulers. The ladies are sent out openly—such was the case with Herzeloyde, Parzival's mother—but the men are sent out secretly.

The "templars," as Wolfram calls the Grail knights, are not allowed to marry or have a love relationship with women while guarding the Grail. Only the Grail king may be married, but Anfortas, the current king, had defied that stipulation and, performing chivalric deeds in the service of a lady, had been wounded in the groin by a poisoned spear. The wound cannot be healed, and his sufferings are intense, yet he cannot die because of the presence of the Grail. At length, a message appears on the Grail, stating that a stranger will come to the Grail castle who is to ask the question that will release Anfortas. No one must inform him of the situation, and he must ask the question on the first night, otherwise he will lose the opportunity to become king, and Anfortas will not be healed.

Parzival, of course, is the one chosen by the Grail to free Anfortas. He had been raised far from courtly life: after the tragic death of his father, Gahmuret, his mother had purposely kept him away from court, but the genetic inheritance from his adventure-loving father is not to be denied, and Parzival goes out into the world, dressed as a fool, seeking King Arthur in order to become a knight. He eventually does become one, but only after killing a relative unwittingly in the process. He rescues and marries the beautiful Condwiramurs, whom he then leaves to visit his mother, only to arrive at the Grail castle. Mindful of all he had been taught about knightly behavior, Parzival sees the Grail procession and the bloody spear and hears the lamenting of the people. He receives a sword from Anfortas, who is obviously suffering. He remains silent, however, and on the next morning the Grail company has mysteriously disappeared. Two days later, Parzival arrives at Arthur's court and is accepted as a knight of the Round Table. At this crowning moment of his knightly career, Parzival suffers the bitter humiliation of being cursed publicly by the ugly Grail messenger, Cundrie, for having failed to ask the question.

The narrative then divides, with Gawan occupying the foreground in his quest for four queens and 400 maidens held captive in Schastel Merveile; yet Parzival hovers in the background, angry with God and determined to find the Grail again. Gawan's adventures are interrupted in the middle when the narrative returns to Parzival on Good Friday, to his meeting with his hermit uncle, Trevrizent, who tells him about his family, his relationship to Anfortas and the Grail, about his mother's death and the murder of his relative. He hears Parzival's confession and gives him insight into God and His ways with man, so that Parzival loses his anger toward God, yet he still hopes to find the Grail.

Gawan eventually succeeds in freeing the queens. He gains the hand of the proud Orgeluse and arranges for Arthur to come to see his culminating duel with Gramoflanz. Parzival, however, intervenes, fights first with Gawan (unaware of his identity), then in Gawan's stead with Gramoflanz. King Arthur is left with the problem of reconciling Gramoflanz with Gawan successfully, and Parzival leaves the ensuing joyous celebration, only to encounter his heathen half-brother, Feirefiz, in combat that almost costs Parzival his life before his brother magnanimously reveals his identity first. Parzival, having learned to know God and having proven himself, is now ready to be called to the Grail by Cundrie. Accompanied by Feirefiz, he is conducted to the Grail; asks what ails his uncle, Anfortas, who is then miraculously cured; and assumes the kingship of the Grail, his wife and twin sons joining him shortly thereafter.

Wolfram's story clearly deals with two realms, the Arthurian world of preeminent chivalry, with Gawan, the perfect knight, as its leading figure, and the Grail-world, a transcendent realm with a definite relationship to God, one that demands a suitable electus as its savior and new leader. Both Parzival and Gawan are exemplary knights in the eyes of the world, and both succeed in their quests, but it is Parzival who must undergo the purification process that will enable him to assume his rightful heritage. The courtly world of Arthur, implicit in the first two books in the life of Parzival's father, is sought at first by Parzival in his ignorance. It is a world of the highest courtly virtues, but Parzival must learn that for him it is not sufficient. He has a higher calling.

King Arthur does not appear in Wolfram's *Willehalm*, an unfinished tragic romance of some 13,000 lines, yet the spirit of courtly love and chivalry is very much present. It is remarkable that here Wolfram portrays not only the Christians but also the heathens as noble knights in the service of ladies, and he lavishes praise on the heroes of both sides, quite in contrast to his Old French source, *Aliscans*.

The *Titurel* fragments, also placed in a courtly setting, are likewise without the presence of King Arthur. They are composed in strophes of four long lines each, similar to those of the *Nibelungenlied*. The two groups of fragments, comprising approximately 170 strophes (there are questions about the authenticity of some strophes), present the love story of two young people, Schionatulander and Sigune. The first group describes the development of their love; the second tells of a hunting dog with a magnificent long leash that has an artistically worked story on it. The hound tears itself loose from Sigune's hands, but she wishes to learn the whole story and asks Schionatulander to retrieve it, saying that she will not grant him her love until he does. Here, the fragment breaks off, but we know from Wolfram's *Parzival* that Schionatulander meets his death in the attempt and that Sigune spends the rest of her life doing penance and grieving over the body of her lover.

Titurel was continued and brought to a conclusion in an enormous work, known as *Der jüngere Titurel*, by a certain Albrecht (possibly Albrecht von Scharfenberg), who actually passes himself off initially as Wolfram. Thus, Wolfram was generally considered to be the author throughout the fourteenth and fifteenth centuries. If one adds *Der jüngere Titurel* to his *Parzival* and *Willehalm*, one should not be surprised that Wolfram was highly regarded by his successors. He is even credited with participation in the famous singing contest at the Wartburg, and his style was consciously imitated by other poets. Today, he is viewed as a highly individualistic artist who transformed his sources with masterful skill into new creations and imbued them with an ethical and spiritual dimension that was unique in his time. [SMJ]

�763 *Wolfram von Eschenbach*, ed. Karl Lachmann. Berlin, 1833; 6th ed. Berlin: de Gruyter, 1926 (repr. 1965).

Wolfram von Eschenbach (edition of *Parzival*), ed. Albert Leitzmann. Halle, 1905–06. 5 vols.; 6th ed. Wilhelm Deinert. Tübingen: Niemeyer, 1965.

Wolfram von Eschenbach. *Willehalm*, ed. Werner Schröder. Berlin and New York: de Gruyter, 1978.

―――. *Parzival*, trans. A.T. Hatto. Harmondsworth and New York: Penguin, 1980.

Bumke, Joachim. *Wolfram von Eschenbach*. Stuttgart: Metlzer, 1964; 5th ed. 1981.

Poag, James F. *Wolfram von Eschenbach*. New York: Twayne, 1972.

Sacker, Hugh D. *An Introduction to Wolfram's "Parzival."* Cambridge: Cambridge University Press, 1963.

WORDSWORTH, WILLIAM (1770–1850). In "The Egyptian Maid," Merlin, "provoked to envious spleen" by a lovely ship that seems to float in the air, destroys the ship; an Egyptian princess is cast ashore. At the instruction of Nina, Lady of the Lake, Merlin takes the innocent and unconscious princess to Arthur's court. The maid's father, earlier freed by Arthur, had promised to become a Christian and betroth his daughter to one of Arthur's knights. One by one, the knights touch her hand; at Galahad's touch, she returns from death and the two are married. Wordsworth changes the traditional characters Merlin and Galahad to create a symbolic account of his own turning from youthful freedom toward moral responsibility. As such, the poem is much less successful than the "Immortality" ode. [JW]

�734 Wordsworth, William. *The Poetical Works of William Wordsworth*, ed. E. de Selincourt. 5 vols. Oxford: Clarendon, 1940–49.

Merriman, James D. *The Flower of Kings: A Study of the Arthurian Legend in England Between 1485 and 1835.* Lawrence: University Press of Kansas, 1973.

WORKSHOP MOOSACH, a German experimental and alternative theatrical group founded in 1977 in Moosach near Munich, is best known for the dramatic piece *Flechtungen: Der Fall Partzifall* ("Weavings: The Partzifall Case"). The "case" of Parzival (in the Wolfram version) is here joined to a modern story of a schizophrenic, using associative techniques. Common to both, the authors and players (Ulrike Doepfer, Rudi Roth, Axel Tangerding) believe, is the abnormality of the protagonists. The play was produced with great success between 1978 and 1981 in Germany, Austria, Yugoslavia, Canada, and the United States (at the La Mama Theater in New York). [UM/WCM]

&❧ Müller, Ulrich. "Parzival 1980." In *Mittelalter-Rezeption II*, ed. Jürgen Kühnel, Hans-Dieter Mück, Ursula Müller, and Ulrich Müller. Göppingen: Kümmerle, 1982.

WRAKE VAN RAGISEL, DE ("The Avenging of Ragisel"), a Middle Dutch adaptation of the Old French *La Vengeance Raguidel*, dating from the first half of the thirteenth century. The Middle Dutch poet increases the tension of certain situations in a courtly fashion (Walewein is depicted as a courtly lover, more so than Gauvain in the *Vengeance*). Of this adaptation, about 900 lines have been preserved. The fragments, from two manuscripts, are preserved in Düsseldorf (Landes- und Stadtsbibliothek F. 26a and F. 26b) and Cologne (Historisches Archiv W. f°. 317). One of the two manuscripts dates from 1260–80.

The *Lancelot-Compilatie* includes a greatly abridged version of the Middle Dutch adaptation that numbers 3,414 lines. The compiler of the *Lancelot-Compilatie* inserted two chapters in his abbreviation and, moreover, followed it with two more chapters. One of the two inserted chapters completes two fabliaulike stories with an antifeminist moral. The other three chapters are intended to adjust the *Wrake* adaptation on the one hand to the compositional properties of the *Lancelot-Compilatie* (such as putting the figure of Lancelot back into prominence) and on the other hand to the narrative technique of the historical Arthurian romances (narrative threads have to be brought to a logical and compositionally justified end). [BB]

&❧ Gerritsen, W.P., ed. *Die Wrake van Ragisel*. 2 vols. Assen: van Gorcum, 1963.

WRIGHT, S(IDNEY) FOWLER (1874–1967), composed three poems based on Malory. *The Ballad of Elaine* (1926) in six-line stanzas presents a whitewashed Lancelot whose refusal to marry Elaine of Astolat depends not on his love for Guenevere but on his vow of chastity. *The Riding of Lancelot* (1929) is a blank-verse narrative in twenty-four parts from Malory's *Morte Darthur*, Book VI. *Scenes from the Morte d'Arthur* (1930) shows Tennysonian influence in its form, treatment of nature, and comprehensiveness. Of nineteen parts, the most extensive are "Uther and Igraine" and "Gareth and Lionore." [MAW]

&❧ Wright, S. Fowler. *The Ballad of Elaine*. London: Merton, 1926.
———. *The Riding of Lancelot*. London: Merton, 1929.
———. *Scenes from the Morte d'Arthur*. London: Merton, 1930.

WYETH, N.C.: *see* BOOK ILLUSTRATION (AMERICAN).

WYNKYN DE WORDE. The first illustrated edition of Malory's *Le Morte Darthur* was published in London in 1498 by Wynkyn de Worde. Jan van

Wynkyn, from Worth in Alsace, had been William Caxton's foreman in Bruges. He moved to England with Caxton in 1476 and took over the press when Caxton died in 1491. Wynkyn moved the press from Westminster to Fleet Street and finally to St. Paul's churchyard, the center of London's new printing trade. There he worked until his death in 1534–35.

In spite of the intention of the printers to produce books in relatively large numbers for profitable commercial distribution, only one copy of Wynkyn de Worde's illustrated Malory survives (John Rylands Library, Manchester). Caxton had published the original edition of the *Morte* in 1485. Wynkyn now added illustrations at the heading of each chapter for his 1498 edition. Woodblocks, about 4 by 5 inches, are rather crudely cut, with heavy angular lines and shading created by blocks of parallel strokes. Elongated figures move like puppets, but in the best illustrations, such as Lancelot's madness, the birth of Tristram, and the enchantment of Merlin, a childlike directness carries considerable power. In early woodblocks, the drawing and the cutting of the block were not necessarily done by the same person, and here the inventiveness is not matched by skill in cutting. Deep spatial settings suggest the artist's debt to Flemish painting; landscapes with distant towns, castles, and even windmills spread out under skies filled with flying birds. Wynkyn reissued the Malory in 1529 and also re-used some of the blocks in later books, such as the *Recuyles of ye Hystories of Troye* (1502). [MS]

Hind, Arthur M. *An Introduction to a History of Woodcut.* London: Constable, 1935, Vol. 2, pp. 728–29; fig. 463.

Loomis, Roger Sherman, and Laura Hibbard Loomis. *Arthurian Legends in Medieval Art.* London: Oxford University Press, 1938, pp. 143–44; figs. 415–20.

YDER, a French romance of 6,769 lines, extant in one manuscript; it was probably composed in the second quarter of the thirteenth century. The illegitimate Yder attempts to win the love of Queen Guenloie by deeds of arms. He rescues an ungrateful Arthur, then joins Arthur's enemy, Talac de Rougemont, and is treacherously wounded by Kay. Cured by Guenloie and reconciled to Arthur, he joins the Round Table and rescues Guenièvre from a bear. When Guenièvre claims that she would have preferred Yder to Arthur if she had had the choice, Arthur tries in vain to kill the hero. Yder fulfills all of Guenloie's conditions, marries her, and then legitimizes his own birth with the wedding of his mother and his father, Nuc. The romance is noteworthy for its portrayal of an odious Arthur and Kay and for its links with an old tradition according to which Yder was the lover of Guenièvre, for whose sake he kills a bear. [KB]

🙦 Adams, Alison, ed. *Yder*. Cambridge: Boydell and Brewer, 1983.

YSAÏE LE TRISTE, a fourteenth-century French romance providing a sequel to the Prose *Tristan* and recounting the adventures of Ysaïe, the son of Tristan and Isolde. In this work, Arthurian chivalry is shown to be something of an anachronism, and themes and motifs are inverted (e.g., the traditionally evil dwarf becomes an ally) in a frequently humorous play on Arthurian conventions. [NJL]

   L'Histoire d'Isaie le Triste. Paris: Galliot du Pré, 1522.

     Zeidler, Julius. "Der Prosaroman *Ysaÿe le Triste.*" *Zeitschrift für Romanische Philologie*, 25 (1901), 175–214, 472–89, 641–68.

YVAIN (IVAIN, OWEIN, YWAIN), the son of Urien. He appears in the Book of Taliesin and then in *The Dream of Rhonabwy,* in which he plays a game with Arthur. The major developments of his character occur in Chrétien de Troyes's *Yvain* (*Le Chevalier au lion*) and in the Welsh *Owein*; in those works he kills a woman's husband, marries her, loses and eventually regains her love. Yvain also appears in a number of later romances, and his prominence in the *Mort Artu* is indicated by the fact that he is one of the last knights to die (at Mordred's hand) before the death of the King himself. (*See also* OWEIN; CHRÉTIEN DE TROYES.) [NJL]

YVAIN: *see* CHRÉTIEN DE TROYES; *YVAIN IN PROSE.*

YVAIN IN PROSE, an episodic French romance preserved in a single manuscript from the fourteenth century. The work consists of seven separate episodes, only the first of which concerns Yvain directly (although he is mentioned in others). The first part recounts the rescuing of the lion, and the details of the adventure do not differ substantially from those given by Chrétien de Troyes. The other sections relate a series of adventures of various knights, including Gawain, Tristan, and Lancelot. The fifth episode contains an interesting debate concerning the relative merits of various knights of Uther's and Arthur's courts. Although the work as a whole is historically interesting, the talent of the author is decidedly deficient. [NJL]

   Muir, Lynette. "A Reappraisal of the Prose *Yvain* (National Library of Wales MS. 444-D)." *Romania*, 85 (1964), 355–65.

YWAIN AND GAWAIN, a clear adaptation from Chrétien de Troyes's *Yvain* (*Le Chevalier au lion*). *Ywain and Gawain* is the only one of Chrétien's romances to survive in an English version (the Middle English *Sir Perceval de Galles* does not go back to the *Perceval*). Preserved in a single manuscript of the early fifteenth century, it was probably composed some hundred years earlier, in the north. The uniqueness of the text and of the manuscript appears to confirm the impression, created by the lack of references to Chrétien in Middle English poetry and the slight influence of his works, that Chrétien was far less popular with speakers of English than with French-speaking audiences. The English adapter reduced the number of lines by approximately a third (6,808 against

4,032). Most of Chrétien's long and penetrating musings on the workings of love have been clipped or completely discarded by the English poet, who instead concentrates on the more realistic elements of the story, such as Ywain's chivalric exploits and his heroic qualities. Women, the goddesses to men in truly courtly poetry, have been reduced to a position of inferiority, as if the adapter were writing for a male audience more interested in life's realities than in love's ideals. Also, high chivalric notions expressed by such words as *enor* 'honor' or *honte* 'shame' do not play a part in the English *Ywain*; the words for honor and shame do not even occur in it. However, the changes show a coherent pattern and were apparently deliberately introduced by an adapter whose aims or audience must have been different from Chrétien's. His skillful control of the story, the swift succession of events, the powerful diction, the often lively colloquial language, as well as the competent handling of the octosyllabic line, explain why the poem has been called one of the most successful romances in Middle English. [ESK]

🐦 Friedman, Albert B., and Norman T. Harrington, eds. *Ywain and Gawain*. London: Oxford University Press, 1964.

ZAUBERER MERLIN: *see* STUCKEN, EDUARD.

ZAUBERLEHRLING, DER: *see* GOETHE, JOHANN WOLFGANG.

ZAUBERMANTEL, DER: *see* VAN DER VELDE, CARL FRANZ.

ZELAZNY, ROGER, makes extensive use of many legends in his science fiction and fantasy. Lancelot appears briefly in *The Guns of Avalon* (1972), then again in "The Last Defender of Camelot" (1979). Here, he fights against intolerance when he forms an untraditional alliance with Morgan le Fay to prevent a reawakened Merlin from imposing his will upon a new age. [RHT]

  Zelazny, Roger. *The Guns of Avalon.* New York: Doubleday, 1972.
    Yoke, Carl. *Roger Zelazny.* Westlinn, Ore.: Starmont, 1979.

ZIFAR (OR CIFAR), LIBRO DEL CABALLERO, the first indigenous Spanish romance of chivalry, composed circa 1300, perhaps by Ferrán Martínez, Archdeacon of Madrid in the church of Toledo. The *Zifar*'s debt to Arthurian romance is nebulous, although there are specific allusions (e.g., Arthur's fight with the Cath Palug as found in the Vulgate *Merlin*, and the figure of Yván, son of King Orián, recalling Chrétien de Troyes's hero Yvain) as well as distinct parallels (e.g., the accusation of adultery and the sentencing to the stake of Grema, the hero Zifar's wife, as happens to Guenevere in the Grail cycle, and the supernatural adventures of the Caballero Atrevido, or Bold Knight, involving a Lady of the Lake and those of Zifar's son Roboan, who travels to the Islas Dotadas, recalling Geoffrey of Monmouth's Insulae Fortunae). Critics have also pointed to the possible influence of various French lais. In general, however, the work is essentially a Byzantine romance with a strong didactic and religious (but not mystical) tone, revealing oriental and epic influences, as well as much in common with the Placidas/St. Eustace legend. [HLS]

González Muela, Joaquín, ed. *Libro del caballero Zifar*. Madrid: Castalia, 1982.

González, Cristina, ed. *Libro del Caballero Zifar*. Madrid: Cátedra, 1983.

Olsen, Marilyn A., ed. *Libro del Cauallero Çifar*. Madison: Hispanic Seminary of Medieval Studies, 1984.

ZUMSTEEG, JOHANN RUDOLF: *see* WERTHES, FRIEDRICH AUGUST CLEMENS.

809.9335 A791e

The Arthurian encyclopedia

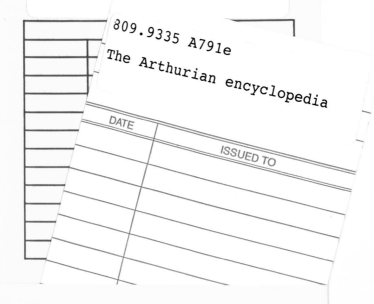

809.9335 A791e

The Arthurian encyclopedia

DATE	ISSUED TO	